HISTORICAL DICTIONARIES OF EUROPE
Edited by Jon Woronoff

1. *Portugal,* by Douglas L. Wheeler. 1993. *Out of print. See No. 40.*
2. *Turkey,* by Metin Heper. 1994. *Out of print. See No. 38.*
3. *Poland,* by George Sanford and Adriana Gozdecka-Sanford. 1994. *Out of print. See No. 41.*
4. *Germany,* by Wayne C. Thompson, Susan L. Thompson, and Juliet S. Thompson. 1994
5. *Greece,* by Thanos M. Veremis and Mark Dragoumis. 1995
6. *Cyprus,* by Stavros Panteli. 1995
7. *Sweden,* by Irene Scobbie. 1995
8. *Finland,* by George Maude. 1995
9. *Croatia,* by Robert Stallaerts and Jeannine Laurens. 1995. *Out of print. See No. 39.*
10. *Malta,* by Warren G. Berg. 1995
11. *Spain,* by Angel Smith. 1996
12. *Albania,* by Raymond Hutchings. 1996. *Out of print. See No. 42.*
13. *Slovenia,* by Leopoldina Plut-Pregelj and Carole Rogel. 1996
14. *Luxembourg,* by Harry C. Barteau. 1996
15. *Romania,* by Kurt W. Treptow and Marcel Popa. 1996
16. *Bulgaria,* by Raymond Detrez. 1997
17. *United Kingdom: Volume 1, England and the United Kingdom; Volume 2, Scotland, Wales, and Northern Ireland,* by Kenneth J. Panton and Keith A. Cowlard. 1997; 1998
18. *Hungary,* by Steven Béla Várdy. 1997
19. *Latvia,* by Andrejs Plakans. 1997
20. *Ireland,* by Colin Thomas and Avril Thomas. 1997
21. *Lithuania,* by Saulius Suziedelis. 1997
22. *Macedonia,* by Valentina Georgieva and Sasha Konechni. 1998
23. *The Czech State,* by Jiri Hochman. 1998
24. *Iceland,* by Guðmundur Hálfdanarson. 1997
25. *Bosnia and Herzegovina,* by Ante Cuvalo. 1997
26. *Russia,* by Boris Raymond and Paul Duffy. 1998
27. *Gypsies (Romanies),* by Donald Kenrick. 1998
28. *Belarus,* by Jan Zaprudnik. 1998
29. *Federal Republic of Yugoslavia,* by Zeljan Suster. 1999
30. *France,* by Gino Raymond. 1998
31. *Slovakia,* by Stanislav J. Kirschbaum. 1998
32. *Netherlands,* by Arend H. Huussen Jr. 1998
33. *Denmark,* by Alastair H. Thomas and Stewart P. Oakley. 1998
34. *Modern Italy,* by Mark F. Gilbert and K. Robert Nilsson. 1998

35. *Belgium,* by Robert Stallaerts. 1999
36. *Austria,* by Paula Sutter Fichtner. 1999
37. *Republic of Moldova,* by Andrei Brezianu. 2000
38. *Turkey, 2nd edition,* by Metin Heper. 2002
39. *Republic of Croatia, 2nd edition,* by Robert Stallaerts. 2003
40. *Portugal, 2nd edition,* by Douglas L. Wheeler. 2002
41. *Poland, 2nd edition,* by George Sanford. 2003
42. *Albania, New edition,* by Robert Elsie. 2004
43. *Estonia,* by Toivo Miljan. 2004
44. *Kosova,* by Robert Elsie. 2004
45. *Ukraine,* by Zenon E. Kohut, Bohdan Y. Nebesio, and Myroslav Yurkevich. 2005

Historical Dictionary of Ukraine

Zenon E. Kohut
Bohdan Y. Nebesio
Myroslav Yurkevich

Historical Dictionaries of Europe, No. 45

The Scarecrow Press, Inc.
Lanham, Maryland • Toronto • Oxford
2005

SCARECROW PRESS, INC.

Published in the United States of America
by Scarecrow Press, Inc.
A wholly owned subsidiary of
The Rowman & Littlefield Publishing Group, Inc.
4501 Forbes Boulevard, Suite 200, Lanham, Maryland 20706
www.scarecrowpress.com

PO Box 317
Oxford
OX2 9RU, UK

Copyright © 2005 by Zenon E. Kohut, Bohdan Y. Nebesio,
and Myroslav Yurkevich

All rights reserved. No part of this publication may be reproduced, stored in a retrieval system, or transmitted in any form or by any means, electronic, mechanical, photocopying, recording, or otherwise, without the prior permission of the publisher.

British Library Cataloguing in Publication Information Available

Library of Congress Cataloging-in-Publication Data
Kohut, Zenon E.
  Historical dictionary of Ukraine / Zenon E. Kohut, Bohdan Y. Nebesio, and Myroslav Yurkevich.
    p. cm. — (Historical dictionaries of Europe ; no. 45)
  Includes bibliographical references.
  ISBN 0-8108-5387-6 (hardcover : alk. paper)
  1. Ukraine—History—Dictionaries. I. Nebesio, Bohdan Y. II. Yurkevich, Myroslav, 1950– III. Title. IV. Series.
DK508.444.K64 2005
947.7'003—dc22
                                                              2004027284

∞™ The paper used in this publication meets the minimum requirements of American National Standard for Information Sciences—Permanence of Paper for Printed Library Materials, ANSI/NISO Z39.48-1992.
Manufactured in the United States of America.

Contents

Editor's Foreword *Jon Woronoff*	vii
Acknowledgments	ix
Note on Transliteration, Terminology, and Dates	xi
Acronyms and Abbreviations	xv
Maps	xxiii
Chronology	xxxiii
Introduction	1
THE DICTIONARY	15
Bibliography	743
About the Authors	853

Editor's Foreword

Ukraine, like most other "new" states in central and eastern Europe, is exceedingly fortunate to have recovered its independence. In this case, even more than the others, "lucky" is not the correct word, since its people have fought for the right to govern themselves for centuries, and for centuries have been subjected to others—worse, to various combinations of others—with various parcels of territory under the control of stronger, predatory neighbors including Poland-Lithuania, Germany, Austria-Hungary, the Ottoman Empire, and, of course, Russia or the Union of Soviet Socialist Republics, which preserved a Ukrainian entity in its own interests and still does not want to give up its claim entirely. For obvious reasons, the "new" Ukraine, which has undergone many metamorphoses over its long history, is not in an enviable position, owing to inexperience in governing a state, economic imbalance and a decayed infrastructure, and lack of national unity—the result of long-term Russification and provincialization. One thing Ukraine has clearly gotten right is its decision to forsake nuclear weapons, the only country ever to do so. But there still remain any number of problems and challenges that are important not only for the Ukrainians but for all of Europe, since Ukraine is one of the largest countries on the continent in both size and population.

So this *Historical Dictionary of Ukraine* fills a particularly large gap in the series of Historical Dictionaries of Europe. It informs us of what has been happening over many centuries in "the Ukraine," the expression used before Ukraine became a state of its own. And it tells us something about present-day Ukraine. In so doing, it also describes the situation further afield, including information on many other polities, kingdoms, and empires. Considerable attention is devoted to the Ukrainian Cossacks, who, unlike their Russian counterparts, played a major nation-building role in the early modern period. There are thus, in this very large and readable volume, hundreds of entries—nearly 700, to be more precise—on significant persons; places; events; institutions; and economic, social, and cultural aspects that will be of interest to Ukrainians, persons of Ukrainian extraction, and the general reader interested either in Ukraine or the whole region. Meanwhile, through its extensive bibliography, the dictionary provides access to numerous other sources on all these matters.

This volume was written by a team of three: Zenon E. Kohut, Bohdan Y. Nebesio, and Myroslav Yurkevich. They are all associated with the Canadian Institute of Ukrainian Studies (CIUS) at the University of Alberta, of which Dr. Kohut has been director for a decade. Earlier, he taught at the University of Pennsylvania and Michigan State University and was a long-term associate of the Harvard Ukrainian Research Institute. Dr. Kohut has written widely on early modern Ukraine, historiography, and the development of Ukrainian identity. His book, *Russian Centralism and Ukrainian Autonomy: Imperial Absorption of the Hetmanate*, was published in 1988 (revised Ukrainian version, 1996). Dr. Nebesio teaches in the film/media studies program at the University of Alberta and serves as assistant editor of *Canadian Slavonic Papers*. His articles and reviews on the history of film theory and the Ukrainian and East European cinema have appeared in film and Slavic studies journals. Myroslav Yurkevich is senior editor of the Canadian Institute of Ukrainian Studies Press and has participated in the CIUS project to translate Mykhailo Hrushevsky's monumental *History of Rus'-Ukraine* since its inception.

It should also be mentioned that this book has benefited from its authors' association with a project undertaken by scholars at the Institute of Historical Research, Lviv University, who produced the first post-Soviet Ukrainian historical dictionary. The present work, the first of its kind in English focusing on Ukrainian history (as compared with the much broader range of subjects covered in the *Encyclopedia of Ukraine*), makes a remarkable contribution to our knowledge of an old but little-known country and its new state.

Jon Woronoff
Series Editor

Acknowledgments

Our thanks go first and foremost to Lada Hornjatkevyč, who worked as a research assistant on this project for more than three years. With skill, resourcefulness, and dedication far beyond the call of duty, she translated and researched reams of material for the entries and compiled the initial versions of the chronology and bibliography. This volume could not have been produced without her.

Our work on this project was carried out under the auspices of the Kowalsky Program for the Study of Eastern Ukraine at the Canadian Institute of Ukrainian Studies (CIUS), University of Alberta, and was supported entirely by the Michael and Daria Kowalsky Endowment Fund.

During the early stages of compilation, the authors collaborated closely with the Lviv University project that produced the three-volume *Dovidnyk z istoriï Ukraïny* (Handbook of Ukrainian History; Kyiv: Heneza, 1993–99), edited by Ihor Pidkova and Roman Shust and subsequently published in a one-volume revised edition (Heneza, 2001). We greatly appreciate their assistance.

Valuable advice on church history was provided by Dr. Serhii Plokhy, associate director of the Peter Jacyk Centre for Ukrainian Historical Research at CIUS. Dr. Yuri Shapoval, director of the Institute of Political and Ethnonational Studies, National Academy of Sciences of Ukraine, gave us the benefit of his extensive knowledge of the Stalin regime. Andrij Makuch, a researcher in the Encyclopedia of Ukraine Project at CIUS, supplied useful data for entries on political dissidents. We are also grateful to Tetiana Narozhna, who researched and drafted some of the entries on present-day Ukraine. With Roman Shyian, Ms. Narozhna checked the entries on the Cossack era; Mr. Shyian also worked on early versions of some general entries. We alone, however, assume responsibility for all statements of fact and opinion expressed in this volume.

It was a pleasure to work with Jon Woronoff, Kim Tabor, and Niki Averill of Scarecrow Press, who gave us prompt and helpful advice. We also wish to thank Peter Matilainen of CIUS Press, who resolved a host of computer-related problems and formatted the text of the dictionary.

We gratefully acknowledge the permission of the University of Toronto Press to reproduce maps 2, 6, 7, and 8 from the *Encyclopedia of Ukraine*, ed. Volodymyr Kubijovyč and Danylo Husar Struk, 6 vols. (Toronto, 1984–2001) and map 5 from Paul R. Magocsi, *A History of Ukraine* (Toronto, 1996). Map 4 is reproduced from Zenon E. Kohut, *Russian Centralism and Ukrainian Autonomy: Imperial Absorption of the Hetmanate, 1760s–1830s* (Cambridge, Mass.: Harvard Ukrainian Research Institute, 1988). Maps 1 and 9 were drawn for this volume by Wendy Johnson of Johnson Cartographics, Edmonton, Canada. Map 3, also drawn by Ms. Johnson, is reproduced from vol. 9, pt. 1, of Mykhailo Hrushevsky's *History of Ukraine-Rus'* (Edmonton and Toronto: Canadian Institute of Ukrainian Studies Press, 2005).

Note on Transliteration, Terminology, and Dates

The present work seeks to give the reader an orientation in Ukrainian history through a combination of general articles on population, geography, economy, politics, and culture; descriptions of major events, institutions, and cultural monuments; and biographical sketches of key individuals in politics, the arts and sciences, the church, and the military. It could not have been undertaken without the factual, interpretative, and terminological foundation established by a number of encyclopedic works about Ukraine and its history. These works, as well as the general English-language literature on Ukrainian history, are discussed in the introduction to the bibliography.

In the text of the dictionary, the modified Library of Congress system is used to transliterate Ukrainian and other East Slavic words and names. Initial iotated vowels are rendered with a "y" (e.g., Yaroslav, Yevhen, Yurii). In individual words and titles of publications, but not personal or geographic names, the soft sign (ь) is marked with a prime ('). In surnames, the masculine ending -ий is simplified to -y (e.g., Khmelnytsky, not Khmel'nyts'kyi) and the soft sign is rendered with an "i" (thus Khvyliovy, not Khvylovy, as in the *Encyclopedia of Ukraine*). Titles of East Slavic publications are transliterated according to the strict Library of Congress system (ligatures omitted). For details of these transliteration systems, the reader may consult the *ALA-LC Romanization Tables* (available online at www.loc.gov/catdir/cpso/roman.html) or the *Encyclopedia of Ukraine*, vol. 1, pp. xi–xiii.

Ukrainian personal names are transliterated from their Ukrainian forms. This practice also applies to the names of political and ecclesiastical figures of Kyivan Rus', which most English readers are accustomed to seeing in their Church Slavonic or Russian forms. Both spellings are given on first mention in biographical entries about these individuals, with the Ukrainian form taking precedence, e.g., Riuryk (Riurik), Oleh (Oleg), Ihor (Igor), Volodymyr (Vladimir), and so on. The Ukrainian form alone appears in cross-references. Nineteenth- and 20th-century East Slavic printed sources typically give initials instead of first names of individuals, making it difficult or impossible to establish the first names of lesser-known persons.

The names of geographic features, cities, towns, and villages on the territory of present-day Ukraine are transliterated from their modern Ukrainian forms (e.g., Dnipro, Dnister, Kharkiv, Kyiv, Lviv, Odesa). The spelling of toponyms with double consonants in Ukrainian is simplified according to the usage of the *Encyclopedia of Ukraine* (e.g., Podilia, Polisia, Trypilia, Zaporizhia). A few prominent Ukrainian toponyms have traditional English spellings derived from Russian (Dnieper, Kharkov, Kiev, Odessa); these are supplied in parentheses as appropriate. Given the focus of this dictionary on Ukrainian history, Ukrainian forms of toponyms on historical or present-day Ukrainian ethnic territory precede forms used in other languages; hence Chornobyl (Chernobyl), Kholm (Chełm), Lviv (Lwów), Peremyshl (Przemyśl), and so on. An exception is made (again, following the *Encyclopedia of Ukraine*) for the names of three regions (Crimea, Galicia, Volhynia) that are well established in English; these spellings take precedence, while their Ukrainian forms (Krym, Halychyna, Volyn) are supplied in parentheses as required. The headwords of entries on geographic regions are followed by their Ukrainian names in parentheses. Places located in present-day Belarus are transliterated from their Belarusian forms (e.g., Hrodna, Mahilioŭ, Mazyr), not from the Russian forms prevalent in the English-language literature.

In articles devoted to organizations and political parties, their names are given in English translation, followed by their Ukrainian names (in strict LC transliteration) and acronyms, which are used in further references within the relevant articles. In the case of the Communist Party of Ukraine, which figures in many articles on 20th-century history, its English acronym (CPU) is used instead of the Ukrainian version (KPU). The same applies to the Ukrainian Soviet Socialist Republic (UkSSR) and several other institutions.

Ukrainian terms used in the text are italicized, and their plurals are given in their Ukrainian forms (e.g., *povit, povity*). However, a number of frequently used terms have been naturalized and are treated as English words: duma (epic song of the Cossack period), hetman, otaman (Cossack commanding officers), haidamaka, opryshok (insurgents of the early modern period), hromada (community), kobzar (minstrel), kurin (Cossack infantry unit or company), raion, oblast (administrative divisions roughly corresponding to "district" and "province"), Sich (Cossack headquarters), and sobor (Eastern Church council).

In English-language writings on pre-independence Ukraine, the definite article was invariably used to denote Ukraine's regional, non-autonomous status (cf. the Argentine, the Lebanon, the Sudan). This practice drew incessant protests from independence-minded Ukrainians in the West, who considered that the Ukrainian People's Republic had established an independent state, aspired to revive it, and insisted that it be treated in English-language references as a country, not as a region. (Some writers have cited "the Netherlands" and "the United States" as justification for writing "the Ukraine," but these are plurals.) Scholarly (and most journalistic) writing on Ukraine in English published since 1991 conventionally omits the definite article.

The name of the Ukrainian Academy of Sciences (est. 1918) was changed three times in the 20th century (since 1993, its official name has been "National Academy of Sciences of Ukraine"), but the original name is generally used in references throughout the dictionary, with occasional references to the academy's later names as required by context.

Another problem of consistency is posed by references to the Ukrainian Catholic Church, established in 1596 as the Uniate Church and renamed the Greek Catholic Church by Empress Maria Theresa of Austria in 1774 in order to distinguish this Byzantine-rite institution from the Roman Catholic Church of Poland. To avoid the misleading implication that this is an ethnically Greek church, it is termed the "Ukrainian Catholic Church" in this dictionary, but readers should note that its current official name is "Ukrainian Greek Catholic Church."

In the central and eastern Ukrainian lands, the Julian calendar, which lagged behind the Gregorian calendar (10 days in the 17th century, 11 in the 18th, 12 in the 19th, and 13 in the 20th), was used until 1 March 1918 and is still employed by the traditional Ukrainian churches for ritual purposes. The Gregorian calendar was introduced on 1 March 1918 by the government of the Ukrainian People's Republic. Consequently, earlier dates are cited according to both calendars, with the new (Gregorian) style preceding the old (Julian) style and the latter date in parentheses. Because the sources are not always explicit, it is sometimes impossible to determine whether a given date is old (Julian) or new (Gregorian) style. In Galicia and Bukovyna, which came under Habsburg rule in 1772–74, the Gregorian calendar was generally used for secular purposes, and developments there are dated accordingly.

Acronyms and Abbreviations

ABN	Antybol'shevyts'kyi blok narodiv—Anti-Bolshevik Bloc of Nations
AK	Armia Krajowa—Home Army (Poland)
AN UkSSR	Akademiia nauk (Academy of Sciences) of the Ukrainian SSR
ARA	American Relief Administration
CC	Central Committee
Cheka	Chrezvychainaia komissiia po bor'be s kontrrevoliutsiei i sabotazhem—Extraordinary Commission for Fighting Counterrevolution and Sabotage (Soviet Russia)
CIS	Commonwealth of Independent States
CIUS	Canadian Institute of Ukrainian Studies
CP(B)	Communist Party (Bolshevik)
CPSU	Communist Party of the Soviet Union
CPU	Communist Party of Ukraine—Komunistychna partiia Ukraïny (KPU)
EU	European Union
FNIe	Front natsional'noï iednosty—Front of National Unity
GPU	Gosudarstvennoe politicheskoe upravlenie—State Political Administration (Soviet Union)

GULAG	Glavnoe upravlenie lagerei—Main Administration of Labor Camps (Soviet Union)
GUUAM	Georgia, Ukraine, Uzbekistan, Azerbaijan, and Moldova
HURI	Harvard Ukrainian Research Institute
KGB	Komitet gosudarstvennoi bezopasnosti—Committee for State Security (Soviet Union)
Komsomol	Lenins'ka komunistychna spilka molodi Ukraïny—Leninist Communist Youth League of Ukraine
KPRP	Komunistyczna Partia Robotnicza Polski—Communist Labor Party of Poland
KPSH	Komunistychna partiia Skhidnoï Halychyny—Communist Party of Eastern Galicia
KPU	*See* CPU
KPZU	Komunistychna partiia Zakhidnoï Ukraïny—Communist Party of Western Ukraine
KRNS	Katolyts'kyi rus'ko-narodnyi soiuz—Catholic Ruthenian People's Union
LNV	*Literaturno-naukovyi visnyk*—Literary and Scientific Herald
MASSR	Moldavian Autonomous Soviet Socialist Republic
MP	Moskovskaia Patriarkhiia (Ukr. Moskovs'kyi Patriarkhat)—Moscow Patriarchate
MVD	Ministerstvo vnutrennikh del—Ministry of Internal Affairs (Soviet Union)
NANU	Natsional'na akademiia nauk Ukraïny—National Academy of Sciences of Ukraine
NATO	North Atlantic Treaty Organization

NBU	Natsional'nyi bank Ukraïny—National Bank of Ukraine
NDP	Natsional'no-demokratychna partiia—National Democratic Party
NKVD	Narodnyi komissariat vnutrennikh del—People's Commissariat of Internal Affairs (Soviet Union)
NTSh	Naukove tovarystvo imeny Shevchenka—Shevchenko Scientific Society
OGPU	Ob"edinennoe glavnoe politicheskoe upravlenie—United State Political Administration (Soviet Union)
OUN	Orhanizatsiia ukraïns'kykh natsionalistiv—Organization of Ukrainian Nationalists
OUN(B)	OUN (Bandera faction)
OUN(M)	OUN (Melnyk faction)
POW	prisoner of war
RA	Red Army
RCP(B)	Russian Communist Party (Bolshevik)
RKU	Reichskommissariat Ukraine
RM	Rada Ministriv—Council of Ministers
RNK	Rada Narodnykh Komisariv—Council of People's Commissars
ROC	Russian Orthodox Church
RSDLP	Russian Social Democratic Labor Party
RSFSR	Rossiiskaia Sovetskaia Federativnaia Sotsialisticheskaia Respublika—Russian Soviet Federative Socialist Republic
RUP	Revoliutsiina ukraïns'ka partiia—Revolutionary Ukrainian Party

SHD	Soiuz het'mantsiv-derzhavnykiv—United Hetman Organization
SSSR	Soiuz Sovetskikh Sotsialisticheskikh Respublik—Union of Soviet Socialist Republics (USSR)
SU	Soiuz ukraïnok—Union of Ukrainian Women
SUM	Spilka ukraïns'koï molodi—Ukrainian Youth Association
SVU	Soiuz vyzvolennia Ukraïny—Union for the Liberation of Ukraine (1914)
SVU	Spilka vyzvolennia Ukraïny—Union for the Liberation of Ukraine (1930)
TseSUS	Tsentral'nyi soiuz ukraïns'koho studentstva—Central Union of Ukrainian Students
TUP	Tovarystvo ukraïns'kykh postupovtsiv—Society of Ukrainian Progressives
UAN	Ukraïns'ka akademiia nauk—Ukrainian Academy of Sciences
UAOC	Ukrainian Autocephalous Orthodox Church—Ukraïns'ka Avtokefal'na Pravoslavna Tserkva
UCC	Ukrainian Canadian Congress—Kongres ukraïntsiv Kanady
UCC	Ukrainian Catholic Church—Ukraïns'ka Katolyts'ka Tserkva
UCCA	Ukrainian Congress Committee of America—Ukraïns'kyi kongresovyi komitet Ameryky
UDKhP	Ukraïns'ka demokratychno-khliborobs'ka partiia—Ukrainian Democratic Agrarian Party
UDRP	Ukraïns'ka demokratychno-radykal'na partiia—Ukrainian Democratic Radical Party

Acronyms and Abbreviations • xix

UHA	Ukraïns'ka halyts'ka armiia—Ukrainian Galician Army
UHA	Ukraïns'ka hel'sins'ka asotsiiatsiia—Ukrainian Helsinki Association
UHH	Ukraïns'ka hel'sins'ka hrupa—Ukrainian Helsinki Group
UHVR	Ukraïns'ka holovna vyzvol'na rada—Supreme Ukrainian Liberation Council
UKNP	Ukraïns'ka katolyts'ka narodna partiia—Ukrainian Catholic People's Party
UKP	Ukraïns'ka komunistychna partiia—Ukrainian Communist Party
Ukrainian SSR UkSSR	Ukrainian Soviet Socialist Republic—Ukraïns'ka Radians'ka Sotsialistychna Respublika
UN	United Nations
UNDO	Ukraïns'ke natsional'no-demokratychne ob'iednannia—Ukrainian National-Democratic Alliance
UNDS	Ukraïns'kyi natsional'no-derzhavnyi soiuz—Ukrainian National-State Union
UNK	Ukraïns'kyi natsional'nyi komitet—Ukrainian National Committee
UNO	Ukraïns'ke natsional'ne ob'iednannia—Ukrainian National Alliance
UNP	Ukraïns'ka narodna partiia—Ukrainian People's Party
UNP	Ukraïns'ka natsional'na partiia—Ukrainian National Party
UNR	Ukraïns'ka Narodna Respublika—Ukrainian People's Republic
UNRada	Ukraïns'ka natsional'na rada—Ukrainian National Rada

UNS	Ukraïns'ka narodna samooborona—Ukrainian People's Self-Defense
UNS	Ukraïns'kyi natsional'nyi soiuz—Ukrainian National Union
UOC	Ukrainian Orthodox Church—Ukraïns'ka Pravoslavna Tserkva
UOC-KP	Ukrainian Orthodox Church, Kyiv Patriarchate—Ukraïns'ka Pravoslavna Tserkva (Kyïvs'kyi Patriarkhat)
UPA	Ukraïns'ka povstans'ka armiia—Ukrainian Insurgent Army
UPNR	Ukraïns'ka partiia natsional'noï roboty—Ukrainian Party of National Work
UPP	Ukraïns'ka partiia pratsi—Ukrainian Party of Labor
UPSF	Ukraïns'ka partiia sotsiialistiv-federalistiv—Ukrainian Party of Socialist Federalists
UPSR	Ukraïns'ka partiia sotsiialistiv-revoliutsioneriv—Ukrainian Party of Socialist Revolutionaries
UPSS	Ukraïns'ka partiia sotsiialistiv-samostiinykiv—Ukrainian Party of Socialist Independentists
URDP	Ukraïns'ka revoliutsiino-demokratychna partiia—Ukrainian Revolutionary Democratic Party
URP	Ukraïns'ka radykal'na partiia—Ukrainian Radical Party
URSR	Ukraïns'ka Radians'ka Sotsialistychna Respublika—Ukrainian Soviet Socialist Republic. *See* Ukrainian SSR.
USDP	Ukraïns'ka sotsiial-demokratychna partiia—Ukrainian Social Democratic Party
USDRP	Ukraïns'ka sotsiial-demokratychna robitnycha partiia—Ukrainian Social Democratic Labor Party

Acronyms and Abbreviations • xxi

USKhD	Ukraïns'kyi soiuz khliborobiv-derzhavnykiv—Ukrainian Union of Agrarian Statists
USS	Ukraïns'ki sichovi stril'tsi—Ukrainian Sich Riflemen
USSR	Union of Soviet Socialist Republics
UTsK	Ukraïns'kyi tsentral'nyi komitet—Ukrainian Central Committee
UVAN	Ukraïns'ka vil'na akademiia nauk—Ukrainian Academy of Arts and Sciences
UVO	Ukraïns'ka viis'kova orhanizatsiia—Ukrainian Military Organization
UVU	Ukraïns'kyi vil'nyi universytet—Ukrainian Free University
UVV	Ukraïns'ke vyzvol'ne viis'ko—Ukrainian Liberation Army
UWC	Ukrainian World Congress—Svitovyi kongres ukraïntsiv
VPTsR	Vseukraïns'ka pravoslavna tserkovna rada—All-Ukrainian Orthodox Church Council
VR	Verkhovna Rada—Supreme Council
VRNH	Verkhovna Rada narodnoho hospodarstva—Supreme Council of the National Economy
VUAN	Vseukraïns'ka akademiia nauk—All-Ukrainian Academy of Sciences
VUFKU	Vseukraïns'ke foto-kinoupravlinnia—All-Ukrainian Photo-Cinema Administration
VUTsVK	Vseukraïns'kyi tsentral'nyi vykonavchyi komitet—All-Ukrainian Central Executive Committee
ZCh OUN	Zakordonni chastyny Orhanizatsiï ukraïns'kykh natsionalistiv—Foreign Sections of the Organization

of Ukrainian Nationalists

ZO UNR   Zakhidna Oblast' Ukraïns'koï Narodnoï Respubliky—Western Province of the Ukrainian People's Republic

ZUNR   Zakhidno-Ukraïns'ka Narodna Respublika—Western Ukrainian People's Republic

Maps

1. Kyivan Rus'
2. Lands of the Polish-Lithuanian Commonwealth, 16th–18th Centuries
3. Cossack Ukraine ca. 1650
4. The Cossack Hetmanate, 1750s
5. Ukrainian Lands in the 19th Century
6. The Ukrainian People's Republic, 1917–20
7. Interwar Ukraine
8. Ukraine in World War II
9. Present-Day Ukraine

Map 1. Kyivan Rus'

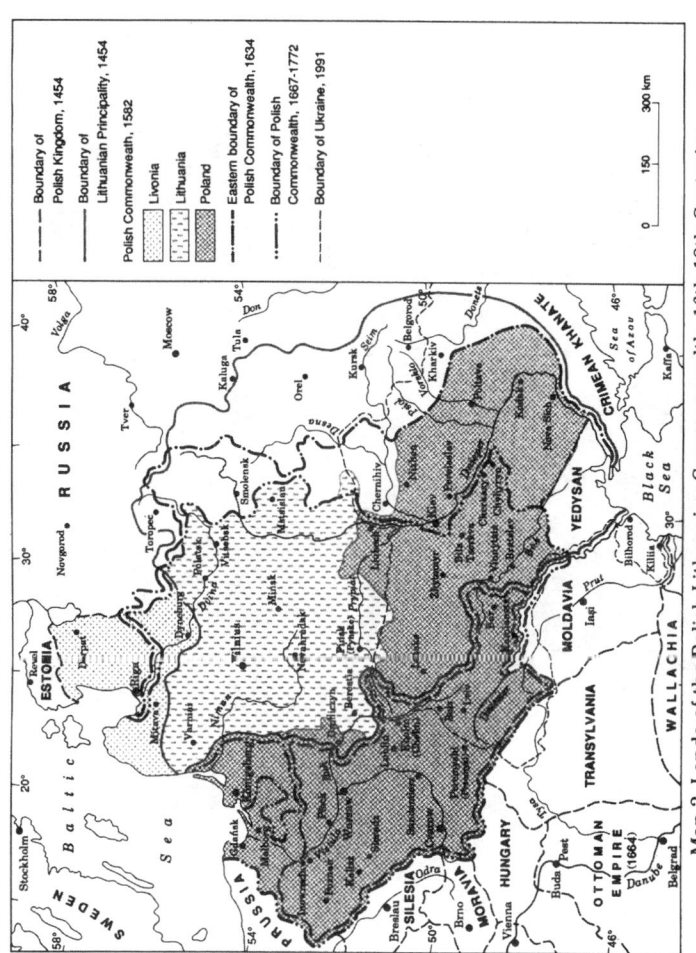

Map 2. Lands of the Polish-Lithuanian Commonwealth, 16th-18th Centuries

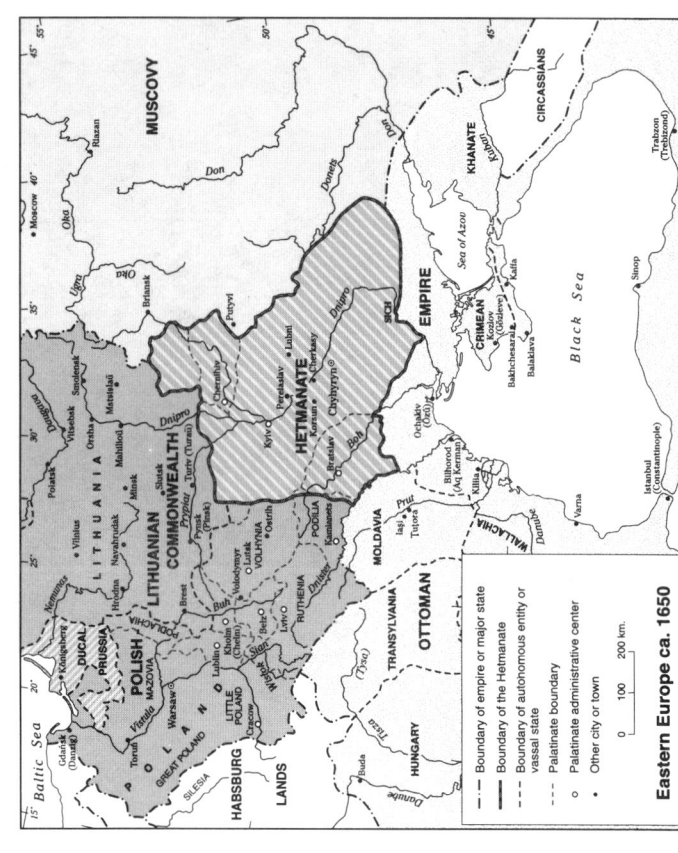

Map 3. Cossack Ukraine ca. 1650

Map 4. The Cossack Hetmanate, 1750s

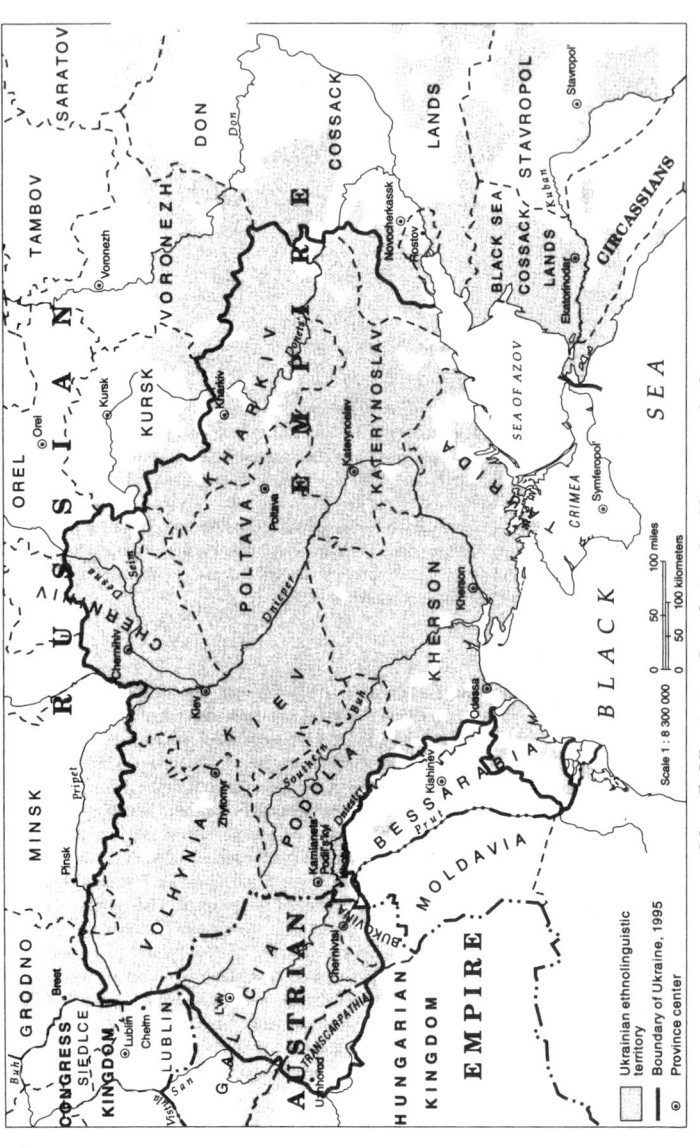

Map 5. Ukrainian Lands in the Nineteenth Century

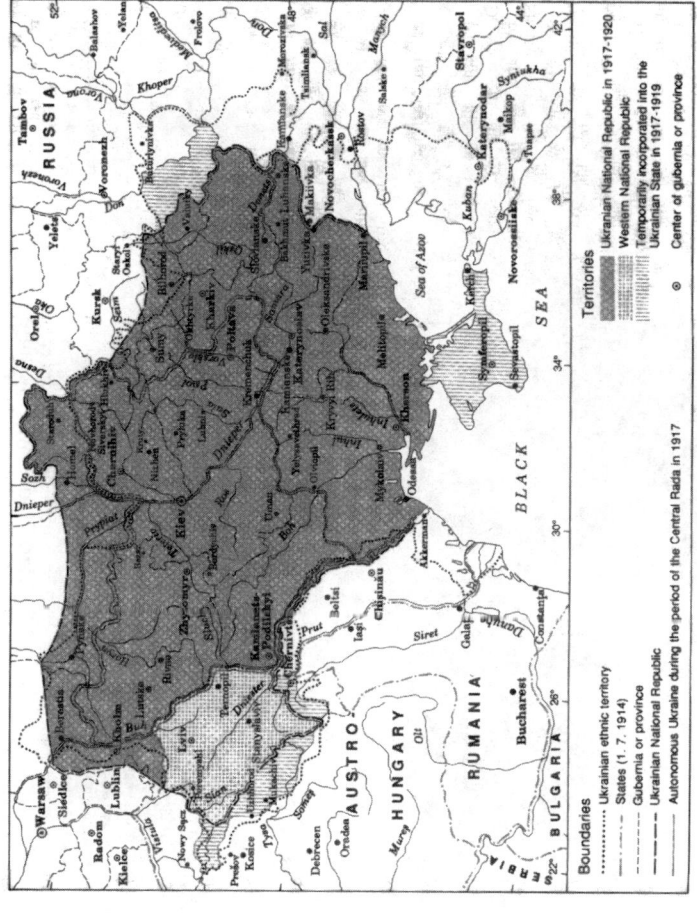

Map 6. The Ukrainian People's Republic, 1917-20

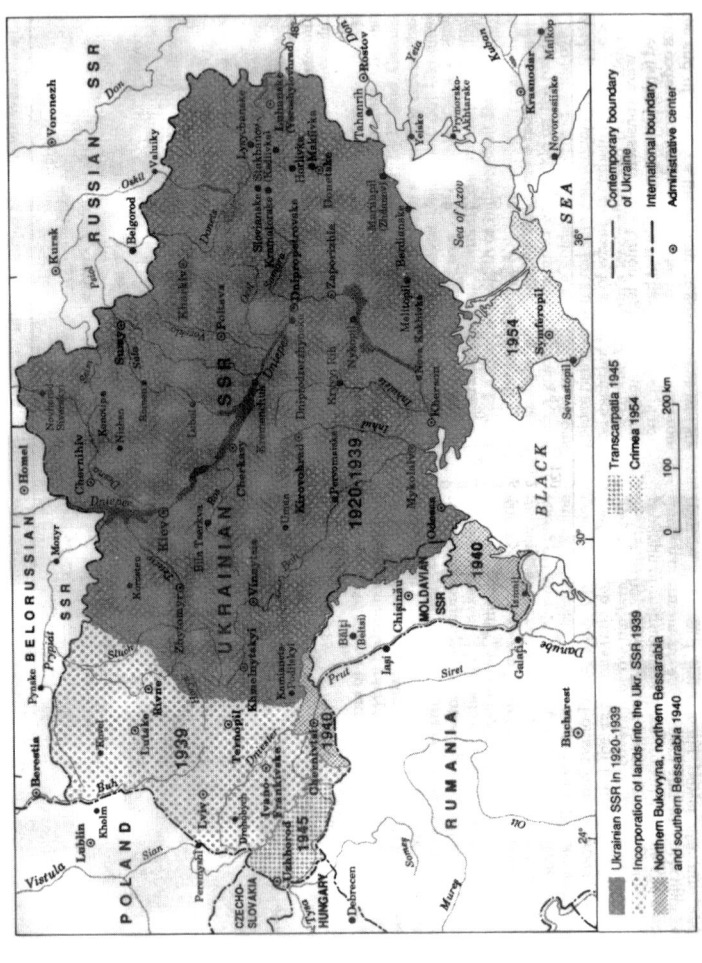

Map 7. Interwar Ukraine

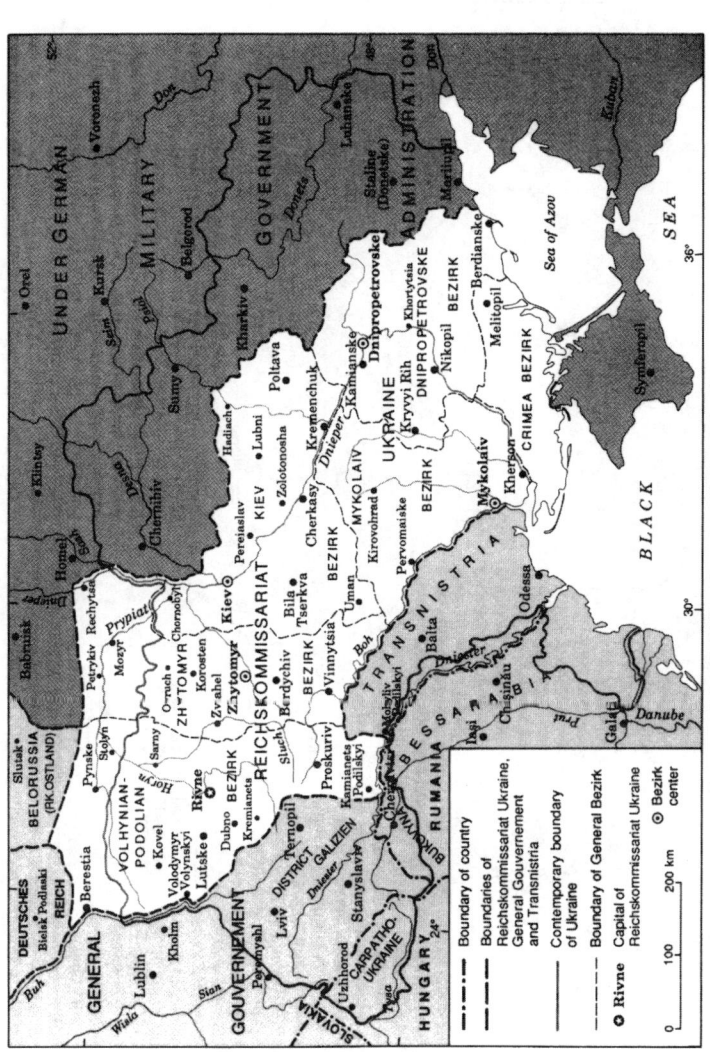

Map 8. Ukraine in World War II

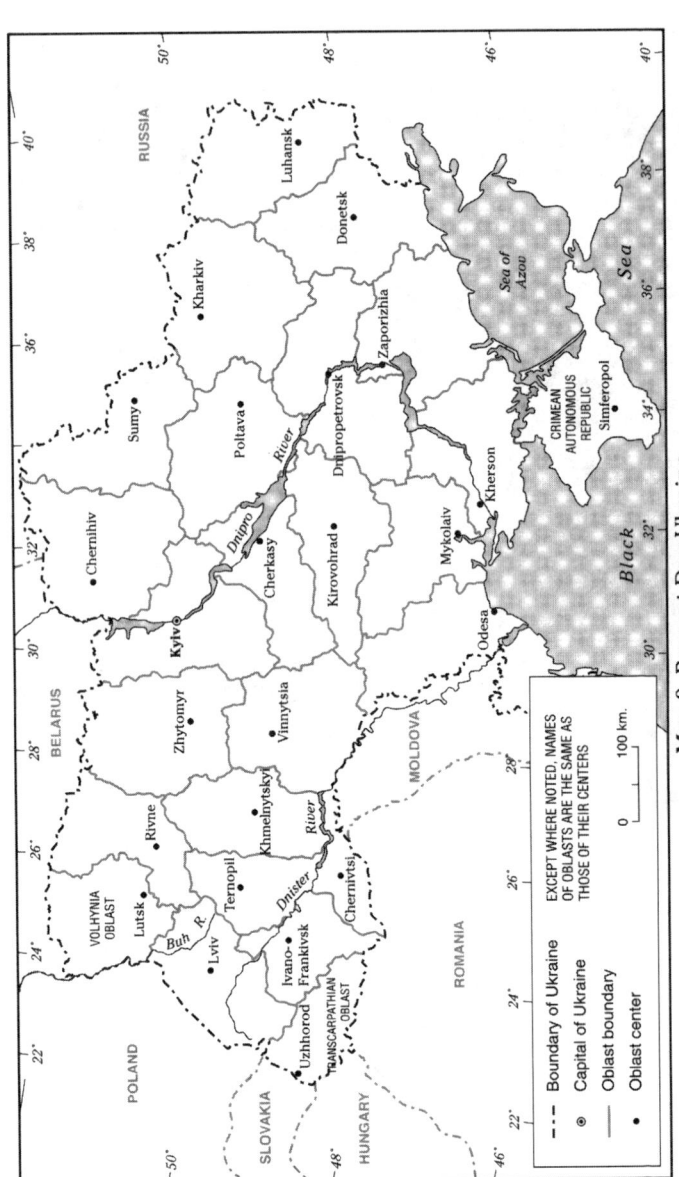

Map 9. Present-Day Ukraine

Chronology

6th–7th centuries	Formation of Rus' Land in middle Dnipro region, centered in Kyiv
8th–9th centuries	Formation of Kyivan Rus'
862	Traditional date of Slavic tribes' "invitation to the Varangians" (Riuryk, Sineus, and Truvor) to rule over them
882	Oleh's arrival in Novgorod; murder of Askold and Dir; beginning of Riuryk line in Kyiv
912–945	Ihor's reign in Kyiv
945–969	Olha's regency in Kyiv
mid-950s	Olha's conversion to Christianity
969–972	Reign of Sviatoslav Ihorevych in Kyiv
980–1015	Reign of Volodymyr the Great in Kyiv
988	Christianization of Kyivan Rus'
989–996	Construction of Church of the Tithes in Kyiv
1015–1019	Internecine struggle for Kyivan throne
1019–1054	Reign of Yaroslav the Wise in Kyiv; compilation of first Rus' law code, the *Ruskaia Pravda*, begins
1037 (or 1017)	Construction of St. Sophia's Cathedral begins in Kyiv
1049	Marriage of Yaroslav's daughter, Anna Yaroslavna, to Henry I of France
1051	Ilarion consecrated metropolitan of Kyiv without sanction of the patriarch of Constantinople
1054	Great Schism leads to separation of Orthodox and Catholic churches
1056–1057	Copying of Ostromir's Evangeliary (oldest dated East Slavic manuscript)
1097	Liubech congress of princes attempts to establish principle of succession to Kyivan throne
1108–1113	Construction of St. Michael's Golden-Domed Monastery in Kyiv
1113–1125	Reign of Volodymyr Monomakh in Kyiv

1117	Compilation of Monomakh's *Poucheniie* (Instruction)
1125–1132	Reign of Mstyslav Volodymyrych in Kyiv
1187	First use of the term "Ukraine" (in Kyiv Chronicle) to identify southern Kyiv and Pereiaslav regions
1199	Unification of Galicia and Volhynia; founding of the Principality of Galicia-Volhynia
late 12th century	Writing of *Tale of Ihor's Campaign*
1203–1205	Reign of Roman Mstyslavych in Kyiv
1238–1264	Reign of Danylo Romanovych in Halych and Kholm
1239	Danylo Romanovych extends his rule to Kyiv
November 1240	Destruction of Kyiv by Golden Horde
early 13th century	Compilation of Kyivan Cave Patericon
1253	Coronation of Danylo Romanovych by delegates of Pope Innocent IV
1303	Establishment of Halych metropolitanate
1349	Poland annexes most of Galicia-Volhynia
1352	Partition of Galicia-Volhynia between Poland and Lithuania
1354	Patriarchal council in Constantinople sanctions transfer of Kyiv metropolitanate to Vladimir on the Kliazma
1362	Definitive annexation of Kyiv and Pereiaslav regions, Volhynia, and Podilia by Grand Duchy of Lithuania; Chernihiv annexed later in 14th century
ca. 1371	Restoration of Halych metropolitanate
1385	Union of Krevo between Poland and Lithuania
1387	Official introduction of Catholicism in Lithuania
1434	Galicia fully incorporated into Poland; Orthodox nobility in Poland and Lithuania granted equal rights with Catholic nobility
1439	Church Union of Florence; not recognized by Orthodox Church in East Slavic lands
1443	Crimean Khanate secedes from Golden Horde; establishment of Giray dynasty
1471	Abolition of Kyiv principality
1475	Crimean Khanate becomes a vassal of Ottoman Empire
1482	Kyiv raided by Crimean khan Mengli Giray

Chronology • xxxv

1483	Printing, in Rome, of first book by a Ukrainian author: Yurii Kotermak-Drohobych's *Judicium prenosticon Magistri Georgii Drogobicz de Russia*
1492	Earliest documentary mention of the Cossacks
1507–1508	Mykhailo Hlynsky's uprising against Sigismund I of Poland
1529	Earliest documentary mention of opryshoks
ca. 1552	Founding of Zaporozhian Sich on island of Khortytsia below Dnipro Rapids
ca. 1552–1563	Dmytro Vyshnevetsky's hetmancy
1556–1561	Translation of Peresopnytsia Gospel
1569	Union of Lublin between Grand Duchy of Lithuania and Kingdom of Poland
1569–1795	Polish-Lithuanian Commonwealth
1574	Ivan Fedorov prints first book in the Ukrainian lands, the *Apostol*
1581	Publication of Ostrih Bible
1587	Lviv Dormition Brotherhood receives right of stauropegion
December 1591–May 1593	Cossack rebellion against Polish rule led by Kryshtof Kosynsky
July 1594–May 1596	Cossack rebellion led by Severyn Nalyvaiko
6–10 (16–20) October 1596	Union of Brest establishes Uniate Church
1606–1622	Petro Sahaidachny's hetmancy
1619	Meletii Smotrytsky publishes *Hrammatiki slavenskiia pravilnoe syntagma*, systematizing Church Slavonic
17 (27) September–29 September (9 October) 1620	Battle of Cecora: Turco-Tatar forces defeat Polish army
October 1620	Patriarch Theophanes of Jerusalem consecrates new Orthodox hierarchy in Kyiv
22 August (1 September)–18 (28) September 1621	Battle of Khotyn: Cossack and Polish forces defeat Turco-Tatar army
September–October 1625	Cossack rebellion led by Marko Zhmailo
1630s	Mass settlement of Sloboda Ukraine begins
March–May 1630	Cossack rebellion led by Taras Fedorovych
1632–1647	Petro Mohyla leads Orthodox revival as metropolitan of Kyiv; Kyiv Mohyla Academy founded

March 1633	Polish Diet ratifies Measures for the Accommodation of the Ruthenian Nation
1637	Cossack rebellion led by Pavlo Pavliuk
March–July 1638	Cossack rebellion led by Yakiv Ostrianyn
24 April 1646	Union of Uzhhorod establishes Uniate Church in Transcarpathia
1648–1657	Khmelnytsky Uprising; Bohdan Khmelnytsky's hetmancy
1648–1782	The Hetmanate
8 (18) August 1649	Treaty of Zboriv between Cossacks and Polish-Lithuanian Commonwealth
8 (18) January 1654	Pereiaslav Agreement: Cossack Host led by Bohdan Khmelnytsky accepts Muscovite protectorate
14 (24) March 1654	Articles of Bohdan Khmelnytsky issued in Moscow
1657–1687	The Ruin
6 (16) October 1657	Treaty of Korsun between Hetmanate and Sweden
6 (16) September 1658	Treaty of Hadiach provides for a Grand Duchy of Rus' in Polish-Lithuanian Commonwealth; not implemented
28–29 June (8–9 July) 1659	Battle of Konotop; Cossack forces defeat invading Muscovite army
17 (27) October 1659	Yurii Khmelnytsky signs Pereiaslav Articles
1660–1663	Yakym Somko's acting hetmancy in Left-Bank Ukraine
1663–1665	Pavlo Teteria's hetmancy in Right-Bank Ukraine
17–18 (27–28) June 1663	Black council in Nizhyn elects Ivan Briukhovetsky hetman of Left-Bank Ukraine (to 1668)
11 (21) October 1665	Briukhovetsky signs Moscow Articles
1665–1676	Petro Doroshenko's hetmancy in Right-Bank Ukraine
30 January (9 February) 1667	Truce of Andrusovo divides Ukraine between Muscovy and Polish-Lithuanian Commonwealth
1669–1672	Demian Mnohohrishny's hetmancy in Left-Bank Ukraine
1672–1687	Ivan Samoilovych's hetmancy in Left-Bank Ukraine
1673–1676	Turco-Polish War for control of Right-Bank Ukraine

1677–1681	Turco-Muscovite War for control of Right-Bank Ukraine
1685	Kyiv metropolitanate subordinated to patriarch of Moscow
6 (16) May 1686	Eternal Peace between Muscovy and Polish-Lithuanian Commonwealth signed in Moscow
1687–1708	Ivan Mazepa's hetmancy in Left-Bank Ukraine
June 1699	Polish Diet outlaws Cossackdom in Right-Bank Ukraine
1700–1721	Northern War between Russia and Sweden
1702–1704	Cossack rebellion in Right-Bank Ukraine led by Semen Palii
1707	Mazepa begins secret negotiations with Charles XII of Sweden
1708–1722	Ivan Skoropadsky's hetmancy in Left-Bank Ukraine
27 June (8 July) 1709	Battle of Poltava; forces of Peter I defeat Charles XII and Mazepa
5 (16) April 1710	Constitution of Bendery
1710–1742	Pylyp Orlyk's hetmancy-in-exile
1714	Tsarist ukase forbids export of goods from Hetmanate
1715	First documentary mention of haidamakas
1720	Tsarist ukase forbids printing of books in Ukrainian
16 (27) May 1722	Office of hetman abolished by tsarist ukase; first Little Russian Collegium rules Hetmanate until September 1727
1722–1723	Pavlo Polubotok's acting hetmancy in Left-Bank Ukraine
1727–1734	Danylo Apostol's hetmancy in Left-Bank Ukraine
January 1734	Office of hetman abolished
1734–1738	First major haidamaka insurrection
1738–1745	Opryshok movement under leadership of Oleksa Dovbush
1743	Code of Laws of 1743
1750	Office of hetman restored; Kyrylo Rozumovsky's hetmancy in Left-Bank Ukraine
1753–1785	Hryhorii Skovoroda writes *Sad bozhestvennykh pisnei*
10 (21) November 1764	Catherine II abolishes hetmancy; second Little Russian Collegium (until August 1786)
May–July 1768	Koliivshchyna Rebellion

5 August 1772	First partition of Poland, as a result of which Galicia becomes part of Habsburg Monarchy
4–5 (15–16) June 1775	Destruction of Zaporozhian Sich by order of Catherine II
1782	Creation of Kyiv, Chernihiv, and Novhorod-Siverskyi vicegerencies puts an end to the Hetmanate
1784	Lviv University founded
1788	Formation of Black Sea Cossacks
17 August 1793	Polish Diet ratifies treaty with Russian Empire, which annexes Right-Bank Ukraine (second partition of Poland)
24 October 1795	Third partition of Poland leads to incorporation of Volhynia into Russian Empire
1805	Kharkiv University founded
1807	Halych metropolitanate restored as Catholic church province
1813–1835	Peasant insurgency led by Ustym Karmaliuk
1834	Kyiv University founded
1837	Ruthenian Triad publishes *Rusalka Dnistrovaia*
1840	First publication of Taras Shevchenko's *Kobzar*
December 1845–March 1847	Cyril and Methodius Brotherhood in Kyiv
13 March 1848	Beginning of Revolution of 1848 in Habsburg Monarchy
16 April 1848	Abolition of serfdom in Galicia
2 May 1848	Supreme Ruthenian Council established in Lviv
1857	Panteleimon Kulish's published grammar normalizes Ukrainian orthography
1859–1861	Alphabet War in Galicia
19 February (3 March) 1861	Emancipation Manifesto abolishes serfdom in Russian Empire
18 (30) July 1863	Valuev circular forbids publication of books in Ukrainian
8 December 1868	Prosvita Society founded in Lviv
13 (25) February 1873	Southwestern Branch of Imperial Russian Geographic Society founded in Kyiv
11 December 1873	Shevchenko Scientific Society founded in Lviv
18 (30) May 1876	Ems Ukase forbids publication or import of Ukrainian-language books in Russian Empire
early 1870s	Beginning of mass emigration to United States
14 January 1880	*Dilo*, first Ukrainian daily newspaper in Galicia, begins publication in Lviv

1884	Nataliia Kobrynska establishes first Ukrainian women's organization, the Society of Ruthenian Women, in Stanyslaviv
summer 1891	Brotherhood of Taras, a clandestine independentist organization, established in Russian-ruled Ukraine
1891	Beginning of mass emigration to Canada
1895	Publication of Yuliian Bachynsky's *Ukraïna Irredenta*
1898	First issue of *Literaturno-naukovyi visnyk*; first volume of Mykhailo Hrushevsky's *History of Ukraine-Rus'*
29 January (11 February) 1900	Revolutionary Ukrainian Party founded
1900	Publication of Mykola Mikhnovsky's *Samostiina Ukraïna*
1903	First complete publication of the Bible in Ukrainian
9 (22) January 1905	Bloody Sunday marks beginning of Revolution of 1905
14 (27) June–25 June (8 July) 1905	Mutiny on battleship *Potemkin*
October 1905	Union of the Russian People (Black Hundreds) founded
24 November (7 December) 1905	Temporary lifting of ban on publishing in Ukrainian and of censorship restrictions in Russian Empire
27 April (10 May)– 8 (21) July 1906	First Russian State Duma
20 February (5 March)– 2 (15) June 1907	Second Russian State Duma
1907–1909	Publication of Borys Hrinchenko's dictionary of Ukrainian language
1 (14) November 1907–9 (22) June 1912	Third Russian State Duma
May 1908	Duma rejects bill concerning Ukrainian-language instruction in primary schools
March 1909	First issue of *Ukraïns'ka khata* published in Kyiv
15 (28) November 1912–26 February (11 March) 1917	Fourth Russian State Duma

summer 1913	Debate in State Duma concerning restrictions on Ukrainian language
February 1914	Mass protests against ban on celebrating 100th anniversary of Taras Shevchenko's birth
1914–1918	World War I
31 July (13 August) 1914	Ukase imposing military censorship and ban on Ukrainian publishing in Russian Empire
1 August 1914	Supreme Ukrainian Council established in Lviv
6 August 1914	Formation of Ukrainian Combat Board, leadership of Ukrainian Sich Riflemen, in Lviv
1914–1916	Publication in St. Petersburg of two volumes of first (Russian-language) Ukrainian encyclopedia, *Ukrainskii narod v ego proshlom i nastoiashchem*
2 (15) March 1917	Tsar Nicholas II abdicates; Russian Provisional Government formed
1917–1921	Ukrainian Revolution
7 (20) March 1917	Presidium of Ukrainian Central Rada elected in Kyiv
10 (23) June 1917	First universal of Central Rada, declaring Ukrainian autonomy within Russian state
3 (16) July 1917	Second universal of Central Rada, announcing its compromise with Russian Provisional Government
7 (20) November 1917	Third universal of Central Rada, declaring establishment of Ukrainian People's Republic within a federal Russian state
11–12 (24–25) December 1917	First All-Ukrainian Congress of Soviets in Kharkiv declares formation of People's Secretariat of Ukraine; first Bolshevik invasion of Ukraine begins
9 (22) January 1918	Fourth universal of Central Rada declares independence of Ukrainian People's Republic
27 January (9 February) 1918	Treaty of Brest-Litovsk signed, leading to German and Austrian occupation of Ukraine; Donets-Kryvyi Rih Soviet Republic proclaimed in Kharkiv
12 (25) February 1918	Ukrainian People's Republic adopts Gregorian calendar as of 16 February (1 March), Central European time zone, and trident as official coat of arms
9 March 1918	Central Rada returns to Kyiv following expulsion of Bolshevik troops

24 March 1918	Ukrainian People's Republic publishes law making Ukrainian official language
26 April 1918	Ukrainian forces in Kyiv disarmed by German troops
29 April 1918	All-Ukrainian Agrarian Congress declares Pavlo Skoropadsky hetman; Central Rada deposed
21 May 1918	Ukrainian National-State Union established
2 June 1918	Germany and Austria-Hungary recognize Skoropadsky regime
16 October 1918	Austria proclaimed a federal state
18 October 1918	Ukrainian National Rada established in Lviv
30 October–11 November 1918	Collapse of Austria-Hungary
1 November 1918	Ukrainian National Rada declares Ukrainian state in Lviv; Ukrainian troops seize government buildings
1 November 1918–16 July 1919	Ukrainian-Polish War in Galicia
6 November 1918	Bukovyna joins Ukrainian People's Republic
11 November 1918	Romanian forces take Chernivtsi and proceed to occupy Bukovyna
13 November 1918	Western Ukrainian state formally constituted as Western Ukrainian People's Republic; Ukrainian Galician Army formed
15 November–14 December 1918	Anti-Skoropadsky rebellion
20 November 1918	Provisional Workers' and Peasants' Government of Ukraine established; second Bolshevik invasion of Ukraine begins
21 November 1918	Polish forces take Lviv
27 November 1918	Ukrainian Academy of Sciences established
14 December 1918	Skoropadsky resigns
15 December 1918	Directory of Ukrainian People's Republic takes power
18 January 1919	Paris Peace Conference begins
22 January 1919	Act of Union between Ukrainian People's Republic and Western Ukrainian People's Republic proclaimed in Kyiv
23–28 January 1919	Labor Congress of Ukraine
5 February 1919	Bolshevik forces take Kyiv
11 February 1919	Symon Petliura becomes head of Directory
8 May 1919	Central Ruthenian People's Council declares voluntary union of Transcarpathia with Czechoslovakia

9 June 1919	Yevhen Petrushevych appointed dictator of Western Ukrainian People's Republic
18 June 1919	Delegates from Azerbaijan, Estonia, Georgia, Latvia, North Caucasus, Belarus, and Ukraine protest decision of Paris Peace Conference to recognize Gen. Aleksandr Kolchak as head of Russian government and demand recognition of their independence
August 1919	White armies drive Bolsheviks out of Ukraine
10 September 1919	Treaty of Saint-Germain concerning dissolution of Austria-Hungary
6 December 1919–6 May 1920	First Winter Campaign of Army of Ukrainian People's Republic
8 December 1919	Curzon Line established as eastern border of Poland
December 1919	Third Bolshevik invasion; Kharkiv becomes capital of Soviet Ukraine
12 January 1920	Red Ukrainian Galician Army established
16 January 1920	Entente calls off economic blockade of Soviet government
21 April 1920	Treaty of Warsaw between Poland and Ukrainian People's Republic
25 April 1920	Beginning of Polish-Soviet War
6 May 1920	Ukrainian and Polish forces enter Kyiv
June–July 1920	Ukrainian and Polish forces retreat from Kyiv across Zbruch River
10 August 1920	Treaty of Sèvres awards Bukovyna to Romania
September 1920	Ukrainian Military Organization established in western Ukraine
17 January 1921	Ukrainian Free University opened in Vienna
18 March 1921	Treaty of Riga between Poland and Soviet Russia
8 May 1921	Transcarpathia annexed by Czechoslovakia
14–30 October 1921	Ukrainian Autocephalous Orthodox Church founded at First All-Ukrainian Orthodox Church Sobor in Kyiv
November 1921	Second Winter Campaign of Army of Ukrainian People's Republic
Autumn 1921–Summer 1923	Man-made famine in southern Ukraine claims between 1.5 and 2 million lives
30 December 1922	Soviet Union established
April 1923–November 1933	Ukrainization policy in effect in Ukrainian SSR

14 March 1923	Conference of Allied Ambassadors approves Poland's annexation of Galicia
31 July 1924	Polish government forbids use of Ukrainian in government institutions in Galicia
12 October 1924	Moldavian ASSR established within Ukrainian SSR
1925–1928	Literary discussion concerning modernization of Ukrainian literature and Ukraine's relations with Russia and Europe
1925–1931	Mass emigration from western Ukraine to South America
January 1926–28 January 1928	Vaplite literary organization active in Kharkiv
26 April 1926	Communist Party begins campaign against "national deviationism"
25 May 1926	Symon Petliura assassinated in Paris
29 September 1926	Kyivan Cave Monastery designated a national museum
2–9 December 1927	Communist Party congress in Moscow announces collectivization of agriculture
18 May–6 July 1928	Shakhty Trial in Moscow
September 1928	New standardized Ukrainian orthography adopted by Council of People's Commissars
28 January–3 February 1929	Organization of Ukrainian Nationalists established at founding congress in Vienna
1930	Beginning of official persecution of intelligentsia in Ukrainian SSR
28–29 January 1930	Ukrainian Autocephalous Orthodox Church abolished in Ukrainian SSR
9 March–19 April 1930	Show trial of Union for the Liberation of Ukraine in Kharkiv
8 April 1930	Premiere of Oleksander Dovzhenko's film *Zemlia*
21 September–16 October 1930	Repressive "Pacification" campaign in western Ukraine
April 1932–November 1933	Man-made famine kills 4–5 million in Ukrainian SSR and more than 1 million in North Caucasus
10 October 1932	Opening of Dnipro Hydroelectric Power Station in Zaporizhia; scientists at Kharkiv Physico-Technical Institute effect first nuclear reaction in USSR
January 1933	Pavel Postyshev takes over Communist Party of Ukraine as Stalin's personal representative; massive purge follows

13 May 1933	Former Vaplite leader Mykola Khvyliovy commits suicide
7 July 1933	Ukrainian communist leader Mykola Skrypnyk commits suicide
6 May 1934	Institute of Red Professors publicly criticized for failing to eliminate "Ukrainian bourgeois nationalism" from educational programs; purge of higher educational institutions follows
10 June 1934	Formation of GULAG (Main Administration of Labor Camps); in 1937–38, the GULAG had more than 10 million prisoners and accounted for 14 percent of Soviet industrial production
24 June 1934	Kyiv becomes capital of Ukrainian SSR
18 September 1934	USSR joins League of Nations; expelled on 14 December 1939
1934	Institute of Physical Chemistry first in USSR to produce heavy water
27–28 March 1935	Closed session of military collegium of USSR Supreme Court sentences a number of prominent Ukrainian writers to prison terms for allegedly creating a "counterrevolutionary underground organization of Borotbists"
19 July 1935	Communist Party of Ukraine orders removal of Zinovievite, Trotskyist, and nationalist literature from libraries
1937–1939	Height of Stalin regime's political terror
1 January 1938	Ukrainian government newspapers begin publishing in Russian
28 January 1938	Nikita Khrushchev appointed first secretary, Communist Party of Ukraine
20 April 1938	Study of Russian made obligatory in all schools in Ukrainian SSR
11 October 1938	Carpatho-Ukraine becomes autonomous
15 March 1939	Carpatho-Ukraine declares independence
15–18 March 1939	Hungary occupies Carpatho-Ukraine
23 August 1939	Molotov-Ribbentrop Pact of German-Soviet nonaggression
1 September 1939	Nazi Germany's invasion of Poland begins World War II
17 September 1939	Red Army invades Poland
26–28 October 1939	Western Ukraine annexed to Ukrainian SSR
28–30 June 1940	Red Army occupies Bessarabia and Bukovyna
22 June 1941	Nazi Germany invades USSR

Chronology • xlv

30 June 1941	Organization of Ukrainian Nationalists (Bandera faction) proclaims Ukrainian state in Lviv
1 August 1941	Distrikt Galizien established
30 August 1941	Transnistria established
1 September 1941–10 November 1944	Reichskommissariat Ukraine administered by Erich Koch in Rivne
19 September 1941	Red Army retreats from Kyiv after 72 days of fighting
29–30 September 1941	Beginning of mass execution of civilians by Nazis in Babyn Yar (Kyiv); more than 100,000 Jews, Ukrainians, and Russians killed
6 March–24 July 1942	First mass deportation of *Ostarbeiter* to Germany
22 June 1942	"Match of Death" between soccer team of German Luftwaffe and Dynamo Kyiv, which Dynamo won by a score of 5–3; after the match, four Dynamo players were arrested and executed
14 October 1942	Formation of Ukrainian Insurgent Army
1942–1944	Ukrainian-Polish conflict in western Ukrainian lands; tens of thousands of civilians killed
28 April 1943	Recruitment of Division Galizien begins in Lviv
3–13 November 1943	Red Army recaptures Kyiv with 417,000 casualties
18 January 1944	First major clash between Ukrainian Insurgent Army and NKVD forces
18 May 1944	Crimean Tatars deported from the Crimea
17–22 July 1944	Battle of Brody; Division Galizien largely destroyed by Red Army
26 November 1944	Transcarpathia annexed to Ukrainian SSR
4–11 February 1945	Yalta Conference
11 April 1945	Hierarchy of Ukrainian Catholic Church arrested
25 April–26 June 1945	Founding congress of United Nations Organization in San Francisco; Ukrainian SSR among founding members
9 May 1945	Surrender of Nazi Germany to USSR ends World War II in East European theater
8–10 March 1946	Council of Ukrainian Catholic Church organized by Soviet authorities in Lviv approves annulment of Union of Brest and union with Russian Orthodox Church
Autumn 1946–Summer 1947	Man-made famine in Ukrainian SSR claims more than 1 million lives
1946–48	Wave of official repression in literature, art, and scholarship

28 April–30 July 1947	Operation Vistula; some 140,000 Ukrainians deported to northwestern Poland
29 August 1949	Supreme Ukrainian Liberation Council orders cessation of struggle by Ukrainian Insurgent Army; sporadic resistance continues until mid-1950s
1949–1995	Shevchenko Scientific Society in Sarcelles, France, publishes 14-volume Ukrainian-language *Encyclopedia of Ukraine*
5 March 1950	Gen. Roman Shukhevych, commander in chief of Ukrainian Insurgent Army, killed in battle with Soviet secret police units near Lviv
5 March 1953	Death of Stalin
19 February 1954	The Crimea becomes part of Ukrainian SSR
26 March 1954	Oleksii Kyrychenko becomes first secretary, Communist Party of Ukraine, the first ethnic Ukrainian to hold that post since Dmytro Manuilsky (1921–22)
12 May 1954	Ukrainian SSR joins UNESCO and International Labor Organization
14–25 February 1956	Twentieth Congress of CPSU in Moscow; Nikita Khrushchev's secret speech denouncing Stalin's cult of personality
March–April 1956	Exiled Crimean Tatars form first groups to petition for right to return to their homeland
August 1956	Beginning of official rehabilitation of executed, exiled, and silenced Ukrainian activists
17 July 1958	Council of Ministers closes eight of the 40 active monasteries in Ukrainian SSR
15 October 1959	Nationalist leader Stepan Bandera assassinated by KGB agent in Munich
1959–1968	Publication of first edition of *Ukrainian Soviet Encyclopedia*
11–15 February 1963	Conference of scholars in Kyiv appeals to government to make Ukrainian the official language of Ukrainian SSR
1–2 July 1963	Petro Shelest becomes first secretary, Communist Party of Ukraine
14 October 1964	Nikita Khrushchev removed as first secretary of CPSU and replaced by Leonid Brezhnev
August–September 1965	First wave of arrests of Ukrainian intelligentsia (60 people arrested for "anti-Soviet" activities)

4 September 1965	Premiere of Serhii Paradzhanov's film *Shadows of Forgotten Ancestors* in Kyiv, accompanied by protests against arrests of Ukrainian intellectuals
December 1965	Ivan Dziuba sends copies of *Internationalism or Russification?* to heads of party and state (published in the West in 1968)
January–April 1966	Trials of 18 human-rights activists
20 April 1967	Viacheslav Chornovil completes compilation of *Lykho z rozumu* about Ukrainian political prisoners (published in the West in 1968)
April 1968	Letter of protest submitted by 139 scholars, scientists, writers, and artists to top government bodies against new wave of political repression
1970	Petro Shelest publishes *Ukraïno nasha Radians'ka* in Kyiv
1970–1980	Eleven-volume dictionary of Ukrainian language published in Kyiv
January–May 1972	More than 200 Ukrainian dissidents arrested
25 May 1972	Petro Shelest deposed as first secretary, Communist Party of Ukraine; replaced by Volodymyr Shcherbytsky
June 1973	Ukrainian Research Institute established at Harvard University
1 July 1976	Canadian Institute of Ukrainian Studies established at University of Alberta
9 November 1976	Ukrainian Helsinki Group founded in Kyiv
19–20 April 1978	New constitution of Ukrainian SSR adopted
15 August 1978	Council of Ministers of USSR issues resolution concerning enforcement of passport controls, providing for repressive measures against Crimean Tatars attempting to return to their homeland
1984–1985	Ukrainian SSR a member of UN Security Council
11 March 1985	Mikhail Gorbachev elected general secretary of CC CPSU; beginning of *glasnost* and *perestroika*
26 April 1986	Disaster at Chornobyl nuclear power plant
10 June 1988	State commission to study demands of Crimean Tatars announces lifting of all restrictions
June–August 1988	Celebration of millennium of Christianization of Kyivan Rus'
8–10 September 1989	Founding congress of Popular Movement of Ukraine (*Rukh*)

28 September 1989	Volodymyr Shcherbytsky deposed as first secretary, Communist Party of Ukraine; replaced by Volodymyr Ivashko
28 October 1989	Verkhovna Rada of Ukrainian SSR gives Ukrainian status as official language
16 July 1990	Declaration of State Sovereignty of Ukraine
23 July 1990	Leonid Kravchuk elected head of Verkhovna Rada of Ukrainian SSR, replacing Volodymyr Ivashko, who resigned
2–4 August 1990	Celebration of 500th anniversary of Ukrainian Cossackdom
2–17 October 1990	Hunger strikes in Kyiv by students demanding political reform
23 October 1990	Verkhovna Rada of Ukrainian SSR abolishes article 6 of constitution concerning leading role of Communist Party in society and accepts resignation of Vitalii Masol, chairman of Council of Ministers
16 January 1991	Pope John Paul II reestablishes Ukrainian Catholic and Roman Catholic ecclesiastical hierarchies in Ukraine
12 February 1991	Restoration of Crimean ASSR
27 June 1991	Verkhovna Rada of Ukrainian SSR postpones discussion of agreement concerning Union of Sovereign Republics proposed by Mikhail Gorbachev to study its compatibility with Ukraine's Declaration of State Sovereignty
19–21 August 1991	Attempted coup by hard-line communist officials in Moscow
24 August 1991	Ukraine declares independence
24 October 1991	Ukraine declares its intention to become a non-nuclear state
1 December 1991	Referendum on independence: 90.3 percent of electorate in favor; Leonid Kravchuk elected president
8 December 1991	Belarus, Russia, and Ukraine establish Commonwealth of Independent States, bringing USSR to an end
1 January 1992	Introduction of *kupon* as provisional currency
30 January 1992	Ukraine joins Organization for Security and Cooperation in Europe
10 March 1992	Ukraine joins North Atlantic Cooperation Council

Chronology • xlix

5 April 1992	Presidential decree proclaims Black Sea Fleet a constituent of Ukraine's armed forces
5 May 1992	Crimean parliament declares independence
6 May 1992	Crimean parliament ratifies Constitution of Republic of the Crimea, sections of which conflict with Constitution of Ukraine
September 1992	Crimean constitution brought into conformity with Constitution of Ukraine
13 October 1992–21 September 1993	Government of Prime Minister Leonid Kuchma
9 July 1993	Supreme Soviet of Russia lays claim to Sevastopol as a Russian city
20 July 1993	UN Security Council declares that Russia's claim to Sevastopol has no legal basis
3 September 1993	Massandra Protocol concerning division of Black Sea Fleet; accord not ratified by Verkhovna Rada
18 November 1993	Verkhovna Rada ratifies START-1 and Lisbon Protocol (with reservations)
14 January 1994	Ukraine, Russia, and United States sign agreement concerning elimination of nuclear weapons in Ukraine
3 February 1994	Verkhovna Rada withdraws its reservations concerning START-1
8 February 1994	Ukraine joins NATO Partnership for Peace program
23 March 1994	Agreement concerning partnership and cooperation between Ukraine and European Union
27 March 1994	Elections to Verkhovna Rada
15 April 1994	Ukraine joins CIS Economic Union as associate member
20 May 1994	Crimean parliament restores its constitution (6 May 1992 redaction); Verkhovna Rada gives Crimean parliament 10 days to bring its constitution into conformity with Constitution of Ukraine
16 June 1994–4 April 1995	Government of Prime Minister Vitalii Masol
10 July 1994	Leonid Kuchma elected president
7 September–5 October 1994	Crimean constitutional crisis
5 December 1994	Ukraine signs Nuclear Non-Proliferation Treaty
17 March 1995	Verkhovna Rada and president annul Crimean constitution and abolish post of president of the Crimea

l • Chronology

1 June 1995	Signing of provisional trade agreement between Ukraine and European Union (EU)
8 June 1995–27 May 1996	Government of Prime Minister Yevhen Marchuk
9 June 1995	Ukrainian-Russian summit concerning division of Black Sea Fleet
19 October 1995	Ukraine joins Council of Europe
28 May 1996–2 July 1997	Government of Prime Minister Pavlo Lazarenko
30 May 1996	Last strategic warheads removed from Ukraine
28 June 1996	New constitution adopted
2 September 1996	New currency—the *hryvnia*—introduced
28 May 1997	Accord concerning division of Black Sea Fleet gives Russia 82 percent of ships and use of two naval bases in the Crimea
31 May 1997	Ten-year political treaty signed between Ukraine and Russia, whereby Russia recognizes Ukraine's territorial integrity
9 July 1997	Ukraine and 16 NATO leaders sign charter on "Distinctive Partnership between NATO and Ukraine"
16 July 1997–22 December 1999	Government of Prime Minister Valerii Pustovoitenko
16 September 1997	Minister of Foreign Affairs Hennadii Udovenko elected president of UN General Assembly
24 September 1997	New electoral law passed, instituting election of one-half of Verkhovna Rada deputies in single-mandate districts and the other half by proportional vote from party lists
19 November 1997	Astronaut Leonid Kadeniuk participates in flight of Columbia space shuttle
14 January 1998	Verkhovna Rada ratifies Treaty of Friendship, Cooperation and Partnership with Russia
1 March 1998	Partnership and Cooperation Agreement between EU and Ukraine comes into effect
29 March 1998	Elections to Verkhovna Rada
22 April 1998	Former National Bank head Vadym Hetman assassinated
19 February 1999	Former prime minister Pavlo Lazarenko arrested in United States
3 March 1999	Ukraine joins CIS Inter-Parliamentary Assembly
25 March 1999	Opposition leader Viacheslav Chornovil killed in automobile accident

14 October 1999	Ukraine elected to two-year term on UN Security Council (2000–1)
14 November 1999	Leonid Kuchma reelected president
3 December 1999	Presidential decree abolishing collective farms
22 December 1999–28 May 2001	Government of Prime Minister Viktor Yushchenko
January 2000	Parliamentary crisis
22 February 2000	Death penalty abolished
16 April 2000	Referendum on constitutional amendments gives president greater powers
16 September 2000	Abduction of investigative journalist Heorhii Gongadze, later found to have been murdered
15 December 2000	Chornobyl nuclear power plant closed
25 January 2001	Council of Europe condemns lack of freedom of expression in Ukraine
3 February 2001	Ukraine's last TU-160 strategic bomber decommissioned
9 March 2001	Violent antigovernment demonstrations in Kyiv calling for resignation of President Kuchma
29 May 2001–16 November 2002	Government of Prime Minister Anatolii Kinakh
7 June 2001	Signing of GUUAM charter
23–27 June 2001	Pope John Paul II visits Ukraine
25 October 2001	Land Code legalizes private ownership of land as of 1 January 2005
30 October 2001	Last ICBM missile silo destroyed
31 March 2002	Elections to Verkhovna Rada
18 April 2002	Poland officially expresses regret over Operation Vistula
16 September 2002	Mass antigovernment protests in connection with Gongadze case
21 November 2002	Viktor Yanukovych appointed prime minister
22 November 2002	New NATO-Ukraine action plan introduced
28 January 2003	Delimitation of Russo-Ukrainian land border completed
9 March 2003	Mass antigovernment protests
11 March 2003	European Commission adopts Communication on Wider Europe-Neighborhoods, outlining foreign-policy strategy for countries sharing borders with EU following its expansion in 2004
11 July 2003	Joint Polish-Ukrainian commemoration of 60th anniversary of atrocities in Volhynia

19 September 2003	Agreement on proposed creation of Common Economic Space encompassing Belarus, Kazakhstan, Russia, and Ukraine
31 October 2003	Mobs prevent Viktor Yushchenko's bloc, Our Ukraine, from holding rally in Donetsk
10 November 2003	Twenty-six UN member states cosponsor declaration commemorating famine of 1932–33
24 November 2003	By unconstitutional show of hands, Verkhovna Rada approves bill coauthored by Viktor Medvedchuk and Petro Symonenko giving parliament the right to elect the president of Ukraine
3 February 2004	Following protests by deputies and criticism by Parliamentary Assembly of the Council of Europe, Verkhovna Rada withdraws provision for parliamentary election of president of Ukraine
3 March 2004	Radio Kontynent, Kyiv affiliate of Radio Free Europe/Radio Liberty, abruptly closed by Ukrainian authorities
9 March 2004	Mass demonstration for freedom of the press held in Kyiv; Viktor Yushchenko and Yuliia Tymoshenko address crowd
19 March 2004	Verkhovna Rada passes law on presidential elections, imposing spending limits and reducing length of campaign
15 April 2004	Ernest Nuser declared mayor of Mukacheve following election marked by intimidation and fraud
28 May 2004	Ernest Nuser resigns as mayor of Mukacheve, citing threats against himself and his family
14 June 2004	Major steel producer Kryvorizhstal sold to consortium headed by Rinat Akhmetov and Viktor Pinchuk amid allegations that foreign bidders were shut out
4 July 2004	Viktor Yushchenko announces his presidential candidacy in Kyiv before crowd of almost 50,000
31 October 2004	First round of voting in presidential election. Central Electoral Commission announces plurality for Yushchenko (39.87 percent)

21 November 2004	Runoff election between Viktor Yushchenko and Viktor Yanukovych. Massive electoral fraud reported; Yushchenko camp calls for national strike
22 November 2004	Orange Revolution begins. Huge crowds gather in central Kyiv to protest electoral fraud. Occupation of Khreshchatyk and Independence Square by demonstrators begins. Pro-Yushchenko demonstrations begin in other cities and towns
24 November 2004	Central Electoral Commission announces victory for Yanukovych (49.46 percent to Yushchenko's 46.61 percent). Demonstrators denounce result as fraudulent and refuse to disperse. Major Western governments refuse to accept results. President Vladimir Putin of Russia congratulates Yanukovych on victory before announcement of results
26 November 2004	European mediators, led by Javier Solana (EU head of foreign and security policy) and President Aleksander Kwaśniewski of Poland, meet with Kuchma, Yanukovych, and Yushchenko. Draft agreement on constitutional reform approved
3 December 2004	Supreme Court unanimously upholds Yushchenko's appeal against electoral fraud and decrees repeat of runoff election
8 December 2004	Verkhovna Rada approves changes to electoral law intended to combat fraud; adopts constitutional reforms reducing presidential powers and increasing those of the prime minister
26 December 2004	Runoff election repeated under scrutiny of unprecedented numbers of observers. Yushchenko wins 51.99 percent of vote; Yanukovych takes 44.20 percent (results officially announced on 10 January 2005)
31 December 2004	Viktor Yanukovych resigns as prime minister
23 January 2005	Viktor Yushchenko inaugurated as third president of independent Ukraine

Introduction

The name "Ukraine" (*Ukraïna*), which means "borderland," is first encountered in a chronicle reference to a 12th-century military campaign. It did not become a generally accepted designation for the whole territory inhabited by Ukrainians until the early 20th century. As late as 1944, the American journalist William Henry Chamberlin could write in *The Ukraine: A Submerged Nation*: "There is a Ukrainian language, a Ukrainian culture, a Ukrainian historical tradition. . . . But efforts to organize an independent Ukraine . . . have always been frustrated."

Almost half a century later, in August 1991, Ukraine proclaimed its independence, which was overwhelmingly ratified by referendum in December of that year. The Soviet Union, of which the Ukrainian SSR had been a constituent since its establishment in 1922, had been foundering since the late 1980s; at the end of 1991, the Union formally ceased to exist. The new Ukrainian Republic, with a territory of 603,700 sq. km, was now the largest state on the continent of Europe, exceeded in size only by European Russia.

To much of the world, the appearance of a Ukrainian state was a political novelty; indeed, a recent survey by an English scholar refers to Ukraine as an "unexpected nation." Yet the political and ethnocultural roots of Ukraine reach back more than a thousand years. Kyivan Rus', the medieval state with which Ukrainian history begins (and from which Belarus and Russia also claim descent) flourished as a Slavic branch of Byzantine Christian civilization. It was founded in the ninth century along the middle course of the Dnipro River, and the city of Kyiv became its center. The grand princes of Kyiv brought many of the East Slavic tribes under their authority, extending their rule over a wide area. After initial conflicts with the Byzantine Empire, they established commercial relations with it, and in the late ninth century Prince Volodymyr formally accepted Byzantine Christianity as the religion of the Kyivan state. Rus' reached its apogee under Prince Yaroslav the Wise (1019–54), who established dynastic ties with major European powers, initiated the codification of Rus' law, promoted Kyivan learning, and began the construction of the great Cathedral of St. Sophia. No adequate system of succession to the Kyivan throne was developed after Yaroslav's death. Rus' entered a period of decline and succumbed to the Mongol conquest of the mid-13th century. The western Principality of Galicia-Volhynia continued Rus' traditions for another century, but it was divided between Poland and Lithuania in the 1340s.

Over the next two centuries, Poland and Lithuania contended for supremacy in eastern Europe, with Poland emerging as the senior partner of the Polish-Lithuanian Commonwealth (established by the Union of Lublin in 1569). Although the Rus' chancery language and legal traditions continued under Lithuanian rule, this was a period of decline for Rus' society, culture, and religion. The Rus' nobiliary elite assimilated to Polish culture and Roman Catholicism in large numbers. It was the rise of Cossackdom in the 16th century, as well as an Orthodox revival, that laid the foundations for the emergence of early modern Ukraine.

The Ukrainian Cossacks, who included peasants, townsmen, seasonal workers, and nobles without property, developed into a military caste that defended the Ukrainian lands against the incessant raids of the Crimean Tatars and the Ottoman Turks. The Cossacks built their headquarters beyond the Dnipro Rapids (in Ukrainian, *za porohamy*, from which the name "Zaporozhian Cossacks" is derived). The Polish authorities sought to control the Cossacks by establishing a register of those in official service, but their numbers were dwarfed by the constant influx of new recruits, mainly peasants escaping the harsh conditions of Polish serfdom. From the late 16th century, Cossack revolts against Polish rule gathered strength. The largest of them, led in 1648 by Bohdan Khmelnytsky, ended Polish rule on the Left (east) Bank of the Dnipro and established a new Cossack polity, the Hetmanate, which remained semi-autonomous until the late 18th century. Khmelnytsky's need for allies against the Poles led him to conclude the Pereiaslav Agreement (1654) with Tsar Aleksei Mikhailovich, whereby Cossack Ukraine came under a Muscovite protectorate. Khmelnytsky himself found this arrangement restrictive, and his successors sought alliances by turns with the Ottomans, the Crimean Khanate, Poland, and Sweden in an effort to maintain their independence.

The fate of the Cossacks was closely intertwined with that of the Orthodox Church. The Counter-Reformation, led in Poland by the Jesuits, produced strong assimilative pressure on the Ukrainian Orthodox, leading to the church Union of Brest in 1596. Under its terms, part of the Orthodox hierarchy agreed to the establishment of a Uniate Church under the authority of Rome. Although it was theoretically equal in rights with the Roman Catholic Church, in practice such equality was never recognized, while Orthodoxy was effectively proscribed. The Union of Brest split the Orthodox community, whose defenders produced an extensive polemical literature and organized church brotherhoods, but it was not until 1620, at the initiative and under the protection of the Cossacks, that a new Orthodox hierarchy was consecrated in Kyiv. The Polish government found itself constrained to recognize the revived Orthodox Church and permit the appointment of a new metropolitan, Petro Mohyla (1633–47), who led a major reform of Orthodox doctrine and ecclesiastical literature. He also established a school that grew into the Kyiv Mohyla Academy, a major center of East European learning. But Mohyla and his circle of learned clergymen, strongly influenced by Jesuit education and Western religious trends, never reached an entente with the Cossacks. In 1685, the Ukrainian Orthodox Church came under Russian ecclesiastical authority and remained subject to it until 1918.

In the wake of Khmelnytsky's death, as contending powers maneuvered for control of Ukraine and backed rival Cossack hetmans, the Ukrainian lands were divided along the Dnipro River by the Truce of Andrusovo (1667), whereby Muscovy took the Left Bank and Poland the Right. The last armed insurrection intended to win the sovereignty of the Hetmanate was led in 1708–9 by Hetman Ivan Mazepa, who allied himself with Charles XII of Sweden. The Cossack and Swedish forces were defeated by Peter I at the Battle of Poltava, and Mazepa was formally anathematized by the Orthodox Church. Muscovy, which formally became the Russian Empire in 1721, proceeded to strengthen its hold on the Hetmanate, abolishing the office of hetman and establishing the Little Russian Collegium as its ruling body. Controls over the Hetmanate's administration and economy were tightened, and even the printing of Ukrainian books became subject to Russian censorship. By means of official appointments and land grants, the Cossack officer elite was largely integrated into the Russian nobility. Catherine II destroyed the Zaporozhian Cossack fortress in 1775 and abolished the Hetmanate in the 1780s, subjecting the Ukrainian peasantry to serfdom. This period also saw the imperial conquest of the Crimea and the beginning of the large-scale settlement of southern Ukraine, partly by immigrants such as Germans, Serbs, and Greeks.

The three partitions of Poland (1772, 1793, 1795) brought most of Ukraine under Russian control, while Austria took over the western Ukrainian lands of Galicia and Bukovyna. Seeking to curtail the strong Polish influence in western Ukraine, the Habsburg rulers Maria Theresa and Joseph II promoted the revival of the Uniate Church (renaming it the Greek Catholic Church because of its Byzantine rite) and established institutions to educate its clergy. In the course of the 19th century, the Greek Catholic Church and its clergy became the mainstay of a new Ukrainian national movement in Galicia; Bukovyna, which remained Orthodox, evolved more slowly in that regard. The Revolution of 1848 in Galicia led to the formation of the Supreme Ruthenian Council, which called for the administrative division of Galicia into western (Polish) and eastern (Ukrainian) provinces. This became a standard programmatic demand of the national movement in Galicia, which developed strongly and became increasingly secular after 1867, when the Habsburg Monarchy introduced a constitutional regime. Educational and scholarly societies, cooperatives, newspapers, publishing houses, and paramilitary associations promoted the Ukrainian cause in the course of the half-century preceding World War I.

In the Ukrainian lands under Russian rule, by contrast, the leadership of the national movement passed from the largely Russified Cossack elite to the intelligentsia (writers of the Kharkiv school; the Cyril and Methodius Brotherhood), only to encounter official suppression. The Valuev circular (1863) and the Ems Ukase (1876) forbade publishing in Ukraine, while Russian became the language of schooling and administration. The rapid industrialization of Russian-ruled Ukraine in the late 19th century, notably the development of coal mining in the Donets Basin and the production of iron ore near Kryvyi Rih, was accompanied by an influx of Russian workers; Russians were also dominant in the cities. Many Ukrainian peasants preferred to migrate thousands of miles east in order to farm unoccupied land than face the highly exploitative conditions of factory work. Not until 1905, when popular revolt forced the tsarist government to proclaim a constitution, was the Ukrainian national movement able to develop in the Russian Empire—a development cut short less than a decade later by World War I.

At the outbreak of war, the Galician Ukrainians overwhelmingly took the Austrian side, and their volunteer military formation, the Ukrainian Sich Riflemen, fought in the Austrian ranks in the hope of establishing a distinct Galician crown land (if not an independent state). When the Habsburg Monarchy collapsed in late 1918, the Galicians founded the Western Ukrainian People's Republic (ZUNR), and the Ukrainian Galician Army fought greatly superior Polish forces until mid-1919 for the republic's independence. In the east, the revolution of February 1917 in Petrograd and the downfall of the Romanov dynasty led to the formation of a representative body, the Ukrainian Central Rada, in Kyiv, but it was not supported by a social consensus of the kind that prevailed in Galicia. The Central Rada favored a federalist reform of the Russian Empire, but the Bolshevik coup of October 1917, followed soon afterward by a Bolshevik invasion of Ukraine, led the Rada to declare the independence of the Ukrainian People's Republic (UNR) in January 1918. The attempt of Bukovynian Ukrainians to join the UNR was cut short by a Romanian invasion. An act of union between the UNR and the ZUNR in January 1919 proved more a declaration of intent than a true political merger.

The short-lived republic was followed by the German-sponsored regime of Hetman Pavlo Skoropadsky (April-November 1918), which in turn was overthrown by a Directory that revived the UNR. But the Directory's armed forces, composed mainly of peasants, soon dispersed to their villages. The peasants, whose principal demand was landownership, were influenced more by independent warlords than by the Directory; they were also swayed by Bolshevik promises of ending the landlords' dominance. This chaotic situation was further complicated by the Russian White armies, which sought to restore the imperial order. It took two more Bolshevik invasions, in 1918 and 1919, to establish a Soviet regime on the Ukrainian territories of the former Russian Empire. The Polish-Soviet War of 1920 brought the Red Army almost to the gates of Warsaw, raising the possibility that the western Ukrainian lands would also be Sovietized, but the subsequent Polish victory staved off that prospect for almost two decades. Under the terms of the Treaty of Riga (1921) between Poland and Soviet Russia, Galicia and western Volhynia (the latter a tsarist possession after the partitions of Poland) were annexed to the Second Polish Republic. The overwhelming majority of the Ukrainian lands were constituted as the Ukrainian Socialist Soviet Republic (as it was known until 1937, when the middle terms of the name were reversed), while Bukovyna remained under Romanian rule, and Transcarpathia became part of the new Czechoslovak Republic.

During the 1920s, the Ukrainian SSR enjoyed considerable autonomy within the newly established Union of Soviet Socialist Republics. The revolution had produced an upsurge of nationalism throughout the non-Russian areas of the former tsarist empire, and the Soviet authorities in Moscow compromised with it by adopting a policy of "indigenization" (*korenizatsiia*) in the non-Russian republics. In the Ukrainian SSR, where this policy was known as "Ukrainization," it amounted to nation-building under communist auspices. The party and government in Kharkiv (which remained the Soviet Ukrainian capital until 1934) adopted measures that sharply increased the Ukrainian presence in cities and institutions; education, publishing, and the mass media were also Ukrainized at a rapid rate. Ukrainization was even tolerated by Joseph Stalin (a centralist by conviction, as he had made plain in the debates leading up to the formation of the Soviet Union), because he needed the support of the Ukrainian party apparatus during his struggle for power in Moscow.

In 1928, when Stalin became sufficiently powerful to revoke his tacit compromise with the Ukrainian party, his regime launched a two-pronged counterattack on Ukrainization. The collectivization of agriculture—a protracted struggle to do away with individual peasant farms—was ultimately enforced by a man-made famine that took the lives of some five million Ukrainian peasants in 1932–33. Since the peasantry was also the principal source of cadres for the national movement, the famine was a crushing blow to Ukrainization. The other aspect of Stalin's policy was the destruction of autonomous Ukrainian institutions, ranging from the

Ukrainian Orthodox Church to the Communist Party of Ukraine, accompanied by the wholesale slaughter of Ukrainian intellectuals on charges of anti-Soviet activity. By the late 1930s, a policy of Russification was in place, and the existence of the Ukrainian SSR was so tenuous that there was talk in Stalin's circles of abolishing it entirely as an administrative unit.

In Galicia, official efforts to Polonize the Ukrainian population were strongly resisted by society at large and by an armed underground, the Ukrainian Military Organization, which was succeeded in 1929 by the highly influential Organization of Ukrainian Nationalists (OUN). Since the ultimate goal of the OUN was the establishment of an independent Ukrainian state, a cause to which the Western democracies were indifferent or opposed, the organization looked to Germany as its likeliest source of support. That hope was dashed after the outbreak of the Nazi-Soviet conflict in June 1941, when the Germans reacted to the OUN's declaration of Ukrainian independence by arresting its leaders and hunting down its cadres. In western Ukraine, the OUN gave rise to the Ukrainian Insurgent Army, which fought both German and Soviet forces in a struggle described by the American political scientist John A. Armstrong as "very probably . . . the most important example of forceful resistance to Communist rule." A self-defeating aspect of the conflict was the intense Ukrainian-Polish struggle for control of western Ukraine, which took the lives of many thousands of innocent civilians. Ultimately, forced postwar transfers of population eliminated this fundamental source of enmity between Poland and Ukraine. Political dissidents who supported independence for the two countries came to realize their need for cooperation in putting an end to Soviet rule.

For the Ukrainian SSR, the Second World War was a disaster even worse than that of the 1930s. Ukraine was the main battleground of the war in the east, suffering tremendous destruction as the German and Soviet armies advanced and retreated across its territory by turns. Ukrainian civilian and prisoner-of-war deaths have been estimated at 5.2 million, while Red Army casualties in Ukraine totaled some 3.5 million, with Ukrainians accounting for 50–70 percent of them. After the war, the Stalin regime was intent on annexing all Ukrainian territory to the Ukrainian SSR so as to eliminate any possible base for the independence movement: western Ukraine, Transcarpathia, and Bukovyna were accordingly detached from Poland, Czechoslovakia, and Romania. Ukraine and Belarus also became founding members of the United Nations as a result of Stalin's bid to increase Soviet voting power in the organization.

The post-Stalin regime in Moscow treated the Ukrainian SSR as a reliable subordinate well integrated into the USSR (with the exception of the newly acquired western territories). Stalin's successor, Nikita Khrushchev, had headed the Communist Party of Ukraine for 11 years and continued to rely on it as a source of support. The 300th anniversary of the Pereiaslav Agreement was celebrated with great pomp in 1954 as marking the "reunion of Ukraine with Russia," and the Crimea was transferred from Russian to Ukrainian jurisdiction in the same year, apparently for economic reasons.

Fissures began to appear in the 1960s, when the rapidly expanding Communist Party of Ukraine, led by the assertive Petro Shelest, sought a greater share of authority and resources. A significant number of Ukrainian intellectuals, emboldened by the cultural "thaw" of the Khrushchev period, demanded an end to Russification and called on the party to promote the Ukrainian language and culture. The more prominent dissidents were arrested and sentenced to terms of imprisonment and forced labor, but Khrushchev's successor, Leonid Brezhnev, remained apprehensive about Shelest's intentions. When Shelest celebrated the achievements of his republic and party in a book titled *O Ukraine, Our Soviet Land*, published exclusively in Ukrainian in a press run of 100,000 copies, Brezhnev abruptly replaced him with the pliable Volodymyr Shcherbytsky, who made a point of using only Russian in his public pronouncements. Shcherbytsky's appointment was accompanied by a thoroughgoing purge of "nationalists" in Ukrainian institutions. Even the advent of Mikhail Gorbachev's *perestroika* did not shake the Shcherbytsky regime: concerned about the stability of Ukraine, Gorbachev kept the aged first secretary of the Ukrainian party in power until 1989.

Gorbachev's political reforms had the unintended effect of destabilizing the Soviet Union, provoking a desperate attempt to overthrow him in August 1991. Ukraine declared its independence on 24 August, in the immediate aftermath of the unsuccessful coup. Alarmed by the possibility of further attempts at centralization, Ukraine's ruling elite made haste to cut its ties with Moscow and take over the mantle of national leadership from the dissident movement. Once the declaration of independence was ratified by referendum in December, the former head of the ideology department of the Communist Party of Ukraine, Leonid Kravchuk, was elected president. He went on to represent himself as a guarantor of Ukraine's national security and stability, thereby coopting part of the dissident movement and dividing his opposition. This sudden about-face by the Ukrainian party and government, so rigidly subordinate to Moscow until 1989, highlights one of post-communist Ukraine's major political problems—the continuing dominance of its Soviet-era elite. Unused to autonomous decision-making or to democratic procedures, and lacking serious commitment to a distinct Ukrainian identity, the former Soviet apparatus has clung to its old practices, hindering the development of an independent nation and state. Although a number of prerequisites to democratic rule have been put in place—a national parliament, the Verkhovna Rada; a constitution; a national currency and state bank; a judicial system, and so on—the presidential administration holds the plenitude of power, while civil society is having a difficult time establishing itself. This conflict was dramatized by the murder of the investigative journalist Heorhii Gongadze in the autumn of 2000, an unsolved case in which Kravchuk's successor, President Leonid Kuchma, was implicated, leading to widespread demands for his impeachment. The political opposition in Ukraine, as well as foreign governments, human-rights organizations, and media, have expressed continuing concern about the suppression of press freedom, electoral fraud, and governmental corruption.

The state of the Ukrainian economy presents another barrier to democratization. The fall of the Soviet Union was accompanied by large-scale illegal "privatization" of resources on the part of well-placed individuals and groups, leading to tremendous economic disparity. Like the Russian economy, that of Ukraine is dominated by a few very rich "oligarchs" and their associated "clans," while the average professional subsists on an official salary of some U.S. $150 per month. Given the chronic nonpayment of taxes, the treasury of independent Ukraine has lacked resources to guarantee the regular payment of civil-service salaries and old-age pensions or to supply basic social services; thus, the population of Ukraine declined from 51.9 million in 1989 to 48.4 million in 2001. There are two principal compensating factors: after a period of galloping inflation in the latter part of Kravchuk's mandate, the Kuchma government introduced the *hryvnia* as the national currency and managed to keep its value relatively stable; moreover, in the last several years, Ukraine's GDP has grown very significantly, attaining 5.9 percent in 2000, 9.2 percent in 2001, and 4.6 percent in 2002 according to official figures. Yet even official sources acknowledge the existence of widespread corruption and legal irregularities that make it difficult for legitimate businesses to function and discourage foreign investment. Thus, Ukraine lacks the well-established middle class indispensable to a democratic political order.

A third obstacle to Ukraine's functioning as a modern democratic state is its lack of national unity. As a result of three centuries of Russian rule over most of its territory, including some 50 years of mass Russification under the Stalin regime and its successors, eastern and southern Ukraine is largely Russian-speaking, even though more than three-quarters of the general population (77.8 percent, according to the 2001 census) consists of ethnic Ukrainians. As a result of the historical factors noted above, western Ukraine is the most culturally Ukrainian part of the country, followed by the central region. The constitution of 1996 established Ukrainian as the country's sole official language, despite insistent appeals to give Russian equal status, and Ukrainian-language education is making headway, but the electronic and print media function overwhelmingly in Russian, given Russia's greatly advantageous economy of scale and unrestricted access to the Ukrainian market. Citing the need for "ethnic harmony," the government has shown little interest in promoting the Ukrainian language and culture so as to bring its actual condition into line with its constitutional status.

As the 21st century begins, it appears increasingly likely that the evolution of Ukrainian politics and society will be determined by the trend of developments in Europe. The accession of Poland, Slovakia, and Hungary to the European Union in 2004 brought Ukraine into direct contact with the EU, strengthening pressure on the government to translate its declared commitment to Ukraine's "European choice" into political action. Ukraine's increasing openness to foreign contacts and information, as well as the aspiration of its people to a European standard of living, are breaking down the isolation that has long held the country's progress in check.

* * *

This book had been submitted for publication when Ukraine was overtaken by the Orange Revolution of November and December 2004, which focused unprecedented world attention on this nation. The revolution hinged on the presidential election of autumn 2004, in which the leading candidates were the incumbent prime minister, Viktor Yanukovych, and the former head of the National Bank of Ukraine, Viktor Yushchenko, who had also served as prime minister (1999–2001). Yushchenko's campaign color gave the revolution its name.

The first round of voting, held on 31 October, produced no majority for any candidate, although the Central Electoral Commission announced on 10 November that Yushchenko had taken 39.87 percent of the vote as compared with 39.32 percent for Yanukovych. Yushchenko's support was concentrated mainly in the west and center of the country, including the capital, while Yanukovych dominated the east and south. The International Election Observation Mission reported that the election "did not meet a considerable number of OSCE [Organization for Security and Cooperation in Europe], Council of Europe and other European standards for democratic elections."

The critical runoff election between Yushchenko and Yanukovych was held on 21 November. It was immediately apparent from many observers' reports that there had been massive electoral fraud in eastern and southern Ukraine, intended to secure a victory that Yanukovych, the candidate of the "party of power," was unable to obtain at the ballot box. (Yanukovych was backed by the outgoing president, Leonid Kuchma, as well as by President Vladimir Putin of Russia.) The OSCE statement issued on 22 November concluded that, as in the first round, the state executive authorities and the Central Electoral Commission had shown a lack of will to conduct a genuine democratic election. Among the abuses noted in that statement were intimidation, attempts to influence voters, the use of absentee voter certificates and a higher incidence of mobile voting than in the first round (to increase the Yanukovych vote), dismissal of election observers, interference in electoral procedures by unauthorized officials (including police and local government representatives), inattention to ballot security and counting procedures, and isolated incidents of violence. Other observers reported the destruction of ballots or the use of disappearing ink to mark them, multiple voting, pressure on civil servants, workers, and students by their superiors in order to influence their vote, inaccurate voter lists, busloads of people being driven to various locations to vote several times, electricity shutoffs, beatings of media representatives, and the like.

Yushchenko and his supporters announced a national strike to prevent the electoral fraud from succeeding. In scale, immediacy, and determination, the public response dwarfed anything seen in the late 1980s and early 1990s, when the demise of the Soviet Union and the birth of Ukrainian independence had been attended by a great deal of spontaneous public activity. There had also been major antigovernment demonstrations during Kuchma's second term, but these, too, paled in comparison with the massive protest of 2004. A crowd estimated at 100,000 promptly filled the main street of Kyiv, Khreshchatyk, and its focal point, Independence Square (*Maidan Nezalezhnosty*). A tent city went up on Khreshchatyk and occupied it for almost two months. Independence Square became the scene of continuous political speeches, rock concerts, and crowds chanting "Yu-shchen-ko," while the wave of demonstrators continued to swell (at their peak, their numbers were estimated at half a million). Demonstrations in support of Yushchenko also took place in many western and central towns, as well as in Kharkiv, Sumy, Poltava, Dnipropetrovsk, Mykolaiv, and Odesa. Yushchenko symbolically took the oath of presidential office on 23 November; his supporters surrounded government buildings, interrupting official business and forcing Leonid Kuchma to withdraw to a villa in Koncha-Zaspa, a recreational area south of Kyiv.

The government sought to end the crisis quickly by having the head of the 15-member Central Electoral Commission announce on 24 November that Yanukovych had won the election with 49.46 percent of the vote to Yushchenko's 46.61 percent (four commission members refused to endorse the result). When this had no effect on the crowds, the use of force may have been contemplated and perhaps even ordered. According to the *Financial Times* (London, 13 December), on 28 November both Viktor Medvedchuk, the head of the presidential administration, and Viktor Yanukovych urged President Kuchma to use troops, who were issued live ammunition, to disperse the crowds. The *New York Times* (17 January 2005) reported that on the night of 28 November more than 10,000 Interior Ministry troops wielding shields and clubs (3,000 of them carrying guns) scrambled to end the demonstration, but the plan was foiled by powerful dissident elements in the Security Service of Ukraine. Whatever the accuracy of these reports, no violent clash took place, although riot police came out in full force to seal off key government buildings.

The Kuchma administration came under increasing international pressure as the European Union and the governments of such countries as the United States, Canada, and Australia denounced the election as fraudulent. The political crisis was defused with the help of a mission comprised of five foreign mediators: Javier Solana, head of foreign and security policy for the EU; Jan Kubis, secretary general of the OSCE; President Aleksander Kwaśniewski of Poland; President Valdas Adamkus of Lithuania; and Boris Gryzlov, head of the Russian State Duma. Their joint meeting with Kuchma, Yanukovych, and Yushchenko on 26 November laid the basis for a compromise involving a rebalancing of powers between the presidency and the Verkhovna Rada (Supreme Council or parliament).

Before parliament met to consider the constitutional reform, Yushchenko won a stunning legal and political victory: on 3 December, the Supreme Court unanimously upheld his appeal against election fraud in the second round and decreed a repeat of the runoff to be held on 26 December. The Verkhovna Rada met on 8 December and enacted reforms to Ukraine's electoral laws in order to help prevent fraudulent practices. By an overwhelming majority, it also adopted a package of constitutional amendments (to take effect in late 2005) that significantly reduced the powers of the presidency and increased those of the prime minister, who would now be in a position to control the legislative and budgetary agenda of parliament. The presidential veto, which can be overridden by a two-thirds majority of the Verkhovna Rada, remains in effect.

This constitutional reform package was based on one that President Kuchma had unsuccessfully attempted to push through the Verkhovna Rada a year earlier, apparently in the expectation that Yanukovych would be elected president in 2004, leaving Kuchma in a position to return to office as a powerful prime minister. Kuchma would then have been guaranteed immunity against prosecution in the murder of Heorhii Gongadze, a long-running scandal that had cast a huge shadow on the president and some members of his administration for most of his second term. The option of a political comeback was foreclosed, but before the Supreme Court handed down its decision on repeating the runoff election, Kuchma pressed for a wholly new presidential election instead. Such an arrangement would have given him about three months to sponsor a more attractive presidential candidate with a serious chance of defeating Yushchenko. When that option, too, was denied him, Kuchma stated in a wide-ranging interview (5 December) that if he were in Yanukovych's position, he would not stand as a candidate in the runoff.

Once the rift between Kuchma and his prime minister became public, Yanukovych's electoral prospects began to dim. Even earlier, he had been deserted by his campaign manager, Serhii Tyhypko, the head of the National Bank; that defection was followed by others. Yanukovych made strenuous efforts to rebuild his image by dissociating himself from the Kuchma administration, and his new campaign manager went so far as to claim that Kuchma and his immediate circle had worked against Yanukovych during the election. In this situation, Yanukovych was no longer perceived as the favorite, and the Russian backing that had been so prominent in October and November was no longer in evidence. Moreover, Yanukovych took an official leave of absence from his government post for the duration of the runoff, limiting his access to the "administrative resources" that had promoted his victory in the second round.

Other developments worked in Yushchenko's favor. If Yushchenko had been steadily attacked by the state-controlled media during the previous campaign, with backing only from certain Internet sites, newspapers, and the independent television channel 5, coverage was now quite different in tone and official censorship was greatly diminished. In the course of the Orange Revolution, many journalists had refused to report managed news, and some had come forward to tell their audiences that they would no longer present false information, as they had done in the past. Yushchenko also gained sympathy because he was poisoned with dioxin (an action widely attributed to the Kuchma administration and its Russian backers, although the case remains unsolved) during the summer of 2004. On 6 September Yushchenko fell ill with severe abdominal pain and lesions on his face and trunk; four days later, he was rushed to the elite Rudolfinerhaus clinic in Vienna for treatment. After further tests at the same clinic, doctors confirmed on 7 December that an extremely high dose of dioxin had been administered to Yushchenko, probably in food or drink, in an attempt to kill him. A third factor helping Yushchenko's cause was the world attention focused on the December runoff and the participation of unprecedentedly high numbers of observers—more than 300,000 Ukrainians and 12,000 from abroad—making this election one of the most intensely monitored in history. By the early morning of 27 December, it was apparent from the official vote count that Yushchenko had prevailed by a convincing margin. On 10 January the Central Electoral Commission announced that Yushchenko had won the election with 51.99 percent of the vote, while Yanukovych had obtained 44.20 percent. Although Yanukovych resigned as prime minister on 31

December, he dragged out the transfer of power until mid-January 2005, appealing unsuccessfully to the Central Electoral Commission and the Supreme Court with alleged election irregularities. Yushchenko was finally inaugurated on 23 January.

For Ukraine, the immediate significance of the Orange Revolution was a fundamental change in social attitudes. By their resolute show of civil disobedience, Ukrainians declared in overwhelming numbers that they would no longer tolerate a corrupt regime and demanded to be treated as citizens to whom the government was accountable. The fear and passivity that had previously dominated public life were broken.

The revolution was not, however, unanimously endorsed throughout the country. Although the Western media greatly exaggerated the prospect of political disintegration or civil war in Ukraine—a prospect dismissed by every competent authority—long-standing historical differences between eastern and western Ukraine came to the surface and made for considerable tension. If western and central Ukraine was largely Ukrainian-speaking, embraced the national idea, oriented itself toward Europe, and was actively involved in political and economic development, the east and south were largely Russified, still heavily influenced by the Soviet past, politically oriented on Russia, and resigned to making do with an obsolete coal-and-steel economy that had to be propped up by subsidies from the central government. This clash of orientations was reflected in the electoral platforms of the two presidential candidates. A week after the Orange Revolution began, on 28 November, regional leaders in Donetsk, Luhansk, and Kharkiv oblasts sponsored a congress in Severodonetsk to show support for Yanukovych and discuss the prospect of regional autonomy. The congress was attended by some 3,500 local councillors from 15 oblasts, as well as by Yanukovych and the mayor of Moscow, Yurii Luzhkov. The Yushchenko camp responded with calls for decisive presidential action against any threat to the country's integrity, and there was subsequently much backing away from talk of political devolution. Nevertheless, the sentiments expressed at the congress and the substantial vote for Yanukovych on 26 December indicated the depth of disaffection with which the Yushchenko administration would have to deal.

On the international scene, the Orange Revolution was a diplomatic defeat for Vladimir Putin, who had invested very heavily in the Yanukovych candidacy. It was widely reported that the Yanukovych campaign had cost the equivalent of US $600 million, half of it raised in Ukraine and half from a variety of Russian business sources—almost as much as George W. Bush had spent on his reelection in the United States, whose GDP was 50 times greater than that of Ukraine. Putin had visited Ukraine twice before the presidential election to signal support for Yanukovych; he also congratulated Yanukovych on winning the second round of voting even before the official results were announced. When Kuchma paid a brief visit to Putin in Moscow on 2 December, the latter compounded his previous faux pas by dismissing the prospect of another runoff, which "could be conducted a third, a fourth, a 25th time, until one side gets the results it needs." On 1 December, the Russian foreign minister, Sergei Lavrov, made a heavy-handed offer to help bring the situation in Ukraine under control, given the "excessive involvement of certain European representatives" whose behavior was "provoking tension." Statements of this kind had the general effect of confirming Ukrainian and Western fears that Russia was determined to reassert its Soviet-era control over Ukraine. They also provoked widespread speculation that the authoritarian governments of Russia and Belarus were concerned about the spread of democratic ideas among their own subjects.

In Europe, the most determined support for the Orange Revolution came from Poland, for reasons most frankly expressed by President Kwaśniewski in an interview given on 22 December: "Russia is reasserting its status in the world, which is normal. But why should it avail itself of 50 million Ukrainians?" Other heads of government were circumspect, as was the European Union, although its rhetoric became more encouraging after Yushchenko's election. On 13 January, the European Parliament overwhelmingly endorsed a resolution to give Ukraine "a clear European perspective, possibly leading to EU membership." More generally, the Orange Revolution brought Ukraine into European consciousness as never before, raising the prospect that the eastward shift of Europe's borders begun in 1989 and continued in 2004 might still have some distance to go.

The Dictionary

A

ACT OF UNION. On 1 December 1918, a preliminary agreement concerning the unification of the **Western Ukrainian People's Republic** (ZUNR) and the **Ukrainian People's Republic** (UNR) was signed in Fastiv by a delegation of the **Lviv**-based **Ukrainian National Rada** and representatives of the **Directory** of the UNR. This agreement was approved by the Rada on 3 January 1919. On 22 January 1919, the Act of Union between the ZUNR (**Galicia, Bukovyna,** and **Transcarpathia**) and the UNR (**eastern Ukraine**) was officially proclaimed in **Kyiv.** Pursuant to the law "Concerning the Form of Rule in Ukraine" adopted by the **Labor Congress,** the ZUNR acquired the name "Western Province of the Ukrainian People's Republic." Owing to chaotic international and domestic circumstances, the unification of the two Ukrainian states was never implemented: their administrative bodies maintained virtual independence and followed different policies.

ADMINISTRATIVE DIVISIONS OF UKRAINE. The principalities of **Kyivan Rus'** were the first administrative units established on Ukrainian territory. These principalities—**Kyiv**, Chernihiv, Siversk, Pereiaslav, **Volhynia,** and **Galicia**—all belonged to the Kyivan state, as did some smaller territories, notably the Polianian (Rus'), Turiv-Pynsk (Turaŭ-Pinsk), and Derevlianian lands. The principalities were divided into *volosti*, with towns or cities as their administrative centers. Kyivan Rus' was a monarchy; its ruler, the grand prince of Kyiv, held the plenitude of legislative, executive, judicial, and military power. Representatives of his family or viceroys and *tysiats'ki* (commanders) were appointed to the highest administrative posts. The *dvirs'kyi* or *dvorets'kyi* (courtier) was the principal administrator.

After the fall of Kyivan Rus' in the mid-13th century, its political and cultural traditions were continued by the Principality of **Galicia-**

Volhynia, which united most of the **western Ukrainian** lands from the 13th to the mid-14th century, when individual towns obtained rights of self-government under **Magdeburg law**. The first town to acquire that status was Sianik (Sanok, 1339), followed by **Lviv**, Kamianets-Podilskyi, Lutsk, and other towns. In the second half of the 14th century, most of the Ukrainian lands were annexed by Poland and Lithuania. Initially, they enjoyed a significant degree of autonomy; Volhynia, Kyiv, Novhorod-Siverskyi, Chernihiv, and **Podilia** constituted **appanage principalities** ruled by **princes** who maintained the same administrative offices as in Kyivan Rus'. After 1470, the principalities became provinces of the **Grand Duchy of Lithuania**, and the Kyiv, Bratslav, and Volhynia voivodeships (palatinates) were created, each administered by a *voivode* (vicegerent) of the grand duke. The voivodeships consisted of *povity* (counties), which in turn consisted of *volosti*. **Galicia** was annexed by Poland in 1349, remaining autonomous until 1434.

After the **Union of Lublin** (1569), most Ukrainian lands came under the direct control of the Kingdom of Poland. This territory was divided into palatinates: Rus', Belz, Podilia, Bratslav, Volhynia, Kyiv, and Chernihiv-Siverskyi (the latter ceded by Muscovy in 1618). The Berestia and **Podlachia** palatinates were incorporated into Lithuania. The administration of Ukrainian lands within the **Polish-Lithuanian Commonwealth** was based on the **Lithuanian Statute** of 1588 and the norms of Polish law. A significant number of Ukrainian towns were ruled according to Magdeburg law, with an elected municipal council headed by a *viit* (magistrate). **Transcarpathia** was annexed by Hungary in the 13th century and divided into seven *komitats* (counties): Szepes, Zemplén, Sáros, Ung, Ugocsa, Bereg, and Maramureş. The head of the *komitat* was the *zhupan*, who was appointed by the king. In the early 16th century, most of Transcarpathia came under the rule of Transylvania and, after 1699, of Austria.

The territory of contemporary **Bukovyna** was part of Kyivan Rus' and then belonged to the Galician-Volhynian principality. From the mid-14th to the 15th century, Bukovyna was constituted as the **Shypyntsi land**. Then, as part of **Moldavia**, Bukovyna was divided into three *volosti*: Chernivtsi, Khotyn, and Suceava. In 1514, Moldavia, including its Bukovynian territory, came under Turkish rule. In 1774, Bukovyna (with the exception of the Khotyn *raya*) became part of Austria and was annexed to Galicia in 1787. The Khotyn *raya* was conquered by the Russian Empire from the Turks and annexed in 1812.

The **Black Sea littoral** and the **Crimea** were a battleground between the Rus' princes and nomadic tribes. The Taman peninsula and the lands surrounding the Sea of Azov, Kuban, and the eastern

Crimea formed the Tmutorokan Principality, which became part of the Kyivan state in the early 11th century. In the 13th century, the littoral and the Crimea were conquered by the **Tatars**, who established the Crimean Khanate (1440s–1783).

The **Zaporozhian Host**, a **Cossack** military and political organization, was established to the south of the Dnipro Rapids in order to provide a defense against Tatar and Turkish aggression. In the second half of the 16th century, the Host developed a distinct administrative system divided into regiments led by colonels. Regiments were divided into *kureni* (battalions) headed by kurin otamans (commanders), and kurins were further subdivided into companies. An elected **hetman** led the Cossack Host. His executive officer was the otaman. The supreme ruling body was the Council of the Host, which chose or removed the otaman and **Cossack officers** and made decisions on all important matters. The **Khmelnytsky Uprising** (1648–57) extended Cossack control to a large portion of Ukrainian ethnic territory, for which a new administrative system based on the traditions of the Zaporozhian Host was created. The **Hetmanate**, based in the former Kyiv, Chernihiv, and Bratslav palatinates, covered a territory of approximately 200,000 sq. km. The new state was led by the hetman, who exercised military, political, administrative, and judicial power, ruling through the General Chancellery. His immediate aides were the Cossack officers (*starshyna*): chancellor (*pysar*), judge (*suddia*), aide-de-camp (*osavul*), flag-bearer (*khorunzhyi*), treasurer (*pidskarbii*), quartermaster (*oboznyi*), and standard-bearer (*bunchuzhnyi*). The highest judicial body was the General Court. The town of Chyhyryn, where **Bohdan Khmelnytsky** resided, became the capital of the Hetmanate, which was divided into 20 regiments (1650). Local administration was carried out by Cossack councils. Towns with Magdeburg law (Kyiv, Nizhyn, Chernihiv, Pereiaslav, Starodub, Hlukhiv, **Poltava**, Baturyn, and others) were governed by elected magistrates, while the rest had limited self-government.

Following the period of **Ruin** in the second half of the 17th century, Ukraine was divided between Muscovy and Poland. According to the **Truce of Andrusovo** (1667), the territory of **Left-Bank Ukraine**, along with Kyiv and Zaporizhia, came under Muscovite rule, while **Right-Bank Ukraine** remained part of the Polish-Lithuanian Commonwealth. In 1699 Podilia, which had been under Turkish rule, was annexed by Poland. The Ukrainian lands under Muscovy retained relative autonomy throughout the 17th and 18th centuries, although it was severely curtailed after the revolt of Hetman **Ivan Mazepa** (1709). The territory of the Hetmanate (present-day Chernihiv, Poltava, western Sumy, **Kharkiv**, and eastern Kyiv oblasts) was divided into 10 military and administrative regiments. It ceased to exist as a separate entity in 1782, when its territory was integrated into the Russian Empire.

At the end of the 17th century and throughout the 18th, most of Right-Bank Ukraine (Podilia, Volhynia, Galicia, the **Kholm region**, Podlachia, and the **Sian region**) was under Polish rule. Fearful of growing Ukrainian resistance, the Polish authorities abolished the Cossack regiments in 1699 and then did away with the Cossack administrative system, reestablishing the former palatinates. When Poland itself was partitioned by Austria, Prussia, and Russia (1772, 1793, 1795), the Ukrainian lands were incorporated into the Habsburg Monarchy, the Russian Empire, and the Ottoman Empire. In 1772, the Rus' palatinate (with the exception of the Kholm land) was incorporated into Austria, followed by Bukovyna (except for the Khotyn *raya*) in 1774. The Austrian government turned the annexed territories into a crown land, the Kingdom of Galicia and Lodomeria, with its administrative center in Lviv. The governor of the crown land held executive power and was appointed by the emperor. Locally, administrative and judicial power belonged to the *viit* (magistrate). Towns were governed by municipal councils, which included the magistrate, burgomaster, councillors, and town-court judges. With the creation of the Austro-Hungarian Empire in 1867, eastern Galicia and Bukovyna remained under Austria, while Transcarpathia came under the direct rule of Hungary.

Following the destruction of the Zaporozhian Sich in 1775, the Russian government created two gubernias, Azov and New Russia, on its territory. The administrative system of the Hetmanate was also abolished in 1781 and replaced by the Kyiv, Kharkiv, Chernihiv, Novhorod-Siverskyi, and Katerynoslav vicegerencies (1781–83). Further Russian expansion in southern Ukraine culminated in the annexation of the Crimean Khanate in 1783 and the creation of the Tavriia gubernia, centered in Simferopol. After the second and third partitions of Poland, the palatinates of Kyiv, Bratslav, and Volhynia became part of the Russian Empire, and, as a result, the Podilia, Bratslav, and Volhynia gubernias were established. At the beginning of the 19th century, there were nine gubernias in Ukraine: Kyiv, Poltava, Chernihiv, Kharkiv, Katerynoslav, Kherson, Tavriia, Podilia, and Volhynia. In 1815, the Kholm region and Podlachia were annexed by the Russian Empire, and in 1831 they became part of the Siedlce, Lublin, and Hrodna gubernias. The Kholm gubernia, encompassing most of the Ukrainian lands in Russian-ruled Poland, was established in 1912.

During the **Ukrainian Revolution** (1917–21), several governments succeeded one another. The **Ukrainian People's Republic**

(UNR), which declared its independence in January 1918, established its western and southwestern borders under the terms of the **Treaty of Brest-Litovsk** (February 1918) with the Central Powers. At the beginning of March 1918, the UNR adopted a law on the administrative system of Ukraine based on new units called *zemli* (lands). Local executive power belonged to gubernia and county commissioners appointed by the **Ukrainian Central Rada**. Supreme judicial authority resided in the General Court and appellate courts.

When Hetman **Pavlo Skoropadsky** took power in a coup on 29 April 1918, the **Ukrainian State** was proclaimed in place of the UNR. The Council of Ministers became its supreme executive and administrative body, and the posts of gubernatorial and county starostas (elders) were introduced in local administration. Municipal administrations were headed by otamans, with the capital otaman in Kyiv. The supreme judicial body was the State Senate. Some territories in the Mahilioŭ, Kursk, Voronezh, and Minsk gubernias where Ukrainians constituted the majority of the population were annexed to the Ukrainian State.

Skoropadsky was overthrown in December 1918 by the **Directory** of the UNR, whose laws, including the law on territorial administration, were restored. Local administration was entrusted to labor councils (representing the "toiling masses") that were unable to function in time of war; accordingly, military otamans and commissars of the Directory served as administrators. The territory of the restored UNR was divided into a Western (Western Province of the UNR) and an Eastern oblast. The latter consisted of the Kyiv, Kharkiv, Poltava, Chernihiv, Katerynoslav, Kherson, Zhytomyr, Kamianets, and Kholm gubernias. The capital of the UNR was Kyiv, but the Directory was unable to hold it against Bolshevik forces and retreated to Vinnytsia and Kamianets-Podilskyi.

With the approaching defeat of the Central Powers, the Ukrainian population of Austria-Hungary spoke out for the creation of a Ukrainian state. On 13 November 1918, the **Western Ukrainian People's Republic** (ZUNR) was declared. Its supreme executive and administrative body was the State Secretariat. The ZUNR included Ukrainian ethnic territory in Galicia, Bukovyna, and Transcarpathia (total area 70,000 sq. km). Local administrative and financial functions were carried out by county commissioners appointed by the State Secretary of Internal Affairs. Military functions were entrusted to county military commandants. District courts were created for judicial proceedings. In January 1919, through the **Act of Union**, the ZUNR was formally united with the UNR and became its Western Province.

The defeat of the Ukrainian Revolution led to the partition of Ukrainian ethnic territory between four states—the USSR, Poland,

Czechoslovakia, and Romania—during the interwar period. In the 1920s, the Ukrainian Socialist Soviet Republic (renamed the Ukrainian Soviet Socialist Republic in 1937) was divided into 12 gubernias (nine gubernias after October 1922): Volhynia, Donetsk, Zaporizhia, Katerynoslav, Kyiv, Kremenchuk, Mykolaiv, **Odesa**, Podilia, Poltava, Kharkiv, and Chernihiv. In the early 1920s, parts of the Chernihiv, Kursk, and Voronezh gubernias, where Ukrainians constituted an absolute majority, were annexed by Russia. In 1923, okruhs (regions) and raions (districts) replaced *volosti* and counties, and in 1925 the division into gubernias was abolished. The Ukrainian okruhs of Tahanrih and Shakhty were ceded to Russia in 1924. The Moldavian Autonomous Socialist Soviet Republic, which included a portion of Ukrainian ethnic territory, was created on 12 October 1924 as part of the **Ukrainian SSR** (a status that it retained until 2 August 1940, when the Moldavian SSR was established). The first oblasts of the Ukrainian SSR were established in 1932: Chernihiv, Dnipropetrovsk, Donetsk, Kyiv, Odesa, and Vinnytsia. In 1934, the capital of Ukraine was moved from Kharkiv to Kyiv, and in 1937 the Mykolaiv, Poltava, Zhytomyr, and Kamianets-Podilskyi (after 1954, Khmelnytskyi) oblasts were added. The Donetsk oblast was divided in 1938 into the Stalin (renamed Donetsk in 1961) and Voroshylovhrad (renamed Luhansk in 1961) oblasts. The Kirovohrad, Sumy, and Zaporizhia oblasts were created in 1939.

Following the dissolution of Austria-Hungary, Romania and Hungary annexed a significant portion of Ukrainian ethnic territory in 1918–19. Romania occupied the Khotyn, Izmail, and Akkerman counties of Bessarabia, northern Bukovyna, and the Ukrainian portion of the Maramureş region. The western Ukrainian lands occupied by Poland were officially annexed in 1923, pursuant to a decision of the Council of Allied Ambassadors. These lands included the Polisia, Volhynia, Lublin, Lviv, Stanyslaviv, and Ternopil districts, officially named "Eastern Little Poland." The districts were divided into counties and *gminy*. **Subcarpathian Rus'** became part of the new Czechoslovak state.

World War II brought about further changes in the administration of the Ukrainian lands. As anticipated by the secret protocol of the Molotov-Ribbentrop Pact, the Red Army occupied western Ukraine in September 1939 and northern Bukovyna and Khotyn, Akkerman, and Izmail counties in June 1940. Six oblasts were created in western Ukraine in 1939: Lviv, Stanyslaviv (Ivano-Frankivsk as of 1962), Ternopil, Volhynia, Rivne, and Drohobych (merged with Lviv oblast in 1959). Ukrainian ethnic lands covering an area of 16,000 sq. km (the **Lemko region**, Sian region, Kholm region, and Podlachia) that came under German occupation were annexed to the **General-**

gouvernement, administered from Cracow. In 1941, the entire territory of Ukraine was divided by the Germans and their allies into zones of occupation. Galicia (approx. 50,000 sq. km) was constituted as a district and united with the Generalgouvernement. The **Reichskommissariat Ukraine**, based in Rivne and covering an area of about 340,000 sq. km, was created in order to administer the rest of Ukraine. Its territory consisted of six general districts: Volhynia, Zhytomyr, Kyiv, Tavriia, Dnipropetrovsk, and Mykolaiv, which were divided into *Generalbezirke* (general districts) and *Kreise* (districts). The **Donets Basin** was placed under military administration. In the same year, the Romanian army occupied the Chernivtsi, Izmail, Odesa, southern Vinnytsia, and western Mykolaiv oblasts, creating the administrative unit of **Transnistria**.

After the retreat of Hitler's armies and their allies at the end of 1944, the prewar Soviet administrative system was restored in the Ukrainian SSR. The postwar treaties involving the Soviet Union, Poland, and Czechoslovakia established the southwestern and western borders of Ukraine, which retained the Soviet wartime annexations and added Transcarpathia. Between the 1950s and 1980s, the administrative system of Ukraine did not change significantly. In 1954, the Crimean oblast was transferred from the Russian Federation to the Ukrainian SSR, apparently for economic reasons.

After Ukraine declared its independence in 1991, the borders of Ukrainian SSR became the state borders of Ukraine. Subsequent treaties between Ukraine and its neighbors have resulted in some minor adjustments to existing borders. The administrative division into oblasts has remained intact. Present-day Ukraine is divided into 24 oblasts and the Republic of the Crimea, which has autonomous status within Ukraine (*see* GOVERNMENT).

AGRICULTURE. Ukraine has been popularly known for centuries as the "breadbasket of Europe," and agriculture was the main component of its economy until the first half of the 20th century. Ukraine's mainly temperate continental **climate**, with some subtropical features on the **Black Sea littoral**, offers favorable weather conditions for crop cultivation and animal husbandry. Most of the Ukrainian lands are flat, with very rich soil—the country possesses one-third of the world's fertile "black earth."

Land cultivation and animal husbandry have been practiced on what are now the Ukrainian lands since the Mesolithic period (ca. 12,000–ca. 5000 B.C.). Agriculture expanded considerably during the Neolithic era and particularly during the middle period of **Trypilian culture** (3500–2750 B.C.). In the middle of the first millennium B.C., **Scythian** tribes settled in present-day southern and southeastern

Ukraine, and later in the southern **Crimea**. They were composed of two groups, farmers (the "Scythian plowmen" of Herodotus) and nomads. The former grew wheat, rye, millet, beans, hemp, onions, garlic, and other vegetable crops. Along with Egypt and Sicily, Scythia was one of the main breadbaskets of the ancient world.

Over time, farming methods advanced as the early tribes absorbed techniques practiced by other peoples. From the Celts they borrowed the iron hoe; from the Goths they learned to build separate shelters for livestock; and from the Germanic tribes they acquired a plow fitted with metal shares. Numerous archaeological finds indicate a well-developed system of agriculture among the **Slavs** throughout the ancient and princely eras. Most scholars maintain that the short-fallow system, with two- and three-field crop rotation, was dominant in **Kyivan Rus'**. It was more intensive than the Scythian long-fallow system. Almost all the crops known to the agriculture of the period were cultivated in Rus': spring and winter grains, beans, hemp, and garden produce.

The export of Ukrainian wheat to Western Europe began in the 16th century and continued until the mid-17th, when it was interrupted by the incessant warfare of the **Ruin**. It resumed intensively in the 18th century with the development of agriculture in southern Ukraine. The construction of seaports and railroads reestablished Ukraine as a major grain exporter. In the years 1909–13, eastern and southern Ukraine produced 8 percent of the world's output of wheat (20 percent of world export), 45 percent of its rye (21 percent of world export), and 3 percent of its corn (10 percent of world export).

Historically, from the times of Kyivan Rus' to the **Ukrainian Revolution** (1917–21), land in Ukraine was privately owned, and all social strata defined their place in the social hierarchy on the basis of their relation to land: freeholders, who held land on condition of military or civil service, peasant landowners, and the landless (seasonal workers, servants, serfs, leaseholders, etc.) (*see* PEASANTS). The abolition of serfdom in the Habsburg Monarchy (1848) and the Russian Empire (1861) turned many former serfs into hired laborers. In **western Ukraine**, agrarian overpopulation made farming unprofitable, leading to mass peasant emigration in the late 19th and early 20th centuries (*see* DIASPORA).

After the establishment of Soviet rule, an abortive attempt to collectivize agriculture ("war communism") gave way to the New Economic Policy, which briefly restored free enterprise. The **collectivization** of Soviet agriculture, undertaken by the Stalin regime in 1928, was a catastrophe for the Ukrainian peasantry. Resistance to collectivization was broken by the man-made **famine of 1932–33**, which took millions of lives. In the 1930s, a system of collective farms (*kolhospy*) and state farms (*radhospy*) was established in the **Ukrainian SSR** and throughout the Soviet Union. An internal passport system drastically curtailed the movement of peasants to the cities, and in many respects peasants reverted to the status of serfs. As peasant apathy grew, production plummeted. Under **Nikita Khrushchev**, private plots made something of a comeback but were repeatedly banned in the 1960s and 1970s. During the Soviet period, Ukraine produced almost a quarter of the USSR's agricultural output in spite of state regulation and the general inefficiency of the collective farm system. By the 1970s, Soviet agriculture was in crisis, and even wheat had to be imported from abroad.

In independent Ukraine, state and collective farms were turned into collective agricultural enterprises (CAEs) in 1992, but this produced no substantial change. In October 2001, the Verkhovna Rada adopted a land code that permitted the purchase and sale of land beginning on 1 January 2005. While the private sector currently accounts for a mere fraction of arable land reserves and the 16–million-strong rural population, it produces 60 percent of Ukraine's meat, dairy and poultry products, 50 percent of its fruit, and 83 percent of its vegetables.

More than half of cultivated land is used for cereal crops. In 2003, the Ukrainian grain harvest was the lowest since 1945—20.2 million tons (including 3.6 million tons of wheat). After wheat, barley and corn are the predominant grain cultures. Peasants and farmers also grow sugar beets, sunflowers, potatoes, cabbages, carrots, onions, tomatoes, and cucumbers. The southern Ukrainian lands provide almost 90 percent of the country's pumpkin, melon, watermelon, and squash crops.

Animal husbandry is developed in the Carpathian Mountains, in western Ukraine (a total of 550,000 ha), the Crimean plateau (350,000 ha), and the arid steppelands of southern Ukraine. This sector, too, has shown a huge decrease in output, dropping from 24.6 million head in 1991 to 12.7 million in 1998. The production of pork, veal, beef, and mutton fell by 11 percent (1998). The declining output of primary agriculture, bad weather, increased competition from imports, and the loss of traditional markets have all contributed to the drop in Ukraine's food production, turning the country from a major food exporter into an importer of agricultural products. *See also* COOPERATIVE MOVEMENT; ECONOMY; FAMINE OF 1921–23; FAMINE OF 1946–47.

AKHMETOV, RINAT (b. 21 September 1966). Reputed economic oligarch from Donetsk, head of the so-called Donetsk clan, the richest and most influential of the three major Ukrainian clans (the others are based in Dnipropetrovsk and Kyiv). Akhmetov, a **Tatar** by ethnic origin, was born in Donetsk into the family of a coal miner. In the early 1990s, he graduated from the economics department of Donetsk State University. He established the Donetsk City Bank in 1995, becoming one of the youngest bankers in independent Ukraine. Until the mid-1990s, Akhmetov remained in the shadow of other leaders of the Donetsk clan. He then became chief executive officer of the Industrial Union of the Donbas (*see* DONETS BASIN) and of System Capital Management (est. 2000), which control most economic activity in eastern Ukraine. Akhmetov is also a major shareholder of the Azovstal, Alchevsk, Yenakiieve, and Kerch **metallurgical** plants, the Avdeev and MarkoKhim coal and chemical plants, the Vostokenergo power company, the DCC cellular communications provider, the First Ukrainian International Bank, the Sarmat brewery, the ASKO insurance company, the Segodnia publishing group, the Ukraine television company, the Donbas Palace Hotel, and the two largest machine-building plants in Ukraine, Azovmash and Kuibyshev. One of Akhmetov's close business associates is **Viktor Pinchuk**, the son-in-law of President **Leonid Kuchma**. Akhmetov is also known as a long-standing friend of **Viktor Yanukovych**, who was governor of Donetsk oblast from 1997 to 2002 and became prime minister of Ukraine in November 2002.

Since 1995, Akhmetov has been president of the leading soccer team Shakhtar Donetsk. Little is known of his private life or business dealings, as he is quite reclusive. In 2002, the Polish magazine *Wprost* (Point-Blank) listed Akhmetov as the sixth-richest person (out of 50) in Central and Eastern Europe and the richest Ukrainian, with estimated capital of U.S. $1.7 billion. According to an estimate in the Ukrainian newspaper *InvestGazeta* (2004), Akhmetov's wealth exceeds U.S. $2.9 billion.

ALPHABET WAR. Struggle of **Galician** Ukrainians in 1859–61 against attempts by the Austrian government to introduce a Latin script for the Ukrainian alphabet. The use of Latin script was first suggested by the Ukrainian philologist Yosyp Lozynsky in 1834, drawing opposition from western Ukrainian intellectuals, notably **Markiian Shashkevych**. In 1859, attempts by Agenor Gołuchowski, the governor-general of Galicia, to introduce the Latin alphabet provoked widespread protest. The public outcry, supported by the eminent Slavists Pavol Šafařík and Fran Miklošić, forced the government to abandon the project.

ANDRUKHOVYCH, YURII (b. 13 March 1960). Writer. Born in Stanislav (now Ivano-Frankivsk) in western Ukraine, Andrukhovych graduated from the Ukrainian Institute of Printing in 1982. He began as a poet, publishing the collections *Nebo i ploshchi* (Sky and Squares, 1985), *Seredmistia* (Downtown, 1989), and *Ekzotychni ptakhy i roslyny* (Exotic Birds and Plants, 1991). In 1985, he became a cofounder of the postmodern literary group **Bu-Ba-Bu**, and from 1991 to 1996 he was coeditor of the first Ukrainian postmodern literary journal, *Chetver* (Thursday), based in Ivano-Frankivsk.

Andrukhovych is best known for his innovative novels and essays. His first collection of stories, *Zliva, de sertse* (On the Left, Where the Heart Is, 1989), was a quasi-documentary rendering of his period of military service. He came to general notice with the novel *Rekreatsiï* (Recreations, 1992; English translation, 1998), which appeared in the first issue of the journal ***Suchasnist'*** to be published in Ukraine. This satirical account of a "Festival of the Resurrecting Spirit" (based on the highly popular music, folk, and religious festivals of the late 1980s), set in mythical Chortopil (Devilsburg), became something of a *succès de scandale*. Andrukhovych ridiculed not only the remains of the Soviet system but also the solemn, exaggerated patriotism associated with the **populist** tradition and the **diaspora**. He was equally irreverent in dealing with the traditional cult of the poet as conscience of the nation, a role that could not possibly be ascribed to the novel's antihero, Rostyslav Martofliak, "the hope of Ukrainian poetry." Andrukhovych's inclination toward satire, parody, and the grotesque, as well as his preoccupation with wordplay, were reflected in his next two novels, *Moskoviada* (The Moscoviad, 1993), which deals with the legacy of Soviet colonialism, and *Perverziia* (Perversion, 1996; English translation, 2004), in which a postcolonial Ukrainian intellectual confronts the world and his own death in Venice.

Another genre that Andrukhovych has cultivated is the essay, especially the literary travelogue, which serves as a basis for broader cultural, political, and historical reflection. His first collection in this vein was *Dezorientatsiia na mistsevosti* (Disorientation toward Places, 1999), followed by *Moia Ievropa* (My Europe, 2001), a joint publication with the Polish writer Andrzej Stasiuk that also appeared in Polish and German. Andrukhovych's essay collection *Das letzte Territorium* (2003) gained considerable public and critical attention in Germany. His work has been widely translated in Europe, making him Ukraine's best-known postmodern writer.

ANDRUSOVO, TRUCE OF. Armistice signed between the **Polish-Lithuanian Commonwealth** and Muscovy on 30 January (9 February) 1667 in the village of Andrusovo near Smolensk that remained in force until June 1680. According to its terms, the Polish-

Muscovite War (1654–67) was terminated. **Left-Bank Ukraine**, the Siverian land (including Chernihiv and Starodub) and Smolensk remained under Muscovite control, while **Right-Bank Ukraine** and Belarus, including Vitsebsk, Polatsk, and Dvinsk, remained part of the Commonwealth. Kyiv, on the Right Bank, was turned over to Muscovy for two years, after which it was to revert to Poland (Muscovy never implemented this provision). The **Zaporozhian Sich** came under the joint jurisdiction of Poland and Muscovy, both of which were to protect Ukraine against **Tatar** raids. The provisions of the truce were subsequently confirmed by the **Eternal Peace of 1686**. Since the truce was negotiated without Ukrainian participation and amounted to a de facto partition of the **Hetmanate** along the Dnipro River, it aroused opposition in Ukrainian society, culminating in a rebellion headed by Hetman **Ivan Briukhovetsky**.

ANNA YAROSLAVNA (b. between 1024 and 1032, d. after 1075). Daughter of **Yaroslav the Wise** and queen of France after 1049. On 4 August 1049, in Reims, she married Henry I of France, who was seeking Yaroslav's support in his struggle with the Holy Roman Empire. After the death of her husband in 1060, Anna Yaroslavna ruled as regent for her young son, Philip I. It appears that in 1062 she married the Count of Valois and Crépy, but the marriage was never legalized. Anna Yaroslavna is depicted in a sculpture on the portal of St. Vincent's Church in Senlis, France. Documents with her signature, the oldest examples of Rus' writing, have been preserved. According to some sources, Anna Yaroslavna brought the so-called Reims Gospel from Kyiv to France. It was used for taking the royal oath during the coronation of French kings. *See also* KYIVAN RUS'.

ANTES (Greek: *Antae*). Tribal alliance of the fourth to seventh centuries A.D. that inhabited the territories between the Dnipro and Dnister Rivers. The Antes are known from the writings of the Gothic historian Jordanes and Byzantine writers of the sixth and seventh centuries. Their identity remains controversial; some historians consider them **Sarmatians**, while others maintain that they were Eastern **Slavs**. **Mykhailo Hrushevsky** regarded the Antes as the first ethnic Ukrainians.

The Antes were successful warriors who fought the Goths in the fourth century A.D.; they also attacked and settled Byzantine possessions in the Balkans during the sixth century. They established themselves in what is now northwestern and north-central Ukraine, founding numerous villages and engaging in agriculture, livestock breeding, pottery-making, and ironworking, as well as trade with the Romans and Byzantines. Toward the end of the sixth century the

Antes were overwhelmed by the incursion of the Avars and became extinct.

ANTHEM. Official song performed at formal celebrations, state functions, military parades, political events, church rituals, and the like. The Ukrainian national anthem, "Ukraine Has Not Yet Perished" (*Shche ne vmerla Ukraïna*), was composed in the 1860s. The lyrics were written by the poet, ethnographer, and folklorist **Pavlo Chubynsky** (1839–84). It was first published in 1863 and quickly became popular among the intelligentsia and students throughout Ukraine. The **music** was written by the Ukrainian Catholic priest, composer, and conductor Mykhailo Verbytsky (1815–70). Other composers, notably Kyrylo Stetsenko, also set the text to music. By the late 19th century, "Ukraine Has Not Yet Perished" was the most widely used anthem; it became even more popular during the **Ukrainian Revolution** of 1917–21. Banned during the period of Soviet rule, it was adopted after 1991 as the official national anthem.

Throughout the 19th and 20th centuries, other songs were also considered national anthems in the Ukrainian lands, especially **Taras Shevchenko's** "Testament," which was frequently performed on formal occasions. In **Galicia**, the song "We Bring All of You Peace, Brothers" (lyrics by Ivan Hushalevych, music by Denys Sichynsky) was adopted during the **Revolution of 1848** as the anthem of Galician Ukrainians. In **Transcarpathia**, Ukrainians used the anthem "I Was a Ruthenian" and "Subcarpathian Ruthenians" (lyrics by Oleksander Dukhnovych). The latter was the official anthem of Transcarpathia under the Czechoslovak administration (until 1939). Independent **Carpatho-Ukraine** declared "Ukraine Has Not Yet Perished" its official anthem.

Diaspora Ukrainians generally used "Ukraine Has Not Yet Perished" as their anthem; in North America, the songs "For You, Ukraine" (lyrics by Vasyl Shchurat, music by **Stanislav Liudkevych**) and "We Live For You, Ukraine" (lyrics by Ostap Hrytsai, music by Liudkevych) were also sung as anthems.

ANTI-BOLSHEVIK BLOC OF NATIONS/ANTYBOL'SHE-VYTS'KYI BLOK NARODIV (ABN). Coordinating center for European and Asian anticommunist political organizations. It was founded at the initiative of the **Organization of Ukrainian Nationalists (Bandera** faction) at the first Conference of Subjugated Peoples of Eastern Europe and Asia, held near Zhytomyr on 21–23 November 1943, in which 39 delegates from 13 nations participated (Armenians, Azeris, Bashkirs, Belarusians, Chuvash, Circassians, Georgians, Kabardians, Kazakhs, Ossetians, **Tatars**, Ukrainians, Uzbeks). The conference was attended by the commander in chief of the **Ukrainian Insurgent Army**, **Roman Shukhevych**.

In 1946, the ABN became an émigré organization headed by **Yaroslav Stetsko**. It organized anticommunist demonstrations and press conferences and sent appeals to parliaments of various countries regarding **human-rights** violations and the persecution of political and religious **dissidents** in the USSR. After 1986, the organization was headed by **Slava Stetsko**.

ANTONOV-OVSIIENKO, VOLODYMYR (9 [21] March 1883–February 1938). Bolshevik military commander and diplomat. He was born in Chernihiv into an impoverished gentry family that had adopted Russian culture. In 1897, the family moved to Warsaw. Antonov-Ovsiienko entered an infantry school in St. Petersburg in 1902 and joined the Russian Social Democratic Labor Party (1903). Arrested for organizing a revolt of two regiments in 1906, he was condemned to death, but the sentence was commuted to 20 years' imprisonment. Antonov-Ovsiienko managed to escape and lived as a revolutionary in Finland, St. Petersburg, and Moscow. From 1910 to 1917, he lived in France and associated with Mensheviks; it was there that the pseudonym Antonov was added to his surname. On returning to Russia, he joined the Bolsheviks and became secretary of the St. Petersburg Military Revolutionary Committee. He played a prominent organizational role in the October Revolution.

In late 1917, Antonov-Ovsiienko was placed in charge of the Bolshevik offensive against the Don Cossack forces of Aleksei Kaledin. Since the **Ukrainian Central Rada** had halted the export of grain to Russia, Antonov-Ovsiienko turned against it as well, mobilizing the **Red Cossacks** and other forces for an assault on **Kyiv** that began on 18 (31) January 1918. His chief of staff, Mikhail Muraviev, became notorious for his brutality when, after taking Kyiv, he ordered mass executions of supporters of Ukrainian independence. Antonov-Ovsiienko valued Muraviev's military prowess and defended him against protests from Soviet authorities in Ukraine and Russia.

When Soviet Russia signed the **Treaty of Brest-Litovsk** with Germany on 3 March 1918, the presence of Russian troops on Ukrainian soil became illegal. In order to get around this, Lenin arranged for the **Ukrainian SSR** to be declared a sovereign republic and appointed Antonov-Ovsiienko commander of its armed forces, noting that he should use only the Ukrainian form of his name, Ovsiienko. His army was soon forced out of Ukraine, and he resigned as supreme commander on 4 April.

In November 1918, as the **Skoropadsky** regime was on its last legs, Antonov-Ovsiienko commanded the second Bolshevik invasion of Ukraine, raising about 25,000 troops and taking a quarter of its territory by February 1919. By April, his forces had routed the **Directory** of the **Ukrainian People's Republic**, taking most of Ukraine. Antonov-Ovsiienko's success was due in part to his reversal of earlier Bolshevik policy; he halted forced requisitions of food and called for cooperation with Ukrainian socialists, who had great influence with the **peasantry**. He also established good relations with the peasant otamans **Nestor Makhno** and **Nykyfor Hryhoriiv**.

In June 1919, the armed forces of the Ukrainian SSR were fully subordinated to those of Russia, and Antonov-Ovsiienko, blamed for a White breakthrough on the Soviet front, was removed from his post. After holding a variety of administrative offices, he served as a diplomatic representative in Czechoslovakia, Lithuania, Poland, and Spain. In 1937, he was accused of espionage and shot soon thereafter. His wartime activity in Ukraine was detailed in his *Zapiski o grazhdanskoi voine* (Notes on the Civil War, 4 vols., 1924–33).

ANTONOVYCH, VOLODYMYR (18 [30] January 1834–8 [21] March 1908). Historian, archaeologist, and ethnographer. Antonovych was born in the village of Makhnivka, **Kyiv** gubernia (now the village of Komsomolske, Vinnytsia oblast), into an impoverished Polish gentry family. He graduated from the medical (1855) and then from the historical and philological (1860) faculties of Kyiv University. Breaking with Polish circles in the early 1860s, he dedicated himself to the Ukrainian cause. A **populist**, Antonovych was an organizer and head of the Kyiv **Hromada** and the ideologue of the *khlopoman* ("peasant-lover") movement. From 1863 to 1880, he was editor in chief of the Kyiv Archaeographic Commission and oversaw the publication of 15 volumes of *Arkhiv Iugo-Zapadnoi Rossii* (Archive of Southwestern Russia), which included materials on the history of **Right-Bank Ukraine** from the 16th to the 18th century. For 30 years (1870–1900), he was professor of history at Kyiv University. Antonovych was the founder of the Kyiv historical school, which consisted of his students **Dmytro Bahalii**, Mytrofan Dovnar-Zapolsky, **Mykhailo Hrushevsky**, Ivan Kamanin, Ivan Lynnychenko, and others. As a historian, Antonovych concentrated on the collection of sources and on the documentary research of discrete historical problems rather than on works of synthesis. His publications, numbering more than 300, included studies of the **Grand Duchy of Lithuania**, the city of Kyiv from the 14th to the 16th century, the **Union of Brest** and its effect on the Orthodox Church, the origins of the Ukrainian **nobility**, and topics in the history of the Ukrainian **Cossacks**, **haidamakas**, and **peasants**. Antonovych initiated systematic archaeological studies in Ukraine and produced detailed archaeological maps of the Kyiv and **Volhynia** gubernias. In his last years, he did extensive documentary research in the Vatican archives.

In addition to his work as a scholar, Antonovych was a Ukrainian community leader for half a century. Much of his work in this area involved cooperation with the Ukrainian movement in **Galicia**. In the early 1890s, Antonovych helped establish the **Shevchenko Scientific Society** and initiate the agreement between the Galician populists and Austro-Polish political circles that came to be known as the "New Era." In 1893, he was invited to take the newly established chair of Ukrainian history at **Lviv** University but declined because of ill health and successfully recommended Hrushevsky for the position.

APOSTOL, DANYLO (4 [14] December 1654–17 [28] January 1734). Military leader and **hetman** of **Left-Bank Ukraine** (1727–34). He was born into a **Cossack officer** family in the village of Velyki Sorochyntsi (**Poltava** region). As colonel of the Myrhorod regiment (1683–1727), he took part in campaigns against the Turks and **Tatars** and distinguished himself in the Northern War (1700–21). Initially a supporter of the autonomist policies of **Ivan Mazepa**, he switched sides in November 1708 and joined Peter I. In 1722, he headed a Cossack regiment of 10,000 men in the Russian campaign against Persia. A close associate of acting hetman **Pavlo Polubotok**, Apostol opposed the restriction of the **Hetmanate's** autonomy by the **Little Russian Collegium**. When he helped initiate the Kolomak Petitions (1723), which called for the abolition of the collegium, he was arrested together with Polubotok and others and incarcerated at the SS. Peter and Paul Fortress.

In 1727, to secure Cossack support in the approaching Russo-Turkish War, Peter II abolished the collegium and permitted the election of a new hetman. Apostol was elected at a **Cossack council** in Hlukhiv on 1 (11) October 1727. In 1728, he submitted a petition concerning the reinstatement of Ukrainian autonomy on the basis of the **Articles of Bohdan Khmelnytsky** (1654). In response, the Russian government issued the Authoritative Ordinances of 1728, which restricted the hetman's authority while allowing for a semi-autonomous Hetmanate. Apostol systematized the Hetmanate's administration, reorganized its finances, and conducted a general survey of landholdings (1729–31) in an attempt to recover state lands appropriated by private landholders. In 1728, he established the commission that produced the **Code of Laws of 1743**; in 1730, he issued an "Instruction to Ukrainian Courts" that established appellate procedures in judicial cases. Apostol demanded changes to the discriminatory commercial system established by Peter I and sought the abolition of restrictions on the export of Ukrainian goods. He reclaimed the right to appoint the General Military Chancellery and Cossack colonels, reduced the number of Russians in his administration and Russian regiments in the Hetmanate, and forbade Russians from buying land there. Apostol transferred the city of **Kyiv** from the jurisdiction of the Russian governor-general to that of the hetman, secured the return of Cossacks living since 1708 under the authority of the **Crimean** Khanate (Oleshky Sich) to the hetman's rule, and obtained permission to establish the **New Sich** (1734). He was buried in his native village.

APPANAGE PRINCIPALITIES. Princedoms formed as a result of the disintegration of **Kyivan Rus'** after the mid-11th century. Following the death of **Yaroslav the Wise**, the Rus' lands were divided among his sons; hence the Kyiv, Chernihiv, and Pereiaslav lands became separate appanages. Appanage **princes** were vassals of the grand prince of Kyiv (a title adopted in the 11th century), but that dependence was often nominal. The **Liubech congress of princes** (1097), convoked to put an end to internecine conflicts, legalized appanages as a way of resolving disputes over succession. The process of disintegration was temporarily halted by **Volodymyr Monomakh** and his son Mstyslav Volodymyrych, but by the 12th century, the principalities of Kyiv, Chernihiv, Pereiaslav, **Volhynia**, and **Galicia** were separate entities, with each prince controlling his own administrative apparatus, currency, and army. While the formation of the Principality of **Galicia-Volhynia** represented a unifying trend, dependence on the **Golden Horde** and later on Lithuania and Poland hampered unification and preserved the appanage system. Appanages were abolished in Polish-ruled Galicia in the first half of the 15th century and in most Rus' lands under Lithuanian rule in the second half of the century. The last appanage principality, that of Kyiv, was eliminated in 1471.

ARCHIPENKO, ALEXANDER (ARKHYPENKO, OLEKSANDER) (18 [30] May 1887–25 February 1964). Eminent **sculptor** and **painter**. Born in **Kyiv**, he studied at the Kyiv Art School (1902–5), from which he was expelled for participation in the Ukrainian student movement. In 1906, Archipenko organized his first exhibit near Kyiv. In 1907, he studied at the Moscow School of Painting, Sculpture, and Architecture, and, from 1908, at the École des Beaux-Arts in Paris. He founded his own school in Paris (1910) and subsequently in Berlin and New York (1923–64). Archipenko was a brilliant representative of cubism, constructivism, and abstractionism, producing more than 1,000 sculptures and paintings. Among his best-known works are *Adam and Eve* (1908), *The Kiss* (1910), *Dance* (1912), *Woman*

Combing Her Hair (1914), a series of female torsos (1909–16), portraits of **Taras Shevchenko** (1923–35), **Ivan Franko** (1925), and the conductor Willem Mengelberg (1925), *Madonna* (1936), *Zarathustra* (1948), *Cleopatra* (1957), and *King Solomon* (1963).

ARCHITECTURE. Traces of early architectural constructions in Ukraine date back to the Paleolithic period. Remnants of **Trypilian culture** from the late Neolithic period attest to a well-developed tradition of building among local tribes. The **Black Sea colonies** of the first millennium B.C. introduced structures built in the Greek style. From the sixth to the third century B.C., **Scythian** tribes built fortified settlements, as exemplified by the well-preserved ruins of their capital, Neapolis, in the **Crimea**. With the introduction of **Christianity**, stone churches based on the Greek-cross form were built on the ruins of the Greek colonies.

Kyivan Rus' adopted Christianity from Constantinople and assimilated Byzantine architecture in the process, synthesizing it with local traditions of wood construction and with a number of Western elements. **Volodymyr the Great** built the first important stone shrine, the Church of the Tithes (989–96), whose plan and construction were copied throughout Rus'. Only its foundations have survived. **Yaroslav the Wise** encircled Kyiv with defensive walls (remnants of the **Golden Gate** still exist) and built **St. Sophia's Cathedral** (begun 1037), modeled on Hagia Sophia in Constantinople. Many churches of the period survived into the 1930s and 1940s, only to be destroyed by the Soviet authorities. The most notable of these were the Cathedral of St. Michael's Golden-Domed Monastery (1108–13, rebuilt in the late 1990s) and the Dormition Cathedral of the **Kyivan Cave Monastery** (1078; also rebuilt). Several medieval churches survived in Chernihiv, and others have been preserved in Ovruch, Volodymyr-Volynskyi, Kaniv, and Halych (St. Panteleimon's Church, which displays Romanesque elements).

The invasion of the **Golden Horde** was followed by the decline of Ukrainian architecture from the late 13th to the 16th century. It revived during the Renaissance, mainly in **western Ukraine**, where Italian, German, and French architects introduced the new style. The best examples of Renaissance architecture in Ukraine include the church of the **Lviv Dormition Brotherhood**, the Black Building in Lviv, and the castle in Pidhirtsi. The unique and varied architecture of the Crimean peninsula during that period included Genoese fortresses, Armenian monasteries and churches, **Tatar** mosques, and the palace of the Crimean khan in Bakhchesarai.

During the **baroque** period, the center of Ukrainian cultural life shifted back to **eastern Ukraine**. The synthesis of Western baroque and Byzantine-Ukrainian traditions produced a style characterized by a three-nave Greek-cross church fused with the basilica. Under the leadership of Metropolitan **Petro Mohyla** and the subsequent patronage of Hetman **Ivan Mazepa**, many medieval churches, including St. Sophia's Cathedral, the Dormition Cathedral of the Kyivan Cave Monastery, and the churches of St. Michael's Monastery and the Vydubychi Monastery in Kyiv, were rebuilt and crowned with distinctive cupolas. Important churches built during the period include the church of the **Kyiv Epiphany Brotherhood** Monastery (1693) and St. Nicholas's Military Cathedral (1696), both of which were demolished in the 1930s.

The oldest surviving wooden churches in Ukraine date back to the 16th and 17th centuries. They have distinctive regional traits. Boiko churches are notable for their tripartite construction, in which each frame is topped with a tiered pyramidal roof. Ukrainian baroque wooden churches, particularly of the Dnipro school, create an impression of great inner height through the use of inwardly inclined walls, with each tier narrower than the one below. The most important of these churches is Yakym Pohrebniak's Trinity Church in Novomoskovsk (1773–78), which has nine frames with nine cupolas rising to a height of 65 meters.

During the mid-18th century, the more decorative rococo style flourished in Ukraine. Its most notable examples are St. George's Cathedral in Lviv (1744–64), St. Andrew's Church in Kyiv (1747–53, designed by Bartolomeo Rastrelli), and the belfry of the Kyivan Cave Monastery (1731–45).

By the early 19th century, rococo had given way to the official Empire classicist style, known for its eclecticism. Old cities such as Kyiv, Chernihiv, **Kharkiv**, and **Poltava** were reconstructed, while towns in southern Ukraine developed rapidly after the expulsion of the Turks from the Black Sea region. Notable architectural achievements of the period include the Potemkin steps in **Odesa** (1837–41), the palaces of **Kyrylo Rozumovsky** in Pochep (1796) and Baturyn (1799), and a number of surviving churches in Kharkiv and Poltava. Other outstanding examples include the Catholic Church of St. Nicholas in Kyiv, built in the pseudo-Gothic style (1897–1900); the residence of the metropolitan of Bukovyna, now the University of Chernivtsi (1864–82); the pseudo-Byzantine St. Volodymyr's Cathedral in Kyiv (1862–82); the Odesa Opera House (1884–87); the Kyiv National Bank, built in the style of the Venetian Renaissance (1902–5); and the Trinity Cathedral in Pochaiv (1906), built in the Old Rus' style.

At the beginning of the 20th century, Vasyl Krychevsky pioneered a revived Ukrainian style, exemplified in the zemstvo building in Poltava (1905–9). Other important buildings of the period include the Pedagogical Museum in Kyiv (1911–13) and the tsar's palace in Livadiia in the Crimea (1910–11). The Society of Ukrainian Architects and the Ukrainian Architectural Institute were established in Kyiv in 1918. Ukrainian architects incorporated baroque motifs and elements of wooden folk architecture into their work. By the 1930s, however, many of them were accused of propagating a "national style" and persecuted. From the mid-1920s, many buildings were designed in the constructivist style, coinciding with rapid industrialization and the **collectivization** of **agriculture**. Soon, however, the modernist tendencies were criticized, and in the mid-1930s architects developed the pompous Stalinist style, which combined the St. Petersburg Empire style with pseudomonumentalism. New architectural ideas began to emerge only in the 1960s, with a generation of postwar architects inspired by American reinforced steel-and-concrete constructions.

Architecture in Ukraine today concerns not so much the construction of new public edifices as the rebuilding of structures, particularly churches, demolished by the Soviets, as well as the renovation of older buildings. *See also* SCULPTURE.

ARMED FORCES. With the breakup of the **USSR** in 1991, all Soviet forces deployed in Ukraine were placed under the jurisdiction of the Defense Ministry of Ukraine. Ukraine inherited one of the largest armies in Europe, consisting of nearly 800,000 personnel, 6,500 tanks, 7,000 armored vehicles, 1,500 combat aircraft, and more than 350 ships. Furthermore, Ukraine's arsenal of **nuclear weapons** totaled some 5,000 strategic and tactical weapons. Ukraine became the first nation in history voluntarily to relinquish its nuclear arsenal, and by 1996 no nuclear warheads remained on its territory.

The Ukrainian Armed Forces are divided into four branches: Army, Navy, Air Force, and Air Defense Force. Other forces under different jurisdictions include Internal Troops, the Civil Defense Force, and Border Troops. The army, or the land force, is the largest division of the armed forces, with about 150,700 personnel divided among the Western command, based in **Lviv**; the Southern command, based in **Odesa**; and the Northern command, based in Chernihiv. It comprises five army corps, 11 tank and mechanized divisions, seven mechanized brigades, two artillery divisions, two training divisions, and 40 service brigades. The Ukrainian Navy emerged from the partition of the **Black Sea Fleet** and is staffed by about 13,500 personnel. It includes warships, submarines, naval aviation, coastal missile and artillery troops, marines, and support units. The navy's main base is Sevastopol; others include Odesa, Ochakiv, Chornomorske, Novoozerne,

Mykolaiv, Yevpatoriia, and Feodosiia. The Ukrainian Air Force was formed on the basis of four Soviet air force armies stationed in Ukraine in 1992, which had more than 120,000 servicemen (subsequently reduced to 70,000). The air force operates fighters, bombers, attack aircraft, and reconnaissance and transport planes. With headquarters in Vinnytsia, the air force includes two corps (Lviv and Odesa), long-range and transport aviation, and educational and training centers. The air defense force, with headquarters in **Kyiv**, consists of three corps deployed in Lviv, Odesa, and Dnipropetrovsk. It includes air-defense missile troops and radio-technical troops, as well as fighter aviation and other specialized services, with a total of 49,100 servicemen.

Military service in Ukraine is mandatory for men 18 years of age and lasts 18 months. Since 1991, the armed forces have reduced their personnel to 315,000 (2000). Ukraine is committed to reduce its armed forces even further and replace conscription with the recruitment of about 260,000 professional servicemen by 2010. Chronic underfunding has led to the deterioration of equipment and military performance, resulting in a number of accidents. On 20 April 2000, an errant missile hit an apartment building in the Kyiv suburb of Brovary, killing three residents and leaving 91 people homeless. On 4 October 2001, a Russian passenger plane was shot down by a missile during training exercises on the Black Sea, killing all 78 people on board. On 27 July 2002, 76 people were killed when a military jet crashed during an air show at the Skynyliv aerodrome near Lviv.

Throughout history, Ukrainian military formations were created during periods of independence, while Ukrainians under alien rule served in foreign armies. **Kyivan Rus'** had a military force initially comprised of **Varangian** mercenaries, who in time were replaced by local troops loyal to the **princes**. A unique military formation, the **Cossacks**, emerged on the steppe frontier in the 15th and 16th centuries. The Cossacks served the **Hetmanate** in the 17th and 18th centuries. They eventually became part of the Russian imperial army and lost their distinctive character. In Austria-Hungary, Ukrainians served in Austrian forces on their territory, and in 1914 they formed the **Ukrainian Sich Riflemen**—a Ukrainian legion in the Austrian army. With the disintegration of imperial armies at the end of World War I, Ukrainian soldiers joined new national military formations: the Army of the **Ukrainian People's Republic**, the **Ukrainian Galician Army**, and various insurgent groups. In **western Ukraine** during the interwar period, Ukrainians were drafted into the Polish, Hungarian, Romanian, and Czechoslovak armies. In **World War II** about 4.5 million Ukrainians served in the Red Army, while inhabitants of western Ukraine were drafted into various national forces. The Germans established several Ukrainian units, including the **Division Galizien** and the **Ukrainian Liberation Army**, the latter recruited from Red Army prisoners of war. The independent **Ukrainian Insurgent Army** fought German, Soviet, and Polish forces in its struggle to establish a sovereign state.

ARTICLES OF BOHDAN KHMELNYTSKY. A set of documents that defined the political and legal status of the **Hetmanate** after the **Pereiaslav Agreement** (1654). In the course of negotiations leading to the agreement, the Muscovite ambassador, the **boyar** Vasilii Buturlin, refused to swear an oath on the tsar's behalf guaranteeing the rights and privileges of the **Zaporozhian Host**, the Ukrainian **nobility**, the Orthodox clergy, and the burghers. To secure a written guarantee, Hetman **Bohdan Khmelnytsky** and his officers drew up the so-called Soliciting Articles to the tsar, which were taken to Moscow by a delegation headed by the general judge of the Zaporozhian Host, Samiilo Bohdanovych-Zarudny, and the colonel of Pereiaslav, **Pavlo Teteria**.

The document consisted of articles on the privileges, rights, and liberties of the Zaporozhian Host and the Ukrainian nobility and clergy, the establishment of a **Cossack** register of 60,000, the payment of officers' salaries and the financing of the Host, the maintenance of the local administration and its right to collect taxes, the granting of the Chyhyryn region for the hetman's use, the right of the Host to choose its **hetman**, the hetman's right to conduct foreign relations, the noninterference of Muscovite authorities in the affairs of the Hetmanate, defense against the Poles and **Tatars**, and the maintenance of a Cossack garrison at the Kodak fortress.

As a result of negotiations in Moscow (February 1654), the Cossack terms were reduced and the document ratified by the tsar and the boyar council on 14 (24) March, becoming known as the "March Articles." It established a Cossack register of 60,000, fixed salary amounts for officials, granted the use of mills to the **Cossack officers**, confirmed the property rights of the **Kyiv metropolitan** and the clergy, pledged that the Muscovite government would declare war on Poland in the spring of 1654, and arranged the stationing of Muscovite armies on the border between the Hetmanate and the **Polish-Lithuanian Commonwealth**. It further provided that in the event of a Tatar attack, the Hetmanate and Muscovy would mount a joint campaign.

The articles became the defining document in Russo-Ukrainian relations. Some variant of them was used whenever a new hetman took office. From the Ukrainian viewpoint, the articles embodied the contractual relationship between the Hetmanate and the tsar.

The original articles of 1654 were substantially altered in 1659, when Muscovy obtained the right to establish garrisons in all major towns and the hetman's authority to conduct foreign relations was curtailed (*see* KHMELNYTSKY, YURII). Although the Hetmanate's autonomy was whittled down considerably, the practice of confirming Cossack "rights and liberties" continued until 1687.

ASKOLD (OSKOLD) AND DIR. Semilegendary rulers of **Kyivan Rus'** in the mid-ninth century. According to various sources, they were either descendants of **Kyi** or retainers in the forces of the **Varangian** prince **Riuryk**. The *Tale of Bygone Years* relates that Askold and Dir took control of **Kyiv**, led an unsuccessful expedition against Constantinople in 860, and continued to rule Kyiv afterward. Many sources mention their baptism. According to **chronicle** accounts, they were murdered in Kyiv in 882 by **Oleh**, who accused them of usurping power. The *Tale* states that Askold was buried on Uhorska Hill (the site of "Askold's Grave" in Kyiv, now part of a park on the right bank of the Dnipro River), while Dir was buried at the church of Oryna (Iryna) in Kyiv.

B

BACHYNSKY, LEV (14 July 1872–4 October 1930). Politician and lawyer. He was born in Serafyntsi, **Galicia**. After completing his legal studies, he worked as a lawyer in Stanyslaviv (now Ivano-Frankivsk). Bachynsky was a leading member of the **Ukrainian Radical Party** and served as a deputy to the Austrian Reichstag from 1907 to 1918. In August 1914, he became a member of the **Supreme Ukrainian Council**, and from May 1915 he was a vice president of **Kost Levytsky's** General Ukrainian Council. He also served as vice president of the **Ukrainian National Rada** of the **Western Ukrainian People's Republic** (ZUNR). Bachynsky wrote the constitutional law of 3 January 1919 on the unification of the ZUNR with the **Ukrainian People's Republic**, as well as the land reform law of 14 April 1919. In January 1919, he headed the delegation of representatives from Galicia, **Bukovyna**, and **Transcarpathia** that took part in the ceremonial **Act of Union** of the two Ukrainian states. After the **Ukrainian Galician Army** retreated across the Zbruch River in 1919, Bachynsky remained in Polish-occupied Stanyslaviv. He supported the efforts of President **Yevhen Petrushevych** to restore the independence of the ZUNR by diplomatic means. From 1924 to 1930, Bachynsky headed the Ukrainian Radical Party (renamed the Ukrainian Socialist Radical Party in 1926). From 1928, he was a member of the Polish

Diet and leader of the Socialist-Radical Club, which cooperated with the Ukrainian Parliamentary Representation.

BACHYNSKY, YULIIAN (28 March 1870–6 June 1940). Civic leader and publicist. He was a member of the **Ukrainian Radical Party** and then of the **Ukrainian Social Democratic Party** (from 1899). In 1895, Bachynsky published *Ukraïna irredenta*, in which he argued the case for Ukrainian political independence along Marxist lines. He saw the development of capitalism as leading to the formation of a multi-ethnic bourgeoisie on Ukrainian territory that would lead a drive for Ukrainian independence in its own economic interest; this in turn would lead to a conflict between the Ukrainian bourgeoisie and proletariat. The book, published shortly before the fourth congress of the Ukrainian Radical Party, led it to adopt independence as part of its platform—the first such instance in modern Ukrainian history.

After visiting North America in 1905–6 to study Ukrainian immigrant communities, Bachynsky published his findings in a monograph (1914). In 1918, he was a member of the **Ukrainian National Rada** of the **Western Ukrainian People's Republic**. In 1919, he became a representative of the **Ukrainian People's Republic** in Washington. He spent the 1920s in Vienna and Berlin. Having adopted pro-Soviet views, Bachynsky settled in the **Ukrainian SSR** (November 1933), where he worked on the editorial board of the *Ukrainian Soviet Encyclopedia*. A year later he was arrested on a trumped-up charge of "counterrevolutionary nationalist activity." He died in a forced-labor camp.

BAHALII, DMYTRO (26 October [7 November] 1857–9 February 1932). Historian and civic figure, academician of the **Ukrainian Academy of Sciences** (from 1919). Bahalii was born in **Kyiv** into a burgher family. He received his higher education at the historical and philological faculties of Kyiv and **Kharkiv** universities. In 1876, with the assistance of the linguist **Oleksander Potebnia**, Bahalii helped establish the Kharkiv Historical and Philological Society, which collected and published historical sources. After graduating from Kyiv University and completing three further years of study at the faculty of Russian history at Kharkiv University, he became a lecturer at the faculty in 1883 and professor in 1887. From 1906 to 1910, he was rector of Kharkiv University. In 1906, and again from 1910 to 1914, Bahalii was elected a delegate to the State Council from the Imperial Academy of Sciences. From 1914 to 1917, he was head of the Kharkiv city council. In 1918, Bahalii was among the founders of the Ukrainian Academy of Sciences. He became chairman of its historical and philological division in 1919 and subsequently a member of its presidium. He was highly active in the organization of scholarly research and in establishing the academy's library. During the 1920s and 1930s, Bahalii lectured in Ukrainian history at the Kharkiv and **Poltava** Institutes of Education and headed the Research Chair of Ukrainian History in Kharkiv, the Institute of the History of Ukrainian Culture, the **Shevchenko** Institute, and the Central Archive of the **Ukrainian SSR**.

As a historian, Bahalii was influenced by the **populist** views of his teacher, **Volodymyr Antonovych**. He wrote more than 200 works devoted primarily to the history of **Sloboda**, **Left-Bank**, and Southern Ukraine from the 15th to the 18th century, especially on the settlement of the steppe frontier. He also wrote on **Magdeburg law** in Ukraine, the history of Kharkiv and its university, the philosopher **Hryhorii Skovoroda** (whose complete works were first edited by Bahalii), and Ukrainian socioeconomic history and historiography.

BANDERA, STEPAN (1 January 1909–15 October 1959). Revolutionary; leader of the **Organization of Ukrainian Nationalists** (OUN). He was born in the village of Uhryniv Staryi, Stanyslaviv region (now Ivano-Frankivsk oblast) into the family of a Ukrainian Catholic priest. From 1919 to 1927, Bandera studied at the Stryi gymnasium. In 1922, he became a member of **Plast** and later of a clandestine student organization. From 1928 to 1932, he studied agronomy at the Higher Polytechnical School in **Lviv**. In 1928, having become a member of the **Ukrainian Military Organization**, Bandera was assigned to its intelligence and propaganda sections. He joined the newly established OUN in the following year, becoming a member of its Western Ukrainian Territorial Executive in 1931. In June 1933, at an OUN conference in Berlin, Bandera was confirmed as head of the organization in **western Ukraine**. In 1933, he planned and directed a student anti-Polonization campaign. To protest the man-made **famine of 1932–33** in the **Ukrainian SSR**, he assigned Mykola Lemyk to assassinate the Soviet consul in Lviv. In 1934, carrying out a resolution of the Berlin conference, Bandera planned the assassination of the Polish foreign minister, Bronisław Pieracki, a leading organizer of the **Pacification**. Bandera was arrested in June 1934 and sentenced to death at a trial of OUN leaders in Warsaw (1935–36). The sentence was commuted to life imprisonment at a second trial in Lviv in 1936. Along with other OUN leaders, Bandera was incarcerated at the Holy Cross Prison in Warsaw.

With the outbreak of **World War II**, Bandera gained his freedom. Arriving in Lviv, he planned the development of an OUN network throughout Ukraine. For generational and ideological reasons, Bandera and his supporters did not recognize the election of **Andrii**

Melnyk as head of the OUN. On 10 February 1940, the Revolutionary OUN Leadership was established in Cracow, and Bandera was confirmed as leader at a congress in April 1941. The OUN(B), which commanded the loyalty of most OUN cadres, saw the war as an opportunity to assert Ukrainian independence. On 30 June 1941, in Lviv, the Bandera faction proclaimed Ukrainian statehood and formed the **Ukrainian State Administration**, headed by **Yaroslav Stetsko**.

On 6 July 1941, Bandera was arrested by the Germans and, after refusing to rescind the proclamation, was imprisoned in the Sachsenhausen concentration camp. At the same time, Bandera's brothers, Vasyl and Bohdan, were imprisoned in Auschwitz, where they perished in 1942. Bandera and Stetsko were freed on 25 September 1944, as the Germans hoped to exploit them in the **Ukrainian National Committee**. After the war Bandera settled in Munich, was elected to the leadership of the OUN in Ukraine, and assumed the leadership of the Foreign Sections of the OUN (ZCh OUN) in February 1946. A protracted conflict developed between the ZCh OUN and OUN emissaries from Ukraine over the major revision of OUN ideology that had been approved in Ukraine in 1943, while Bandera was still incarcerated. Bandera rejected this evolution toward pluralism and social democracy, seeing it as a betrayal of integral nationalism. In 1953 and 1955, Bandera was reelected leader of the OUN(B), while the dissidents, led by Zynovii Matla and **Lev Rebet**, constituted themselves in 1956 as the OUN Abroad. In 1959, the KGB agent Bohdan Stashynsky, who had killed Rebet in 1957, assassinated Bandera. He turned himself in to the American authorities in Berlin on 13 August 1961 and was tried for both crimes in Karlsruhe (8–16 October 1962), receiving an eight-year sentence. The court found that Stashynsky had been operating under the direct instructions of the head of the KGB, Aleksandr Shelepin. Bandera was buried in Munich.

BANKING. Banks in Ukraine, as in the Russian Empire generally, appeared only at the end of the 18th century, while the West European banking system evolved as early as the 16th and 17th centuries. Until Ukraine gained its independence in 1991, banks in the Ukrainian lands were entirely dependent on the central banking systems of the Russian and Austro-Hungarian empires, and subsequently on the centralized banking policy of the Soviet Union.

Banks in the Russian Empire provided loans for land purchases by the nobility and, from 1882, by the peasantry. On Ukrainian territory, banks operated as branches of central institutions until private commercial banks were established in the early 1870s. On the eve of **World War I**, the Russian-ruled Ukrainian lands had 22 branches of the State Bank, 55 branches of the International Bank of

St. Petersburg, 31 branches of the United Bank, 23 branches of the Azov-Donets Bank, five branches of the State Bank for the Nobility, and two branches of the Peasant Land Bank. Many needs of the general population were served by a network of credit **cooperatives**, small land and mortgage banks, and small city banks. In **Galicia**, private Ukrainian banks were established in the late 19th century and, together with cooperative banks and credit unions, served the population until the outbreak of **World War II**.

Under Soviet rule, financial institutions in the **Ukrainian SSR** enjoyed some degree of independence in the early 1920s. The Ukrainbank (est. 1917) was a central financial coordinating body for Ukrainian credit and agricultural cooperatives. By 1926, it served 5,800 credit cooperatives through a system of 50 regional branches. With the Soviet Union's adoption of five-year plans, the Ukrainbank was subordinated to the central bank in Moscow and ultimately closed down in 1936. Subsequently, the banking needs of Ukraine were served by a republic office and regional branches of the State Bank, as well as by branches of specialized banks dealing with **agriculture**, construction, and trade.

The formation of the banking system of independent Ukraine began in March 1991 with the adoption of legislative documents by the Verkhovna Rada. The system consists of the National Bank of Ukraine (NBU) and commercial banks of various types. The NBU serves as the country's central bank, responsible for monetary policy and supervision of commercial banks. In 1996, Ukraine adopted the *hryvnia* (UAH) as its official monetary unit.

Commercial banks in Ukraine are formed as joint-stock or private companies. In 2003, there were 179 registered commercial banks. Of these, seven banks had entirely foreign capital and another 20 were partly capitalized from abroad. The total authorized capital of all banks was 7.32 billion UAH. The major banks are Prominvestbank, PryvatBank, Aval, Ukrsotsbank, and two state-owned institutions, the Savings Bank of Ukraine and the Export-Import Bank. Since 1998, the banking system in Ukraine has been using international accounting and statistical standards. *See also* ECONOMY.

BAROQUE. Ukrainian baroque **literature**, which began in the first quarter of the 17th century with the works of **Meletii Smotrytsky**, Kyrylo Stavrovetsky-Tranquillon, and **Ivan Vyshensky**, ended in the late 18th century with **Hryhorii Skovoroda**. A peculiarity of the genre in Ukraine was that religious works outnumbered secular ones. The latter consisted of a relatively small quantity of poetry, epics, tales, and historical **chronicles**, while plays and treatises remained almost exclusively religious. Writers of the period were predominantly members of the clergy, while secular patrons were few. There were no secular schools of higher learning, and many Ukrainians turned to writing in Latin or Polish. The literary language of the period was not standardized; the church used the Ukrainian redaction of Church Slavonic, while the language of nonreligious works often absorbed Polish elements, but the extent of vernacular or foreign borrowings in particular works depended on the writer. In the 18th century, elements of Russian entered the literary language. Ukrainian baroque literature, for its part, exerted considerable influence on Russian literature of the 17th and 18th centuries.

Ukrainian baroque art and **architecture** emerged in the 17th century. Because Ukrainian baroque architecture coincided with the **Cossack** period, this style is often referred to as Cossack baroque. In contrast to the decorative style prevalent in Western Europe, Ukrainian baroque architecture preferred moderate ornamentation and simpler forms. Since the Orthodox Church discouraged **sculpture**, Ukrainian artists instead produced ornate carvings, particularly elaborate, multi-tiered iconostases. During the baroque period, **painting** became more realistic and Byzantine iconographic traditions gave way to secular elements, three-dimensional forms, and the illusion of movement. Nevertheless, painting remained predominantly religious in character.

BARVINSKY, OLEKSANDER (8 June 1847–25 December 1926). Civic and political activist, pedagogue and historian, full member of the **Shevchenko Scientific Society** from 1899. Barvinsky was born in the village of Shliakhtyntsi, Ternopil region, into a clerical family. From 1857 to 1865, he studied at the Ternopil gymnasium, and in 1865 he enrolled at **Lviv** University, where he studied history and Ukrainian language and literature. During his student years, he was active in the Lviv **Hromada**, working with the periodicals *Pravda*, *Meta*, and *Rusalka*. From 1868, Barvinsky taught at the Berezhany and Ternopil gymnasiums. In 1888, he became a professor at the State Teachers' Seminary in Lviv. He was a member of the **Galician** School Council (1893–1918), headed the Ukrainian Pedagogical Society (1891–96), and was vice president of the Lviv **Prosvita Society** (1889–95). In 1886, he began issuing the *Ruthenian Historical Library* (24 volumes). Together with **Oleksander Konysky** and **Volodymyr Antonovych**, he initiated the reorganization of the Shevchenko Literary Society as the Shevchenko Scientific Society, which he directed (1893–97).

Barvinsky was active in politics, helping to initiate the short-lived understanding with Austrian government and Polish political circles known as the "New Era" (1890). From 1891 to 1907, he was a deputy to the Austrian Reichstag, becoming a life member of the upper chamber in 1917. From 1894 to 1904, he was a deputy to the Galician

Diet. In 1896, Barvinsky founded the **Catholic Ruthenian People's Union**, renamed the Christian Social Party in 1911. In 1918–19, he headed the State Secretariat of Education and Religious Affairs in **Kost Levytsky's** government. After the Polish annexation of Galicia (1923), he abandoned political life. Barvinsky wrote and published several literature textbooks for Ukrainian primary and secondary schools.

BASARAB, OLHA (24 July 1899–12/13 February 1924). Civic and political activist in **Galicia**. She was born in the village of Pidhoroddia, Rohatyn region (now in Ivano-Frankivsk oblast). She studied at the Peremyshl (Przemyśl) Lyceum and then at the Academy of Commerce in Vienna. During her student years, Basarab became active in the Ukrainian national movement. At the beginning of **World War I**, with Olena Stepaniv, she organized the first **women's** platoon of the **Ukrainian Sich Riflemen**. During the war, Basarab conducted charitable and educational work for the Ukrainian Women's Committee to Aid Wounded Soldiers in Vienna and in the Ukrainian community of that city. In 1918, she was secretary of the **Ukrainian People's Republic** mission to Finland and later worked with the government-in-exile of the **Western Ukrainian People's Republic**. She was a founder and treasurer of the **Union of Ukrainian Women**. Arrested by the Polish police on 9 February 1924 for belonging to the **Ukrainian Military Organization**, Basarab died under torture. She was buried at the Yaniv Cemetery in **Lviv**. Her martyrdom made her a cult figure of the nationalist movement in **western Ukraine**.

BASILIAN ORDER. Religious order established in Byzantium, guided by a rule compiled ca. 362 by St. Basil the Great of Caesarea. In the 11th century, monasteries subject to the Basilian rule began to be established in **Kyivan Rus'**. After the **Union of Brest** (1596), Metropolitan **Yosyf Veliamyn Rutsky** reorganized monastic life in the Ukrainian lands, placing Basilian monasteries under the authority of a protoarchimandrite. Each monastery was governed by a hegumen (appointed for four years) and an archimandrite (appointed for life). The new rule for the Basilian Order was confirmed by Pope Urban VIII in 1631. In the 17th century, the Eastern branch of the order was active mainly in Belarus, where its novitiate and school of philosophy were located; Basilians studied theology in West European papal colleges. According to a papal decree of 1635, it was obligatory for Eastern-rite Catholic bishops to be Basilians.

Once the **Galician** eparchies adhered to the Union (ca. 1700), the Basilian Order propagated Catholicism there. After the Synod of Zamostia (Zamość) in 1720, all Eastern-rite monasteries were required to join the Basilian Order, and in 1743, on the instructions of Pope Benedict XIV, an Order of Basilian Monks for the Ukrainian and Belarusian lands was created at an assembly in Dubno. In 1780, the Order was divided into four provinces—Lithuania, Belarus, Ruthenia, and Galicia—comprising approximately 1,235 monks in 155 monasteries. Its major activities were propagating the faith, education, and publishing. The Basilians administered schools (noted for their high level of instruction) in many Ukrainian towns and had colleges in Buchach, Hoshcha, Liubar, Ostrih, Sharhorod, Uman, and Volodymyr-Volynskyi, as well as schools for the sons of impoverished nobles. Their main publishing centers were Pochaiv in **Volhynia** and Univ near **Lviv**; between 1733 and 1800, Pochaiv alone published more than 100 works in Ruthenian.

After the partitions of Poland, when all the Basilian provinces except Galicia came under Russian rule, the Order was persecuted and ultimately abolished by the tsarist authorities. In Galicia, Joseph II of Austria closed most of the monasteries and secularized their properties. Not until 1882, when Pope Leo XIII entrusted the reform of the Order to the Jesuits, did it begin to revive in Galicia. The Basilians reached out to young people through the Marian societies (more than 20,000 members).

During the interwar period, a seminary was established in Lviv and a junior gymnasium in Buchach. In Zhovkva, the Basilian publishing center, the journals *Misionar* and *Nash pryiatel'* (Our Friend) and the scholarly *Zapysky Chyna sv. Vasyliia Velykoho/Analecta Ordinis S. Basilii Magni* were issued. The Basilians also extended their mission to **Transcarpathia**. By the 1930s, the Order had 22 monasteries: 16 in Galicia (Buchach, Dobromyl, Krystynopil [now Chervonohrad], Lviv, Peremyshl, Zolochiv, and others), three in Transcarpathia, and one each in Hungary, Romania, and Canada. In 1946, with the suppression of the **Ukrainian Catholic Church** by the Soviet authorities, the Order ceased to exist in Ukraine. It shifted its activities to the Americas, where Ukrainian Basilians had first arrived in the late 19th century. Provinces of the Order were established in the United States, Canada, and Brazil, with a vice-province in Argentina. In 1989, the Basilian Order returned to Ukraine, resuming its activities in Lviv, Uhniv, Zhovkva, and other centers.

BENDERY, CONSTITUTION OF (Constitution of Pylyp Orlyk, Pacta et Constitutiones Legum Libertatumque Exercitus Zaporoviensis). The first written Ukrainian constitution, signed on 5 (16) April 1710 at the election of **Pylyp Orlyk** as **hetman** of Ukraine. It was drafted by Orlyk, Hryhorii Hertsyk, Andrii Voinarovsky, and Kost Hordiienko in Latin and Ruthenian (Ukrainian). Its official title is

Pacts and Constitution of Laws and Liberties of the Zaporozhian Host.
Based on an agreement between the hetman, the **Cossack officers**, and the **Zaporozhian Host**, the constitution comprised a preamble and 16 paragraphs. The preamble presented a schema of the history of the Ruthenian (Ukrainian) people and the Zaporozhian Host, asserting that the "Cossack people" were the founders of **Kyivan Rus'** and that the Host was obliged to defend the rights of the Ukrainian people. The Swedish king, Charles XII, "guardian and protector" of Ukraine, confirmed the conditions and proceedings of the hetman's election and became guarantor of an independent Ukraine. Orthodoxy was proclaimed the state religion, and the church was to be subject to the patriarchate of Constantinople, not Moscow. The Hetmanate's border with the **Polish-Lithuanian Commonwealth** was to be the one established by the Treaty of Zboriv (1649). The constitution confirmed the return of Trakhtemyriv, Kodak, and adjoining lands to the Zaporozhian Host and stressed the importance of destroying the Muscovite fortress at the **Zaporozhian Sich**.

All important state affairs were to be decided by the hetman together with the General Officer Staff, colonels, and general councillors from each regiment. The General Military Council was to meet at the hetman's residence three times a year (at Christmas, Easter, and the Feast of the Holy Protection). All important judicial matters were to be reviewed by the General Military Court. The general treasurer was to manage revenue with the hetman's assent. The hetman would be paid out of income from estates in Sheptaky county and part of the lands of the Zaporozhian Host. The same applied to colonels. The hetman was to supervise the administrative bodies and ratify the elections of higher officials and colonels, as well as to prevent the abuse of rank-and-file **Cossacks** and commoners by officers. Widows and orphans of Cossacks and some other strata of the population were exempt from taxation. A good deal of attention was devoted to financial, economic, and military matters (surveying state land, introducing fixed tariffs and revenue collection, canceling leases on mercenaries' and guardsmen's quarters, etc.). The constitution was in force in **Right-Bank Ukraine** until 1714.

BERESTIA LAND (Ukr. *Beresteis'ka zemlia*). Ukrainian ethnic territory bounded by the Buh, Prypiat, Yaselda, and Narev Rivers. Its total area is 32,300 sq. km, and its largest towns are Brest, Kobryn, and Kamianets. In the 10th century, it became part of **Kyivan Rus'**. From 1080, it belonged to the Principality of Turiv-Pynsk (Turaŭ-

Pinsk). In 1150, it became part of the Volhynian Principality and was incorporated into the Principality of **Galicia-Volhynia** in 1199. In 1320, the Berestia land was taken over by the Principality of Trakai (Lithuania) and became part of the Brest palatinate of the **Polish-Lithuanian Commonwealth** (1569–1795). After the third partition of Poland (1795), the Berestia land was annexed to the Russian Empire. It is now in Belarus.

In 1940, Brest oblast had 58 schools with Ukrainian-**language** instruction, 127 **Prosvita** reading rooms, and a Ukrainian library. Today there are no schools with Ukrainian-language instruction. The Ukrainian Community-Cultural Alliance, founded in Brest in 1990, has made consistent efforts to obtain official status for the population of the Berestia land as a Ukrainian ethnic minority.

BEREZIL THEATER. Theater founded in 1922 by **Les Kurbas**, who recruited a group of actors of the former Young Theater (est. 1917). The name comes from the first month of spring, *berezen'* (March). The theater was based in **Kyiv** until 1926 and in **Kharkiv** from 1926 to 1933. Berezil evolved from Kurbas's belief that **theater** should not imitate life but shape the basic principles of society. His creative practices were influenced by expressionism and constructivism. Berezil staged works by Ukrainian and foreign playwrights; the productions of **Mykola Kulish's** plays *Maklena Grassa*, *Narodnyi Malakhii* (The People's Malakhii), and *Myna Mazailo* were particularly successful. Notable actors included Danylo Antonovych, Amvrosii Buchma, Valentyna Chystiakova, Mariian Krushelnytsky, Oleksander Serdiuk, Stepan Shahaida, Nadiia Tytarenko, and Nataliia Uzhvii. Because of its clearly defined national and artistic program, Berezil was constantly charged with nationalism and resistance to the policies of the Communist Party. Following the arrest of Kurbas at the end of 1933, Berezil was reformed and renamed the Kharkiv **Shevchenko** State Dramatic Theater.

BEREZOVSKY, MAKSYM (16 (27) October 1745–22 March (2 April) 1777). Composer. Born in Hlukhiv (now in Sumy oblast), he studied at the **Kyiv Mohyla Academy**, where he began writing **music**. Berezovsky was invited to join the court choir in St. Petersburg in 1758. In 1762, he became a soloist with an Italian opera company in Oranienbaum near the Russian capital. While living in Italy (1765–74), Berezovsky completed his musical studies with the music theoretician Giuseppe Martini and was elected to the Bologna Philharmonic Academy (1771). His opera *Demofonte* was staged with great success in Livorno in 1773. Depressed by court intrigues and unable to find an outlet for his creativity upon his return to St. Petersburg, Berezovsky committed suicide. He is best known for numerous sacred concertos ("Do Not Forsake Me in My Old Age," Lord's Prayer, Credo), which are influenced by Ukrainian **folk music** and Kyivan church singing. Berezovsky was a prominent founder of Ukrainian classical music and the choral concerto.

BESSARABIA (Ukr. *Bessarabiia*). Historical region bounded by the Prut and Dnister Rivers and the Danube estuary. The larger portion of Bessarabia belongs to Moldova, while lands at the southern and northern ends of Bessarabia belong to Ukraine. In ancient times, Bessarabia was settled by **Scythians**, Getae, Dacians, **Antes** (from the fourth century), Ulychians, and Tivertsians. In the 10th and 11th centuries, it was part of **Kyivan Rus'** and later belonged to the Principality of **Galicia-Volhynia**. Bessarabia was annexed to the Moldavian Principality in the mid-14th century, and both became subject to the Ottoman Turks in 1514. During the mid-16th century, Bessarabia was the site of **Cossack** campaigns led by **Dmytro Vyshnevetsky** (1553, 1563), Ivan Svyrhovsky (1574), **Ivan Pidkova** (1577), and Severyn Nalyvaiko (1594). During the **Khmelnytsky Uprising** (1648–57), two campaigns took place in **Moldavia** (1650 and 1652). After the destruction of the **Zaporozhian Sich** (1775), Cossacks founded the **Transdanubian Sich** in southern Bessarabia. Following the Russo-Turkish War of 1806–12, the Ottomans ceded Bessarabia to the Russian Empire.

The February Revolution of 1917 resulted in the flowering of the Ukrainian national movement in Bessarabia, including the establishment of Ukrainian schools and the organization of **Prosvita societies**. The Ukrainian population of that part of Bessarabia where Ukrainians constituted the majority appealed for union with the **Ukrainian People's Republic** (UNR). In mid-January 1918, taking advantage of Ukraine's difficult international circumstances, Romanian forces occupied Bessarabia. On 25 November 1918, the Bessarabian National Council (Sfatul Ţărei) declared the union of Bessarabia with Romania and dissolved itself. Ukrainian deputies who opposed the decision were arrested and executed. Ukrainian inhabitants protested the annexation at mass meetings in Akkerman, Izmail, the western Odesa region (southern Bessarabia), and Khotyn (northern Bessarabia). At the beginning of January 1919, a Ukrainian rebellion in the Khotyn region was suppressed by Romanian forces. The Tatarbunary rebellion of September 1924 ended in bloody reprisals against the participants, some of whom were shot without trial. The leaders were tried in Chişinău in 1925 and sentenced to imprisonment or punitive labor.

During the interwar period, Ukrainian national and cultural life in Bessarabia developed poorly because of Romanian assimilationist policies. There was a small number of Prosvita societies, reading rooms, and theatrical groups. According to the Romanian census of 1930, Ukrainians accounted for 36.6 percent of the population in northern Bessarabia and 74.2 percent in the south. In June 1940, Bessarabia and northern **Bukovyna** were taken over by the Red Army. They were annexed to the **USSR** on 2 August, and the Akkerman, Izmail, and Khotyn counties of Bessarabia were incorporated into the **Ukrainian SSR**.

BEZBORODKO, OLEKSANDER (14 [25] March 1747–6 [17] April 1799). Diplomat and prince of the Russian Empire, descended from a **Cossack** family. He was born in Hlukhiv and graduated from the **Kyiv Mohyla Academy**. In 1765, he began serving in the chancellery of the governor-general of **Little Russia**, **Petr Rumiantsev**. Bezborodko took part in the drafting of the Treaty of Küçük Kaynarca (1774) with the Ottoman Empire. In 1775, he became a personal secretary to Catherine II. He joined the Collegium of Foreign Affairs in 1780, and from 1784 he was its virtual head. In 1791, he signed the Treaty of Iaşi with the Ottomans. Bezborodko's advancement coincided with the abolition of Ukrainian autonomy, in which he actively participated as an imperial functionary. He did, however, express local patriotism in encouraging the writing of Little Russian history.

BLACK COUNCIL (Ukr. *chorna rada*). **Cossack council** that included not only rank-and-file **Cossacks** and officers but also **peasants** and townspeople (these lower estates were known as *chern'*, hence the council's name). Black councils were called when some Cossack faction or foreign power wanted to stir up the "rabble" and gain its support. The best-known black council convened on 17–18 (27–28) June 1663 in the vicinity of Nizhyn to elect the **hetman** of Left-Bank Ukraine.

After **Yurii Khmelnytsky** abdicated as hetman (January 1663), a civil war, known as the **Ruin**, divided Ukraine along the **Right** and **Left Banks** of the Dnipro River. The **Polish-Lithuanian Commonwealth** attempted to influence developments on the Right Bank, while the Left Bank was under Muscovite control. In January 1663, **Pavlo Teteria** was elected hetman with the approval of the Polish king, but the Cossack regiments on the Left Bank and in Zaporizhia did not recognize Teteria's authority. Acting hetman **Yakym Somko** and the Nizhyn colonel Vasyl Zolotarenko sought the hetmancy with the support of the northern regiments and

Cossack officers. **Ivan Briukhovetsky**, the hetman of Zaporizhia, who relied on demagoguery, found support among the impoverished segments of Ukrainian society. He was also supported by the tsarist government. Elected hetman at the black council of June 1663, Briukhovetsky ordered the arrest of Somko and Zolotarenko, accused them of ties with the Polish aristocracy, and had them executed in Borzna (now in Chernihiv oblast) in September 1663.

BLACK HUNDREDS. Popular name for Russian chauvinist and ultranationalist organizations that arose in reaction to the **Revolution of 1905**. The most prominent was the Union of the Russian People (St. Petersburg), which drew its membership from among landlords, bureaucrats, intellectuals, and clergymen. It enjoyed official support and collaborated with the tsarist secret police. The Black Hundreds supported the principle of tsarist autocracy, which had been shaken by the revolution, and the concept of an all-Russian nationality (which entailed a refusal to recognize Ukrainians and Belarusians as distinct peoples). Anti-Semitism was an important element of their program.

In Ukraine, the Black Hundreds were well organized, with centers in **Kharkiv**, **Kyiv**, **Odesa**, and Yelysavethrad. They mobilized support among Russians, Russified Ukrainians, and the Orthodox clergy (notably at the **Pochaiv Monastery**), which was generally loyal to the tsarist regime. Their strong-arm squads organized pogroms against **Jews** in Kyiv, Odesa, Yalta, and other cities in 1906–7. The more moderate Russian Assembly had branches in Kharkiv, Kyiv, and Odesa, while the Odesa Union of the Russian People had 10 branches in southern Ukraine. In 1906, the Black Hundreds established a common front in Kyiv known as the United Russian People, and a similar front, the Russian (White) Two-Headed Eagle, existed in Odesa in 1907–8. Such organizations exploited **peasant** resentment against Polish landlords on the Right Bank, taking all the seats for the Kyiv and **Volhynia** gubernias in the elections to the Third Duma (1907). In 1908, a splinter group organized the Union of the Archangel Michael in Kyiv, Odesa, and Kherson, and the Southern Monarchist Union was founded in Odesa in 1910. In 1913, the Black Hundreds took over the Odesa city council through electoral fraud and banned the city's **Prosvita Society**.

The Black Hundreds provoked the trial of Mendel Beilis, which took place in Kyiv in September-October 1913. Beilis, a Jew, was accused of the ritual murder of a Christian boy, and his trial became the pretext for an anti-Semitic campaign. Despite official pressure from the ministries of justice and the interior, the jury of Ukrainian peasants acquitted Beilis. Early in 1914, reacting to **Shevchenko** commemorations in Ukraine, members of the Black Hundreds threatened to hang Ukrainians from lampposts as soon as war broke out. After the February Revolution of 1917, the Black Hundreds dissolved or were abolished.

BLACK RUS' (Ukr. *Chorna Rus'*). Ancient name of indeterminate origin for the lands of northwestern Belarus in the upper Neman River basin. Its major centers were Haradzen (now Hrodna), Navaharodak (now Navahrudak), Vaŭkavysk, Slonim, Zdzitaŭ (now Zdzitava), Lida, and Niasvizh (all now in Belarus). From the 10th century, Black Rus' was part of **Kyivan Rus'**. In the 13th century, the **Grand Duchy of Lithuania** and the Principality of **Galicia-Volhynia** fought for control of it, with Lithuania taking it over in the 1240s (according to some historians, as early as 1219). In approximately 1255–58, Roman Danylovych, son of **Danylo Romanovych** of Halych, ruled the area as a vassal of the Lithuanian prince Mindaugas. Black Rus' came under Lithuanian rule in the 1270s.

BLACK SEA COLONIES. Between the seventh and fifth centuries B.C., Greeks fleeing overpopulation and civil strife established colonies on the northern shore of the Black Sea. In time, the colonies developed into city-states. The most prominent was Olbia on the Buh estuary, which dominated the grain trade with Greece. Situated on the Crimean peninsula were Chersonesus (near present-day Sevastopol), Theodosia (now Feodosiia), and Panticapaeum (now Kerch); Phanagoria was located across the Strait of Kerch. Panticapaeum was the capital of the Bosporan Kingdom, an alliance of Greek city-states that flourished from ca. 480 B.C. to 370 A.D. The city-states traded primarily in grain, fish, and wine; crafts were also well developed. In 63 B.C., the Roman Empire defeated the Bosporan Kingdom, gaining control of the Black Sea littoral. A period of stability ensued until the invasions of the Goths and Huns (third–fourth centuries A.D.) destroyed the Greek cities, putting an end to the hybrid civilization that had evolved from Greek interaction with the **Scythians** and **Sarmatians**. During the reign of the Byzantine emperor Justinian (527–65 A.D.), the Greek coastal cities were revived and fortified, with Chersonesus as their new administrative center. Under Byzantine rule, the **Crimea** became an important center of Christian influence. *See also* BLACK SEA LITTORAL.

BLACK SEA COSSACKS. Army recruited by the Russian government from the former **Zaporozhian Cossacks** in late 1787 and early 1788. The Army of Loyal Cossacks, subsequently the Black Sea

Cossack Host, commanded by *kish* otaman Sydir Bily, was established in 1788 to support Russian forces at war with the Ottoman Empire. It received the Zaporozhian **Cossack insignia** (April-May 1788) confiscated during the destruction of the **Sich** in 1775. The Host restored the previous officer ranks, the division into kurins (companies), and Cossack dress. In 1788, it was granted territory between the Southern Buh and Dnister Rivers. After the death of Bily in a naval battle near Ochakiv (June 1788), the army was led by a new otaman, Zakhar Chepiha, and a military judge, Antin Holovaty.

After the Russo-Turkish War (1787–91), in which some 15,000 **Cossacks** took part, they petitioned St. Petersburg for provisions and a new place to settle. In 1792, the Russian government moved them to the Kuban region to consolidate its position in the North Caucasus. The Cossacks were settled along the Black Sea Border Line, from the Laba River along the right bank of the Kuban River to the Sea of Azov. In 1792–93, approximately 25,000 Cossacks were resettled there and allotted a territory of 30,000 sq. km. The former Zaporozhians comprised 40 kurins, renamed *stanytsi* in the mid-19th century, with headquarters in Katerynodar (now Krasnodar). In the Kuban, the Cossacks retained the right to elect their military administration and maintain their kurin names. The army grew thanks to the resettlement of former **registered** and **Sloboda** Cossacks, as well as veterans of the reorganized Ukrainian Cossack armies. The major resettlement campaigns took place in 1809–11, 1821–25, and 1848–50. By 1860, the Kuban Cossacks numbered approximately 200,000. They participated in Russian military campaigns in the Caucasus and in the Crimean War (1853–56). In 1860, the Black Sea Cossack Host was incorporated into the Kuban Cossack Host. The Cossacks engaged in cattle herding and fishing, as well as in **agriculture** from the mid-19th century. Their landholdings were considerable, and they played an important role in the economic development of the Kuban region.

BLACK SEA FLEET. A part of the tsarist Russian and Soviet navies, the Black Sea Fleet is now divided into Russian and Ukrainian sections, both based at the Ukrainian port of Sevastopol in the **Crimea**. An integral part of the Ukrainian Navy since 1992 (*see* ARMED FORCES), the fleet comprises some 40 combat ships and more than 40 auxiliary vessels, as well as 60 aircraft and about 13,500 personnel. The navy also uses ports in **Odesa**, Ochakiv, Chornomorske, Novoozerne, Mykolaiv, Yevpatoriia, and Feodosiia as bases.

The dispute between Ukraine and Russia over the Black Sea Fleet that emerged after the breakup of the Soviet Union was partly resolved in 1997 by an agreement allowing the larger, Russian part of the fleet to lease Sevastopol harbor for 20 years as its main base. The assets of the fleet were divided between the two countries.

The Black Sea Fleet was created in the 1780s by Prince Grigorii Potemkin, who combined the Azov, Dnipro, and Danube flotillas. It was first put to the test in the Turco-Russian War of 1787–91. After the Treaty of Paris (1856), the Black Sea was demilitarized, and Russia lost the right to have a fleet there and build fortresses and naval bases. Russia denounced the treaty in 1870 and reestablished its naval presence on the Black Sea. On the eve of **World War I**, the fleet, manned by more than 36,000 officers and sailors, consisted of battleships, cruisers, destroyers, and submarines. During the **Ukrainian Revolution** (1917–21), the **Ukrainian Central Rada** claimed the section of the fleet that declared itself Ukrainian, and the **Ukrainian State** took over the entire fleet in November 1918. But the fleet changed hands very often, flying tsarist, Bolshevik, French, and German flags at various times. In the aftermath of Entente intervention, the fleet was interned at the French naval base in Tunisia and later incorporated into the French navy or sold for scrap.

The Soviet government rebuilt the Black Sea Fleet by 1928. Although it suffered great losses at the hands of the German air force at the beginning of **World War II**, the fleet contributed to the Soviet war effort by defending coastal towns and evacuating personnel. It was substantially enlarged after the war and established a Soviet military presence on the Mediterranean Sea. At the disintegration of the Soviet Union the fleet, according to various estimates, comprised more than 400 combat and support ships, with a complement of more than 200 warplanes and transport aircraft. The Caspian flotilla was considered part of the Black Sea Fleet.

BLACK SEA LITTORAL. The Black Sea coast is divided among Ukraine, the Russian Federation, Georgia, Turkey, Bulgaria, and Romania. With the exception of the **Crimea**, the Ukrainian portion of the coast is fairly even, low, and intersected by rivers, the largest of which are Danube, Dnister, Southern Buh, and Dnipro.

The northern Black Sea coast has long had close ties with the Mediterranean lands. Ancient Greek pirates and traders established trading posts on the northern coast as early as the beginning of the first millennium B.C. Greek **Black Sea colonies**, which began to appear between the seventh and fifth centuries B.C., soon became city-states, the largest of which were Chersonesus (now Sevastopol), Theodosia (now Feodosiia), and Panticapaeum (now Kerch). A union of city-states known as the Bosporan Kingdom controlled the

Black Sea littoral from ca. 480 B.C. to ca. 370 A.D. The Greeks established trade relations with the **Scythians** and **Sarmatians** to the north. After a period of decline, the Bosporan Kingdom was taken over by the Roman Empire in 63 B.C., securing its prosperity for more than three centuries. The invasions of the Goths and Huns in the third and fourth centuries, as well as the migration of Turkic-Mongolian tribes into the Black Sea steppes, led to the destruction of the Greek cities. They were rebuilt in the ninth century, when the Byzantine Empire took control of the Crimea.

A number of Slavic tribes, including the **Antes**, Ulychians, and Tivertsians, settled the western part of the Black Sea region. **Kyivan Rus'** expanded its access to the Black Sea by attacking Constantinople in 860, 912, and 945. The link between Rus' and the Black Sea was severed as a result of nomadic invasions from the east by **Pechenegs**, Torks, and **Cumans** in the 10th and 11th centuries. With the destruction of Rus' by the **Golden Horde** in 1240, direct access to the Black Sea was lost. European goods and cultural influences continued to reach the Rus' lands through Genoese and Venetian colonies on the northern Black Sea coast that recognized the authority of the Golden Horde. The Lithuanian prince Vytautas campaigned on the Black Sea coast in the late 14th century, but it remained in the hands of the **Tatars**, who established the Crimean Khanate in the 1440s and became vassals of the Ottoman Turks in 1475.

As Ukrainian settlements moved further away from the Black Sea coast to avoid frequent Tatar incursions, parts of the steppe lay abandoned. The **Cossacks** protected the Ukrainian population and ventured into Tatar territory, raiding coastal fortresses and towns. Muscovy's southward expansion to the Black Sea coast began in the late 17th century. After protracted wars, the Russian Empire took over the Crimea in 1783. In 1812, Russian control was extended to **Bessarabia** and the coastal lands between the Dnister and Danube Rivers. Throughout the 19th century, the Black Sea littoral was colonized by Ukrainians, Russians, Bulgarians, Germans, and Greeks.

The strategic importance of the Black Sea littoral and the **Black Sea Fleet** was recognized by the warring factions during the **Ukrainian Revolution** (1917–21). Before it was captured by the Bolsheviks, the coast was held by the Army of the **Ukrainian People's Republic** (1918), French expeditionary forces, the White armies of Generals Anton Denikin and Petr Wrangel, and various Ukrainian insurgents. With the formation of the Soviet Union, the Crimea became part of the Russian SFSR, the remainder of the northern coastal region went to the **Ukrainian SSR**, and Bessarabia was annexed by Romania until its takeover by Soviet forces in 1940. The Crimea was transferred to the Ukrainian SSR in 1954. Since 1991, the northwestern Black Sea coast has been the natural southern border of independent Ukraine.

BLAKYTNY, VASYL (31 December 1893 [12 January 1894]–4 December 1925). Actual surname: Ellansky. Political activist and writer. He was born in the village of Kozly, Chernihiv gubernia, and studied at the Chernihiv seminary and the **Kyiv** Commercial Institute. In 1917, Blakytny joined the **Ukrainian Party of Socialist Revolutionaries**; a year later, he helped initiate a split within the party and the creation of its left faction, the **Borotbists**. He edited its newspaper, *Borot'ba* (Struggle). After the forced merger of the Borotbists with the **Communist Party of Ukraine** (CPU), Blakytny became a member of the Central Committee of the CPU (1920–25). In 1921, he was appointed head of the State Publishing House and editor of the newspaper *Visti VUTsVK* (News of the All-Ukrainian Central Executive Committee). Blakytny founded and edited the journals *Shliakhy mystetstv* (Paths of the Arts), *Chervonyi perets'* (Red Pepper, 1922–25), and *Vsesvit* (Universe, 1925). He was also a founder of two unions of "proletarian" writers in Ukraine: Borot'ba (1919) and Hart (1923–25). Blakytny was well known as a poet (pseud. Vasyl Ellan), prose writer (pseud. A. Ortal), satirist (pseud. Valer Pronoza), and parodist (pseud. Markiz Popeliasty). In the 1930s, Blakytny's works were banned as "nationalist" and the monument to him in **Kharkiv** was destroyed. *See also* LITERATURE.

BODIANSKY, OSYP (31 October [12 November] 1808–6 [18] September 1877). Philologist and Slavist, historian and writer. He was born in the village of Varva, **Poltava** gubernia (now in Chernihiv oblast), into a clerical family. In 1834, he graduated from Moscow University, and from 1837 to 1842 he traveled on research expeditions to the west and south Slavic lands, becoming acquainted with leading literary figures there. A founder of Slavic studies in Russia, Bodiansky was a professor at Moscow University (1842–68), and from 1845 he was secretary of the Moscow Society of History and Antiquities at the university. He edited its periodical, *Readings of the Moscow Society of Russian History and Antiquities* (1846–48, 1858–77), in which he published much valuable material on Ukrainian history and folk songs. Bodiansky also published scholarly works on Slavic folk poetry and problems of early Slavic linguistics. A **romantic** enthusiast of **Cossack** Ukraine, he maintained that Ukrainians and Russians had different origins and contrasted the "despondency" of Russian folk songs with the "dramatic" quality of Ukrainian ones. In 1846, he published the *Eyewitness Chronicle* and *Istoriia Rusov* for the first time and initiated the publication of **Yakiv Holovatsky's** *Folk Songs of Galician and Hungarian Ruthenia*. He wrote the poetical work *Nas'ki ukraïns'ki kazky* (Our Ukrainian Tales, 1835) and other works based on Ukrainian folklore. Bodiansky was a friend of **Nikolai Gogol, Mykhailo Maksymovych,** and **Taras Shevchenko.**

BOHOMOLETS, OLEKSANDER (12 [24] May 1881–19 July 1946). Pathophysiologist, full member of the **Ukrainian Academy of Sciences** from 1929 and its president from 1930 to 1946; full member of the Academy of Sciences of the USSR from 1932 and its vice president from 1942. Born in **Kyiv**, Bohomolets graduated from the medical faculty of **Odesa** University in 1906. He lectured at the universities of Odesa, Saratov, and Moscow and was director of the Moscow Institute of Hematology and Transfusion (1928–31). In 1931, he returned to Kyiv, where he founded the Institute of Experimental Biology and Pathology and the Institute of Clinical Physiology. In 1953, these institutes were reformed as the Oleksander Bohomolets Institute of Physiology of the Academy of Sciences of the **Ukrainian SSR.**

Bohomolets founded an influential school whose work encompassed pathophysiology, endocrinology, the autonomic nervous system, the theory of constitution and diathesis, metabolism, immunity, shock, allergy, oncology, blood transfusion, the physiology and pathology of connective tissue, and longevity. His best-known hypothesis links the course of a disease and recovery not only to its causal agent but also to the resistance of the organism, which depends mainly on the condition of the nervous system and the connective tissue. Antireticular cytotoxic serum, a stimulant discovered by Bohomolets, offers an effective method of changing the condition of connective tissue.

BOHUN, IVAN (Fedorenko, Fedorovych; d. 17 (27) February 1664). **Cossack** military leader and colonel of **Podilia**, later of Kalnyk (Vinnytsia) and Pavoloch. A descendant of the Ukrainian **nobility**, he took part in the **Cossack rebellions** of 1637–38 and the **Khmelnytsky Uprising** (1648–57). In March 1651, with Semen Vysochan, he led the defense of Vinnytsia. As acting **hetman**, he successfully organized the defense of the Cossack encampment and the army's breakout from encirclement in the Battle of Berestechko (1651). He led fierce battles against Polish regiments at Monastyryshche in 1653 and a heroic defense of Uman in 1655. In January 1654,

Bohun and **Ivan Sirko** refused to swear allegiance to the Muscovite tsar. Three years later, Bohun helped suppress the Russian-backed uprising of Martyn Pushkar and Yakiv Barabash (1657–58). Committed to the autonomy of the **Hetmanate**, Bohun opposed both the Russian and Polish orientations of various Ukrainian hetmans and criticized **Yurii Khmelnytsky** for signing the Pereiaslav Articles (1659). Imprisoned by the Poles at the Marienburg fortress in 1662, he was released by King John Casimir in 1663 and assigned to command the **Right-Bank** Cossack regiments. In 1663–64, he took part in Hetman **Pavlo Teteria's** campaign into **Left-Bank Ukraine**. Bohun was accused of treason by the Poles in February 1664 and executed near Novhorod-Siverskyi.

BOICHUK, MYKHAILO (30 October 1882–13 July 1937). Monumentalist painter and teacher; a founder of Ukrainian monumental art. Boichuk was born in the village of Romanivka in the Ternopil region. After studying art in Cracow, Vienna, Munich, and Paris, he became a professor at the **Ukrainian State Academy of Arts** (1917) and at the Art Institute of **Kyiv** (1924). Boichuk founded a school of monumentalist artists, the so-called Boichukists (Tymofii Boichuk, Kyrylo Hvozdyk, Serhii Kolos, Ivan Padalka, Oksana Pavlenko, Mykola Rokytsky, **Vasyl Sedliar**, and others). His art combined Byzantine influences with traditional elements of Ukrainian visual arts. Boichuk supervised the **painting** of the Lutsk Barracks in Kyiv (1919), the All-Ukrainian Central Executive Committee sanatorium in **Odesa** (1928), and the Chervonozavod Theater in **Kharkiv** (1933–35). He also painted portraits, illustrated books, and designed sets for productions of **Les Kurbas's** Young Theater in Kyiv (1918). In 1937, he was arrested by the Soviet authorities and sent into exile. He died in a concentration camp.

BOOKS OF GENESIS OF THE UKRAINIAN PEOPLE/KNYHY BYTIIA UKRAÏNS'KOHO NARODU. Main programmatic document of the **Cyril and Methodius Brotherhood**, written in 1846 primarily by **Mykola Kostomarov**. It is known in two slightly different versions. In documents from the police investigation of the brotherhood it is called the *Divine Law*. The *Books of Genesis* were influenced by the historical and political conceptions of *Istoriia Rusov,* the poetry of **Taras Shevchenko**, the ideology of **Panslavism**, and the ideas of European romanticism, utopianism, and Christian socialism. The title and style of the *Books of Genesis* were borrowed from Adam Mickiewicz's *Books of the Polish People and of the Polish Pilgrimage* (1832). The essence of the *Books of Genesis* is its fusion of Christian ideals of justice, freedom, and equality with Ukrainian patriotism. The *Books of Genesis* developed the idea of Ukrainian messianism: the Ukrainian people, as the most oppressed and abused among the **Slavs** and, simultaneously, the most freedom-loving and democratic, would free the Russians of their despotism and the Poles of their aristocratism. The political ideal advanced in the *Books of Genesis* was a federal union of the Slavic peoples with its capital in **Kyiv**. The *Books of Genesis* also propagated a radical social program that included the abolition of serfdom and popular self-government. Although the first unabridged text of the *Books of Genesis* was not published until 1918, its egalitarian and **populist** orientation remained dominant in Ukrainian politics until the **Ukrainian Revolution** of 1917–21.

BORETSKY, IOV (secular name: Ivan; d. 2 [12] March 1631). Ecclesiastical, political, and pedagogical figure. Born in the village of Bircha in **Galicia** (now in Lviv oblast), Boretsky taught at the **Lviv Dormition Brotherhood** School and was its rector in 1604–5. In 1615, he helped establish the **Kyiv Epiphany Brotherhood** School, of which he also became the first rector. In 1620, when the hierarchy of the **Ukrainian Orthodox Church** was reestablished under **Cossack** protection, Boretsky was consecrated metropolitan of **Kyiv** and served in that capacity until his death. He wrote polemical works in defense of Orthodoxy: *Protestatsiia* (Protestation, 1621) and *Iustyfikatsiia* (Justification, 1622). Negotiating in the 1620s with his Uniate counterpart (*see* UKRAINIAN CATHOLIC CHURCH), Metropolitan **Yosyf Rutsky**, Boretsky sought to reconcile the Ukrainian Orthodox and Catholic churches, but these plans did not materialize, largely because of Cossack opposition.

BOROTBISTS. Popular name of the Ukrainian Party of Socialist Revolutionary Borotbists (Communists), created by the left faction of the **Ukrainian Party of Socialist Revolutionaries** (UPSR), which split at its fourth congress (13–16 May 1918). The left faction, headed by Panas Liubchenko, included **Vasyl Blakytny**, Hryhorii Hrynko, Levko Kovaliv, Hnat Mykhailychenko, Mykhailo Poloz, Antin Prykhodko, **Oleksander Shumsky**, and others. They shared the Bolshevik view of socialism as class-based nonparliamentary democracy and advocated an underground struggle and armed uprising against the **Ukrainian State** and its successor, the **Directory**. The left faction came to be known as Borotbists after their newspaper, *Borot'ba* (Struggle).

As internationalists, the Borotbists denounced competing parties for placing Ukrainian independence ahead of the cooperation of Ukrainian and Russian workers. But they also considered themselves

Ukrainians and sought to lead the **Ukrainian Revolution** by establishing their own Soviet regime with the support of the **peasant** otaman **Nykyfor Hryhoriiv**. When the invading Bolsheviks ignored this regime and set up their own, headed by **Georgii Piatakov**, the Borotbists submitted to it, even when Hryhoriiv revolted against the Bolsheviks. In August 1919, the Borotbists merged with a small group of pro-Bolshevik dissidents who had broken with the **Ukrainian Social Democratic Labor Party** (USDRP) to form the **USDRP (Independentists)**. As the Borotbists came from a **populist** background, the merger with social democrats made it possible for them to adopt Marxist socialism as their official ideology, reconstitute themselves as the Ukrainian Communist Party (Borotbists), and apply for membership in the Third International (Comintern). At this time, their membership was approximately 15,000.

In their memorandum to the Comintern, the Borotbists argued that the collapse of the Piatakov regime was due to its hostility to the peasantry, from which it forcibly requisitioned food, and its disdain for Ukrainian culture, which alienated the Ukrainian intelligentsia. Although the Borotbists' application to the Comintern was rejected, Lenin was sufficiently swayed by their influence among the peasants to promise an independent **Ukrainian SSR** on condition that the Borotbists merge with the Moscow-controlled **Communist Party of Ukraine** (CPU). They complied in March 1920. Approximately 4,000 Borotbists were accepted into the CPU and played a vital role in its policy of **Ukrainization**. In the 1930s, many of them fell victim to Stalin's **political terror**.

BOROVETS, TARAS (9 March 1908–15 May 1981). Political and military figure. He was born in the village of Bystrychi, **Volhynia**, and worked for a time as a stone-cutter. A member of the **Organization of Ukrainian Nationalists** (OUN), Borovets was arrested by the Polish police and imprisoned at Bereza Kartuzka (1934–35). In 1937, he was forbidden to live in Poland's eastern borderlands and moved to the interior. Following the German invasion of the **USSR**, which Borovets considered Ukraine's principal enemy, he organized an underground detachment under the name Polisian Sich and took the nom de guerre "Taras Bulba" (from **Gogol**'s novel about the **Cossacks**). After disarming the Soviet police in the town of Sarny, he attacked retreating Red Army units. He then established relations with the **Melnyk** faction of the OUN. In November 1941, Borovets attempted to gain German recognition for the Polisian Sich in return for a campaign against Soviet partisans, but his offer was refused and the Sich was forced underground. It adopted the name "Ukrainian Insurgent Army" (UIA).

From April to June 1942, the UIA (whose strength was estimated by the Germans at between 10,000 and 20,000 men) attacked German installations to obtain supplies but avoided killing any Germans. Repeated offers were made to Borovets to join the German forces, but the Germans would not satisfy his demand to recognize Ukrainian independence. An expeditionary group of the **Bandera** faction of the OUN, led by Ivan Mitringa, was active in the UIA and developed a political program for it. This resulted in yet another change of name to the Ukrainian People's Revolutionary Army (UNRA) in July 1943. Together with Mitringa, Borovets established the Ukrainian National Democratic Party, which declared itself a party of Ukrainian workers and peasants fighting for national and social liberation.

In late 1942 the OUN(B), led by **Mykola Lebed**, established its own **Ukrainian Insurgent Army** (UPA) and demanded in mid-1943 that Borovets subordinate himself to it. Following his refusal, the UPA forcibly disbanded the UNRA and incorporated those who surrendered to it. According to Borovets's memoirs, his wife was interrogated by the UPA and died under torture, with Lebed subsequently claiming that she was a Polish spy who had been duly tried and executed. (In his *UPA* [1946], Lebed states that she was a faithful member of the OUN(B), never tried or persecuted by the UPA.)

Borovets made one more effort to reach an understanding with the Germans but was tricked into going to Berlin in November 1943. There he was arrested and incarcerated in Sachsenhausen. The Germans released him in October 1944, hoping to exploit him as a Ukrainian resistance leader against the Red Army. Borovets lacked sufficient prestige to attract a significant following but cooperated with the **Ukrainian National Committee** and recruited a brigade for the nascent Ukrainian National Army commanded by **Pavlo Shandruk**. In 1948, Borovets emigrated to the USA, where he lived as a private citizen. His memoirs, *Armiia bez derzhavy* (An Army without a State), were published posthumously in Winnipeg in 1981.

BOROVYKOVSKY, VOLODYMYR (24 July [4 August] 1757–6 [18] April 1825). Painter. He was born in Myrhorod into a **Cossack** family and first studied **painting** with his father and uncle, both iconographers. In 1788, Borovykovsky moved to St. Petersburg, where he worked under Dmytro Levytsky, eventually becoming the city's leading portrait painter. He became an academician in 1795 and a councillor of the Academy of Fine Arts in 1802. He painted in the spirit of West European classicism, producing close to 400 portraits, among them Col. Pavlo Rudenko (1780s), the Mother of

God Enthroned, King David (1785), **Vasyl Kapnist** (1790), Levytsky (1796), Mariia Lopukhina (1797), Ekaterina Arsenieva (1799), Emperor Paul I (1800), and Countess Bezborodko and her daughters (1803). He also painted iconostases, churches, and cathedrals in Myrhorod, Kobyntsi in the **Poltava** region, Kherson, and St. Petersburg.

BORTNIANSKY, DMYTRO (1751–28 September [10 October] 1825). Composer and choral conductor born in Hlukhiv (now in Sumy oblast). Because of his beautiful singing voice, he was invited to join the court choir in St. Petersburg in 1758. He studied with the Italian composer Baldassare Galuppi, who took him to Italy to continue his musical education (1769–79). Bortniansky's operas *Creonte* (1776), *Alcide* (1778), and *Quinto Fabio* (1779) were performed on the Italian stage. Upon his return to Russia (1779), he conducted court choirs, taught **music**, and wrote the operas *Le faucon* (1786) and *Le fils-rival* (1787), the pastoral comedy *La fête du seigneur* (1786), a ballet, and a concert symphony (1796). From 1796 to 1825, he directed the court choir in St. Petersburg. Bortniansky wrote more than 100 choral works (including nearly 50 choral concertos and two liturgies), which drew liberally on Ukrainian folk motifs. Among Bortniansky's best-known choral concertos are "O Lord, in Your Strength," "Glory to God in the Highest," "This Is the Day," and "Hear My Voice, O God." Bortniansky's choral style is distinguished by its solemnity and lyricism.

BOYARS. Representatives of the ruling stratum in **Kyivan Rus'** whose power was second to that of the **princes**. Some scholars derive *boyar* from the Old Slavic *boi* (warrior) or *bolii* (large), others from the Turkic *boiar* (lord, wealthy man) or from the Old Icelandic *boaermen* (distinguished person).

During the emergence of the Kyivan state, the boyars were divided into two large groups: landed boyars, descendants of the earlier clan leadership, who constituted the social elite, and the prince's boyars, members of the princely retinue and court officials. The two groups merged in the course of the 11th century. The boyars were vassals of the prince, obliged to serve in his army in exchange for grants of land. They were not a closed estate—burghers, clergymen, and even **peasants** could join their ranks—and they could change allegiance from one prince to another. The boyars occupied the most important positions at court and in the provincial administration. Their power was exercised through the boyar council, an advisory body to the prince.

In the 14th century, as the Rus' lands came under the rule of the **Grand Duchy of Lithuania** and the Kingdom of Poland, most boyars entered the service of the Lithuanian grand dukes and Polish kings and were included in the closed noble estate. The most distinguished among them obtained the title of prince (**Ostrozky**, **Vyshnevetsky**, Zbarazky, and others). Boyars of average and poorer means lost a measure of privilege and went into military service, the bureaucracy, and other dependent positions. In the **Polish-Lithuanian Commonwealth**, the lower stratum of boyars and petty nobility waged a protracted struggle for legal equality with the nobiliary elite, which they obtained in the 16th century. As this did not eliminate social disparities, some of the impoverished boyars joined the **Cossack** movement.

In Romania, **Moldavia**, and Ukrainian lands ruled by those states, large landowners were known as boyars. The boyar estate was formed in the 13th and 14th centuries. In later centuries, the boyars played a leading political role and engaged in the Romanianization of their Ukrainian possessions. Following the annexation of northern **Bukovyna** to the **Ukrainian SSR** (1940), the boyar estate was abolished, as it was in Romania in 1945.

BREST, UNION OF. Union of the Ruthenian (Ukrainian-Belarusian) Orthodox Church of the **Polish-Lithuanian Commonwealth** with the Holy See. The union was prompted by a number of pressures on Ruthenian society. As a result of the Counter-Reformation, Orthodoxy became increasingly viewed by the Polish clergy and state authorities as not only schismatic but subversive. Roman Catholic religious and political pressure was accompanied by a flowering of Polish culture, resulting in the Polonization of many Ruthenian nobles. In this crisis, some of the Ruthenian elites, both nobles and clergy, began looking for ways of defining a Ruthenian cultural and religious identity that would find acceptance in the Commonwealth. One idea was to negotiate a church union whereby the Ruthenian Church would recognize papal supremacy but retain its Eastern Christian traditions. The concept found support in Polish government and ecclesiastical circles and among members of the Orthodox hierarchy who sought equality with their Catholic counterparts.

Discussions about a union began in 1590; in 1595 most Orthodox bishops signed a letter to Pope Clement VIII supporting the idea and authorizing Bishops **Ipatii Potii** and Kyryl Terletsky to go to Rome for further negotiations. After lengthy discussions, the two bishops were received by Pope Clement in December 1595 and made a profession of faith in the Roman Catholic Church.

Subsequently, a document establishing the rights and privileges of the Ruthenian Church was issued. On 6–10 (16–20) October 1596, a church council was held in Brest for the official proclamation of the union by the metropolitan of Kyiv, **Mykhail Rahoza**, and King Sigismund III of Poland. However, strong opposition developed. The Orthodox **brotherhoods** rebelled against their hierarchs, and the most prominent Orthodox layman, Prince **Kostiantyn Ostrozky**, insisted on the inclusion of the patriarch of Constantinople and the Muscovite Orthodox Church in any ecclesiastical union. Opponents of the union, led by Ostrozky and Nikephoros, the representative of the patriarch of Constantinople, joined by the bishop of **Lviv**, Hedeon Balaban, and the bishop of Peremyshl, Mykhailo Kopystensky, held a separate Orthodox council, concurrently with the official one, condemning the union.

Metropolitan Rahoza and bishops loyal to him conducted their council and concluded the union with the Holy See. Attended by five bishops, a segment of the clergy and nobility, and representatives of the Roman Catholic Church, the council ratified the act of union, which was announced in several epistles by the metropolitan. Under the conditions of the union, the Ukrainian church preserved its Eastern rite, the Church Slavonic liturgical language, the right to appoint metropolitans and bishops, the old (Julian) calendar, and the lower clergy's right to marry. It recognized the primacy of the pope and accepted the dogmas of the Catholic Church as defined at the Council of Florence (1439).

In theory at least, the Orthodox clergy that acceded to the union gained equal rights with the Roman Catholic clergy and was exempted from taxation and other obligations; bishops were promised seats in the Commonwealth Diet (a promise that was not fulfilled); and nobles and burghers were granted equal rights with Latin-rite Catholics, as well as the right to hold posts in state and local government. Following the Council of Brest, six of eight bishops of the **Kyiv metropolitanate** accepted the union (Kyiv, Volodymyr-Volynskyi, Turiv-Pynsk, Lutsk, Kholm, and Polatsk). The Peremyshl and Lviv eparchies acceded to the union only in 1692 and 1700, respectively. However, in 1620 the Orthodox hierarchy of the Kyiv metropolitanate was reconstituted, dividing the Ruthenian Church into Orthodox and Catholic branches. The **Ukrainian Catholic Church** is the successor of the part of the old Ruthenian Church that accepted union with Rome.

BREST-LITOVSK, TREATY OF. Peace treaty between the **Ukrainian People's Republic** (UNR) and the Central Powers—Germany, Austria-Hungary, Turkey, and Bulgaria—signed on 27 January (9

February) 1918 in Brest (Berestia, Brest-Litovsk). The Bolsheviks, desperate for peace in order to consolidate their rule, initiated talks with the Central Powers, beginning with representatives of the Austro-German bloc at German army headquarters in Brest-Litovsk on 20 November (3 December) 1917. On 2 (15) December, they signed a 28-day cease-fire. Peace negotiations between Soviet Russia and Germany and its allies began in Brest on 9 (22) December. The Soviet delegation, led by Adolf Ioffe, announced that it would represent the interests of all the peoples of the former Russian Empire.

The **Ukrainian Central Rada**, then at war with the Bolsheviks, decided to send its own delegation to represent Ukrainian interests. The UNR delegation, chosen at a council of the **Ukrainian Party of Socialist Revolutionaries** and the **Ukrainian Social Democratic Labor Party**, included Vsevolod Holubovych (head), Mykhailo Poloz, Mykola Levytsky, Mykola Liubynsky, and **Oleksander Sevriuk**. Prior to its departure, the delegation received detailed instructions from **Mykhailo Hrushevsky**, head of the Rada. The delegation was to strive for the inclusion of Ukrainian lands under Austria-Hungary (eastern **Galicia**, **Bukovyna**, and **Transcarpathia**) into the UNR, as well as Ukrainian ethnic territory (**Podlachia**; **Kholm** and **Sian** regions) that had been part of the Russian Empire. If Austria-Hungary refused to cede the territories it occupied, the delegation was to demand that they be constituted as a separate crown land with broad autonomy.

On 25 December 1917 (7 January 1918), the Ukrainian delegation, which the Central Powers recognized as the "independent and duly authorized representative of the Ukrainian People's Republic," joined the negotiations. Questions concerning eastern Galicia, Bukovyna, and Transcarpathia were removed from discussion at the request of the Austro-Hungarian delegation. It was acknowledged, however, that the Kholm region, Podlachia, and the Sian region should be united with the UNR. A recess was declared, and the Ukrainian delegation departed for Kyiv.

After the proclamation of Ukrainian independence in the Fourth Universal of the Central Rada on 9 (22) January 1918, the Ukrainian delegation, now led by Sevriuk, returned to Brest. On 17 (30) January 1918, prior to the resumption of talks, the Russian delegation (headed by Leon Trotsky) refused to recognize the authority of the UNR delegation, citing the change in the political situation in Ukraine and the presence of representatives of the **Kharkiv** Bolshevik government at the talks. On 19 January (1 February), at a plenary session, participants were briefed on the contents of the Fourth Universal. The Central Powers were anxious for good relations with the UNR in order to obtain Ukrainian grain and relieve the pressure on the Eastern front. Accordingly, Count Ottokar Czernin, the Austro-Hungarian foreign minister, announced the recognition of the UNR as an independent and sovereign state.

On the night of 26–27 January (8–9 February), a peace treaty consisting of 10 articles was signed between the UNR and the Central Powers. The border between the Austro-Hungarian Empire and the UNR was established along the prewar boundary between the Russian Empire and Austria-Hungary. A mixed mission was created for the definitive establishment of the border with Poland. The treaty provided for the evacuation of occupied regions, the establishment of diplomatic and consular relations, the mutual renunciation of war reparations, and the return of prisoners of war and interned civilians. It regulated economic relations and the exchange of goods between Ukraine and the Central Powers. An additional condition concerned military assistance from the Central Powers to the UNR against the Bolsheviks and a loan of one million *karbovantsi* to the Ukrainian government. At Brest the UNR and Austria-Hungary also signed a secret agreement on the consolidation of eastern Galicia and Bukovyna into a single crown land. Under Polish pressure, however, Austria-Hungary annulled the agreement on 4 July under the pretext that Ukraine had not delivered the quantity of grain stipulated by the treaty. The signing of the treaty was the first act of recognition of Ukraine as an independent state in modern times. The Central Powers signed a separate treaty with Russia on 3 March. *See also* WORLD WAR I.

BRIUKHOVETSKY, IVAN (d. 8 (18) June 1668). **Hetman** of **Left-Bank Ukraine** (1663–68). He served as chief domestic at **Bohdan Khmelnytsky's** residence and carried out some diplomatic assignments for the hetman. After the 1659 hetman elections, in which he rallied support for **Yurii Khmelnytsky**, Briukhovetsky remained at the **Zaporozhian Sich** and was elected *kish* otaman (1659–63). A capable orator, Briukhovetsky appealed to the **Cossack** rank and file, proposing lower taxes and restrictions on the landholdings of officers. Supported by the Zaporozhians, peasants, townspeople, and a Muscovite army, he was elected hetman of Left-Bank Ukraine at a **black council** in Nizhyn in June 1663. After his election, he signed the Baturyn Articles (1663) with Muscovy, becoming the first Ukrainian hetman to visit Moscow and to be granted the title of **boyar**, as well as landholdings in the Chernihiv region (1665). In October he signed the **Moscow Articles**, allowing Russian garrisons to be stationed in Ukraine's largest towns and the tsar's voevodas to perform various functions, e.g., collecting taxes for the tsar's treasury and consigning grain for the Muscovite armies. Together with a survey of landholdings in Left-Bank Ukraine (1666), these developments provoked general dissatisfaction with Briukhovetsky that reached its climax after the signing of the **Truce of Andrusovo** (1667). In early 1668, Briukhovetsky changed his pro-Muscovite orientation. He entered into talks with **Petro Doroshenko**, hetman of **Right-Bank Ukraine,** who had accepted Ottoman protection, and sent a delegation to Istanbul. In May 1668, Briukhovetsky's armies, having driven Muscovite garrisons from a number of Ukrainian towns, set out to liberate the border town of Kotelva, which was besieged by a Muscovite army commanded by Grigorii Romodanovsky. In early summer, Right-Bank regiments commanded by Doroshenko entered Left-Bank Ukraine to meet Briukhovetsky's forces near Opishnia (now in Poltava oblast). Upon learning that Doroshenko's armies were approaching, the Left-Bank Cossacks rebelled against Briukhovetsky and killed him. He was buried in Hadiach.

BRODSKY, OLEKSANDER (7 [19] June 1895–21 August 1969). Physical chemist and full member of the **Ukrainian Academy of Sciences** from 1939. Born in Katerynoslav (now Dnipropetrovsk), Brodsky graduated from Moscow University in 1922. In 1927, he began working at the Institute of Physical Chemistry of the All-Ukrainian Academy of Sciences, becoming its director in 1939. His research was devoted to the thermodynamics and electrochemistry of solutions, and he developed a general theory for isolating isotopes. Brodsky was the first in the Soviet Union to produce heavy water (1934), as well as concentrates of heavy oxygen (1937) and heavy nitrogen (1949).

BROTHERHOOD OF TARAS/BRATSTVO TARASIVTSIV. Political organization established at the grave of **Taras Shevchenko** in Kaniv. According to most sources, the brotherhood was founded in the summer of 1891 by four students: Mykola Baizdrenko, Mykhailo Bazkevych, Vitalii Borovyk, and Ivan Lypa. Other sources give 1892 and name different founders. Young intellectuals in **Kharkiv, Kyiv, Odesa, Poltava,** and Lubny, including **Borys Hrinchenko, Mykhailo Kotsiubynsky,** and **Mykola Mikhnovsky,** soon joined the brotherhood. Its program, written by Lypa and published in the Lviv newspaper *Pravda* under the title "*Profession de foi* of Young Ukrainians," called for political autonomy for Ukraine, as well as the development of Ukrainian "national feeling" and the dominance of the Ukrainian **language**. It asserted the ethnic unity of Ukrainians in the Russian Empire and Austria-Hungary. The older **Ukrainophile** generation was severely criticized for limiting itself to cultural concerns and failing to develop a political consciousness. As its social ideal, the program advanced a classless "all-Ukrainian national family."

Since the brotherhood made little effort to conceal its activities, which included organizing events in honor of Shevchenko and illegally disseminating Ukrainian literature (*see* EMS UKASE), the imperial police proceeded to arrest a number of its members in 1893. Several were imprisoned; one member, Mykola Yatsenko, contracted tuberculosis in prison and died. Other members remained active until 1898. The work of the brotherhood was continued in a nationalist vein by Mikhnovsky and the **Ukrainian People's Party**, while its social concerns were taken up by the **Revolutionary Ukrainian Party**.

BROTHERHOODS. Religious, cultural, and educational organizations of Ukrainian burghers, active from the 15th to the early 18th century. Initially engaged only in religious and charitable activity, in the late 16th century the brotherhoods acquired civic, national, and cultural significance and gained more influence among all strata of Ukrainian society: tradesmen, guild craftsmen, merchants, and the Orthodox nobility. Brotherhoods were supported by the few existing Ukrainian magnates, such as **Kostiantyn Ostrozky** and Adam Kysil. They opened schools and publishing houses and established libraries. The oldest and best-known organization was the **Lviv Dormition Brotherhood**, founded ca. 1585. In the late 16th and early 17th centuries, brotherhoods were active in Lutsk, Ostrih, Peremyshl, Rohatyn, Ternopil, and other Ukrainian towns. The membership of the **Kyiv Epiphany Brotherhood**, founded ca. 1615 at the Epiphany Monastery, included not only Kyiv burghers and Ukrainian noblemen but the whole **Zaporozhian Host**, led by Hetman **Petro Sahaidachny**. In 1632, the Kyiv Brotherhood School was merged with the school of the **Kyivan Cave Monastery**, ultimately becoming the **Kyiv Mohyla Academy**. Leading activists of the brotherhoods included eminent scholars, churchmen, and political activists of the time, such as Ivan Krasovsky, Yurii Rohatynets, Stepan Zyzanii, **Iov Boretsky**, and Pamva Berynda. Active throughout the 17th century, the brotherhoods declined in the early 18th century and became exclusively religious organizations.

BU-BA-BU. First postmodern literary group in Ukraine, established in **Lviv** in April 1985 by **Yurii Andrukhovych**, Oleksandr Irvanets, and Viktor Neborak. Its name was derived from the words *burlesk* (burlesque), *balahan* (farce), and *bufonada* (buffoonery). The group cultivated self-parody, establishing a mock literary academy in which Andrukhovych figured as patriarch, Irvanets as bursar, and Neborak as prosecutor. Bu-Ba-Bu was most active in the years 1987–91, giving more than 20 readings in western Ukraine. Its climactic literary event was the staging of a "poetic opera," *Chrysler Imperial*, at the Lviv Opera House on the nights of 1–4 October 1992 (the Chrysler motif was borrowed from Andrukhovych's novel *Rekreatsii*). The group celebrated its centennial, calculated by adding the ages of its three members, with the publication of the poetry collection *Bu-Ba-Bu. T.v.o.[...] ry* (Bu-Ba-Bu. W.o.r.[...] ks, 1995).

The performances staged by Bu-Ba-Bu were a carnivalesque reaction to the fall of the Soviet Union and its stultified, rigidly controlled official literary culture. The three writers also mocked the earnestness and narrow-mindedness of **populism**, which had left a profound imprint on the Ukrainian national movement. Explicitly acknowledging the influence of the Russian literary theorist Mikhail Bakhtin and his writings about the carnival tradition, Andrukhovych described Bu-Ba-Bu as "an attempt to melt this iceberg of lenten undereducated seriousness that weighs upon everything Ukrainian."

BUKOVYNA. Historical name of Ukrainian ethnic territory located between the middle course of the Dnister River and the main range of the Carpathian Mountains in the valley of the upper Prut and Seret Rivers. Today this territory is divided between Ukraine (northern Bukovyna—Chernivtsi oblast) and Romania (southern Bukovyna [Rom. Bucovina]—Suceava and Botoşani districts). The name "Bukovyna," which first appears in historical sources in 1392, is derived from the great beech (*buk*) forests that cover a significant portion of its territory.

The first traces of human settlement in Bukovyna date back to the Paleolith (Babyn, Bila, and Mliiv sites). During the Neolithic era (fourth–third centuries B.C.), the area was settled by tribes of the **Trypilian culture** and later by the Getae and Dacians. Slavic tribes appeared in Bukovyna between the fourth and seventh centuries as part of the clan alliance of the **Antes**. In the ninth century, the area was settled by Slavic tribes of Tivertsians and White Croatians. During the 10th and 11th centuries, Bukovyna was part of **Kyivan Rus'**, then passed to the Galician Principality from the 12th to the first half of the 14th century and subsequently to the Principality of **Galicia-Volhynia**. After the invasion of the **Golden Horde**, ties between Bukovyna and the Galician-Volhynian lands weakened. This resulted, in the first half of the 14th century, in the formation of the separate **Shypyntsi land** on these territories, which recognized the supremacy of the Mongols. In the 1340s–50s, Bukovyna was ruled by Hungary. King Louis appointed as his deputy the voivode Dragoş, who subsequently facilitated the migration of Romanians from Transylvania and the **Maramureş region** to Bukovyna.

In the 1360s, after the creation of an independent Moldavian principality, Bukovyna became part of that state and remained so until 1774. From 1387 to 1497, **Moldavia** recognized the supremacy of Poland, and in 1514 it became a vassal of the Ottoman Empire. At the end of the 16th century, Moldavia became a Turkish province. The active Romanianization of the Bukovynian lands began in this period, particularly after 1564, when the capital was moved from Suceava to Iaşi. From 1490 to 1492, Bukovyna and **Galicia** were swept by the Mukha Rebellion against Polish rule. During the 16th and 17th centuries, the Ukrainian **Cossacks** were frequently involved in armed engagements against Turkish and **Tatar** invaders on Moldavian territory. In the 1570s, these military campaigns were led by **Ivan Pidkova**.

During the **Khmelnytsky Uprising** (1648–57), a significant number of Bukovynians joined the Cossack and **peasant** armies, forming their own regiment, which took part in the siege of **Lviv** in 1648. In 1650, **Bohdan Khmelnytsky** led a campaign into Moldavia that resulted in an alliance with its *hospodar*, Vasile Lupu. From the 16th to the 18th century, Bukovyna maintained cultural ties with other Ukrainian lands. Moldavian *hospodars* founded a number of churches in Ukraine, and many natives of Bukovyna studied in **Kyiv** and Lviv.

As a result of Russian and Austrian military action against Turkey, Bukovyna was seized by Austria in 1774. It remained part of the Habsburg Monarchy until 1918. From 1787 to 1849, Bukovyna was attached to Galicia but was made a separate crown land after the **Revolution of 1848**. The Ukrainian national movement began to develop after 1848 and gained strength with the founding of the Ruska Besida Society in Chernivtsi (1869). By the 1890s, Ukrainians were represented in the regional diet and the Vienna parliament, led by **populists** such as **Stepan Smal-Stotsky**. The populists published the first Ukrainian-language periodical in the region, *Bukovyna* (1885–1918), and lobbied for ethnocultural autonomy and the division of the crown land into Ukrainian and Romanian sections. Bukovyna was home to the distinguished Ukrainian writers **Yurii Fedkovych** and **Olha Kobylianska**. Adverse economic conditions resulted in the emigration of some 50,000 peasants, primarily to North America, between 1891 and 1910.

During **World War I**, Bukovyna was occupied by Russian armies until the summer of 1917 and suffered great destruction. After the collapse of Austria-Hungary, Bukovyna joined the

Western Ukrainian People's Republic (November 1918) but was immediately occupied by Romanian forces. The postwar treaties of Saint-Germain (1919) and Sèvres (1920) ceded Bukovyna to Romania. During the period of Romanian rule (1918–40), Bukovyna's autonomy was abolished, and it was reduced to an ordinary Romanian province. From 1918 to 1928, and again from 1937 to 1940, Bukovyna was subject to martial law. The Ukrainian language was suppressed; educational and cultural institutions, newspapers, and magazines were closed. Ukrainian place names and surnames were Romanianized. The **Ukrainian Orthodox Church** was persecuted.

As a result of a secret protocol to the Molotov-Ribbentrop Pact between the **USSR** and Germany (1939), as well as a Soviet ultimatum to Romania, Romanian authorities withdrew from northern Bukovyna in June 1940 and were replaced by Soviet armies of occupation. Chernivtsi oblast was created as part of the **Ukrainian SSR**. The region was again taken over by Romanian forces in June 1941 and occupied by them until early 1944. Following the Soviet reoccupation (1944), the borders of 1940 were reestablished and Bukovyna was once again incorporated into the Ukrainian SSR.

BUNIAKOVSKY, VIKTOR (4 [16] December 1804–30 November [12 December] 1889). Mathematician. Born in Bar, **Podilia** (now in Vinnytsia oblast), Buniakovsky completed a doctorate in Paris in 1826. He spent the rest of his life in St. Petersburg, where he taught at various institutions of higher learning. In 1830, he was elected to the St. Petersburg Academy of Sciences and was its vice president from 1864 to 1889. He wrote more than 150 works on mathematics and mechanics, particularly mathematical analysis, number theory, geometry, applied mechanics, hydrostatics, and the theory of probability and its applications in demography, statistics, and inequality theory. He is best known for discovering the Schwarz inequality, which he published in 1859, 25 years before Karl Schwarz. He also gave a new proof of Johann Carl Friedrich Gauss's law of quadratic reciprocity. Among Buniakovsky's inventions are the planimeter, the pantograph, and a device for adding squares.

C

CABINET OF MINISTERS/KABINET MINISTRIV. Supreme executive body of the Ukrainian government, created in 1991 by the renaming of the Soviet-era **Council of Ministers**. Its legal status is regulated by chapter 6 of the 1996 **Constitution**. The cabinet includes the prime minister, first deputy prime minister, three deputy prime ministers, and individual ministers. The prime minister is appointed by the president of Ukraine with the approval of a majority of the **Verkhovna Rada** (VR) of Ukraine. The cabinet is appointed by the president on the recommendation of the prime minister and tenders its resignation to a newly elected president. The passing of a VR resolution of nonconfidence results in the cabinet's dissolution. Within the limits of its authority (defined by art. 116 of the Constitution), the cabinet issues binding decisions and decrees (*see also* CONSTITUTION; GOVERNMENT).

Since October 1990, the following individuals have held the post of prime minister of Ukraine: **Vitold Fokin** (23 October 1990–1 October 1992), Valentyn Symonenko (2–12 October 1992), **Leonid Kuchma** (13 October 1992–21 September 1993), **Yukhym Zviahilsky** (22 September 1993–15 June 1994), **Vitalii Masol** (16 June 1994–4 April 1995), **Yevhen Marchuk** (8 June 1995–27 May 1996), **Pavlo Lazarenko** (28 May 1996–2 July 1997), Vasyl Durdynets (acting p.m., 2–15 July 1997), **Valerii Pustovoitenko** (16 July 1997–22 December 1999), **Viktor Yushchenko** (22 December 1999–28 May 2001), **Anatolii Kinakh** (29 May 2001–16 November 2002), and **Viktor Yanukovych** (21 November 2002–31 December 2004).

CANADIAN INSTITUTE OF UKRAINIAN STUDIES (CIUS). Established at the University of Alberta in Edmonton in July 1976 as a publicly funded national institute with a project office at the University of Toronto, CIUS promotes Ukrainian and Ukrainian-Canadian studies through research grants, publications, scholarships, seminars, and conferences. It coordinates scholarly activity and facilitates Ukrainian-content programs at Canadian universities. CIUS Press has published more than 125 books, 65 research reports, and 50 issues of the *Journal of Ukrainian Studies*. Its publications include the six-volume English-language *Encyclopedia of Ukraine*, prepared jointly with the **Shevchenko Scientific Society** in Sarcelles, France. The Peter Jacyk Centre for Ukrainian Historical Research, established in 1989, is issuing an English translation of **Mykhailo Hrushevsky's** 10-volume *History of Ukraine-Rus'*, as well as other historical publications in English and Ukrainian. The Ukrainian Language Education Centre prepares curriculum aids for the teaching of Ukrainian in bilingual school programs.

CARPATHIAN SICH (Carpathian Sich National Defense Organization). Armed force of autonomous **Carpatho-Ukraine**, formed in November 1938 on the basis of the Ukrainian National Defense, which was established in Uzhhorod (August 1938) at the initiative of the **Organization of Ukrainian Nationalists** (OUN). Its name was derived from the historical **Sich** of the Ukrainian **Cossacks**. It was headed by Dmytro Klympush (commander), Ivan Roman (deputy), Ivan Rohach (general secretary), Stepan Rosokha (attaché to the government of Carpatho-Ukraine), and Col. Mykhailo Kolodzinsky (chief of staff). The Carpathian Sich held mass meetings (the largest, attended by several thousand people, took plaçe in Khust in February 1939). It also engaged in cultural and educational work among local Ukrainians and published the weekly *Nastup* (Advance, ed. Rosokha). Many young **Galicians**, primarily OUN members, crossed the border illegally to join the Carpathian Sich, eager to defend the first Ukrainian polity to have emerged since the demise of the **Ukrainian People's Republic**. There were volunteers from other Ukrainian lands as well.

The dominance of the OUN in the command of the Carpathian Sich led to friction with local Ukrainians. According to the memoirs of Vincent Shandor, who represented the Carpatho-Ukrainian government to the Prague authorities, the latter were prepared to provide weapons, supplies, and training to the Carpathian Sich, but the command would not accept an offer that might have compromised its exclusive control of the Sich.

Following Hitler's liquidation of Czechoslovakia in early March 1939, Hungary invaded Carpatho-Ukraine on 14 March in order to annex its territory. Carpatho-Ukraine was declared independent on 14 March by its premier, **Avhustyn Voloshyn**, who appointed Stepan Klochurak minister of defense and Col. Serhii Yefremov commander in chief. The poorly armed and untrained Carpathian Sich, whose strength was about 2,000 men, fought the Hungarians until 17 March. Some members of the Sich took refuge in Romania. Of these, 373 were extradited to Hungary; some were executed and others interned. The Hungarians also handed over 40 Galician members of the Sich to Poland, some of whom were shot at the border. Sporadic resistance to the Hungarian occupation continued in the Carpathian Mountains until mid-April.

CARPATHO-UKRAINE (Ukr. *Karpats'ka Ukraïna*). Independent Ukrainian state proclaimed in **Transcarpathia** on 14 March 1939. Unofficially, the name Carpatho-Ukraine was used before 1939 to designate the Transcarpathian region, which was settled largely by Ukrainians. After the dissolution of Austria-Hungary (1918), Transcarpathian Ukrainians campaigned for union with other Ukrainian lands. On 21 January 1919, at the People's (Ruthenian) Council in Khust, where more than 400 delegates from all of Transcarpathia gathered, the union of Carpatho-Ukraine with the **Ukrainian People's Republic** (UNR) was approved. Nevertheless, a contending movement for union with Czechoslovakia prevailed. On the basis of the treaties of Saint-Germain (1919) and Trianon (1920), Carpatho-Ukraine became an autonomous region of Czechoslovakia, officially designated **Subcarpathian Rus'**. During the interwar period, Ukrainian national consciousness and cultural institutions developed rapidly in the region.

Following the Munich Pact (29 September 1938), which initiated Germany's dismemberment of Czechoslovakia, the Prague authorities were forced to grant autonomy to Subcarpathian Rus' (11 October). Its first prime minister, Andrii Brodii, was removed as an agent of Hungary and replaced on 26 October by **Avhustyn Voloshyn**, who headed an all-Ukrainian government. Hungary, which had ruled the region until 1918, demanded its return, and the Vienna arbitration, conducted on 2 November by Germany and Italy, awarded Hungary the southwestern part of Subcarpathian Rus', including its capital, Uzhhorod, and its two largest towns, Mukacheve and Berehove. Voloshyn's government reacted by moving its capital to Khust and creating the **Carpathian Sich** as a defense force against Hungarian and Polish incursions. The state administration, educational system, and publishing were Ukrainized. Elections to the Diet on 12 February 1939 resulted in an overwhelming victory for the one-party slate of the Ukrainian National Alliance, which took 92.4 percent of the vote.

The Voloshyn government was dependent on the good will of Germany, the only major power involved in the region, which promised economic assistance. Accordingly, it permitted fascist organizational activity among German residents and banned anti-Nazi propaganda. At the beginning of March 1939, Hitler proceeded with the complete liquidation of Czechoslovakia amid rumors that Germany was planning to create a greater Ukraine, beginning with an autonomous Transcarpathia. In a speech on 10 March, Stalin ridiculed such a prospect as "merging an elephant with a mosquito." Satisfied that the USSR would not intervene, Hitler tacitly acquiesced in Hungary's invasion of Subcarpathian Rus', which began on 14 March. On the same day, Voloshyn proclaimed Carpatho-Ukraine an independent state, calling upon Germany to intervene with Budapest and halt the invasion.

On 15 March, the Diet ratified the constitution, which designated the name of the state (Carpatho-Ukraine), the form of government (a presidential republic), and the official language (Ukrainian). The state adopted a coat of arms (a bear on a red field on the left with four blue and three yellow stripes on the right, and a **trident** with a cross in the center), the yellow-and-blue flag, and the Ukrainian national **anthem**. Voloshyn was elected president and appointed Yuliian Revai prime minister. The Hungarian forces soon overwhelmed the Carpathian Sich, and Hungary ruled the region until 1944. It was annexed to the **Ukrainian SSR** in 1945.

CATHOLIC RUTHENIAN PEOPLE'S UNION/KATOLYTS'KYI RUS'KO-NARODNYI SOIUZ (KRNS). Conservative political organization established in Lviv on 14 October 1896 under the leadership of **Oleksander Barvinsky**, with the support of the Greek Catholic hierarchy and Metropolitan **Sylvestr Sembratovych** (*see* UKRAINIAN CATHOLIC CHURCH). From 1897 to 1914, it published the daily *Ruslan*. Of nine Ukrainian delegates from **Galicia** elected to the Austrian parliament in 1897, six were representatives of the KRNS. They formed the Ruthenian Delegates' Club, and on 1 April 1897, with like-minded deputies from Bohemia, Slovenia, Croatia, and Serbia, the Slavic Christian National Club. The KRNS was also represented in the Galician Diet. It opposed the local Polish administration but was loyal to the imperial throne and the Austrian monarchy. The party advocated the establishment of a Ukrainian crown land in the Habsburg Monarchy and a future sovereign Ukrainian state. It called for tax and land reform, equal administrative status for the Ukrainian **language** in Galicia, and the establishment of Ukrainian primary and secondary schools. The KRNS was sharply critical of the **Russophiles**. It defended the Catholic Church against attacks by members of the Radical and Social Democratic parties.

In the parliamentary elections of 1907, the KRNS failed to win any seats, which led to its reorganization in 1911 as the Christian Social Party. Its nine-man executive was led by Barvinsky, and the party consisted of sections based on professional, social, and other interests. Party members included peasants and workers, but most belonged to the intelligentsia (teachers, priests). A small organization, it was often criticized by other parties, especially the Radicals, for its clericalism, conservatism, and relations with Polish political circles. At the outbreak of **World War I** the party abandoned active politics and, after a brief revival in the early 1920s, dissolved itself. Most of its active members gravitated toward the **Ukrainian National Democratic Alliance**.

CECORA (ȚUȚORA), BATTLE OF. Conflict in September-October 1620 between Polish and Turco-**Tatar** forces near Iași (now in Romania). In the summer of 1620, a large Turco-Tatar army led by Iskander Pasha entered Wallachia and **Moldavia**. In early September, it was met by the Polish army, led by Crown Hetman Stanisław Żółkiewski, and a small **Cossack** detachment (including the colonel of Chyhyryn, Mykhailo Khmelnytsky, and his son **Bohdan Khmelnytsky**). The Moldavian *hospodar*, Gaspar Graţiani, and his regiment (600 men) came to Żółkiewski's aid. The opposing forces clashed near the village of Cecora. Unable to withstand the continuous assault, the Polish army began a disorderly withdrawal. The Polish camp near Mohyliv-Podilskyi was surrounded by the Turco-Tatar forces and completely routed. Żółkiewski and Mykhailo Khmelnytsky died in battle, while Bohdan Khmelnytsky, Field Hetman Stanisław Koniecpolski, and other Polish commanders were taken prisoner. The Turks and Tatars took advantage of their victory to ravage **Podilia** and **Galicia**. In the following year, a Ukrainian-Polish force defeated a huge Turco-Tatar army at the **Battle of Khotyn**.

CENTRAL UNION OF UKRAINIAN STUDENTS/TSENTRAL'NYI SOIUZ UKRAÏNS'KOHO STUDENTSTVA (TseSUS). Coordinating body of Ukrainian students outside the **USSR**. TseSUS was founded in 1922 and based in Prague for the first 12 years of its existence. Its membership was highest in the early years, with 4,650 students from 18 organizations in 1923. In the following year, North American student clubs joined TseSUS, but membership fell to 3,364 and declined steadily thereafter. Initially, various ideological tendencies were represented in TseSUS, but Sovietophile students left in 1924 to establish the short-lived Working Alliance of Progressive Students, and by the early 1930s nationalism had become dominant. In 1934, TseSUS moved its head office to Vienna. It was active in informing non-Ukrainians about the problems of Ukrainian students and the political situation in Ukraine. TSeSUS joined the Confédération Internationale des Etudiants and belonged to the International Students' Service aid organization. When the German authorities began to restrict TseSUS activities, it decided to transfer its head office to Rome, but the outbreak of hostilities made that impossible. In 1941, the Nationalist Organization of Ukrainian Students took over responsibility for Ukrainian student organizations in Germany.

TseSUS resumed activity in 1946, but rivalries between factions of the **Organization of Ukrainian Nationalists** led to dissension. The conflict was settled with a merger in 1947. In that year, TseSUS represented 33 student clubs from 10 countries, with a membership of 2,721. Membership declined as Ukrainians emigrated in large numbers from Western Europe to North America, and much TseSUS work was taken over by national student organizations. In 1967, TseSUS was reactivated by students born in the **diaspora** and initiated a campaign in defense of political **dissidents** in Ukraine

(1971). Ideological rivalries reemerged, however, and TseSUS became inactive after 1977.

CHEKHIVSKY, VOLODYMYR (19 July 1876–ca. 1938). Political and ecclesiastical figure; ideologue of the **Ukrainian** Autocephalous **Orthodox Church** (UAOC). Chekhivsky was born in Horokhuvatka, **Kyiv** region, into the family of a priest. He graduated from the Kyiv Theological Seminary in 1896 and the Kyiv Theological Academy in 1900. From 1901 to 1903, he was assistant inspector of the Kamianets-Podilskyi Theological Seminary. He was transferred to the Kyiv Theological Seminary in 1904 with a warning against his activity in the national movement. In 1905–6, Chekhivsky taught Russian, literary history and theory in Cherkasy. He joined the **Ukrainian Social Democratic Labor Party** (USDRP) in 1905. Owing to his political and civic activities, Chekhivsky was under constant police surveillance. In 1906, he was elected to the First State Duma; in the same year he was arrested for his work in the national movement and exiled to Vologda gubernia. He returned to Ukraine in 1907.

From 1908 to 1917, Chekhivsky lived in **Odesa**, teaching history, psychology, and logic in city high schools. He took part in the local **Hromada** and **Prosvita** societies and edited the newspaper *Ukraïns'ke slovo* (Ukrainian Word). In 1917, he moved to Kyiv, where he was a leader of the USDRP and represented Odesa in the **Ukrainian Central Rada**. From April 1918, Chekhivsky was director of the department of religious affairs of the **Ukrainian People's Republic** (UNR). Under the **Ukrainian State** of Hetman **Pavlo Skoropadsky**, he directed the general affairs department of the Ministry of Religious Confessions. In the autumn of 1918, he helped plan an uprising against Skoropadsky. From 26 December 1918 to 11 February 1919, as a member of the UNR **Directory**, Chekhivsky headed the Council of Ministers and the Ministry of Foreign Affairs. Thanks to his initiative, the UNR proclaimed the autocephaly of the UAOC on 1 January 1919. In 1919–20, he was professor of cultural history at the Ukrainian State University in Kamianets-Podilskyi.

From 1920, Chekhivsky worked closely with the All-Ukrainian Orthodox Church Council (VPTsR), which led the All-Ukrainian Union of Orthodox Parishes and made preparations for an All-Ukrainian Orthodox Church Sobor. At the first sobor (14–30 October 1921), he chaired the ideology commission; he also founded and headed the Brotherhood of Workers of the Word. From 1921 to 1924, Chekhivsky was a member of the VPTsR presidium, an evangelist of the UAOC, and an organizer and instructor of pastoral courses in Kyiv. He chaired the second All-Ukrainian sobor (17–30 October 1927). On 29 July 1929, Chekhivsky was arrested and accused of membership in the **Union for the Liberation of Ukraine**, an organization invented by the secret police. At the show trial of the Union in 1930, Chekhivsky was sentenced to death. The sentence was commuted to 10 years' imprisonment, which he spent at the Kharkiv and Yaroslavl isolation camps. In 1933, he was transferred to the Solovets Islands. His sentence was extended by 20 years in 1936, and he was transferred to strict-regime camps, where he died. In the course of his career, Chekhivsky published numerous works on religious and church topics (some under the pseudonym Illia Bratersky).

CHORNOBYL NUCLEAR DISASTER (Russ. Chernobyl). The worst accident in the history of atomic energy generation, which occurred on 26 April 1986 at Unit Four of the Chornobyl Power Station, 104 km north of Kyiv. An explosion blew off the heavy lid of the reactor and started a fire in the graphite reactor core that resulted in the release of large amounts of radioactive material into the atmosphere. Radioactive particles were spread by winds over Ukraine, Belarus, and Russia, and then throughout Europe. The Soviet government initially attempted a cover-up but admitted the accident once high levels of radiation were registered abroad. On 2–3 May, some 45,000 people from a 10-km radius of the plant were evacuated. More than 30 individuals, mainly firefighters, lost their lives immediately after the accident, and dozens more died as a result of radiation sickness. As a temporary measure, the reactor was enclosed in a steel and concrete sarcophagus. In subsequent years, some 210,000 people were resettled from an exclusion zone of 4,300 sq. km to less-contaminated areas.

The causes of the accident are associated with design flaws of the reactor, disregard for safety, and poorly trained personnel. The remaining reactors of the power plant were closed down in 1991, 1997, and 2000. It is estimated that some 1.8 million people still live in parts of Ukraine contaminated by the accident. Deformations in newborn livestock, radiation-induced illnesses in humans, and an increase in cancer deaths, particularly thyroid cancer in children, are linked directly to the accident. The long-term consequences of exposure to radiation are not known. *See also* ENVIRONMENT.

CHORNOVIL, VIACHESLAV (24 December 1937—25 March 1999). Journalist, **human-rights** activist, and politician. He was born in the village of Ierky (now in Cherkasy oblast). A Communist Youth League activist for 10 years, Chornovil graduated from the journalism department of **Kyiv** University in 1960 and worked in the press, radio, and television in **Lviv** and Kyiv until 1965. Assigned to cover the trials of several *shistdesiatnyky* in the autumn of 1965, Chornovil was outraged by the courts' flagrant procedural irregularities. He was dismissed from his job for refusing to testify at the closed trial of **Mykhailo Osadchy**. In 1967, Chornovil compiled materials about 20 political dissidents under the title *Lykho z rozumu* (literally, "Woe from Wit," an allusion to Aleksandr Griboedov's play of 1824) that was published in the West as *The Chornovil Papers* (1968) and circulated in the underground. Arrested in August 1967, he was sentenced in Lviv to three years' imprisonment for "anti-Soviet agitation and propaganda" (the term was reduced by half owing to an amnesty). After his release, Chornovil lived in Lviv and edited the underground *Ukraïns'kyi visnyk* (Ukrainian Herald). Rearrested in January 1972, he was sentenced to six years' imprisonment and three years' exile, which he served in the strict-regime labor camps of Mordovia and then in Yakutia. In 1979, he joined the **Ukrainian Helsinki Group**. He was rearrested in April 1980 on a trumped-up charge of rape and sentenced to five years' imprisonment, but was released in 1983 following a protest by the procurator of the Yakutian ASSR.

Returning to Lviv in 1985, Chornovil plunged into political activity and renewed the publication of *Ukraïns'kyi visnyk* in August 1987. He was among the founders of **Rukh**. Elected head of the Lviv Oblast Council of People's Deputies in April 1990, he oversaw the democratization of political life in the region in 1990–91. Chornovil ran for president of Ukraine in December 1991, taking second place with 23.27 percent of the vote. In March 1992, he was elected one of the three leaders of Rukh; following the organization's split, Chornovil became its sole head in December 1992 and turned it into a political party. He was killed in an automobile accident shortly before the presidential elections of 1999, which led to widespread allegations of foul play. Chornovil was buried at the Baikove Cemetery in Kyiv. A posthumous collection of his essays and speeches appeared under the title *Pul's ukraïns'koï nezalezhnosti* (Pulse of Ukrainian Independence, 2000).

CHRISTIANIZATION OF RUS'. As early as the first century A.D., Christianity won converts in the Greek **Black Sea colonies**. The *Tale of Bygone Years* recounts the legend of the apostle Andrew's mission to the coastal settlements and his blessing of the site of present-day **Kyiv**.

In the third century, the Goths began migrating southward, adopting Arian Christianity in the fourth century. Remnants of their fourth- and fifth-century churches have been excavated in the **Crimea**. However, the invasion of the Huns in 375 halted the spread of Christianity on what is now Ukrainian territory for several centuries.

During the era of **Kyivan Rus'**, Princes **Askold and Dir** are said to have adopted Christianity after conquering Kyiv (860). The reign of Prince **Oleh** witnessed a pagan revival, although Christianity did not disappear entirely. Christianity also came to Rus' from the West, propagated by the Moravian disciples of SS. Cyril and Methodius. After the death of Prince **Ihor** in 945, his widow, Princess **Olha**, converted to Christianity (between 954 and 957). Her son, Prince **Sviatoslav Ihorevych**, remained a pagan. **Volodymyr the Great** decided that the adoption of Byzantine Christianity would strengthen relations with his Christian neighbors. He was baptized ca. 987 and ordered his people baptized in 988–89. According to the *Tale of Bygone Years*, the baptism of Kyiv's residents took place in August 988. Christianization met with the greatest resistance in northern towns such as Novgorod, Suzdal, and Belozersk, now in Russia. Volodymyr assigned one-tenth of the state's property to the church and recognized the rights of the clergy. The first known metropolitan of Kyiv was the Greek Theopemptos (1037–48).

The baptism of Rus' was followed by the diffusion of Christian literature and culture, facilitated by the adoption of a Slavonic liturgy. Along with religious unity, Kyivan Rus' gained general acceptance as a Christian power, as evidenced by Volodymyr's successor, **Yaroslav the Wise**, whose wives were Swedish and Byzantine princesses. His daughters married into the royal lines of France, Hungary, and Norway. Despite the survival of many pagan traditions in popular culture, Christianity became firmly established as the dominant religion in Ukraine. *See also* CHURCHES AND RELIGIOUS COMMUNITIES; PAGANISM.

CHRONICLES. Historical works of **Kyivan Rus'** and later of Ukrainian, Belarusian, and Russian lands. Chronicle entries were composed in the form of annual records, beginning with the words *v lito* (in the year), whence the term *litopys* (chronicle). The earliest Rus' chronicles date back to the ninth or 10th centuries. The first collection of chronicles to be preserved, the *Tale of Bygone Years*, was compiled and edited at the beginning of the 12th century. It was preceded by several collections from **Kyiv** and Novgorod. New chronicles arose as summaries and continuations of previous entries. The Rus' chronicles, which are the principal sources for the study of early medieval Ukrainian history, contain narratives concerning the settlement of the Eastern **Slavs** and neighboring peoples and the founding and development of the Kyivan state, its international relations, religion, and culture.

In the 12th and 13th centuries, as Kyivan Rus' began to disintegrate, the chronicles assumed a more local character. They were written in monasteries and at the courts of **princes** and bishops. The Kyivan and Galician-Volhynian chronicles date from this period. During the 14th and 15th centuries, chronicles concerning the Rus' lands in general were once again compiled (e.g., the Laurentian and Hypatian redactions of the *Tale of Bygone Years*) and have survived in later copies. The Belarusian-Lithuanian chronicles of the 14th to 16th centuries are a continuation of the Rus' chronicle tradition. They include the Suprasl, Bykhovets, and Barkulabovo chronicles.

A number of 17th-century Ukrainian chronicles survive, most notably the Hustynia, **Lviv**, Mezhyhiria, and Ostrih chronicles, as well as the collection titled Chroniclers of **Volhynia** and Ukraine. They describe the struggle against the Ottoman Empire and the **Crimean** Khanate, the emergence of the **Cossacks** and their military campaigns and rebellions, town life and the policies of the **Polish-Lithuanian Commonwealth** in the Ukrainian lands, and the international relations of the **Hetmanate**. The last chronicles identified as such (though not compiled in the form of annual records) were written by Cossack officers in the 17th and early 18th centuries, notably the Eyewitness Chronicle and the chronicles of **Hryhorii Hrabianka** and Samiilo Velychko. They concern the **Khmelnytsky Uprising** of 1648–57 and other Cossack wars of the period.

CHUBAR, VLAS (10 [22] February 1891–26 February 1939). Soviet party and state figure. Chubar was born in Fedorivka (now Chubarivka, Zaporizhia oblast) and studied at the Oleksandrivsk (now Zaporizhia) mechanical and technical school (1904–11). He participated in the **Revolution of 1905** and joined the Bolshevik Party in 1907. After completing his education, he worked in factories in Kramatorsk, Mariupol, **Kharkiv**, Petrograd, and Moscow. During the October Revolution (1917), Chubar was commissar of the revolutionary committee of the main artillery administration in Petrograd. After the Bolshevik victory, he was a member of the Supreme Council of the National Economy (1918–19).

From December 1919, Chubar worked in Ukraine. He headed the Supreme Council of the National Economy of Ukraine (from late 1920) and directed the central administration of the coal industry in the **Donets Basin** (from December 1921). After Stalin recalled **Khristian Rakovsky** from Ukraine, Chubar became the first ethnic Ukrainian to head the government of the **Ukrainian SSR** as chairman of the **Council of People's Commissars** (1923–34). He supported the **Ukrainization** policy and, shortly before the **famine of 1932–33**, argued that **collectivization** was proceeding too quickly and grain-collection plans were unrealistic. In his defense of Ukrainian interests, Chubar never went so far as to oppose the policies of the all-Union Communist Party. In 1934, he was transferred to Moscow and served as deputy chairman of the **USSR Council of People's Commissars** (1934–37). He was arrested in 1937 and shot in 1939.

CHUBYNSKY, PAVLO (15 [27] January 1839–14 [26] January 1884). Ethnographer, folklorist, and civic activist. Chubynsky was born near Boryspil in the **Kyiv** region. He graduated from the faculty of law at St. Petersburg University (1861) and contributed to the journal *Osnova*. He was a founder and active member of the Kyiv **Hromada**. Along with other Hromada members, Chubynsky conducted propaganda among the peasantry and taught in **Sunday schools**. In 1862, he wrote the poem that would become the national **anthem** of Ukraine, "Shche ne vmerla Ukraïna" (Ukraine Has Not Yet Perished). In October of that year, he was arrested for participating in the Ukrainian national movement, accused of seditious activity, and exiled to Pinega, Arkhangelsk gubernia, then to Arkhangelsk. Following his release (1869), Chubynsky was elected to the Russian Geographic Society, under whose auspices he conducted ethnographic expeditions to Ukraine, Belarus, and **Moldavia** (1869–70). He studied Ukrainian folkways, customs, folklore, dialects, and beliefs. The findings of this research, *Trudy étnografichesko-statisticheskoi èkspeditsii v Zapadno-russkii krai* (Works of the Ethnographic and Statistical Expedition to the West Russian Region, 7 vols., 1872–79), were published under his editorship. Together with **Mykhailo Drahomanov**, **Mykola Lysenko**, and **Fedir Vovk**, Chubynsky edited *Kievskii telegraf* (Kyiv Telegraph), the unofficial newspaper of the Kyiv Hromada. He was a founder and managing director of the **Southwestern Branch of the Imperial Russian Geographic Society** in Kyiv (1873). Owing to the **Ems Ukase** (1876), he was exiled from Ukraine and worked in St. Petersburg (1877–79).

Chubynsky was awarded gold medals for his research by the Russian Geographic Society (1873) and the International Geographic Congress (Paris, 1875); he also received the Uvarov Prize (1879). In the spring of 1879, he returned to Kyiv, where he died after a long illness. Chubynsky made an important contribution to the study of Ukrainian customary law, which he considered to be based on a strong tradition of individualism. In addition to his ethnographic works, he wrote the poetry collection *Sopilka Pavlusia* (Pavlus's

Flute, 1871). Petro Yefymenko published a bibliography of Chubynsky's works in *Kievskaia starina* (Kyivan Antiquity, May 1884).

CHURAI, MARUSIA. Legendary folk poetess and singer. According to the Ukrainian oral tradition, she was born to a **Cossack** family in **Poltava** and lived from 1625 to 1653. Her father, Hordii Churai, supposedly participated in the Pavliuk rebellion (*see* COSSACK REBELLIONS) and was executed in Warsaw together with other Cossack leaders (1638). According to the same tradition, Marusia Churai is credited with the authorship of such folk songs as "Oi, ne khody, Hrytsiu" (Do Not Go to Parties, Hryts), "Zasvit vstaly kozachen'ky" (The Cossacks Rose at Dawn), and "Kotylysia vozy z hory" (The Wagons Rolled Downhill). "Oi, ne khody, Hrytsiu" ostensibly related the tragic love affair between Churai and Hryhorii Bobrenko, a standard-bearer of the Poltava regiment. The song inspired many literary works, including **Mykhailo Starytsky's** drama of the same name, **Olha Kobylianska's** *V nediliu rano zillia kopala* (On Sunday Morning She Gathered Herbs, 1909), and Lina Kostenko's verse novel *Marusia Churai* (1979). The song was also translated into French and German in the 19th century. *See also* FOLK MUSIC AND DANCE.

CHURCHES AND RELIGIOUS COMMUNITIES. On the history of the traditional Christian churches, which remain dominant in Ukraine, *see* CHRISTIANIZATION OF RUS'; UKRAINIAN ORTHODOX CHURCH; UKRAINIAN CATHOLIC CHURCH; PROTESTANT CHURCHES IN UKRAINE.

After the declaration of Ukrainian independence in 1991, official persecution of religion came to an end. The Verkhovna Rada ratified a law on freedom of religion in April 1991. Nevertheless, relations between politics and religion remain uneasy. Although art. 5 of the law on freedom of religion states that "religious organizations do not participate in the activities of political parties, do not support political parties financially, do not nominate candidates for government positions, and do not engage in agitation or funding of election campaigns for government posts," politicians continue to lobby religious organizations, believing that the church can mobilize popular support.

The law on religious freedom was amended in August 1996. A significant number of changes and additions were related to the ratification of the **Constitution**, as well as to the problem of church ownership of property and the registration of religious organizations, particularly those run by foreign churches. Art. 7 of the law outlaws religious organizations that propagate war, violence, ethnic, racial or religious conflict, that pose a threat to life, health, freedom or dignity, or disrupt the civil order. The law prohibits conscientious objection to state or military service but makes provision for alternative (nonmilitary) service.

In 1997, the cabinet approved measures pertaining to the commemoration of the second millennium of Christianity, including the convening of several congresses, assistance to charitable projects and pilgrimages, and the completion of restoration projects, including St. Michael's Golden-Domed Cathedral, the Church of the Theotokos of Pyrohoshcha, the Dormition Cathedral of the **Kyivan Cave Monastery**, and the Cathedral of St. Volodymyr in Sevastopol.

The All-Ukrainian Council of Churches and Religious Organizations, established in late 1996, includes leaders of more than 92 percent of all religious communities in Ukraine. It is an ecumenical consultative body created to coordinate the efforts of religious and civic organizations and state institutions to realize social and cultural projects, as well as to resolve problems in state-church relations.

In recent years, the number of religious organizations in Ukraine has grown: by 2003, there were 27,347. Of these, 96.1 percent (26,271 communities) had registered their statutes with the government. Of the registered communities, 344 were monasteries with 5,846 monks and nuns, 153 were educational institutions with 18,048 students, and 9,969 were Sunday schools. At the beginning of 2003, there were also 25,871 members of the clergy in Ukraine (including 688 foreigners) and 249 missions. Ukrainian Catholic communities grew most rapidly (12.1 times between 1988 and 1998), followed by nontraditional organizations (8.3 times) and Roman Catholic communities (7.1 times).

Currently, the Roman Catholic Church has seven dioceses and 840 communities in Ukraine, 477 priests, 78 monasteries (564 monks and nuns), seven educational institutions, three missions, two brotherhoods, and three periodicals. Most of its communities are located in western Ukraine. Clergy are trained at the Vatican, in Poland, and in Lithuania. The head of the church in Ukraine is Cardinal Marian Jaworski.

Ukraine is home to numerous Protestant churches represented in the All-Ukrainian Union of Evangelical Baptists, other evangelical communities, the All-Ukrainian Union of Pentecostal Christians, the Jehovah's Witnesses of Ukraine, the Seventh-Day Adventists, and others. The largest numbers of Protestant communities are located in **Transcarpathia**, Donetsk, Chernivtsi, Rivne, **Volhynia**, and Vinnytsia oblasts. The All-Ukrainian Union of Evangelical Baptist

Communities includes 2,230 communities, 39 educational institutions, 2,925 ministers, 77 missions, and two brotherhoods. The union is headed by Hryhorii Komendant.

The All-Ukrainian Union of Pentecostals incorporates 1,366 communities, 14 educational institutions, 2,081 ministers, and 51 missions. The union is headed by Mykola Melnyk.

The Church of Seventh-Day Adventists has 970 communities, three educational institutions, two missions, and 1,143 ministers (including six foreigners). Its head is Volodymyr Krupsky.

The number of German religious communities has also grown considerably. At the start of 2003, there were 71 communities of the German Evangelical Lutheran Church in Ukraine. It has one educational institution, 31 Sunday schools, and 60 ministers, including 8 foreigners.

In recent years, the Native Ukrainian National Faith (RUN Vira) has grown, with 36 communities at the beginning of 1998. It also has three Sunday schools and 42 priests. Based on pre-Christian foundations, it regards Dazhboh as chief among the gods. Its first synod took place in Chicago in 1972.

The number of Jewish religious communities has risen sharply to 233, with five educational institutions, 81 Saturday schools, two missions, and 119 rabbis (50 foreign). The largest concentrations are in Cherkasy and **Kharkiv** oblasts and in the city of **Kyiv**. The chief rabbi of Kyiv and all Ukraine is Jacob Dov Bleich (*see also* JEWS).

Ukraine is also home to Islamic religious communities (*see* ISLAM IN UKRAINE).

The spread of Buddhism in Ukraine is a recent phenomenon. In 1992, Ukrainian Buddhists formed their own organization and held a congress in Donetsk. Fourteen Buddhist communities have been established.

More recently, the Hare Krishna, Taoists, Vedantists, and other religious groups have emerged in Ukraine. The greatest number of religions per capita is to be found in Rivne, Volhynia, Chernivtsi, and Kherson oblasts and in the **Crimea**. Historically, these regions have been subject to frequent changes of political regime and migrations of various nationalities. The lowest number of religions per capita is to be found in **Lviv**, Dnipropetrovsk, Donetsk, Luhansk, and Kharkiv oblasts. In the eastern oblasts, this is indicative of prolonged **Russification** and generally low religious adherence. In Lviv oblast, the most religious of Ukraine's regions, the low level of diversity is the result of conservatism and a strong Catholic tradition.

The current territorial status of religions in Ukraine is exceptionally dynamic and likely to change. Religious life in western

Ukraine is very intensive, while Kyiv is growing in importance as a center for many religions. If at the start of 1993 Ukraine had 2.7 religious communities per 10,000 inhabitants, at the beginning of 2003 it had 5.8 per 10,000. In 1993, the number was lowest (0.5–1.0) in the Crimea and in Donetsk, Luhansk, Kharkiv, **Poltava**, Dnipropetrovsk, and Zaporizhia oblasts, lower than average (2.1–4.0) in Zhytomyr, Cherkasy, and Chernihiv oblasts, higher than average (4.1–8.0) in Vinnytsia, Khmelnytskyi, Rivne, Ivano-Frankivsk, and Chernivtsi oblasts, and highest (more than 8.0) in Transcarpathia, Lviv, and Ternopil oblasts. By early 2003, the situation had changed considerably. The lowest ratio of religious communities per 10,000 people (up to 4) was to be found in Donetsk, Dnipropetrovsk, Kharkiv, Luhansk, and Zaporizhia oblasts and the city of Kyiv, while the highest ratio (more than 10) was in Chernivtsi, Khmelnytskyi, Lviv, Rivne, Ternopil, Transcarpathia, and Volhynia oblasts.

Analysis of the available data indicates that Ukraine may be divided into four religious regions: west, central, east, and south. Each region comprises several oblasts with similar religious characteristics.

The western region consists of nine oblasts, with Lviv as the religious center. Lviv is home to the Lviv archdiocese of the Roman Catholic Church, the hierarchy of the Armenian Apostolic Church in Ukraine, and the Consistory of the Ukrainian Autocephalous Orthodox Church. Until 2004, it was also the seat of the metropolitanate of the Ukrainian Catholic Church, which is being transferred to Kyiv. The recently established Ukrainian Catholic University is located in Lviv, as is the Museum of Religion (founded in 1970) and the Logos publishing house, which has produced more than 100 handbooks, textbooks, brochures, and catalogs.

The western region also has other religious centers, including the **Pochaiv Monastery** and the Hoshiv Monastery. The western region has best preserved the material base of religious life, particularly its various places of worship, and the base is expanding intensively.

The central religious region includes seven oblasts centered around Kyiv, home of the patriarchal chancellery of the Ukrainian Orthodox Church (Kyiv Patriarchate), the metropolitanate of the Ukrainian Orthodox Church (Moscow Patriarchate), and the Old Believers' Eparchy of Kyiv and All Ukraine. Kyiv is also the home of Ukraine's primary religious shrines (**St. Sophia's Cathedral** and the Kyivan Cave Monastery) and theological seminaries. Its other religious centers are Mezhyhiria, Vyshhorod, Mhar, and Liubech. The region is characterized by moderate participation in religious life.

The eastern religious region consists of five oblasts centered around Kharkiv (with the Dormition and Holy Protection cathedrals). Its religious centers include Slovianohirsk (the Stohirsk Dormition Monastery in Donetsk oblast) and Novomoskovsk (Samara Monastery in Dnipropetrovsk oblast). The region is characterized by very low religious participation, conditioned by intensive industrialization and Soviet-era atheism.

The southern religious region consists of Kherson, Mykolaiv, and Odesa oblasts and the Crimea. Its religious centers are **Odesa** (Trinity Church and the Odesa Theological Seminary, which trained priests under all regimes) and Old Crimea (the mosque of Khan Uzbek and Bakhchysarai). The region is also home to a number of shrines.

For many **Galicians**, Volhynians, Transcarpathians, and **Bukovynians**, the church remains an integral part of their lives and social interaction, whereas these functions have largely been lost in the eastern regions. As two-thirds of Sunday schools are located in the west, this situation seems likely to continue.

CHYKALENKO, YEVHEN (9 [21] December 1861–20 June 1929). Civic and cultural figure, patron of culture, and agronomist. Chykalenko was born in Pereshory, Kherson gubernia. He studied at the faculty of natural science of **Kharkiv** University. Arrested in 1884 for participating in the student **hromada** and the **Drahomanov** circle, he was sentenced to five years of internal exile in his native village. Chykalenko moved to **Odesa** in 1894 and to **Kyiv** in 1900. In 1897, he began publishing his five-volume *Rozmovy pro sil's'ke khaziaistvo* (Conversations on Farming), a popular guide to **agriculture**. He helped establish the **Ukrainian Democratic Radical Party** in 1905. In 1908, following the ban on Ukrainian organizations, Chykalenko became a founder and unofficial head of the **Society of Ukrainian Progressives**. Together with Vasyl Symyrenko and Leonid Zhebunev, he financed the publication of the Kyiv Ukrainian dailies *Hromads'ka dumka* (Public Opinion, 1906) and *Rada* (Council, 1906–14)—the only Ukrainian daily newspapers in **eastern Ukraine** at the time—and the Lviv newspaper of the **Revolutionary Ukrainian Party**, *Selianyn* (Peasant). He also donated honoraria and prizes for the best historical, scholarly, and literary works in *Kievskaia starina* (Kyivan Antiquity). He donated 25,000 rubles for the construction of the Academic Home (a student residence) and Ukrainian courses in Lviv. During **World War I**, Chykalenko was persecuted by the Russian authorities and went into hiding in Finland and Moscow. In April 1917, he became a member of the **Ukrainian Central Rada**, representing the Union of

Ukrainian Autonomist Federalists. After the establishment of Bolshevik rule in 1919, Chykalenko emigrated to **Galicia**, then to Czechoslovakia and Austria. He lived in difficult circumstances on a small stipend from the Ukrainian Civic Committee. In 1925, he settled in Poděbrady, where he headed the terminological commission of the Ukrainian Husbandry Academy. Chykalenko published his memoirs for the years 1861–1907 (1925–26) and his diary for the years 1907–17 (1931), which are important sources for the history of the Ukrainian national movement.

CHYZHEVSKY, DMYTRO (Čiževsky, Tschyževskyj, 23 March [4 April] 1894–18 April 1977). Slavist and intellectual historian. He was born in Oleksandriia, Kherson gubernia, and studied at the universities of St. Petersburg (1911–13) and **Kyiv** (1913–17, 1919). During the **Ukrainian Revolution**, he was a member of the **Ukrainian Central Rada** and its executive body, the Little Rada. In 1921, Chyzhevsky emigrated to Germany, where he continued his studies at the universities of Heidelberg (1921–22) and Freiburg (1922–24). He studied philosophy with Karl Jaspers, Edmund Husserl, and Martin Heidegger. His dissertation on Hegel's influence in Russia was published in 1934. Chyzhevsky served as professor at the Ukrainian Higher Pedagogical Institute in Prague, the **Ukrainian Free University**, and the universities of Halle, Jena, Marburg, Heidelberg, and Cologne; he was also a visiting professor at Harvard University (1949–53). Chyzhevsky was a full member of the Heidelberg Academy, a founder of the **Ukrainian Academy of Arts and Sciences** in the United States, and a recipient of several honorary degrees. He died in Heidelberg.

Chyzhevsky wrote more than 1,000 scholarly works on Slavic studies, the history of **literature**, philosophy, and intellectual history. They include *Filosofiia na Ukraïni* (Philosophy in Ukraine, 1926), *Narysy z istoriï filosofiï na Ukraïni* (Essays on the History of Philosophy in Ukraine, 1931), *Ukraïns'kyi literaturnyi barok* (The Ukrainian Literary Baroque, 3 vols., 1941–44), *Geschichte der altrussischen Literatur: Kiever Epoche* (1948, English trans. 1960), *Istoriia ukraïns'koï literatury vid pochatkiv do doby realizmu* (1956; English trans., *A History of Ukrainian Literature*, 1975, 2d ed., 1997), *Vergleichende Geschichte der slavischen Literaturen* (1968; English trans., 1971), and **Skovoroda:** *Dichter, Denker, Mystiker* (1974).

CIMMERIANS. First known settlers of what is now Ukraine, who inhabited the southern steppes between the 12th and seventh centuries B.C. They are mentioned in Homer's *Odyssey* and

Herodotus's *History*. The Cimmerians' origin is uncertain, but linguistic evidence suggests that they were Iranians. The Cimmerians were nomadic horsemen whose main occupation was warfare; they used iron implements and weapons. Driven from the steppes by the **Scythians** in the seventh century B.C., the Cimmerians conquered Sardis, the capital of Lydia, in 652 B.C. A number of historical toponyms associate the Cimmerians with the Kerch and Taman peninsulas, suggesting that some of them remained in the **Crimea** and became ancestors of the Taurians.

CLIMATE. Located at a great distance from the Atlantic Ocean and close to the Asian continent, Ukraine lies in the central part of the northern temperate zone and has a moderate continental climate on most of its territory. Four climatic regions can be distinguished. The cold snow-forest climate covers western and northern Ukraine north of a line running from Chișinău in Moldova through **Kharkiv**. In the forest and forest-steppe belts, precipitation is highest in summer, which is conducive to the growth of forest plants. The steppe climate extends from the southern boundary of the forest zone to the Black Sea. In this area of moderate rainfall, evaporation exceeds precipitation; hence droughts and dry winds are frequent. The fertile "black-earth" soil of the steppe belt is intensively cultivated, with irrigation provided by the melting snow cover—the main source of water for rivers in this area. The Carpathian and **Crimean** mountains have a mountain meadow climate, with lower temperatures and the highest precipitation, while the southern coast of the Crimea has a Mediterranean climate. Average annual temperatures range from 5.5–7°C in the north to 11–13°C in the south. The average temperature in July, the hottest month, is 18°C in the northwest and 23°C in the southwest, where maximum temperatures can reach 36–39°C. The average temperature in January, the coldest month, is -3°C in the southwest and -8°C in the northeast, where the temperature may drop as low as -42°C. Precipitation, which is greater in summer than in winter, exceeds 500 mm per year in most areas of Ukraine and is conducive to agriculture. The Carpathian Mountains experience the highest precipitation (1,500 mm), while the **Black Sea littoral** and the northern Crimea have the least (300 mm). Sudden jumps in precipitation occasionally cause floods and the expansion of marshlands, particularly in western regions, where precipitation exceeds evaporation. In winter, most of Ukraine has snow cover, which is deepest in February. Its depth ranges from 70–80 cm in the Carpathians to 5–10 cm in the steppe belt. The southern coast of the Crimea experiences winter rainfall and is the only region of Ukraine where precipitation is higher in winter than in summer.

COAT OF ARMS. Emblem or distinctive hereditary device, designed according to the rules of heraldry, combining figures and objects that have symbolic significance and reflect historical tradition. Coats of arms may be divided into the following categories: state, territorial, municipal, corporate, and familial. They are depicted on flags, coins, armor, weapons, buildings, and in books, either handwritten or printed.

The oldest prototypes for coats of arms were totemic depictions of animals, the protectors of a clan or a family, during the period of tribal social organization. They can also be traced to symbolic figures and tribal signs of ownership. In the Ukrainian lands, the **Slavs** used a variety of symbolic signs during that period, including the square, rhombus, circle, stars, crescent moon, and heraldic animals and birds such as unicorns and eagles. During the disintegration of the tribal order, such signs of ownership were widely used to brand cattle and work utensils and to mark boundaries. In **Kyivan Rus'**, the princely **Riuryk line** used the bident and later the **trident** (*tryzub*), initially as a sign of ownership and later as the state coat of arms. During the disintegration of the Kyivan state, the trident was modified to a bident and later went out of use. Territorial coats of arms, such as St. Michael the Archangel in the **Kyiv** region, emerged in its place.

Following the annexation of Ukrainian lands by Poland, the coats of arms of individual noble families whose lineages dated back to ancient Rus' (the princes Ostrozky, Koretsky, Vyshnevetsky, and others) came to be widely used. Coats of arms of individual historical lands were adopted during this period, and municipal coats of arms, reproduced on seals, flags and the like, came into general use.

Created in 1572, the **registered Cossack** army obtained its heraldic symbol, a depiction of a Cossack holding a musket, which was widely used on its seals and then adopted by the **Zaporozhian Sich** and Ukrainian **hetmans** in the 17th and 18th centuries.

During the mid-19th-century Ukrainian revival in **Galicia**, the symbol of the Principality of **Galicia-Volhynia**, a golden lion on an azure background, was used as an emblem of many western Ukrainian political, cultural, and educational organizations, as well as military formations (e.g., the **Ukrainian Sich Riflemen**). The lion on a blue background facing right was ratified as the coat of arms of the **Western Ukrainian People's Republic** (ZUNR) on 12 November 1918.

In the same year, the **Ukrainian Central Rada** adopted as Ukraine's coat of arms a gold trident on a blue background, designed by Vasyl Krychevsky. The trident remained the official coat of arms under the **Hetmanate** (1918) and after the union of the **Ukrainian People's Republic** with the ZUNR (1919).

During the interwar period, the trident was widely used in **western Ukraine**: the **Organization of Ukrainian Nationalists** modified it, with the central arm resembling a sword, while Christian organizations turned the central arm into a cross. In 1920, the depiction of a bear to the right of a heraldic shield with blue and yellow stripes was ratified as the territorial coat of arms of **Transcarpathia** (then part of Czechoslovakia). On 15 March 1939, the parliament of **Carpatho-Ukraine** proclaimed independence and added the trident to its territorial coat of arms.

The coat of arms of the **Ukrainian SSR** was a modified version of that of Soviet Russia: a gold hammer and sickle illuminated by the sun's rays against a red background bordered by sheaves of wheat, surmounted by a red five-pointed star. It bore the motto "Proletarians of All Countries, Unite!" This depiction, which contained no elements of Ukrainian national or historical tradition, was frequently but not significantly modified. In 1992, following Ukraine's declaration of independence, the Verkhovna Rada of Ukraine adopted the depiction of a gold trident on a blue background as the official coat of arms.

CODE OF LAWS OF 1743. Compilation of laws used in 18th-century **Left-Bank Ukraine**. According to the **Articles of Bohdan Khmelnytsky** (1654), the Ukrainian lands were exempt from the Muscovite judicial system. Consequently, customary law, Polish-Lithuanian legislation, and **Magdeburg law** were observed in the **Hetmanate**. Often contradictory, they allowed Ukrainian legal bodies to resort to different legislation for similar cases, leading to inconsistencies and legal abuses. In response to a tsarist ukase to have the laws of the Hetmanate codified and translated into Russian, Hetman **Danylo Apostol** established a codification commission in 1728. In 15 years the commission produced an extensive collection titled *The Laws by Which the Little Russian People Are Judged* (1743). The codex consisted of 30 sections, 531 articles, and 1,716 points. It included the instructions to the Codification Commission, a list of military and civil service ranks in the Hetmanate, explanations of citations in the text, and an index.

The codex of 1743 dealt with ownership and possession, servitudes, and mortgage law; it distinguished between personal, hereditary, and acquired property rights, as well as between contractual obligations and those pertaining to reparations. It contained detailed provisions for agreements of purchase and sale, exchange, loans, deposit, guaranty, and custody. Criminal investigation was defined as an essentially private matter. The **court** determined penalties depending on the wishes of the victim or, in his absence, on the demands of his family. In time, the courts increased their investigative initiative. The codex enumerated crimes against religion, "the honor and authority of the monarch," life, personal security, property, and sexual morality.

The criminal law grew in complexity, distinguishing between criminal intent and commission, between the chief perpetrator and accomplices, and so on. The following penalties were imposed: capital punishment, mutilation and corporal punishment, imprisonment, dishonor (branding), exile, dismissal from one's position, confiscation and sale of property, ecclesiastical penalties (the most common of which was binding the felon's neck or right hand in an iron ring that was chained to the external wall of a church or bell tower), as well as imprisonment in a monastery, forced marriage (in cases of rape), and censure. To act as a deterrent, the punishments were carried out in public. An appellate court system was developed.

The General Military Court was responsible directly to the **Cossack hetman**. Most judicial matters were decided by regimental, company, and village courts and rarely adjudicated by the hetman, although he had the right to issue pardons and confirm all death sentences. Towns without Magdeburg law had town courts, while those with Magdeburg law had magistrate courts. Only formally elective, the judges performed both judicial and administrative functions. A fairly clear distinction was drawn between civil and criminal cases. Civil suits were subject to the adversary principle, while criminal cases were governed by the investigative process. "Distinguished honest persons," the insane, people over 70 years of age, and pregnant women were exempt from torture. Court decisions and decrees could be appealed to a higher court, except for indisputable obligations and verdicts based on confessions.

Although never confirmed by the Russian imperial authorities, the code of 1743 was used extensively in the Hetmanate until its abolition in the late 18th century. Elements of the code were incorporated into subsequent amendments of imperial law and remained in effect in the 19th century.

COLLECTIVIZATION. Communist policy of subjecting **agriculture** to state control. The first efforts at collectivization in Ukraine were made by the invading Bolsheviks in the course of the **Ukrainian Revolution** (1917–21). They encountered strong **peasant** resistance, as the tradition of individual landholding was deeply entrenched in Ukraine (*see* INSURGENT MOVEMENT). Lenin compromised by introducing the New Economic Policy (1921), which restored private property and market relations.

Collectivization was reintroduced by Stalin as part of the first Five-Year Plan of industrialization in 1928. In order to feed the vast new armies of proletarians required for the state-sponsored industrialization drive, the Soviet authorities needed an unlimited supply of agricultural produce. They also had to export grain in order to obtain the hard currency essential for the import of modern machinery. It was therefore imperative that the state become independent of the individual peasant farmer, who responded to low prices or high taxes by producing only enough for his own needs. Ukraine, as the traditional breadbasket of the Russian Empire, came under particularly strong pressure to collectivize its agriculture. Moreover, Soviet planners explicitly referred to Ukraine as a "colossal laboratory" for the development of the rural economy. The secret police prepared for collectivization by removing weapons from peasant households and strictly forbidding all voluntary peasant associations. In 1929, Stalin unleashed a campaign to "eliminate the *kulak* (Ukr. *kurkul'*, exploiter of peasant labor) as a class." The definition of a *kulak* was completely elastic, and the term was frequently applied to peasants only slightly better off than their neighbors.

Grain quotas were imposed on villages, which were collectively responsible for fulfilling them. Peasants who did not fulfill their quotas were fined five times the value of the quota; if they could not pay, their property was seized and auctioned. They were also forced to live apart from other villagers and denied essential services. Class antagonism was encouraged by giving poor peasants (i.e., those who did not protest collectivization) part of the proceeds of fines and auctions, as well as by assigning them additional plots of land outside the collective.

It was planned to collectivize the whole **Ukrainian SSR** within a year, by the autumn of 1930. In February, when party activists began taking peasant livestock, there was tremendous resistance, and peasants slaughtered up to half their farm animals. By 10 March, only 2.5 percent of Ukrainian peasant households (almost 62,000) had actually been collectivized. Stalin issued an article titled "Dizziness with Success" (2 March 1930), in which he blamed local authorities for forcing the pace of collectivization and declared it a voluntary process. By autumn, half the collectivized households had left the collective farms. A new campaign began immediately, forcing peasants back into the collectives by means of exorbitant taxes on their produce. By the end of 1932, about 70 percent of Ukrainian peasant households (and four-fifths of Ukraine's arable land) had been collectivized.

"Dekulakization" was carried out with great brutality. Gangs of so-called "25,000ers" (mostly workers from Russia fanatically dedicated to communism; in the Ukrainian villages, there was only one communist per thousand peasants) were employed to expropriate the Ukrainian peasants, who in turn revolted against the authorities. Their uprisings ranged from women's riots (*babs'ki bunty*) to pitched battles involving regular army and secret police units. The number of insurgents in 1930 has been estimated at 40,000.

According to official statistics, some 352,000 peasant households were dekulakized in Ukraine (1928–31). A great many peasant families were deported to Siberia, where they were thrown off trains and left to fend for themselves: it is estimated that approximately a third of the deportees died, especially children and the elderly.

The newly collectivized peasants worked poorly, as the authorities gave them no incentive; almost all their produce was appropriated by the state. Given the failure of collectivization to satisfy the state's ever-increasing appetite for grain, Stalin and his associates proceeded to engineer the **famine of 1932–33** in order to force the peasantry to meet their demands.

COMMUNIST PARTY OF UKRAINE (CPU)/KOMUNISTYCHNA PARTIIA UKRAÏNY. Known until 1952 as the Communist Party (Bolshevik) of Ukraine. Branch of the Communist Party of the Soviet Union (est. 1898 as the Russian Social Democratic Labor Party [RSDLP]; renamed Russian Communist Party [Bolshevik] in 1918; All-Union RCP[B], 1925; CPSU, 1952).

The CPU developed from two sources. The first consisted of Bolshevik-dominated RSDLP cells in Ukraine made up of members of the intelligentsia and workers, predominantly of Russian origin. They had no separate territorial organization, since the Bolsheviks, like all other Russian parties, considered Ukraine an integral part of Russia. The other source, inspired largely by Ukrainian **populism**, consisted of the **Borotbists**, who split off in 1918 from the peasant-based **Ukrainian Party of Socialist Revolutionaries**, and the **Ukrainian Communist Party** (Ukapisty), which broke in 1919 with the **Ukrainian Social Democratic Labor Party**, whose membership consisted largely of socialist intellectuals.

Following the unsuccessful Soviet invasion of Ukraine in December 1917 (*see* UKRAINIAN SSR), the Bolsheviks of Ukraine held a conference at Taganrog (18–20 April 1918), where they accepted **Mykola Skrypnyk**'s proposal to establish the CPU as an independent party. At the behest of Lenin and the largely Russian membership of the CPU, this decision was reversed at the first congress of the CPU in Moscow in July 1918, and the CPU was declared an integral part of the RCP(B). A second Soviet invasion in November 1918 led to the establishment of the **Provisional Workers' and Peasants' Government of Ukraine**. The first secretary of the CPU was **Georgii Piatakov**. This government collapsed in August 1919, having alienated the Ukrainian **peasantry** with its ruthless grain requisitions and the intelligentsia by its contemptuous treatment of the national question. The CPU declared itself dissolved and placed its members at the disposal of the RCP(B).

The CPU resumed activities in late 1919, when a third Soviet invasion, backed by the resources of the million-man Red Army, established a Soviet regime in Ukraine. Bolshevik policies toward Ukraine grew more cautious, given its resistance to direct rule from Moscow. In early 1919, two Ukrainian communists, Vasyl Shakhrai and Serhii Mazlakh, produced a pamphlet titled *On the Current Situation* in which they addressed Lenin directly with the demand to recognize the CPU as an independent party. The CPU gained a significant Ukrainian contingent through the incorporation of the Borotbists (1920); the Ukapisty followed in 1925. Both parties initially sought recognition by the Comintern as independent entities. In 1920, the CPU consisted of 53.6 percent Russians, 13.6 percent **Jews**, and 19 percent Ukrainians. The vast majority were Red Army soldiers and functionaries of proletarian origin; only 2 percent spoke Ukrainian.

After the formation of the **USSR** in December 1922, the RCP(B), recognizing that the non-Russian republics were poorly integrated, adopted a policy of "indigenization" (1923). Its largely Russian cadres were to master the languages of the non-Russian republics and conduct official business in those languages. This policy, known in the Ukrainian SSR as **Ukrainization**, presented an opportunity for former Borotbists and Ukapisty, as well as nationally conscious Bolsheviks, to build a republic that was at once politically communist and culturally Ukrainian. Over the next decade, such "national communists" as Skrypnyk, **Mykola Khvyliovy**, **Oleksander Shumsky**, and **Mykhailo Volobuiev** emerged as leaders, while the Ukrainian SSR became less a Russian province and more a Ukrainian polity.

As long as Stalin needed the support of the CPU in the struggle for power in Moscow, he was prepared to compromise with it: in 1925 he appointed his personal representative, **Lazar Kaganovich**, first secretary of the CPU to enforce the demand that officials speak Ukrainian. But the issue soon went beyond **language** and became a tug of war between Moscow and **Kharkiv**. Stalin and Kaganovich denounced Khvyliovy, Shumsky, and Volobuiev as "national deviationists" for seeking to loosen ties with Moscow. Stalin compromised again in 1928 by recalling Kaganovich, leaving Skrypnyk, the strongest proponent of Ukrainization, in power. By 1927, Ukrainians accounted for 52 percent of the CPU membership, but no more than a quarter of the Central Committee.

By the late 1920s, Stalin was strong enough to revoke his compromise. He unleashed a campaign of **political terror** against the Ukrainian elite that eliminated Skrypnyk and Khvyliovy, the leading "national communists," while the **famine of 1932–33** destroyed the Ukrainian village, the nation's traditional social base. Stalin's representative **Pavel Postyshev**, who became second secretary of the CPU in January 1933, rode roughshod over the first secretary of the CPU, **Stanislav Kosior**, and purged 235,000 members from the CPU, many of whom were shot or sent to forced-labor camps. A large number of vacancies were filled by cadres from Russia. At the November 1933 plenum of the CPU, Ukrainian nationalism was declared the main ideological threat to Ukraine; up to that point, Russian imperialist nationalism had been officially designated as the principal danger. This marked the end of Ukrainization, followed in 1937–38 by the destruction of the top echelons of the CPU (including Postyshev himself). In August 1937, a committee consisting of Viacheslav Molotov, **Nikita Khrushchev**, and Nikolai Yezhov was dispatched by Stalin to demand the resignations of Kosior and the heads of the Ukrainian government. When they refused to comply, the entire CPU Politburo was summoned to Moscow; its members were arrested there or shortly after their return to Kyiv. Only two leaders of the CPU were left alive. Khrushchev, who oversaw this purge, became first secretary of the CPU in January 1938.

During **World War II**, the debilitated CPU was unable to organize effective resistance to the Nazi invasion; until the summer of 1942, the Soviet partisans numbered only about 2,000. Party officials remaining on occupied territory showed little dedication to Soviet rule and readily informed on the resistance network when interrogated.

By 1949, the CPU had regained its prewar numbers, but 90 percent of it consisted of new members—predominantly Ukrainians—recruited during the war. By 1951, the party's top echelons were 71.4 percent Ukrainian, although Russians continued to dominate the Politburo. For the first time since 1923, an ethnic Ukrainian, Oleksii Kyrychenko, became first secretary of the CPU (1954). This tendency continued; in 1954, Ukrainian representation in the CPU Central Committee increased to 72 percent, and all eight Politburo members were Ukrainians. The 300th anniversary of the

Pereiaslav Agreement, celebrated with tremendous pomp in 1954 as marking the "reunion of Ukraine with Russia," indicated that in Moscow's opinion, the CPU was now solidly integrated with the CPSU and had become a trusted junior partner in Soviet affairs.

That judgement appeared well justified until the early 1960s, when tensions developed over the centralization of the Soviet **economy**. Given the significant Ukrainian contribution to Soviet industry, the CPU apparatus began to push for greater economic autonomy and express resentment at the continuing influx of Russian officials into Ukraine. Khrushchev, as first secretary of the CPSU, alienated the CPU (led by **Mykola Pidhorny**, 1957–63) by demanding ever higher quotas of **agricultural** production. Autonomist tendencies in the CPU increased after 1963, when **Petro Shelest** became first secretary. The party grew rapidly (from 1.1 million members in 1958 to 2.4 million in 1971) and began to play a prominent role in all-Union politics (Ukrainians constituted 20 percent of the CC CPSU by 1961). Ukrainian cultural activists and political dissidents attempted to make use of the CPU's self-assertion to counteract **Russification** (*see* DISSIDENT MOVEMENT; DZIUBA, IVAN; *SHISTDESIATNYKY*), leading to two waves of political arrests in 1965 and 1967–68. Although Shelest was no nationalist, the Moscow authorities considered him inefficient in the suppression of dissent and charged him with "economic autarchism." After his peremptory removal from office in 1972, there was a purge of many Ukrainian institutions and an exchange of party cards that reduced CPU membership by 1.5 percent. Shelest's successor, **Volodymyr Shcherbytsky**, was a good economic manager who sought to improve Ukraine's standard of living while following a rigidly conformist line in politics and culture. He remained in office until 1989, stubbornly opposed to Mikhail Gorbachev's *perestroika*. Party control over society was seriously undermined in Shcherbytsky's last years; the **Chornobyl nuclear disaster** (1986) created tremendous social unrest, and more than 1,900 senior CPU officials were retired or dismissed in 1987–88.

Shcherbytsky's own forced retirement in September 1989 led the CPU to seek a rapprochement with the opposition (*see* RUKH) and present itself as a defender of Ukrainian national interests. The new first secretary, Volodymyr Ivashko, found himself leading a divided party; in elections to the **Verkhovna Rada** in March 1990, many CPU deputies were elected as part of the Democratic Bloc, while on 1 June the communist hard-liners formed a caucus "For a Sovereign Soviet Ukraine" led by **Oleksandr Moroz** (popularly known as the "group of 239"). When offered the post of CPSU deputy secretary, Ivashko availed himself of it and abruptly left for Moscow on 11 July. His successor, the stalwartly pro-Moscow Stanislav Hurenko, served as first secretary until the CPU, like the CPSU itself, was outlawed in the aftermath of the attempted coup of 19–21 August 1991.

Part of the former CPU reemerged under Moroz's leadership in October 1991 as the Socialist Party. Other elements of the CPU illegally reestablished the party on 19 June 1993, with the former secretary of the Komsomol (Communist Youth League), **Petro Symonenko**, becoming its leader. The revived CPU was officially registered on 5 October 1993 and became Ukraine's largest party, although its declining electorate consisted largely of senior citizens. President **Leonid Kuchma**, first elected in 1994, made skillful use of the CPU as a foil to attract support from the political right and center.

COMMUNIST PARTY OF WESTERN UKRAINE/KOMUNISTYCHNA PARTIIA ZAKHIDNOÏ UKRAÏNY (KPZU). Established by a group of **Borotbists** in February 1919 in Stanyslaviv (now Ivano-Frankivsk), it was known until 1923 as the Communist Party of **Eastern Galicia** (KPSH). Its predecessor was the International Revolutionary Social Democracy, a small youth organization inspired by the thought of **Mykhailo Drahomanov** that functioned illegally during **World War I**. The first secretary of the KPSH was the former Borotbist Karlo Savrych (pseud. Maksymovych). Another source of KPSH membership was the **Ukrainian SSR**, where former Galician prisoners of war established committees in the **Communist Party of Ukraine** (CPU). In 1920, the KPSH applied to the Comintern for recognition as an autonomous section of the CPU. After the definitive occupation of Galicia by Poland and the signing of the **Treaty of Riga** (1921), a dispute arose between the KPSH and the Communist Labor Party of Poland (KPRP), which formed its own Galician branch. This split the KPSH into two factions, one of which supported union with the KPRP, while the other, led by Osyp Krilyk (pseud. Vasylkiv), defended the independence of the Ukrainian organization (*Vasylkivtsi*). Not until 1923 did the *Vasylkivtsi* join the KPRP as an autonomous branch.

The KPSH, which extended its activities into **Volhynia**, the **Kholm region**, **Podlachia**, and a portion of **Polisia**, was renamed the KPZU. It held congresses (1924, 1928, and 1934), elected its own Central Committee, and held a place in the Comintern within the Polish delegation. In 1924, it had close to 1,700 members (1,326 Ukrainians, 227 **Jews**, and 146 Poles). During the 1920s, the influence of the KPZU grew, owing to the success of the NEP and

Ukrainization in the Ukrainian SSR. It called for the union of all Ukrainian lands with the Soviet Ukrainian republic. In 1926, the KPZU created Sel-Rob (Ukrainian Peasant-Worker Socialist Alliance) as a legal party that could take part in elections. At its height (1928) it had about 10,000 members and seven seats in the Polish Diet; it was abolished by the Polish authorities in 1932. The official periodical of the KPZU was *Nasha pravda* (Our Truth, 1923–35). In addition, the newspapers *Nove zhyttia* (New Life, 1928–30), *Svitlo* (Light, 1925–28), *Sel'-Rob* (1927–32) and the journals *Vikna* (Windows, 1927–32), *Kul'tura* (Culture, 1923–31) and *Novi shliakhy* (New Paths, 1929–32) were published at the party's initiative.

In 1927, the majority of the KPZU supported **Oleksander Shumsky**'s "national deviation" within the CPU. In response, the first secretary of the CPU, **Lazar Kaganovich**, called for the removal of the KPZU leadership. The party split into a majority ("Shumskyists") and a minority (those who accepted the official CPU line, supported by Stalin in Moscow and **Mykola Skrypnyk** in Kharkiv). On 18 February 1928, the majority faction, led by Krilyk and Roman Kuzma (pseud. Turiansky), was expelled from the Comintern. It dissolved itself in October 1928. Its leaders acknowledged their "errors" and most emigrated to the Ukrainian SSR, where they perished in Stalin's purges.

With the onset of Stalin's **political terror** and the end of Ukrainization, the KPZU's influence began to decline. In 1933, its leaders, Myron Zaiachkivsky (pseud. Kosar) and Hryhorii Ivanenko (pseud. Baraba), were recalled to the **USSR** and executed following the "Ukrainian Military Organization" show trial. In 1938, the Comintern passed a resolution concerning the dissolution of the Communist Party of Poland, including the communist parties of western Ukraine and western Belarus. This decision was rationalized with a trumped-up charge that the leadership of those parties had been infiltrated by fascist agents. Almost all members of the KPZU who found themselves within the USSR as a result of the Soviet occupation of **western Ukraine** (1939) were persecuted or killed by the Stalin regime.

CONSTITUTION. Basic law adopted by Ukraine's parliament, the **Verkhovna Rada** (Supreme Council, VR), on 28 June 1996. Its enactment was the result of a lengthy process. According to the law on legal succession (12 September 1991), the Constitution of the **Ukrainian SSR** (1978) remained in force until the ratification of a new one. A constitutional commission headed by the chairman of the VR, Ivan Pliushch, and President **Leonid Kravchuk** was established in 1992. It issued official drafts for public discussion in 1992 and 1993, neither of which was accepted by the VR. The main bone of contention was the president's wish for a strong executive, which was resisted by the communist majority in the VR. The constitutional process ground to a halt in October 1993, and more than 200 amendments were made to the 1978 constitution in an attempt to bring it up to date.

Following the election of President **Leonid Kuchma**, a new constitutional commission was formed. As Kuchma's relations with the VR were adversarial, he forced the adoption of the Law on Power (18 May 1995), an attempt to establish presidential supremacy in **government**. The resulting tensions were eased by a constitutional agreement with the VR (7 June 1995) that somewhat expanded presidential power while restricting that of the VR and local councils. A draft constitution was tabled in the VR on 20 March 1996. This led to further controversy centering on the separation of powers, security of private property, symbols of statehood, the role of the Russian **language**, and the status of the **Crimea**. When Kuchma threatened to break the deadlock by calling a referendum (in which he was likely to prevail), the VR held an extraordinary all-night session on 27–28 June and adopted a new constitution.

The Constitution of Ukraine consists of 15 chapters: 1. general principles; 2. rights, freedoms, and obligations of individuals and citizens; 3. elections and referenda; 4. the VR; 5. the president; 6. the **Cabinet of Ministers** and other executive bodies; 7. the procuracy; 8. the justice system; 9. territorial structure; 10. the Autonomous Republic of the Crimea; 11. local self-government; 12. the Constitutional Court; 13. the constitutional amending process; 14. final provisions; 15. temporary provisions. Chapters one through 14 contain 161 articles. The chapter on temporary provisions includes 14 points on the gradual introduction of particular sections of the constitution. In order to maintain stability, amending procedures are fairly complex. Amendments to the foundations of the constitutional order (chapter one), the electoral system (chapter two), and procedures for amending the constitution (chapter 13) require a two-thirds majority of the VR for adoption. Amendments intended to eliminate or restrict individual rights and freedoms, or to abolish the independence or territorial integrity of Ukraine, are inadmissible.

The constitution defines Ukraine as a sovereign, independent, democratic, social, law-based, and unitary republic (with an exception for Crimean autonomy). Sovereignty is vested in the people of Ukraine. Almost one-third of the constitutional provisions are concerned with civil rights, freedoms, and duties. The constitution establishes the inalienable right of every citizen to life, dignity, privacy, security of person and domicile, confidentiality of communications, and citizenship or change thereof. Ukrainian is established as the sole official language.

The most problematic issue in the constitution is the separation of powers, which represents an uneasy compromise between the models of a presidential republic (strict separation of powers) and a parliamentary one (partial separation of powers). The president, who may hold office for a maximum of two terms, is vested with extensive power to form and lead the government without accountability to the VR, thereby diminishing the authority of the prime minister, while the VR has the power to adopt laws without interference from the executive branch. Kuchma's second term gave strong evidence of his determination to establish presidential supremacy in government (*see* KUCHMA, LEONID).

The constitution also establishes an independent judiciary and an institution without precedent in Ukrainian jurisprudence—the Constitutional Court, whose function is to ensure the legal supremacy of the constitution and interpret its provisions.

In recognition of the importance of the new constitution, the day of its adoption was declared an annual public holiday.

COOPERATIVE MOVEMENT. The cooperative movement in Western Europe developed in response to the needs of industrial workers. By contrast, the Ukrainian cooperative movement emerged in the late 1860s to serve the socioeconomic needs of the recently emancipated **peasantry**. It was also a means of social and economic self-defense and became an integral part of the struggle for national independence. In addition to strengthening the economic power of the populace, it taught the masses social responsibility and trained large numbers of civic leaders.

Mykola Ballin established the first Ukrainian consumer cooperative in **Kharkiv** in 1866. The first credit cooperative was founded in Hadiach in 1866, and the second was formed by **Hryhorii Galagan** in Sokyryntsi, **Poltava** gubernia, in 1869. Until the 1890s, cooperatives in Ukraine developed slowly, given the absence of relevant legislation. The number of cooperatives in Russian-ruled Ukraine grew from 130 in 1880 to 290 by 1895. The Poltava, Kyiv, and **Podilia** gubernias had more consumer cooperatives than any other gubernias in the Russian Empire. National aspirations, especially the demand for cooperative associations independent of Russian organizations, increased markedly within the Ukrainian cooperative movement. By 1913, Kyiv was the center of that movement and the seat of the Nasha Kooperatsiia (Our Cooperation) society. The number of cooperative organizations, primarily consumer cooperatives and credit unions, grew from 450 in 1900 to 820 in 1905, 2,100 in 1910, and 6,510 in 1914.

In Austrian-ruled **western Ukraine**, the cooperative movement emerged in the 1870s through the efforts of the clergy, later augmented by the **Prosvita** society. Truly viable enterprises, such as the Narodna Torhovlia consumer cooperative in Lviv, were founded under the Austrian law of 1873 on commercial trade associations. Credit unions developed rapidly, and in 1898 they formed the first Ukrainian association of credit cooperatives, the Provincial Credit Union (Tsentrobank). Agricultural cooperatives formed the Provincial Union of Farming and Trade Associations in 1911, which was renamed Tsentrosoiuz (Association of Cooperative Unions) in 1924. In 1909, the Educational Economic Congress in Lviv, attended by representatives from all regions of Ukraine, adopted a set of common ideological and organizational principles for coordinated action. By 1914, the Provincial Audit Union represented 609 cooperatives, of which nearly 61 percent were credit unions. An additional 106 cooperatives belonged to the **Russophile** Audit Union of Ruthenian Cooperatives, and some 400 small credit unions were supported by the **Galician** Diet. In **Bukovyna**, about 150 credit unions formed the Selianska Kasa (Peasant Bank) association in 1903 under the leadership of **Stepan Smal-Stotsky**.

During **World War I**, Ukrainian cooperatives in the Russian Empire expanded their activities. As Ukraine began to separate from Russia politically in 1917, Ukrainian cooperatives withdrew from Russian associations and formed their own. Leaders of the Ukrainian movement envisioned the cooperative network as the economic basis of the new Ukrainian state. By the early 1920s, there were some 20,000 cooperatives and 270 credit unions. The movement had six million members, and nearly 60 percent of the population participated in consumer cooperatives. The system was headed by the Ukrainian Central Cooperative Committee.

Conversely, the Galician cooperative movement declined during this period and began to recover only after the adoption of the Polish cooperative law in 1920. The Provincial Audit Union expanded its activities into **Volhynia** and **Polisia**, and by 1925 it represented 1,029 cooperatives—almost twice as many as before the war. By 1939, it represented 3,455 cooperatives with a membership of 643,000. Cooperative membership was proportionally twice as high among Ukrainians as among the general population of the Second Polish Republic. However, the union was financially weaker than before the war, and a new Polish law adopted in 1934 increased government control over the cooperative movement, restricting the union's activities.

In the **Ukrainian SSR**, cooperatives developed rapidly during the NEP period, acting as the primary economic intermediary between the state and peasant farmers. In 1929, more than 60 percent of the peasantry belonged to cooperatives. As many activists of the pre-Soviet period returned to the cooperative movement, making it an important source of national consciousness, the authorities resolved to bring it under control.

Beginning in 1927, cooperative activities began to be restricted. By 1930, the government had begun to set prices on goods sold or manufactured by cooperatives and to tax them heavily. Peasants were forced to buy manufactured goods only from cooperatives in exchange for their produce, which was priced very low (*see* COLLECTIVIZATION). The cooperatives' share of retail trade dropped from 86 percent in 1930 to 42 percent in 1934 and 29 percent in 1940. After the Soviet occupation of western Ukraine, its cooperative system was brought into line with that of the rest of the **USSR**. By 1960, manufacturing cooperatives were abolished, and the network consisted primarily of rural consumer cooperatives specializing in **agricultural** products.

COSSACK COUNCIL (**Sich** Council, Military Council, General Military Council). Administrative body of the **Zaporozhian Host**, the registered **Cossack** armies, and the **Hetmanate** (16th-18th centuries). It was the supreme legislative, administrative, and judicial institution of the Zaporozhian **Sich**. The council's decisions represented the opinion of the whole Host and, as such, were binding on all Cossacks. The council determined internal and foreign policy, elected officers, and punished the most serious crimes. Participants in the council formed a circle with the **Cossack officer** staff in the center—the *kish* otaman (camp commander), quartermaster, chancellor, and *osavuly* (aides-de-camp)—with the latter acting as intermediaries between the council and the officers. The Cossacks voted with loud cries or by throwing their hats into the air. Other than councils of the entire Sich encampment, kurin (company) councils were convened to consider secret and urgent matters, border disputes, and the organization of minor campaigns. Occasionally they preceded the general council. The **registered Cossack** army also conducted general, regimental, and company councils. Their decisions required confirmation from the Polish government.

After the **Khmelnytsky Uprising** (1648–1657) and the emergence of the Hetmanate, Cossack councils were incorporated into the new administrative structure. The General Military Council, which included rank-and-file Cossacks and officers, was called primarily for the formal election of a new **hetman**. Most important decisions were made at the officers' council, which evolved into a rudimentary parliament of the Hetmanate's elite by the 1760s. Regional and local affairs were deliberated at regimental and company councils.

COSSACK INSIGNIA. Military emblems and regalia of the Ukrainian Cossacks used in the 16th-19th centuries. Originally granted to the **Zaporozhian Host** by King Stephen Batory of Poland (1576), they included the *khoruhva* (banner), *bunchuk* (standard), *bulava* (mace), and *pechatka* (seal); later they were supplemented by the *pernach* (mace), *litavry* (kettle-drum), *znachok* (pennant), and *palytsia* (rod). The *bulava*, carried by the hetman and *kish* otaman (camp commander), was the highest symbol of authority. From 1648, **Bohdan Khmelnytsky** carried a gold-plated silver *bulava* decorated with precious stones. Cossack colonels carried smaller, ribbed *bulavas*, called *pernachi*. A round silver seal depicted a Cossack wearing a pointed hat and a buttoned mantle, with a sheathed sword at his side and a musket. It bore the inscription "Seal of the Illustrious Lower Dnipro Zaporozhian Army." A crimson *khoruhva* with an embroidered coat of arms, saint, cross, etc., was issued to the whole Zaporozhian Host. The *litavra*, a large copper caldron covered with a stretched hide, was used for transmitting signals (e.g., summons to council; signaling danger).

Each insignia was issued only to designated members of the Cossack officer staff. The *bulava* was given to the *kish* otaman; the *bunchuk* was issued to the *kish* otaman or hetman but was carried by the standard-bearer or his deputy; the great seal was issued to the military judge, while the kurin or *palanka* (subunit) seal was issued to the kurin otaman or *palanka* colonel; the *pernach* was issued to colonels and the *litavra* to the entire army, although it was the responsibility of the *dovbysh* (drummer); the *palytsia* was issued to the aide-de-camp, and emblems were assigned to all 38 Zaporozhian kurins but placed in the care of Cossacks holding the rank of notable military fellows. All Cossack insignia, with the exception of *litavra* poles, were kept in the treasury of the Church of the Holy Protection at the **Sich**. The *litavra* poles were kept in the kurin of the military *dovbysh*. Occasionally Cossack insignia included the *kalamar* (a large silver ink-pot), the attribute of the chancellor of the Zaporozhian Host.

The insignia of the Zaporozhian Host remained in use in the Hetmanate until its abolition in the 1780s. Similar insignia were used in the **Transdanubian Sich** and by the Kuban Cossacks.

COSSACK OFFICERS (Ukr. *kozats'ka starshyna*) represented the military and administrative leadership of the **Zaporozhian Host**, the **registered Cossack** army, the **Hetmanate**, and **Sloboda Ukraine**. This stratum emerged during the formation of Ukrainian Cossackdom in the 16th century. With the development of the Zaporozhian **Sich**, the officer cohort expanded to some 150 individuals, including the *kish* otaman (camp commander), military judge, military *osavul* (aide-de-camp), deputy *osavul*, military chancellor (*pysar*) and kurin (company) otamans; an undersecretary, the *bulavnychyi* (hetman's mace-bearer), flag-bearer, standard-bearer, *pernachnyi* (colonel's mace-bearer), drummer, assistant drummer, gunner, cannoneer, interpreter, stewards, *kantarzhii* (weights master), clerks, and field and *palanka* (subunit) commanders: colonel, secretary, undersecretary, and deputy *osavul*. The officer staff controlled the administration, judicial system, and finances, led the army, and represented the Sich in the international arena. Staff members were elected at a **Cossack council** by the entire Cossack community.

The officer staff of the registered Cossack army, created in 1572, elected the **hetman** with the approval of the Polish government at a general council. The nobleman Jan Badowski is believed to have been the first hetman of the registered army. The registered officer staff consisted of two (later four) *osavuly*, a quartermaster, military judge, military chancellor, and a varying number of colonels and captains. The officer staff swore allegiance to the king and received privileges for performing military service, but the government of the **Polish-Lithuanian Commonwealth** kept limiting those privileges. In 1625, the government introduced the post of *regimentar*, the deputy of the Crown Hetman, who led the registered Cossack army. After suppressing the **Cossack rebellion** of 1638, the Polish Diet transferred the hetman's functions to a government commissioner. Until the **Khmelnytsky Uprising** (1648–57), officer ranks above captain could be held only by the Polish and Polonized nobility.

In the course of the uprising, the Cossack officers were hierarchically differentiated into general, regimental, and company officers. The General Officer Staff, which functioned as the government of the Hetmanate, included the general quartermaster, general judge, general chancellor, two general *osavuly*, general treasurer, general flag-bearer, and general standard-bearer. According to tradition, these supreme officials were to be elected, but by the 18th century they were increasingly appointed by the hetman and the tsarist authorities.

The regimental officer staff, headed by a colonel, served as the military and civilian administration of Cossack regiments in the 17th and 18th centuries. The other staff members were the regimental chancellor, regimental *osavul*, and regimental flag-bearer. Formally, the regimental staff should have been elected at regimental councils, but it was often appointed by the hetman with the approval of the tsar's commissioners. The company officer staff consisted of the captain, company otaman, secretary, *osavul*, and flag-bearer. The lowest-ranking members of the Cossack officer staff were the town and village (kurin) otamans. Active representatives of the officer staff enjoyed use of the so-called rank estates, the profits from which served as salary. With the abolition of Ukrainian autonomy in the 1780s, a segment of the officer stratum was incorporated into the Russian nobility.

COSSACK REBELLIONS (1590s–1640s). As the Ukrainian **Cossacks** gained experience in defending the steppe frontier against the **Tatars**, making the region more settled and stable, the Polish authorities and magnates began exerting greater pressure to subordinate the Cossacks and impose labor obligations on the **peasants**. Such pressure gave rise to simmering unrest, frequent uprisings, and a number of large-scale rebellions.

Kosynsky Rebellion (1591–93). In December 1591, a **Zaporozhian** unit led by Kryshtof Kosynsky captured the castle and town of Bila Tserkva, where the rebels acquired cannon, gunpowder, and military supplies. By 1592, the insurgent movement had engulfed the palatinates of **Kyiv**, **Volhynia**, Bratslav, and part of **Podilia**. Cossack units seized Trypilia, Bohuslav, Pereiaslav, and the Kyiv castle. In late 1592 and early 1593, a large insurgent army led by Kosynsky operated in Volhynia. In Kostiantyniv, the Polish nobility assembled a large army under the leadership of the palatine of Kyiv, Prince **Kostiantyn Ostrozky**. The Cossack forces were defeated near Piatka and forced to retreat to Zaporizhia. However, in May 1593 a unit of 2,000 Cossacks led by Kosynsky set forth from the Zaporozhian **Sich** and captured the castle of the Cherkasy starosta, Oleksander Vyshnevetsky. The Cossacks were later crushed by Vyshnevetsky's forces, and Kosynsky himself was killed.

Nalyvaiko Rebellion (1594–96). In July 1594, the Cossack Severyn Nalyvaiko persuaded the Zaporozhians to rebel against Polish domination. Joined by Hryhorii Loboda and his unit, the Cossack army numbered 12,000 men. By early 1596, the insurgency had spread to Podilia, the Kyiv region, Volhynia, part of **Galicia**, and Belarus. A Cossack squadron led by **Hetman** Matvii Shaula joined the rebels in Belarus. In December 1595, the Polish government assigned Crown Hetman Stanisław Żółkiewski to quell the rebellion. On 23 March (2 April) 1596, units led by Nalyvaiko, Shaula, and Loboda crushed the advance units of the Polish nobles at Bila Tserkva. During the decisive battle at Hostryi Kamin near Trypilia, the rebels were forced to retreat to the Lubny region. In the spring of 1596, the rebels, surrounded at the Solonytsia River near Lubny by the larger Polish army, resisted for nearly two weeks. Żółkiewski promised amnesty to the registered Cossacks if they surrendered. Suspected of treason, Loboda was executed. On 28 May (7 June) 1596, some of the Cossack officers surrendered Nalyvaiko, Shaula, and other leaders of the rebellion to the Poles. During negotiations, the Polish army attacked the Cossack camp, killing thousands of rebels and their dependants. Only a small squadron of Cossacks managed to escape to Zaporizhia. Nalyvaiko and six other leaders of the rebellion were tortured and executed in Warsaw on 11 (21) April 1597.

Zhmailo Rebellion (1625). The Polish government, alarmed by the growth of Cossack opposition, sent an army of some 30,000 men, led by Field Hetman Stanisław Koniecpolski, to the Kyiv region in September 1625. The Cossacks were forced to retreat, first to Cherkasy and later to the mouth of the Tsybulnyk River. Marko Zhmailo, who brought Zaporozhian reinforcements with artillery, assumed general leadership of the rebels. The 20,000-strong insurgent army inflicted significant losses on the Poles at a battle near the village of Taboryshche (now in Kirovohrad oblast), but the stronger Polish army drove the rebels back to Lake Kurukove near Kremenchuk. After an unsuccessful attempt to capture the Cossack encampment, Koniecpolski entered into negotiations. Given the Cossacks' encirclement and lack of provisions, moderate Cossack officers deposed Zhmailo, who advocated the continuation of hostilities (26 October [5 November] 1625). There is no record of Zhmailo's fate, but in all likelihood he was executed. Mykhailo Doroshenko was elected hetman and signed the Kurukove Agreement (1625) with the Polish command.

Fedorovych Rebellion (1630). A new rebellion against Polish rule was led by Taras Fedorovych (Triasylo), hetman of the unregistered Cossacks. In early March 1630, some 10,000 unregistered Cossacks approached Cherkasy, captured Hryhorii Chorny, the progovernment hetman of the registered Cossacks, and tried and executed him. Peasants and townspeople joined the rebel units, attacking and destroying the estates of noble landowners. Some of the rebels joined the Zaporozhians, while others acted independently. By April and May, the rebellion had engulfed a significant portion of the Kyiv and **Poltava** regions. In late April, the Cossack army moved to the **Left Bank**. For three weeks, battles between the rebels and Polish forces commanded by Crown Hetman Stanisław Koniecpolski raged in the vicinity of Pereiaslav. After the victory of the Ukrainian army at the Battle of Korsun, the Polish command initiated peace talks. On 29 May (8 June) 1630, Koniecpolski and the Cossack officers signed the Pereiaslav Agreement (1630). Tymofii (Tymish) Orendarenko was soon elected hetman. Fedorovych and those Cossacks who were dissatisfied with the agreement returned to Zaporizhia.

Pavliuk Rebellion (1637). In the summer of 1637, a Zaporozhian unit led by Pavlo But (Pavliuk) captured Korsun and seized the artillery of the registered Cossacks. In August, Pavliuk issued a proclamation exhorting the Ukrainian people to join the insurgent units. Soon the rebellion spread across Left-Bank Ukraine. The insurgents attacked estates, destroyed nobiliary castles, and captured towns and fortresses. On 6 (16) December, the insurgent army was defeated near Kumeiky. The rebels retreated to Borovytsia (near Cherkasy), where they were surrounded and forced to surrender. Pavliuk was seized by Polish soldiers and executed in Warsaw on 19 April 1638.

Ostrianyn Rebellion (1638). An uprising led by the Zaporozhian hetman Yakiv Ostrianyn began in March 1638. Units commanded by Ostrianyn, Karpo Skydan, and Dmytro Hunia captured Kremenchuk, Khorol, and Omelnyk. In early May, they crushed Polish units near Hovtva and headed for Zhovnyn (now in Cherkasy oblast), where they made camp. A ferocious battle with the Polish army, commanded by Mikołaj Potocki, ensued on 3 (13) June, resulting in a Cossack defeat. Ostrianyn retreated to **Sloboda Ukraine** with some of the rebels, but those remaining at the camp did not surrender. Hunia was elected the new hetman. Under his leadership the Cossacks built a fortified camp and held out for nearly two months. On 28 July (7 August), exhausted and lacking provisions, they surrendered. The insurgent army was obliged to give up its weapons, cannon, and military insignia, as well as to recognize the Ordinance of 1638. The defeat of this rebellion marked the beginning of a "golden peace" for the **Polish-Lithuanian Commonwealth** that ended in 1648 with the outbreak of the **Khmelnytsky Uprising**.

COSSACKS (Ukr. *kozaky*). 1. From the 15th to the first half of the 17th century, professional military estate on Ukrainian lands in the Kingdom of Poland and the **Grand Duchy of Lithuania** (after 1569, the **Polish-Lithuanian Commonwealth**). The term "Cossack," which probably derives from the Turkish *qazaq* (freebooter; raider), initially denoted freemen settled in the southern Ukrainian steppes. Because of increasing national and social oppression, many Ukrainian peasants, townspeople, and seasonal workers (*ukhodnyky*) headed beyond the Dnipro Rapids. Ukrainian noblemen without property also joined the ranks of the Cossacks. Cossackdom developed as a military force because of the urgent need for defense; from the founding of the Crimean Khanate in the 1440s through the end of the 16th century, there were no fewer than 110 Tatar-Turkish raids on Ukrainian territory. In the first half of the 17th century, the Ukrainian population was depleted by 300,000. The **Zaporozhian Sich** was established south of the Dnipro Rapids as a fortified Cossack camp. Ca. 1552 (in 1554–55 or 1556, according to other sources), **Dmytro Vyshnevetsky** built the first fortifications on the island of Mala **Khortytsia**. Subsequently, the Sich became the political center of Cossackdom.

The Polish-Lithuanian Commonwealth employed the Cossacks to defend its borders. In the 16th century a second category, town Cossacks, was organized by the border starostas: Ostafii Dashkovych and Semen Polozovych of Cherkasy, Przecław Lanckoroński of Khmilnyk, Bernard Pretwicz of Bar, and the magnates Dmytro Vyshnevetsky (founder of the Sich), Bohdan Ruzhynsky, and Samuel Zborowski. The Polish government strove to exert control over the Zaporozhians. By his decree of 5 June 1572, King Sigismund II Augustus established a register that designated Cossack status. By 1578, it numbered 600 Cossacks. A royal proclamation of 1590 increased the register to 1,000 Cossacks. Led by a **hetman** elected with the government's consent, the **registered Cossacks** were comprised of six regiments divided into companies (1625): Bila Tserkva, Kaniv, Cherkasy, Korsun, Pereiaslav, and Chyhyryn. During the first half of the 17th century, the number of registered Cossacks grew to 6,000 in 1625 and 8,000 in 1631. In the late 16th and early 17th centuries, the Cossacks staged several revolts (*see* COSSACK REBELLIONS). In 1638, after the defeat of the Ostrianyn Rebellion, the Polish government transferred command over the registered Cossacks to a Polish commissioner, thereby excluding most Cossacks from the register and leaving them in danger of enserfment. From the 16th to the 18th century, individual magnates in Ukraine maintained their own armies of private Cossack guards.

By establishing a distinct military estate, playing a significant economic role in the settled area along the Dnipro, and identifying themselves with the revival of the **Ukrainian Orthodox Church**, the Cossacks became the stratum that most clearly defined Ukrainian identity in the early modern period.

2. A privileged estate formed in Ukraine during the **Khmelnytsky Uprising** (1648–57). The **Hetmanate** inherited the territorial organization of Cossackdom, which comprised 16 (at times, as many as 22) regiments. The Zaporozhian Sich formed a separate military and administrative unit. During the **Ruin**, Ukrainian Cossackdom

was divided between Muscovy, the Commonwealth, and the Ottoman Empire. Cossack support for **Ivan Mazepa** during the Northern War (1700–21) led to wholesale repression by the Russian autocracy; at the command of Peter I, the hetman's capital of Baturyn was destroyed (1708), as was the Chortomlyk Sich (1709). After Mazepa's defeat at the **Battle of Poltava** (1709), some Cossacks emigrated and elected **Pylyp Orlyk** as their hetman. In the early 18th century, Ukrainian Cossack regiments were pressed into service to build cities, military fortifications, and canals (particularly the Ladoga Canal) in the Russian Empire. In 1722, the Russian government established the **Little Russian Collegium** in the Hetmanate and forbade the elections of hetmans. From 1734 to 1750, **Left-Bank Ukraine** was ruled by a Russian-controlled administration of the Hetman government. During the administration of Hetman **Kyrylo Rozumovsky**, Catherine II abolished the office of hetman (10 [21] November 1764). Rule over Left-Bank Ukraine passed to the president of the second Little Russian Collegium, **Petr Rumiantsev**. In June 1775, the Russian army of Gen. Petr Tekeli destroyed the Zaporozhian Sich.

In **Right-Bank Ukraine**, which passed to the Commonwealth under the terms of the **Eternal Peace of 1686**, the Cossack register was revived until 1699, while the Cossack movement continued until 1714. An assigned hetman commanded the Korsun, Bratslav, and Bila Tserkva (Fastiv) regiments, while the general population was subject to direct Polish rule. In the mid-17th century, Cossackdom emerged in **Sloboda Ukraine** (Ostrohozk, Sumy, Okhtyrka, **Kharkiv**, and Balakliia regiments), but was abolished by order of Catherine II on 28 July (8 August) 1765.

3. After the destruction of the Sich (1775), approximately 5,000 Zaporozhian Cossacks founded the **Transdanubian Sich** in the Ottoman Empire. Another group settled in the Banat territory of the Austrian monarchy (Banat Cossacks). In the late 18th century, **Cossack officers** in Left-Bank Ukraine acquired equal rights with the Russian nobility. Some Cossacks were recruited for military service, others reduced to the status of free peasants, and the remainder enserfed. More than 15,000 **Black Sea Cossacks**, organized by the tsarist government, took part in the Russo-Turkish War (1787–91). Individual Cossacks obtained lands in the basin of the Southern Buh and Dnister Rivers (Buh Cossack Army). In 1792, the Russian government resettled the Black Sea Cossacks (approx. 25,000) along the right bank of the Kuban River. The Kuban Cossacks founded 40 towns. During the Russo-Turkish War of 1828–29, some Transdanubian Cossacks, led by Yosyp Hladky, also settled in the

Kuban region, coming under the jurisdiction of the Russian Empire in May 1828. They were recruited into the Azov Cossack Army.

4. A military estate in Muscovy based primarily on its borders or in areas of active Russian colonization. The Don Cossacks, recruited in the 15th century from among the local population and immigrants from Muscovy and the Ukrainian lands, often acted in tandem with the Zaporozhian Cossacks against the expansion of the Ottoman Empire and the Crimean Khanate. They signed a mutual assistance pact in 1632. The Zaporozhians participated in Don Cossack revolts led by Stepan Razin (1670–71), Kondratii Bulavin (1707–9), and Emelian Pugachev (1773–75). In 1671, the Don Cossacks swore allegiance to the Muscovite tsar, and in 1775 their autonomy was eliminated by Catherine II. The number of Ukrainian settlers in the Don region increased during the 18th century. According to the census of 1782, Don Cossack *stanytsi* (villages) included 7,456 Ukrainian households. The Ural and Terek Cossacks were recruited mainly from among the Don Cossacks, including a significant number of Ukrainians.

5. In 1917, the **Free Cossacks** were formed as volunteer units to maintain order and defend the **Ukrainian People's Republic**; they fought Bolshevik forces in the winter of 1918. They were opposed by the pro-Bolshevik **Red Cossacks**. Under Soviet rule, the Cossack estate was abolished, but during **World War II**, there were Cossack units in the Red Army.

6. Community organizations of descendants of Ukrainian Cossacks, formed in many Ukrainian oblasts in the late 1980s, seek to revive Cossack traditions and restore monuments of Ukrainian history and culture. **Viacheslav Chornovil** was an elected hetman of the Ukrainian Cossacks.

COUNCIL OF MINISTERS/RADA MINISTRIV (RM). Principal executive and administrative body of the **Ukrainian SSR** (1946–91), successor to the **Council of People's Commissars** (as of 25 March 1946; the change of name was adopted throughout the **USSR**). The organization, structure, competence, and agenda of the RM of the UkSSR were defined by the constitutions of the USSR and the UkSSR, notably the 1978 redactions. The RM was formally elected at the first session of each convocation of the UkSSR **Verkhovna Rada** (VR) and was officially responsible to it. It included a chairman, first deputy and deputy chairmen, ministers, and heads of state committees. The RM was formally authorized to decide all matters of state administration pertaining to the UkSSR, insofar as these were not under the jurisdiction of the VR and its presidium. Theoretically a collegial body adopting decisions by majority vote, the RM was in practice subordinate to its presidium and to the **Communist Party of Ukraine**. Moreover, all significant matters concerning the UkSSR were decided in Moscow.

Within the limits of its competence, the RM supervised economic and sociocultural policy (art. 118 of the 1978 constitution), produced and executed plans for the development of science and technology and the use and protection of the **environment**, and administered economic policy (prices, wages, social security, and the like). Its authority was greatest in 1957–62, when regional economic administration was introduced in the USSR. Chairmen of the RM included Oleksii Vatchenko, **Volodymyr Shcherbytsky**, and **Vitalii Masol**. In 1991, the RM was renamed the **Cabinet of Ministers**.

COUNCIL OF PEOPLE'S COMMISSARS/RADA NARODNYKH KOMISARIV (RADNARKOM, RNK). Government of the **Ukrainian SSR** (1919–46). Modeled on the first Soviet government of Russia, it was formed through the reorganization of the **Provisional Workers' and Peasants' Government of Ukraine** (29 January 1919). Named in imitation of the **Council of People's Ministers** of the **Ukrainian People's Republic**, it consisted of 12 commissariats, as well as the Supreme Council of the National Economy (VRNH) and the Supreme Socialist Inspection. Its members included **Volodymyr Antonov-Ovsiienko**, **Yurii Kotsiubynsky**, and **Volodymyr Zatonsky**. According to the UkSSR constitution of March 1919, the RNK was appointed by the All-Ukrainian Central Executive Committee (VUTsVK), reporting to it and to the All-Ukrainian Congress of Soviets. The RNK was chaired by **Khristian Rakovsky** (1919–23), **Vlas Chubar** (1923–34), Panas Liubchenko (1934–37), Mykhailo Bondarenko (1937), Demian Korotchenko (1938–39), Leonid Korniiets (1939–44), and **Nikita Khrushchev** (1944–46).

The RNK acted under the control of the **Communist Party of Ukraine** (CPU) but was in fact subordinate to the RNK of the Russian SFSR and to the Russian Communist Party (Bolshevik) (RCP[B]). Pursuant to an agreement on military and economic union between the UkSSR and the RSFSR (28 December 1920), several joint commissariats were established (defense, foreign trade, finance, labor, transportation, postal and telegraph services, and the VRNH), effectively subordinating the economy and government bodies of the UkSSR to Moscow. After the formation of the **USSR**, the RNKs were divided into all-Union, Union-republican, and republican commissariats. Only six of these—public health, **agriculture**, internal affairs, **education, social welfare**, and justice—were left to the republics.

In the 1930s, the All-Union RNK became influential in most spheres of UkSSR government activity, as the All-Union CP(B) found it a useful transmission belt for its policies. According to the 1937 UkSSR Constitution, the Ukrainian RNK was elected by the newly established **Verkhovna Rada** of the UkSSR and responsible to it and to its Presidium. The UkSSR RNK continued to exist until 25 March 1946, when it was reformed as the **Council of Ministers**.

COUNCIL OF PEOPLE'S MINISTERS/RADA NARODNYKH MINISTRIV. Executive branch of the **Ukrainian People's Republic** (UNR). The General Secretariat, which governed Ukraine from 15 (28) June 1917, was reformed as the Council of People's Ministers on 9 (22) January 1918. The council was active until the demise of the UNR (29 April 1918) and again during the rule of the **Directory**. Controlling all levels of state administration, the council was formed on a coalition basis and confirmed in office by the **Ukrainian Central Rada**. The organization, membership, jurisdiction, and agenda of the Council were defined by articles 50–59 of the Constitution of the UNR (until 29 April 1918), the laws passed by the **Labor Congress**, and articles 15–19 of the laws "On the Provisional Supreme Administration and the Legislative Agenda in the UNR" and "On the State People's Council" (12 November 1920).

The first council (January 1918) included **Volodymyr Vynnychenko** (chairman and minister of internal affairs), deputy chairmen Ivan Kraskovsky, Leonid Abramovych, and Oleksander Karpynsky, **Oleksander Shulhyn** (foreign affairs), **Mykola Porsh** (defense and labor), Oleksander Zhukovsky (deputy minister), Dmytro Antonovych (naval affairs), Vsevolod Holubovych (industry and trade), Mykola Kovalevsky (food supply), Vadym Yeshchenko (communications), **Mykyta Shapoval** (postal and telegraph services), Ivan Steshenko (education), Petro Kholodny (deputy minister of education), Vasyl Mazurenko (acting minister of finance), Dmytro Odynets (Russian affairs), Moshe Zilberfarb (Jewish affairs), Mieczysław Mickiewicz (Polish affairs), Aleksandr Zolotarev (state comptroller), and Ivan Mirny (state secretary).

Bolshevik aggression against the UNR and interparty discussions on defense measures led to a government crisis that resulted in the resignation of Vynnychenko's cabinet on 15 (28) January 1918. On 18 (31) January, the Central Rada instructed Holubovych to form a new government. This cabinet included Holubovych (premier and minister of foreign affairs), **Pavlo**

Khrystiuk (internal affairs), Ivan Nemolovsky (military affairs), Antonovych (naval affairs), Mykhailo Tkachenko (justice), Stepan Perepelytsia (finance), Yevhen Sokovych (communications), Hryhorii Sydorenko (postal and telegraph services), Kovalevsky (food supply), Nykyfor Hryhoriiv (education), and Arystrakh Ternychenko (agriculture).

After the liberation of Kyiv from the Bolsheviks and the return of the Central Rada and government to the capital, the Council of People's Ministers was reorganized (24 March) and now included Holubovych (premier and minister of foreign affairs; according to other sources, Mykola Liubynsky was minister of foreign affairs), Zhukovsky (defense), Tkachenko (internal affairs), Kovalevsky (land affairs; postal and telegraph services, according to other sources), Serhii Shelukhyn (justice), Petro Klymovych (finance; Perepelytsia, according to other sources), Sydorenko (postal and telegraph services), Viacheslav Prokopovych (education), Sokovych (and Yeshchenko, communications), Leonyd Mykhailiv (labor), Ivan Feshchenko-Chopivsky (trade and industry), Dmytro Koliukh (food supply), Oleksander Lototsky (state comptroller; Dmytro Symoniv, according to other sources), Mickiewicz (Polish affairs), and Khrystiuk (state secretary).

According to section 5 of the Constitution, the Council of People's Ministers was declared the "supreme executive authority of the UNR." Its official publication was *Visnyk Rady Narodnykh Ministriv UNR* (Herald of the Council of People's Ministers of the UNR).

After Hetman **Pavlo Skoropadsky** came to power, the "Proclamation to the Whole Ukrainian People" (29 April 1918) dissolved the council and transferred its functions to the Council of Ministers of the **Ukrainian State**.

In December 1918, as a result of an antihetman rebellion, the Directory took power. The UNR was restored on 26 December, and after lengthy consultations with representatives of Ukrainian political parties, the Council of People's Ministers was formed. The political configuration of the coalition government was similar to that of the **Ukrainian National-State Union**, with the participation of ministers from socialist parties: the **Ukrainian Social Democratic Labor Party**, the **Ukrainian Party of Socialist Revolutionaries**, the **Ukrainian Party of Socialist Federalists**, and the nationalist **Ukrainian Party of Socialist Independentists**. **Volodymyr Chekhivsky** was appointed premier and minister of foreign affairs (26 December). The cabinet included Oleksander Mytsiuk (internal affairs), Shapoval (land affairs), Mykhailo Bilynsky (naval affairs), I. Shtefan (postal and telegraph services), Borys Martos (food supply), Serhii Ostapenko (industry and trade), Borys Matiushenko (public health), Antonovych (culture), Oleksander Osetsky (acting minister of military affairs), Kholodny (acting minister of education), Shelukhyn (acting minister of justice), Mazurenko (acting minister of finance), Mykhailiv (acting minister of labor), Pylyp Pylypchuk (director of the ministry of communications), Ivan Lypa (head of the administration of religious affairs at the Ministry of People's Education), Dmytro Symoniv (state comptroller), I. Snizhko (acting secretary of state), and **Osyp Nazaruk** (head of the press bureau). In January 1919, the council changed somewhat. Oleksander Hrekov took charge of military affairs, **Ivan Ohiienko** was made acting minister of education, Abraham Revutsky became minister of Jewish affairs, and Mykhailo Korchynsky became acting state secretary.

The Labor Congress (January 1919) established the temporary constitutional status of the Council of People's Ministers as the supreme executive body of the UNR, declaring that the government was "responsible to the Labor Congress and to the Directory of the UNR between Congress sessions." A new Bolshevik invasion forced the Directory and the Council of People's Ministers to abandon Kyiv and move to Vinnytsia (February 1919). In order to facilitate negotiations for military support from the Entente, which viewed the Ukrainian government as "communist," Ukrainian socialist parties withdrew their members from the council. At the same time, Vynnychenko resigned from the Directory and was replaced by **Symon Petliura**. A new council was formed in Vinnytsia under the leadership of Ostapenko (13 February 1919). It included Kost Matsiievych (foreign affairs), Shapoval (military affairs), Pavlo Chyzhevsky (internal affairs), Stepan Fedak (finance), Feshchenko-Chopivsky (economy), Yevhen Arkhypenko (land affairs), Dmytro Markovych (general procurator), Pylypchuk (communications), Ohiienko (education), Lypa (religious affairs), Ovksentii Korchak-Chepurkivsky (health), Bilynsky (naval affairs), Revutsky (Jewish affairs), Nazaruk (press and propaganda), Symoniv (state comptroller), and Korchynsky (state secretary). After Fedak was imprisoned by the Polish authorities, Martos and then Mykhailo Kryvetsky acted as ministers of finance; the ministry of labor was eliminated.

Following the defeat and withdrawal of Entente forces from Ukraine, Ostapenko's government, having lost its purpose and subject to pressure from leftist political forces, resigned. On 9 April 1919, a new socialist-dominated council was formed in Rivne, including Martos (premier and minister of finance), **Andrii Livytsky** (deputy premier and minister of justice), **Isaak Mazepa** (internal affairs), Volodymyr Temnytsky (foreign affairs), Kovalevsky (land affairs), Hryhorii Syrotenko (acting minister of defense), Antin Krushelnytsky (people's education; succeeded by Hryhoriiv), Mykola Shadlun (communications), Leontii Shramchenko (national economy; succeeded by Teofan Cherkasky), Yosyp Bezpalko (labor), Oleksa Bilous (health; succeeded by Dmytro Odryna), M. Myrovych (religious affairs), Pinkhas Krasny (Jewish affairs), Ivan Lyzanivsky (press and propaganda; acting secretary of state), and Ivan Kabachkiv (state comptroller). The council was reorganized in Kamianets-Podilskyi under the leadership of Mazepa (27 August 1919). Some minor reappointments to the cabinet were made: Shadlun became minister of the national economy; Cherkasky headed the bureau of press and propaganda; Serhii Tymoshenko became minister of communications; Ohiienko headed the ministry of religious affairs; and Volodymyr Salsky became head of the ministry of defense (November 1919).

The conditions of the **Treaty of Warsaw** (1920), whereby western Ukrainian lands were ceded to Poland, caused a profound crisis in Ukrainian politics and forced Mazepa's government to resign. The new Council of People's Ministers, the last government of the UNR in Ukraine, was formed by Prokopovych on 26 May 1920. It included Livytsky (deputy premier and minister of justice), Andrii Nikovsky (foreign affairs), Oleksander Salikovsky (internal affairs), Mazepa (land affairs), Salsky (defense), Arkhypenko (national economy), Khrystofor Baranovsky (finance), Tymoshenko (communications), Kholodny (education), Ohiienko (religious affairs), Ilarion Kosenko (postal and telegraph services), Stanisław Stempowski (public health), and I. Onikhimovsky (secretary of state). From the end of 1920, the Council of People's Ministers acted in exile.

COURT SYSTEM. In **Kyivan Rus'**, courts did not exist as separate bodies. **Princes**, their *posadnyky* (lieutenants), and *volosteli* (chiefs of rural districts) acted as judges. The most serious cases were tried by the prince together with the *viche*. **Boyars** acted as judges of their vassals. With the **Christianization of Rus'** (988), church courts were established for ecclesiastical matters and those involving subjects of the church. After Lithuania and Poland took control of the Ukrainian lands, the Polish-Lithuanian court system was introduced in Ukraine. Its dominant characteristics were the merging of judicial functions with administrative ones and the establishment of separate courts for different social estates: magnates, **nobles**, townspeople, clergy, and **peasants**.

During the **Khmelnytsky Uprising** (1648–57), **Cossack** courts were established on the basis of the court system of **Zaporizhia** and that of the **registered Cossacks** (the latter existed until the Ordinance of 1638). In the 17th and 18th centuries, the supreme court of the **Hetmanate** was the General Military Court. The **hetman's** administration included an arbitration court that facilitated the peaceful resolution of civil cases. The General Court acted as an appellate body against decisions made by the arbitration court. Regimental courts decided the majority of cases. The regimental system also included market courts consisting of a single judge. They were located in the most important trading centers (Starodub, Nizhyn, Krolevets) and adjudicated only civil cases. Company courts heard cases arising on the territory of the company and consisted of representatives of the company officer staff. They adjudicated civil and criminal cases and, like the regimental court, acted as courts martial. Cossack otamans (captains) and village magistrates also performed judicial functions. Cases involving both Cossacks and peasants were adjudicated jointly by the captain and the magistrate. Cities with **Magdeburg law** had *lava* (bench) courts, while other towns had magistrate courts. Verdicts rendered by local courts could be appealed to the regimental court or the hetman. After the court reform of 1760–63, the General Military Court was reorganized as the supreme body exercising judicial supervision over local courts; it also served as the supreme appellate court. The judicial functions of the General Military Chancellery were annulled, and the land, chamberlain, and town courts were reorganized.

Following the abolition of the Hetmanate's autonomy (1782), the Russian gubernial system was introduced. Courts were based on social estates: county courts and a supreme land court for the nobility, town and gubernia magistracies for townspeople, and penal bodies for state peasants. Serfs were judged by their landowners. Each gubernia had a "court of conscience" to review some civil cases, criminal cases involving minors and the insane, and grievances. In addition, each gubernia had a second chamber of civil and criminal courts that acted as appellate and review bodies. After the emancipation of the serfs (1861), a *volost'* (district) court for peasants was established. In 1864, the tsarist government introduced a reform creating a two-tiered court system: local judicial bodies (courts administered by justices of the peace and their county councils) and general judicial bodies (district court and the court chamber). The Senate became the supreme court, and the jury system was introduced.

After the incorporation of the western Ukrainian lands into the Habsburg Monarchy (1772–74), the previous Polish court system continued to exist virtually unchanged (town, land, chamberlain, ecclesiastical, and domanial courts). In 1784, the Austrian court reform of 1782 was extended to **Galicia** and **Bukovyna**. Patrimonial or domanial courts tried peasants, townspeople were subject to magistrate courts, and the nobility and other privileged groups had two land courts (called nobiliary courts) in Lviv and Stanyslaviv. The court of second resort was the Appellate Court in **Lviv**. All courts in Austria were subject to the Supreme Court in Vienna, which briefly included a separate Galician chamber. After the **Revolution of 1848**, the court system was separated from the administration. Several county courts were established in each administrative county. District courts acted as courts of first resort, while higher land courts were courts of second resort. Unlike other Austrian crown lands, Galicia and Bukovyna had two higher land courts, in Lviv (for eastern Galicia and Bukovyna) and Cracow (for western Galicia). The highest courts of appeal in the Austrian lands were the Supreme Court and the Cassation Tribunal in Vienna.

During the **Ukrainian Revolution** (1917–21), a national court system was created. Having proclaimed the **Ukrainian People's Republic** (UNR), the **Ukrainian Central Rada** established a General Court consisting of three departments: civil, criminal, and administrative. All judges of the general and appellate courts were elected by the Central Rada. The court system of the **Ukrainian State** (1918) was significantly different; gubernia and county courts were established, while the State Senate became the supreme judicial and administrative body. The Senate, headed by a president, was divided into general courts: administrative, civil, and criminal. All general judges were appointed by the hetman. The **Directory** reinstated all UNR legislation, including its court system.

The **Western Ukrainian People's Republic** (ZUNR), established in 1918, took the Austrian model as the basis of its court system. Its territory was divided into 12 judicial districts and 130 judicial counties. Their corresponding courts were county courts, district courts, and a Supreme Court. Courts martial were also created: the Supreme Military Tribunal, provincial courts martial (Lviv, Stanyslaviv, and Ternopil), and district courts martial. After the occupation of **Eastern Galicia** (1923), the Polish court system was introduced in western Ukraine. In the late 1920s that system was reformed, introducing the following courts: an appellate court in Lviv, 10 district courts, and municipal courts (several in each judicial district). In 1931, the Polish government created emergency courts, similar to military tribunals, in order to combat the Ukrainian national movement (*see* PACIFICATION). In 1939, when western Ukraine was annexed to the **Ukrainian SSR**, its courts were eliminated and the Soviet court system introduced.

Under Soviet rule, courts were modeled on the Russian system. They included people's courts and revolutionary tribunals. The latter, along with the Cheka *troika* (collegium of three), an extrajudicial body, were responsible for fighting "counterrevolution." The system was revised in 1922 and 1925 according to changes in the Russian model.

The court system was reformed on the all-Union level in 1958 and in the Ukrainian SSR two years later. It consisted of people's courts, oblast courts, and the Supreme Court of the Ukrainian SSR. Raion (or municipal) people's courts had jurisdiction over basic civil and criminal cases. Oblast courts tried civil and criminal cases and acted as appellate courts against decisions of the people's courts. The Supreme Court of the Ukrainian SSR, primarily a court of appeal against decisions reached in oblast courts, also tried civil and criminal cases of particular importance, heard protests by procurators-general against lower court rulings, and reviewed lower court decisions. The Supreme Court of the **USSR** had supervisory jurisdiction over all courts.

Judges of people's courts were elected for five-year terms from among candidates nominated by the Communist Party or party-controlled organizations. Oblast and Supreme Court judges were elected for five-year terms by the oblast soviets and the Supreme Soviet, respectively. Although judges were "accountable to their constituents," they could be recalled if their decisions "failed to conform to the policies of the party and the government," casting doubt on their independence. "People's assessors" (lay judges) were also elected to sit on people's and oblast courts, according to the same procedures. While Soviet law provided for open courts, most criminal cases were actually tried behind closed doors. In practice, rights to defense counsel and to the use of one's native language in court were also restricted.

Some civil and criminal cases were adjudicated by bodies other than courts. Disputes between state institutions or enterprises were decided by government arbitration. Within enterprises, housing projects, and collective farms, disputes were resolved by comrades' courts authorized to punish minor violations of the law. An act of 5 November 1934 (never repealed) empowered the NKVD (later KGB) to punish persons deemed socially and politically dangerous without recourse to the judicial system.

The court system of independent Ukraine has three branches. The Constitutional Court (18 judges appointed in equal numbers by the president, the Verkhovna Rada, and the Supreme Court) adjudicates cases related to the **Constitution**. The General Court, at the head of which stands the Supreme Court of Ukraine, consists of more than 800 raion (city and district) courts and 27 oblast courts (one for each oblast, with separate courts for Kyiv and Sevastopol) and is responsible for criminal, civil, and administrative jurisprudence. The Court of Specialization (arbitration court) settles disputes over contracts, payments, and services. Although the constitution provides for an independent judiciary, in practice there has been considerable interference from the executive branch, and the rule of law is hampered by corruption and inefficiency.

CRAFTS. At the beginning of the first millennium A.D., crafts began to differentiate themselves from farming as a separate endeavor on what is now Ukrainian territory. At the time, there were two basic forms of craft manufacture—iron-making and pottery. In **Kyivan Rus'**, urban crafts were more complex and of higher quality than their rural counterparts. Craftsmen in the larger towns practiced nearly 60 distinct crafts. They belonged to three social ranks: free rural tradesmen, bondsmen working on the estates, and free urban craftsmen, who made up the largest group. Practitioners of a craft generally lived in one district or on one street, and urban tradesmen established associations to protect their interests.

The decline of crafts as a result of the Mongol-Tatar invasions, which severed links with markets, lasted until the 14th century. Their revival begun in the Principality of **Galicia-Volhynia**. In towns governed by **Magdeburg law**, craftsmen organized themselves into **guilds** that regulated their economic activities, protected them from magnates and civic authorities, and restrained competition from rural craftsmen who were moving into the towns. **Lviv** and **Kyiv** were the largest craft centers in Ukraine. Most of the wealthy masters were Poles, Germans, or Armenians. Few Ukrainians in **western Ukraine** were guild members, either because they were excluded from certain guilds or were not permitted to become journeymen or masters. To defend their rights, Ukrainian craftsmen and burghers organized **brotherhoods**.

With the decline of the towns and the burgher class in general in the second half of the 17th century, crafts deteriorated in western Ukraine and **Right-Bank Ukraine** alike. They fared better in Kyiv and **Left-Bank Ukraine**, where they were commonly practiced by **Cossacks** and villagers. The Russian guild law was extended in 1785 to include the Left Bank and, in 1840, Right-Bank Ukraine as well. Craft councils were formed in 1852 and forbade unregistered craftsmen to direct craft enterprises. The development of factory manufacture and the building of railways in the second half of the 19th century entailed the further weakening of crafts. The guilds declined in importance, and their abolition began in 1900. Rural cottage industries proved more resilient, and some attempts were made to organize cottage **cooperatives**. At the turn of the 20th century, crafts and cottage industries remained the primary source of consumer and food products, and more workers were employed in those industries than in large-scale **manufacturing**.

In the early 1920s, crafts became more important in the **Ukrainian SSR** because of the heavy losses suffered by factory manufacture as a result of war and revolution. However, all enterprises were eventually nationalized, and crafts declined as factory production developed. Crafts and cottage industries were reorganized into manufacturing cooperatives, which were abolished in 1960. Although not regulated by the government, these industries did not disappear entirely, and their products were sold at markets. They continued to satisfy local demand for furnishings, clothing, and footwear in rural areas. *See also* ECONOMY.

CRIMEA (Ukr. *Krym*). Constituted since 1991 as the Republic of the Crimea, autonomous within Ukraine and occupying the Crimean Peninsula. In the north, the Crimean Peninsula is joined to the East European Plain by the Perekop Isthmus. The eastern tip of the Crimea is the Kerch peninsula, separated from the Taman peninsula (Caucasus) by the Kerch Strait (4–15 km), which links the Black Sea with the Sea of Azov. The length of the peninsula from north to south is 200 km, and its maximum width is 320 km. The Crimea's total area is 25,881 sq. km, and its population is 2,413,200 (2001). The capital of the republic is the city of Simferopol (Symferopil). Other major cities include Sevastopol, Kerch, Feodosiia, and Yalta.

Topologically, the Crimean Peninsula is divided into three zones: the Crimean Mountains, the northern and central Crimean steppe, and the foothills of the Kerch Peninsula. There is a narrow coastal plain with a Mediterranean climate once known as the "Soviet Riviera." Roman-Kosh (1,543 m) is the highest peak of the Crimean Mountains. The Crimea's mineral resources include iron ores, salts, medicinal clays, and mineral water springs. Its soils include chernozem, mountain forest, and mountain meadow varieties. The climate varies from continental in the northern steppe to arid on the Kerch peninsula. The Crimea's principal rivers include the Chorna, Belbek, Alma, and Salhyr, and its principal lakes are Saky, Sasyk, and Kyiatske. Given their favorable location, the lands of the Crimea were among the first in Ukraine to be settled.

In antiquity the Crimean peninsula was known as Tauris (Tavriia) and was settled by the **Cimmerians**, a nomadic tribe also called Taurians. During the first millennium B.C., the steppe region of the Crimea was conquered by the **Scythians**, who founded a polity with its capital in Neapolis. In the seventh to sixth centuries B.C., Greek colonies appeared on the **Black Sea littoral** and were later united within the Bosporan Kingdom. The most important of these city-states was Chersonesus (now Sevastopol), whose economy flourished when the Crimea became the major source of wheat for ancient Greece, especially during the fourth to second centuries B.C. In the mid-first century B.C., the Crimea fell under the influence of the Pontic king Mithradates VI Eupator, and later came under Roman rule.

Beginning in the second century A.D., nomadic peoples began invading the peninsula. The first to arrive were the Goths, who in turn were pushed out by the Huns at the end of the fourth century. The Huns destroyed the Scythian and Bosporan kingdoms and forced a segment of the Goths into the Crimean Mountains, where their small state continued to exist until the end of the 15th century. During the fifth century, a significant portion of the Crimea came under the influence of the Byzantine Empire, followed by the **Khazars** from the sixth to the eighth century. In the mid-11th century, the **Cumans** took control of the eastern shore of the peninsula. Byzantium retook the coast of the Crimea and maintained its influence there until the 13th century.

From the sixth century, Slavic tribes built settlements in the Crimea. The spread of **Christianity** to **Kyivan Rus'** also originated there. Prince **Sviatoslav Ihorevych** of Kyiv attempted to conquer the Crimea, and **Volodymyr the Great** led a campaign that resulted in the capture of Chersonesus in 989. From the 10th to the 12th century, the eastern Crimea was the site of the Tmutorokan Principality—a part of the Kyivan state. From 1204, Venetian and, later, Genoese settlements were founded on the coast, with Kaffa (Caffa, Kefe, now Feodosiia) as the most important trading port. These settlements fell when the Turks cut them off from their metropolis; in 1475 they took over Kaffa and the Crimean coast. To the north the Turks encountered the **Tatar** Crimean Khanate, which had controlled the Crimean steppe since its separation from the **Golden Horde** in the early 1440s.

The Crimean Tatars, who engaged in nomadic herding, agriculture, and trades, were ruled by the Giray dynasty until its demise in 1783. Incessant Tatar raids into the Ukrainian lands wreaked great destruction and resulted in the capture of large numbers of inhabitants, who were sold into slavery. Such raids were a major stimulus to the development of the Ukrainian **Cossacks**. Although Cossack **hetmans** sometimes sought Tatar military assistance during the 17th century, the latter proved unreliable allies.

Following protracted Russo-Turkish wars, the Crimea was taken over by the Russian Empire in 1783. The Tatar population then declined steeply, and the Crimea was colonized by immigrants from various countries. In 1897, Ukrainians and Russians constituted 45 percent of the population, with Germans at 5.8 percent, **Jews** at 5.3 percent, and Greeks at 3.1 percent.

In the course of the **Ukrainian Revolution** (1917–21), the Crimea changed hands several times. In April 1918, Ukrainian armies drove out the Bolsheviks, taking Simferopol and Bakhchesarai. They were forced to abandon the Crimea under German pressure. The Germans established an occupation regime that lasted until November 1918, when power passed to a government supported by Entente armies based on the peninsula. The Bolsheviks returned in April 1920. On 18 October 1921, Lenin signed a decree establishing the Crimean Autonomous Soviet Socialist Republic as part of the Russian SFSR. Russian and Crimean Tatar were proclaimed the official languages.

During the 1920s, a policy of Tatarization was adopted in the Crimea, but it was reversed by Stalin in 1928. Mass repression was instituted against the Tatars, and all remnants of Crimean autonomy were eliminated. During **World War II**, the Crimea was occupied by German armies (1941–44). After the Soviet reoccupation, more than 188,000 Tatars were deported (18–20 May 1944) to Kazakhstan and Central Asia on charges of collaboration. The Soviet government also deported other nationalities from the Crimea: Germans in 1941 and Greeks, Armenians, and Bulgarians in 1944. The Crimea was subsequently settled by immigrants from Russia, Belarus, and Ukraine. In the postwar period, its population increased tenfold.

In 1945, the autonomy of the Crimean ASSR was abolished and the peninsula became an oblast of the Russian Federation. On 19 February 1954, the Crimean oblast was transferred to Ukraine because of its territorial proximity and close economic and cultural ties. The primary motive for the transfer appears to have been economic; the government of the **Ukrainian SSR** was to assume the burden of rebuilding the war-shattered Crimean economy, thereby relieving pressure on the all-Union budget. In the postwar years, the Crimea became a favorite vacation spot for the ruling elite of the USSR and countries of the Soviet bloc; former party, state, and military figures and their families settled there upon retirement.

In 1989, fewer than 10 percent (some 28,000) of Crimean Tatars resided in the Crimea. In the same year, the Soviet government condemned the wartime deportation and permitted their return. By September 1993, 260,000 Tatars had returned to the Crimea. On 12 February 1991, Crimean autonomy was restored within the

Ukrainian SSR. Although 54 percent of the Crimea's population supported Ukrainian independence during the referendum of 1 December 1991, the Russian-speaking majority continued to support complete or partial separation from Ukraine. Such tendencies were often fueled by the claims of Russian government officials and aggravated by the presence of the Russian **Black Sea Fleet** in Sevastopol. Tensions were alleviated by a Russo-Ukrainian treaty of 1997 that partitioned the fleet. Earlier, in 1995, the **Kuchma** administration took advantage of divisions within the Russian political elite of the Crimea to suspend the Crimean constitution and abolish its presidency. The amended Crimean constitution (1999) reaffirms the peninsula's status as an autonomous republic, but also defines it as an "integral component of Ukraine" with no sovereignty or citizenship of its own.

CULTURE. *See* ARCHITECTURE; DESIGN, GRAPHIC; EDUCATION; FILM; FOLK CUSTOMS AND RITES; FOLK MUSIC AND DANCE; ICON; LITERATURE; MEDIA; MUSIC; PAINTING; PUBLISHING; SCULPTURE; SHEVCHENKO SCIENTIFIC SOCIETY; SPORT; THEATER; UKRAINIAN ACADEMY OF ARTS AND SCIENCES; UKRAINIAN ACADEMY OF SCIENCES.

CUMANS (Polovtsians). Medieval nationality of the Turkic group. The large territory over which the Cumans migrated stretched from the Tien-Shan Mountains to the Danube River. From the 11th to the 15th century, this territory was known as the Dasht-i-Kipchak or Cuman Steppe. The Cumans first approached the southeastern borders of **Kyivan Rus'** in 1055. Late in the 11th century, they settled on permanent winter grounds in the basin of the Donets River and began to attack Rus', especially the **Kyiv**, Pereiaslav, and Chernihiv lands. To protect their borders, Rus' princes campaigned against the Cumans, especially under the leadership of **Volodymyr Monomakh**, who led three successful expeditions in 1103, 1107, and 1111. A prince of Novhorod-Siverskyi, Ihor Sviatoslavych, was held captive by the Cumans after the defeat of his troops in the Battle of the Kaiala River (1185), immortalized in the ***Tale of Ihor's Campaign***. In the early 13th century, the Cumans were defeated on several occasions by the **Golden Horde**, most decisively at the Kalka River (1223). Some Cuman clans subsequently migrated to the Danube region and Hungary. Most remained in the steppes north of the Black Sea, joined the Golden Horde, and were assimilated.

CURRENCY AND COINS. From the earliest times, various goods functioned as money: animal furs, metal axes, cowrie shells, and the like. However, thanks to their physical properties, precious metals (gold and silver) became the most widely used media of exchange. In time, they began to circulate in the form of coins. The oldest coins minted in the Ukrainian lands were those of the Greek **Black Sea colonies**. They were issued from the sixth century B.C. to the fourth century A.D. Coins minted in Greece proper were also in circulation.

Coins of ancient Rome were found much more frequently in the Ukrainian lands. These were primarily silver denarii from the imperial period, particularly those dating from the reigns of Emperors Trajan, Hadrian, Lucius Verus, Marcus Aurelius, and Commodus (second century A.D.). These coins circulated until the fifth century. During the sixth and seventh centuries, a small number of Byzantine coins made of silver, bronze, and, less frequently, gold, appeared in the Ukrainian lands. From the eighth to the 11th century, Arab dirhams, minted at the courts of the Arabian Caliphate in Central Asia, Iran, North Africa, the Middle East, and even in the Pyrenees, dominated the money market of the Kyivan state.

The **princes** of **Kyivan Rus'** began minting their own coins. **Volodymyr the Great** (980–1015) circulated the so-called *zlatnyky* and *sribliaky* (gold and silver coins, respectively). They depicted the prince in his regalia on the face and his coat of arms, the **trident**, on the reverse. Later, Princes Sviatoslav Yaropolkovych (1015–19), **Yaroslav the Wise** (1019–54), and possibly Oleh-Mykhail, prince of Tmutorokan, minted silver coins.

During the second half of the 11th century, Kyivan Rus' entered the so-called coinless period, which resulted from the massive influx of foreign coins and the absence of native silver stocks. It has been suggested that animal furs, primarily of the marten and squirrel, were used as a medium of exchange concurrently with Arab coins. Written sources mention the currency units of the day: *kuna, nogata, rezana, veksha,* and *hryvnia*. During the 12th and 13th centuries, silver bars (*hryvni*) were widely used for large transactions.

In the 14th century, coining resumed in the Ukrainian lands. After the Poles conquered **Galicia**, Casimir the Great (1333–70) began circulating the so-called *kwartnik* (silver half-grosz) and the copper *puło*. The earliest emission bears the coat of arms of Galicia, a lion rampant, and the inscription "moneta Ruscie." Coins of this type were minted in **Lviv** by Casimir's successors, Louis of Hungary (1370–82) and his deputy in Galicia, Władysław of Opole (1372–78), as well as during the reign of Władysław Jagiełło (1386–1434). Jagiełło also coined the so-called Lviv *kwartnik*, a half-grosz coin with the inscription "moneta Lemburgensis," which was distributed until 1414. After the establishment of Lithuanian rule over most of the Ukrainian lands in the mid-14th century, the Kyiv **appanage principality** under Prince Volodymyr (1362–94), son of Algirdas, minted its own coins. In addition, Prince Dmytro Korybut minted coins in the Chernihiv region.

From the second half of the 14th century through the 15th, Czech currency, the *Grossi Pragenses*, dominated the money market. These were coins minted in large quantities by the Czech kings, beginning in 1300. Most widely circulated in Ukraine were the coins of Wenceslas IV (1378–1419). The last coins of this kind date from the first half of the 16th century. In addition to Czech money, hoards of this period contain coins produced by Poland, Lithuania, the **Golden Horde**, and Muscovy. Gold ducats (3.48 g), mainly of Hungarian origin, were used for large financial transactions. Currency denominations included the *kopa*, used in the **Grand Duchy of Lithuania**, which equaled 60 *grosz* pieces (1 *grosz* = 10 dinars or *pieniądze*). The *hryvnia* (48 *grosz* pieces, 1 *grosz* = 18 dinars) was prevalent in Galicia.

During the 16th century, as a result of the monetary reforms of Sigismund I (1526–28), the monetary system in Ukraine changed fundamentally. New denominations appeared on the market: the *szóstak*, which equaled 6 *grosz* pieces; the *trojak*, which equaled 3 *grosz* pieces; the *trzeciak*, equaling 3 dinars; and the *solid* (*szeląg*), equaling 6 dinars. The *złoty*, which equaled 30 *grosz* pieces, became the basic unit of currency. The number and assortment of large coins also increased, notably the silver *taler* (approximately 28 g) and its fractions, the halves and quarters. They were coined primarily in Holland, the southern Netherlands, various German territories and, less frequently, Poland. Gold ducats from Holland and Hungary were dominant, as well as Venetian sequins.

New denominations appeared in the 17th century: the *ort* (1/4 taler) and *półtorak* (1.5 talers). Other coins included low-grade *tynfy*, which were nominally worth one *złoty* (30 *grosz* pieces), but in reality never exceeded 12 *groszy*, and copper *solidy*, known as *boratynki*. This period saw the establishment of the **Lviv** mint, which operated between 1656 and 1663. Following the **Truce of Andrusovo** (1667), the currency system in the Ukrainian lands under Poland remained unchanged. In lands annexed by Muscovy, Russian coins went into immediate circulation, although they were spurned by the population. It was only after the **Battle of Poltava** (1709) that Peter I forbade the use of foreign coins in the **Hetmanate**, although they continued to be used up to the 1730s. From the 18th century to the Revolution of 1917, the market was dominated by the Russian ruble and kopeck (1/100 ruble). In Austrian-ruled **western Ukraine** (after 1772), the government introduced its own monetary system: one *gulden* (*florin*) equaled 60 *kreuzers*. For a time, coins were minted in Galicia in denominations of one *schilling* and three *kreuzers*. From 1857, one *gulden* equaled 100 *kreuzers*. As a result of the monetary reform of 1892, the gold standard was introduced in Austria-Hungary, and the basic monetary unit became the *krone*, which was divided into 100 *hellers* (*fillers*).

The renewal of Ukrainian sovereignty in 1917 necessitated a native currency. In December of that year, the **Ukrainian Central Rada** issued its first credit notes, with a nominal value of 100 *karbovantsi*. This was the first paper currency to feature the state emblem of Ukraine, the trident, and inscriptions in the Ukrainian language. The bank notes of this emission also featured inscriptions in Russian, Yiddish, and Polish. In March 1918, the *hryvnia* became the basic monetary unit. It was worth half a *karbovanets'* and divided into 100 *shahy*. Bills in denominations of 10, 25, 50, 100, 250, and 1,000 *karbovantsi* and 2, 5, 100, 500, 1,000, and 2,000 *hryvni* were put into circulation. Small change, the *shah*, was produced in the form of postage stamps with nominal values of 10, 20, 30, 40, and 50 *shahy*. During **World War I** and the Revolution, the absence of small change precipitated the appearance of large numbers of local and regional monetary tokens, the so-called *bony*, *cheky*, and exchange tokens.

After the establishment of the Soviet regime, Soviet money was introduced in the **Ukrainian SSR**. During the interwar period, the western Ukrainian lands used the currencies of the states into which they had been incorporated. The Polish mark was used in Galicia, followed in 1924 by the *złoty*, which equaled 100 *groszy*. The Czechoslovak crown, which equaled 100 *hellers*, was used in **Transcarpathia**, and the Romanian *leu*, divided into 100 *bani*, was used in **Bukovyna**.

After Ukraine's declaration of independence in 1991, the *kupono-karbovanets'* was introduced as a temporary currency in 1992, initially taking the form of ration coupons. It was replaced by the *hryvnia* (UAH) in 1996.

CURZON LINE. Eastern border of Poland, designated by the Entente on 8 December 1919 in its *Declaration of the Supreme Council of Allied and United States Concerning the Eastern Border of Poland.* The line passed from Hrodna through Jałówka, Brest-Litovsk,

Dorohusk-Ustyluh, east of Hrubieszów, through Kryłów, to the west of Rava-Ruska, east of Przemyśl, and on to the Carpathian Mountains. The Curzon Line did not correspond to Poland's ethnic boundaries but took in a significant portion of Ukrainian ethnic territory (**Sian region**, **Podlachia**, and the **Kholm** and **Lemko** regions). This was emphasized by the delegation of the **Ukrainian People's Republic** (UNR) to the Paris Peace Conference (1919–20). In July 1920, following the collapse of a joint Polish-Ukrainian drive against the Bolsheviks (*see* TREATY OF WARSAW), Poland appealed to the Entente for assistance. On 10 July, the Entente proposed that Poland recognize the line of 8 December as its eastern border. On 12 July, the British foreign secretary, Lord George Curzon, proposed to Moscow that the Red Army also halt at that line (hence the name). Neither side accepted the proposal. As a result of fighting in September-October 1920 and subsequent negotiations (**Treaty of Riga**, 1921), the border between the **Ukrainian SSR** and Poland was established a considerable distance east of the Curzon Line. By decision of the **Yalta Conference** (1945), the Curzon Line became the basis of the Polish-Soviet boundary after **World War II**. An agreement between the USSR and Poland signed in Moscow on 16 August 1945 established the Soviet-Polish border to the benefit of Poland, 17–30 km east of the Curzon Line. The Ukrainian ethnic territory claimed by the UNR in 1919–20 remained within Poland.

CYRIL AND METHODIUS BROTHERHOOD/KYRYLO-METODI-ÏVS'KE BRATSTVO. Clandestine political society established in December 1845–January 1846 in **Kyiv**; the first Ukrainian political organization in modern times. Its initiators were **Mykola Kostomarov** and Mykola Hulak, while members included Heorhii Andruzky, Vasyl Bilozersky, **Panteleimon Kulish**, Opanas Markovych, Oleksander Navrotsky, Ivan Posiada, Dmytro Pylchykov, Mykola Savych, and **Taras Shevchenko**. The society was named after the ninth-century Greek missionaries to the **Slavs**, SS. Cyril and Methodius.

Its program was expounded in the *Books of Genesis of the Ukrainian People* and the *Statute of the Slavic Society of SS. Cyril and Methodius,* written primarily by Kostomarov, and a *Note* on the statute by Bilozersky. These documents drew on the ideas of Ukrainian autonomism (especially as reflected in *Istoriia Rusov*), **Panslavism**, Polish romantic nationalism, and the Decembrist movement (*see* SOCIETY OF UNITED SLAVS). The brotherhood's ideal was a society based on Christian morality, with justice, equality, and freedom for all. Serfdom and corporate estates were to be abolished, democratic rights and freedoms guaranteed, and education promoted. The society looked forward to the creation of a democratic federation of Slavic peoples, led by Ukraine, with its capital in Kyiv. While the society's members generally shared the same sociopolitical views, they differed in the approach to their realization, from the moderate reformism of Kostomarov, Bilozersky, and Kulish to the revolutionary radicalism espoused by Shevchenko. For the Ukrainian national movement, the brotherhood's programmatic documents marked a crucial transition from autonomism based on memories of the **Cossack Hetmanate** to a democratic egalitarianism informed by the language, culture, and aspirations of the common people.

The Cyril and Methodius Brotherhood was in existence for 14 months. In March 1847, it was denounced to the police by the provocateur Aleksei Petrov, and 10 of its members were arrested. An investigation of the brotherhood was held in St. Petersburg in the spring of 1847, and all 10 members were found guilty of clandestine activity. Shevchenko received the harshest sentence, being assigned to military service in the Orenburg Special Corps, where he was forbidden to write or draw. Hulak was imprisoned at the Schlüsselburg Fortress for three years, Kostomarov for a year, and Navrotsky for six months at the Viatka prison. Other members were exiled to distant gubernias of the empire.

D

DANYLO ROMANOVYCH (1201–64). Prince of **Volhynia** and **Galicia**, king of Rus' (from 1253). He was the son of **Roman Mstyslavych**, founder of the Principality of **Galicia-Volhynia**, and was proclaimed prince of Galicia after the death of his father (1205). However, owing to internal strife, Danylo, his mother, and his brother, Vasylko Romanovych, took refuge in Poland and Hungary. Danylo sought to regain his patrimony in the 1230s, finally winning Halych in 1238 establishing himself as ruler of Galicia-Volhynia. In 1239, he extended his rule to Kyiv, and his military commander led the defense of the city against the **Golden Horde** in 1240.

Danylo devoted considerable effort to strengthening the western borders of Galicia-Volhynia. In 1238, he stopped the advance of the Teutonic Knights, who had captured the town of Dorohychyn. On 17 August 1245, he defeated Hungarian and Polish forces and Galician **boyar** rebels at Yaroslav (now Jarosław), consolidating his control of Galicia (his brother Vasylko was in charge of Volhynia). Subsequently, Danylo established good relations with Poland and Hungary.

Relations with the Mongols were Danylo's major political preoccupation. In 1246, he was summoned to Sarai, the capital of the Golden Horde, where he acknowledged the suzerainty of Khan Batu and received confirmation of his right to rule Galicia-Volhynia. Dissatisfied with his vassal status, Danylo sought to create a broad European coalition against the Mongols comprising the Holy See, the Teutonic Order, Hungary, Poland, and Lithuania. In order to promote that goal, he agreed to a church union with the Holy See. The understanding with Rome was sealed by a delegation from Pope Innocent IV that crowned Danylo King of Rus' in Dorohychyn in 1253. When the anti-Mongol coalition failed to materialize, Danylo began military action independently. He was able to drive the Mongols out of **Podilia** and Volhynia, but in 1259 Khan Burundai forced Danylo to recognize the horde's supremacy and dismantle the fortifications of his towns.

Partly because of the peace established by the Mongols, Danylo's reign was relatively stable. He revived the Galician salt trade and promoted commerce, inviting skilled immigrants— Armenians, Germans, **Jews**, and Poles—to settle in Galicia-Volhynia. He devoted particular attention to the building of towns, founding Kholm (Chełm, ca. 1237), **Lviv** (1256), and others. Danylo moved his capital from Halych, which had been destroyed by the Tatars, to Kholm, where he was buried.

DASHKEVYCH, YAROSLAV (b. 13 December 1926). Historian. Dashkevych was born in **Lviv** into the family of a lawyer who served as a general in the army of the **Ukrainian People's Republic**; his mother, a scholar, fought in the ranks of the **Ukrainian Galician Army**. Since he and his family were so closely identified with the national movement, Dashkevych was arrested by the Soviet authorities in 1949 and imprisoned in the Karaganda concentration camp in Kazakhstan until 1956. Upon his return to Lviv, he worked as a bibliographer at the Institute of Social Sciences, **Ukrainian Academy of Sciences**. In 1967, Dashkevych became head of the ethnography department of the Lviv Museum of Ethnography and Crafts, from which he was dismissed in 1972 because of the official campaign against "nationalism" that accompanied the downfall of **Petro Shelest**. Dashkevych managed to obtain a position at the Lviv Central State Historical Archive (1974–78), only to be dismissed once again as politically unreliable, and was unable to gain official employment until the Soviet Union was on its last legs. Since 1990, Dashkevych has headed the Lviv department of the **Mykhailo Hrushevsky** Institute of Ukrainian Archaeography and Source Studies.

The author of some 950 scholarly works, Dashkevych has worked mainly in three areas: bibliography, archaeography, and the history of paper; the development of Ukrainian towns and cities, notably in **Podilia** and the **Black Sea littoral**; and Armenian settlement in Ukraine. Dashkevych published monographs on the latter subject in the 1960s, and his collected papers on Armenian-Ukrainian relations appeared under the title *Virmeniia i Ukraïna* (2000). Dashkevych is also well known as a commentator on historical and political issues. In 2002, when the vice-premiers of Russia and Ukraine agreed to establish a commission in charge of producing history textbooks acceptable to both countries, Dashkevych led a successful public protest against it, maintaining that Russian historiography generally continues to ignore or contradict salient facts of Ukrainian history.

DESIGN, GRAPHIC. From the 11th to the 16th century, manuscript books produced in the Ukrainian lands were ornamented with headpieces, initials, tailpieces, and illuminations. Greek and Bulgarian manuscripts served as models for illuminations in **Ostromir's Evangeliary** (1056–57) and the *Izbornik* of Sviatoslav Yaroslavych (1073), which are decorated in the vivid Byzantine style. The Byzantine-Romanesque style of additions to the Trier Psalter (1078–87) suggests that it originated in **western Ukraine**. The finest 14th-century work is the **Kyiv** Psalter of 1397, which displays neo-Byzantine and Balkan influences. The 15th-century Radziwiłł Chronicle, which includes 618 miniatures, copies the achievements of the **Kyivan Rus'** masters. Manuscripts of the 16th century, notably the **Peresopnytsia Gospel** (1556–61), show distinct evidence of Renaissance influences. The elaborate **baroque** style appeared in the mid-17th century, for example, in the **Kyivan Cave Patericon**.

Lviv became the center of Ukrainian printing and graphic design after **Ivan Fedorov** established his print shop there in 1573. Woodcuts were the primary medium for the illustration of books such as Fedorov's *Apostol* (1574) and the **Ostrih Bible** (1580–81). The **Kyivan Cave Monastery** Press was founded in 1615 and remained the largest press in Ukraine until the mid-19th century. At the end of the 17th century, it established a shop for copper engraving, which became the dominant illustrative medium of the 18th century. During the baroque period, graphic design was first used for purposes other than book publishing. New allegorical and symbolic themes appeared in illustrations, as did *tezy*—large graphics on paper or silk incorporating portraits of political and church leaders with elaborate poetic dedications.

At the turn of the 18th century, the first engraved landscapes and engravings on historical themes began to appear. Lithography was introduced in the early 19th century, and etching was made popular by **Taras Shevchenko** through his album *Zhivopisnaia Ukraina* (Picturesque Ukraine). The prohibitions against Ukrainian-language publishing (the **Valuev circular** of 1863 and the **Ems Ukase** of 1876) were also detrimental to the development of Ukrainian graphic design.

In the early 20th century, Vasyl Krychevsky developed a new style combining traditional Ukrainian graphics with folk motifs and photomechanical methods of reproduction. The most important Ukrainian graphic artist of the century was **Heorhii Narbut**, who blended Ukrainian baroque graphics with modern linearity. The bank notes, postage stamps, and seals that he designed for the **Ukrainian People's Republic** are among the finest in the history of Ukrainian graphic design. Some contemporary Ukrainian postage stamps are still based on his designs.

Other artists who fostered the development of graphic design were **Mykhailo Boichuk**, who combined Byzantine traditions with modern forms; Vasyl Kasiian, whose work was highly influential in the development of socialist realist graphic design; and Pavlo Kovzhun, who became renowned for his cubist and constructivist book designs. The finest émigré graphic artist was **Jacques Hnizdovsky**, who specialized in woodcuts. After **World War II**, graphic art in Ukraine had to conform to the official style of socialist **realism**. Favoring woodcuts and linocuts, graphic artists of the 1960s began presenting folk themes in a more abstract cubist style. Noteworthy postwar graphic artists include Anatolii Bazylevych, Oleksandr Hubariev, and Ivan Ostafiichuk.

DIASPORA. Mass emigration from Ukraine began in the last quarter of the 19th century, primarily because of the oversettlement of arable land. Transoceanic emigration, which began in 1871, was directed primarily toward the United States, where the emigrants worked mainly in industry and construction. In the 1890s, Ukrainian peasants began emigrating to Canada's prairie provinces, Brazil (state of Paraná), and Argentina (Misiones province). Prior to **World War I**, some 500,000 Ukrainians emigrated to the Americas, of whom 350,000 settled in the United States, 100,000 in Canada, and 50,000 in Brazil and Argentina. On the American continent, Ukrainians created a network of religious, economic, educational, civic, sport, and political organizations, helping them maintain their national distinctiveness and ties with their native land.

The Ukrainian diaspora in the Russian Empire (particularly in Asia) was predominantly agrarian. After 1861, emigration from Ukraine was directed toward the Volga region and the Ural Mountains. In the last quarter of the 19th century, when no vacant land remained in European Russia, Ukrainians began moving to western Siberia, neighboring Central Asia, and later to the Far East—the so-called Green Wedge. According to the census of 1897, the Ukrainian diaspora in the Russian Empire consisted of 1.56 million people. By 1914, approximately 3.4 million Ukrainians in the Russian Empire lived outside Ukrainian ethnic territory, including almost two million in Asia. Unlike emigrants to the West, these emigrants had few Ukrainian institutions and tended to assimilate more quickly.

World War I and the defeat of the **Ukrainian Revolution** (1917–21) resulted in the first mass political emigration from Ukraine. It augmented the existing Ukrainian labor diaspora with politicians, scholars, economists, and cultural figures, providing it with intellectual leadership. The primary centers of the new emigration were Czechoslovakia, France, Germany, Poland, Austria, Romania, and Yugoslavia. A new diaspora center was established in Harbin, China. In the postwar years, the transoceanic emigration of workers from **western Ukraine** resumed, though on a much smaller scale than before. Altogether the western diaspora consisted of 1.7–1.8 million people (USA: 700,000–800,000; Canada: 200,000; Argentina: 100,000–200,000; Brazil: 80,000; Romania: 350,000; Poland: 100,000; France: 40,000; Yugoslavia: 40,000; Czechoslovakia: 35,000; other countries of Western and Central Europe: 15,000–20,000). According to the census of 1926, there were 3.4 million Ukrainians in the Soviet Union living outside the **Ukrainian SSR**.

The size and geographical distribution of the Ukrainian diaspora expanded considerably after 1945. A new wave of political emigrants found themselves in Displaced Persons' camps in Germany and Austria after the war (approx. 200,000 people). In the late 1940s and early 1950s, they settled on various continents. New Ukrainian settlements appeared in Australia and Venezuela, while existing communities in the United States, Canada, Brazil, Argentina, and Paraguay were augmented. Approximately 550,000 Ukrainians remained in Europe, establishing new communities in Great Britain and reinforcing existing ones in France, Belgium, and the Netherlands. Today the Ukrainian diaspora in Europe includes some 300,000–350,000 people in Poland, 250,000–280,000 in Romania, 80,000–100,000 in Slovakia, 40,000–60,000 in the Czech Republic, 40,000–45,000 in France, 30,000–35,000 in Great Britain, 30,000 in Serbia, 20,000–25,000 in Germany, 6,000 in Croatia, 5,000 in Bosnia-Herzegovina, 4,000–5,000 in Austria, and 3,000–5,000 in

Belgium. There are 1.2–1.5 million in the United States, 800,000–900,000 (of multiple origin) in Canada, 200,000 in Argentina, 150,000 in Brazil, 10,000 in Paraguay, 10,000 in Uruguay, 2,000 in Chile, 2,000 in Venezuela, and 35,000 in Australia and New Zealand.

The western diaspora is home to a variety of political, scholarly, educational, and cultural organizations. Ukrainians born abroad have become integrated into their countries of residence and strive to preserve their ethnic identity as a distinct cultural heritage. The eastern diaspora living on the territory of the former **USSR** finds itself in significantly inferior circumstances. There are 2.94 million Ukrainians living in the Russian Federation (2002), approximately 700,000 in Kazakhstan, 112,000 in Uzbekistan, 120,000 in Kyrgyzstan, 507,000 in Moldova, and 133,000 in Belarus. Although the eastern diaspora does not enjoy guarantees of minority rights or Ukrainian institutions, it experienced something of a resurgence in the late 1980s and early 1990s. In 1989, a Ukrainian **language** society was established in Moscow, and Ukrainian educational and cultural organizations were founded in the Far East, Kazakhstan, Kyrgyzstan, Uzbekistan, Belarus, and Moldova. *See also* CANADIAN INSTITUTE OF UKRAINIAN STUDIES; HARVARD UKRAINIAN RESEARCH INSTITUTE; POPULATION; UKRAINIAN ACADEMY OF ARTS AND SCIENCES; UKRAINIAN CANADIAN CONGRESS; UKRAINIAN CONGRESS COMMITTEE OF AMERICA; UKRAINIAN FREE UNIVERSITY; UKRAINIAN WORLD CONGRESS.

***DILO*/THE DEED.** Oldest and for many years the only Ukrainian daily newspaper in **Galicia**, published in **Lviv** from 1880 to 1939 (twice weekly from 1880 to 1882, three times weekly from 1883 to 1887, and daily beginning in 1888). *Dilo* was founded by a group of **populists** led by Yuliian Romanchuk. Its first editor in chief was Volodymyr Barvinsky. Between 1881 and 1906 *Dilo* published *Biblioteka naiznamenytishykh povistei* (Library of the Best Short Novels, 74 vols.), followed by *Biblioteka "Dila"* (*Dilo* Library) in 1936–39 (48 vols.). Established as an alternative to the **Russophile** *Slovo* (Word), *Dilo* was the mouthpiece of the Galician populists. Although it was never an official party organ, *Dilo* supported the political line of the **National Democratic Party** (from 1899), the Ukrainian Labor Party (from 1919), and the **Ukrainian National Democratic Alliance** (from 1925).

DIRECTORY OF THE UKRAINIAN PEOPLE'S REPUBLIC/DYREKTORIIA UKRAÏNS'KOÏ NARODNOÏ RESPUBLIKY. Revolutionary body created on 14 November 1918 by the

Ukrainian National Union to overthrow the **Ukrainian State** headed by Hetman **Pavlo Skoropadsky**. Preparations for an uprising began in late October under the auspices of the National Union, and a final meeting was held in **Kyiv** on 13 November. The participants—representatives of Ukrainian political parties, the Peasant Union, the railway workers' union, and the command of the **Ukrainian Sich Riflemen**—ratified a plan of action and elected a Directory to lead the revolt and restore the **Ukrainian People's Republic** (UNR). The Directory consisted of Chairman **Volodymyr Vynnychenko** (**Ukrainian Social Democratic Labor Party** [USDRP]) and members **Symon Petliura** (USDRP), Opanas Andriievsky (**Ukrainian Party of Socialist Independentists**), Fedir Shvets (Peasant Union), and Andrii Makarenko (nonpartisan, chosen by the railway workers' union). Petliura, elected in absentia, was to lead the Directory's military forces. The Directory's manifesto, drafted by Vynnychenko, called on the Ukrainian people to join the uprising in order to restore the "social and political gains of revolutionary democracy." The Directory created a temporary government, the Executive Council for State Affairs, and a Military Revolutionary Committee (Mykhailo Avdiienko, **Volodymyr Chekhivsky**, Andrii Richytsky, Zynovii Vysotsky, Mykola Halahan, N. Zahorodny, and M. Marchenko). On 15 November, the members of the Directory departed for Bila Tserkva, the base of their main military force, the Sich Riflemen.

The Sich Riflemen took Bila Tserkva and Fastiv on 16 November and then set out for Kyiv. The hetman's formations were crushed at Motovylivka (18 November). On 21 November, republican forces began their siege of Kyiv. Land-hungry **peasants** flocked to insurgent units led by local commanders (otamans) such as Danylo Zeleny, **Nykyfor Hryhoriiv**, and Anhel. In December, the Directory's forces numbered some 48,000 men. As the world war had ended on 11 November, a German withdrawal from Kyiv was imminent. The Directory arranged safe conduct for the departing Germans; Skoropadsky abdicated on 14 December and also left for Germany. The Directory entered Kyiv on 19 December.

On 26 December, the restoration of the UNR was proclaimed and a government led by Chekhivsky, the **Council of People's Ministers**, was established. It abolished much of the Hetman government's legislation and restored the laws of the UNR. It also proclaimed the restoration of workers' rights and the imminent distribution of land to the peasants, especially those who had taken part in the uprising, while "nonlaboring, exploiting classes" were to be disenfranchised. A **Labor Congress** was to convene in Kyiv and take over the functions of government. On 22 January 1919, an **Act** of Union between the **Western Ukrainian People's Republic** (ZUNR) and the UNR was solemnized at St. Sophia's Square in Kyiv. Although the Labor Congress convened on 23 January, the Bolshevik advance on Kyiv prevented it from exercising its functions. The congress provisionally transferred power to the Directory, whose leader performed the functions of head of state.

The Directory was unprepared for war with the Bolsheviks, whose advance on Ukraine had begun on 6 December 1918. A Soviet Ukrainian government had been formed on 20 November (*see* PROVISIONAL WORKERS' AND PEASANTS' GOVERNMENT OF UKRAINE). When the Directory demanded the cessation of hostilities, Moscow replied that the Soviet Ukrainians were acting on their own initiative. Not until 16 January 1919, after lengthy attempts by the Directory's radical socialists (including Vynnychenko, Chekhivsky, and **Mykyta Shapoval**) to reach a diplomatic settlement with Moscow, did it declare war on Russia. The Bolsheviks took Kyiv on 5 February, forcing the evacuation of the Directory to **Podilia**. The Directory also faced the hostility of the anti-Bolshevik White forces, which were bent on restoring the Russian Empire and opposed concessions to the non-Russian peoples.

In its struggle against these enemies, the Directory looked to the victorious Entente for support, but the Entente sought the restoration of a united Russia and opposed separatist movements. When French forces took **Odesa** on 18 December, they allied themselves with Russian Whites in the city. The Directory continued to seek their support, sending its representatives to Odesa for negotiations. The French demanded that Vynnychenko and Petliura be expelled from the government because of their radicalism; Vynnychenko resigned on 11 February and settled in Vienna, while Petliura gave up his membership in the USDRP and assumed the leadership of the Directory. A centrist government, from which the USDRP and the **Ukrainian Party of Socialist Revolutionaries** voluntarily excluded themselves, was formed on 13 February under the leadership of Serhii Ostapenko. These efforts at rapprochement with the French proved unsuccessful, as the latter continued to insist on an anti-Bolshevik coalition between the Directory and the Whites. When the French forces were attacked by Nykyfor Hryhoriiv, they withdrew from Odesa (6 April).

Lacking a professional army and support from the Entente, the Directory had to rely on the undisciplined peasant forces of the otamans, which it could not control. These forces discredited the Directory's cause when they engaged in anti-Jewish pogroms (*see* JEWS). Following its expulsion from Kyiv, the Directory established itself in Rivne, and a new left-leaning government was formed on 9 April, with Borys Martos as premier. This provoked an attempted coup by Andriievsky and others, supported by Otaman Volodymyr Oskilko. The coup failed, as did another led by Otaman Petro Bolbochan, and in June the Directory, driven out of Rivne by the Bolsheviks, moved to Kamianets-Podilskyi, where it remained until mid-November.

Relations with the western Ukrainians became confrontational when **Yevhen Petrushevych**, who had joined the Directory as their representative after the Act of Union, was given dictatorial powers by the ZUNR (9 June) to deal with the Ukrainian-Polish war in **Galicia**. Maintaining that this was incompatible with democracy, the Directory expelled Petrushevych and established a separate ministry for the Western Province of the UNR. The advancing Poles drove the **Ukrainian Galician Army** (UHA) out of western Ukraine, and it initially contemplated seeking asylum in Romania, but the Romanian authorities would not admit it. Petrushevych then negotiated a merger with the Directory's forces on condition that the Martos government be dismissed, a platform of parliamentary democracy be adopted, and the separate ministry be abolished.

Given the critical situation, the Directory accepted these conditions. On 12 August, it issued a declaration to the effect that the UNR should be based on all strata of the population and that a Ukrainian parliament based on universal, equal, and proportional representation should be elected by secret ballot. A new government led by **Isaak Mazepa** was formed on 27 August. The combined forces of the UNR, which now numbered some 80,000 men under the command of Gen. Mykola Yunakiv, advanced simultaneously on Kyiv (to retake the capital) and Odesa (to establish contact with the Entente). Although Kyiv was taken on 30 August, the UNR forces were promptly expelled by the Whites. The UNR army then became fully engaged in conflict with the White forces led by the Ukrainophobe Gen. Anton Denikin. This conflict again divided the eastern and western Ukrainians; the easterners regarded Denikin as their principal enemy and even contemplated an alliance with the Bolsheviks to defeat him, while the westerners hoped for an understanding with Denikin, whom they saw as a representative of the Entente. The forces of the UHA were drastically reduced by a typhus epidemic, and, lacking medicine and ammunition, it established a truce with Denikin on 6 November. The last plenary meeting of the Directory was held on 15 November. At that session Shvets and Makarenko were given plenipotentiary powers and went abroad (later to be expelled from the Directory for malfeasance), and Petliura became head of state. Kamianets-

Podilskyi was taken by Polish forces on the following day, and Petliura retreated to northern Volhynia. There he decided to undertake partisan warfare and dispatched a force of 5,000 men on the first **Winter Campaign**.

On 5 December, Petliura fled to Warsaw with the remains of his forces, which were disarmed and placed in internment camps. After the failure of the winter campaign, Petliura made a further effort to reestablish himself in Kyiv by means of an alliance with Józef Piłsudski, head of the restored Polish Republic. The **Treaty of Warsaw**, signed on 21 April 1920, provided for Polish recognition of the Directory as the government of Ukraine, as well as military assistance; in return, the Directory ceded most of western Ukraine to Poland. The joint Polish-Ukrainian campaign against the Bolsheviks led to the recapture of Kyiv on 7 May, but requisitions and looting by the Polish forces antagonized the Ukrainian peasantry. The Bolshevik counteroffensive drove the Polish forces back to the gates of Warsaw, and Piłsudski arranged a separate peace with Russia and the **Ukrainian SSR** by means of the **Treaty of Riga** (18 March 1921) over the protests of the Directory.

Petliura went into exile in Paris, where he continued to work for Ukrainian independence. Following his assassination in 1926, leadership passed to the head of the UNR government-in-exile, **Andrii Livytsky**. The government-in-exile continued to exist until 1992, when its powers were formally transferred to President **Leonid Kravchuk**.

DISSIDENT MOVEMENT. Post-Stalin social movement (late 1950s to 1980s) for civil, national, cultural, and religious rights. Largely but not exclusively identified with the postwar intelligentsia, this movement included a variety of currents, almost all of which were linked by a commitment to democratic values and open expression of their demands according to procedures established by Soviet law. Because the dissidents' demand for the rule of law would have limited the Soviet authorities' absolute power, the latter made little effort to compromise with them and responded with a variety of repressive measures.

Beginning in 1957, a number of clandestine groups were active in **western Ukraine**, holding secret meetings and circulating underground literature. They included the "Association," the Ukrainian National Committee, the Ukrainian National Front, and the Union of Ukrainian Youth of **Galicia**. The Ukrainian Workers' and Peasants' Union (1959–60), led by **Levko Lukianenko**, advocated Ukraine's legal secession from the **USSR**. The secret police uncovered all these groups, whose members were tried (generally in camera) and sentenced to terms in prison or forced-labor camps; a few were sentenced to death.

The early 1960s saw the flourishing of the *shistdesiatnyky*, a diverse group of artists and intellectuals who worked to revive Ukrainian culture and combat **Russification**. The most notable political document produced by this movement was **Ivan Dziuba**'s monograph *Internationalism or Russification?* (1965), which demanded a return to "Leninist norms" of nationality policy and called on the authorities to promote the Ukrainian **language** and culture. When some 20 dissidents were arrested in 1965, their colleagues protested, notably at the Ukraina film theater in Kyiv (4 September), where Dziuba and others spoke. Many of those who spoke out were dismissed from their jobs. The journalist **Viacheslav Chornovil**, outraged by arbitrary practices at trials of the dissidents that he covered, compiled materials about 20 "criminals" that circulated in the underground (as *samvydav* or "self-published" literature) and appeared in the West as *The Chornovil Papers* (1968).

Under the administration of **Petro Shelest**, first secretary of the **Communist Party of Ukraine**, the dissidents were given some leeway to voice their demands, which were supported by a number of establishment figures. Of these, the most notable was the writer Oles Honchar, whose novel *Sobor* (The Cathedral, 1968) condemned the destruction of the Ukrainian cultural tradition; it was removed from circulation. Moscow's concern that Shelest was losing control of Ukraine led to his peremptory dismissal and a major wave of arrests (January-April 1972), followed by a thorough purge of Ukrainian institutions and a series of trials that handed down harsher sentences (imprisonment, forced labor, and internal exile) than those of the 1960s. Some dissidents, such as **Leonid Pliushch**, were deliberately misdiagnosed as mentally ill and incarcerated in psychiatric hospitals, where they were tortured with drugs; others were arrested on trumped-up charges of criminal activity.

The next major manifestation of political dissent was the formation of the **Ukrainian Helsinki Group** (1976), initially led by the writer Mykola Rudenko, which issued dozens of memoranda on official **human-rights** violations. By 1983 it had 37 members, most of whom were sentenced to forced labor, while a few were allowed to emigrate.

Samvydav documents noted that several thousand individuals were directly involved in dissident activity. According to Amnesty International, in the 1970s and early 1980s there were at least 10,000 political prisoners in the USSR; Ukrainian dissident sources estimated that some 40–50 percent of these were Ukrainians. (The

All-Ukrainian Association of Political Prisoners, established in Kyiv on 3 June 1989, claimed a membership of 40,000.) The numbers of those sympathizing with the dissidents were much greater, and dissent was not limited to the political and cultural spheres. The 1960s and 1970s saw a number of economically motivated labor strikes and protests, as well as an attempt to form an independent trade union in Donetsk (1977–78). Religious dissent was particularly strong in **western Ukraine**, where the banned **Ukrainian Catholic Church** continued to function in the underground. In 1982, Yosyp Terelia organized the Committee for the Defense of the Ukrainian Catholic Church to demand its legalization. Protestant sects (Baptists, Pentecostals, Adventists, and Jehovah's Witnesses) also put up determined resistance to official persecution. The Rev. **Vasyl Romaniuk** was the most prominent dissident representing the largely quiescent **Ukrainian Orthodox Church**.

Ukrainians in the West agitated on behalf of the dissidents and translated their writings; the Baltimore-based Smoloskyp publishing house was particularly active in that regard. Western intellectuals signed petitions on behalf of dissidents, who were also defended by a variety of ad hoc committees and by Amnesty International. Among the dissidents who attracted Western attention were **Valentyn Moroz** (atypical of the dissident movement in his dedication to integral nationalism), **Danylo Shumuk** (the world's senior prisoner of conscience), and Leonid Pliushch (defended by a committee of French mathematicians).

Following Mikhail Gorbachev's accession to power (1985), political prisoners in the USSR were released. The Ukrainian Helsinki Group, which renamed itself the Ukrainian Helsinki Union in 1988, became the basis for the formation of the Ukrainian Republican Party (1990). **Rukh**, also formed in 1988, mobilized those who favored Ukrainian sovereignty and played an important role in bringing about Ukraine's independence.

DIVISION GALIZIEN/DYVIZIIA "HALYCHYNA" (14. Waffen-Grenadier-Division der SS, Galizische Nr 1, later First Ukrainian Division of the Ukrainian National Army). **Galician** military formation that fought on the side of Nazi Germany in **World War II**. Its formation began in April 1943, after the German defeat at Stalingrad, which forced the Nazis to revise their earlier prohibitions on allowing "non-Aryans" to bear arms (thus, 19 of the 38 Waffen-SS divisions were non-German). The **Ukrainian Central Committee** (UTsK), which represented Ukrainians in the **Generalgouvernement**, saw the formation of the division as a means of halting the ongoing recruitment of Ukrainians to German formations as cannon fodder. Moreover, it anticipated that the impending German defeat might lead to a period of instability in which the existence of a properly trained and armed Ukrainian military formation could be a significant asset to the Ukrainian cause. Negotiations on the division's formation were held primarily between the UTsK leader, **Volodymyr Kubijovyč**, and the governor of Galicia, Otto Wächter. The major Ukrainian demands—that the division be designated as Ukrainian, attached to the Wehrmacht, and staffed by Ukrainians—were ignored. In order not to breach Nazi racial doctrine, the division was given the regional "Galician" designation; it was attached to the Waffen-SS, and all its officers, down to the noncommissioned level, were Germans. Gen. Fritz Freitag was appointed its commander, and the soldiers were trained in Neuhammer in occupied Poland. The Ukrainians received assurances that the division would not be deployed against the Western Allies, and Ukrainian Catholic priests were allowed to minister to the soldiers. Wächter gave Kubijovyč to understand that if the UTsK resisted the division's recruitment, it would be dissolved, effectively depriving Ukrainians in the Generalgouvernement of economic and social assistance.

An official announcement of the division's formation was made in **Lviv** on 28 April 1943. The call for recruits met with an overwhelming response; some 80,000 men volunteered, inspired mainly by determination to help prevent a Soviet reoccupation of **western Ukraine** (the occupation of 1939–41 had resulted in mass arrests, deportations, and executions). Of these, some 16,000 were enlisted. The **Melnyk** faction of the **Organization of Ukrainian Nationalists**, whose underground forces were small, did not oppose recruitment. The **Bandera** faction, which controlled the **Ukrainian Insurgent Army** (UPA), expressed overt opposition to recruitment in its propaganda but unofficially encouraged prospective recruits to obtain training in the division and desert to the UPA.

The division was deployed against the advancing Red Army, and in the course of a battle near Brody (Lviv oblast) on 17–22 July 1944, it was surrounded and destroyed. About 3,000 survivors broke out of encirclement and retreated west; some of them joined the ranks of the UPA. At the end of 1944, a new division of 18,000 men was formed. In late 1944 and early 1945, the division was involved in the suppression of the Slovak military uprising and fought Soviet and Yugoslav communist forces in Austria and Slovenia.

In March 1945, on instructions of the German-sponsored **Ukrainian National Committee**, the division was formally separated from the Waffen-SS and incorporated into the nascent

Ukrainian National Army commanded by Gen. **Pavlo Shandruk**. On 25 April, the division's soldiers took an oath of allegiance to Ukraine. Most of the division surrendered to British forces in Austria on 8 May; a small portion surrendered to the Americans. After the war, its soldiers were interned at camps in Feldkirchen (Austria), Bellaria, and Rimini (Italy), where they successfully resisted insistent Soviet efforts to "repatriate" them. In May 1947, the Ukrainian POWs were taken to Great Britain and released after a period of contract labor. Most emigrated to North America; a veterans' organization was established in 1950.

The division was consistently denounced in postwar Soviet propaganda for alleged criminal collaboration with the Germans, and there have been sporadic allegations from other quarters as well, but none has been substantiated. A Canadian government investigation of alleged war criminals in 1986 found no evidence of wrongdoing on the part of the division's members.

DONETS BASIN. Also known as the Donets Coal Basin or Donbas. Major fuel source and industrial region of Ukraine. Best known for its coal reserves, the Donbas is also home to ferrous-metallurgy, machine-building, chemical, and construction industries. The basin extends through the Donetsk and Luhansk oblasts of southeastern Ukraine and part of the Rostov oblast of southwestern Russia, covering an area of 23,000 sq. km. In the 1960s, the coalfields were extended westward to eastern Dnipropetrovsk oblast.

From the 11th to the 13th century, the territory along the Donets River belonged to the sphere of influence of the Principality of Pereiaslav. Like the southern steppelands in general, however, it was controlled by nomadic hordes and not permanently settled. The first permanent settlements in the Donbas were established by the Don Cossacks. In the second half of the 17th century, Muscovy built fortifications on the Donbas frontier with the Ottoman Empire. In the mid-18th century, both banks of the Donets were settled by Serbian colonists, and the region was known as **Sloviano-Serbia**. Subsequently, when many Serbs left the area, the Russian government began settling Ukrainian **peasants** there. At the time, the southwestern part of the region was controlled by the **Zaporozhian Host**, the southeastern part by the Don Cossacks, and the northern part by **Sloboda Ukraine**. After the destruction of the **Sich** (1775) and the Russian Empire's expansion to the Black and Azov seas, the western Donbas was incorporated into the Katerynoslav vicegerency, while the eastern part remained under the control of the Don Cossack Host.

Initially the region's economy focused on animal husbandry, and by the 1830s it also involved commercial grain growing. Coal was discovered in the Donbas in 1721, but its exploitation did not begin until the early 19th century. Full-scale industrial development commenced after 1869, when the Donbas was linked to central Russia and the sea by rail. In the last two decades of the 19th century the region was industrialized rapidly, in large part because of French, British, German, Belgian, and Russian investment. By 1913, the Donets Basin was producing 87 percent of the Russian Empire's coal (*see* ENERGY; MINING).

In 1872, the first successful ironworks were established in Yuzivka (now Donetsk), and by 1900 the Donbas became the principal iron- and steel-producing region of the Russian Empire. By 1913, it was producing 74 percent of all the pig iron in the empire. Despite extensive damage in **World War II**, the area remains one of the world's major metallurgical and heavy-industry complexes (*see* METALLURGY). Iron ore is mined nearby in Kryvyi Rih and in Kerch in the Crimea; manganese mines are located in Nykopil and Marhanets on the Dnipro River. Luhansk, Kramatorsk, and the region's iron- and steel-producing centers are also home to a range of heavy industries. The chemical industry is based on coke by-products and rock salt mined near Artemivsk.

Today, the Donbas is the most densely populated region of Ukraine, with 93 percent of its residents in urban centers. The largest cities include Donetsk (1998 pop. 1,065,400), Mariupol (1998 pop. 499,800), and Luhansk (1998 pop 475,300). It is also the most **Russified** area of the country. At the beginning of the region's industrial boom, most workers came from central Russia rather than Ukraine. When revolution broke out in 1917, most workers in the Donbas were under the sway of Russian parties, particularly the Bolsheviks. In December 1917, a Soviet Ukrainian government was proclaimed in Kharkiv with the support of Donbas Bolsheviks, and in 1918 the **Donets-Kryvyi Rih Soviet Republic** briefly existed as a distinct polity. The Donbas was recaptured by the Bolsheviks in December 1919. Despite attempts by local and Moscow communists to form a separate polity, the region was incorporated into the **Ukrainian SSR**.

The **Ukrainization** of the 1920s was less successful in the Donbas than elsewhere. Today, ethnic Ukrainians make up a slim majority in the region, constituting roughly half the urban population but maintaining a clear majority in rural areas. However, significant numbers of ethnic Ukrainians in the Donbas now consider Russian their first language. In addition to economic decline, the region faces serious ecological problems. Chemical pollution has caused a shortage of clean water, and there is greater air pollution than in any other part of the country. *See also* ENVIRONMENT.

DONETS-KRYVYI RIH SOVIET REPUBLIC/DONETS'KO-KRYVORIZ'KA RADIANS'KA RESPUBLIKA. Short-lived political formation (February-March 1918) in the regions of Sumy, **Kharkiv**, Donetsk, Katerynoslav, Kherson, and a portion of the Don Cossack Oblast, including Taganrog and Aleksandro-Grushevskii (now Shakhty, Russia). It was proclaimed in Kharkiv at the fourth oblast congress of the Councils of People's Deputies of the Donets and Kryvyi Rih basins on 27–30 January (9–12 February) 1918. The congress elected the republic's government, the Council of People's Commissars, which included Artem (Fedor Sergeev; head), Abram Kamensky, Boris Magidov, Valerii Mezhlauk, Musii Rukhymovych, Mikhail Zhakov, and others. The initiative for the republic's formation came from the Katerynoslav (now Dnipropetrovsk) wing of the Bolsheviks in Ukraine, led by Emmanuil Kviring, who wanted to deny the **Ukrainian People's Republic** and the German army access to the heavy industry of the Kryvyi Rih and Donbas regions (*see* BREST-LITOVSK, TREATY OF). The Bolshevik leadership in Moscow opposed the creation of the republic as a breach in the "united front" against enemy forces. At the urging of **Mykola Skrypnyk**, Lenin ordered the republic's leaders to participate in the Second All-Ukrainian Congress of Soviets in Katerynoslav (17–19 March), where the republic was abolished. Its leaders joined the **Provisional Workers' and Peasants' Government of Ukraine.**

DONTSOV, DMYTRO (17 [29] August 1883—30 March 1973). Prominent publicist and literary critic; ideologue of Ukrainian integral nationalism. Dontsov was born in Melitopol (now in Zaporizhia oblast). He studied at St. Petersburg University (1900–1907, with interruptions). Dontsov belonged to the **Ukrainian Social Democratic Labor Party**, for which he was arrested (1905 and 1907). In 1908, persecuted by the tsarist authorities, he emigrated and studied at the University of Vienna (1909–11). In 1913, at the Second Ukrainian Student Congress in **Lviv**, Dontsov gave a speech on "The Current Political Situation of the Nation and Our Tasks," condemning the **Little Russian mentality** and calling for an independent state. He was the first head of the **Union for the Liberation of Ukraine** (1914), which he soon left because of political differences. In 1918, Dontsov headed the Ukrainian Telegraph Agency and the Press Bureau of the **Ukrainian State**. He also headed the Ukrainian Press Bureau in Bern (1919–21). From 1922, he lived in Lviv, where he became a founder of the **Ukrainian Party of National Work** and edited its journal, *Zahrava* (1923–24). From 1922 to 1932, Dontsov was editor in chief of

Literaturno-naukovyi visnyk (renamed *Visnyk* in 1932 and run by Dontsov as a private enterprise).

After 1939, Dontsov lived abroad, in Germany, Czechoslovakia, and France. In 1947, he settled in Canada, where he taught Ukrainian **literature** at the University of Montreal (1949–52). Dontsov's most important writings include *Moderne moskvofil'stvo* (Modern Russophilism, 1913), *Istoriia rozvytku ukraïns'koï derzhavnyts'koï ideï* (The History of the Development of the Ukrainian State Idea, 1917), *Pidstavy nashoï polityky* (The Foundations of Our Politics, 1921), *Natsionalizm* (Nationalism, 1926), *De shukaty ukraïns'kykh tradytsii* (Where to Seek Ukrainian Traditions, 1938), and *Dukh nashoï davnyny* (The Spirit of Our Antiquity, 1944). He also wrote literary criticism: *Poetka ukraïns'koho risordzhimenta: Lesia Ukraïnka* (The Poetess of the Ukrainian Risorgimento, **Lesia Ukrainka**, 1922), *Nasha doba i literatura* (Our Age and Literature, 1937), *Tuha za heroïchnym. Postati i ideï literaturnoï Ukraïny* (Yearning for the Heroic: The Figures and Ideas of Literary Ukraine, 1952), and *Poetka vohnennykh mezh. Olena Teliha* (The Poetess of Fiery Extremes, **Olena Teliha**, 1953).

Dontsov underwent several ideological reorientations, moving from socialism to a complete rejection of it and from rejection of religion to extreme conservative Christian militancy. He consistently defended Ukrainian independence and opposed Russian imperialism in all its manifestations. Dontsov was most influential during the interwar period in **western Ukraine**, where his writings greatly weakened the influence of communist ideology and **Russophilism**. A virulent critic of the democratic and socialist currents that he held responsible for the failure of the **Ukrainian Revolution**, Dontsov promoted the authoritarian and fascist movements of the 1930s in his writings, calling for a dictatorial political movement to liberate Ukraine. His advocacy of voluntarism and "active idealism," which had a huge impact on western Ukrainian youth, was the intellectual source of the relentless commitment to the national cause that characterized the **Organization of Ukrainian Nationalists**, especially its **Bandera** faction.

DOROSHENKO, DMYTRO (8 April 1882–19 March 1951). Historian, civic figure, and politician. He was born in Vilnius, Lithuania, a descendant of a **Cossack officer** family from the Hlukhiv region that had produced **Hetmans** Mykhailo Doroshenko and **Petro Doroshenko**. He studied at the historical and philological faculties of the universities of Warsaw, St. Petersburg, and **Kyiv**. In 1903, Doroshenko headed the Ukrainian Student **Hromada** in St. Petersburg. He became involved in politics as a member of the **Revolutionary Ukrainian Party** and later the **Society of Ukrainian Progressives** (TUP). In 1897, he began contributing to political publications in **Galicia**, and in 1905–7 he wrote for newspapers and journals of a national-democratic orientation in **eastern Ukraine**: *Rada*, *Ukrainskii vestnik*, *Ukrainskaia zhizn'*, and *Ukraïna*. Between 1910 and 1913, he edited the periodical *Dniprovi khvyli* (Dnipro Waves) in Katerynoslav (now Dnipropetrovsk).

During **World War I**, Doroshenko was a representative of the All-Russian Union of Towns on the southwestern front (from 1915), directing relief efforts for Ukrainians in Russian-occupied Galicia and **Bukovyna**. After the reorganization of the TUP (renamed the **Ukrainian Party of Socialist Federalists** in June 1917), Doroshenko joined the new organization. As of April 1917, he was a member of the **Ukrainian Central Rada**. That month, he was appointed commissar (with the powers of governor-general) of Galicia and Bukovyna by the Russian Provisional Government. He returned to Kyiv in August after the Russian armies retreated from Galicia. Later that month, Doroshenko was asked to form the new government (General Secretariat) of the **Ukrainian Central Rada**. Owing to political differences with the head of the Rada, **Mykhailo Hrushevsky**, he declined. From August to December 1917, Doroshenko served as commissar of Chernihiv gubernia.

After the coup that brought Hetman **Pavlo Skoropadsky** to power, Doroshenko returned to Kyiv. On 20 May 1918, he became minister of foreign affairs of the **Ukrainian State**. Under his leadership the ministry established diplomatic missions in Romania, Poland, Switzerland, and Finland, as well as a number of consulates. Foreign consulates were also opened in Kyiv. In mid-August 1918, in response to hostile policies of the **Crimean** administration, Doroshenko proposed an economic blockade of the peninsula. Partial implementation of the blockade obliged the Crimean leadership to enter into talks concerning the peninsula's unification with Ukraine. Doroshenko often acted as an intermediary in attempts to reach an understanding between Skoropadsky and political forces associated with the **Ukrainian People's Republic**. In October 1918, he attempted to enter into negotiations with Entente representatives in Berne. After the fall of the Ukrainian State in December 1918, he lectured at the Kamianets-Podilskyi State Ukrainian University.

From 1920, Doroshenko lived abroad. In that year, together with **Viacheslav Lypynsky**, Serhii Shemet, and other activists of the Hetmanite movement, he helped establish a monarchist alliance, the Ukrainian Union of Agrarian Statists. From 1921 to 1951, he was professor of history at the **Ukrainian Free University**. Doroshenko headed the Ukrainian Scientific Institute in Berlin (1926–31) and was the first president of the **Ukrainian Academy of Arts and Sciences** (1945–51). He was one of the founders of the statist school in Ukrainian historiography and wrote nearly 1,000 works on Ukrainian history, culture, and the church in Ukraine. His most important works are: *Narys istoriï Ukraïny* (Outline History of Ukraine, 2 vols., 1932–33, English trans., *A Survey of Ukrainian History*, 1975), *Istoriia Ukraïny 1917–1923 rr.* (History of Ukraine, 1917–23, 2 vols., 1930–32), *Ohliad ukraïns'koï istoriohrafiï* (A Survey of Ukrainian Historiography, 1923), *Pravoslavna tserkva v mynulomu i suchasnomu zhytti ukraïns'koho narodu* (The Orthodox Church in the Past and Present Life of the Ukrainian People, 1940), and monographs on **Mykola Kostomarov**, **Panteleimon Kulish**, **Volodymyr Antonovych**, and Hetman **Petro Doroshenko**. His memoirs, *Moï spohady pro davnie-mynule, 1901–1914* (My Memoirs of the Distant Past, 1901–1914, 1949) and *Moï spohady pro nedavnie-mynule, 1914–1920* (My Memoirs of the Recent Past, 1914–20, 1923–24), are a valuable record of the period.

DOROSHENKO, PETRO (1627–9 [19] November 1698). **Hetman** of Ukraine (1665–76). Born in Chyhyryn into an old **Cossack** family (grandson of Hetman Mykhailo Doroshenko), Petro Doroshenko was secretary of the Chyhyryn regiment during the **Khmelnytsky Uprising** (1648–57) and conducted negotiations with the Polish and Swedish governments. An opponent of union with Muscovy, he supported Hetman **Ivan Vyhovsky**. In 1660, as colonel of Chyhyryn, Doroshenko traveled to Moscow in an unsuccessful attempt to cancel certain provisions of the **Articles of Bohdan Khmelnytsky**. In 1663–64, he served as general aide-de-camp to Hetman **Pavlo Teteria**. As colonel of Cherkasy (from 1665), Doroshenko was elected acting hetman of **Right-Bank Ukraine** on 1 (10) October 1665. His election was ratified in January 1666 by a **Cossack council** in Chyhyryn.

Doroshenko implemented a series of reforms. He created a standing army of 20,000 mercenaries, the so-called *serdeniata* (serdiuks), subordinated directly to himself. He collected customs duties and began minting his own coins. Doroshenko established the Torhovytsia regiment on the steppe frontier to promote colonization of free lands. He was very active in foreign affairs, striving for the union of Left- and Right-Bank Ukraine under his leadership. After the **Truce of Andrusovo**, Doroshenko allied himself with the **Crimean** Khanate and placed Ukraine under an Ottoman protectorate. In September 1667, together with the Crimean **Tatars**, he successfully fought Polish forces and forced Poland to recognize broad autonomy for Right-Bank Ukraine.

In the early summer of 1668, Doroshenko supported an anti-Muscovite rebellion on the **Left Bank** and was declared hetman of all Ukraine on 8 (18) June 1668, following the murder of Hetman **Ivan Briukhovetsky**. His rule was short-lived. Alarmed by Doroshenko's increasing strength, the Crimean Tatars supported the **Zaporozhian** secretary, Petro Sukhovii, for the hetmancy. Having appointed **Demian Mnohohrishny** acting hetman of the Left Bank, Doroshenko, aided by **Ivan Sirko**, defeated Sukhovii and the Crimean Tatars in 1669. Allying himself with the Ottoman Empire in the autumn of 1669, Doroshenko fought **Mykhailo Khanenko**, whom the Poles recognized as hetman of the Right Bank (1670). With Turkish assistance, Doroshenko crushed Khanenko's forces near Chetvertynivka in **Podilia** (July 1672). As a result, on 18 (28) October, the Poles signed the Treaty of Buchach, abandoning claims to part of Right-Bank Ukraine. Muscovy saw this as an opportunity to seize those territories, and, with Muscovite backing, **Ivan Samoilovych** was declared hetman of all Ukraine in June 1674. A Muscovite army, together with Cossack regiments led by Samoilovych, laid siege to Doroshenko's capital, Chyhyryn. With the assistance of a Turco-Tatar army, Doroshenko's rule over the Right Bank was restored. However, incessant warfare destroyed towns and villages on the Right Bank, and Turkish looting contributed to the growth of popular dissatisfaction with Doroshenko and his policies.

In the autumn of 1675, disillusioned with the Turks, Doroshenko surrendered the hetman's insignia at a **Cossack council** in Chyhyryn but refused to capitulate to Muscovy. In 1676, a Muscovite army supported by Samoilovych's forces again besieged Chyhyryn. Doroshenko abdicated and was soon exiled to Moscow. From 1679 until his death in 1698, he lived in Viatka and Yaropolche (now Yaropolets) near Moscow.

DOVBUSH, OLEKSA (1700–13 (24) August 1745). Leader of the Carpathian **opryshok** (brigand) movement during the 1730s–40s. He was born in the village of Pechenizhyn (now in Ivano-Frankivsk oblast) into a **peasant** family. The first mention of his activity dates from 1738. Dovbush's band of 30–50 opryshoks, based on Mt. Chornohora in the Carpathian Mountains, was active in **Subcarpathia**, **Transcarpathia**, and **Bukovyna** from 1738 to 1745, taking property from landlords, moneylenders, and merchants to give it to the poor. All attempts by the Polish military to destroy the band were unsuccessful. Dovbush was betrayed and killed in the village of Kosmach (now in Ivano-Frankivsk oblast) by one of his followers, Stefan Dzvinchuk. Numerous folk songs and tales were composed about him. Certain sites are named after him: mountains in the Carpathians, a cave on Mount Hoverlia, and a cliff near Yaremcha. He has also been depicted in literature (**Hnat Khotkevych's** play *Dovbush*), in music (*Khustka Dovbusha* [Dovbush's Kerchief], a ballet by Anatol Kos-Anatolsky), in the visual arts (Olena Kulchytska's engraving *Dovbush*), and in **film** (*Oleksa Dovbush*, directed by Viktor Ivanov).

DOVZHENKO, OLEKSANDER (29 August [10 September] 1894–25 November 1956). **Film** director, writer, and artist. He was born in Sosnytsia (Chernihiv region) and graduated from the Hlukhiv teachers' college in 1914. He continued his studies at the **Ukrainian State Academy of Arts** in **Kyiv** (1917–19) and with Erich Heckel in Berlin, where he worked in the Ukrainian consulate (1922–23). Dovzhenko began his career as a cartoonist for the newspaper *Visti VUTsVK* in **Kharkiv** but switched to film in 1926. He wrote screenplays and directed films at the **Odesa** film studio (1926–28) and at the Kyiv studio (1929–32). To avoid being persecuted as a "nationalist" during Stalin's **political terror**, Dovzhenko moved to Moscow in 1932, where he spent the rest of his life working for the Mosfilm studio and teaching.

After directing two short comedies, Dovzhenko made a feature-length debut with *Sumka dypkur'iera* (The Diplomatic Pouch, 1927), a spy thriller. The film that established his reputation in Ukraine was *Zvenyhora* (1927), an epic tale hailed by critics as the founding work of the Ukrainian national cinema. *Arsenal* (1929), Dovzhenko's most complex film, remains one of the strongest pacifist statements in the history of the cinema. *Zemlia* (Earth, 1930), whose subject was the transition to **collectivized agriculture**, became Dovzhenko's best-known work and cemented his international reputation as a "poet of the cinema." His last film in Ukraine was *Ivan* (1932), the first Ukrainian-language motion picture with sound.

Outside Ukraine, Dovzhenko was allowed to make only three feature films, *Aerograd* (1935), ***Shchors*** (1939), and *Michurin* (1948), which hardly matched his earlier efforts. During **World War II**, he completed the documentary films *Bytva za nashu Radians'ku Ukraïnu* (The Battle for Our Soviet Ukraine, 1943) and *Peremoha na Pravoberezhnii Ukraïni* (Victory in Right-Bank Ukraine, 1945). Dovzhenko's films were severely criticized in the Soviet Union for their "nationalist deviations" but received wide recognition and praise abroad, especially in Western Europe.

Forbidden to make films, Dovzhenko turned to **literature**. He wrote short stories, including "Maty" (Mother), "Pered boiem" (Before the Battle); the plays *Zhyttia v tsvitu* (Life in Bloom) and *Potomky zaporozhtsiv* (Descendants of the Zaporozhians); and the "cinenovels" *Zacharovana Desna* (The Enchanted Desna, 1954) and *Poema pro more* (Poem about the Sea, 1956).

DRACH, IVAN (b. 17 October 1936). Poet, translator, and civic activist. He was born in Telizhyntsi (**Kyiv** oblast) and studied at the faculty of philology at Kyiv University (1959–63). In 1964, he completed advanced scriptwriting courses in Moscow. He worked on the editorial boards of the newspaper *Literaturna Ukraïna* (Literary Ukraine) and the journal *Vitchyzna* (Fatherland), as well as for the script department of the **Dovzhenko** Film Studio in Kyiv. In the 1960s, Drach became a prominent poet and leading figure among the *shistdesiatnyky*. Widely regarded as a spokesman for Ukrainian culture, he became a founder of **Rukh** and was elected president at its founding and second congresses (1989, 1990) and copresident at its third congress (1992). In March 1990, he was elected to the **Verkhovna Rada**. Drach is head of the Council of the Society for Ties with Ukrainians outside Ukraine (since 1991) and chairman of the presidium of the Congress of the Ukrainian Intelligentsia (since 1995). His collections of poetry include *Soniashnyky* (The Sunflowers, 1962), *Protuberantsi sertsia* (Protuberances of the Heart, 1965), *Balady budniv* (Everyday Ballads, 1967), *Do dzherel* (To the Sources, 1972), *Soniachnyi feniks* (The Solar Phoenix, 1978), *Amerykans'kyi zoshyt* (American Notebook, 1980), *Kyïvs'kyi oberih* (The Kyiv Talisman, 1983), *Khram sontsia* (Temple of the Sun, 1988), and *Vohon' iz popelu* (Fire from Ashes, 1995). His screenplays made into **films** include *Krynytsia dlia sprahlykh* (A Well for the Thirsty, 1967), *Propala hramota* (The Lost Charter, 1971), and *Kaminnyi khrest* (The Stone Cross, 1968). Drach was awarded the **Shevchenko** State Prize in 1976. *See also* LITERATURE.

DRAHOMANOV, MYKHAILO (6 [18] September 1841–8 [20] June 1895). Civic leader, historian, folklorist, publicist, and political thinker. Drahomanov was born in Hadiach, **Poltava** region, into an impoverished gentry family of **Cossack** descent. He was educated at the Hadiach county school and the Poltava gymnasium. When he defended a friend who had been unjustly treated, he was expelled during his final year and denied the right to enter any other educational institution. However, thanks to the intervention of the curator of the **Kyiv** school district, Drahomanov was allowed to take the gymnasium examinations extramurally. In 1859, he was admitted to the faculty of history and philology of Kyiv University, from which he graduated in 1863. In 1870, he successfully defended his dissertation on "The Question of the Historical Significance of the Roman Empire and Tacitus." He spent the next four years studying in central Europe and visited **Galicia** on two occasions. In 1873, he became a lecturer in ancient history at Kyiv University. At the same time, Drahomanov was a member of the Kyiv **Hromada** and of the **Southwestern Branch of the Imperial Russian Geographic Society**.

In 1875, Drahomanov was accused of advocating Ukraine's secession from the Russian Empire, and by decision of Alexander II (*see* EMS UKASE) he was dismissed from the university. In order to prevent Drahomanov's arrest, the Kyiv Hromada sent him abroad to propagate the Ukrainian cause. In 1876, Drahomanov and his supporters, including Antin Liakhotsky, Serhii Podolynsky, **Fedir Vovk**, and later **Mykhailo Pavlyk**, established a publishing house in Geneva and began to issue the journal *Hromada* (five issues, 1878–82). It was the first modern Ukrainian political periodical and coincided with the emergence of the first Ukrainian group of a socialist orientation, led by Drahomanov. In 1886, he broke with the Kyiv Hromada, which was displeased with his socialist views and feared that continuing political activity might provoke increased repression of the Ukrainian movement. To support himself, Drahomanov accepted a position at the newly established Sofia University (Bulgaria), becoming professor of history in 1889. He died in 1895 and was buried in Sofia.

Drahomanov was the leading Ukrainian political thinker of the late 19th century and the one who most strongly insisted that the Ukrainian movement had to expand its concerns beyond **language** and culture. His syncretic social, political, and philosophical views were formed under the influence of the **Cyril and Methodius Brotherhood**, **Taras Shevchenko**, Pierre-Joseph Proudhon, English liberal thinkers, and others. His ideal society was a voluntary association to be achieved through federalism and local self-government. Switzerland, the United States, and Great Britain were contemporary approximations of the society to which he aspired. Drahomanov maintained the priority of individual freedom over economic, social, and class interests, as well as the primacy of international and universal cultural values over national particularism. He advocated the separation of church and state and the secularization of civic and cultural life. His socialism grew out of his opposition to tyranny and injustice; he rejected Marxism and materialism.

For all his hostility to collectivism, Drahomanov had a positive attitude toward nationality and promoted the movement for

Ukraine's national and cultural emancipation. He favored a federal restructuring of the Russian Empire, for which he drafted a proposal in *Vol'nyi soiuz/Vil'na spilka* (Free Union, 1884). Drahomanov did not call for Ukrainian national statehood, both because of his predisposition to federalism and because he considered independence an unrealistic political goal. He favored the consolidation and union of the progressive forces of Eastern Europe but cautioned against their complete organizational coalescence.

Drahomanov's political program had a pan-Ukrainian character, embracing all Ukrainian ethnic territory from **Transcarpathia** to the Kuban. He promoted cooperation among Ukrainian activists across contemporary state borders, maintaining that Galicia should be their organizational center, given the favorable conditions created by Austrian constitutionalism. Nevertheless, Drahomanov was a severe critic of Galician provincialism and clericalism.

Drahomanov devoted considerable attention to contemporary Russian, Polish, and Balkan politics. He criticized Polish "historical" patriotism, whose adherents advocated the renewal of the Polish state within the prepartition borders of 1772, as well as the centralizing policies of the Russian Empire. He studied the problem of national minorities in Ukraine, advocating national and cultural autonomy for them (*see* JEWS).

Drahomanov's major political works are "Perednie slovo do 'Hromady'" (Introduction to *Hromada*, 1878), "Propashchyi chas—ukraïntsi pid Moskovs'kym tsarstvom, 1654–1876" (The Lost Epoch: Ukrainians under the Muscovite Tsardom, 1654–1876, written ca. 1878, pub. 1909), "Shevchenko, ukraïnofily i sotsiializm" (Shevchenko, the **Ukrainophiles**, and Socialism, 1879), *Istoricheskaia Pol'sha i velikorusskaia demokratiia* (Historical Poland and Great Russian Democracy, 1881–82), *Liberalizm i zemstvo v Rossii* (Liberalism and the Zemstvo in Russia, 1889), *Chudats'ki dumky pro ukraïns'ku natsional'nu spravu* (Eccentric Thoughts on the Ukrainian National Cause, 1891), and *Lysty na Naddniprians'ku Ukraïnu* (Letters to Dnipro Ukraine, 1893).

Drahomanov also made notable contributions to Ukrainian ethnography and folklore: *Istoricheskie pesni malorusskogo naroda* (Historical Songs of the Little Russian People; 2 vols., 1874–75, with **Volodymyr Antonovych**), *Malorusskie narodnye predaniia i rasskazy* (Little Russian Folk Legends and Tales, 1876), *Novi ukraïns'ki pisni pro hromads'ki spravy* (Recent Ukrainian Songs on Social Topics, 1881), and *Politychni pisni ukraïns'koho narodu XVIII-XIX st.* (Political Songs of the Ukrainian People, 18th and 19th Centuries, 2 vols., 1883–85).

In Galicia, Drahomanov's impact was particularly strong among representatives of the **Ukrainian Radical** and **National Democratic** parties. He also influenced individual activists in **eastern Ukraine**, where "Drahomanov circles" were established. His emphasis on federalism and cultural autonomy for minorities was reflected in the program of the **Ukrainian Party of Socialist Federalists** and the policies of the **Ukrainian Central Rada**.

DZIUBA, IVAN (b. 26 July 1931). Critic, literary scholar, and political dissident. He was born in Mykolaivka, Donetsk oblast. After graduating from the Donetsk Pedagogical Institute (1953), Dziuba studied at the Institute of **Literature** in **Kyiv** and worked on the editorial boards of journals, newspapers, and publishing houses. He headed the literary-criticism section of the journal *Vitchyzna* (Fatherland, 1957–62) but was dismissed for "ideological errors." Dziuba was a leader of the *shistdesiatnyky* and became active in the **dissident movement** in the mid-1960s. On 4 September 1965, he protested the arrests of dissidents at a demonstration in the Ukraina film theater in Kyiv, for which he was dismissed from his position. On 29 September 1966, at a commemoration of the mass execution of **Jews** by the Nazis in Babyn Yar, Dziuba made a speech denouncing official anti-Semitism and calling for mutual respect between Ukrainians and Jews.

Dziuba's major accomplishment in this period was the writing of *Internatsionalizm chy rusyfikatsiia?* (Internationalism or Russification?, 1965). This indictment of the **Russification** of Ukrainian culture and public life, addressed to the leaders of the **Communist Party of Ukraine** (CPU), became well known as a fundamental document of Ukrainian political dissent. The book was published abroad in Ukrainian (1968) and translated into English (1968), Italian (1970), Chinese (1972), and French (1980). Dziuba worked as a proofreader of a biochemical journal (1966–69) and an editor at the Dnipro publishing house (1969–72). In 1969, to avoid expulsion from the Writers' Union, he issued a statement dissociating himself from Ukrainian nationalism and from those who had published his book in the West. For this "betrayal," he was severely criticized in an essay by the dissident **Valentyn Moroz**. Official harassment of Dziuba began in January 1972 as part of the wave of repression associated with the dismissal of **Petro Shelest** as CPU first secretary. Dziuba was arrested and expelled from the Writers' Union in April 1972 and sentenced in May 1973 to a five-year term for "anti-Soviet activity." He was subjected to intense pressure to disavow his political views and was released in November 1973 after signing a recantation that was published in the Soviet press. In

1978, he published *Hrani krystala* (Facets of a Crystal), a repudiation of *Internationalism or Russification?* Denied work in his profession, Dziuba supported himself as a correspondent for the newspaper of the Kyiv airplane factory.

Volodymyr Shcherbytsky's efforts to improve official relations with the intelligentsia made possible Dziuba's reinstatement in the Writers' Union (1980), and in 1982 he returned to literary criticism and writing about cultural issues. In the 1980s, he reemerged as an authoritative spokesman for Ukrainian culture and was involved in the formation of **Rukh**. In November 1992, Dziuba became an academician of the **Ukrainian Academy of Sciences**. He was president of the National Association of Ukrainian Studies (1989–91) and minister of culture (1992–94). Since 1991, Dziuba has served as editor in chief and coeditor of the journal *Suchasnist'*. His books include *Zvychaina liudyna chy mishchanyn?* (An Ordinary Human Being or a Philistine?, 1959), *Na pul'si doby* (On the Pulse of the Age, 1981), *Avtohrafy vidrodzhennia* (Autographs of Rebirth, 1986), *Sadriddin Aini* (1987), *U kozhnoho svoia dolia* (To Each His Own Fate, 1989), *Zastukaly serdeshnu voliu* (They Stole upon a Wretched Freedom, 1995), and *Mizh kul'turoiu i politykoiu* (Between Culture and Politics, 1998). He was awarded the Shevchenko State Prize in 1991.

E

EASTERN GALICIA. Semiofficial designation of Ukrainian lands within the Austrian Empire between 1772 and 1918. They constituted the eastern portion of what the Austrians termed the Kingdom of Galicia and Lodomeria, which essentially corresponded to historical **Galicia**, with the exception of a portion of the northern **Kholm region** that was incorporated into the Russian Empire. Western Galicia was the name applied by the Austrians to mainly Polish territory (west of the San and Wisłok Rivers) that never belonged to the Galician principality. The use of these terms was intended to legitimize the Habsburgs' territorial annexations. After the fall of the Habsburg Monarchy (1918) and the short-lived independence of the **Western Ukrainian People's Republic**, the term "Eastern Galicia" continued to be widely used during the interwar period with reference to Galicia, which was incorporated into the Second Polish Republic in 1923. The official Polish designation for Galicia was "Małopolska Wschodnia" (Eastern Little Poland).

EASTERN UKRAINE (Ukr. *Skhidna Ukraïna*). Conventional designation for Ukrainian ethnic territory drained by the Dnipro River (hence also known as *Naddniprianshchyna* or Dnipro Ukraine) that was part of the Russian Empire and subsequently of the **Ukrainian People's Republic** (excluding the Western Province of the UNR). This territory constituted the **Ukrainian SSR** until 1939, when **western Ukraine** was annexed to it.

ECONOMY. Proximity to the Black Sea, fertile soil, moderate **climate**, a diverse mineral base, and a well-developed **transportation** network made Ukraine an economic powerhouse of the Soviet Union. Although only 16 percent of Soviet investment funds were spent in Ukraine (1980s), one-fifth of the income of the **USSR** came from the republic. The strength of the Ukrainian economy was in **agriculture** and industry; close to 40 percent of Soviet advanced technology was located in Ukraine.

Independent Ukraine inherited an inefficient and inflexible planned economy. Independent-minded managerial culture was absent, and the economy relied on an administrative bureaucracy traditionally dependent on decision-making in Moscow. Moreover, Ukraine's economic structure was ill-suited to the free market. Soviet priorities lay with heavy industry, followed by light industry, with consumer goods coming last. Consequently, Ukraine entered a period of steep economic decline in 1993. Deteriorating standards of living, hyperinflation, sharp price increases for food and accommodations, and rising unemployment took their toll on the population. The slow progress of market reforms and outdated legislation drove commerce underground, and the barter economy thrived. More than half the population was growing its own food.

Despite these setbacks, the Ukrainian economy has a modern structure, with the major exception of its large agricultural sector. According to World Bank estimates (2002), agriculture employs 24 percent of the labor force and produces 16.9 percent of gross domestic product (GDP); industry contributes 39.3 percent of GDP, employing 32 percent of the labor force, while 43.8 percent of GDP is generated in services, where 44 percent of the labor force is employed.

Prior to 1991, Ukraine's agriculture contributed about 25 percent of GDP, but its share has been reduced considerably in the ensuing decade. While the country has one of the most fertile soils in the world, agriculture remains hamstrung by acute structural problems, including the slow dismantling of large, inefficient collective farms, administrative stalling on land **privatization**, and the lack of an infrastructure to support individual farmers.

The strength of Ukrainian industry lies in metal processing, machine building, and the chemical and petrochemical sectors. The country's **metallurgical** sector is one of the world's largest, accounting for nearly a quarter of Ukraine's industrial output. Rich natural and mineral resources contribute to a well-developed **mining** sector. Ukraine's **manufacturing** is devoted mainly to producer goods: machine-building, metal-working, transport and power-generating equipment, and the aerospace industry are its most advanced sectors. Ukraine's **energy** needs are satisfied mainly by imports of natural gas and oil, as well as by domestic coal mining. The transportation network is also well developed. Ukraine's system of pipelines for the transit of gas and oil to Central Europe is an important source of revenue.

The Ukrainian labor force of about 22 million is relatively well trained. The Soviet-era **education** system was geared toward science and technology to support the USSR's industrial complex; hence Ukraine has an abundance of scientists, engineers, and skilled workers, but lacks qualified managerial cadres. Although the official unemployment rate is quite low (3.5 percent in 2003), there is a large number of unregistered or underemployed workers, pushing the unofficial unemployment rate to nearly 12 percent. **Population** shrinkage, the result of a low birth rate and high migration, has led to the contraction of the labor force at an annual rate of 0.4 percent (1993–2003).

The Ukrainian **banking** system consists of the National Bank of Ukraine, which is responsible for monetary policy, and a network of commercial banks. The introduction of Ukraine's own currency, the *hryvnia* (UAH), in September 1996 had a positive impact on the economy. The *hryvnia*, which was trading at 5.31 to the U.S. dollar in July 2004, has resisted inflation quite successfully. Following a brief period of hyperinflation (10,200 percent in 1993), inflation was held to about 8 percent per annum. Ukraine's external debt of 10.5 billion dollars is well serviced. Since 1992, Ukraine has been a member of the International Monetary Fund and the World Bank, as well as of the European Bank for Reconstruction and Development. The government is also working to meet conditions for Ukraine's admission to the World Trade Organization.

After nearly a decade of decline, Ukraine's economy began to show signs of recovery at the end of 1999. The year 2000 represented the first full year of positive GDP growth since independence. Growth was export-driven and reflected an increase of 13 percent in industrial output. A number of factors contributed to the failure of economic reform in Ukraine during the first eight years of independence. Its industry, like that of the USSR in general, was militarized or worked for the military complex; hence many enterprises failed to find new markets for their products or were unable to convert to the production of consumer goods. Although Ukraine remains one of the world's largest producers and exporters of arms, its share of the market cannot sustain the overcapacity of the industry. The lack of investment incentives and competition during the Soviet period led to the obsolescence of equipment in many sectors, making Ukrainian products less attractive to consumers. As a result, they fare badly on international markets. Furthermore, Ukraine's prolonged isolation from the West has left its industry bereft of the expertise and aggressiveness required to compete internationally. Finally, the state does not provide the economic support and incentives existing elsewhere, while the **privatization** process has been very slow and inefficient. *See also* CRAFTS; CURRENCY AND COINS; FORESTRY; SOCIAL WELFARE; TRADE.

EDUCATION. In **Kyivan Rus'**, education was closely associated with the acceptance of the Cyrillic script and Orthodox liturgy from Bulgaria and the adoption of **Christianity** via Byzantium. Initially limited to the clergy, education and literacy were extended to the princely courts and to the urban population, including **women**. West European influence on Ukrainian education is apparent in the Principality of **Galicia-Volhynia**, where Latin was used at the princely court.

After the fall of the Kyivan state, elementary education was widely accessible through parochial schools, while wealthier families employed private tutors. A significant number of Ukrainians sought higher education in Cracow and Prague. The 16th and 17th centuries saw the aggressive expansion of Protestant and Catholic, particularly Jesuit, schools into Ukraine, with Polish and Latin as the languages of instruction. In an attempt to counter their influence, Prince **Kostiantyn Ostrozky** established Orthodox schools that imitated the Protestant and Catholic models. The most prominent was the **Ostrih Academy** (est. ca. 1576), where students learned Church Slavonic, Greek, and Latin, in addition to theology and other subjects. **Brotherhood** schools, an important force in Orthodox education, were initially supported by Greek patriarchs and emphasized the teaching of Greek, but by the mid-17th century Latin and Polish became the main languages of instruction. The **Kyiv Epiphany Brotherhood** School (est. 1615) merged in 1632 with a school established at the **Kyivan Cave Monastery** by Metropolitan **Petro Mohyla** and developed into the **Kyiv Mohyla Academy**, which gained a high reputation in Eastern Europe. The brotherhoods also initiated the publication of Church Slavonic and Ukrainian grammars that were used as textbooks.

By the mid-17th century, elementary education in Ukraine offered through parishes was accessible to the general population.

Students acquired basic reading skills and learned prayers and hymns used in church services. Following the **Truce of Andrusovo** (1667), brotherhood schools in **Right-Bank Ukraine** went into decline. At the same time, leading scholars abandoned **Left-Bank Ukraine** for new opportunities in Muscovy. In the **Hetmanate**, Orthodox academies went through periods of decline and revival, but the network of parochial schools taught by local or itinerant tutors was well established.

After the decline of the Orthodox Church in Right-Bank Ukraine at the turn of the 18th century, the Uniate Church (*see* UKRAINIAN CATHOLIC CHURCH) assumed responsibility for education. Most schools were run by the **Basilian Order**, and students were taught Church Slavonic, Polish, and Latin, among other subjects.

Changes to the educational system were introduced after the annexation of Right-Bank Ukraine by Russia in 1793–95. Polish-language schools continued to operate until the Polish revolt of 1830, when they were replaced by Russian schools. In 1804, four-year gymnasiums were opened in gubernial centers and placed under the jurisdiction of universities. **Kharkiv** University (est. 1805) and Kyiv University (est. 1834) became the first universities in Russian-ruled Ukraine. Other institutions of higher learning included lyceums, with the Nizhyn Lyceum (est. 1825) and the Richelieu Lyceum in **Odesa** (est. 1817) the most prestigious. The secondary educational system also included cadet schools, finishing institutes for daughters of the nobility, and boarding schools.

Zemstvo schools, organized by bodies of local self-government, began as elementary schools and developed into secondary and vocational institutions. They were established after the tsarist agrarian reforms of 1864 and existed until 1917. In Ukraine there were 3,117 zemstvo schools in 1898 and nearly 4,700 on the eve of **World War I**. An important role was played by **Sunday schools**, which provided tuition-free general and vocational education. Higher technical schools, such as polytechnical and veterinary institutes, began to appear in Ukraine in the 1870s, and by 1915 there were 19 such schools. In general terms, the level of education declined under Russian rule; the high level of literacy prevailing in Ukraine in 1654 fell to 26 percent in 1897.

In **Galicia**, Austrian annexation in 1772 brought a temporary halt to the Polonization of the curriculum. Three types of state-run schools were introduced: the six-grade normal, the four-grade major, and trivium schools. German was the language of instruction in the first two types, while Polish and Ruthenian were used in the trivium schools, which were open to everyone. Education became compulsory and universal in 1781. A seminary for Uniate priests was founded in Vienna in 1774, and the Greek Catholic Theological Seminary opened in **Lviv** in 1783. Lviv University, with Latin as its language of instruction, opened its doors in 1784. After a period of decline, the school system was revived in 1818 and entrusted to the Ukrainian Catholic clergy, with Ruthenian as the language of instruction. In 1843, there were 2,130 schools in eastern (i.e., Ukrainian) Galicia; of these, 921 were Ukrainian, 190 Polish, 81 German, and 938 mixed.

In 1867, control over Galician affairs was effectively transferred to the Poles. Consequently, the Ukrainian language could be used for instruction only in the lower grades. Six years of schooling became compulsory for all children, but most villages could afford only one- and two-grade schools. Although 97 percent of Ukrainian children attended Ukrainian-language schools in Galicia on the eve of World War I, educational opportunities were limited by economic circumstances, and 30 percent of the population over the age of nine was illiterate. A highly influential self-educational association, the **Prosvita Society**, was founded in 1868.

During the **Ukrainian Revolution** (1917–21), various Ukrainian and foreign regimes assumed responsibility for education. Despite political instability, a limited number of Ukrainian schools were open, and institutions of higher learning were established. With the consolidation of Soviet power, religious instruction was banned in 1919 and a new system of education introduced in the **Ukrainian SSR**. In order to transform Ukraine from an agrarian into an industrial society, emphasis was placed on technical education and political indoctrination at the expense of the social sciences and humanities. Access to education was improved, however, and it was easier for Ukrainians to obtain higher education.

The **Ukrainization** of the schools in the 1920s proceeded more quickly in the countryside than in the cities. Some 81.9 percent of rural schools and 43.8 percent of urban schools became Ukrainian-speaking in 1925–26. By 1933, enrollment in Soviet Ukrainian schools had increased to 88.5 percent of the total population of student age. A four-grade school was compulsory for all children in 1925, and a seven-grade education became compulsory (for city children only) in 1930. The school system underwent frequent changes designed to strengthen political control: for example, two-year workers' faculties were introduced to train politically reliable cadres, and many vocational schools were placed under the jurisdiction of various branches of industry.

A new Union-wide school system was introduced in 1936. It included four-year primary schools, "incomplete" seven-year schools, and complete 10-grade secondary schools. In 1938, the Russian language became a compulsory subject of study at all levels. Two years later, Ukrainian was used to teach some subjects in only 44 percent of institutions of higher learning (*see* RUSSIFICATION). At the same time, military training became part of the school curriculum.

In the Polish-ruled Ukrainian territories between the wars, an Austrian school system was maintained until 1921, when it was replaced by a unified system for the whole Polish Republic. Six-grade education became compulsory. Legislation introduced in 1924 unified Polish and Ukrainian schools into bilingual institutions in which the language of instruction was to be determined by referendum. The law and its numerous abuses helped promote Polonization. As a result, by 1939 the number of Ukrainian schools declined from 2,420 to 352 in Galicia and from 443 to eight in **Volhynia**. All Ukrainian teachers' colleges were closed down.

The Soviet annexation of **western Ukraine** in 1939 was followed by the introduction of the Soviet school system. During **World War II**, there were various forms of Ukrainian schooling under the German occupation. After the war, the educational system was geared toward the elimination of labor shortages. Correspondence and night schools became the main focus of the system; at its lowest point, in 1965–66, the proportion of day students fell to 38.7 percent. The emphasis was on training in industrial occupations, engineering, and the military, with comparatively small numbers of students enrolled in the social sciences and humanities.

The educational system has undergone reforms as a result of Ukrainian independence. A 12-year system of secondary education is being implemented. Ukraine's higher educational system consists of 938 institutions: 327 technical vocational schools, 216 vocational schools, 117 colleges, 149 institutes, two conservatories, 48 academies, and 81 universities. Most of these are run by the state (806), with the remainder privately owned but state-regulated. A total of 1.7 million students attend postsecondary institutions (1998–99). The curriculum of the most successful contemporary institutions, such as the Kyiv Mohyla Academy National University, is designed to reflect the values of Western liberal arts education. *See also* LVIV (UNDERGROUND) UKRAINIAN UNIVERSITY; RIDNA SHKOLA SOCIETY; UKRAINIAN FREE UNIVERSITY.

EMS UKASE. Decree of the tsarist government intended to suppress Ukrainian publications, signed by Tsar Alexander II on 18 (30) May 1876 in Ems, Germany. It supplemented the provisions of the **Valuev circular** (1863). The decree was issued in response to a memorandum sent to the tsar by the deputy curator of the **Kyiv** school district, Mikhail Yuzefovich, in which he accused Ukrainians of desiring "a free Ukraine in the form of a republic, led by a **hetman**." Accordingly, the decree became popularly known as the "Yuzefovich ukase." It forbade the import of Ukrainian books into the Russian Empire (notably from **Galicia**) and the publication of original works, translations from foreign languages, and musical texts in Ukrainian. It also banned Ukrainian theatrical performances and public readings. Local administrations were ordered to prevent Ukrainian-**language** instruction in primary schools and remove Ukrainian books from school libraries. **Ukrainophile** teachers were to be transferred to Russia. On the basis of the Ems Ukase, the **Southwestern Branch of the Imperial Russian Geographic Society**, the newspaper *Kievskii telegraf*, and the **hromadas** were closed. Furthermore, **Mykhailo Drahomanov** and **Pavlo Chubynsky** were exiled as "incorrigible agitators." In 1878, at the Paris International Literary Congress, Drahomanov condemned the ukase, publishing the brochure *La littérature oukrainienne, proscrite par le gouvernement russe* (Geneva, 1878). The provisions of the ukase remained in effect until the **Revolution of 1905**.

ENERGY. The Ukrainian economy is heavily dependent on oil and gas supplies from the Russian Federation and natural gas from Turkmenistan to meet its energy requirements. Coal is the main fuel used in Ukraine (48 percent in 2001), followed by natural gas (41 percent) and oil (11 percent).

Petroleum deposits are concentrated in the Carpathian, Dnipro-Donets, and Crimean-Caucasus region. Although oil drilling in **Galicia** began in the early 17th century, its industrial development followed the discovery of a distilling process and the invention of the naphtha lamp in the mid-19th century. The Drohobych-Boryslav region became the main production center, including an oil refinery. At its peak in 1909, Galicia produced 5 percent of world oil output. The exploitation of oil fields in central and eastern Ukraine began in the 1950s. The industry's output grew steadily until it peaked in the early 1970s and then began to decline as a result of the depletion of resources and a decrease in new exploration. Pipelines linked Ukraine with oil-producing regions of the **USSR** (*see* TRANSPORT). Today, Ukraine has proven oil reserves of 395 million barrels, located mainly in the Dnipro-Donets basin. The country's production further declined in the 1990s from 95,000 barrels per day (bbl/d) in 1992 to 86,500 bbl/d in 2001. During the same period, the consumption of oil fell even more rapidly, from 813,000 bbl/d to 341,000 bbl/d. To satisfy its needs, Ukraine imports close to 70 percent of its oil, mainly from Russia. Six oil refineries operate in Ukraine, with a total capacity of just under 1.1 million bbl/d of crude-oil refining. In 2003, they were operating at 41.4 percent of capacity.

The commercial extraction and processing of natural gas in Ukraine began in 1924 in the Dashava gas field in the **Lviv** region. Following the Soviet takeover, the operation was expanded, and a pipeline linked Dashava with **Kyiv** (1948) and Moscow (1951). Gas exploration in central and eastern Ukraine began only after **World War II**. The Shebelynka gas field in **Kharkiv** oblast was one of the largest in Europe, accounting for 30 percent of Soviet output by the late 1960s. In 1975, Ukraine's gas output peaked at 69 billion cu m, or 45 percent of total Soviet output. Rising production costs and the development of gas fields in other parts of the USSR resulted in production decline. In 1988, Ukraine produced 32.4 billion cu m of gas, and by 2003 only 19.5 billion cu m. Natural gas consumption also fell from 109.6 billion cu m in 1993 to 76.4 billion cu m in 2003. Domestic production thus satisfies only about 25.5 percent of the country's demand (in 2003, 57 percent of gas imports came from Turkmenistan and 43 percent from Russia). Gas reserves in Ukraine are estimated at 1.12 trillion cu m (2002).

The Ukrainian coal industry (extraction, enrichment, and bricketing of anthracite and lignite coal) is located mainly in the **Donets Basin**, while the Lviv-**Volhynia** Coal Basin and the Dnipro Lignite Coal Basin produce only 13 percent of Ukraine's coal. The Donets Anthracite Coal Basin was discovered in the first half of the 18th century, but its large-scale commercial exploitation began only in 1876. Accelerated growth started in 1900, when the metallurgical and coke industries developed in southern Ukraine. By 1913, the basin produced 87 percent of the total coal output of the Russian Empire. Before the 1917 revolution, the industry was managed and financed by Russian and West European industrial concerns. Coal production grew steadily in spite of setbacks caused by two world wars and the revolution. From 28.7 million tons in 1916, Ukraine's production of coal reached its peak in 1976, when 218.2 million tons were extracted. Soviet dependence on Ukrainian coal diminished at that time, as new coal basins outside Ukraine went into production. By 1977, Ukraine's share of USSR coal production was only 21.9 percent. The extraction of Ukrainian coal also became very expensive, because new seams were sought at greater depths (70 percent of industrial-quality coal lies at depths of 800 to 1,000 meters). The industry underwent intensive modernization between the 1960s and 1980s, when modern extraction machinery and technology were introduced. At the same time, the number of mines and miners was reduced.

Coal production in independent Ukraine decreased because of economic contraction and the collapse of domestic demand. In 1991, Ukraine produced 146 million tons of coal, and in 2003 only 79.3 million tons. The industry is still plagued by high inefficiency and low productivity. Moreover, it accumulated huge debts because of consumer nonpayments. Labor strikes over unpaid wages and unsafe working conditions are common. Ukrainian coal mines are among the most dangerous in the world; there are close to 300 **mining** fatalities every year. Coal reserves in Ukraine exceed 34 billion tonnes, which is a sufficient amount for 20 more years of commercial production.

The production of electricity in Ukraine began in the last decade of the 19th century. The first electric-power stations opened in Kyiv (1890) and Lviv (1900). In 1913, Ukrainian electric-power stations had a capacity of 304 megawatts (MW) and produced 543 million kilowatt-hours (kWh) of electricity annually. Generating capacity expanded in the Soviet period, especially during the industrialization drive of the 1930s. Thermoelectric stations formed the backbone of Ukrainian power generation, and in 1932 the Dnipro Hydroelectric Station, the largest in Europe at the time, was constructed. The total capacity of electric power stations in the **Ukrainian SSR** grew from 295 MW in 1926 to 2,051 MW in 1937, and production increased from 900 million kWh to 9.5 billion kWh. Power stations in **western Ukraine** under Poland produced 147 million kWh in 1937. After World War II, the industry underwent further expansion; new thermoelectric power stations were built and existing ones enlarged. The construction of six hydroelectric stations along the Dnipro River formed the Dnipro Cascade of Hydroelectric Stations and added to overall power capacity. In 1977, Ukraine's first nuclear power station was completed in Chornobyl, and several others went into production in the following decade. In 1982, Ukraine had a total generating capacity of 47,286 MW and produced 238.3 billion kWh.

Today, thermoelectric and nuclear power stations each produce about 45 percent of electric power in Ukraine, with the balance generated by hydroelectric and experimental power stations. In 2003, Ukraine had a generating capacity of 52,600 MW and produced 179.6 billion kWh of electricity. At the same time, the consumption of power amounted to 174.7 billion kWh. However, the country is not a major power exporter, for much power is lost in an inefficient transmission and distribution network. Of all Ukraine's energy industries, the transition to a market economy is most advanced in the electric power sector. The **privatization** of generation and distribution companies began in 1997 and was amplified in 1999 by new regulations.

Industrial development at the expense of **environmental** protection in the Soviet Union has had devastating consequences for Ukraine. The **Chornobyl nuclear disaster** of 1986 focused global attention on the scale of environmental neglect. In addition to the effects of radiation, Ukraine faces dangerous levels of air (carbon emissions) and water pollution.

ENVIRONMENT. Ukraine consists almost entirely of steppe, along with a belt of highlands in **Podilia** and a short section of the Carpathian Mountains in the west, and the **Crimean** Mountains in the south. It is **forested** in the west and northwest.

Soviet policies of rapid industrialization and forced **collectivization** of **agriculture** in the late 1920s and 1930s did serious damage to one of the world's most fertile regions, the "black-earth" belt of humus-rich soil in the Dnipro River basin. The construction of the Dnipro hydroelectric station in 1932, with a dam 800 meters in length, flooded hundreds of villages. As part of the Soviet plan of total electrification, six reservoirs were created along the Dnipro, flooding 709,900 ha of fertile land and ecological heritage areas. The rapid development of the coal and steel industry in eastern Ukraine (*see* ENERGY; MINING), especially in the **Donets Basin**, created one of the most polluted areas in the world. Industrial runoff into the Dnipro has contributed to the pollution and degeneration of the Black Sea.

After **World War II**, the government sought to prevent environmental degradation by creating a network of reserve lands that now consists of 15 nature and four biosphere reserves, eight national parks, 228 sanctuaries, 132 nature heritage areas, 17 botanical gardens, seven zoological parks, 19 dendrological parks, 88 national landscape parks, and smaller regional and local protected areas.

On 26 April 1986, northern Ukraine was the scene of the **Chornobyl nuclear disaster**, the world's worst accident in the history of atomic energy generation. Radiation spread over a wide area, and the long-term consequences are yet to be determined.

When Ukraine gained its independence, the depth of the environmental crisis, long concealed by Soviet officials and media, became apparent. In 1992, the government appropriated funds for environmental protection. The **Verkhovna Rada** adopted the Land (1992), Forest (1994), Mineral Resources (1994), and Water (1995) Codes, as well as laws "On Environmental Protection" (1991), "On Reserve Lands" (1992), "On Wildlife" (1993), "On Environmental Testing" (1995), "On the Utilization of Nuclear Power and Nuclear Safety" (1995), "On Handling Radioactive Waste" (1995), "On

Waste" (1998), and "On Flora" (1999). The **Constitution** proclaims the state's responsibility to ensure ecological safety and maintain ecological balance (art. 16), confirms the right of free and unrestricted access to information on environmental issues (art. 50), and makes all citizens responsible for preserving the environment and providing compensation for any harm caused by their actions (art. 66).

In March 1998, official policy on the environment was formulated in a document titled "Main Aspects of National Policy on Environmental Protection, Use of Natural Resources, and Guarantees of Environmental Safety." The long-term strategy includes measures against nuclear radiation; amelioration of the Dnipro River basin, city environments in the Donets-Dnipro region, and the quality of drinking water; construction of new municipal sewage-treatment works; measures to alleviate the pollution of the Black and Azov Seas; progress toward the balanced use of natural resources; and protection of biological and landscape diversity.

An environmental issue that arose in 2004 resulted from the dredging of the Danube–Black Sea ship canal in the Danube delta, which killed thousands of unhatched terns and threatens more than 233 bird species. Protests were lodged by Ukrainian conservationists and the Romanian government.

ETERNAL PEACE OF 1686. Peace treaty between the **Polish-Lithuanian Commonwealth** and Muscovy signed on 6 (16) May 1686 in Moscow. The text, consisting of a preamble and 33 points, was based on the **Truce of Andrusovo** (1667). The Commonwealth recognized Muscovy's control over **Left-Bank Ukraine, Kyiv**, the **Zaporozhian Sich**, and the Chernihiv-Siverian land, including the towns of Chernihiv and Starodub. Poland received compensation of 146,000 rubles for relinquishing its claims to Kyiv. The Bratslav and southern Kyiv regions were designated an unpopulated neutral zone. The northern Kyiv region, **Volhynia**, and **Galicia** became part of Poland. **Podilia** remained under Ottoman control (but was annexed to Poland in 1699). Muscovy annulled its previous treaties with the Ottoman Empire and the **Crimean** Khanate, joining the anti-Ottoman Holy League (Poland, the Holy Roman Empire, and Venice) and obliging itself to make war on the Crimean Khanate (such campaigns took place in 1687 and 1689). Although the terms of the Eternal Peace came into force immediately, the Polish Diet did not ratify it until 1710. The treaty confirmed the division of Ukrainian lands between Poland and Muscovy, which remained in effect until the late 18th-century partitions of Poland.

F

FAMINE OF 1921–23. Famine in the southern gubernias of Ukraine, the Volga region, and the North Caucasus that the Soviet authorities attributed exclusively to the drought of 1921. The severity of the famine was greatly increased by state-imposed grain requisitions, which led **peasants** in areas unaffected by the drought to sow much less grain than in previous years. The Soviet government decided to prevent a famine in its power base, central Russia, by taking as much grain as possible from Ukraine. On 6 August 1921, Lenin informed the Ukrainian **agriculture** commissar, Miron Vladimirov, that troops would be used to requisition grain; instructions were also given to take hostages who would be executed if grain quotas were not met.

Offers of assistance to the hungry from the Norwegian philanthropist Fridtjof Nansen and from the American Relief Administration (ARA), led by Herbert Hoover, were initially rebuffed, as the Soviet government did not wish to be beholden to the "international bourgeoisie." Nevertheless, the ARA was admitted to Russia on 20 August, while the famine in Ukraine was officially covered up. Not until 16 January 1922, after countless protests from local Ukrainian authorities had been received and the famine discussed at the sixth conference of the **Communist Party of Ukraine**, was the Ukrainian agriculture commissariat allowed to request foreign assistance, which was provided by the ARA and the Nansen mission (active in Ukraine from March 1922 to June 1923). In 1922, Moscow took a further 10 million tonnes of Ukrainian grain for export in order to obtain foreign currency, falsely claiming that the harvest of 1922 had sufficed to overcome the famine. No official statistics were kept, but, according to various estimates, the famine took between 1.5 and 2 million lives in Ukraine.

The famine also played a role in the Soviet authorities' struggle with the Ukrainian **insurgent movement**. More peasant military leaders gave themselves up in the latter half of 1921 than ever before, and **Nestor Makhno**, finding no support in the famine-stricken Don and Volga regions, was obliged to move west and ultimately to emigrate. The anti-insurgency campaign appears to have reinforced official determination to deprive the southern Ukrainian peasants of their grain supplies.

FAMINE OF 1932–33. Famine created by the Stalin regime to break peasant resistance to the **collectivization** of **agriculture**. Although the famine affected not only the **Ukrainian SSR** but also the North Caucasus, the Volga region, and Central Asia, it hardly touched central Russia (Stalin's power base), as the long Russian tradition of collective landholding greatly lowered resistance to Soviet-era collectivization.

Although some 70 percent of peasant households had been collectivized in the **Ukrainian SSR** by the end of 1932, Ukrainian **peasants** strongly resisted the exorbitant grain requisitions for the state that Stalin proclaimed the "first commandment" of collectivized agriculture. On almost all collective farms, peasants underreported the results of the harvest and concealed grain for their own use. Moreover, much of the grain appropriated by the state was lost because of poor transportation and storage facilities. There was a serious shortage of draft animals, many of which had been slaughtered in earlier resistance to collectivization, and many of the tractors produced to replace them were of such poor quality that they broke down almost immediately.

As a result of these factors, almost one-third of the grain harvested in 1931 was lost, leading to mass starvation in 44 counties of Ukraine. This stage of the famine did not end until the harvest of 1932. Stalin's reaction was to force the peasants to yield all the grain they could possibly produce in order to make them totally dependent on the state for their survival. On 7 August 1932, the Moscow authorities enacted a law drafted by Stalin himself that established the death penalty (or, under extenuating circumstances, 10 years' imprisonment) for theft of collective-farm property. It became popularly known as the "law on five ears of grain," as many peasants were shot for taking even a handful of grain to feed their starving families.

In July 1932, the Third Congress of the **Communist Party of Ukraine** (CPU) was attended by Stalin's personal emissaries, **Lazar Kaganovich** and Viacheslav Molotov, who demanded a grain-procurement quota of 356 million puds from Ukraine. Since the losses registered in 1931 amounted to 120–200 million puds (out of a total of 380 million), CPU officials objected that such a quota was unrealistic. Molotov insisted that the losses were due to "errors in deliveries" and demanded fulfillment of the quota. The harvest of 1932 yielded only 156 million puds. At the end of October, Stalin dispatched Molotov to head a special grain-procurement commission in Ukraine. It offered a token concession, lowering the official quota by 70 million puds, but proceeded to extract 105 million puds of grain between 1 November 1932 and 1 February 1933. This was done by gangs of party activists who searched peasant households and removed every scrap of food. Peasants were reduced to eating leaves, grass, bark, and animals; there were numerous instances of cannibalism. Armed guards were posted to prevent peasants from taking foodstocks destined for Russia or from crossing the Ukrainian border in search of food. Cities continued to be supplied with food, leading peasants to break the law that forbade them to leave their collectives. They would beg for food on city streets or leave their children in the cities, where there was at least a chance of obtaining food. Stalin forbade any mention of the famine, which was not registered even in minutes of CPU Politburo meetings.

In January 1933, Stalin dispatched **Pavel Postyshev** to Ukraine to take charge of the CPU. On 23 February, Postyshev quietly issued a decree authorizing the release of government grain stocks for seeding purposes in Ukraine and the North Caucasus. Previous pleas to this effect from the CPU had been ignored; the political point was that relief from the famine depended on the good will of Moscow. Postyshev also took special measures to feed children, who would supply the next generation of collective farmers, and families of Red Army soldiers. There were no such measures for the peasantry in general.

No general statistics of **population** loss resulting from the famine were kept. The USSR census results of 1937 were covered up on Stalin's orders; as they revealed a drastic population loss, those responsible for the census were shot. The **Kyiv** historian **Stanislav Kulchytsky**, a leading authority on the famine, estimates Ukraine's direct population losses at approx. 150,000 in 1932 and approx. 3–3.5 million in 1933. The figure rises to 5 million if the unborn are included. The demographer Arnold Perkovsky has estimated Ukraine's losses at 4 million. More Ukrainians perished outside Ukraine; in the North Caucasus, where Kaganovich headed the procurement committee, the heavily Ukrainian Kuban region suffered most, and total population losses exceeded 1 million.

The famine did not result in the complete subjugation of the peasantry, as fixed grain-procurement quotas were established from 1933 onward, with the surplus remaining in peasant hands. But collective farming remained in place and market relations were not restored, as they had been with the New Economic Policy, preventing the peasantry from becoming an independent economic force. Moreover, the traditional Ukrainian village was destroyed as a social unit, and the peasant resistance so strongly manifested in the **insurgent movement** during the **Ukrainian Revolution** of 1917–21 and the early 1920s was broken; from this point on, local party and government officials established firm control over rural Ukraine. Villages declined as younger peasants migrated to the cities and submitted to **Russification**. The **Ukrainization** movement of the 1920s, which depended on a steady influx of Ukrainian-speaking peasants to the cities, came to an end. The famine was accompanied by a broad campaign of **political terror**, carried out by Postyshev and his accomplices, against the entire Ukrainian elite; taken together, these measures seriously compromised the viability of Ukrainian nationhood. Consequently, the famine has recently been termed genocidal in intent; a declaration to that effect was adopted by the **Verkhovna Rada** in 2003, and statements using the word "genocide" were issued in the same year by the Canadian Senate (June) and the U.S. House of Representatives (October).

The famine of 1932–33 did not come to world attention until the 1980s. While the British and American governments were informed of it, they chose not to disturb their relations with the USSR. The *New York Times* reporter Walter Duranty, who was well aware of the famine, kept silent about it (he was awarded a Pulitzer Prize in 1932 for insightful writing on Soviet affairs). The Soviet authorities arranged propaganda tours for such prominent Western figures as George Bernard Shaw, Sidney and Beatrice Webb, and Edouard Herriot in order to demonstrate the absence of a famine and continued to deny it until the last years of the USSR, while émigré accounts were dismissed as nationalist fabrications. In 1986, Robert Conquest's scholarly study *The Harvest of Sorrow* and a film based upon it focused attention on the famine, as did a commission of the U.S. Congress that gathered survivor accounts and did research under the direction of the historian **James E. Mace** (1986–90). For Ukrainians, the famine ranks as a national tragedy without parallel. In 1998, President **Leonid Kuchma** declared the fourth Saturday in November an annual day of mourning, and a monument to famine victims was erected in Kyiv.

FAMINE OF 1946–47. Famine caused by relentless state grain requisitions during the drought of 1946 (southern Ukraine was also subject to drought in 1947). After **World War II**, the Stalin regime accumulated large grain reserves for a number of reasons: for use in the event of a new war with the Western powers, to feed its newly acquired East European satellites, and to sell on the world market in order to build up its military-industrial complex. In 1946, only 77.2 percent of Ukraine's prewar arable land was sown, and drought cut the yield by some 20 percent; the labor force was greatly reduced by the war (more than 80 percent of collective farm workers were **women**, child labor was used extensively, and more than a million collective farmers were unfit for labor); and state investment accounted for only 15 percent of collective farm capital. **Nikita Khrushchev**, head of the **Communist Party of Ukraine**, appealed to Stalin in the autumn of 1946 to reduce grain requisitions in Ukraine (340 million puds, increased to 362 million in the summer) in order to prevent a famine. Stalin accused Khrushchev of lying about Ukraine's production capacity and replaced him as first secretary of the CPU with **Lazar Kaganovich**, one of the organizers of the **famine of 1932–33**. Kaganovich, who held the post from March to December 1947, used personnel assigned by Moscow to collect all available grain so as to fulfill 101.3 percent of Ukraine's assigned quota (as he and Khrushchev reported to Stalin on 10 October 1947). Overall, grain deliveries in 1947 exceeded those of 1946 by 206.4 million puds, hence the state could easily have distributed sufficient grain to prevent the famine had it chosen to do so. Approximately 1.7 million tonnes of grain were exported from Ukraine in 1946 alone; part of it was sent to satellite countries as "international assistance." Thousands of tonnes rotted in Ukraine because of poor storage facilities.

The famine, which also extended to **Moldavia** and parts of central and southern Russia, began in early 1946, reaching its peak in the winter and spring of 1947. On 22 June 1946, many oblast party committees were allowed to increase requisition quotas by 50 percent and, from 17 August, by 100 percent. A total of 1,312 heads of collective farms (one in 16) were sentenced for "incompetence" and "wrecking." Raion committees submitted daily reports to oblast committees on grain deliveries. Not only did some 400,000 government agents scour peasant households for foodstuffs, but peasants were forced to pay extremely heavy taxes in kind, even on produce from their private plots, and to buy large quantities of government bonds (accounting for 30–40 percent of average peasant income) that would not be redeemed until the 1970s and 1980s. As of 1 October 1946, 3.6 million individuals were denied ration cards, yielding a 30 percent savings in grain distribution by the state. Between 1 and 20 July 1947 alone, 1,426 individuals were charged with the "theft" of small quantities of grain to feed their families (such cases accounted for 90 percent of all court proceedings in Ukraine in 1947). Sentences ranged from 5 to 10 years, while those who took 2–3 kg. of grain could be shot.

Western Ukraine, where **collectivization** was only beginning, became a haven for many thousands of famine refugees not only from eastern Ukraine but also from Belarus, Moldavia, and the Voronezh, Kursk, Orel, Tambov, and other oblasts of Russia. In the last third of June 1946 alone, the **Lviv** police arrested 97,633 individuals who reached the city by train. The **Ukrainian Insurgent Army** (UPA) called for resistance to collectivization and grain deliveries to the state, as well as for assistance to hungry refugees. In 1947, official statistics recorded 906 confrontations between UPA units and Soviet officials requisitioning grain in eight oblasts of

Ukraine. There was also sporadic resistance in eastern Ukraine, where several heads of collective farms and village soviets were killed, and scores of leaflets calling for a boycott on grain deliveries were distributed.

Not until the spring of 1947, faced with the necessity of sowing a new grain crop, did the state begin to provide assistance to collective farms, imposing 10 percent interest on distributed grain (to be paid back from the 1947 harvest). In 1946–47, the UN Relief and Rehabilitation Administration provided U.S. $189 million worth of relief to offset Ukraine's wartime devastation, but the famine remained officially unacknowledged. The state declined offers of assistance from organizations such as the Society of Friends.

In 1946–47, more than 3 million people in Ukraine went hungry. As of 20 June 1947, according to official figures, there were some 1.1 million cases of dystrophy (with peasants accounting for about 80 percent). Total deaths from the famine (including the unborn) have been estimated at more than a million; about one-third of the dead were children. As in 1933, peasants took their children to cities and abandoned them in the hope that they would be fed (between January and July 1947, the number of orphanages in Ukraine increased from 85 to 148, housing 132,400 children). The authorities registered 130 cases of cannibalism.

The famine was completely covered up while it was taking place, although state archives accumulated more than 44,000 written complaints of famine conditions and nonpayment of collective-farm wages. The subject remained taboo until 1988, when previously closed archives became accessible. A documentary volume, *Holod v Ukraïni, 1946–1947* (Famine in Ukraine, 1946–47), was published in 1996, and two collections of articles edited by the historian Oleksandra Veselova appeared in 1998 and 2000. *See also* AGRICULTURE; COLLECTIVIZATION; POPULATION.

FEDKOVYCH, YURII (8 August 1834–11 January 1888). Writer, translator, folklorist, civic and cultural activist. He was born in Storonets-Putyliv (now Putyla, Chernivtsi oblast) in **Bukovyna**, descended from a gentry family. He studied at the Chernivtsi Lower Technical School (1846–48), after which he pursued his education independently. Writing initially in German, Fedkovych switched to Ukrainian while serving in the Austrian army as a second lieutenant (1852–63) and participating in the Italian campaigns. He returned to his native village, where he worked as a bailiff and school inspector. In 1866, he prepared a *Bukvar* (Primer) for elementary schools. Fedkovych called for Ukrainian-**language education** at all levels, as well as the conversion of the German university in Chernivtsi into a Ukrainian one. From 1871 he lived in **Lviv**, working as an editor at the **Prosvita** publishing house. He then settled permanently in Chernivtsi (1876), where he edited the newspaper *Bukovyna* (1885–88).

Works published during Fedkovych's lifetime include collections of poetry in German and Ukrainian: *Poeziï* (Poems, 1862), *Gedichte von I. Fedkowicz* (1865), *Poeziï* (Poems, 3 vols., 1867–68), as well as the prose works *Liuba-zhuba* (Love Is Fatal, 1863), *Kazky dlia rus'koho narodu* (Fables for the Ruthenian People, 1873), and *Dnistrovi kruchi* (The Dnister Ravine, 1885). Fedkovych's plays include the comedy *Tak vam i treba* (You Deserve It!, 1865), the drama *Dovbush* (1869, 1876), the melodrama *Kermanych* (The River Pilot, 1876), and the historical tragedy *Bohdan Khmel'nyts'kyi* (1886–87). His work was influenced by West European **romanticism**, fused with mystical motifs of Bukovynian folklore and problems of contemporary life, especially in the military. He translated works from German and English, as well as the *Tale of Ihor's Campaign*, into Ukrainian. As a folklorist he collected, systematized, and published Bukovynian songs and stories. A memorial museum in honor of Fedkovych was opened in Chernivtsi (1945), and a memorial house was established in Putyla (1974). *See also* LITERATURE.

FEDOROV (FEDOROVYCH), IVAN (ca. 1525–5 [15] December 1583). Founder of book printing and publishing in Muscovy and Ukraine. In the 1550s, together with Petr Mstsislavets, he headed the Muscovite state print shop and published the first precisely dated books in Moscow: the *Apostol* (Acts and Epistles of the Apostles, 1564) and two editions of the *Chasovnik* (Horologion, 1565). In 1569–70, he published two books at the printshop of the Belarusian magnate Ryhor Khadkevich in Zabludiv (now Zabłudów, Poland). During his last years, he worked in **Lviv** (ca. 1572–75 and 1583), Derman (now in Rivne oblast, 1575–76), and Ostrih (1577–82). In 1574, with the help of Lviv tradesmen, he published the first printed books in Ukraine: the *Apostol* and *Azbuka* (Primer). He founded the Ostrih printing house, where under his direction a Greek-Church Slavonic primer (1578), the New Testament with an index (1580), Andrii Rymsha's *Khronolohiia* (Chronology, 1581), and the **Ostrih Bible** (1581) were published. Fedorov edited and designed books, wrote afterwords, and was a gifted innovator in the field of printing technique. After his death, Fedorov's press and equipment became the property of the **Lviv Dormition Brotherhood** print shop and was utilized until the 19th century.

FILARET DENYSENKO (secular name: Mykhailo; b. 23 January 1929). Patriarch of the **Ukrainian Orthodox Church** (Kyiv Patriarchate). He was born into a working-class family in Blahodatne, Donetsk oblast, and studied at the **Odesa** Theological Seminary and the Moscow Theological Academy. In 1950, he was tonsured and awarded the degree of candidate of theology. He became a hieromonk in 1951 and an archimandrite in 1958. In 1960, Filaret was appointed head of the Ukrainian Exarchate of the Russian Orthodox Church (ROC) and superior of St. Volodymyr's Cathedral in **Kyiv**. In 1962, he became bishop of Luga and vicar of the Leningrad eparchy; two years later he was appointed bishop of Dmitrov and rector of the Moscow Theological Academy. From May 1966, Filaret was archbishop of Kyiv and Halych, becoming metropolitan in 1968—the first ethnic Ukrainian to hold that post in 150 years. A Soviet establishment figure and a consistent critic of Ukrainian nationalism, he frequently carried out diplomatic missions on behalf of the Moscow Patriarchate (MP). After the death of Patriarch Pimen of Moscow, he was elected *locum tenens* of the MP (3 May 1990). From October 1990, when the UOC (MP) received the right of self-government, Filaret held the title of Metropolitan of Kyiv and All Ukraine.

Despite his position as *locum tenens*, Filaret was not elected patriarch of Moscow. Following Ukraine's declaration of independence, he initiated an appeal of the clergy of the Ukrainian Exarchate of the ROC to the new patriarch, Aleksii II, requesting autocephaly for the UOC. In response, the council of bishops of the ROC stripped Filaret of all his ecclesiastical ranks on 11 June 1992. Later that month, Filaret, who did not recognize the legitimacy of the council's decision, defected from the ROC. At the All-Ukrainian Orthodox Sobor (25–26 June 1992), which adopted a resolution merging the two largest Ukrainian Orthodox churches (the UOC and the Ukrainian Autocephalous Orthodox Church [UAOC]) into a single Ukrainian Orthodox Church (Kyiv Patriarchate), Patriarch **Mstyslav Skrypnyk** of the UAOC was elected head of the new church, and Filaret was chosen as his deputy. Skrypnyk died in 1993, and on 20 October 1995 Filaret was elected patriarch of Kyiv and all Rus'-Ukraine. He was excommunicated and placed under anathema by the ROC in 1997 but did not acknowledge the decision, maintaining that he had left one national church for another.

FILATOV, VLADIMIR (15 [27] February 1875–30 October 1956). Ophthalmologist and surgeon, academician of the **Ukrainian Academy of Sciences** (from 1939) and the Academy of Medical Sciences of the USSR (from 1944). Born in Mikhailovka (now in Penza oblast, Russia), Filatov graduated from the medical faculty of Moscow University (1897). He became professor and head of the department of eye diseases at Novorossiisk University in **Odesa** (1911) and professor at the Odesa Medical Institute (1921). In 1936, he established the Odesa Scientific Research Institute of Eye Diseases and Tissue Therapy, which he directed until his death. It was renamed after him in 1965. Filatov is best known for introducing methods of complete and partial cornea transplants (1927–38), including a method of transplanting corneas from corpses (1931). He also proposed new methods of treating glaucoma, trachoma, and ophthalmia. He invented special surgical instruments for many treatments. Filatov discovered biogenic stimulants and developed a method of medical tissue therapy. He also contributed to the field of plastic surgery by inventing the so-called Filatov pedicle, a tubed pedicle flap.

FILM. The first motion pictures seen in Ukraine were the films of the Lumière brothers, shown in **Odesa** and other cities in 1896. In the same year, Alfred Fedetsky began making short films in **Kharkiv**. Several film studios were established in **Kyiv**, Kharkiv, and Odesa before **World War I**, and occasional adaptations of Ukrainian literary classics were produced. After the **Ukrainian Revolution**, the cinema was nationalized, and its production was initially limited to documentaries and propaganda films.

In 1922, the All-Ukrainian Photo-Cinema Administration (VUFKU) was formed, initiating the most productive period in the development of the Ukrainian cinema. The vertically integrated VUFKU controlled the production, distribution, and exhibition of films in Ukraine. A large film studio was established in Odesa and a smaller one rented in Yalta until one of largest and most modern studios in Europe was built in Kyiv (1928). The number of feature films released grew from five in 1923 to 25 in 1928, in addition to an annual output of more than 50 documentaries and educational films. The number of permanent movie theaters also increased from 265 in 1914 to 5,394 in 1928. The outstanding film directors of the period included Petr Chardynin, Heorhii Stabovy, **Oleksander Dovzhenko**, Dziga Vertov, and **Ivan Kavaleridze**. The attempt to build a national cinema in Ukraine coincided with the policy of **Ukrainization**, and studios employed many well-known writers and artists. Film actors came from the ranks of **theater** stars who had worked in film before the 1917 revolution, as well as actors of the **Berezil Theater**. The finest works of Ukrainian silent film were Dovzhenko's trilogy, *Zvenyhora* (1927), *Arsenal* (1929), and *Earth* (1930), as well as Vertov's documentary classic *The Man with a*

Movie Camera (1929). Also noteworthy was the work of Dovzhenko's cinematographer Danylo Demutsky. However, many films on Ukrainian themes were attacked for "national deviations" and banned in the early 1930s. Kavaleridze's experimental *Downpour* (1929) came under especially severe criticism.

The end of the silent film era coincided with the onset of Stalin's **political terror**. In 1930, VUFKU lost its independence: it was renamed Ukrainfilm and subordinated to Moscow. The output of the Odesa and Kyiv film studios dropped significantly, and films lost their Ukrainian character. With the exception of Dovzhenko's first sound film, *Ivan* (1932), the films of the 1930s were unimaginative, concerned above all to implement the official socialist **realist** style. Ukrainian themes were limited to a few screen adaptations of literary classics and operettas. State-sanctioned epics such as Dovzhenko's *Shchors* (1939) and Ihor Savchenko's *Bohdan Khmelnytsky* (1941), released on the eve of **World War II**, were meant to secure Ukrainian support for the Soviet war effort.

After the war and throughout the 1950s, the output of the Ukrainian studios was limited to a few films per year. Because of the growing campaign against "bourgeois nationalism" and increasing **Russification**, Ukrainian filmmakers were transferred to Moscow, and Ukrainian studios employed Russian-speaking personnel from other republics. In line with the cult of Stalin, a genre of biographical epics gained in popularity. ***Taras Shevchenko*** (1951) by Ihor Savchenko, the most talented director of the period, and ***Hryhorii Skovoroda*** (1959) by Kavaleridze are the finest examples of this trend.

The *shistdesiatnyky* movement made a strong impact on cinema in the 1960s with the release of **Serhii Paradzhanov's** *Shadows of Forgotten Ancestors* (1964). The film was instrumental in rekindling the traditions of Dovzhenko's poetic cinema, which were later evident in the films of the director and cinematographer Yurii Illienko, the director Leonid Osyka, and the director and actor Ivan Mykolaichuk. Other notable directors of the time included the documentarist Ihor Hrabovsky and Kira Muratova of the Odesa Film Studio. The Soviet regime remained hostile to their work, blocking the production of many scripts and banning certain films until the mid-1980s.

After independence, the economic crisis limited production at Ukraine's film studios, a problem exacerbated by the virtual absence of a domestic distribution network. This has led to the prevalence of Hollywood movies on the Ukrainian market. During the 1990s, films by Kira Muratova and Viacheslav Kryshtofovych received some international recognition. Today, Ukraine has two feature film studios in Kyiv and Odesa, as well as studios specializing in documentaries and animation, both located in Kyiv. *See also* STUPKA, BOHDAN.

FLAG. The oldest Ukrainian flags were triangular pennants. At the turn of the 14th century, rectangular flags with pennants along the free side appeared. The most frequently used color was red, followed by white, azure, and, less frequently, yellow. Parti-colored flags were also in use. The images most often depicted on flags were crosses, celestial bodies, and dynastic **tridents** and bidents. The flag of **Kyivan Rus'** was mainly red, along with the gold trident or bident of the individual grand principality. Later on, the Principality of **Galicia-Volhynia** used an azure banner depicting a golden lion.

During the **Cossack** period, crimson flags made their appearance. Most Cossack flags were rectangular or oblique (trapezoid). The most important emblems of state were the two standards of the **hetman**: the first was red and depicted a white Archangel Michael, while the second featured the hetman's **coat of arms**. The general standard-bearer was in charge of the flags. In the 17th century, the **Hetmanate** used parti-colored flags, although the color red predominated. In the 18th century, the most frequently used flags were azure with a gold or yellow coat of arms and, occasionally, other signs, such as celestial bodies, weapons, and SS. Michael and George. The right side of regimental and company banners and standards featured the national emblem: a Cossack with a musket on a gold or yellow shield against an azure background. The left side displayed the regimental or company emblem in an appropriate color. The great banner of the **Zaporozhian Sich** was red. On the right side it depicted the Archangel Michael, and on the left a white Greek cross surrounded by a golden sun, crescent moon, and stars. The flags of Cossack subunits were predominantly crimson, with a depiction of the Archangel Michael, or yellow-azure with a white cross. Zaporizhia also gave birth to Ukrainian naval ensigns, which were originally white, with a depiction of St. Nicholas.

With the abolition of the Hetmanate and the annexation of central and **western Ukraine** to the Russian and Austrian empires respectively, Ukrainian flags became disused. The yellow-azure flag reappeared in **Galicia** in the early 20th century as the emblem of the **Ukrainian Sich Riflemen**. That combination was also used on the flag of the **Ukrainian People's Republic**. In January 1918, the Little Rada adopted the ensign of the Ukrainian navy, which consisted of two stripes, yellow above and blue below, the blue stripe bearing the golden emblem of **Volodymyr the Great**, the trident, with a cross on the central arm. During the rule of Hetman

Pavlo Skoropadsky, the order of the colors was reversed. The azure-yellow flag was adopted by the **Western Ukrainian People's Republic** (13 November 1918) and **Carpatho-Ukraine** (15 March 1939). Between 1945 and 1949, disagreements arose in the **diaspora** between advocates of the azure-yellow or yellow-azure color combination. A resolution of the **Ukrainian National Council** in exile (27 June 1949) stated that until the national emblem was established by an independent government of Ukraine, the national flag would be azure-yellow.

The first flag of the **Ukrainian SSR**, adopted in March 1919, was red and bore the initials *YCPP* (Ukrainian Socialist Soviet Republic) in a red gold-bordered canton. After the republic's adhesion to the **USSR**, it received a new red flag with a crossed golden hammer and sickle and the Cyrillic initials *YPCP*. On 21 November 1949, the Presidium of the **Verkhovna Rada** of the Ukrainian SSR approved a new flag: a red upper horizontal stripe, comprising two-thirds of the flag, and a lower azure stripe. The upper portion displayed the golden hammer and sickle surmounted by a red gold-bordered five-pointed star. The Ukrainian SSR did not have its own naval or merchant marine flags.

The matter of national symbols, especially the flag, was frequently broached by democratic forces in the late 1980s. On 12 December 1989, it was raised at the Second Congress of People's Deputies of the USSR. On 23 March 1990, the first session of the Ternopil City Council of People's Deputies (21st convocation) passed a resolution concerning national symbols, including a decision to raise the Ukrainian national flag at the city council building alongside the flag of the Ukrainian SSR. A similar decision was made by the **Lviv** oblast Council of People's Deputies on 28 April, and the **Kyiv** city council followed suit on 24 July. Following the declaration of Ukrainian independence, the Verkhovna Rada adopted the azure-yellow flag as the state flag of Ukraine (28 January 1992), a decision reflected in the **Constitution** (1996). The state flag is a rectangular cloth consisting of two horizontal stripes of equal width, the upper stripe azure and the lower one yellow. The ratio of the flag's width to length is 2:3.

FOKIN, VITOLD (b. 25 October 1932). Soviet bureaucrat and first prime minister of independent Ukraine. He was born into the family of a teacher in the village of Novomykolaivka, Zaporizhia oblast. Fokin graduated from the Artem Mining Institute in Dnipropetrovsk and from the Moscow Mining Institute. In 1954, he began his career as an assistant section manager at a colliery in Luhansk and, following several promotions, became head of the Sverdlovantratsyt mining complex (1963). In 1971, Fokin moved to Kyiv, where he worked in the State Planning Committee (Derzhplan) of the **Ukrainian SSR**, serving as its head for three years (1987–90). Fokin was then appointed deputy head of the **Council of Ministers** and, in October 1990, became acting head of the council.

In April 1991, Fokin became head of the Council of Ministers and retained his post after Ukraine's proclamation of independence in August 1991. He also served as prime minister of Ukraine (from 23 October), implementing economic policies generally consistent with those of the Soviet period. Fokin became known as the "father of the coupon" (ersatz currency that circulated until the introduction of the *hryvnia*). Facing accusations of corruption, Fokin resigned his post on 1 October 1992. In the same year, he was elected to the **Verkhovna Rada** and served as a deputy until 1995. Two years later, he was appointed an economic advisor to the president of Ukraine. He is also president of the International Foundation for Humanitarian and Economic Relations between Ukraine and the Russian Federation, as well as head of the supervisory board of the Devon international oil company.

FOLK CUSTOMS AND RITES. Ukrainian folk customs can be divided into three categories: calendar customs, which are tied to seasonal and religious celebrations; rites of passage, which consist of birth, marriage, and burial rites; and communal customs, which mark events in the life of the community. With the rise of urban culture and the political changes of the 20th century, Ukrainian folk customs have changed greatly. Although they are now practiced mainly in rural areas, folk traditions that were discouraged by the Soviet regime are being revived in cities as well.

The Ukrainian folk calendar was originally based on a lunar year of 13 months. In time, folk feasts and rites were combined with Christian holidays and grouped in four cycles. The spring cycle begins with the "meeting of winter and spring," which coincides with the Feast of the Purification of the Mother of God (15 February). The Feast of the Annunciation (7 April) marks the day cattle are driven out "for the spring" and girls perform the first spring dance, known as the "crooked dance," around the churchyard. On the last Sunday before Easter, called "Willow Sunday," pussy-willow branches are blessed in church. They are used to drive the cattle to pasture, and people tap one another with them as a token of health and prosperity.

Easter is the principal spring festival and the major religious festival of the year. Celebrated according to the Julian calendar in Ukraine, it combines pagan and Christian elements. The former are closely related to agriculture, the cult of the dead, and the marriage season. Easter celebrations, which last three days, begin with Easter matins and a solemn liturgy. Inasmuch as Easter marks the end of a lengthy fast, an important part of the celebration is the blessing of *pasky* (Easter breads), Easter eggs, and dairy products and meats of various descriptions that make up the family feast. The holiday is accompanied by the ringing of church bells and the singing of *vesnianky* (spring songs). In western Ukraine, girls perform choral dances called *haïvky* or *hahilky*, which predate the *vesnianky*. Easter eggs are a pre-Christian element, going back to the **Trypilian culture**, that figures prominently in the celebration. The cult of the dead is observed during the Easter period, beginning on Maundy Thursday. On the Sunday following Easter, people gather in the church cemetery for a commemorative feast.

The third major spring festival is St. George's Day, celebrated on 5 May. St. George is the protector of agriculturalists and the patron of animals. His festival often includes the blessing of fields, and purification rituals are performed to protect the cattle from "unclean spirits."

The summer cycle begins fifty days after Good Friday with Pentecost, known in Ukraine as *Zeleni sviata* (Green Holidays). Prior to the main celebration, houses are cleaned and whitewashed, and both churches and houses are decorated with greenery. On Pentecost Sunday, young people engage in song-games, the ritual decorating and stripping of a birch tree a day later, and the plaiting of wreaths that are later floated on the water. The festival also includes a commemoration of the dead; graveyards are decorated with tree boughs and sometimes with candles.

The end of the summer solstice and the beginning of midsummer is commemorated with the Kupalo festival, a celebration of pagan origin. After the introduction of **Christianity**, the church tried to suppress the tradition, replacing it with the Feast of St. John the Baptist (7 July). However, it persisted as the festival of Ivan (from St. John) Kupalo, who is believed to be the god of love and the harvest, as well as the personification of the earth's fertility. Kupalo Eve was the only time of the year that the earth was believed to reveal its secrets and the only time when free love was sanctioned. Unmarried young people gathered outside the village, where they built bonfires around which they performed ritual dances and songs, often erotic in content. They leaped over the fires and bathed in nearby water as acts of purification. Among the rituals that experienced a revival at the end of the 20th century, Kupalo, in restrained form, was one of the most popular and widespread.

The customs and rites associated with the harvest are now mostly concentrated in a single harvest feast, the *obzhynky*. The harvest ritual was identical throughout Ukraine: women wove a wreath from stalks of grain and placed it on the head of the young woman they selected as the most beautiful. She led a procession to the master of the house for whom they were harvesting, and a feast took place at his home. The harvest coincides with three religious feasts: the Feast of St. Elijah (2 August), who is associated with Perun, the pagan god of thunder; the Feast of the Maccabees (14 August); and *Spas* (the Feast of the Transfiguration of the Lord, 19 August). All heavy agricultural work is completed before the Feast of the Assumption of the Mother of God (28 August).

The autumn cycle is associated primarily with marriage ceremonies. The most important holiday of the period is the Feast of the Holy Protectress or *Pokrova* (14 October), as she was considered the patron of the **Zaporozhian Sich**. The Feast of St. Demetrius (8 November) ushers in the beginning of winter and is preceded by the autumn commemoration of the dead. The Archangel Michael, the patron saint of **Kyiv**, is commemorated on 21 November, while the Feast of the Apostle Philip or *Pylypivka* (27 November) marks the beginning of the pre-Christmas fast.

The winter cycle is dominated by Christmas and the New Year. It begins with the Feast of the Presentation of the Mother of God (4 December), associated with protective rites against illness and witchcraft. The Feast of the Apostle Andrew (13 December) is of particular significance to young people, who tell their fortunes by pouring hot wax into water and engage in elaborate dating rituals. Children receive presents on the Feast of St. Nicholas (19 December).

Christmas celebrations begin on Christmas Eve (*Sviat-Vechir*), celebrated on 6 January according to the Julian calendar. It originated as an agricultural festival related to the cult of the family and the commemoration of ancestors. The "Holy Supper" served on Christmas Eve consists of 12 meatless and milkless dishes containing the most important products of the field, garden, and orchard. Traditionally, it was accompanied by an elaborate ceremony. The head of the household took the first spoonful of *kutia* (cooked whole grains, honey, and ground poppy seeds) outside and invited the "frost to eat *kutia*." On reentering the house, he threw a spoonful to the ceiling; adhesion augured a good harvest and a good swarming of bees. He then took food from every dish and carried it out for the cattle to eat. Dead ancestors are believed to participate in the celebration, and their presence is signified by a sheaf of wheat (*didukh*) placed under the icons. Caroling, sometimes accompanied by a puppet theater, is characteristic of Christmas, while the religious festival, which lasts three days, involves Christmas liturgies.

A week after Christmas, New Year's Eve, called *Malanka* or "Generous Eve" (*Shchedryi Vechir*), is celebrated (13 January). It involves rituals to ensure a bountiful harvest and the family's health and happiness. The key rituals include the eating of *kutia*, the singing of special carols called *shchedrivky*, usually by children, fortune-telling and weather forecasting for the next year, and the symbolic sowing of wheat. According to superstition, animals are able to speak at midnight, and buried treasures burn with a blue flame. The Christmas season ends on 19 January with Epiphany, called *Vodokhreshchi* (Blessing of Water) or *Yordan* (Jordan River). Its principal ceremony consists of a solemn outdoor blessing of waters, usually at a river or well, where a cross made of ice is erected. Epiphany is followed by *Miasnytsi*, a new marriage period that lasts until Lent. It ends with the *kolodka* party on the Monday before the fast.

Rites of passage concern birth, marriage, and death. Customs related to birth involve the actual birth, during which rites are performed to protect the child from evil, the acceptance of the newborn into the community through baptism and a family reception, and purification rituals for the mother and midwife, who are considered unclean after the birth. Marriage customs include elaborate ceremonies of matchmaking, betrothal, and wedding preparations. The marriage ceremony consists of a church wedding (*vinchannia*) and a ritual wedding (*vesillia*), after which the bride leaves her own family for that of the groom. In the past, wedding celebrations lasted several days, but village weddings today seldom extend past two or three days. Burial rites are concerned primarily with driving the soul of the deceased from the house. The dead cannot be left unattended; coffins are usually made of maple or pine, since these woods are believed to drive away spirits and vampires; and when the deceased is carried from the house, precautions are taken to prevent the return of its spirit.

Communal customs are more abridged now than in the past, when unmarried young people performed ritual functions, with young men responsible for the preparation of religious festivals and young women organizing social gatherings, notably evening parties called *vechornytsi*. Other communal rituals included the rite of the first sowing (*zasiv*), the first driving of the herd to pasture, and rites associated with the construction of new houses.

FOLK MUSIC AND DANCE. Although they vary greatly from one region to another, Ukrainian folk songs can be divided into four basic groups: ritual songs, such as carols, spring songs, and Kupalo songs; harvest and wedding songs; historical and political songs, such as dumas (epic songs) and ballads; and lyrical songs, which concern love, the family, and society. In folk songs, nature manifests human emotions: poetic images or symbols derived from the animal and plant world are common devices. Folk songs have inspired many Ukrainian composers, such as **Semen Hulak-Artemovsky**, **Mykola Leontovych**, Borys Liatoshynsky, **Stanislav Liudkevych**, **Mykola Lysenko**, Yevhen Stankovych, and Kyrylo Stetsenko, as well as foreign composers such as Beethoven, Dvořák, Mussorgsky, and Tchaikovsky.

Instrumental folk **music** is used primarily to accompany dancing and marching. Ukrainian folk musical instruments include string instruments, such as the bandura or kobza, violin (*skrypka*), bass viol (*basolia*), hurdy-gurdy (*lira*), and hammer dulcimer (*tsymbaly*); wind instruments, including the reed flute (*sopilka*), bagpipe (*duda* or *koza*), and *trembita* (a type of alpine horn used primarily for communication); and percussion instruments, such as the frame drum (*bubon* or *taraban*), tambourine (*resheto*), and kettledrum (*tulumba* or *litavry*). The classic folk ensemble, known as *troïsti muzyky* (trio musicians), arose in the early 17th century. It consisted of a violin, bass viol, and frame drum. In western Ukraine, the hammer dulcimer was commonly used in place of the bass viol, and on occasion the reed flute replaced the violin as the lead instrument. In **Polisia** and **Podilia**, brass orchestras were also popular. Today there are many professional ensembles of folkloric music in Ukraine, including choirs, bandura ensembles, and folk instrument orchestras, as well as departments of folk music performance at Ukraine's music conservatories. Authentic vocal and instrumental folk music is still performed in rural areas.

Ukrainian folk dances show great regional variation. Unlike dances of other nations, Ukrainian folk dances were not influenced by court dances and preserved their original character. With roots in agricultural dance games, folk dances maintained the basic form of the circle, associated with the cult of the sun. Other ritual dances included spring *khorovody* (circular choral dances), dances of the Kupalo festival, and dances performed during Whitsuntide celebrations and the harvest feast. Most Ukrainian folk dances are circular in form but incorporate other figurative patterns, such as the cross, chain, and rows. They unfold horizontally, except for the vertical dances of mountain people. **Women's** dances are generally lyrical and graceful. Some dances, such as the *metelytsia*, *dribushka*, *horlytsia*, and *volynianka*, were originally performed by women only but are now performed by men and women together. Male dances include the *chumak*, *zaporozhets'*, and *arkan*. The most popular

Ukrainian dance, the *hopak*, was originally a male display of physical strength and acrobatic agility but is now a group dance for both men and women. In time, folk dance became a form of pure entertainment. The effect of Ukrainian dance is augmented by colorful folk costumes and melodious musical accompaniment. What is commonly known as Ukrainian folk dance today is actually a professional art form. The dances are choreographed, greatly embellished, and presented in frontal rather than circular fashion, while the performers exhibit a very high degree of technical proficiency.

FOLKLORE. See FOLK CUSTOMS AND RITES; FOLK MUSIC AND DANCE; LITERATURE; PAGANISM; POPULISM.

FOREIGN POLICY. Under the Union Treaty of 1922, the **Ukrainian SSR** was technically a sovereign state with the right to conduct its own foreign relations—a theoretical right somewhat reinforced by Stalin's acquisition of separate seats for Ukraine and Belarus at the **United Nations**. In practice, however, all decisions were made in Moscow, and until the late 1980s the two republics functioned merely as additional instruments of Soviet foreign policy. In July 1990, as the Soviet Union began to totter, the Verkhovna Rada in **Kyiv** issued a declaration of sovereignty announcing Ukraine's intention to become a neutral and nonnuclear state. On 24 August 1991, Ukraine declared its independence, overwhelmingly ratified by national referendum on 1 December 1991. The most important step toward implementing independence was taken in Belavezha, Belarus, in early December, when Russia, Ukraine, and Belarus abrogated the 1922 Union Treaty, effectively dissolving the **USSR**. Beginning in late 1991, Ukraine developed a foreign-affairs infrastructure and sought recognition of its independence. Since 1990, the following have served as foreign ministers of Ukraine: **Anatolii Zlenko** (1990–94, 2000–2003), **Hennadii Udovenko** (1994–98), **Borys Tarasiuk** (1998–2000), and **Kostiantyn Hryshchenko** (since 2003).

In order to function as an independent state, Ukraine had to disengage itself from the former USSR and the Russian Federation (RF). This proved very difficult, as Russia was ambivalent about Ukrainian statehood, either viewing it as a temporary phenomenon or, at the very least, attempting to preserve regional dominance. As president of the RF, Boris Yeltsin participated in the dissolution of the USSR because it allowed him to marginalize the Soviet president, Mikhail Gorbachev. The tension between the assertion of Ukrainian sovereignty and Russian insistence on superior regional status colored all issues, including the nature of the Commonwealth of Independent States (CIS), the status of the **Black Sea Fleet**, the

Crimea, and Sevastopol, recognition of Ukraine's borders, and the enlargement of the North Atlantic Treaty Organization (NATO).

Russia has tried to dominate the CIS as a political, economic, and military bloc, while Ukraine has sought to use it as a means to achieve a "civilized divorce" and turn it into a loose mechanism of economic cooperation. Russia's attempts to create a CIS security system and alliance have proved unavailing. Moreover, Ukraine has been instrumental in splitting the CIS into two groupings, the more Western-oriented GUUAM (Georgia, Ukraine, Uzbekistan, Azerbaijan, and Moldova) and the Russian-dominated remainder of CIS.

Russia and Ukraine have periodically clashed over the status of the Black Sea Fleet, the Crimea, and the city of Sevastopol. Ukraine maintained that in splitting up Soviet property, each republic was entitled to whatever was on its territory. Russian politicians argued that the fleet and the Crimea had been historically Russian and should therefore be under Russian control. Russia procrastinated in signing a state-to-state treaty with Ukraine in the hope of wresting concessions on these issues. In June 1992, Russia and Ukraine agreed to divide the fleet, and subsequently Ukraine sold most of its portion to Russia. However, Ukraine insisted on retaining sovereignty over Sevastopol, where the fleet was based. Only after the signing of the Treaty of Friendship and Cooperation with Russia (May 1997) was agreement reached on a 20-year Russian lease of the port facilities at Sevastopol.

Since the 1997 treaty officially recognized the "immutability of existing borders," Russo-Ukrainian relations have continued to improve. Ukraine has designated Russia a "strategic partner" and continues to placate it while trying to maintain a cordial relationship with the United States and the West. Nevertheless, pressure has continued on Ukraine to join the "Slavic core" of the former USSR, particularly since the Belarus-Russia Union of April 1997.

After declaring independence, Ukraine sought close ties with the United States, which alone could provide sufficient political and economic assets to counter pressure from Russia. Until 1994, however, Ukraine's relations with the United States were somewhat strained. While Ukrainians believed that the United States would welcome Ukrainian independence, Americans viewed it as a nuisance and danger, supporting political reform in the USSR and, except for the Baltic states, opposing independence for the republics. When this proved unworkable, the United States adopted a "Russia first" policy. American policy toward Ukraine consisted mainly of applying pressure to give up the nuclear arsenal that Ukraine had inherited from the former USSR. Such pressure, which did not address Ukraine's security concerns, only strengthened the hand of those who wanted to keep Ukraine's **nuclear weapons** or use them as bargaining chips. By late 1993, American policy began to shift. As relations with Russia soured, the United States attached greater importance to an independent Ukraine, realizing that political and economic incentives were needed to bring about nuclear disarmament, which in turn required cooperation between Ukraine, Russia, and the United States. The resulting Trilateral Statement of January 1994 committed Ukraine to the elimination of all strategic nuclear missiles on its territory, which was completed by June 1996. The ratification of the SALT-1 Treaty by the **Verkhovna Rada** in February 1994 and of the Nuclear Non-Proliferation Treaty in November 1994 removed the nuclear issue as an irritant in U.S.-Ukrainian relations.

After 1994, the United States backed economic reforms in Ukraine, making it the third-largest recipient of U.S. foreign assistance (after Israel and Egypt). In 1996, the two counties set up a binational commission, chaired by President **Leonid Kuchma** and Vice President Al Gore, whose purpose was to develop a "strategic partnership" between Washington and Kyiv.

Ukraine has consistently attempted to forge closer relations with Central European states, particularly its neighbors. The central Europeans, for their part, do not consider Ukraine an integral part of their region and are wary of encroaching on Russia's "sphere of influence." In April 1993, Ukraine proposed a central European security zone that would have included Ukraine, Belarus, the Baltic states, Moldova, and the East European members of the Warsaw Pact, but this was rebuffed by the central European and Baltic states, which were eager to join the European Union (EU) and enter NATO.

Ukraine was much more successful in establishing bilateral relations with its western neighbors. In May 1992, it signed a treaty of friendship and cooperation with Poland that affirmed the inviolability of borders and renounced all territorial claims. In May 1997, that relationship was deepened by the signing of a "Declaration of Understanding and Unity," which sought to alleviate historical grievances and provide a basis for reconciliation, as between Poland and Germany. Ukraine was able to establish good relations with Hungary, Slovakia, and the Czech Republic. Relations with Romania, however, were marred by territorial disputes over northern **Bukovyna**, southern **Bessarabia**, and Serpent Island. In June 1997, after four years of negotiations, Ukraine and Romania signed a Treaty of Cooperation that recognized the inviolability of borders and minority rights, making special provisions for a demilitarized Serpent Island.

Relations with the United States and the EU deteriorated after 2000, when President Kuchma was implicated in the murder of the investigative journalist **Heorhii Gongadze**; more generally, restrictions on press freedom in Ukraine became a diplomatic issue. Under President George W. Bush, American aid to Ukraine was drastically reduced, partly because of commercial disputes involving U.S. firms. In 2002, the Bush administration accused Ukraine of having sold the Kolchuga antiaircraft radar system to Iraq; the issue faded in 2003, when Ukrainian troops participated in the postwar occupation of Iraq and no Kolchugas were found there. Nevertheless, isolation by the West was an important factor in the Kuchma administration's rapprochement with Russia.

While successfully establishing bilateral relations with its western neighbors, Ukraine has had difficulty in dealing with Western multinational structures, particularly the EU and NATO. In June 1994, Ukraine signed a partnership agreement with the EU, but the bulk of EU aid has been associated with the closure of the **Chornobyl** nuclear power plant and has done little to reform Ukraine's **economy** or facilitate its access to EU markets. Indeed, the EU increasingly views Ukraine as a potential source of unwanted cheap agricultural, textile, and steel products, uncontrolled immigration, and crime, prompting it to establish barriers rather than integrate Ukraine into Europe. As Ukraine's western neighbors gain access to the EU, they are required to extend such barriers to Ukraine, negating some of the benefits of bilateral relations (e.g., travel without visas).

Ukraine finds itself in a similar position with regard to security and NATO. At first, Ukraine tried to obtain a security arrangement that would eliminate the presence of NATO on its borders. Those efforts failed completely, as Ukraine's western neighbors were eager to join NATO and opposed any other security arrangement. Thus, from 1995, Ukraine sought to make a virtue of necessity and dropped its opposition to NATO enlargement, while attempting to strike the best possible deal for itself. It was the first CIS state to participate in the NATO Partnership for Peace program. Ukraine's relations extended well beyond the parameters of the program, and its efforts at rapprochement culminated in the signing of the Ukraine-NATO Charter on Distinctive Partnership at the Madrid Summit in July 1997. While the charter does not offer any security guarantees, it establishes a mechanism for consultation if Ukraine feels that its security is threatened. The charter made Ukraine's NATO ties the most extensive of any non-NATO member except Russia. Nevertheless, NATO's own reluctance, internal Ukrainian opposition, lack of Ukrainian progress on democratic reforms required by NATO and the EU, and Russian pressure make it unlikely that Ukraine will actually join NATO. Despite Ukraine's best diplomatic efforts, it seems destined to remain a nonbloc buffer between NATO and Russia, its "strategic partner" to the east. *See also* TRADE.

FORESTRY. Ukraine's geographic location between the humid regions of Europe and the dry steppes of Asia determines the variety, density, and degree of its forestation. Most densely forested is **Polisia** in the northwest, with 39 percent of Ukrainian forests. The main tree species there are pine (60 percent), oak (15 percent), and birch (12 percent). The forest-steppe belt that extends through the north-central parts of Ukraine accounts for about 33 percent of its total forest area (the main tree species are oak, pine, and hornbeam). The steppe-belt forests of southeastern Ukraine (17.2 percent of total forest area) are dominated by oak and pine. Spruce, beech, and oak are the main tree species in the forests of the Carpathian Mountains (8.2 percent of total forest area), while oak and beech are predominant species in the **Crimean** Mountains (2.6 percent of total forest area). The forest area of Ukraine is 9.9 million ha (1988), of which 8.6 million ha are covered with trees. On the average, 16.4 percent of Ukraine's territory is forested. Fifty-two percent of trees are deciduous (74 species) and 48 percent coniferous (15 species).

Forests in Ukraine have two main economic functions: protective (water-retaining, soil-protecting, field-shielding, and green belts) and exploitable, with the latter accounting for 56.7 percent of forests. Despite a relatively small forested area, the Carpathians provide about half of Ukrainian timber, and Polisia another third. The balance comes from the forest-steppe and steppe regions and from the Crimea, where forests have mainly a protective function. The average age of Ukrainian forests is relatively young—under 40 years—as a result of excessive exploitation in the past. Inadequate protection and often neglectful management accompanied rapid Soviet-era industrialization. Merciless tree-cutting during 20th-century wars led to a further reduction in the general forest area. The shortening of cutting cycles, lowering of harvesting age, and reforestation with fast-growing tree species all contributed to a reduction in the quality of Ukrainian forests.

Wood and pulp and paper industries in Ukraine amount to 2.3 percent of total industrial output (2000). In 1995, forest-related industries employed 216,000 people, with 46,000 employed in harvesting and forest management and 23,000 in the pulp and paper industry. The largest sector of the industry, woodworking, which employed 232,000 workers in 1985, when it relied on raw materials imported from Russia, was reduced to 145,000 workers by 1995. Most forest-related industries are located close to forested areas, although woodworking factories can be found in all industrial centers.

FRANKO, IVAN (27 August 1856–28 May 1916). Writer and civic figure who dominated the late 19th and early 20th centuries in **western Ukraine**. He was born in Nahuievychi, Sambir county (now Ivan Franko, Drohobych raion, **Lviv** oblast), into a peasant family. His father, Yakiv Franko (d. 1865), the village blacksmith, was descended from German colonists. Franko's mother, Maria Kulczycka (d. 1873), came from the Polish petty gentry. He studied at the elementary school in Yasenytsia-Silna (1862–63) and at the **Basilian** school in Drohobych (1864–67). He graduated from the Drohobych gymnasium (1875) and began studies at the philological faculty of Lviv University. Arrested for socialist activity in 1877, Franko resumed his studies in the autumn of 1880. Subsequently he studied at the universities of Chernivtsi (1890) and Vienna (1890–93), obtaining his doctorate at the latter.

Franko was the first Ukrainian writer to make his living from **literature**. His rich and varied creative legacy includes approximately 4,000 literary, publicistic, and scholarly works. Franko wrote fluently in three languages (Ukrainian, Polish, German) and translated from 14 languages. He helped establish the **realist** style in Ukrainian prose and is generally considered the most significant Ukrainian poet after **Taras Shevchenko**. His best-known works include the poems "Kameniari" (The Stonecutters, 1878), "Vichnyi revoliutsioner" (The Eternal Revolutionary, 1880), "Ne pora, ne pora" (This Is Not the Time, 1880, which later became a national anthem), and *Moisei* (Moses, 1905), the novels *Boa Constrictor* (1878), *Boryslav smiiet'sia* (Boryslav Is Laughing, 1881), *Zakhar Berkut* (1883), *Osnovy suspil'nosty* (The Foundations of Society, 1895), *Dlia domashn'oho ohnyshcha* (For the Family Hearth, 1897), and *Perekhresni stezhky* (Crossed Paths, 1900), the drama *Ukradene shchastia* (Stolen Happiness, 1893), and the children's narrative poem *Lys Mykyta* (Fox Mykyta, 1890). Franko published the poetry collections *Z vershyn i nyzyn* (From Heights and Depths, 1887), *Ziv'iale lystia* (Withered Leaves, 1896), *Mii izmarahd* (My Emerald, 1898), *Iz dniv zhurby* (From Days of Sorrow, 1900), and *Semper tiro* (1906) and the prose collections *Halyts'ki obrazky* (Galician Pictures, 1885) and *U poti chola* (In the Sweat of the Brow, 1890).

A significant portion of Franko's output consists of scholarly works. He published scores of historical studies, sources, reviews, etc., including the first biographical study in Ukrainian historiography, *Zhyttia Ivana Fedorovycha ta ioho chasy* (The Life of Ivan Fedorovych and His Times, 1883; *see* FEDOROV, IVAN).

Franko worked as an editor for many Ukrainian and Polish publications, including the journals *Druh* (Friend), *Hromads'kyi druh* (Friend of the Community, 1878), *Svit* (World, 1881), *Zoria* (Star, 1883–86), **Pravda** (Truth, 1888), *Tovarysh* (Comrade, 1888), *Narod* (People, 1890–95), *Hromads'kyi holos* (Community Voice, 1895), *Zhytie i slovo* (Life and Word, 1894–97), and **Literaturno-naukovyi visnyk** (Literary and Scientific Herald, 1898–1907) and the newspapers **Dilo** (Deed, 1883–86), *Przyjaciel ludu* (Friend of the People, 1886), *Kurjer Lwowski* (Lviv Courier, 1887–97), *Przegląd społeczny* (Social Review, 1886), and *Khliborob* (Farmer, 1891). Franko contributed regularly to the Warsaw journals *Prawda* (Truth) and *Głos* (Voice), *Kievskaia starina* (Kyivan Antiquity) and *Die Zeitung* (Vienna), the newspapers *Severnyi kur'ier* (Northern Courier, St. Petersburg), *Arbeiter Zeitung* (Vienna), and others. From 1878 to 1886, he was on the editorial board of *Praca* (Labor), the first socialist newspaper in **Galicia**, and belonged to the Polish-Ukrainian-Jewish socialist committee organized around it. He conducted socialist propaganda among the workers of Lviv, Boryslav, and Drohobych and among Galician **peasants** (1878–86). Because of his propaganda work, he was arrested and imprisoned on four occasions: June 1877–March 1878 in Lviv, March-June 1880 in Kolomyia, August-October 1890 in Lviv, and March 1893 in Lviv. Franko's socialism alienated him from the conservative **populists** who dominated Ukrainian civic and political life in Galicia. As a result, he spent a decade (1887–97) working as an editor for Polish journals and newspapers. He was also barred from a university appointment because of his political views. In October 1890, Franko, **Mykhailo Pavlyk**, Viacheslav Budzynovsky, Yevhen Levytsky, and others founded the first political party in Ukraine, the Ruthenian-Ukrainian Radical Party (*see* UKRAINIAN RADICAL PARTY). Franko was its first leader (until 1898) and one of its main ideologues. As its representative he ran unsuccessfully for the Austrian parliament in 1895, 1897, and 1898.

In 1899, Franko left the Radicals and helped establish the **National Democratic Party**. His defection was prompted in part by changes in the leadership of the Ukrainian national movement in Galicia following the arrival of **Mykhailo Hrushevsky** in Lviv (1894). In 1899, with Hrushevsky's support, Franko became a full member of the **Shevchenko Scientific Society** (NTSh). He abandoned active politics in 1904, largely because of his heavy involvement with the NTSh. Franko headed its philological section (1898–1901, 1903–12), as well as its ethnographic commission (1898–1900, 1908–13). He edited many of the society's publications, notably *Literaturno-naukovyi visnyk*, with Hrushevsky and Volodymyr Hnatiuk (1899–1907). Although his health began to decline in 1908, he continued to work productively.

In the course of his lifetime, Franko's world view underwent a complex evolution. Influenced by **Mykhailo Drahomanov**, he and other students in the Lviv Academic Circle adopted **populist** views (early 1876). Franko's first arrest (June 1877) and trial (January 1878) led to his ostracism by virtually all his former associates. Following his release, Franko turned to socialism and was a principal author of the political program of the Polish and Ukrainian socialists of Eastern Galicia (1881). His outlook at the time combined a variety of European socialist influences that he sought to adapt to Galician conditions. He was never an orthodox Marxist; the Galician proletariat was numerically small, and Franko always saw it as his task to promote the welfare of the Galician peasantry. By the late 1890s, he had also become critical of what he considered the propensity of Marxism to develop into a tyrannical statism. Franko expressed his critical views in such articles as "Sotsiializm i sotsiial-demokratiia" (Socialism and Social Democracy, 1897), his review of Anatolii Faresov's book *Narodniki i marksisty* (The Populists and the Marxists, 1899), "Shcho take postup" (What Is Progress, 1903), and "Do istoriï sotsiialistychnoho rukhu" (On the History of the Socialist Movement, 1904).

During this period, Franko critically reassessed his association with Polish socialists and democrats, who were becoming increasingly dedicated to the Polish national cause. By the elections of 1897, there was open conflict between Polish and Ukrainian socialists. In the same year, Franko published an inflammatory article about Adam Mickiewicz ("Ein Dichter des Verrates") that resulted in a complete break with Polish circles. By the late 1890s, Franko had also come to support of the idea of a politically independent Ukraine (his 1895 review of **Yuliian Bachynsky's** *Ukraïna Irredenta* and the article "Poza mezhamy mozhlyvoho" [Beyond the Limits of the Possible, 1900]). This shift was associated with Franko's reaction against the influence of Drahomanov following the latter's death in 1895. Franko's former rationalist and positivist views were modified by irrational and voluntarist elements that bore some resemblance to interwar Ukrainian nationalism. The climactic expression of his philosophical views, as well as his political testament, was the poem *Moisei* (1905), in which the story of Moses leading the Israelites out of the wilderness serves as an allegory of Ukraine's national and social liberation.

The most complete editions of Franko's works appeared in 30 volumes (Kyiv, 1924–31), 20 volumes (Kyiv, 1950–56), 20 volumes (New York, 1956–62), and 50 volumes (Kyiv, 1976–86). Soviet editions of his works were heavily censored. Franko's archive is housed in the Manuscript Division of the Institute of Literature, National Academy of Sciences of Ukraine.

FREE COSSACKS. Volunteer military and militia units established to maintain law and order and defend the Ukrainian state. The first unit, commanded by Semen Hryzlo, was formed in Zvenyhorod county, **Kyiv** region (April 1917). It was initiated by Khresant Smoktii, a **peasant** from Husakiv, Zvenyhorod county. By August, there were Free Cossack units in the Kyiv, **Poltava**, Chernihiv, and Katerynoslav regions, drawn mainly from the middle and well-to-do peasantry. Their main task was to defend village communities against military deserters and looters. The basic unit was the company, which varied in size. Companies of a single *volost'* (community) comprised a kurin, kurins made up a regiment, and all the regiments of a county were joined in a *kish*. One of the strongest units was the **haidamaka** kurin in the Kherson region, consisting of approximately 8,000 men.

An all-Ukrainian Congress of Free Cossacks was held in Chyhyryn (3–7 [16–20] October 1917), attended by 200 delegates representing 60,000 free Cossacks. The congress established the General Council of Free Cossacks, consisting of 12 members. Gen. **Pavlo Skoropadsky**, commander of the First Ukrainian Corps, was elected otaman of the Free Cossacks, and Bila Tserkva became their headquarters. In October 1917, the Free Cossacks began publishing the daily *Vil'nyi kozak* (Free Cossack). With the Bolshevik advance, the General Secretariat of Military Affairs of the **Ukrainian Central Rada** ordered the reorganization of the Free Cossacks into regular army units, the Registered Free Cossacks (January 1918). Throughout the winter of 1918, the Free Cossacks resisted the advancing Bolshevik armies. Companies commanded by Mykhailo Kovenko particularly distinguished themselves in battle against stronger Bolshevik forces approaching Kyiv (late January-early February). The territory of Zvenyhorod county, whose regiment was commanded by Yurii Tiutiunnyk, was cleared of Bolshevik forces. In March and April 1918, when German forces occupied Ukraine, the Free Cossacks were disarmed and disbanded. However, many kept their weapons and subsequently joined the Army of the **Ukrainian People's Republic**. *See also* RED COSSACKS.

FRONT OF NATIONAL UNITY/FRONT NATSIONAL'NOÏ IEDNOSTY (FNIe). Political organization of a right-radical orientation in **western Ukraine**. It opposed both the policy of "normalization" with the Polish authorities conducted by the **Ukrainian National Democratic Alliance** (UNDO) and the tactics of political terror espoused by the **Organization of Ukrainian Nationalists** (OUN). The Front was initiated by Dmytro Paliiv, a founder of the **Ukrainian Party of National Work** who joined UNDO and was expelled from it in 1933 for opposing "normalization."

The first congress of the FNIe, held in **Lviv** on 20 September 1936, was attended by 150 delegates, most of whom were **peasants**. The FNIe described its ideology as one of "creative nationalism" and favored a corporatist social order with the family, based on Christian principles, as its basic unit. It was influenced by European totalitarian movements, especially German national socialism and Italian fascism (charismatic leadership, organization in cohorts, form of greeting, etc.). The FNIe was the first nonsocialist organization in western Ukraine to attract workers. It gained a youth following through its sports sections and extended its activities into **Volhynia**. The FNIe also attracted former followers of **Pavlo Skoropadsky** and others who were drawn to its hierarchical, conservative orientation. It opposed the Polish state and boycotted elections to upper legislative bodies and city administrations.

From 1937, the leadership of the FNIe advocated the consolidation of Ukrainian political and community forces, participating in the Contact Committee (1937–39). Paliiv remained leader of the FNIe throughout its existence. Other executive members included Ivan Hladylovych, Volodymyr Kokhan, Yurii Krokhmaliuk, Mykola Shlemkevych, and Stepan Volynets. The front published the ideological quarterly *Peremoha* (Victory, 1933–39, ed. Shlemkevych), the weekly *Bat'kivshchyna* (Fatherland, 1933–39, ed. Paliiv and others), with its supplement, *Nova molod'* (New Youth), and the daily *Ukraïns'ki visti* (Ukrainian News, 1935–39, ed. Hladylovych). The FNIe had a publishing house, Batkivshchyna, in Lviv. Following the Soviet occupation of western Ukraine, the FNIe terminated its activities.

G

GALAGAN, HRYHORII (3 [15] August 1819–13 [25] September 1888). Civic leader. A descendant of an old **Cossack** family from Chyhyryn, Galagan owned large estates in the **Poltava** and Chernihiv regions. He was acquainted with **Volodymyr Antonovych**, **Panteleimon Kulish**, **Mykhailo Maksymovych**, and **Taras**

Shevchenko and corresponded with them. In his birthplace, the village of Sokyryntsi, Galagan opened the first **peasant** savings and loan association in Ukraine and established a museum of Ukrainian folk life. As a government official, he implemented the abolition of serfdom in 1861 and, from 1882, was a member of the imperial State Council, where he defended the interests of Ukrainian peasants. In 1871, he founded a private school in Kyiv, the Pavlo Galagan Collegium (named after his deceased son). At his initiative and with his financial support, a gymnasium in Pryluka, trade schools in Ichnia and Pryluka counties, and a number of elementary schools were opened. Galagan was president of the **Southwestern Branch of the Imperial Russian Geographic Society** (1873–75). He supported the first general-interest Ukrainian journal, *Osnova*, as well as the historical journal *Kievskaia starina* and other Ukrainian publications; he also promoted the development of **architecture**, **theater**, and choral singing. Galagan published *Iuzhnorusskie pesni s golosami* (South Russian Songs for Voices, 1857) and *Opisanie malorusskikh vertepnykh dram s prilozheniem not* (A Description of Little Russian *Vertep* Dramas, Including Musical Notes, 1862).

GALICIA (Ukr. *Halychyna*). Western Ukrainian historical region north of the Carpathian Mountains in the basins of the upper and middle Dnister, upper Western Buh, and upper Sian Rivers. Its territory encompasses the **Lviv**, Ivano-Frankivsk, and Ternopil (excepting its northern section) oblasts of Ukraine and, historically, a number of Polish provinces: Przemyśl (Peremyshl), Rzeszów, Zamość (Zamostia), Chełm (Kholm), and others.

The Galician lands were inhabited during the Paleolithic period and actively colonized in the periods that followed. Galicia's archaeological map is particularly rich, indicating that conditions for settlement were favorable. In the second half of the ninth century, the area was settled by White Croatians, Dulibians (Buzhanians, Volhynians), and Tivertsians, who maintained relations with the **princes** of **Kyivan Rus'**. As a consequence of Prince **Volodymyr the Great's** war with the Poles, Galicia was incorporated into Rus' (981). After the collapse of Kyivan Rus', Galicia became the site of the Galician Principality (based in the town of Halych) and subsequently of the Principality of **Galicia-Volhynia**.

In the 14th century, Galicia became a zone of contention between Poland, Hungary, and Lithuania. In 1349, Casimir III annexed Galicia to Poland as a distinct Kingdom of Rus'. In 1434, that kingdom was fully incorporated into Poland, bringing Galicia's autonomy to an end. Rus' law and administrative practices were abolished, and the Galician **boyars** gained equal rights with the

Polish *szlachta* (nobility). The Rus' palatinate, centered in Lviv, was established in 1434. It consisted of five lands (counties): Sianik (Sanok), Peremyshl (Przemyśl), Lviv, Halych, and Kholm (Chełm). The Belz palatinate was established in 1462.

Religious **brotherhoods** arose in the 16th century to defend Orthodoxy and oppose the advance of the Counter-Reformation and its concomitant Polonization; they also served as cultural and educational organizations. The most prominent was the **Lviv Dormition Brotherhood** (1586). At the turn of the 17th century, there was a national revival in Galicia; Ukrainian schooling, publishing, literature, and art flourished. Prominent figures from Galicia included the **Cossack hetman Petro Sahaidachny** and the churchmen **Iov Boretsky, Yelysei Pletenetsky,** Zakhariia Kopystensky, **Kasiian Sakovych,** Pamva Berynda, and Lavrentii and Stepan Zyzanii. The ecclesiastical **Union of Brest**, which gave rise to the **Ukrainian Catholic Church,** was initiated in Galicia. Intensely controversial at a time when the overwhelming majority of Ukrainians were Orthodox, the union made slow headway. The eparchy of Peremyshl did not accept it until 1692; the Lviv eparchy accepted the union in 1700, followed by the Lviv Brotherhood in 1708.

The late 17th and early 18th centuries were a time of economic and cultural decline in Galicia, the result of continual warfare, nobiliary despotism, and the weak central leadership of the **Polish-Lithuanian Commonwealth**. After the first partition of Poland (1772), Galicia was incorporated into the Austrian Empire as a separate province, the Kingdom of Galicia and Lodomeria, that comprised the Ukrainian lands of eastern Galicia and southeastern Poland, including Cracow (western Galicia), as well as **Bukovyna** (1787–1849). The Austrian government carried out a number of reforms intended to improve socioeconomic conditions: the rights of landlords were curtailed and peasant labor obligations limited, a new judicial system introduced, and educational institutions provided for the Ukrainian population. Lviv University was established in 1784 and the **Halych metropolitanate** restored as a Ukrainian Catholic jurisdiction in 1808.

A Ukrainian national revival began in Galicia in the early 19th century, led by representatives of the Catholic clergy. Important steps in this process included the founding of the Clerical Society in Peremyshl, the educational initiatives of Metropolitan Mykhailo Levytsky, and especially the cultural activity of the **Ruthenian Triad**. The **Revolution of 1848** precipitated the awakening of national consciousness among the Ukrainian populace. The Supreme Ruthenian Council, established in Lviv in 1848, promulgated the idea of the unity of all Ukrainian lands and proposed the creation of a separate crown land within the Austrian Empire consisting of Ukrainian eastern Galicia, Bukovyna, and **Transcarpathia**. The abolition of serfdom in Galicia (1848) helped integrate peasants into political life but did not improve economic conditions. Galicia remained an internal colony of Austria, serving as a source of cheap agricultural produce and timber. Its small industrial enterprises were unable to compete with those of Austria's better-developed western provinces. The Galician petroleum industry was the only sector capable of attracting foreign investment. Most peasants subsisted on small holdings. Rapid population growth in the second half of the century exacerbated land hunger and resulted in the emigration of some 380,000 Galicians to the Americas between the 1880s and 1914.

With the creation of Austria-Hungary in 1867, political power in Galicia was assumed by the Poles, which led to strong Ukrainian-Polish antagonism. Nevertheless, Austrian constitutionalism provided an opportunity for the active development of Ukrainian national and cultural organizations in Galicia: the **Prosvita Society** (1868), the **Shevchenko Scientific Society** (1873), cooperative societies, and paramilitary sport associations such as Sich and Sokil. Eminent Ukrainian activists of the time, including **Ivan Franko**, **Mykhailo Pavlyk**, and Yuliian Romanchuk, worked in Galicia. From 1894, the historian **Mykhailo Hrushevsky** worked in Lviv, playing a vital role in the development of Ukrainian cultural, scholarly, and political life.

During **World War I**, the Legion of **Ukrainian Sich Riflemen** was established in Galicia, subsequently becoming the first military formation of the **Ukrainian Galician Army**. As Austria-Hungary collapsed, the **Western Ukrainian People's Republic** (ZUNR) was proclaimed on 1 November 1918 in Galicia and Bukovyna. The union between the ZUNR and the **Ukrainian People's Republic** (UNR) in January 1919 failed after Galicia was occupied by Polish forces. The official decision concerning Galicia's incorporation into the Second Polish Republic was made by the Council of Allied Ambassadors in March 1923, with the provision of Galician autonomy—a condition that was never honored.

Under Polish rule (1919–39) the region was actively Polonized, and Ukrainians were subject to linguistic, religious, economic, and political discrimination. Galicia was colonized by immigrants from indigenous Polish lands. These conditions brought about the underground struggle of the **Ukrainian Military Organization** and the **Organization of Ukrainian Nationalists**, which, in turn, provoked the Polish policy of **Pacification** and other repressive measures. Even under these circumstances, Galicia's Ukrainians developed cultural, educational, and **cooperative** organizations. Metropolitan **Andrei Sheptytsky**, who led the Ukrainian Catholic Church in this period, was also a very prominent cultural and political figure.

As a result of the Molotov-Ribbentrop Pact, Galicia was occupied by the Red Army in September 1939 and incorporated into the **Ukrainian SSR**. Four oblasts were created in Galicia: Lviv, Stanyslaviv (renamed Ivano-Frankivsk in 1962), Ternopil, and Drohobych (merged with Lviv oblast in 1959). During **World War II**, Galicia was occupied by the Germans and administered as a district of the **Generalgouvernement**. It was the only area of Ukraine where the Germans tolerated a Ukrainian representative body, the **Ukrainian Central Committee**, and recruited an indigenous military unit, the **Division Galizien**, to fight on the eastern front.

The postwar Soviet reoccupation of Galicia was accompanied, as in 1939–41, by mass arrests and deportations deep into the territory of the **USSR**. **Agriculture** was forcibly **collectivized**. Wartime resistance to the Nazi and Soviet occupations, led by the **Ukrainian Insurgent Army**, continued into the early 1950s. The Ukrainian Catholic Church was forcibly merged with the Russian Orthodox Church in 1946; it was restored in the late 1980s.

Industrialization, which proceeded slowly during the interwar period, became significant in the Galician **economy** during the Soviet period. The major industrial sectors are machine building and metalworking, food processing, light industry (mainly clothing and textiles), chemicals, forest products, and building materials. Nevertheless, Galicia remains one of the least urbanized (52 percent) and least economically developed regions of Ukraine. Contemporary Galicia (Lviv, Ivano-Frankivsk, and Ternopil oblasts) occupies 8.2 percent of Ukraine's territory and is home to 10.4 percent of its population.

Galicia's leading role in the development of Ukrainian institutions and national consciousness has given it the sobriquet "Piedmont of Ukraine." It is frequently contrasted with eastern and southern Ukraine, where the legacy of **Russification** and totalitarian rule has greatly hindered Ukrainian nation-building.

GALICIA-VOLHYNIA, PRINCIPALITY OF. Polity established by **Roman Mstyslavych**, who united the **Galician** and **Volhynian** principalities in 1199. It was the largest and most powerful of the **appanage principalities** that emerged after the demise of **Kyivan Rus'**. At various times, it consisted of the Halych, Peremyshl (Przemyśl), Zvenyhorod, Terebovlia, Volodymyr-Volynskyi, Lutsk, Belz, Berestia (Brest), and other principalities. In 1203, Roman

Mstyslavych briefly extended his rule to the **Kyiv** and Pereiaslav regions. For nearly 40 years after his death (1205), Galicia-Volhynia was rent by civil war among the Galician **boyar** elite and some appanage princes, as well as by intervention on the part of Hungary and Poland.

The first to vie for power in the Galician principality were Volodymyr, Sviatoslav, and Roman, sons of Ihor Sviatoslavych, the prince of Novhorod-Siverskyi depicted in the *Tale of Ihor's Campaign*. They maintained their position for nearly six years (1206–12), but were ultimately defeated in their confrontation with the boyar elite. The boyar Volodyslav Kormylchych assumed the throne of Halych (1213). After his removal, the rulers of Hungary and Poland partitioned the Galician lands (1214).

Following a lengthy struggle that ended in 1221, the foreigners were expelled and the throne taken by Mstyslav the Able (Mstyslavych), a descendant of lesser Kyivan princes who had previously ruled Novgorod. During his reign (1221–28), the Galician and Volhynian armies took part in the Battle of the Kalka River (1223) against the Mongols. In 1228, the boyars forced Mstyslav to abandon the Galician Principality, which was transferred to the king of Hungary.

Having established himself in Volhynia, **Danylo Romanovych** of Halych began his struggle for the other half of the principality. He restored its unity by taking Halych in 1238. At the Battle of Yaroslav (Jarosław) on 17 August 1245, Danylo and his brother Vasylko defeated the Hungarians and Poles, and Danylo took complete control of Galicia-Volhynia.

The principality's golden age followed. Its borders were secured and good relations established with Poland and Hungary. Danylo Romanovych defeated the Teutonic Knights at Dorohychyn (1238) and thwarted their designs on Rus' lands for an extended period. Danylo was forced to recognize the supremacy of the **Golden Horde** but received confirmation of his right to rule Galicia-Volhynia. He promoted commerce, established new towns, and invited foreign artisans and traders to settle in his realm. Danylo agreed to a church union with Rome and was crowned King of Rus' by a papal representative in 1253. This greatest of the Galician-Volhynian princes died in 1264 and was buried in his new capital, Kholm (Chełm).

After Danylo's death, the Galician-Volhynian lands formally remained a single state, but rivalry developed between Volhynia, ruled by Vasylko Romanovych (until 1269; and by his son Volodymyr from 1269 to 1288), and Galicia, ruled by Lev Danylovych (1264–1301). At the beginning of the 14th century, the unity of Galicia-Volhynia was restored under the rule of Yurii I, son of Lev Danylovych. His major accomplishment was the creation of a separate **Halych metropolitanate** (1303). After Yurii's death, the Galician-Volhynian principality passed to his sons Andrii and Lev, who allied themselves with the Teutonic Order and fought the Mongols.

The last prince of Galicia-Volhynia was **Yurii II Boleslav**, who ruled from 1323 to 1340. He promoted the growth of towns and introduced **Magdeburg law**, thereby provoking dissatisfaction among the boyars, who poisoned him. With Yurii's death, the Romanovych dynasty became extinct.

After a few years of oligarchical rule by the boyar Dmytro Dedko (1340–49), the Galician-Volhynian principality ceased to exist. In 1349, Casimir III of Poland took Galicia, followed by the Kholm region and the Belz land. In 1340, Volhynia came under the rule of Liubartas, son of the Lithuanian prince Gediminas, and was annexed to the **Grand Duchy of Lithuania**.

GENERALGOUVERNEMENT. Administrative unit created on 12 October 1939 by Nazi Germany in east-central Poland. Its administrative center was Cracow. It also included Ukrainian ethnic lands: **Podlachia**, the **Lemko** region, and part of the **Sian** and **Kholm** regions (total area 16,000 sq. km). On 1 August 1941, **Galicia**, which had been ruled by Austria for a century and a half and was thus considered "German" territory, was incorporated into the Generalgouvernement as the Distrikt Galizien. The Generalgouvernement, ruled by Governor-General Hans Frank, was divided into districts (Kreishauptmannschaften) and individual "free cities" (Kreisfreistädte) administered by a *Stadthauptmann*. Galicia was subdivided into 16 districts, with the city of **Lviv** and its surrounding area constituting a separate district. The occupation regime in Galicia was less harsh than in the **Reichskommissariat Ukraine**, given the prominence of Galician Germans in its administration and the recognition of the **Ukrainian Central Committee** as a representative body. An important consideration in annexing Galicia to the Generalgouvernement (as attested by Frank's diary entries for 11 March and 15 August 1942) was to secure German rule by promoting Polish-Ukrainian antagonism. *See also* WORLD WAR II.

GOGOL, NIKOLAI (HOHOL, MYKOLA) (20 March [1 April] 1809–21 February [4 March] 1852). The most prominent Russian writer of Ukrainian origin. Born in Velyki Sorochyntsi near Myrhorod, he graduated from the Nizhyn gymnasium and went to St. Petersburg in 1828, hoping to make a literary career. His first collections of stories, *Vechera na khutore bliz Dikan'ki* (Evenings on a Farm near Dykanka, 1831–32) and *Mirgorod* (Myrhorod, 1835), based on Ukrainian village life and folklore, brought him immediate fame. Gogol's stories intermingled fantastic elements with realistic incidents, becoming increasingly satirical. His comic play *Revizor* (The Inspector-General, 1835), a scathing depiction of the empire's corrupt bureaucracy, was first performed by special order of the tsar in 1836. In the same year, Gogol left the Russian Empire, living mainly in Rome until 1849. It was there that he wrote most of his masterpiece, the comic novel *Mertvye dushi* (Dead Souls, 1842), which describes a landowner's elaborate scheme to make a fortune by pawning recently deceased serfs (known as "souls"). This theme allowed Gogol to depict the iniquities of Russian serfdom and gained him a following among liberal intellectuals bent on social reform. Gogol, however, turned increasingly toward religion as a remedy for evil and sought to continue *Dead Souls* as a kind of *Divine Comedy*, pointing the way toward moral regeneration through the acceptance of divinely established authority. His *Vybrannye mesta iz perepiski s druziami* (Selected Passages from Correspondence with Friends, 1847), which eulogized the tsarist regime and the official Orthodox Church, consolidated Gogol's reputation as a political reactionary. The liberal Russian critic Vissarion Belinsky attacked him in an open letter as a "preacher of the knout, a defender of obscurantism and of darkest oppression." Returning to Moscow in 1849, Gogol came under the influence of a fanatical priest who persuaded him to burn the manuscript of the second volume of *Dead Souls*. He died 10 days later.

In the 19th century, Gogol's work was regarded as the fountainhead of the Russian realist tradition. The short story "Shinel'" (The Overcoat, 1842), which details the tribulations of a petty official robbed of the overcoat that has come to symbolize his identity, was the key work underlying that interpretation. According to Fedor Dostoevsky, all Russian realists had "emerged from under Gogol's overcoat." Gogol's influence, however, was apparent not so much in the works of such classic realists as Ivan Turgenev and Leo Tolstoy as in the more obsessive and idiosyncratic productions of such writers as Dostoevsky himself and the later Russian symbolists. Twentieth-century criticism, notably that of the Russian Formalists, has tended to focus on the nonrealist aspects of Gogol's art. His influence has remained seminal in Russian culture, not only in **literature** but also in **film** and **painting**.

Gogol's decision to make his career in the imperial capital and write exclusively in Russian has made him a controversial figure in Ukrainian literary history. The outstanding modern study of the issue, George Luckyj's *Between Gogol' and Ševčenko* (1971), contrasts Gogol with **Taras Shevchenko**, who chose to elevate Ukrainian from the status of a despised peasant dialect to a vehicle of full-fledged literary expression. In the 1920s, such critics as **Serhii Yefremov** and Yevhen Malaniuk condemned Gogol as a representative of the **Little Russian mentality**. Their interpretations were countered by Pavlo Fylypovych and Volodymyr Doroshenko, who stressed the importance of the Ukrainian element in Gogol's work and his contribution to modern Ukrainian identity. Since Ukraine's attainment of independence, there has been a tendency to reestablish a place for Gogol in the Ukrainian literary tradition.

GOLDEN GATE. Main gate of **Kyiv** dating from the era of **Kyivan Rus'**. It was built in 1037, during the reign of **Yaroslav the Wise**, at the southern entrance to Kyiv as part of the city's fortifications. It was constructed of brick and stone, and a small Church of the Annunciation was built above its vaulted passage. The gate or the chapel dome may have been gilded, whence the gate's name. It was partially destroyed during the Mongol invasion of 1240. In 1648, **Bohdan Khmelnytsky** and his army made their ceremonial entrance into Kyiv through the gate. In 1743–50, during work on the city's fortifications, the gate was covered with earth. The ruins were excavated by the archaeologist Kindrat Lokhvytsky in 1832, and in 1837–38 they were reinforced with brick. The gate was reconstructed in the 1980s.

GOLDEN HORDE. Western portion of the Mongol Empire (13th-14th centuries) that extended from Central Asia to Eastern Europe. It emerged in the 1230s as a result of the campaigns of Batu Khan. In 1237–40, he sacked Pereiaslav, Chernihiv, and **Kyiv**, destroying **Kyivan Rus'**. Subsequently, Rus' principalities were not territorially part of the Golden Horde but were vassals to it, paying tribute and providing military assistance. In the 1240s, **Danylo Romanovych** of Halych led the struggle against the Horde in the southwestern Rus' lands but was ultimately forced to recognize the supremacy of the khan. From the second half of the 14th century, the Horde declined as a result of internal conflicts. It then disintegrated into a number of independent units, including the **Crimean** Khanate (1440s).

GONGADZE, HEORHII (1969–2000). Investigative journalist. A native of Tbilisi, Georgia, Gongadze received his higher education at the department of foreign languages of **Lviv** University. In 1989, he created the independent information service of the People's Front of Georgia. Upon his return to Ukraine, Gongadze worked for the Lviv section of **Rukh** and, from 1991, as a journalist associated with the Lviv newspaper *Post-Postup* and Lviv State Television. He moved to Kyiv in the mid-1990s, working as an anchor for the Internews International Media Center and Gravis Television.

A strong critic of President **Leonid Kuchma's** administration, Gongadze took part in a television debate with Kuchma during the 1999 presidential campaign, criticizing the minister of the interior. On a visit to the United States at the beginning of 2000, Gongadze issued a statement (signed by 60 journalists) denouncing restrictions on the press in Ukraine. He organized a demonstration against these restrictions in **Kyiv** on 3 May and campaigned against Kuchma's referendum on strengthening presidential powers. On 17 April, Gongadze launched the online Kyiv newspaper *Ukraïns'ka pravda* (Ukrainian Truth), which focused on the business activities of **Oleksandr Volkov**, a close friend of Kuchma's and a sponsor of his presidential campaign. In the summer of 2000, Gongadze complained to the authorities that he was being threatened and shadowed by persons unknown because of his journalistic work. On 16 September, he was abducted while on his way home. His headless corpse was discovered by a farmer near Tarashcha, a small town in the Kyiv region, on 2 November. Not until 10 December was the journalist's widow, Myroslava Gongadze, allowed to see the body; she made a positive identification.

The Gongadze case became a major political scandal on 28 November 2000, when the leader of the Socialist Party, **Oleksandr Moroz**, released tape recordings purportedly made in the president's office by a police officer, Mykola Melnychenko. The recordings, apparently reproducing conversations between Kuchma and senior government officials, dealt with means of eliminating Gongadze. Melnychenko took refuge in the United States, where he was granted political asylum. Well into 2002, demonstrations in Ukraine ranging in size from a few dozen to several thousand protesters called for a "Ukraine without Kuchma"; some of these involved clashes with police. Foreign governments, **human-rights** groups, and media called for independent investigations of the murder. In the spring of 2001, Myroslava Gongadze and her two children obtained political asylum in the United States.

After an initial period of stonewalling, Leonid Kuchma acknowledged that the voice on the Melnychenko tapes was his but maintained that the recordings had been doctored to create the appearance of guilt. This remained the government's official position. In June 2004, the office of Ukraine's prosecutor-general announced that an individual identified as "K." had confessed to murdering Gongadze and was in custody. The announcement was met with widespread skepticism at home and abroad.

GONTA (HONTA), IVAN (d. 1768). Leader of the **Koliivshchyna Rebellion** (1768) in **Right-Bank Ukraine**. He was born in the village of Rosishky (Uman region). Initially a **Cossack**, Gonta was later a captain in the household militia of Count Franciszek Potocki of Uman. In 1768, he and his men went over to the **haidamaka** army led by **Maksym Zalizniak**. On 9–10 (20–21) June 1768, the joint haidamaka forces captured Uman and slaughtered its inhabitants. The expansion of the rebellion to the **Kyiv**, Bratslav, and **Podilia** regions aroused concern in the Russian government that it might spread into **Left-Bank Ukraine**. Tsarist armies engaged on the Right Bank against the Confederation of Bar helped the Polish nobility quell the rebellion. On 27 June (8 July) 1768, Russian armies surrounded the rebel camp. Zalizniak and Gonta were arrested and their squadrons disarmed, while other units were destroyed in the battle. The Russian command delivered Gonta to the Polish authorities. After brutal torture, Gonta was hacked to pieces at the command of Crown Hetman Ksawery Branicki. Numerous folk legends about Gonta have been preserved. He was depicted by **Taras Shevchenko** in the poem "Haidamaky" (The Haidamakas).

GOVERNMENT. The contemporary republic of Ukraine takes its origin from the Declaration of Independence of Ukraine, passed by the **Verkhovna Rada** (VR, Supreme Council) of Ukraine on 24 August 1991 and overwhelmingly ratified by referendum on 1 December 1991. The 24th of August is celebrated as Independence Day. However, the first step toward independence was the Declaration of State Sovereignty (16 July 1990), defined as the "supremacy, independence, plenitude and indivisibility of the power of the republic within its territory, and independence and equality in foreign relations." The document declared the principle of the separation of powers between legislative, executive, and judicial branches.

On 12 September 1991, the law on legal succession was passed, according to which Ukraine would continue to abide by the constitution and laws of the **Ukrainian SSR** insofar as they did not contradict postindependence laws. The borders of the Ukrainian SSR were recognized as those of Ukraine, and Ukraine pledged to fulfill international agreements made by the Ukrainian SSR.

On 28 June 1996, the VR adopted a new **Constitution** that defines Ukraine as a unitary republic (the **Crimea** is recognized as autonomous). Administratively, Ukraine is divided into oblasts, raions, cities, city raions, towns, and villages. The state consists of the Autonomous Republic of the Crimea and 24 oblasts (Cherkasy, Chernihiv, Chernivtsi, Dnipropetrovsk, Donetsk, Ivano-Frankivsk, Kharkiv, Kherson, Khmelnytskyi, Kirovohrad, Kyiv, Luhansk, Lviv, Mykolaiv, Odesa, Poltava, Rivne, Sumy, Ternopil, Transcarpathia, Vinnytsia, Volhynia, Zaporizhia, and Zhytomyr), as well as the cities of Kyiv and Sevastopol, which have special status.

Ukraine recognizes single citizenship. The basis for its acquisition and renunciation is defined by the citizenship law (passed 8 October 1991; amended 16 April 1997). Ukrainian citizenship was granted to all those residing permanently in Ukraine at the moment independence was declared, regardless of nationality or race, except citizens of another state.

The supreme legislative body of Ukraine is the Verkhovna Rada, which consists of 450 deputies elected by secret ballot to four-year terms. All citizens of Ukraine 18 years of age and older have the right to vote. A citizen over the age of 21 who has resided in Ukraine for at least five years may serve as a deputy.

The head of state and commander in chief of Ukraine is its president, elected by secret ballot to a five-year term in universal, equal, and direct elections. He is limited to two terms of office. The supreme executive body is the **Cabinet of Ministers**, headed by the prime minister, who is appointed by the president and confirmed in office by a majority of the VR. All other cabinet members are appointed by the president on the advice of the prime minister. The newly formed cabinet submits its program to the VR for approval. The VR may adopt a resolution of nonconfidence to force the resignation of the cabinet.

The local executive bodies are oblast, raion, and municipal administrations. Their heads are appointed and dismissed by the president on the recommendation of the cabinet. Representative bodies of local self-government are village, town, city, raion, and oblast councils of deputies elected to four-year terms. In addition, residents of a given community elect the head of their village, town, or city to a four-year term. On the judiciary, *see* COURT SYSTEM.

GRAVE, DMITRII (25 August [6 September] 1863–19 December 1939). Mathematician and full member of the **Ukrainian Academy of Sciences** (from 1919) and the **Shevchenko Scientific Society** (from 1923). Born in Kirillov, Novgorod gubernia, Russia, Grave completed his doctorate at St. Petersburg University in 1897. He was a professor at **Kharkiv** University (until 1899), **Kyiv** University (until 1939), and director of the Institute of Mathematics at the Academy of Sciences of the **Ukrainian SSR** (1934–39). His most important contributions were in Galois theory, the theory of ideals, number theory, the three-body problem, and equations of the fifth degree. Grave founded the Kyiv school of algebra, which became the leading center of algebraic studies in the **USSR**.

GUILDS (Ukr. *tsekh*). Closed corporations of free craftsmen working either in a single trade or in several related **crafts**. Guilds guaranteed their members professional and personal independence, a monopoly over a given trade, and a privileged place in a city's market. They regulated the purchase of raw materials, manufacturing, and the sale of goods. Guilds were also political organizations that opposed encroachments by the gentry; military units that defended the city; and religious and charitable organizations that assisted the poor and the widows and orphans of craftsmen. Although precursors of guilds existed in **Kyivan Rus'**, guilds on the West European model appeared in Ukraine with the introduction of **Magdeburg law**. The earliest guilds were established in **Galicia** in the 14th century. Ukrainian guilds reached their peak in the 16th and 17th centuries, by which time the guild system had begun to decline in Western Europe. Less exclusive than its Western counterparts, the Ukrainian guild structure consisted of master craftsmen, journeymen, and apprentices. Guilds were headed by elected masters and had their own statutes and treasuries. In order to become a master craftsman, a journeyman was required to travel to large towns to perfect his skills, produce a "masterpiece," and host a reception for guild members. Guilds had their own courts and were subject to the local city council. In the late 17th and 18th centuries, guild members in the **Hetmanate** included not only townsmen but also **Cossack** and village craftsmen.

H

HADIACH, TREATY OF. Treaty between Hetman **Ivan Vyhovsky** and the Polish government signed on 6 (16) September 1658 in Hadiach. According to its terms, a Grand Duchy of Rus' consisting of the palatinates of **Kyiv**, Chernihiv, and Bratslav was to become an equal partner with the Kingdom of Poland and the **Grand Duchy of Lithuania** in a federative expansion of the **Polish-Lithuanian Commonwealth**. Supreme legislative power in the duchy was to be vested in a congress of deputies. Executive power and supreme military command would belong to the **hetman**, elected for life and confirmed in office by the king. Candidates for hetman were to be chosen jointly by the **Cossacks**, nobles, and clergy. The posts of chancellor, marshal, and treasurer, as well as a higher judicial tribunal, were to be created. All official business was to be conducted in Ruthenian. The army of the Grand Duchy was to consist of 30,000 Cossacks and 10,000 mercenaries, and Polish forces were to be barred from its territory. In the event of war, Polish armies operating in the Grand Duchy would come under the command of its hetman. The rights and privileges of the Cossacks were guaranteed. Up to one hundred Cossacks from each regiment were to be granted nobiliary status annually. The Orthodox were granted equal rights with Roman Catholics, and the Uniate Church (*see* UKRAINIAN CATHOLIC CHURCH) was preserved. The **Kyiv Mohyla Academy** obtained the same rights as Cracow University, and a second university was to be founded in another Ukrainian town. The treaty provided for the establishment of as many gymnasiums, collegiums, and publishing houses "as necessary."

The Polish side refused to include the palatinates of **Volhynia**, Belz, **Galicia**, **Podilia**, Pynsk, Starodub, and Ovruch in the Grand Duchy of Rus', provoking dissatisfaction among the Cossack rank and file. Although the treaty was favored by the Cossack officers and ecclesiastical elites, it gained no mass support, and, owing to Vyhovsky's political demise in 1659, was not implemented. *See also* NEMYRYCH, YURII.

HAIDAMAKAS. Anti-Polish insurgents in **Right-Bank Ukraine** in the 18th century. The haidamaka movement emerged in **Volhynia** and western **Podilia**, spreading to the **Kyiv** and Bratslav regions after 1725 (some sources give 1712–14). The first mention of the haidamakas dates from 1715. The term comes from the Turkish *hajda* (chase, pursue). Initially used by the Polish nobility, the name was adopted by the rebels themselves. Detachments of 200–300 rebels ravaged the estates of Polish magnates and nobles, seized their property, and murdered particularly hated landowners. Led by **Zaporozhian Cossacks**, haidamaka units included peasants and townspeople.

The first large haidamaka rebellion erupted in 1734, engulfing the Kyiv, Podilia, and Volhynia regions. After the death of Augustus II of Poland, Russian armies and **Hetmanate** regiments entered Right-Bank Ukraine to ensure the succession of Augustus III. A rumor spread that Tsarina Anna had issued a decree calling for the destruction of the nobility. A unit led by Verlan, consisting of 1,500 men, was the primary force of the uprising. The detachments of

Hryva, Holy, Zhyla, Medvid, Pysarenko, and others were also active. The haidamakas took Zhvanets, Brody, and Zbarazh, besieged Kamianets-Podilskyi, and approached Lviv. At the end of 1738, Russian and Polish armies, assisted by the turncoat Sava Chaly, destroyed the main rebel force, compelling the haidamakas to retreat into **Moldavia**. A resurgence of the haidamaka movement in the winter of 1750 was crushed by joint Polish and Russian armies.

The haidamaka struggle reached its apogee in 1768, when the **Koliivshchyna Rebellion** erupted. It was sparked by the arrival in Right-Bank Ukraine of Russian armies, perceived by the Ukrainian population as allies in the struggle against Polish rule. Led by the Zaporozhian **Maksym Zalizniak**, a haidamaka detachment captured Zhabotyn, Smila, Cherkasy, Korsun, Kaniv, and Lysianka (May 1768). On 9–10 (20–21) June, Zalizniak's haidamakas and a group led by **Ivan Gonta** captured Uman. Simultaneously, the rebel units of Bondarenko, Zhurba, Nezhyvy, and Shvachka were active in the Kyiv and Bratslav regions, slaughtering the Polish and **Jewish** inhabitants of the captured towns. On 27 June (8 July), the rebellion was crushed by Russian and Polish forces near Uman. Zalizniak, Gonta, and other rebel leaders were captured. In July and August, most haidamaka detachments were destroyed and the rebels brutally punished.

Despite its defeat, the haidamaka movement entered folk memory through songs and legends. The movement was favorably depicted in a poem by **Taras Shevchenko** and by later Ukrainian writers and **populist** historians, as well as by members of the Ukrainian school in Polish literature.

HALYCH METROPOLITANATE. Church province established in 1303 in the Principality of **Galicia-Volhynia** through the efforts of Princes Lev Danylovych and Yurii I (1301–8). The bull and charter concerning the elevation of the bishop of Halych to the rank of metropolitan and his independence of the **Kyiv metropolitanate** were signed, respectively, by Emperor Andronicus of Byzantium and Patriarch Athanasius of Constantinople. The Halych metropolitanate included six eparchies: Halych, Peremyshl (Przemyśl), Volodymyr, Kholm (Chełm), Lutsk, and Turiv (Turaŭ). Its first metropolitan was Niphont (1303–5), a Greek. His successor was Petro, a **Galician** monk, who subsequently moved to Moscow. Other known metropolitans of Halych were Havryil (1326–29) and Teodor (1331–47). The metropolitanate was abolished by the Byzantine emperor John Cantacuzenus at the insistence of **Kyiv** and Moscow (1347). It was reinstated through the efforts of Casimir III of Poland, who was concerned to offset Lithuanian influence, and Bishop Antonii was consecrated metropolitan in 1371 (d. 1391). In 1401, the Halych metropolitanate was subordinated to Kyiv and soon ceased to exist. The eparchy of Halych was reestablished in 1539 under Makarii Tuchapsky, whose see was in Lviv. In 1700, the eparchy accepted the church **Union of Brest**.

Following the partitions of Poland, Austria took over Galicia and promoted the revival of the Uniate Church. Pope Pius VII renewed the Halych metropolitanate with two eparchies, Lviv and Peremyshl (1807), and Bishop Antonii Anhelovych was consecrated as metropolitan (1808–14). Among subsequent metropolitans were Mykhailo Levytsky (1816–58), **Sylvestr Sembratovych** (1885–98), **Andrei Sheptytsky** (1901–44), and **Yosyf Slipy** (1944–84). After the revival of the **Ukrainian Catholic Church** in 1989, the Halych metropolitanate was headed by **Myroslav Ivan Liubachivsky**, who was succeeded by **Lubomyr Husar** (2001).

HARVARD UKRAINIAN RESEARCH INSTITUTE (HURI). Research institute at Harvard University in Cambridge, Massachusetts, established in June 1973 to support research, publishing, and teaching in Ukrainian studies. It conducts seminars, holds conferences, undertakes special research projects, sponsors research associates, and publishes monographs, conference proceedings, series such as the *Harvard Library of Early Ukrainian Literature*, and the journal *Harvard Ukrainian Studies*. The institute's programs receive support from three endowed professorships in Ukrainian studies in the Departments of History and Slavic Languages and Literatures. The institute also maintains a reference library and archives. In conjunction with the Harvard Summer School, HURI offers courses in Ukrainian history, **language**, **literature**, and culture. Financial support for HURI is provided by the Ukrainian Studies Fund.

HEALTH CARE. In early Ukraine, health care was identified with medical practitioners, most notably the so-called *tsyrul'nyky* (phlebotomists), who were active from the 12th century. They established a professional guild in **Kyiv** in the 15th century, and one of their larger guilds was founded in **Lviv** in 1512. In the 16th and 17th centuries, church **brotherhoods** played a crucial role in the development of health care by establishing hospitals. The development of a health-care network was facilitated by the accumulation of medical knowledge, which increased with the founding of the **Kyiv Epiphany Brotherhood** (ca. 1615) and medical schools in Kyiv, Chernihiv, Pereiaslav, and **Kharkiv**.

The **Kyiv Mohyla Academy** played a decisive role in organizing the medical service of the Russian army in the 18th century. Its graduates studied at the Moscow Medical School, upon completion of which they served as regimental doctors. In the course of the 19th century, a network of hospitals developed in the Ukrainian lands within the Russian Empire: on the eve of **World War I** there were 3,933 doctors (1911) and 1,145 hospitals (1915). Health-care facilities were concentrated in urban areas; the rural population had to depend on zemstvo clinics. In the western Ukrainian lands under Austrian rule, health care was administered by physicians in private practice working for the Ministry of the Interior; for the poor, there were hospitals funded by municipalities and charitable organizations. A Ukrainian Physicians' Society was established in Lviv in 1912. Austria's first health ministry, established in 1917, was headed by the Ukrainian **Ivan Horbachevsky**.

Between the world wars, responsibility for the provision of health care in the **Ukrainian SSR** was divided between the state, workers' treasuries, and voluntary associations. The system was badly overloaded, and poor living conditions made for a low level of public health. In western Ukraine under Poland, the health-care system was better developed, with state-owned and private facilities supplemented by voluntary societies and **cooperatives**. **Transcarpathia** under Czechoslovakia also had good facilities, while **Bukovyna**, under Romanian rule, had inferior medical care.

After 1940, Ukraine's health-care network grew considerably. This growth, however, was not accompanied by quality service. For example, the increase in number of hospital beds was accomplished through the simple addition of beds in existing hospitals, often placed in corridors. In 1940, Ukraine had only 2,500 medical facilities with a total of 157,600 beds. By 1960, the number of medical facilities had doubled to 5,000, with 343,800 beds, but in the 1970s, it was cut back to 3,900. Between 1940 and 1995, the number of hospital beds in Ukraine increased 4.1 times. Nevertheless, the system's capacity to serve the population remained substandard. In 1990–95, the number of hospital beds fell from 700,300 to 638,900, or nearly 9 percent. In 1995, Ukraine's hospitals had 12.5 beds per 1,000 people, which satisfied only 88 percent of demand. As many medical establishments were located in adapted or unsuitable facilities, the availability of adequate medical care was in fact even lower, and in some cases corresponded to only 40–50 percent of demand.

At present, Ukraine has a centrally administered health-care system including a progressive diagnosis system and treatment by category. The first level of treatment is first aid, administered at nursing and midwifery centers in rural areas or clinics in urban centers. As a rule, treatment is administered in the patient's area of residence; that is, within the territorial boundaries of the first-level network. The second level consists of primary specialized (therapeutic, surgical, pediatric, and gynecological-obstetric) treatment administered at polyclinics and hospitals. Such treatment is provided in clearly defined regions of the second-level network. The third level consists of specialized and consultative facilities in urban centers that service both rural and urban dwellers within their territorial zone, usually including one or several administrative regions. The fourth level consists of comprehensive specialized treatment in oblast hospitals or oblast consultative clinics. The fifth level consists of highly specialized treatment administered in regional centers or in the capital.

There are severe regional disparities between the distribution of medical facilities and the needs of the population. Rural dwellers have considerably less access to health care than the urban population. This disproportion is also apparent in the distribution of hospitals and medical personnel. Oblasts with specialized secondary and postsecondary medical schools (e.g., Kyiv, Kharkiv, Lviv, Vinnytsia) are better staffed with medical personnel.

As government funding decreased in the 1990s, the health-care system deteriorated. In 1997, the network of medical facilities in Ukraine, excluding sanatoriums and health resorts, consisted of 3,211 hospitals and 6,384 clinics. The total included 625 city hospitals, 109 city pediatric hospitals, 134 specialized hospitals, 27 oblast hospitals, 488 central raion hospitals, 1,047 regional hospitals, 87 psychiatric and narcological hospitals, 379 dispensaries, and 87 obstetrical hospitals. The total number of hospital beds was 472,450, or 9.4 beds per 1,000 people. There were 205,000 doctors in Ukraine and nearly 10.2 secondary medical practitioners per 1,000 people.

Medical personnel in Ukraine are trained at 15 institutions of higher learning, which graduated 8,375 specialists (7,587 doctors and 789 pharmacists) in 1997, and at specialized medical secondary schools, which graduated 24,376 medical workers. Despite the relatively well-developed network of medical facilities, its main problems include low wages for medical staff, the lack of certain types of medical establishments in parts of Ukraine, the nonproportional distribution of medical facilities in rural and urban areas, reduced facility expansion in the 1990s, and reduced production of medical supplies. *See also* SOCIAL WELFARE.

HETMAN. "Leader," from Ger. *Hauptmann* and Pol. *hetman*. From the second half of the 15th century, the royally appointed commander of armed forces in the Kingdom of Poland (i.e., the Crown) and the **Grand Duchy of Lithuania**. The post of Crown Grand Hetman and, later, Grand Hetman of Lithuania became permanent (1503) and lifelong (1581).

From 1572, the **registered** Ukrainian **Cossack** army was led by hetmans. Their authority was limited, and the government of the **Polish-Lithuanian Commonwealth** avoided this title, referring instead to the "elder of His Royal Majesty's Zaporozhian Host," and often eliminated the post.

After the **Khmelnytsky Uprising** (1648–57), the hetman became head of state, holding the plenitude of executive, legislative, and judicial power in the **Hetmanate**, conducting external relations, and influencing church affairs. Following the signing of the **Articles of Bohdan Khmelnytsky** with Muscovy (1654), the hetman's authority was restricted. He was formally elected at a General Military Council with the approval of the tsarist government. In the 18th century, the hetman was appointed by the tsar and signed a special agreement with Russia. He headed the General Officer Staff, which governed the Hetmanate. Together with the regimental colonels, the Officer Staff formed the Council of Officers and had considerable influence on state affairs. In Russian-controlled **Left-Bank Ukraine**, the post of hetman existed until 1764 (with interruptions in 1722–27 and 1734–50). His residence was located successively in Chyhyryn, Hadiach, Baturyn, and Hlukhiv.

The post of hetman also existed under Polish control in **Right-Bank Ukraine** (**Pavlo Teteria**, **Petro Doroshenko**, and **Mykhailo Khanenko**, 1663–74). **Pylyp Orlyk** was hetman of Ukraine in the emigration (1710–42).

From April to December 1918, the head of the **Ukrainian State**, **Pavlo Skoropadsky**, held the title of hetman.

HETMAN, VADYM (12 July 1935–22 April 1998). Banker and politician. He was born in the village of Snityn, **Poltava** oblast, into the family of a teacher. In 1956, Hetman graduated from the **Kyiv Institute of Economics and Finance**. From 1970, he worked in various departments of the Zaporizhia Oblast Executive Committee, including price regulation, finance, and planning bodies. Hetman was appointed first deputy head of the **Ukrainian SSR** State Committee on Price Regulation (1975). In 1987, he was elected chairman of the Agroprombank. From 1992, Hetman served as a member of the Ukrainian Economic Reforms Coordinating Council and for almost two years, from March 1992 to December 1993, headed the National Bank of Ukraine. It was in this post that Hetman made initial preparations for the introduction of the *hryvnia* as Ukraine's national currency, which was to be carried out in 1996 by his protégé, **Viktor Yushchenko**. During Hetman's tenure as chairman of the National Bank, Ukraine joined the International Monetary Fund and the European Bank for Reconstruction and Development.

In late 1993, believing that the introduction of a new national currency was risky and detrimental, given the unstable economic climate in Ukraine, and having failed to reach agreement with President **Leonid Kravchuk's** administration on monetary reform, Hetman resigned. He was promptly elected chairman of the Ukrainian interbank currency exchange. In July 1994, Hetman became a deputy to the **Verkhovna Rada** and headed the Independent parliamentary group. In 1996–97, an all-Ukrainian awards program named him best parliamentary deputy and best financier.

On 22 April 1998, as Hetman was entering his apartment building, he was assassinated. The murder, which the police immediately termed a contract killing, has not been solved. There was speculation to the effect that Hetman controlled financial resources to support Yushchenko, his successor as chairman of the National Bank, in a bid for the presidency in the 1999 elections. On 7 February 2004, the prosecutor-general of Ukraine charged ex–Prime Minister **Pavlo Lazarenko** with ordering the assassination.

HETMANATE/HET'MANSHCHYNA, HET'MANS'KA DERZHAVA. Ukrainian polity (1648–1782) that emerged as a result of the **Khmelnytsky Uprising**. The Muscovite government referred to it in official documents as Little Russia. At various times, the capitals of the Hetmanate were Chyhyryn, Hadiach, Baturyn, and Hlukhiv.

Initially, the Hetmanate was nominally dependent on the **Polish-Lithuanian Commonwealth** and its territory limited to the **Kyiv**, Chernihiv, and Bratslav palatinates. However, the authority of the **hetman** also extended across part of the **Volhynian** and Belarusian lands. The political order of the Hetmanate was characterized by a distinct **Cossack** military and administrative system, the election of the hetman and of the general, regimental, and company officer staff, a unified tax, court, and financial system, and diplomatic relations with foreign states.

After the **Pereiaslav Agreement** (1654) and the signing of the **Articles of Bohdan Khmelnytsky**, the Muscovite government converted the Hetmanate into a semiautonomous territory. In 1669, relations with foreign states were forbidden. The 1666–68 tax collection was conducted by Muscovite officials and the revenue sent to Moscow. From the early 18th century, the hetman was virtually appointed by the tsar.

In 1663, the Hetmanate was divided along the Dnipro River into the **Left Bank** (Muscovite-controlled) and the **Right Bank** (controlled by the Commonwealth). From 1657 to 1687—a period known as the **Ruin**—Left- and Right-Bank hetmans fought one another incessantly, devastating Ukrainian territory in the process. The partition of the Ukrainian lands between Poland and Muscovy, without regard to Cossack wishes, was confirmed by the **Truce of Andrusovo** (1667) and the **Eternal Peace** (1686). The Right Bank came under direct Polish rule, while the truncated Hetmanate remained in existence on the Left Bank.

Administratively and territorially, the Hetmanate was divided into regiments and companies. On the Right Bank, the Cossack regimental-company system existed until 1714; on the Left Bank, until 1782. The number of regiments and companies changed frequently. Towns in the Hetmanate enjoyed self-government and were administered by *magistrat* and *ratush* councils. The social structure of the Hetmanate included Cossacks, nobles, burghers, and peasants. Cossack officers and nobles formed the Council of Officers.

The tsarist government steadily limited the autonomy of the Hetmanate. The first **Little Russian Collegium**, which supervised the actions of the hetman and his government, was active in the years 1722–27. From 1734 to 1750, the hetmancy was suspended and eventually abolished by decree of Catherine II (10 [21] November 1764). The Hetmanate was then ruled by the second Little Russian Collegium, led by **Petr Rumiantsev**. With the creation of the Kyiv, Chernihiv, and Novhorod-Siverskyi vicegerencies (1782), the Hetmanate ceased to exist.

The Hetmanate was also the name applied to the **Ukrainian State**, led by Hetman **Pavlo Skoropadsky**, which existed from 29 April to 14 December 1918.

HLUSHKOV (GLUSHKOV), VIKTOR (24 August 1923–30 January 1982). Specialist in cybernetics, computer science, and control theory; full member of the **Ukrainian Academy of Sciences** from 1961 (and its vice president from 1962) and the Academy of Sciences of the **USSR** from 1964. Born in Rostov-na-Donu, Russia, he graduated from the university there in 1948. In 1956, he began working for the Institute of Mathematics at the Academy of Sciences of the **Ukrainian SSR**, and in the following year he became director of its Computing Center, reorganized as the Institute of Cybernetics in 1962. Hlushkov did seminal work in modern algebra, automata theory, digital computers, automatic control systems, and artificial intelligence. He made outstanding contributions to the development of computing science, computer manufacturing, and the automatization of manufacturing in the USSR. The Dnipro and Mir computer systems were designed and constructed under his supervision. A general theory of automata that he developed was widely used in computer and automatic-machine construction. Hlushkov was also the first to propose a new system of computer-assisted economic planning. The Institute of Cybernetics of the National Academy of Sciences of Ukraine is named after him.

HLYNSKY, MYKHAILO (ca. 1460–15 [24] September 1534). Prince, statesman, and leader of an anti-Polish rebellion. He was a descendant of the ancient princely Hlynsky family that ruled Hlynske, **Poltava**, and Hlynnytsia. Raised at the court of the German emperor Maximilian, he served Prince Albert of Saxony. While in Italy, he converted to Catholicism. From 1499 to 1507, he was marshal at the court of the **Grand Duchy of Lithuania**. Accused of designs on the throne and removed from his posts, he and his brothers, Vasyl and Ivan, led an uprising of Ukrainian and Belarusian nobles against Sigismund I of Poland (1507–8). After their defeat, the Hlynsky brothers fled to Muscovy. Mykhailo entered the service of Prince Vasilii III Ivanovich, obtaining large landholdings and the title of **boyar**. A distinguished military commander in battles against the **Tatars**, he was imprisoned (1514–26) for attempting to switch allegiance to the Lithuanian side during the Lithuanian-Muscovite War (1512–22). During the regency of his niece Elena, the mother of Ivan IV, he served as her principal advisor. Accused of trying to seize power, Hlynsky was again incarcerated in 1534 and died in prison.

HNIZDOVSKY, JACQUES (YAKIV) (27 January 1915–8 November 1985). Graphic artist, sculptor, and painter. He was born in Pylypche (**Podilia** region) and studied at the Chortkiv gymnasium. While continuing his education at the School of Applied Art in Lviv, he submitted his drawings to children's and youth publications, as well as to the humor magazine *Komar* (Mosquito). In 1938, Hnizdovsky enrolled at the Warsaw Academy of Art and, following the outbreak of **World War II**, at the Academy of Arts in Zagreb, Croatia. Before settling in the United States in 1949, he was art editor of the journal *Arka* (Ark) in Munich (1946–47). The first large-scale exhibition of his works was held in New York (1954). Hnizdovsky worked in graphic art (woodcuts), painting, ceramics, and small-scale sculpture, employing a style that he termed "simplified realism." He illustrated many books, including a jubilee edition of the *Tale of Ihor's Campaign* (1950), *Ukrainian Folk Tales* (1964), and *Poems of Samuel Taylor Coleridge* (1967). His works were exhibited in Tokyo, London, West Berlin, Munich, Prague, and Moscow and are included in the permanent collections of many of the world's museums. He died in New York. In 1987, a posthumous catalogue raisonné of Hnizdovsky's works was published in New Orleans. A monograph and catalog of his graphic art was published in New York at the same time. Among Hnizdovsky's most important works are *Death* (1944), *Academy* (1944–45), *Displaced Persons* (1948), *Dance* (1953), *An Hour without Meetings* (1956), *Metro— Closed Gate* (1957), *Fanny* (1960), *The Bronx* (1960), *Field* (1962), and *Stump* (1966). See also DESIGN, GRAPHIC.

HOLOVATSKY, YAKIV (17 October 1814–13 May 1888). Poet, literary historian, ethnographer, and pedagogue. He was born in Chepeli, **Lviv** region (now in Lviv oblast). He graduated from Lviv University in 1841 and became a Catholic priest in 1843. As a result of the **Revolution of 1848**, he was appointed the first professor of **Ruthenian** (Ukrainian) **language** and **literature** at Lviv University, serving as the university's rector in 1864–66. A member of the **Ruthenian Triad**, he helped publish the literary miscellany *Rusalka Dnistrovaia* (Dnister Nymph, 1837), which included several of his poems. In 1846–47, he published 20 Serbian songs in Ukrainian translation in the anthology *Vinok rusynam na obzhynky* (A Garland for Ruthenians at the Harvest Feast). With the onset of political reaction, Austria began to support the Poles in Galicia, and the disillusioned Holovatsky, influenced by Mikhail Pogodin, adopted a **Russophile** orientation. After being dismissed from the university because of his views, he moved to the Russian Empire in 1867. He lived in Vilnius, where he headed the archaeographic commission. Holovatsky wrote literary and ethnographic studies, his most important work being *Narodnye pesni Galitskoi i Ugorskoi Rusi* (Folk Songs of Galician and Hungarian Ruthenia, 4 vols., 1878).

HORBACHEVSKY, IVAN (15 May 1854–24 May 1942). Biochemist, epidemiologist, full member of the Czech Academy of Sciences and the **Ukrainian Academy of Sciences** (from 1925). Born in Zarubyntsi, Zbarazh county, **Galicia**, Horbachevsky graduated from Vienna University in 1875. A professor at Prague University from 1883 to 1917 and its rector in 1902–3, he founded the Prague Institute of Physiology. Horbachevsky was a member of the Austrian House of Lords from 1908 and served as Austria's first minister of health in 1917–18. In 1919, he helped establish the **Ukrainian Free University** in Vienna and served as its rector twice after its move to Prague.

Horbachevsky was one of the first scientists to isolate amino acids and determine that they are components of proteins. In 1882, he synthesized uric acid from carbamide and glycine. He established how uric acid is formed in the body and studied uremia. In 1889–91, he discovered xanthineoxidase. Horbachevsky also devoted considerable effort to the development of Ukrainian scientific terminology.

HORSKA, ALLA (18 September 1929–28 November 1970). Artist and **human-rights** activist. Born in Yalta, she survived the blockade of Leningrad during **World War II**. Horska studied at the State Art Institute in **Kyiv**. Along with **Vasyl Stus**, **Vasyl Symonenko**, and **Ivan Svitlychny**, she became an organizer and active member of the Club of Creative Youth in Kyiv (1961–65), a center of *shistdesiatnyky* activities. She helped organize literary and artistic evenings, as well as annual commemorations honoring **Taras Shevchenko**. Horska was a prolific artist, producing a number of monumental works. In 1964, she was expelled from the Artists' Union for her role in producing a stained-glass panel of Shevchenko for the vestibule of Kyiv University. (The panel was destroyed.) Reinstated in the Artists' Union, she was again expelled and persecuted by the secret police for protesting the arrests of Ukrainian human-rights activists (**Viacheslav Chornovil**, Bohdan and Mykhailo Horyn, Sviatoslav Karavansky, **Valentyn Moroz**, Opanas Zalyvakha, and others) in 1965–68. In April 1968, she signed a letter to the Soviet leaders from 139 scholars and cultural figures protesting the arrests and closed trials of **dissidents**. Horska was murdered in Vasylkiv near Kyiv on 28 November 1970 under circumstances indicating KGB involvement. Her funeral became a demonstration of protest against the regime. Her works include *Self-Portrait with Son* (1960), *Portrait of My Father* (1960), *Alphabet* (1960), *By the River* (1962–63), and *Portrait of Vasyl Symonenko* (1963). A memorial volume, *Chervona tin' kalyny* (Red Shadow of Viburnum), appeared in 1996.

HRABIANKA, HRYHORII (d. ca. 1738). **Cossack** chronicler, judge, quartermaster, and colonel of the Hadiach Cossack regiment. He joined the Cossack Host (1686) and participated in the Crimean campaigns (1687 and 1689), the Azov campaigns (1695–96) and the Northern War (1700–21). In 1723, Hrabianka was imprisoned at the SS. Peter and Paul Fortress for seeking the abolition of the **Little Russian Collegium** and the reinstatement of an elective **hetmancy** (Kolomak Petitions of 1723). After the death of Peter I (1725), he returned to Ukraine. He died in the course of the Russo-Turkish War (1735–39).

Hrabianka wrote a major historical chronicle: *Diistviia prezil'noi i ot nachala poliakov krvavshoi nebyvaloi brani Bohdana Khmelnytskoho, hetmana Zaporozhskoho s poliaky* (The Events of the Most Bitter and Most Bloody War since the Origin of the Poles between Bohdan Khmelnytsky, the Zaporozhian Hetman, and the Poles, 1710). Based on previous Polish and Ukrainian **chronicles**, the work deals with the history of Ukraine from ancient times to 1709, focusing primarily on Cossackdom and the **Khmelnytsky Uprising** (1648–57). Hrabianka's theme, reflecting the ideology of the **Cossack officers**, is the struggle against alien oppression and the assertion of the **Hetmanate's** autonomy. The manuscript has not survived, but the chronicle is known to exist in more than 50 copies.

HRINCHENKO, BORYS (27 November [9 December] 1863–23 April [6 May] 1910). Writer, civic and political activist, linguist, and pedagogue. He was born on the Vilkhovyi Yar homestead in the **Kharkiv** region (now in Sumy oblast). Hrinchenko studied at a technical high school in Kharkiv and taught in elementary schools in the Kharkiv and Katerynoslav regions. From 1884 to 1900, he worked in the Chernihiv zemstvo and cooperated with the local **hromada**. There he established a publishing house that produced popular-education books in spite of severe restrictions (*see* EMS UKASE). In 1891 or 1892, Hrinchenko helped initiate the patriotic **Brotherhood of Taras**. From 1902, he lived and worked in **Kyiv**. In 1904, he became a founder of the Ukrainian Democratic Party (UDP). Later that year he assumed leadership of the left faction of the UDP, which became the Ukrainian Radical Party (URP). He edited the *Slovar' ukraïns'koï movy* (Dictionary of the Ukrainian Language, 4 vols., 1907–9), the most complete general Ukrainian dictionary until the 1970s. Hrinchenko became coeditor of the *Hromads'ka dumka* (Civic Thought) newspaper and editor of the journal *Nova hromada* (New Community, 1906). He also served as president of the Kyiv **Prosvita Society** (1906–9). Hrinchenko was one of the most distinguished representatives of Ukrainian **populism**. He defined his political views in the program of the **Ukrainian Democratic Radical Party**, which he wrote when the UDP merged with the URP in 1905, and in *Lysty z Ukraïny Naddniprians'koï* (Letters from Dnipro Ukraine, printed in the newspaper *Bukovyna*, 1892–93).

Hrinchenko began his literary activity in the 1880s. He wrote poems and nearly 50 short stories focusing on social questions, especially relations between the intelligentsia and the **peasantry**. His dramas also took up these problems, as well as historical themes. Hrinchenko compiled and published three large volumes of ethnographic material from the Chernihiv region and neighboring areas. He also compiled anthologies of folk culture and produced the first bibliographic guide to Ukrainian folklore, covering publications from 1777 to 1900. He was active in Ukrainian-**language education** and wrote a number of school textbooks. He died in Ospedaletti, Italy, and was buried in Kyiv.

HROMADA (Community). Organizations of the Ukrainian intelligentsia in the second half of the 19th and early 20th centuries in Ukraine. Hromadas were active in national, cultural, civic, and political life. As they were often subject to official persecution, much of their activity was clandestine. The first hromada, which arose in the late 1850s in St. Petersburg, consisted mainly of former members of the **Cyril and Methodius Brotherhood**, including **Mykola Kostomarov, Panteleimon Kulish, Taras Shevchenko**, and Vasyl Bilozersky. They established the first general-interest Ukrainian journal, *Osnova*. In 1861, a hromada was established in **Kyiv**, and from the 1870s to the 1890s it was a major center of national and cultural activism in Ukraine. Its members included **Volodymyr Antonovych, Pavlo Chubynsky, Mykhailo Drahomanov, Mykola Lysenko**, Ivan Nechui-Levytsky, **Mykhailo Starytsky**, and **Fedir Vovk**. Hromada members worked to promote **education** and develop national consciousness among the Ukrainian **peasantry**. They operated **Sunday schools**, published Ukrainian popular and scholarly **literature**, and collected ethnographic and folkloric materials. They were also active in the **Southwestern Branch of the Imperial Russian Geographic Society** (1873–76) and debated current issues in the newspaper *Kievskii telegraf* (Kyiv Telegraph). The **Ems Ukase** (1876) condemned the Kyiv Hromada and outlawed its activities. As a result of this repression, *Kievskii telegraf* had to cease publication, the Geographic Society branch was closed, and Chubynsky and Drahomanov were exiled. A number of hromada members, led by Drahomanov, emigrated and published the journal *Hromada* in Geneva (1878–82). In the 1880s, hromada members in Kyiv founded the major historical journal *Kievskaia starina* (Kyivan Antiquity, 1882–1906).

In the late 1870s, as younger activists began to establish their own hromadas, the Kyiv organization came to be known as the Old Hromada. During the next two decades, hromadas were active in Chernihiv, **Kharkiv, Odesa**, and **Poltava**, and, outside Ukraine, in Dorpat, St. Petersburg, and Warsaw. In 1897, at the initiative of Antonovych and **Oleksander Konysky**, a congress of hromada members was held in Kyiv to establish the General Ukrainian Non-Party Democratic Organization. It united hromadas in 20 Ukrainian cities whose activities continued until the February Revolution of 1917.

HRUSHEVSKY, MYKHAILO (17 [29] September 1866–25 November 1934). Historian and statesman. Hrushevsky was born in Kholm (now Chełm, Poland) into the family of a teacher and Slavist. He came from an old clerical family, the Hrushivs (later the Hrushevskys of the Chyhyryn district). Soon after his birth, the Hrushevsky family moved to Stavropol and subsequently to the Caucasus. Hrushevsky studied at the Tbilisi gymnasium (from 1880) and at the faculty of history and philology of **Kyiv** University (1886–90). In May 1894, he defended his dissertation on the Bar starosta region and obtained his master's degree. On the recommendation of his teacher, **Volodymyr Antonovych**, Hrushevsky was appointed professor of the newly established chair of Ukrainian history (officially termed a chair of East European history) at **Lviv** University (1894). From 1897 to 1913, Hrushevsky was president of the **Shevchenko Scientific Society** (NTSh) in Lviv. He was extremely active in reorganizing the society along the lines of a European academy of sciences, establishing its publications, collecting historical sources, and creating a library and museum. He edited *Zapysky NTSh* (Memoirs of the NTSh, 1895–1913). In Lviv, Hrushevsky established a school of Ukrainian historians that included **Myron Korduba**, **Ivan Krypiakevych**, **Stepan Tomashivsky**, Ivan Dzhydzhora, Vasyl Herasymchuk, and Omelian Terletsky. The first volume of his monumental *Istoriia Ukraïny-Rusy* (History of Ukraine-Rus') was published in Lviv in 1898. Its publication continued in Lviv and Kyiv (1899–1936).

Hrushevsky became involved in **Galician** politics as a founder of the **National Democratic Party** (1899). With the **Revolution of 1905**, he reestablished himself in Kyiv, where he organized and directed the Ukrainian Scientific Society (1907). In 1908, Hrushevsky became a founder and leader of the mainstream **Society of Ukrainian Progressives**. During this period, he published a series of works on the Ukrainian question: *Z bizhuchoï khvyli* (On the Present Moment, 1906), *Vyzvolennia Rosiï i ukraïns'ke pytannia* (The Liberation of Russia and the Ukrainian Question, 1907), and *Nasha polityka* (Our Politics, 1911).

The outbreak of **World War I** found Hrushevsky in Galicia. In November 1914, traveling via Austria, Italy, and Romania, he managed to return to Kyiv. He was arrested by the Russian authorities, who had long been monitoring his activities, accused of "Austrophilism," and exiled to Siberia. On 14 (27) March 1917, after the fall of the tsarist regime, Hrushevsky returned to Kyiv, where he was elected head of the **Ukrainian Central Rada**. The political situation in Ukraine changed swiftly, leading Hrushevsky and the Rada to abandon their demands for autonomy in favor of a declaration of Ukrainian independence (January 1918). On 29 April 1918, Hrushevsky was elected president of the **Ukrainian People's Republic**. When **Pavlo Skoropadsky** came to power in a coup d'état on the same day, Hrushevsky abandoned his direct involvement in politics.

Hrushevsky emigrated to Czechoslovakia (March 1919) and later to Austria, where he was active as a scholar and publicist. He founded the Ukrainian Sociological Institute in Vienna (1919), and from 1920 to 1922 he edited *Boritesia-Poborete!* (Struggle, You Will Overcome!), the publication of the **Ukrainian Party of Socialist Revolutionaries**, and the periodicals *Skhidna Evropa* (Eastern Europe) and *Nash stiah* (Our Banner). On 7 March 1924, after lengthy deliberation and negotiations with the Soviet authorities, Hrushevsky returned to Kyiv. That year he was elected a member of the **Ukrainian Academy of Sciences** (VUAN), taking over the chair of Ukrainian history. He participated in the publication of the journals *Ukraïna* (Ukraine), *Zapysky istoryko-filolohichnoho viddilu VUAN* (Memoirs of the Historical-Philological Department of VUAN), *Naukovyi zbirnyk* (Scholarly Collection), and others. He edited *Ukraïns'kyi arkheolohichnyi zbirnyk* (Ukrainian Archaeological Collection), *Pam'iatky ukraïns'koho pys'menstva* (Monuments of Ukrainian Literature), and *Studiï z Ukraïny* (Studies from Ukraine). In 1929, Hrushevsky was elected an academician of the Academy of Sciences of the USSR. He was arrested shortly thereafter on a trumped-up charge of leading a so-called Ukrainian National Center but was soon released. In March 1931, he was exiled to Moscow. The scholarly institutions that he had created were abolished, and his coworkers and students were arrested. All this had an adverse effect on his health. Hrushevsky died under dubious circumstances in Kislovodsk, where he was undergoing medical treatment. He was buried at the Baikove Cemetery in Kyiv.

Hrushevsky wrote more than 2,000 scholarly works, most notably *Istoriia Ukraïny-Rusy* (10 vols., 1898–1937; English translation being issued by the **Canadian Institute of Ukrainian Studies**, 1997ff.), *Narys istoriï ukraïns'koho narodu* (Survey History of the Ukrainian People, 1904), *Iliustrovana istoriia Ukraïny* (Illustrated History of Ukraine, 1911), *Pochatky hromadianstva* (Origins of Society, 1921), and *Istoriia ukraïns'koï literatury* (History of Ukrainian Literature, 5 vols., 1923–27). Hrushevsky was an editor of the multilingual documentary series *Zherela do* *istoriï Ukraïny* (Sources for the History of Ukraine), published in Lviv.

Hrushevsky's historical views were formed under the influence of Antonovych, **Mykola Kostomarov**, and **Mykhailo Drahomanov**. His scholarly and civic life was dominated by the ideas of **populism** and federalism, leading him to stress the primacy of social interests over those of the nation and state. This view also led him to challenge the statist interpretation of Russian history, which denied that Ukrainians were a distinct nation. By stressing the continuity of popular traditions and institutions, Hrushevsky developed a view of Ukrainian history as a continuous process, regardless of periods of statelessness. As he studied Ukrainian history and participated in civic and political life, Hrushevsky came to place greater emphasis on the national factor. His pioneering accomplishments as a historian, along with his tremendous organizational work and political role during the **Ukrainian Revolution** (1917–21), rank him among the most important figures in Ukrainian history.

HRYHORIIV, NYKYFOR (MATVII) (c. 1885–27 July 1919). **Peasant** military leader. He was born in Zastavia, **Podilia** gubernia. Having fought in the Russo-Japanese War and in **World War I**, he attained the rank of captain in the Russian army and was decorated for distinction in battle. In 1917, Hryhoriiv became associated with **Symon Petliura**, who enlisted his aid in the uprising against Hetman **Pavlo Skoropadsky** (November 1918). Accordingly, he led a partisan force in the Oleksandriia region in support of the **Directory**. In January 1919, Hryhoriiv broke with the Directory when it forbade him to attack Entente forces that had landed in **Odesa**. When the Directory was driven out of **Kyiv** by the invading Bolsheviks, Hryhoriiv aligned himself with the latter, although he maintained that "the permanent government will not be formed by us or by you, but by the people." With an army of 15,000, he led an offensive against Entente and White forces, taking Kherson (10 March), Mykolaiv (12 March), and Odesa (5 April). When the Bolsheviks ordered Hryhoriiv to help save Béla Kun's Soviet government in Hungary, he refused and issued a manifesto to the Ukrainian people (9 May) calling for struggle against Bolshevik requisition squads and commissars, as well as for the creation of representative councils at all levels. Hryhoriiv's rebellion was crushed by the Red Army at the end of May. In the summer of 1919, Hryhoriiv sought to join forces with **Nestor Makhno**. Seeing Hryhoriiv as a rival for power, Makhno arranged his murder and informed Lenin about it in an effort to patch up his relations with the Bolsheviks.

HRYSHCHENKO, KOSTIANTYN (b. 28 October 1953). Professional diplomat, minister of foreign affairs of Ukraine. Hryshchenko was born into the family of a civil servant in **Kyiv**. In 1975, he graduated from the international law department of the Moscow State Institute of International Relations. He then took a **United Nations** (UN) training course in interpreting in Moscow. Hryshchenko is fluent in English and French. He began his diplomatic career in 1976 as a staff member of the UN Secretariat in New York. From 1981 to 1985, Hryshchenko was attaché and then third secretary of the consular administration of the **USSR** Ministry of Foreign Affairs. He served as vice-consul and later consul at the consulate of the USSR in Montreal, Canada (1985–90). In 1990, Hryshchenko became first secretary of the department of arms reduction and disarmament of the Soviet Ministry of Foreign Affairs.

From 1992 to 1995, Hryshchenko was a staff member and then head of the department of arms control and disarmament at Ukraine's Foreign Ministry. He was a member of delegations that negotiated Ukraine's participation in the START-1 and ABM treaties (*see* NUCLEAR WEAPONS). Hryshchenko also played a leading role in negotiations with Russia on dividing the **Black Sea Fleet**. In 1995, he was appointed deputy foreign minister. His responsibilities included European security, arms control and disarmament, Russian and CIS affairs, border delimitation with Russia, Belarus, and Moldova, and bilateral relations with Asian, Pacific, African, and Middle Eastern countries. From May 1998 to January 2000, he served as Ukraine's ambassador to Belgium, the Netherlands, and Luxembourg, head of Ukraine's mission to the North Atlantic Treaty Organization, and permanent representative of Ukraine to the Organization for the Prohibition of Chemical Weapons (Brussels).

In January 2000, Hryshchenko was appointed ambassador to the United States. He is credited with improving Ukraine's relations with the United States following the scandal surrounding the murder of **Heorhii Gongadze** and allegations that Ukraine had sold anti-Stealth Kolchuga radar systems to Iraq. No Kolchugas were found in Iraq, and Ukraine joined the U.S.-led coalition there in 2003, reportedly at Hryshchenko's urging. On 2 September 2003, Hryshchenko was appointed minister of foreign affairs. He has the reputation of a pro-Western politician and a strong advocate of Ukraine's "European choice."

HRYTSAK, YAROSLAV (b. 1 January 1960). Historian. Born in the village of Dovhe in **Lviv** oblast, Hrytsak studied at Lviv University and obtained his doctorate at the Institute of Archaeography, **Ukrainian Academy of Sciences** (1996). In 1992 he became director of the newly established Institute of Historical Research at Lviv University. One of Hrytsak's abiding research interests has been the life and work of the major **Galician** writer **Ivan Franko**, the subject of his first monograph (1990). He edited and annotated a two-volume collection of the essays of a leading émigré historian, Ivan L. Rudnytsky (1994). Hrytsak is best known for his *Narys istoriï Ukraïny: Formuvannia modernoï ukraïns'koï natsiï XIX-XX st.* (An Outline History of Ukraine: The Formation of the Ukrainian Nation, 19th and 20th Centuries), first published in 1996 (a revised edition and a Polish translation appeared in 2000; the earlier centuries were covered in a companion volume by **Natalia Yakovenko**). Hrytsak's was the first post-Soviet survey of modern Ukrainian history to draw widely on Western-language historical literature and employ analytical approaches derived from the intensive Western study of nationalism in recent decades. In his history, Hrytsak propounded the view that for all the difficulties encountered by the Ukrainian national movement, Ukraine's evolution toward nationhood was essentially "normal," since it was shaped by the same modernizing forces that transformed other countries from hierarchical agrarian societies into industrial democracies, nationalizing them in the process. Widely used as a student text, Hrytsak's survey has influenced the teaching of history in Ukrainian schools and universities. Since the mid-1990s, Hrytsak has frequently served as visiting professor at Central European University in Budapest and has taught at Columbia and Harvard universities in the United States.

HRYVNIA. Monetary unit. The *hryvnia* was a unit of weight, counting, and exchange in **Kyivan Rus'** and other Slavic lands. In central and northern Europe it was called the mark. The term *hryvnia* comes from gold and silver ring-shaped jewelry worn around the nape of the neck (*zahryvok*). According to other historians, the term initially referred to heads of cattle, which used to function as a unit of equivalent worth. Later, *hryvnia* referred to a unit of weight (the silver *hryvnia*). The Rus' *hryvnia*, first mentioned in a 10th-century treaty between Rus' and Byzantium, was equivalent to five-twelfths of a Byzantine *litra* (136.44 g) or, according to other historians, half that quantity (68.22 g). Inasmuch as that quantity of silver could be represented by several coins of equal value, the *hryvnia* was divided into smaller units. A *hryvnia* consisting of a certain number of coins known as *kuny* was called the *hryvnia kuna*, a monetary and numerical unit used in Rus' from the 10th to the early 15th century. In the 10th and 11th centuries, the *hryvnia kuna* was worth 68.22 grams of silver; in the 12th and early 13th centuries, 51 g of silver;

in the 13th and 14th centuries, 20 g of silver. Some historians believe that the different denominations were actual silver coins, while others suggest that they were represented by marten and squirrel furs. The silver *hryvnia* (unit of weight) and the *hryvnia kuna* (numerical unit) both came to be used as currency in Kyivan Rus', with the silver *hryvnia* becoming equivalent to several *hryvni kuny*.

Coin *hryvni* were not standardized. Based on variations in form and weight, they are classified as **Kyiv**, Chernihiv, Novgorod, Lithuanian, and **Tatar** *hryvni*. Kyivan *hryvni*, which appeared in the 11th and early 12th centuries, are named after their place of manufacture. Hexagonal in shape, with a weight of 140–60 g of high-quality silver, they remained in circulation until the invasion of the **Golden Horde**. Chernihiv *hryvni*, so called because the largest hoards were found in that city, were used in the 12th and 13th centuries. They were similar to Kyivan *hryvni*, except for their flattened ends, and their weight was close to that of the Novgorod *hryvnia*. The latter was a sticklike coin with triangular incisions, weighing approximately 204 g, that circulated from the 12th to the 15th century. From the 13th century, the term *rubl'* was used along with *hryvnia* and eventually replaced it (*rubl'* strips were equal in weight to the Novgorod *hryvnia*).

The *hryvnia* is also the monetary unit of present-day Ukraine. Introduced under the **Ukrainian People's Republic** (March 1918), it was equivalent to half a *karbovanets'* and divided into 100 *shahy*. Its gold content was 0.387 g. Paper denominations of 2, 10, 100, and 500 *hryvni* were printed in Berlin. Under the **Ukrainian State** (1918), denominations of 1,000 and 2,000 *hryvni* were issued. The 5-*hryvnia* note was printed in Stanyslaviv (now Ivano-Frankivsk). **Heorhii Narbut**, Vadym Modzalevsky, Fotii Krasytsky, Anton Sereda, and others helped design the currency. Owing to military and political circumstances, the government was unable to issue coins. *Shahy*, or monetary tokens similar in appearance to postage stamps, were issued in denominations of 1, 2, 5, 10, 15, 25, and 50.

After Ukraine's declaration of independence in 1991, the government took steps to reintroduce the *hryvnia* (UAH) as the national currency (1996). The Luhansk mint issued coins in denominations of 1, 2, 5, 10, 15, 25, and 50 *kopiiky*. One *hryvnia* equals 100 *kopiiky*. Commemorative coins in denominations of 2 *hryvni* (copper-nickel alloy), 10 and 20 *hryvni* (silver), and 75, 150, 200, 250, and 500 *hryvni* (gold) are also issued. Paper bills are issued in denominations of 1, 2, 5, 10, 20, 50, and 100 *hryvni*. The printing of *hryvni* and the minting of coins is centered in Kyiv.

Some commemorative and circulating coins are prepared at mints in Austria, Great Britain, and Poland. *See also* CURRENCY AND COINS; ECONOMY.

HULAK-ARTEMOVSKY, SEMEN (4 [16] February 1813–5 [17] April 1873). Composer and opera singer (baritone). Born in Horodyshche, **Kyiv** gubernia, he studied at the Kyiv Theological School (1824–30) and seminary (1835–38) and sang in the city's church choirs. He continued his vocal studies in St. Petersburg and in Italy. In 1841, Hulak-Artemovsky made his debut at the Florence opera house. In the following year he joined the St. Petersburg opera, where he spent most of his performing career (1842–64); he later sang in Moscow (1864–65). Hulak-Artemovsky had a voice of exceptional beauty, power, and range. His musical interpretations were noted for their dramatic mastery. Among his 51 operatic roles were Ruslan in Glinka's *Ruslan and Liudmila*, Masetto in Mozart's *Don Giovanni*, Antonio and Enrico Ashton in Donizetti's *Linda di Chamounix* and *Lucia di Lammermoor*.

Hulak-Artemovsky began composing in 1851, writing incidental music to *Kartiny stepovoi zhizni tsyganov* (Pictures from the Steppe Life of Gypsies) and the vocal-choreographic divertissement *Ukraïns'ke vesillia* (Ukrainian Wedding). He wrote **music** to the vaudeville *Nich na Ivana Kupala* (St. John's Eve, to his own text, 1852) and to the drama *Korablerazrushiteli* (The Corsairs, 1853). To his own libretto Hulak-Artemovsky composed the comic opera *Zaporozhets' za Dunaiem* (**Zaporozhian Cossack** beyond the Danube, 1862), which soon became a classic of the Ukrainian repertoire.

HUMAN RIGHTS. Ukraine's human-rights record since 1991 has been mixed. The pervasiveness of connections between government officials and the criminal underworld has often blurred the distinction between political and criminal acts. Politicians, businessmen, and journalists have been attacked under circumstances suggesting political motives. The high-profile murders of the businessman Arkadii Tabachnyk (1997); the former head of the National Bank, **Vadym Hetman** (1998); the deputy head of the **Crimean** government, Oleksandr Safontsev (1998); and the investigative journalists **Heorhii Gongadze** (2000) and Ihor Aleksandrov (2001) remain unsolved. Abuse and ill-treatment of detainees, prisoners, and conscripts by police, prison officials, and fellow soldiers remains common and sometimes results in death. In 1998, there were 1,901 deaths in prisons and detention facilities, which was more than three times the death rate of the general population. The **United Nations** (UN) Committee against Torture has noted many deficiencies in

Ukraine's penal system, including lack of clarity regarding detainees' rights to counsel, medical examination, and contact with family.

The Security Service of Ukraine, police, and the prosecutor-general's office have generally not been aggressive in dealing with corruption; numerous cases have been dropped for lack of incriminating evidence. Anticorruption statutes are enforced selectively against lower-level officials for political ends. The former government officials Petro Shkudun, Mykola Syvulsky, and Vasyl Koval have all claimed that charges against them were politically motivated because of their ties with ex–Prime Minister **Pavlo Lazarenko**. The court system, which lacks sufficient staff and funds, is subject to political interference. Criminal elements are also widely alleged to influence court decisions. The Ministry of Justice reported that in 1997 135 judges were disciplined, 22 dismissed, and five prosecuted for bribery.

In violation of the **Constitution** and a law of 1991 on freedom of speech and of the press, the government owns or controls most of the national radio and television channels and interferes with freedom of the press through tax inspections, libel cases, subsidies, *temnyky* (guidelines on what to cover), and harassment of journalists. The Committee on Protection of State Secrets enjoys broadly defined powers over all **media**. In 1997, the **Cabinet of Ministers** adopted a regulation that further defined state secrets to include information on executions, the state of prisons, pretrial detention blocks, and centers for the forcible treatment of alcoholics. In 1999, the newspaper *Kievskie vedomosti* (Kyiv News) suspended publication after months of government pressure against it and resumed publication only when the presidential ally **Hryhorii Surkis** bought the newspaper and replaced its editor. Four television stations lost their broadcasting licenses in 2002. In October 2002, the staff of UNIAN, an independent news agency, issued a statement denouncing the "fierce pressure" they had encountered.

The European Union and the Organization for Security and Cooperation in Europe have noted Ukraine's progress toward international standards for democratic elections, particularly greater transparency. However, international observers have indicated significant flaws involving abuse of state resources by incumbent candidates and preference given to certain candidates in the use of state facilities, an imbalance in the distribution of election commission chairmanships, with some 70 percent drawn from propresidential parties in the elections of 2002, and incidents of violence, intimidation, and inappropriate influencing of voters.

In January 2003, Ukraine acceded to the 1951 UN Refugee Convention and its 1967 Protocol. In 2001–2, hundreds of migrants without appropriate documents were detained under inhumane conditions in the newly established Pavshyno camp on Ukraine's western border. According to the U.S. Committee for Refugees, in 2001 Ukrainian border guards allowed only three of 4,620 refugees, many of whom were Afghans escaping from the Taliban, to claim asylum.

The Constitution prohibits discrimination on the basis of race, sex, and other grounds, but the court system is less than efficient in enforcing these provisions. Violence against **women** is reportedly pervasive. In 1997, the last year for which statistics are available, 1,510 criminal cases were opened for rape, 822 for sexual abuse, and three for sexual coercion. Ukraine remains an origin and transit country for girls and women involved in the international sex trade. The U.S. State Department has placed Ukraine on its list of countries not yet in compliance with minimum standards for the elimination of trafficking, despite some official efforts to improve the situation. The government has approved a comprehensive program for 2002–5 designed to combat trafficking through increased investigative efforts, as well as to improve services for victims, including counseling and shelter.

HUSAR, LUBOMYR (b. 26 February 1933). Cardinal and major archbishop of the **Ukrainian Catholic Church** (UCC). Husar was born in **Lviv**. He and his parents were interned by the Germans in the course of **World War II**, reached the American zone of occupation after the war, and immigrated to the United States in 1949. Following studies at St. Basil's Ukrainian Catholic Seminary (Stamford, Conn.) and the Catholic University of America, Husar was ordained a priest (1958) and served as a pastor in Kerhonkson, N.Y. He earned a master's degree in philosophy at Fordham University (1967) and a doctorate in theology at the Pontifical Urbaniana University in Rome (1972). Husar became a Studite monk and was elected superior of the Studite monastery at Grottaferrata near Rome. In April 1977, he was secretly ordained a bishop of the church in Ukraine by Cardinal **Yosyf Slipy**. Following the declaration of Ukrainian independence, Husar returned to Lviv (1993), serving as administrator of Lviv diocese under Cardinal **Myroslav Liubachivsky**. Husar was elected head of the Ukrainian Catholic Church by an episcopal synod in January 2001, shortly after Liubachivsky's death, and nominated to the College of Cardinals in the following month.

Husar began the transfer of the headquarters of the UCC from Lviv to the Ukrainian capital of **Kyiv** in April 2004—a critically important development for a church that had been identified with

western Ukraine (and thus considered regional) for some three centuries. Concurrently with the transfer, the Cathedral of the Holy Resurrection is being built in Kyiv. On the long-standing issue of establishing a Ukrainian Catholic patriarchate, which Husar has described as "the normal way of doing church business in the Eastern tradition," he faces the inveterate opposition of the Orthodox patriarchs of Moscow and Constantinople, which makes the Vatican reluctant to grant the UCC patriarchal status. Following a UCC synod in Rome in June 2004, Pope John Paul II stated, "I share your aspiration, well-founded in the canonical and conciliar discipline, to have full juridical and ecclesiastical configuration." The pontiff appealed for patience while "your request is being seriously studied."

I

ICON. A painted, mosaic, or low-relief depiction of Jesus Christ, the Mother of God (Theotokos), the saints, or biblical events. Icons emerged in the Eastern Church in the second century, and their veneration was sanctioned at the seventh ecumenical council in Nicaea (787). They were painted according to an established technique and traditional prescriptions. A thin piece of canvas was stretched over a linden, oak, or cypress panel and covered with several layers of gesso (alabaster and glue), polished, and painted in a specific order: the image was traced first, then gold leaf was applied, followed by egg tempera paints, and the icon was ultimately covered with varnish. The first icons in **Kyivan Rus'** were of Byzantine origin. Among icon painters of the 11th and 12th centuries at the **Kyivan Cave Monastery**, the best-known was Olimpii. The oldest surviving icons date back to that period. Some icons in Ukraine, renowned for their purported miraculous powers, became objects of presentation or war booty. Among the most famous of these are the Vyshhorod Theotokos (later known as the Vladimir Theotokos, 11th–12th cent.), Ihor's Theotokos (13th cent.), the Chernihiv Theotokos (12th cent.), the Theotokos of the Caves (13th cent.), the Mother of God Hodegetria (Lutsk, 13th–14th cent.), and the Zaporozhian Protectress (17th cent.).

After the fall of Kyivan Rus', icon painting continued in the Principality of **Galicia-Volhynia**. **Lviv** emerged in the 16th century as the principal center of Ukrainian icon painting, with regional schools in Rybotychi and Sudova Vyshnia. With the Orthodox revival of the early 17th century, the church and the **Cossacks** began to patronize icon painting in Kyiv and other centers in **eastern Ukraine**. The art form was supplanted in the late 18th century by paintings on biblical themes but was revived in neo-Byzantine style in the early 20th century, notably by **Mykhailo Boichuk**. Subsequently, icon painting flourished in the Ukrainian **diaspora**.

IHOR (Norse Ingvar; Russ. Igor, d. 945). Descendant of **Riuryk** and prince of **Kyiv** (912–45). He continued the expansionist policies of his predecessor, **Oleh**, subjugating the Derevlianians and Ulychians and forcing them to pay tribute. The first **Pecheneg** attacks on Kyiv occurred during Ihor's rule (915, 920); he later signed a peace treaty with them. Ihor mounted a campaign against Byzantium in which his fleet was destroyed by "Greek fire" (941). The new peace treaty, signed in 944, was much less favorable than the one obtained by Oleh; moreover, the prince of Kyiv was obliged not to attack Byzantine colonies in the **Crimea** and forbidden to maintain garrisons at the Dnipro estuary. In the same year, Ihor waged a successful campaign on the Caspian coast. He was killed by the Derevlianians after demanding excessive tribute and was avenged by his wife, **Olha**.

ILARION. Church figure and writer of the 11th century; first native (non-Greek) metropolitan of **Kyiv**. He was a priest at the princely village of Berestove near Kyiv. According to the wishes of **Yaroslav the Wise**, Ilarion was consecrated metropolitan in 1051. Nothing is known of him after 1055. Ilarion wrote the renowned *Slovo o zakoni i blahodati* (Sermon on Law and Grace) between 1037 and 1050. It lionized **Volodymyr the Great** for introducing Christianity to **Kyivan Rus'** and glorified the native land and church as equal in status to Byzantium, the preeminent power of the day. The *Slovo*, preserved in more than 50 copies dating from the 15th and 16th centuries, influenced Ukrainian and other Slavic literatures.

INSURGENT MOVEMENT (1917–22). Armed struggle of the Ukrainian **peasantry** for political and economic freedom. In the **Kyiv** region, the **Free Cossacks** arose in 1917 to defend the local population against roving soldiers returning from the front. These units also resisted the Bolshevik offensive against Kyiv in January-February 1918.

In 1918, peasant revolts broke out against German occupying forces and the government of Hetman **Pavlo Skoropadsky** in response to food requisitions and the return of estates to their landlords. The Tarashcha uprising in southern Kyiv gubernia was put down with the help of German forces. In November and December, the **Ukrainian National Union** organized the overthrow of the Skoropadsky regime with the support of 100,000 peasant insurgents.

In 1919, the insurgent movement grew rapidly, to the point where some partisan units held the balance of power. **Nykyfor Hryhoriiv's** insurgents undertook a successful offensive against the Whites and Entente forces in southern Ukraine. Danylo Zeleny's revolt against the **Directory** weakened its control of the Kyiv, Chernihiv, and **Poltava** regions. **Nestor Makhno,** allied with the Directory and the Bolsheviks by turns, played a major role in the defeat of Gen. Anton Denikin's White army. At the height of his power, Makhno commanded 80,000 men and controlled much of southern Ukraine.

The Bolshevik invasions of Ukraine encountered strong peasant resistance because of food requisitioning, forced imposition of collective farming, and the **political terror** of the Cheka. According to **Khristian Rakovsky,** there were 328 anti-Bolshevik revolts in Ukraine between 1 April and 15 June 1919. The reactionary policies of the White armies also provoked spontaneous revolts. Unsuccessful efforts were made by **Ukrainian Party of Socialist Revolutionaries** and **Ukrainian Social Democrats** to coordinate the peasant forces; between December 1919 and May 1920, the first **Winter Campaign** of the Army of the **Ukrainian People's Republic** (UNR) also attempted to organize a peasant revolt against the Bolsheviks.

In 1920, the Red Army imposed Soviet rule on Ukraine, but it was largely confined to the towns. That summer there were 11 peasant revolts in June, 51 in July, and 106 in August in Kyiv gubernia alone, while in **Poltava** gubernia there were 76, 99, and 98, respectively. In October, Lenin had to admit that Soviet power in Ukraine was only formal, since the countryside belonged to the insurgents.

In 1921, there were some 460 insurgent bands in Ukraine, their numbers varying from 20 to 500 men. At the end of that year, the UNR attempted a second Winter Campaign that also ended in failure. Ultimately, the Soviet authorities overcame the insurgents by concentrating large masses of troops in Ukraine (in October 1920, their units accounted for 46 percent of the contending forces). Unable to coalesce around a political center, the insurgents were destroyed, although individual bands continued to operate into the late 1920s.

The peasant insurgents were opposed to all urban-based governments, which they saw as a threat to their anarchist ideal. They made tactical alliances with socialist regimes of various stripes, only to switch their allegiance as circumstances required. The Soviet authorities overcame peasant resistance to their policies by means of forced **collectivization** and the **famines** of 1921–23 and 1932–33.

ISAIEVYCH, YAROSLAV (b. 7 March 1936). Historian. Isaievych was born in the village of Verba in **Volhynia**. His father, an economist, was a diplomat in the service of the **Ukrainian People's Republic**. Isaievych studied at **Lviv** University under the distinguished historian **Ivan Krypiakevych**, specializing in the medieval and early modern periods. His first monograph was a pioneering work on religious **brotherhoods**, *Bratstva ta ïkh rol' u rozvytku ukraïns'koï kul'tury XVI-XVIII st.* (Brotherhoods and Their Role in the Development of Ukrainian Culture, 16th-18th Centuries, 1966; a revised English translation is forthcoming from the **Canadian Institute of Ukrainian Studies** Press). Isaievych then focused on the development of Ukrainian print culture, becoming an outstanding authority on the subject. He published studies of the first printer in Ukraine, **Ivan Fedorov**, and of Yurii Drohobych, the 15th-century rector of Bologna University who became the first Ukrainian to publish a book abroad. With Yakym Zapasko, Isaievych produced the three-volume *Pam'iatky knyzhkovoho mystetstva* (Monuments of the Art of the Book, 1981–84), an annotated catalog of Ukrainian books published between 1574 and 1800. He has also studied the Principality of **Galicia-Volhynia** and the medieval history of **Podlachia** and the **Kholm region**.

A research scholar at the Lviv-based Institute of Social Sciences of the **Ukrainian Academy of Sciences** since 1958, Isaievych became its director in 1993, when it was renamed the Krypiakevych Institute of Ukrainian Studies. Isaievych became an academician of the Academy of Sciences (1992) and secretary of its division of history, philosophy, and law (1993–98). A frequent visitor to the **Harvard Ukrainian Research Institute** since 1988, Isaievych has also served as president (1993–99) of the International Association for Ukrainian Studies (est. 1989).

ISLAM IN UKRAINE. Islam was introduced into **Kyivan Rus'** in the first half of the 10th century from the Volga Bulgar region and Khwārezm, whose merchants successfully promulgated Islam among the Turkic peoples of Rus'. The Mongol invasion of 1237–40, the subsequent conversion of the **Golden Horde** to Islam, and its eventual replacement by the **Crimean** Khanate facilitated the growth of Sunni Islam, including forced conversion, in southern Ukraine. The khanate's vassalage to the Ottoman Empire prompted the formation of the **Zaporozhian Sich**, which fought the Turks and **Tatars**. However, many Muslim Tatars served Ukrainian **princes**. Prince **Kostiantyn Ostrozky** went so far as to build a mosque for the Muslims in his service.

Persecution of the Tatars and Islam began after the Russian

Empire's annexation of the **Crimea** in 1783. As a consequence, more than 160,000 Crimean Tatars left their homeland in the 19th century. Nevertheless, in 1917, one-third of the Crimean population was Muslim. Islam was suppressed by the Soviet regime and further crippled by Stalin's deportation of the Tatars from the Crimea (1944). In the early 1990s, large numbers of Tatars began returning to the Crimea, revitalizing Islam on the peninsula.

Today, most Muslims in Ukraine are Crimean Tatars, who generally follow a more secular way of life than more recent Arab immigrants to Ukraine. Islamic communities in Ukraine also include immigrants from the former **USSR**, many of whom live in the **Donets Basin**. Most officially registered Muslim communities belong to the moderate Religious Administration of Muslims of the Crimea, headed by Emirali Ablaiev. It generally aligns itself with the Kyiv Patriarchate of the **Ukrainian Orthodox Church** (UOC), since both regard the UOC (Moscow Patriarchate) as their main adversary. The Religious Administration of Ukrainian Muslims, headed by Tamim Akhmed Muhamed Mutakh, includes most of the non-Tatar Muslims in Ukraine. A number of Islamic states are funding the reconstruction of historic mosques in Ukraine and have provided financial assistance to many Crimean Tatars undertaking the Hajj. New mosques are also being built in the Crimea, and construction of the large Al-Rahmah mosque is under way in Kyiv. Currently, there are 452 Islamic communities in Ukraine, with 436 imams (21 foreign), more than 150 mosques, and six educational institutions.

***ISTORIIA RUSOV*/HISTORY OF THE RUS' PEOPLE.** Most important Ukrainian historical work of the late 18th and early 19th centuries. It was first published in Moscow in 1846 by **Osyp Bodiansky**. The author of the work is unknown, although it has been attributed to many individuals (**Oleksander Bezborodko**, **Heorhii Konysky**, **Hryhorii Poletyka**, Prince Nikolai Repnin, and others). *Istoriia Rusov* traces the historical development of Ukraine from the earliest times to 1769, focusing primarily on the **Cossack** movement, the **Khmelnytsky Uprising** (**Bohdan Khmelnytsky** is the work's central figure), and the **Hetmanate**. It is not a work of professional historiography but a political tract that glorifies the struggle to preserve Cossack liberties and Ukrainian autonomy against Polish and Russian encroachments. Written in Russian with a large admixture of Ukrainian, *Istoriia Rusov* probably originated in the Novhorod-Siverskyi region and circulated in manuscript. It became extremely popular among the Ukrainian **nobility**, which was descended from the **Cossack officer** estate. But *Istoriia Rusov* was also strongly marked by the antityrannical and egalitarian motifs of the French and American revolutions, with their emphasis on the right to life, liberty, and property. The work thus exercised a strong influence on Ukrainian writers who came of age in the 1840s and had few ancestral ties with the Hetmanate, among them **Nikolai Gogol**, **Mykola Kostomarov**, **Panteleimon Kulish**, and **Taras Shevchenko**.

J

JEWS. The first Jewish settlements on what is now Ukrainian territory were established in the **Crimea** and on the **Black Sea littoral** during the fourth century B.C. Jews were not numerous in **Kyivan Rus'** but were prominent in the city of **Kyiv**, where they resided in the western and southern sections of the affluent *Kopyriv kinets*. This area was looted in 1113 in connection with a succession crisis following the death of Prince Sviatopolk II. Although that event has been characterized as a pogrom, the Harvard historian Omeljan Pritsak concluded (1990) that it was a political conflict between Rus' factions in an area that still bore its traditional Jewish name, but in which wealth had largely changed hands.

A large wave of Jewish settlement in Ukraine followed the expulsion of Jews from Western and Central Europe between the 13th and 15th centuries. Between the **Union of Lublin** (1569) and the **Khmelnytsky Uprising** (1648), the number of Jews in the Ukrainian palatinates (**Volhynia**, **Podilia**, Kyiv, and Bratslav) of the **Polish-Lithuanian Commonwealth** increased from approx. 4,000 to approx. 52,000. Like East European Jews generally, they spoke Yiddish and lived in ghettos in urban areas or in small rural settlements called shtetls. Many Jews, however, lived in mixed areas; a minority were frontiersmen who trained for military action against **Tatar** invasions and took part in the **Cossack** campaign against Muscovy in 1610.

Jews, usually in service to Polish landlords, were active in moneylending and commerce, buying agricultural produce, and supplying manufactured and imported goods. They also served as leaseholders of large estates, tax collectors, and estate stewards administering justice, including the death penalty. Jews held leases on individual villages or enterprises such as inns, dairies, fish ponds, mills, and lumberyards. Landlords held a monopoly on distilling liquor, which **peasants** were forbidden to produce and had to buy from Jewish leaseholders. Since many Polish landlords were non-residents, the peasants regarded the Jews as their immediate overlords, while in the towns the Orthodox Christians viewed them as competitors in trade and sought to restrict their commercial activities.

The growing dissatisfaction of the enserfed peasants and the Orthodox burghers placed Jews in a vulnerable position. The Cossacks, who increasingly identified themselves with the **Ukrainian Orthodox Church** after its revival in 1620, opposed the spread of Jewish leaseholds in their areas of settlement during the 1630s–40s. Anti-Jewish writings and practices of the Counter-Reformation, generally mediated through Poland, also had their effect in Ukraine. Together with Polish landowners and Catholics, Jews became victims of the **Khmelnytsky Uprising** in 1648. Modern scholarship does not accept the figures of scores of thousands of victims given in contemporary Jewish chronicles; Jaroslaw Pelenski (University of Iowa, 1990) estimates that some 10,000 Jews were killed in the uprising, while Shaul Stampfer (Hebrew University, 2003) gives an estimate of 18–20,000 victims out of a total Jewish population of some 40,000 in Ukraine. The 17th-century Jewish chronicles, of which the best known is Nathan Hanover's *Abyss of Despair*, register the trauma experienced by a community that saw many of its settlements wiped out in a sudden wave of violence.

In the Cossack **Hetmanate**, which was dependent on Moscow, Jewish settlement was banned beginning with the reign of Peter I. Nevertheless, the **Cossack officers** recognized the value of Jewish commercial activity and sometimes waived the prohibition. Most Jews (about 300,000 in the latter half of the 18th century), continued to live in **Right-Bank Ukraine**, which was part of the Polish-Lithuanian Commonwealth until 1772. Ukrainian peasants rebelled against economic, ethnic, and religious oppression, directing their anger against Poles and Jews. According to the late Shmuel Ettinger (Hebrew University), the **haidamaka** rebels killed 27 Jews in Korsun (1734), 35 in Pavoloch, and 14 in Pohrebyshche (1736); there were other massacres in 1738, 1742, and 1750. The Uman massacre of 1768, which was part of the **Koliivshchyna Rebellion**, is traditionally said to have taken some 20,000 Polish and Jewish lives, but Jaroslaw Pelenski's research (1980) indicates that the figure could not have exceeded 2,000.

Following the partition of Poland in 1772, the Russian Empire found itself with more than 900,000 Jewish subjects, whom it confined to a Pale of Settlement until 1915. In Ukraine, the Pale included most of the Right Bank, as well as the Chernihiv and Poltava gubernias on the Left Bank, the Kyiv and New Russia gubernias, and **Bessarabia**. Jews were subject to numerous restrictions (e.g., compulsory military service, bans on the public use of Yiddish and Hebrew, aggressive assimilation measures), especially during the reign of Nicholas I. Although some restrictions were loosened under Alexander II, Jews were never emancipated in the Russian Empire, and the vast majority lived in poverty.

Ukraine was the cradle of major developments in Jewish religious and secular culture. Hasidism, a mystical religious movement that challenged orthodox Judaism, arose in Podilia in the 18th century under the leadership of Israel Ba'al Shem Tov. It developed strongly in Right-Bank Ukraine before spreading to the Russian Empire. The modernizing *Haskalah* (Enlightenment) movement, which originated in the late 18th century, was an important influence on Zionism. Major Jewish writers of the 19th and 20th centuries in Ukraine included Shalom Aleichem (Rabinovitz), Isaak Babel, Hayyim Nahman Bialik, and Saul Tchernikowsky.

In the early 19th century, Jews prospered most in southern and eastern Ukraine, where they engaged in the grain trade and were active in commercial centers such as **Odesa**, Kremenchuk, and Berdychiv. In 1817, some 30 percent of factories in Russian-ruled Ukraine were owned by Jews. By the early 1870s, Jews accounted for 90 percent of those engaged in distilling and 32 percent of those in the sugar industry in Ukraine.

In Austria-Hungary, Jews were emancipated in 1868. In the mid- and late 19th century, Jews made up about 11 percent of the population of **Galicia**. Here, economic stagnation and sharp differences in occupational structure made for antagonism between Jews and Ukrainians; more than 60 percent of Jews were engaged in trade and commerce, while 94 percent of Ukrainians were peasants. Consequently, Ukrainian **cooperatives** competed with Jewish shopkeepers and moneylenders. Politically, Jews were mainly allied with the dominant Poles, although there was a growing tendency toward Jewish-Ukrainian electoral cooperation, especially after the introduction of universal manhood suffrage in 1907. **Ivan Franko**, the most prominent Ukrainian public figure of the period in Galicia, called on Jews to avoid isolation and participate fully in politics, as well as to support the Ukrainian national movement. Franko's poetic masterpiece, *Moisei* (1905), used the story of Moses to convey his view of the Ukrainian situation.

Ukrainian **populists** and early socialists in the Russian Empire (e.g., **Mykola Kostomarov**, Serhii Podolynsky) tended to be anti-Jewish, both because of religious prejudice and because of their endorsement of popular protest, even if it took violent forms. **Mykhailo Drahomanov**, however, urged full emancipation for Jews, the creation of a Jewish socialist movement, and the socioeconomic equalization of Ukrainians and Jews in order to eliminate sources of conflict. He advocated a multicultural society in Ukraine in which all minorities, notably Jews, would enjoy constitutional guarantees for their languages and cultures. Franko's contemporaries in the Russian Empire tended to see the Ukrainian and Jewish movements as parallel forces for social emancipation and thus at least potential allies—a perception expressed in such works as Hnat Khotkevych's *Lykholittia* (Hard Times), **Mykhailo Kotsiubynsky's** "Vin ide" (He Is Coming), **Volodymyr Vynnychenko's** *Dysharmoniia* (Disharmony), all published in 1906, and **Lesia Ukrainka's** poem "I ty kolys' borolas', mov Izrail'" (And you [Ukraine] once battled like Israel, 1904). This was also the approach of the leading historian **Mykhailo Hrushevsky**, who called for the abolition of the Pale of Settlement and promoted Ukrainian-Jewish political cooperation.

Before **World War I**, there were two waves of anti-Jewish pogroms in the Russian Empire. In 1881–84, pogroms were carried out in Ukrainian cities, mainly by migrant laborers, with victims numbering in the dozens; there were also pogroms in Warsaw and in Belarusian and Lithuanian towns. The second wave of pogroms, in 1903–6, was instigated by the **Black Hundreds** and claimed victims in the low thousands. Again, these pogroms were largely an urban phenomenon, with workers, shopkeepers, and artisans as the main perpetrators. Many Jews abandoned the Russian Empire and emigrated to North America as a result.

For the intellectuals who led the **Ukrainian Central Rada** in 1917 and went on to establish the **Ukrainian People's Republic** (UNR), it was crucial to obtain the support of urbanized minorities, notably the Jews, since the government could not function without institutions staffed by qualified professionals. (According to the 1897 census, 80 percent of Jews in the Russian Empire lived in cities and towns, compared to less than 6 percent of Ukrainians.) Consequently, the UNR adopted a law on national-personal autonomy for ethnic minorities (January 1918), and Moshe Zilberfarb became head of the UNR Ministry of Jewish Affairs, the first such institution in the modern world. It had scant opportunity to function, as the **Skoropadsky** regime supplanted the UNR for seven months, but the **Directory** of the UNR reinstated the ministry at the end of the year. It was headed initially by Solomon Goldelman and then by Abraham Revutsky.

In the course of 1919, as the Directory fought the Red Army and the Russian Whites for control of the country, Ukraine descended into anarchy. The troops on whom the Directory relied were, for the most part, peasant irregulars mobilized by warlords who shifted allegiance as their interests dictated. Since funds to pay soldiers were in short supply, all parties to the conflict robbed and victimized the defenseless Jewish population. At least 30,000 Jews were killed in the pogroms of 1919. According to figures compiled at the time by Nakhum Gergel, a prominent activist on behalf of Jewish refugees and the most authoritative source on the matter, 40 percent of the pogroms were perpetrated by troops of the Directory, 25 percent by independent warlords such as **Nykyfor Hryhoriiv**, **Nestor Makhno**, and Zelenyi, 17 percent by White troops, and 8.5 percent by Red Army units. **Symon Petliura**, the head of the Directory, Oleksander Hrekov, the commander in chief of its forces, and **Andrii Melnyk**, its chief of staff, issued orders to stop the pogroms and established tribunals to punish those responsible. Although courts-martial were held and individual perpetrators shot, the government and military command did not have sufficient control to enforce its orders against pogroms. Jewish historians (most recently Henry Abramson, 1999) have argued that Petliura did not sufficiently chastise his troops for pogroms, fearing that they would rebel against the Directory. Taras Hunczak (1969) points out, by contrast, that Petliura was well aware of the presence of anti-Semitic elements in the Directory's forces and took advantage of a period of respite in Galicia (May-June 1919) to disband partisan forces and create a smaller but more reliable regular army.

An idea raised in 1917 and supported by Petliura (then secretary for military affairs in the Central Rada) was to form Jewish self-defense units to prevent pogroms. This was voted down by the Jewish socialist parties, both on ideological grounds (opposition to ethnically based military units) and for fear of antagonizing the Rada's Ukrainian units. The idea was later revived by the Zionist leader Vladimir Jabotinsky, who had argued from the turn of the century that Jewish interests required an understanding with the rising Ukrainian national movement. In September 1921, Jabotinsky signed an agreement with his old friend Maksym Slavinsky, who represented the Directory, to organize a Jewish gendarmerie that would accompany the Directory's forces into Ukraine in the event of an anti-Soviet offensive. (Owing to the failure of the Second **Winter Campaign** in November 1921, no such offensive was mounted.)

An important consequence of the pogroms was the growing rapprochement between Jews and the Bolshevik Party, given that the Red Army was better able to prevent pogroms than any of its opponents. Prior to the 1917 revolution, Jews had overwhelmingly supported Zionist and social-democratic parties; now they appeared in the unprecedented role of government officials, Cheka operatives, and prominent Bolshevik leaders, making Jewish-Ukrainian relations generally more antagonistic.

The violence of 1919 again came to public attention in 1926, when Petliura was assassinated in Paris by Shalom Schwartzbard, a

Bessarabian Jew who claimed to be avenging the victims of the pogroms. Schwartzbard's lawyer, Henri Torrès, managed to focus the sensational trial (which lasted more than a year) on the pogroms rather than on the assassination. When the jury exonerated Schwartzbard and Petliura's family was ordered to pay court costs, the cause that Petliura represented was severely compromised in world opinion. Most Ukrainians, who regarded Petliura and the Directory as the leaders of their struggle for independence, maintained that Schwartzbard was a Soviet agent exploited to discredit the Ukrainian national movement because of its potential to destabilize the Soviet Union.

The **Western Ukrainian People's Republic** (ZUNR), supported by a well-developed national movement and operating under legal norms shaped by a half-century of Austrian constitutionalism, presented a sharp contrast with eastern Ukraine. The **Ukrainian Galician Army**, which fought the **Ukrainian-Polish War** (1918–19) on behalf of the ZUNR, carried out no pogroms against the substantial Jewish population (12 percent) on its territory and incorporated a Jewish battalion in its ranks.

In the **Ukrainian SSR**, Jewish culture flourished under the policy of indigenization (1923–33). In an attempt to change the traditional Jewish occupational structure, the Soviet authorities promoted Jewish agricultural colonies in southern Ukraine during the 1920s. These proved a failure; most Jews abandoned them in the 1930s, either for the cities or for the Birobidzhan Jewish Autonomous Oblast, established in the Soviet Far East in 1934. Jews accounted for approximately 13.6 percent of the membership of the **Communist Party of Ukraine** in 1922, a figure that declined as more Ukrainians were recruited. After 1933, when the Stalin regime did away with the **Ukrainization** policy and began a broad campaign of **political terror** and **Russification**, Jewish cultural and community activists suffered the same fate as their Ukrainian counterparts. In western Ukraine under Polish rule, Ukrainian and Jewish political parties supported each other in electoral blocs, while in the economic sector the cooperative movement competed with established Jewish enterprises.

There were about three million Jews living in the Ukrainian lands shortly before **World War II**, constituting 60 percent of the Jewish population of the Soviet Union and about 20 percent of world Jewry. Of these, according to various estimates, between 0.9 and two million were murdered by the Nazi occupation regime during the war (the figure of one million is generally accepted). The Ukrainian auxiliary police recruited by the Germans was employed to round up Jews, drive them into concentration camps, and execute them. This police force was by no means exclusively Ukrainian but included Russians, Belarusians, and recruits from the Caucasus; in eastern Ukraine, it helped the Germans combat the Ukrainian nationalist underground. Many policemen and members of other auxiliary formations were recruited from among Red Army POWs, who saved their lives by means of such collaboration. The number of Ukrainians involved in carrying out the Germans' policy of extermination has been estimated by Stefan T. Possony (1974, on the basis of documentation in the Israeli war-crimes investigation bureau) at 11,000. This figure is dwarfed by the number of Ukrainians who fought against the Germans in the Red Army (approx. 4.5 million) and in the **Ukrainian Insurgent Army** (UPA; tens of thousands).

Ukrainian wartime attitudes toward Jews were influenced by the widespread identification of the latter with the Soviet regime. This was particularly true in western Ukraine, which had just endured a brutal Soviet occupation (1939–41). The program of the majority Bandera faction of the **Organization of Ukrainian Nationalists** (OUN), adopted in April 1941, identified the Jews as the "most dedicated base of support for the ruling Bolshevik regime and the vanguard of Muscovite imperialism in Ukraine." When the Germans occupied western Ukraine and local Ukrainians discovered the corpses of thousands of people tortured and executed by the retreating Soviets, they vented their rage on local Jews. According to estimates of Jewish historians, between 2,000 and 6,000 Jews were killed in a pogrom in Lviv in early July 1941.

Nazi propaganda constantly emphasized the "Jewish-Bolshevik" motif, hoping to stir up spontaneous anti-Jewish violence, but Raul Hilberg (1964), the outstanding authority on the Holocaust, points out that it took the arrival of Nazi *Einsatzgruppen* to organize or provoke such outbreaks. The overwhelming majority of the population in occupied Ukraine, preoccupied with its own survival, remained passive in the face of mass murder, especially as the penalty for assisting or hiding Jews was death.

In spite of the danger, considerable numbers of people risked their lives to help Jews; in Galicia alone, 100 people were executed for such assistance, and Yad Vashem has recognized 1,755 Ukrainians as "Righteous among the Nations." Metropolitan **Andrei Sheptytsky** not only protested to Himmler in February 1942 against the mass murder of Jews and the employment of the Ukrainian auxiliary police for that purpose but also organized assistance through the **Ukrainian Catholic Church**, which hid hundreds of Jews and provided them with baptismal certificates. Sheptytsky also issued the pastoral letter "Thou Shalt Not Kill" (November 1942), condemning all murder, especially for political ends, and demanding that murderers be treated as social outcasts.

More than the pogroms of 1919, the Holocaust established the widely held Western view of Ukrainians as inveterate anti-Semites. Several reasons may be adduced for this. Once the German invasion of the **USSR** brought Stalin's collaboration with Hitler to an end, making the Soviet Union an ally of the Western powers, those who fought the Soviets for any reason, such as the OUN, UPA, and the **Division Galizien,** were taken to be ideological sympathizers of Nazi Germany—an impression incessantly reinforced by Soviet propaganda during the postwar decades. Moreover, once the concept of the Holocaust became well established in the 1960s, some Jewish historians and writers began extending it to earlier periods; in the Ukrainian case, such thinking produced an image of unrelieved anti-Semitism extending from the 17th to the 20th century. The hunt for war criminals who had allegedly taken shelter in the West polarized Jewish and East European communities, producing media-fueled controversies that encouraged stereotyping and hostility.

After the war, severe restrictions on Jewish culture and religion continued in the USSR, and domestic anti-Semitism (in the guise of anti-Zionism) was tacitly encouraged. As part of their campaign to discredit Ukrainian nationalism in the West, the Moscow authorities were at pains to associate Soviet Ukrainian institutions with anti-Semitic publications; the best-known instance was Trokhym Kichko's *Iudaïzm bez prykras* (Judaism without Embellishment), issued in 1963 under the aegis of the **Ukrainian Academy of Sciences.** The Six-Day War of 1967, in which the USSR sided with Syria and Egypt, set off a movement for Jewish emigration to Israel that was given strong impetus by the political détente of the 1970s. From more than 776,000 in 1970, the Jewish community in Ukraine was reduced to some 486,000 in 1989 and 103,600 in 2001 (0.2 percent of the general population). Recent emigration has been driven mainly by poor economic conditions.

The **dissident movement** of the 1960s–80s produced a breakthrough in Jewish-Ukrainian relations, as activists from both communities worked to promote democratic values, advance **human rights,** and defend their cultures. **Ivan Dziuba's** speech at Babyn Yar in Kyiv (the site of mass executions of Jews in 1941) on 29 September 1966, condemning anti-Semitism and calling on Ukrainians and Jews to show mutual respect, was the first step in this process. Subsequently, the clandestine *Ukrainian Herald* reported on the persecution of Jewish dissidents, and Ukrainian activists such as **Viacheslav Chornovil,** Petro Hryhorenko (Grigorenko), Sviatoslav Karavansky, **Leonid Pliushch,** and Yevhen Sverstiuk worked with Jewish dissidents, including Semen Gluzman, Mikhail Kheifets,

Avraam Shifrin, Yakov Suslensky, and Yosyf Zisels.

With Ukrainian independence, a law on ethnic minorities was adopted (1992) guaranteeing equality of rights and respect for the "languages, cultures, traditions, customs, and religious identity of the Ukrainian people and all national minorities." There has since been a revival of Jewish religious and cultural life in Ukraine. The Solomon University opened in Kyiv in 1992, in addition to some 75 Jewish schools throughout the country. The Institute of Jewish Studies in Kyiv conducts historical research, holds conferences and exhibitions, and issues publications. The Jewish community publishes several journals and newspapers and produces a weekly program aired on state television. Many synagogues confiscated by the Soviet regime have been returned to Jewish communities. The Federation of Jewish Communities of Ukraine and the All-Ukrainian Jewish Congress act as umbrella organizations for Jewish activities.

K

KAGANOVICH, LAZAR (10 [22] November 1893–26 July 1991). Soviet party and state official. Kaganovich was born in Kabany, **Kyiv** gubernia, into a **Jewish** family. From 1907, he worked as a shoemaker in Kyiv. Kaganovich joined the Bolshevik Party in 1911 and held leading positions in Bolshevik organizations in Belarus (1917), Russia (1918–20), and Turkestan (1920–21). In the years 1922–25, he was a department head in the Russian Communist Party (Bolshevik). Kaganovich was devoted to Stalin, who appointed him general secretary of the **Communist Party of Ukraine** (CPU) (1925–28), replacing Emmanuil Kviring, whom Stalin considered a potential opponent. Kaganovich resolutely implemented the official policy of **Ukrainization**, but his high-handed style of administration brought him into conflict with such leading Ukrainian communists as **Vlas Chubar**, **Oleksander Shumsky**, and **Volodymyr Zatonsky**. In 1925, Shumsky proposed to Stalin that Kaganovich be replaced by Chubar and that a former **Borotbist**, Hryhorii Hrynko, become head of the Ukrainian government. As this would have meant surrendering Moscow's control of Ukraine to the CPU, Stalin reacted by supporting Kaganovich, who forced Shumsky out of Ukraine. In 1928, when Stalin was battling Nikolai Bukharin and the "Right Opposition" for control of the party, he recalled Kaganovich to Moscow and made him his second-in-command as secretary of the All-Union CP(B). **Stanislav Kosior** replaced Kaganovich in Ukraine, and **Mykola Skrypnyk**, the strongest supporter of Ukrainization, emerged as the dominant CPU official; this, allegedly, was the price of the Ukrainian party's support for Stalin in his struggle for power in Moscow.

Kaganovich returned to Ukraine with Viacheslav Molotov in July 1932 to enforce Moscow's demands for high grain-procurement quotas, which led to the **famine of 1932–33**. Kaganovich also headed the grain-procurement committee in the North Caucasus, where the famine of 1933 took more than a million lives, especially in the Kuban, which was predominantly settled by Ukrainians. From March to December 1947, Kaganovich replaced **Nikita Khrushchev** as head of the CPU, carrying out a purge of the "nationalist" intelligentsia and leading the Soviet offensive against the **Ukrainian Insurgent Army**. His ruthless enforcement of grain-procurement quotas was largely responsible for the **famine of 1946–47**, of which Khrushchev had warned Stalin. Kaganovich spent the next decade in Moscow and, in 1957, was involved in an attempted coup against Khrushchev. For this he was removed from his government and party posts and, in 1962, expelled from the party. He was allowed to live out the rest of his life in Moscow; his memoirs appeared posthumously in 1996.

KAPNIST, VASYL (12 [23] February 1758–28 October [9 November] 1823). Writer; civic and political activist. He was born in Obukhivka (now Velyka Obukhivka, **Poltava** oblast). Kapnist served in the military and was comptroller of the main postal administration in St. Petersburg (1782–83). In 1783, he returned to Ukraine and served as director of specialized schools in Poltava gubernia. Highly regarded by the Ukrainian **nobility**, he was elected marshal ot the nobility of Myrhorod county (1782, prior to his departure for St. Petersburg) and **Kyiv** gubernia (1785–87). He was elected general judge of Poltava gubernia (from 1802) and was marshal of the nobility in Poltava (from 1820). Kapnist began publishing in 1780, writing odes, elegies, and Anacreontic poetry. In 1783, he wrote "Oda na rabstvo" (Ode on Slavery, published 1806), in which he protested growing Russian centralism in Ukraine, particularly the definitive abolition of Cossack regiments (1783) and the introduction of serfdom in **Sloboda** and **Left-Bank Ukraine**. In 1787, Kapnist and a group of aristocratic autonomists proposed the renewal of **Cossack** formations in Ukraine, which was rejected by the tsarist government despite the support of **Petr Rumiantsev** and Grigorii Potemkin. In April 1791, Kapnist and his brother Petro were sent to Berlin by Ukrainian patriotic circles. He conducted negotiations with representatives of the Prussian government, including the foreign secretary of Prussia, Ewald Friedrich von Hertzberg, concerning potential aid to the Ukrainian movement in the event of armed rebellion against Russian autocracy. In 1798, Kapnist published the poem "Iabeda" (Calumny), in which he sharply criticized Russian centralism in Ukraine. He translated the *Tale of Ihor's Campaign* into Russian, adding a commentary in which he emphasized the work's Ukrainian origin and qualities.

KARAZYN, VASYL (30 January [10 February] 1773–4 [16] November 1842). Scientist, inventor, educator, and reformer. He was born of noble descent in Kruchyk, **Kharkiv** region, and studied at a private boarding school in Kharkiv and the Institute of Mining in St. Petersburg. He invented steam heating and drying machines, **agricultural** equipment, and machines for saltpeter extraction. Karazyn wrote more than 60 articles in such fields as agronomy, genetic selection, climatology, and meteorology. From 1811 to 1818, he headed the Philotechnical Society, established for the dissemination of scientific, technological, and industrial achievements. Karazyn briefly served as director of schools in the Russian imperial ministry of education (1801–4) and sought to reform the system according to West European standards. He initiated the founding of Kharkiv University in 1805. For his outspoken criticism of the empire's political and economic backwardness, Karazyn was imprisoned at the Schlüsselburg Fortress (1820–21) and subsequently confined to his estate under police surveillance. He died in Mykolaiv, where he was buried. A monument to Karazyn was erected in Kharkiv in 1905.

KARMALIUK, USTYM (27 February [10 March] 1787–10 [22] October 1835). Also known as Karmeliuk. Folk hero and leader of the insurgent movement against national and social oppression in **Podilia**. He was born in Holovchyntsi, Podilia gubernia (now Karmaliukove, Vinnytsia oblast) into an enserfed **peasant** family. Sent to the army by his landowner, Pigłowski, he escaped from his lance regiment in Kamianets-Podilskyi (1813) and took command of an insurgent movement against the Russian administration and nobility in Lityn, Liatychiv, and Olhopil counties (1814). Karmaliuk's movement, which united some 20,000 rebels, engulfed Podilia, neighboring regions of **Bessarabia**, and the **Kyiv** region (1830–35). Over a period of 23 years, the rebel units conducted approximately 1,000 raids on landed estates. Seized money and property were distributed among poor peasants. In November 1833, the Russian government created the Haluzyntsi Commission to counter the rebels. Karmaliuk was arrested four times, sentenced to hard labor, and exiled to Siberia. Each time he escaped, returned to Podilia, and again took command of the rebel movement. He was killed in an ambush by the nobleman Rutkowski in the village of Shliakhovi Korychyntsi (now in the Khmelnytskyi region). Karmaliuk was depicted as an avenger of the people's wrongs in works by **Taras Shevchenko**, **Mykhailo Starytsky**, Marko Vovchok, and others.

KAVALERIDZE, IVAN (14 [26] April 1887–3 December 1978). Sculptor, **film** director, and playwright. Born on the Ladany homestead (now in Sumy oblast), he studied at the **Kyiv** Art School (1907–9), then in St. Petersburg (1909–10) and Paris (1910–11). Kavaleridze's sculptures include a bust of Fedor Chaliapin (1909), a monument to Princess **Olha** in Kyiv (1911, destroyed in 1934, restored in 1996), monuments to **Taras Shevchenko** in Romny (1919), **Poltava** (1925), and Sumy (1926), monuments to **Hryhorii Skovoroda** in Lokhvytsi (Poltava oblast, 1922) and Kyiv (1977), a model for a monument to **Yaroslav the Wise** (1944–60), and the group compositions *Amvrosii Buchma in the Role of Mykola Zadorozhny* (1954) and *Prometheus* (1962).

Kavaleridze worked in the cinema as a set designer (1911–15) and from 1928 as a director and screenwriter at the **Odesa** and Kyiv film studios. In 1957, he became a director at the Kyiv **Dovzhenko** Film Studio. He wrote and directed a number of highly stylized monumental costume films that were frequently accused of having a nationalist slant. They included *Zlyva* (Downpour, 1929), *Perekop* (1930), *Koliivshchyna* (1933), and *Prometei* (Prometheus, 1936). He also adapted for the screen two Ukrainian operas, *Natalka Poltavka* (1936) and *Zaporozhets' za Dunaiem* (**Zaporozhian Cossack** beyond the Danube, 1937). After **World War II**, he completed a biographical film about the philosopher *Hryhorii Skovoroda* (1958) and adapted literary classics such as *Poviia* (Strumpet, 1961).

KHANENKO FAMILY. Cossack officer family in **Left-Bank Ukraine** that included a number of statesmen and cultural activists of the 17th to 20th centuries. Mykhailo Khanenko (ca. 1620–1680) was **hetman** of **Right-Bank Ukraine** (1669–74). He took part in the **Khmelnytsky Uprising** (1648–57) and was colonel of the Uman regiment from 1656. He received nobiliary status from King John Casimir of Poland (1661) and was elected hetman of Right-Bank Ukraine at a **Cossack council** in Uman (September 1669). Khanenko and *kish* otaman **Ivan Sirko** conducted successful campaigns into the **Crimea** and Turkish possessions (1670–71). Under the Ostrih Treaty, Khanenko and the **Zaporozhians** came under a Polish protectorate (September 1670). He fought for control over the Right Bank with **Petro Doroshenko** (autumn 1670) and was defeated at

Chetvertynivka (July 1672) and at Stebliv (1673), subsequently seeking aid from Hetman **Ivan Samoilovych**. Khanenko resigned the hetmancy at a Cossack council in Pereiaslav and swore allegiance to the Muscovite tsar (19 March 1674), receiving in exchange lands in Left-Bank Ukraine. In 1677–78, accused of secret contacts with Poland, he was imprisoned in Baturyn. Mykola Khanenko (26 November [6 December] 1693–27 January [7 February] 1760) was a politician, diplomat, and diarist. He studied at the **Kyiv Mohyla Academy** and the **Lviv Dormition Brotherhood** School (1710). He was on military service until 1717. In May 1723, acting hetman **Pavlo Polubotok** dispatched Khanenko to St. Petersburg to seek the restoration of the practice of electing hetmans. At the command of Peter I, Khanenko and Polubotok were imprisoned at the SS. Peter and Paul Fortress. Khanenko returned to Ukraine in 1726. He was judge, quartermaster, and acting colonel of the Starodub regiment (1727–38). In 1735–39, he participated in the Russo-Turkish War. In recognition of his military service, he was appointed general flag-bearer (1738) and general standard-bearer (1741). He worked on the commission that compiled the **Code of Laws of 1743**. Under Hetman **Kyrylo Rozumovsky**, he was a leading figure in the General Military Chancellery. Khanenko's *diariush* of daily entries for January–early July 1722 and a diary for the years 1727–53 are valuable historical sources. Oleksander Khanenko (1805–1895) was a historian and civic and cultural activist. In the 1840s, he was marshal of the nobility in Surazh county, Chernihiv gubernia. He wrote works on the Chernihiv gubernia (1887) and the Khanenko family (1889). Bohdan Khanenko (11 [23] January 1848–26 May [8 June] 1917) was a collector of Ukrainian antiquities, archaeologist, and patron of the arts. He sponsored archaeological digs in the Kyiv region and published the collection *Drevnosti Podneprov'ia* (Antiquities of the Dnipro Region, 1899–1907). He donated his collection of archaeological finds and art works to the Museum of Art in Kyiv (now the Kyiv Museum of Western and Eastern Art).

KHARKIV. Second-largest city in Ukraine (1998 pop. 1,521,400), capital of Kharkiv oblast, historical capital of **Sloboda Ukraine**, and a major industrial, scientific, and cultural center. Kharkiv's location at the hub of trade routes between Russia, central Ukraine, the Caucasus, and the Black Sea has promoted its commercial and industrial growth. The city's name is probably derived from the Kharkiv River, although popular tradition traces it to a **Cossack** named Kharko.

The environs of Kharkiv have been settled since the second millennium B.C., and evidence of Bronze Age, **Scythian**, and

Sarmatian culture has been discovered there. From the 12th to the 17th century, the area was a wild steppe dominated by the **Cumans** and then by the **Tatars**. In the early 17th century it was acquired by Muscovy, which established frontier garrisons and lines of fortifications to protect the region from Tatar incursions. With the eastward expansion of the **Polish-Lithuanian Commonwealth**, Cossacks and peasants seeking relief from labor obligations began to settle the area.

Modern Kharkiv developed on the basis of a fortified settlement established in 1654–55 by Ukrainian Cossacks. During the **Hetmanate** of the 17th and 18th centuries, the Kharkiv regiment, one of the major Cossack administrative and military units, was based there. Kharkiv continued to function as a defensive outpost for the Russian Empire, with Russian soldiers, merchants, and artisans based in the fortress, while the Cossacks, who lived in the expanding *slobody*, engaged in farming, animal husbandry, and barter.

In the course of the 18th century, as the empire's borders shifted southward, Kharkiv became more of a commercial, cultural, and administrative center. Its annual fairs were frequented by merchants from central Ukraine, Russia, and Eastern Europe. The Kharkiv Collegium, one of the empire's most important religious secondary schools, was established in 1734 and succeeded by Kharkiv University, founded in 1805. In 1765, following the abolition of the Cossack regimental system, Kharkiv became the capital of the new Sloboda Ukraine gubernia (1765–80, restored from 1796 to 1835) and then of Kharkiv gubernia (1835–1925). During the 19th century, many new buildings were erected in the imperial style. The Kharkiv eparchy of the Orthodox Church was constituted in 1799. Throughout the 19th century, Kharkiv was the center of a military district, with a large number of army personnel. By mid-century it had 212 small manufacturing enterprises, but their number and size increased rapidly following the emancipation of the peasants in 1861, given the proximity of the **Donets Basin** coalfield and the arrival of a railway line in 1868. By 1900, Kharkiv had 259 factories and plants, with a notable concentration on machine-building and metal-working, manned by some 12,000 workers.

From the early 19th century, Kharkiv became an important center of the Ukrainian cultural renaissance. The classicist writer **Hryhorii Kvitka-Osnovianenko** lived and worked there, as did the writers of the Kharkiv **romantic** school, who laid the foundations of modern Ukrainian **literature**. Many of the early Ukrainian miscellanies were published there, as well as the first periodicals in Russian-ruled Ukraine, including *Ukrainskii vestnik* (1816–19) and *Ukrainskii zhurnal* (1824–25). The first professional **theater** troupe in Ukraine was established in Kharkiv in 1789, and the earliest modern Ukrainian plays were performed there. A clandestine **hromada** functioned in the city from the early 1860s, and a **Prosvita** branch was active after the **Revolution of 1905**. **Mykola Mikhnovsky**, one of the earliest advocates of Ukrainian independence, worked as a lawyer in Kharkiv, and his program provided the basis for the **Revolutionary Ukrainian Party**, established in the city in 1900. The eminent historian **Dmytro Bahalii** was rector of Kharkiv University and head of the city council.

During the **Ukrainian Revolution** (1917–21), Kharkiv was held only intermittently by Ukrainian forces. Its proximity to the Russian border made it a base of Bolshevik operations, and on 12 (25) December 1917 the People's Secretariat of the Ukrainian Soviet Republic was proclaimed there. In February 1918, Kharkiv became the capital of the **Donets-Kryvyi Rih Soviet Republic**; it was briefly held by the **Ukrainian State** and the **Ukrainian People's Republic** before being recaptured by the Bolsheviks. From 1920 to 1934, Kharkiv was the capital of the **Ukrainian SSR**. This period, which coincided with the rise and fall of the **Ukrainization** policy, saw an explosion of Ukrainian cultural activity in Kharkiv; the State Publishing House of Ukraine, as well as the cooperative publishers Knyhospilka and Rukh, were based there, as was the **Berezil Theater** and virtually every important writers' and artists' organization of the period. Kharkiv's status as capital of Ukraine also led to its intensive redevelopment and expansion in the 1920s and 1930s. This was accompanied by the destruction of many buildings of historical importance, especially the city's **baroque** churches. Stalin's industrialization drive of the 1930s led to the establishment of such huge enterprises as the Kharkiv Tractor Plant, Machine-Tool Plant, and Turbine Plant.

Under German occupation in **World War II**, Kharkiv was devastated; approximately 100,000 of its inhabitants were killed and 60,000 forcibly transported to Germany as *Ostarbeiter*. The city was rebuilt after the war as an industrial and administrative center, with broad streets and large apartment subdivisions to house a greatly expanded labor force. Today, Kharkiv has more than 250 industrial enterprises, led by the machine-building and metal-working sectors. Diesel locomotives, mining machinery, tractors, generators, and turbines, as well as a wide variety of foodstuffs and consumer goods, are the major products of Kharkiv's enterprises. The city is the largest railway junction in Ukraine, is well connected by highways to major cities in Russia and Ukraine, and has a large airport.

In **education** and scientific research, Kharkiv is second in importance only to **Kyiv**. There are more than 20 postsecondary educational institutions, with a strong emphasis on engineering and industry, and a number of scientific research institutes. The city supports a philharmonic hall, circus, and a number of theaters, including an opera house. Because of Kharkiv's political and economic importance and proximity to Russia, it has been subject to intense **Russification** since the 1930s. Although the number of Ukrainians in the city has risen steadily from 29 percent (1897) to 38 percent (1926) and 64.1 percent (1959), Russian remains the dominant language.

KHAZARS. Nomadic Turkic people who established themselves on the territory between the lower Don and Volga Rivers and the Kuban and Terek river valleys in the mid-seventh century A.D. Their capital was Itil on the Volga, which became the center of a large commercial empire that traded with the Middle East and Byzantium. The Khazar kaganate, the first state in Eastern Europe, was ruled by a supreme kagan and a vicegerent, who was the actual administrator. From the mid-seventh to the mid-ninth century, the *pax Chazarica* ensured stability and prosperity throughout the kaganate and surrounding territory. The Khazars maintained good relations with the Byzantines, their major trading partners, and divided the **Crimea** into a Byzantine coastal region and a Khazar-dominated hinterland. In the late eighth century, the Khazars, originally Shamanists, converted to Judaism.

Several Slavic tribes, including the Radimichians, Severians, and Viatichians, became vassals of the Khazar kaganate. In the late ninth century, the Khazars encountered a major adversary, the **Pechenegs**, whose raids seriously weakened the kaganate. Subsequently, **Kyivan Rus'** emerged as the Khazars' principal opponent. According to **chronicle** accounts, the Kyivan prince **Oleh** ended the dependence of the Polianians and Sivierianians on the Khazars, while **Ihor** led campaigns through Khazar lands (913–14, 943–44). Prince **Sviatoslav Ihorevych** destroyed Itil and Semender, annexing part of the kaganate to Rus' (964–65). Subsequently, the Khazars fell under Khwārezm rule and converted to Islam. The kaganate ceased to exist in the late 10th century, and the Khazars assimilated with Turkic and **Cuman** tribes.

KHLOPOMANY. Adherents of a **populist** trend in **Right-Bank Ukraine** in the 1850s–60s. The name of the movement came from the Polish word *chłop* (peasant) and meant "lovers of the peasantry." Its adherents strove to develop national consciousness among the **peasants** and defend their social and cultural interests. The movement was established by students of Kyiv University who were descendants of Polish or Polonized Ukrainian families: **Volodymyr Antonovych**, Kostiantyn Mykhalchuk, Borys Poznansky, Tadei Rylsky, Anatol Svydnytsky, Pavlo Zhytetsky, and others.

The ideologue of the movement was Antonovych, who formulated its program. He rejected the appeal of the Polish revolutionaries of 1863 to restore the Polish state in its prepartition boundaries, as much of that territory was settled by a Ukrainian peasant population. Antonovych maintained that the Polish nobility had to expiate, "by means of tireless labor and love, the evil done to the Ukrainian people by their class." The *khlopomany* rejected revolutionary struggle and engaged in cultural and educational work, conversing exclusively in Ukrainian and wearing traditional dress. They regularly visited villages (a practice known as "going to the people"), where they studied the way of life, customs, and oral tradition of the peasants and established **Sunday schools**. They were active members of the Kyiv **Hromada** and supported the journal *Osnova*. The authorities suspected them of harboring separatist aims: even though Antonovych publicly disavowed such motives, Ukrainian activities were officially suppressed (*see* VALUEV CIRCULAR), and the *khlopomany* had to disband. Their influence continued to be felt in the populist movement and in the historical school established by Antonovych.

KHMELNYTSKY, BOHDAN (ca. 1595–27 July [6 August] 1657). Military commander, **Cossack hetman** (1648–57), and founder of the **Hetmanate**. Born into the family of Mykhailo Khmelnytsky, an officer in the Chyhyryn starosta district, probably on his father's homestead in Subotiv, he received his primary education in Chyhyryn and **Kyiv** and studied at the **Lviv** (or Jarosław) Jesuit college. He was fluent in Polish and Latin and well-versed in history. Khmelnytsky joined the Chyhyryn company of **registered Cossacks** (after 1618). In 1620, his father fell at the **Battle of Cecora**, while Khmelnytsky himself was captured and spent two years as a prisoner in Istanbul. After being freed (possibly ransomed by his mother), he served in the Chyhyryn regiment. Khmelnytsky's activities in the 1620s–30s are poorly documented, but by 1637 he had attained the office of military chancellor, and his signature appeared on the instrument of surrender following the **Cossack rebellion** of 1637. In 1646, Khmelnytsky went to Warsaw with a Cossack delegation and met with Władysław IV of Poland in an attempt to restore traditional Cossack liberties.

In the spring of 1647, the Chyhyryn vice-starosta Daniel Czapliński seized the Subotiv homestead and severely mistreated Khmelnytsky's family, leading to the deterioration of the latter's relations with the royal administration. In November, Khmelnytsky was arrested on allegations of plotting rebellion. Freed through the intervention of his friends, Khmelnytsky, his son Tymish, and a small unit of Cossacks established a camp at Tomakivka Island (late 1647–early 1648). At the **Zaporozhian Sich**, Khmelnytsky was elected hetman in early February. He embarked on a revolt against Polish rule (*see* KHMELNYTSKY UPRISING) that made him the ruler of most of the Ukrainian lands and ultimately obliged him to seek military assistance from Muscovy. The **Pereiaslav Agreement** (1654), which established a Muscovite protectorate over Ukraine, made more stringent by the **Articles of Bohdan Khmelnytsky**, marked a decisive reorientation of Ukrainian politics from the **Polish-Lithuanian Commonwealth** to Muscovy.

Khmelnytsky's greatest achievement was the establishment of the **Hetmanate**, the first Ukrainian polity of early modern times, administered by a **Cossack officer** elite, which remained autonomous until the late 18th century. The hetman's last years were marked by increasing conflict with Muscovy and a search for new alliances that was cut short by his death in 1657. He was buried in St. Elijah's Church in Subotiv (23 August [2 September]). According to **chronicle** records, in 1664 the Polish commander Stefan Czarniecki desecrated Khmelnytsky's grave, scattering his remains to the winds.

A defining figure in Ukrainian history, Khmelnytsky has been regarded by most Ukrainians as a liberator, and his state-building activity has been praised by such historians of the "statist school" as **Viacheslav Lypynsky, Dmytro Doroshenko,** and **Ivan Krypiakevych**. It has also been greatly emphasized since Ukraine's declaration of independence in 1991. His critics have included the outstanding poet **Taras Shevchenko**, who saw the Pereiaslav Agreement as the beginning of Ukraine's submission to Russia, and **Panteleimon Kulish**, who denounced the Cossacks as an anarchic, destructive force. During the Soviet period, Khmelnytsky was officially praised for promoting the "reunification" of Ukraine with Russia. His monument on **St. Sophia** Square in Kyiv, erected in 1888, is one of the best-known landmarks in the Ukrainian capital.

KHMELNYTSKY UPRISING (1648–57). Revolt against the **Polish-Lithuanian Commonwealth** led by **Bohdan Khmelnytsky**.

The failure of the **Cossack rebellions** of the late 16th and early 17th centuries resulted in the restriction of Cossack self-rule and intensified exploitation of the Ukrainian **peasantry**, as well as greater religious and ethnic discrimination against Ukrainians in general. At the same time, the **Cossack officers** sought the restoration of their former rights and privileges.

Elected **hetman** of the **Zaporozhian Host** in February 1648, Khmelnytsky mustered a Cossack army, negotiated with Khan Islam Giray III of the **Crimea** for support against Poland, and began corresponding with Crown Hetman Mikołaj Potocki, demanding that the Ordinance of 1638 be repealed and the Crown Army withdrawn from Cossack lands. In April 1648, Potocki dispatched 2,500 **registered Cossacks** and 1,500 soldiers, led by his son, Stefan, to quell Khmelnytsky's rebellion. The registered Cossacks joined the rebels and the **Tatar** horde of Tughay Bey, crushing the Polish forces near Zhovti Vody and Korsun (May 1648). The populace joined the Cossack ranks en masse. Rebel units commanded by Petro Holovatsky (Siverian region), Semen Vysochan (**Galicia**), Tryfon of Bershad (Bratslav region), Ivan Hanzha (Uman region), and **Maksym Kryvonis** (areas owned by the Wiśniowiecki family) also joined Khmelnytsky's army.

Władysław IV died in May 1648, and Chancellor Jerzy Ossoliński and the Orthodox magnate Adam Kysil began negotiations with Khmelnytsky. Both sides used this period to reorganize their forces. Prompted by radical lieutenants, Khmelnytsky advanced to Pyliavtsi, where the Cossacks scored a decisive victory (12 [22] September 1648). On 15 (25) October, units led by Kryvonis captured the commanding heights of **Lviv** and continued westward to Zamostia (Zamość).

The Cossack uprising influenced the election of Poland's new king. Khmelnytsky supported the candidacy of John Casimir, who was subsequently elected. However, the dominant magnate faction demanded revenge for the defeats of 1648. In December, greeted by Patriarch Paisios of Jerusalem; Metropolitan **Sylvestr Kosiv**; ambassadors from **Moldavia**, the Ottoman Empire, Transylvania, and Wallachia; and by Ukrainian Cossacks, peasants, and burghers, Khmelnytsky triumphantly entered **Kyiv** and declared that his goal now was to liberate all of Ukraine from Polish rule, establishing Cossack authority as far as Lviv, Kholm (Chełm), and Halych.

In early 1649, battles began in **Volhynia** and **Podilia**. By summer, Khmelnytsky had mustered an army of 150,000, against which the Commonwealth fielded its Crown Army of 18–20,000. In mid-August, Khmelnytsky engaged the Polish army near Zboriv. However, Ossoliński managed to establish contact with Islam Giray III, whose mediation between Khmelnytsky and John Casimir saved the Poles from catastrophic defeat. The Treaty of Zboriv restricted Khmelnytsky's **Hetmanate** to the Kyiv, Bratslav, and Chernihiv palatinates, established a register of 40,000 Cossacks, granted amnesty to participants in the uprising, and provided for the return of landed property to the nobility. Its terms dissatisfied the peasants, who began to abandon the army and directly attacked Polish landowners, Catholic clergymen, and Jewish leaseholders; innocent civilians also perished.

Warfare resumed in 1651. In March, Colonel **Ivan Bohun** halted the Polish advance near Vinnytsia and forced the Poles to retreat to Kamianets. In mid-June 1651, as a result of Islam Giray's desertion, the Cossack army found itself in dire straits near Berestechko in Volhynia and was forced to retreat. In August, Khmelnytsky signed the treaty of Bila Tserkva, which reduced the size of the Cossack register to 20,000 and restricted the Hetmanate to the territory of the Kyiv palatinate. The Polish Diet rejected the treaty, and armed conflict resumed in 1652. Khmelnytsky's son Tymish led part of the Cossack army into Moldavia to force its ruler, Vasile Lupu, to fulfill his military obligations. Tymish defeated a 20,000-strong Polish force at the Battle of Batih (22–23 May [1–2 June]), in which some 8,000 Polish soldiers were killed. The Moldavian campaign ended with the marriage of Tymish to Lupu's daughter, Rozanda. Opposed by a powerful anti-Ukrainian coalition in Moldavia, Tymish was killed in the Battle of Suceava (September 1653), forcing the Cossack army to retreat.

Throughout 1653, battles continued in the Bratslav region, with Bohun defeating the army of Stefan Czarniecki at Monastyryshche. In the autumn, the surrounded Crown Army was saved by the Tatars near Zhvanets on the Dnister River. Bribed by King John Casimir, Islam Giray III signed a treaty with Poland.

On 8 (18) January 1654, in Pereiaslav, Khmelnytsky and his officers swore allegiance to the Muscovite tsar in return for military assistance. However, many Cossack officers, burghers, Zaporozhian Cossacks, and clergymen, led by Metropolitan Kosiv, refused to swear allegiance, fearing Muscovite encroachment in Ukraine. The conditions of the **Pereiaslav Agreement** were confirmed in Moscow in March 1654 by the **Articles of Bohdan Khmelnytsky**, affirming the independence of the Hetmanate but restricting the hetman's freedom of action in foreign policy. In the spring, Muscovy declared war on the Commonwealth. Together with the Muscovite army, the Cossacks captured Smolensk, Minsk, and Vilnius. In the autumn, the Commonwealth signed a treaty with the Crimean Khanate and directed its armies, commanded by Stanisław Potocki, into Podilia and the Bratslav region, where they faced stiff resistance from the local population and Cossack regiments.

In early 1655, a fierce battle at Okhmativ (Kyiv region) between the Cossack-Russian army and Polish forces ended in stalemate. In

August and September, Khmelnytsky led a successful campaign into Galicia. By November, the Cossacks were laying siege to Lviv, but the Tatars again entered Ukraine, forcing Khmelnytsky to withdraw to the Dnipro region.

In October 1656, Muscovy and the Commonwealth signed the Treaty of Vilnius. The Cossack delegation was barred from the negotiations; hence Khmelnytsky intensified diplomatic ties with King Charles X Gustav of Sweden and relations with Moldavia, Wallachia, Transylvania, and Brandenburg. However, divergent interests and misunderstandings between members of the potential coalition, as well as Khmelnytsky's untimely death in July 1657, put an end to the Polish-Cossack War. Ultimately, Muscovy and Poland settled their differences by means of the **Truce of Andrusovo** (1667) and the **Eternal Peace of 1686**. The Hetmanate established by Khmelnytsky maintained its autonomy until the 1780s.

KHMELNYTSKY, YURII (ca. 1641–1685). Younger son of **Bohdan Khmelnytsky**, **hetman** of Ukraine (1657, 1659–63) and of **Right-Bank Ukraine** (1677–81; possibly 1685). He was born on his father's homestead in Subotiv (now in Chyhyryn raion) and studied at the **Kyiv Mohyla Academy**. In April 1657, at a **Cossack council** called by his father, the 16-year-old Yurii was proclaimed hetman of Ukraine. Following Bohdan Khmelnytsky's death, a Cossack council in Chyhyryn confirmed Yurii's election (23 August [2 September] 1657). As he was still a minor, he temporarily resigned the position, and the General Military Council proclaimed General Chancellor **Ivan Vyhovsky** hetman (15 [25] October 1657). Vyhovsky's attempted union with Poland (*see* HADIACH, TREATY OF) and the intrigues of **Yakym Somko** resulted in Vyhovsky's removal (11 [21] September 1659). Aided by pro-Moscow officers, Khmelnytsky was reelected hetman at a council in Bila Tserkva. After Muscovite armies led by Prince Aleksei Trubetskoi captured **Left-Bank Ukraine** (October 1659), Khmelnytsky was prevailed upon to sign the Pereiaslav Articles of 1659, which greatly curtailed the autonomy of the **Hetmanate**. In 1660, Cossack forces under his command participated in a new war between Poland and Muscovy. The **Volhynian** campaign of the Muscovite army led by Vasilii Sheremetiev, joined by a Cossack corps on Khmelnytsky's instructions, ended in a crushing defeat near Chudniv (Zhytomyr region).

On 17 (27) October 1660, Khmelnytsky signed the Treaty of Slobodyshche with Poland, restoring a political union with the **Polish-Lithuanian Commonwealth** under the terms of the Treaty of Hadiach. Incited by Moscow, the Nizhyn, Chernihiv, and Pereiaslav regiments challenged Khmelnytsky's policies. Following the election of Somko as acting hetman of Left-Bank Ukraine (Kozelets council, spring 1662), conflict broke out between supporters of the two hetmans. In January 1663, Khmelnytsky resigned the hetmancy and took monastic orders under the name Hedeon. He lived in monasteries in **Kyiv**, Korsun, Smila, and Chyhyryn, was imprisoned by the Polish government in Marienburg (1664–67), and went to the Uman monastery after his release. In 1670 or 1673, Khmelnytsky was captured by the **Crimean Tatars**, taken to Istanbul, and held at the Edichkul prison. Subsequently, he settled in a Greek monastery, becoming its archimandrite.

During the Chyhyryn campaigns of 1677–78, the Turkish government exploited Khmelnytsky's name, proclaiming him hetman and "prince of Little Russia–Ukraine" beholden to the Ottomans. He chose Nemyriv (now in Vinnytsia oblast) as his capital and issued proclamations signed "Prince of Sarmatia, Little Russia–Ukraine, leader of the Zaporozhian Host." In 1678–79, with the help of Turco-Tatar forces, he attempted to establish rule over Left-Bank Ukraine. After the Treaty of Bakhchesarai (1681) with Muscovy, Khmelnytsky was removed from the hetmancy and executed in Kamianets by the Ottoman authorities.

KHOLM REGION (Ukr. *Kholmshchyna*). Historical region that occupies the territory west of the middle course of the Western Buh River (now in Poland). It is named after the town of Kholm (now Chełm), founded in the mid-1230s by Prince **Danylo Romanovych** of the Principality of **Galicia-Volhynia**. The Kholm region occupies a portion of the Volhynian-Lublin Upland, bordered on the east and north by the Western Buh, on the north by the **Podlachian** Lowland, and on the southwest by the Sian Lowland. The western border of the Kholm region partially follows the Wieprz River, a right tributary of the Vistula. Its total area is approximately 6,500 sq. km.

The Kholm region was settled during the Upper Paleolithic period (ca. 40,000 B.C.). During the early medieval period, it was populated by Slavic tribes mentioned in the **chronicles**, the Dulibians and Buzhanians, who controlled the Cherven towns. From the 980s, the Kholm region was part of **Kyivan Rus'**. From the early 13th century, it belonged to the Volodymyr principality, and from the mid-13th century to 1340 it was part of the Principality of Galicia-Volhynia, of which Kholm was the capital in the 1230s–60s. The Kholm region was attacked by the **Golden Horde** from the mid- to late 13th century. In the years 1340–77, it was ruled by Lithuania. Volhynian, Polish, and Lithuanian princes fought for control of the Kholm lands. In the decade 1377–87, the area was subject to Hungary. In 1387, it definitively passed to Poland, where it remained until 1795. From the 15th century, the Kholm land (Kholm and Krasnystaw counties) was part of the Rus' palatinate. The armies of **Bohdan Khmelnytsky** fought there in 1648. At the turn of the 18th century, it was the site of armed engagements between Poland and Sweden. Following the third partition of Poland (1795), the Kholm region was annexed to the Austrian Empire. It was part of the Duchy of Warsaw (1809–14) and the Congress Kingdom of Poland (1815–32); after the Polish revolt of 1830, it was under direct Russian rule (1832–1917).

The church played an important role in maintaining Ukrainian consciousness in this region; the Kholm eparchy, created by Prince Danylo, was based in Kholm from 1240. The region was home to church **brotherhoods** and schools, as well as a theological seminary. The Uniate Church (*see* UKRAINIAN CATHOLIC CHURCH) in the Kholm region was subject to the metropolitan of Halych and later directly to Rome (from 1839). Strong anti-Catholic pressure developed under Russian rule. In 1875, the Kholm eparchy was incorporated into a newly created Kholm-Warsaw Orthodox eparchy. Ukrainian Catholic priests who did not convert to Orthodoxy were persecuted by the tsarist administration. Following the **Revolution of 1905**, more than 200,000 Ukrainians in the Kholm region converted from Orthodoxy to Roman Catholicism because the Uniate Church was outlawed.

From 1885 to 1917, the Kholm Orthodox **Brotherhood** was especially active in the cultural life of the region. It issued periodicals and was crucial in the establishment of elementary **education**. Pedagogical seminaries operated in Kholm and Biała Podlaska. At the initiative of the Kholm Brotherhood, the Russian State Duma passed a law establishing the Kholm gubernia, incorporating counties of the Lublin and Siedlce gubernias populated mainly by Ukrainians (1912). The Kholm gubernia was to be administered directly by the imperial ministry of internal affairs, but the law was not implemented because of the outbreak of **World War I**.

During the war, the Kholm region was the site of battles between Austro-Hungarian and Russian armies (summer 1915). The Russian army forcibly evacuated some 120,000 Ukrainians from the Kholm region and Podlachia to the eastern regions of the empire, destroying many villages and cultural monuments. Approximately 30,000 Ukrainians stayed behind. The Austro-Polish administration, ignoring requests by the General Ukrainian Council, forbade Ukrainians to conduct cultural and educational work.

The Kholm region and Podlachia were declared parts of the **Ukrainian People's Republic** (UNR) on 14 (27) November 1917 by the **Ukrainian Central Rada**, a decision confirmed by the

Treaty of **Brest-Litovsk** (1918). However, Polish forces occupied the Kholm region and Podlachia in November 1918. Most of the local population deported to Russia returned to the region after the war.

During the interwar period, the Kholm region was part of Poland, whose rule was legalized by the **Treaty of Riga** (1921). The Poles hindered Ukrainian activities, schooling was conducted in Polish, and many Ukrainian churches were closed or destroyed. In response, the Ukrainian population continued to demand its rights. The cultural and educational society Ridna Khata was founded and numerous **cooperatives** were active, as were houses of worship (the authorities forbade the opening of churches).

From September 1939 to June 1944, the Kholm lands were under German occupation and administered as part of the **Generalgouvernement**. Ukrainian schools, cultural and educational organizations, and Orthodox churches were opened between 1939 and 1941. The Ukrainian Relief Committee, established in Kholm, directed Ukrainian cultural and national life in the region, coordinating its activities with the **Ukrainian Central Committee** in Cracow. The Orthodox cathedral in Kholm was returned to the Ukrainian community in 1940, and the activities of the **Ukrainian** Autocephalous **Orthodox Church** and the Kholm eparchy resumed. In the years 1942–44, the armed Polish underground (later the Polish Home Army) became active in the Kholm region. With the support of the German-Polish administration, it conducted mass terror against residents of Ukrainian villages and the intelligentsia. The Ukrainian population of Hrubeshiv (Hrubieszów) county organized self-defense units that later joined the **Ukrainian Insurgent Army**.

In July 1944, Soviet armies occupied the region and established the Polish Committee of National Liberation in Kholm. The border between the Polish People's Republic and the **Ukrainian SSR** was drawn in August 1945 along the **Curzon Line**, leaving the Kholm region within Poland. Some 193,000 people were resettled from the Kholm region and Podlachia to the Ukrainian SSR at the end of the war. The remaining Ukrainians (approximately 30,000) were deported to newly created Polish provinces in 1947 (*see* OPERATION VISTULA). In the 1960s, approximately 12,000 of the deportees returned. Today, the religious and cultural life of the small Ukrainian population there centers around the Polish Orthodox Autocephalous Church.

KHOMYSHYN, HRYHORII (25 March 1867–24 December 1947). Bishop of the **Ukrainian Catholic Church**. He was born in Hadynkivtsi, **Galicia**. Khomyshyn studied theology in **Lviv** and Vienna, obtained a doctorate in theology (1899), and was ordained a priest

(November 1893). He served as rector of the Lviv Theological Seminary (1902–4), then became bishop of Stanyslaviv (1904) and founded a theological seminary there (1907). Khomyshyn facilitated the activities of religious organizations and sponsored the Ukrainian Catholic People's Party (UKNP). He initiated the publication of a clerical quarterly, *Dobryi pastyr* (The Good Pastor, 1931–39). He also influenced the newspaper *Nova zoria* (New Star), the organ of the UKNP, and established the Skala network of reading rooms, excluding publications not under his control. Devoting considerable attention to charity work, Khomyshyn established the cooperative organization Sviashchenycha Pomich (Priestly Assistance), the Diocesan Fund, and the Society of John the Merciful. In the interwar period, he favored the normalization of relations with Poland on condition that Ukrainian lands be granted autonomy. Given the obduracy of the Polish government, Khomyshyn subsequently changed his views. Favoring the Latinization of church practices, he attempted unsuccessfully to introduce the Gregorian calendar (1916) and decreed obligatory celibacy for Greek Catholic priests in his eparchy (1920). In 1945, he was arrested by the Soviet authorities and sentenced to 10 years' forced labor for "antipopular activity." He died in a **Kyiv** prison.

KHORTYTSIA. Island on the Dnipro River, now part of the city of Zaporizhia. The island is 12 km long and 2.5 km wide, with a total area of some 2,650 ha. It was first mentioned by Constantine VII Porphyrogenitus in *De administrando imperio* (mid-10th century) as the island of St. Gregory. In the times of **Kyivan Rus'**, Khortytsia was an important trading post with Constantinople and Greek colonies. The ***Tale of Bygone Years*** mentions Khortytsia under the year 1103 as the place where Rus' retinues met prior to their campaigns against the **Cumans**. The island of Mala (Small) Khortytsia was located to the north of Khortytsia, near the Dnipro rapid of Vilnyi. Ca. 1552, **Dmytro Vyshnevetsky** founded the first **Zaporozhian Sich** on Mala Khortytsia. In the summer of 1557, a joint Turkish-Tatar army destroyed the **Cossack** fortification there. From 1596 to 1648, Khortytsia was garrisoned by **registered Cossacks**. **Bohdan Khmelnytsky** routed a Polish military detachment on the island (1648). Until the destruction of the Zaporozhian Sich by imperial Russian forces in 1775, Khortytsia was included in its lands. During the Russo-Turkish War, a fortification was built on the island (1735–39), the remains of which have survived to this day. On 18 September 1965, the island was declared a historical and cultural preserve. It is home to a museum of Zaporozhian Cossack history.

KHOTKEVYCH, HNAT (19 [31] December 1877–8 October 1938). Writer, art scholar, musician, actor, **theater** director, and activist of the Ukrainian national movement. He was born in **Kharkiv** and graduated from the Kharkiv Technological Institute as an engineer (1900). Khotkevych played a significant role in reviving the bandura as a folk instrument, staging performances by **kobzars** and *lirnyky*. He founded and directed amateur **peasant** and workers' Ukrainian theaters in the Kharkiv region. At the beginning of the 20th century, Khotkevych established and headed a Ukrainian publishing commission attached to the Kharkiv Literacy Society and helped establish publishing cooperatives. Because of his revolutionary activities, he was obliged to emigrate to **Galicia** (1906), where he organized the Hutsul Theater, which toured Galicia, **Bukovyna**, and Poland. Upon his return to Kharkiv in 1912, he edited the journal *Visnyk kul'tury i zhyttia* (Herald of Culture and Life), lectured, and organized theatrical activity. Although Khotkevych opposed the Bolshevik occupation, he became an active participant in Soviet cultural life of the 1920s and early 1930s, teaching Ukrainian **literature** and bandura playing and organizing the **Shevchenko** State Bandura Capella. Arrested in 1938, Khotkevych was executed at the Kharkiv NKVD headquarters.

Khotkevych began writing in 1897, and his first collection of stories appeared in Kharkiv in 1902. Subsequently, he wrote numerous short-story collections and plays for the Hutsul Theater. His finest prose work is the lyrical neoromantic novella *Kaminna dusha* (The Stone Soul, 1911). His works also include essays on historical themes, teachers' manuals on history and art, and translations of literary classics into Ukrainian. In addition, Khotkevych composed **music**, wrote scholarly studies of Ukrainian music, and published a bandura player's manual.

KHOTYN, BATTLE OF. A campaign fought by Polish and **Zaporozhian Cossack** forces against the Turkish army of Sultan Osman II throughout the month of September 1621. Approximately 30,000 Poles and 40,000 Cossacks faced the 150,000-strong Ottoman army invading Ukraine, Poland, and Central Europe.

To some extent, the invasion was precipitated by the raids of Zaporozhians led by Hetman **Petro Sahaidachny** against the Turks (1614–18) and by the Poles' inability to prevent such raids. The Turks retaliated with a war against the **Polish-Lithuanian Commonwealth**, destroying the Crown army at the **Battle of Cecora** in 1620. In 1621, a strong Turkish army marched into **Moldavia**. Emboldened by these successes, the sultan began an invasion intended to conquer Central Europe. Polish forces were greatly outmatched, forcing the Polish government to plead with the Zaporozhian Cossacks for help. On 5–7 (15–17) June, a **Cossack council** at Sukha Dibrova (now in Cherkasy oblast) agreed to come to Poland's assistance and sent a delegation to Warsaw to negotiate privileges for the Cossacks and the **Ukrainian Orthodox Church**. The delegation was led by Sahaidachny, who convinced the Diet to accept the Cossack conditions. At the same time, the Zaporozhian Host under the command of Hetman Yakiv Borodavka was attempting to slow down the Turkish advance through Moldavia, but Borodavka would not commit his forces in support of the Poles. At a council near Mohyliv-Podilskyi, Sahaidachny had Borodavka overthrown and subsequently executed. As the new hetman, Sahaidachny marched to Khotyn with the whole Cossack Host (some 40,000 men) to relieve the surrounded Polish army. Following his successful breakthrough on 22 August (1 September), the combined Polish and Cossack forces repeatedly withstood the Turkish onslaught, counterattacking near the end of the month. The campaign ended on 18 (28) September, with Sultan Osman obliged to negotiate. The battle prevented the Turks from penetrating Central Europe and demonstrated the growing military and political might of the Zaporozhian Cossacks.

KHRUSHCHEV, NIKITA (3 [15] April 1894–11 September 1971). Soviet party and government leader; general secretary of the Central Committee, Communist Party of the Soviet Union (CC CPSU; 1953–64). He was born in Kalinovka, Kursk gubernia (now in Kursk oblast, Russia), into a Russian peasant family. In 1908, his family moved to the **Donets Basin** and settled near Yuzivka (now Donetsk). In 1909, Khrushchev began working as a metal fitter at a mine near Yuzivka. He participated in labor strikes (1912–16), headed the local metalworkers' union (1917), and joined the Bolshevik Party (1918). It was in Yuzivka that Khrushchev first met **Lazar Kaganovich**, who would become his patron in the 1930s. In 1918–20, he fought in the civil war. He studied at the labor faculty of the Yuzivka Mining Technical School (1922–25) and at the Moscow Industrial Academy (1929–30). Khrushchev was a party official in the Donbas (1923–27), **Kharkiv**, and **Kyiv** (1928–29). From 1931, he worked in the Moscow party organization, becoming first secretary of the Moscow city and oblast committees in 1935.

In January 1938, Stalin appointed Khrushchev first secretary of the **Communist Party of Ukraine** (CPU), a post that he retained until December 1949 (with an interruption between March and December 1947). In that capacity, Khrushchev was involved in carrying out purges that took some 168,000 lives (1938–40). At the

15th Congress of the CPU in June 1938, Khrushchev announced the obligatory study of Russian in Ukrainian schools, a policy that greatly contributed to the **Russification** of Ukraine. (The same policy was applied throughout the non-Russian republics.) During **World War II**, Khrushchev held a variety of defense posts, including membership in the Kyiv Special Military Council. After the victory over Germany, Khrushchev oversaw punitive actions of Soviet security agencies against the population of **western Ukraine** during the struggle against the **Organization of Ukrainian Nationalists** and the **Ukrainian Insurgent Army**.

Khrushchev became involved in a serious altercation with Stalin during the **famine of 1946–47** in Ukraine, when he appealed for lower grain-requisition quotas. Stalin reacted by sending Kaganovich to "strengthen" the CPU apparatus and replace Khrushchev as first secretary of the CPU. He remained head of the **Council of Ministers** of Ukraine. Once Ukraine had fulfilled the grain requisitions to Stalin's satisfaction, he recalled Kaganovich to Moscow, and Khrushchev resumed his post as head of the CPU. Following Stalin's death, Khrushchev emerged as first secretary of the CC CPSU (September 1953). His "secret speech" at the 20th Congress of the CPSU in February 1956 condemned Stalin's "cult of personality" and provided an ideological justification for freeing many thousands of political prisoners, as well as posthumously "rehabilitating" victims of Stalin's purges. The text of the speech was not published in the **USSR** until 1989. In it Khrushchev claimed that the Ukrainians would have become one of the peoples that Stalin deported to the Soviet interior, had it not been that "there were too many of them." In 1957, Khrushchev survived an attempt by Stalinist hard-liners, including Kaganovich, to depose him.

Khrushchev's political record remains controversial. Highly energetic, bombastic, and impulsive, he undertook a number of vastly ambitious agricultural and industrial projects that ended in failure. He also implemented administrative reforms that made party cadres fear for the stability of their posts, ultimately turning the party leadership against him. Khrushchev's break with Stalinist ideology was by no means complete; he sent troops to crush the Hungarian Revolution in 1956 and made public statements to the effect that Stalin's role in Soviet life had been generally positive. His subsequent tirades against ideological nonconformism were highly reminiscent of the campaigns undertaken against the intelligentsia during the Stalin era. In December 1958, the Khrushchev administration imposed a law that allowed parents to choose the language in which their children would be educated. Given the political and cultural dominance of Russian, the law virtually guaranteed the decline of other languages in the USSR. It aroused opposition in Ukrainian society, as well as from senior CPU officials.

Because Khrushchev was so closely associated with the CPU and relied on its support during the post-Stalin struggle for power, his rise to supremacy heightened the status of the Ukrainian party. Nevertheless, his reprimands to the CPU for failing to meet economic production targets were among the factors that alienated **Mykola Pidhorny**, who headed the CPU from 1957 to 1963. Pidhorny plotted with Leonid Brezhnev to depose Khrushchev, and they drew **Petro Shelest**, Pidhorny's successor as first secretary of the CPU, into the plot. In October 1964, the Presidium of the CC CPSU removed Khrushchev from his post and allowed him to live out his last years in Moscow—a period in which he secretly tape-recorded his memoirs, which were first published in the West in 1971. Khrushchev died in Moscow and was buried at the Novodevichii Cemetery.

KHRYSTIUK, PAVLO (1880–28 September 1941). Civic figure, politician, and publicist. He was born in Yelysavethrad *stanytsia*, Krasnodon region (now in Russia), into the family of a Kuban **Cossack** (*see* BLACK SEA COSSACKS). Khrystiuk studied at the **Kyiv** Polytechnical Institute, contributed to the newspapers *Rada* (Council) and *Borot'ba* (Struggle), and took part in the **cooperative movement**. During the **Ukrainian Revolution** (1917–21), he was active in civic life and politics. In April 1917, Khrystiuk became a founder of the **Ukrainian Party of Socialist Revolutionaries** (UPSR) and was a member of its central committee. From April 1917, he and Mykola Kovalevsky edited the nonpartisan newspaper *Narodna volia* (People's Will). Khrystiuk's work among the **peasantry** helped the UPSR take the leadership of the Peasant Union. He was elected a member of the **Ukrainian Central Rada** and the Little Rada. In June 1917, he became a member of the first General Secretariat of the **Ukrainian People's Republic** (UNR) as general chancellor. He was minister of internal affairs (from January 1918), state secretary of the UNR (from February 1918), and coauthor of the Central Rada's law on land reform. When the UPSR split (May 1918), Khrystiuk joined the centrist group and helped publish the party's newspaper, *Trudova hromada* (Labor Community). Under the **Directory**, Khrystiuk was deputy minister of internal affairs in the government of Vsevolod Holubovych.

From 1919, Khrystiuk lived in Vienna, where he was a member of the Foreign Delegation of the UPSR. He was coeditor of the journal *Boritesia—poborete!* (Struggle, You Will Overcome!, 1920–

22) and belonged to the Union of Ukrainian Writers and Journalists. In the emigration, he prepared and published a work in four volumes, *Zamitky i materiialy do istoriï ukraïns'koï revoliutsiï 1917– 1920 rr.* (Notes and Materials on the History of the Ukrainian Revolution of 1917–1920, 1922), which still stands as the most detailed account. Encouraged by the **Ukrainization** policy, Khrystiuk returned to Ukraine in 1923 and became an inspector of the Ukrainian Bank. He then joined the State Publishing House of Ukraine (1925–28) and worked for the People's Commissariat of Finance (1928–31), where he was assistant head of economic planning (from 1930). In **Kharkiv**, he helped establish the Ukrainian Society of Workers of Science and Technology for the Facilitation of Socialist Construction (1928) and directed its cultural and educational section. In March 1931, Khrystiuk was arrested on a trumped-up charge of belonging to a "counterrevolutionary organization," the Ukrainian National Center. Sentenced to five years' imprisonment (July 1931), Khrystiuk was exiled to the Russian North (1935). After a brief period of freedom (November 1936), he was rearrested and sentenced to eight years' imprisonment (September 1937). He died in 1941 in Sevvostlag, Arkhangelsk oblast (Russia).

KHVOIKA, VIKENTII (1850–20 October [2 November] 1914). Archaeologist of Czech origin. He was born in Semin, Bohemia, and graduated from a commercial school. In 1876, he moved to **Kyiv**, where he worked as a teacher. In the 1890s, Khvoika became interested in archaeology and began conducting excavations, studying the late Paleolithic settlement on Starokyivska Hora in Kyiv (1893–1903). In 1896, he discovered the first settlements of the **Trypilian culture** in the Kyiv region. He studied Bronze and Iron Age tumuli in the middle Dnipro Basin (Pastyrske and Motronynske sites) and discovered remnants of the Zarubyntsi culture (1899) and the Cherniakhiv culture (1900–1). Khvoika studied remnants of the princely era in Kyiv, Vytachiv, and the Chernihiv region. In 1899, he became a founder of the Kyiv City Museum of Antiquities and Arts (now the National Historical Museum), where he directed the archaeological division from 1904. In his numerous works, Khvoika propagated the theory that the East Slavic inhabitants of the middle Dnipro Basin were autochthonous.

KHVYLIOVY, MYKOLA (1 [13] December 1893–13 May 1933). Writer and publicist. He was born Nikolai Fitilev in the village of Trostianets, **Kharkiv** gubernia (now in Sumy oblast) into a family of teachers and graduated from the Bohodukhiv gymnasium (1916).

During **World War I**, Khvyliovy fought in the Russian army. He joined the **Communist Party of Ukraine** (CPU) in 1919, moved to Kharkiv in 1921, and began publishing in the same year. The collection *Syni etiudy* (Blue Studies, 1923) brought him immediate acclaim. Khvyliovy published the poetry collections *Molodist'* (Youth, 1921) and *Dosvitni symfoniï* (Dawn Symphonies, 1923), the short-story collection *Osin'* (Autumn, 1924), and the novels *Val'dshnepy* (The Woodcocks), *Sanatoriina zona* (Sanatorium Zone), and *Sentymental'na istoriia* (A Sentimental Story). A founder of the literary organization **Vaplite** (1926–28), Khvyliovy promoted lofty aesthetic ideals rather than mass participation in the new proletarian culture (as opposed to the policies advocated by the proletarian writers' association, Hart, and the Union of Peasant Writers, Pluh). In that vein, he initiated the literary discussion of 1925–28 with his publicistic and critical works *Kamo hriadeshy* (Whither Goest Thou, 1925), *Dumky proty techiï* (Thoughts against the Current, 1926), and *Apolohety pysaryzmu* (Apologists of Scribbling, 1926). Khvyliovy insisted that the new Ukrainian **literature** must stop imitating Russian models and orient itself on "psychological Europe." He believed that European primacy in global culture would yield to an "Asiatic renaissance" in which Ukrainian culture would play a central role. Ukrainian "national communists," the literary neoclassicists led by Mykola Zerov, and broad segments of the nationally conscious Ukrainian intelligentsia supported Khvyliovy's position.

In a letter to **Lazar Kaganovich** and other Politburo members (26 April 1926), Stalin identified Khvyliovy's statements as a manifestation of growing anti-Russian sentiment in Ukraine. The letter prompted harsh criticism of Khvyliovy by Russian and Ukrainian party leaders (speeches and articles by Kaganovich, **Vlas Chubar**, Andrii Khvylia, and Hryhorii Petrovsky). Together with **Oleksander Shumsky** and **Mykhailo Volobuiev**, Khvyliovy was treated as a leading ideologue of "national deviationism" within the CPU. Attempting to rescue Vaplite from dissolution, Khvyliovy acknowledged his "errors" (1926) and agreed to his expulsion from the organization (1927). He traveled to Berlin and Vienna (December 1927–March 1928). In January 1928, prior to his return to Ukraine, he condemned his slogan "Away from Moscow" in a letter to the newspaper *Komunist* (Communist). Despite this forced recantation, Khvyliovy attempted to continue the previous orientation of Vaplite in the journals ***Literaturnyi iarmarok*** (1928–30) and *Prolitfront* (1930–31), which he established. When both were shut down, Khvyliovy made an effort to write according to the "party line" but found himself completely isolated from literary life by the regime. As an act of protest against the **famine of 1932–33** and the **political terror** against the Ukrainian intelligentsia, Khvyliovy committed suicide. His death symbolized the defeat of Ukrainian "national communism" and the end of the cultural renaissance of the 1920s. Khvyliovy's name and works continued to be banned until the final years of the Soviet regime.

KINAKH, ANATOLII (b. 4 August 1954). Eleventh prime minister of independent Ukraine. He was born in the village of Bratuşani, **Moldavia**, into a worker's family. In 1978, Kinakh graduated from the Leningrad Shipbuilding Institute as an engineer. After working in shipbuilding in Leningrad and Tallinn, he moved to the Okean Shipbuilding Plant in Mykolaiv, where he advanced from foreman to head of the production department. In 1990, he was elected to the **Verkhovna Rada** (VR). From March 1992 to July 1994, Kinakh was presidential representative in the Mykolaiv region, and in 1994–95 he headed the Mykolaiv Oblast Council of People's Deputies. A close ally of President **Leonid Kuchma**, Kinakh was appointed deputy prime minister for industrial policy in July 1995. In September of that year, he succeeded Kuchma as president of the Ukrainian Economic Council of Industrialists and Entrepreneurs. In March 1998, Kinakh was reelected to the VR, where he headed the Committee on Industrial Policy.

After the government of **Viktor Yushchenko** was ousted on a vote of nonconfidence, President Kuchma appointed Kinakh prime minister (29 May 2001). With Ukraine's **foreign policy** shifting toward an eastern orientation, Kinakh was seen as a compromise candidate who, unlike the pro-Western Yushchenko, would not oppose the change. Although Kinakh promised to continue the reforms initiated by Yushchenko, he adhered in practice to the agenda of the presidential administration. Following his appointment, Kinakh signed a decree on administrative reform that established the posts of secretaries of state. Appointed by the president, they oversee the activities of the **Cabinet of Ministers** and government ministries, controlling budgets, staff, and appointments to key positions, thereby strengthening presidential power. The Kinakh government failed in its attempts to enact a new tax code and promote **privatization**; it also had difficulty in obtaining a consensus on the state budget. Kinakh was dismissed by President Kuchma in November 2002 and succeeded by **Viktor Yanukovych**.

KOBYLIANSKA, OLHA (27 November 1863–21 March 1942). Writer. She was born in Gura Humora, **Bukovyna** (now Gura Humorului, Romania). From 1891, she lived in Chernivtsi. Kobylianska completed a four-year German school, after which she studied independently. Raised under the influence of German culture, she wrote her first literary works in German. Subsequently, inspired by Ukrainian **literature** and meetings with writers, Kobylianska became involved in the Ukrainian **women's** movement and started to write in Ukrainian. Her writing was notably influenced by impressionism and neoromanticism (*see* MODERNISM). In her works, she often explored women's emancipation and created a cult of the strong woman of "aristocratic character": *Liudyna* (A Person, 1894), "Valse mélancolique" (1894), *Vin i vona* (He and She, 1895), *Tsarivna* (The Princess, 1895), *Shcho ia liubyv* (That Which I Loved, 1896), *Nekul'turna* (The Uncultured One, 1897), *Pokora* (Submission, 1898), *Nioba* (Niobe, 1905), and others. Kobylianska depicted the lives of Bukovynian **peasants** in short stories and in one of her best novels, *Zemlia* (Land, 1902). The novel *U nediliu rano zillia kopala* (On Sunday Morning She Gathered Herbs, 1909; English translation, 2001), a love story based on a well-known folk song, focuses on relations between the heroine and the mother of the man she loves, who is also the source of the herbs that poison him. Kobylianska wrote a series of antiwar short stories (1915–23); during the interwar period, she wrote short stories about folk life. She died in Chernivtsi, where a memorial museum dedicated to her was opened in 1944.

KOBZARS. Folk bards, performers of historical dumas (epic songs), who accompanied themselves on the kobza or bandura. In the 16th and 17th centuries, they were participants in **Cossack** campaigns and **haidamaka** uprisings, using their songs to exhort the masses to battle against invaders and raise the morale of the Cossack army. The kobzars formed brotherhoods with their own customs and laws. The most famous 19th- and 20th-century kobzars were Ostap Veresai, **Hnat Khotkevych**, Mykhailo Kravchenko, Hnat Honcharenko, Yehor Movchan, and Pavlo Nosach. *See also* MUSIC.

KOLESSA, FILARET (17 July 1871–3 March 1947). Folklorist, composer, musicologist, literary scholar, full member of the **Shevchenko Scientific Society** (from 1909) and the **Ukrainian Academy of Sciences** (from 1929), and founder of Ukrainian ethnographic musicology. Born in Tatarske (now Pishchane, **Lviv** oblast), Kolessa studied at the University of Vienna under Anton Bruckner (1891–92) and graduated from Lviv University (1896). He taught at gymnasiums in Lviv, Stryi, and Sambir, and at various times he worked with **Ivan Franko**, **Mykola Lysenko**, and **Lesia Ukrainka**. In 1918, he obtained his doctorate from the University of Vienna.

Kolessa studied the rhythmics of **Galician, Volhynian,** and **Lemko** folk songs. In 1939, he was appointed professor at Lviv University. In the following year, he became director of the State Museum of Ethnography in Lviv and the Lviv Branch of the Institute of Fine Arts, Folklore, and Ethnography of the Academy of Sciences of the **Ukrainian SSR**. He died and was buried in Lviv. Kolessa wrote important works on Ukrainian folk songs, dumas (epic songs), and oral literature. He also wrote choral works and arrangements of Ukrainian folk songs. *See also* FOLK MUSIC AND DANCE.

KOLIIVSHCHYNA REBELLION. Large-scale revolt against Polish rule in **Right-Bank Ukraine** that marked the apogee of the **haidamaka** movement (1768). The term *koliivshchyna* probably derived from the words *kil* (pike, the weapon used by some of the rebels), *koloty* (to pierce), and *kolii* (butcher). After King Stanisław Poniatowski of Poland signed a treaty that granted Orthodox and Protestant believers equal rights with Catholics in the **Polish-Lithuanian Commonwealth** (February 1768), a large portion of the Polish nobility formed the Confederation of Bar to defend Catholicism and free Poland from subservience to the Russian Empire. They abused the Ukrainian population and destroyed Orthodox churches and monasteries in the **Kyiv** region, **Podilia**, and **Volhynia**. The Russian government responded by sending an army into Right-Bank Ukraine to fight the confederates. A rumor that Catherine II had issued a "golden charter" calling for the destruction of the Polish nobility spread among the Ukrainian population. These factors provoked the haidamaka rebellion in Right-Bank Ukraine. The historian Jaroslaw Pelenski estimated (1990) that the revolt involved some 500–600 Cossacks and 4,000–5,000 peasants.

The rebels elected a **Zaporozhian Cossack, Maksym Zalizniak**, as their leader at Kholodnyi Yar near Chyhyryn (spring 1768). The haidamakas captured the towns of Zhabotyn, Smila, Cherkasy, Bohuslav, Kaniv, and Lysianka and approached Uman, which belonged to the magnate Franciszek Potocki. A regiment of Potocki's household militia led by **Ivan Gonta** joined the rebels and helped capture Uman, where the rebels massacred the Polish and **Jewish** inhabitants.

In June and July 1768, nearly 30 units were active on the Right Bank, threatening to engulf indigenous Polish lands, **Left-Bank Ukraine**, and Zaporizhia. In late June, Russian and Polish forces jointly initiated punitive actions. On 27 June (8 July), Russian divisions destroyed haidamaka units and captured Zalizniak, Gonta, and Nezhyvy. Polish troops dealt brutally with the rebels, who were hanged, decapitated, and impaled. Gonta was tortured and executed in the village of Serby. Zalizniak and other rebels, considered subjects of the Russian Empire, were sentenced to corporal punishment and hard labor in Nerchinsk. Other rebel detachments remained active until the late spring of 1769. **Taras Shevchenko** devoted one of his poems, "Haidamaky," to the rebellion.

KONDRATIUK, YURII (9 [21] June 1897–1941 or 1942). Scientist and inventor; pioneer in rocketry and space technology. Born Oleksander Sharhei in **Poltava**, he studied briefly at the St. Petersburg Polytechnical Institute after graduating from the Second Poltava Gymnasium in 1916. After serving as an officer in the tsarist army, he assumed the identity of Yurii Kondratiuk in 1921. Kondratiuk worked as a structural and electrical engineer in Poltava, **Kyiv**, the northern Caucasus, and Novosibirsk. In 1930, he was imprisoned for allegedly sabotaging a grain-storage project in western Siberia. After his release in 1932, he returned to Ukraine and worked as a designer of the world's largest wind-powered generating station in the **Crimea**. At the beginning of **World War II** he was drafted into the army and died under unknown circumstances.

In 1919, Kondratiuk published *To Those Who Will Read in Order to Build*, which was later expanded into *The Conquest of Interplanetary Space* (1929). In it he formulated the essential equations for rocket propulsion, calculated optimal flight trajectories, designed and explained multistage rockets, and proposed the use of new fuels, including the boron fuels used in rockets today. He recommended that orbiting support bases be used to supply spacecraft, that small expedition vehicles be used to land astronauts on planets and return them to spaceships, and that the gravitational fields of celestial bodies be used for accelerating and stopping spaceships. Kondratiuk's concepts and equations are widely used in space travel today. A crater on the far side of the moon is named after him.

KONOTOP, BATTLE OF. Victory of a Ukrainian **Cossack** army led by Hetman **Ivan Vyhovsky** over Muscovite forces at Konotop (now in Sumy oblast). In the early spring of 1659, a Muscovite army of 100,000 men commanded by Aleksei Trubetskoi and Grigorii Romodanovsky was held back near Konotop by Cossacks of the Nizhyn and Chernihiv regiments. In late March, the Cossack units took refuge in the town of Konotop, which was besieged by the Muscovites. The defenders, led by the colonel of Nizhyn, Hryhorii Hulianytsky, held out for three months, allowing Vyhovsky to prepare for battle, whereas the Muscovites lost approximately 10,000 men in the unsuccessful siege. At the decisive battle on the banks of the Sosnivka River near Konotop (28–29 June [8–9 July]), the Muscovite army was crushed, losing 30,000 men, with an additional 5,000 taken prisoner. The remaining Muscovite forces retreated to Kursk. Vyhovsky, facing internal dissent and a subsequent renewal of the Muscovite advance, was unable to profit from his victory and abdicated the hetmancy in September 1659.

KONOVALETS, YEVHEN (14 June 1891–23 May 1938). Military and political leader. He was born in Zashkiv (now in **Lviv** oblast) and studied at the Academic Gymnasium in Lviv (1901–9). In 1909, he began studies at the law faculty of Lviv University. Konovalets was active in the struggle to establish a Ukrainian university in Lviv (1910–11). In 1911, he began working in **Prosvita** and was an executive member of the Ukrainian Students' Union. He soon joined the **National Democratic Party**. In August 1914, Konovalets was mobilized by the Austrian army, and in May 1915, during the Battle of Makivka Mountain, was captured by Russian forces. He spent the remainder of 1915 and early 1916 in a POW camp near Tsaritsyn (now Volgograd). After the February Revolution (1917), Konovalets and other **Galician** officers, including **Andrii Melnyk**, engaged in organizational and propaganda activity among the Ukrainian prisoners. Konovalets escaped in September 1917 and soon reached **Kyiv**.

In October and November 1917, Konovalets helped initiate the formation of the Galician-**Bukovynian** Battalion of **Ukrainian Sich Riflemen**, made up of western Ukrainian POWs, which soon became one of the most battle-ready units of the Army of the **Ukrainian People's Republic** (UNR). In January 1918, he was chosen commander of the battalion, now reorganized as the First Battalion of Sich Riflemen. In late January and early February 1918, the Sich Riflemen distinguished themselves in battle against Bolshevik armies approaching the city. Under the **Ukrainian Central Rada**, the Sich Riflemen led by Konovalets acted as a national guard. His forces helped drive the Bolsheviks out of Kyiv at the beginning of March 1918.

When Hetman **Pavlo Skoropadsky** came to power, the Sich Riflemen were disarmed and demobilized at the insistence of the German command (1 May 1918). In mid-August, Konovalets obtained permission from Skoropadsky to reorganize the Riflemen in Bila Tserkva. They supported the **Directory** in its anti-Skoropadsky revolt and, at the Battle of Motovylivka (17–19 November), crushed the hetman's forces. The Sich Riflemen fought for the Directory until its forces, greatly outnumbered by the Soviets and Whites, were disbanded in December 1919, and Konovalets was interned at a Polish POW camp in Lutsk. Released in the spring of 1920, he emigrated to Czechoslovakia.

In July 1921, Konovalets took command of a new revolutionary underground in Galicia, the **Ukrainian Military Organization** (UVO), and also headed its successor, the **Organization of Ukrainian Nationalists** (OUN, est. 1929). In the mid-1920s, his dedication to the revival of the UNR and his extensive political activity in Galicia brought Konovalets into conflict with **Yevhen Petrushevych**, head of the government-in-exile of the **Western Ukrainian People's Republic**. At one point, Petrushevych even attempted to assassinate his rival but was ultimately forced out of the UVO. In 1923, like other leaders of the Ukrainian underground, Konovalets emigrated in order to escape arrest by the Polish authorities and lived successively in Berlin, Geneva, and Rome. He established contacts, especially in Germany and Lithuania, to support the underground, organized political and press bureaus abroad, and rallied Ukrainian émigré support. As a result, OUN centers and related organizations were established in France, Belgium, the United States, and Canada. Konovalets's attempts to develop a nationalist underground in the **Ukrainian SSR** concerned Stalin sufficiently to order his assassination. He was killed in Rotterdam by a package bomb given to him by a Soviet secret police operative, Pavel Sudoplatov. Konovalets was buried at the Crooswijk Cemetery in Rotterdam.

KONYSKY, HEORHII (9 [20] November 1717–2 [13] February 1795). Writer, churchman, and cultural figure. He was born in Nizhyn (now in Chernihiv oblast) into a noble family, received his education at the **Kyiv Mohyla Academy** (1728–43), served as a professor of poetics, rhetoric, and philosophy (1745) and, in 1751, became rector of the academy. He was the Orthodox bishop of Mahilioŭ (1755) and later archbishop of Belarus (1783). He founded the Mahilioŭ seminary (1757). Konysky wrote poetry, and his drama *Voskreseniie mertvykh* (Resurrection of the Dead), which included five intermedia based on everyday life, employed the Ukrainian vernacular and native Ukrainian humor. Konysky wrote many sermons, a course on poetics, and two manuscripts of a course in philosophy. He also wrote historical works, including *Prawa i wolności obywatelów Korony Polskiej i Wielkiego Księstwa Litewskiego* (Rights and Freedoms of the Citizens of the Kingdom of Poland and the Grand Duchy of Lithuania, 1767), *Istoricheskoe izvestiia o Belorusskoi eparkhii* (Historical Information about the Belarusian Eparchy, 1776), and *Zapiska o tom, chto v Rossii do kontsa XVI veka ne bylo nikakoi unii s Rimskoi Tserkov'iu* (A Note on the Fact That until the

End of the 16th Century There Was No Union with the Roman Church in Russia, published in 1847). Opposed to the legacy of the **Union of Brest**, Konysky attempted to convert Uniates to Orthodoxy. While his poems are written in **baroque** style, his sermons use the more straightforward classical style. Konysky's works were published in St. Petersburg in two volumes (1835); his sermons appeared separately (1892). Some historians attribute the *Istoriia Rusov* to him. He died in Mahiliou̯.

KONYSKY, OLEKSANDER (6 [18] August 1836–29 November [12 December] 1900). Writer, publicist, pedagogue, and civic activist of a liberal orientation. He was born in Perekhodivka (now in Chernihiv oblast). Konysky's civic activities were numerous and varied. He organized **Sunday schools** in **Poltava** and wrote textbooks for them. He published articles on church affairs and participated in the Kyiv **Hromada**, organizing Sunday schools. As a member of the **Kyiv** city council, he attempted to introduce Ukrainian-**language** schooling. A victim of tsarist persecution of Ukrainian activists (1863), Konysky was exiled to Vologda and later to Totma. From 1865, he lived abroad, maintaining close contacts with Ukrainian activists in **Galicia** and **Bukovyna**. Returning to Kyiv in 1872, he worked for *Kievskii telegraf*, the Kyiv Hromada's unofficial newspaper. He was a founder of the Shevchenko Society in Lviv (1873) and later helped initiate its reorganization as the **Shevchenko Scientific Society**. Konysky worked closely with the historian **Volodymyr Antonovych** to promote cooperation with Galician Ukrainians and establish the General Ukrainian Non-Party Democratic Organization in Kyiv (1897), whose aim was to unite Ukrainian activists throughout the Russian Empire.

Konysky began writing in 1858. In his poetry, novellas, dramas, and short stories, many of them published under pseudonyms, he defended the Ukrainian national movement, advocated incremental reform, and depicted folk life. In the novellas *Semen Zhuk i ioho rodychi* (Semen Zhuk and His Relatives) and *Iurii Horovenko*, he portrayed Ukrainian educators and cultural activists. Konysky wrote a fundamental biographical study of **Taras Shevchenko** (1898–1901). He died in Kyiv.

KOPYNSKY, ISAIA (d. 5 [15] October 1640). Orthodox metropolitan of **Kyiv**. Born in **Galicia**, he studied at the **Lviv Dormition Brotherhood** School. Kopynsky was a monk at the **Kyivan Cave Monastery** and later hegumen of the Mezhyhiria Transfiguration and **Kyiv Epiphany Brotherhood** monasteries; he helped establish a school attached to the latter monastery in 1615. With the financial support of Princess Raina Vyshnevetska, Kopynsky completed the building of the Hustynia Trinity Monastery near Pryluky and established the Mhar Transfiguration Monastery near Lubny in 1619. With the renewal of the Orthodox metropolitanate (1620), Kopynsky was consecrated bishop of Peremyshl (Przemyśl) and Sambir by Patriarch Theophanes of Jerusalem, but the Polish authorities prevented him from taking up his post. He was appointed archbishop of Smolensk and Chernihiv in 1628. After the death of **Iov Boretsky** in 1631, Kopynsky was elected Orthodox metropolitan of Kyiv, enjoying **Cossack** support as a staunch opponent of conciliation with the Uniate Church (*see* UKRAINIAN CATHOLIC CHURCH). Following the legalization of the Orthodox Church in the **Polish-Lithuanian Commonwealth** in 1632, Kopynsky was forced to relinquish his post to **Petro Mohyla**, who ceded St. Michael's Golden-Domed Monastery to him in return for a promise of noninterference in the affairs of the **Kyiv metropolitanate**. Kopynsky spent the last years of his life in **Polisia** (from 1635) and Kyiv (from 1638).

KORDUBA, MYRON (2 March 1876–2 May 1947). Historian; full member of the **Shevchenko Scientific Society** from 1903 and director of its historical and philosophical section from 1923. He was born in Ostriv (now in Ternopil oblast) and studied at the universities of **Lviv** (1893–95, under **Mykhailo Hrushevsky**) and Vienna (1895–98). Korduba worked as a teacher in gymnasiums in Chernivtsi (1900–18), Lviv, and Kholm (Chełm) and was a professor at Warsaw University (1929–39). He was appointed professor and chairman of South and West Slavic history at Lviv University (1944). Korduba wrote works on the history and historical geography of ancient and medieval Ukraine; he also focused on Ukrainian-Polish relations in the 16th and 17th centuries, especially the **Khmelnytsky** period. In the 1920s and 1930s, Korduba wrote a number of historiographic works in French, as well as numerous articles and reviews on Ukrainian historical and geographical themes. He also wrote popular historical works, of which *Istoriia Kholmshchyny i Pidliashshia* (History of the **Kholm Region** and **Podlachia**, 1941) is particularly well-known. He was a coauthor of the *Cambridge History of Poland* (vol. 1, 1950).

KOROLIOV, SERHII (KOROLEV, SERGEI) (30 December 1906 [12 January 1907]–14 January 1966). Aeronautical engineer; designer of spacecraft and guided missiles; full member of the Academy of Sciences of the **USSR** (from 1953). Born in Zhytomyr, Koroliov studied at the **Kyiv** Polytechnical Institute and the Bauman Technological Institute in Moscow. In 1931, he cofounded the

Group for the Study of Jet Propulsion, which launched the first Soviet liquid-fuel rocket, the GIRD-09, in 1933. From 1934, Koroliov led a department of the Jet Scientific Research Institute, which developed a series of rocket-propelled missiles and gliders. In 1937, he was arrested and sent first to a concentration camp and later to a special prison design bureau for scientists, where he worked on rocket boosters for military aircraft. Released after the war, he tested and improved German V-2 missiles. Under **Nikita Khrushchev**, Koroliov led research and design teams developing intercontinental ballistic missiles, launch vehicles, and spacecraft. Responsible for the Soviet space program, Koroliov launched the Vostok and Voskhod manned spacecraft and the Elektron, Kosmos, and Molniia earth satellites, as well as the first space stations. Rockets designed by him launched the first artificial earth satellite (Sputnik), the first astronauts in earth orbit, the first probes to the moon, Mars, and Venus, and the first unmanned soft landing on the moon. Koroliov's name was kept secret during his lifetime, and he was referred to only as the Chief Designer. A large crater on the far side of the moon is named after him.

KORSUN, TREATY OF. Treaty between the **Hetmanate** and Sweden signed on 6 (16) October 1657 at a **Cossack council** in Korsun. Its terms were worked out by Ivan Kovalevsky, **Ivan Bohun**, and **Yurii Nemyrych** on the Ukrainian side, with Gustaf Liliencrona acting for Sweden. The treaty provided for a Ukrainian-Swedish military and political alliance to guarantee the independence and territorial integrity of the Hetmanate. Under its terms, King Charles X Gustav of Sweden pledged to obtain Polish recognition of the Hetmanate, which was to incorporate the western Ukrainian lands and the Berestia (Brest) and Polatsk palatinates, then controlled by the **Polish-Lithuanian Commonwealth**. The outbreak of war between Sweden and Denmark and the difficult internal political situation in the Hetmanate prevented the implementation of the treaty and obliged Hetman **Ivan Vyhovsky** to sign the **Treaty of Hadiach** (1658).

KOSHYTS, OLEKSANDER (31 August [12 September] 1875–21 September 1944). Also known as Alexander Koshetz. Choral conductor and composer. He was born in Romashky (now in **Kyiv** oblast) and graduated from the Kyiv Theological Academy (1901). Koshyts continued his studies at the **Lysenko** Music and Drama School (1906–10); upon graduation, he taught singing in Kyiv schools and conducted the Kyiv University choir and other student choirs. He was choirmaster and later conductor at Mykola Sadovsky's **theater** (1912–16) and conductor and chief choirmaster at the Kyiv Opera (1916–17). In January 1919, together with Kyrylo Stetsenko, Koshyts organized the Ukrainian Republican Capella, renamed the Ukrainian Republican Choir in 1920. The capella was sent on tour by the **Ukrainian People's Republic** to propagate Ukrainian **music** abroad and performed with great success throughout Western Europe and the Americas. After 1926, Koshyts lived in the United States and Canada, where he taught choir conducting and performed. He composed liturgies and arranged folk songs, which he also collected and published. Koshyts died in Winnipeg; his memoirs were published in two volumes (1948–52).

KOSIOR, STANISLAV (18 November 1889–26 February 1939). Soviet government and party official. A Pole by nationality, he was born in Węgrów, Poland. Kosior became a metal worker in the **Donets Basin** and joined the Bolshevik Party in 1907. He was secretary of finance in the People's Secretariat of the **Ukrainian SSR** (March-April 1918) and an organizer of the **Communist Party of Ukraine** (CPU), serving as secretary of its central committee (1919–20). After holding a variety of party and government posts, he became general secretary of the CC CPU (1928–38; first secretary from 1934). Kosior took part in Stalin's **political terror** against the Ukrainian intelligentsia, condemning **Mykola Skrypnyk** and endorsing the purge of Ukrainian cultural, academic, and scientific institutions in the early 1930s. Kosior was also deeply implicated in the **famine of 1932–33**, expressing the hope that it would "knock sense" into the **peasantry** (as early as 1930, he had threatened peasant opponents of **collectivization** with famine). But Stalin did not trust the CPU to oversee the famine, and **Pavel Postyshev**, whom he dispatched from Russia to take over the CPU, openly ignored Kosior. A CPU instruction signed by Kosior on 29 November 1932 attempted to mitigate the collection of grain reserves by attaching numerous conditions to it.

In 1937, when Stalin decided on a complete purge of the CPU, its central committee refused to vote nonconfidence in Kosior. He was transferred to Moscow in 1938. Arrested in 1939, he was accused of belonging to the "Polish Military Organization" and shot.

KOSIV (KOSOV), SYLVESTR (d. 13 [23] April 1657). Orthodox metropolitan of **Kyiv**; cultural and educational figure descended from the petty Orthodox gentry of the Vitsebsk region in Belarus. For many years, he taught at the Vilnius and **Lviv Dormition Brotherhood** schools and the **Kyivan Cave Monastery** school. Along with **Petro Mohyla**, he was a founder of the Kyiv Collegium

(1632). Kosiv was consecrated bishop of Mstsislaŭ, Mahilioŭ, and Orsha (1634) and elected metropolitan of Kyiv after Mohyla's death in 1647. His tenure as metropolitan coincided with the uprising against Poland led by Hetman **Bohdan Khmelnytsky**, with whom Kosiv's relations were often strained; like Mohyla before him, he favored a Western orientation. Kosiv was strongly opposed to a rapprochement with Muscovy. He condemned the **Pereiaslav Agreement** (1654) and subsequently resisted attempts to subordinate the **Kyiv metropolitanate** to the patriarch of Moscow. He wrote theological and polemical works such as *Didaskaliia* (a study of the sacraments, 1637) and *Exegesis* (a defense of Orthodox schools, 1635).

KOSTOMAROV, MYKOLA (4 [16] May 1817–7 [19] April 1885). Historian, ethnographer, and writer. He was born in Yurasovka, Voronezh gubernia (now in Voronezh oblast, Russia). The illegitimate son of a Russian landowner and a Ukrainian serf girl, Kostomarov was forced into serfdom after the murder of his father. Kostomarov's mother bought his ransom in the early 1830s. He studied at the Voronezh gymnasium and graduated from the historical and philological faculty of **Kharkiv** University (1836). Following military service, Kostomarov passed his master's examinations in history. He submitted his first dissertation, "On the Reasons and Character of the Union in Western Rus'" (1842), but owing to protests from church authorities, who claimed that Kostomarov had slandered the Orthodox clergy, it was rejected and destroyed (*see* BREST, UNION OF). He successfully defended his second dissertation, "On the Historical Significance of Rus' Folk Poetry" (1844). Kostomarov taught at the Rivne and First **Kyiv** gymnasiums (1844–46), after which he became an adjunct professor of the Chair of Russian History at St. Vladimir's University in Kyiv.

Inspired by **Panslavism** and by his study of folklore, Kostomarov became a Ukrainian patriot devoted to "the poor peasant, [who] seems not to exist for history." In 1846, he initiated the founding of the clandestine **Cyril and Methodius Brotherhood** and became the principal author of its programmatic document (*see BOOKS OF GENESIS OF THE UKRAINIAN PEOPLE*). When the brotherhood was uncovered, Kostomarov was imprisoned for a year and exiled to Saratov (1847), where he served as a clerk in the gubernia statistical committee. In 1857, he received permission to move to St. Petersburg, where he was appointed adjunct professor at the university (1859–62) but then forced to resign because of his heterodox political views. Kostomarov was a member and editor of the St. Petersburg Archaeographic Commission (1860–85), an editor of the journal *Osnova*, and editor of the collection *Akty, otnosiashchiesia k istorii Iuzhnoi i Zapadnoi Rossii* (Documents Pertaining to the History of Southern and Western Russia). He was elected an associate member of the Russian Academy of Sciences (1876), an honorary member of the Serbian Scientific Society (1869), and a member of the South Slavic Academy (1870). He died in St. Petersburg and was buried at the Volkov Cemetery (11 [23] April 1885).

Kostomarov was the author of some 300 works of history, ethnography, and journalism. His historical research concentrated on the **Cossack** era (16th to 18th centuries), and one of his best-known works was a biography of **Bohdan Khmelnytsky**. Kostomarov founded the **populist** school of Ukrainian historiography, which remained dominant until the early 20th century. In his influential essay "Dve russkie narodnosti" (Two Rus' Nationalities, 1861) he argued that the democratic, freedom-loving Ukrainians differed fundamentally in political culture from the autocratic Russians. Kostomarov's ethnographic work focused on the Ukrainian folk-song tradition. His literary works, inspired by the **romantic** school, depict events from the times of **Kyivan Rus'**, the Khmelnytsky era, and the **Hetmanate**.

KOTLIAREVSKY, IVAN (29 August [9 September] 1769–29 October [10 November] 1838). Poet, dramatist, and initiator of modern Ukrainian **literature**; one of the foremost exemplars of the Enlightenment in the Ukrainian lands. Kotliarevsky was born in **Poltava**, where he attended the theological seminary (1780–89). He worked as a clerk (1789–93) and private tutor for landowning families (1793–96) before serving in the Russian army (1796–1808). In 1810, he was appointed a trustee at the Institution for the Education of the Children of Impoverished Nobles. In 1812, Kotliarevsky mustered the Fifth Ukrainian **Cossack** Regiment in Poltava gubernia to fight Napoleon. He was director of the Poltava Theater (1817–21) and directed a number of charitable institutions (1817–35). He died in Poltava.

Kotliarevsky began writing ca. 1794. He was the author of *Eneïda* (1798, three sections; 1842, complete posthumous edition), the first work of modern Ukrainian literature. A travesty of Virgil's *Aeneid*, Kotliarevsky's poem depicted various strata of the Ukrainian society of his day, featuring local color and matchless ethnographic detail. With *Eneïda*, the Ukrainian literary language shed older bookish forms in favor of a masterfully versified vernacular. In 1819, Kotliarevsky wrote the operetta *Natalka Poltavka* (Natalka from Poltava, first published in 1838) and the vaudeville *Moskal'-*

charivnyk (The Muscovite Sorcerer, published 1841) for the Poltava **Theater**. These works laid the foundations for a new Ukrainian dramaturgy. Kotliarevsky's writings exerted great influence on subsequent Ukrainian writers, notably **Taras Shevchenko**, but *kotliarevshchyna* became a pejorative term for third-rate literary provincialism. Monuments to Kotliarevsky were erected in Poltava (1903) and **Kyiv** (1973), and the Kotliarevsky Literary Memorial Museum was established in Poltava in 1952.

KOTSIUBYNSKY, MYKHAILO (5 [17] September 1864–12 [25] April 1913). One of the most prominent Ukrainian **modernist** writers. He was born in Vinnytsia and educated at the Sharhorod Theological School and the Kamianets-Podilskyi Theological Seminary. For his involvement in the **populist** movement, Kotsiubynsky was expelled from the seminary in 1882 and placed under secret police surveillance, which continued for the rest of his life. To support himself, he worked as a private tutor and teacher; he also held various government appointments. He traveled extensively throughout Europe and was well acquainted with Ukrainian writers in the Russian Empire and in **Galicia**. Kotsiubynsky began publishing his works in **Lviv** journals. In 1897, he moved to Chernihiv, becoming president of the **Prosvita Society** (1906–8) and organizing community events. He died in Chernihiv.

Kotsiubynsky's early works were influenced by populist ideas. They are mainly concerned with the daily life and problems of **peasants**, emphasizing the responsibilities of the Ukrainian intelligentsia to the masses. From such ethnographic realism he evolved toward a more subtle impressionism. In the works *V putakh shaitana* (In Satan's Clutches, 1899), "Lialechka" (The Little Doll, 1901), "Tsvit iabluni" (Apple Blossom, 1902), "Na kameni" (On the Rock, 1902), "Pid minaretamy" (Beneath the Minarets, 1904), and "Intermezzo" (1908), Kotsiubynsky masterfully portrayed the psychological state of his protagonists, rendering changes in mood and capturing momentary impressions. National and social oppression in Ukraine was one of Kotsiubynsky's preoccupations, especially in "Vin ide" (He Is Coming, 1906), "Smikh" (Laughter, 1906), "Persona grata" (1907), and *Fata morgana* (1903–10). The works of his final years, notably *Tini zabutykh predkiv* (Shadows of Forgotten Ancestors, 1911) and "Na ostrovi" (On the Island, 1913), are permeated with great humanism and lyricism. Kotsiubynsky's prose has been translated into many languages. A number of **films** have been adapted from his short stories and novels, including the internationally acclaimed *Tini zabutykh predkiv* (1964), directed by **Serhii Paradzhanov**. Museums dedicated to Kotsiubynsky were opened in Vinnytsia (1927) and Chernihiv (1934). *See also* LITERATURE.

KOTSIUBYNSKY, YURII (25 November [7 December] 1896–8 March 1937). Soviet state, party, and military figure. He was born in Vinnytsia, the son of the distinguished writer **Mykhailo Kotsiubynsky**, and studied at the Chernihiv gymnasium. He joined the Bolshevik party in 1913 and participated in the Bolshevik coup in Petrograd (October 1917). Kotsiubynsky became a member of the People's Secretariat of the **Ukrainian SSR**, first as assistant secretary, then as acting secretary for military affairs (December 1917). In January 1918, he was appointed commander in chief of the Soviet armed forces in Ukraine, which fought the **Ukrainian People's Republic**. Following the second Soviet invasion of Ukraine in November 1918, he was a member of the **Provisional Workers' and Peasants' Government of Ukraine**. After working in government and party institutions in Chernihiv and **Poltava**, Kotsiubynsky was a diplomat in Austria (1921–22, 1925–27) and Poland (1927–30). He was deputy chairman (from February 1930) and chairman (from February 1934) of the State Planning Commission, as well as deputy chairman of the Soviet People's Commissariat of the Ukrainian SSR. He was also a member of the All-Ukrainian Central Executive Committee.

In November 1934, during the purge of the **Communist Party of Ukraine**, Kotsiubynsky was relieved of his posts and expelled from the party. He was arrested in February 1935, accused of anti-Soviet activity, and sentenced to six years' exile in western Siberia. He was rearrested while in exile, taken to **Kyiv** (October 1936), and charged with organizing and running a counterrevolutionary Trotskyist organization in Ukraine on the instructions of **Georgii Piatakov**. Sentenced to death by the Supreme Court of the **USSR** on 8 March 1937, Kotsiubynsky was shot the same day. He was officially rehabilitated in December 1955. The literary scholar **Serhii Yefremov** wrote a well-known "open letter" to Kotsiubynsky, accusing him of committing vicious crimes against his own people.

KOVPAK, SYDIR (14 [26] May 1887–11 December 1967). Soviet partisan commander and major-general (from 1943). He was born in Kotelva (now in **Poltava** oblast). He led a partisan unit that fought Anton Denikin and later, as part of the Red Army, the forces of Petr Wrangel (1918–20). Kovpak joined the Bolshevik Party in 1919 and served as a Red Army commissar (1921–26). He then became an administrator, heading the Putyvl executive committee in

Sumy oblast (1937–41). During **World War II**, he commanded the Putyvl partisan unit and later an expanded partisan detachment. Kovpak's detachment conducted raids in the Sumy, Kursk, and Briansk oblasts (1941–42), **Right-Bank Ukraine** (1942–43), and the Carpathian Mountains (July-August 1943). The main object of the Carpathian raid—the destruction of the Drohobych oil field—was partly achieved, as was the goal of showing the Soviet flag in **western Ukraine** two years after the rout of Soviet forces there. Since the local population was hostile, Kovpak had to fight formations of the **Ukrainian People's Self-Defense** and units of the **Ukrainian Insurgent Army** as well as German forces. Having sustained heavy losses, Kovpak retreated to the northern marshlands with about 300 men. In 1944, his detachment was renamed the S. A. Kovpak First Ukrainian Partisan Division (commanded by Petro Vershyhora). In 1946, Kovpak headed the short-lived postwar defense ministry of the **Ukrainian SSR**. He was deputy chairman of the Presidium of the **Verkhovna Rada** of the UkSSR (1947–67). His memoirs are titled *Ot Putivlia do Karpat* (From Putyvl to the Carpathians, 1952; Ukrainian ed. 1968).

KOZLOVSKY, IVAN (11 [24] March 1900–21 December 1993). Singer (lyric tenor) and People's Artist of the **USSR** (from 1940). He was born in Marianivka (now in Hrebinky raion, **Kyiv** oblast). After singing with the choir of the **Kyivan Cave Monastery**, Kozlovsky joined the troupe of the National Home. In 1917, he was admitted to the Lysenko Music and Drama Institute on the recommendation of **Oleksander Koshyts**. He did military service and performed with the **Poltava** Touring Music and Drama Theater (1919–24). Kozlovsky joined the **Kharkiv** Opera in 1924 and the Sverdlovsk Opera the following year. He made triumphant appearances at the Bolshoi Theater in Moscow (1926–54) and directed a Moscow chamber opera ensemble (1938–41). Kozlovsky had an exceptionally beautiful voice of gentle timbre and wide range. His most successful roles included Levko and Petro in **Mykola Lysenko's** *Utoplena* (The Drowned Maiden) and *Natalka Poltavka* (Natalka from Poltava), Andrii in **Semen Hulak-Artemovsky's** *Zaporozhets' za Dunaiem* (Zaporozhian Cossack beyond the Danube), Lensky in Tchaikovsky's *Eugene Onegin*, the Holy Fool in Mussorgsky's *Boris Godunov*, the title role in Gounod's *Faust*, Alfredo and the Duke of Mantua in Verdi's *La traviata* and *Rigoletto*, and the title role in Wagner's *Lohengrin*. Throughout his career he propagated Ukrainian vocal **music**, performing romances, folk songs, and carols with great feeling, ease, and warmth. He died in Moscow.

KRAVCHUK, LEONID (b. 10 January 1934). Politician; president of Ukraine (1991–94). Born in Velykyi Zhytyn (now in Rivne oblast), he studied at the Rivne Cooperative Technical School (1949–53) and graduated from the economics department at Kyiv University (1958). He joined the **Communist Party of Ukraine** (CPU) in 1958. Kravchuk lectured at the Chernivtsi Financial Technical School and, in 1960, became a lecturer and later director of the department of propaganda and agitation of the Chernivtsi oblast committee of the CPU. He graduated from the Academy of Social Sciences in Moscow (1970) with a candidate degree in economics and was immediately employed in the CC CPU apparatus. Kravchuk became director of the division of propaganda and agitation (1980) and was appointed director of the ideology department (1988). In October 1989, he became secretary of ideology of the CC CPU and a candidate member of the Politburo.

Elected chairman of the **Verkhovna Rada** (VR) of Ukraine on 23 July 1990, Kravchuk aligned himself with the prosovereignty wing of the CPU. Following the attempted coup of August 1991, to which Kravchuk reacted with circumspection, Ukraine declared its independence, overwhelmingly ratified in a referendum on 1 December 1991. Presidential elections, contested by six candidates, were held on the same day, with Kravchuk taking 61.6 percent of the vote. A week later, Kravchuk met with Boris Yeltsin and Stanislaŭ Shushkevich to dissolve the **USSR**, establishing the Commonwealth of Independent States (CIS) in its place.

As president, Kravchuk was widely praised for his role as a consensus politician who managed Ukraine's transition to independence with a minimum of civil unrest. He introduced Ukrainian as the **language** of administration, taking care not to antagonize Ukraine's ethnic minorities. He asserted Ukrainian sovereignty, resisting pressure to integrate Ukraine into a Russian-dominated CIS and overseeing the formation of Ukraine's defense ministry. In January 1994, Ukraine acceded to the Trilateral Agreement with Russia and the United States, giving up its **nuclear weapons** in exchange for assurances of security and territorial integrity. In February 1994, Ukraine became the first CIS country to join the "Partnership for Peace" of the North Atlantic Treaty Organization.

In domestic policy, Kravchuk sought to expand presidential power at the expense of the VR and the **Cabinet of Ministers**, creating a strong presidential administration consisting of key advisors. Two other initiatives along this line—the formation of an advisory council known as the State Duma and the appointment of presidential representatives as de facto oblast governors—ended in failure. Kravchuk's nemesis was the Ukrainian **economy**, which declined precipitously after the dissolution of the USSR. Successive prime ministers adopted contradictory remedies: **Vitold Fokin** followed the traditional Soviet practice of subsidizing unprofitable enterprises, which led to hyperinflation in 1992–93, while **Leonid Kuchma** attempted unsuccessfully to introduce strict monetary controls. This dismal economic record left Kravchuk at a disadvantage when he ran for reelection in 1994 against Kuchma; his attempt to portray Kuchma as a pro-Russian politician who might compromise Ukraine's sovereignty also proved unavailing.

Following his loss of the election (in the second round, Kravchuk took 45 percent of the vote to Kuchma's 52 percent), Kravchuk remained politically active. He has served as a deputy to the VR since 1994. In 1998, he joined the leadership of the (United) Social Democratic Party of Ukraine.

KRUSHELNYTSKA, SOLOMIIA (23 September 1872–16 November 1952). Also known as Salomea Krusceniski. Singer (lyric-dramatic soprano) and pedagogue. She was born in Bilivyntsi (now in Buchach raion, Ternopil oblast). In 1893, she graduated from the **Lviv** Conservatory, where she studied with Walery Wysocki, and made her debut at the Lviv Opera in Donizetti's *La favorita*. She studied with Fausta Crespi in Milan (1893–96) and in Vienna (1895). Krushelnytska had exceptional vocal and dramatic gifts and a mastery of the *bel canto* style. She sang with great success at the world's leading theaters, including the opera houses of Lviv, **Odesa** (1896–97), Warsaw (1898–1902), St. Petersburg (1901–2), the Paris Grand Opera (1902), Naples (1903–4), Cairo (1904), Alexandria (1904), Rome (1904–5), La Scala in Milan (1898, 1904, 1907, 1909, 1915), and Buenos Aires (1906, 1908, 1910–13). Her repertoire consisted of some 60 roles in operas such as **Semen Hulak-Artemovsky's** *Zaporozhets' za Dunaiem* (Zaporozhian Cossack beyond the Danube); Verdi's *Aïda*, *Il trovatore*, and *Otello*; Puccini's *Tosca*; Wagner's *Lohengrin*, *Tannhäuser*, *Götterdämmerung*, *Siegfried*, and *Tristan und Isolde*; Strauss's *Salome* and *Elektra*; and Tchaikovsky's *Eugene Onegin* and *Queen of Spades*. Her greatest role was Puccini's *Madama Butterfly*. She also propagated Ukrainian **folk music** and works by Ukrainian composers abroad. In 1939, she returned to Ukraine, where she taught at the Lviv Conservatory, becoming a professor in 1946. She died in Lviv.

KRYMSKY, AHATANHEL (3 [15] January 1871–25 January 1942). Orientalist, historian of Ukrainian **language** and **literature**, writer, full member of the **Shevchenko Scientific Society** (from 1903) and the **Ukrainian Academy of Sciences** (from 1918). He was born in

Volodymyr-Volynskyi (now in **Volhynia** oblast) and studied in Ostrih and **Kyiv**, then at the Pavlo Galagan College in Kyiv (1885–89). He went on to the Lazarev Institute of Oriental Languages in Moscow (1889–92) and the department of philology at Moscow University (1892–96). Krymsky had a phenomenal linguistic talent and mastered some 60 languages and dialects. He was active in Ukrainian affairs and corresponded with eminent cultural figures, including Oleksander Ohonovsky, **Borys Hrinchenko**, and **Ivan Franko**. At the turn of the century he engaged in a lengthy debate with the linguist Aleksei Sobolevsky, a proponent of Mikhail Pogodin's hypothesis that the ancient Kyivans were Russians who had migrated northward because of the invasion of the **Golden Horde**. Krymsky conducted field research in Syria and Lebanon (1896–98). He taught Arabic, Persian, Turkish, and the history of the Islamic East at the Lazarev Institute (1898–1918), becoming a professor (1901). After the establishment of the **Ukrainian People's Republic** (1918), he returned to Ukraine and became a professor at Kyiv University, remaining there, with interruptions, until 1941. In 1918, Krymsky, **Volodymyr Vernadsky**, **Mykola Vasylenko**, and others organized the **Ukrainian Academy of Sciences**. Krymsky was its permanent secretary, as well as chairman of its department of history and philology and de facto director (until 1928). He was also director of the Institute of the Ukrainian Scientific Language (1921–29). In May 1928, following Krymsky's reelection as secretary of the Academy of Sciences, the Soviet government refused to confirm his appointment. During the **political terror** of the 1930s, Krymsky was removed from scholarly and pedagogical activity. He was briefly rehabilitated (1938–40). On 20 July 1941, he was arrested by the NKVD, accused of anti-Soviet activity, and held in an NKVD prison in Kustanai (now in Kazakhstan). He died there of exhaustion and numerous illnesses.

Krymsky wrote many works on the history and cultures of Arab countries, Semitics, and Islam. He prepared literary-historical monographs about the *Hamāsah* of Abū Tammām, Hāfiz, and Paul of Aleppo. He also wrote a great deal on the history of the Ukrainian language and literature, folklore, and ethnography. As a writer, Krymsky is known for his poems on Oriental themes, short stories, and the novel *Andrii Lahovs'kyi* (1905, published in its entirety in 1972). He translated many works, including the *Romance of Antar* and the poetry of Omar Khayyam, Saadi Hāfiz, Mihri Hatun, Ferdowsī, and a number of West European poets.

KRYPIAKEVYCH, IVAN (25 June 1886–21 April 1967). Historian, full member of the **Shevchenko Scientific Society** (NTSh) from

1911, and academician of the **Ukrainian Academy of Sciences** from 1958. Born in **Lviv** into a clerical family, Krypiakevych studied with **Mykhailo Hrushevsky** at Lviv University (1904–9), obtaining his doctorate in 1911. As a student, he was active in the struggle for the establishment of a Ukrainian university and organized classes for young workers and peasants. In 1905, he began publishing articles in *Zapysky NTSh* (Memoirs of the NTSh). Krypiakevych lectured in history at the Academic Gymnasium in Lviv (1912–14) and subsequently at Polish gymnasiums in Lviv, Rohatyn, and Zhovkva (to 1939). He also taught at the Kamianets-Podilskyi Ukrainian State University (1918–19), the **Lviv (Underground) Ukrainian University**, and the Catholic Theological Academy in Lviv (1934–39). He was secretary (from 1920) and then director (1934–39) of the historical section of the NTSh and editor of *Zapysky NTSh* (from 1934).

Krypiakevych was among the founders of the statist school in Ukrainian historiography. During the interwar period, he published a series of pioneering studies on the **Cossack** polity of **Bohdan Khmelnytsky**. He also wrote on the socioeconomic and cultural history of early modern **Galicia** and published many popular historical surveys. He was the author of more than 500 works.

Following the Soviet occupation of **western Ukraine**, Krypiakevych was appointed to the chair of Ukrainian history at the newly Ukrainized Lviv University (October 1939), becoming a full professor in 1941. During the Nazi occupation, he was editor of scholarly publications at the Ukrainian publishing house in Lviv. In the immediate postwar years, he was persecuted as a "bourgeois nationalist." Krypiakevych and other Lviv scholars were transferred to **Kyiv** (1946). He worked as a senior research associate at the Institute of Ukrainian History at the Academy of Sciences (AN UkSSR). In 1948, he was allowed to return to Lviv, where he became a department head at the AN UkSSR Institute of Social Sciences in Lviv (1951) and then director of the institute (1953–62). His biography of Bohdan Khmelnytsky, censored to meet official requirements for the 300th anniversary of the **Pereiaslav Agreement**, was published in 1954. The original text was issued in 1990.

KRYVONIS, MAKSYM (ca. 1600–November 1648). Also known as Perebyinis and Vilshansky. Military commander, close associate of **Bohdan Khmelnytsky** (1648–57), and colonel of Cherkasy. Most probably, he was born in Vilshana (now in Cherkasy oblast). According to other sources, he was a townsman from Ostrih or Mohyliv-Podilskyi. He became a **Zaporozhian Cossack** and distinguished himself in campaigns against the Turks and **Tatars** (1630s–

40s). Kryvonis headed Cossack units in Khmelnytsky's battles of 1648, including the cavalry that was decisive in the victory at Korsun. In June 1648, he commanded rebel units in the **Podilia** and Bratslav regions, taking Tulchyn, Vinnytsia, Uman, and Bratslav in **Right-Bank Ukraine**. At Nemyriv, Makhnivka, and Starokostiantyniv, he routed the household troops of the Polish magnates Jeremi Wiśniowiecki and Władysław Dominik Zasławski. In July, Cossacks commanded by Kryvonis captured Berdychiv, Mezhybizh, Bar, and other towns. After the Battle of Pyliavtsi, Kryvonis organized the pursuit of the retreating enemy. In mid-September, he was badly wounded in battle with German mercenary units near Starokostiantyniv. Before he recovered, Kryvonis participated in the campaign into **Galicia** and, on 15 (25) October, his units captured Vysokyi Zamok, the primary fortification of **Lviv**. He died in mid-November 1648 of a plague that broke out in the Cossack army during the siege of Zamostia (Zamość).

KUBIJOVYČ, VOLODYMYR (23 September 1900–2 November 1985). Civic activist, geographer, demographer, and full member of the **Shevchenko Scientific Society** (NTSh, from 1931). Kubijovyč was born in Nowy Sącz, Poland, into a Ukrainian-Polish family. He studied at the Jagiellonian University in Cracow (1918–23), obtaining a doctorate in geography. During the **Ukrainian-Polish War** (1918–19), he served in the **Ukrainian Galician Army**. Kubijovyč was a lecturer at the Jagiellonian University (1928–39). He studied the anthropogeography of the Carpathians and demographic problems on Ukrainian ethnic territory in Poland and elsewhere. He engaged in a scholarly debate (that later assumed a political character) with the noted Polish geographers Jerzy Smoleński and Eugeniusz Romer, accusing them of falsifying statistical data in their research. Dismissed from his university post (1939) for his Ukrainian sympathies, Kubijovyč became a professor at the **Ukrainian Free University** in 1940. In June of that year, he assumed the leadership of the **Ukrainian Central Committee** in Cracow, which provided economic and social assistance to Ukrainians in the **Generalgouvernement**. He was a leading organizer of the **Division Galizien** in 1943. After 1945, Kubijovyč lived in Germany and France, where he engaged primarily in scholarship. He was general secretary of the NTSh abroad (1947–63) and president of its European branch (from 1952). He died in Sarcelles, France.

Kubijovyč wrote approximately 80 scholarly works on the geography and demography of Ukraine and prepared numerous maps of Ukraine and Galicia, as well as an atlas and geography of

Ukraine and adjacent lands. He was editor in chief of the Ukrainian-language *Encyclopedia of Ukraine* (Sarcelles and New York, 1949–84), writing many of its entries himself. His memoirs include *Meni 85* (I am 85, 1985) and *Ukraïntsi v Heneral'nii Huberniï, 1939–41* (Ukrainians in the Generalgouvernement, 1939–41, 1975).

KUCHMA, LEONID (b. 9 August 1938). Engineer, politician, and president of Ukraine (since 1994). He was born in Chaikyne, Chernihiv oblast, and graduated from Dnipropetrovsk University (1960) as a mechanical engineer specializing in rocketry. Kuchma worked as a senior engineer and designer at the Pivdenne (Southern) Design Bureau (1960–75). From 1972 to 1975, he was a technical supervisor of rocket testing at the Baikonur Cosmodrome (Kazakhstan). Kuchma became secretary of the **Communist Party of Ukraine** (CPU) primary organization at Pivdenne (1975–80) and director of the world's largest rocket factory, Pivdenmash (Southern Machine Building Factory, 1986–92).

From 1990 to 1994, Kuchma was a deputy to the **Verkhovna Rada** (VR) of Ukraine and served as prime minister in the administration of **Leonid Kravchuk** (13 October 1992–21 September 1993). He attempted to resolve Ukraine's severe economic crisis by introducing strict controls but resigned when political support for his policy was not forthcoming. In 1993, Kuchma was president of the Ukrainian Union of Manufacturers and Businessmen. In 1994, he ran against Kravchuk for the presidency of Ukraine, promising to introduce economic reforms and make Russian a state **language**. He was elected in the second round of voting on 10 July, taking 52 percent of the votes cast.

On taking office, Kuchma delivered his inaugural speech in Ukrainian and shelved his commitment regarding the official status of Russian. He announced a program of radical economic reform leading to the adoption of a market economy but encountered overwhelming opposition from powerful oligarchs unwilling to give up their control of key economic sectors, as well as from the VR; the revived CPU opposed **privatization** and a free market on ideological grounds, while national-democratic forces, such as **Rukh**, feared that Russian business would avail itself of market reforms to take over Ukrainian industry. Like his predecessor, Kuchma responded by asserting the superiority of the presidential administration over the CPU-dominated VR. The president's views were embodied in the Law on Power (18 May 1995), which aroused strong CPU opposition and led to a political stalemate that Kuchma threatened to resolve by calling a referendum. Since the Ukrainian public, weary of economic and political crisis, was likely to support the president, the VR responded by adopting the **Constitution** (1996), which ended the Soviet era of Ukrainian legislation without resolving the tension between the executive and legislative branches of **government**. In the same year, Ukraine's new **currency**, the *hryvnia*, was introduced; unlike the previous *karbovanets'*, it did not succumb to runaway inflation. To these major stabilizing measures, Kuchma added a third; taking advantage of a political conflict in the **Crimea**, he abolished the office of Crimean president and pushed through a new constitution whereby the restive Crimean parliament acknowledged its subordination to the **Kyiv** authorities (May 1996).

In **foreign policy**, Kuchma exploited Ukraine's rapprochement with the United States (largely a result of Ukraine's decision to send its **nuclear weapons** to Russia for destruction) to stabilize relations with Russia. In the mid-1990s, Ukraine expanded its relations with the North Atlantic Treaty Organization (NATO), participating in joint maneuvers in the Crimea and western Ukraine and signing a NATO-Ukraine charter in Madrid (9 July 1997). Russia's concern about these closer relations with the West led Boris Yeltsin to sign a treaty with Kuchma recognizing the integrity of Ukraine's borders and putting to rest the long-simmering issue of the division of the **Black Sea Fleet** and the status of Sevastopol, Russia's naval base in the Crimea (1 June 1997).

Despite these signal achievements, Ukraine's **economy** continued to deteriorate, and the government grew increasingly dependent on loans from the International Monetary Fund and the World Bank. The economic crisis dimmed Kuchma's prospects of reelection in 1999, but he managed to overcome this handicap through near-total control of the media and a Western-style advertising campaign funded by powerful business interests. In the final round of voting, Kuchma was pitted against the CPU leader, **Petro Symonenko**, whom he successfully depicted as a reactionary.

Having won the election with 56 percent of the vote, Kuchma sought to secure his dominance over the VR. In 2000, he maneuvered the noncommunist majority of the VR into uniting in order to depose the procommunist speaker, Oleksandr Tkachenko, as well as other powerful left-wing deputies. On 16 April 2000, Kuchma staged a constitutional referendum whose procedures were widely regarded as fraudulent. He obtained a large majority for his proposals to amend the constitution so as to establish a bicameral parliament that the presidential administration could more easily control by means of appointments, as well as to deprive deputies of immunity from prosecution (thereby leaving them open to possible blackmail) and to reduce the number of seats in the VR from 450 to 300. Since the enactment of these amendments required a two-thirds majority in the VR, they remained in abeyance. In November 2000, Kuchma was implicated in the murder of an investigative journalist, **Heorhii Gongadze**, which led to a campaign for his impeachment and a lengthy controversy over the investigation of the case, leaving his presidency under a cloud. In the parliamentary elections of March 2002 the pro-Kuchma bloc, For a United Ukraine, was challenged by his former prime minister, **Viktor Yushchenko**, a reformist who had been brought down in the spring of 2001 by a parliamentary coalition representing the CPU and economic oligarchs. Yushchenko's bloc, Our Ukraine, took almost one-quarter of the vote, which proved insufficient to overturn the dominance of the propresidential bloc.

KULCHYTSKY, STANISLAV (b. 10 January 1937). Historian. A native of **Odesa**, Kulchytsky graduated from Mechnikov University of Odesa in 1959 and obtained his doctorate at the Institute of History, **Academy of Sciences of Ukraine** (1972), specializing in 20th-century Ukrainian economic history. Since 1990 he has served as deputy director of the Institute of History; he is also professor of history at the **Kyiv Mohyla Academy** National University. Kulchytsky is the author or coauthor of more than 1,000 publications in his field, including 29 books. He is noted as Ukraine's foremost authority on the interwar period and the **famine of 1932–33**. His monograph *Tsina "velykoho perelomu"* (The Cost of the "Great Break," 1991) was the first to present a detailed analysis of the **collectivization** of Ukrainian agriculture. It also offered the first estimate of the number of victims of the famine calculated on the basis of summary results of the 1937 **USSR** census that were discovered in the Leningrad state archives in 1988. Kulchytsky went on to publish a study of the Communist Party's socioeconomic policy in the preceding period under the title *Komunizm v Ukraïni: pershe desiatyrichchia (1919–1928)* (Communism in Ukraine: The First Decade [1919–1928], 1996), drawing heavily on previously restricted archival sources. A survey encompassing the whole interwar period appeared in 1999: *Ukraïna mizh dvoma viinamy, 1921–1939* (Ukraine between the Wars, 1921–1939). Kulchytsky has also been a prominent commentator on historical issues of public interest, publishing in such leading Kyiv newspapers as *Den'* (The Day) and *Dzerkalo tyzhnia* (Weekly Mirror).

KULISH, MYKOLA (6 [18] December 1892–3 November 1937). Playwright. He was born in Chaplyntsi, Tavriia gubernia, and studied at the Oleshky (now Tsiuriupynsk, Kherson oblast) eight-year school, then at a gymnasium. He enrolled in the **Odesa** school for ensigns (1913) and fought in **World War I**. In early 1918, Kulish became head of the Oleshky soviet of workers' and **peasants'** deputies. He served in the military (1919–21) and fought Anton Denikin's White forces. In 1920, he became commander of the Dnipro peasant regiment. After demobilization, Kulish worked as an educational administrator in Oleshky county; he also edited the newspaper *Chervonyi shliakh* (Red Path) in Zinovievsk (now Kirovohrad). In 1924, he wrote the play *97*, in which he described the **famine of 1921–23** in the Kherson region. The stage productions of that work and *Komuna v stepakh* (Commune in the Steppes) in **Kharkiv** brought him general acclaim. In 1925, he moved to Kharkiv, where he befriended **Mykola Khvyliovy** and **Les Kurbas**. In the 1920s, Kulish belonged to the literary organizations Hart and **Vaplite**, serving as president of the latter (November 1926–January 1928). He was an editor of *Chervonyi shliakh* (1926–28) and became a presidium member of Prolitfront (1929), which succeeded the banned Vaplite.

Kulish was a founder of the new Ukrainian **theater**. His first plays, *97* (1924) and *Komuna v stepakh* (1925), are mainly realistic and prosaic in character, while the farce *Khulii Khuryna* (1926) has expressionistic features. *Zona* (The Zone, 1926) is a pointed satire on party careerists, while the comedy *Otak zahynuv Huska* (And So Died Huska, 1927) has elements of symbolism. Kulish's masterpieces are the plays *Narodnyi Malakhii* (The People's Malakhii, 1928) and *Myna Mazailo* (1929), which deal with the political conflicts attending the Ukrainian revival of the 1920s. *Sonata pathétique* (1929) depicts the struggle between communists, White Guards, and Ukrainian republicans in 1917–18. Kulish combined the devices of contemporary experimental theater with traditional Ukrainian drama (the *vertep*). Most of his plays were staged at Kurbas's **Berezil Theater**. Kulish's works were censured by official critics. He was arrested in December 1934 and sentenced to 10 years at the Solovets Islands concentration camp, but was shot on orders of the NKVD in 1937.

KULISH, PANTELEIMON (27 July [8 August] 1819–2 [14] February 1897). Writer, historian, ethnographer, literary critic, and translator. Kulish was born of **Cossack**-gentry stock in Voronizh, Chernihiv gubernia (now in Sumy oblast) and studied at the Novhorod-Siverskyi gymnasium. He audited classes at **Kyiv** University, where he was not permitted to enroll because of his non-noble origin. Kulish was profoundly influenced by **Mykhailo Maksymovych**, whose collection of folk songs and epic dumas inspired his devotion to Ukrainian culture. Kulish attended Maksymovych's classes and obtained a teaching post in Lutsk (1842) on the latter's recommendation. He soon moved to Kyiv, where he also taught and did ethnographic research, collecting folk songs, legends, and stories. He established friendships with Vasyl Bilozersky, Mykola Hulak, **Mykola Kostomarov**, and **Taras Shevchenko**, with whom he founded the clandestine **Cyril and Methodius Brotherhood** in 1845. Kulish was arrested upon the discovery of the brotherhood and imprisoned at the SS. Peter and Paul Fortress in St. Petersburg. After lengthy interrogation, Kulish was exiled to Tula. He pleaded with the authorities to be allowed to return to St. Petersburg, and his request was granted in 1850.

Kulish proceeded to publish a major ethnographic collection, *Zapiski o Iuzhnoi Rusi* (Notes on Southern Rus', vols. 1–2, 1856–57), a historical novel about the Cossack era, *Chorna rada* (Black Council, 1857), and a grammar textbook for use in **Sunday schools**. He developed his own orthography, which became known as the *kulishivka* and served as a basis for modern Ukrainian orthography. Eager to promote popular **education**, Kulish established a printing press and published approximately 40 low-priced books under the series title *Sil's'ka biblioteka* (Village Library). He was a founder of the journal *Osnova*, to which he frequently contributed. Following the official prohibition on Ukrainian publishing in 1863 (*see* VALUEV CIRCULAR), Kulish took up a bureaucratic appointment in Warsaw. In 1867, owing to his connections with political activists in **Galicia** and his contributions to Ukrainian publications there, he was forced to resign from government employment. He lived abroad, primarily in Galicia, where he was involved in politics and worked with Ukrainian **populists** (1868–71). He maintained close ties with the physicist **Ivan Puliui** and the writer **Oleksander Barvinsky**. In 1871, Kulish returned to St. Petersburg, where he worked for the Ministry of Transport and edited its official journal.

In the 1870s, Kulish turned to historical studies, publishing his *Istoriia vossoedineniia Rusi* (History of the Reunification of Rus', 3 vols., 1874–77). In this and other works, he bitterly attacked the Cossack and **haidamaka** movements that had inspired his friends Kostomarov and Shevchenko. Kulish regarded Cossackdom as an anarchic force that had destroyed the political and cultural achievements of the Ukrainian elite—the **nobility** and the **Cossack officer** stratum. Kulish's rejection of populism, contemptuous references to Shevchenko's "half-drunken muse," and praise of Russian absolutism estranged him from most Ukrainian intellectuals of the day. The **Ems Ukase** (1876), which banned virtually all Ukrainian publications, undercut Kulish's program of compromise with the imperial government in return for the opportunity to develop Ukrainian culture. He protested the ukase, contemplated moving to Galicia, and came close to renouncing his imperial citizenship. In the end, Kulish retired to his homestead of Motronivka near Borzna (now in Chernihiv oblast), where he continued extremely intensive literary work. He wrote a three-volume study of the **Khmelnytsky Uprising**, as well as poetical works. He translated works of Shakespeare, Byron, Goethe, Heine, and Schiller. Together with Puliui and Ivan Nechui-Levytsky, he produced the first complete Ukrainian translation of the Bible. Kulish died and was buried at the Motronivka homestead. His literary achievements remained influential well into the Soviet period; **Mykola Khvyliovy** was particularly attracted by Kulish's orientation toward European elite culture. *See also* LITERATURE.

KURBAS, LES (25 February 1887–3 November 1937). **Theater** director. He was born in Sambir (now in **Lviv** oblast) into the family of an actor and educated at the Ternopil gymnasium, the University of Vienna (1907–8), and Lviv University (1910). In 1911, he was invited to join **Hnat Khotkevych's** Hutsul Theater as one of its directors. He also acted in the theater of the Ruska Besida society (1912–14) and organized the Ternopil Theatrical Evenings troupe (1915). In 1916, Kurbas joined the Sadovsky Theater in **Kyiv** and moved on to the Young Theater (1917–19), where he introduced modern European repertoire and acting styles. In June 1920, Kurbas and a group of actors established Kyivdramte (Kyiv Dramatic Theater), among whose offerings was a Ukrainian-language production of Shakespeare's *Macbeth* with Kurbas in the title role. Kurbas began to create an all-Ukrainian theatrical academy, the Berezil Artistic Association, which consisted of actors' studios, a directors' lab, research committees, and a large number of actors. In the early 1920s, Kurbas also made the **films** *Vendetta*, *Macdonald*, and *Arsenal'tsi* (Fighters of the Arsenal) at the **Odesa** film studio.

Kurbas's work at the **Berezil Theater** in Kyiv (1922–26) and Kharkiv (1926–33) marked the most experimental and creative period of his career. The theater staged a series of highly innovative, often controversial productions, including *Jimmy Higgins* (based on a work by Upton Sinclair), Fernand Crommelynck's *Tripes d'or*, **Mykola Kulish's** *Narodnyi Malakhii* (The People's Malakhii), *Myna Mazailo*, and *Maklena Grassa*, and Ivan Mykytenko's *Dyktatura* (Dictatorship). Berezil detached itself from the old **realist**, ethnographic style of Ukrainian theater and introduced works influenced by expressionism and constructivism. This new intellectual theater reduced the role of the spoken word and focused on images that combined rhythm, movement, and other visual devices, such as montage.

By 1927, Kurbas's work had provoked attacks and accusations of nationalism, formalism, remoteness from Soviet reality, and the like. A production of Georg Büchner's *Woyzeck* was forbidden, and Kulish's *Sonata pathétique* also failed to reach the stage. An orchestrated campaign to discredit and harass Kurbas began in 1931. After he refused to condemn the activities of **Mykola Khvyliovy** and **Mykola Skrypnyk**, Kurbas was dismissed as artistic director of the Berezil Theater and stripped of the title of People's Artist of the **Ukrainian SSR**, which he had received in 1925. He was arrested in Moscow in 1933 and sentenced to forced labor in the North. He was executed in 1937.

KURKOV, ANDREI (b. 23 April 1961). Writer. Born in the village of Budogoshch in Leningrad oblast, Russia, Kurkov moved to Ukraine with his parents and graduated from the **Kyiv** State Pedagogical Institute of Foreign Languages in 1983. Calling himself "a Ukrainian of Russian origin," Kurkov has become a highly successful Russian-language novelist—the first in post-Soviet Ukraine to make his living from writer's royalties—with a considerable following in Europe. Employing the conventions of the suspense and crime novel, Kurkov explores social breakdown in post-Soviet Ukraine and the corruption resulting from it. Among the best-known of his novels are *Smert' postoronnego* (1996; trans. *Death and the Penguin*, 2001); *Piknik na l'du* (Picnic on the Ice, which sold over 150,000 copies, more than any other book by a contemporary Ukrainian author); *Igra v otrezannyi palets* (2000; trans. *The Case of the General's Thumb*, 2003), and *Zakon ulitki* (2002; trans. *Penguin Lost*, 2004). Asked to explain the penguin motif in his recent fiction, Kurkov responded that penguins act collectively, not individually, a trait shared by the protagonists of his novels, whose consciousness took shape under Soviet conditions. Kurkov has also written scenarios for several **films**, most notably *Priiatel' pokoinika* (A Friend of the Deceased, 1997), directed by Viacheslav Kryshtofovych.

KVITKA-OSNOVIANENKO, HRYHORII (18 [29] November 1778–8 [20] August 1843). First major prose writer of modern Ukrainian **literature**. He was born in Osnova (now a suburb of **Kharkiv**) into a family of **Cossack officer** origin and received his education at home. At the age of 23, he briefly entered the Kuriazh Monastery but returned to secular life. He was a commissar in the militia, a county marshal of the **nobility** (1817–28), and later president of the

Kharkiv chamber of the criminal court. Kvitka-Osnovianenko was prominent in the civic and cultural life of Kharkiv. He was elected to the Scientific Society at Kharkiv University and was a founder of the Kharkiv Professional **Theater** (and its director from 1812), the Society of Benevolence (1812), the Institute for Noble Girls (1812), and the Kharkiv gubernia library (1838). Kvitka-Osnovianenko propagated folk themes in literature, with an emphasis on "writing from nature" and subjects drawn from everyday life. He wrote in both Ukrainian and Russian.

Continuing the literary tradition begun by **Ivan Kotliarevsky** and drawing on folk songs and folk humor, Kvitka-Osnovianenko wrote the comedy *Svatannia na Honcharivtsi* (Matchmaking at Honcharivka, 1835), popular to this day, and *Shel'menko-denshchyk* (Shelmenko the Orderly, 1837). His Ukrainian prose includes literary travesties such as "Saldats'kyi patret" (A Soldier's Portrait), the first short story in Ukrainian literature; "Mertvets'kyi velykden'" (Dead Man's Easter), "Ot tobi i skarb" (There's a Treasure for You), *Parkhymove snidannia* (Parkhym's Breakfast), *Pidbrekhach* (The Second Matchmaker), *Konotops'ka vid'ma* (The Witch of Konotop); and the sentimental stories "Marusia" (1834), "Kozyr-divka" (Lively Wench, 1838), and "Serdeshna Oksana" (Poor Oksana, 1841). Kvitka-Osnovianenko's Russian-language publications include historical and ethnographic surveys. His better works were among the first to represent Ukrainian literature to a European audience. "Serdeshna Oksana" was first published in French in 1854, while other works were translated into Polish, Bulgarian, and Czech. Kvitka-Osnovianenko's narratives, whose plots avoid social conflict and depict ideally honorable and pious protagonists, are typical examples of sentimentalism. His writing significantly influenced the development of Ukrainian literature, particularly the "ethnographic school."

KYBALCHYCH, MYKOLA (19 [31] October 1853–3 [15] April 1881). Inventor and revolutionary. Kybalchych was born in Korop, Chernihiv gubernia, and received his secondary education at the Novhorod-Siverskyi Gymnasium. While studying at the St. Petersburg Institute of Railroad Engineers and then at the Medical-Surgical Academy, he became active in the revolutionary movement and was incarcerated for three years at the Lukianivka Prison in **Kyiv** (1875). In 1879, he joined the People's Will (*see* POPULISM), for which he built the bomb used to assassinate Tsar Alexander II in 1881. He was arrested, tried, and executed at the SS. Peter and Paul Fortress in St. Petersburg. While awaiting execution, Kybalchych outlined his design for an aircraft able to fly beyond the earth's atmosphere. The project included a design for a solid-fuel jet engine and a rocket navigation system—the first recorded proposal of its kind. His ideas, while simple, are fundamental to jet propulsion and space technology. A crater on the far side of the moon is named after him.

KYI, SHCHEK, KHORYV, AND LYBID. Three brothers and a sister who, according to the *Tale of Bygone Years*, founded **Kyiv**. Archaeological digs confirm the existence of fifth-century settlements on the Shchekavytsia and Khoryvytsia hills mentioned in the **chronicles**, and the Lybid River runs through Kyiv. Some historians maintain that Kyi was a historical person, a prince of the Polianian tribe who lived from the fifth to the early sixth century. According to the *Tale*, Kyi dealt with a Byzantine emperor (identified by some as Justinian), who received him "with honor."

KYIV (Kiev). Political, religious, scientific, and cultural capital of Ukraine. It is also Ukraine's largest city (2001 pop. 2,611,300), a major industrial center, and an important **transport** and communications hub. The city stands on the Dnipro River, 951 km north of its mouth in the Black Sea. Kyiv was initially located only on the high right bank of the Dnipro, but since **World War II** it has spread to the low, flat left bank.

The oldest human traces on the territory of Kyiv date from the late Paleolithic era. Traces of the Neolithic **Trypilian culture**, as well as Copper, Bronze, and Iron Age settlements, are also numerous. According to the *Tale of Bygone Years*, the city's founders were the brothers **Kyi, Shchek, and Khoryv**. Although the account is probably legendary, archaeological evidence suggests that Kyiv was founded in the sixth or seventh century. With the arrival of Prince **Oleh** and the founding of **Kyivan Rus'** in the second half of the ninth century, Kyiv became the capital of the state.

Following the **Christianization of Rus'** by Prince **Volodymyr the Great** in 988, Kyiv became a major religious center. Under his son **Yaroslav the Wise**, the city reached its zenith. Yaroslav further extended the boundaries of Kyiv, constructing fortifications and the **St. Sophia Cathedral**. Kyiv maintained diplomatic relations with Byzantium and the major West European powers and became a center of scholarship, writing, and painting. Its population reached 50,000–100,000 by the 12th century.

The city also engaged in a series of wars against nomadic tribes such as the **Khazars**, **Pechenegs**, and **Cumans**, who lived in the steppes to the south. A greater threat came from internecine conflicts for the Kyivan throne that began after Yaroslav's death (1054): Andrei Bogoliubsky of Suzdal sacked Kyiv in 1169, as did Riuryk

Rostyslavych in 1203. In 1240, much of the city was destroyed by the **Golden Horde**. In 1362–63, Algirdas of Lithuania annexed the Kyivan land as an **appanage principality**, and his descendants ruled the city until 1470. In 1471, Kyiv became the capital of the Kyiv voivodeship and was governed by Lithuanian viceroys until 1569. At the time, Kyiv was reduced to a minor market town on the Lithuanian-**Tatar** frontier. The city suffered greatly from Tatar raids, particularly the attack of 1482 by Khan Mengli Giray, an ally of Ivan III of Muscovy, after which the upper city lay in ruins for more than a century. After the **Union of Lublin** (1569), Kyiv came under Polish rule.

In the early 17th century, Kyiv experienced a renaissance, becoming the political, religious, and cultural center of Ukraine. The **Kyiv Epiphany Brotherhood** and the **Kyivan Cave Monastery Press** were established. Metropolitan **Petro Mohyla**, in particular, did much to make Kyiv an important cultural center, initiating and funding the restoration of many of the city's churches and establishing the school that would become the **Kyiv Mohyla Academy**. **Bohdan Khmelnytsky** cleared the city of Polish forces in 1648, but the Polish-Lithuanian army struck back in 1651. After the **Pereiaslav Agreement** (1654), a Muscovite fortress was built in Kyiv, and the **Truce of Andrusovo** (1667) granted the city to Muscovy for two years. The Muscovites, however, managed to take control of Kyiv, sealing their acquisition by means of the **Eternal Peace of 1686**. Kyiv's architecture and culture developed significantly under the patronage of Hetman **Ivan Mazepa**. After Mazepa's defeat at the **Battle of Poltava** (1709), Kyiv's autonomy was progressively eliminated and restrictions were imposed on Ukrainian merchants, while Russians and others received preferential treatment. In 1782, the **Cossack** regimental system of administration was abolished, and Kyiv became the capital of a vicegerency encompassing several **Left-Bank** regiments. The vicegerency was abolished in 1796 and replaced by the Kyiv gubernia in the following year.

The Polish uprising of 1830 led to intensive government-directed **Russification** measures in Kyiv and **Right-Bank Ukraine**. The city's right of **Magdeburg law** was officially rescinded, and Russian merchants were encouraged to settle in Kyiv. The Russification of religion was fostered at the Kyiv Theological Academy, which replaced the Mohyla Academy in 1819. Kyiv University was founded in 1834 with an eye to curbing Polish influences. Despite such measures, a Ukrainian national movement arose in the city, evident in the activities of the **Cyril and Methodius Brotherhood**, the *khlopoman* movement, the Kyiv **Hromada**, the **Southwestern Branch of the Imperial Russian Geographic Society**, and

Ukrainian-**language** teaching in **Sunday schools**. As tsarist persecution intensified in the mid-19th century, however, the Ukrainian movement gravitated toward Austrian-ruled **Lviv** (*see also* VALUEV CIRCULAR; EMS UKASE).

Kyiv grew rapidly in the second half of the 19th century. In 1869–70, it was connected to Moscow and Odesa by rail and became the main market of the sugar industry in the Russian Empire. In the liberal period after the **Revolution of 1905**, Kyiv became the focal point of Ukrainian cultural, scholarly, publishing, and political activity.

During the **Ukrainian Revolution** (1917–21), Kyiv was the seat of the **Ukrainian Central Rada** and the capital of the **Ukrainian People's Republic**. Subsequently it was also the capital of the **Ukrainian State** and the **Directory**. Ukrainian, White, and Bolshevik forces fought for control of the city, with the Bolsheviks definitively taking control in June 1920. Since Kyiv was associated with the Ukrainian national movement, the Bolsheviks established **Kharkiv**, a short distance from the Russian border, as the capital of the **Ukrainian SSR**. Once Stalin's **political terror** had done away with the **Ukrainization** policy of the 1920s, the capital was moved back to Kyiv in 1934. While new buildings and squares were being designed, more than two dozen ancient churches and landmarks were destroyed between 1934 and 1936.

After the German invasion of the USSR, German forces occupied Kyiv on 19 September 1941. Soviet mines began detonating the following day, and the city burned for a week and a half. During the occupation, at least 200,000 residents of Kyiv, mostly **Jews**, were executed at Babyn Yar. About 100,000 Ukrainians were sent from Kyiv to Germany as *Ostarbeiter*, and some 100,000 Soviet soldiers died in prisoner-of-war camps in the city. By the time the Red Army recaptured Kyiv on 6 November 1943, 80 percent of the city's residents were homeless, and the population had been reduced from 930,000 (1940) to 305,000.

After the war, Kyiv grew rapidly into a major industrial center, but was politically overshadowed by Moscow. With Ukraine's declaration of independence in 1991, Kyiv returned to the political stage. As the capital of Ukraine, Kyiv today performs major administrative functions, has a vibrant cultural life, and leads Ukraine's scientific and educational activity. The city's strong industrial complex, concentrated in its western sections and on the Left Bank, includes a variety of engineering (metal, machinery, tools, aircraft, electrical instruments), chemical (resins, fertilizers, plastics, and fibers), construction materials, and consumer goods industries. Kyiv is also a major **publishing** and **media** center.

As the cultural and academic center of Ukraine, Kyiv is the base of the **Ukrainian Academy of Sciences** and more than 20 institutions of higher education, including Kyiv University, the Kyiv Mohyla Academy (reopened in 1992 as a national university), and the Polytechnical Institute (established in 1898), as well as a **music** conservatory and agricultural, medical, pedagogical, art, **theater**, and economics institutes.

Kyiv is home to the National Opera, National Drama Theater, National Philharmonia, and several other large auditoriums and "palaces of culture." Among the city's music ensembles, the most prominent are the National Symphony Orchestra, the Dumka National Choral Capella, the **Lysenko** String Quartet, the National Bandura Capella, and the Veriovka Song and Dance Ensemble. Kyiv also has a permanent circus and is home to the **Dovzhenko** Film Studio. The city has museums of history, natural history, Ukrainian art, Ukrainian folk art, Western and Eastern art, Russian art, Ukrainian literature, and the Second World War. Other significant museums are located at St. Sophia's Cathedral and the Kyivan Cave Monastery. Kyiv's religious prominence is also exemplified by St. Michael's Golden-Domed Cathedral, St. Volodymyr's Cathedral, and the churches of St. Cyril and St. Andrew.

KYIV COSSACKS (1855). **Peasant** revolt in **Kyiv** gubernia. It began with the publication of a manifesto by Tsar Nicholas I during the Crimean War (1853–56) calling for the formation of a popular militia. A rumor circulated among the peasants of the Kyiv region that by enlisting in the militia (the "**Cossacks**"), they could gain emancipation and take over the lands and property of estate owners. The peasants compiled lists of "free Cossacks," refused to perform corvée labor or obey the commands of the local administration, and created their own representative bodies (village *hromadas*). The peasant movement began in Vasylkiv county (February 1855) and soon engulfed eight of the Kyiv gubernia's 12 counties (more than 400 villages and 180,000 peasants). Twenty-five cavalry squadrons and nine infantry companies were dispatched to quell the revolt. The largest clashes with peasant rebels occurred in the towns of Korsun and Tahancha (Kaniv county) and the villages of Berezna (Skvyra county), Bykova Hreblia (Vasylkiv county), and Yablunivka. The revolt manifested strong popular opposition to serfdom and an attachment to the tradition of **Cossack** and **haidamaka rebellions** against nobiliary oppression. In 1856, there was another large wave of unrest among the peasants of the Katerynoslav, Kherson, **Poltava**, Chernihiv, and **Kharkiv** gubernias, with many of the rebels attempting to escape to the **Crimea**.

KYIV EPIPHANY BROTHERHOOD. Religious organization established ca. 1615 at the initiative of Orthodox clergymen from **western Ukraine**. It was located at the **Kyiv** Epiphany **Brotherhood** Monastery, built on lands donated by the noblewoman Yelysaveta Hulevychivna. Hetman **Petro Sahaidachny** and the whole **Cossack** Host enrolled in the brotherhood in 1620, saving it from official repression at a time when Orthodoxy had been outlawed in the **Polish-Lithuanian Commonwealth** by the **Union of Brest**. In 1620–21, when Patriarch Theophanes of Jerusalem visited Kyiv, he consecrated a new Orthodox hierarchy and granted the right of stauropegion (autonomy from the rule of local bishops) to the brotherhood. At the behest of the local **nobility**, the brotherhood was given a royal charter in 1629. From 1615, it operated a school of Church Slavonic, Greek, and Latin-Polish studies (Kyiv Brotherhood School). In 1632, the brotherhood school merged with the school of the **Kyivan Cave Monastery** established by Metropolitan **Petro Mohyla** to form the **Kyiv Mohyla Academy**. As the Orthodox Church gained strength under Mohyla's leadership, the lay membership of the Epiphany Brotherhood, consisting largely of burghers, was relegated to a secondary role, and the organization declined after the 1640s.

KYIV METROPOLITANATE. First central church organization on Ukrainian territory, established under the jurisdiction of the patriarchate of Constantinople after the **Christianization of Rus'** (988). Its early history is obscure. According to one version of events, the first hierarch was a Greek named Michael. Other scholars maintain that the first metropolitan was Leon or Leontios (d. 1004) or Bishop Nastasios of Korsun (Chersonesus). The first metropolitan of **Kyiv** mentioned in historical documents was a contemporary of Prince **Yaroslav the Wise**, the Greek Theopemptos (1037–48). The jurisdiction of the Kyiv metropolitanate expanded to include the 16 eparchies created on the territory of **Kyivan Rus'**. Twenty-two Kyivan metropolitans from the pre-Mongol period are known, most of them Greeks sent by the patriarch of Constantinople. Metropolitans **Ilarion** (consecrated 1051), Yefym (1089–97), Klym Smoliatych (1141–54), and Kyrylo II (1233–36) were natives of the Kyivan state. The Kyiv metropolitanate enjoyed considerable autonomy within the patriarchate.

After the invasion of the **Golden Horde** (1237–40), the metropolitans of Kyiv decided to relocate their residence to Vladimir on the Kliazma. This led to the weakening of their ties with the Rus' lands and obliged the **Galician-Volhynian** princes to create a separate **Halych metropolitanate**. In the 14th and 15th centuries,

Ukrainian and Belarusian lands within the **Grand Duchy of Lithuania** were under the jurisdiction of metropolitans who resided in Moscow but continued to use the title "Metropolitan of Kyiv and All Rus'." Kyivan metropolitans of the second half of the 15th century supported union with Rome on terms established at the Council of Florence (1439), while the Muscovite church declared its autocephaly in 1448 (recognized by Constantinople in 1589).

In the 16th century, the Kyiv metropolitanate entered into a period of deep crisis, resulting in the **Union of Brest** (1596), which established the Uniate Church (*see* UKRAINIAN CATHOLIC CHURCH) under the authority of Rome. From 1596 to 1620, the only metropolitanate in Kyiv was Uniate; King Sigismund III of Poland transferred the rights and privileges of the Kyiv metropolitanate to the Uniate Church. Nevertheless, an Orthodox church continued to exist. With the support of the **Cossacks**, led by Hetman **Petro Sahaidachny**, an Orthodox hierarchy was restored in Ukraine (1620), and **Iov Boretsky** became metropolitan of Kyiv (1620–31). The Orthodox metropolitanate of Kyiv was recognized by the Polish government in 1632. In the 17th century, the post was held by **Isaia Kopynsky** (1631–33), **Petro Mohyla** (1633–47), **Sylvestr Kosiv** (1647–57), Dionisii Balaban (1657–63), and **Yosyf Tukalsky-Neliubovych** (1663–75). From 1675 to 1685, the *locum tenens* of the Kyiv metropolitan's cathedral was Lazar Baranovych, archbishop of Chernihiv.

The Uniate metropolitans of Kyiv after the Union of Brest were **Mykhail Rahoza** (1596–99), **Ipatii Potii** (1599–1613), **Yosyf Rutsky** (1614–37), Rafail Korsak (1637–42), Antonii Seliava (1642–55), Havryil Kolenda (1655–74), Kypriian Zhokhovsky (1674–93), and Lev Zalensky (1694–1708). After the **Khmelnytsky Uprising** (1648–57), the Uniate Church was increasingly identified with the Polish-ruled Ukrainian lands. By the early 18th century, the Uniate metropolitanate of Kyiv included nine eparchies: Kyiv, Polatsk, Smolensk, Turiv-Pynsk (Turaŭ-Pinsk), Berestia (Brest)-Volodymyr, Kholm (Chełm)-Belz, Peremyshl (Przemyśl)-Sambir-Sian (which adhered to the Union in 1692), Lviv-Halych-Kamianets (adhered in 1700), and Lutsk-Ostrih (adhered in 1702). After the second and third partitions of Poland (1793, 1795), the Uniate Church was confined to **Galicia** in the Habsburg Monarchy and renamed the "Greek Catholic Church." The Halych metropolitanate, restored in 1808, continued to claim jurisdiction over Kyiv, but in the course of the 19th century the Uniate Church was abolished in the Russian Empire.

The Orthodox metropolitanate of Kyiv lost its autonomy in 1685, when **Hedeon Sviatopolk-Chetvertynsky** became metropolitan (1685–90). Consecrated in Moscow by Patriarch Ioakim, he swore an oath of allegiance to Muscovy. In 1688, the use of the title "Metropolitan of Kyiv, Halych, and all Rus'" was forbidden. Under Tsar Peter I, the Kyiv metropolitanate was reduced to the status of a regular eparchy of the Moscow patriarchate (1721), no longer headed by metropolitans but by archbishops (until 1743). While most metropolitans of Kyiv in the 18th century were of Ukrainian descent, Russians were dominant in the 19th century.

After the formation of the **Ukrainian** Autocephalous **Orthodox Church** (UAOC) during the **Ukrainian Revolution** (1917–21) and the confirmation of its autocephaly by an all-Ukrainian church council (1921), its head was named "Metropolitan of Kyiv and all Ukraine." That title was employed by metropolitans **Vasyl Lypkivsky** (1921–27) and Mykola Boretsky (1927–30). The UAOC was destroyed by the Soviet authorities in the 1930s, and the Kyiv metropolitanate was again subordinated to the Moscow patriarchate. After **World War II**, the metropolitanate became an exarchate of the Russian Orthodox Church (ROC) in Ukraine. In 1990, the UAOC reestablished itself in Ukraine and renewed its Kyiv metropolitanate. In the same year, the Russian Orthodox Church granted its Ukrainian exarchate metropolitan status (autonomy). In 1992, when the ROC in Ukraine split and the Ukrainian Orthodox Church (Kyiv Patriarchate) was established, its head adopted the title "Metropolitan of Kyiv and all Ukraine."

KYIV MOHYLA ACADEMY/KYIEVO-MOHYLIANS'KA AKADEMIIA. One of the first and most prominent schools of general learning in Eastern Europe. It began with the founding of the **Kyiv Epiphany Brotherhood** School (1615). In 1632, it was merged with the school of the **Kyivan Cave Monastery** (founded in 1631) to form the Kyiv Brotherhood Collegium, or, to honor its founder, **Petro Mohyla**, the Kyiv Mohyla Collegium. Thanks to the efforts of Hetman **Ivan Mazepa**, the collegium obtained the status of an academy (university) in 1694, although the name "Academy" was not officially confirmed until 1701.

Mohyla modeled his collegium on Polish Jesuit schools, which were introducing Renaissance learning to Eastern Europe. As metropolitan of the newly revived **Ukrainian Orthodox Church**, he adopted the most advanced educational methods and curricula available to him. Throughout its existence, the academy remained primarily an ecclesiastical institution, little influenced by secular culture.

The number of students at the academy in 1700 approached 2,000 and later fluctuated between 500 and 1,200. Many of them were sons of townspeople, **Cossacks**, and **peasants**. The academy was divided into seven grades or schools (eight in the 18th century). In the first five grades, pupils studied Latin, Polish, and Slavonic grammar. The next two grades stressed Latin and Polish rhetoric, followed by a three-year course of Aristotelian philosophy and a four-year program of theology. Lectures were given primarily in Latin.

The academy was strongly supported by the **Cossack officer** stratum and flourished particularly during Mazepa's rule. Its professors included such distinguished educators as Inokentii Gizel, **Teofan Prokopovych**, Stefan Yavorsky, Mykhail Kozachynsky, and **Heorhii Konysky**. In the 17th century, branches of the academy were active in Vinnytsia, Hoshcha, Kremianets, and Iaşi. Collegiums in Chernihiv (1701), **Kharkiv** (1726), and Pereiaslav modeled themselves on the academy. In the 18th century, its traditions influenced the establishment of secondary and postsecondary schools in Russia. Its graduates contributed to the development of education in Belarus, **Moldavia**, and the South Slavic countries. Closed by the Russian imperial authorities in 1817, the academy was replaced by a school of theology. The institution was revived in 1992 as an elite school, the Kyiv Mohyla Academy National University.

KYIVAN CAVE MONASTERY/KYIEVO-PECHERS'KA LAVRA. One of the largest and oldest Orthodox monasteries in Ukraine. It was founded in Berestove near Kyiv, on the right bank of the Dnipro River (ca. 1051). **St. Anthony of the Caves** is considered its founder. The first hegumen mentioned in historical documents was the monk Varlaam (1061), who was succeeded by **St. Theodosius of the Caves**. The monastery was the preeminent religious and cultural center of **Kyivan Rus'** (11th–13th centuries). In the 12th century, it was designated a *lavra* (a Greek term denoting a major monastery of the Eastern Church). The monastery was the site of **chronicle** writing and book copying, a hospice for the poor and crippled, and a workshop producing mosaics and jewelry. It was destroyed on several occasions: by **Cuman** hordes (1096), by the armies of Andrei Bogoliubsky of Vladimir-Suzdal (1169), by the forces of Riuryk Rostyslavych and the princes of Chernihiv (1203), by the **Golden Horde** (1240), and by the Crimean **Tatars** (1482). However, the monastery was rebuilt each time and became even better established. In 1598, it was granted the right of stauropegion (independence of the local metropolitan) by the patriarch of Constantinople.

After the **Union of Brest** (1596), a lengthy dispute ensued between Catholics and Orthodox over ownership of the monastery, with the Orthodox retaining control. During this period, the monastery was the center of the Orthodox religious and cultural revival. The **Kyivan Cave Patericon** was compiled there. **Yelysei Pletenetsky**, archimandrite of the monastery, established a printing press in 1615. In the 17th century, the monastery published more than 100 works, including writings by **Petro Mohyla**, Inokentii Gizel, Lazar Baranovych, and Ioanikii Galiatovsky. In 1631, Mohyla opened a school at the monastery whose merger with the **Kyiv Epiphany Brotherhood** School resulted in the creation of the **Kyiv Mohyla Academy**.

Following the **Pereiaslav Agreement** (1654) with Muscovy, the patriarch of Moscow began encroaching on the monastery's rights, and it was subordinated to him in 1688. The tsarist government forbade the printing of books in the Ukrainian variant of Church Slavonic (1720), resulting in a significant loss of income for the monastery. In 1786, the monastery's extensive properties were secularized and it became dependent on the state. Its ancient custom of electing a council of elders as its governing body was abolished, and the **Russification** of church life in Ukraine proceeded apace. After the establishment of the Soviet regime, the monastery was persecuted by the authorities. In 1921–22, most of its treasures and art works were confiscated.

During its long existence, the monastery developed an impressive array of buildings. The oldest were the Dormition Cathedral (1073–78, destroyed by the retreating Soviets on 3 November 1941; restored by the Kyiv city authorities in 2000) and the Trinity Church above the Main Gate (1108). A number of churches were built in the 17th and 18th centuries, funded by Ukrainian **hetmans** and **Cossack** officers. The monastery's Great Bell Tower (96.5 m high) was built by Johann Gottfried Schädel (1731–44). A number of buildings were designed by the monastery's 18th-century architect, Stepan Kovnir. On 29 September 1926, the monastery was declared a state historical and cultural preserve, and all its treasures were nationalized. Its grounds (22 ha) contain more than 80 buildings and a number of prominent museums, including the Museum of Historical Treasures of Ukraine. After **World War II**, most of its buildings were rebuilt and restored. In the late 1980s, a portion of the monastery's territory and buildings was returned to the church. Currently, the monastery is the residence of the head of the **Ukrainian Orthodox Church** (Moscow Patriarchate).

KYIVAN CAVE PATERICON/KYIEVO-PECHERS'KYI PATERYK. Celebrated work of church **literature** dating from the first half of the 13th century. It is a collection of tales about the history of the **Kyivan Cave Monastery** and its first monks. Begun on the model of patericons compiled in several centers of Eastern Orthodoxy, it has been preserved in three 15th-century redactions: Arsenian (1406), First Cassian (1460), and Second Cassian (1462). The patericon is based on correspondence between Bishop Simon of Vladimir-Suzdal and the cave monk Polikarp (ca. 1223–33), to which various materials, including a life of **St. Theodosius**, hegumen of the Cave Monastery, were added. It celebrates the builders, iconographers (especially Olimpii), and individual monks of the monastery. The work contains a wealth of historical information about the monastery and **Kyiv** in general, the attitude of Kyivan princes toward the monastery, the cultural role of the **Varangians**, and the libraries and reading habits of monks. There are also tales of miracles, encounters with devils, and the like. The patericon was first published by the monastery's printing press in 1635 (in Polish translation) and 1661 (in the original Church Slavonic). A critical edition appeared in Kyiv in 1930, and the first complete English translation, by Muriel Heppell, was published in 1989.

KYIVAN RUS'. The first East Slavic state, centered in **Kyiv**. It emerged in the mid-ninth century after a lengthy process of consolidation among East Slavic tribal principalities. At its zenith, Kyivan Rus' extended from the Baltic Sea in the north to the Black Sea in the south, and from the Sian River in the west to the Volga and Oka Rivers in the east (approx. 800,000 sq. km). It was destroyed by the invasions of the **Golden Horde** in the mid-13th century. The history of Kyivan Rus' may be divided into three periods:

1. The establishment and evolution of state structures from the late eighth century through the 10th. Alliances of Slavic tribes evolved into tribal principalities (sixth–eighth centuries). Arab writers of the time name three prestate formations of East Slavs: Kuiaviia, Slaviia, and Artaniia. Present-day researchers equate Kuiaviia with the Kyiv land, Slaviia with Pereiaslav, and Artaniia with Tmutorokan, Chernihiv, or Peremyshl (Przemyśl). The evolution of tribal principalities along the middle course of the Dnipro River during the eighth and mid-ninth centuries resulted in the formation of the Rus' Land (*Rus'ka zemlia*), which initially incorporated Polianian, Derevlianian, and Siverianian lands. According to **chronicle** accounts, Kyiv was ruled in the 860s–80s by Princes **Askold and Dir**, who traced their descent to **Kyi**. In the northern lands of Rus', the process of state-building developed after three brothers, **Riuryk, Sineus, and Truvor**, were invited to rule the territory in 862 (**Norman theory**). After the death of Riuryk (879), his successor,

Oleh, killed Askold and Dir (882) and made Kyiv his capital. According to tradition, he declared that Kyiv would be "the mother of Rus' cities." Oleh's rule extended to the peripheral territories of Rus'. In 907, he organized a campaign against the Byzantine Empire, the preeminent political and cultural power of the time, which resulted in a commercial treaty favorable to Rus' (911). Riuryk's descendant **Ihor** subjugated the Ulychians and Derevlianians and led a successful campaign to the Caspian Sea. During his reign, the **Pechenegs** first attacked Rus' (915). Ihor was killed while collecting tribute in the Derevlianian lands (945). His wife, Princess **Olha**, crushed the Derevlianian rebellion and standardized the collection of tribute from lands annexed to Kyiv. Olha visited Constantinople (950s) and became the first Kyivan ruler to convert to **Christianity**.

Grand Prince **Sviatoslav Ihorevych** conducted a series of successful campaigns against the Viatichians, Volga Bulgars, the Khazar kaganate, Alans, and Kasogians (964–67) and into the Balkans (968–71). He wished to move the capital of Rus' to the town of Pereiaslavets on the Danube; however, following his defeat at Dorostolon (Silistra), he was forced to return to Rus'. He died in battle against the Pecheneg kagan Kuria near the Dnipro Rapids (972).

2. The period of the greatest flowering and development of Kyivan Rus' (late 10th–11th century). After a lengthy internecine war between Sviatoslav's sons, **Volodymyr the Great** took the Kyivan throne. He curbed the power of the tribal princes and initiated the practice of placing his sons in charge of various Rus' lands. Volodymyr established defenses along the southern borders of the state and repelled Pecheneg attacks. After attempting to reform pagan beliefs, he introduced Christianity as the state religion (988–89). The reign of **Yaroslav the Wise** (1019–54) was marked by a series of important reforms, notably the establishment of a code of laws known as the *Ruskaia Pravda*. Yaroslav conducted an active foreign policy, arranging a number of advantageous dynastic marriages between his children and European rulers. He also appointed the first native metropolitan, **Ilarion**, and promoted the development of scholarship and culture. Shortly before his death, Yaroslav attempted to introduce a system of succession by primogeniture to the throne of the grand prince. Kyivan Rus' attained the pinnacle of its development under Yaroslav.

3. The political disintegration of Kyivan Rus' (late 11th–mid-13th century). Yaroslav's demise was followed by a period of internecine strife. An attempt to resolve the problem of succession at the **Liubech congress of princes** (1097), where the principle of patrimonial succession was adopted, proved futile. Centrifugal

tendencies increased, and the authority of the Kyivan prince became nominal. Only **Volodymyr Monomakh** and his son Mstyslav Volodymyrych were successful in maintaining the unity of the Rus' lands. In the latter half of the 12th century, disagreements between individual principalities resulted in frequent civil wars. The Rus' principalities were briefly united under the rule of the Galician-Volhynian princes **Roman Mstyslavych** and his son **Danylo Romanovych**. The attack of the Golden Horde (1237–40) completed the destruction of Kyivan Rus'.

The Rus' economy was dominated by **agriculture**. In forest-steppe zones, farmers used the slash-and-burn method, while crop rotation was practiced in the steppe regions. Early farmers used the plow, harrow, spade, scythe, and sickle. They planted cereal and nonfood cultures. Animal husbandry developed extensively; hunting, fishing, and beekeeping were common occupations. Most peasant farmers were freemen, but from the late 11th century, princely landholdings expanded. This led to the impoverishment of freemen, who had to work on the estates. There were more than 60 specialized trades during this period. Numerous trade routes passed through Kyivan Rus': "from the Varangians to the Greeks," linking Rus' with Scandinavia and the countries of the Black Sea basin, the "salt route" (from **Galicia** to the **Crimea**), the "iron route" (into the Caucasus), and Kyiv-Regensburg (into Western Europe). Rus' began minting its own coins, *sribnyky* (silver coins) and *zlatnyky* (gold coins). The number of towns grew from 20 in the ninth–10th centuries to 32 in the 11th century and some 300 in the 13th century (many of these were small fortified settlements).

The political and administrative structure of Kyivan Rus' was headed by the prince and his retinue (*druzhyna*) and an urban elite known as the **boyars**. The major institution of urban and rural self-government was the *viche* (popular assembly). Vicegerents (*posadnyky*) were entrusted with the administration of individual *volosti* (towns and their surrounding villages), towns, and lands. The home guard (*voi*) was organized according to a decimal system. A *tysiacha* (thousand), subdivided into hundreds and tens, was the basic military unit.

The population of Kyivan Rus' has been variously estimated at 3 to 12 million. Below the prince and the boyars was the urban elite (*liudy* or people), consisting primarily of well-to-do merchants, while the *molodshi liudy* (younger people) made up the bulk of the urban population (shopkeepers, artisans, craftsmen, etc.). Most of the population consisted of peasants (*smerdy*). The *chern'* was the stratum of hired manual laborers, while the *kholopy* and *cheliad'* were slaves. The **Kyiv metropolitanate** was under the jurisdiction of the patriarch of Constantinople. Bishoprics existed in all lands, and each was divided into parishes. Between the 11th and 13th centuries, scores of monasteries were founded, most notably the **Kyivan Cave Monastery**.

In addition to the **Slavs**, more than 20 other nationalities lived on Kyivan Rus' territory: Pechenegs, **Cumans**, Torks, Berendeis, and Kara-Kalpaks in the south; Lithuanians and Yatvingians to the northeast; and the Chud, Vepsians, Meria, Muroma, Mordva, Cheremis, Permiaks, and other Finno-Ugric tribes to the north and northeast. There were urban colonies of Germans, Poles, **Jews**, Armenians, Goths, and **Varangians**.

Kyivan Rus' attained a high degree of cultural development, greatly influenced by Byzantium. The Cyrillic alphabet, developed on the basis of Greek script, came into use in the late 10th century. Birch bark and parchment were used for writing. Outstanding examples of Rus' writing are **Ostromir's Evangeliary** (1056–57) and the *Izbornik* of Sviatoslav Yaroslavych (1073). During the reign of Volodymyr the Great, the first schools were established in Kyiv, Novgorod, and other towns. Yaroslav the Wise promoted the collection and copying of manuscripts. The first Kyivan chronicle was compiled in 1037–39, and the *Tale of Bygone Years* was also compiled in Kyiv. Notable works of **literature** include Metropolitan Ilarion's *Sermon on Law and Grace*, Volodymyr Monomakh's *Instruction*, and the *Tale of Ihor's Campaign*. Among the major ecclesiastics of Kyivan Rus' were Ilarion, Klymentii Smoliatych, Cyril of Turiv, **St. Theodosius of the Caves**, and Luka Zhydiata.

Architecture held a leading place among the arts of Kyivan Rus'. Distinguished examples of church architecture (cross-shaped, domed, multiple-nave churches) included the Church of the Tithes (989–96), the Cathedral of the Transfiguration in Chernihiv (1036), and the cathedrals of **St. Sophia** in Kyiv (begun in 1037), Novgorod (1045), and Polatsk (mid-11th century). In the 12th century, original architectural schools arose in Kyiv, Halych, Novgorod, and Suzdal. Churches were extensively decorated with frescoes and mosaics. A distinguished master of iconography was Olimpii of the Caves. Kyivan artisans mastered many techniques of jewelry, including granulation, filigree, niello, and enameling. **Music** was also important; a number of string, wind, and percussion instruments are known to have been in use. The art of jesters and bards had wide currency, and there was a well-developed oral literature.

The Principality of **Galicia-Volhynia** was the most direct successor to the political and cultural traditions of Kyivan Rus' following the Mongol invasions.

L

LABOR CONGRESS. Legislative assembly of the **Ukrainian People's Republic** (UNR). The congress, convened by the **Directory** of the UNR soon after its accession to power, took place in **Kyiv** on 23–28 January 1919. Elections to the congress, conceived as the national representative body of the "toiling masses," proceeded according to instructions issued by the Directory (26 December 1918). **Andrii Livytsky** was appointed head of the electoral commission. The elections were held on 12–15 January 1919 in curiae of workers, **peasants**, and the intelligentsia, excluding landowners and business elements, who were deemed exploiters. The right to vote was granted to all citizens of the UNR over 21, except those stripped of civil rights by judicial means and military servicemen in the republican army. The congress was to consist of 593 elected delegates from the Kyiv region (67 delegates), **Podilia** (59), **Kharkiv** region (65), Kherson region (52), **Volhynia** (60), Chernihiv region (54), **Poltava** region (58), Katerynoslav region (46), Tavriia (18), **Kholm region, Podlachia, Polisia** district (total of 19), and the **Western Ukrainian People's Republic** (ZUNR, 65), as well as representatives from professional organizations: the All-Ukrainian Railway Congress (20) and the All-Ukrainian Postal Congress (10). Of the 528 eastern Ukrainian delegates to be elected, 377 were to be peasants, 118 workers, and 33 representatives of the intelligentsia. Owing to the **Ukrainian-Polish War in Galicia** (1918–19), elections to the Labor Congress did not take place in the ZUNR, but a delegation of 36 representatives of the **Ukrainian National Rada** who took part in the **Act of Union** between the UNR and the ZUNR were invited to participate.

The Labor Congress opened at the Kyiv opera house on 23 January 1919, by which time 400 delegates had arrived. All Directory members were elected to the congress, with the exception of **Symon Petliura**, who was ineligible as a representative of the military. The congress was dominated politically by the **Ukrainian Party of Socialist Revolutionaries** and the **Ukrainian Social Democratic Labor Party**. It ratified the Act of Union and a draft provisional constitution (28 January) before the Bolshevik advance into Kyiv forced its suspension. After transferring its powers to the Directory, the congress ratified a proclamation "To the Ukrainian People" and a note "To the Peoples of the World" that declared the right of the Ukrainian people to representation at the Paris Peace Conference. It protested the Bolshevik advance into Ukraine and called on the army of the UNR to defend the state. In order to prepare bills for its next session, 30 delegates were elected and assigned to six commissions: defense, land reform, budget, foreign affairs, supply, and culture and **education**. Because of the UNR's failure to reestablish itself in Kyiv, a session of commission members chaired by Semen Vityk passed a resolution putting an end to their activities (Kamianets-Podilskyi, 11 July 1919).

LANGUAGE. Ukrainian is the second-most widely spoken Slavic language, a member of the Indo-European family of languages. Traditionally classified as East Slavic, Ukrainian borders on West Slavic languages and, historically, on Bulgarian, a South Slavic language. Ukrainian comprises several dialects, but the divisions between them are weaker than those in English or German. Standard Ukrainian, taught in schools and used in **literature**, is a superstructure developed mainly on the basis of the **Poltava** and **Kyiv** dialects.

The proto-Ukrainian language (sixth to mid-11th centuries A.D.) emerged as tribes inhabiting regions west of the middle Dnipro Basin developed speech characteristics that were not shared with bordering Slavic dialects. The accumulation of such features led to the evolution of Ukrainian as a separate language. From Common Slavic the proto-Ukrainian dialects inherited a complex system of declension and conjugation. The integration of dialects took place during the period of **Kyivan Rus'** and the subsequent migrations caused by invasions of various Turkic tribes.

The linguistic features of the Old Ukrainian (mid-11th to late 14th centuries) spoken in Kyivan Rus' are well documented by the surviving Rus' **chronicles**. Its morphological system did not undergo significant change, despite simplifications introduced by speakers, but the phonetic system was notably altered. The Old Ukrainian vocabulary was expanded with many loanwords as a result of extensive contacts with Central Europe and the Turkic steppe peoples. The Byzantine Empire exerted a strong political and religious influence on Rus', which led to the large-scale borrowing of Greek words and phrases. Such borrowings, however, did not penetrate the spoken language of the illiterate majority; they were eliminated after Constantinople lost its influence and Ukrainian culture reoriented itself toward Western Europe. This period of language development ended in the late 14th century, when Polish supremacy over **Galicia** and Lithuanian supremacy over the other Ukrainian lands were firmly established.

The consolidation of the Lithuanian-Ruthenian state and the rise of the **Cossacks** provide the background to the development of Early Middle Ukrainian (late 14th to late 16th centuries). Threatened by incessant Crimean **Tatar** raids, the Ukrainian population was driven west and northwest. As a result, Ukrainian speakers were confined to a relatively small area. Subsequently, when they began to settle the central and, later, eastern and southern regions of Ukraine, their language preserved a relative uniformity across that large territory. The early middle period saw changes in the phonetics, morphology, and syntax of Ukrainian and the expansion of its vocabulary, which distanced itself from Russian and Church Slavonic, drawing closer to West Slavic. Loanwords from Polish and Latin, as well as from German and Czech via Polish, often entered the basic vocabulary but were most apparent in administrative, commercial, and cultural terminology. At the same time, trade and military terminology adopted some Turkic borrowings through encounters with neighboring Crimean Tatars.

The Middle Ukrainian period reflects the language of Cossackdom from the **Union of Lublin** (1569) to the loss of Ukrainian autonomy under Russian rule in the 18th century. The period was marked on the one hand by increased Polonization of the Ukrainian **nobility** and on the other by the linguistic resistance of the church. As ideological leadership in Ukraine was assumed by the clergy, a restored version of Church Slavonic became the vehicle for the continuation of the Greco-Byzantine tradition. The development of a vernacular-based Ukrainian literary language was hindered by the political and cultural decline of the Ukrainian towns. As a result, the literary medium of the Cossack **Hetmanate** of the 17th and early 18th centuries was an eclectic language based on Church Slavonic.

The decline and secularization of **baroque** culture coincided with the efforts of the tsarist government to censor the language of Ukrainian printed books and the ensuing **Russification** of the Cossack officer elite. The printing of works in the literary language of the 17th century came to an end when the Cossack officers and the higher Orthodox clergy consolidated their position in the service of the Russian Empire. The use of the vernacular was prescribed by the classicist theory of low style and allowed only in satirical, humorous, intimate, or lyrical works.

Romanticism in Ukraine acquired a distinctly **populist** character, changing the prevailing attitude to the vernacular. Various writers preferred historically based folklore to colloquial speech as a source of the literary language and demonstrated the possibility of a serious, full-fledged **literature** based on the vernacular. The poetry of **Taras Shevchenko** first met the challenge of synthesizing the historical and geographical dimensions of the Ukrainian language into a pan-Ukrainian idiom. This new form of Ukrainian established itself as the language of literary expression and scholarship in the early 1860s, but its development was interrupted by the **Valuev**

circular (1863) and the **Ems Ukase** (1876), which proscribed Ukrainian-language **publishing** in the Russian Empire.

Only in the **Ukrainian People's Republic** of 1917–20 and in the **Ukrainian SSR** of the 1920s could Standard Ukrainian extend to all social spheres. With the requisite state support, the language underwent normalization and codification, and literature expanded its generic and formal limits. When the policy of **Ukrainization** was abolished by Stalin in the early 1930s, bureaucratic restrictions were imposed on Ukrainian, and its sphere of use was greatly reduced. A renewed policy of Russification focused on bringing Ukrainian closer to Russian. Western Ukrainianisms and European loanwords present in Ukrainian but not in Russian were removed. The language was reoriented toward the eastern Ukrainian dialects, spelling was revised to conform to Russian patterns, and Russian vocabulary and grammar were imposed.

The extent of Russification became evident with Ukrainian independence. Since the 1930s, Russian, not Ukrainian, has been the most widely used language in Ukrainian cities, with the exception of the western regions. Russian is the mother tongue not only of the sizable Russian minority but also of a portion of the ethnic Ukrainian **population** (14.8 percent, according to 2001 census results). The use of *surzhyk*, a Russo-Ukrainian creole spoken by less-educated Ukrainians, is also significant. Although the **Constitution** of 1996 made Ukrainian the sole official language, efforts have been made to reintroduce Russian in an official capacity. The **Kravchuk** administration of the early 1990s emphasized the use of Ukrainian in the public service, **education**, and the media, but subsequent government policy has been one of laissez-faire, effectively allowing Russian to remain dominant in eastern and southern Ukraine. The 2001 census registered a decline in the number of Russians in Ukraine (from 22.1 percent in 1989 to 17.3 percent), indicating a shift in the self-identification of ethnic Ukrainians, which was accompanied by a decline in linguistic proficiency; the number of ethnic Ukrainians giving Russian as their mother tongue increased from 12.3 percent (1989) to 14.8 percent. The number of citizens giving Ukrainian as their mother tongue increased from 64.7 to 67.5 percent, while the number of native Russian speakers declined from 32.8 to 29.6 percent. *See also* SHEVELOV, GEORGE YURII.

LAZARENKO, PAVLO (b. 23 January 1953). Seventh prime minister of independent Ukraine. He was born in the village of Karpivka, Dnipropetrovsk oblast, into a family of collective farmers. In 1978, Lazarenko graduated from the Dnipropetrovsk Agricultural Institute with a diploma in agronomy; he obtained a doctorate in economics in 1997. From 1979, Lazarenko headed the Mikhail Kalinin Collective Farm in Dnipropetrovsk oblast. Between 1985 and 1990, he was head of the Agriculture Department of the **Communist Party of Ukraine** committee for Dnipropetrovsk oblast. President **Leonid Kravchuk** appointed him presidential representative in Dnipropetrovsk in 1992. Lazarenko neutralized the political opposition by dismissing almost all incumbent deputy chairmen and appointing leaders of major parties and civic organizations as advisors. He was active in the development of numerous regional enterprises and accumulated wealth by trading oil and gas contracts. In June 1994, Lazarenko was elected head of the Dnipropetrovsk Oblast Council of People's Deputies; a month later, he was elected a deputy to the **Verkhovna Rada** (VR).

In September 1995, President **Leonid Kuchma** appointed Lazarenko first deputy prime minister in the government of **Yevhen Marchuk**, and on 28 May 1996, following Marchuk's dismissal, the VR confirmed Lazarenko's appointment as prime minister. Already a wealthy man, Lazarenko became a multimillionaire while in office. On 16 June 1996, as Lazarenko was making his way to the airport for a working visit to Canada, a radio-controlled bomb exploded near his car—an indication of the ruthless struggle between Ukraine's underworld "clans." (Lazarenko's son was badly injured in a suspicious car accident two years later.) On 19 June, in the wake of an announcement that Lazarenko had fallen ill a day after returning from Canada, President Kuchma appointed First Deputy Prime Minister Vasyl Durdynets as acting prime minister. Lazarenko resigned his office on 1 July. His dismissal from government coincided with his rise as leader of the Hromada Party (elected September 1997) and his decision to run for the presidency. The Hromada Party managed to overcome the 4 percent entry barrier and constituted a faction in the VR after the elections of 1998. Lazarenko formed a shadow cabinet, with **Yuliia Tymoshenko** as shadow prime minister.

On 14 September 1998, the prosecutor-general's office charged Lazarenko with large-scale misappropriation of state property, and he fled the country for "medical procedures" in Greece. A few weeks later, he was arrested in Switzerland and sentenced to 1.5 years' imprisonment, with a fine of 10.6 million Swiss francs, on charges of laundering money in Swiss banks (he was released on bail of $3 million). The VR stripped Lazarenko of his parliamentary immunity on 17 February 1999. Two days later, he was arrested at Kennedy Airport in New York on a charge of attempting to enter the United States without a valid visa. Lazarenko was subsequently imprisoned in California and charged with 29 counts of money-laundering through U.S. banks (involving a sum of $114 million) and transportation of stolen property. He was convicted on all charges by a San Francisco court on 3 June 2004. Lazarenko, having repeatedly claimed that the charges were politically motivated, announced his intention to appeal the verdict. Earlier, on 7 February 2004, the prosecutor-general of Ukraine charged Lazarenko with ordering the contract killings of **Vadym Hetman**, head of the National Bank of Ukraine, and Yevhen Shcherban, a Donetsk businessman.

LAZAREVSKY, OLEKSANDER (8 [20] June 1834–31 March [13 April] 1902). Historian. He was born in Hyrivka, Chernihiv gubernia (now Shevchenkove in Sumy oblast), and graduated from the faculty of history and philology of St. Petersburg University (1858). Lazarevsky worked in the judicial institutions of the Chernihiv and **Poltava** regions and joined the Kyiv Judicial Chamber (1880). He was a member of the Historical Society of **Nestor** the Chronicler and a founder of the major historical journal *Kievskaia starina* (Kyivan Antiquity). Lazarevsky wrote nearly 450 works and articles, primarily on the history of **Left-Bank Ukraine** in the 17th and 18th centuries. He concentrated on the history of the **peasantry**, the **Cossack officers** and the Ukrainian **nobility**, colonization and land tenure, and the administrative and judicial system of the **Hetmanate**. Lazarevsky published many important documents, including the diary of **Mykola Khanenko** (1884), the Sulyma archive (1884), the Motyzhynsky archive (1890), the diary of the Cossack general treasurer Yakiv Markovych (1893–97), and the Liubech archive of Count Mykhailo Myloradovych (1898). Lazarevsky's historical views were based on **populism**. In analyzing the exploitation of the Ukrainian peasantry by the Cossack officers, he became unsympathetic to the Hetmanate and its leaders. His collection of manuscripts and books is preserved at the V. I. **Vernadsky** National Library of Ukraine.

LEAGUE OF UKRAINIAN NATIONALISTS/LEGIIA UKRAÏNS'KYKH NATSIONALISTIV. Organization established at a meeting in Poděbrady, Czechoslovakia, of representatives of the Ukrainian National Alliance, the Union for the Liberation of Ukraine, and the Union of Ukrainian Fascists (12 November 1925). Its members were predominantly émigrés from eastern Ukraine. **Mykola Stsiborsky** was elected president of the league, which sought to continue the struggle for Ukrainian statehood waged by the **Ukrainian People's Republic** (UNR). While a minority proposed that the league orient itself on contemporary nationalist movements, especially Italian fascism, Stsiborsky prevailed against this trend. Since the league supported only the UNR's tradition of sovereignty, while rejecting its socialist ideology, it was attacked by such émigré UNR politicians as **Isaak Mazepa**. The league proposed an All-Ukrainian National Political Alliance to promote Ukrainian independence. It was active in Poděbrady, Prague, Berlin, Vienna, Paris, and Luxembourg. Two issues of its journal, *Derzhavna natsiia* (Sovereign Nation), appeared in 1927. In 1929, the league was absorbed by the **Organization of Ukrainian Nationalists**.

LEBED, MYKOLA (23 November 1909–19 July 1998). Underground resistance leader. He was born in Novi Strilyshchi (now in Lviv oblast), the son of a tailor. A member of **Plast**, Lebed organized youth groups of the **Organization of Ukrainian Nationalists (OUN) in western Ukraine** and directed their clandestine training in the Carpathian Mountains (1930–32). He served as liaison between the OUN National Executive and the OUN leadership abroad (1932–34). In 1934, he helped plan the assassination of the Polish minister of internal affairs, Bronisław Pieracki. Lebed escaped to Germany but was arrested and turned over to the Polish authorities. At the Warsaw trial of the OUN (1935–36) he was sentenced to death, which was later commuted to life imprisonment. Lebed escaped from prison at the outbreak of **World War II**.

In 1940, during the split within the OUN, Lebed supported **Stepan Bandera**, becoming deputy leader of the OUN(B). Appointed minister of state security in the **Ukrainian State Administration**, he managed to avoid arrest by the Germans and became the OUN(B)'s chief organizer of anti-Nazi resistance. Lebed headed the OUN(B) in western Ukraine until early 1943 and played a leading role in the formation of the **Ukrainian Insurgent Army (UPA)**. He organized and conducted three OUN-B conferences in Ukraine (September 1941, April 1942, and February 1943). Lebed participated in the Third Extraordinary Great Assembly of the OUN(B) (August 1943), which elected him head of its Chief Council. In 1944, he became a founder of the **Supreme Ukrainian Liberation Council**. As its general secretary for foreign affairs, he left Ukraine to establish contacts with the Western Allies. Lebed was a member of the Foreign Sections of the OUN(B) until 1948. From December 1949, he lived in the USA. Breaking with the OUN(B) to associate himself with the OUN (Abroad), Lebed founded and headed the Prolog Research Corporation (1952–74), served as its vice president (1982–85), and was a member of its executive council (from 1974). He published a documentary memoir titled *UPA* (1946, 2d ed. 1987).

LEFT-BANK UKRAINE (Ukr. *Livoberezhna Ukraïna, Livoberezhzhia*). Historical and geographical name for the portion of Ukrainian lands that encompasses present-day Chernihiv, **Poltava**, western Sumy, eastern Kyiv (including the city of **Kyiv**), and eastern Cherkasy oblasts. In Russian official documents of the late 17th to early 20th centuries, Left-Bank Ukraine was called Little Russia. With the **Pereiaslav Agreement** (1654), the Left Bank became a protectorate of Muscovy. This dependent status was confirmed by the **Truce of Andrusovo** (1667), the Treaty of Bakhchesarai (1681), and the **Eternal Peace of 1686** between Muscovy and the **Polish-Lithuanian Commonwealth**. To the north and east, Left-Bank Ukraine bordered Muscovite territory and **Sloboda Ukraine**; to the south lay the wild steppe and the **Zaporozhian Sich**; and its western border was formed by the Dnipro River, as well by as the city of Kyiv and its environs on the Right Bank.

The **Cossack** military and administrative system was introduced on the Left Bank during the **Khmelnytsky Uprising** (1648–57). The Left Bank was divided into the Chernihiv, Hadiach, Kropyvnia, Kyiv, Lubny, Myrhorod, Nizhyn, Pereiaslav, **Poltava**, Pryluky, and Starodub regiments, each of which was subdivided into 10–20 companies (late 17th and 18th centuries).

Within the Muscovite state (the Russian Empire from 1721), the Left Bank, constituted as the **Hetmanate**, preserved a degree of political autonomy, progressively restricted by the tsarist government. **Cossack councils**, which elected the **hetman**, continued to be held on the Left Bank, although the hetman was later confirmed in office by the tsar. The hetman was obliged to gain approval for his actions from the Little Russian Bureau and the first **Little Russian Collegium** (1722–27). Towns on the Left Bank were either of the *magistrat* (with **Magdeburg law**) or *ratush* (without Magdeburg law) type. *Magistrat* towns included Chernihiv, Kyiv, Nizhyn, Novhorod-Siverskyi, Pereiaslav, Poltava, and Starodub. *Ratush* towns were subject to **Cossack officer** administration. With the introduction of town dumas (councils), urban administration was brought into conformity with the Russian imperial model (1785). Between 1734 and 1750, authority over the Left Bank was held by the Administration of the Hetmanate Government. Once the post of hetman was abolished in 1764, the Little Russian Collegium (1764–86), headed by **Petr Rumiantsev**, was reinstated. The Kyiv, Chernihiv, and Novhorod-Siverskyi vicegerencies were established on the Left Bank, their boundaries determined without consideration for the previous administrative system (1781). In 1796, the Left-Bank vicegerencies were combined by ukase into the Little Russia gubernia, which was divided in 1802 into the Chernihiv and Poltava gubernias.

By ukase of Catherine II (3 [14] May 1783), serfdom was introduced on the Left Bank, while the Cossack officers acquired the rights of the Russian nobility (1785). The Left-Bank economy developed within the imperial market. The elimination of internal customs barriers (1754) led to the reorientation of industry and trade toward Russia.

In response to increased national and social oppression, the Ukrainian population of Left-Bank Ukraine staged a number of uprisings in the 17th and 18th centuries, including the Pereiaslav rebellion (1666), the Klishchyn rebellion (1767–70), the Turbai rebellion (1789–93), and the **haidamaka** movement (1730s–60s). After the second partition of Poland (1793) and the incorporation of **Right-Bank Ukraine** into the Russian Empire, the term "Left-Bank Ukraine" came to denote a geographic rather than an administrative concept.

LEMKO REGION (Ukr. *Lemkivshchyna*). Territory populated since early times by an ethnically Ukrainian group, the Lemkos. It is located in the Ukrainian Carpathian Mountains (on both sides of the Eastern Beskyd) between the Sian (San) and Poprad Rivers within the borders of present-day Poland, and northwest of the Uzh River in **Transcarpathia** up to the Poprad River in Slovakia. Its total area is approximately 3,500 sq. km. In the opinion of some scholars, the ancestors of the Lemkos were the White Croatians, who settled the Carpathian region between the seventh and 10th centuries. In the Middle Ages, the Lemko region was part of **Kyivan Rus'** and the Principality of **Galicia-Volhynia**. Subsequently, the southern Lemko lands were annexed by Hungary, and in the 1340s the entire Lemko region was incorporated by Casimir III into Poland, where it remained until 1772. The eastern Lemko region comprised the Sianik (Sanok) land of the Rus' palatinate, while the western section belonged to the Cracow palatinate. Between the 14th and 16th centuries, the Lemko region was overwhelmingly Ukrainian. By the end of the 16th century, the Lemko dialect of the Ukrainian **language** was in use and became established in the region as it existed until 1946. In the religious sphere, the Lemko region belonged to the Peremyshl (Przemyśl) eparchy, and most of its population was Ukrainian Catholic.

By the early 20th century, the predominant orientation in Lemko sociopolitical life was **Russophilism**, propagated primarily by the local Orthodox clergy. The Ukrainian national movement, whose main centers were the towns of Nowy Sącz and Sianik (Sanok), began to develop in the late 19th and early 20th centuries. After the collapse of Austria-Hungary, the East Lemko Republic was proclaimed, and in 1918–19 it established the Sianik Commissariat of the **Western Ukrainian People's Republic** (ZUNR), based in Komancha. It was overwhelmed by Polish forces (mid-February 1919). After the fall of the ZUNR, the Warsaw government, striving to impede the development of the national movement, supported the Russophile tendency and made efforts to turn the Lemkos into a regional group with a Polish national consciousness. In order to splinter the Ukrainian movement in the Lemko region, the area was divided from the Peremyshl (Przemyśl) eparchy (1934), and a separate Lemko Apostolic Administration with a Russophile hierarchy was created. During the interwar period, the Polish government eliminated Ukrainian schooling, banned the publication of Ukrainian periodicals, closed almost all **Prosvita** reading rooms, and arrested or exiled nationally conscious Ukrainians. To counter such policies, a Lemko commission that engaged in cultural and educational work among the populace was formed in **Lviv**. The newspapers *Nash lemko* (Our Lemko) and *Biblioteka Lemkivshchyny* (Library of the Lemko Region) were published in Lviv and distributed both in **Galicia** and in the Lemko region (1934–39). In order to assist the Lemko-Ukrainian movement, the Organization for the Defense of the Lemko Region was founded in the United States (1936).

During **World War II**, the Ukrainian movement in the Lemko region became more active. A number of secondary schools, a teachers' college, and a Ukrainian educational society were established. In the course of the war, the Polish underground killed Lemkos in the region and assassinated prominent individuals. After the region was occupied by Soviet forces (1944–45), under Polish pressure, some 80 percent of the Lemko population was resettled to the **Ukrainian SSR**. The remaining Lemkos were deported to western Poland in the course of **Operation Vistula** (1947). The deportations were opposed by the **Ukrainian Insurgent Army**, which conducted military operations in the region (1944–47). As a result of these expulsions, the Lemko region, home to 160,000 Ukrainians in 1939, was left without autochthonous residents.

In western Poland, the Lemkos were dispersed and forbidden to form communities. Not until the late 1950s were some deportees allowed to return home. Ukrainian cultural and educational life in the region revived gradually. The Ukrainian Social and Cultural Society in Poland (est. 1956) had a branch devoted to Lemko culture and published *Lemkivs'ke slovo* (Lemko Word) as a supplement to the Warsaw weekly *Nashe slovo* (Our Word). Since 1983, the Vatra festival of folklore and ethnography has been held in the Lemko region. The Lemko Alliance was formed in 1990, and a Lemko branch is active within the Alliance of Ukrainians in Poland.

LEONTOVYCH, MYKOLA (1 [13] December 1877–23 January 1921). Composer, conductor, and teacher. He was born in Monastyrok (now in Vinnytsia oblast) into the family of a priest and graduated from the Kamianets-Podilskyi Theological Seminary (1899). He continued his studies at the court capella in St. Petersburg and passed extramural examinations as a choirmaster (1903–4). Leontovych taught **music** and other subjects and conducted choirs at schools in the **Kyiv**, Katerynoslav, and **Podilia** gubernias before moving to Kyiv in 1918. In 1918–19, he lectured in choral music at the conducting department of the **Lysenko** Institute of Music and Drama in Kyiv and later at the music department of the Committee on Elementary Education. His musical legacy includes classic arrangements of Ukrainian folk songs (more than 150 choral arrangements and four choral compositions), choral poems, and church music. Leontovych was murdered, allegedly by a Soviet secret police agent, in 1921. His opera *Na rusalchyn velykden'* (On the Water Nymph's Easter), based on a story by **Borys Hrinchenko**, was completed, edited, and orchestrated by Myroslav Skoryk (1978).

LEVYTSKY, KOST (18 November 1859–12 November 1941). Civic leader, politician, lawyer, journalist, and full member of the **Shevchenko Scientific Society** (from 1899) and the **Prosvita Society**. Born in Tysmenytsia (now in Ivano-Frankivsk oblast) into the family of a priest, he graduated from the Stanyslaviv gymnasium (1878) and studied law at the universities of Lviv and Vienna, obtaining a doctorate in 1884. From 1890, he practiced law in Lviv. Facilitating the advancement of Ukrainian business in **Galicia** at the turn of the century, he helped create and was actively involved in a whole series of important economic institutions: Narodna Torhovlia, the Dnister Insurance Company, the Regional Credit Union (later Tsentrobank, which he directed from 1898 to 1939), and the Audit Union of Ukrainian Cooperatives (which he headed from 1904 to 1914). Levytsky greatly expanded Prosvita's activities in the economic sphere. He established and edited the *Chasopys pravnychyi* (Legal Gazette, 1889–1900) and was president of the Society of Ukrainian Lawyers in Lviv for many years. In 1899, he became a founder of the **National Democratic Party**, which he headed from 1907. He was elected to the Austrian Reichstag (1907) and the Galician Diet (1908), leading the Ukrainian parliamentary caucus in both institutions.

Levytsky became head of the **Supreme Ukrainian Council** in Lviv (August 1914) and of the General Ukrainian Council in Vienna (from May 1915). During **World War I**, because of his connections in the Austrian government, Levytsky expected to realize the long-standing Ukrainian demand for Galician autonomy within Austria-Hungary, but on 4 November 1916 Austria announced the establishment of an autonomous Galicia under Polish control. Levytsky became the scapegoat for the failure of Ukrainian aspirations and was removed from the leadership of the Ukrainian caucus in the Reichstag. Nevertheless, with the establishment of the **Western Ukrainian People's Republic** (ZUNR) in November 1918, Levytsky became head of its State Secretariat. After the Polish occupation of Galicia (1919), he was a member of the ZUNR government-in-exile (Vienna, 1920–23) in charge of press and propaganda, and later of foreign affairs (from 1921). In 1923, he returned to Galicia, where he continued his civic and scholarly activities. He belonged to the **Ukrainian National Democratic Alliance**. In the 1920s and 1930s, he was head of the Union of Ukrainian Lawyers, a member of the Supreme Council of Lawyers in Warsaw (1935–39), editor of *Zhyttia i pravo* (Life and Law), and director of Tsentrobank. Levytsky was arrested by the NKVD in 1939 and released after two years' imprisonment. In July 1941, he became a founder and head of the **Ukrainian National Council**, which was intended to represent the interests of western Ukrainians before the German occupation regime. Levytsky died in Lviv. His writings include valuable historical works on Ukrainian politics in Galicia.

LITERATURE. The oral tradition in Ukrainian literature can be traced to pre-Christian times. Its **pagan** ritual songs were subsequently adopted and modified for various church feasts (*see* FOLK CUSTOMS AND RITES). Medieval heroic epics (*bylyny*) were sung until the 16th century, when they were replaced by dumas—epic songs of early modern **Cossack** Ukraine.

Written literature developed in **Kyivan Rus'** after the official adoption of **Christianity** in 988. In addition to translations from the Greek and adaptations of Balkan Slavic religious texts, the Kyivan period produced original collections of sermons and saints' lives. The *Izbornik* of Sviatoslav Yaroslavych (1073) was the most significant example of such compilations. The 11th-century sermons of **Ilarion**, the first native metropolitan of Kyiv, and the 12th-century sermons of **Volodymyr Monomakh** and Cyril of Turiv marked the heights of the genre, while the **Kyivan Cave Patericon** was the outstanding hagiographic collection of the period.

Chronicles combining fact and fiction have been regarded as both historical documents and literary monuments. The *Tale of Bygone Years* or Primary Chronicle, traditionally attributed to the Kyivan monk **Nestor**, described events up to the time of its writing in the early 12th century. The Kyiv Chronicle, written by anonymous scribes, dealt with events occurring from 1118 to 1190, while the **Galician-Volhynian** Chronicle covered events from the beginning of the 13th century to 1292. Unique among Kyivan Rus' writings was the *Tale of Ihor's Campaign*, a 12th-century epic written in an ornate style and permeated with vivid imagery.

Literary activity declined after the invasion of the **Golden Horde**, which destroyed Kyivan Rus' in 1240. Without the traditional patronage of the church and the court, no major literary works were produced in the 14th and 15th centuries. A revival, known as the **Cossack** or Middle period of Ukrainian literature, began when the Ukrainian lands were part of the **Polish-Lithuanian Commonwealth**. Western influences, especially those of the Renaissance and Reformation, brought an emphasis on learning. Orthodox **brotherhoods** were pivotal in establishing schools that served as hubs of literary activity. The founding of the first printing press in Lviv by **Ivan Fedorov** in 1574 was followed by the development of other printshops run by the brotherhoods. They contributed to the rise of literary culture, first manifested in printed vernacular editions of the Gospels.

The **Union of Brest** (1596), which brought considerable numbers of Orthodox believers into communion with the Catholic Church, stirred up a religious controversy that resulted in a flood of polemical literature. Works expressing opposition to the Union and Catholicism in general included the anonymous *Perestoroha* (Warning, 1605) and *Protestatsiia* (Protestation, 1620). The writings of Metropolitan **Ipatii Potii**, who defended the Union, and of **Meletii Smotrytsky** on the Orthodox side were notable for their literary skill. The most prominent place in polemical literature, however, was occupied by **Ivan Vyshensky**, a defender of Orthodoxy and Eastern asceticism. The art of sermonizing, known for its complex formal structure and rich, often fantastic, imagery, also developed in this period. The allegorical style of sermons demanded of its practitioners a vast knowledge of folk tales, literature in translation, and apocryphal writings, which were interwoven into this mainly oratorical genre. Smotrytsky, Lazar Baranovych, **Dymytrii Tuptalo**, Kyrylo Stavrovetsky-Tranquillon, and Ioanikii Galiatovsky were acknowledged masters of homiletics.

An interest in history was manifested initially through the publication of saints' lives and fostered the development of the historiographic genre. The compilation titled *Synopsis* (1674) provided the first synthetic survey of Ukrainian and East European history. Historical writing of the period was best represented by the Cossack chronicles. The anonymous Eyewitness Chronicle and chronicles by **Hryhorii Hrabianka** (1710) and Samiilo Velychko (ca. 1720) did not have an immediate influence but inspired romantic writers a century later.

The dominant style of 17th- and 18th-century Ukrainian literature, as in Europe generally, was **baroque**, with its copious adornment and linguistic invention. These traits were most evident in poetry and drama, which remained predominantly religious in the Ukrainian context. **Kasiian Sakovych** and Ivan Velychkovsky were the major poets of the era, while **Teofan Prokopovych** was the major dramatist. An outstanding figure was **Hryhorii Skovoroda**, a philosopher, poet, and teacher who wrote religious and moralizing poetry. His theocentric philosophy found its best expression in the collection *Sad bozhestvennykh pesnei* (Garden of Divine Songs, 1753–85).

Literary expression in Ukraine did not rely on the use of vernacular Ukrainian alone but often adapted Polish, Russian, and Church Slavonic for the concepts it required (*see* LANGUAGE). With the rise of the Cossack **Hetmanate** in the mid-17th century, the vernacular became more prominent. It receded again in the 18th century as the Hetmanate was absorbed into the Russian Empire and many Ukrainians wrote in Russian.

The return to vernacular Ukrainian in the last decade of the 18th century marked the beginning of modern Ukrainian literature. *Eneïda* (1798) by **Ivan Kotliarevsky**, a classicist poet and playwright, was a travesty of Virgil's *Aeneid* that turned its heroes into Ukrainian Cossacks. The surprising popularity of this work demonstrated that colorful popular idioms combined with syllabo-tonic metrics had a distinct expressive potential. Encouraged by Kotliarevsky's success, **Hryhorii Kvitka-Osnovianenko** sought to employ the vernacular for "serious" subjects in short prose. His sentimentalist *Malorosiiskie povesti* (Little Russian Novelettes, 1834–37) were based on both the literary and the oral traditions.

Ukrainian **romanticism** developed in three centers. The **Kharkiv** romantic school of the 1830s was initially influenced by Izmail Sreznevsky's ethnographic research and collections of folk legends, as well as by folk-song collections published by **Mykhailo Maksymovych**. Levko Borovykovsky emerged as the most prominent poet of the group, while Amvrosii Metlynsky wrote nostalgic poems about the glory of the Cossack past. In **western Ukraine**, the collection *Rusalka Dnistrovaia* (Nymph of the Dnister, 1837) marked the emergence of the **Ruthenian Triad**. This group of Lviv seminarians was led by **Markiian Shashkevych**, its most talented poet. The peak of the Ukrainian romantic movement was reached in Kyiv during the 1840s; the **Cyril and Methodius Brotherhood** united poets and thinkers whose ideology was reflected in Kostomarov's *Books of Genesis of the Ukrainian People* (1846), which envisioned the creation of a free, democratic Ukraine within a Slavic federation.

Taras Shevchenko was the most prominent and influential Ukrainian poet of the 19th century. Beginning with *Kobzar* (The Bard, 1840), a collection in the romantic vein, he moved on to longer historical poems such as *Haidamaky* (The **Haidamakas**, 1841). His poetry, which combined folk-like simplicity, social and political protest, moral reflection, and biblical paraphrases, evolved continually toward broader, humanistic themes. **Panteleimon Kulish** established himself as a renowned poet, translator, and prose writer whose *Chorna Rada* (Black Council, 1857) became the first Ukrainian historical novel.

Shevchenko's death in 1861 signaled the end of the romantic era and the onset of **realism**, with its positivist philosophy. The short stories of Marko Vovchok, the first major female writer, combined ethnographic romanticism with socially conscious depictions of village life. The poetry of Stepan Rudansky and Leonid Hlibov made use of folklore for realist purposes. Realism had its greatest impact on the development of prose. The novelist Ivan Nechui-Levytsky expressed his **populist** world view in works describing the life of the peasants—*Kaidasheva sim'ia* (Kaidash's Family, 1879)—and of the intelligentsia—*Khmary* (The Clouds, 1908). The novels of Panas Myrny added a psychological dimension to tales of social injustice, especially in his *Khiba revut' voly, iak iasla povni?* (Do the Oxen Low When the Manger Is Full? 1880).

By means of the **Valuev circular** (1863) and the **Ems Ukase** (1876), the tsarist regime proscribed publishing in Ukrainian until 1905. As a result, many novels were published too late to have an impact on the development of the genre. Tsarist censorship made writers turn to the **theater**, which allowed their positivist message to reach a wider audience. The plays of **Mykhailo Starytsky**, Marko Kropyvnytsky, and Ivan Karpenko-Kary (Tobilevych) integrated ethnographic romanticism with realism.

Nineteenth-century literature contributed greatly to the development of Ukrainian national consciousness. The ban on publications shifted the center of Ukrainian publishing to **Galicia**, where the dominant figure was **Ivan Franko**. A prolific poet, dramatist, prose writer, critic, and scholar, Franko not only promoted new genres and themes but also endowed Ukrainian literature with a sense of civic duty peculiar to the realist tradition.

The realist tendency lost its appeal in the last decade of the 19th century in favor of a wealth of Western-inspired **modernist** trends. **Mykhailo Kotsiubynsky** introduced impressionism to Ukrainian prose. **Vasyl Stefanyk** mastered the genre of very short impressionist stories with dramatically charged plots expressing human anguish. **Olha Kobylianska** and **Hnat Khotkevych** turned to folklore for inspiration and wrote neoromantic novels often reflecting the modernist interest in women and their sexuality. The moral dilemmas and psychological experiences of the Ukrainian intelligentsia were the basis of the novels and dramas of **Volodymyr Vynnychenko**, one of the most prolific writers of his generation. Decadent and symbolist trends dominated the poetry of **Moloda Muza** in Galicia and the work of writers associated with the journal *Ukraïns'ka khata* in Kyiv. **Lesia Ukrainka**, the finest woman writer of the day, excelled in poetic dramas; her *Kaminnyi hospodar* (The Stone Host, 1912) was an early feminist reflection on the Don Juan motif.

In the aftermath of the **Ukrainian Revolution** (1917–21), literature enjoyed unprecedented freedom and growth. The stimulus of the **Ukrainization** policy resulted in the emergence of numerous literary groups, such as Hart, MARS, Pluh, Nova Generatsiia, and **Vaplite**, which had the support of a nationalized **publishing** industry. Espousing numerous modernist trends, these groups published quality journals, such as *Literaturnyi iarmarok* and *Nova generatsiia*, and engaged in a "literary discussion" on the development of modern Ukrainian culture. The symbolist **Pavlo Tychyna** was the most innovative poet of his generation. Neoclassicism produced outstanding poets in **Maksym Rylsky**, Mykola Zerov, and Mykhailo Drai-Khmara. The Futurists were led by poet **Mykhail Semenko**, while the expressionists found their proponent in Mykola Bazhan. Other notable poets included **Volodymyr Sosiura, Vasyl Blakytny**, Maik Yohansen, and Dmytro Zahul.

Mykola Khvyliovy, the single most important writer of the period, initiated the "literary discussion," insisting that Ukrainian culture should orient itself on Europe. His prose combined a romantic sensibility with an expressionist style. The lyrical stories and novels of **Yurii Yanovsky** were conspicuously neoromantic, while **Valeriian Pidmohylny** introduced the modern urban novel in neorealist fashion. Other prose writers of note were Borys Antonenko-Davydovych, Oleksa Slisarenko, and the impressionist Hryhorii Kosynka. The outstanding playwright **Mykola Kulish** raised Ukrainian drama to new heights.

The literary and cultural renaissance of the 1920s ended with the Communist Party's imposition of socialist realism at the beginning of the 1930s. Independent literary organizations were abolished, and writers became prime targets during Stalin's **political terror**. By the end of the 1930s, many writers succumbed to party control, while others were imprisoned or killed. The bleak literary atmosphere of the 1930s–50s was exemplified by the conformist novels of **Mykhailo Stelmakh** and the dramas of Oleksander Korniichuk.

The process of de-Stalinization in Ukrainian literature and the rehabilitation of the victimized writers of the 1920s was initiated by an autobiographical novel, *Zacharovana Desna* (The Enchanted Desna, 1954), by the film director **Oleksander Dovzhenko**. A new generation of writers, known as the *shistdesiatnyky*, rejected socialist realism and revitalized all literary genres. The revival was led by the poets **Ivan Drach, Dmytro Pavlychko**, Lina Kostenko, Vitalii Korotych, **Vasyl Symonenko**, Vasyl Holoborodko, Ihor Kalynets, and **Vasyl Stus**. Among prose writers, the most prominent were Yevhen Hutsalo, Hryhir Tiutiunnyk, Oles Honchar, and Pavlo Zahrebelny. **Ivan Dziuba** contributed to the revival of literary and cultural criticism. After several years of relative freedom, new repressions against Ukrainian writers began in the mid-1960s. Many ceased to publish, while others conformed or were incarcerated.

The revival of Ukrainian literature that followed the breakup of the Soviet Union was spearheaded by writers whose work had been suppressed in the 1970s and 1980s. For the first time, many proscribed older works also became available to Ukrainian readers. Emerging writers found themselves competing for reader attention with writers hitherto consigned to "blank spots" of literary history. They frequently resorted to postmodern parody and satire, as reflected in the works of urban avant-garde groups such as **Bu-Ba-Bu** and LuHoSad (Ivan Luchuk, Nazar Honchar, Roman Sadlovsky).

Young writers and poets have faced the task of breaking down colonial stereotypes and raising the prestige of Ukrainian literature. For many, literature has reflected a search for personal and national identity lost under foreign rule, as exemplified by the seriocomic novels of **Yurii Andrukhovych** and the taboo-breaking prose of the feminist Oksana Zabuzhko. Other well-known literary figures include the once-banned philosophical writer Valerii Shevchuk, Volodymyr Dibrova, Yevheniia Kononenko, Yurii Vynnychuk, and Serhii Zhadan. Among poets, Vasyl Herasymiuk, Oleh Lysheha, and Ihor Rymaruk led the way. The revitalization of Ukrainian literature that began in the late 1980s has been accomplished, for the most part, by writers who emerged after Ukraine gained its independence.

***LITERATURNO-NAUKOVYI VISNYK* (LNV)/LITERARY AND SCIENTIFIC HERALD.** Literary, artistic, scholarly, and sociopolitical monthly journal. It was founded in **Lviv** in 1898 as a continuation of *Zoria* (Star), published by the **Shevchenko Scientific**

Society (NTSh), and *Zhytie i slovo* (Life and Word, 1894–96), edited by **Ivan Franko**. The *LNV* was published by the NTSh (1898–1905; editorial board in 1898: Oleksander Borkovsky, **Mykhailo Hrushevsky**, Osyp Makovei, and Franko; in 1899–1905: Volodymyr Hnatiuk, Hrushevsky, and Franko). Individual members of the NTSh disapproved of the journal's position on various civic and political issues, especially its criticism of **Galician** parties, as a result of which it was turned over to the Ukrainian-Ruthenian Publishing Company (1905). After the **Revolution of 1905**, Hrushevsky transferred the *LNV* to **Kyiv**, and until 1913 it was published in two editions appearing in Kyiv and Lviv (edited by Hrushevsky). Its publication was interrupted by **World War I**, but the *LNV* was revived in Kyiv (1917–19) until its prohibition by the Soviet authorities in 1920. In 1922, it was again revived in Lviv with the financial support of former **Ukrainian Sich Riflemen**. At the initiative of **Yevhen Konovalets**, **Dmytro Dontsov** was appointed editor in chief. Dontsov's nationalist ideological line alienated some contributors, and financial difficulties led to the demise of the *LNV* at the end of 1932. Dontsov then published his own journal under the title *Vistnyk* (1933–39). In its day, the *LNV* was the leading forum for the discussion of Ukrainian politics and culture. *See also* LITERATURE.

LITERATURNYI IARMAROK/LITERARY FAIR. Literary and artistic almanac based in **Kharkiv** (1928–30). It published 12 issues under the editorship of **Mykola Khvyliovy**. Officially nonpartisan, the almanac was actually the organ of writers who had formerly belonged to **Vaplite**. It represented one of the last organized attempts to resist the communist ideological leveling of **literature** under the slogan of socialist **realism**. *Literaturnyi iarmarok* published, inter alia, the plays of **Mykola Kulish**, the satires of Khvyliovy, Volodymyr Gzhytsky's novel *Chorne ozero* (Black Lake), poetry and prose by Vasyl Mysyk, Oleksa Vlyzko, and Maik Yohansen, and humorous pieces by Ostap Vyshnia. It was frequently attacked by official critics, who objected even to the cover design (which combined **modernist** influences with the traditional forms of the Ukrainian *vertep*). After *Literaturnyi iarmarok* was forced to cease publication, its leading contributors founded the Prolitfront literary group and a journal under that name (April 1930).

LITHUANIA, GRAND DUCHY OF. United under the rule of Mindaugas, the majority of Lithuanian tribes formed the Grand Duchy of Lithuania in the early 13th century. Carrying the policy of expansion toward the south and east, Mindaugas's successor, Gediminas, added to his realm the Brest and **Podlachia** regions of **Volhynia**, the Polatsk principality, and the Turiv-Pynsk principality, assuming the title "King of Lithuania and Rus'." By the mid-14th century, all the Rus' principalities except **Galicia** had come under the political control of the Grand Duchy. The Lithuanians proved respectful of local customs and, at least initially, changed little in the conquered lands. Ruthenian became the official language of the Duchy, and the legal system continued the traditions of **Kyivan Rus'**. The fusion of Lithuanian and Rus' practices was so extensive that scholars often refer to the Grand Duchy of that period as the Lithuanian-Rus' (Ruthenian) state. However, the dynastic Union of Krevo (1385) brought Polish influences, including the official adoption of the Roman Catholic faith. An internal struggle between Polish and Lithuanian-Ruthenian orientations continued until the 16th century, provoking several armed conflicts. The **Union of Lublin** (1569) created the **Polish-Lithuanian Commonwealth**, signaling not only the victory of the Polish orientation but also Polish political dominance. As a result of the union, the Ruthenian lands of the Grand Duchy were divided. Most of them, except for parts of Podlachia and **Polisia**, were annexed by the Kingdom of Poland. Virtually all the Belarusian lands remained within the Grand Duchy, accelerating the differentiation of Ruthenians into Ukrainians and Belarusians. The Grand Duchy remained part of the Commonwealth until the partition and abolition of the latter in the late 18th century.

LITHUANIAN STATUTE. Medieval law code of the **Grand Duchy of Lithuania**, also employed in Ukraine from the 16th to the early 19th century. Three Lithuanian Statutes, issued in 1529 (Old), 1566 (**Volhynian**), and 1588 (New), drew upon common law, court decisions, German, Polish, and Roman law, and the customary law of Lithuania, Poland, and **Kyivan Rus'**. The statute increased the privileges of landlords by obliging **peasants** to perform corvée labor. The statute of 1588 preserved the foundations of Kyivan Rus' law and was in effect until 1840, particularly in the Kyiv, **Podilia**, and **Volhynia** gubernias. It created a single estate of serfs by merging enserfed servants with other categories of dependent peasants. Contracts, most commonly those of purchase and sale, loans, and property rent, were in written form, and, when necessary, registered in court in the presence of witnesses. To ensure the execution of obligations, a system of collateral was utilized. The right of inheritance belonged to sons; daughters were entitled to no more than one-quarter of their fathers' property as a dowry. Perpetrators were held responsible for deliberate crimes, and murder was punishable by death; a *holovshchyna* (fine) and other expenses related to material damage were levied on the murderer's property. In the event of manslaughter, the guilty party was obliged only to pay the *holovshchyna* to the victim's family. Minors were exempt from criminal responsibility. The criminal code distinguished between degrees of direct and accessory perpetration. Crimes against individual and property rights were punished mainly by fines paid to the victim and the grand duke. Theft was punished severely; horse theft and repeat offenses were punishable by hanging. However, noblemen were punished less severely than commoners. Bodily harm committed by one nobleman against another was punishable by having the perpetrator's hands cut off. For a similar crime against a commoner, the nobleman was assessed a monetary fine. In the event of a commoner's inflicting bodily harm on a nobleman, capital punishment applied. The Lithuanian Statute was used as a source in the drafting of the **Code of Laws of 1743**.

LITTLE RUSSIAN COLLEGIUM/MALOROSIIS'KA KOLEHIIA.

(Russ. *Malorossiiskaia kollegiia*). Central Russian administrative body in **Left-Bank Ukraine** in the 18th century. The first collegium was established in Hlukhiv by a ukase of Tsar Peter I (16 [27] May 1722) shortly before the death of Hetman **Ivan Skoropadsky** and was headed by Brigadier Stepan Veliaminov-Zernov. In civil matters, the collegium was subject to the Senate, while in military affairs it was responsible to Mikhail Golitsyn, commander in chief of Russian armies in Ukraine. On the tsar's instructions, the collegium assumed responsibility for overseeing the actions of the hetman and his staff, collecting taxes for the tsarist treasury, supplying the Russian army, controlling the activities of the General Military Chancellery, and allotting lands to officers. The collegium acted as an appellate court in cases tried by the General Military Court and Left-Bank regimental and town courts.

The first Little Russian collegium held office from 1722 to 1727. In an attempt to win the support of the **Cossack officers** and because of impending warfare with the Ottoman Empire, the Russian government chose to eliminate the collegium (September 1727). The second Little Russian Collegium was established in Hlukhiv by Catherine II after the forced resignation of the last hetman, **Kyrylo Rozumovsky** (10 [21] November 1764). It was headed by Count **Petr Rumiantsev**, who was also the governor-general of Little Russia. Administratively subject to Rumiantsev's chancellery until his death in 1796, the collegium gradually usurped all powers previously exercised by the Cossacks. The Russian government abolished the Cossack company-regimental system in Left-Bank Ukraine (1781), turned Left-Bank Cossack regiments into regular carbine cavalry units of the Russian army (1783), and introduced vicegerencies (1780–83), thereby absorbing Ukrainian lands into the imperial administrative system. The Little Russian Collegium was ultimately eliminated by tsarist ukase on 20 (31) August 1786.

LITTLE RUSSIAN MENTALITY. An indifferent or negative attitude toward Ukrainian national traditions and aspirations, often accompanied by active support of Russian culture and imperial policies. In the course of the 19th century, as most of the Ukrainian lands were assimilated into the Russian Empire, the early modern distinction between Great Rus' (Muscovy) and Little Rus' (Ukraine) turned into a hierarchical relationship between a dominant Great Russia and a subordinate Little Russia. According to **Mykhailo Drahomanov**, the "Little Russian mentality" (*malorosiistvo*) was characteristic of Russified Ukrainians, whose national character was formed under imperial influence. **Viacheslav Lypynsky** called that mentality a "disease of statelessness." As 19th- and 20th-century Ukrainian leaders and political writers (notably **Symon Petliura, Dmytro Dontsov,** and Yevhen Malaniuk) strove to promote a distinct national identity, they condemned the "Little Russian mentality" as provincial truckling to imperial Russia.

LIUBACHIVSKY, MYROSLAV IVAN (24 June 1914–14 December 2000). Head of the **Ukrainian Catholic Church** (UCC). Liubachivsky was born in Dolyna (now in Ivano-Frankivsk oblast), graduated from the First Stryi State Gymnasium (1933), and entered the **Lviv Theological Academy**, where he studied philosophy and theology. He then studied at the Catholic University in Innsbruck (1936–39) and obtained his doctorate at the University of Sion, Switzerland (1941). Liubachivsky was ordained a priest on 21 September 1938 by Metropolitan **Andrei Sheptytsky**. In May 1947, he immigrated to the United States and taught at St. Basil's Seminary in Stamford. He served as professor and catechist at St. Josaphat's Seminary in Washington (from 1968) and St. Basil's Academy in Philadelphia (from 1971). Liubachivsky became archbishop of Philadelphia (12 November 1979). On 27 March 1980, he was made coadjutor and successor to Archbishop Major **Yosyf Slipy**. Following Slipy's death, Liubachivsky became archbishop major of the UCC (7 September 1984). On 25 May 1985, Pope John Paul II elevated him to the rank of cardinal. With the legalization of the UCC in Ukraine, Liubachivsky took up residence at St. George's Cathedral in Lviv (30 March 1991) and worked to rebuild the church. He was succeeded in January 2001 by **Lubomyr Husar**.

LIUBECH CONGRESS OF PRINCES. Meeting of **princes** of **Kyivan Rus'** held at the initiative of **Volodymyr Monomakh** in Liubech (now in Chernihiv oblast) on the Dnipro River in 1097. The six princes present decided to end the internecine warfare that had prevailed since the death of **Yaroslav the Wise**, who had attempted to establish a principle of lateral succession based on primogeniture. The congress resolved that each prince should rule the lands inherited from his father (*otchyna* or patrimony). Sviatopolk Iziaslavych, as the eldest, received **Kyiv** and the title of grand prince; Monomakh received the Pereiaslav principality; Oleh and Davyd Sviatoslavych received Chernihiv; Davyd Ihorevych received Volodymyr-Volynskyi; Vasylko Rostyslavych and his brother, Volodar, received Terebovlia and Peremyshl (Przemyśl). The princes decided to convene similar congresses to resolve common problems and organize a joint campaign against the **Cumans**. The congressional resolutions were confirmed by a collective oath.

The congress failed to prevent conflict among the princes. The blinding of Vasylko of Terebovlia by Davyd Ihorevych (with Sviatopolk's endorsement) resulted in a new internecine war. Volodymyr Monomakh called the Vytychiv congress (1100) to end the war, and the princes subsequently mounted successful campaigns against the Cumans. Monomakh himself violated the terms of the Liubech congress by accepting the Kyivan throne in 1113. Thus, neither the system of primogeniture nor that of patrimonial succession was established, and Kyivan Rus' disintegrated into competing **appanage principalities**.

LIUDKEVYCH, STANISLAV (STANYSLAV) (24 January 1879–12 September 1979). Composer, musicologist, folklorist, and teacher. He was born in Jarosław (now in Poland) and received his musical education in **Lviv** and Vienna, where he wrote his doctoral dissertation on program **music**. Liudkevych taught music at various schools before he was appointed director of the **Mykola Lysenko** Institute of Music, professor at the Lviv Conservatory (1939), and director of the Musicology Commission of the **Shevchenko Scientific Society** (1936). He was the first professional composer in **western Ukraine**. His works include a cantata-symphony, choral works, symphonic poems, operas, and numerous arrangements of folk and riflemen's songs. Liudkevych died and was buried in Lviv.

LIVYTSKY, ANDRII (27 March [9 April] 1879–17 January 1954). Civic leader, politician, and president of the **Ukrainian People's Republic** (UNR) in exile (1926–54). He was born in Lypliava, **Poltava** gubernia, and educated at the Pavlo Galagan College and the faculty of law at **Kyiv** University. He worked as a lawyer and judge in Lubny, Kaniv, and Zolotonosha. Livytsky was active in the Ukrainian movement, heading the student **hromada** in Kyiv. He joined the **Revolutionary Ukrainian Party** in 1901 and headed its branch in Lubny. In 1905, he was arrested and convicted for his political activity. Livytsky was a leading member of the **Ukrainian Social Democratic Labor Party** (1905–20). He became a member of the **Ukrainian Central Rada** and the Peasant Union (March 1917). That summer he was appointed the UNR commissioner of Poltava gubernia. In 1918, he belonged to the **Ukrainian National Union**, which opposed the rule of **Pavlo Skoropadsky**. After the establishment of the **Directory**, Livytsky was an organizer and leader of the **Labor Congress** of Ukraine. In April 1919, he became minister of justice and deputy premier of the UNR government and, in August, foreign minister in **Isaak Mazepa's** government. From October 1919, Livytsky headed the UNR diplomatic delegation in Warsaw, seeking an alliance against Soviet Russia; he signed the **Treaty of Warsaw** (1920).

After the defeat of the **Ukrainian Revolution**, Livytsky emigrated. In 1920–21 and 1922–26, he headed the UNR government-in-exile. Following the assassination of **Symon Petliura** (May 1926), Livytsky succeeded him and headed the UNR government-in-exile until his death. While living in Warsaw, where he was under constant police surveillance, Livytsky helped initiate the anti-Soviet émigré Prometheus Movement. After **World War II**, he lived in Germany. He reactivated the UNR government's activities in May 1945. In order to consolidate political forces in the **diaspora** and reorganize the State Center of the UNR in exile, Livytsky and Mazepa established the **Ukrainian National Council** (1947). Livytsky died in Karlsruhe and was buried in Munich. His remains were later transferred to South Bound Brook, New Jersey.

LUBLIN, UNION OF. Treaty that united the Kingdom of Poland and the **Grand Duchy of Lithuania** into a single state, the **Polish-Lithuanian Commonwealth**. Negotiations on the conditions of union began in January 1569 at a joint Polish-Lithuanian assembly in Lublin. Lithuanian magnates demanded a separate senate and diet, putting a stop to negotiations (March 1659). Supported by Lithuanian and Ruthenian nobles, the Polish Diet sanctioned King Sigismund II Augustus's annexation of lands formerly belonging to **Kyivan Rus'** (**Podlachia**, **Volhynia**, Bratslav, **Podilia**, and **Kyiv**). Lithuania's military reverses in the Livonian War (1558–83) and its efforts to obtain military assistance from Poland against Muscovy forced the Lithuanian magnates to reopen talks. The Union of Lublin was signed on 28 June 1569 and ratified separately by the Polish and Lithuanian diets on 1 July. The head of the united state was a monarch bearing the titles "King of Poland" and "Grand Duke of Lithuania." He was to be elected by a joint Polish-Lithuanian assembly and crowned in Cracow. Poland and Lithuania shared a diet and senate, and a common currency was introduced. The Grand Duchy of Lithuania preserved a separate legal code, court system, army, and administration. Poland became the senior partner in the Commonwealth, and Rus' lands incorporated into Poland were divided into the Volhynia, Podilia, Bratslav, and Kyiv palatinates.

LUKIANENKO, LEVKO (b. 24 August 1927). Lawyer, **human-rights** activist, and politician. He was born into a **peasant** family in Khrypivka, now in Chernihiv oblast. Lukianenko fought in **World War II** and remained in the Red Army until 1953. He then studied at Moscow State University, graduating in law in 1958; he practiced law in **Lviv** oblast. In 1959, with several western Ukrainian acquaintances, Lukianenko organized the clandestine Ukrainian Workers' and Peasants' Union and wrote its political program, which called for the exercise of Ukraine's constitutional right to secede from the USSR. When the group was uncovered, Lukianenko was convicted of treason and sentenced to death (January 1961), commuted to 15 years' imprisonment. The "jurists' case," as the trial of Lukianenko and his associates became known, was the first important manifestation of the **dissident movement** in postwar Ukraine. He spent five years in Vladimir Prison and 10 in the strict-regime labor camps of Mordovia and Perm oblast. Lukianenko renounced Marxism during his imprisonment and became a religious believer, remaining committed to political change by legal means. Following his release in 1976, he became a founding member of the **Ukrainian Helsinki Group**.

Rearrested in December 1977, Lukianenko was charged with anti-Soviet agitation and propaganda and sentenced to another 15-year term in July 1978. He then renounced Soviet citizenship. He served 10 years in Mordovian and Perm oblast camps and was released in November 1988. While still in exile in Tomsk oblast, he was elected head of the Ukrainian Helsinki Union (March 1988), which reconstituted itself as the Ukrainian Republican Party (URP) in April 1990. Lukianenko headed the party until May 1992, when he was appointed Ukraine's first ambassador to Canada. Owing to disagreement with Ukrainian government policy, he resigned his ambassadorial post in November 1993 and returned to Ukraine, where he became a leading figure in the URP. Lukianenko was elected to the **Verkhovna Rada** in 1990 and 1994. His political writings have been collected in *Viruiu v Boha i v Ukraïnu* (I Believe in God and in Ukraine, 1991) and *Ne dam zahynut' Ukraïni!* (I Shall Not Let Ukraine Perish!, 1994). In 1998, Lukianenko became head of the Association of Ukrainian **Famine** Researchers.

LVIV (Lat. Leopolis, Pol. Lwów, Ger. Lemberg, Russ. Lvov). Historical capital of **Galicia** and **western Ukraine**; administrative center of Lviv oblast (1998 pop. 793,700). Lviv is located at the intersection of important historical trade routes: the north-south route from the Baltic Sea to the Black Sea and the east-west route from **eastern Ukraine** to Poland and Western Europe. The city was founded by Prince **Danylo Romanovych** in the mid-13th century and named after his son Lev. Although the site had been inhabited since the 10th century, Lviv is first mentioned in the Galician-Volhynian **Chronicle** under the year 1256. Under the reign of Prince Lev Danylovych, Lviv became the capital of the Principality of **Galicia-Volhynia**. With a population of two to three thousand, the city had 10 Orthodox, three Armenian, and two Catholic churches.

In the mid-14th century, Lviv was annexed to Poland by Casimir III. Initially autonomous, with its own currency and laws, in 1356 Lviv was granted the rights prevailing under **Magdeburg law**. Since the law applied only to Catholics, German and Polish merchants soon took control of municipal affairs, while the Ukrainian population was marginalized. From 1434 to 1772, Lviv was the capital of the Rus' palatinate. Initially German in character, the city acquired Polish features in the early 16th century, by which time most of the resident Germans and Armenians had been Polonized. To protest ethnic and religious discrimination, the Ukrainians of Lviv established the **Lviv Dormition Brotherhood** (1586) and other Orthodox **brotherhoods**, which maintained Lviv's reputation as an important Ukrainian cultural center. The city's economy, which had been based on farming, **crafts**, and commerce in the princely era, turned to manufacturing, and Lviv became an important trade center.

With the first partition of Poland in 1772, Lviv came under Austrian rule, the capital of the crown land of Galicia and Lodomeria and an important administrative, commercial, and cultural center. The expansion of railways in the second half of the 19th century made Lviv one of the largest railway junctions in Austria-Hungary and stimulated its rapid industrial development. Food processing, textiles and clothing, construction, and metalworking were the major industries prior to **World War I**.

The suppression of Ukrainian culture in the Russian Empire reoriented Ukrainian political and cultural life toward the Habsburg Monarchy, with its liberal political climate, social reforms, and tolerant cultural policies. Lviv became the center of the Ukrainian national and cultural revival in the late 19th century and home to political organizations and the Ukrainian **cooperative movement**. Major cultural institutions such as the **Prosvita Society** (1868) and the **Ridna Shkola Society** (1881) were based in Lviv. A chair of Ukrainian studies at Lviv University and the **Shevchenko Scientific Society** (1873) made great contributions to Ukrainian learning. Lviv also became the center of Ukrainian **publishing**, with more than 70 percent of periodical and nonperiodical publications originating there. Important newspapers such as *Pravda* (1867–96) and *Dilo* (1880–1939), as well as journals such as *Literaturno-naukovyi visnyk* (1898–1906, 1922–32), were published in Lviv.

Lviv also became more significant as a center of Polish life in the 19th century. Political influence within the Austrian government gave the Poles privileged status in Galicia, and Lviv became an arena of struggle between Ukrainians and Poles, with violence erupting on occasion. With the collapse of the Austro-Hungarian Empire, Lviv was proclaimed the capital of the **Western Ukrainian People's Republic** on 1 November 1918. The ensuing **Ukrainian-Polish War in Galicia** resulted in the capture of Lviv by Polish forces by the end of the same month. Lviv and Galicia were incorporated into Poland by decision of the Council of Allied Ambassadors in 1923, with a provision of Ukrainian autonomy that was never honored.

During the interwar period (1919–1939), Lviv lost its status as the capital of a large province and became a regional Polish center. The political and economic isolation of the **Ukrainian SSR** reduced Lviv's role as a trade hub between east and west. Organized resistance to Polish rule was conducted by the **Ukrainian Military Organization** and the **Organization of Ukrainian Nationalists**, while the **Lviv (Underground) Ukrainian University** defied discriminatory policies in **education**.

In the aftermath of the Molotov-Ribbentrop Pact, Soviet forces occupied Lviv between September 1939 and June 1941. Under the subsequent Nazi occupation (June 1941 to July 1944), the city became a district center within the **Generalgouvernement**, where Ukrainian interests were represented by the **Ukrainian Central Committee**. Soviet forces recaptured the city without a battle on 27 July 1944.

Postwar Lviv grew rapidly and underwent a number of major changes. The ethnic composition of the city changed from predominantly Polish (50 percent in 1931) and **Jewish** (31.9 percent in 1931) to mostly Ukrainian (79.1 percent in 1989) and Russian (16 percent in 1989). As a result of rapid industrialization, Lviv's economy was reoriented from food industries (60 percent in 1939; 20 percent in 1991) to machine building (40 percent in 1991). Buses, farm implements, loading machinery, bicycles, and television sets are the main products manufactured in Lviv, in addition to a wide range of consumer goods and foodstuffs. Lviv remains an important transportation center, with nine railways intersecting in the city.

After the war, Lviv lost its role as the major center of Ukrainian national and religious life linked to the West. Prewar cultural institutions and the **Ukrainian Catholic Church** were suppressed, not to be revived until the late 1980s. Although there was a strong **dissident movement** in the city, it was held in check by severe official repression. Today Lviv ranks second only to **Kyiv** as a center of Ukrainian life. Although it lacks the splendor and significance of national institutions, it has again become an important cultural center. The Ukrainian Catholic Church and its teaching institutions returned to Lviv in 1991. The city's **architecture** is relatively well preserved, and its opera house, five main **theaters**, and 10 large museums offer diverse programming. Lviv is also the center of scholarly research in western Ukraine. A number of institutes of the **Ukrainian Academy of Sciences** are located there, in addition to 11 postsecondary educational institutions.

LVIV DORMITION (STAUROPEGION) BROTHERHOOD/L'VIVS'KE USPENS'KE (STAVROPIHIIS'KE) BRATSTVO. Organization of Orthodox and, from 1708, Greek Catholic burghers in **Lviv**. The **brotherhood** grew out of a long-established association of Orthodox caretakers of the Dormition Church and the St. Onuphrius Monastery in the Lviv suburb of Pidzamche. By 1585, a group of Ukrainian burghers (Yurii and Ivan Rohatynets, Ivan and Demyd Krasovsky, Lesko Maletsky, and others) prepared the brotherhood's statute and submitted it for approval to Patriarch Joachim IV of Antioch (January 1586). The statute established the brotherhood's supremacy over other brotherhoods and its right to oversee the clergy, including bishops. Soon the Lviv brotherhood obtained the right of stauropegion, i.e., independence from local bishops. Its statute became a model for many brotherhoods in **Right-Bank Ukraine**.

Pamva Berynda, **Iov Boretsky**, Kyrylo Stavrovetsky-Tranquillon, Lavrentii and Stepan Zyzanii, and other Ukrainian cultural and educational figures were active in the brotherhood, which was supported by Orthodox magnates, including **Kostiantyn Ostrozky**. The brotherhood opposed the **Union of Brest** (1596) and defended the political rights of Ukrainian burghers. It maintained close ties with religious and cultural centers in Orthodox countries. The brotherhood attempted to establish municipal self-government in Lviv, independent of the city administration and Polish rule. It owned a printing press, maintained a school, and funded the construction of the Dormition Church in Lviv. The brotherhood devoted considerable attention to the development of Ukrainian visual arts. It established a hospice for the unemployable and provided financial assistance to its impoverished members. In the mid-17th century, its leadership passed to wealthy merchants. Persecution by Polish nobles and the destruction of the brotherhood's premises by Swedish forces (1704) led to the decline of its sociopolitical and cultural activity. In 1708, the brotherhood accepted the Union of Brest. It was dissolved, along with all brotherhoods under Austrian rule, in 1788.

LVIV (UNDERGROUND) UKRAINIAN UNIVERSITY/L'VIVS'KYI (TAIEMNYI) UKRAÏNS'KYI UNIVERSYTET. Clandestine Ukrainian institution of higher learning established at the initiative of the **Shevchenko Scientific Society** (NTSh), the Mohyla Scholarly Lectures Society, and the Stauropegion Institute. After the Polish occupation of **Lviv** (1918), the bilingual (Polish-Ukrainian) Emperor Francis University was Polonized and renamed in honor of King John Casimir. All eight Ukrainian chairs were abolished, and the university's 14 Ukrainian professors were dismissed. By order of the university's rector (14 August 1919), only Polish citizens who had done military service were to be admitted as students. This made the university virtually inaccessible to Ukrainians. A similar decision was made by the rectorate of the Lviv Polytechnical Institute. Under the circumstances, the NTSh announced the establishment of Ukrainian university courses (20 September). This and all subsequent attempts by Ukrainian civic and scholarly institutions to organize a postsecondary educational program for **Galician** youth were forbidden by the Polish administration. Despite the official ban and persecution, clandestine university courses were organized through the joint efforts of Ukrainian scholars and Galician youth (autumn 1920). Later, these courses were reorganized along the lines of West European universities.

The decision to establish the underground university was reached in July 1921, and it began operations in mid-September. Lectures took place at the NTSh, the **Prosvita** and **Ridna Shkola** societies, the National Museum, the basement of St. George's Cathedral, and the homes of lecturers and students. In the first year of its existence, the university had three departments: arts, law, and medicine. Later, a technical department was added, leading to the establishment of the Ukrainian (Underground) Higher Polytechnical School in Lviv (1922–25). In 1924, an art department under the direction of **Oleksa Novakivsky** and the protectorate of Metropolitan **Andrei Sheptytsky** was added. The university had 1,028 registered students (235 in arts, 608 in law, and 185 in medicine). In addition, it had 230 special students, bringing the total to 1,258. The technical department had 150 students.

The university's first rector was the literary scholar Vasyl Shchurat, and it was administered by a senate (nine members). Viktor Luchkiv was rector of the Higher Polytechnical School. In 1924–25, the university's three departments had 58 positions: 22 in arts, 26 in law, and 10 in medicine. The program in the faculties of philosophy and law lasted four years; study at the medical and technical faculties lasted two years, after which students could continue their programs in Prague, Vienna, or Gdańsk. The university's faculty included such noted scholars as Stepan Balei, Leonid Biletsky, Mykola Chubaty, Mykhailo Halushchynsky, Yuliian Hirniak, **Myron Korduba**, **Ivan Krypiakevych**, Volodymyr Levytsky, **Kyrylo Studynsky**, and **Ilarion Svientsitsky**. Despite the exigencies of its clandestine existence, the university offered a high level of instruction and professional training. Its students founded numerous organizations, including the Ukrainian Students' Union, the Academic Community, the Medical Community, the Lawyers' Group, and the Regional Student Council. The historians published the journal *Istorychnyi visnyk* (Historical Herald). The university received material support from Ukrainian community and financial institutions, as well as from émigrés in Czechoslovakia, the United States, and Canada. Its lecturers and students were constantly harassed by the Polish authorities. Attempts by Ukrainian civic and political organizations and Ukrainian deputies to the Polish Diet to legalize the underground university were unsuccessful. Persecution and arrests of students and professors, lack of funds, the government ban forbidding civil servants from teaching at the university, and discrimination against graduates forced the university to cease operations in 1925. *See also* EDUCATION.

LYPA, YURII (5 May 1900–20 August 1944). Civic and political activist, writer, and physician. He was born in **Odesa**, the son of the writer Ivan Lypa. In 1917, he volunteered for a marine unit of the Army of the **Ukrainian People's Republic** (UNR). Lypa began studying law at the University of Kamianets-Podilskyi (summer of 1919) but was obliged to join the UNR émigrés in Poland. In the 1920s, he organized the Sontsesvit literary group. He graduated from the faculty of medicine of Poznań University (1929) and worked as a physician in Warsaw. From the early 1930s, Lypa was also active in writing and **publishing**. He established the Tank literary group with Yevhen Malaniuk, and his works appeared in numerous periodicals. In 1943, Lypa moved to Yavoriv (now in Lviv oblast) and became active in the medical service of the **Ukrainian Insurgent Army**. He was arrested by the Soviet secret police on 19 August 1944 and tortured to death.

Lypa began writing in 1919, publishing verse collections, short stories, and literary criticism. His works on healing plants were highly popular in **western Ukraine**, as were his nationalist political writings, which advocated Ukraine's development as a Black Sea power: *Ukraïns'ka doba* (The Ukrainian Age, 1936), *Pryznachennia Ukraïny* (The Destiny of Ukraine, 1938), *Chornomors'ka doktryna* (The Black Sea Doctrine, 1940, 1942, 1947), and *Rozpodil Rosiï* (The Partition of Russia, 1941, 1954).

LYPKIVSKY, VASYL (7 [19] March 1864–27 November 1937). Cofounder and leader of the **Ukrainian** Autocephalous **Orthodox Church** (UAOC) and metropolitan of **Kyiv** and all Rus' (1921–27). Born in Popudnia, Vinnytsia region, Lypkivsky received his education at the Uman Theological School and the Kyiv Theological Seminary and Academy. He was ordained in 1891. From 1903 to 1905, he taught canon law at the Kyiv Church Teachers' School but was dismissed for his support of an independent Ukrainian church. Later he was dean of the Solomianka parish in Kyiv and worked as a schoolteacher. From early 1917, Lypkivsky became a leader of the movement to gain autocephaly for the Ukrainian Orthodox Church. He was an initiator of the Brotherhood of the Resurrection and the All-Ukrainian Orthodox Church Sobor. On 9 May 1919, he celebrated the first Ukrainian-language liturgy at the St. Nicholas Military Cathedral in the Pechersk district of Kyiv. In October 1921, the All-Ukrainian Church Sobor ratified the autocephaly of the Ukrainian Orthodox Church (initially proclaimed on 1 January 1919) and elected Lypkivsky its first metropolitan (installed on 23 October 1921). Since the Russian Orthodox Church (ROC) denounced the election and refused to consecrate Lypkivsky, the council resorted to the Alexandrine tradition of the "laying on of hands" to perform the ceremony. This noncanonical consecration provoked criticism of Lypkivsky by the ROC and some of the Ukrainian faithful.

Despite the resistance of pro-Muscovite clergymen, Lypkivsky promoted the Ukrainization of the church and the translation of ecclesiastical **literature** into Ukrainian. He visited some 500 parishes, thereby enhancing the authority of the UAOC. Lypkivsky championed lay participation in church affairs at a time when most bishops advocated the supremacy of the clergy. His work in strengthening and expanding the autocephalous church, as well as his moral influence on the clergy and faithful, aroused the hostility of the Soviet authorities. Using threats and intimidation, they arranged Lypkivsky's dismissal at the All-Ukrainian Church Sobor of October 1927. In the years that followed, Lypkivsky was under constant surveillance by Soviet agents and was arrested and imprisoned several times. Arrested yet again on 22 October 1937, he was sentenced to death by an extraordinary *troika* of the Kyiv NKVD and summarily executed.

LYPYNSKY, VIACHESLAV (5 [17] April 1882–14 June 1931). Historian, civic and political figure, publicist, full member of the **Shevchenko Scientific Society** (from 1914), and ideologue of Ukrainian conservatism. He was born in Zaturtsi, **Volhynia**, into a Polish nobiliary family and christened Wacław Lipiński. He graduated from the **Kyiv** classical gymnasium and served in a dragoon regiment in Kremianets. Lypynsky studied agronomy, philosophy, and history at the Jagiellonian University in Cracow, then sociology at the University of Geneva. He returned to Ukraine in 1908, settled at his ancestral estate of Rusalivski Chahary near Uman, and devoted himself to scholarship. During this period, he produced his first works: *Danylo Bratkovs'kyi* (1909) and *General artyleriï Velykoho Kniazivstva Rus'koho. Z arkhivu Nemyrychiv* (Artillery General of the Grand Duchy of Rus'. From the **Nemyrych** Archive, 1909). Like **Volodymyr Antonovych** and the 19th-century *khlopomany*, Lypynsky believed that Ukrainian-born Poles should devote themselves to the Ukrainian cause; unlike them, he was oriented on the **nobility** and opposed to **populism**. In his *Szlachta na Ukrainie* (The Gentry in Ukraine, 1909), Lypynsky substantiated the decisive role of the gentry in the establishment of the 17th-century **Hetmanate** and exhorted its descendants to work for the rebirth of Ukraine. At a clandestine meeting with political émigrés from **eastern Ukraine** in 1911, Lypynsky declared himself in favor of a constitutional monarchy. The participants, mainly socialists, went on to establish the **Union for the Liberation of Ukraine** in 1914. In 1912, Lypynsky published his monumental work *Z dziejów Ukrainy* (From the History of Ukraine), which included the studies *Nazwy Ruś i Ukraina i ich znaczenie historyczne* (The Names Rus' and Ukraine and Their Historical Significance), *Stanisław Michał Krzyczewski*, *Szlakiem Bohdanowym* (On Bohdan's Path), and *Dokumenty Ruiny* (Documents of the **Ruin**).

During **World War I**, Lypynsky was mobilized by the Russian army, serving as commander of a reserve unit because of illness. While in **Poltava**, Lypynsky Ukrainized his regiment and offered its services to the **Ukrainian People's Republic** (UNR) but was rebuffed because of his nobiliary background (1918). He helped establish the **Ukrainian Democratic Agrarian Party** (June 1917) and wrote its program, which advocated the formation of an independent state and the preservation of private land ownership (October 1917). In 1918, Hetman **Pavlo Skoropadsky** appointed Lypynsky ambassador of the **Ukrainian State** in Austria, a post he briefly continued to hold under the **Directory**. He later lived in the Austrian and German emigration.

In 1920, Lypynsky published the monograph *Ukraïna na perelomi 1657–59* (Ukraine at the Turning Point, 1657–59), in which he analyzed the historical process of Ukrainian state-building from the 15th to the 17th century, praising the statesmanship of **Bohdan Khmelnytsky**. In February 1920, he organized the Ukrainian Union of Agrarian Statists (USKhD), becoming the main ideologue and leader of the hetmanite movement. From 1920 to 1925, Lypynsky published the irregular collection *Khliborobs'ka Ukraïna* (Agrarian Ukraine), in which he first issued his best-known work, *Lysty do brativ-khliborobiv* (Letters to Fellow Landowners). He worked at the Ukrainian Scientific Institute in Berlin (1926–27). An ideological conflict with Skoropadsky led to the dissolution of the USKhD in 1930. Along with Mykola Kochubei, Vasyl Kuchabsky, and others, Lypynsky formed a new organization, the Brotherhood of Ukrainian Classocrat Monarchists. He died at the Wienerwald sanatorium near Vienna and was buried in Zaturtsi.

Central to Lypynsky's thought was his criticism of the weaknesses of the Ukrainian movement that had led to the downfall of the UNR and his search for a resolution to Ukraine's political crisis. He criticized the leaders of the **Ukrainian Central Rada** and the Directory for attempting to base the national-liberation struggle on socialist ideas and seeking support only among the proletarian and semiproletarian peasantry, workers, and populist intelligentsia, rejecting the state-building potential of "landowners" (wealthy peasants, estate owners, Ukrainian bureaucrats and bourgeois). Lypynsky maintained that an independent state could be established only under the leadership of the "landowning elite." This process was to involve the conversion of the Russified and Polonized Ukrainian elite to the Ukrainian national cause. The unity of the Ukrainian movement would be ensured by a legitimate Ukrainian monarch, since Lypynsky believed that a hereditary monarchy could provide the requisite legitimacy, continuity, and political impartiality.

Although Lypynsky was a critic of democracy in principle, he affirmed liberal values and opposed totalitarian tendencies in 20th-century Ukrainian political thought.

LYSENKO, MYKOLA (10 [22] March 1842–24 October [6 November] 1912). Composer, conductor, pianist, ethnographer, and civic figure. He was born in Hrynky, **Poltava** region, a descendant of the Lysenko **Cossack officer** family. Lysenko studied at the universities of **Kharkiv** and **Kyiv**. He studied **music** in Leipzig (1867–69) and in St. Petersburg under Nikolai Rimsky-Korsakov (1874–75). From 1869, he lived in Kyiv, where he worked as a piano teacher and established a school of music and drama (1904). Lysenko was at the center of Ukrainian national, musical, and cultural life in Kyiv. He appeared as a concert pianist and organized choirs with which he performed in Kyiv and throughout Ukraine. He established himself as a leading figure in the Kyiv **Hromada**, organized **Sunday schools**, and was involved in the work of the **Southwestern Branch of the Imperial Russian Geographic Society**. He organized annual **Taras Shevchenko** memorial concerts and, along with **Oleksander Koshyts**, founded the Boian Musical Society (1905). The Ukrainian composers Porfyrii Demutsky, Lev Revutsky, Kyrylo Stetsenko, and Ostap Lysenko received their initial musical education in Lysenko's choir.

Lysenko's ethnographic works include studies of the **kobzar** Ostap Veresai, as well as works on the torban and folk musical instruments. He wrote classic arrangements of folk songs and more than 80 vocal and piano works. Settings of texts by Shevchenko hold an especially important place in Lysenko's compositional legacy. His operas *Rizdviana nich* (Christmas Eve), *Utoplena* (The Drowned Maiden), *Taras Bul'ba*, and *Eneïda* (The Travestied Aeneid); the children's operas *Koza dereza*, *Pan Kotsky*, and *Zyma i vesna* (Winter and Spring); and the operetta *Chornomortsi* (Black Sea Cossacks) were among the founding works of Ukrainian opera. Lysenko died and was buried in Kyiv.

LYTVYN, VOLODYMYR (b. 28 April 1956). Historian and politician. Lytvyn was born in the village of Sloboda-Romanivska, Zhytomyr oblast, into a family of collective farmers. In 1978, he graduated from **Kyiv** University with an honors degree in history. He earned his candidate of sciences degree in 1984 and his doctorate in 1995 with a dissertation on Ukrainian political elites. Until the breakup of the Soviet Union in 1991, Lytvyn taught at the university level and worked in the apparatus of the **Communist Party of Ukraine**. From 1986 to 1989, he served as a department head in the Ministry of

Higher and Secondary Specialized Education. He became professor of Ukrainian history at Kyiv State University in 1996. When **Leonid Kuchma** was elected president of Ukraine in 1994, Lytvyn worked as an assistant to him and was quickly promoted to deputy head of the presidential administration (November 1995). Until 1999, Lytvyn served as the president's principal assistant and chief speechwriter. In November of that year, he was appointed head of the presidential administration and a member of the National Security Council. Implicated in the scandal resulting from the murder of the journalist **Heorhii Gongadze** in 2000, Lytvyn denied any involvement.

In January 2002, Lytvyn found himself in the midst of a plagiarism scandal when it was revealed that he had copied excerpts of the article "Civil Society" by Thomas Carothers from the journal *Foreign Policy* (Winter 1999/2000 issue), translated them, and published under his own name in the newspaper *Fakty i komentari* (Facts and Comments). In March of the same year, President Kuchma appointed Lytvyn to lead his electoral bloc, For a United Ukraine. The bloc formed the majority in the **Verkhovna Rada**, and in May 2002 Lytvyn was elected speaker (by a majority of one). In June 2004, he became head of the People's Agrarian Party of Ukraine.

LYTVYN, YURII (26 November 1934–5 September 1984). Poet, journalist, and **human-rights** activist. Lytvyn was born in Ksaverivka near **Kyiv**, studied at the mining school in Shakhty, and subsequently worked in the **Donets Basin**. As a youth, he became interested in Ukrainian literature and culture. In 1953–55, he spent his first period of imprisonment on the construction of the Kuibyshev hydroelectric station. Soon after his release, Lytvyn was rearrested (14 April 1956) and accused of forming a secret nationalist organization, the Group for the Liberation of Ukraine, while incarcerated. For this he was sentenced to 10 years' imprisonment, served at camps in Medyn and Vikhorevka (Ozerlag, Irkutsk oblast) and in Mordovia. While imprisoned, Lytvyn wrote poems in Ukrainian and Russian and completed *Tragicheskaia galereia* (Tragic Gallery, 1965), a narrative about the crimes of the totalitarian system; it appeared in the posthumous collection *Peredchuttia* (Presentiment, 1991). Subsequently, all his poems were confiscated.

After his release (June 1965), Lytvyn was forced to move to Krasnoiarsk. He was rearrested on 14 November 1974 and convicted of defamation of the Soviet state and social order. Immediately after his release (November 1977), he joined the **Ukrainian Helsinki Group**. In April 1979, he completed the article "Pravozakhysnyi rukh v Ukraïni. Ioho zasady i perspektyvy" (The Civil Rights Movement in Ukraine: Its Principles and Prospects), in which he developed the political program of the Ukrainian human-rights movement. On 5 July 1979, Lytvyn, then gravely ill, was arrested again, accused of "anti-Soviet agitation and propaganda," and sentenced to 10 years' imprisonment and five years' exile. From May 1982, he was incarcerated in the hard-labor camps (Kuchino, Polovinka, and Vsesviatsk, Perm oblast) where most members of the Ukrainian human-rights movement were imprisoned. He was found in his cell on 24 August 1984 with his abdomen cut open and died shortly thereafter.

On 19 November 1989, the remains of Lytvyn, **Vasyl Stus**, and **Oleksii Tykhy** were transferred to Kyiv and reburied at the Baikove Cemetery. Lytvyn's writings include "Rabochee delo" (The Workers' Cause), "Bezumets" (The Madman), and "Poėma o podsnezhnikakh" (Poem about Snowdrops). A posthumous collection, *Liubliu—znachyt' zhyvu* (I Love, Therefore I Live), appeared in 1999.

LYZOHUB FAMILY. Cossack officer family in the Chernihiv and **Poltava** regions whose representatives held high government posts. Ivan Lyzohub (Kobyzenko; d. 1662 or 1663) was colonel of Kaniv (1659, 1662) and Uman (1659–61), serving as **Ivan Vyhovsky's** envoy to the Muscovite government (1658). He was executed by order of **Yurii Khmelnytsky**. Yakiv Lyzohub (d. 9 [19] August 1698) was colonel of Kaniv (1666–69). In 1667, he participated in **Ivan Briukhovetsky's** mission to the Muscovite tsar. During the hetmancy of **Petro Doroshenko**, Lyzohub was general aide-de-camp (1669–74) and acting **hetman** (1670, 1673). He entered the service of Hetman **Ivan Samoilovych** (1674), was colonel of Chernihiv (1687–98), and participated in the Chyhyryn campaigns (1677–78) and the **Crimean** campaigns (1687–89). During the conquest of Azov (1696), he was acting hetman. Yukhym Lyzohub (d. 1704) was general standard-bearer (1688–90), general flag-bearer (1694–98), and colonel of Chernihiv (1698–1704). Yakiv Lyzohub (1675–1749) studied at the **Kyiv Mohyla Academy** and served as general quartermaster (1728–49). As acting hetman, he led a force of 10,000 Ukrainians stationed in Poland against King Stanisław Leszczyński (1733–34). A Russo-Ukrainian army under the command of Burkhardt Minikh and Lyzohub captured Perekop (20 [31] May 1736), Kozlov (Yevpatoriia; 5 [16] June), and Bakhchesarai (17 [28] June). From 1728 to 1744, Lyzohub headed the commission that compiled the **Code of Laws of 1743**. He was a member of an officer delegation that strove for the restoration of the hetmancy

(1745–49; *see* ROZUMOVSKY, KYRYLO). Some scholars consider him the author of the Lyzohub Chronicle (ca. 1742). Andrii Lyzohub (1804–64) was a close friend of **Taras Shevchenko**, who visited his estate at Sedniv (now in Chernihiv oblast) in 1846 and 1847. He corresponded with the poet in exile and provided him with material assistance. In 1850, he petitioned the government to reduce Shevchenko's sentence. Dmytro Lyzohub (1850–10 [22] August 1879) took part in the **populist** movement of the 1870s. Born in Sedniv, the son of Andrii Lyzohub, he graduated from the faculty of law at St. Petersburg University. In 1873–74, he participated in the Chaikovsky group and became a founder of the clandestine populist organization Land and Freedom. He was arrested in 1878, accused of plotting the assassination of Alexander II, and executed in Odesa. Fedir Lyzohub (1851–1928), a brother of Dmytro Lyzohub, was counselor of the Chernihiv zemstvo assembly (1888–97) and chairman of the Poltava zemstvo executive (1901–15). He initiated the erection of a monument to **Ivan Kotliarevsky** and the publication of his works, as well as the opening of a museum in Poltava. A member of the Octobrist Party, after the February Revolution of 1917 he headed the department of foreign subjects at the Russian Ministry of Foreign Affairs. On 3 May 1918, he was appointed minister of internal affairs (until 8 July) of the **Ukrainian State**; a week later, he also became its otaman (premier). When forming a new cabinet, Lyzohub strove to compromise with mainstream parties, including the **Ukrainian National Union**. He resigned after **Pavlo Skoropadsky** announced Ukraine's federation with a future non-Bolshevik Russia (14 November 1918). Lyzohub died in the emigration in Yugoslavia.

M

MACE, JAMES E. (18 February 1952–3 May 2004). Historian. Born in Muskogee, Oklahoma, Mace studied at the University of Oklahoma and obtained his doctorate at the University of Michigan (1981). His monograph, *Communism and the Dilemmas of National Liberation: National Communism in Soviet Ukraine, 1918–1933*, was published in 1983 by the **Harvard Ukrainian Research Institute**. Mace's chief subject of research was the **famine of 1932–33** in Ukraine. As researcher and discussant, he made a major contribution to the first English-language monograph on the famine, Robert Conquest's *Harvest of Sorrow* (1986). From 1986 to 1990, Mace served as staff director of the United States Congress Commission on the Ukraine Famine. In that capacity, he wrote the commission's *Report to Congress* (with Olya Samilenko, 1988) and edited its three-volume *Oral History Project* (with Leonid Heretz, 1990).

Mace's contention (now generally accepted) that the famine had been man-made was controversial in American historical circles at the time, and he was unable to obtain an academic position in the United States. He moved to Ukraine in 1993 and settled in Kyiv, where he continued his research and writing on the famine and became professor of political science at the **Kyiv Mohyla Academy** National University. He was also a consultant to the leading Kyiv newspaper *Den'* (The Day), for which he wrote a weekly column of historical and political commentary.

In one of his last articles, "Is the Ukrainian Genocide a Myth?" (2003), Mace cited a newly discovered letter in which Stalin insisted to **Lazar Kaganovich** (11 September 1932) that "If we do not now correct the situation in Ukraine, we could lose Ukraine. . . . Set yourself the task of turning Ukraine in the shortest possible time into a fortress of the **USSR**, into the most inalienable republic." The man-made famine, wrote Mace, was the instrument whereby the Soviet leaders sought to wipe out a distinct Ukrainian identity and integrate Ukraine permanently into the Soviet Union. That made the famine genocidal, argued Mace; Raphael Lemkin, the Jewish jurist from Poland who coined the word "genocide," had written that "criminal intent to destroy or cripple permanently a human group" was part of the definition of the term.

The sudden death of James Mace was mourned not only by his professional colleagues but also by Ukraine's civic elite, whose public statements lauded his dedicated scholarly work and personal integrity as a model for their countrymen. Mace was buried at the Baikove Cemetery in Kyiv, which is now reserved for those who have made outstanding contributions to Ukraine.

MAGDEBURG LAW. Medieval municipal legal code that freed cities from the administrative and judicial authority of large landowners, creating bodies of local self-government. Enhancing the rights of townspeople (merchants, burghers, and tradesmen), it was a juridical manifestation of their successful struggle against the feudal lords. Adopted in the 13th century in the city of Magdeburg (Germany), the law established election procedures and functions of local self-government, courts, trade associations, and **guilds**, regulated trade relations, welfare, and inheritance, and defined punishments for various types of crimes. In the 13th and 14th centuries, Magdeburg law spread to Bohemia, Hungary, and Lithuania, and from there to the territory of Belarus and Ukraine. Ukrainian towns received the law from Lithuanian princes, Polish kings, and Ukrainian **hetmans**. Towns in the Principality of **Galicia-Volhynia** were the first in Ukraine to receive Magdeburg law. Sianok (Sanok), now in Poland, received the law in 1339, followed by **Lviv** (1356), Kamianets (1374), Berestia (1390), **Kyiv** (1494–97), and Stanyslaviv (1663). Between the 15th and 17th centuries, most towns in Ukraine came under Magdeburg law. In some towns, especially in **western Ukraine**, its introduction was accompanied by increased Polish and German colonization at the expense of the rights of the Ukrainian population. Influenced by local conditions and the norms of customary law, Magdeburg law in **Right-** and **Left-Bank Ukraine** differed significantly from the law as applied in Western Europe, notably in the organization of *magistraty* (bodies of local self-government). In smaller *ratush* towns, **Cossack officers** administered Cossack affairs, while an elected municipal authority governed the townspeople. The norms of Magdeburg law were incorporated into every official and informal codification of laws in Ukraine in the 18th and early 19th centuries, including the **Code of Laws of 1743**. Following the **Pereiaslav Agreement** (1654) and the subsequent restriction of Left-Bank autonomy, Magdeburg law remained in force in only a few "privileged towns" in Ukraine. It ceased to function after the introduction of gubernias (1781) and the establishment of a new court system. In 1831, Tsar Nicholas I abolished Magdeburg law in Ukraine, with the exception of the city of Kyiv, where it was in effect until 1835. In western Ukrainian towns that passed to Austria after the first partition of Poland (1772), local administrations and courts created under the law initially continued to function. Subsequently, the Austrian government restricted the rights of those bodies. The application of the law in Lviv ended in 1786.

MAKARENKO, ANTON (1 [13] March 1888–1 April 1939). Pedagogue and writer. Born in Bilopillia (now in Sumy oblast), Makarenko was trained as a teacher in Kremenchuk (1905), studied at the **Poltava** Pedagogical Institute (1914–17), and taught in Poltava and **Kharkiv**. In 1920, he established the Gorky Labor Colony for homeless children near Poltava. He then headed the Dzerzhinsky Children's Commune for young offenders near Kharkiv (1927–35), many of whose inmates were orphaned by the **famine of 1932–33**. For two years (1935–37), Makarenko held important posts in the NKVD labor-colony system, first as deputy head of the labor-colony division in Kyiv and later as director of a labor colony in Brovary.

He then moved to Moscow, where he continued writing pedagogical works and fiction. Makarenko's most important works, all written in Russian, are *Marsh 30 goda* (The March of 1930, 1932), *Pedagogicheskaia poèma* (Pedagogical Poem, 1933–35; often titled *The Road to Life* in English translation), and *Kniga dlia roditelei* (Book for Parents, 1937).

Makarenko's pedagogical theories were based on the principle of **education** through the collective. In the colonies that he headed, children were organized into brigades that competed with one another and engaged in collective criticism of misbehavior. Uniforms and daily routines were compulsory; duty to the collective and to Soviet society was constantly stressed. This educational system was wholly in keeping with the strong pressure for conformity characteristic of the Stalin regime. Makarenko's theories gained considerable popularity; his works were translated into 58 languages, and centers specializing in the study of his thought were established in Bulgaria, Czechoslovakia, England, Germany, Italy, and Japan.

MAKHNO, NESTOR (15 [27] October 1888–25 July 1934). Prominent **peasant** warlord. He was born in Huliai-Pole, Katerynoslav gubernia (now in Zaporizhia oblast), and attended the local elementary school. In 1906, he became a member of a local anarchist organization, the Union of Indigent Agrarians. Arrested repeatedly on charges of political assassination and expropriation, Makhno was sentenced to death by the **Odesa** military district court in March 1910, but this was commuted to life imprisonment because he was a minor. From 1911 to 1917, Makhno was incarcerated at the Butyrki Prison in Moscow, where he came under the strong influence of the Russian anarchist Petr Arshinov.

After the February Revolution, Makhno returned to the Katerynoslav (now Dnipropetrovsk) region, where he became an organizer of the Peasant Union and of the labor union of metal and carpentry workers. He established himself as a leader of peasant bands that took over estates and redistributed the land. In 1918, Makhno led peasant revolts against Hetman **Pavlo Skoropadsky** and the German occupation forces, in addition to raiding private estates. This campaign brought him to prominence, and his land-hungry peasant followers gave him the sobriquet *bat'ko* (father), traditionally applied to Zaporozhian **Cossack** and **haidamaka** leaders. It became Makhno's practice to seek tactical alliances with contending forces—the **Directory** of the **Ukrainian People's Republic** and the Bolsheviks—in order to obtain arms and supplies from them, thereby holding the balance of power in southern Ukraine. His most effective forces were light cavalry units supported by machine-gun carriages (*tachanky*).

Makhno obtained arms from the Bolsheviks in the spring of 1918 and met with Lenin that summer. In December 1918, he accepted an offer of alliance with the Directory, only to turn against it after obtaining military supplies. In the same month, he helped the Bolsheviks take Katerynoslav—an engagement that demonstrated his inability to go over from guerrilla to regular warfare. The Directory's forces counterattacked, and Makhno was driven out of the city with heavy losses on 31 December. In January 1919, fighting both the Directory and the Whites under Gen. Anton Denikin, Makhno allied himself with the Bolsheviks, and his units were incorporated into the Red Army as the Third Trans-Dnipro Brigade. By the end of January, his forces numbered some 20,000. In the spring, Makhno was joined by members of the Nabat Confederation of Anarchist Organizations, who saw his army as the basis of an anarchist revolution. Their relations remained difficult, and no coherent political program was ever worked out. Makhno attracted a peasant following that aspired to partition the landlords' estates and pursue an independent agrarian existence, free of entanglement with urban regimes of any political stripe.

When Denikin's forces broke through the Makhnovite-Bolshevik front in May 1919, the Bolshevik commissar of war, Leon Trotsky, blamed Makhno and declared an all-out campaign against him. Makhno strengthened his forces by arranging the murder of his strongest rival, Otaman **Nykyfor Hryhoriiv**. Augmented by most of Hryhoriiv's rebels and deserters from the Red Army, Makhno's forces continued to fight Denikin until his defeat late in 1919. On 20 September, Makhno concluded another short-lived alliance with the Directory, of which he took advantage to obtain ammunition and transfer ill and wounded troops to **Galicia**. In the latter half of 1919, commanding a force of approximately 80,000 and holding much of southern Ukraine, Makhno reached the apex of his strength. Since Makhno's forces remained a major obstacle to the establishment of Soviet rule in Ukraine, Trotsky sought to eliminate him once again, and Soviet troops began operations against Makhno in November 1919. Throughout most of 1920, Makhno waged a struggle against the Bolsheviks, destroying local soviets and executing communists. The advance of Gen. Petr Wrangel's Whites forced Makhno into a final alliance with the Soviets, concluded in October 1920. Once Wrangel was defeated, Soviet troops surrounded Huliai-Pole on 26 November, hoping to put an end to Makhno, but he escaped and conducted a series of guerrilla campaigns against them along the Azov coast, the Don River, and in the Volga region. These campaigns continued until Makhno's forces were exhausted and Makhno himself severely wounded.

On 28 August 1921, Makhno and his remaining 83 men crossed the border into Romania. He settled in Bucharest and later in Warsaw. In late October 1922, he was arrested by the Polish authorities. During his trial, Makhno was accused of plotting with Soviet diplomats to incite an anti-Polish rebellion in **western Ukraine** so as to unite it with the **Ukrainian SSR**. Makhno refuted the charge, claiming that he had saved Poland in 1920 by refusing to join the Soviet offensive against it and by delaying the advance of Semen Budenny's First Cavalry Army. Acquitted on 27 November, Makhno spent more than a year in Poland under police surveillance. In April 1925, he settled in the Vincennes district of Paris. There he was provided with a modest income by European and American anarchists and published articles in *Anarkhicheskii vestnik* (Anarchist Herald) and *Delo truda* (The Cause of Labor). His incomplete Russian-language memoirs appeared in three volumes. Makhno died in Paris, and an urn containing his ashes was interred in the Wall of the Communards at the Père Lachaise Cemetery.

MAKSYMOVYCH, MYKHAILO (3 [15] September 1804–10 [22] November 1873). Biologist, historian, folklorist, ethnographer, and writer. He was born on the Tymkivshchyna homestead in **Poltava** gubernia (now Bohuslavets, Cherkasy oblast). In 1819, he graduated from the Novhorod-Siverskyi gymnasium and went on to study at the philological and natural sciences departments of Moscow University, defending his dissertation in 1827. He lectured at Moscow University and was director of the botanical gardens. In 1833, Maksymovych became a professor of botany, and in 1834–35 he was appointed the first rector of **Kyiv** University and dean of the faculty of arts. He hoped to employ **Nikolai Gogol**, **Mykola Kostomarov**, and **Taras Shevchenko** as faculty members. In 1845, he resigned his post because of ill health. Subsequently he lived on his estate, Mykhailova Hora, near Prokhorivka (now in Kaniv raion, Cherkasy oblast) and engaged in scholarship. He attempted repeatedly to return to teaching, but the imperial ministry of education, wary of his **Ukrainophile** views, prevented his return to the academy, and he did not become a corresponding member of the St. Petersburg Academy of Sciences until 1871. Maksymovych maintained close ties with Yevhen Hrebinka, Petro Hulak-Artemovsky, Kostomarov, Mikhail Shchepkin, Shevchenko, Adam Mickiewicz, and other distinguished figures of scholarship and culture. He was elected a member of Moscow, St. Petersburg, and Novorossiisk universities and many learned societies.

Maksymovych was a scholar of encyclopedic range, from history to botany. As a historian, he was partial to the prevailing currents of **romanticism** and **populism**. He defended the thesis of continuity between the princely and **Cossack** periods in Ukrainian history and refuted Mikhail Pogodin's assertion that the Kyiv region had been populated by "Great Russians" during the princely era. Maksymovych's numerous works on the history of **Kyivan Rus'**, Cossackdom, the **Hetmanate**, and the **haidamaka** movement were important for the development of Ukrainian historical scholarship. He wrote valuable works on archaeology and initiated Ukrainian folklore studies. **Panteleimon Kulish** avowed that he and Kostomarov had become Ukrainian patriots as a result of reading Maksymovych's second collection of folk songs, *Ukrainskie narodnye pesni* (1827), which also influenced Gogol, Shevchenko, and Aleksandr Pushkin. Maksymovych's folklore publications aroused considerable interest in Ukrainian folklore among other Slavic peoples. As a linguist, he published a series of articles on the classification of the Slavic languages. He founded and published the almanacs *Dennitsa* (Morning Star, 1830–34), *Kievlianin* (The Kyivan, 1840, 1841, 1850), and *Ukrainets* (The Ukrainian, 1859, 1864). Maksymovych prepared verse translations of the ***Tale of Ihor's Campaign*** in Ukrainian and Russian. He also published and researched the oldest literary monuments of Kyivan Rus', the ***Ruskaia Pravda*** and the ***Tale of Bygone Years***. He published the texts of many historical charters, proclamations, and other documents. Maksymovych translated the Book of Psalms into Ukrainian and wrote poetry. He devised a Ukrainian orthography, the so-called *maksymovychivka*. His extensive work in biology made him a founder of the discipline in Ukraine.

MALEVICH, KAZIMIR (11 [23] February 1878–15 May 1935). Painter; founding figure of abstract art. He was born in **Kyiv** and lived in **Podilia** (Yampil), the **Kharkiv** region (Parkhomivka, Bilopillia), and the Chernihiv region (Vovchok, Konotop) until the age of 17. He studied drawing with Mykola Pymonenko at the Kyiv Art School (1895–97). In 1904, Malevich moved to Moscow, where he studied at the School of **Painting**, Sculpture, and Architecture (1904–5) and at the studio of Ivan Rerberg (1905–10). In his early paintings, he attempted to combine principles of cubism, futurism, and expressionism. He participated in the exhibitions of the artistic associations Jack of Diamonds (1910), Donkey's Tail (1912), and others, at which he displayed works painted in a neoprimitivist (*Peasant Women in Church*, 1911–12, and *Rye Harvest*, 1912) and cubo-futurist style (*An Englishman in Moscow*, 1914). In 1915,

Malevich launched the suprematist movement (*Black Square*; *Black Rectangle, Blue Triangle*) and went on to publish the journal *Supremus* (1916). He taught at an art school in Vitsebsk (1919–22) and was director of the Institute of Artistic Culture in Leningrad (1923–27). In 1927, Malevich moved to Kyiv, where **Mykola Skrypnyk** endeavored to provide him with suitable working conditions. He published articles on art in the journal *Nova generatsiia* (New Generation, 1928–29) in Kharkiv. In 1927–30, he lectured at the Kyiv Art Institute, but Stalin's **political terror** against the intelligentsia in Ukraine forced him to return to Leningrad. He died in Leningrad and was buried near Moscow. Notable works by Malevich include *The Woodcutter* (1912), *Eight Red Rectangles* (1915), *Suprematist Painting* (1915), *Boy with Knapsack—Color Masses in the Fourth Dimension* (1915), *Yellow and Black (Supremus No. 58)* (1916), *White Square on White* (1918), *Going to the Harvest* (ca. 1928), *Girls in the Field* (ca. 1928), and *Self-Portrait* (1933).

MANIAVA HERMITAGE/SKYT MANIAVS'KYI. Monastery founded in 1611 near the village of Maniava (now in Ivano-Frankivsk oblast) by the monk Yov Kniahynytsky. In 1621, a stone wall with three defensive towers was built around the monastery. It was used by neighboring villagers during Turkish and Crimean Tatar raids. The monastery became a center of cultural life in **Galicia**. It had a large library, a school of church music, and a famous iconostasis by Yov Kondzelevych, which was later moved to a church in Bohorodchany (preserved at the Ukrainian National Museum in **Lviv** since 1923). The monastery was closed in 1785 by the Austrian government. Only the fortress walls and the ruins of the main church survived. In 1980, following a restoration project, a historical and architectural museum was opened at the hermitage.

MANUFACTURING. Until the 19th century, **western Ukraine** and **Right-Bank Ukraine** under Polish rule were mainly **agricultural** areas, and the need for goods was satisfied either by imports or by local artisans (*see* CRAFTS). **Left-Bank Ukraine** was more propitious for industrial development because of its higher standard of living, which resulted in a greater demand for manufactured goods. Large enterprises manufacturing textiles, tobacco, and gunpowder were established there in the early 18th century.

Modern industrial development began in the late 18th century with the establishment of factories owned by the tsarist government and by the local landowning nobility. Plants processing agricultural products, such as sugar refineries, distilleries, and flour mills, opened in Right-Bank Ukraine. By 1860, there were 2,709 mechanized plants employing 85,800 workers in the nine Ukrainian gubernias of the Russian Empire. The abolition of serfdom in 1861 and the construction of railways, which began in the 1870s, contributed to the growth of heavy industry, especially ferrous **metallurgy**. The railways also stimulated exports of agricultural and industrial products. Foreign investors, mainly French, British, and Belgian, owned many of Ukraine's industrial enterprises, while others were locally owned. For example, in 1913 the machine-building sector was entirely in foreign hands, while the sugar industry belonged largely to Ukrainian families. The transition from manufacturing producer goods to consumer goods contributed to the expansion of Ukrainian industry at the beginning of the 20th century. By 1914, the number of workers in Ukraine had grown to more than 600,000.

The unbalanced structure of Ukrainian industry in the last decades of the Russian Empire persisted throughout the 20th century. The extractive and industrial-materials branches of the industry (*see* ENERGY; MINING) and the food-products branch were favored over the manufacture of finished goods. Soviet industrialization efforts were concentrated in the resource-rich **Donets Basin** and Dnipropetrovsk region, as well as in **Kharkiv** and **Kyiv**—two politically important metropolitan areas. During the most intensive period of industrialization, the number of workers increased from 855,000 in 1929 to 2.2 million in 1940.

During **World War II**, more than 500 Ukrainian plants were dismantled in advance of the German forces and evacuated to other parts of the Soviet Union. More than 16,000 enterprises were destroyed or considerably damaged by the Germans and Soviets alike. Industry was quickly rebuilt after the war and surpassed its prewar level of production by 1950, but industrial growth rates declined considerably in Ukraine and in the **USSR** as a whole, particularly during the 1970s. If between 1950 and 1965 Ukrainian industry grew 11.1 percent annually on average, the growth rate for the period 1965–85 was only 5.7 percent per annum.

The economic crisis following the breakup of the Soviet Union severely affected the manufacturing sector. In 1990, industrial production in Ukraine began to decline, sinking to a rate of -27.3 percent in 1994. By 1996, Ukrainian enterprises were utilizing only between 10 and 50 percent of their capacity. Industry began to grow again in 1999 at an average annual rate of 3.4 percent. In 2003, production increased by 15.8 percent over the previous year.

As in the Soviet period, the strength of Ukrainian manufacturing lies in producer rather than consumer goods. Machine-building, instrument-making, and metalworking are the largest components of the industrial sector. Plants producing heavy mining and metallurgical equipment are located close to the industries they serve, mainly in the Donets Basin. Machinery for the agricultural sector is built mainly in Kyiv, **Odesa**, Kirovohrad, and Kharkiv. One of the largest tractor plants in the world is also located in Kharkiv. In the transportation sector, ships, railway cars, and locomotives, as well as automobiles, are built in Ukraine. The Ukrainian space industry is also well developed. Large Antonov transport airplanes are designed and built in Kyiv and Kharkiv. Rockets and rocket boosters manufactured in Dnipropetrovsk are used around the world to launch satellites. Heavy equipment used for the generation and transmission of electrical energy, such as turbines, generators, and high-voltage transmission lines, is also manufactured in Ukraine.

A large portion of the Ukrainian manufacturing sector still serves the defense industry, and Ukraine is a major armaments producer. Sophisticated weaponry manufactured in Ukraine includes tanks, rockets and missiles, aircraft and sea vessels, air defense radar systems, and a variety of small arms. *See also* ECONOMY.

MARAMUREŞ REGION (Ukr. *Marmaroshchyna*). Historical and geographic region in the basin of the Tysa (Tisa) River. Its name is derived from the Mara River, and its total area is 10,300 sq. km. The northern portion of the region is a Ukrainian ethnic territory that constitutes the eastern part of Ukrainian **Transcarpathia**. In 1910, Ukrainians comprised 45 percent of the region's population of 360,000, Romanians 24 percent, and **Jews** 16 percent. The term "Maramureş region" first appears in a document dating from 1199. Until the end of the 13th century, the region was virtually uninhabited. From the 14th century it was colonized by Ukrainians from **Galicia** and Romanians from Transylvania. In 1385, the region became a county within the Kingdom of Hungary. In 1526, it was annexed to Transylvania, and in 1733 it passed to Austria. With the collapse of Austria-Hungary (1918), the northern part of the Maramureş region became part of Czechoslovakia (1919) and the southern part was claimed by Romania. The process of Romanianization was countered by the **Ukrainian Catholic Church**, which had 11 parishes in the area. In March 1939, the Ukrainian population of the region assisted refugees from **Carpatho-Ukraine**. After 1945 the southern Maramureş region became part of Romania, where it comprises the Sighetul and Vişeu regions of Maramureş district. In 1960, more than 30,000 Ukrainians lived in the region, most of them in villages, as well as in the towns of Cîmpulung, Sighetul-Marmaţiei, Baia Sprie, and Baia Mare.

MARCHUK, YEVHEN (b. 28 January 1941). Politician; sixth prime minister of independent Ukraine. Marchuk was born in the village of Dolynivka, Kirovohrad oblast, into a family of collective farmers. In 1963, he graduated from the Kirovohrad Pedagogical Institute with a diploma in linguistics (Ukrainian and German). Marchuk earned his second degree in law and embarked on a career as a law-enforcement officer in Kirovohrad. From 1965 to 1988, he moved up through the ranks from KGB operations officer to senior officer, deputy department head, and head of an inspectorate. In 1988, Marchuk was appointed head of the **Poltava** oblast KGB administration. From 1990, he served as first deputy head of the KGB of the **Ukrainian SSR**.

In 1991, shortly before Ukraine's declaration of independence, Marchuk was appointed minister of defense, national security, and emergency situations. From November 1991 to July 1994, he headed the Security Service of Ukraine, which replaced the KGB. Marchuk was appointed deputy prime minister on 1 July 1994 by President **Leonid Kravchuk**. Following the dismissal of **Vitalii Masol**, Kravchuk's successor, **Leonid Kuchma**, appointed Marchuk prime minister (June 1995). Almost a year later, in May 1996, Marchuk was faulted for the slow pace of market reforms and inability to cooperate with the **Verkhovna Rada** (VR); he was dismissed "for actively building a personal political image" and replaced by **Pavlo Lazarenko**.

In June 1996, Marchuk resumed his duties as deputy to the VR, to which he had been elected in 1995. He was reelected in 1998 as a member of the (United) Social Democratic Party but left it when the party's political bosses, **Viktor Medvedchuk** and **Hryhorii Surkis**, declined to support his presidential campaign in 1999. Marchuk took part in the presidential race, finishing fifth in the first round. Prior to the second round, he supported Leonid Kuchma, who appointed him secretary of the National Security Council. In June 2003, he became Ukraine's minister of defense and embarked on a program of staff reductions and large-scale replacement of military appointees with civilian specialists.

MARGOLIN, ARNOLD (17 November 1877–29 October 1956). Activist of the Ukrainian Jewish community. Born in **Kyiv**, Margolin graduated from the law faculty of Kyiv University (1900). He was general secretary of the South Russian Branch of the Union for Equal Rights for **Jews** in Russia (1905–17). He was also a founder and president of the Jewish Territorial Organization (1906–18). As a member of the Russian College of Lawyers, Margolin often defended the interests of the Jewish minority at anti-Semitic show trials. In 1911–13, he participated in the investigation and trial of Mendel Beilis, who was falsely accused of ritual murder and exonerated by a jury of Ukrainian **peasants**. From 1918, Margolin was a member of the **Ukrainian Party of Socialist Federalists**, and in March 1918 he became a judge of the General Court of the **Ukrainian People's Republic** (UNR). Under the **Directory**, he was deputy minister of foreign affairs in the governments of **Volodymyr Chekhivsky** and Serhii Ostapenko. Margolin supported the policies of the Directory and its efforts to prevent pogroms. He published numerous articles in the foreign press refuting blanket accusations of Ukrainian anti-Semitism (1919) and emphasizing the Directory's struggle against pogrom organizers. In early 1919, he was a member of the Ukrainian delegation at negotiations with the Entente in **Odesa** and took part in the UNR diplomatic mission to the Paris Peace Conference (1919–20). Subsequently, he was the UNR ambassador to Great Britain.

From 1922, Margolin lived in the United States, where he engaged in scholarly and community activities. He was a corresponding member of the **Ukrainian Academy of Arts and Sciences** in the United States and professor of the Ukrainian Technical Institute in New York. He died in New York. In his numerous works, including *Ukraina i politika Antanty* (Ukraine and the Policy of the Entente, 1921; English trans., 1977), *Zapiski evreia i grazhdanina* (Notes of a Jew and a Citizen, 1922), *The Jews of Eastern Europe* (1926), *From a Political Diary: Russia, the Ukraine, and America, 1905–1945* (1946), Margolin defended the cause of Ukrainian independence and the reputation of the Directory's leader, **Symon Petliura**.

MARTOS, IVAN (1754–5 [17] April 1835). Sculptor. He was born in Ichnia (now in Chernihiv oblast) into a **Cossack** family. Martos was educated at the St. Petersburg Academy of Arts (1764–73) and at the Academy of Arts in Rome, where he studied and copied sculptures of antiquity (1774–79). After his return to St. Petersburg, he became a prominent classicist. He served as professor at the St. Petersburg Academy of Arts (1794) and as its rector (1814). Martos produced a number of monumental and decorative works in Ukraine and Russia, notably the burial monuments of **Kyrylo Rozumovsky** in Baturyn (1803–5), **Petr Rumiantsev** in **Kyiv** (1797–1805), and Paul I in Pavlovsk (1807), as well as monuments to Kuzma Minin and Dmitrii Pozharsky in Moscow (1804–18), Armand Richelieu in Odesa (1823–28), Mikhail Lomonosov in Arkhangelsk (1826–29), and Grigorii Potemkin in Kherson (1829–35).

MASOL, VITALII (b. 14 November 1928). Soviet bureaucrat and fifth prime minister of independent Ukraine. Masol was born in the village of Olyshivka, Chernihiv oblast, into the family of a teacher. After graduating from the Kyiv Polytechnical Institute in 1951 with a degree in mechanical engineering, he worked at the Novokramatorsk Machine-Building Plant as a foreman's assistant, was promoted to foreman, and became head of the technical development office. Masol then rose to deputy head engineer and, in 1963, became director of the plant. This was followed by a year's service as director-general of the Kramatorsk Production Association of Heavy Industry Plants (1971). In September 1972, Masol became first deputy head of the State Planning Committee of the **Ukrainian SSR**. He was promoted to deputy chairman of the **Council of Ministers** in January 1979 and subsequently headed the State Planning Committee. In July 1987, Masol was appointed chairman of the Council of Ministers.

Shortly after Ukraine's declaration of sovereignty in July 1990, students gathered in Kyiv and organized a mass hunger strike to protest the policies of the Council of Ministers and demand Masol's resignation. In October, Masol became the first high-level Soviet bureaucrat to quit his post under public pressure. He continued to serve as a deputy to the **Verkhovna Rada** (elected 1989). Shortly before the 1994 presidential elections, on 16 June 1994, President **Leonid Kravchuk** appointed Masol prime minister, hoping to gain votes among the procommunist sector of the electorate. Nine days later, ex–Prime Minister **Leonid Kuchma** was elected president of Ukraine. In an attempt to speed up the pace of his promised economic reforms, Kuchma brought a team of promarket officials into his administration. The antireformist Masol was now out of place, and Kuchma managed to obtain his de facto resignation at the beginning of March 1995. Masol was succeeded by **Yevhen Marchuk**.

MAZEPA, ISAAK (16 August 1884–18 March 1952). Civic and political figure. He was born in Kostobobriv, Chernihiv gubernia. Mazepa studied at St. Petersburg University and was active in the Ukrainian student association (1904–10). In 1905, he became a member of the **Ukrainian Social Democratic Labor Party** (USDRP) and a leader of the Ukrainian social-democratic movement. From 1911 to 1917, Mazepa worked as an agronomist. After the February Revolution (1917), he became a member of the Katerynoslav (now Dnipropetrovsk) City Duma and the Katerynoslav Council of Workers' and Peasants' Deputies. In April 1918, he headed the Katerynoslav Gubernia Revolutionary Council. During the rule of **Pavlo Skoropadsky**, Mazepa coedited the USDRP newspaper *Nasha sprava* (Our Cause). In January 1919, he was a deputy to the **Labor Congress** of Ukraine. In April, he became minister of internal affairs of the **Ukrainian People's Republic** (UNR) in the government of Borys Martos. From 27 August 1919 to 25 May 1920, Mazepa was premier of the UNR. In May and June 1920, he served as the UNR minister of **agriculture**. He participated in the First **Winter Campaign** (1919–20).

From 1920, Mazepa lived in **Lviv**, where he edited the USDRP newspaper *Vil'na Ukraïna* (Free Ukraine). Emigrating to Prague in 1923, he worked at the Ukrainian Institute of Sociology. During the interwar period, Mazepa was a leading member of the Foreign Delegation of the USDRP. He represented Ukrainian interests at many social-democratic conferences and was a member of the executive committee of the Labor and Socialist International. After 1945, he lived in Austria and Germany, serving as a professor of the Ukrainian Technical and Husbandry Institute in Munich. He was a coorganizer of the **Ukrainian National Council** in exile (1947) and was elected the first chairman of its Executive Organ (until January 1952). In 1950, Mazepa became a founding member of the Ukrainian Socialist Party. He died in Augsburg. Mazepa wrote a number of historical works, including *Bil'shovyzm i okupatsiia Ukraïny* (Bolshevism and the Occupation of Ukraine, 1922), *Pidstavy nashoho vidrodzhennia* (Foundations of Our Rebirth, 1946), and *Ukraïna v ohni i buri revoliutsiï* (Ukraine in the Fire and Storm of Revolution, 1941, 1950–52).

MAZEPA, IVAN (most probably 20 [30] March 1639–21 September [2 October] 1709). **Hetman** of Ukraine. He was born in Mazepyntsi, **Kyiv** region, into an Orthodox family of the petty gentry. He obtained his education at the Kyiv **Mohyla** Collegium and at the Jesuit college in Warsaw (or Polatsk). In 1656–59, he studied gunnery in Holland and visited Germany, Italy, and France. From 1659 to 1663, Mazepa was in the service of King John Casimir of Poland. He returned to Ukraine in 1663 and soon attained the office of cupbearer of Chernihiv (1665). Following John Casimir's resignation, Mazepa became a squadron commander in the service of the **Right-Bank** hetman **Petro Doroshenko** (1669), then his general chancellor. On various occasions, Mazepa represented the **Hetmanate** in negotiations with Muscovy, the **Crimean** Khanate, the Ottoman Empire, and the **Polish-Lithuanian Commonwealth**.

In 1674, while on a diplomatic mission, Mazepa was captured by the **Zaporozhian** otaman **Ivan Sirko**, who handed him over to Doroshenko's **Left-Bank** rival, **Ivan Samoilovych**. Mazepa established himself as an influential official on Samoilovych's staff and gained the confidence of Peter I. After the failure of a Crimean campaign (1687), Samoilovych was deposed as hetman and exiled to Siberia. Mazepa was elected to succeed him at the Kolomak Council (25 July [4 August] 1687). He strove to unite all Ukrainian lands into a single polity. Mazepa promoted the formation of an aristocratic elite, granting large estates and new privileges to the **Cossack officers**, thereby provoking dissatisfaction among the lower orders. A number of decrees intended to protect the Cossacks (1691), burghers, **peasants** (1701), and clergy (1690–94) did not suffice to overcome social tensions. Moreover, during the first years of the Northern War (1700–21), tsarist exploitation of the Hetmanate grew more intense. In 1700, more than 17,000 Cossacks were sent to the Baltic region to engage the Swedish army; many others were dragooned into large-scale construction projects, such as the building of Peter I's new capital, St. Petersburg. The deployment of Muscovite armies in the Hetmanate dissatisfied the Cossack officers.

In 1704, on the instructions of Peter I, Mazepa extended his rule into Right-Bank Ukraine. Concerned to establish his authority and put a stop to the tsar's exactions and limitations on the traditional rights of the Hetmanate, he entered into secret negotiations with King Stanisław Leszczyński of Poland, an ally of Charles XII of Sweden. In 1709, Charles XII, Mazepa, and the Zaporozhian otaman Kost Hordiienko signed an agreement providing for Swedish assistance to rid the Hetmanate and Zaporizhia of Russian rule. As Swedish forces advanced through Ukrainian territory, Mazepa openly switched his allegiance to Charles XII (autumn 1708), provoking large-scale punitive actions by Muscovite armies against the Ukrainian population. The hetman's capital of Baturyn, the Zaporozhian **Sich**, and other sites were destroyed. On 27 June (8 July) 1709, the Swedish and Hetmanate armies were defeated by Peter I at the **Battle of Poltava**. Charles XII and Mazepa were forced to retreat to Ottoman territory, and Mazepa settled in a suburb of Bendery. He died soon afterward and was buried at St. George's Monastery in Galați (now in Romania).

Mazepa was an eminent patron of culture and **education** in Ukraine. Thanks to his efforts, the Kyiv Mohyla Collegium obtained the status of an academy in 1694 (*see* KYIV MOHYLA ACADEMY). During his administration, a number of monumental structures were built or restored in the Ukrainian **baroque** style. Mazepa was also a patron of **literature**. He wrote a number of poems himself and sponsored the work of **Dymytrii Tuptalo**, Stefan Yavorsky, and Ivan Maksymovych. Mazepa also donated icons, books, bells, and treasures to numerous churches and monasteries.

Mazepa's striking career made him a favorite subject of **romantic** art; Byron, Pushkin, and Słowacki wrote poems about him, while Liszt, Tchaikovsky, and others devoted musical compositions to him. Lauded by the Ukrainian national movement as a symbol of independence, Mazepa was particularly reviled in the Russian Empire. On the orders of Peter I, he was formally anathematized by the Orthodox Church, and until the **Ukrainian Revolution** the word *mazepinets* was a common Russian term of abuse for Ukrainian patriots. This tradition continued under Soviet rule, when official reference works termed Mazepa a "traitor to the Ukrainian people."

MEASURES FOR THE ACCOMMODATION OF THE RUTHENIAN NATION. Act issued by King Władysław IV of Poland (and ratified by the Diet of the **Polish-Lithuanian Commonwealth** in March 1633) that legalized the existence of the **Ukrainian Orthodox Church** in the Ukrainian lands. Following the death of Sigismund III (April 1632), the **Cossack officers** demanded the right to participate in the election of a new king, which was denied, as well as guarantees of national and religious rights. Provincial dietines in Ukraine and the **brotherhoods** of **Lviv** and Vilnius made similar demands to restore the rights of the Orthodox faithful that had been taken away following the church **Union of Brest** (1596). Those demands, expressed in a work titled *Synopsis: A Brief Description of Rights and Freedoms*, were supported by the Orthodox hierarchy, led by the archimandrite of the **Kyivan Cave Monastery**, **Petro Mohyla**. Inasmuch as Protestants were also demanding the restoration of their rights, Mohyla was supported by the Lithuanian **hetman**, Prince Krzysztof Radziwiłł. At the Convocation Diet in Warsaw, the Orthodox and Protestants jointly submitted their demands (June 1632). A commission formed at the Election Diet prepared the Measures (September 1632). According to the document, the Orthodox Church was officially granted the right to its own hierarchy, headed by a metropolitan and four bishops (Lviv, Lutsk, Peremyshl [Przemyśl], and Mstsislaŭ), to conduct services freely, and to maintain its own churches, monasteries, print shops, schools, and brotherhoods. Mohyla was elected Orthodox metropolitan of **Kyiv**. The Measures did not resolve the religious question in Ukraine. Following his election, Władysław IV annulled a number of points under pressure from the Roman Catholic Church and the Polish nobility. Continued oppression of the Orthodox Church became one of the causes of the **Cossack rebellions** of the 1630s and the **Khmelnytsky Uprising** (1648).

MEDIA. Historically, information media in Ukraine have mainly served the interests of political regimes that were not Ukrainian. A Ukrainian-**language** press began to develop during the **Revolution of 1848** in Austrian-ruled **western Ukraine** and during the **Revolution of 1905** in the Russian Empire. **Galician** newspapers and periodicals assumed a national character in the 19th century, particularly after the ban on Ukrainian **publishing** in the Russian Empire (*see* VALUEV CIRCULAR; EMS UKASE). One of the most influential general-interest periodicals at the time was *Pravda* (1867–96), published in **Lviv**. From the 1870s, many periodicals established themselves as organs of political groups, including radical and socialist parties. Moderate newspapers such as *Dilo* (1880–1939), influential scholarly periodicals such as *Zapysky Naukovoho Tovarystva im. Shevchenka* (est. 1892), published by the **Shevchenko Scientific Society**, and literary and cultural journals such as *Literaturno-naukovyi visnyk* (1898–1932) were all founded in Lviv. In the Russian Empire, the first regular Ukrainian-language periodical, *Osnova* (1861–62), appeared in St. Petersburg. The relaxation of censorship after 1905 paved the way for Ukrainian dailies such as *Rada* (1906–14) and literary monthlies such as *Ukraïns'ka khata* (1909–14), in addition to specialized journals.

Following the **Ukrainian Revolution** (1917–21), the Soviet regime in the **Ukrainian SSR** gradually eliminated noncommunist newspapers. Literary and scholarly periodicals, such as *Literaturnyi iarmarok* (1928–30) and *Ukraïna* (1914–30), flourished throughout the 1920s under the policy of **Ukrainization**. Nearly all non-newspaper periodicals were closed down after 1933, and newspaper publishing was centralized. In western Ukraine during the interwar period, Ukrainian periodicals were plagued by official Polish prohibitions and strict censorship.

Postwar periodicals and newspapers in Ukraine served purposes established in Moscow: centralization, unconditional party control, and **Russification**. Despite the large number of newspapers published and their high press runs, readers found little diversity of opinion. In 1955, there were 1,192 newspapers and 245 periodicals published in Ukraine; in 1990, there were 1,476 newspapers and 185 periodicals. As a result of the centralized distribution system, the Ukrainian press was overshadowed by more readily available Russian-language periodicals.

The declaration of Ukrainian independence brought an influx of new titles and diversity of opinion to the periodicals market. At the beginning of 2000 there were 2,551 newspapers and 1,374 magazines published in Ukraine. Although the number of publications grew, total circulation dropped by some 30 percent as compared with the Soviet period. Most publications are registered as bilingual, meaning that some have separate Ukrainian and Russian editions, while others cater to the Russian-speaking population. As compared with Western democracies, the Ukrainian government is highly involved with the press; 9 percent of the print media were established by the state.

Radio broadcasts in Ukraine began in **Kharkiv** in 1924, and a radio network was initiated in 1928. Throughout the Soviet period, radio broadcasting used wired transmitters and receivers. The relatively small number of wireless radios had to be registered with the authorities, and their use was limited to the larger cities, where foreign broadcasts were jammed. Ukrainians own 45 million radios (1997), and broadcasting is carried by 134 AM stations, 289 FM stations, and four short-wave stations (1998). State-owned wire radio broadcasting still accounts for a large part of the network and includes close to 10 million radio points.

Television broadcasting in Ukraine began in 1939, and the country's first television center was built in **Kyiv** (1949). From the early 1950s, viewers began to receive high-clarity telecasts in all major Ukrainian cities. In 1962, a second channel of broadcasts from Moscow was added. Centralized Ukrainian broadcasting from Kyiv was initiated in 1965, and color broadcasting began in 1969. Today, Ukrainians own 18 million (1997) television sets, and broadcasting originates from at least 33 stations (in addition to 21 repeater stations that relay broadcasts from Russia). There are 791 television and radio organizations registered in Ukraine (2000), with only 28 of them state-owned. The aggregate amount of television and radio broadcasts is 8,366 hours per day. The most popular national television channels are the private Studio 1+1 and Inter and the state-owned UT-1. The total number of regular TV viewers exceeds 60 percent of the Ukrainian population.

Ukrainian participation in the Internet began in 1990, and the domain *.ua was registered in 1992. In 2003, there were 260 Internet service providers in Ukraine; the number of regular users was estimated at about 8 percent of the population. Most central newspapers have electronic copies available on their Internet sites. The number of publications and news services that have no print versions is also growing rapidly.

Although most media in Ukraine are privately owned, their freedom is curbed by government interference. Despite significant growth in the number of Ukrainian-language publications, television programs, and radio broadcasts, Russian-language media still account for the overwhelming majority of the market.

MEDVEDCHUK, VIKTOR (b. 7 August 1954). Lawyer, politician, and reputed economic oligarch. Medvedchuk's father was convicted in 1944 of heading the Zhytomyr cell of the **Organization of Ukrainian Nationalists** and exiled to Siberia. Medvedchuk was born in the village of Pochet (Krasnoiarskii krai); the family moved to the **Kyiv** region in 1962. In 1978, Medvedchuk graduated from Kyiv University with a diploma in law. He earned a candidate of laws degree in 1996 and a doctorate in law in 1997. In 1978, he began his career as a lawyer with the Kyiv City Bar Association. In December 1979, he was the state-appointed defender of the political **dissident Yurii Lytvyn** and, in October 1980, of the poet **Vasyl Stus**. Both were convicted of "anti-Soviet activity" and died in forced-labor camps. From 1989, Medvedchuk worked as head of the Legal Advice Office in the **Shevchenko** district of Kyiv. In 1990, he founded and was elected president of the Lawyers' Association of Ukraine and became a board member of the Lawyers' Association of the **USSR**. In 1991, he established the Ukrainian-American-Israeli BIM law firm and became its first president; a year later, with other members of the so-called Kyiv clan, he founded the Ometa XXI Century Trust, the Ukrainian Credit Bank, and the Dynamo Kyiv Soccer Club Stock Company. In 1994, after the financial collapse of Ometa XXI, Medvedchuk and his business partners renamed it the Slavutych Industrial and Financial Concern, which trades extensively in gas and oil.

Medvedchuk became involved in politics in 1994–95 as a member of the Social Democratic Party of Ukraine (SDPU; later the [United] SDPU), of which he was elected deputy head in 1996. From 1994 to 1999, he was a member of the presidential Coordinating Committee against Corruption and Organized Crime. From 1996 to 2000, Medvedchuk was an adjunct consultant to President **Leonid Kuchma** on tax policy. Elected to the **Verkhovna Rada** (VR) in 1997, he worked in the Committee on Law and Order, serving concurrently as a member of the presidential Coordinating Council on Legal Reform and of the Supreme Economic Council. In October 1998, Medvedchuk was elected head of the (United) SDPU, which includes some of Ukraine's richest and most influential figures. Reelected to the VR in the same year, he served as deputy speaker (2000–1). Medvedchuk is believed to have been the driving force behind the vote of nonconfidence that led to the resignation of **Viktor Yushchenko** as prime minister in 2001. In 2002, Medvedchuk was elected to the VR on the (United) SDPU election list and headed its parliamentary faction. In June of the same year, he was appointed head of the presidential administration and a member of the National Security Council.

MELNYK, ANDRII (12 December 1890–1 November 1964). Military and political figure, colonel of the Army of the **Ukrainian People's Republic** (UNR) and leader of the **Organization of Ukrainian Nationalists** (OUN). He was born in Volia Yakubova, **Lviv** region. In 1914–16, he commanded a company of the **Ukrainian Sich Riflemen** on the Austro-Russian front that distinguished itself in the Battle of Makivka. On 4 September 1916, during the Battle of Lysonia, Melnyk was taken prisoner by the Russian forces. In captivity he became closely associated with **Yevhen Konovalets**, with whom he organized the **Galician-Bukovynian** battalion of Sich Riflemen in the autumn of 1917, becoming second in command to Konovalets. From January 1919, he was chief of staff of the Army of the UNR. Following its demobilization in December 1919, Melnyk was interned by the Polish authorities in Rivne. Subsequently, in 1920–21, he was a military attaché for the UNR in Prague and Vienna. In 1922, he returned to Galicia, where he became a cofounder and home commander of the **Ukrainian Military Organization**. Arrested by the Polish police in April 1924, he was sentenced in March 1925 to four years' imprisonment.

After his release, Melnyk remained active in the underground while continuing his civic activities. He was head of the Orly Catholic Association of Ukrainian Youth (1933–38), as well as a member of the Moloda **Hromada** Society of Ukrainian Veterans. Following the assassination of Konovalets, Melnyk became head of the Leadership of Ukrainian Nationalists (11 October 1938) and was formally elected leader in Rome on 27 August 1939. The younger majority of the OUN, led by **Stepan Bandera**, did not recognize the election and established its own Revolutionary Leadership, splitting the organization. During **World War II**, the Germans kept Melnyk under house arrest. Later in the war he was taken to Sachsenhausen concentration camp (26 February 1944), where Bandera and other nationalist leaders were also held, and was the spokesman in negotiations that led to the formation of the **Ukrainian National Committee**. After the war, Melnyk lived in Luxembourg. In 1947, at the Third Great Council of the OUN (Melnyk faction), he was reelected leader, a post he held until the end of his life. Melnyk dedicated himself to the consolidation of the **diaspora**. In 1957, he proposed the creation of a Ukrainian world congress, realized in 1967 with the creation of the World Congress of Free Ukrainians (*see* UKRAINIAN WORLD CONGRESS). Melnyk died in Clervaux and was buried in the city of Luxembourg.

MERCENARY REGIMENTS. Volunteer cavalry regiments, known as *kompaniis'ki polky*, and infantry units, known as *serdiuts'ki polky*—

the only full-time standing military units in the **Hetmanate** in the late 17th century. They performed military and police functions, acted as guards and scouts, and took part in military engagements. Unlike *kompaniis'ki polky*, which **peasants** and town **Cossacks** were not allowed to join, *serdiuk* regiments consisted largely of peasants, non-Ukrainians, and defecting **registered Cossacks**. Mercenary regiments were divided into companies, which in turn were divided into kurins. They were commanded by a colonel and the regimental officer staff, who took orders directly from the **hetman**. There were six to seven mercenary regiments at any one time, each consisting of 400–600 Cossacks. The regiments received salaries, provisions, and ammunition from the Hetmanate government. The tsarist government abolished *serdiuk* regiments in 1726, while the *kompaniitsi* were reformed as regular cavalry regiments in 1776.

METALLURGY. The inhabitants of what is now Ukraine developed a practical knowledge of extracting and refining metals from their ores beginning in the sixth century B.C. They learned to utilize copper, silver, and gold to make functional and ornamental objects. The iron industry in Ukraine can be traced back to the fifth century B.C., when iron was produced from bog iron ore. The practice of ore enrichment was introduced in the ninth century, and in the 14th century the production of steel began in blacksmiths' foundries. The production of ferrous metals on an industrial scale started in 1872 in Yuzivka (now Donetsk) and in 1887 in Katerynoslav (now Dnipropetrovsk). By 1913, there were 21 metallurgical plants in Ukraine employing some 90,000 workers and producing more than half of all the pig iron, steel, and rolling stock in the Russian Empire. Some 90 percent of the metallurgical industry was owned by Western corporations.

The destructive effects of **World War I**, the 1917 revolution, and the ensuing Soviet nationalization of industry greatly reduced the capacity of the metallurgical industry in Ukraine. Its prewar production figures were matched only in 1928. During the industrialization drive of the 1930s, the industry grew rapidly, with large new plants opening in Zaporizhia and Mariupol. In 1935, more than 153,000 workers were engaged in metallurgy. **World War II** left the sector in ruins. The industry was rebuilt and reached its prewar capacity by 1950. During the 1970s, metallurgical plants were modernized extensively to increase their efficiency. Although Ukrainian output grew steadily, its share of Soviet output declined because of rapid industrial expansion in the Urals.

The nonferrous metallurgical industry developed in Ukraine only after 1930. An aluminum plant utilizing inexpensive hydroelectric energy opened in Zaporizhia in 1933, and a larger plant in Mykolaiv began production in 1980. Other facilities included a zinc plant established in 1931 and a magnesium plant that went into production in 1935. Growth continued after the war, but production data was not made public, as nonferrous metals were used mainly for military applications.

In independent Ukraine, metallurgy is one of the main branches of the economy, and its products constitute a significant portion of the country's exports. Together with **mining**, the Ukrainian metallurgical industries make up 23.2 percent of the industrial sector and contribute up to 40 percent of the country's hard-currency earnings. Between 1992 and 1998, Ukraine's steel production shrank from 41.8 to 23.5 million tons, yet the country continued to hold 10th place among world producers, mainly because of reduced production volumes worldwide. In 2003, the metallurgical and mining enterprises of Ukraine produced 29.6 million tons of pig iron, 36.9 million tons of raw steel, 29.2 million tons of rolled steel (including 2.1 million tons of steel pipe), and 63 million tons of iron ore. Ukraine was ranked the seventh largest steel producer in the world. *See also* ECONOMY; MANUFACTURING.

MIKHNOVSKY, MYKOLA (1873–23 May 1924). Civic and political activist; first ideologue of Ukrainian nationalism. Mikhnovsky was born in Turivka, **Poltava** gubernia. From 1890, he studied at the faculty of law of **Kyiv** University; upon graduation, he worked as a lawyer in **Kharkiv**. Mikhnovsky was a member of the **Brotherhood of Taras**, a patriotic organization established in 1891. His speech at the **Taras Shevchenko** commemorations in Poltava and Kharkiv in 1900 was published in **Lviv** in the same year by the **Revolutionary Ukrainian Party** (RUP), the first Ukrainian political party in **eastern Ukraine**, under the title *Samostiina Ukraïna* (Independent Ukraine). In proclaiming the ideal of Ukrainian independence, Mikhnovsky broke with the dominant **populist** current in Ukrainian political thought, which was federalist, egalitarian, and hostile to the tradition of **Cossack** autonomism, regarding the **Cossack officers** as exploiters of the Ukrainian **peasantry**. Citing the precedent of the 17th-century **Hetmanate** established by **Bohdan Khmelnytsky**, Mikhnovsky argued that Moscow had violated the freedoms guaranteed in the **Articles of Bohdan Khmelnytsky**, rendering the **Pereiaslav Agreement** of 1654 null and void.

This postulate found little acceptance in eastern Ukraine and was rejected by most members of the RUP. In 1902, Mikhnovsky left the RUP and helped establish the **Ukrainian People's Party**

(UNP), which united advocates of an independent nation-state. In his "Desiat' zapovidei" (Ten Commandments, 1903), Mikhnovsky set forth his political creed. There was to be "a unitary, indivisible, independent, free Ukrainian Democratic Republic from the Carpathians to the Caucasus." Universal brotherhood was an ultimate ideal, but Russians, Poles, and **Jews** were to be regarded as enemies as long as they ruled over Ukrainians and exploited them. Mikhnovsky called for national solidarity under the watchword "Ukraine for Ukrainians." He sought to popularize these ideas in a number of short-lived publications: *Samostiina Ukraïna* (1905), *Khliborob* (Agrarian, 1905), *Zaporizhzhia* (Zaporizhia, 1906), *Slobozhanshchyna* (Sloboda Region, 1906), and *Snip* (Sheaf, 1912–13).

At the outbreak of **World War I**, Mikhnovsky was drafted into the imperial army with the rank of lieutenant. In March 1917, he became the first to agitate for the creation of a Ukrainian national army. At his initiative, the Hetman **Pavlo Polubotok** Ukrainian Military Club and the Military Organizing Committee were founded in Kyiv with the aim of creating Ukrainian military formations. The First Hetman Bohdan Khmelnytsky Ukrainian Cossack Regiment was formed on 18 April (1 May) 1917 with Mikhnovsky's participation. In 1917, he became a member of the **Ukrainian Central Rada** and the Ukrainian General Military Committee. Mikhnovsky's blatant militarism antagonized the social-democratic majority of the Rada, and an abortive attempt by the Polubotok Regiment to seize power (5 [18] July 1917) led to his arrest. He was dispatched to the Romanian front, from which he returned in the autumn of 1917. Mikhnovsky was associated with the **Ukrainian Democratic Agrarian Party**. He was at odds with both the Hetman government and the **Directory**, and in 1919 he barely avoided execution by the advancing Bolsheviks. Mikhnovsky moved to Novorossiisk in early 1920 and attempted unsuccessfully to emigrate abroad. Subsequently he lived in the Kuban region, working as a teacher and an employee of **cooperatives**. In the spring of 1924, he returned to Kyiv, where he either committed suicide or, more probably, was executed by the secret police. Mikhnovsky's militant nationalism was subsequently taken up by **Dmytro Dontsov** and the **Organization of Ukrainian Nationalists**.

MINING. Ukraine has an estimated 5 percent of the world's mineral resources, with nearly 90 kinds of minerals concentrated in more than 7,700 deposits, of which more than half are commercially exploited. The country possesses the world's largest supply of titanium, the third largest deposit of iron ore, and some 30 percent of the world's manganese ore. There are also commercially viable deposits of mercury, uranium, and nickel. Other minerals located in Ukraine include salt, sulphur, graphite, kaolin, and phosphorus. The mining sector employs about 3 percent of the labor force and accounts for 10 percent of GNP.

The management of natural resources during the Soviet era was ideologically motivated and rarely based on economic rationality. Most resources were considered "free" and their utilization was geared toward the fulfillment of production quotas and five-year plans. As a result, some resources were quickly depleted. For example, once a major producer of oil and natural gas, Ukraine became an importer of hydrocarbons (*see* ENERGY).

Before the 19th century, the principal mineral resources exploited in Ukraine included bog iron ore, potter's clay, building stone, amber, and salt. More intense exploration and industrial production began in the 19th century. Although coal had been extracted since the late 18th century, its large-scale commercial exploitation began in 1876. Commercial mining for iron ore in the Kryvyi Rih area began in 1881, and for manganese ore in the Nykopil area in 1886. The extraction of oil in **western Ukraine** dates even further back, to the 1850s. The most developed sectors are coal, iron ore, and manganese mining, which traditionally account for nearly 90 percent of the mined resources by value.

Coal mines are located mainly in the **Donets Basin**. Coal production has declined since the mid-1970s from well over 200 million tons to 79 million tons in 2003, which still makes Ukraine the eighth-largest coal producer in the world. Despite long exploitation, the Donbas still has large coal reserves. Proved reserves number 34.1 billion tons, about a quarter of which is anthracite, while probable reserves total another 63.5 billion tons, with 76.2 billion tons possible. However, nearly 330 coal-bearing seams are thinner than one meter, and only 40 seams are suitable for commercial exploitation today. Because most of the thicker seams have been worked out, mining is now deep. The average mining depth is 350–400 m, but bituminous and anthracite coals are mined as deep as 1,800 m. At present, the Donbas coal mines are among the most dangerous in the world, taking the lives of an average 300 miners per annum. Between 1996 and 2002, an average of 304 Donbas miners died in industrial accidents every year.

There are 79 iron ore deposits in Ukraine. The largest are located in Kryvyi Rih (Kryvbas), Kremenchuk, Bilozerske, and Kerch in the **Crimea**. In 2003, Ukraine produced 63 million tons of iron ore and remains one of the top producers in the world. Most iron ore is consumed locally by ferrous **metallurgy** industries.

Manganese ore deposits (of which Ukraine has the world's second-largest reserves) are located in Nykopil and Tokmak in the Trans-Dnipro manganese ore basin. The production of manganese declined from 7.1 million tons in 1985 to 2.5 million tons in 2003. Most manganese ore is consumed by the metallurgical industry and used for steel production. Major deposits of titanium ores are located in the Zhytomyr and Dnipropetrovsk regions. In 2002, Ukraine produced 740,000 tons of ilmenite and rutile titanium ores, making it the world's third-largest producer. *See also* ECONOMY; MANUFACTURING.

MINORITIES. The primary autochthonous **population** of Ukraine is made up of Ukrainians (77.8 percent in 2001), as well as descendants of Russians, Belarusians, and other immigrants who settled long ago on the territory of what is now Ukraine. Today, more than 130 ethnic groups are represented among Ukraine's minorities. According to the census of 2001, ethnic minorities constituted 10.9 million people (22.2 percent of Ukraine's population). **Slavs** account for nearly 9 million of this total.

Russians are the second-largest ethnic group in Ukraine (8.3 million, 17.3 percent of the population). The largest Russian settlements were established between the 15th and 17th centuries in **Sloboda Ukraine**, and later in the **New Russia gubernia**, **Bessarabia**, and **Bukovyna**. The early 20th century saw the mass immigration of Russian workers to large industrial centers in the Dnipro region and the **Donets Basin**. Most Russians in Ukraine live in cities (88 percent), mainly in the large industrial centers of southern and eastern Ukraine. They constitute the majority of the population in the **Crimea** (58.3 percent). Russians in Ukraine have ample cultural facilities (13 state theaters, radio and television broadcasts, the training of Russian language and literature specialists at 11 universities and 20 pedagogical institutes, 7 civic associations, etc.). The Russian minority, like all others, is officially protected against discrimination.

The oldest settlements of Belarusians in Ukraine are located on the border of Ukrainian-Belarusian ethnic territory (Rokytne raion, Rivne oblast). Belarusians settled in the eastern regions of Ukrainian **Polisia** and Sloboda Ukraine after the first partition of Poland. In the 19th century, Belarusians established military settlements in the New Russia gubernia, and Belarusian peasants settled in southern Ukraine. Today, there are 275,800 Belarusians in Ukraine, mainly in the urban centers of the Donets Basin, the southern oblasts, and the Crimea. Very few remain in the territory bordering Belarus. Most arrived as workers after **World War II**.

There are 204,600 Bulgarians in Ukraine. They began to establish colonies in southern Ukraine at the turn of the 19th century, especially during the Russo-Turkish War, when Bulgarians fled Ottoman persecution. They founded large settlements in southern Bessarabia, the **Odesa** region, the Crimea, Kherson, and Mykolaiv. Today, most Bulgarians in Ukraine live in the western regions of Odesa oblast and on the Azov coast of Zaporizhia oblast. More than half of them live in urban areas (Bolhrad and Izmail). Bulgarians in Ukraine are working to revive their national and cultural life. Their language is taught at schools in Odesa oblast, as well as in Zaporizhia and Mykolaiv oblasts. Bulgarian language and literature are studied at Odesa University, and a Bulgarian-Ukrainian gymnasium operates in Bolhrad. Bulgarian teachers are trained at the Izmail Pedagogical Institute and **Lviv** University.

Poles, who now number 144,100, are one of the oldest ethnic minorities in the country, having settled primarily on the **Right Bank** and in eastern **Galicia**. Polish colonization followed the annexation of the Principality of **Galicia-Volhynia** in the 14th century and extended into **Left-Bank Ukraine** from the turn of the 17th century until the early 20th century. During the interwar period (1918–39), the greatest number of Poles lived in Lviv and its vicinity. In 1939–41, several hundred thousand Poles were deported by the Soviet regime from western Ukraine to the eastern regions of Ukraine, Siberia, and Kazakhstan. Today, most Poles in Ukraine live in ethnically mixed settlements in Zhytomyr, Khmelnytskyi, and Lviv oblasts. They have established cultural and educational societies, Polish schools, and Polish-language newspapers and radio programs. Roman Catholic religious life is also being revived. Other smaller groups of Slavs living in Ukraine include Czechs, Slovaks, Serbs, and Croats.

Of the non-Slavic minorities, the most numerous today are the **Moldavians**, numbering 258,600 (0.5 percent of the population). (*See also* entries on JEWS and TATARS.) The largest migration of Moldavian serfs into Ukraine took place in the 16th and 17th centuries, when they fled the oppression of Moldavian *hospodars* and Ottoman invaders. Most Moldavians in Ukraine today live in Odesa, Chernivtsi, and Mykolaiv oblasts, almost a third of them in cities. Odesa oblast is home to Moldavian-language schools, and teachers of Moldavian are trained at several Ukrainian universities. Romanians in Ukraine are settled in the southwestern sections of Chernivtsi and Transcarpathia oblasts. The oldest Romanian villages in Ukraine were established in the 13th century in the present-day Tiachiv and Rakhiv raions of **Transcarpathia** oblast and in parts of southern Bukovyna. Today, Ukraine's Romanian population of

151,000 lives mainly in villages. Romanian interests are represented by cultural and educational societies. There are Romanian-language preschools, schools, teacher-training courses, and radio and television facilities in Chernivtsi, Transcarpathia, and Odesa oblasts.

Almost all of the 156,600 Hungarians in Ukraine live in Transcarpathia oblast (97 percent). In the sixth and seventh centuries, Hungarians lived in the Azov steppes. They settled Transcarpathia in the 11th century, displacing the local Slavic inhabitants. The size of Ukraine's Hungarian population varied according to socioeconomic conditions. In recent years, Hungarians have begun migrating from Ukraine to Hungary. A Hungarian consulate opened in Uzhhorod in 1993. The largest civic association of Hungarians in Ukraine is the Society of Hungarian Culture of Transcarpathia. The region has Magyar-language radio and television and a system of Magyar-language education, and the department of Magyar language and literature at Uzhhorod University prepares teachers for the school system.

The first Armenian colonies appeared in the Crimea in the 10th and 11th centuries, after Armenia was invaded by Arabs and Turks. In the 11th and 12th centuries, Armenian colonies were established in western Ukraine, the Right Bank, and the Crimea; the largest communities were located in Lviv, Kamianets-Podilskyi, Volodymyr, Lutsk, Stanyslaviv, and Brody. Armenians exercised self-government and had their own courts and church, as well as trading rights. However, most Armenian colonies disintegrated in the 19th century. Today there are nearly 100,000 Armenians in Ukraine, living primarily in urban centers such as Donetsk, **Kharkiv**, Dnipropetrovsk, and Odesa. Armenians have their own national and cultural organizations throughout Ukraine (*see* DASHKEVYCH, YAROSLAV).

Greeks founded urban settlements in southern Ukraine between the seventh and fifth centuries B.C. (*see* BLACK SEA COLONIES). Later there were Greek communities in Nizhyn, **Kyiv**, and other towns. After the establishment of the Crimean Khanate, Greeks founded settlements in the Azov region. Today there are 91,500 Greeks in Ukraine, 85 percent of whom live in Donetsk oblast. In recent years, Greeks have begun emigrating to their ethnic homeland.

Roma, members of the Indo-Iranian language family, live alongside Ukrainians in the southern and western oblasts, numbering 47,600. Most Roma in Ukraine originate from Bessarabia, Romania, and the Balkans. Transcarpathia oblast accounts for 29.4 percent of Roma in Ukraine. They are primarily urban dwellers, while rural residents live mainly in Odesa and Mykolaiv oblasts. Other sizeable minorities in Ukraine include Azeris (45,200), Georgians (34,200), Germans (33,300), and Gagauzy (31,900). The remaining minorities add up to 177,000 people.

MNOHOHRISHNY, DEMIAN (ca. 1630–after 1701). **Hetman** of **Left-Bank Ukraine** (1669–72). A participant in the **Khmelnytsky Uprising** (1648–57), Mnohohrishny, born to a **peasant** family near Konotop, was first mentioned in the Zboriv register (ca. 1649) as a **Cossack** aide-de-camp. He served as colonel of Chernihiv in the late 1650s and early 1660s. Opposed to the **Truce of Andrusovo**, he participated in the anti-Muscovite rebellion of 1668 and entered the service of Hetman **Petro Doroshenko**. Forced to retreat to the **Right Bank**, Doroshenko appointed Mnohohrishny acting hetman of Left-Bank Ukraine (1668). In 1669, Mnohohrishny signed the Hlukhiv Articles with Muscovy, which somewhat limited Muscovite control over the **Hetmanate**. He was proclaimed hetman of Left-Bank Ukraine at a **Cossack council** in Hlukhiv (9 [19] March 1669). He successfully pressed for the inclusion of **Kyiv** and its environs in Left-Bank Ukraine despite the provisions of the Truce of Andrusovo. Supported by mercenary regiments, Mnohohrishny strove to strengthen the hetman's powers and gradually limited the influence of the **Cossack officers**, whom he also alienated with his blatant nepotism. He conducted secret negotiations with Doroshenko concerning a possible Ottoman protectorate over Left-Bank Ukraine, a policy that dissatisfied some Cossack officers and the Muscovite government. On the night of 12 (22) March 1672, Cossack officers, supported by the commander of the Muscovite garrison, arrested Mnohohrishny in Baturyn. Accused of treason, he was tortured in Moscow and sentenced to exile for life. He was incarcerated at the Irkutsk prison. In 1682, Mnohohrishny was released and transferred to military service in Selenginsk. In 1696, he entered a monastery, where he died. He was buried at the Church of the Savior in Selenginsk.

MODERNISM. An artistic current that developed in the late 19th century, mainly as a challenge to the prevailing **realism**. Modernism rejected the traditional representation of reality by stressing the subjective world of the senses and emotions. The term has come to encompass various tendencies toward abstraction, including symbolism, impressionism, expressionism, cubism, constructivism, futurism, and surrealism. All these currents have influenced the development of the arts in Ukraine.

Ukrainian poets came under the influence of French and Russian symbolists in the last decade of the 19th century. They did not form a unified movement but committed themselves to the revival of poetry by rejecting utilitarian **literature**. The first major proponent of symbolism was Mykola Vorony, with his almanac *Z-nad khmar i dolyn* (From Above the Clouds and Valleys, 1903), which promoted the notion of "pure art" in poetry. There were self-conscious symbolist overtones in the works of the poets who formed **Moloda Muza** in **Lviv** in 1906. The poetry of Vasyl Pachovsky and Petro Karmansky and the prose of Mykhailo Yatskiv best reflect the group's fascination with symbolist and decadent trends. After the **Ukrainian Revolution**, symbolist tendencies were revived in **Kyiv** by an artistic group that published the journal *Muzahet* (Musagète). Members of Muzahet included **Pavlo Tychyna**, Dmytro Zahul, Oleksa Slisarenko, Yakiv Savchenko, and Klym Polishchuk.

Impressionism had a strong influence on Ukrainian **painting**. The first Ukrainian impressionists were graduates of the Cracow Academy of Fine Arts at the end of the 19th century. They included **Oleksa Novakivsky**, who later embraced symbolic expressionism, and **Ivan Trush**, who worked with muted colors and adopted impressionism only in part. Other leading exponents of impressionism included Oleksander Murashko, Vasyl and Fedir Krychevsky, and Petro Kholodny, Sr. **Mykhailo Parashchuk** was a major impressionist sculptor.

Impressionism also influenced Ukrainian **music** and literature. Vasyl Barvinsky was a typical representative of the trend in music, which strove to convey intimate and subtle moods. Literature written in this vein sought to capture impressions of reality and often focused on registering the sensations of its characters rather than attempting to interpret them. Outstanding impressionist writers included **Mykhailo Kotsiubynsky**, **Vasyl Stefanyk**, Hryhorii Kosynka, and the poet Oleksander Oles. Literary impressionism was often associated with symbolism and neoromanticism.

Ukrainian expressionism, unlike the subjective, emotional, and strident movement in Germany and Austria, was moderate. Ukrainian expressionist artists included the painters Oleksa Novakivsky, Anatol Petrytsky, Oleksii Hryshchenko, Mykola Butovych, and Myroslav Radysh, and, to some extent, the sculptor **Alexander Archipenko**.

In literature, the expressionist movement, which favored imagery, language, and sound over content, was fairly short-lived. The most important expressionist writer was **Mykola Khvyliovy**, who combined expressionism with neoromanticism. The poets Mykola Bazhan, **Todos Osmachka**, and Valeriian Polishchuk were influenced by expressionism, as was the playwright **Mykola Kulish**.

The cubist movement had little influence on the arts in Ukraine but was successfully combined with the functionalism of the constructivists. Favoring simple geometric forms, constructivism in Ukraine had its greatest impact in **architecture**. From the early 1920s, factorylike buildings of concrete, glass, and metal with minimal decoration were built throughout the country. The style survived well into the 1960s, replacing the pseudoclassicism of the Stalin era after **World War II**. Government buildings, "palaces of culture," hotels, theaters, and apartment complexes were designed in the constructivist style. In painting, cubist-inspired constructivists employed combinations of lines, objects, and planes in their abstract compositions. The most prominent were Archipenko, **Kazimir Malevich**, and Alexandra Exter, as well as the sculptor and **filmmaker Ivan Kavaleridze**.

Constructivism was the dominant style of Ukrainian stage design throughout the 1920s and early 1930s. Its main advocate was Vadym Meller, whose work at the **Berezil Theater** was a synthesis of architecture, painting, and sculpture. Several theaters in Kyiv, **Kharkiv**, and Odesa employed constructivist designers. In film, a world masterpiece of constructivist cinema, Dziga Vertov's *The Man with a Movie Camera*, was made in Ukraine in 1929.

Ukrainian futurism reached its height with a group of artists and writers associated with the Kharkiv journal *Nova generatsiia* (New Generation, 1927–30). They proclaimed the death of traditional peasant and bourgeois aesthetic sensibilities, exalting technology, industry, and cosmopolitan themes. **Mykhail Semenko** was the driving force behind the movement and its celebrated poet. The futurist destruction of form in the constructivist rather than anarchist tradition also appealed to the poets Geo Shkurupii and Mykola Bazhan, theoreticians Oleksii Poltoratsky and Leonid Skrypnyk, and artists Oleksander Bohomazov and Anatol Petrytsky.

Surrealism, which strove to combine the world of dreams and fantasy with realism, had little impact on the Ukrainian arts and was limited to Artes, a left-leaning group in Lviv during the 1920s. The main proponent of this style in painting was Roman Selsky. In the 1960s and 1970s, surrealist elements were reintroduced in the works of nonconformist graphic artists.

With the imposition of socialist realism in the 1930s, modernist trends in the **Ukrainian SSR** were condemned as "formalist" and decadent. Modernist artists fell victim to political persecution. Many perished in labor camps or were executed, while others conformed to the official cultural line.

MOHYLA, PETRO (31 December 1596 [10 January 1597]–1 [11] January 1647). Outstanding church leader and cultural figure of the 17th century; Orthodox metropolitan of **Kyiv**. He was the son of

Simeon Movilă, *hospodar* of Wallachia (1600–1) and **Moldavia** (1606–7). After the murder of his father, Mohyla fled to his magnate relatives in **western Ukraine**. According to traditional accounts, he was educated at the **Lviv Dormition Brotherhood** School and at the Jesuit academy in Zamość. He served in the Polish army and fought in the battles of **Cecora** (1620) and **Khotyn** (1621). Under the influence of **Iov Boretsky**, Mohyla became a monk in 1625. In 1627, he was elected archimandrite of the **Kyivan Cave Monastery**. Well connected in Polish official circles and oriented toward Polish and Latin culture, Mohyla was favored by the government to head the **Kyiv metropolitanate** when the **Ukrainian Orthodox Church** was officially reinstated in 1632. He was consecrated as metropolitan in Lviv in 1633 despite opposition from the **Cossacks**, who supported **Isaia Kopynsky**.

Mohyla established a circle of scholars and cultural activists, the so-called Mohyla Atheneum (**Sylvestr Kosiv**, Atanasii Kalnofoisky, Isaia Kozlovsky-Trofymovych, Tarasii Zemka, and others). Under his leadership, they conducted a reform of the church and produced the first Orthodox catechism, ratified by church councils in Kyiv (1640) and Iași (1641) and by the Eastern patriarchs in 1643. Mohyla set strict organizational and dogmatic guidelines for the church and systematized its liturgical practice by issuing new editions of service books, notably the *Sluzhebnyk* (Leiturgiarion, 1639) and *Trebnyk* (Sacramentary, 1646). He also participated in the writing of a major work of polemical literature, the treatise *Lithos, albo kamien* (Lithos, or Stone, 1644). Written in Polish, it was published under the pseudonym Evsebii Pimin.

In reforming Orthodox learning, Mohyla was strongly influenced by the Jesuit schools established in Poland during the Counter-Reformation, taking over much of their curriculum. In 1631, he opened a school at the Cave Monastery that merged with the **Kyiv Epiphany Brotherhood** School in 1632 to form the Kyiv Brotherhood Collegium, later known as the **Kyiv Mohyla Academy**. It became prominent in Eastern Europe during the 17th century. Mohyla sponsored the restoration of **St. Sophia's Cathedral** and the buildings of the Kyivan Cave Monastery; in 1635 he authorized the excavation of the Church of the Tithes, destroyed by the **Golden Horde**. In 1640, Mohyla helped found the first Romanian school of higher learning, the Slavonic-Greek-Latin Academy in Iași, directed by Sofronii Pochasky, a former rector of the Kyiv Brotherhood Collegium. He also established printing presses in Cîmpulung (1635) and Iași (1641). Mohyla died in Kyiv and was buried at the Cave Monastery.

MOLDAVIA. Official name: Republic of Moldova. State in southern Europe located in the basin of the Dnister and Prut Rivers. To the northeast and south it borders Ukraine, and to the west it borders Romania. Its territory encompasses 33,700 sq. km, its population numbers 4,394,000 (1992), and its capital is Chişinău. Moldavia declared its independence from the **USSR** on 27 August 1991.

Bessarabia, which had been part of Moldavia in the early modern period, was occupied by Romanian forces in January 1918 and incorporated into Romania later the same year. That decision was not recognized by the Soviet Union, which supported pro-communist elements there. In 1924, a **peasant** uprising for unification with the **Ukrainian SSR** took place in the vicinity of Tatarbunary and was crushed by Romanian forces. The Soviet leaders developed the idea of promoting Moldavian autonomy within the Ukrainian SSR in order to gain the loyalty of Bessarabian Moldavians, who might then favor integration into the USSR. The leadership of the Ukrainian SSR, especially **Mykola Skrypnyk**, opposed the plan but came under pressure from Moscow to agree to its implementation. The Moldavian Autonomous Socialist Soviet Republic (MASSR), including parts of the Balta, Tulchyn, and **Odesa** regions (area of 8,300 sq. km), was created on 12 October 1924. In 1926, its population totaled 572,000, of whom only 30.1 percent were Moldavians, while Ukrainians comprised 48.5 percent. Other nationalities in the MASSR included Russians and Jews. The republic's capital was Balta and later Tiraspol (from 1929). In 1925, Moldavian-language instruction was introduced in the schools. Forced **collectivization**, dekulakization, and the **famine of 1932–33** affected the MASSR as well.

Before the outbreak of **World War II**, Bessarabia's fate was decided by the Molotov-Ribbentrop Pact (1939). In a secret protocol to the agreement, Germany granted the Soviet Union freedom of action in Bessarabia. On 26 June 1940, the USSR issued an ultimatum to Romania demanding the immediate surrender of Bessarabia and **Bukovyna**. In the absence of support from its German ally, Romania was obliged to capitulate. Soviet armies occupied Bessarabia on 29 June 1940. All political parties and community organizations there were dissolved. On 2 August 1940, the Supreme Soviet of the USSR passed a law creating the Moldavian SSR (MSSR), which incorporated six raions of the former MASSR and six central counties of Bessarabia. Eight raions of the MASSR, Akkerman county, and most of Izmail and Khotyn counties (areas populated by Ukrainians) were incorporated into the Ukrainian SSR.

Soon after the German invasion of the USSR in June 1941, Moldavia was occupied by German and Romanian armies. The

German leadership returned Bessarabia and northern Bukovyna, as well as lands between the Dnister and Southern Buh Rivers, to Romania, which occupied them during the war (*see* TRANSNISTRIA). Between March and August 1944 the Red Army drove its opponents out of Moldavia, and the Soviet regime was restored in the MSSR. **Russification** resumed, and attempts to protect Moldavian culture and historical traditions were suppressed. Other nationalities living in Moldavia (Ukrainians, Jews, Gagauzy, Bulgarians) had little opportunity for sociocultural development.

The Moldavian national movement began to gather strength in the late 1980s, gaining considerable support for closer ties with Romania, especially in the cultural sphere. It demanded that the Latin script replace the Cyrillic alphabet, which was accomplished in 1989. There was strenuous debate about national identity; some viewed the Moldavian people as a separate nation, while others considered them part of the Romanian people. In June 1990, the republic's Supreme Soviet declared the sovereignty of the MSSR.

National minorities were negatively disposed toward the pro-Romanian tendency in the Moldavian national movement. This opposition was especially strong on the left bank of the Dnister, with its largely Russian and Ukrainian population, and in the southern regions of the republic, populated by the Gagauzy. Moscow supported these elements as an opposition to the Moldavian national movement. After the collapse of the attempted coup in Moscow (August 1991), the Supreme Soviet of the MSSR declared the independence of the Republic of Moldova. Left-Bank separatists among the pro-Moscow communist bureaucrats responded by declaring an independent Trans-Dnister Moldavian Republic based in Tiraspol.

The Republic of Moldova received international recognition, established close ties with Romania, and instituted diplomatic relations with Ukraine (1992). The Trans-Dnister Republic was not recognized by any state. The Moldovan leadership in Chişinău used force in an attempt to destroy the separatist movement, provoking resistance from Trans-Dnister residents, who were supported by the 14th Russian Army. Armed conflict continued through 1992 but was halted by international mediation, although a separatist regime continues to exist. The Gagauzy, who have demanded autonomy and even independence, are another source of tension. In 1994, an agreement granting Gagauz autonomy was reached. The Ukrainian population of Moldova consists of some 600,000 people (13.8 percent of the republic's total population in 1989).

MOLODA MUZA/YOUNG MUSE. Literary group of western Ukrainian writers and artists founded in 1906, based on the Moloda

Muza publishing house (1906–9) and the journal *Svit* (World) in **Lviv**. It was not a formal organization but an association of likeminded individuals whose motto was "Art for art's sake" and who oriented themselves on West European literature. Its work was characterized by a cult of pure art, individualism, pessimism, mysticism, and attention to form. The best-known members of Moloda Muza were Stepan Charnetsky, Petro Karmansky, Bohdan Lepky, Ostap Lutsky, Vasyl Pachovsky, and Sydir Tverdokhlib, the prose writers Volodymyr Birchak, Mykhailo Yatskiv, and Osyp Turiansky, the composer **Stanislav Liudkevych**, and the sculptor **Mykhailo Parashchuk**. Vasyl Shchurat and the literary critics Mykhailo Rudnytsky and Mykola Yevshan were also close to the group. Moloda Muza was one of the first attempts to modernize Ukrainian **literature**. It provoked heated discussion at the time and was later adamantly rejected by official Soviet criticism.

MOLODA UKRAÏNA/YOUNG UKRAINE. Alliance of student groups in **Galicia** and **Bukovyna** (1899–1903). Its members included university and senior high-school students who met to exchange ideas and discuss social and political problems. The organization's leading members were Stepan Baran, Mykhailo Halushchynsky, Semen Horuk, Yevhen Kosevych, Antin Krushelnytsky, Teofil Melen, **Volodymyr Starosolsky**, and **Lonhyn Tsehelsky**. The alliance established close ties with students in **Kharkiv**, **Kyiv**, and **Poltava**. Subsequently, members of Moloda Ukraïna became leading figures in Galician and Bukovynian political parties.

The organization's journal, *Moloda Ukraïna*, was the first Ukrainian student weekly, published from January 1900 to March 1903 (with interruptions) in **Lviv** (33 issues in all). *Moloda Ukraïna* was the unofficial organ of the Academic **Hromada** (Community). It propagated Ukrainian independence, opposed Polonization, and advocated the establishment of Ukrainian institutions of higher **education**. Among the contributors were Stepan Charnetsky, Vasyl Shchurat, **Lesia Ukrainka**, and Mykhailo Yatskiv. *Moloda Ukraïna* ceased publication owing to financial difficulties. It was revived briefly as a monthly in Lviv (1905) under the editorship of Vasyl Paneiko and produced four issues.

Moloda Ukraïna was also the name of the first Ukrainian children's magazine in **eastern Ukraine**, published as a monthly supplement to the periodical *Ridnyi krai* (Native Land). It was published in Kyiv (1906, 1908–12) and Hadiach (1912) by Olena Pchilka; 64 issues appeared. The periodical printed works by Khrystia Alchevska, Stepan Rudansky, **Maksym Rylsky**, Ukrainka, and Stepan Vasylchenko, as well as many translations of foreign literature for children.

MOROZ, OLEKSANDR (b. 29 February 1944). Politician, leader of the Socialist Party of Ukraine. Moroz was born in the village of Buda, **Kyiv** oblast, into the family of a carpenter. In 1965, he graduated from the Ukrainian Agricultural Academy as a mechanical engineer. He obtained a political science diploma from the Advanced Party School, **Communist Party of Ukraine** (CPU), in 1985.

Moroz began his career in 1965 as an **agricultural** engineer in Zhytomyr oblast. In 1976, he became senior engineer of the Kyiv Oblast Agricultural Machinery Association. Moroz embarked on a career in the CPU in the same year, serving in various agriculture-related posts in the Kyiv Oblast Committee. In the 1980s, he worked in the Kyiv oblast CPU trade-union council and served as first secretary of the Kyiv Party Committee of Oblast Organizations and Institutions. In 1990, Moroz was elected to the **Verkhovna Rada** (VR), where he headed the communist majority until the unsuccessful putsch of August 1991 in Moscow, after which the Communist Party was outlawed. Moroz and a number of soft-line ex-communists circumvented the ban by founding the Socialist Party of Ukraine (October 1991), of which Moroz was elected president. In May 1994, he was elected speaker of the VR (until 1998), where he actively opposed President **Leonid Kuchma's** policy of market-oriented reform and attempts to strengthen presidential control over parliament. (Moroz was a presidential candidate in the 1994 elections, finishing third, with 13 percent of the vote.) Moroz was reelected to the VR in 1998 and again stood for president in 1999, losing in the first round of voting.

On 28 November 2000, Moroz disclosed tape recordings purporting to show that President Kuchma and two of his top aides had been involved in the murder of the investigative journalist **Heorhii Gongadze**. The president denounced the tapes and launched an investigation of Moroz's alleged "insults and slander" against the presidency. Moroz then spearheaded the "Ukraine without Kuchma" movement, which launched a turbulent but ultimately unsuccessful campaign for impeachment. After the 2002 elections to the VR, Moroz formed the parliamentary opposition to the presidential bloc together with the right-of-center leaders **Viktor Yushchenko** and **Yuliia Tymoshenko**. Their major goals were to block Leonid Kuchma from running for a third term and to support Yushchenko in his presidential bid. Prior to the 2004 elections, however, Moroz left the ad hoc coalition and entered the presidential race as a representative of his party.

MOROZ, VALENTYN (b. 15 April 1936). Political **dissident**. Born into a **peasant** family in the village of Kholoniv, **Volhynia**, Moroz graduated from **Lviv** University in 1958 with a degree in history. He taught in the Lutsk and Ivano-Frankivsk pedagogical institutes (1964–65). Moroz was arrested in September 1965 for reading and disseminating underground literature, charged with "anti-Soviet agitation and propaganda," and sentenced to five years' imprisonment, which he served in Vladimir Prison and strict-regime labor camps in Mordovia. While in prison, and during a brief period of freedom in 1970, Moroz wrote a number of striking essays about the persecution of political dissidents and the crimes of Soviet officialdom; they were widely disseminated in the underground and published abroad in two English-language collections: *Boomerang* and *Report from the Beria Reserve* (both 1974). A leitmotif of Moroz's essays was obsessive dedication (*oderzhymist'*) to the Ukrainian cause and uncompromising struggle against the Soviet regime—characteristics that identified him with the ideological tradition of the **Organization of Ukrainian Nationalists**. In one of his essays, Moroz severely criticized his fellow dissident **Ivan Dziuba** for yielding to official pressure. Released in September 1969, Moroz was rearrested nine months later and sentenced to nine years' imprisonment and five years' exile. In July 1974, while incarcerated in Vladimir Prison, he began a five-month hunger strike to protest his mistreatment. This attracted international attention and prompted agitation for his release by Ukrainians in the **diaspora**. Transferred to Mordovia in 1976, Moroz renounced his Soviet citizenship. As a result of Soviet-American negotiations, Moroz and four other dissidents were flown to the United States on 27 April 1979 in exchange for two Soviet spies.

Moroz's relations with much of the Ukrainian community in the West quickly deteriorated. After a term at the **Harvard Ukrainian Research Institute** (1979–80), he published a journal, *Anabasis* (1980–91), and ran a weekly radio program in Toronto (1986–91). He also attempted to establish a youth organization known as the Knights of Sviatoslav (an allusion to **Sviatoslav Ihorevych**). He obtained a doctorate in history from the **Ukrainian Free University** in 1982. Following Ukraine's declaration of independence, Moroz returned to Lviv and was appointed professor in the Ukrainian studies department of the State Institute of Physical Culture in 1993.

MOROZOV, KOSTIANTYN (b. 3 June 1944). First defense minister of independent Ukraine. He was born in the town of Brianka, Luhansk oblast. In 1967, he graduated from the **Kharkiv** Military Aviation College and served as a pilot, commanding a fighter detachment of the Northern Group. In 1975, he graduated from the

Military Aviation Academy and became a pilot instructor. Morozov quickly rose to the rank of air base commander in the Turkestan military district. In 1981–84, he served as lieutenant commander and then commander of an air force division of the Southern Group. After two years at the General Staff Military Academy (1984–86), Morozov became chief of staff and lieutenant commander of the 46th air army in Smolensk. In 1990, he was appointed commander of the 17th air army in **Kyiv**.

Morozov became defense minister of Ukraine on 3 September 1991. He managed a large-scale reduction of Ukraine's **armed forces**, taking control of Soviet conventional and **nuclear weapons** on Ukrainian soil. After two years in office, he resigned in the wake of harsh criticism of President **Leonid Kravchuk** concerning the division of the **Black Sea Fleet**. From October 1993, Morozov was a reserve officer. At the same time, he was a senior research fellow at the Kennedy School of Government and the **Harvard Ukrainian Research Institute**, which subsequently published his memoirs (*Above and Beyond: From Soviet General to Ukrainian State Builder*, 2000). From 1994 to 1996, Morozov was a consultant to the Committee on Defense and State Security of the **Verkhovna Rada**. He entered the political arena in 1995, coordinating the Ukraine Democratic Association. From 1996 to 1998, he served at the embassy of Ukraine in Brussels as minister-counsellor for relations with the North Atlantic Treaty Organization, and then as deputy head of the Ukrainian mission to NATO (1998–2000). In April 2000, Morozov was appointed ambassador to Iran. He retired on 15 June 2001 and became president of the Military Institute at the Interregional Management Academy in Kyiv.

MOSCOW ARTICLES. Agreement signed in Moscow by Hetman **Ivan Briukhovetsky** and representatives of the Muscovite government (11 [21] or 12 [22] October 1665) that significantly restricted the political rights of the **Hetmanate**. The articles placed Ukrainian towns and lands under the direct control of the tsar, and the Hetmanate was forbidden to enter into diplomatic relations with foreign states. The election of the **hetman** was to be followed by his official confirmation in Moscow. In addition to the primary regimental towns, Muscovite garrisons were now stationed in **Poltava**, Kremenchuk, Novhorod-Siverskyi, Kaniv, and even the **Cossack** headquarters at Zaporizhia (the Kodak fortress). Tax collection was carried out by Muscovite voevodas, and all the proceeds were to be deposited in the tsar's treasury. The **Ukrainian Orthodox Church** came under the jurisdiction of the Moscow patriarchate. Only the Cossack estate preserved its autonomy, and royal charters granting **Magdeburg law** to Ukrainian towns were restored (they had been confiscated by the tsar). The privileges of the **Cossack officers** were guaranteed, as Briukhovetsky, abandoning his earlier populist rhetoric, had decided to base his rule on the support of the tsar and the Cossack elite. The Moscow Articles provoked great dissatisfaction in Ukrainian society, leading to an anti-Muscovite rebellion that culminated in the murder of Briukhovetsky.

MURAVIEV-APOSTOL FAMILY. Noble family of statesmen and Decembrists. Ivan Muraviev-Apostol (1770–12 [24] March 1851), a grandson (on his mother's side) of Hetman **Danylo Apostol**, served in the Collegium of Foreign Affairs (from 1784) and as Russian ambassador in Hamburg, Copenhagen, and Madrid (1796–1805). He engaged in scholarship and literature, translated works by foreign authors, and wrote *A Journey Through Taurida in 1820* (1823), one of the first works on the history and geography of the **Crimea**. In 1801, he received permission to use the Muraviev-Apostol surname and inherited the Apostol estates in the Myrhorod region. He was the father of the Decembrists Ippolit, Matvei, and Sergei Muraviev-Apostol. Ippolit Muraviev-Apostol (1806–3 [15] January 1826) was born in St. Petersburg. On 13 (25) December 1825, he was sent to Ukraine by the Northern Society of Decembrists to inform the Southern Society of the outbreak of the St. Petersburg rebellion and reach agreement on joint action. Upon learning of the rebellion's defeat, he and his brothers participated in the uprising of the Chernihiv Regiment. On 3 (15) January 1826, he was wounded in battle against a punitive squadron near Kovalivka (now in **Kyiv** oblast) and shot himself rather than fall into enemy hands. His brothers, Matvei and Sergei Muraviev-Apostol, were educated at private schools in Hamburg and Paris and subsequently graduated from the St. Petersburg Institute of Railway Engineers. They participated in the War of 1812 and later were the founders of the Union of Salvation (1816), as well as members of the Union of Welfare (1818) and the Southern Society of Decembrists (1821). Matvei (25 April [6 May] 1793–21 February [5 March] 1886) conducted negotiations on the merger of the Southern and Northern Societies (May 1823–August 1824). He was arrested in January 1826 and sentenced to death (later commuted to 15 years' hard labor). After the amnesty of 1856, he settled in Moscow gubernia. He dictated his memoirs three years before his death. Together with Mikhail Bestuzhev-Riumin, Sergei Muraviev-Apostol (b. 28 September [9 October] 1776) assumed the leadership of the Vasylkiv executive of the Southern Society (1823) and wrote the revolutionary *Orthodox Catechism* (the popular version of the Southern Society's program), which was read to soldiers. He established ties between the Southern Society and the Polish Patriotic Society, and in September 1825 he facilitated the merger of the Society of United Slavs with the Southern Society. He participated in Decembrist congresses and councils in Kyiv, Tulchyn, and Kamianka (1822–25), advocating the overthrow of the autocratic regime through military revolution and the establishment of a republican order in the Russian Empire. On 29 December 1825 (10 January 1826), Lt.-Col. Sergei Muraviev-Apostol led the Chernihiv Regiment uprising. Badly wounded, he was arrested on 3 (15) January 1826 after a battle near Kovalivka and hanged on 13 (25) July 1826 at the SS. Peter and Paul Fortress.

MUSIC. During the Middle Ages, three kinds of music developed in **Kyivan Rus'**: the music of the princely courts, performed by resident musicians or by *skomorokhy* (wandering musicians and actors); church music, which initially came from Byzantium and Bulgaria; and folk songs (*see* FOLK MUSIC AND DANCE). In the late 11th century, the **Kyivan Cave Monastery** became the center of religious music in Rus'. Characterized by a cappella singing and monophony, its melodies were recorded in two types of nonlinear notation, *znamenna* and *kondakarna*.

Between the 14th and 17th centuries, church **brotherhoods** played an important role in the development of Ukrainian music, as brotherhood schools emphasized the study of church music and music theory. Polyphonic singing was introduced into church services, leading to the development of *kyïvs'ke znam'ia* notation. In 1675, the composer and musicologist Mykola Dyletsky wrote a "musical grammar," a comprehensive treatise on polyphonic music that remained a basic theoretical text in Eastern Europe through the 18th century. A favorite musical form of the time was the polyphonic concert for a cappella choir.

Western influences brought a new level of sophistication to Ukrainian music in the 18th century, but Ukrainian musical talent was increasingly absorbed into Russian musical development, especially after the **Rozumovsky** family established itself at the St. Petersburg court. Ukraine's primary centers of musical education were the **Kyiv Mohyla Academy** and the Hlukhiv Singing School. The century saw the emergence of three remarkable composers, **Maksym Berezovsky**, **Dmytro Bortniansky**, and **Artem Vedel**, best known for their religious choral music. Berezovsky and Bortniansky studied and worked in Italy, where they wrote the first known operatic and chamber music by Ukrainian composers.

By the 19th century, Ukrainian musicians were still being recruited to work in Russia, but with the exception of the Italian opera, they had lost their dominant position. In Ukraine itself, musical life was restricted to traveling **theater** companies performing comic operas, notably **Semen Hulak-Artemovsky's** *Zaporozhian Cossack beyond the Danube*. The development of orchestral music was also retarded by the Orthodox Church's ban on instrumental music.

In the late 19th century, considerable efforts were made to develop a Ukrainian national school comparable to those established by the Poles, Czechs, and Russians. The key figure in this movement was **Mykola Lysenko**, who collected and studied Ukrainian folk songs in order to establish their cultural specificity. Orchestral music still lagged behind, and the development of Ukrainian opera was thwarted by the restrictions of the **Ems Ukase**, which forbade public performances in Ukrainian. The development of the Ukrainian national school reached a high point in the years 1917–22 with the establishment of the Ukrainian Republican Capella in Kyiv and through the work of the composers **Mykola Leontovych**, Kyrylo Stetsenko, and Yakiv Stepovy.

The 1920s saw important advances in Ukrainian music. The **Galician** composers Vasyl Barvinsky and **Stanislav Liudkevych** were the first to produce significant orchestral works. Lev Revutsky and Borys Liatoshynsky (author of the first Ukrainian music drama) developed into Ukraine's first distinguished symphonists under the tutelage of Reinhold Glière in Kyiv, and Viktor Kosenko wrote exceptional chamber music. The establishment of the Soviet regime proved a mixed blessing for Ukrainian music. State support strengthened the music **education** system, financed the publication of music journals, and provided steady employment for musicians, composers, and music scholars. However, the imposition of socialist **realism** as the sole officially sanctioned artistic style and an atmosphere of ideological conformity frequently resulted in the production of mediocre works. The state commissioned music in great quantity, notably operas, from composers such as Kostiantyn Dankevych, Anatol Kos-Anatolsky, Vitalii Kyreiko, Yulii Meitus, Heorhii Maiboroda, and Mykhailo Verykivsky.

The 1960s saw the emergence of a new generation of composers known as the "Kyiv Avant-Garde": Leonid Hrabovsky, **Valentyn Sylvestrov**, Volodymyr Zahortsev, and Volodymyr Huba. Other younger composers of note included Myroslav Skoryk, Lesia Dychko, Yevhen Stankovych, and Ivan Karabyts, who fused elements of folk music with contemporary techniques. Although ideological pressures eased during this period, the work of those artists was still frowned upon by the Union of Composers, and, as under Stalin, much of it was subject to revision or banned from public performance.

Today, the development of Ukrainian music is hindered mainly by economic difficulties. Notable composers who have emerged recently include Viktor Stepurko, Yurii Laniuk, and Hanna Havrylets.

Music is taught in Ukraine mainly through a state-run network of 1,201 children's music schools, 28 cultural educational high schools, and 33 music high schools, including four elite schools. Postsecondary music institutions include the Kyiv, **Odesa**, and **Lviv** conservatories, the **Kharkiv** Institute of Arts, and the Donetsk Music Pedagogical Institute. Music departments also exist at a number of pedagogical institutes.

Each of Ukraine's 25 oblast centers has a concert hall with resident instrumental and vocal ensembles, as does the state radio and television company. The largest symphony orchestras are based in Kyiv, Kharkiv, Dnipropetrovsk, Odesa, Donetsk, Zaporizhia, Lviv, Luhansk, and Yalta. Ukraine's six major opera houses, each with its own ballet company, are located in Kyiv, Kharkiv, Dnipropetrovsk, Odesa, Donetsk, and Lviv. There are operetta theaters in Kyiv, Kharkiv, and Odesa, and Kyiv is home to an opera and ballet theater for juvenile audiences. An additional 22 cities have theaters that perform both musical and dramatic works. Ukraine's distinguished choral tradition is reflected in its large number of choirs. *See also* KOBZARS.

N

NARBUT, HEORHII (YURII) (25 February [9 March] 1886–23 May 1920). Graphic artist. He was born on the Narbutivka estate near Hlukhiv (now in Sumy oblast) and received his initial art education independently. He continued his studies in St. Petersburg and Munich. In St. Petersburg, Narbut became a member of the World of Art association. In 1910–12, he illustrated the stories of Hans Christian Andersen, the fables of Ivan Krylov, and folk tales. Being well acquainted with early Ukrainian art and heraldry, Narbut drew countless **coats of arms** and illustrated and designed books on Ukrainian heraldry (by Vladislav Lukomsky and Vadym Modzalevsky, 1914), the coats of arms of Ukrainian **hetmans** (1915), the ancient architecture of **Galicia** (by Georgii Lukomsky, 1905), the old villas of **Kharkiv** gubernia (1917), and others. Narbut traveled to Hlukhiv every summer to study monuments of Ukrainian antiquity. He signed his own coat of arms "*Mazepynets* [i.e., follower of **Ivan Mazepa**], Chernihiv regiment, Hlukhiv company, son of **Cossack** officers, designer of coats of arms and emblems" (1912). In March 1917, Narbut moved to **Kyiv**, where he became a professor of graphic art and rector of the newly established **Ukrainian State Academy of Arts**. During this period, Narbut designed a series of banknotes, postage stamps, and charters for the **Ukrainian People's Republic**. Later he contributed to the journals *Nashe mynule* (Our Past), *Zori* (Stars), *Solntse truda* (Sun of Labor), *Mystetstvo* (Art), and others. Narbut's students and disciples included Pavlo Kovzhun, Marko Kyrnarsky, Robert Lisovsky, Les Lozovsky, and Antin Sereda. *See also* DESIGN, GRAPHIC.

NATIONAL DEMOCRATIC PARTY/NATSIONAL'NO-DEMOKRATYCHNA PARTIIA (NDP). Leading Ukrainian political party in **Galicia** in the early 20th century. It was established in **Lviv** on 26 December 1899 as the result of a merger between the right wing of the **Ukrainian Radical Party** (Viacheslav Budzynovsky, **Ivan Franko**, Yevhen Levytsky, Volodymyr Okhrymovych) and most of the Galician **populists** (**Mykhailo Hrushevsky**, **Kost Levytsky**, Teofil Okunevsky, Yevhen Olesnytsky, Iuliian Romanchuk). The party sought to consolidate Ukrainian forces in Galicia and posited the creation of a sovereign Ukrainian state as its ultimate goal. More immediately, it advocated autonomy for the Ukrainian lands of Austria-Hungary, the development of Ukrainian **education**, and the establishment of a Ukrainian university. Because its activists were influential in cultural, educational, and economic institutions, the NDP soon emerged as the dominant Ukrainian political party in Galicia. It was headed by Romanchuk (1899–1907) and Levytsky, and its publication was the weekly *Svoboda* (Liberty, 1897–1939); the newspapers *Dilo* and *Bukovyna* also supported the NDP platform.

The NDP won 17 of the 27 seats taken by Ukrainian deputies to the Austrian Reichstag in the election of 1907 (the first conducted on the basis of universal male suffrage). It changed its name to the Ukrainian National Democratic Party in 1914 and played a leading role in the establishment of the **Western Ukrainian People's Republic** in 1918. In the following year, it changed its name to the Ukrainian Labor Party, which split in 1923. These factions in turn became the basis of the **Ukrainian National Democratic Alliance**, the dominant Galician party of the interwar period.

NAZARUK, OSYP (31 August 1883–31 March 1940). Journalist; civic and political activist. He was born in Buchach (now in Ternopil oblast) and attended the Buchach and Zolochiv gymnasiums. Nazaruk studied law at the universities of **Lviv** and Vienna, obtaining a doctorate (1908). From 1905 to 1919, he belonged to the **Ukrainian Radical Party** and was a member of its chief executive, as well as editor of its newspaper *Hromads'kyi holos* (Civic Voice, 1916–18). During **World War I**, Nazaruk headed the press bureau of the **Ukrainian Sich Riflemen**, organized Ukrainian schools, and did cultural and educational work in **Volhynia** (1916) and **Podilia** (1918). From December 1918 to June 1919, he was director of press and propaganda with ministerial rank in the government of the **Ukrainian People's Republic** (UNR). From mid-1919, he directed the press bureau of the **Ukrainian Galician Army** and edited the newspaper *Strilets'* (Rifleman). In 1920–22, he was a member of the government-in-exile of the **Western Ukrainian People's Republic** in Vienna. From September 1922 to October 1923, at the commission of that government, he led the National Defense bond drive in Canada. Nazaruk's wartime disenchantment with the UNR led him to abandon his socialist ideas. During his stay in Canada, he became a champion and propagandist of Ukrainian monarchism, and from 1924 he was a disciple and close associate of the monarchist ideologue **Viacheslav Lypynsky**. After moving to the United States (November 1923), Nazaruk became an organizer of the **United Hetman Organization**. He edited the weekly *Sich* (Chicago, 1923–26) and *Ameryka* (America, Philadelphia, 1926–27). In August 1927, Nazaruk returned to Lviv, where he joined the leadership of the Ukrainian Christian (later Catholic) Organization and became editor of its newspaper, *Nova zoria* (New Star, 1928–39). This led to a falling out with Lypynsky, who opposed both clericalist politics and an accommodation with Poland. From 1930, Nazaruk was an organizer and leader of the Ukrainian Catholic People's Party (1930; later the Ukrainian People's Renewal). He died in Cracow. He wrote numerous works on sociopolitical themes and the history of the Ukrainian Sich Riflemen, as well as historical novels, travelogues, and memoirs.

NEMYRYCH, YURII (ca. 1612–August 1659). Diplomat and military figure. Descended from a Ukrainian noble family, Nemyrych studied at the Socinian Academy in Raków and at the universities of Leiden and Basel, as well as in England, France, and Italy. A leader of the Ukrainian **Protestants** (Socinians), Nemyrych was a founder of the Socinian Academy in Kyselyn (**Volhynia**) and defended Socinian rights at the Lublin tribunal (1636) and the Polish Diet (1637–39). He owned large latifundia in **Right-** and **Left-Bank Ukraine**. Nemyrych commanded a private army during the Polish-Muscovite

War (1632–34) and in the war against Sweden. As an adherent of Socinianism, Nemyrych was stripped of a significant portion of his estates and sentenced to exile from the **Polish-Lithuanian Commonwealth** (1646). Nevertheless, during the **Khmelnytsky Uprising** (1648–57) he fought on the side of Poland. In 1655, he joined the army of Charles X Gustav of Sweden and participated in military actions in Transylvania and Poland.

Nemyrych changed sides in 1657 and became a supporter of **Bohdan Khmelnytsky**. He conducted lengthy negotiations with the Swedish government that culminated in the **Treaty of Korsun** (1657), whereby Sweden recognized the **Hetmanate**. In the summer of 1657, Nemyrych converted to Orthodoxy, received the title of colonel, and reclaimed his Left-Bank properties. After Khmelnytsky's death, he supported **Ivan Vyhovsky** and helped draft the **Treaty of Hadiach** (1658), which was intended to establish an autonomous Grand Duchy of Rus' within the Commonwealth. Nemyrych headed the Ukrainian delegation to the Diet during the ratification of the treaty (1659). He served as chancellor of the short-lived Grand Duchy of Rus' (1658–59) and fought in the **Battle of Konotop** (1659). Nemyrych was killed by peasant insurgents near Nizhyn.

NESTOR (ca. 1056–ca. 1114). Writer and chronicler of **Kyivan Rus'**. He was a monk and hierodeacon at the **Kyiv Cave Monastery** (1074–78). In his life of the murdered **princes** (and Orthodox saints) Borys and Hlib, written in the 1070s or early 1080s, Nestor praised them for having accepted death in the spirit of Christian humility. He also wrote the life of Theodosius, hegumen of the Cave Monastery (1080s). Nestor has traditionally been regarded as the author of the major **chronicle** of Kyivan Rus', the *Tale of Bygone Years* (ca. 1111–13). Modern scholarship posits the participation of other compilers and distinguishes Nestor the Hagiographer from Nestor the Chronicler.

NEW RUSSIA GUBERNIA. 1. Administrative unit created by the tsarist government as a military district for defense against the Ottoman Empire and the Crimean Khanate (1764). It consisted of **New Serbia**, **Sloviano-Serbia**, the Ukrainian Line, and 39 companies of the **Poltava**, Myrhorod, Lubny, and Pereiaslav regiments. Its administrative center was Kremenchuk. The population consisted of military colonists from hussar and lancer regiments, Ukrainian and Russian **peasants**, **Cossacks**, Serbs, Montenegrins, Hungarians, and other foreigners who received land subsidies for settling in the area. Most settlements in the gubernia had military garrisons. The gubernia's primary industries were agriculture and animal husbandry. There was a factory near Kremenchuk that processed imported sugar cane, a distillery, a brick factory, a leather shop in Novomyrhorod, and a salt factory in Bakhmut. Having lost its military and strategic importance after the annexation of the **Crimean** Khanate, the New Russia gubernia was abolished and merged with the Katerynoslav vicegerency (1783).

2. Administrative unit consisting of 12 counties, created by a ukase of Paul I (12 [23] December 1796), that included most of the former Katerynoslav vicegerency. Its administrative center was Novorossiisk (now Dnipropetrovsk). It was divided in 1802 into the Mykolaiv (Kherson, after 1803), Katerynoslav, and Tavriia gubernias.

NEW SERBIA. Administrative unit established by the Russian government on **Zaporozhian** lands in 1751 to defend southern Ukraine against Ottoman and **Tatar** raids and establish greater control over the Zaporozhian **Cossacks**. The government allowed Serbian and Hungarian colonists from Austria led by Col. Ivan Horvat, followed by Bulgarians, Vlachs, and Greeks from the Ottoman Empire, to settle on the territory between the Dnipro River in the east and the Syniukha River in the west, and from the headwaters of the Inhul and Inhulytsia Rivers in the north to the Velyka Vysa and Omelnyk Rivers in the south. In 1752, this region was named New Serbia. Two regiments, which simultaneously became administrative units, were recruited from the local population (a pandour infantry and a hussar regiment). The regiments were combined into corps headquartered in Novomyrhorod. In 1754, the St. Elizabeth Fortress was established in New Serbia (the town of Yelysavethrad from 1755, now Kirovohrad) and became the region's administrative center. That year, Cossacks from **Left-Bank Ukraine** were resettled in New Serbia, forming the Novosloboda regiment. Most of New Serbia's population consisted of Ukrainian Cossacks and emigrant **peasants** from Right- and Left-Bank Ukraine. In March 1764, the military settlements in New Serbia were eliminated, and, together with **Sloviano-Serbia**, the territory was incorporated into the newly created **New Russia gubernia**.

NEW SICH. Last **Zaporozhian Sich** established on Ukrainian lands (1734–75), also known as the Pidpilna, Pokrova, and Krasnokut Sich. After the destruction of the Zaporozhian (Old or Chortomlyk) Sich at the command of Peter I (1709), a number of **Cossacks** established the Oleshky and Kamianets Sich in **Tatar** domains. Difficult economic circumstances and Tatar persecution forced them to petition the tsar for permission to return to Ukraine. In late March 1734, given the need to strengthen the southern borders of the Russian Empire, the Cossacks were allowed to return and establish the New Sich on the Pidpilna River (a tributary of the Dnipro).

By government order, a citadel staffed with a Russian garrison was built to keep watch over the Zaporozhians (1735). The whole territory of the New Sich was surrounded by a high bulwark, numerous watchtowers, trenches, and other defenses. Assigned mainly to defend Zaporizhia against Ottoman and Tatar raids, the Zaporozhian infantry, cavalry, and fleet also fought in the Russo-Turkish wars (1735–39 and 1768–74). Their ranks were filled primarily by **peasants** escaping serfdom. Despite constant demands by the tsarist administration, the **Hetmanate** government, and landowners, the officer staff of the New Sich did not surrender runaway peasants. The Zaporizhia region experienced considerable economic growth, and the **Cossack officers'** landholdings increased.

The New Sich was subject to the governor-general of Kyiv. The Novosich retrenchment (1735) and numerous forts housing Russian military garrisons (1740s–50s) were built close to the Sich. **New Serbia** was established in 1752, and Zaporozhian lands up to the Inhul River were included in the **New Russia gubernia** (1764). In 1775, at the command of Catherine II, an army led by Gen. Petr Tekeli destroyed the New Sich (4–5 [15–16] June). The arrested officer staff was accused of treason and exiled to Siberia or the Solovets Islands. The Sich treasury and property were confiscated, and Zaporozhian lands were incorporated into the New Russia and Azov gubernias. Some of the dispossessed Zaporozhians settled in the Ottoman-ruled Dobrudja, where they founded the **Transdanubian Sich**.

NIKON (d. after 1088). Monk and chronicler of **Kyivan Rus'**. He entered the **Kyivan Cave Monastery** before 1058 and became an associate of **St. Anthony of the Caves**. Owing to a political dispute, he moved to Tmutorokan, where he founded a monastery. Nikon returned to **Kyiv** in 1068, then went back to Tmutorokan in 1073 to escape internecine strife. Upon his second return to Kyiv, he became hegumen of the Cave Monastery (1078–88). He is thought to have continued the Kyiv Chronicle of 1037 and edited the Cave Monastery Compilation of 1073, one of the sources of the *Tale of Bygone Years*. Some scholars believe that Nikon introduced the narrative about the contest between Prince Mstyslav Volodymyrovych of Tmutorokan and the Kasogian prince Rededia into the chronicle (entry for 1022). They also surmise that he developed the narrative about Princess **Olha's** reprisals against the Derevlianians (946 entry), the so-called Korsun version of the baptism of **Volodymyr the Great** (entry for 922), and others.

NOBILITY (Ukr. *shliakhta*; Pol. *szlachta*). A privileged and usually titled elite that emerged from the feudal order in Europe. Ukraine's domination by Poland and then by Russia impeded the formation of a native aristocracy. Nevertheless, a native nobility did exist in certain areas of Ukraine and periods of Ukrainian history. The nobility of the Lithuanian-Ruthenian state (14th–15th centuries) originated in the ruling and military elite of **Kyivan Rus'**. It constituted a distinctive group within the ruling class of the **Grand Duchy of Lithuania** and was represented by local **princes**, who ruled certain palatinates (e.g., the Olelkovychi in the Kyiv palatinate), as well as by **boyars** (magnates) and the petty gentry. As Lithuania became more closely associated with Poland, the Polish aristocratic order was gradually introduced. This trend was accelerated by the **Union of Lublin** (1569), which brought the palatinates of **Volhynia**, **Podilia**, Kyiv, and Bratslav under direct Polish rule. Nevertheless, the Ukrainian nobility continued to be distinguished from its Polish counterpart by its adherence to Orthodoxy and by a more hierarchical structure (princes, lower *shliakhta*, military retainers). Under the impact of the Counter-Reformation and the flowering of Polish culture, Ukrainian nobles began converting to Roman Catholicism and adopting the Polish language and culture. Some of the princes resisted and exercised their leadership role. For example, Prince **Kostiantyn Ostrozky** sponsored the printing of the **Ostrih Bible** and founded the **Ostrih Academy**, which generated cadres for an Orthodox revival. However, by the mid-17th century, princely families became extinct or Polonized, while the lesser nobility sided either with the Poles or the Ukrainian **Cossacks**. The *shliakhta* ceased to be an identifiable leading stratum of Ukrainian society.

The **Khmelnytsky Uprising** of 1648 and the establishment of a Cossack polity, the **Hetmanate**, marked the end of nobiliary rule. Many of the nobles were either killed or fled, while others joined the uprising. However, those nobles who joined the Cossacks could hardly continue to be an exclusive elite. At best, they could hope to fuse with an existing elite—the **Cossack officers** (*starshyna*)—and the notables. Because of constant warfare, the formation of a new elite proved long and difficult. During the rule of **Hetmans Ivan Samoilovych** (1672–1687) and **Ivan Mazepa** (1687–1709), a fairly cohesive landed elite emerged, approximating the gentry in social status and way of life. This new gentry included descendants of the *shliakhta* and of established Cossack officers, as well as deserving new recruits. It had a formal organization known as the Society of Notable Military Fellows (*znachne viis'kove tovarystvo*), which was divided into three social categories by the mid-18th century. With the abolition of the Hetmanate in the late 18th century, most of this elite was incorporated into the Russian nobility (*dvorianstvo*).

NORMAN THEORY. Scholarly theory that laid the foundations of Normanism, a trend in historiography of the 18th to 20th centuries. It asserts that the Normans or **Varangians** of Scandinavia were the founders of East Slavic statehood, including **Kyivan Rus'**. The Norman theory was developed by the German historians Gottlieb Siegfried Bayer, Gerhard Friedrich Müller, and August Ludwig Schlözer, who worked at the St. Petersburg Academy of Sciences in the 18th century. Their assessment of the Scandinavian origin of Rus' (the state and the name) was based on their interpretation of written sources, primarily the entry for 862 in the *Tale of Bygone Years*, which described the **Slavs'** invitation to three Varangian princes, **Riuryk, Sineus, and Truvor**, to rule over them. The Norman theory was based on a conception of nation-building by distinguished historical personages. Initially, it had a political subtext, suggesting that the Eastern Slavs were incapable of creating their own state.

In the 19th century, the Norman theory was developed by the Russian historians Nikolai Karamzin, Sergei Soloviev, and Mikhail Pogodin, as well as the Danish Slavist Vilhelm Thomsen. Twentieth-century research focused on the word Rus' and its derivation from Scandinavian roots, notably *Ruotsi*, the Finnish term for Swedes. Attempts were also made to identify the original Rus' homeland.

Scholarly criticism of the Norman theory (anti-Normanism) began in the second half of the 18th century with Mikhail Lomonosov. In the early 19th century, the theory was opposed by Decembrists and Slavophiles, and later by such Russian historians as Stepan Gedeonov, Dmitrii Ilovaisky, and Vasilii Vasilevsky, who proposed alternative theories about the Baltic-Slavic, Lithuanian, and Gothic origins of Rus'. Soviet historiography initially reflected the significant influence of the Norman theory, but anti-Normanism became politically obligatory from the 1930s.

Ukrainian historiography generally opposed the Norman theory. The author of *Istoriia Rusov* believed that the term Rus' and the Kyivan state had local origins. **Mykola Kostomarov** posited the Lithuanian origin of Rus', while **Volodymyr Antonovych** and his school did not give serious consideration to Normanism. The distinguished historian **Mykhailo Hrushevsky** acknowledged only a limited influence of the Varangian military organization on the unification of the Rus' lands under Kyivan rule. Hrushevsky's students and disciples shared his assessment, although representatives of the "state school" in western Ukrainian historiography of the 1920s–30s (**Stepan Tomashivsky**, **Myron Korduba**, Mykola Chubaty, and Borys Krupnytsky) accepted individual tenets of the Norman theory. **Dmytro Bahalii** and Volodymyr Parkhomenko, who worked in the scholarly institutions of the **Ukrainian SSR**, took anti-Normanist positions.

Present-day scholarship in Ukraine and elsewhere generally accepts such major elements of the Norman theory as the Scandinavian origins of the ruling **Riuryk line** and the term Rus', as well as the crucial role of the Varangians in the political and commercial development of Kyiv.

NOVAKIVSKY, OLEKSA (2 [14] March 1872–29 August 1935). Painter and teacher. Born in Slobodo-Obodivka (now in Vinnytsia oblast), he received his art education from F. Klymenko in **Odesa** (1888–92) and at the Cracow Academy of Fine Arts (1892–1900) under Leon Wyczółkowski and Jan Stanisławski. Novakivsky's style, initially based on impressionism, became increasingly expressionist. He worked for an extended period in the village of Mogiła near Cracow. With the assistance of his patron, Metropolitan **Andrei Sheptytsky,** Novakivsky moved to **Lviv** in 1913, where he founded an art school that became prominent in **western Ukraine** and trained a number of well-known artists, including Leonid Perfetsky, Roman Selsky, Sofiia Zarytska, Stepan Lutsyk, Hryhorii Smolsky, and Mykhailo Moroz. In 1924–25, Novakivsky headed the faculty of art of the **Lviv (Underground) Ukrainian University**. He died in Lviv, where a memorial museum dedicated to him was opened in 1972. His works include *Children* (1905), *Caroling* (1907–10), *Spring* (1909), *Self-Portrait* (1911), the panels *Folk Art* and *Scholarship* (both 1915–16), *Spring in the Village of Mogiła*, *Awakening* (1912), *St. George's Cathedral* (1925), *Music* (1929), *Dovbush* (1931), and portraits of Dmytro Levytsky, Metropolitan Sheptytsky, and **Oleksander Barvinsky**. *See also* PAINTING.

NUCLEAR WEAPONS. After the disintegration of the **USSR**, Ukraine found itself in possession of the world's third-largest nuclear arsenal—176 ICBM launchers with some 1,240 warheads. Concentrated in Khmelnytskyi and Pervomaisk, they belonged to the 43rd Missile Army of the USSR Defense Ministry. This force consisted of 130 "Stiletto" SS-19s (six warheads each) and 46 "Scalpel" SS-24s (10 warheads each). Fourteen SS-24s were not operationally deployed. In addition, Ukraine was a base for 42 strategic nuclear-capable bombers (based in Pryluky and Uzyn) armed with some 600 air-launched missiles, along with gravity bombs. The number of cruise missiles in storage was estimated at 700 units. Finally, as many as 3,000 tactical nuclear weapons rounded out an arsenal totaling approximately 5,000 strategic and tactical weapons.

For the United States, an independent Ukraine possessing nuclear weapons was the ultimate nuclear-proliferation nightmare. Even though all theater warfare missiles were controlled from Russian military installations, the United States, which favored Russia at the time, feared that Ukraine's claim to its nuclear arsenal might provoke a conflict or even a preventive strike by Russia. Moreover, there were great fears that Ukraine possessed the know-how to override or reprogram the Moscow-controlled codes, particularly for tactical nuclear weapons. The United States therefore accelerated an ongoing program to reduce such weapons and, with Ukraine's consent, helped Russia remove all tactical nuclear weapons from Ukraine in 1992.

From the first days of independence and despite domestic opposition from some politicians, Ukraine affirmed its intention not to accept, manufacture, or acquire nuclear weapons. At no time did Ukraine attempt to obtain operational control of any nuclear weapons. Nevertheless, as with all property on its territory, Ukraine claimed ownership of the weapons and sought to assume "administrative" control over them. It held that the weapons were part of assets to be divided in any post-Soviet settlement. While Ukraine was unwilling to challenge Russia and the United States on the removal of tactical nuclear weapons, the ICBMs could not readily be removed without Ukraine's active participation.

Ukrainian society was significantly divided on the "nuclear issue." Although most Ukrainians were wary of nuclear power of any kind after the **Chornobyl nuclear disaster**, a broad coalition of nationalist and ex-communist forces dominating the Verkhovna Rada tended to see the possession of nuclear weapons as a way of asserting Ukrainian independence. That attitude changed gradually with the realization that Ukraine could not maintain nuclear weapons on its own and that an attempt to do so would make it a pariah in the world community. Even so, the Ukrainian authorities used the weapons as a lever to force both Russia and the United States to treat Ukraine as an independent state and extract (very vague) security assurances from the United States. Finally, there was the complicated issue of compensation. On 31 August 1992, the United States and Russia signed an agreement calling for the United States to purchase some 500 MTf weapons-grade uranium acquired from the former Soviet stock. Price estimates ranged from U.S. $5 to 10 billion. Washington urged Russia to share the proceeds of the sale with Belarus and Ukraine, but official Moscow was reluctant to do so. Ukraine felt disadvantaged, since it would not benefit under that scheme, whereas it appeared that Russia would earn billions of dollars from the sale of material from Ukrainian warheads. Moreover, Ukraine was dependent on Russian nuclear fuel to run its five nuclear plants. Official **Kyiv** was therefore determined not to transfer its strategic warheads without compensation, arguing that it had made a significant contribution to the Soviet nuclear arsenal.

The trilateral agreement signed in Moscow on 14 January 1994 by the United States, Russia, and Ukraine resolved some of these issues. Under the agreement, Russia undertook to send 100 tons of fuel to Ukraine for its nuclear-power plants. The United States agreed to pay $60 million to Russia in support of the process. For its part, Ukraine agreed to transfer 200 nuclear warheads over a 10-month period. Ukraine announced in June 1996 that all warheads had been removed from the country. In May 1997, Ukraine agreed to destroy its SS-24s, in addition to SS-19s, silos, and launch sites, utilizing $47 million provided through the Nunn-Lugar Cooperative Threat Reduction program. All ICBM silos and launch sites were to be liquidated by 4 January 2001.

The 11 strategic bombers and 600 air launch missiles supplied by Ukraine to Russia in exchange for its gas debt were transferred in mid-February 2000. Three TU-95MS and six TU-160 bombers were transferred to the Russian airbase at Engels in October 1999 in fulfillment of the intergovernmental agreement. Thus, Ukraine disposed not only of all nuclear weapons on its territory but also of the means of their delivery. *See also* ARMED FORCES; FOREIGN POLICY.

O

ODESA (Odessa). Fifth-largest city in Ukraine (1998 pop. 1,027,400), capital of Odesa oblast, and the country's largest seaport, as well as a major commercial, cultural, and administrative center and transportation terminal. It is located on a large, virtually ice-free bay on the Black Sea near the mouths of the Danube, Dnister, Southern Buh, and Dnipro Rivers.

In prehistoric and early historical times, the site of present-day Odesa was settled by various peoples, including **Cimmerians**, **Scythians**, **Sarmatians**, and Greeks. During the period of **Kyivan Rus'**, it was inhabited by the Ulychians and Tivertsians. The settlement that arose on the site in the 14th century was fortified by Grand Duke Vytautas of Lithuania. In 1480, the fortress was captured by the Turks, who named it Hadzhybei (Khadzhybei) and held it for three centuries. The Russian army and Zaporozhian

Cossacks captured the settlement in 1789, and it was ceded to the Russian Empire by the Treaty of Iaşi (1792). Hadzhybei was immediately rebuilt as a fortress and naval port and renamed Odesa in 1795 on the mistaken assumption that the site had once been occupied by the Greek colony of Odessos.

In the 19th century, as the steppe regions of Ukraine underwent rapid colonization, Odesa was the capital of the New Russia gubernia (1803–74). The city soon became a major port and commercial center; by 1815, it handled more than half the freight passing through the Black and Azov Seas, and by the mid-1870s it was the largest wheat-exporting center in Europe. Odesa was Ukraine's largest city by the mid-1830s, a status that it maintained until 1918. It was also the least ethnically Ukrainian of the large cities in Ukraine; according to the 1897 census, Ukrainians accounted for 5.7 percent of the population, while Russians (50.8 percent), Jews (32.5 percent), Poles, Germans, and Greeks (all under 5 percent) made up the majority. A Ukrainian plurality developed only after **World War II**; by 1959, Ukrainians made up 41 percent of Odesa's population.

The building of railways in southern Ukraine in the 1860s–70s and the opening of the Suez Canal in 1869 led to an explosion of commercial activity in Odesa. By the early 20th century, it was second only to St. Petersburg among the ports of the Russian Empire, handling almost a quarter of the empire's exports (mainly grain and sugar) and almost 10 percent of its imports (petroleum products, coal, and cement). In the late 19th century, the processing of agricultural products developed into a major industry involving flour, sugar, tea, and tobacco.

Since Odesa was regarded as the Russian Empire's southern window on Europe, great care was lavished on its appearance. The city was laid out on a grid plan by Franz de Voland (1794), its major buildings constructed in the classical style, and the great staircase to the port built in 1837–41. In the course of the 19th century, Odesa also became an important cultural center. The Richelieu Lyceum, named for the first governor-general of New Russia, was founded in 1817 and became Odesa University in 1865. The Odesa Archaeological Museum, the first municipal institution of its kind in Ukraine, was established in 1825, and the Odesa Society of History and Antiquities was organized in 1839. The Odesa Opera and Ballet Theater was built in 1810, a philharmonic society was formed in 1839, and the Odesa Conservatory was founded in 1913 on the basis of an earlier **music** school. Ever since, the city has been prominent in the musical life of Ukraine and the former **USSR**. Science also flourished in Odesa; an astronomical observatory was built in 1871, the empire's first bacteriological laboratory organized in 1886, and an agricultural institute established in 1918. The Russian-language *Odesskii vestnik* (1827–93) was the first daily newspaper in Ukraine.

Ukrainian culture, represented by the Odesa **Hromada** (late 1860s) and the **Prosvita Society** (established 1906), did not begin to flourish until the **Ukrainization** of the 1920s. New educational institutions were established, the Russian-language *Odesskii listok* became a large-circulation Ukrainian newspaper, *Chornomors'ka komuna*, and the Odesa branch of the State Publishing House issued many Ukrainian books. The region's favorable climate helped establish Odesa as a major **film** production center, and the Odesa Film Studio began to function in 1919. The Odesa Ukrainian Music and Drama Theater was founded in 1925. All this activity ceased with the **political terror** and renewed **Russification** of the 1930s.

More than any other Ukrainian city, Odesa was devastated by fighting in the course of the **Ukrainian Revolution** (1917–21) and the **famine of 1921–23**, which halved its prewar population. During **World War II**, it became the administrative center of Romanian-ruled **Transnistria** and also suffered heavy damage. Under Soviet rule, the city became an important industrial center. Today, its wide range of engineering industries (machine tools, cranes, and plows) and its chemical industry (fertilizers, paints, and dyes) account for about one-third of Odesa's industrial output. The city has an oil refinery and is the point of origin of the Odesa-Brody pipeline. Although less prominent than in the past, food industries account for about one-quarter of the city's industrial output. With its ports and railways, Odesa is an important **transportation** hub. To increase its capacity, a new port was built in 1957–58 at Illichivsk, 20 km to the southwest. Today, the city's ports handle almost half the freight moving through Ukrainian ports.

Odesa has 14 higher **educational** institutions, and the Southern Scientific Center of the **Ukrainian Academy of Sciences** is based there. It remains an important health-resort center, a function it has fulfilled since the 1820s. The best known of its medical research centers is the **Filatov** Institute of Eye Diseases. Odesa has six major theaters, a film studio, a philharmonic orchestra, an opera house, and a variety of museums. Ukrainian culture remains a minority presence in the city. Odesa has long been the center of Ukraine's largest Jewish community (*see* JEWS), which nurtured such well-known writers as Isaak Babel, Ilia Ilf, and Evgenii Petrov. A distinctive Russian-Jewish slang has also developed in Odesa and become part of the city's cultural fabric.

OHIIENKO, IVAN (14 January 1882–29 March 1972). Monastic name: Ilarion. Church and civic figure, Ukrainian Orthodox metropolitan, church historian, teacher, and full member of the **Shevchenko Scientific Society** (from 1922). He was born in Brusyliv, **Kyiv** region, and graduated from Kyiv University in Slavic philology and literature (1909). Later, he completed the Higher Pedagogical Courses and worked at the Kyiv Commercial Institute. From 1915, Ohiienko lectured in **language** and **literature** at Kyiv University. He belonged to the **Ukrainian Party of Socialist Federalists**. In 1917–18, he promoted the Ukrainization of higher learning. Ohiienko became a professor in the department of the history of Ukrainian culture at the Kyiv Ukrainian State University in 1918. On 9 (22) January 1918, he spoke at the All-Ukrainian Church Sobor in Kyiv, arguing for the right of the Ukrainian church to an independent existence. That summer, he became a founder and first rector of the Kamianets-Podilskyi Ukrainian State University (opened 22 October).

In early 1919, Ohiienko was appointed minister of education of the **Ukrainian People's Republic** (UNR) in the governments of **Volodymyr Chekhivsky** and Serhii Ostapenko. He was minister of religious affairs in the governments of **Isaak Mazepa** and Viacheslav Prokopovych (1919–20). In October 1920, after the retreat of the **Directory** from Kamianets-Podilskyi, Ohiienko became the principal representative of the government. The Bolshevik capture of Kamianets-Podilskyi forced him to emigrate, and from 1920 he lived in Tarnów, Poland. He was a member of the Council of the Republic (1921) and minister of religious affairs in the UNR government-in-exile (until 1924). Ohiienko lectured on the Ukrainian language at the Lviv Teachers' College (from 1924) and was professor of Church Slavonic at the department of theology of Warsaw University (1926–32). In Warsaw, he founded and edited the journals *Ridna mova* (Native Language) and *Nasha kul'tura* (Our Culture), which popularized Ukrainian culture, advocated standard linguistic norms among Ukrainians outside the **Ukrainian SSR**, and opposed **Russification**. In October 1940, he was consecrated archbishop of **Kholm** (Chełm) and **Podlachia** (under the name Ilarion) and began to Ukrainize the church there. He was appointed metropolitan of Kholm and Podlachia in March 1944.

Ohiienko emigrated to Switzerland in the summer of 1944 before moving to Winnipeg, Canada, in September 1947. He was elected head of the Ukrainian Greek Orthodox Church of Canada and metropolitan of Winnipeg at an extraordinary council in August 1951. Ohiienko invested a great deal of effort in the organization and development of Ukrainian national, cultural, and religious life in Canada. He founded the Theological Society (now the Metropolitan

Ilarion Theological Society), established St. Andrew's College at the University of Manitoba (which trains Orthodox priests for Ukrainian communities world-wide), engaged in scholarly research and publishing, and continued editing *Nasha kul'tura* (1951–53; renamed *Vira i kul'tura* [Faith and Culture] in 1954). He died in Winnipeg.

Ohiienko wrote numerous scholarly works on Ukrainian linguistics, church history, culture, and canon law. He translated the Bible into Ukrainian (1962).

OHLOBLYN, OLEKSANDER (24 November [6 December] 1899–16 February 1992). Historian; full member of the **Shevchenko Scientific Society** (from 1947; honorary member from 1988). He was born in **Kyiv**, a descendant of the Lashkevych and Savytsky **Cossack** families. Ohloblyn graduated from Kyiv University (1919) and was professor of Ukrainian economic history at the Kyiv Archaeological Institute (1921–22), lectured at the Kyiv Institute of People's Education (1920–33), and held the chair of Ukrainian national economy at the Kyiv Institute of the National Economy (1928–30), as well as the chair of Ukrainian history at the University of **Odesa** (1939–41). Ohloblyn was a senior research associate of the **Ukrainian Academy of Sciences** (1926–33, 1935–41), serving as director of its commission on Ukrainian socioeconomic history (1930–34). In 1930, he was arrested on ideological grounds and imprisoned for four months by the Soviet authorities; in 1933–35, during Stalin's **political terror**, he was stripped of all of his official posts. In the autumn of 1941, during the German occupation, Ohloblyn headed the Kyiv municipal administration and was a member of the **Ukrainian National Council**. He lived in **Lviv** in 1943 and emigrated in 1944, first to Czechoslovakia and West Germany and then to the United States (1951). He was a professor of the **Ukrainian Free University** (UVU) in Prague (from 1944) and Munich (from 1945). He was also a professor and senator (1946–51) of the Theological Academy of the **Ukrainian** Autocephalous **Orthodox Church**. Ohloblyn was a full member of the **Ukrainian Academy of Arts and Sciences** (UVAN), whose historical section he headed from 1951, and president of the Ukrainian Historical Association from 1965. He was visiting professor of Ukrainian history (1968–70) and thesis advisor (1970–73) at Harvard University. He died in Ludlow, Massachusetts.

Ohloblyn wrote approximately 700 works, including 30 monographs, primarily on socioeconomic development in Ukraine (he published a three-volume history of Ukrainian industry), the Cossack era, and the development of Ukrainian historiography.

OLD RUTHENIANS. Clerical leaders of the Ukrainian movement in **Galicia** in the mid-19th century. They were also known as the "St. George party" after St. George's Cathedral in **Lviv**, the seat of the Lviv Greek Catholic eparchy (*see* UKRAINIAN CATHOLIC CHURCH). The Old Ruthenians first came to prominence in the **Revolution of 1848**, when Bishop Hryhorii Yakhymovych headed the Supreme Ruthenian Council, which served as the Ukrainian representative body. Other important figures were the canon of Lviv eparchy, Mykhailo Kuzemsky, and the clerical administrator and Reichstag deputy Mykhailo Malynovsky. Their policy was one of loyalty to the Habsburg Monarchy, both because the Greek Catholic Church owed its revival to the Habsburg rulers and because the monarchy was their only defense against the Polish nobiliary elite that dominated Galicia. As social and political conservatives, they were opposed to the younger Ukrainian intelligentsia (*see* RUTHENIAN TRIAD), which was oriented toward **populism**. In the **Alphabet War** (1859–61), the Old Ruthenians defended the Church Slavonic orthography, which the populists had long abandoned for the civil script (*hrazhdanka*). The patriarchal outlook of the Old Ruthenians inclined them against the democratic nationalism represented by the Revolution of 1848; they thought of the **Ruthenian** nation either as embodied in the Ukrainian subjects of the Habsburgs or, increasingly, as related to tsarist Russia (*see* RUSSOPHILES). As Austrian power declined in the 1860s, leading to the formation of Austria-Hungary and subsequent autonomy for Galicia under de facto Polish rule, the political foundations of the Old Ruthenian orientation were undermined, and most of its adherents were assimilated into the Russophile movement.

OLEH (Norse Helgi, Russ. Oleg, d. 912 or 922). Semilegendary **Kyivan Rus'** prince of **Varangian** descent. From 879, he ruled in Novgorod, where, according to the *Tale of Bygone Years*, he was regent after the death of **Riuryk** and guardian of the young Prince **Ihor**. In 882, Oleh took control of Smolensk and Liubech with a large retinue. Having arranged the murder of **Askold and Dir**, he proclaimed himself prince of Kyiv. In 883–85, Oleh subjugated the Derevlianians, Radimichians, Siverianians, and other Slavic tribes. He also ended the dominance of the **Khazars** in the middle Dnipro region. In 907, he led a successful campaign against Constantinople, obtaining a favorable economic and political agreement with the Byzantine Empire in 911. The treaty established friendly relations, exempted Rus' merchants from customs duties, and gave them the right to live free of charge in a suburb of Constantinople for up to six months. Oleh died in 912, according to the *Tale*, or 922, according to the Novgorod I Chronicle. Modern scholarship questions the *Tale*'s chronology of Oleh's reign and differentiates "Oleh the Seer" of the *Tale* from the Kyivan prince who concluded the treaty with Byzantium.

OLHA (Norse Helga, Russ. Olga, d. 969). Princess of **Kyiv** (from 945), wife of Prince **Ihor** and regent for her son, **Sviatoslav Ihorevych**. Olha dealt severely with the Derevlianians in retaliation for their murder of her husband in 945. She regularized the collection of tribute in the Kyiv region and in the Derevlianian and Novgorod lands. Sometime between 954 and 957 she traveled to Constantinople, where she converted to Christianity—the first ruler of **Kyivan Rus'** to do so—and took the name Helena. Although the conversion raised Kyiv's prestige, the commercial advantages that Olha sought from Byzantium did not materialize. In 959, Olha asked Emperor Otto I to provide a bishop and priests for Rus'. The resulting mission of Bishop Adalbert ended in failure. Olha's religious and diplomatic initiatives were subsequently taken up with great success by the Kyivan princes **Volodymyr the Great** and **Yaroslav the Wise**.

OLZHYCH, OLEH (8 July 1907–10 June 1944). Pseudonym of Oleh Kandyba. Archaeologist, poet, and political figure. He was born in Zhytomyr, the son of the poet Oleksander Oles, and studied at a high school in Pushcha-Vodytsia near **Kyiv** (1917–23). In 1923, he emigrated to Czechoslovakia with his parents. Olzhych studied at Charles University in Prague and at the literary and historical faculty of the Ukrainian Pedagogical Institute (1924–29). He also studied archaeology at the **Ukrainian Free University** (UVU). In the autumn of 1930, he defended his doctoral dissertation on the neolithic painted ceramics of **Galicia**. Olzhych was an assistant at the chair of archaeology at the UVU (1930–31). As a staff member of the archaeological division of the Czech National Museum (1926–32), he conducted scientific expeditions in western Ukraine, Austria, and Yugoslavia, participated in archaeological conferences, and published works on anthropology and archaeology. In 1938, he lectured at Harvard University. In the early 1930s, Olzhych also emerged as a poet. His works appeared in the Lviv periodicals *Literaturno-naukovyi visnyk* (Literary and Scientific Herald), *Visnyk* (Herald), *Obriï* (Horizons), and *Naperedodni* (On the Eve), as well as in the Prague-based *Students'kyi visnyk* (Student Herald) and *Proboiem* (By Force).

Olzhych joined the **Organization of Ukrainian Nationalists** (OUN) in 1929 and assumed the leadership of its cultural and educational branch in 1937. He was coeditor of the journal *Samostiina dumka* (Independent Thought) in Chernivtsi. Olzhych was active in establishing the independence of **Carpatho-Ukraine** (1938–39). Following the split in the OUN, he sided with **Andrii Melnyk** and became his second-in-command. After the German invasion of the **USSR**, Olzhych moved to Kyiv, where he organized the underground network of the OUN(M), as well as the **Ukrainian National Council**. With the beginning of Nazi persecution of Ukrainian nationalists, Olzhych moved to Lviv. In May 1942, the Pochaiv conference of the OUN(M) elected Olzhych its deputy chairman and head of the leadership in Ukraine. Following Melnyk's arrest (January 1944), Olzhych assumed the leadership of the OUN(M). He was arrested by the Gestapo in Lviv (25 May 1944) and imprisoned at the Sachsenhausen concentration camp, where he died under torture.

OMELCHENKO, OLEKSANDR (b. 9 August 1938). Mayor of **Kyiv**. Omelchenko was born in the village of Zoziv, Vinnytsia oblast, into a family of collective farmers. He studied at the Kyiv Construction College (1956–59) and graduated from the Kyiv Engineering and Construction Institute (1974) and the Kyiv Institute of the National Economy (1978). In 1959, Omelchenko began work as a concrete placer at the construction factory of the Kyiv Oblast Construction Trust, where he rose to the position of chief engineer (1980). From 1980 to 1987, he was chief engineer of the General Kyiv City Construction enterprise. He then served as a construction advisor in Afghanistan (1987–89). In 1989–90, he was a department head at Ukraine's State Construction Ministry.

Omelchenko's political career began in 1990–92, when he was deputy head of Kyiv city council. From August 1996, he headed the Kyiv city administration, becoming mayor in May 1999. His rise to that office involved a protracted confrontation with the prominent "oligarchs" **Viktor Medvedchuk** and **Hryhorii Surkis**. He is also president of the Association of Ukrainian Cities and head of the Unity Party. Known for his close connections with President **Leonid Kuchma** and members of the **Verkhovna Rada**, Omelchenko is a highly influential politician and the most powerful municipal administrator in Ukraine.

OPERATION VISTULA/AKCJA "WISŁA." Concluding phase of the **Ukrainian-Polish Conflict** (1943–47), entailing the deportation of Ukrainians from their ancestral lands in the **Lemko, Sian, Podlachia**, and **Kholm** regions to the western and northern territories of Poland that belonged to Germany prior to 1945. Almost half a million Ukrainians were deported to the **Ukrainian SSR** between 1944 and 1946 under the terms of a population exchange, leading the Polish authorities to believe that very few Ukrainians remained in the country and that the **Ukrainian Insurgent Army** (UPA), then operating in southeastern Poland, would wither for lack of a popular base. In 1947, when the numbers of Ukrainians who had avoided deportation were found to be greater than previously believed, the Polish chief of staff, Gen. Stefan Mossor, recommended their dispersion in western and northern Poland in order to assimilate them. The death of the Polish deputy minister of defense, Gen. Karol Świerczewski, at the hands of the UPA on 28 March 1947 served as a pretext to implement Mossor's plan in order to "resolve the Ukrainian problem in Poland once and for all," as stated in the official resolution. On 28 April, five infantry divisions and internal security units (approx. 17,900 men) surrounded areas populated by Ukrainians. Simultaneously, divisions of the NKVD and the Czechoslovak army blocked the eastern and southern approaches to Poland from Brest to Nowy Sącz. The inhabitants of Ukrainian villages were given a few hours to prepare and herded onto trains for Lublin and Oświęcim (Auschwitz), whence they were dispatched to northwestern Poland. In the process, villages were burned and their inhabitants killed or beaten; more than 170 Ukrainians were summarily executed for collaborating with the UPA. Operation Vistula, commanded by Mossor and terminated on 30 July 1947, resulted in the deportation of some 140,000 Ukrainians. About 4,000 passed through the Jaworzno concentration camp in Silesia, where typhus epidemics, food shortages, and routine beatings caused the death of at least 150 inmates. By the end of 1947, the evacuated areas were resettled by approximately 14,000 Poles.

The organized Ukrainian community in Poland did not gain official recognition until 1956 (as the Ukrainian Social and Cultural Society). A few thousand Ukrainians were allowed to resettle in southeastern Poland. On 3 August 1990, the Polish Senate formally condemned Operation Vistula, but the measure proved unpopular: many Polish organizations protested, citing the mass murder of Poles in **Volhynia** by Ukrainian nationalists in 1943. A draft bill to recognize the Ukrainian deportees as victims of communist rule was defeated in 1995. In April 2002, President Aleksander Kwaśniewski addressed a letter to participants in a conference on Operation Vistula, expressing regret to all who had been wronged by the operation.

OPRYSHOKS. Social brigands active in the Carpathian Mountains (**Galicia, Bukovyna,** and **Transcarpathia**) between the 16th and early 19th centuries. The first mention of the opryshoks dates from

1529, although the phenomenon was prompted earlier by the increased oppression of **peasants** and demand for corvée labor. Small units of peasants and poor townsmen attacked nobiliary estates, castles, tavern keepers, and moneylenders; some of the booty was distributed to the poor. Their weapons typically included rifles, pistols, pikes, knives, and spears. Hatchets, used to swear oaths upon joining a unit, were symbols of courage. In the 16th and early 17th centuries, the opryshoks were active in **Pokutia** and the Peremyshl (Przemyśl) region. During the **Khmelnytsky Uprising** (1648–57), they fought the Polish nobility. In 1648, they participated in the rebellion led by Semen Vysochan, and in 1653 they assisted Tymish Khmelnytsky's forces in **Moldavia**. The opryshok movement reached its apogee in the years 1738–59 under the leadership of **Oleksa Dovbush**, Vasyl Baiurak, and Ivan Boichuk. The opryshoks also participated in the 18th-century **haidamaka** rebellions in **Right-Bank Ukraine**. In the first half of the 19th century, more than 50 opryshok units were active in **western Ukraine**. Thanks to the abolition of serfdom during the **Revolution of 1848**, the Austrians succeeded in eliminating the movement.

The struggle of the opryshoks is described in many folk songs, legends, and tales. They inspired such writers as **Markiian Shashkevych**, **Ivan Vahylevych**, **Yurii Fedkovych**, Mykola Ustyianovych, and **Ivan Franko**. Scholarly works about them were written by Kazimierz-Władysław Wójcicki, Antoni Prochaska, Yuliian Tselevych, **Ivan Krypiakevych**, and others. In the Carpathian Mountains, certain mountains, cliffs, and rivers are named after opryshok leaders.

ORGANIZATION OF UKRAINIAN NATIONALISTS/ORHANIZATSIIA UKRAÏNS'KYKH NATSIONALISTIV (OUN). Revolutionary political movement formed through the merger of the **Ukrainian Military Organization** (UVO), the Group of Ukrainian National Youth (Prague and Berlin), the **League of Ukrainian Nationalists** (Poděbrady), and the Union of Ukrainian Nationalist Youth (**Lviv**) at the First Congress of Ukrainian Nationalists in Vienna (28 January–3 February 1929). The congress elected a Leadership of Ukrainian Nationalists headed by **Yevhen Konovalets**, who had commanded the UVO; its members were Dmytro Andriievsky, Dmytro Demchuk, Gen. Mykola Kapustiansky, Leonid Kostariv, Petro Kozhevnykiv, Volodymyr Martynets, **Mykola Stsiborsky**, and Yuliian Vassyian. In its founding declaration, the OUN set itself the goal of establishing an independent state on Ukrainian ethnic territory. This was to be accomplished by means of a national revolution led by a dictatorship that would proceed to establish a representative government and a mixed economy. The OUN defined itself as a movement, not a party, and criticized legal Ukrainian political parties for their "collaborationist" policies. Rejecting the socialist policies of the **Ukrainian People's Republic** that it held responsible for the failure of the **Ukrainian Revolution** (1917–21), the OUN promoted national solidarity, a strong political elite, and self-reliance.

In the 1930s, the OUN carried out hundreds of acts of sabotage against the Polish regime in **Galicia** and **Volhynia**. These included an incendiary campaign against Polish landowners that helped provoke the **Pacification** (1930), boycotts of Polish-language schools and Polish tobacco and liquor monopolies, holdups to obtain funds, and some 60 assassinations. The OUN's most prominent victims included a department head of the Polish foreign ministry, Tadeusz Hołówko; the Polish interior minister, Bronisław Pieracki; a Soviet consular official in Lviv, Aleksei Mailov (in retaliation for the **famine of 1932–33**); and the director of the Ukrainian Academic Gymnasium in Lviv, Ivan Babii (accused of collaboration with the Polish police).

The OUN membership consisted overwhelmingly of students and young people radicalized by the wartime struggle to establish an independent state and by the discriminatory policies of the interwar Polish regime. The OUN "decalogue," which required total dedication to the national cause, and the writings of **Dmytro Dontsov**, who condemned "decadent" socialism and propounded a cult of voluntarism, had a strong appeal to young OUN recruits, whose numbers have been estimated at 20,000 (1939). The OUN published a number of journals for its cadres, of which the most important was *Rozbudova natsiï* (Nation-Building, 1928–34). It also made strenuous efforts to disseminate its ideology and establish its organizational presence in society at large.

In order to escape arrest, most leaders of the OUN lived abroad, while the Western Ukrainian Territorial Executive (headed, most notably, by **Stepan Bandera**) carried out OUN activity. In 1934, the Polish police gained access to OUN records and arrested many of its leaders, who were subsequently tried and imprisoned until the outbreak of **World War II**. Although the OUN did not penetrate the **Ukrainian SSR**, the Stalin regime was sufficiently concerned about its potential to order the assassination of Konovalets in 1938.

His death prompted a succession crisis that split the OUN along generational and ideological lines. The émigré leaders, older men with a generally traditionalist, authoritarian outlook, were shouldered aside by the younger cadres, more sympathetic to fascist ideology, who felt that their assumption of the risks of revolutionary activity entitled them to leadership. The leadership attempted to meet this challenge by electing one of Konovalets's closest associates, **Andrii Melnyk**, at the Second Grand Assembly of the OUN (Rome, 27 August 1939) and endowing him with the title of *vozhd'* (chieftain, equivalent to *Führer*), implying dictatorial power. Bandera and his followers, who emerged from imprisonment after the outbreak of war, treated Melnyk's election as an empty gesture and established their own Revolutionary Leadership on 10 February 1940; they held a congress in Cracow in April 1941 and elected Bandera leader. Most of the OUN membership accepted Bandera's legitimacy, and the rift became permanent, splitting the organization into the OUN(M), "Melnykites," and OUN(B), "Banderites"; the latter faction was also known as the Revolutionary OUN. There was bitter infighting between them, including assassinations.

Both factions saw the impending conflict between Germany and the USSR as an opportunity to establish an independent Ukraine and sought a tactical alliance with the Germans. The OUN(B) formed two battalions of about 600 men, Nachtigall and Roland, which it considered the nucleus of a future army. Both factions also recruited expeditionary groups to follow the invading Germans into Ukraine. On 30 June 1941, the OUN(B) proclaimed Ukrainian independence in Lviv, with Bandera as head of state and **Yaroslav Stetsko** as premier (*see* UKRAINIAN NATIONAL COUNCIL [LVIV, 1941]; UKRAINIAN STATE ADMINISTRATION). The OUN(M) established a **Ukrainian National Council** in Kyiv in September. In both cases, the Germans reacted by imprisoning the OUN leaders and undertaking a campaign to wipe out the organization (*see* LEBED, MYKOLA; OLZHYCH, OLEH; TELIHA, OLENA). In the autumn of 1942, both factions organized armed units in **western Ukraine** to fight the Germans; the stronger OUN(B) ultimately consolidated these into the **Ukrainian Insurgent Army** (UPA), which fought German, Polish, and Soviet forces until the early 1950s.

OUN members who penetrated **eastern Ukraine** found the population unreceptive to their program of national dictatorship after the devastation wrought by Stalin's totalitarian regime. Considering a revision of its ideology imperative, the OUN(B) held a Third Extraordinary Grand Assembly (21–25 August 1943) at which it condemned "internationalist and fascist national-socialist programs and political concepts," as well as "Russian-Bolshevik communism," and expressed support for "a system of free peoples and independent states." The OUN(B) social program was revised along the lines of West European social democracy, with an emphasis on social services, civil rights, and an end to ethnic discrimination. A three-man OUN Leadership Bureau was elected, consisting of **Roman**

Shukhevych, Zynovii Matla, and Dmytro Maivsky. In July 1944, an OUN(B)-dominated **Supreme Ukrainian Liberation Council** was formed to coordinate the armed struggle.

In the autumn of 1944, the Germans released Bandera, Melnyk, and other leaders in a futile attempt to obtain their support (*see* UKRAINIAN NATIONAL COMMITTEE). At the end of the war, Bandera and Stetsko were elected to the OUN(B) leadership in Ukraine. The Foreign Sections of the OUN(B) (ZCh OUN) were formed in Munich in 1946 under Bandera's leadership, while Stetsko established the **Anti-Bolshevik Bloc of Nations** to consolidate the struggle against Soviet imperialism. When OUN(B) emissaries from Ukraine (Lebed et al.) were sent to establish contact with the ZCh OUN, a conflict developed over the ideological revision of 1943, which Bandera and his émigré followers rejected. After a protracted conflict, those supporting the revision established the OUNz (OUN Abroad) in 1956 under the leadership of Zynovii Matla and **Lev Rebet**. Melnyk resumed his post as leader of the OUN(M), which developed a conservative corporatist ideology after the war.

Following the reoccupation of Ukraine in 1944, the Soviet authorities waged a protracted armed struggle against the OUN and UPA. This was accompanied by an extensive propaganda campaign to defame the nationalists as collaborators with the Nazis. The KGB assassinated Rebet (1957) and Bandera (1959). As late as the mid-1980s, there were trials and executions in Ukraine of individuals accused of membership and criminal activity in the OUN and UPA.

Through their community organizations, youth groups (*see* UKRAINIAN YOUTII ASSOCIATION), and publications, all three factions of the OUN exercised considerable influence in the Ukrainian **diaspora** after **World War II**. As the most powerful group, the OUN(B) sought to dominate émigré life, establishing the World Ukrainian Liberation Front (1973) and taking over the **Ukrainian Congress Committee of America** (1980). The OUN(M), whose presence in the diaspora dated back to the 1930s (it established organizations abroad, as well as the newspapers *Novyi shliakh* [New Pathway] in Canada in 1930 and *Ukraïns'ke slovo* [Ukrainian Word] in France in 1933), also continued its activity. Mykola Plaviuk, who became head of the OUN(M) in 1981, was also president in exile of the Ukrainian People's Republic, whose powers he formally transferred to **Leonid Kravchuk** on 24 August 1992. The OUNz established the Prolog Research Corporation in New York, which issued more than 200 books and published the mainstream journal *Suchasnist'*.

After 1990, the OUN(B) and OUN(M) both became politically active in Ukraine and began issuing publications there. The OUN(B) established the Congress of Ukrainian Nationalists in 1992 under the leadership of **Slava Stetsko**, while the Leadership of Ukrainian Nationalists held its 12th congress in Irpin in 1993, electing Plaviuk as its leader. Neither organization is a significant influence in present-day Ukrainian politics.

ORLYK, PYLYP (11 [21] October 1672–26 May 1742). **Hetman** of Ukraine in the emigration (1710–42); coauthor of the **Constitution of Bendery**. Born in Kosuta, near Vilnius, into a Lithuanian-Czech family, Orlyk studied at the Jesuit college in Vilnius and at the **Kyiv Mohyla Academy**. He was secretary to the metropolitan of **Kyiv** (1698–1700), senior military chancellor of the **Cossack** Host, and later regent (superintendent) of the General Military Chancellery (1700–6). In 1706, he became general chancellor and the closest advisor to Hetman **Ivan Mazepa**. In 1708–9, Orlyk and Mazepa attempted to create an anti-Muscovite coalition with Sweden to guarantee the independence of the **Hetmanate**. Their defeat at the **Battle of Poltava** (1709) forced Orlyk to emigrate. Following Mazepa's death, Orlyk was elected hetman (5 [16] April 1710) and recognized by the king of Sweden and the sultan of the Ottoman Empire. During Orlyk's election, the hetman, officer staff, and **Zaporozhian** Cossacks signed the Constitution of Bendery.

Striving to free the Hetmanate from Muscovite rule, Orlyk formed an alliance with Sweden (10 [21] May 1710) and the **Crimean** Khanate (23 January [3 February] 1711). Backed by the Ottoman Empire, Orlyk led a force of 16,000, including a **Tatar** detachment, into **Right-Bank Ukraine** against the Muscovite administration. The Tatars, however, pillaged the area and took many Ukrainian captives. Finally, the Ukrainian-Turkish coalition broke up after Muscovy and the Ottoman Empire signed the Treaty of Prut near Iaşi (12 [23] July 1711).

In 1711–14, Orlyk unsuccessfully attempted to organize a new anti-Muscovite coalition. He moved to Sweden in 1714 with a number of Cossack officers at the invitation of Charles XII. In 1720, they relocated to Germany and subsequently to France. In 1722, Orlyk settled in Salonika at the demand of the Turkish government, and from 1734 he lived in Budzhak and later in **Moldavia**. Orlyk frequently requested assistance for the renewal of Ukrainian sovereignty from France, England, the German states, Poland, and the Holy See. He attempted to establish his own armed forces, including the Zaporozhian Cossacks. Orlyk died in Iaşi on 26 May 1742 (other dates also appear in the sources). He was the last hetman openly to advocate the sovereignty of the Hetmanate. Orlyk wrote works dedicated to Ivan Mazepa, political manifestos, and the *Diariusz podrożny* (Travel

Diary, 1720–32). The *Diariusz* was published by the **Harvard Ukrainian Research Institute** in two volumes (1988–89).

OSADCHY, MYKHAILO (22 March 1936–5 July 1994). Poet, prose writer, and **human-rights** activist. Honorary member of the Swiss section of PEN International from 1979. Osadchy was born in Kurmany, Sumy oblast, and graduated from the journalism department of **Lviv** University (1958), later lecturing and pursuing graduate studies at the university (1960–65). His first collection of poetry, *Misiachne pole* (The Moonlit Field), was published in 1965. In the same year, he was arrested for the possession of underground **literature** and sentenced in 1966 to two years' imprisonment. **Viacheslav Chornovil** refused to testify at Osadchy's closed trial; as a consequence, in 1967, Osadchy was forced to testify at Chornovil's trial. Osadchy's account of life in Soviet labor camps, *Bil'mo* (Cataract), was written after his release in 1968. The book was published in the West and translated into French (1974) and English (1976). In 1972, Osadchy was rearrested and sentenced to seven years' hard labor and three years' exile. He was incarcerated in Mordovia and exiled to the Komi ASSR. In 1988, he edited *Kafedra* (Cathedral), the popular underground publication of the Ukrainian Association of the Independent Creative Intelligentsia. In 1990, he returned to lecturing in journalism at Lviv University. He died in Lviv and was buried at the Lychakiv Cemetery. Osadchy wrote the verse collections *Quos ego* (1979), *Skyts'kyi oltar* (Scythian Altar, 1990), and *Yrii* (Southern Climes, 1993). A collection of his scholarly and journalistic writings appeared under the title *Ukraïnotsentryzm* (Ukrainocentrism, 2001).

OSMACHKA, TEODOSII (TODOS) (3 May 1895–7 September 1962). Writer and translator. He was born in Kutsivka, Cherkasy region. After graduating from the **Kyiv** Institute of People's Education (1923), he worked as a teacher in Kyiv. Osmachka's first literary works date from 1916. In the 1920s, he belonged to the literary groups Aspys, Lanka, and MARS, which soon came to be regarded as "counterrevolutionary." Like other members of those associations, Osmachka was persecuted and arrested by the NKVD (1934). The ordeal drove him to feign insanity so as to escape execution and left him with a lifelong persecution complex. After being released, he attempted to cross the border but was stopped and sent to the Kyrylivka psychiatric hospital. During **World War II**, he lived in Lviv, where he published the poetry collection *Suchasnykam* (To My Contemporaries, 1943). At the end of the war, he moved to Germany, where he published the epic *Poet* (1946) and his first prose work, *Starshyi boiaryn* (The Best Man, 1946). Subsequently he lived in France, Yugoslavia, Canada, and the United States. He died on Long Island, New York. Osmachka wrote numerous collections of verse, and his prose works include *Plan do dvoru* (Annihilation, 1951) and *Rotonda dushohubtsiv* (Rotunda of Assassins, 1956). He also translated works of Byron, Shakespeare, and others into Ukrainian. *See also* LITERATURE.

***OSNOVA*/FOUNDATION.** Sociopolitical, scholarly, and literary monthly published from January 1861 to October 1862 in St. Petersburg (22 issues). A portion of its contents appeared in Russian. It was edited by Vasyl Bilozersky, **Mykola Kostomarov**, and **Panteleimon Kulish**; Oleksander Kistiakovsky was its secretary. Financial support was provided by two wealthy Ukrainians, **Hryhorii Galagan** and Vasyl Tarnovsky. *Osnova* was the first modern general-interest Ukrainian journal; it championed the distinctiveness of the Ukrainian **language** and **literature**, serving as a forum for prominent Ukrainian writers of the day and provoking opposition from the Russian press. It published literary works, historical studies, bibliographies, documents, memoirs, literary criticism, and reviews. *Osnova* was the first publication to print many works by **Taras Shevchenko** (more than 70 poems), Leonid Hlibov, Kulish, **Oleksander Lazarevsky**, Stepan Rudansky, Tadei Rylsky, and Pavlo Zhytetsky.

OSTARBEITER. German term (meaning "eastern worker") for people taken by the Nazis from occupied eastern territories to Germany as forced laborers during **World War II**. Although this policy was not anticipated in Nazi occupation plans, the forced deportation of workers to Germany began in November 1941, when it became clear that there would be no rapid victory on the Eastern Front. In the years 1941–44, the total number of *Ostarbeiter* was approximately 2.8 million, of whom the vast majority—2.2 million—were from Ukraine. In Germany, the *Ostarbeiter* lived at approximately 20,000 special camps under strict police surveillance. As they were easily replaced, *Ostarbeiter* were poorly fed and often forced to work 14–16 hours per day. Some were assigned to work for German farmers, who tended to treat them more humanely than the industrial enterprises in which the great majority were employed. Most of their wages, which constituted 30 percent of the wages paid to German workers, were deducted to pay for food and lodging. Attempts to escape were punishable by death or imprisonment in concentration camps. *Ostarbeiter* were forced to wear the discriminatory badge "Ost." In June 1944, the term *Ostarbeiter* was abandoned and national symbols (the **trident** for Ukrainians) were added to uniforms, but the "Ost" badge remained compulsory.

After the war, approximately 150,000 *Ostarbeiter* from Ukraine remained in the West, but 1.85 million made their way back to the **USSR** (1942–50). As they walked back, they were usually jeered and sometimes mistreated by Red Army soldiers, who regarded them as collaborators. Soviet repatriation officials at the border treated *Ostarbeiter* with the greatest suspicion, and some were deported to concentration camps for alleged collaboration.

In 1994, the German government allocated funds to compensate former *Ostarbeiter*. This was followed on 12 August 2000 by the establishment of a German government foundation called Remembrance, Responsibility, and the Future to provide financial compensation to *Ostarbeiter* and other victims of Nazism. By mid-2004, it had distributed compensation payments of some 3 billion Euros and expected to complete its operations by mid-2005.

OSTRIH ACADEMY/OSTROZ'KA AKADEMIIA. Institution of higher learning established ca. 1576 in Ostrih at the initiative of Prince **Kostiantyn Ostrozky**. The academy focused on promoting the Orthodox tradition. Its curriculum consisted of Church Slavonic, Greek, Latin, theology, philosophy, grammar, mathematics, astronomy, rhetoric, and logic. The writer Herasym Smotrytsky became its first rector; many of its instructors were distinguished Ukrainian and foreign teachers such as Demian Nalyvaiko, Khrystofor Filaret, Jan Latos, and Cyril Lucaris. The academy worked closely with the Ostrih press. It greatly influenced the development of pedagogical thought and served as a model for Orthodox **brotherhood** schools in **Lviv**, Lutsk, and Volodymyr-Volynskyi. The school existed until ca. 1636.

OSTRIH BIBLE/OSTROZ'KA BIBLIIA. First complete edition of the Bible in Church Slavonic. It was published in 1581 by **Ivan Fedorov** in Ostrih (whence its title). The publication was funded by Prince **Kostiantyn Ostrozky** and included verses in praise of him by Herasym Smotrytsky. In preparing the Ostrih Bible, canonical Church Slavonic and Greek texts were collected from monasteries throughout the Orthodox East, especially the complete text of the Bible compiled by Archbishop Gennadii of Novgorod (1499).

OSTROHRADSKY, MYKHAILO (OSTROGRADSKY, MIKHAIL) (12 [24] September 1801–20 December 1861 [1 January 1862]). First Ukrainian mathematician of world renown; member of scientific academies in St. Petersburg (from 1831), New York (from 1834), Turin (from 1841), Rome (from 1853), and Paris (from

1856). Descended from a **Cossack officer** family, Ostrohradsky was born in Pashenna, **Poltava** gubernia. He studied at the Poltava Gymnasium, **Kharkiv** University (1816–20), and the Collège de France in Paris (1822–28). From 1828, he taught mathematics at several St. Petersburg institutions, including the Naval Academy, the Main Engineering School, and the Main Artillery Academy. Ostrohradsky wrote textbooks on analytical mechanics, algebra, differential and integral calculus, and analytical geometry. He contributed to diverse fields of applied mathematics, including ballistics, hydromechanics, hydrodynamics, potential theory, heat, elasticity, and astronomy. He is considered the founder of theoretical mechanics in imperial Russia.

Ostrohradsky is best known for his contributions to mathematical analysis, especially his work on the transformation of multiple integrals. His most famous theorem concerns the reduction of an integral over an n-dimensional space to one over its boundary. A special case for this theorem applied to three-dimensional space is known as Gauss's theorem (a.k.a. *théorème d'Ostrogradsky* in French). It forms a basis for the modern study of partial differential equations, variational calculus, theoretical mechanics, and electromagnetism. Ostrohradsky was also the first to prove a theorem in linear differential equations known as Abel's theorem.

OSTROMIR'S EVANGELIARY/OSTROMYROVE IEVANHELIIE. Oldest dated East Slavic manuscript and the most important Old Church Slavonic literary monument. It contains the gospel readings for Sundays and holy days. The evangeliary was copied for Ostromir, the vicegerent of Novgorod, by the scribe Grigorii (1056–57), most probably in **Kyiv**; it was written in uncial script on 294 sheets of parchment. The manuscript was kept in St. Sophia's Cathedral in Novgorod and transferred to the St. Petersburg Public Library (now the National Library of Russia) in 1896.

OSTROZKY FAMILY. Princely family of the 14th to early 17th centuries, descended from the Turiv-Pynsk (Turaŭ-Pinsk) **appanage** princes. The largest landowners in Ukraine at the time, the Ostrozkys owned the towns of Ostrih, Iziaslav, and Korets. It is believed that the family was founded by Prince Danylo Ostrozky, who participated in a revolt against Casimir III of Poland and built a castle in Ostrih. Danylo's son Fedir Ostrozky (1360–1446) was starosta of Lutsk and a supporter of the Lithuanian prince Švitrigaila. Toward the end of his life, he became a monk of the **Kyivan Cave Monastery** and was later canonized. Vasyl Ostrozky (d. ca. 1453), vicegerent of Turiv, fought with Švitrigaila against Poland.

Vasyl's grandson Kostiantyn Ostrozky (ca. 1460–1530) was marshal of **Volhynia**, palatine of **Kyiv**, and grand **hetman** of Lithuania. He participated in the Lithuanian-Muscovite wars (1500–12). **Cossack** units commanded by Ostrozky campaigned successfully against **Crimean Tatars** raiding southern Ukrainian lands. He was buried at the Kyivan Cave Monastery. Kostiantyn-Vasyl Ostrozky (1526–23 February [5 March] 1608) was a distinguished political and cultural leader and the most celebrated member of the family. He owned large latifundia in Volhynia, the Kyiv region, **Podilia**, and **Galicia**. Ostrozky was starosta of Volodymyr-Volynskyi, marshal of Volhynia (from 1550), palatine of Kyiv (from 1559), and a senator (from 1569). He was a candidate for the Polish throne after the death of Sigismund II Augustus (1572) and for the Muscovite throne following the death of Tsar Fedor I (1598). While maintaining strong ties with the Cossacks, he opposed the Kosynsky and Nalyvaiko **Cossack rebellions**. Ostrozky founded schools in Turiv (1572) and Volodymyr-Volynskyi (1577), as well as the **Ostrih Academy** and printing press (ca. 1576). At his initiative, a group of distinguished Ukrainian cultural figures, including Herasym Smotrytsky, Lavrentii Zyzanii, and Demian Nalyvaiko, was formed in Ostrih. In 1581, he financed the first complete printing of the Bible in Church Slavonic. Ostrozky was a leading opponent of the **Union of Brest** (1596). His son Janusz Ostrogski (1554–1620) was starosta of Bila Tserkva, palatine of Volhynia, and a convert to Catholicism. With his death, the Ostrozky line came to an end. Its huge latifundia passed to the Zasławski princes, then to the Sanguszko princes and other Polish noble families.

P

PACIFICATION. Official name for the massive campaign of repression against the Ukrainian population of **Galicia** conducted in the autumn of 1930 by the Polish government, led by Prime Minister Józef Piłsudski and Minister of Internal Affairs Gen. Felicjan Sławoj-Składkowski. It was prompted by numerous acts of anti-Polish sabotage, such as the burning of property owned by Poles and the sabotage of communications. According to official Polish data, 62 homes, 87 barns, 78 farm buildings, and 112 grain stacks were burned in the summer of 1930. The Polish authorities laid the responsibility for these acts on the Ukrainian underground: the **Organization of Ukrainian Nationalists** (OUN) and its paramilitary arm, the **Ukrainian Military Organization** (UVO). The underground acknowledged its participation in sabotage as a form of protest against official anti-Ukrainian policies. The campaign, which lasted from 21 September to 16 October, was intended to "pacify" Galicia, weaken Ukrainian political forces, and secure maximum success for the government in the parliamentary elections (November 1930). It was preceded by the arrest of Ukrainian deputies to the Polish Diet (Osyp Kohut, Ivan Lishchynsky, Dmytro Paliiv, Volodymyr Tselevych, and Oleksander Vyslotsky) and of the regional commander of the UVO, Yuliian Holovinsky, who was shot, allegedly while trying to escape.

In order to conduct the punitive measures, the government utilized special police detachments (17 companies, totaling more than 1,000 men) and army units (10 cavalry squadrons), as well as local (county and district) police. They carried out countless searches of private buildings and facilities of Ukrainian cultural, educational, and financial establishments, accompanied by the destruction of buildings, furniture, cultural objects, and foodstuffs. A total of 970 individuals were arrested, most of whom were later released. Beatings and physical abuse of Ukrainian peasants, teachers, and priests became a common feature of the Pacification (seven people died as a result). This was often accompanied by humiliation and ridicule. The **Plast** youth organization, the Luh and Sokil sport associations, **Prosvita** branches, and **cooperatives** were closed, as were Ukrainian gymnasiums in Drohobych, Rohatyn, and Ternopil. In the course of the campaign, more than 30 former parliamentarians, including virtually the entire leadership of the **Ukrainian National Democratic Alliance** and leaders of the **Ukrainian** Socialist **Radical Party**, were arrested. This prevented their participation in the elections, while their constituents were strong-armed into voting for the government ticket.

Ukrainian parties condemned the Pacification, although they were also opposed to the sabotage campaign of the Ukrainian underground. Metropolitan **Andrei Sheptytsky** traveled to Warsaw in an unsuccessful attempt to meet with Piłsudski and put a stop to the operation. Ukrainian efforts to have the Polish Diet investigate the Pacification proved unavailing, but appeals to public opinion, especially in Great Britain, as well as in France and Germany, resulted in denunciations of the Polish government. The League of Nations convened an investigative committee that ultimately justified the Polish campaign as a response to sabotage. The Pacification heightened Polish-Ukrainian antagonism in Galicia and led to increasingly strained relations, as well as retaliatory actions by the OUN.

PAGANISM. General term for pre-Christian polytheistic religions. In **Kyivan Rus'**, pagan beliefs evolved from primitive animism to the worship of fertility gods (Rod, creator of the world, and the *rozhanytsi* or Fates). The cult of Svaroh, god of the sky, sun, and thunder, emerged near the beginning of the first millennium B.C. Svaroh was the precursor of the major Slavic deity Perun, the god of thunder. Veles, the god of cattle, wealth, and trade, was another of the principal pagan gods. In addition to gods who were thought to control the forces of nature, the pagan **Slavs** worshipped a host of deities who "inhabited" forests, fields, and bodies of water. Individual tribes, clans, and families had gods of their own. Sacrifices and rituals were performed to propitiate these gods. There was no priestly caste among the pagans, nor did they erect temples or statues.

In an unsuccessful attempt to promote **Kyiv's** primacy, Prince **Volodymyr the Great**, who was to Christianize Kyivan Rus' in 988, erected a pantheon of pagan gods in the Kyiv citadel in 980. Besides Perun, the pantheon included representations of Khors and Dazhboh (sun gods), Simarhl (god of the earth and the underworld), Stryboh (god of the winds), and Mokosh (goddess of fertility and households). These statues were destroyed with Kyiv's adoption of Christianity.

The **Christianization of Rus'** was a lengthy process that involved compromise with existing pagan beliefs. Pagan seasonal festivals were assimilated to feasts of the Christian calendar, and attributes of pagan deities came to be associated with Christian saints. Dualism persisted for centuries, with many traces of pagan rituals preserved in **folk customs** associated with Christian feasts.

PAINTING. Frescoes and murals discovered at archaeological sites among the Greek **Black Sea colonies** (first millennium B.C.) are the oldest surviving paintings in Ukraine. The **Kyivan Rus'** legacy is preserved in fragments of frescoes at the Cathedral of the Transfiguration in Chernihiv and **St. Sophia's Cathedral** and St. Michael's Golden-Domed Monastery in **Kyiv**. Stylistically, these 11th-century frescoes resemble Middle Byzantine art. More realist Balkan influences are apparent in the 12th-century frescoes of the church of St. Cyril's Monastery in Kyiv. According to the *Tale of Bygone Years*, portable icons were being painted by the 10th and 11th centuries, but none from that period have survived in Ukraine. The best-known Kyivan iconographer of the time was Olimpii. Examples of medieval Ukrainian painting are also to be found in illuminated manuscripts (*see* DESIGN, GRAPHIC).

In the 13th century, the Principality of **Galicia-Volhynia** emerged as the leading political and cultural center of the Ukrainian lands. The surviving achievements of Ukrainian iconographers of that period are preserved in churches of the Wawel Castle in Cracow and the Holy Cross Church in Łysa Góra (14th century) in works commissioned by the Polish kings Casimir III and Władysław II Jagiełło. The 15th and 16th centuries saw the emergence of a distinctive school of Galician icon-painting in which the Byzantine style was modified by local variations and Western influences. During the Renaissance, icons became more realistic, but secular themes were introduced only in the 17th century, when Byzantine traditions gave way to the **baroque**. Two of the better-known iconographers of the time were Ivan Rutkovych and Yov Kondzelevych, whose work was influenced by Western religious painting. Some of the finest examples of baroque painting are to be found in the Holy Trinity Church of the **Kyivan Cave Monastery**.

Portrait painting as a separate genre developed in the 16th century, but portraits used for nonreligious purposes did not appear until the 17th century. In time, Ukrainian painting came to encompass a variety of portraits, battle scenes, genre depictions, and historical compositions. As the autonomy of the **Hetmanate** was circumscribed by the Russian authorities in the 18th century, local painters found opportunities increasingly limited. While art in Ukraine declined, Ukrainians such as **Volodymyr Borovykovsky** and Dmytro Levytsky became leading figures of the St. Petersburg classical school of painting.

In many ways, the poet **Taras Shevchenko** is considered the father of modern Ukrainian painting, since he devoted most of his works to Ukrainian themes. His followers adopted that approach and gave rise to the Ukrainian ethnographic school of art. At the end of the 19th century, realist artists such as **Ilia Repin** came under the influence of the Peredvizhniki Society in St. Petersburg.

Movements inspired by **modernism** influenced the style of numerous artists. **Ivan Trush**, Mykola Burachek, and Oleksander Murashko painted in the impressionist vein, Mykola Hlushchenko adopted the postimpressionist style, and **Oleksa Novakivsky** and Oleksa Hryshchenko (Alexis Gritchenko) were inspired by expressionism. The early 20th-century avant-garde was strongly felt in Ukraine, particularly in the work of **Kazimir Malevich**, Oleksander Bohomazov, Davyd Burliuk, Vladimir Tatlin, and Alexandra Exter. The resurgence of Ukrainian national traditions after 1917 is best exemplified by the monumentalism of **Mykhailo Boichuk**, Ivan Padalka, and **Vasyl Sedliar**, who combined Ukrainian, Byzantine, and modern Western influences in a revived form of fresco. Boichuk was a particularly influential teacher at the **Ukrainian State Academy of Arts**, which he helped establish in 1917. In the 1920s, Ukrainian painting was part of a thriving artistic culture in a variety of styles, including cubo-futurism, abstraction, and symbolism.

In the 1930s, officially mandated socialist **realism** became the only permissible style, and the development of avant-garde painting in the **Ukrainian SSR** came to an end. Painting was limited to naturalistic depictions glorifying Soviet life. Landscape and still-life painting was discouraged, and deviations from socialist realism were condemned as "formalist." The confines of socialist realism were broadened somewhat during the de-Stalinization of the late 1950s and early 1960s. Painters returned to abstraction, surrealism, and expressionism, as well as to Ukrainian folk themes, more vibrant colors, and flattened planes. The curtailment of artistic freedom in the late 1960s was an obstacle to the careers of such painters as Opanas Zalyvakha and Ivan Marchuk; it gave rise to nonconformist tendencies best exemplified by Feodosii Humeniuk and Volodymyr Makarenko. Among émigré artists, **Jacques Hnizdovsky** was a prominent painter in the neorealist style.

The introduction of *glasnost* and *perestroika* in the **USSR** in the mid-1980s resulted in greater creative freedom and a proliferation of styles, among which surrealism gained special popularity. Artists whose work had been suppressed gave solo exhibitions. Today, Ukrainian artists are rejoining the international artistic mainstream. Smaller independent art galleries promoting a variety of styles and genres flourish in all major cities.

PALII, SEMEN (1640s–January 1710). Actual surname: Hurko. Colonel of Bila Tserkva (Fastiv) and leader of the anti-Polish struggle in **Right-Bank Ukraine**. Born in Borzna, Chernihiv region, into a **Cossack** family, Palii received his education at the **Kyiv Mohyla** Collegium. In the 1670s, he distinguished himself in military and organizational affairs in the **Zaporozhian Host**. In 1685, after the Polish Diet confirmed Cossack rights, Palii assisted in the formation of the Fastiv and Bohuslav Cossack regiments on the sparsely populated territory of the southern **Kyiv** region and helped revive regiments in Bratslav and Korsun. Together with **Left-Bank** Cossacks, he battled the forces of the Ottoman Empire and the **Crimean** Khanate (1680s–90s). In the late 1680s, striving for the liberation of Right-Bank Ukraine from Polish rule and its unification with the **Hetmanate**, Palii and his associates led a large-scale struggle against the Polish nobility. The abolition of the Right-Bank Cossack regiments by the Polish Diet (1699) provoked a major uprising under Palii's leadership (1702–4) that engulfed the Kyiv and Bratslav palatinates, as well as part of **Podilia**. Unable to secure help from the Hetmanate or Muscovy, the rebels were defeated by the Polish forces. Palii then sought allies among Polish magnates who supported Charles XII of Sweden. He attempted to rally the Zaporozhians against **Ivan Mazepa**, who ordered Palii's arrest (July 1704). In 1705, Palii was exiled to Tobolsk, Siberia. After Mazepa's breach with Peter I, Palii was released from exile and served as colonel of the Bila Tserkva regiment until his death. He was buried at the **Kyivan Cave Monastery**.

PANSLAVISM. Cultural and political movement among the Slavic peoples based on a conception of their ethnic and linguistic affinity and the necessity of their political union. The idea developed in the late 18th and early 19th centuries. (The term "Panslavism" was first used in Bohemia in 1826 by Ján Herkel.) The ideals of the French Revolution and German **romanticism** influenced the Slavic cultural and political revivals of the early 19th century, promoting ideas of Slavic unity and cultural mutuality among the West and South Slavic intelligentsia (the Czech Josef Dobrovský, the Slovaks Pavol Šafařík and Jan Kollár, the Croat Ljudovit Gaj, the Serb Vuk Karadžić, and others). The successes of the Russian Empire in its wars against the Ottoman Empire and Napoleon led some Slavic activists, such as Dobrovský, Gaj, and Josef Jungmann, to propose a political and linguistic union of the **Slavs** under Russia. Some of them later changed their views on the subject (Gaj, Karel Havlíček-Borovský, and L'udovít Štúr). Other supporters of Panslavism, represented by the Czech historian František Palacký, advocated the transformation of the Habsburg Monarchy into a federation of Slavs, Austrians, and Hungarians (in 1867, when the formation of Austria-Hungary rendered this plan obsolete, Palacký attended the Slavic Congress organized by Russian Panslavists in Moscow). Among the Poles, whose ideal was the restoration of Poland in its pre-1772 boundaries, Panslavism developed both pro-Russian and anti-Russian trends. Representatives of the latter believed that Poland should play the principal role in Slavic unification.

In Russia itself at the end of the 1830s, the works of Mikhail Pogodin proclaimed the superiority of Slavs over other peoples and Russia's mission to lead the Slavic world. Russian Slavophiles of the 1840s and 1850s (e.g., Konstantin Aksakov, Aleksei Khomiakov, and Ivan Kireevsky) opposed the Orthodox Slavic world to a "diseased" and heathen Europe. The Russian defeat in the Crimean War (1853–56), the Polish Uprising of 1863–64, and the escalation of the Eastern Question mobilized the Russian Panslavists, who attained the height of their political influence in the Russo-Turkish War (1877–78), when the government intervened in the Balkans on behalf of the Bulgarians, Romanians, and Serbs.

In Ukraine, Panslavic ideas proliferated in the first quarter of the 19th century (*see* SOCIETY OF UNITED SLAVS). Their influence was clearly apparent in the program of the **Cyril and Methodius Brotherhood**, among Ukrainian scholars of the mid-19th century (e.g., **Osyp Bodiansky** and **Mykhailo Maksymovych**), and in the liberal segment of the Ukrainian gentry (e.g., **Hryhorii Galagan** and Nikolai Rigelman), whose representatives participated in the Slavic committees of Kyiv and Odesa in the 1850s–70s. As in other Slavic lands, a **Galician**-Ruthenian *matytsia* (cultural institution) was founded in **Lviv** in 1848. During the **Revolution of 1848**, Galician Ukrainians established contacts with Slavic activists in the Habsburg Monarchy and participated in the Slavic Congress in Prague (June 1848).

With the establishment of independent Slavic states in the late 19th and early 20th centuries, Russia came to be seen as a competitor and potential oppressor, diminishing the appeal of Panslavism. Subsequent attempts to reanimate it were made shortly before **World War I**, as Russia revived its claims to Ukrainian territory under Austrian rule, and in the 1940s, when the **USSR** sought to mobilize Slavic support against Nazi Germany and then against the West. There have also been Panslavic stirrings in Russia since the collapse of the USSR.

PARADZHANOV, SERHII (9 January 1924–21 July 1990). Armenian name: Sarkis Paradzhanian. Armenian and Ukrainian **film** director, People's Artist of the **Ukrainian SSR** (1990), and laureate of the **Shevchenko** State Prize (posthumously, 1991). He was born in Tbilisi, Georgia. After graduating from the Moscow State Institute of Cinema Arts (class of Ihor Savchenko) in 1951, Paradzhanov was assigned to work at the **Dovzhenko** Film Studio in **Kyiv**. He made several short and documentary films, including *Nataliia Uzhvii*, *Zoloti ruky* (Golden Hands), *Dumka* (all 1957), *Pershyi khlopets'* (First Boy, 1958), *Ukraïns'ka rapsodiia* (Ukrainian Rhapsody, 1961), and *Kvitka na kameni* (Flower on Stone, 1962). His screen adaptation of **Mykhailo Kotsiubynsky's** novella *Tini zabutykh predkiv* (Shadows of Forgotten Ancestors, 1964) brought him international acclaim and numerous awards. The production became an important event for the ***shistdesiatnyky*** generation. The film also initiated an influential movement known as the Ukrainian poetic cinema.

For his involvement in protests against political arrests in Ukraine (1965–68), Paradzhanov was persecuted by the Soviet authorities. In 1973, he was arrested and sentenced to a lengthy term of imprisonment on trumped-up charges but released in 1977 thanks to an international protest campaign. Barred from living in Ukraine, he settled in Tbilisi. Outside Ukraine, Paradzhanov completed *Sayat Nova* (The Color of Pomegranates, 1969), *Legend of Surami Fortress* (1984), and *Ashik Kerib* (1988). *Lebedyne ozero. Zona* (Swan Lake: The Zone), based on Paradzhanov's screenplay and directed by Yurii Illienko, was released in 1990. Paradzhanov died in Yerevan, Armenia.

PARASHCHUK, MYKHAILO (16 November 1878–24 December 1963). Sculptor and civic activist. He was born in Varvaryntsi, Ternopil region, and studied at the Cracow School of Fine Arts and the **Lviv** Polytechnic, as well as at the Académie Julian and the studio of Auguste Rodin in Paris (1907–9). He worked in Lviv, Warsaw (1902–5), Munich (1908–11), and **Kyiv** (1911–13). During **World War I**, Parashchuk was an active member of the **Union for the Liberation of Ukraine**. He organized courses in sculpture, pottery, and wood carving for Ukrainian soldiers in the Russian army interned in Austrian POW camps (1915–18). After returning to Ukraine in 1918, Parashchuk served as secretary and later head of the diplomatic mission of the **Ukrainian People's Republic** in Estonia. In 1923, he settled in Sofia, Bulgaria, where he opened an art school and participated in the community life of the Ukrainian **diaspora**. He died and was buried in Sofia.

Parashchuk executed some 30 sculptural portraits of distinguished Ukrainian cultural figures, including **Vasyl Stefanyk**, **Stanyslav Liudkevych** (both 1906), **Taras Shevchenko** (1912), **Ivan Franko** (1913), **Mykola Lysenko** (1913), **Mykhailo Hrushevsky**, **Symon Petliura** (1936), Metropolitan **Andrei Sheptytsky**, Oleksander Oles, Bohdan Lepky, and **Yevhen Petrushevych**, and Bulgarian political figures (Khristo Botev [1922], Georgi Dimitrov [1927]). He created monuments to Adam Mickiewicz in Lviv (with Antoni Popiel) and to the POWs who died in the Wetzlar and Rastatt camps, and sculpted the burial monument of **Mykhailo Drahomanov** in Sofia (1932). He also executed a series of monumental and decorative sculptures for buildings in the Bulgarian capital. Parashchuk's early works display a tendency toward Rodin's impressionism and psychologism, while his Bulgarian period is dominated by the academic style.

PATON, BORYS (b. 27 November 1918). Metallurgist; full member (from 1958) and president (from 1962) of the **Ukrainian Academy of Sciences**. Born in **Kyiv**, the son of **Yevhen Paton**, he graduated from the Kyiv Industrial Institute in 1940. In 1942, he began working at the Institute of Electric Welding at the Academy of Sciences, becoming its director in 1953. Paton's scientific contributions are in modern welding methods, including electric-arc, electron-beam, and plasma welding; welding in space; and seamless pipes.

PATON, YEVHEN (4 March 1870–12 August 1953). Welding scientist and civil engineer; full member of the **Ukrainian Academy of Sciences** from 1929. Born in Nice, France, Paton graduated from the Dresden Polytechnical Institute (1894) and the St. Petersburg Institute of Civil Engineers (1896) and was a professor at the **Kyiv** Polytechnical Institute from 1904 to 1939 (with interruptions). He formulated basic principles of bridge design and bridge testing and published textbooks and monographs in the field. Between 1896 and 1929 he designed more than 35 bridges and viaducts, including a large bridge across the Dnipro River (1924). Paton's major scientific contributions were in electric welding and include arc welding and automation, welding apparatus designs, and strength calculations of welded joints. In 1934, the electric welding laboratory that Paton organized at the Academy of Sciences became the Institute of Electric Welding, which he headed until his death. Today the institution bears his name. In 1964, the Academy of Sciences established the Paton Prize for outstanding contributions to materials science, particularly welding technology.

PAVLYCHKO, DMYTRO (b. 28 September 1929). Poet, translator, and diplomat. Born in Stopchativ (now in Ivano-Frankivsk oblast), he graduated from **Lviv** University (1953). Pavlychko began to publish poetry in the 1950s; in the 1970s and 1980s, he worked as a journalist in Lviv and **Kyiv**. He was editor in chief of the journal *Vsesvit* (Universe, 1972–79) and secretary of the Union of Writers of both Ukraine and the **USSR** (1986–90). A founder of **Rukh**, he was also president of the **Taras Shevchenko** Ukrainian Language Society (1989–90). Pavlychko was a deputy to the Verkhovna Rada of Ukraine (1990–94), in which he headed the parliamentary faction of the Democratic Party of Ukraine and the commission on **foreign affairs**. In 1995, he was appointed ambassador to Slovakia, and in 1999, he became ambassador to Poland. He has written many poetry collections, articles of literary criticism, **film** scripts, and children's books. Pavlychko has been awarded the **Shevchenko** State Prize (1977) and the Pavol Hviezdoslav Literary Prize of Slovakia. Pavlychko's daughter Solomiia (1958–99) was noted as a literary critic, translator, and cofounder of the Osnovy publishing house in Kyiv.

PAVLYK, MYKHAILO (17 September 1853–26 January 1915). Civic and political figure, publicist, and writer. He was born in Monastyryske, Kolomyia region, and studied at gymnasiums in Kolomyia and **Lviv**. After enrolling at Lviv University (1874), he joined the Academic Circle. Pavlyk contributed to the journal *Druh* (Friend), where he became acquainted with **Ivan Franko**. Under the influence of **Mykhailo Drahomanov**, he became a **Ukrainophile** socialist, helping to change the orientation of the Academic Circle away from **Russophilism**. Pavlyk and Franko published the journal *Hromads'kyi druh* (Friend of the Community, 1878) and the almanacs *Dzvin* (Bell) and *Molot* (Hammer) and participated in a Polish-Ukrainian socialist committee. Because of his political views, Pavlyk was imprisoned five times and tried on nearly 30 occasions. In order to escape further arrest, he emigrated to Geneva (1879), where he published the journal *Hromada* (Community) with Drahomanov and Serhii Podolynsky (until 1882). After returning to Lviv, he edited the **populist** newspaper *Bat'kivshchyna* (Fatherland) in 1889. With Franko, he became a founder of the **Ukrainian Radical Party**, publishing its periodicals *Narod* (People, 1890–95), *Khliborob* (Agrarian, 1891–95), and *Hromads'kyi holos* (Community Voice, 1898–1903); he led the party from 1899 to 1914. Pavlyk was a full member of the **Shevchenko Scientific Society** and its first librarian (1897–1904). In 1914, he became vice president of the **Supreme Ukrainian Council**. He wrote novels, numerous short stories, and works on the Ukrainian movement in **Galicia**. He also published Drahomanov's letters and works.

PEASANTS. In **Kyivan Rus'**, peasants lived in relatively autonomous settlements where they worked together. They belonged to the stratum of *smerdy*, most of whom enjoyed the rights of freemen. With the onset of Polish and Lithuanian rule in the mid-14th century, peasants generally lost their freedom and became serfs dependent on landowners. Beginning in the late 15th century, a new form of serfdom was established requiring peasants to labor for their landlords as a form of rent, often four or five days a week. They also had their own small plots that provided for their families. With the eastward expansion of the Polish state in the 16th century, peasants were encouraged to settle in the eastern and southern territories, where labor obligations were not so onerous. Over time, however, they steadily increased.

Peasant serfs who escaped from their landlords' estates often settled in the steppes of southern and **Sloboda Ukraine**, where they became **Cossacks**. In the aftermath of the **Khmelnytsky Uprising** (1648–57), when enserfed peasants joined the Cossack forces, the emerging **Hetmanate** abolished serfdom, only to reinstate it later. By 1730, about half the peasant population of **Left-Bank** and Sloboda Ukraine was enserfed. With the suppression of Cossackdom by the Muscovite and Polish authorities, the status of the peasants declined even further, resulting in the **haidamaka** revolts of the mid-18th century. The Russian empress Catherine II officially reinstated serfdom in Left-Bank and Sloboda Ukraine in 1783.

In the first half of the 19th century, serfs constituted the most oppressed stratum in the Russian Empire. Entirely dependent on their gentry landlords, serfs could be tried, exiled to Siberia, impressed into military service, and subjected to corporal punishment. They also needed the landlord's permission to marry and could be sold as individuals or as entire families. Labor obligations were established by the landlord. Rising unrest in the countryside and the loss of the **Crimean** War led in 1861 to reforms that included the abolition of serfdom in the Russian Empire.

In **Galicia**, under Austrian rule from 1772, peasants fared somewhat better owing to the reforms of Empress Maria Theresa and Emperor Joseph II. Legal protection was introduced, and the landlords' traditional rights were restricted: labor obligations were limited to three days per week, personal servitude was abolished, and a form of peasant landownership was legally defined. However, the reforms had only a limited impact, as landlords undermined their implementation and political reaction set in. The established order began to crumble with the **Revolution of 1848**, which led to the abolition of serfdom in Galicia, **Bukovyna**, and **Transcarpathia**.

Peasant emancipation in Russian-ruled Ukraine brought personal freedom but entailed heavy financial obligations in the form of redemption payments to landlords. Part of the land was sold to village communes, to be repaid in installments over a lengthy period. Individual peasant holdings were small, averaging 7.3 ha per household. Land hunger resulted in the migration of about 1.6 million Ukrainian peasants to the Russian Far East between 1896 and 1914.

In Austrian-ruled Ukraine, the average size of peasant landholdings declined rapidly, owing to a tradition of dividing land among all children in the family. By the end of the 19th century, more than half of peasant plots were smaller than two ha, forcing peasants to emigrate to North America and elsewhere. During the 1860s, the Austrian government introduced compulsory **education** for peasant children, which considerably raised the cultural level of the western Ukrainian peasantry.

The revolutionary upheaval of 1917–21 saw the redistribution of land owned by the state and the landlords to peasants. Farms became larger, and the production of grain and livestock increased considerably. This growth was curtailed by Soviet appropriation detachments that confiscated grain and livestock to feed the urban population and the Red Army. As a result, peasants decreased production—a policy that, combined with drought and official malfeasance, resulted in the **famine of 1921–23**. The Soviet authorities relented, introducing the New Economic Policy (NEP), under which peasants were allowed to lease land and hire labor. Shortly thereafter, agricultural production surpassed the prerevolutionary level.

Stalin abruptly reversed the NEP in 1928, introducing the **collectivization** of **agriculture**. This provoked mass resistance, with peasants slaughtering their livestock and refusing to join collectives. The regime responded by arresting large numbers of peasants, deporting them to the Soviet north, and confiscating their property. When this did not suffice, the man-made **famine of 1932–33** was imposed to break peasant resistance; all grain and livestock were confiscated, and the death penalty was imposed for any theft of food from collective farms. Between four and one-half and five million peasants starved as a result. Collectivization and the famine drastically changed the social psychology of the Ukrainian village; since there was scant economic incentive to produce and a higher standard of living was available in the cities, the rural sector became depressed for decades to come. The **famine of 1946–47** claimed an additional million lives when, in the wake of **World War II**, the Soviet authorities imposed high grain-requisition quotas in the drought-stricken Ukrainian countryside.

With the Soviet reoccupation of western Ukraine after the war, western Ukrainian peasants were forced to join collective farms, although they were able to retain some animals and small plots of land around their houses. The yield of these gardens was sufficient to feed peasant families and supply cities with potatoes, vegetables, and milk. However, the food shortages of the 1970s and 1980s exposed the inefficiency of collective farming and the declining productivity of private plots.

Ukraine's independence brought no immediate improvement, and agricultural production declined for several years. Land is still effectively owned by the state and collective agricultural enterprises, although privately owned farms produce more than half of Ukraine's meat, fruit, and vegetables from less than 15 percent of the arable land. Land **privatization** is proceeding slowly, with a target date of January 2005 established for the free-market purchase and sale of land.

PECHENEGS. *Be-ča-nags* in Turkic and Patzinaks in West European and Byzantine chronicles. Alliance of Turkic and other tribes in the trans-Volga steppes in the eighth and ninth centuries. In the 890s, the Pechenegs moved into the steppes north of the Black Sea. Reaching the Danube estuary, they forced out other tribes, notably the Magyars. The Pechenegs are first mentioned in the *Tale of Bygone Years* under the year 915. Prince **Ihor** signed a treaty with them, after which they migrated to the borders of Byzantium and Hungary. In 920, Ihor led a campaign against the Pechenegs, but in 944 they participated in his campaign against Byzantium.

The Pechenegs first attacked **Kyiv** in 915. They crushed the retinue of **Sviatoslav Ihorevych** near the Dnipro Rapids, killing the prince in battle (972). In the late 10th and early 11th centuries, Pecheneg attacks on Rus' became more frequent. **Volodymyr the Great** engaged in ferocious battles with the Pechenegs (988–97) and built fortifications as a defense against them. Subsequently, the Pechenegs were involved in internecine wars between Volodymyr's sons Sviatopolk (whom they supported) and **Yaroslav the Wise**, who dealt them a crushing defeat in 1036.

Those Pechenegs who continued their nomadic existence on the Black Sea steppes entered into a tribal union with the **Cumans** in the second half of the 11th century. At the end of that century, the Pechenegs began attacking Byzantine lands. Some of them recognized the authority of the Kyivan princes and settled in **Kyivan Rus'**, particularly in the basin of the Ros River. The Pechenegs were last mentioned in 1168 as members of Turkic tribes known in the **chronicles** as the Black Hats.

PEREIASLAV AGREEMENT. Political arrangement whereby **Cossack Ukraine**, or the **Hetmanate**, recognized the suzerainty of the Muscovite tsar. After the **Khmelnytsky Uprising** (1648) against the **Polish-Lithuanian Commonwealth**, Hetman **Bohdan Khmelnytsky** established an autonomous polity, the Hetmanate, whose existence was threatened by continuing hostilities with Poland. Khmelnytsky sought a military alliance with Muscovy. In October 1653, Muscovy declared war on the Commonwealth, and the Assembly of the Land decided to accept Cossack Ukraine into the Muscovite state. A large delegation of Muscovite officials went to Pereiaslav (on the Dnipro River) to proclaim the new arrangement officially. Negotiations between Khmelnytsky and the Muscovite **boyar** Vasilii Buturlin began in Pereiaslav in early January 1654. The **hetman** first called an officers' council and subsequently a general military council to the ratify the proposed agreement. Then the hetman and the officers were to pledge allegiance to their new sovereign, the Muscovite tsar. However, Khmelnytsky demanded that the Muscovite officials first swear on behalf of the tsar that he would uphold all their rights and liberties. Buturlin refused, declaring it unthinkable that an autocrat should swear an oath to a subject, but assured the Ukrainian elite that the tsar's word was equivalent to an oath. The Ukrainian side suspended the ceremony and held a new council. In the end, Khmelnytsky and most of the Cossack elite swore allegiance to the tsar on 8 (18) January, although some key officers and clergymen refused to do so. Insisting on a written agreement, Khmelnytsky sent the general judge of the Hetmanate, Samiilo Bohdanovych-Zarudnyi, and the colonel of Pereiaslav, **Pavlo Teteria**, to Moscow with the "Soliciting Articles" for confirmation by the tsar. The conditions specified in the document were reduced and ratified by the tsar and the boyar council on 14 (24) March (*see* ARTICLES OF BOHDAN KHMELNYTSKY).

The "March Articles" were modeled on treaties between the Cossacks and the Commonwealth signed at Zboriv (1649) and Bila Tserkva (1651). The Muscovite government undertook to declare war on Poland, respect the hetman's right to conduct domestic and foreign policy (except for relations with Poland and the Ottoman Empire), and maintain a 60,000-strong Cossack army and administration with taxes collected in the Hetmanate. These terms were modified whenever a new hetman took office so as to establish greater Muscovite control. Subsequently, historians differed greatly in interpreting the treaty; some believed that it signaled the incorporation of Ukraine into Russia, others saw it as establishing a protectorate over an autonomous Hetmanate, and still others viewed it merely as a military alliance. However the agreement is interpreted, there is a consensus that it marked the beginning of centuries of Russian dominance in Ukraine.

PERESOPNYTSIA GOSPEL/PERESOPNYTS'KE IEVANHELIIE. Vernacular Ukrainian translation of the New Testament from the Polish and Czech (1556–61). The translation was done by Archimandrite Hryhorii of the Monastery of the Theotokos in Peresopnytsia (**Volhynia**). The scribe was probably Mykhailo Vasyliovych of Sianik (Sanok). In 1837, the manuscript was discovered by **Osyp Bodiansky**; it is now preserved at the **Volodymyr Vernadsky** National Library of Ukraine in **Kyiv**. Since 1991, the gospel has been used in presidential inauguration ceremonies.

PETLIURA, SYMON (10 May 1879–25 May 1926). Journalist; military and political leader. Petliura was born in a suburb of **Poltava**, descended from old **Cossack** and clerical families. After completing a boarding school, he studied at the Poltava Theological Seminary (1895–1901). He was expelled for membership in a clandestine Ukrainian **hromada** and for inviting the composer **Mykola Lysenko** to the seminary. In 1900, Petliura became a member of the **Revolutionary Ukrainian Party** (RUP), part of which was reorganized as the **Ukrainian Social Democratic Labor Party** (USDRP) in 1905. To avoid arrest, he moved to the Kuban region (1902), where he worked as a teacher and archivist (cataloguing the archives of the Kuban Cossacks). Arrested for his RUP activities, Petliura went to **Lviv** in 1904 to edit the RUP monthly *Selianyn* (Peasant) and returned to **Kyiv** after the general amnesty of 1905. In early 1906, he edited the USDRP monthly *Vil'na Ukraïna* (Free Ukraine) in St. Petersburg. Later in 1906 he became secretary of the Kyiv daily *Rada* (Council) and coedited the social democratic monthly *Slovo* (Word, 1907–9). From 1912, Petliura edited the Russian-language monthly *Ukrainskaia zhizn'* (Ukrainian Life) in Moscow, which published works by **Mykhailo Hrushevsky**, **Dmytro Dontsov**, Sofiia Rusova, **Serhii Yefremov**, and Maxim Gorky.

During **World War I**, Petliura worked for the All-Russian Union of Zemstvos and Towns and represented the Ukrainian Military Committee of the Western Front in Minsk. In the declaration "Viina i ukraïntsi" (The War and the Ukrainians, July 1914), Petliura argued that Ukrainians were faithfully carrying out their obligations to the Russian state and expressed his hope that the postwar Russian leadership would take a more liberal attitude on the Ukrainian question. After the February Revolution of 1917, he became deeply involved in military affairs. He was a member of the **Ukrainian Central Rada** (from March 1917), head of the Ukrainian General Military Committee (May), and general secretary of military affairs in the Rada (June). In December 1917, Petliura resigned in protest against the policies of the head of government, **Volodymyr Vynnychenko**. In January and February 1918, he formed the **Haidamaka** Battalion of **Sloboda Ukraine** and helped put down a Bolshevik revolt in Kyiv. Under the **Ukrainian State**, he headed the Kyiv Gubernia Zemstvo and the All-Ukrainian Union of Zemstvos. He arranged the restoration of **Taras Shevchenko's** grave and Chernecha Mount in Kaniv. Petliura was arrested in July for a manifesto of the Union of Zemstvos denouncing the policies of **Pavlo Skoropadsky**. During the November uprising against Skoropadsky, Petliura was released from prison and elected to the Directory.

From November 1918, Petliura was supreme otaman of the Army of the **Ukrainian People's Republic** (UNR). In February 1919, he resigned from the USDRP (an attempt to appease the Entente) and became head of the Directory. For the next 10 months, he commanded the armed forces of the UNR (*see* DIRECTORY). When these forces were defeated by the Bolsheviks and Whites, Petliura signed the **Treaty of Warsaw** (21 April 1920) with Poland, initiating a joint military campaign against the Bolsheviks at the price of renouncing sovereignty over the western Ukrainian lands. After the failure of the campaign, Petliura headed the UNR government-in-exile in Poland. On 31 December 1923, he departed for Austria, then moved to Hungary and Switzerland. In October 1924, Petliura settled in Paris, where he organized the publication of the weekly *Tryzub* (Trident) and continued performing the duties of head of the Directory and supreme otaman of the UNR. He was murdered by Shalom Schwartzbard, a Bessarabian **Jew** who claimed to be avenging the victims of the pogroms of 1919 in Ukraine. Petliura was buried in Montparnasse Cemetery in Paris.

Petliura's uncompromising dedication to the cause of Ukrainian independence made him a leading symbol of the struggle for statehood. This was particularly true after his assassination, when his controversial role in arranging the Treaty of Warsaw was overshadowed by what most Ukrainians regarded as a martyr's death. Although Petliura has been accused of responsibility for the pogroms of 1919, there is abundant evidence that, like Ukrainian social democrats in general, he was personally opposed to anti-Semitism and condemned pogroms by irregulars acting in the name of the UNR. Ever since Petliura's death, there has been a widespread belief among Ukrainians that Schwartzbard was a Soviet agent hired to kill the leading representative of the Ukrainian independence struggle and compromise the Ukrainian cause in world opinion.

PETRUSHEVYCH, YEVHEN (3 June 1863–29 August 1940). President and dictator of the **Western Ukrainian People's Republic** (ZUNR). He was born in Busk (now in **Lviv** oblast) into a priest's family and educated at the Academic Gymnasium in Lviv and the faculty of law at Lviv University, where he obtained a doctorate. After opening his law practice in Sokal, Petrushevych became head of the local **Prosvita Society** branch and the County Savings Bank. An executive member of the **National Democratic Party**, he was a deputy to the Austrian parliament and vice-chairman of the Ukrainian Parliamentary Caucus (1907–17). From 1910, Petrushevych was a deputy to the Galician Diet and worked for electoral reform. During **World War I**, he was a member of the **Supreme Ukrainian Council** and the General Ukrainian Council.

In 1917–18, Petrushevych chaired the Ukrainian Parliamentary Caucus in Vienna. On 19 October 1918, as president of the **Ukrainian National Rada** (UNRada), he proclaimed the creation of a Ukrainian state within Austria-Hungary. He was elected president of the Rada in Stanyslaviv (now Ivano-Frankivsk), making him de facto president of the ZUNR (4 January 1919). By decision of the **Labor Congress**, Petrushevych became a member of the **Directory** after the proclamation of the **Act of Union** between the ZUNR and the **Ukrainian People's Republic** (UNR; 22 January 1919). On 9 June 1919, at a critical point in the **Ukrainian-Polish War in Galicia**, the UNRada appointed Petrushevych dictator of the ZUNR. The Directory refused to approve this act, ousted Petrushevych, and established a separate ministry for the ZUNR. Although the breach was papered over with the formation of a new government led by **Isaak Mazepa**, the acute political differences between Petrushevych and **Symon Petliura**, the president of the UNR, were never resolved (*see* UKRAINIAN GALICIAN ARMY).

On 15 November 1919, Petrushevych abandoned Kamianets-Podilskyi, where the UNR government was based, and established himself in Vienna. When Petliura signed the **Treaty of Warsaw** (21 April 1920), which ceded most of western Ukraine to Poland in return for military assistance against the Bolsheviks, Petrushevych declared the act legally invalid and took charge of the diplomatic struggle for the self-determination of the ZUNR. In August 1920, he formed a government-in-exile of the ZUNR that functioned until 15 March 1923, a day after the decision of the Council of Allied Ambassadors to place Galicia under Polish administration. Petrushevych settled in Berlin. He adopted Sovietophile views in the 1920s but abandoned them after the defeat of the **Ukrainization** policy in the **Ukrainian SSR**. He died in Berlin and was buried in the cemetery of St. Hedwig's Cathedral.

PIATAKOV, GEORGII (6 August 1890–30 January 1937). Russian Bolshevik leader in Ukraine. He was born in Horodyshche, **Kyiv** gubernia, and educated at St. Petersburg University. Piatakov joined the Bolshevik Party in 1910 and lived abroad for an extended period. In 1917, he became chairman of the Kyiv committee of the Bolshevik Party and a member of the executive committee of the Kyiv Soviet of Workers' Deputies. Until the beginning of 1918, Piatakov was a Bolshevik representative in the **Ukrainian Central Rada**; from August to November 1917 he belonged to the Little Rada and the Regional Committee for the Defense of the Revolution in Ukraine. His membership in those bodies was dictated by tactical considerations. Piatakov condemned virtually all the policies of the Central Rada, accusing it of "Ukrainian chauvinism" and declaring that "there is no reason for us to support the Ukrainians, as this movement does not benefit the proletariat."

On 27 October (9 November) 1917, Piatakov became a member of the Bolshevik Revolutionary Committee that attempted unsuccessfully to take over Kyiv in December. At the July 1918 congress of the **Communist Party of Ukraine**, he was elected secretary of its

Central Committee. In November 1918, Piatakov became a member of the Ukrainian Revolutionary Military Council (Joseph Stalin, **Volodymyr Zatonsky**, and **Volodymyr Antonov-Ovsiienko**) that planned and prepared the invasion of Ukraine that month. Piatakov headed the **Provisional Workers' and Peasants' Government of Ukraine** until January 1919. In that capacity, he oversaw the forced **collectivization** of **peasant agriculture** and the requisition of food for Russia. He opposed compromise with Ukrainian socialist parties, especially the **Borotbists**. Replaced as head of government by **Khristian Rakovsky**, Piatakov headed the Extraordinary Military Revolutionary Tribunal (from June 1919) and belonged to the Revolutionary Military Council of the 13th Workers' and Peasants' Red Army.

From 1920, Piatakov was a supporter of Leon Trotsky. He directed the Central Administration of the Coal Industry in the **Donets Basin** (1920–23) and was vice-chairman of the **USSR** Supreme Council of the National Economy (1923–27) and later of the USSR State Bank. He was one of the authors of the first Five-Year Plan and advocated the rapid industrialization of Ukraine. In 1923–27 and 1930–37, Piatakov was a member of the Central Committee of the All-Union Communist Party (Bolshevik). Arrested in Stalin's purge of 1936, Piatakov was accused of heading a secessionist "Ukrainian Trotskyist center" and summarily executed.

PIDHORNY, MYKOLA (PODGORNY, NIKOLAI) (5 [18] February 1903–11 January 1983). Soviet party leader. He was born in Karlivka (now in **Poltava** oblast), where he worked as a laborer from 1918. He was secretary of the Karlivka raion committee of the Communist Youth League (1921–23). Pidhorny completed a workers' school (1926) and graduated from the **Kyiv** Technological Institute of the Food Industry (1931). From 1930, he was a member of the **Communist Party of Ukraine** (CPU). After working as a sugar production engineer in the 1930s, he became deputy minister of the Ukrainian food industry (1939–40, 1944–46). He was also in charge of resettling Ukrainians from Poland to the **Ukrainian SSR** (1944–46; *see* UKRAINIAN-POLISH CONFLICT). From 1946, Pidhorny was the permanent representative of the **Council of Ministers** of the **Ukrainian SSR** to the **USSR** government. He was first secretary of the **Kharkiv** oblast committee (1950–53), then second secretary (from 1953) and first secretary (1957–63) of the CC CPU. During Pidhorny's tenure as first secretary, **Nikita Khrushchev** severely criticized the CPU for failing to meet his exceptionally high agricultural production targets. In line with these demands, Pidhorny blamed his subordinates for mismanagement and promised that the targets would be met. In June 1963, Khrushchev nominated him secretary of the Central Committee of the Communist Party of the Soviet Union (CPSU). In that post, Pidhorny plotted with Leonid Brezhnev and others dissatisfied with Khrushchev's leadership to remove him from office. Pidhorny convinced key members of the CPU leadership to support the coup, which was carried out in October 1964. From December 1965, Pidhorny chaired the Presidium of the USSR Supreme Soviet, becoming a member of the CPSU Politburo in April 1966. A close associate of **Petro Shelest**, his successor as CPU first secretary, Pidhorny lost favor after the latter's removal from office. In 1977, he was relieved of his government and party posts. He died and was buried in Moscow.

PIDKOVA, IVAN (POTCOAVĂ, IOAN) (d. 16 June 1578). **Cossack** leader and *hospodar* of the Principality of **Moldavia** (1577–78). He lived for an extended period at the **Zaporozhian Sich** and participated in a number of Cossack campaigns. In 1577, Pidkova intervened in the struggle over the Moldavian throne. Calling himself the brother of the Moldavian *hospodar* Ioan Vodă (d. 1574) and supported by a Cossack force led by Otaman Yakiv Shakh, Pidkova fought the Turkish candidate, Petru Şchiopul. His units seized Iaşi, and Pidkova was proclaimed *hospodar* of Moldavia, but in 1578, with the advance of a large Ottoman-Moldavian army under Sultan Murâd III, Pidkova's Cossacks retreated into Ukraine. He was seized in Nemyriv (Kamianets-Podilskyi, according to other sources) by Polish soldiers on the orders of Janusz Zbaraski, the palatine of Bratslav, and taken to Warsaw. By decision of the Polish Diet, Pidkova was executed in **Lviv** on 16 June 1578. His corpse was abducted by the Cossacks, who took it to a monastery in Kaniv for burial. He is eulogized in **Taras Shevchenko's** poem "Ivan Pidkova."

PIDMOHYLNY, VALERIIAN (20 January [2 February] 1901–3 November 1937). Writer and translator. He was born in Chapli, Katerynoslav region (now in the city of Dnipropetrovsk). Pidmohylny graduated from the Katerynoslav technical school in 1918 and briefly studied at **Kyiv** University. He worked as a teacher in Katerynoslav, Pavlohrad, and Vorzel, and then for the Knyhospilka **publishing** house in Kyiv. Pidmohylny's stories were first published in the Katerynoslav journal *Sich*; his first book, *Tvory. Tom pershyi* (Works: Volume One), appeared soon afterward. He contributed to the literary almanac *Vyr revoliutsiï* (Vortex of the Revolution, 1921) and to the journals *Zhovten'* (October), *Nova hromada* (New

Community), and *Zhyttia i revoliutsiia* (Life and Revolution). In the 1920s, he belonged to the literary organizations Aspys, Lanka, and MARS. As part of Stalin's campaign against the Ukrainian intelligentsia, Pidmohylny was dismissed from his editorial post in 1930 and arrested in 1934. He was imprisoned in a camp on the Solovets Islands and later executed.

Pidmohylny was one of the most notable Ukrainian novelists of the 20th century. He wrote a number of short-story collections and the novel *Ostap Shaptala* (1922), which depicted the revolutionary events in Ukraine in 1917–21, the fate of the Ukrainian village during the period of "war communism," the **famine of 1921–23**, and the postwar life of the Ukrainian intelligentsia. His best-known work is the novel *Misto* (The City), a psychological work that explores the complex relations between the city and the village in the 1920s. The novel was denounced by official critics, who accused Pidmohylny of disparaging the new Soviet culture and deliberately opposing the village to the city. Pidmohylny's final work, the novel *Nevelychka drama* (A Little Touch of Drama), was published in 1930. His *Povist' bez nazvy* (Untitled Novella) remained unfinished. Pidmohylny was also a prolific translator of French **literature** into Ukrainian.

PINCHUK, VIKTOR (b. 14 December 1960). Politician, reputed economic oligarch. He was born in **Kyiv** into the family of a civil servant. Pinchuk graduated from the Dnipropetrovsk Metallurgical Institute in 1983 as an engineer. After graduation, he worked as a scientist at the Dnipropetrovsk Research Institute of the Pipe Industry. At the same time, he cofounded a number of successful businesses. The most prominent of them—Interpipe, established in 1990—became one of the largest pipe producers in Europe. In 1997, after quitting his research job in Dnipropetrovsk, Pinchuk became president of Interpipe and began to expand his business, acquiring holdings in metallurgy and oil and gas in Ukraine, Belarus, and Russia, and becoming a major supplier to the Russian firm Gazprom, the world's largest gas and oil company. He also took over a number of sugar refineries, the major television channels ICTV and STB, the newspaper *Fakty i komentari* (Facts and Comments), and the banks Finansy i Kredyt and Kredyt-Dnipro, the latter headed by his first wife, Olena Arshava.

In 1998, Pinchuk was elected to the **Verkhovna Rada** (VR). Although he avoided the parliamentary limelight, he was actively involved in the reelection of President **Leonid Kuchma**, enlisting some of Boris Yeltsin's former image-makers in the campaign. In April 1998, the Labor Ukraine faction in the VR was established under Pinchuk's patronage; in the summer of 1999, it became a political party under the same name. A leader of the so-called Dnipropetrovsk clan, Pinchuk recruited as allies **Serhii Tyhypko** (later head of the National Bank of Ukraine), the young businessman Andrii Derkach (whose father headed the Security Service of Ukraine), and the former head of the presidential administration, **Dmytro Tabachnyk**. Pinchuk became even more influential in 2002, when he married Leonid Kuchma's daughter, Olena Franchuk. She gained international attention by establishing a fund in her name to fight HIV/AIDS, based on Pinchuk's contributions and additional fund-raising.

Cultivating the image of a reputable international businessman and civic leader, Pinchuk cooperated with the American philanthropist George Soros, initiating a network of free legal-advice centers in major Ukrainian cities. In 2004, he held meetings with Kofi Annan at **United Nations** headquarters in New York, former U.S. national security advisor Zbigniew Brzezinski, and former U.S. President George H. W. Bush in Kyiv. In an effort to distance himself from the Dnipropetrovsk clan, Pinchuk left the Labor Ukraine Party in the summer of 2004 to sit as an independent in the VR. He is known for his generous donations to museums, art galleries, orchestras, and **theaters**, as well as for his activities in the All-Ukrainian **Jewish** Congress.

PLAST. Children's and youth organization based on the principles of Lord Baden-Powell's scouting movement, dedicated to developing leadership abilities and nurturing Ukrainian patriotism. Its symbol is a trident intertwined with a *fleur-de-lis*. St. George is considered the organization's patron. Plast members greet one another with the word *skob*, the name of an eagle that lives near large bodies of water. The four letters of *skob* are interpreted as initials of the words *syl'no* (strongly), *krasno* (beautifully), *oberezhno* (carefully), and *bystro* (quickly), each of which has its own symbol (an oak leaf, a cluster of guelder-rose berries, a toadstool, and a lightning bolt).

The first Ukrainian scouting organization was established at the Academic Gymnasium in **Lviv** (1911) by Oleksander Tysovsky. It immediately adopted the name Plast (among **Zaporozhian Cossacks**, *plastuny* were scouts who followed enemy movements in border-area swamps). The movement soon spread throughout **western Ukraine**, and many Plast members joined the **Ukrainian Sich Riflemen**. The Plast movement assumed mass proportions in **Galicia** after the publication of the first Ukrainian scouting handbook, *Zhyttia v Plasti* (Life in Plast, 1921), edited by Tysovsky. Because of its Ukrainian patriotic ethos, the Polish authorities sought to eradicate Plast; its leaders were arrested, its assets confiscated, and the organization itself driven underground (from 1930) and then abroad (after 1939). National Plast organizations were established in most countries of the Ukrainian **diaspora**. In the 1990s, Plast activities were renewed in Ukraine, the Lviv city council being the first to grant the organization legal status.

PLETENETSKY, YELYSEI (1550–29 October [8 November] 1624). Orthodox church leader. Born in Pletenychi (now in **Lviv** oblast), he was archimandrite of the Leshcha Monastery in the Pynsk (Pinsk) region (1595–99). From 1599 to 1624, he served as archimandrite of the **Kyivan Cave Monastery**, winning the right of stauropegion (independence from local bishops) for it. Supported by the **Cossacks** and Hetman **Petro Sahaidachny**, Pletenetsky reclaimed monastic properties assigned by Sigismund III of Poland (1614) to the Uniate Church (*see* UKRAINIAN CATHOLIC CHURCH). In 1615, Pletenetsky established a press at the monastery that issued original works, as well as literature translated from Polish, Latin, and other languages. Between 1616 and 1624 he published 11 major religious, historical, and polemical works for which he wrote introductions, notably *Chasoslov* (Menaion, 1617), *Antologion* (1619), *Nomocanon* (1620 and 1624), a service book (1620), and a number of school texts. Pletenetsky established a paper factory in Radomyshl, assisted **brotherhood** schools, and sought to improve monastic life. By attracting leading ecclesiastical and cultural figures to **Kyiv**, Pletenetsky facilitated its transformation into the leading cultural and political center of Ukraine.

PLIUSHCH, LEONID (b. 26 April 1939). Mathematician, **human-rights** activist, and literary critic. Born in Naryn, Kirgizia, Pliushch grew up loyal to the Soviet regime—as an adolescent, he applied for admission to a KGB school. He turned against officialdom after the revelations of **Nikita Khrushchev's** "secret speech" (1956), while remaining a neo-Marxist by political conviction. Pliushch graduated from the University of **Kyiv** in 1963 and worked at the Institute of Cybernetics, **Ukrainian Academy of Sciences**, until 1968. **Ivan Dziuba**'s book *Internationalism or Russification?* prompted Pliushch to reexamine Soviet nationalities policy and begin speaking Ukrainian. He lost his position after taking part in an unofficial commemoration of the poet **Taras Shevchenko** and joined the Moscow-based Initiative Group for the Defense of Human Rights in 1969. Arrested in 1972 for writing articles and signing protests against human-rights violations, Pliushch (like other **dissidents** of the 1970s) was declared insane and imprisoned in the Dnipropetrovsk Special Psychiatric Hospital (July 1973), where he was subjected to depressants that rendered him immobile. His wife, Tatiana Zhitnikova, conducted a campaign in his defense that ultimately involved Amnesty International and a committee of French mathematicians. In January 1976, the Pliushch family was permitted to leave the **USSR** and settled in Paris. Pliushch was active in the foreign representation of the **Ukrainian Helsinki Group**.

Pliushch's autobiography, *U karnavali istoriï* (History's Carnival), was published in French (1977), English (1979), Russian (1979), and Ukrainian (1980). In the 1980s, he turned to literary criticism, publishing the study *Ekzod Tarasa Shevchenka* (Taras Shevchenko's Exodus, 1987).

POCHAIV MONASTERY/POCHAÏVS'KYI MONASTYR. Orthodox monastery in Pochaiv (now in Ternopil oblast), the second-largest men's monastery in Ukraine, first mentioned in a written source dated to 1527. In 1597, the noblewoman Anna Hoiska donated large properties to the monastery, which established a printing press and published its first book in 1618. Its Holy Trinity Church was built under the patronage of Fedir and Yevdokiia Domashevsky in 1649, and in the course of the 17th century the monastery was repeatedly attacked by Turks and **Tatars**. In 1675, it was reputedly saved from such an attack by a celebrated apparition of the Mother of God. In the early 18th century, it joined the Uniate Church (*see* UKRAINIAN CATHOLIC CHURCH), becoming a major center of the **Basilian Order**. After the defeat of the Polish Uprising of 1830–31, the Russian government transferred the monastery to the Orthodox clergy, and it became a stronghold of **Russification** in **Volhynia**. From 1887, the monastery published the journal *Pochaevskii listok* (Pochaiv Leaflet), which became an organ of the **Black Hundreds** in 1906. During the interwar period, the monastery was subject to the Orthodox metropolitan of Warsaw. Following the incorporation of **western Ukraine** into the **USSR**, it became an object of Soviet antireligious policies. The number of monks fell drastically from 200 in 1939 to approximately 12 in 1970. An attempt to close the monastery in 1964 was prevented by local and international protests. Today it is an Orthodox men's monastery under the jurisdiction of the **Ukrainian Orthodox Church** (Moscow Patriarchate). Its architectural ensemble consists of the Dormition Cathedral (1771–91, architect Gottfried Hoffman; sculptures by Matvii Poleiovsky, 1781–86), the **baroque** refectory (18th century), the classical bell tower (1860), and the Trinity Cathedral (1910–13, architect Aleksei Shchusev), built in imitation of the Novgorod style of the 12th and 13th centuries.

PODILIA (Ukr. *Podillia*). Historical and geographic region of Ukraine that occupies the basin between the Southern Buh River and the left tributaries of the Dnister River, encompassing the territories of present-day Vinnytsia, Khmelnytskyi, Ternopil, and parts of Ivano-Frankivsk and **Lviv** oblasts. In the Galician-Volhynian **Chronicle**, this territory was named Ponyzia. The term Podilia first appears in documents of the 14th century. In the 1360s, Podilian lands taken by Lithuanian princes became part of the **Grand Duchy of Lithuania**. Grand Duke Algirdas appointed Prince Fedir Koriatovych vicegerent of the region. In 1430, there was a Polish campaign into Podilia. The Bakota rebellion against Polish overlordship erupted in 1431–34. After it was quelled, western Podilia, including the towns of Kamianets, Smotrych, Bakota, and Skala, was incorporated into Poland. The Polish administrative system was introduced into western Podilia in 1434, creating the Podilia palatinate (based in Kamianets), which consisted of Kamianets, Letychiv, and Chervonohorod counties. Eastern Podilia remained part of the Grand Duchy of Lithuania. Podilian autonomy was abolished by Poland in the mid-15th century, and in 1566 the Bratslav palatinate, incorporating Bratslav, Vinnytsia, and Zvenyhorod counties, was established. Until 1598, its administrative center was Bratslav, later succeeded by Vinnytsia.

After the **Union of Lublin** (1569), the territory of eastern and western Podilia became part of the **Polish-Lithuanian Commonwealth**. These lands suffered great devastation at the hands of Crimean **Tatar** hordes and Ottoman feudal lords using the so-called Black and Kuchman routes. In the second half of the 15th century alone, no fewer than 33 raids were conducted in Podilia, followed by 35 in the 16th century. In the 15th and 16th centuries, there were numerous uprisings in Podilia, the largest of which were led by Mukha and Severyn Nalyvaiko (*see* COSSACK REBELLIONS).

During the **Khmelnytsky Uprising** (1648–57), the **Cossack** administrative system was established in Podilia. Regiments were formed in Bratslav (22 companies) and Kalnyk (later Vinnytsia; 19 companies). As a result of the **Truce of Andrusovo** (1667), Podilia again became part of the Commonwealth. In 1672, it was attacked by the Ottoman Turks, who established the Podilia eyalet, based in Kamianets, on the captured territory. Podilia was not returned to the Commonwealth until after the Treaty of Karlowitz (1699). In the 18th century, the Ukrainian population of Podilia staged a number of uprisings, including the **Palii** rebellion of 1702–4 and the **haidamaka** movement, which eventually grew into the **Koliivshchyna Rebellion**.

As a result of the first partition of Poland (1772), part of western Podilia was incorporated into Austria. In 1793, the remainder of Podilia was annexed by the Russian Empire, which established the vicegerencies of Podilia (seven counties) and Bratslav (nine counties). By a ukase of 12 (23) December 1796 they were merged into the Podilia gubernia (12 counties), based in Kamianets (1797). In the 1820s and 1830s, Podilia was the site of peasant uprisings led by **Ustym Karmaliuk**.

During **World War I**, Podilia became a major battleground, as a result of which its economy and population suffered great losses. Under the **Ukrainian People's Republic** (UNR), Kamianets, Proskuriv, Ushytsia, Liatychiv, and most of Mohyliv and Starokostiantyniv counties were incorporated into the Podilia land (administered from Kamianets), while Vinnytsia, Bratslav, Lityn (partially), Lypovets, Mohyliv, and Yampil counties were included in the Bratslav land (with its administrative center in Vinnytsia). The government of the UNR was briefly headquartered in Vinnytsia and Kamianets-Podilskyi.

After the defeat of the **Ukrainian Revolution** (1917–21), part of Podilia was incorporated into the **Ukrainian SSR**. In place of the Podilia gubernia, abolished in 1925, Vinnytsia oblast was created (1932), followed by Zhytomyr oblast (1937). The territory of Podilia west of the Zbruch River became part of Poland (1921–39). After **World War II**, all of Podilia was incorporated into the Ukrainian SSR. Today its territory consists of 61,000 sq. km, and its population numbers approximately 4.6 million.

PODLACHIA (Ukr. *Pidliashshia*). Historical province occupying the territory between the **Kholm region** to the south, the Narev River to the north, Mazovia (Poland) to the west, and **Polisia** to the east. Its name comes from the word *liakh* (Pole; "land near the Poles"). Podlachia, along with other Ukrainian ethnic territories (Kholm, **Sian**, and **Lemko** regions), is now part of Poland. In the ninth and 10th centuries, its territory was settled primarily by East Slavic tribes: Derevlianians, Buzhanians, and Drehovichians. From the 10th century, Podlachia was part of **Kyivan Rus'** and formed the western part of the **Berestia land** (known from the 12th century as the Dorohychyn land). In 1238, Prince **Danylo Romanovych** annexed the Dorohychyn land to the Principality of **Galicia-Volhynia**. At the time, the largest towns in Podlachia were Dorohychyn, Bilsk (Bielsk), and Melnyk. In 1253, Danylo was crowned king in Dorohychyn.

With the decline of the Galician-Volhynian state, Princes Gediminas and Kęstutis annexed Podlachia to the **Grand Duchy of Lithuania** in the early 14th century. In 1520, a separate palatinate, administered from Dorohychyn, was created in Podlachia. It consisted of the Dorohychyn, Bilsk, and Brest lands. In 1566, the Berestia land was incorporated into the newly created Brest-Lithuanian palatinate, while the Podlachian palatinate was divided into the Dorohychyn, Melnyk, and Bilsk lands.

After the **Union of Lublin** (1569), Podlachia became part of the **Polish-Lithuanian Commonwealth**. As a result of the three partitions of Poland (1772, 1793, and 1795), southern Podlachia was incorporated into Austria (up to the Buh River), while northern Podlachia (Bilsk region) was annexed to Prussia. During the Napoleonic Wars, northern Podlachia was incorporated into Russia (part of the Hrodna gubernia from 1842). Southern Podlachia became part of the Duchy of Warsaw (1809) and the Kingdom of Poland (1815). Throughout the 19th and early 20th centuries, the Ukrainian church and schooling were subject to increased official pressure intended to promote Polonization and then **Russification**. In 1874, the Russian government outlawed the Uniate Church (*see* UKRAINIAN CATHOLIC CHURCH) in Podlachia and introduced Orthodoxy, which prompted part of the Ukrainian population to adopt Roman Catholicism. In the early 20th century, Podlachian lands were part of the Hrodna, Siedlce, and Kholm gubernias of the Russian Empire.

During **World War I**, the tsarist government deported approximately 120,000 people from Podlachia and the Kholm region to the east. According to the **Treaty of Brest-Litovsk** (1918), Podlachia was to be included in the **Ukrainian People's Republic**, but in early November 1918 Polish forces took over Podlachia and the Kholm region, previously occupied by German armies. During the interwar period, the Polish government continued efforts to Polonize Ukrainians living in the region. After **World War II**, the autochthonous population of Podlachia suffered the same fate as Ukrainians in other ethnically Ukrainian lands that remained part of Poland. By agreement between the **USSR** and Poland, a significant number of Podlachian Ukrainians were resettled to the **Ukrainian SSR**, while the remainder were deported to northwestern Poland in the course of **Operation Vistula**.

POKUTIA (Ukr. *Pokuttia*). Historical province of Ukraine, the eastern portion of present-day Ivano-Frankivsk oblast. In documents of the 17th and 18th centuries, the region was referred to as the *kut* (corner) of **Galicia** (whence its name). It is located between the Dnister and Cheremosh Rivers and the Carpathian Mountains, including the Hutsul region. Since the 19th century, "Pokutia" has referred only to the flat portion of this territory. In 1387, Pokutia came under Polish control, and in 1772 it was taken over by Austria. Pokutia was a base of the Mukha rebellion (1490–92) against Polish magnate rule. From the 16th to the 18th century, **opryshok** units were active in the region. Pokutia again came under Polish rule in 1919. In 1939, along with other western Ukrainian lands, Pokutia was incorporated into the **Ukrainian SSR**.

POLAND. *See* BREST, UNION OF; COSSACKS; CURZON LINE; GALICIA; GALICIA-VOLHYNIA, PRINCIPALITY OF; HAIDAMAKAS; KHMELNYTSKY UPRISING; KHOLM REGION; LEMKO REGION; LUBLIN, UNION OF; LVIV; OPERATION VISTULA; ORGANIZATION OF UKRAINIAN NATIONALISTS; PACIFICATION; PODLACHIA; POLISH-LITHUANIAN COMMONWEALTH; POLISIA; RED RUS'; REVOLUTION OF 1848; RIGA, TREATY OF; SHEPTYTSKY, ANDREI; SIAN REGION; UKRAINIAN CATHOLIC CHURCH; UKRAINIAN MILITARY ORGANIZATION; UKRAINIAN-POLISH CONFLICT (1943–47); UKRAINIAN-POLISH WAR IN GALICIA (1918–19); VOLHYNIA; WARSAW, TREATY OF.

POLETYKA FAMILY. Cossack officer family in **Left-Bank Ukraine**. Ivan Poletyka, a Cossack of the Lubny company (1649), was the founder of the family. Pavlo Poletyka (d. 1709) was a fellow of the banner of the Lubny regiment. Andrii Poletyka (ca. 1692–1773) was the mayor of Romny (1727–29) and a fellow of the banner and fellow of the standard (from 1749) of the Lubny regiment. Andrii's son Hryhorii Poletyka (1725–27 November [8 December] 1784) was a political figure and writer. After graduating from the **Kyiv Mohyla Academy** (1745), he worked as a translator at the Academy of Sciences in St. Petersburg. He was the chief inspector of the nobiliary corps (1764–73). In 1767, upon his election to Catherine II's Legislative Council, Poletyka defended the autonomous order of Left-Bank Ukraine and the rights of the Ukrainian **nobility**. He wrote *Sbornik prav i privilegii malorossiiskogo shliakhetstva* (Collection of the Rights and Privileges of the Little Russian Nobility) and an essay on the origins of his *alma mater*. He translated Aristotle and compiled a six-language dictionary of Russian, Greek, Latin, French, German, and English (1763). In the opinion of some historians (**Oleksander Lazarevsky**, Vasyl Horlenko, and Illia Borshchak), Poletyka and his son, Vasyl, wrote the *Istoriia Rusov*. Andrii's son Andrii Poletyka (ca. 1741–ca. 1798) was a military chancellor (from 1758), assistant to the general standard-bearer, and a fellow of the standard (from 1767). In 1784 and 1797–98, he was marshal of the nobility of Romny county and Chernihiv gubernia (1785–88). He wrote *Dnevnik prebyvaniia Ekateriny II v Kieve v 1787 g.* (Diary of the Visit of Catherine II to Kyiv in 1787). Andrii's son Ivan Poletyka (18 [29] August 1726–22 April [3 May] 1783) was a physician and scientist. He studied in Kiel and Leiden and later became a professor at Kiel University

(1754–56). From 1756, he directed the St. Petersburg Infantry Hospital and Medical School. In 1763, he became director of the Vasylkiv Quarantine Service and worked at the Kyiv Quarantine Hospital. He distinguished himself while fighting an epidemic of the plague. Vasyl Poletyka (1765–1845), a son of Hryhorii Poletyka, was a historian and civic figure. After graduating from Vilnius University, he served in the military (until 1790). In 1802 and from 1805 to 1812, he was marshal of the nobility of Romny county. Involved in **education**, he wrote a work on the history of the ancient East and collected documentary materials for a history of Ukraine from the 16th to the 18th century. Ivan's son, Mykhailo Poletyka (1768–1824), was secretary to Empress Maria Fedorovna. He wrote the philosophical work *Essais philosophiques sur l'homme, ses principaux rapports et sa destinée, fondés sur l'expérience et la raison, suivis d'observations sur le beau* (published in 1818 and 1822). His brother Petro Poletyka (1778–1849) was a career diplomat. From 1798, he served in the College of Foreign Affairs in St. Petersburg. He was chancellor of Russian missions in Stockholm (1802–3) and Naples (1803–5) and advisor to missions in Philadelphia (1809–11), Rio de Janeiro (1812–14), and London (1816–17). In 1817–22, he was a special envoy and minister plenipotentiary to the United States. From 1822, he belonged to the American Philosophical Society in Philadelphia. He later became a senator and worked for the Ministry of Foreign Affairs. His *Sketch of the Internal Conditions of the United States and Their Political Relations with Europe* (1826) and memoirs were published in *Russkii arkhiv* (vol. 3, 1855). Hryhorii Poletyka (ca. 1735–1798) was a diplomat and cousin of Hryhorii Poletyka Sr. He graduated from the **Kyiv** and Moscow academies and worked for the College of Foreign Affairs as a translator. He became secretary of the Russian legation in Rome (1762) and advisor to the Russian embassy in the Austrian Empire (1770). Emperor Joseph II granted Poletyka nobiliary status. His article on the **Zaporozhian Cossacks** was published in Vienna (1788). Volodymyr Poletyka (1886–?) was a civic figure and diplomat who served as a zemstvo official in the **Poltava** region. In 1918–19, he was first secretary of the Ukrainian mission to Austria.

POLISH-LITHUANIAN COMMONWEALTH/*RZECZPOSPOLITA*, from the Latin *res publica*. The **Union of Lublin** (1569) joined Poland and Lithuania into a single Commonwealth that existed until the third partition of Poland (1795). It was headed by a king elected by a nobiliary diet. While the rights and privileges of the Polish nobility in the Lithuanian lands expanded, some elements of autonomous administration were preserved in the **Grand Duchy of Lithuania**. Poland emerged as the senior partner in the new state.

The political structure of the Commonwealth took final shape under King Henri de Valois (1573–74), who signed the *Pacta conventa* with the Diet (*Sejm*) and the Henrician Articles. They obliged the king to execute the decisions of the Diet unconditionally and granted the nobility the right not to submit to royal authority, even including the right to armed opposition (known as "confederation"). This distinctive form of estate monarchy, dubbed "nobiliary democracy," adversely affected the social circumstances of other estates (burghers, **peasants**), as well as the status of non-Polish peoples in the Commonwealth.

The Diet was the supreme administrative body of the Commonwealth. It consisted of a Senate, comprised of the king and senior administrative and church officials, and a Chamber of Delegates from the provincial nobiliary dietines. The Diet was called into session biennially to decide all state affairs, from the election of the king to the ratification of laws ("constitutions"). The king ruled the state under the control of 16 senators appointed by the Diet. The requirement of unanimous consent, with each delegate having the right of *liberum veto*, paralyzed the activities of the Diet in the 18th century.

POLISIA (Ukr. *Polissia*). A geographic region on both sides of the Ukrainian-Belarusian border. It is a large flat lowland with extensive marshes and considerable areas of sand. Polisia has a dense network of rivers and lakes and large reserves of ground water. It is part of the mixed-forest subzone of the East European broad-leaved forest zone. Ukrainian Polisia includes **Volhynia**, Rivne, and Zhytomyr oblasts, as well as the northern parts of **Kyiv** and Chernihiv oblasts.

Substantial parts of Polisia belong to the historical region of Volhynia and share its history. Initially part of **Kyivan Rus'**, Polisia was annexed to the Principality of **Galicia-Volhynia** in 1199. After the collapse of the principality in the mid-14th century, Polisia was taken over by Lithuania. The **Union of Lublin** (1569) divided Polisia between the **Grand Duchy of Lithuania** in the north and the Kingdom of Poland in the south. With the partitions of Poland in the late 18th century, Polisia became part of the Russian Empire. The **Treaty of Brest-Litovsk** (1918) transferred Polisia to the **Ukrainian People's Republic**, but the **Treaty of Riga** (1921) divided it again between Poland and the **USSR**. When the Red Army occupied the Polish western part of Polisia in September 1939, most of it was annexed to the Belarusian SSR.

Polisia's inaccessible terrain shielded its inhabitants in times of conflict and isolated them from foreign influences. As a result, they have never developed a strong sense of national identity. Speakers of Ukrainian dialects inhabit Ukrainian Polisia, as well as the southern parts of Belarusian Polisia. By the late 1980s, the population of Ukrainian Polisia was estimated at 4.7 million. It is the least populated region of Ukraine (43 people per sq. km) and has the lowest level of urbanization (under 50 percent). As one of the poorest regions of Ukraine, Polisia has attracted few foreign settlers. The largest decline in the proportion of Ukrainians occurred in the second half of the 19th century. Ukrainians constituted 71 percent of the population, Jews 15 percent, Poles 7 percent, and Russians 4 percent. Today, Ukrainian Polisia is inhabited by Ukrainians (more than 90 percent), and Russians are the largest minority (5 percent).

The Polisian economy has depended for centuries on forest and wetland resources. Its industry is relatively weak and involves **forestry**, agricultural products, and minerals. Since the end of the 18th century, lumber has been an important export and has stimulated local industrial development. Mills, furniture factories, pulp and paper plants, and wood-chemical plants are well established. Although only the drier parts of the region are suitable for **agriculture**, food industries account for a significant share of gross production. Alcohol distilling, the processing of dairy products, meat packing, and fruit canning are the main branches of the agricultural sector. Various minerals are mined and used in the **manufacturing** of building materials (cement, bricks, tiles, and glass) and in the porcelain industry. Beginning in the 1960s, other industries were established as well. Machine-building includes agricultural and chemical machinery, as well as a tractor factory, while the chemical industry produces fertilizers, synthetic fibers, plastics, and petroleum products. Light industry is represented mainly by linen manufacturing and clothing factories.

Compared to other parts of Ukraine, Polisia has the lowest density of roads and railways, and its waterways are an important part of the **transportation** system. The Prypiat River and its tributaries connect Polisia with the Black Sea via the Dnipro River, and the Dnipro-Buh Canal links it with the Baltic Sea. The Polisia Nature Reserve was established in 1968 to preserve the region's distinctive landscape, flora, and animal species.

POLITICAL PARTIES SINCE 1991. The development of a multiparty political system in Ukraine became possible in October 1991, when the **Verkhovna Rada** (VR, Ukraine's parliament) abolished art. 6 of the **Ukrainian SSR** constitution, which guaranteed the **Communist Party of Ukraine** (CPU) a monopoly of political power. At that point, the principal opposition to the CPU came from **Rukh**, a mass movement for the revival of Ukrainian culture and sovereignty that became a political party in 1993. This reorganization led to a split in Rukh that gravely weakened the "national democratic" forces committed to Ukrainian nation-building. Other parties in the national-democratic camp included the Ukrainian Republican Party, whose origins went back to the **Ukrainian Helsinki Group**, the Kharkiv-based Ukrainian Party of Democratic Revival, and the Democratic Party of Ukraine, whose initiators included such prominent writers as **Ivan Drach** and **Dmytro Pavlychko**. On the far right was the Ukrainian National Assembly and its paramilitary affiliate, the Ukrainian National Self-Defense, based in **Galicia**, which had a negligible following.

The CPU, outlawed after the attempted coup of August 1991, was revived in two stages. In October 1991, former communists established the Socialist Party, led by **Oleksandr Moroz**, which had a membership of some 90,000. Two years later, in June 1993, the CPU itself was reestablished under the leadership of **Petro Symonenko**. With a membership in excess of 120,000, it was by far the largest political party in Ukraine (most parties had only a few thousand followers, and in the mid-1990s, aggregate party membership in Ukraine did not exceed 400,000). Until the parliamentary elections of March 2002, the CPU was the largest party in the VR, but its strength was sapped by its commitment to an obsolete ideology, and its electorate, which consisted mostly of impoverished pensioners, kept shrinking.

The Green Party, led by Yurii Shcherbak, grew out of the ecological movement (*see* ENVIRONMENT) of the 1980s and gained prominence because of widespread concern about the consequences of the **Chornobyl nuclear disaster**. A variety of social-democratic groupings formed the Ukrainian Social Democratic Party in 1990; in the course of the decade, it evolved into a center-right party of powerful established interests, among whose leaders was the former president of Ukraine, **Leonid Kravchuk**. It was renamed the (United) Social Democratic Party of Ukraine.

Representing the Ukrainian elite—popularly known as the "party of power" and consisting of highly placed former Soviet bureaucrats, enterprise directors, and regional oligarchs—was a host of small parties whose names had a deceptively populist ring: the Hromada (Community) Party, the Liberal Party, the Peasant Party (representing directors of collective farms), the Revival of Regions Party, and others.

The proliferation of small parties, which numbered more than 70 by the end of the 1990s, led to the adoption of a requirement (first implemented in the parliamentary elections of 1998) that a party obtain at least 4 percent of the total vote in order to gain representation in the VR. Even earlier, parties had consolidated into blocs in order to contest elections. In the 2002 elections, six blocs and parties overcame the 4 percent barrier. The bloc "For a United Ukraine," which supported the incumbent president, **Leonid Kuchma**, took 12 percent of the vote, while the "Our Ukraine" bloc, led by his principal opponent, **Viktor Yushchenko**, gained 23.6 percent, and the Fatherland Party, also aligned against Kuchma, obtained 7 percent. The CPU took 20 percent of the vote and the Socialist Party 7 percent, while the (United) Social Democratic Party gained 6 percent.

POLITICAL TERROR (Ukrainian SSR). The use of terror as an instrument of political rule goes back to the origins of the Soviet state. Writing in 1918 in *Red Terror*, the periodical of the Cheka (Extraordinary Commission for Fighting Counterrevolution and Sabotage), one of its leaders, Martin Latsis, proclaimed that "We are not waging war against individual persons. We are exterminating the bourgeoisie as a class. . . . In this lies the significance and essence of the Red Terror." Lenin, who established the origins of what would become the Main Administration of Labor Camps (GULAG), exiled thousands of opponents of the October Revolution to Siberia. Even after introducing the New Economic Policy—a concession to popular dissatisfaction with the Bolsheviks—Lenin wrote to Lev Kamenev that "It is a tremendous error to think that the NEP put an end to terror. We shall yet return to terror, as well as to economic terror" (3 March 1922).

In Ukraine, the Cheka was established in December 1918 by decree of the **Provisional Workers' and Peasants' Government of Ukraine** and was headed by Latsis in 1919. It fought the **Directory** and the **insurgent movement**, killed politically active members of the Ukrainian intelligentsia, and committed atrocities, notably in **Kharkiv, Kyiv, Odesa,** and the **Donets Basin**. In 1922, the Cheka was reformed as the State Political Administration (GPU) and subordinated to the Commissariat of Internal Affairs. With the founding of the **USSR**, the GPU became the OGPU (United State Political Administration, 1923). The GPU of the **Ukrainian SSR**, headed from 1924 to 1937 by Vsevolod Balytsky, organized the show trial of the fictitious **Union for the Liberation of Ukraine** (1930), deported *kulaks* during the **collectivization** of agriculture (1929–33), helped organize the **famine of 1932–33**, and eliminated many others identified as opponents of the Soviet regime. The **Ukrainian Academy of Sciences** was largely closed down,

Political Terror (Ukrainian SSR) • 437

including **Mykhailo Hrushevsky's** "historical institutions," while Hrushevsky himself was exiled to Moscow. The **Ukrainian Autocephalous Orthodox Church** was forced to dissolve itself in 1930, and most of its clergy was sent to the GULAG.

In the midst of this wave of terror, which destroyed much of the pre-Soviet Ukrainian intelligentsia and broke the **peasantry** as a political force, Stalin sent **Pavel Postyshev** to Kyiv as his personal representative (January 1933). Postyshev oversaw a devastating purge of the **Communist Party of Ukraine** (CPU), as well as of the Ukrainian intelligentsia and its institutions. The CPU was purged of some 235,000 members. More than 15,000 officials were purged from every significant Ukrainian institution on accusations of "nationalism." More than 300 writers were incarcerated, executed, or forced into silence. Many of Postyshev's victims perished in the GULAG.

In 1934, the OGPU was subordinated to the People's Commissariat of Internal Affairs (NKVD). After this point, as Stalin strove to eliminate his last remaining rivals for power, the terror became self-perpetuating; in order to keep itself supplied with victims, the NKVD forced those arrested to "confess" who had recruited them and whom they had recruited. Entire categories of people (e.g., *kulaks*, immigrants from Western Ukraine, those with relatives abroad, former members of non-Soviet organizations) were targeted for destruction. In Ukraine alone, the NKVD fabricated cases against 10 major "anti-Soviet centers," ranging from the Polish Military Organization to the Ukrainian White Guard Terrorist Center. Those accused were given summary sentences by so-called *troikas* (first secretary of the oblast party committee, head of the oblast NKVD, and the oblast procurator) and shot, or sent to the GULAG.

In 1937–38, the top echelons of the Ukrainian party, government, and armed forces were destroyed. Of the CPU leaders, only two—Oleksander Boichenko and Hryhorii Petrovsky—remained alive, while in 1938 the Ukrainian government was purged twice. Postyshev was arrested in 1937 on charges of tolerating Trotskyism and shot two years later. Overseeing this purge was **Nikita Khrushchev**, who became first secretary of the CPU in January 1938. His rule marked the beginning of large-scale **Russification** in Ukraine. The demographer Aleksandr Babyonyshev has estimated Ukraine's total population loss from political terror (1927–38) at no less than 4.4 million lives.

While Stalin's great terror ended in 1938, and many of its perpetrators were themselves killed once the authorities considered them no longer useful, political terror remained the basis of Soviet rule until Stalin's death. During **World War II**, NKVD battalions followed advancing Soviet troops in order to kill anyone trying to desert. Many thousands who had spent the war under the Nazi occupation or performing forced labor in Germany (*see OSTARBEITER*) were shot or sent to the GULAG for alleged treason to the USSR. After the war, Stalin and Andrei Zhdanov launched new campaigns against "ideological enemies." In western Ukraine, large-scale terror against the population was used to destroy the **Ukrainian Insurgent Army**.

After Stalin's death (March 1953), his political successors acted immediately to prevent the secret police from becoming a threat to them. Lavrentii Beria, the former head of the NKVD (renamed the Ministry of Internal Affairs or MVD in 1946), was executed, and the Committee for State Security (KGB) was established as a separate agency in 1954 in order to rein in the MVD. Many prisoners in the GULAG were amnestied and allowed to return to their homes.

The era of mass political terror was over, but the Soviet authorities continued to persecute citizens on ideological grounds until the 1980s (*see* DISSIDENT MOVEMENT). The last political prisoners were freed by Mikhail Gorbachev in the latter half the 1980s. No one was ever brought to trial for the numerous crimes perpetrated under the rubric of political terror.

POLONSKA-VASYLENKO, NATALIIA (31 January [13 February] 1884–8 June 1973). Historian; full member of the **Shevchenko Scientific Society** (from 1947) and the **Ukrainian Academy of Arts and Sciences** (from 1948). She was born in **Kharkiv** into a gentry family, the daughter of the historian Dmytro Menshov. She graduated from the **Kyiv** Fundukleev-Mariinsky Women's Gymnasium (1890) and studied at the historical and philological division of the Higher Women's Courses in Kyiv (1905–11). Having become interested in archaeology, she worked on an expedition under the direction of **Vikentii Khvoika** in 1909. Polonska-Vasylenko taught history and geography at Kyiv gymnasiums (1910–24). She was an assistant (1912–16) and professor (1916–18) at the chair of Russian history at the Higher Women's Courses. In 1915, she completed her master's examinations at Kyiv University, where she lectured (1916–20). Polonska-Vasylenko was one of the first female professors at Kyiv University.

With the establishment of Soviet rule, higher **education** was reorganized and all the institutions at which Polonska-Vasylenko had taught were closed. She rejected opportunities to work at the universities of Moscow and St. Petersburg. Polonska-Vasylenko quickly mastered the Ukrainian **language** and from then on published exclusively in Ukrainian. She worked at the Kyiv Archaeological Institute (1918–25) and at the **Ukrainian Academy of Sciences** (1924–41, with the exception of 1934–38, when she was dismissed from her post) and was a professor at the Kyiv Art Institute (1927–32). In 1923, she married **Mykola Vasylenko**, who was arrested soon afterward by the secret police, accused of belonging to a counterrevolutionary organization, and sentenced to 10 years' imprisonment. Polonska-Vasylenko worked tirelessly for a year and a half to obtain an amnesty for her husband. Having defended her doctoral dissertation, she became one of the first **women** in the **Ukrainian SSR** to be awarded a doctorate in history (1940). During the German occupation, she was director of the Institute of Archaeology of the Academy of Sciences (October-December 1941) and the Kyiv Central Archive of Old Documents (December 1941–September 1943). She then left Kyiv and, from October 1943, was in charge of cultural activity at the **Ukrainian Central Committee** in **Lviv**. In 1944, she lectured at the **Ukrainian Free University** (UVU) in Prague. She was a professor at the UVU in Munich (from 1945) and vice president of the Ukrainian Historical Association (from 1965). In 1966, she became dean of the UVU faculty of arts. She died in Dornstadt near Ulm, Germany.

Polonska-Vasylenko wrote numerous historical works, notably on the **Khmelnytsky Uprising**, **Ivan Mazepa**, Zaporizhia in the 18th century, the settlement of southern Ukraine, the history of the Ukrainian church, and the two-volume *Istoriia Ukraïny* (History of Ukraine, Munich, 1973–76; Kyiv, 1992). She was a leading representative of the statist school of Ukrainian historiography.

POLTAVA. City (1998 pop. 317,300) on the right bank of the Vorskla River, administrative center of Poltava oblast, and a major industrial and communications center. First mentioned in the Hypatian **Chronicle** under the year 1174, the site was inhabited as early as the seventh or sixth century B.C. Destroyed by the **Golden Horde** in 1240, Poltava came under the rule of the **Grand Duchy of Lithuania** in the second half of the 14th century and passed to the **Polish-Lithuanian Commonwealth** in 1569. During the **Hetmanate**, Poltava flourished as a **Cossack** regimental center. In 1709, the city withstood a two-month siege by Swedish and Ukrainian forces (*see* POLTAVA, BATTLE OF). In the 17th century, Poltava obtained the rights of **Magdeburg law**, and in the late 18th century it became a gubernia center.

Only a small number of the city's historical monuments survived **World War II**, and present-day Poltava is largely new. The city's economy depends on industrial enterprises developed since the late 1920s. Because of Poltava's location in a fertile agricultural region, food processing is its largest branch of industry, followed by the textile and clothing industries. Machine building and chemical plants are also important to the local economy. Higher **education** is provided by five institutes: pedagogical, civil engineering, agricultural engineering, cooperative, and medical; there are also several research establishments. Poltava supports two theaters and six museums and is considered one of the greenest cities in Ukraine.

POLTAVA, BATTLE OF. Large-scale engagement between the armies of Sweden and Muscovy that took place on 27 June (8 July) 1709 near **Poltava** during the Great Northern War (1700–21). After successful military engagements on the territory of the **Polish-Lithuanian Commonwealth** and Saxony, the army of Charles XII of Sweden began its advance through Belarusian lands to Smolensk and on to Moscow (spring 1708). However, as a result of secret negotiations between Charles XII, King Stanisław Leszczyński of Poland, and Hetman **Ivan Mazepa**, the initial battle plan was altered.

In October 1708, when the Swedish army entered Ukrainian territory, Mazepa openly switched allegiance to the Swedish side. However, the absence of most **Cossack** armies from Ukraine did not allow him to give the Swedes any meaningful assistance. The severe winter of 1708–9 and the failure of the **Crimea**, the Ottoman Empire, and Poland to deliver promised assistance weakened Charles's army. Only the support of Kost Hordiienko, the otaman of the **Zaporozhian Sich**, who brought a force of 8,000 Cossacks, improved the situation. Charles XII decided to begin his advance on Moscow via **Kharkiv** and Kursk.

The most significant obstacle in his path was Poltava, defended by a Russian garrison of 4,300 men and by 2,600 of the city's inhabitants. In early May 1709, an unsuccessful assault on Poltava forced the Swedish armies to begin a lengthy siege of the city that resulted in major casualties (more than 6,000 killed). It also allowed the Muscovite command to prepare for a full-scale battle. Peter's army numbered 42,500 men with 102 cannon. The Ukrainian Cossack army loyal to Peter, commanded by **Ivan Skoropadsky**, cut off a possible Swedish retreat toward the Dnipro River. The Swedish army consisted of 31,000 men with six cannon. Mazepa's forces defended the Swedish flank and participated in the siege of Poltava, preventing the Muscovite army from encircling Charles's forces. Having learned of the possible arrival of a force of 40,000 **Tatars** to assist Peter, Charles decided to attack first. Previously wounded, he entrusted command of the army to Field Marshal Carl Gustaf

Rehnskiöld. On 27 June (8 July), the Swedish infantry assault was halted by cannon fire, and the Swedes were forced to retreat toward the Budushcha Forest. The renewed battle ended with the defeat of the Swedish army, which lost 9,234 men, with another 2,874 wounded. Rehnskiöld and many generals and officers were taken prisoner. Russian losses totaled 1,345 dead and 3,290 wounded. The remainder of the Swedish army retreated along the Vorskla River toward the Dnipro but was surrounded near Perevolochna and forced to surrender on 30 June (11 July). Charles XII, Mazepa, Hordiienko, approximately 50 Cossack officers, and Swedish and Cossack units (approx. 3,000 men) crossed the Dnipro into Ottoman-controlled territory. Ukrainian Cossacks in the Swedish army were turned over to the Muscovite command. Most of them were immediately executed and the remainder exiled to Siberia. As a result of the battle, the **Hetmanate's** autonomy was severely curtailed.

POLTAVA, PETRO (24 February 1919–22 December 1951). Pseud. of Petro Fedun. Military and political figure, publicist, and major of the **Ukrainian Insurgent Army** (UPA). He was born in Shnyriv (now in **Lviv** oblast). Poltava graduated from the Brody gymnasium (1938) and later studied at the medical faculty of Lviv University. In 1940, he was mobilized by the Red Army and participated in the Soviet-Finnish War. At the beginning of the Soviet-German War (1941–45), he was captured by the Germans but soon released. Poltava was an organizer and leader of the youth wing of the **Organization of Ukrainian Nationalists** (OUN) and edited the underground publication *Iunak* (Youth, 1942–43). He headed the political division of the UPA-West headquarters (1944–46) and directed the political education division at UPA headquarters (1946–49). From 1946 to 1951, Poltava directed the information bureau of the **Supreme Ukrainian Liberation Council** (UHVR), becoming a member of the council in 1950. He was deputy chairman of the General Secretariat of the UHVR (1950–51) and a member of the OUN leadership (1948–51). The circumstances of his death are unknown.

Poltava was one of the leading publicists of the Ukrainian underground, helping to turn the OUN-UPA away from integral nationalism. He was noted for his essays on Ukrainian statehood, in which he argued for a democratic polity, a mixed economy, and a world order based on cooperation among independent nation-states. Poltava's works were reissued in Munich as *Zbirka pidpil'nykh pysan'* (A Collection of Underground Writings, 1959).

POLUBOTOK, PAVLO (ca. 1660–18 [29] December 1724). Acting **hetman** of **Left-Bank Ukraine** (1722–23). Descended from a

Cossack officer family, he received his education at the **Kyiv Mohyla** Collegium. Polubotok served in the **Cossack** Host, attaining the rank of notable military fellow (1689). In 1691, he was arrested for conspiring against Hetman **Ivan Mazepa**, stripped of his property, and barred from government posts for an extended period. He became colonel of Chernihiv in 1706. After the **Battle of Poltava** he was a candidate for the hetmancy, but because of Peter I's distrust, **Ivan Skoropadsky** was elected hetman. During this period, Polubotok received significant landholdings in the Chernihiv, Lubny, and other regiments. As acting hetman after Skoropadsky's death (1722), Polubotok attempted to restrict the powers of the newly established **Little Russian Collegium**. He reorganized the courts, established appeal procedures, combated bribery and red tape, and appointed inspectors to ensure that his resolutions were carried out. His opposition to the collegium president, Stepan Veliaminov-Zernov, aroused the dissatisfaction of the Russian government. In the summer of 1722, Polubotok, General Chancellor Semen Savych, and General Judge Ivan Charnysh submitted a new petition to Peter I concerning the restoration of the **Hetmanate's** traditional right of self-government. Following the submission of the Kolomak Petitions of 1723, which had the same purpose, Polubotok and several Cossack officers, including **Danylo Apostol**, **Mykola Khanenko**, and **Yakiv Lyzohub**, were arrested and imprisoned at the SS. Peter and Paul Fortress, where Polubotok either died of natural causes or was executed.

POPULATION. Population in Ukraine can be determined for the 17th century and later. It has been estimated that between five and six million people inhabited Ukraine in 1629. Until the late 18th century, population growth was hampered by frequent wars, epidemics, famines, and slavery. There were more than eight million inhabitants in 1764–74, 18.7 million in 1870, and 28.4 million in 1897. Ensuing overpopulation in the rural areas induced mass emigration (1896–1914) to other regions of the Russian Empire (1.6 million) and to the New World (some 500,000), reducing population growth (*see* DIASPORA). The period was characterized by high fertility and mortality rates. Life expectancy at birth in Ukraine was 36 years for men and 37 years for women. In 1913, Ukraine had 35.2 million inhabitants.

The upheavals of **World War I** and the **Ukrainian Revolution** (1917–21) reduced the population by at least three million between 1914 and the early 1920s. Some stabilization was achieved in the 1920s during the period of the New Economic Policy, which was characterized by a high fertility rate and a decline in mortality. In

1926–27, life expectancy increased to 44 years for men and 48 years for women.

The greatest demographic cataclysms occurred between 1929 and the late 1940s, when Ukraine lost between 15.8 and 17 million inhabitants. The man-made **famine of 1932–33**, together with the **political terror** and deportations of the 1930s, cost Ukraine between seven and nine million lives. Deportations of western Ukrainians, the German-Soviet war of 1941–45, and the ensuing population transfers, as well as the **famine of 1946–47** and the guerrilla war in western Ukraine (*see* UKRAINIAN INSURGENT ARMY) were responsible for the balance.

The fertility rate has been decreasing rapidly in Ukraine since 1989. The number of deaths has continuously exceeded the number of births since 1991. In 1995, for example, population decline occurred in 92.4 percent of rural administrative districts. The overall fertility rate fell to 1.3 children per couple (1.1 in urban settlements and 1.8 in rural areas). Young mothers are giving birth to an ever larger proportion of infants; in 1996, 84.7 percent of children were born to mothers under the age of 30. Average life expectancy in Ukraine is 67 years (61.7 for men and 72.8 for women)—about 10 years less than in Western Europe. The population structure is also indicative of the aging process. In 1999, children up to 14 years of age constituted 18.4 percent of the total population, while those over 65 years of age made up 13.8 percent.

The total population of Ukraine is 48.45 million (2001). Ukraine is populated by representatives of more than 130 ethnic groups, with ethnic Ukrainians constituting 77.8 percent. Historically prominent **minorities** include Russians (17.3 percent), Crimean **Tatars** (0.5 percent), Poles (0.3 percent), and **Jews** (0.2 percent).

POPULISM. Ideology and political movement promoted by members of the intelligentsia in the Russian Empire during the 1860s–80s. Populists espoused the ideal of a **peasant** democracy, combining radical opposition to serfdom with utopian socialism. The best-known populist ideologues of the 1870s were Mikhail Bakunin, Petr Lavrov, and Petr Tkachev. They regarded the Russian peasant as having conserved the ancient foundations of communal ownership, the *mir*, which they saw as the basis for Russia's transition to socialism, circumventing the capitalist stage of development.

In the 1860s, populist activity was sporadic, but in 1874 populist groups undertook to "go to the people" on a mass scale with the notion of organizing the first socialist socioeconomic cells. The campaign encompassed 37 gubernias of European Russia, including almost all the Ukrainian gubernias. Most peasants, however, maintained a naive faith in the tsar and generally upheld patriarchal values. Many helped turn in their would-be deliverers to the authorities, who arrested more than 1,000 populist propagandists. The most active were sentenced at the Trial of the 193 (1877–78).

Numerous Russian populist groups of varying inclinations (Bakuninites, Chaikovskyites, Lavrovites, and others) operated in Ukraine in the 1860s. In **Kyiv**, groups of Chaikovskyites (1872–74), the Kyiv Commune (1873–74), and the Insurrectionists were active. The **Odesa** populists were led by Feliks Volkhovsky (1872). There were other groups in **Kharkiv**, Chernihiv, **Poltava**, Kherson, and Mykolaiv. In 1876, the populists created the revolutionary group Land and Freedom. Abandoning the notion of change through evolution, it began planning a peasant uprising. In 1875–76, the most active populist group in Ukraine was the Southern Insurgent group, led by Volodymyr Debohorii-Mokriievych. Its members planned to incite a rebellion with the help of peasant units but were soon dispersed by the police.

In the late 1870s, populists split over the issue of political violence. Those who supported the use of terror took the name People's Will, while the "official populists" established the Black Repartition, which briefly organized the South Russian Workers' Union (1880–81). With the emigration of Georgii Plekhanov and other leaders in the early 1880s, the Black Repartition virtually ceased to exist.

The People's Will expanded its activities. In Ukraine, it had organizations and groups in Kyiv, Kharkiv, Nizhyn, Odesa, Poltava, and other cities. In May 1878, Hryhorii Popko murdered the police adjutant Gustav Geiking. In February 1879, the governor of Kharkiv, Prince Dmitrii Kropotkin, was assassinated. After the assassination of Tsar Alexander II by a member of People's Will (March 1881), the tsarist administration began to attack the organization openly, and the trials of the 1880s completed its eradication.

Many Ukrainians belonged to Russian populist organizations (Mykola Kuliabko-Koretsky, **Mykola Kybalchych**, **Dmytro Lyzohub**, Sofiia Perovska, Andrii Zheliabov, and others), depriving the Ukrainian movement of potential cadres. Russian populists used the Ukrainian language only occasionally for propaganda purposes, particularly in Volkhovsky's exhortation "Pravdyve slovo khliboroba do svoïkh zemliakiv" (The True Word of an Agrarian to His Countrymen, 1875).

Aside from the political movement, populism had a very strong cultural dimension. Beginning with the **Cyril and Methodius Brotherhood** (1845–46) and the *khlopomany* of the 1850s–60s, the Ukrainian intelligentsia dedicated itself to the social and cultural emancipation of the peasant masses. The populist ideal was a peasant-based Ukraine "without serf or lord," in the words of the poet **Taras Shevchenko**. Such 19th-century writers of **eastern Ukraine** as Pavlo Hrabovsky, Ivan Karpenko-Kary, Ivan Manzhura, Panas Myrny, and Ivan Nechui-Levytsky were greatly influenced by populism, as were many **Galician** Ukrainian writers, notably **Ivan Franko**, **Mykhailo Pavlyk**, and Ostap Terletsky (*see also* REVOLUTION OF 1848; RUTHENIAN TRIAD).

Populism was in part a reaction to the gentry-led Ukrainian autonomism of the 18th century, which petered out as descendants of the **Cossack officer** stratum became integrated into the Russian nobility. Such populist historians as **Mykola Kostomarov**, **Volodymyr Antonovych**, Oleksandra Yefymenko, **Oleksander Lazarevsky**, Orest Levytsky, and **Mykhailo Hrushevsky** tended to view Ukrainian nobles and Cossack officers as traitors to the national cause who had assimilated to the dominant Polish and Russian cultures and exploited the peasant masses for their own benefit. Populism was the dominant trend in Ukrainian political and social thought until the defeat of the **Ukrainian Revolution** (1917–21), when it was challenged by the conservatism of **Viacheslav Lypynsky** and the nationalism of **Dmytro Dontsov**. Much of Ukrainian political and cultural life in the 20th century may be interpreted as a protracted conflict between the enduring influence of populism, with its insistence on local patriotism, collectivist values, and popular taste, and varieties of elitism, inspired by Western or Russian models, which have sought to overcome Ukrainian "provincialism."

PORSH, MYKOLA (19 October 1879–16 April 1944). Politician, economist, and political writer. Born in Lubny (now in **Poltava** oblast), he was descended from a German-**Jewish** family. Porsh was an organizer and leading member of the **Revolutionary Ukrainian Party** (RUP), editing its newspaper, *Pratsia* (Work; **Lviv**, 1904–5), with Dmytro Antonovych. He consistently defended the principle of Ukrainian independence and the need for a Ukrainian social democratic party separate from the Russian. In 1904–5, Porsh engaged in covert organizational and propaganda work in **Kyiv** and Nizhyn. In 1906, he became the leader of the **Ukrainian Social Democratic Labor Party**, which issued from the split of the RUP in 1904. Together with Viktor Domanytsky and Valentyn Sadovsky, Porsh promoted the development of the **cooperative movement** in **eastern Ukraine**.

With the advent of the 1917 revolution, Porsh became a member of the **Ukrainian Central Rada** and its Little Rada. In

September 1917, polemicizing with **Volodymyr Vynnychenko** and Borys Martos, he argued the incompatibility of Ukrainian and Russian economic interests and advocated independence for Ukraine. On 30 October (12 November), he was appointed general secretary of labor, and at the end of December, following the resignation of **Symon Petliura**, he became general secretary of military affairs. Porsh initiated measures to establish a Ukrainian militia and recruit officers for a national army. After the fall of the Central Rada, Porsh opposed the **Ukrainian State** of **Pavlo Skoropadsky** and was arrested with Petliura in June 1918. Following the restoration of the **Ukrainian People's Republic** by the **Directory**, Porsh became ambassador to Germany (1919–20). After the defeat of the **Ukrainian Revolution**, he remained in the emigration and abandoned politics for scholarship, analyzing the Russian Empire's exploitation of the Ukrainian economy. Under the pseudonym "Hordiienko," he polemicized with the prominent Russian statesman Petr Struve (also an émigré) on the problems and prospects of Ukrainian economic development. Porsh translated Karl Marx's *Zur Kritik der politischen Ökonomie* into Ukrainian (1923). He died and was buried in Berlin.

POSTYSHEV, PAVEL (6 [18] September 1887–26 February 1939). Soviet party and state official. He was born in the village of Ivano-Voznesensk, Vladimir guberniia, Russia. Postyshev joined the Bolshevik Party in 1904 and became a party organizer in the Far East. Transferred to the milder climate of Ukraine in 1923 because of ill health, he served as secretary of the Central Committee of the **Communist Party of Ukraine** (CPU; 1926–20). Openly opposed to **Ukrainization**, Postyshev gained Stalin's trust as a reliable enforcer of Moscow's policies. From July 1930, he was secretary of the Central Committee of the All-Union Communist Party (Bolshevik) in charge of propaganda and organization, helping Stalin consolidate power.

In January 1933, Stalin sent Postyshev to Ukraine as his personal representative, with a large staff of Russian cadres. Elected second secretary of the CPU in March, Postyshev openly flouted the authority of the first secretary, **Stanislav Kosior**. When Postyshev arrived in Ukraine, the **famine of 1932–33**, organized at Stalin's behest over the protests of CPU leaders, was reaching its height. Postyshev released grain supplies to ensure the success of the spring planting (a measure for which CPU officials had pleaded in vain) and took measures to feed dependents of the Red Army and children, but not politically unreliable categories of the population. At the same time, he replaced thousands of local officials. These actions indicated that the CPU's authority in Ukraine was being superseded by the direct control of Moscow. Over the next two years Postyshev oversaw a massive purge of the CPU, including a campaign of defamation against its leading figure, **Mykola Skrypnyk**, that drove him to suicide. Postyshev also directed a thoroughgoing campaign of **political terror** against the Ukrainian intelligentsia and its institutions that abolished the Ukrainization policy. He became popularly known as the "hangman of Ukraine."

In 1935–36, Postyshev appears to have attempted to become a strongman in Ukraine in order to prevent his own destruction by the all-powerful secret police. He took to wearing a Ukrainian embroidered shirt, evinced an unwonted interest in Ukrainian culture, and promoted an influx of Ukrainians into the CPU. At the March 1937 plenum of the All-Union CP(B), he headed a group opposed to committing Nikolai Bukharin to trial—a final effort to limit the extent of Stalin's terror. That month, Postyshev was transferred from Ukraine and appointed first secretary of the Kuibyshev regional party committee (1937). In February 1938, he was expelled from the party and soon arrested. He was executed a year later.

POTEBNIA, OLEKSANDER (10 [22] September 1835–29 November [11 December] 1891). Philologist. He was born near Havrylivka (now Hryshyne, Sumy oblast) into the family of a small landowner. Potebnia graduated from **Kharkiv** University (1856), obtaining master's (1860) and doctoral (1874) degrees. He was a professor at Kharkiv University (from 1874) and president of the Kharkiv Historical and Philological Society. In the early 1860s, he was active in the Kharkiv Ukrainian student community and took part in folklore expeditions in **eastern Ukraine**.

In his book *Mysl' i iazyk* (Thought and Language, 1862), his doctoral dissertation, *Iz zapisok o russkoi grammatike* (From Notes on Russian Grammar, 1874), and his article "Iazyk i narodnost'" (Language and Nationality, published posthumously in 1895), Potebnia made a major contribution to the philosophy of **language**. Inspired by German scholarship of the period, he argued that the form of words is shaped by individual and national experience. Words, whose internal form often develops out of myth, serve as a bridge to the symbols that animate folklore. These ideas were expressed in Potebnia's master's thesis and in his major work, *Ob'iasneniia malorusskikh i srodnykh narodnykh pesen* (Explanations of Little Russian and Related Folk Songs, 1883–87). Potebnia's view of language as an individual or national way of interpreting experience led him to denounce linguistic assimilation in general and the **Russification** of Ukrainians in particular as an assault on national integrity. He made important discoveries in Ukrainian historical phonetics and etymology. Potebnia also did extensive work in Slavic dialectology and comparative historical syntax, reorienting the field from cataloguing linguistic constructions as encountered in discrete literary monuments to explaining their historical development as a result of changes in ways of thinking. Potebnia produced an important annotated edition of the *Tale of Ihor's Campaign*, edited the works of **Hryhorii Kvitka-Osnovianenko**, Petro Hulak-Artemovsky, and Ivan Manzhura, and began a translation of Homer's *Odyssey* into Ukrainian. In 1945, the Institute of Linguistics of the **Ukrainian Academy of Sciences** was named after him.

POTII, IPATII (12 August 1541–18 [28] July 1613). Secular name: Adam. Uniate metropolitan of **Kyiv** and **Halych**. He came from Rozhanky in **Podlachia**, a descendant of the Ukrainian gentry. After graduating from Cracow University, Potii entered the service of Prince Radziwiłł the Black and was later secretary to King Sigismund II Augustus of Poland (until 1572). He was judge of Brest until 1588 and later became a castellan and senator. A close friend of Prince **Kostiantyn Ostrozky**, Potii belonged to the group of writers and publicists associated with the **Ostrih Academy**. Having been widowed, he took monastic orders, and in 1593 he became bishop of Volodymyr and Brest. In 1595, Potii and Kyryl Terletsky, bishop of Lutsk, were dispatched to Rome to negotiate the terms of the church **Union of Brest** (1596). Following the death of Metropolitan **Mykhail Rahoza**, Potii became metropolitan of Kyiv (1599–1613). He worked to establish the legal equality of the Uniate Church (*see* UKRAINIAN CATHOLIC CHURCH) with the Roman Catholic Church in the **Polish-Lithuanian Commonwealth** and sought converts among the clergy and nobility. Because of Potii's role in persecuting the Orthodox, an attempt was made on his life in 1609. A noted polemicist, Potii defended the Union in such works as *Uniia* (1595) and *Antirysis* (Anti-Discourse, 1599). He also founded a seminary in Vilnius and a Uniate school in Brest.

***PRAVDA*/TRUTH.** Literary, scholarly, and political periodical. It was published in **Lviv** three times monthly in 1867, four times monthly in 1868–70, semimonthly in 1872–78, monthly in 1879, irregularly in 1880, as one volume edited by Volodymyr Barvinsky and **Ivan Franko** in 1884, monthly in 1888–93, and semimonthly in 1894–96. The journal received financial support from **Panteleimon Kulish** and **Oleksander Konysky**. Prior to the establishment of *Dilo* (The Deed, 1880), *Pravda* was the leading organ of the **populists** in **Galicia**. In the 1860s and 1870s, nearly all important civic and cultural figures and writers from Galicia and **eastern Ukraine**

contributed to *Pravda,* including Franko, **Oleksander Barvinsky, Mykhailo Drahomanov, Yurii Fedkovych,** Ivan Nechui-Levytsky, and **Mykhailo Starytsky.** *Pravda's* editorial board was headed by Lonhyn Lukashevych (1867, 1876), I. Mykyta, Anatol Vakhnianyn (1869–70), Oleksander Ohonovsky (1872–76), and V. Barvinsky (1876–79). After a four-year hiatus (1884–88), publication resumed at the initiative of **Volodymyr Antonovych** and Konysky in anticipation of the abortive attempt at a Polish-Ukrainian understanding in Galicia ("New Era").

In the 1890s, the journal propagated the ideology of the right wing of the populist movement. Its editors were Yevhen Olesnytsky (1888), Ivan Stronsky (1889), Pavlo Kyrchiv (1890–91), and A. Berezynsky (1891–96). Its publisher and editor in chief was O. Barvinsky. Contributors during this period included **Borys Hrinchenko, Mykhailo Kotsiubynsky, Ahatanhel Krymsky,** Osyp Makovei, and Yuliian Romanchuk. *See also* MEDIA.

PRINCES. Heads of principalities or political unions. In **Kyivan Rus'** before the ninth century, princes were military leaders of tribes or tribal alliances who performed judicial and administrative functions. In the ninth century, with the creation of the Kyivan state, princely rule assumed a more monarchic character. The Kyivan princes and the rulers of the **Grand Duchy of Lithuania** bore the title of grand prince. In the **appanage principalities** that developed as a result of the disintegration of Kyivan Rus', princes often had to share power with **boyar** councils and with the *viche* (popular assembly). In the 14th century, most Rus' lands were taken over by the Grand Duchy of Lithuania, and Rus' princes became vassals of the grand prince of Lithuania. In the 15th and 16th centuries, they lost state power and became territorial magnates.

PRIVATIZATION. The privatization of state property emerged as an issue on Ukraine's political agenda in 1992. The government identified privatization as a vital aspect of transition to the market and an indispensable source of revenue for the state treasury. In 1994, the presidential decree "On a Unified System of Privatization Institutions in Ukraine" established the State Property Fund to supervise the process of privatization. The government expected to achieve transparency and create demand for assets on the part of both domestic and international investors, to maximize utilization of the Ukrainian capital-market infrastructure, and to attract private investors with long-term interests and good management skills. The State Property Fund began to turn state-owned enterprises into joint-stock companies and sell them off.

Also in 1994, the government signed a memorandum of understanding with the World Bank, the USAID agency, and the European Union to oversee Ukraine's program of mass privatization. The government agreed to distribute shares rapidly and free of charge to all citizens of Ukraine, develop capital markets, and create a critical mass of privately owned enterprises. Mass privatization was intended to place a great percentage of shares (from 25 to 100 percent of each enterprise) into the hands of a large number of investors (employees and the public) in exchange for privatization certificates. The decision to undertake it was based on optimistic expectations of rapid economic reform. Privatization was supposed to make possible the recovery and growth of the Ukrainian economy, support private-sector investment, and reduce corruption.

Official efforts to implement mass privatization met with opposition from managers of state-owned enterprises, bureaucrats and politicians who controlled state assets, the communist majority in the **Verkhovna Rada**, and oligarchic groups. There was also opposition from large numbers of senior citizens and the most vulnerable groups of employees in state enterprises, who realized that they might well lose their jobs in newly privatized enterprises, while the government was unlikely to provide sufficient compensation in the form of **social welfare** benefits. This negative attitude was expressed by the term *prykhvatyzatsiia* (literally, privatization by seizure). The public complained that privatization had not generated any significant new revenue, attracted strategic investors, or produced efficient entrepreneurs.

In March 1996, a law "On the Foreign Investment Regime" extended fairly minimal guarantees of favorable treatment for all types of foreign investment in the hope of generating an inflow of cash from abroad. The results were disappointing, given the failure to create a supportive investment climate through such measures as reducing red tape, establishing a transparent and equitable regulatory regime, land privatization, effective protection of shareholder rights, and entrenchment of the rule of law.

Privatization in Ukraine did not hit its peak until 1996–98. Only then did privatization measures begin to have positive effects; salaries increased, and wage arrears at privatized companies were paid off more quickly and in greater amounts than at state-owned enterprises. Tax revenues from privatized companies also exceeded those from nonprivatized ones.

According to the State Property Fund, 66,077 enterprises had been privatized by 1 January 2000. The government invited major international consulting firms to advise it on issues of privatization, the rule of law, and transparency. In October 2000, Prime Minister

Viktor Yushchenko stressed that Ukraine had approximately 500 enterprises worth at least several billion dollars, but the investment climate remained unattractive, given lack of progress on the obstacles to investment identified in the mid-1990s and Yushchenko's resignation, engineered by antireform forces in 2001.

PROKOPOVYCH, TEOFAN (8 [18] June 1681–8 [19] September 1736). Secular name: Eleazar. Ecclesiastical and civic figure, writer, and scholar. He graduated from the **Kyiv Mohyla Academy**, then studied philosophy and theology in Poland and at the St. Athanasius Greek College in Rome. Returning to Ukraine in 1702, he took monastic orders under the name Teofan (Russ. Feofan). From 1704, he taught at the **Kyiv** Academy. He was a supporter of **Ivan Mazepa**, the dedicatee (along with Tsar Peter I) of his historical drama *Vladimir* (1705), which depicted Mazepa as **Volodymyr the Great**. In numerous sermons, Prokopovych eulogized Mazepa and described Kyiv as the "second Jerusalem."

After the **Battle of Poltava** and the demise of Mazepa, Prokopovych became a favorite of Peter I. In 1711, he was appointed rector of the Kyiv Academy. He moved to St. Petersburg at the tsar's invitation (1716), becoming his advisor on church reform. In the *Dukhovnyi reglament* (Spiritual Statute, 1721), he established a new system of church administration that turned the church into a department of state. Prokopovych became bishop of Pskov (1718), vice president of the Holy Synod (1721), and archbishop of Novgorod (1725). In his political and philosophical treatises, Prokopovych promoted enlightened absolutism. He helped reform education in the Russian Empire and participated in the organization and establishment of the Imperial Academy of Sciences. Prokopovych was among the first scholars in the empire to conduct scientific observations with the aid of the microscope and the telescope. His *Philosophia peripatetica* was a compendium of 17th-century European science and political philosophy; he introduced mathematics and geometry into the curriculum of the Kyiv Mohyla Academy.

As a poet, Prokopovych was influenced by classicism. He wrote a history of Peter's reign. Prokopovych's library (some 30,000 volumes) was bequeathed to the Imperial Academy of Sciences. He was buried at St. Sophia's Cathedral in Novgorod.

PROSVITA SOCIETY/TOVARYSTVO "PROSVITA." Cultural and educational society founded in **Lviv** by a group of **populists** (8 December 1868). Its primary task was to promote **education** in cultural, political, and economic matters. Prosvita (Enlightenment) was initially limited to the Main Branch in Lviv. In 1869, the society obtained financial assistance from local endowments for the publication of Ukrainian books, was involved in the founding of Ukrainian schools despite the **Galician** Diet's establishment of Polish as the official **language** (1868), and petitioned the government for a chair of Ukrainian history at Lviv University. Its new statute of 1870 allowed the organization to establish branches in the counties (the first branch was opened in Bortnyky in 1875). In the 1880s, Prosvita took charge of reading rooms in the counties, revising its statute in 1891 in order to connect them into a network. In 1914, Prosvita reading rooms were active in 75 percent of Ukrainian settlements in Galicia; by 1939, they covered 85 percent of the western Ukrainian lands. (In 1914, there were 75 branches, 2,944 reading rooms, and approx. 200,000 members; in 1939, there were 83 branches, 3,075 reading rooms, and 360,000 members.)

Prosvita's activities were regulated by statutes ratified at its general meetings. The statute of 1870 changed the society's initial scholarly orientation and allowed it to extend its influence into the regions. The second (1891) directed the society's work toward the economic improvement of the Ukrainian village. In 1924, Prosvita returned to cultural and educational work. Its presidents were prominent Galicians: Anatol Vakhnianyn (1868–70), Yuliian Lavrivsky (1870–73), Volodyslav Fedorovych (1873–77), Oleksander Ohonovsky (1877–94), Yuliian Romanchuk (1896–1906), Yevhen Olesnytsky (1906), Petro Ohonovsky (1906–10), Ivan Kyveliuk (1910–23), Mykhailo Halushchynsky (1923–31), Ivan Bryk (1932–39), and Yuliian Dzerovych (1939). Prosvita was most politicized under the presidency of Lavrivsky, head of the Galician populists, who attempted to bring about an understanding between Ukrainians and Poles, as well as between populists and **Russophiles**. Prosvita also initiated the founding of the populist newspaper *Dilo* (The Deed, 1880), as well as of a political organization, the People's Council (1885). In November 1918, with the establishment of the **Western Ukrainian People's Republic**, Prosvita became the basis of its State Secretariat of Education.

Besides its cultural and educational work, Prosvita played an especially important role in economic development, establishing stores, cooperatives, dairies, and savings-and-loan societies under the auspices of the reading rooms. Its publications fostered the development of theoretical and practical husbandry. Prosvita opened a commercial school in Lviv (1911), a **women's** domestic school in Uhertsi Vyniavski (1912), and a farming school in Mylovannia (1912). The society granted scholarships and opportunities for study in Western Europe. In 1909, it organized the First Ukrainian

Educational and Economic Congress, attended by activists from all Ukrainian lands.

Over 60 years, Prosvita published approximately 1,000 books, mainly of a popular nature. From 1877, it published monthly booklets distributed in exchange for membership dues. With the help of government funding, Prosvita prepared and published 22 textbooks for Ukrainian gymnasiums (totaling 15,100 copies, 1869–76). In 1878, Prosvita published the first Ukrainian prayer book written in the vernacular. In all, it published eight series: Ruthenian Literature (later Ukrainian Literature, 1904–28, 25 vols., totaling 172,000 copies), Prosvita Leaflets (1907–27, eight books, 23,000 copies), Popular Library (1920–27, 38 books, 203,000 copies), General Library (1920–25, eight books), Learn, My Brothers (1921–29, nine books, 45,000 copies), Historical Library (1925–28, 10 books, 48,000 copies), and the Life and Knowledge Library (1925–39, 53 books, 158,000 copies). It also published seven periodicals: *Pys'mo z Prosvity* (Letter from Prosvita, 1876–79, 1891–94, 1907–14, 1921–33), *Chytal'nia* (Reading Room, 1894–96), *Amators'kyi teatr* (Amateur Theater, 1925–27), *Bibliotechnyi poradnyk* (Library Guide, 1925–26), *Narodna Prosvita* (Popular Enlightenment, 1922–27), *Zhyttia i znannia* (Life and Knowledge, 1927–39), and *Prosvita* (1936–39).

Prosvita's books and periodicals were edited by noted civic and cultural figures, including **Ivan Franko, Kost Levytsky,** Volodymyr Levytsky, Petro Ohonovsky, Omelian Partytsky, Romanchuk, Stepan Shakh, and Yaroslav Vesolovsky. The illustrations of Pavlo Kovzhun, Yuliian Pankevych, and **Ivan Trush** gave Prosvita's books artistic value. A library was established at Prosvita headquarters in 1869; more than half of Prosvita reading rooms had their own libraries. Prosvita also organized an extensive book-distribution network; books were mailed out, a mobile book trade was first organized in 1924, and exhibitions of Ukrainian books were held. Despite its own financial difficulties, Prosvita distributed many books as a form of charitable assistance and sent books to distant Ukrainian settlements. In the 1930s, the society opened its own bookstore in Lviv. Prosvita organized a museum and archive at its library, the holdings of which were subsequently donated to the **Shevchenko Scientific Society** and the National Museum.

Prosvita's sources of revenue were membership dues (approx. 30 percent), public donations, provincial and state subsidies, and profits from its businesses. The Polish majority in the Galician Diet impeded government assistance to the society, and after **World War I** all subsidies were blocked. The Polish authorities hindered the registration of new branches and reading rooms and forbade

Prosvita's expansion into northwestern Ukraine. In September 1939, with the Soviet occupation of Galicia, Prosvita was closed and a significant portion of its property and books destroyed.

The activities of the Lviv Prosvita Society prompted great interest in **eastern Ukraine**. The establishment of an analogous society became possible there only after the **Revolution of 1905**. The first Prosvita educational society based on the Galician model was founded in Katerynoslav (now Dnipropetrovsk, October 1905). It opened four branches and began publishing activities (the *Dobra porada* [Good Advice] newspaper). Vasyl Bidnov, **Dmytro Doroshenko**, and **Dmytro Yavornytsky** participated in the society's work. It was closed in the autumn of 1914 for "propagating separatism." Prosvita also became active in **Odesa** (November 1905). The society opened a library, bookstore, and museum, conducted literary and musical evenings, and began publishing the *Narodna sprava* (People's Cause) newspaper. In 1906, Prosvita arranged for **Mykhailo Hrushevsky** to lecture in Ukrainian history at Odesa University. Its activities were banned in 1908. In May 1906, a Prosvita society was opened in **Kyiv** that would subsequently become a headquarters for other societies. Through the efforts of **Borys Hrinchenko**, **Mykola Lysenko**, **Lesia Ukrainka**, **Serhii Yefremov**, and others, the Kyiv Prosvita Society began publishing actively (34 books with a circulation of 163,760 copies). It opened a library/reading room and conducted lectures, concerts, and exhibits. The authorities forced the society to close in 1910. Other branches were active in Kamianets-Podilskyi, Zhytomyr, Chernihiv, Mykolaiv, Melitopol, and elsewhere (1906–11). From 1917 to 1922, Prosvita societies became centers of Ukrainian national life in central and eastern Ukraine. In 1922, more than 4,000 Prosvita branches were closed by the Soviet authorities.

At the beginning of the 20th century, Prosvita was also active in **Podlachia**, the **Kholm** (Chełm) **region**, **Volhynia**, **Transcarpathia**, and in a number of countries in Europe and the Americas. All these branches maintained ties with the Lviv society as best they could and strove to promote the exchange of books. In September 1990, the society renewed its activities in Ukraine under the name **Taras Shevchenko** Society for the Ukrainian Language: Prosvita.

PROTESTANT CHURCHES IN UKRAINE. The ideas of the Protestant Reformation were first brought to Ukraine in the 15th century by Hussite refugees from Bohemia. Subsequently, Calvinism and Antitrinitarianism spread to Ukraine from the **Polish-Lithuanian Commonwealth**, winning converts mainly on the estates of magnate families. Socinianism became well established in **Volhynia**. The Protestant sects had an important cultural impact on Ukraine through their vernacular translations of the gospels. However, Protestantism failed to penetrate the masses and was swept away by the Counter-Reformation and the Orthodox revival of the early 17th century.

Beginning in the late 18th century, German immigrants, including Baptists, Lutherans, and Mennonites, began to colonize the southern Ukrainian steppes. The Baptists, who were particularly strong in the Kherson, Katerynoslav, **Kyiv**, and Volhynia regions, gave rise to an evangelical movement known as Stundism (from the German *Stunde*, the hour devoted to Bible study). They were persecuted by the authorities until a toleration law was enacted as a result of the **Revolution of 1905**; many were deported to Siberia or emigrated to North America. The Mennonites, many of whom were prosperous farmers, also suffered official persecution, as well as pillage and dispossession by peasant revolutionaries (1917–21). As a result, thousands of Mennonites emigrated to Canada in the 1920s, while the remainder perished during Stalin's forced **collectivization** or were resettled during **World War II**.

Under the Soviet regime, Protestant sects (like other religious organizations) were subject to persecution, including the official suppression of churches, show trials, and the sentencing of believers to terms in forced-labor camps. Since Ukraine's declaration of independence, there has been a notable Protestant revival, owing in part to the evangelizing activities of foreign missionaries. If in the past many Protestant sects were German- or Russian-speaking and isolated from Ukrainian society, there is now a trend toward social integration. The largest Protestant grouping is the All-Ukrainian Union of Evangelical Baptists, with 2,230 communities (second only to Great Britain in the European Baptist Federation). There are also Pentecostals (1,366 communities), Seventh-Day Adventists (970 communities), the Subcarpathian Reformed Church (approx. 105 communities), the Lutheran Church (71 communities), and smaller groups such as Jehovah's Witnesses and Mormons.

PROVISIONAL WORKERS' AND PEASANTS' GOVERNMENT OF UKRAINE/TYMCHASOVYI ROBITNYCHO-SELIANS'KYI URIAD UKRAÏNY. Second Soviet government of Ukraine, popularly known as the Piatakov regime. It was established on 20 November 1918 in Kursk, Russia, on instructions of the Russian Bolshevik Party, and its creation was announced in Sudzha (now in Kursk oblast) on 28 November. Its leading members were **Georgii Piatakov** (chairman), Artem (Fedor Sergeev; military affairs), Viktor Averin (internal affairs), Oleksander Khmelnytsky (justice), Emmanuil Kviring (economy), Valerii Mezhlauk (military affairs), Mykola Podvoisky (military affairs), Oleksander Shlikhter (agriculture), Musii Rukhymovych (economy), Kliment Voroshilov (internal affairs), and **Volodymyr Zatonsky** (education). **Yurii Kotsiubynsky** and Iukhym Shchadenko were members of the Military Revolutionary Committee. On 29 November, the government issued a manifesto announcing the overthrow of Hetman **Pavlo Skoropadsky** and the restoration of Soviet rule in Ukraine (the revolt against Skoropadsky had in fact been initiated two weeks earlier by the **Directory** of the **Ukrainian People's Republic**). The manifesto canceled all laws, agreements, and decrees of the Skoropadsky regime and announced the nationalization of industry and the redistribution of landowners' property among the peasants without compensation.

On 6 January 1919, the Provisional Government began using the name Ukrainian Socialist Soviet Republic. After **Sloboda Ukraine** was captured by Bolshevik forces, the government moved to **Kharkiv**, and **Khristian Rakovsky** became its premier. He reorganized the government on the Russian model; departments were renamed people's commissariats, and the government itself was renamed the **Council of People's Commissars**. On 25 January, the government proclaimed the union of the **Ukrainian SSR** with Soviet Russia on the basis of "socialist federalism."

The Piatakov regime soon discredited itself with the Ukrainian **peasantry** by turning many of the old estates into communes instead of parceling them out, as well as by its unrelenting requisition of grain for Russia, carried out by village soviets and committees of poor peasants (*komnezamy*). The number of peasant revolts against the regime rose steadily. Piatakov and Rakovsky also regarded all manifestations of Ukrainian national feeling as reactionary, thereby alienating the Ukrainian intelligentsia. In August, the Piatakov regime came to an end with the evacuation of Kyiv.

PTUKHA, MYKHAILO (26 October [7 November] 1884–3 October 1961). Demographer and statistician; full member of the **Ukrainian Academy of Sciences** (UAN, from 1920) and corresponding member of the **USSR** Academy of Sciences (from 1943). Born in Oster, Chernihiv gubernia, Ptukha began working for the statistics section of the Chernihiv zemstvo bureau as a gymnasium student. He studied at St. Petersburg University (1906–10), in Berlin (1910–12), and London (1914–15), and began teaching statistics at St. Petersburg University in 1913. After moving to **Kyiv** in 1918, he organized the UAN Demographic Institute (1919), the first demographic research center in the world. He headed the institute until its absorption into the Institute of Economics in 1938. Ptukha organized the latter's statistical section, heading it from 1940 to 1950. From 1944 to 1950, he headed the Social Science Section of the Academy of Sciences of the **Ukrainian SSR**. In 1929, he was elected to the International Statistical Institute. The founder of the Ukrainian school of demography, Ptukha wrote 11 books on theoretical and applied statistics, the history of statistics in the Russian Empire, and demography.

PUBLISHING. Early manuscript books in **Kyivan Rus'** were translations of ecclesiastical **literature**, which gave way to original literary work by the end of the 11th century. Book printing developed in Ukraine in the second half of the 16th century, and the mass production of books began in the early 19th century with the introduction of mechanical printing. Beginning in the 16th century, the **Lviv Dormition Brotherhood** distributed religious literature in Church Slavonic throughout Ukraine, and the press of the **Kyivan Cave Monastery** became the country's most significant publisher.

The first book written in the Ukrainian vernacular, **Ivan Kotliarevsky**'s *Eneïda* (Travestied Aeneid), was printed in St. Petersburg in 1798, while the first vernacular publication printed in Ukraine, Petro Hulak-Artemovsky's *Solopii ta Khivria*, appeared in **Kharkiv** in 1819. Kharkiv was the main publishing center in **eastern Ukraine** until Ukrainian-language publishing was almost completely halted by the provisions of the **Valuev circular** (1863) and the **Ems Ukase** (1876). From the 1860s, **Galicia**, especially the city of **Lviv**, became the center of Ukrainian-language publishing. Restrictions eased in the Russian Empire after the **Revolution of 1905**, and 246 Ukrainian books were published there in 1913, but this total still lagged behind that of Galicia, where 326 books were published in the same year. In Galicia, books were distributed through the Stauropegion Institute, the **Prosvita Society**, and the **Shevchenko Scientific Society**. Ukrainian publishing in **Bukovyna** developed slowly, while in **Transcarpathia**, only 22 Ukrainian books appeared in 1913.

During the **Ukrainian Revolution** (1917–21), book production increased rapidly. After the consolidation of the Soviet regime, private publishing activity was eliminated, and the State Publishing House of Ukraine, as well as the Knyhospilka cooperative publishing union, emerged as the country's largest publishers. The proportion of Ukrainian-language books produced in the Soviet Union increased as a result of the **Ukrainization** policy (11.7 percent in 1931) but never reflected the proportion of the Ukrainian **population** (16.5 percent). During Stalin's **political terror** and the concomitant campaign against Ukrainian culture, that proportion fell sharply (4.3 percent in 1939). From the 1930s, scientific and technical books appeared almost exclusively in Russian. Between 1946 and 1975, 190,693 books and pamphlets were published in Ukraine; of these, only 83,319 titles were in Ukrainian. By 1978, 68 percent of publications printed in Ukraine were in Russian. Book distribution was centralized under the auspices of Ukrknyhotorh (Ukrainian Book Trade). The Ukrainian Scientific Institute of Bibliology (1922–36) studied book production, while the Book Chamber of Ukraine (est. 1919) has been responsible for registering and preserving copies of all publications. The Book and Book Printing Museum was established at the Kyivan Cave Monastery in 1972 to preserve rare books and incunabula.

Between the **world wars**, many valuable historical works were published in Galicia. In 1938, book production there reached 476 titles (22 percent of the **Ukrainian SSR's** production). Romanian censorship kept Ukrainian book production in Bukovyna very low; in Transcarpathia, where the regime was far more liberal, more than a thousand Ukrainian titles appeared between the wars.

Since independence, Ukrainian publishing has lost the state support that previously sustained it, and the Soviet-era distribution system has broken down. The number of book titles published in Ukraine declined from 7,046 in 1990 to 4,736 in 1999, while press runs have declined even more drastically, from 170 million copies in 1990 to about 21 million in 1999. The market has been flooded with Russian-language publications; Ukrainian-language publishers cannot hope to match Russia's economy of scale. Nevertheless, a great many books that could not have appeared under Soviet censorship have been published, and there is a constant stream of new publications, many of them with small press runs. *See also* MEDIA.

PULIUI, IVAN (Puluj, Jan; 2 February 1845–31 January 1918). Physicist, electrical engineer, inventor, and translator. Puliui was born in Hrymailiv, **Galicia** (now in Ternopil oblast). He studied theology (1864–69) and physics (1869–72) at Vienna University and completed a doctorate in physics at Strasbourg University (1877). He taught physics at Vienna University, and from 1884 to 1916 he was professor of experimental physics and electrical technology at the Prague Polytechnical Institute, where he served as rector (1899–1900) and first dean of Europe's first electrical technology faculty (from 1902). He was a founding member of the electrical technology societies of Vienna and Prague, serving as head of the latter.

Puliui made major contributions in the study of electrical discharges in gases, molecular physics, and the technology of alternating electrical currents. He is best known for the "Puluj tube," a cathode-ray tube of his own invention, and is credited with the discovery of X-rays in 1883, several years prior to Wilhelm Röntgen's published findings (1895). Puliui also produced many inventions in the fields of thermal measurements, electric incandescent lamps, and telemetry. He wrote more than 50 scientific and technical works.

Puliui was actively involved in Ukrainian civic life, publishing articles in defense of the Ukrainian **language**. With **Panteleimon Kulish**, he translated the Gospels (1871) and the entire New Testament (1880) into Ukrainian. These, along with translations of the Old Testament made with Ivan Nechui-Levytsky, became part of the Ukrainian bible published by the British Bible Society in 1903. Puliui also translated and published the first prayer book in the Ukrainian vernacular (1871).

PUSTOVOITENKO, VALERII (b. 23 February 1947). Ninth prime minister of independent Ukraine. Pustovoitenko was born in the village of Adamivka, Mykolaiv oblast, into a family of collective farmers. After graduation from an industrial school in **Odesa**, he worked as a metal turner at the October Revolution Plant in the city and studied civil engineering. In 1971, Pustovoitenko moved to Dnipropetrovsk, where he became chief engineer and then head (1984) of the Dnipro Construction Mechanization Trust. After serving on various administrative bodies in Dnipropetrovsk, Pustovoitenko became the city's mayor (1989–93), serving concurrently as a deputy to the **Verkhovna Rada** (VR). In 1993, his loyalty to Prime Minister **Leonid Kuchma** was rewarded with an appointment to the **Cabinet of Ministers**. Following Kuchma's resignation, Pustovoitenko was vice president of the Ukrainian State Construction Corporation and deputy head of the Expobank Credit Union. In 1993, he helped establish the Association of Cities of Ukraine and served as its first president. He was reappointed to the Cabinet of Ministers, holding office from July 1994 to July 1997.

Following the dismissal of the discredited **Pavlo Lazarenko** and the very brief tenure of Vasyl Durdynets as acting prime minister, President Kuchma appointed Pustovoitenko to the prime minister's office on 16 July 1997. Pustovoitenko gained attention with an unorthodox effort to collect tax payments from enterprises in default—he assembled executives of large companies for civil-defense training and insisted that they would continue training until the debts of their enterprises were paid. After Kuchma's reelection to the presidency in November 1999, the VR did not support his renomination of Pustovoitenko as prime minister, and **Viktor Yushchenko** was appointed in the following month. After his resignation, Pustovoitenko headed the People's Democratic Party. He returned to government in June 2001 as minister of transportation in the cabinet of Prime Minister **Anatolii Kinakh**. Since 2002, he has been a deputy to the VR.

PYSARZHEVSKY, LEV (1 [13] February 1874–23 March 1938). Inorganic and physical chemist; full member of the **Ukrainian Academy of Sciences** (VUAN; from 1925) and the Academy of Sciences of the **USSR** (from 1930). Born in Chişinău, **Moldavia**, Pysarzhevsky studied at **Odesa** University, where he completed a master's degree in 1903. He was professor at Tartu University (1904–8), the **Kyiv** Polytechnical Institute (1908–11), and the Dnipropetrovsk Mining (1913–30) and Chemical Technology (1930–32) institutes. He cofounded and directed the Ukrainian Physical Chemistry Institute in Dnipropetrovsk (1927–34), the Tbilisi Chemical Research Institute (1929–31), and the VUAN Institute of Physical Chemistry in Kyiv (1934–38), which is now named after him. Pysarzhevsky devoted his research to the structure and properties of peroxides and peracids and studied the influence of solvents on chemical equilibria, the free energy of reactions, and electronic concepts of chemistry. His findings were crucial for shaping current views on the nature of chemical bonding and chemical reaction mechanisms, with special emphasis on the electronic theory of heterogeneous catalysis. In 1926, he advanced a holistic approach to chemistry from the standpoint of electronic interactions.

R

RABYNOVYCH, VADYM (b. 4 August 1953). Businessman, media baron. He was born in **Kharkiv** into the family of an army officer. In 1970, Rabynovych was admitted to the Kharkiv Road Transport Institute but expelled in 1974 after his exclusion from the Communist Youth League. Following military service, he worked as a construction foreman. Rabynovych amassed his starting capital by selling state building materials. He was arrested in January 1980 and convicted on charges of misappropriation of state property, but the charges were dropped following the intervention of the Soviet prosecutor-general. From 1980 to 1982, Rabynovych ran an underground shop in Kharkiv that produced crystal, wooden doors, and calendars. Rearrested in 1982, he was given a 14-year sentence. Rabynovych was released in July 1991 and soon established a new enterprise together with his former prison supervisor, but it proved a failure. In the following years, Rabynovych founded the Ortex consulting firm and worked as a representative of Nordex, a company with ties to Prime Minister Viktor Chernomyrdin of Russia. In this period, Rabynovych obtained Israeli citizenship and worked in Ukraine as a foreign businessman. At the end of 1995, he established the RC Group and entered the media market, acquiring the SuperNova FM radio station, the newspaper *Delovaia nedelia* (Business Week), and shares in People's Television. He also cofounded Studio 1+1, which became the most popular television channel in Ukraine. Together with **Oleksandr Volkov**, Rabynovych established the Ukraine-Israel Chamber of Commerce to attract investments to Ukraine. The project was successful, and the partners channeled more than a billion dollars into the computer and communication industries. This activity helped Rabynovych enter the inner circle of President **Leonid Kuchma** and become one of his advisors on economic affairs. Rabynovych became president of the Stolychni Novyny (Capital News) publishing house, which controlled a number of newspapers, Internet portals, and radio and television stations.

In 1998, Rabynovych sponsored the Green Party of Ukraine, helping the Greens enter the **Verkhovna Rada** and form their own parliamentary faction. He also headed the newly established All-Ukrainian **Jewish** Congress (AUJC) and was awarded an honorary doctorate by Solomon University (established in **Kyiv** in 1992). Rabynovych was obliged to step down as head of the AUJC because of criticism from influential Ukrainian Jews; in April 1999, he established the alternative Main Coordinating Council of the Jewish Community of Ukraine.

In August 1998, the Israeli secret service began an investigation of Rabynovych's alleged underworld connections. In June 1999, the Security Service of Ukraine denied him access to the country for five years. He was also placed on a watch list by the U.S. State Department. Following negotiations with the Kuchma administration, Rabynovych was granted access to Ukraine but lost control of Studio 1+1, selling his shares to the U.S. cosmetics mogul Ronald Lauder. In 2000, he established International Media MIGNews, which included a number of Ukrainian and Israeli mass-media outlets. At a press conference in Kyiv in February 2001, Rabynovych displayed his new Ukrainian passport without explaining whether he had given up Israeli citizenship. In 2004, he bought a Russian radio station in New York and *Novoe russkoe slovo* (New Russian Word), the oldest Russian newspaper in the United States.

RADA/COUNCIL. Newspaper published from 15 (28) September 1906 to 20 July (2 August) 1914 in **Kyiv**. At the time, it was the only

Ukrainian-language daily in the Russian Empire. The newspaper was established by **Borys Hrinchenko** and published by **Yevhen Chykalenko**, with financial support from the industrialist Vasyl Symyrenko and others. Never an official party organ, *Rada* nevertheless supported the policies of the **Society of Ukrainian Progressives**. Its chief editors were Fedir Matushevsky, Metodii Pavlovsky (1907–13), and Andrii Nikovsky (1913–14). One of *Rada's* editorial secretaries was **Symon Petliura**, while **Dmytro Doroshenko**, Oleksander Oles, **Liudmyla Starytska-Cherniakhivska**, and **Serhii Yefremov** were among its editors. Contributors included such prominent figures as **Mykhailo Hrushevsky, Ivan Franko**, and **Volodymyr Vynnychenko**. In covering civic, political, and cultural life, *Rada* played an important role in the formation of national consciousness in **eastern Ukraine**. The newspaper's offices were frequently raided by the authorities, who also imposed fines and confiscated issues. The number of subscribers never rose above 2,000. With the outbreak of **World War I**, the imperial government suspended the newspaper's publication. In March 1917, it was replaced by *Nova rada* (New Council), published until January 1919 (eds. Nikovsky and Yefremov). *See also* MEDIA.

RAHOZA (ROHOZA), MYKHAIL (ca. 1540–1599). Orthodox metropolitan of **Kyiv**. He was born in **Volhynia** (according to other sources, in Belarus) and studied at the Jesuit college in Vilnius. In 1576, he was secretary to Bohush Koretsky, palatine of Vilnius. Subsequently, he was tonsured and entered the **Basilian** Ascension Monastery in Minsk, becoming its archimandrite in 1579. He maintained friendly relations with Prince **Kostiantyn Ostrozky**. In 1588, he was appointed metropolitan of Kyiv by King Sigismund III and consecrated by Patriarch Jeremiah II of Constantinople in 1589. Rahoza supported the ecclesiastical **Union of Brest** (1596), sending Bishops **Ipatii Potii** and Kyryl Terletsky to Rome to negotiate its terms.

RAKOVSKY, KHRISTIAN (1 August 1873–11 September 1941). Bolshevik revolutionary, politician, and diplomat. Born in Gradets, Bulgaria, he lived in Switzerland from 1890 and later studied medicine in Germany and France. He was a founder of social democratic parties in Bulgaria and Romania and became an influential member of the Second International. Rakovsky opposed Bulgaria's participation in **World War I** and was a member of the Central Bureau of the antiwar Revolutionary Balkan Social Democratic Labor Federation. In 1915, he was arrested in Iaşi and imprisoned. Released from prison by Russian soldiers in May 1917, he joined the Bolshevik Party after the October 1917 revolution.

From May 1918, Rakovsky headed the Bolshevik diplomatic delegation at peace negotiations with the **Ukrainian State**. From January 1919 to July 1923 (with interruptions), he was head of the **Provisional Workers' and Peasants' Government of Ukraine** and the government of the **Ukrainian SSR**. Since Rakovsky had no Ukrainian power base, he was dependent on Moscow; Lenin expected him to settle differences between contending Bolshevik factions in Ukraine. He managed to divide the **Borotbist** party, bribing some of its members with government posts and eliminating others with the help of the Cheka. On first being posted to Ukraine, Rakovsky opposed its independence and even questioned the existence of a Ukrainian nationality. By 1921, however, he had begun to function as head of an autonomous government and demanded greater political and economic freedom for the Ukrainian SSR. At the 12th congress of the Russian Communist Party (April 1923), Rakovsky clashed with Stalin on the national question, particularly the latter's proposal to eliminate the sovereignty of the Soviet republics. For this, Rakovsky was removed from the Ukrainian government and appointed Soviet ambassador to Britain (1923–25) and France (1925–27). He was expelled from France for conducting revolutionary activity. After his return to the **USSR**, Rakovsky became an active member of the Left (Trotskyist) Opposition. In December 1927, he was expelled from the party and soon exiled to Astrakhan. In February 1934, with Stalin firmly in control, Rakovsky submitted to party discipline and was permitted to return to Moscow, where he headed the scientific research institute of the Commissariat of Health. He was arrested in December 1936 on charges of anti-Soviet activity and sentenced in March 1938 to 20 years' imprisonment. He was shot at a prison in Orel, Russia.

REALISM. A term referring to various traditions in the arts concerned with the depiction of the material world with as little distortion as possible, directly opposed to stylized or abstract depictions of the visible. As an artistic movement, realism was popularized in the late 19th century in the Russian-ruled Ukrainian lands through the efforts of the Peredvizhniki, a St. Petersburg–based group of artists committed to the idea of enlightenment through traveling exhibitions. Landscapes and scenes of **peasant** life were the preferred subjects of the Peredvizhniki, who strove for social relevance. Several Ukrainian-born artists, such as **Ilia Repin** and Serhii Vasylkivsky, became members of the group or exhibited with them.

The beginnings of realist **literature** in the second half of the 19th century coincided with the prohibition of Ukrainian-**language** publishing in the Russian Empire (*see* VALUEV CIRCULAR; EMS UKASE). As a result, no cohesive realist movement emerged in Ukrainian prose, and eastern Ukrainian writers were obliged to publish their works in **western Ukraine**. The most prominent among them were Ivan Nechui-Levytsky and Panas Myrny, who focused on contemporary social and national issues. Other writers, such as **Oleksander Konysky**, **Borys Hrinchenko**, and Olena Pchilka, were considered ethnographic realists because of their interest in **populist** social issues. In western Ukraine, **Ivan Franko** became a major force in realist prose and drama under the influence of West European naturalists, particularly Emile Zola. Many of his works described the plight of workers and peasants in difficult economic conditions.

Ukrainian drama reached a particularly high level of development during the realist period. Populist plays spiced with ethnographic elements were written by **Mykhailo Starytsky** and Marko Kropyvnytsky. The career of the greatest 19th-century Ukrainian dramatist, Ivan Karpenko-Kary (Tobilevych), culminated in socially critical realist plays (*see* THEATER).

From the early 1930s to the late 1980s, the arts in the Soviet Union, including the **Ukrainian SSR**, were dominated by officially sanctioned "socialist realism." Described as the "true depiction of reality in its revolutionary development," this trend glorified the leadership of the Communist Party. Distinguished by politically correct content and naturalist style, socialist realism strove to conceal its superficiality with upbeat depictions of communist heroes and happy workers and peasants. Departures from the style were criticized as "formalist," "abstractionist," and "modernist." The painters Mykhailo Bozhii and Oleksii Shovkunenko, the dramatist Oleksander Korniichuk, and the novelist **Mykhailo Stelmakh** are considered more talented representatives of socialist realism. *See also* MODERNISM; PAINTING.

REBET, LEV (3 March 1912–12 October 1957). Political leader, journalist, and ideologue of Ukrainian nationalism. He was born in Stryi, **Galicia**, and studied law at **Lviv** University. In 1927, Rebet joined the **Ukrainian Military Organization** and later the **Organization of Ukrainian Nationalists** (OUN). From 1930, he headed the OUN network in Stryi county, then the OUN Territorial Executive in **western Ukraine** (1935–39). Rebet was arrested several times by the Polish police and imprisoned for almost two years. He sided with the OUN faction led by **Stepan Bandera** and was second vice-president of the **Ukrainian State Administration** (Lviv, 1941), headed by **Yaroslav Stetsko**. Following Stetsko's arrest, Rebet took over his functions until 14 September, when he was arrested by the Gestapo and incarcerated in Auschwitz for three years. After his release, Rebet lived in Munich, where he belonged to the Foreign Center of the OUN(B) and was its chief justice.

Rebet advocated democratic reforms within the OUN in accordance with its Third Extraordinary Great Congress (21–25 August 1943). In 1952, he was coopted by the External Representation of the **Supreme Ukrainian Liberation Council** (UHVR) and headed its Council of Representatives. In 1953, at the behest of the OUN leadership in Ukraine, Rebet, Bandera, and Zynovii Matla established a collegium charged with reorganizing the OUN and defining its tasks in the postwar period. In February 1954, having failed to reach an understanding with Bandera, Rebet and Matla established a separate faction that constituted itself as the OUN (Abroad) on 25 December 1956. They were joined by **Mykola Lebed** and other UHVR representatives, and Rebet headed the Political Council of the OUN (Abroad). He worked as a journalist with the political weekly *Ukraïns'ka trybuna* (Ukrainian Tribune, Munich, 1946–49) and the biweekly *Suchasna Ukraïna* (Contemporary Ukraine, Munich, 1951–60). In 1955–57, he was editor in chief of the OUN (Abroad) journal *Ukraïns'kyi samostiinyk* (Ukrainian Independentist). Rebet wrote works on the formation of the Ukrainian nation and on the theory of the nation, as well as a critical study of the OUN. In October 1957, he was assassinated by the KGB agent Bohdan Stashynsky, who killed Bandera two years later. Rebet was buried at the Waldfriedhof Cemetery in Munich.

RED COSSACKS. Military formations created by the Bolsheviks to counteract the **Free Cossacks**. The first regiment of Red Cossacks, commanded by Vitalii Primakov, was formed in **Kharkiv** (28 December 1917 [10 January 1918]) and is considered the first Soviet Ukrainian military unit. The name was chosen to help legitimize the Bolshevik cause by identifying it with the **Cossacks** of early modern Ukraine. Red Cossack regiments fought the Army of the **Ukrainian People's Republic** and Ukrainian insurgents, as well as the White armies of Anton Denikin and Petr Wrangel, German occupying forces (1918), and Polish forces.

RED RUS' (Ukr. *Chervona Rus'*, Lat. *Russia Rubra*, Pol. *Czerwona Ruś*). Historical name for **Galicia** that appears in written sources, primarily foreign, from the 16th to the 19th century. The term was used by the 15th-century Italian cartographer Fra Mauro to designate the lands of the Don River basin. An early 17th-century Polish historian, Szymon Starowolski, used it to describe the Ukrainian lands in general. Gradually it came to be used in historical and geographical literature to denote the territory of the former Galician principality (the Rus' and Belz palatinates, according to the administrative divisions of the 15th to 18th centuries). Red Rus' remained a literary term and was not adopted by the local population. It probably emerged under the influence of the compound geographical names of the Eastern peoples, in which colors were used to distinguish parts of the globe. Some Polish historians used the term to promote the view that the Cherven towns of **Kyivan Rus'** had a "non-Ukrainian character." With a similar purpose in mind, Polish publicists of the 1920s and 1930s used the term *Czerwieńska Ruś* in place of *Czerwona Ruś*. At the turn of the 20th century, some writers of the **Russophile** camp propagated the term "Red Rus'" to distinguish Galicians from the rest of the Ukrainian people. In present-day literature, the terms "Galician land" and "Galician-Volhynian Rus'" are used to denote the southwestern portion of Kyivan Rus' up to the 14th century, while "Galicia" and "western Ukraine" are used to name that territory after the 14th century.

REGISTERED COSSACKS. Cossacks engaged by the **Polish-Lithuanian Commonwealth** for military service whose names were entered in a special register. In June 1572, King Sigismund II Augustus ordered the recruitment of a hired army of 300 Cossacks to protect the southern and eastern borders of the Commonwealth and control the Zaporozhian Cossacks. The Polish nobleman Jan Badowski is believed to have been the first elder (*starshyi*) of the registered Cossacks. The Polish government recognized only registered Cossacks as legitimate (as distinct from the independent **Zaporozhian Host**). In 1578, King Stephen Batory expanded the register to 600 men. Registered Cossacks received the right to their own military, administrative, and judicial jurisdiction and were exempt from taxation and labor obligations. They were given ownership of the town of Trakhtemyriv, where their arsenal and hospital were located. They elected their **hetman** and officers independently at **Cossack councils**. The registered army received several cannon and **Cossack insignia**. In the 1620s and 1630s, the size of the registered Cossack army varied between 3,000 and 8,000 men, with the Cossacks seeking to increase it and the Polish government attempting to restrict it. During the **Cossack rebellions** of the late 16th and early 17th century, registered Cossacks often joined the rebels. In 1648, most joined the army of **Bohdan Khmelnytsky**. In the **Hetmanate**, registered Cossacks came to be known as town Cossacks, and from 1735 they were called elected Cossacks.

REICHSKOMMISSARIAT UKRAINE (RKU). One of two large administrative zones created on German-occupied territories of the **USSR** during **World War II** (the other was the Reichskommissariat Ostland, consisting of Estonia, Latvia, Lithuania, parts of Belarus, and Leningrad oblast). The RKU, established on 1 September 1941, included much of **western Ukraine** (**Galicia** was annexed to the **Generalgouvernement**), while **Carpatho-Ukraine** was taken over by Hungary and **Bukovyna** by Romania. On 2 September 1942, the rest of the **Poltava** region and Dnipropetrovsk, Zaporizhia, and **Kharkiv** oblasts were added to the RKU. At that time, its total area consisted of approximately 340,000 sq. km, with a population of approximately 17 million. Administratively, it was divided into six Generalbezirke (**Volhynia** and **Podilia**, Zhytomyr, **Kyiv**, Dnipropetrovsk, Mykolaiv, and Tavriia), each headed by a *Generalkommissar* appointed by Hitler. Only at the lowest (raion or district) level were Ukrainians appointed to administrative posts. The RKU was administered by Erich Koch, the *Gauleiter* of East Prussia, who described himself as "a brutal dog" appointed "to suck from Ukraine all the goods we can get hold of, without consideration for the feelings or the property of Ukrainians." The RKU was conceived as a purely geographical entity bearing no relation to Ukrainian ethnic territory. In order to emphasize that fact, Koch selected the Volhynian town of Rivne, not Kyiv, as his capital. After the war, the RKU was to be annexed to the German Reich.

Koch destroyed expeditionary groups of the **Organization of Ukrainian Nationalists** operating in the RKU. Hundreds of thousands of Red Army prisoners of war were herded into barbed-wire enclosures and allowed to die of starvation and typhus. About 2.2 million *Ostarbeiter* were shipped from the RKU to the Reich for forced labor. In the winter and spring of 1942, cities in the RKU starved because of German neglect and Wehrmacht food requisitions. Medical services were curtailed to check the "biological power of the Ukrainians," in Koch's words. General education was limited to four grades of primary school, all cultural institutions closed, and the press strictly censored. The hated Soviet collective farms were left intact, and in many areas German-imposed grain quotas were double the Soviet norm of 1941. Of the 6 million tonnes of grain requisitioned from the USSR (1941–44), 5 million came from the RKU.

Alfred Rosenberg, head of the Reich Ministry for the Occupied Eastern Territories, and senior officials of his ministry believed that more could be extracted from Ukraine through concessions than through Koch's brutal policies. They waged a vigorous bureaucratic campaign against Koch, but the latter's thinking was fully endorsed by Hitler. At a meeting held in Vinnytsia on 19 May 1943 to mediate between Rosenberg and Koch, Hitler asserted that "We can never expect the political approval of the Ukrainians for our actions." The minor concessions won by Rosenberg—the reopening of Ukrainian schools and a statute on the privatization of collective-farm property—were rendered ineffective by Koch and his staff.

The brutality of the occupation regime produced a sharp increase in anti-German sentiment and open resistance to the German authorities. By late 1942, such resistance had become so widespread as to oblige the **Bandera** faction of the OUN to begin organizing the **Ukrainian Insurgent Army** in Volhynia. In March 1943, a German official estimated that no more than 10 percent of Ukrainian auxiliary units could be considered reliable, and that summer, more than a million tonnes of grain could not be harvested because of Ukrainian resistance. The RKU was formally liquidated on 10 November 1944, long after the reoccupation of Ukraine by Soviet forces.

REPIN, ILIA (24 July [5 August] 1844–29 September 1930). Painter. Repin was born in Chuhuiv, **Kharkiv** gubernia, into the family of a military settler. He received his first instruction in **painting** at a local **iconography** studio and went on to study at the drawing school of the Society for the Encouragement of the Arts and at the Academy of Fine Arts (1864–71) in St. Petersburg. He also studied in Italy and later in Paris (1873–76). From 1882, Repin lived in St. Petersburg; in 1878 he joined the influential Peredvizhniki (Itinerant) Society of Painters. He was a full member of the St. Petersburg Academy of Fine Arts (from 1893) and teacher to many Ukrainian artists. From 1900 until his death, he lived in Kuokkala, Finland.

Most of Repin's works are genre paintings on peasant and historical themes; he also painted many portraits. Repin's monumental canvases on historical themes are highly dramatic, e.g., *Ivan the Terrible and His Son Ivan* (1875) and *Tsarina Sofia* (1879). His creative and civic activities were closely associated with Ukraine. The subjects of his portraits include such distinguished Ukrainians as **Mykola Kostomarov**, **Taras Shevchenko**, and **Dmytro Bahalii**. Many of Repin's paintings explore Ukrainian themes: *Ukrainian Peasant Woman* (1880), *The Zaporozhian Cossacks Write a Letter to the Turkish Sultan* (1880–91), *Evening Party* (1881), *Black Sea Freebooters* (1908), *Haidamakas* (1902), and *Hopak* (1930). He also illustrated **Nikolai Gogol's** *Taras Bul'ba* and *Sorochinskaia iarmarka* (Sorochyntsi Fair, 1872–82) and **Dmytro Yavornytsky's** *Zaporozh'e v ostatkakh stariny i predaniiakh naroda* (Zaporizhia in Relics of the Past and Folk Tradition, 1887).

REVOLUTION OF 1848. Democratic revolution in a number of European states. In Austria, the revolution began with a popular uprising in Vienna (13 March 1848) that led to the overthrow of Clemens von Metternich's conservative government. Emperor Ferdinand I proclaimed democratic freedoms and convoked a constitutional assembly (Reichstag) in April. Liberals won a majority in the Reichstag elections and passed a compromise resolution emancipating the serfs in exchange for compensation to landowners. No solution was found for chronic disputes among Austria's nationalities. Conservatives took advantage of divisions in the antimonarchist forces to launch an offensive in Hungary (25 August) that ultimately renewed the absolutist regime under a new emperor, Franz Joseph I, who took the throne in December 1848 after Ferdinand's abdication.

The revolution had broad resonance in the western Ukrainian lands under Austrian rule. In **Galicia**, the abolition of serfdom was announced on 16 April, four months earlier than in the rest of the Habsburg Monarchy. This initiative was taken by Governor Franz Stadion in order to prevent a **peasant** revolt and maintain the loyalty of the populace. In the Reichstag, 14 eastern Galician peasant deputies opposed paying compensation to landowners for the elimination of corvée labor. On 17 August, during the debate on the agrarian question, the peasant deputy Ivan Kapushchak gave an impassioned speech in defense of enserfed Galician peasants that was reported in many West European newspapers. He maintained that if anyone was to pay compensation, it should be the landlords, who had long mistreated their serfs. Ultimately, the question was left in abeyance.

The Ukrainian national movement, headed by the local clergy and intelligentsia, became active. Its leaders considered that loyalty to the Habsburgs (which differentiated them from the Poles, dominant in western Galicia) offered the best chance of obtaining concessions. On 19 April, at Stadion's urging, the Ukrainian leaders submitted a petition to the emperor requesting the introduction of the **Ruthenian** (Ukrainian) **language** into the educational and administrative systems of eastern Galicia, access to government posts for Ukrainians, and equalization of Greek Catholic clerics (*see* UKRAINIAN CATHOLIC CHURCH) with the dominant Roman Catholics. The petition was composed on behalf of the Habsburgs' Ukrainian subjects, i.e., "the Galician Ruthenian nation, which numbers 2.5 million." At the insistence of the lawyer Iuliian Lavrivsky, the text was changed to acknowledge that the Galician Ukrainians were part of a nation of 15 million, most of whom lived in the Russian Empire.

The Supreme Ruthenian Council, established on 2 May in **Lviv**, became the nucleus of the national movement and the first legal Ukrainian political organization of modern times. It was led by the bishop of Peremyshl (Przemyśl), Hryhorii Yakhymovych, and composed in roughly equal parts of clergymen and members of the intelligentsia. The council, which had 50 local and 13 regional branches, supported a plan to create a Slavic federation within the empire and sent a delegation to the Pan-Slavic Congress in Prague. That summer, the council appealed for the partition of Galicia along ethnic lines and the creation of a separate province in eastern Galicia with its center in Lviv, hoping thereby to end the dominance of the Polish aristocracy. A memorandum with 200,000 signatures was submitted in support of partition. The project was strongly opposed by the Polish elite, which created its own representative body, the Central National Council, as well as a Polish-sponsored Ruthenian Council to counteract the Supreme Ruthenian Council. The vicegerent of Galicia, Agenor Gołuchowski, and Polish deputies in the Reichstag opposed partition, frightening the government with the prospect that eastern Galicia might secede and join the Russian Empire. The partition plan was rejected but remained on the agenda of the Ukrainian national movement until the collapse of Austria-Hungary in 1918. At the Prague congress, Ukrainian delegates managed to gain recognition as a separate Slavic nationality, and a compromise resolution on education called for the language of instruction in Galicia to reflect the ethnic composition of the population. The Galician Ukrainians also formed two military units, a frontier defense force and the Ruthenian Riflemen, which manifested their loyalty to the monarchy.

The Revolution of 1848 brought a number of significant cultural achievements. The first Ukrainian newspaper, *Zoria halyts'ka* (Galician Star, 1848–57), began publication. It was followed by an explosion of Ukrainian publishing (more than 150 titles in 1848). From 19 to 26 October, the first congress of Ukrainian scholarly, educational, and cultural figures took place in Lviv. A department of Ukrainian language and literature headed by **Yakiv Holovatsky** was established at the University of Lviv. A Galician-Ruthenian *matytsia* (Slavic cultural institution) and a National Home were founded, and Ukrainian amateur theaters were active in Kolomyia, Peremyshl, and other centers.

From the autumn of 1848, with the political defeat of the revolution, the national movement in Galicia lost its mass character. In early 1849, following the introduction of martial law in the region, the most active Ukrainian councils were eliminated. In 1851, the Supreme Ruthenian Council announced its dissolution.

In **Bukovyna**, revolutionary events began with peasant uprisings, and serfdom was abolished in August 1848. The question of compensation to landlords provoked continued dissatisfaction, and a protracted peasant revolt (1848–49) was led by Lukian Kobylytsia, a deputy to the Reichstag, who exhorted the peasants not to yield to the landlords, to establish their own judicial system of elected elders, and to seize forests and pastures. The revolt was put down by Austrian forces and, contrary to the wishes of the Ukrainian population, Bukovyna was separated from Galicia on 4 March 1849 and declared a crown land with its own diet and administration.

In **Transcarpathia**, the small Ukrainian movement was led by a mining engineer, Adolf Dobriansky, who presented a petition to the emperor seeking the unification of Transcarpathia with eastern Galicia. His initiative was supported by the Supreme Ruthenian Council but did not meet with official approval. Dobriansky also had **Russophile** sympathies and served as an Austrian commissioner with the Russian army that suppressed the Hungarian revolt in 1849. The Catholic priest Oleksander Dukhnovych began a cultural revival in Transcarpathia, publishing school textbooks in the vernacular and establishing a literary society.

For the Ukrainian movement, the Revolution of 1848 was a signal event. It eliminated serfdom and introduced democratic freedoms that allowed much of Ukrainian society to participate in politics for the first time. It also strengthened the cultural revival that had begun in the 1830s. Since the Russian Empire lagged far behind the Habsburg Monarchy in these respects, Ukrainian activists there began to develop extensive cooperation with their counterparts in Galicia to attain their political and cultural goals.

REVOLUTION OF 1905. First democratic revolution in the Russian Empire, brought on by social and economic crisis and Russia's defeat in its war with Japan. The revolution was provoked by the events of 9 (22) January 1905 ("Bloody Sunday") in St. Petersburg, when soldiers opened fire on a large peaceful demonstration of workers attempting to deliver a petition to the tsar. More than 200 were killed and several hundred injured, provoking indignation throughout the empire. A wave of strikes followed, including such Ukrainian cities as Katerynoslav (now Dnipropetrovsk), **Kharkiv**, **Kyiv**, Mykolaiv, and **Odesa**. In addition to economic demands, the strikers called for democratic rights. **Peasants** burned landowners' estates and buildings, seized livestock, and divided estates and state properties among themselves. Peasant unrest engulfed more than half the gubernias of Ukraine. Students demanded university autonomy and participated in labor meetings and demonstrations. Oppositional political forces, from associations of zemstvo activists to the Social Democratic and Socialist Revolutionary parties, increased their activity.

On 14 (27) June 1905, mutiny broke out on the battleship *Potemkin* in Odesa. Its leaders included the Ukrainians Hryhorii Vakulenchuk and Opanas Matiushenko. Among the officers who joined the mutiny was Oleksander Kovalenko, a member of the **Revolutionary Ukrainian Party** (RUP). The military ceased to be the reliable prop of autocracy. The government unsuccessfully attempted to put a stop to the revolution with its manifesto convoking a consultative State Duma (6 [19] August). By mid-October, the empire was in the grip of a general strike that included almost two million workers, 120,000 of them in Ukraine. Councils of workers' deputies, which opposition parties attempted to control, emerged during the strike. In Ukraine, workers clashed with the army in Kharkiv, Katerynoslav, and Oleksandrivsk (now Zaporizhia). In Horlivka, there were severe casualties on both sides (approx. 300 workers killed on 17 [30] December).

By the autumn of 1905, the peasant movement encompassed more than a third of the empire's European counties. Between October and December, peasant uprisings in Ukraine occurred in 64 counties (out of 91). More than 300 incidents of destruction of landlords' estates were registered in Ukraine (approx. 150 on the **Left Bank** and more than 100 in the south). One of the largest peasant actions occurred in Velyki Sorochyntsi, **Poltava** gubernia (19–21 December [1–3 January 1906]), where 63 peasants were killed. In October and November, a new wave of unrest swept through military units in Bila Tserkva, Chernihiv, Kyiv, Kharkiv, Poltava, and Sevastopol. Under the circumstances, the tsarist government was forced to compromise. On 17 (30) October, Nicholas II issued a manifesto granting the State Duma legislative powers. The manifesto also extended voting rights and democratic freedoms (of religion, the press, assembly, and association). The liberal opposition formed political parties (the Constitutional Democrats [Cadets] and Octobrists) and attempted to redirect the revolutionary movement onto a peaceful constitutional path, while radical forces, particularly the Bolsheviks, called for armed uprisings (which occurred in Moscow, Nizhnii Novgorod, Krasnoiarsk, and other cities) and refused to participate in the elections. The **Black Hundreds** also became active, organizing anti-**Jewish** pogroms and conducting promonarchist and antisocialist demonstrations.

The October manifesto facilitated the growth of the Ukrainian movement. In March 1905, the Imperial Academy of Sciences had sent a report to the government affirming that Ukrainian was an independent Slavic **language** and recommending that the anti-Ukrainian measures of 1863 and 1876 (*see* VALUEV CIRCULAR; EMS UKASE) be rescinded. In late 1905, Ukrainian periodicals began to appear. In 1906, 24 Ukrainian newspapers and journals were published in Kyiv, Katerynoslav, Kharkiv, Lubny, Odesa, and other Ukrainian cities, as well as in St. Petersburg and Moscow. Some of them, such as the newspaper *Hromads'ka dumka* (Civic Thought, later *Rada*), continued to publish in the years that followed, despite persecution. The cultural and educational organization **Prosvita** established centers in Kyiv, Chernihiv, Katerynoslav, Odesa, Mykolaiv, Nizhyn, and Poltava. Noted cultural figures, including **Borys Hrinchenko**, **Mykhailo Kotsiubynsky**, **Mykola Lysenko**, **Lesia Ukrainka**, and **Dmytro Yavornytsky**, participated in Prosvita's activities, such as organizing libraries and reading rooms for the populace, publishing popular educational literature in Ukrainian, staging plays, concerts, and the like. Political parties also became active. The **Ukrainian Social Democratic Labor Party** was formed (December 1905), declaring itself the sole political organization of the Ukrainian proletariat. The **Ukrainian Democratic Radical Party** was established at the end of 1905. Ukrainian political organizations generally advocated the national and territorial autonomy of Ukraine within the Russian state.

Elections to the First State Duma took place in the shadow of government repression (February to early March 1906). The Cadets won the greatest number of seats (34 percent of the Duma). Peasant deputies were also influential. The activities of the Duma continued for only 72 days, from 27 April (10 May) to 9 (22) July 1906. Of the 62 Ukrainian deputies, 44 formed the Ukrainian Parliamentary Faction. Illia Shrah, a lawyer from Chernihiv, was elected its chairman. The faction's publication was *Ukrainskii vestnik* (Ukrainian Herald, ed. Maksym Slavinsky). The Ukrainian faction was preoccupied with issues of land distribution, education, and literacy. It prepared a bill on Ukrainian autonomy that was never introduced for debate because of the dissolution of the Duma.

Elections to the Second State Duma took place in January and February 1907. This Duma, which included a faction of 47 Ukrainian deputies (half of them peasants), proved even more leftist and oppositional than its predecessor. It began its session on 20 February (5 March) 1907. As before, the agrarian question took center stage and was hotly debated. Demands for Ukrainian autonomy and Ukrainian-language education were also advanced. The Ukrainian faction published the Ukrainian-language periodical *Ridna sprava: Dums'ki visti* (Our Native Cause: News of the Duma, ed. Vasyl Domanytsky). A tsarist manifesto of 3 (16) June 1907 ordering the dissolution of the second Duma marked the government's rejection of reform and the defeat of the revolution. Many of its central issues and individuals who took part in it would again come to the fore in the **Ukrainian Revolution** of 1917–21.

REVOLUTIONARY UKRAINIAN PARTY/REVOLIUTSIINA UKRAÏNS'KA PARTIIA (RUP). First Ukrainian political party in **eastern Ukraine**. It arose in **Kharkiv** as an underground political organization on 29 January (11 February) 1900. The party's founders were Kharkiv Student **Hromada** members Petro Andriievsky, Dmytro Antonovych, Bonifatii Kaminsky, Oleksander Kovalenko, Lev Matsiievych, Mykhailo Rusov, and others. **Mykola Mikhnovsky's** *Samostiina Ukraïna* (Independent Ukraine), which declared the idea of Ukrainian political independence, was the RUP's first programmatic publication. Since it did not address social issues, most members of the RUP were unwilling to accept it as a political program. This led to the departure of the nationalists, who founded the **Ukrainian People's Party** (1902). At almost the same time, the **populists**, headed by **Mykyta Shapoval** and Mykola Zalizniak, left the RUP and joined the Socialist Revolutionaries.

In early 1903, the RUP adopted a social-democratic program that included a demand for Ukraine's national and territorial autonomy. Later that year, the RUP organizations, known as "free hromadas" (in **Kyiv**, Kharkiv, Lubny, Nizhyn, **Poltava**, and Ekaterinodar in the Kuban), were disbanded by the authorities, and many members were arrested. In 1904, the new RUP leader, **Mykola Porsh**, attempted to rebuild the party as a conspiratorial group dedicated to the interests of the Ukrainian proletariat. At the second RUP congress in the summer of 1904, Mariian Melenevsky, Oleksander Skoropys-Yoltukhovsky, and Yevhen Holitsynsky advocated the party's merger with the Russian Social Democratic Labor Party (RSDLP). For them, the social question superseded Ukrainian national interests, and they established the **Ukrainian Social Democratic Spilka**, which became an integral part of the RSDLP and propagated Marxist ideas among Ukrainian workers (it continued to exist until 1913). Most members of the RUP supported Porsh, **Symon Petliura**, and **Volodymyr Vynnychenko**, who advocated Ukrainian autonomy. In December 1905, the party held its final congress, at which the founding of the **Ukrainian Social Democratic Labor Party** was declared.

During the years of its existence, the RUP participated in joint actions with the **Jewish** Bund and the RSDLP, organized strikes and demonstrations, and distributed brochures and leaflets. The party, whose membership numbered in the low hundreds, had considerable influence among the Ukrainian **peasantry**. Tsarist officials considered it partly responsible for the peasant strikes of 1902. The RUP's periodicals were *Haslo* (Slogan, 1902–3, published in Chernivtsi, eds. Antonovych, Holitsynsky, and Vasyl Simovych), *Selianyn* (Peasant, 1903–5, published in Chernivtsi and **Lviv**, eds. Lev Kohut and Antonovych), and *Pratsia* (Work, 1904–5, published in Lviv, eds. Antonovych and Porsh).

RIDNA SHKOLA SOCIETY. Popular name for the Ukrainian Pedagogical Society (known as the Ruthenian Pedagogical Society until 1912). It was founded in **Lviv** in 1881 to help resolve the difficulties faced by Ukrainian-**language education** and provide material and moral support to students. Throughout its existence it was the ideological and organizational center of Ukrainian schooling in **Galicia**. In 1905, it established the Ukrainian Teachers' Mutual Aid Society and began publishing the journal *Uchytel'* (Teacher, 1889–1914). It also published children's **literature**, the journal *Dzvinok* (Bell, 1892–1914), textbooks and readers, and an annual school calendar. Its appeals to the government prompted an increase in the number of Ukrainian-language schools. The society's leading figures up to 1918 included **Oleksander Barvinsky**, Konstantyna Malytska, Tyt Voinarovsky, Amvrosii Yanovsky, and Roman Zaklynsky. By 1906, it had approximately 3,000 members and 33 branches.

During the interwar period, the society fought the Polonization of schooling and organized Ukrainian private schools in Galicia and **Volhynia** in response to the government policy of closing Ukrainian public schools. The society's name was officially changed in 1926 to Ridna Shkola—Ukrainian Pedagogical Society. It was directed by a main executive in Lviv, elected at a general meeting, which supervised local branches. On the eve of **World War II**, the society was financially supporting 12 gymnasiums, 11 lyceums, and approximately 60 elementary schools. It also oversaw three teachers' colleges and more than 600 libraries. From 1932, it published the illustrated journal *Ridna shkola* (Native School). The society was supported by the community at large and by the **Ukrainian Catholic Church**, particularly by Metropolitan **Andrei Sheptytsky**.

RIGA, TREATY OF. Treaty signed by Poland with the Russian SFSR and the **Ukrainian SSR** following the conclusion of the Polish-Soviet War of 1920. Peace talks between the warring sides began in mid-August 1920 in Minsk but were moved in early March to Riga, where they continued until early 1921. A combined Russo-Ukrainian delegation headed by Adolf Ioffe included representatives of the Ukrainian SSR (Dmytro Manuilsky, Emanuil Kviring, and **Yurii**

Kotsiubynsky) and the Galician SSR (V. Baran, N. Khomyn). On 26 September, a delegation from the **Western Ukrainian People's Republic** led by **Kost Levytsky** arrived in Riga and made several declarations and protests defending the right of its people to self-determination. This delegation was not admitted to the talks. The protest of the **Ukrainian People's Republic** (UNR), which had been allied with Poland through the **Treaty of Warsaw**, was also ignored.

On 12 October, Soviet and Polish representatives signed a preliminary treaty. According to the final text, signed on 18 March 1921, both sides were to cease military actions, the Treaty of Warsaw was annulled, and a new border was established, giving Poland western Ukrainian and western Belarusian lands east of the **Curzon Line**. Article 7, which guaranteed cultural, linguistic, and religious rights to Ukrainians and Russians in Poland, as well as to Poles in Ukraine and Russia, remained a dead letter throughout the interwar period. On 14 March 1923, the new border along the Zbruch River was confirmed by the Council of Allied Ambassadors in Paris, effectively providing great-power ratification of the territorial settlement. The treaty remained in effect until the fall of the Second Polish Republic in September 1939.

RIGHT-BANK UKRAINE (Ukr. *Pravoberezhna Ukraïna, Pravoberezhzhia*). Historical and geographical designation of Ukrainian lands on the west bank of the Dnipro River. It encompassed the territory of present-day **Volhynia**, Rivne, Vinnytsia, Zhytomyr, Kirovohrad, and **Kyiv** oblasts and part of Cherkasy and Ternopil oblasts. The term "Right-Bank Ukraine" appears in historical documents from the second half of the 17th century. According to the **Truce of Andrusovo** (1667), Right-Bank Ukraine (with the exception of Kyiv and its environs) remained under the rule of the **Polish-Lithuanian Commonwealth**. As a result of the Treaty of Buchach (1672), the Right Bank was divided into three sections: **Podilia** was occupied by the Ottoman Empire, the Bratslav and southern Kyiv regions were under the jurisdiction of the Right-Bank **Cossack** hetman **Petro Doroshenko**, and the remainder of the territory was ceded to Poland. The Treaty of Bakhchesarai (1681) established the border between Muscovy and the Ottoman Empire along the Dnipro River, as a result of which the southern Kyiv, Bratslav, and Podilia regions came under Ottoman rule. After the defeat of the Turkish army at Vienna (1683) and the signing of the Treaty of Karlowitz (1699), Right-Bank Ukraine in its entirety was annexed by the Commonwealth. The Right Bank was the site of large-scale rebellions against Polish overlordship: the **Palii** rebellion (1702–4), the **haidamaka** rebellions (1730s–60s), and the **Koliivshchyna rebellion** (1768). As a result of the second partition of Poland (1793), Right-Bank Ukraine was annexed by the Russian Empire. In 1921, under the terms of the **Treaty of Riga**, part of the Right Bank (present-day Volhynia, Rivne, and northern Ternopil oblasts) was annexed by Poland, which ruled it until the region was incorporated into the **Ukrainian SSR** (September 1939). *See* LEFT-BANK UKRAINE.

RIURYK LINE. Ruling dynasty of **Kyivan Rus'** descended from the **Varangian** prince **Riuryk** (Russ. Riurik). Major representatives of the dynasty were the Kyivan princes **Ihor**, **Sviatoslav Ihorevych**, **Volodymyr the Great**, **Yaroslav the Wise**, and **Volodymyr Monomakh**. As Kyiv's power declined in the late 11th century, representatives of the Riuryk line began to rule individual principalities, such as Chernihiv, Novhorod-Siverskyi, and Vladimir-Suzdal, where they founded local ruling dynasties (e.g., Monomakhovych, Olhovych, Romanovych). In the late 12th century, the founder of the Romanovych house, **Roman Mstyslavych**, united **Volhynia** with **Galicia** to create one of the strongest Rus' states, the Principality of **Galicia-Volhynia**. **Appanage princes** of the Riuryk line ruled in various Rus' lands until the end of the 15th century. The grand princes and tsars of Muscovy were descendants of the Vladimir-Suzdal Monomakhovych line, which ended with the sons of Ivan IV, the last of whom, Fedor I, died in 1598.

RIURYK, SINEUS, AND TRUVOR. Three **Varangian** princes who, according to the *Tale of Bygone Years*, were invited to rule over the Slavic tribes of the Slovenes, Krivichians, Chud, and Ves in 862. The eldest, Riuryk (Russ. Riurik), first ruled in Ladoga and then in Novgorod. Sineus and Truvor ruled over Beloozero and Izborsk, respectively, but died within two years. Archaeologists have unearthed ruins of a ninth-century settlement at Novgorod now known as Riurikovo Gorodishche (Riuryk's Fortress). According to the *Tale*, Riuryk died in 879 and was survived by a young son, **Ihor**, who ruled Kyiv in the early 10th century after the regency of **Oleh**. Riuryk is traditionally considered the progenitor of the **Riuryk line**, the dynasty of **Kyivan Rus'** princes.

The chronicle entry concerning the invitation to the three princes generated extensive historiographic debate in the 19th and 20th centuries. Most Soviet historians considered Riuryk to have been a historical figure, while his brothers were regarded as legendary. Some have maintained that Riuryk of Novgorod and the ninth-century King Hroerekr of Jutland and Frisia were the same person.

ROKSOLIANA (1505–ca. 1561). Actual name: Nastia Lisovska. Wife of the Ottoman sultan Süleyman the Magnificent (reigned 1520–66). She was born in Rohatyn (now in Ivano-Frankivsk oblast). In the summer of 1520, she was captured during a **Tatar** raid and later sold to the sultan's harem. Contemporaries noted Roksoliana for her beauty, intelligence, and musical ability. As Süleyman's consort, Roksoliana played a significant role in the political life of the Ottoman Empire. She is associated with the building of several historical monuments in Istanbul and its vicinity. Roksoliana's image inspired numerous writers, musicians, and artists. She is depicted in **literature** in the anonymous historical novella *Roksolana ili Anastaziia Lisovskaia* (Roksoliana or Anastasiia Lisovska, 1880), a novella by **Osyp Nazaruk** (1930), Mykola Lazorsky's novel *Stepova kvitka* (Flower of the Steppe, 1965), Pavlo Zahrebelny's novel *Roksolana* (1979), and a novella by Serhii Plachynda and Yurii Kolisnychenko in *Neopalyma kupyna* (The Burning Bush, 1968), among many others. In music, she was the inspiration of Denys Sichynsky's opera *Roksoliana* (1908–9). Among works of visual art, the earliest known painting of Roksoliana is her portrait by an anonymous artist of the late 16th century (now in the **Lviv** State Historical Museum).

ROMAN MSTYSLAVYCH (ca. 1152–1205). Ruler of the Principality of **Galicia-Volhynia** (1199–1205). He was prince of Novgorod (1168–70), Volodymyr-Volynskyi (1170–87, and again from 1188), and Halych (in 1188, and again from 1199). He was the son of Grand Prince Mstyslav Iziaslavych of Kyiv and Agnieszka, daughter of King Bolesław III of Poland. After the death of Volodymyr Yaroslavych, the last prince of the Rostyslavych line (1198), Roman took control of Halych and united the Volhynian and Galician lands into a single principality. In asserting his authority, he struggled with the powerful Galician **boyars** and drove the influential Kormylchych boyar family out of Galicia. He drew support from the Volhynian boyars and burghers. In 1202, he led a campaign into the **Kyiv** principality and took control of the city (from 1203 to 1205, he was effectively grand prince of Kyiv). Thus, for the last time, the principalities of **Kyivan Rus'** briefly came under the rule of a single prince. Roman was renowned for his military prowess; as an ally of Byzantium, he led two large-scale campaigns against the **Cumans** (1201–2, 1203–4). He was active in foreign policy, maintaining contacts with the Teutonic Order, Poland, Hungary, and Lithuania. Roman's territorial ambitions led to a breakdown of his alliance with Poland. He was ambushed near Zawichost (now in Poland) and died in battle against the Poles on 19 June 1205. His consolidating political activity led contemporaries to refer to him as "grand prince" and "autocrat of all Rus'."

ROMANIUK, VASYL (9 December 1925–14 July 1995). **Human-rights** activist, political prisoner, and Orthodox patriarch. He was born in Khomchyn (now in Ivano-Frankivsk oblast). Falsely accused of participating in the Ukrainian nationalist resistance during **World War II**, Romaniuk was sentenced in 1944 to 10 years' imprisonment, which he spent in Kolyma. He studied for the Orthodox priesthood in Ivano-Frankivsk and Moscow and was ordained in 1964. Until 1972, he served as a priest in Kosmach in the Hutsul region of western Ukraine, where he collected Hutsul folk art and called on the faithful to maintain their traditions (activities described in a well-known essay by **Valentyn Moroz**). He also associated with members of the *shistdesiatnyky* movement. Romaniuk's activity in defense of human and religious rights led to his arrest in January 1972. He was sentenced in the same month to seven years' imprisonment and three years' exile, which he spent in the strict-regime camps of Mordovia and Yakutia. He declared a hunger strike in 1975, joined the **Ukrainian** Autocephalous **Orthodox Church** (UAOC) in 1976, and became a member of the **Ukrainian Helsinki Group** in November 1979. A collection of his writings appeared in English under the title *A Voice in the Wilderness* (1980).

Following his release in 1981, Romaniuk resumed his pastoral work in western Ukraine (1984). In 1987, he lectured in Canada, the United States, and Britain. In April 1990, he was consecrated archimandrite of the UAOC (taking the name Volodymyr) and bishop of Uzhhorod and Vynohradiv in **Transcarpathia**. In June 1992, Romaniuk became a founder of the Ukrainian Orthodox Church (Kyiv Patriarchate), and, following the death of **Mstyslav Skrypnyk**, was enthroned as patriarch of the UOC-KP at **St. Sophia's Cathedral** in **Kyiv** (24 October 1993). Romaniuk's sudden death in 1995 led to a spontaneous attempt by his followers to bury him at St. Sophia's Cathedral, even though the government, apparently seeking to maintain neutrality with regard to Ukraine's Orthodox churches, had refused permission for burial at that site. The attempted burial was broken up violently by riot police—an incident that further strained church-state relations. At a memorial service held one year after Romaniuk's death, his remains were interred in a marble sarcophagus, funded by the city of Kyiv, near the gates of St. Sophia's Cathedral.

ROMANTICISM. An artistic and philosophical world view that emerged in **literature**, art, and **music** at the end of the 18th century in Germany, England, and France as a reaction to the rationalism of the Enlightenment and the formal constraints of classicism. In Ukraine, romanticism was initially manifested through enthusiasm for folk art, poetry, and songs, as well as through an intensified historical consciousness. A number of Ukrainian grammars were published in the early 19th century, and collections of folk songs by Nikolai Tsertelev and **Mykhailo Maksymovych** appeared in 1819 and 1827. Petro Hulak-Artemovsky was the precursor of romanticism in literature; his ballads showed that the Ukrainian language could be used for purposes beyond burlesque and travesties, an uncommon view in the Russian Empire.

The development of Ukrainian romanticism was also influenced by the so-called Ukrainian schools in Polish and Russian literatures. Polish writers, such as Antoni Malczewski, Józef Bohdan Zaleski, and Seweryn Goszczyński, and their Russian counterparts, Kondratii Ryleev and Faddei Bulgarin, were fascinated by exotic Ukrainian themes, folklore, and history. They were joined by Ukrainians writing in Russian, including Yevhen Hrebinka and the highly influential **Nikolai Gogol**.

The first phase of Ukrainian romanticism (early 1830s), which reflected ethnographic interests and the use of the Ukrainian vernacular, was represented by two groups. The **Kharkiv** romantic school included the philologist Izmail Sreznevsky, the poets Levko Borovykovsky and Amvrosii Metlynsky, and the historian **Mykola Kostomarov**. In **Galicia**, the **Ruthenian Triad**, composed of **Markiian Shashkevych**, **Ivan Vahylevych**, and **Yakiv Holovatsky**, exemplified the romantic trend.

The second phase, which began in **Kyiv** in the late 1830s and early 1840s, produced a greater variety of poetic works and asserted itself with a political program. The group included two former members of the Kharkiv school, Kostomarov and Metlynsky, as well as the ethnographer Maksymovych, the writer **Panteleimon Kulish**, and the poet **Taras Shevchenko**. The Kyiv romantics were inspired by the programmatic documents of the **Cyril and Methodius Brotherhood**. Shevchenko's messianic poetry revolutionized Ukrainian literature and did much to inspire the national movement.

The third phase of Ukrainian romanticism was associated with the journal *Osnova* (Foundation), published in St. Petersburg in 1861–62. Kostomarov and Kulish were the major forces behind this resurgence of romanticism, followed by Oleksa Storozhenko, a writer of fantastic stories, and the poets Yakiv Shchoholiv and **Yurii Fedkovych**.

A mainly poetic phenomenon, Ukrainian romanticism contributed greatly to the development of national consciousness. It idealized the heroic **Cossack** past and stressed folk poetry at the expense of intimate, personal lyricism. Songlike versification and historically informed epics were prominent features of Ukrainian romantic poetry.

Populist ideology and literary **realism** brought an end to romanticism in the second half of the 19th century. However, romantic elements began to reappear in Ukrainian literature in the first decades of the 20th century. Neoromanticism, with its characteristic return to folk sources, enhanced several currents within **modernism**. Many works of **Mykhailo Kotsiubynsky**, **Lesia Ukrainka**, and **Olha Kobylianska** were inspired by folk motifs. The romantic legacy is also apparent in the poetry and prose of the 1920s. *See also* FOLK MUSIC AND DANCE.

ROZUMOVSKY, KYRYLO (18 [29] March 1728–3 [15] January 1803). Last **hetman** of Ukraine (1750–64), count (1744), and general-field marshal (1764). Born in Lemeshi (now in Chernihiv oblast) into the family of the **Cossack** Hryhorii Rozum, he was the younger brother of **Oleksii Rozumovsky**. After he received an elementary education at home, Empress Elizabeth sent him to study in Berlin, Göttingen, Königsberg, and Strasbourg (1743–45). Upon returning to St. Petersburg, he became a chamberlain. At the age of 18, Rozumovsky was appointed president of the Imperial Academy of Sciences (1746), a position he held for nearly 20 years. In 1747, in response to a petition by the **Cossack officers**, the office of hetman was restored and Rozumovsky was designated to occupy it. In 1750, he was inaugurated as hetman at a **Cossack council** in Hlukhiv. Rozumovsky became the spokesman for the aspirations of the educated and wealthy segment of Ukrainian society. During the early period of his administration, he spent most of his time in St. Petersburg, leaving internal affairs in the care of the **Hetmanate** Chancellery. The Hetmanate was transferred from the jurisdiction of the Russian Senate to the College of Foreign Affairs, and the hetman's authority was extended to the **Zaporozhian Sich** and **Kyiv**.

From 1760, Rozumovsky lived primarily in Ukraine and was actively involved in state affairs. He implemented a judicial reform that resulted in the creation of land, town, and *pidkomors'ki* (chamberlain's) courts (1760–63) for the nobility. He divided the Hetmanate into 20 judicial counties, each with its own land court (for deciding civil cases) and *pidkomors'kyi* court (for deciding land claims). During his administration, the mobility of the **peasantry** was restricted (1760). Rozumovsky reformed the Cossack army according to a plan prepared by Ivan Kuliabka, the colonel of

Lubny. He also introduced obligatory schooling for the children of Cossacks and sought to open a university in Baturyn. In 1762, he took part in the coup that brought Catherine II to power. The Cossack officers appealed to Catherine to restore the Hetmanate's former rights and establish a parliament there analogous to the Polish Diet. Feeling secure at his position at court, Hetman Rozumovsky began agitation for a hereditary hetmancy. Catherine exploited these developments to demand his resignation. An imperial ukase on the abolition of the hetmancy was issued on 10 (21) November 1764, and the second **Little Russian Collegium** was established to administer the Hetmanate. Subsequently, Rozumovsky was a member of the State Council (1768–71); he then retired from state affairs and lived in St. Petersburg, Moscow, and abroad. He spent the last nine years of his life in Baturyn.

ROZUMOVSKY, OLEKSII (17 [28] March 1709–6 [17] July 1771). General-field marshal (1756) and count of the Holy Roman Empire and the Russian Empire (1744). He was born in Lemeshi (now in Chernihiv oblast) into the family of the **registered Cossack** Hryhorii Rozum. From 1731, he sang in the court choir in St. Petersburg. He became a favorite of the Empress Elizabeth and, in 1741, took part in a coup that brought her to power. Rozumovsky received the titles of chamberlain, lieutenant-general, and general-field marshal. He was awarded the Order of St. Andrew and granted large estates in Russia and Ukraine. It is highly likely that Rozumovsky and Elizabeth were secretly married at Baturyn in 1742. He facilitated Elizabeth's trip to Ukraine (1744), during which the **Cossack officers**, supported by Rozumovsky, convinced the empress to restore the hetmancy. With Rozumovsky's participation, the **Kyiv metropolitanate** was restored (1745), and **Kyrylo Rozumovsky**, Oleksii's brother, was appointed hetman (1747). After Elizabeth's death, Rozumovsky resigned his office and lived in the Anichkov Palace in St. Petersburg. Unlike his brother, he did not participate in the coup that brought Catherine II to power. Maintaining a degree of influence at court, he helped defend the rights of the Ukrainian Cossacks. He died in St. Petersburg.

RUDNYTSKY, STEPAN (3 December 1877–3 November 1937). Geographer; full member of the **Shevchenko Scientific Society** (NTSh, from 1901). Founder of Ukrainian scientific geography. Born in Peremyshl (Przemyśl), he graduated from a gymnasium in **Lviv** (1895) and studied at Lviv University under **Mykhailo Hrushevsky**, Isydor Sharanevych, and Ludwik Finkel. Rudnytsky was awarded a doctorate in geography from Lviv University in

1901. From 1902 to 1908, he worked as a teacher in Ternopil and Lviv, and in August 1908 he became a lecturer in geography at Lviv University. He then studied geography and geology in Vienna and Berlin. Rudnytsky conducted research in the Dnister Basin (**Subcarpathia** and **Podilia**, 1903–11) that subsequently became the basis for a number of works on geomorphology. His works of this period included the first Ukrainian-language survey of contemporary trends in geography (1905), as well as a textbook of physical geography (1905), the first dictionary of Ukrainian geographic terminology (1908), and a two-volume geographic survey of Ukraine (1910–14).

In 1914, Rudnytsky became a member of the governing council of the Lviv National Museum. During **World War I**, he worked with the **Union for the Liberation of Ukraine**, which published his *Ukraine, Land und Volk* (1916). This book, published in English in 1918 under the title *Ukraine: The Land and Its People*, was the first modern survey of Ukraine to appear in major Western languages. In 1918, Rudnytsky published the first comprehensive physical maps of Ukraine. In 1918–19, he was an advisor to the government of the **Western Ukrainian People's Republic** on economic and geopolitical affairs. Following its demise, Rudnytsky lived in Vienna and then in Prague. He was a founder of the **Ukrainian Free University** and the first dean of its faculty of arts. He taught geography at Charles University, the Prague German University, and the Ukrainian Husbandry Academy in Poděbrady. From 1920 to 1926, he conducted research in **Transcarpathia** and assisted the **Prosvita** society in Uzhhorod. In 1924, he helped organize the First International Congress of Slavic Ethnographers and Geographers in Prague.

In October 1926, Rudnytsky moved to the **Ukrainian SSR** at the invitation of the Soviet government. He established the Ukrainian Scientific and Research Institute of Geography and Cartography in **Kharkiv** (1927) and became a full member of the **Ukrainian Academy of Sciences** (VUAN) in 1929. In the same year, he was appointed to the newly established chair of geography at the VUAN; he also headed the VUAN Regional Studies Commission and the **Fedir Vovk** Museum of Anthropology and Ethnography. From 1927 to 1933, Rudnytsky conducted research in the Dnipro region and the **Donets Basin**. He was cofounder and coeditor of the *Visnyk pryrodoznavstva* (Herald of Natural Sciences) in Kharkiv.

On 21 March 1933, Rudnytsky was arrested by the secret police on trumped-up charges of sabotage and espionage and then sentenced to five years' imprisonment (23 September). In January 1934, he was expelled from the VUAN as an "overt propagator of fascism in geography," and in the spring of 1935 he was imprisoned on the

Solovets Islands. Rudnytsky was sentenced to death by the Leningrad oblast NKVD on 9 October 1937 and shot on 3 November.

RUIN. Period of the mid-17th century marked by internal struggle, foreign interventions of neighboring states (Poland, Muscovy, and the Ottoman Empire), and the general decay of Ukrainian sovereignty. The term was coined by the historian **Mykola Kostomarov**. In essence, the Ruin resulted from the struggle for succession in the **Hetmanate**, which was established by **Bohdan Khmelnytsky**. After his death in 1657, as Muscovy and Poland vied for control, the Ukrainian lands became divided along the Dnipro River, with separate **hetmans**, administrations, and armies. Those in **Right-Bank Ukraine** were supported by Poland, whereas those in **Left-Bank Ukraine** were backed by Muscovy. Each hetman and his allies sought to eliminate his counterpart and secure control over Ukraine as a whole. A third alternative, unification by means of a **Cossack-Tatar**-Ottoman alliance, only plunged Ukraine into further hostilities involving Poland, the **Crimean** Khanate, the Ottoman Empire, and Muscovy. The 30-year struggle desolated Right-Bank Ukraine. The signing of the **Eternal Peace of 1686** between Muscovy and Poland, followed by the accession of Hetman **Ivan Mazepa** in 1687, marked the end of the Ruin.

RUKH (POPULAR MOVEMENT OF UKRAINE). Civic organization and political party. The impetus to establish the Popular Movement of Ukraine for Restructuring, as it was initially called, developed among leading Ukrainian writers, scholars, **human-rights** activists, and **dissidents** (late 1988). Despite a campaign of harassment by the **Communist Party of Ukraine** (CPU), the first program of Rukh ("movement") was published in the newspaper of the Ukrainian Writers' Union, *Literaturna Ukraïna* (Literary Ukraine, 16 February 1989). The All-Ukrainian Founding Congress of Rukh, held in **Kyiv** (8–10 September 1989), was greeted at the opening ceremonies by the prominent writer Oles Honchar. The president of the organizing committee, the writer Volodymyr Yavorivsky, addressed the congress on the tasks of Rukh. The poet **Ivan Drach** was elected president.

The program adopted at the congress addressed the establishment of Ukrainian sovereignty, the revival of the Ukrainian **language** and culture, the ecological problems facing Ukraine, especially after the **Chornobyl nuclear disaster**, and the need for democratization. Particular emphasis was placed on the rights of ethnic minorities and groups (many Russians, **Jews**, and members of other ethnic groups joined Rukh). During this period, Rukh had approximately 280,000 members. In March 1990, it began publishing the *Narodna hazeta* (People's Newspaper). The largest action organized by Rukh was the "human chain" (21 January 1990) between Kyiv, **Lviv**, and Ivano-Frankivsk commemorating the anniversary of the **Act of Union** between the **Ukrainian People's Republic** and the **Western Ukrainian People's Republic** in 1919. It demonstrated the strength of the newly created organization and symbolized national solidarity. According to various sources, participants numbered between 300,000 and 450,000.

By 1990, Rukh had emerged as Ukraine's largest umbrella organization, with some five million supporters. In that year, it elected its first representatives to the **Verkhovna Rada** (VR). Although defectors from the CPU were initially welcomed in Rukh, its second congress (25–28 October 1990) barred communists from joining and espoused the cause of Ukrainian independence. This led Rukh to become more closely identified with Ukrainian ethnicity and narrowed its political base to nationally conscious western Ukraine. Following Ukraine's declarations of sovereignty and independence, Rukh had to choose between supporting or opposing the country's ruling elite, made up overwhelmingly of former communists. Some leaders of Rukh (especially Drach, **Dmytro Pavlychko**, and Mykhailo Horyn) held that it should remain an alliance of democratic organizations and parties devoted to creating a solid political base for the new Ukrainian state. They wanted Rukh to evolve from opposition to the government and the president to cooperation with them. The opposing faction, led by **Viacheslav Chornovil**, argued that democratic reform was impossible as long as the former communist elite remained in power. Chornovil and his supporters called for Rukh's transformation into an opposition party. Many Rukh members were disenchanted with this difference of opinion, and the organization's membership declined sharply. At the third Rukh congress (28 February–1 March 1992), three leaders—Drach, Horyn, and Chornovil—were elected in order to prevent it from splintering.

At its fourth congress (4–6 December 1992), Rukh made the decision, ratified in 1993, to become a political party, with Chornovil as its sole president. Subsequently, a group of Rukh members seceded to create the Nation-Wide Popular Movement of Ukraine (VNRU, headed by Larysa Skoryk). The organization led by Chornovil numbered approximately 55,000 members. In March 1999, following Chornovil's death in an automobile accident, the organization he had led also splintered. The faction led by the former minister of foreign affairs, **Hennadii Udovenko**, won a court battle to retain the name "Rukh." It is currently headed by **Borys Tarasiuk**. The opposing faction, which constituted itself as Rukh

(Ukrainian People's Movement), was led by the former minister of environmental protection, Yurii Kostenko. It subsequently became the Ukrainian People's Party. Claiming a membership of more than 27,000 and 23 deputies in the VR, it identified its task as representing Ukraine's emerging middle class. On 9 June 2001, the two factions signed a declaration of intent to create a united party. They contested the 2002 parliamentary elections as part of the Our Ukraine bloc led by **Viktor Yushchenko**.

RUMIANTSEV, PETR (4 [15] January 1725–8 [19] December 1796). Russian statesman, general-field marshal, and count. He began his military career in the guards (1740), participating in the Russo-Swedish War (1741–43) and the Seven Years' War (1756–63). In 1764, he was appointed president of the second **Little Russian Collegium** (to 1786) and governor-general of Little Russia. In these posts, Rumiantsev implemented Russian government policies intended to abolish Ukrainian autonomy. He reformed taxation (introduction of the poll tax) and the postal service, conducted a property census of the Left-Bank population, eliminated the **Cossack** company/regimental administrative system (1781), and replaced it with the imperial system (division into vicegerencies, 1780–83). Ukrainian Cossack regiments were replaced by regular carbine regiments on the Russian model. The imperial Charter to the Nobility was introduced in Ukraine (1785), the Ukrainian **peasantry** was definitively enserfed (1783), and monastic properties were secularized (1786). Rumiantsev owned huge estates in **Left-Bank Ukraine**. In 1770, armies under his command crushed Turkish forces at Riaba Kobyla on the Prut River and occupied the left bank of the lower Danube. In 1771 and 1773–74, Rumiantsev led campaigns in Bulgaria that forced the Ottomans to sign the Peace Treaty of Küçük Kaynarca (1774); for this, he was made a count and given the surname "Zadunaisky." During the Russo-Turkish War (1787–91), he led an army (consisting mostly of Ukrainian soldiers), but owing to conflicts with Grigorii Potemkin and the personal disfavor of Catherine II, he was relieved of his command and of the post of governor-general (1789). In 1794, he commanded the Russian armies in Poland. He was buried in the Dormition Cathedral of the **Kyivan Cave Monastery**.

RUSALKA DNISTROVAIA/**THE DNISTER NYMPH.** Literary miscellany published by the **Ruthenian Triad** in Buda, Hungary (1837). It contained Ukrainian folk songs with a preface by **Ivan Vahylevych**, works by **Markiian Shashkevych**, Vahylevych, and **Yakiv Holovatsky**, translations of Serbian folk songs, excerpts from

Václav Hanka's *Rukopis Královédvorský* (Králové Dvůr Manuscript), an annotated index of manuscripts in the library of St. Onuphrius's **Basilian** monastery in **Lviv**, and Shashkevych's review of Yosyp Lozynsky's folklore anthology *Ruskoje wesile* (Ruthenian Wedding). In the preface, Shashkevych described the miscellany as a manifestation of the Ukrainian revival, welcomed the initiative of **eastern Ukraine** in the development of a new **literature**, and called for its further cultivation.

In 1834, the members of the Ruthenian Triad had prepared another miscellany, "Zoria" (Star). It was not issued because, in the eyes of the Austrian government, publications in Ukrainian might inspire a Ukrainian movement that would be exploited by the Russian Empire against the Habsburg Monarchy. The Greek Catholic Church (*see* UKRAINIAN CATHOLIC CHURCH) also opposed it, fearing that such a publication would cast doubt on its loyalty to Austria. Accordingly, the Triad decided to print *Rusalka Dnistrovaia* in Buda, where censorship was more lenient and help was available from Serbian sympathizers. When the Triad attempted to distribute the work in Lviv, it was banned by the provincial censor; 800 of the original 1,000 copies were confiscated and only 200 distributed. The ban was not lifted until the **Revolution of 1848**. Nevertheless, *Rusalka Dnistrovaia* marked the beginning of a vernacular literature in **western Ukraine**, as **Ivan Kotliarevsky's** *Eneïda* had done in the Ukrainian lands of the Russian Empire 40 years earlier. It also showed that there were no substantial differences between the vernacular of both parts of Ukraine, a factor that subsequently promoted unification.

***RUSKAIA PRAVDA*/RUS' TRUTH (LAW).** Collection of legal norms in **Kyivan Rus'**, compiled mainly in the 11th and 12th centuries. It is the most important source for studying the social relations and legal system of Rus'. The original text has not survived, but most historians correlate the "Earliest Pravda" with the reign of **Yaroslav the Wise**. In the second half of the 11th century, Yaroslav's sons expanded and altered the text, creating the so-called *Pravda Yaroslavychiv* (Statute of the Yaroslavychi). Today, 106 copies of the text compiled between the 13th and 17th centuries are known to exist. These are conventionally divided into the short, expanded, and abridged redactions. The short redaction (43 articles) is the oldest (11th century). It consists of the "Earliest Pravda" (articles 1–18, compiled either in 1016 or in the 1030s), the "Statute of the Yaroslavychi" (articles 19–41, dating from the mid-11th century), and two additional articles on the penalty for murder and on revenge.

The norms of the "Earliest Pravda," derived from customary law, reflect the social relations of the early medieval period. They permit revenge killing and specify fines to be paid as compensation for assault, bodily harm, or violation of property. The "Statute of the Yaroslavychi" is concerned almost entirely with defending princely property, the **prince's** lands, and the like. It clearly reflects the hierarchical nature of medieval society: for example, the murder of a **peasant** or a *kholop* (slave) was punishable by a fine of five *hryvni*, while that of a member of the Kyivan retinue entailed a fine of 80 *hryvni*.

The expanded redaction of the *Ruskaia Pravda* (121 articles, dating from the 12th century) includes revised norms of the short redaction. It replaces revenge killing with a system of fines and penalties (*vira* or *prodazha*) payable to the prince. Property rights are defined as pertaining not only to land and accommodations but also to such chattels as horses and equipment. The contractual forms mentioned are exchange, purchase and sale, loan, deposit, and personal hire. The loan contract was the most highly regulated, a result of the rebellion of Kyivan commoners against moneylenders in 1113. **Volodymyr Monomakh**, summoned by the **boyars** to restore order, took steps to regulate interest rates. The *Ruskaia Pravda* treated crimes as "insults," regardless of whether the damage done was material, physical, or moral. All persons, with the exception of slaves, were subject to criminal responsibility. Owners were held responsible for the actions of slaves. The most serious punishment was confiscation of property, with the perpetrator exiled from the community or reduced to slavery. The death penalty is not recorded in the *Ruskaia Pravda*, although **chronicle** entries indicate that it was used to punish treason and revolts against the prince.

The Kyivan state had no separate judicial institutions. Judicial functions were performed by representatives of the administration, including the prince himself. However, there were officials responsible for aiding the judicial process (for example, the *virnyky*, who collected bloodwite). Judicial functions were also performed by the church. Crimes under the jurisdiction of the church court were punishable by epithymy (penance), corporal punishment (blinding, cutting off of noses, ears, etc.), incarceration, and the like.

RUSSIA (Muscovy; renamed the Russian Empire by Peter I in 1721). *See* ANDRUSOVO, TRUCE OF; ANTONOV-OVSIIENKO, VOLODYMYR; BLACK HUNDREDS; BLACK SEA FLEET; COLLECTIVIZATION; COMMUNIST PARTY OF UKRAINE; COSSACKS; EASTERN UKRAINE; EMS UKASE; ETERNAL PEACE OF 1686; FAMINE OF 1921–23; FAMINE OF 1932–33;

FAMINE OF 1946–47; FOREIGN POLICY; GOGOL, NIKOLAI; HETMANATE; KHMELNYTSKY UPRISING; KHRUSHCHEV, NIKITA; LANGUAGE; LITTLE RUSSIAN COLLEGIUM; LITTLE RUSSIAN MENTALITY; MINORITIES; MOSCOW ARTICLES; PANSLAVISM; PEREIASLAV AGREEMENT; POLITICAL TERROR; POLTAVA, BATTLE OF; POPULATION; POPULISM; POSTYSHEV, PAVEL; RUSSIFICATION; RUSSOPHILES; SHEVCHENKO, TARAS; SOCIETY OF UNITED SLAVS; *SYNOPSIS*; UKRAINIAN INSURGENT ARMY; UKRAINIAN ORTHODOX CHURCH; UKRAINIAN REVOLUTION (1917–21); UKRAINIAN SOVIET SOCIALIST REPUBLIC; UKRAINIZATION; UNION OF SOVIET SOCIALIST REPUBLICS; VALUEV CIRCULAR; WORLD WAR I; WORLD WAR II.

RUSSIFICATION. Policy of imposing the Russian language and culture on other nationalities, primarily other Eastern **Slavs** (Ukrainians and Belarusians). Ukraine came under a Muscovite protectorate in 1654 as a result of the **Pereiaslav Agreement**, which was followed by increasing political restrictions on the **Hetmanate** (*see* ARTICLES OF BOHDAN KHMELNYTSKY). The **Ukrainian Orthodox Church** was subordinated to Moscow in 1685. Following the revolt of Hetman **Ivan Mazepa**, which was defeated in 1709, Ukrainian autonomy was severely limited. The printing of books in Ukrainian was forbidden in 1720, and Ukrainian editions of books in Church Slavonic had to conform to Russian practice. Secret instructions were issued to promote the assimilation of Ukrainians through intermarriage. The **Little Russian Collegium** headed by **Petr Rumiantsev** (1764–86) promoted the Russification of **education**, **publishing**, and church life in the Hetmanate, which was abolished and integrated administratively with the rest of the Russian Empire in 1782.

In the 19th century, the imperial doctrine of Orthodoxy, autocracy, and nationality was promoted in an attempt to create one Russian nation; the Ukrainians (Little Russians) and Belarusians (White Russians) were treated as its lesser branches. Ukrainian publishing in the Russian Empire was prohibited by means of the **Valuev circular** (1863) and the **Ems Ukase** (1876). As the Ukrainian gubernias were reduced to provincial status, much of the intelligentsia adopted the Russian language and developed a deferential **Little Russian mentality** vis-à-vis Moscow. Urban life in Russian-ruled Ukraine was almost completely Russified. **Galicia**, under Austrian constitutional rule, developed into the mainstay of the Ukrainian national movement during the late 19th century.

Ukrainian **peasants** in the Russian Empire, little affected by developments in the towns, maintained their **language** and culture. They were mobilized by the Ukrainian **populist** intelligentsia after the **Revolution of 1905**, which loosened restrictions on Ukrainian cultural and political activity. The **Ukrainian Revolution** of 1917–21 produced the first Ukrainian state of modern times, the **Ukrainian People's Republic** (UNR). Although the UNR succumbed to Russian aggression, it took three Bolshevik invasions to establish the **Ukrainian SSR** as part of the Soviet Union; similar struggles were waged against other national movements, and after the Civil War, Moscow recognized the need for concessions to the non-Russian nationalities. Throughout the Soviet Union, this resulted in a policy of "indigenization" (*korenizatsiia*), known in the Ukrainian SSR as **Ukrainization**. This policy raised the prestige of the Ukrainian language and resulted in great gains for Ukrainian education, publishing, and communications.

Ukrainization was abruptly reversed by the Stalin regime in the 1930s as part of a thoroughgoing campaign of **political terror**. Ukrainian autonomy was effectively abolished by the destruction of the republic's institutions, including the **Communist Party of Ukraine** (CPU); the man-made **famine of 1932–33**, which took millions of peasant lives; and the mass execution of the Ukrainian intelligentsia on charges of anti-Soviet activity. So comprehensive was the assault on Ukrainian identity that Stalin and his associates even contemplated the administrative abolition of the Ukrainian SSR. When **Nikita Khrushchev** took over as first secretary of the CPU in 1938, Russian became an obligatory subject of study in all Ukrainian schools (as it did throughout the Soviet Union). Urban life in the Ukrainian SSR was thoroughly Russified, and, in contrast to the prerevolutionary period, even the peasantry began to learn Russian, realizing that social advancement depended on a command of the language. This gave rise to a widespread Russo-Ukrainian creole known as *surzhyk*.

After **World War II**, the Russification drive resumed with great intensity. In 1956, the eminent filmmaker **Oleksander Dovzhenko** noted in his diary that higher education in Ukraine was completely Russified: "There is nothing like this anywhere in the world. I recall Lenin's letters on the national question and think: do not tell me anything else. I have understood everything. . . . If my people has not managed to obtain higher education of its own, then . . . nothing else is now of any value." At the all-Union level, Khrushchev began a campaign to promote Russian-language instruction at the elementary and secondary levels by allowing parents to choose whether their children would attend Russian or non-Russian schools. Given the enormous prestige and practical utility of Russian, this was bound to reduce the number of non-Russian schools; in the Ukrainian SSR, a law establishing the principle of parental choice was passed in 1959. By the 1960s, almost all Ukrainian pedagogical, vocational-technical, and specialized secondary schools were Russified, as was the overwhelming majority of higher educational institutions, where Ukrainian language and literature remained almost the only subject taught in Ukrainian. This situation gave rise to the **dissident movement** of the 1960s–70s, which demanded political democratization and policies to restore the Ukrainian language and culture. The outstanding dissident work on the subject was *Internationalism or Russification?* by the literary critic **Ivan Dziuba**, which was addressed to the party and government leadership.

The authorities responded with a campaign of repression; after 1972, Russification continued unabated under the auspices of the CPU first secretary, **Volodymyr Shcherbytsky**, who made a point of using only Russian in all public pronouncements. By 1987, only 16 percent of schools in **Kyiv** and oblast centers had Ukrainian-language instruction; some major cities, such as Chernihiv, Donetsk, Simferopol, and Voroshylovrad, had no Ukrainian-language schools at all. The dominance of Russian became overwhelming in publishing, library holdings, radio and television broadcasting, and scientific research.

Another Soviet policy that promoted Russification was large-scale resettlement. The proportion of Russians in the Ukrainian population rose from 8.2 percent (1926) to 22.1 percent (1989), partly as a result of planned resettlement, including the transfer of entire villages from the Russian SFSR to Ukraine. Conversely, the 1989 census showed that there were some 6.8 million Ukrainians in other republics of the **USSR**, where they had no facilities to develop their culture and usually succumbed to Russification.

As the USSR began to disintegrate in the late 1980s, a movement for the revival of the Ukrainian language and culture gained strength. The **Taras Shevchenko** Ukrainian Language Society was established in February 1989, and in the same year a Language Act was passed by the **Verkhovna Rada** of the Ukrainian SSR to make Ukrainian the official language, without restricting the use of Russian. The **Constitution** of independent Ukraine (1996) made Ukrainian the country's sole official language, raising its prestige; according to the 2001 census, the percentage of Russians in Ukraine has dropped from 22.1 percent to 17.3, indicating a change of ethnic identification among a substantial number of eastern Ukrainians. Progress has also been made in propagating the Ukrainian language by means of the educational system. Nevertheless, the mass **media** in Ukraine remain overwhelmingly Russian-speaking, and the state bureaucracy, still largely staffed by Soviet-era cadres whose first language is Russian, feels little urgency to promote the Ukrainian language.

RUSSOPHILES. Russophilism was a linguistic, literary, and sociopolitical trend among the Ukrainian population of **Galicia**, **Bukovyna**, and **Transcarpathia** between the early 19th century and the 1930s. It advocated cultural and later political unity with the Russian people and state.

The first manifestations of Russophilism in Transcarpathia occurred in the late 18th and early 19th centuries, when the well-known scholars and civic figures Mykhailo Baluhiansky, Vasyl Kukolnyk, Petro Lodii, and Ivan Orlai moved to Russia, where they assumed senior positions in government and scholarly institutions. Maintaining contact with their homeland, they promoted interest in Russia, especially its culture. After the annexation of Galicia (1772) and Bukovyna (1774) by the Habsburg Monarchy, the Austrian government, aware of cultural similarities between Ukrainians and Russians, was constantly suspicious that the local population was drawn to Russia. This distrust was encouraged by Polish political circles, which claimed that any manifestations of Ukrainian national life were the result of "Muscovite intrigues."

The first propagandist of the "Pan-Russian" idea in Galicia was the **Panslavist** ideologue Mikhail Pogodin, who traveled to **Lviv** to meet the local intelligentsia (1835 and 1839–40). He established close ties with the historian Denys Zubrytsky, who rallied supporters of the Russian language and the unity of "Galician Ruthenia and Great Russia." With the defeat of the **Revolution of 1848**, which restored the alliance between the Austrian government and the Polish and Hungarian political elites at the expense of other nationalities, notably the Ukrainians, much of the clerical and secular intelligentsia in Galicia and Transcarpathia turned to another powerful patron—the Russian autocracy. Unable to engage in overt political activity, the Russophiles shifted their attention to education and culture. Among the greatest advocates of linguistic **Russification** in Galicia in the 1850s were Zubrytsky, Bohdan Didytsky, **Yakiv Holovatsky**, Ivan Holovatsky, Ivan Hushalevych, Mykhailo Malynovsky, Antonii Petrushevych, and Severyn Shekhovych. The Russophiles took control of virtually all cultural and educational institutions: the Stauropegion Institute, the National Home and the Galician-Ruthenian *matytsia* in Lviv, the newspapers *Zoria halyts'ka* (Galician Star), the Lviv and Vienna *Vistnyk* (Herald), *Lada*, and *Simeina biblioteka* (Family Library), the publication of scholarly works and school textbooks, the teaching of "Ruthenian literature" at the university and in gymnasiums, and even the publication of the laws and decrees of state and church authorities.

In the 1850s, similar processes occurred in Transcarpathia, where well-known activists of the national revival (Adolf Dobriansky, Oleksander Dukhnovych, and Ivan Rakovsky) promoted the Russophile idea in close collaboration with their Galician colleagues. The chaplain of the Russian embassy in Vienna, Mikhail Raevsky, greatly facilitated contacts with Russia.

With the introduction of virtual Polish autonomy in Galicia in 1867, the Russophiles became dependent on financial assistance from Russia and found it difficult to maintain their façade of loyalty to the Habsburgs. They also faced competition from the Ukrainian **populists**. To counteract the **Prosvita Society** (1868), the Russophiles established the Kachkovsky Society (1874), which in time developed a parallel network of local branches and reading rooms in Galicia. They also issued many publications in a dialect that the populists derided as *yazychiie*.

The Russophiles paid great attention to the so-called rite question, advocating Russian Orthodoxy under the guise of purging the Greek Catholic rite of Latin influences (*see* UKRAINIAN CATHOLIC CHURCH). In 1882, under Russophile influence, the Greek Catholic parish of Hnylychky in Galicia announced its intention to convert to Orthodoxy. The Austrian administration responded by forcing the resignation of Metropolitan Yosyf Sembratovych and expelling the most active Russophiles from the church leadership. This was followed by a trial of leading Russophiles, known as the trial of Olha Hrabar and her confederates (Dobriansky, Ivan Naumovych, Osyp Markov, Venedykt Ploshchansky, and others), in 1882. Although they were acquitted of treason, the trial was a severe blow to their movement, exposing their dependence on aid from the Russian Empire.

In the mid-1880s, the Russophiles lost their influence in Bukovyna, where the primary cultural and political organizations (Ruska Besida and Ruska Rada) came under populist control. A small group of activists (Vasyl Prodan, Ivan Hlibovytsky, and Hryhorii Kupchanko) maintained their Russophile attitudes, congregating around the newspapers *Pravoslavnaia Bukovina* (Orthodox Bukovyna, 1893–1901), *Bukovynsky vidomosty* (Bukovynian News, 1895–1909), *Pravoslavnaia Rus'* (Orthodox Rus', 1909–10), and *Russkaia pravda* (Russian Truth, 1910–14).

Given the crisis in their ideology and the growth of populism, the Galician Russophiles united as the Ruthenian People's Party (1900). Its radical wing, led by Volodymyr Dudykevych and Dimitrii Markov, advocated outright union with Russia and the adoption of the Russian literary language. This, as well as their cooperation with Polish circles, discredited the Russophiles and led to the defection of moderate activists (Ivan Svientsitsky, Sylvestr Drymalyk, Mykhailo Korol, and others) to the Ukrainian national-democratic camp.

There was something of a Russophile revival before and during **World War I**. The Committee for the Liberation of Carpathian Ruthenia, established in **Kyiv** (August 1914), exhorted Galicians to support the Russian Empire. Following the Russian occupation of Lviv, the committee deferred to the Ruthenian People's Council, led by Dudykevych. Russophile activity led to repressions by the Austro-Hungarian military against the Ukrainian civilian population, including arrests and mass executions of those suspected of assisting the Russian army. Thousands of Ukrainians were interned in the Thalerhof, Theresienstadt, and other concentration camps. The retreat of the Russian army led a number of Russophiles to emigrate to Russia, where many became disenchanted with Russophile ideology and later participated in the **Ukrainian Revolution** (1917–21).

During the interwar period, the small number of Russophiles remaining in Galicia either became pro-Soviet or compromised themselves by collaborating with the Polish authorities. The Russophile position was somewhat stronger in the Lemko region and Transcarpathia. By the late 1930s, however, Ukrainian national consciousness was well established in those areas.

RUTHENIAN TRIAD. Galician literary and cultural group formed among Ukrainian students of **Lviv** University and the Greek Catholic Theological Seminary in the 1830s. It was headed by **Markiian Shashkevych**, **Ivan Vahylevych**, and **Yakiv Holovatsky**, to whom the name "Ruthenian Triad" was first applied in jest. Influenced by **romanticism**, the Polish revolutionary movement, and the general Slavic revival of the early 19th century, the Triad developed Ukrainian literature and culture in Galicia through its work in ethnography, folklore, linguistics, the study of original sources, literary scholarship, journalism, and pedagogy, as well as original writing and translation.

The Triad maintained that Ukrainian writing should be based on vernacular speech, not on the bookish Church Slavonic language, and its activity marked the beginning of modern Ukrainian literature in Galicia. The Triad's ethnographic work produced a number of studies and transcriptions of oral literature, including Holovatsky's four-volume anthology *Narodnye pesni Galitskoi i Ugorskoi Rusi* (Folk Songs of Galician and Hungarian Ruthenia, 1878). The Triad's linguistic interests were reflected in its members' work on a dictionary and grammar of the Ukrainian vernacular. Grammars were published by Vahylevych (1845) and Holovatsky (1849). These were supplemented by Vahylevych's articles on the "Southern Ruthenian" language, written prior to 1843, and Holovatsky's *Rozprava o iazytsi iuzhnorus'kim (malorus'kim) i ioho narichchiakh* (Treatise on the South Russian [Little Russian] Language and Its Dialects, 1849). The Triad's orthographic reforms included replacing the etymological system with a phonetic one and using the civil script (*hrazhdanka*) rather than Church Slavonic letters. They translated literary works from Church Slavonic, Czech, Polish, Russian, Greek, and German into the vernacular and opposed the Latinization of Ukrainian writing, as evidenced by Shashkevych's brochure *Azbuka i Abecadło* (The Alphabet and the Abecedarium, 1836).

The Triad did much to revive interest in **Kyivan Rus'** as the historical source of Ukrainian culture. Vahylevych and Holovatsky discovered valuable monuments of Kyivan jurisprudence—the *kormchi knyhy* (books of rule) of the 12th, 13th, and 15th centuries containing the statutes of **Volodymyr the Great** and **Yaroslav the Wise**, as well as many other documentary sources (decrees, letters, and the like). Vahylevych produced a Polish translation (1840) of the *Tale of Bygone Years*, published jointly with August Bielowski, with the appended "Poucheniie" (Instruction) of **Volodymyr Monomakh**. Holovatsky wrote a biographical sketch of **Nestor** the Chronicler (1848). Shashkevych and Vahylevych were the first to translate the *Tale of Ihor's Campaign* into Ukrainian. Holovatsky published a scholarly study of the poem (1853) and was the first in Galicia to publish an anthology of Church Slavonic and Old Rus' literature (1854).

The Ruthenian Triad was also inspired by the **Cossack** era. Shashkevych often referred to **Bohdan Khmelnytsky** in his writings. Holovatsky edited the Lviv Chronicle, an important source for the history of the Cossack era (excerpts were published in 1871).

National and patriotic themes were sounded in the literary miscellanies of the Ruthenian Triad. The manuscript of "Zoria" (Star, 1834, banned by the censors), which featured a portrait of Khmelnytsky, contained a biography of the **hetman**, short stories about the **opryshoks**, poems by Shashkevych, Vahylevych, and Holovatsky, and cycles of folk songs. Similar themes appeared in *Rusalka Dnistrovaia* (The Dnister Nymph, 1837), the Triad's most important publication. The traditions of the censored "Zoria" and *Rusalka Dnistrovaia* were continued by an anthology compiled by Yakiv Holovatsky and his brother, Ivan, *Vinok rusynam na obzhynky* (A Garland for Ruthenians at the Harvest Feast, 2 vols., 1846–47), a representative selection of Ukrainian literature of the time. The culmination of the Triad's activities was Holovatsky's article "Zustände der Russinen in Galizien" (The Condition of the Ruthenians in Galicia, 1846), which laid the basis for the program of the Supreme Ruthenian Council (*see* REVOLUTION OF 1848).

The activities of the Triad had considerable resonance in Galicia and beyond its borders. Its traditions were continued by **populists** in Galicia and **Bukovyna**. The Triad maintained contacts with Ukrainian scholars in the Russian Empire such as **Osyp Bodiansky** and **Mykhailo Maksymovych**, as well as with representatives of the national movements and cultures of other Slavic peoples. Thanks to these contacts, works by Triad members that encountered censorship in Galicia were published in Buda, Vienna, Prague, Warsaw, Leipzig, Stuttgart, Moscow, and St. Petersburg.

RUTHENIANS (Ukr. *rusyny*). Historical ethnonym for Ukrainians; variants include *rus'ki*, *rusy*, *rusyntsi*, *rusnaky*, *rusaky*, *rosy*, *malorosy*, *pivdennorosy*, *karpatorosy*, and *uhrorosy*. It was employed by the inhabitants of **Kyivan Rus'**, and its Latin form, *Rutheni*, was used in Western Europe and in the **Polish-Lithuanian Commonwealth** to denote Ukrainians and Belarusians throughout the late medieval and early modern periods.

In **eastern Ukraine**, the designations *rus'ki*, *malorosy*, *iuzhnorosy*, and others began to be replaced in the early 19th century by the ethnonym "Ukrainian" (*ukraïnets'*), derived from the ancient name of Ukraine (first encountered in the Kyiv Chronicle entry for 1187). Documents of the **Cyril and Methodius Brotherhood**, the ethnographic works of **Mykhailo Maksymovych**, **Mykola Kostomarov**, and **Volodymyr Antonovych**, the political writings of **Mykhailo Drahomanov**, and subsequent literary works helped consolidate the term "Ukrainian," which applied only to the Ruthenians of the Ukrainian lands, distinguishing them from the Russians (*russkie*, *rossiiane*). This undermined the imperial concept of an "all-Russian" nationality and emphasized the separate identity of the Ukrainian people.

In the **western Ukrainian** lands, following their annexation by Austria (1772, 1774), the term *Ruthenen* came into use as the German equivalent of the Ukrainian *rusyny* and remained the sole official designation until the collapse of Austria-Hungary in 1918. In the late 19th and early 20th centuries, under the influence of usage in eastern Ukraine and extensive transborder collaboration between activists of the national movement, the term "Ukrainian" displaced "Ruthenian" in **Galicia** and **Bukovyna**. Its adoption was also a way of combating the influence of the **Russophile** movement.

In **Transcarpathia** and in the Prešov region of Slovakia, the term "Ruthenian" continued to be used after **World War II** in the local vernacular, although the annexation of Transcarpathia to the **Ukrainian SSR** resulted in official Ukrainization. This is the only region of Ukraine in which an attempt has been made to revive *rusyn* as an ethnonym. In the late 1980s and early 1990s, a movement developed to promote the national and cultural distinctiveness of the Rusyns, and there were calls for separation from Ukraine and union with other countries (Slovakia, Hungary) or the creation of an independent state. In February 1990, the Society of Subcarpathian Ruthenians was founded in Uzhhorod. In 1993, it formed the so-called Provisional Administration of Subcarpathian Ruthenia. In North America, the concept of a distinct Rusyn identity has been propagated by Professor Paul Robert Magocsi of the University of Toronto. In 1995, the Rusyn Renaissance Society in Bratislava declared Rusyn a distinct Slavic language and announced its intention to develop literary and educational materials in Rusyn.

RUTSKY, YOSYF VELIAMYN (1574–5 February 1637). Secular name: Ivan. Uniate metropolitan (*see* UKRAINIAN CATHOLIC CHURCH) of Kyiv. He was born in the village of Ruta near Navahrudak in Belarus and educated at a Calvinist school in Vilnius. In 1590, he enrolled at Charles University in Prague and came under Jesuit influence, converting to Catholicism in 1592. Rutsky continued his theological studies at Würzburg and Rome until 1596, when he converted to the Uniate rite at the behest of Pope Clement VIII. In 1603, Rutsky returned to Vilnius, where he established a school for boys and took monastic orders at the Holy Trinity Monastery (1607). Two years later, the Uniate metropolitan **Ipatii Potii** appointed Rutsky hegumen of the monastery. Rutsky began to administer the **Kyiv metropolitanate** in 1612 and succeeded Potii as metropolitan in 1614. In 1615 he traveled to Rome, obtaining stipends for Ruthenians to study in Western Europe, as well as a guarantee of formal equality between Uniate and Roman Catholic schools. Rutsky carried out a reform of the **Basilian Order** (1616–17) that freed it from the control of local bishops and made it the driving force of a reformed school system. After considerable effort, Rutsky obtained legislation in 1624 that prohibited Uniates in the **Polish-Lithuanian Commonwealth** from converting to the Latin rite. He established new regulations for monastic life (1621) and took measures to improve the education of the village clergy. In the 1620s, he negotiated with **Iov Boretsky**, **Meletii Smotrytsky**, and **Petro Mohyla** concerning a union of churches under a joint Kyivan patriarchate, but the talks proved fruitless. After Rutsky's death, his remains were buried in Vilnius, but they were removed by Muscovite soldiers in 1655 to an undisclosed location. A collection of Rutsky's letters was published in Rome in 1956.

RYLSKY, MAKSYM (7 [19] March 1895–24 July 1964). Poet, translator, cultural and civic activist, and academician of the **Ukrainian Academy of Sciences** (from 1943). He was born in **Kyiv** into the family of Tadei Rylsky, a founder of the **populist** *khlopoman* movement. Rylsky graduated from Volodymyr Naumenko's private gymnasium in Kyiv before entering the medical faculty of Kyiv University. In 1918, he transferred to the faculty of history and philology but did not complete his studies. Throughout the 1920s he taught Ukrainian **language** and **literature** in Kyiv schools before embarking on a literary career in 1929. Rylsky had written poetry since adolescence; he published his first poem in 1907, and his first collection followed in 1910. In the 1920s, he was associated with the neoclassicist group. His poetry collections of this period are characterized by depth and sincerity of feeling, plasticity of imagery, refined expression, and the reinterpretation of classical motifs, themes, and heroes.

Rylsky was the only neoclassicist to survive Stalin's **political terror** and remain a prominent writer. He was obliged, however, to join other writers in eulogizing communist rule. With the outbreak of **World War II**, his poetry became more patriotic. Rylsky helped awaken historical memory and preserve national consciousness during a period of intense **Russification**, for which he was accused of "nationalism." His postwar poetry took the form of meditations on life, art, man, and nature. At its best, his poetry is highly intellectual and refined in form. Rylsky was also a distinguished master of literary translation, noted particularly for his rendering of Adam Mickiewicz's *Pan Tadeusz*. His articles on art and literature were collected in *Vechirni rozmovy* (Evening Conversations) and *Pro mystetstvo* (On Art). Rylsky headed the Writers' Union of Ukraine (1943–46) and directed the Institute of Fine Arts, Folklore, and Ethnography of the Academy of Sciences (1944–64), which was named after him when he passed away.

S

SABODAN, VOLODYMYR (b. 23 November 1935). Secular name: Viktor. Metropolitan of the **Ukrainian Orthodox Church** (Moscow Patriarchate). He was born to a peasant family in the village of Markivtsi (now in Khmelnytskyi oblast). After graduating from the **Odesa** Theological Seminary (1958), Sabodan studied at the

Leningrad Theological Academy, graduating in 1962, and completed his graduate studies at the Moscow Theological Academy (1965). He was consecrated to the priesthood and became a monk in 1962. In 1965, Sabodan became rector of the Odesa Theological Seminary. He served as bishop of Zvenigorod and vicar of the Moscow eparchy (1966), deputy head of the Russian religious mission in Jerusalem and representative to the World Council of Churches (1966–68), bishop of Pereiaslav-Khmelnytskyi and vicar to the Exarch of Ukraine, **Filaret Denysenko** (1968–73), and archbishop of Dmitrov and vicar of the Moscow eparchy (1973–82). In 1982, Sabodan was promoted to the rank of metropolitan and appointed to the see of Rostov and Novocherkassk. He became patriarchal exarch of the Russian Orthodox Church for Western Europe in 1986, and from 1987 to 1992 he was administrator of the Moscow patriarchate. Following the dismissal of Filaret Denysenko, Sabodan was elected Metropolitan of Kyiv and All Ukraine at a hierarchical council (27 May 1992). A six-volume collection of his writings was published in 1997–98. He has received several Ukrainian state awards, including that of Prince **Yaroslav the Wise**. In January 2001, when Pope John Paul II (then 80 years old) was preparing to visit Ukraine, Sabodan wrote to him at the behest of the Holy Synod of the Russian Orthodox Church, requesting that he postpone his trip in order to prevent strain in Orthodox-Catholic relations. When the pope visited Ukraine that summer, there was no formal meeting with hierarchs of the Ukrainian Orthodox Church. Sabodan's residence at the **Kyivan Cave Monastery** has drawn protests from ecclesiastical and secular circles that regard the presence of the Moscow Patriarchate there as an occupation of a Ukrainian shrine.

SAHAIDACHNY, PETRO (1570?–10 [20] April 1622). **Hetman** of the **registered Cossacks**; political and educational figure. He was descended from the Ukrainian Orthodox nobility in the vicinity of Sambir (**Galicia**) and educated at the **Ostrih Academy**. In 1601, he settled at the **Zaporozhian Sich**, where he became renowned for organizing **Cossack** military campaigns against the Ottoman Turks and **Tatars**. Under his leadership, the Cossacks attacked Varna, Ochakiv, Perekop (1607), Sinop, Trabzon, and Kaffa (1616). Sahaidachny joined the Holy League, which intended to fight the Ottoman Empire (1618). In the spring of 1618, Sahaidachny led a Cossack army of 20,000 in the campaign of Władysław IV of Poland against Muscovy.

Sahaidachny was the first Ukrainian hetman to employ Cossack military might in defense of Orthodoxy. Together with the whole **Zaporozhian Host**, he joined the **Kyiv Epiphany Brotherhood**

(1620). Under Cossack protection, Patriarch Theophanes III of Jerusalem consecrated **Iov Boretsky** metropolitan of **Kyiv** (9 [19] October 1620), restoring the Orthodox hierarchy in the **Polish-Lithuanian Commonwealth**. The hetman also financially supported the Kyiv Brotherhood School.

Sahaidachny realistically assessed the military prospects of the Zaporozhian Host and attempted to defend Ukrainian interests through negotiation and compromise with the Polish authorities, provoking dissatisfaction among the Cossacks and leading to the brief tenure of Yakiv Borodavka as hetman.

With the outbreak of the Turco-Polish War (1620–21), Sigismund III and the Commonwealth authorities entreated Cossack assistance. In September 1621, Sahaidachny commanded a Cossack army of 40,000 that played a decisive role in defeating the Turks at the **Battle of Khotyn**, thereby halting Ottoman expansion into Europe. Wounded during the battle, Sahaidachny died in April 1622. He bequeathed his estate to the restoration of the Epiphany Monastery and the maintenance of the Kyiv, **Lviv**, and Lutsk **brotherhood** schools. He was buried at the Kyiv Brotherhood monastery. At a memorial service attended by most of Kyiv's Ukrainian elite, 20 students of the Kyiv Brotherhood School performed the panegyric *Virshi na zhalosnyi pohreb zatsnoho rytsaria Petra Konashevycha-Sahaidachnoho* (Verses on the Sorrowful Obsequy for the Worthy Knight Petro Konashevych-Sahaidachny) by **Kasiian Sakovych**.

ST. ANTHONY (ANTONII) OF THE CAVES (ca. 983–1073). Church figure of **Kyivan Rus'** and founder of the **Kyivan Cave Monastery**. Born in Liubech, he spent some time at Mt. Athos, where he was tonsured. Upon his return, Anthony settled near the prince's summer residence in Berestove on a hill above the Dnipro River (previously the residence of **Ilarion**, who would become metropolitan of **Kyiv**). There in the mid-11th century he founded a monastic community that developed into the Cave Monastery. His life is recounted in the **Kyivan Cave Patericon**.

ST. SOPHIA'S CATHEDRAL. Outstanding religious and artistic monument of **Kyivan Rus'**, named after Hagia Sophia in Constantinople. Its construction began in **Kyiv** during the reign of **Yaroslav the Wise** to commemorate a victory over the **Pechenegs** in 1036 and completed in the late 11th and early 12th centuries. According to the *Tale of Bygone Years*, the cathedral's foundations were laid in 1037, while the Novgorod Chronicle states that construction began in 1017. Along with the **Kyivan Cave Monastery**, the cathedral was the religious and cultural center of the

Kyivan state. For many years, it served as the burial place of distinguished political and church figures, notably Yaroslav, **Volodymyr Monomakh**, and the metropolitans of Kyiv from the 11th to the 19th century. The cathedral is 37 meters long, 35 meters wide, and 29 meters high. Its original form, consisting of five naves, a central dome, and 12 smaller domes surrounded by two rows of open, arched galleries, was preserved until the mid-17th century. From the 13th to the 16th century, the cathedral suffered great damage. In the 1630s–40s, Metropolitan **Petro Mohyla** restored it and established a men's monastery on the site. Between 1685 and 1707, the cathedral was rebuilt in the Ukrainian **baroque** style. In the 18th century, it was augmented by a series of buildings (including a bell tower, metropolitan's residence, and refectory). The building was again restored in the 20th century, and its **architecture** and frescoes were studied.

In the 11th century, the cathedral was decorated with mosaics (*Christ Pantocrator*, the *Mother of God [Oranta]*, and the *Eucharist*) and frescoes (notably a family portrait of Yaroslav the Wise and scenes of hippodrome races, hunting, and entertainment) created by local and Byzantine artists.

In 1934, all religious activity was halted and the cathedral was declared a state architectural and historical preserve. In 1990, UNESCO designated it a world cultural heritage site. The cathedral has remained a state museum since 1991.

ST. THEODOSIUS (TEODOSII [FEODOSII]) OF THE CAVES (ca. 1036–74). Hegumen of the **Kyivan Cave Monastery** He was born in Vasyliv (now Vasylkiv), near **Kyiv**, into a **boyar** family. In 1055, he was initiated into monastic life by **St. Anthony of the Caves**, the founder of Kyivan monasticism. On taking monastic orders, he adopted the name Theodosius (his secular name is unknown). Ca. 1062, he became hieromonk and then hegumen of the Cave Monastery. Theodosius reformed monastic life by introducing the ascetic principles of the Studite Typicon (compiled by St. Theodore, 759–826). He began the construction of the Church of the Dormition (1073–89) and a cell monastery. Theodosius was active in politics during the struggle for the Kyivan throne between the three Yaroslavych brothers (1060s–70s) and was persecuted by Prince Sviatoslav II Yaroslavych. His support of Iziaslav Yaroslavych led to conflict in the Cave Monastery, where some of the monks, led by Anthony, supported Sviatoslav. During Iziaslav's second exile (1073), Theodosius reconciled himself with Sviatoslav. Eleven of Theodosius's works have survived: two epistles to Prince Iziaslav Yaroslavych, eight instructions, and a prayer. He died in Kyiv. In 1091, his remains were transferred to the Dormition Church. He was canonized at the initiative of Prince Sviatopolk Iziaslavych (1108). Theodosius's ideas influenced his successors, particularly **Nestor** the Chronicler, whose *Life of Theodosius* was included in the **Kyivan Cave Patericon**.

SAKOVYCH, KASIIAN (1578–1647). Secular name: Kallist. Church figure and writer. He studied at the academies in Zamostia (Zamość) and Cracow. Upon completing his studies, he was cantor of the Uniate church (*see* UKRAINIAN CATHOLIC CHURCH) in Peremyshl (Przemyśl). Sakovych took Orthodox monastic orders in Kyiv (1620) and became rector of the **Kyiv Epiphany Brotherhood** School (1620–24). He was head of the Lublin Orthodox Brotherhood (1625). Subsequently, he became a Uniate, for which he was excommunicated by the Kyiv Orthodox Sobor (1628). Sakovych was archimandrite of the Dubno Basilian Monastery (1626–39). In 1640, he converted to Roman Catholicism. He died in Cracow.

Sakovych was a noted writer and polemicist. In 1622, he wrote *Virshi na zhalosnyi pohreb zatsnoho rytsera Petra Konashevycha-Sahaidachnoho* (Verses on the Sorrowful Obsequy for the Worthy Knight Petro Konashevych-Sahaidachny), performed by students of the Kyiv Brotherhood School at a memorial service for **Sahaidachny**. His other works, written in Polish, include the philosophical tracts *Aristoteles problemata albo Pytania o przyrodzeniu człowieczym* (Aristotle's Problem, or the Question of Human Nature, 1620) and *Tractat o Duszu* (Tract on the Soul, 1625). These were among the first surveys of Western philosophy published in Ukraine. In *Perspektiwa* (Perspective, 1642), Sakovych justified his conversion to Catholicism and polemicized with the Orthodox and Uniate clergy about ritual and religious practices that he considered superstitious.

SAMOILOVYCH, IVAN (d. 1690). **Hetman** of **Left-Bank Ukraine** (1672–87). The son of a priest, Samoilovych was educated at the **Kyiv Mohyla Academy** and began his service in the **Zaporozhian Host** in the 1660s as a secretary. At a **Cossack council** in Hlukhiv in 1669, he was elected general judge. Following the deposition of **Demian Mnohohrishny**, Samoilovych was elected hetman at a **Cossack officer** council in Koziacha Dibrova (17 [27] June 1672). Basing his rule on the support of the Cossack officers and his own relatives, whom he rewarded with land grants, Samoilovych established the Military Fellows (mainly officers' sons) as part of his entourage. Advocating the unity of the Ukrainian lands, he fought the **Right-Bank** hetman **Petro Doroshenko**. In early 1674,

Samoilovych and the Muscovite voevoda Grigorii Romodanovsky led a campaign into Right-Bank Ukraine. Samoilovych was elected hetman of all Ukraine at a council in Pereiaslav (17 [27] March 1674). Two years later, backed by a Muscovite army, he forced Doroshenko to resign as hetman of the Right Bank. As a result of the Chyhyryn campaigns of the Ottoman Turks to the Right Bank (1677–78) and the signing of the Treaty of Bakhchesarai (1681), Samoilovych lost control of Right-Bank Ukraine. The southern Kyiv region, Bratslav region, and **Podilia** remained under the nominal rule of **Yurii Khmelnytsky**, who recognized the Ottoman protectorate.

Samoilovych's authoritarian rule and the high taxes collected for the maintenance of Muscovite garrisons and regular armies in the **Hetmanate** were heavy burdens for the population and provoked dissatisfaction among the Cossacks. Taking advantage of an unsuccessful Muscovite-Cossack campaign in the **Crimea** in 1687, the Cossack officers accused Samoilovych of secret dealings with the Crimean **Tatars**, as well as of corruption and arbitrary rule. They requested that the tsarist government depose Samoilovych, and on 22 July (1 August) 1687 Muscovite regiments surrounded his headquarters. The hetman was arrested and sent to Moscow with his son, Yakiv. From there he was exiled to Siberia and died in Tobolsk.

SARMATIANS. Group of nomadic Iranian tribes related to the **Scythians**. They migrated from the lower Volga region and settled the steppes north of the Black Sea in the fourth and third centuries B.C. The Sarmatian tribes most prominent in that region were the Roxolani and the Alans. Warfare, in which women played a major role, was the Sarmatians' basic activity; their religion and art emphasized a cult of the sword and fire. Their economy was based on livestock raising, crafts, and extensive trade, notably with the **Black Sea colonies**. After the second century A.D., Sarmatian control of the steppes was broken by invasions of the Goths and Huns. In the 16th and 17th centuries, a cult of "Sarmatism" developed among the nobility of the **Polish-Lithuanian Commonwealth**, which legitimized its status as a ruling warrior caste by claiming descent from the ancient Sarmatians.

SCULPTURE. The oldest three-dimensional representations found in Ukraine date back to the Paleolithic period. Stone stelae and terracotta figures of the **Trypilian culture** have survived from the Neolithic and Bronze ages. The **Scythians** produced impressive relief sculptures and gold jewelry from the middle of the first millennium B.C., and Hellenic sculptures have been found on the northern **Black Sea littoral**. The Zbruch idol, carved in low relief on all four sides of a block of stone, is an example of pre-Christian sculpture of the first millennium A.D. **Kyivan Rus' chronicles** also mention gilded wooden idols, none of which have survived. Freestanding stone *babas* were erected in the Ukrainian steppes by Turkic tribes between the 11th and 13th centuries.

The **Christianization of Rus'** in the 10th century became an obstacle to the development of sculpture. The hostile attitude of the Eastern Church to sculptural images limited the practice of the art to relief carvings. A few Kyivan Rus' sculptures that have come down to the present exhibit Eastern, Greek, and Romanesque influences. Much later, as Renaissance art spread to **western Ukraine**, particularly **Galicia**, sculpture became more common. Memorial tomb sculptures similar to those found in northern Italy appeared, as did carved and gilded wooden iconostases. Secular buildings were often decorated with carved reliefs.

Relief carvings and multitier iconostases reached the peak of their development during the **baroque** period. One of the largest iconostases to survive Soviet destruction was installed in the Transfiguration Church in Velyki Sorochyntsi (**Poltava** region) in 1732. Because the Orthodox Church continued to oppose figural carving, most ecclesiastical sculpture was produced in Galicia, especially for Roman Catholic churches. The **architecture** of **Ukrainian Catholic** churches, such as St. George's Cathedral in **Lviv**, also incorporates sculpture in the round.

The emergence of classicism in the form of the imperial style (early 19th century) coincided with the decline of Ukrainian autonomy. Sculptors such as **Ivan Martos** worked primarily in Russia. However, Martos did erect several monuments in Ukraine, including the statue of the Duke de Richelieu in **Odesa** (1828) and the grave monument of Hetman **Kyrylo Rozumovsky** in Baturyn. Public sculpture, largely unknown in Ukraine until then, was commissioned as a result of the unprecedented growth of civic architecture and city planning during this period. The statue of **Volodymyr the Great** on the right bank of the Dnipro River in **Kyiv** is the best-known sculpture of this type. Most monuments, however, were dedicated to tsars and their officials. In western Ukraine, public statues were erected by sculptors from Central and Western Europe. Among the best-known works of this period are the four fountains in Rynok Square (Lviv).

Romantic and **realist** themes appeared in Ukrainian sculpture during the latter half of the 19th century. Many Ukrainian sculptors studied in Paris, and some, especially **Mykhailo Parashchuk**, were influenced by Auguste Rodin.

Alexander Archipenko is the best-known Ukrainian sculptor. In the 1910s, he created some of the first cubist sculptures, experimented with a variety of materials and abstraction, and revived polychromatic sculpture. Other innovators included Vladimir Tatlin, who spent most of his career in Russia; Vasilii Ermilov, a leading constructivist; and **Ivan Kavaleridze**, who produced cubist sculptures in the 1910s and 1920s before switching to state-imposed socialist realism.

From the 1930s, all the arts in the **Ukrainian SSR** were subject to official guidelines, and sculpture was used primarily to glorify the Soviet state. Stalinist sculpture was especially pompous. Notable sculptors in the socialist realist style were Mykhailo Lysenko, Vasyl Borodai, and Halyna Kalchenko, while later sculptors who deviated from that style include Halyna Sevruk, who works in ceramic relief sculpture, and Mykhailo Hrytsiuk. More recently, many young sculptors in Ukraine have begun to explore new forms and materials, among which terra-cotta, stone, and wood are especially popular.

SCYTHIANS. Group of nomadic Iranian-speaking tribes that inhabited the steppes north of the Black Sea from the seventh to the third century B.C. They are mentioned in Assyrian and Greek sources; Herodotus devoted the fourth book of his *History* to them. Known as fierce warriors, the Scythians withstood an attempted invasion by Darius I of Persia (ca. 513–512 B.C.), establishing themselves in a forest-steppe belt (on the territory of present-day Ukraine) that became known as Great Scythia. The population was made up of so-called Royal Scythians and notables (migrants from the east) and Scythian agriculturalists and plowmen (dependent local tribes). The Scythians attained the height of their power in the mid-fourth century B.C. under King Ateas, who united them and campaigned successfully against the Thracians. He died in battle against the forces of Philip II of Macedon in 339 B.C. Following the appearance of the **Sarmatians** between the Don and Dnipro Rivers and later to the west of the Dnipro, Scythian might began to decline. The successor of Great Scythia was Scythia Minor in the **Crimea**, which continued to exist until the third century A.D.

The Scythians left a rich and varied cultural legacy. First and foremost, it includes several hundred *kurhany* (burial mounds) of the military tribal elite in the Sula River region dating from the sixth century B.C. (Aksiutyntsi, Pustovoika, Budky) and *kurhany* from the fourth century B.C. in the Dnipro region (Chortomlyk, Solokha, Haimanova, and Tovsta Mohyla), as well as in the Crimea (Kul-Oba, Trybratnii, and others). Scythian chieftains were buried with their wives or concubines, servants, horses, and a large assortment of weapons and material possessions. The Scythian economy was based on nomadic herding, agriculture, raids, and the collection of tribute. They also traded extensively with the **Black Sea colonies**. The Scythians excelled in metalworking and manufacturing covered wagons, weapons, and horse harnesses. Scythian culture was based on the traditions of Central Asian Iranian tribes (Śakas, Massagetae), incorporating the so-called animal style in art, numerous myths, and primal religious conceptions. Today, the Scythians are best known for their magnificent golden art objects, many of which have been excavated in the 20th century and widely exhibited.

SEDLIAR, VASYL (1 [12] April 1889–13 July 1937). Painter. Born in Liubech (Chernihiv region), Sedliar studied at the **Kyiv** Art School (1915–19) and the **Ukrainian State Academy of Arts** (1919–22) under **Mykhailo Boichuk**. He taught at the Art and Ceramics Tekhnikum (1923–28) and the Technological Institute of Ceramics (1928–30) in Mezhyhiria and at the Kyiv Art Institute (1930–36). He worked in monumental and easel **painting**, easel and book graphics, and decorative art. Sedliar took part in the painting of murals at the Lutsk regimental barracks in Kyiv (1919), the Kyiv Institute of Plastic Arts (now the Kyiv Art Institute), the Mezhyhiria Art and Ceramics Tekhnikum (both 1924), and the Chervonozavod Theater in **Kharkiv** (1935–36; the murals have not survived). His paintings include *In the Literacy School* (1924–25), *Execution, Portrait of the Artist Oksana Pavlenko* (both 1927), *Peasant Woman*, and *Holiday at Dniprelstan* (1933–34). Sedliar illustrated an edition of **Taras Shevchenko's** *Kobzar* (1931) and worked in pottery (faience and majolica, 1924–29). He was executed by the NKVD during Stalin's **political terror**.

SEMBRATOVYCH, SYLVESTR (3 September 1836–4 August 1898). Catholic metropolitan of **Galicia**, archbishop of **Lviv**, Roman count (1894) and cardinal (1895). He was born in Doshnytsia, **Lemko region**, into the family of a priest. Following studies in Peremyshl (Przemyśl), Lviv, and Vienna, Sembratovych entered the Athanasius College in Rome (1853), where he studied philosophy and theology. He was ordained in 1860 and defended his doctoral dissertation in theology in June 1861. He served as auxiliary priest in Florynka and Tylych (Peremyshl eparchy). In 1862, Sembratovych moved to Lviv, where he worked as a catechist and chaplain in a **Basilian** convent. He was prefect of the Lviv Theological Seminary (LTS, 1863–70), then professor of dogmatics at Lviv University (from 1869) and dean of the theological faculty at the university (1873, 1879). Sembratovych and the Rev. Yuliian Pelesh founded a religious journal, *Rus'kii Sion"* (Ruthenian Zion, 1870), and Sembratovych published a *Euchologion* (with Pelesh and the Rev. Onufrii Lepky) and one of the first prayer books in the Ukrainian vernacular (1879).

In February 1878, he was appointed assistant to his uncle, Yosyf Sembratovych, who was bishop of Lviv. The latter was forced to resign in November 1882 (*see* RUSSOPHILES), and Sembratovych became metropolitan of Halych on 26 March 1885. The Lviv Synod, which he convened in 1891 to reform church practices, considerably increased the metropolitan's powers. Sembratovych was a privy counselor to the emperor, a member of the Galician Diet and twice its chairman, and a member of the House of Lords in Vienna. He devoted considerable attention to training young priests and expanded the LTS (1889). In 1885, he established a separate Stanyslaviv eparchy and completed a reform of the Basilian Order. Sembratovych founded the Society of St. Paul, which helped poor parishes build and repair churches. During his pastoral visits, he paid particular attention to general education and the state of cultural establishments, especially **Prosvita** reading rooms. In 1884, Sembratovych founded a girls' institute in Lviv. He was active in Galician political life, combating Russophile influence and supporting the New Era policy of compromise with the Poles. He was buried in Lviv in the crypt of St. George's Cathedral.

SEMENKO, MYKHAIL (19 [31] December 1892–23 October 1937). Poet. He was born in Kybyntsi (now in **Poltava** oblast), the son of the writer Mariia Proskurivna. Semenko received his education at the Khorol gymnasium and technical schools in Kybyntsi and Kursk. He then took a two-year general course in St. Petersburg and studied at the city's Psycho-Neurological Institute. Semenko organized the Futurist literary groups Kvero (Quaero, 1914), Flamingo (1919), Poet-Futurists' Shock Brigade (1921), Aspanfut (1921), and Nova Generatsiia (New Generation, 1927). He edited the journals *Mystetsvo* (Art), *Katafalk iskusstva* (The Catafalque of Art, 1922), *Semafor u maibutnie* (Semaphore into the Future, 1922), *Bumerang* (Boomerang), *Gong komunkul'tu* (The Gong of Communist Culture), and *Nova generatsiia* (1927–31).

Semenko's first poems were published in *Ukraïns'ka khata* (Ukrainian House) in 1913. Subsequently, he published collections in which he established himself as both a poet and a theoretician of Futurism. The prefaces to those collections were manifestos of exploratory (quaero)-Futurism in which Semenko opposed artistic canonization and cults, such as that of **Taras Shevchenko**. In the years that followed, he published many collections, long poems, and pamphlets. Semenko's early poetry was preoccupied with urban themes, linguistic and formal experimentation, shocking assertions, and the destruction of form. He expanded the thematic range and versification of Ukrainian poetry. Under pressure from the authorities, Semenko abandoned Futurism in the late 1920s and switched to Soviet patriotism. During Stalin's **political terror**, he was arrested on charges of "counterrevolutionary activity" and executed. *See also* LITERATURE.

SERFDOM. See PEASANTS.

SEVRIUK, OLEKSANDER (1893–26 or 27 December 1941). Politician and diplomat. He received his higher education at the Petrograd Technological Institute. There Sevriuk belonged to the Ukrainian student **hromada** and worked in its information bureau. He was a leading activist of the **Ukrainian Party of Socialist Revolutionaries**, which he represented in the **Ukrainian Central Rada**. Sevriuk headed the commission to draft the law creating the Ukrainian Constituent Assembly. In December 1917, at the Congress of Councils of Workers', Peasants', and Soldiers' Deputies in **Kyiv**, Sevriuk proclaimed the resolution (subsequently ratified by the congress) that termed the Bolshevik ultimatum of 4 (17) December an "attack on the **Ukrainian People's Republic** (UNR)."

Sevriuk's most notable achievement was heading the Ukrainian delegation at negotiations with the Central Powers; in February 1918 he was the first to sign the **Treaty of Brest-Litovsk** on behalf of the UNR. He persuaded the Austro-Hungarian representatives to sign a secret agreement on the creation of a separate crown land consisting of eastern **Galicia** and **Bukovyna**. From February to April 1918, Sevriuk was the UNR ambassador in Germany. He then became Ukraine's diplomatic representative in Bucharest, authorized to sign a peace treaty with Romania. From February to July 1919, he headed the Ukrainian mission in Italy, where he was to repatriate Ukrainian POWs, but was dismissed for dereliction of duty. Sevriuk was a member of the Ukrainian delegation at the Paris Peace Conference (1919–20). From 1920, he lived in France. He worked for the newspaper *Ukraïns'ki visti* (Ukrainian News), in which he published a series of articles about the peace talks at Brest-Litovsk. In the 1920s, he adopted Sovietophile views and visited the **Ukrainian SSR** in 1928. In the 1930s, he lived in Germany. He died in a railway accident near Frankfurt an der Oder.

SHAKHTY TRIAL. Officially designated the "Case of the Counterrevolutionary Organization of Engineers and Technicians Who Worked in the Coal Industry of the **USSR**." First show trial in the USSR, involving a large group of coal industry leaders from the **Donets Basin** (Donbas). It took place at the Supreme Court of the USSR in Moscow from 18 May to 6 July 1928. The presiding judge was the future Soviet chief procurator, Andrei Vyshinsky. The defendants (53 engineering and technical workers of the coal industry, including the directors of Donvuhillia, the Administration for New Construction in the Donbas, five directors of mines and ore administrations, five chief mine engineers, four German specialists, and others) were accused of belonging to a "counterrevolutionary organization" active in Shakhty county and other parts of the Donbas, as well as in **Kharkiv** and Moscow (1922–28).

The United State Political Administration (OGPU) or secret police charged the defendants with attempting to destroy the coal industry in the Donbas, the most important fuel-resource region in the USSR, in order to undermine Soviet industrialization. They were accused of destruction and sabotage (blowing up and flooding mines, burning power stations, destroying equipment, and the like) on instructions from Poland and France.

The trial was planned in advance in order to deflect blame from communist officials for the failures of Soviet industrialization. On Stalin's authority, Efim Evdokimov, the OGPU representative in the North Caucasus, conducted mass arrests of specialists in the coal industry. On 13 March 1928, newspapers published an official announcement to the effect that a "counterrevolutionary organization" had been discovered in the Shakhty region.

During the trial, 20 of the accused "acknowledged" their guilt completely (such confessions were extracted by force), 11 acknowledged it partially, and 22 pleaded innocent. Eleven of the accused were sentenced to death by firing squad, three to 10 years' imprisonment with an additional five years of restricted rights and confiscation of property, 21 to terms of four to eight years, and 10 to prison terms of one to three years. Four were sentenced conditionally, and another four (the German specialists) were found not guilty. Later, six death sentences were commuted to 10 years' imprisonment in strict isolation, restricted rights for five years, and confiscation of property.

The trial was widely covered in the press and used to whip up class hostility. Stalin himself warned that "Shakhtyites" were wrecking Soviet industry and called for purges to root them out. The trial thus foreshadowed the mass **political terror** of the 1930s.

SHANDRUK, PAVLO (28 February 1889–15 February 1979). General of the Army of the **Ukrainian People's Republic** (UNR). He was born in Borsuky, **Volhynia**. Shandruk graduated from the Nizhyn

Historical and Philological Institute (1911) and the Aleksei Military School in Moscow (1913). During **World War I**, he commanded a battalion in the Russian army. He participated in the **Ukrainian Revolution** (1917–21), fighting in the Army of the UNR. From April 1920, he commanded a brigade. Shandruk later lived in Poland, where he graduated from the General Staff Academy (1938) and served as a deputy regimental commander. In March 1945, Shandruk headed the **Ukrainian National Committee**, which initiated the formation of a Ukrainian National Army (UNA) under his command. The **Division Galizien** was incorporated as the First Division of the UNA. After the war, Shandruk lived in Germany and, from 1949, in the United States. He died in Trenton, New Jersey. Shandruk published his memoirs, *Arms of Valor* (1959), and edited the collection *Ukraïns'ko-moskovs'ka viina 1920 r. v dokumentakh* (The Ukrainian-Russian War of 1920 in Documents, 1933).

SHAPOVAL, MYKYTA (26 May 1882–25 February 1932). Civic and political leader, writer, and sociologist. He was born to a peasant family in Sriblianka (now in Donetsk oblast) and educated in **Kharkiv**. Shapoval joined the **Revolutionary Ukrainian Party** in 1901 and cofounded the literary journal *Ukraïns'ka khata* (Ukrainian House, 1909–14) in **Kyiv**. In April 1917, he became a founder of the **Ukrainian Party of Socialist Revolutionaries** (UPSR), and in July he joined its central committee. From March 1917, he was a member of the **Ukrainian Central Rada** and, from July, a member of its Little Rada. Following the proclamation of the **Ukrainian People's Republic** (UNR) on 7 (20) November 1917, he was appointed minister of the postal and telegraph service. Together with **Mykhailo Hrushevsky** and **Volodymyr Vynnychenko**, Shapoval drafted the Fourth Universal of the UNR. After the demise of the UNR, Shapoval headed the **Ukrainian National Union**, which opposed the rule of **Pavlo Skoropadsky**. From 26 December 1918 to 11 February 1919, he was minister of agriculture in the **Directory** and drafted legislation to nationalize land.

Forced to emigrate after the Bolshevik takeover of Kyiv, Shapoval became secretary of the Directory's diplomatic mission in Budapest (1919–20) and later lived in Prague. He headed the UPSR in exile, firmly opposing the party's "foreign delegation" in Vienna, which favored compromise with Bolshevik Russia. Along with Nykyfor Hryhoriiv and Mykola Halahan, he initiated the Ukrainian Civic Committee (active until 1925). The organization was involved in the founding, with the assistance of the Czechoslovak government, of the Ukrainian Husbandry Academy in Poděbrady (1922) and the Ukrainian Higher Pedagogical Institute in Prague (1923).

Shapoval edited and published the journal *Nova Ukraïna* (New Ukraine, 1922–28) and headed the Ukrainian Institute of Sociology in Prague. He published some 350 literary, scholarly, and publicistic works.

SHASHKEVYCH, MARKIIAN (6 November 1811–7 June 1843). Writer and leading figure of the national revival in **western Ukraine**. He was born in Pidlysia (now in **Lviv** oblast) into the family of a priest and studied at gymnasiums in Lviv and Berezhany. After graduating from the theological faculty of Lviv University and the Greek Catholic Theological Seminary (1838; *see* UKRAINIAN CATHOLIC CHURCH), he served as a priest in rural **Galicia**. During his student years, Shashkevych inspired, organized, and led the **Ruthenian Triad**, whose activities included collecting and popularizing folklore, compiling a dictionary and grammar of the Ukrainian vernacular, reforming orthography on the phonetic principle, employing the so-called *hrazhdanka* script rather than the Cyrillic, and introducing the vernacular into everyday use by the intelligentsia and clergy. Shashkevych was an innovative **romantic** poet whose works are characterized by patriotism, gentle and lyrical tones, and uncomplicated symbolism. In his works on historical themes he poeticized the Ukrainian past, especially the figure of **Bohdan Khmelnytsky**. In 1834, he wrote a biographical sketch of Khmelnytsky, translated from the Latin Khmelnytsky's fable addressed to the legates of John Casimir of Poland, and published both works in the almanac *Zoria* (Star; banned by the censors). Shashkevych became famous as the coauthor and publisher of the almanac ***Rusalka Dnistrovaia*** (1837) and as the author of *Azbuka i Abecadło* (The Alphabet and the Abecedarium, 1836), which opposed the Latinization of the Ukrainian script. He was among the first to translate selections from the ***Tale of Ihor's Campaign*** and the Scriptures into Ukrainian (1842), and he translated works from Serbian, Czech, Polish, Greek, Latin, and German. Shashkevych died in poverty and was buried in Novosilky Lisni; in 1893, his remains were reburied in Lviv. *See also* LANGUAGE; LITERATURE.

SHCHERBYTSKY, VOLODYMYR (4 [17] February 1918–16 February 1990). Soviet Ukrainian political leader. He was born in Verkhniodniprovsk (Dnipropetrovsk oblast) into a worker's family. In 1934, he became active in the Communist Youth League (Komsomol) and enrolled in the Dnipropetrovsk Chemical Technology Institute in 1937. His withdrawal from Komsomol activity saved him from the thoroughgoing purge of that organization in 1937–39.

In 1941, Shcherbytsky joined the **Communist Party of Ukraine** (CPU) and graduated as an engineer. During **World War II**, he served in Mongolia, where he saw no action. On settling in Dniprodzerzhynsk in 1946, he became a close associate of Leonid Brezhnev, who was then first party secretary of Zaporizhia oblast.

Thanks to Brezhnev's patronage, Shcherbytsky became second secretary of the Dniprodzerzhynsk city party committee (1948–51), where he established his reputation as an efficient and hard-working administrator. By 1955, he had risen to first secretary of the Dnipropetrovsk oblast party committee, and in 1957 he became a member of the CPU Presidium and secretary responsible for industry. In 1961, when the head of Ukraine's **Council of Ministers**, Nykyfor Kalchenko, was demoted for alleged inefficiency, Brezhnev recommended Shcherbytsky to **Nikita Khrushchev** as Kalchenko's replacement. Shcherbytsky held the post for two years, but his relations with the CPU first secretary, **Mykola Pidhorny**, were poor, and he made an enemy of **Petro Shelest** by blocking the latter's bid to succeed him as industry secretary. In June 1963, when Shelest became first secretary of the CPU, Shcherbytsky was demoted to first secretary of the Dnipropetrovsk oblast party committee. He was saved from obscurity by Brezhnev's assumption of power following the removal of Khrushchev. Over Shelest's objections, Brezhnev insisted on restoring "his" appointee to the chairmanship of the Ukrainian Council of Ministers in October 1965. Following his installation, Shcherbytsky waged a protracted bureaucratic struggle with Shelest, appointing his loyalists to major government posts. Shcherbytsky became a member of the Politburo of the CC CPU (from 1966) and of the CC of the Communist Party of the Soviet Union (from 1971).

Shelest's abrupt dismissal and transfer to Moscow in May 1972 (for which he blamed Shcherbytsky's intrigues) resulted in Shcherbytsky's appointment as first secretary of the CPU. He reversed Shelest's autonomism, seeking to integrate Ukraine as fully as possible into the Soviet mainstream. Above all, this meant linguistic and cultural **Russification**. Shcherbytsky demonstratively spoke Russian in carrying out all official functions and presided over the systematic Russification of secondary **education** in Ukraine. Shelest's secretary of ideology, the moderate Fedir Ovcharenko, was replaced in October 1972 by Valentyn Malanchuk (Milman), a relentless campaigner against "Ukrainian nationalism." Under Malanchuk's supervision, a purge of Ukrainian cultural institutions (especially the **media**) and scholarly institutes of history and archaeology) was carried out, with a large number of dismissals and prohibitions on publication. Many historical figures partially rehabilitated in the 1960s again became subject to attack. The 325th anniversary of Ukraine's "reunion" with Russia (see PEREIASLAV AGREEMENT) was officially celebrated in 1979 amid considerable talk of the formation of a Russian-speaking "Soviet people." A wave of arrests of political **dissidents** took place in 1971–72, even before Shelest's dismissal, and Shcherbytsky continued to deal very harshly with dissidents (see UKRAINIAN HELSINKI GROUP).

In 1979–80, Shcherbytsky dismissed a number of key officials associated with the purges of the 1970s, most notably the overambitious Malanchuk. While this reflected a desire to mend fences with the intelligentsia, it was also typical of Shcherbytsky's cadres policy; he had no inner circle, kept his appointees at a strict distance, and disposed of them as his interests required. At the CPU congress of 1976, Shcherbytsky replaced almost all members and candidate members of the party's Politburo.

A technocrat by training and inclination, Shcherbytsky concentrated on economic development, striving to obtain maximum inputs from Moscow and pouring resources into Ukrainian industry, **agriculture**, and **transportation**. He also spurred the development of nuclear energy, giving direct orders to build the Chornobyl nuclear power station without awaiting official ratification of the project and ignoring the warnings of scientific experts. While these measures did not stem long-term economic deterioration or reduce chronic inflation, they kept the economy on a sufficiently even keel to ward off major disturbances. Not until the **Chornobyl nuclear disaster** (1986), which set off a major wave of ecological and political protest, was the stability of Shcherbytsky's regime shaken. Even then, Mikhail Gorbachev left him in office so as to keep Ukraine under control. Shcherbytsky was finally pensioned off with full honors in September 1989 and died shortly thereafter. He was buried at the Baikove Cemetery in Kyiv.

SHCHORS, MYKOLA (25 May [6 June] 1895–30 August 1919). Bolshevik military leader. Born in Snovsk (now Shchors, Chernihiv oblast), Shchors graduated from military schools in **Kyiv** (1914) and **Poltava** (1916). As a captain in the Russian imperial army, he fought in **World War I**. In 1918, he joined the Bolsheviks, and in February of that year he took command of a Red Army unit in the Chernihiv region. In September, Shchors became commander of the **Bohun** Regiment, which he recruited from assorted partisan units. In November, he took command of a brigade of the First Ukrainian Soviet Division, recruited primarily from Red Army regiments, Hungarian internationalists, and Volga **Tatars**. His brigade fought forces of the **Directory** on the Chernihiv-Kyiv route in early 1919.

After the Bolsheviks captured Kyiv, Shchors was appointed commandant of the city. From March 1919, he was commander of the First Uman Soviet Division, and in August he became commander of the Tarashcha 44th Rifle Division of the 12th Army, which fought the **Lviv** brigade of the **Ukrainian Galician Army** near Korosten. According to his official biography, Shchors fell in the Korosten battle; another account maintains that he was murdered by a commissar at the instigation of the 12th Army command. He was buried in Samara, Russia. When Stalin decided that Ukraine needed a counterpart of the Russian revolutionary hero Vasilii Chapaev, Shchors became a favorite subject of Soviet Ukrainian painters, writers, film directors, and composers; monuments were erected to him and a museum opened.

SHELEST, PETRO (1 [14] February 1908–22 January 1996). Soviet Ukrainian political leader. He was born in Andriivka (now in **Kharkiv** oblast) into a **peasant** family. According to his father's stories, his family was descended from a **Cossack** captain, Stepan Shelest. From 1923, Shelest worked as a mechanic and steamfitter in Kharkiv. From 1927, he studied at the Izium party school, joined the **Communist Party of Ukraine** (CPU) in 1928, and became secretary of the Communist Youth League committee in Borova (Kharkiv oblast) in the same year. Shelest then worked at the Mariupol metallurgical factory (1932–36) while studying at the local metallurgical institute, from which he graduated in 1935. Following military service (1935–37), he became chief engineer at the Hammer and Sickle Factory in Kharkiv (1937–40). In 1940, he was appointed defense industry secretary for the city of Kharkiv. During **World War II**, he headed the defense production department in Cheliabinsk and served as deputy secretary of the Saratov party committee for defense production. From 1948 to 1954, Shelest was a director of aircraft factories in Leningrad and **Kyiv**. In 1954, he was chosen second secretary of the Kyiv city party committee and became a member of the CC CPU. From February 1957, he was first secretary of the Kyiv oblast party committee. In December 1962, he became head of the CC CPU Bureau of Industry and Construction. In July 1963, **Nikita Khrushchev** appointed Shelest to succeed **Mykola Pidhorny** as first secretary of the CPU. Soon afterward, Pidhorny and Leonid Brezhnev prevailed upon Shelest to join them in plotting to remove Khrushchev from power. Shelest played a key role in recruiting support for the plot within the CPU, and Khrushchev was deposed in October 1964. In 1966, Shelest became a member of the Politburo of the Central Committee, Communist Party of the Soviet Union (CC CPSU), and of the Presidium of the USSR Supreme Soviet.

The assertive, hard-working Shelest apparently saw no contradiction between his Soviet patriotism and loyalty to his native Ukraine; in his memoirs, he would describe himself as "a Ukrainian, a Soviet man, and a communist." He came to power at a time when the CPU was growing rapidly and seeking to expand its influence, as well as to stem the influx of Russian cadres into Ukraine that resulted from Khrushchev's *sovnarkhoz* reform. An important means of maintaining local control over the CPU was promotion of the Ukrainian **language**; Khrushchev's removal from power meant that his policy of **Russification** was open to challenge. Shelest's minister of education, Yurii Dadenkov, prepared a reform calling for the Ukrainization of government services and **education**. Although the implementation of this reform was prevented by a directive from Moscow, Shelest expressed strong support for the Ukrainian language, notably at the Fifth Congress of the Ukrainian Writers' Union (16–20 November 1966) and at a meeting with Ukrainian students at Kyiv University (3 September 1968), where he stated that all new textbooks in Ukraine should be published in Ukrainian. The intelligentsia began to claim greater freedom; Ukrainian historical studies were revived, and 1967 saw the inauguration of a multivolume reference work on the history of Ukrainian towns and villages. In 1968, the writer Oles Honchar, a member of Shelest's inner circle, published his patriotic novel *Sobor* (Cathedral), which condemned bureaucratic hostility to Ukrainian cultural traditions and became a cause célèbre. The world's first encyclopedia of cybernetics, issued in Kyiv in 1973, came out in Ukrainian, not in Russian.

In such an atmosphere, political **dissidents** concerned about Ukraine's subordination to Russia, for whom communist ideology was less a creed than an obligatory form of public discourse, felt freer to make claims on the government. **Ivan Dziuba**'s *Internationalism or Russification?*, the most important work of 1960s dissident literature, was addressed to Shelest and to the head of the Ukrainian **Council of Ministers**, **Volodymyr Shcherbytsky**. Presenting his case in impeccably Leninist terms, Dziuba called on them to take measures to revive Ukrainian culture. A wave of arrests in 1965 led to the trial and imprisonment of a score of Ukrainian dissidents, raising the question of whether Shelest was fully in control of the republic. The Czechoslovak crisis of 1968 raised that question even more insistently; fearing that the ideas of the "Prague spring" might provoke rampant dissent, especially in neighboring **western Ukraine**, Shelest was among those most insistent on a crackdown by Warsaw Pact forces. This did not suffice to allay Moscow's concerns about Ukraine's political stability; in July 1970, Shelest's associate Vitalii Nikitchenko was replaced as head of the

Ukrainian KGB by Vitalii Fedorchuk. Under the latter's direction, arrests of Ukrainian intellectuals began in February 1971 and expanded into a large-scale campaign in 1972.

Shelest was also insistent on expanding Ukraine's economic prerogatives. During his administration, government officials openly complained that Ukraine was being economically exploited by Moscow and called for greater capital investment in Ukraine, rather than in Siberia. When Shcherbytsky praised Brezhnev's economic policies at the CPSU congress of 1971, Shelest openly contradicted him, maintaining that the **Donets Basin** coal industry required more investment.

In 1970, Shelest's pride in Ukraine's achievements led him to issue a book under his name entitled *Ukraïno nasha Radians'ka* (O Ukraine, Our Soviet Land). Published exclusively in Ukrainian, with a press run of 100,000 copies, the book aroused concern in Moscow about Ukrainian self-assertion. On 19 May 1972, when Shelest was in Moscow attending a plenum of the CC CPSU, Brezhnev abruptly insisted on his transfer to Moscow to become deputy chairman of the USSR Council of Ministers. The new post, in which Shelest was given no significant responsibilities, was a stunning demotion that left him embittered and depressed. As his memoirs make clear, Shelest considered it a direct result of Shcherbytsky's political intrigue—one that exploited the pusillanimity of Brezhnev, whom Shelest characterized as vain and indecisive. In April 1973, Shelest asked Brezhnev to approve his retirement from public life, which was done. In the same month, the party journal *Komunist Ukraïny* (Communist of Ukraine) published a scathing unsigned attack on the "errors" of Shelest's *Ukraïno nasha Radians'ka*. Shelest was accused of idealizing pre-Soviet Ukrainian history and giving it undue prominence; of neglecting the epochal significance of Ukraine's "reunification" with Russia in 1654 (*see* PEREIASLAV AGREEMENT); of playing down the role of the Communist Party and treating the Ukrainian economy and culture in an "autarchic" manner; and of failing to conduct a thoroughgoing attack on Ukrainian bourgeois nationalism. This authoritative condemnation of Shelest's views, accompanied by arrests of political dissidents and a purge of major Ukrainian institutions, indicated that the reasons for Shelest's removal went far beyond personal rivalries. Shcherbytsky, who succeeded Shelest as head of the CPU, was clearly expected to keep Ukraine on a tight leash.

Shelest was forbidden to return to Ukraine and lived under constant surveillance. From 1974 to 1985, he was head of a construction bureau at an aviation factory in Podmoskovie. In 1989, he broke the silence previously imposed on him and began giving public interviews. Shortly before his death, Shelest published his memoirs, *Da ne sudimy budete. Dnevnikovye zapisi, vospominaniia chlena Politburo TsK KPSS* (Lest Ye Be Judged. Diary Entries and Memoirs of a Member of the Politburo of the CC CPSU, 1995). He died in Podmoskovie. On 13 June 1996, his ashes were reinterred at the Baikove Cemetery in Kyiv.

SHEPTYTSKY, ANDREI (29 July 1865–1 November 1944). Metropolitan of the **Ukrainian Catholic Church** (UCC) (metropolitan of Halych, archbishop of **Lviv**, bishop of Kamianets-Podilskyi); outstanding cultural and civic figure. He was born in the village of Prylbychi (now in Yavoriv raion, Lviv oblast). At baptism he received the name Roman Aleksander Maria. Sheptytsky was descended from an old Ukrainian **boyar** family that had been Polonized in the late 18th century. Some of his ancestors had been prominent hierarchs of the UCC, with which he identified himself even though he was brought up as a nationally conscious Polish aristocrat. He received his primary and secondary education at home and at St. Anna's Gymnasium in Cracow. In 1887, Sheptytsky traveled through Ukraine and Russia, meeting with the philosopher Vladimir Soloviev and the historian **Volodymyr Antonovych**. He studied law at the universities of Cracow and Wrocław, receiving his doctorate on 19 May 1888. In the same month, having adopted the Greek rite, he entered the Basilian monastery in Dobromyl, taking the monastic name Andrei. Subsequently he studied philosophy and theology in Cracow, obtaining doctorates in both subjects. On 22 August 1892, Sheptytsky was ordained in Peremyshl (Przemyśl), later serving as master of novices in Dobromyl (1893–96) and becoming hegumen of the St. Onuphrius Monastery in Lviv (1896–97). He was also professor of theology at the monastery in Krystynopil (now Chervonohrad, Lviv oblast).

Sheptytsky was consecrated bishop of Stanyslaviv on 17 September 1899. On 17 December 1900, following the death of Metropolitan Yuliian Sas-Kuilovsky, Sheptytsky was nominated metropolitan of Halych by Pope Leo XIII and enthroned at St. George's Cathedral in Lviv (17 January 1901). As a deputy to the Galician Diet and a member of the Austrian House of Lords in Vienna, Sheptytsky defended the interests of the Ukrainian population of **Galicia**. In January 1906, he headed a delegation to the emperor that sought equal rights for Ukrainians in the Austro-Hungarian Monarchy.

Sheptytsky did much to develop education and culture in the western Ukrainian lands, promoting the growth of Ukrainian national consciousness. In 1901, he supported the secession of Ukrainian students from Lviv University, and in 1910, at a session of the

House of Lords, he demanded the establishment of a Ukrainian university in Lviv. In order to promote professional training for young people, he helped establish a school of **agriculture** in Korshiv and a horticultural school in Mylovashchi. In 1905, Sheptytsky founded an ecclesiastical museum (now the National Museum in Lviv) that amassed one of the largest collections of **icons** in Europe thanks to his efforts. He bought a building to house **Oleksa Novakivsky's** art school and the studios of Modest Sosenko and Osyp Kurylas; he also established scholarships that enabled young Ukrainian artists to study in Western Europe. In 1903, Sheptytsky founded the People's Hospital Society, which later established a large modern hospital in Lviv (1930–38). He was an initiator and founder of the Land Mortgage Bank in Lviv (1910) and supported the activities of the **Prosvita**, **Ridna Shkola**, and Silskyi Hospodar societies.

Sheptytsky contributed greatly to the development of national and religious life in **western Ukraine**. With his assistance, a theological seminary was established in Lviv and a library was founded at the Stanyslaviv Capitula. In 1904, he established the Order of St. Theodore the Studite in Galicia, and in 1913 he invited the Redemptorist Order there; it adopted the Eastern rite and created a Galician branch. Sheptytsky also supported women's monastic communities—the orders of the Holy Family, Studites, Mercy, St. Vincent, St. Joseph, and St. Josaphat. Sheptytsky's ecumenical activities were particularly important. He twice visited Russia (1907, 1912) and Belarus, founding the Russian Catholic Church. He created an apostolic vicarage for the faithful of the Greek Catholic Church in Bosnia, and in 1908 he sent Studite monks there to conduct missionary work. Sheptytsky appointed bishops to serve Ukrainian settlers in the United States (1907) and Canada (1912). In 1910, he participated in the Eucharistic Congress in Montreal and visited Ukrainian settlements in North America. He initiated the Velehrad ecumenical congresses (1907–27) and established an Eastern branch of the Benedictine Order in Belgium.

Following the Russian occupation of Lviv after the outbreak of **World War I**, Sheptytsky was arrested (18 September 1914) and taken first to **Kyiv** and later to Russia, where he was held in Novgorod, Kursk, and Suzdal. After the February Revolution (1917) he was released; in March 1917, he held a synod in Petrograd and appointed the Rev. Leonid Fedorov exarch for Byzantine-rite Catholics in Russia.

In September 1917, Sheptytsky returned to Lviv and immersed himself in the region's political life. On 28 February 1918, he gave a speech in the Austrian House of Lords defending the right of all the peoples of the empire to self-determination and supporting the **Treaty of Brest-Litovsk** with the **Ukrainian People's Republic**. From October 1918, he was a member of the **Ukrainian National Rada** of the **Western Ukrainian People's Republic**. During the **Ukrainian-Polish War in Galicia**, Sheptytsky was interned by the Polish authorities. In December 1920, he traveled to Rome and then visited Ukrainian settlers in North and South America. In his public appearances he defended Ukrainian independence and condemned the Polish occupation of Galicia. After his return, Sheptytsky was arrested for his political activities and interned in Poznań (September 1923). He was released only after a personal appeal from Pope Pius XI and returned to Lviv (January 1924).

During the interwar period, Sheptytsky continued to work on strengthening the UCC. At his initiative, the Lviv Greek Catholic Academy (1928), the Theological Scholarly Society (1929), and the Ukrainian Catholic Institute of Church Unity (1939) were founded. Sheptytsky also strove to consolidate Ukrainian political forces, calling for moderation and condemning the terrorist activity of the **Organization of Ukrainian Nationalists**. He appealed to the government to end the **Pacification** of 1930. On 24 July 1933, Sheptytsky and his bishops issued a letter condemning the manmade **famine** in the **Ukrainian SSR**. He defended the rights of the Orthodox population of **Volhynia**, the **Kholm** (Chełm) **region**, and the **Sian region**; his letter protesting the persecution of Orthodox believers in those areas was issued on 2 August 1938. Following appeals by Sheptytsky and other church leaders to Pope Pius XI, the Polish authorities put a stop to the destruction of Orthodox churches. In March 1939, Sheptytsky welcomed the declaration of independence by **Carpatho-Ukraine**.

Following the Soviet occupation of western Ukraine in 1939, the new regime began persecuting the UCC and closing its institutions. Anticipating increased repression, Sheptytsky secretly consecrated the rector of the Lviv Theological Academy, **Yosyf Slipy**, as his successor (21 December 1939). In October 1939, he appointed exarchs for Catholics of the Byzantine rite in the Soviet Union: Mykola Charnetsky in Volhynia and **Polisia**, his brother Klymentii Sheptytsky for Russia and Siberia, and others.

At the beginning of the Soviet-German conflict, Sheptytsky welcomed the restoration of Ukrainian statehood and the establishment of the **Ukrainian State Administration** led by **Yaroslav Stetsko** (letter of 1 July 1941). He was the patron of the **Ukrainian National Council** (1941). Sheptytsky protested the mass murder of the Jewish population of Galicia to *Reichskommissar* Heinrich Himmler. On his instructions, hundreds of **Jews** were given refuge in Ukrainian Catholic monasteries and in the metropolitan's residence. On 21 November 1942, Sheptytsky issued the epistle "Ne ubyi" (Thou Shalt Not Kill), in which he called for peace among Ukrainian political forces, condemned all killing, and threatened those who organized and performed such acts with excommunication. During **World War II**, he raised the issue of uniting all Christians in Ukraine in a Kyivan patriarchate in union with Rome, but failed to find support among church hierarchs and the Ukrainian intelligentsia. Sheptytsky died on 1 November 1944 and was buried in the crypt of St. George's Cathedral in Lviv. On 5 December 1958, Sheptytsky's beatification process was initiated at the Vatican. A comprehensive bibliography of Sheptytsky's writings (collected in 22 volumes) appears in Andrii Krawchuk's study of his ethical views (1997).

SHEVCHENKO SCIENTIFIC SOCIETY/NAUKOVE TOVARYSTVO IMENY SHEVCHENKA (NTSh). Scholarly and cultural organization that performed the functions of an all-Ukrainian academy of sciences for many years. It was founded in **Lviv** on 11 December 1873 (initially as the Shevchenko Literary and Scientific Society) through the joint efforts of the nationally conscious intelligentsia of **eastern Ukraine** and **Galicia** in response to prohibitions on Ukrainian publishing in the Russian Empire (*see* VALUEV CIRCULAR). The society was named after the outstanding poet **Taras Shevchenko**. The financial basis for its establishment was a donation of 20,000 Austrian crowns by Yelysaveta Myloradovych of Poltava. Other benefactors were Stepan Kachala, **Oleksander Konysky**, Dmytro Pylchykov, and Mykhailo Zhuchenko. The society's aim was to "promote the development of Ruthenian (Little Russian) **literature**." Its first presidents were Kornylo Sushkevych (1874–85), Sydir Hromnytsky (1885–86), and Demian Hladylovych (1886–92). In the first decade of its existence, the society sponsored the publication of two annuals of the journal *Pravda* (Truth) and Omelian Ohonovsky's *Studien auf dem Gebiete der ruthenischen Sprache* (1880). From 1885 to 1898, it published the journal *Zoria* (Star), which became an all-Ukrainian literary forum and was distributed (illegally, following a ban in 1894) in eastern Ukraine.

In the late 1880s, members of the Kyiv **Hromada** (the so-called Austrophiles, led by **Volodymyr Antonovych** and Konysky) proposed to transform the society into a purely scholarly institution. This idea was supported in Galicia by a group of **populists** led by **Oleksander Barvinsky**. Accordingly, the organization was renamed the Shevchenko Scientific Society (1893), whose stated aim was "to nurture and develop scholarship and art in the Ukrainian-Ruthenian language and to preserve and collect the ancient artifacts and scholarly materials of Ukraine-Rus'." Three sections were established: historical and philosophical, philological, and mathematical-natural sciences-medical, each of which formed commissions. The organization of a library and museum was begun. In 1892, the society began issuing its primary publication, *Zapysky NTSh* (Memoirs of the NTSh, vol. 1 edited by Yuliian Tselevych, vols. 2–4 edited by Barvinsky). The first presidents were Tselevych (1892–93) and Barvinsky (1893–97).

The society's greatest period of development began in 1894 with the arrival of **Mykhailo Hrushevsky** in Lviv. He became director of the historical and philosophical section in 1894 and was elected president in 1897. In 1895, he became editor of the *Zapysky NTSh* and assumed control of all NTSh publishing activities. During his presidency, the society published approximately 800 volumes of scholarly works, including 112 volumes of *Zapysky*. Hrushevsky initiated a number of other periodicals, including *Khronika NTSh* (Chronicle of the NTSh, 74 vols., 1900–39), *Zbirnyk filolohichnoï sektsiï* (Collection of the Philological Section, 23 vols., 1898–1937), *Zbirnyk istorychno-filosofs'koï sektsiï NTSh* (Collection of the Historical and Philosophical Section of the NTSh, 17 vols., 1898–1934), *Zbirnyk matematychno-pryrodnycho-likars'koï sektsiï* (Collection of the Mathematical-Natural Sciences-Medical Section, 32 vols., 1897–1939), *Zherela do istoriï Ukraïny-Rusy* (Sources for the History of Ukraine-Rus', 22 vols., 1895–1929), and *Studiï z polia suspil'nykh nauk i statystyky* (Studies in the Social Sciences and Statistics, 5 vols., 1909–38).

Besides Hrushevsky, **Ivan Franko** and Volodymyr Hnatiuk were especially prominent in the NTSh. They headed various structures within the society, edited its serial and individual publications, notably the ***Literaturno-naukovyi visnyk***, and directed the Ukrainian Publishing Alliance. At their initiative, a reform of the society's statute was conducted in 1898, as a result of which the title of "full member" was bestowed solely on the basis of scholarly qualifications. The first academic body of NTSh scholars, elected in 1899, consisted of 32 individuals from both western and eastern Ukraine. In addition to Ukrainian scholars, 19 foreign scholars of international rank were elected to the society between 1903 and 1914, including Jan Baudouin de Courtenay, Vladimir Bekhterev, Aleksander Brückner, Alfred Jensen, Aleksandr Pypin, and Aleksei Shakhmatov.

Questions concerning the further improvement of the NTSh structure came to the fore between 1899 and 1913, leading to a protracted crisis that reflected ideological, political, and personal divergences among the society's full members. As a result of the crisis, Hrushevsky resigned the presidency in 1913. After his departure, the duties of vice president were assumed by **Stepan Tomashivsky** (1913–18) and Vasyl Shchurat (1919–21). During the interwar period, the society's presidents were Shchurat (1921–25), **Kyrylo Studynsky** (1925–32), Volodymyr Levytsky (1932–35), and Ivan Rakovsky (1935–39).

The scope of NTSh activities decreased considerably as the Polish authorities deprived the society of the right to publish Ukrainian school textbooks, one of its primary sources of revenue, and forbade it to organize university courses. The number of NTSh publications in the interwar period dropped to some 350 titles. In response to the ban on working with student youth, the NTSh led the establishment of the **Lviv (Underground) Ukrainian University**. It increased the number of its commissions, created research institutes, and established new serials: *Stara Ukraïna* (Old Ukraine, 1924–25), *S'ohochasne i mynule* (The Present and the Past, 1939), *Likars'kyi visnyk* (Medical Herald, 17 vols., 1920–39; published by the NTSh from 1926), and *Zbirnyk fiziohrafichnoï komisiï* (Collection of the Physiographic Commission, 7 vols., 1915–38). It continued to publish the *Zapysky NTSh,* which was divided into two series: *Pratsi istoryko-filosofs'koï sektsiï* (Works of the Historical and Philosophical Section, ed. **Ivan Krypiakevych**, 1924–37) and *Pratsi filolohichnoï sektsiï* (Works of the Philological Section, eds. Studynsky, 1925–29, Yaroslav Hordynsky, 1935, and Vasyl Simovych, 1937). The NTSh initiated two major publications: *Ukraïns'ka zahal'na entsyklopediia* (Ukrainian General Encyclopedia, 3 vols., ed. Rakovsky, 1935) and *Atlas Ukraïny i sumizhnykh zemel'* (Atlas of Ukraine and Adjacent Lands, 1937), prepared by the geographical commission, which was led by **Volodymyr Kubijovyč**. Foreign members elected to the NTSh included David Hilbert, Felix Klein, Max Planck (all 1924), and Albert Einstein (1929). Between 1899 and 1939, the society consisted of 333 full members (of whom approx. one-third were foreign members), belonging to three sections and 20 commissions. In addition, a Bacteriological and Chemical Institute, an Institute of Normal and Pathological Psychology, and three museums (cultural and historical, natural science, and historical and military) were affiliated with the NTSh. As of 1 January 1939, the NTSh library consisted of 73,000 titles in 200,000 volumes and was one of the finest collections of books on Ukrainian studies.

The society's output between 1873 and 1939 consisted of 1,172 volumes, including 943 volumes of serial scholarly publications. Its most important achievements were in the humanities: history (works of Hrushevsky and his students Ivan Dzhydzhora, **Myron Korduba**, Ivan Krevetsky, Krypiakevych, and Tomashivsky), philology and literary criticism (works of Franko, Ohonovsky, Studynsky, and Mykhailo Vozniak); ethnography, folklore, and art history (publications by Hnatiuk, **Filaret Kolessa**, Volodymyr Shukhevych, and Mykhailo Zubrytsky); anthropology (Rakovsky and **Fedir Vovk**), and bibliography (Volodymyr Doroshenko and Ivan Levytsky).

The NTSh made important contributions to the development of Ukrainian scientific terminology. Major achievements of NTSh members in the exact and natural sciences include **Ivan Puliui's** discovery of cathode rays (later named X-rays), **Ivan Horbachevsky's** synthesis of uric acid, and the contributions of **Stepan Rudnytsky** and Kubijovyč to the study of Ukraine's geography.

The NTSh maintained close ties with the **Ukrainian Academy of Sciences** (VUAN) in Kyiv, a result of the joint efforts of Studynsky and Hrushevsky, who became director of the VUAN chair of Ukrainian history (1924). Stanislav Dnistriansky, Hnatiuk, Horbachevsky, Kolessa, Shchurat, **Stepan Smal-Stotsky**, Studynsky, and Vozniak were elected members of the VUAN. In turn, **Dmytro Bahalii**, **Ahatanhel Krymsky**, **Dmytro Yavornytsky**, and **Volodymyr Vernadsky** became members of the NTSh. In 1927, Studynsky and **Ilarion Svientsitsky** participated in the Kharkiv conference that adopted a new Ukrainian orthography. This orthography was employed in all NTSh publications.

Stalin's **political terror** of the late 1920s and 1930s put an end to this cooperation. Those NTSh members who had moved to the **Ukrainian SSR** in search of employment or for ideological reasons suffered especially (Antin and Ivan Krushelnytsky and Stepan Rudnytsky were shot), and NTSh members were stripped of the rank of academician. In Lviv, this led to the resignation of Studynsky as president, since he had been accused of collaborating with the Soviet authorities.

After Soviet forces occupied western Ukraine, the NTSh was forced to dissolve (14 January 1940), and its institutions and property were turned over to the Academy of Sciences of the Ukrainian SSR (AN UkSSR). Some NTSh members saved themselves by escaping to the German zone of occupation (Rakovsky), while others found employment in the Lviv branch of the AN UkSSR. Several (Petro Franko, Studynsky, and Roman Zubyk) were executed by the NKVD.

During the German occupation, the renewal of the NTSh was forbidden, hence commission and section meetings took place secretly. Scholars from eastern Ukraine who took refuge in Galicia

(**Oleksander Ohloblyn**, Lev Okinshevych, and **Nataliia Polonska-Vasylenko**) participated in NTSh underground activities.

At the war's end, society members living in Germany's western zone of occupation renewed the activities of the NTSh (March 1947). Four centers were established in France, the United States, Canada, and Australia. They continued to publish the *Zapysky NTSh* (52 vols., 1947–88). Between 1949 and 1995, the society published the multi-volume *Entsyklopediia ukraïnoznavstva* (English ed.: *Encyclopedia of Ukraine*).

In October 1989, a congress of scholars renewed the NTSh in Lviv. Oleh Romaniv was elected president of the restored society, while Oleh Kupchynsky was elected academic secretary and editor of the *Zapysky NTSh*. The society began reprinting the Ukrainian-language encyclopedia and conducting scholarly conferences.

SHEVCHENKO, TARAS (25 February [9 March] 1814–26 February [10 March] 1861). Artist, poet, and national bard of Ukraine. Shevchenko was born in Moryntsi (now in Cherkasy oblast) into a large serf family. Orphaned at an early age, he served the precentor Petro Bohorsky, from whom he obtained his primary education. In 1828, he became a servant on the estate of Pavel Engelhardt, an adjutant to the governor of Vilnius. In early 1831, he arrived in St. Petersburg, where he studied with the painter Vasilii Shiriaev. A group of Shevchenko's friends raised enough funds to buy his freedom in 1838. He graduated from the St. Petersburg Academy of Fine Arts in 1845.

Shevchenko began writing poetry in 1836. He published the collection *Kobzar* (Bard) in St. Petersburg in 1840, followed by "Haidamaky" (The **Haidamakas**) in 1841. His first works were written in the spirit of **romanticism** and deal with typical romantic themes: the glorification of the heroic past and sorrow over the ignoble present, the sufferings and death of an abused young **peasant** girl, and celebration of the beauty of nature. Shevchenko, however, gave each of these themes a profoundly national character. The *Kobzar* and "Haidamaky" were well received and brought Shevchenko recognition as an uncommon talent. His subsequent works were strongly influenced by his trips to Ukraine (1843–46), during which he met the leading intellectuals **Mykhailo Maksymovych**, **Panteleimon Kulish**, and **Mykola Kostomarov**. Securing a temporary position with the Kyiv Archaeographic Commission (1845–46), Shevchenko traveled throughout Ukraine collecting ethnographic and historical materials and making sketches of architectural and archaeological monuments. The oppression that Shevchenko witnessed in Ukraine awakened a strong opposition to

Russian overlordship and serfdom. National-liberation motifs pervade the poems in the manuscript collection *Try lita* (Three Years), especially "Rozryta mohyla" (The Plundered Grave, 1843), "Son" (The Dream, 1844), and "Zapovit" (Testament, 1845). The "three-year" period was a turning point for Shevchenko, who subsequently became the generally acknowledged leader of the national revival and was elevated to the status of national bard and prophet.

Shevchenko's political views led to his association with the **Cyril and Methodius Brotherhood** in the spring of 1846. In 1847, he was arrested and, on the basis of "evidence" found in his collection *Try lita*, declared a dangerous political offender. Shevchenko was sentenced to exile as a private in the Orenburg special corps, with an admonition by Tsar Nicholas I that he be held "under the strictest surveillance and forbidden to write or paint." During the initial period of his exile, when the sentence was not strictly enforced, Shevchenko continued to draw and write poetry secretly, hiding the poems in his bootleg (the origin of his so-called bootleg books). Four of the books (1847, 1848, 1849, and 1850) have survived. In exile, Shevchenko wrote philosophical, scenic, and intimate lyrics, as well as poems on historical themes. As a painter he participated in military expeditions to the Aral Sea and the Karatau Mountains. In 1850, Shevchenko was transferred to the Novopetrovskoe Fortress (now Fort Shevchenko), where he endured the most severe period of his punishment. He also wrote 20 novellas in Russian, of which nine have survived. In 1856, he made a series of drawings titled *The Parable of the Prodigal Son* that allegorically reveal the brutality and inhumanity of the tsarist political regime. From April 1857 to July 1858, he kept a diary (*Zhurnal*).

Following the death of Nicholas I, Shevchenko was released from military service (1857) and resettled in St. Petersburg thanks to the efforts of his friends. The publication ban on his works was lifted in 1858 and a new edition of the *Kobzar* was published in 1860, followed by his *Bukvar' iuzhnorusskii* (South Russian Primer, 1861) for **Sunday schools**. The writings of Shevchenko's later period (1857–61) are characterized by a concern with philosophical and biblical themes, some of which (Mary in the poem "Mariia") are treated in an unorthodox manner. In July 1859, Shevchenko received permission to travel to Ukraine, where he planned to settle. However, he was arrested again and required to return to St. Petersburg. The exigencies of a long exile, anxiety over the fate of Ukraine, and illness led to his premature death in St. Petersburg.

Shevchenko played a unique role in the formation of modern Ukrainian identity. His poetic language, based on his local peasant dialect and fused with elements of Church Slavonic, the language of the **Cossack** chronicles, and neologisms, is distinguished by its natural and euphonic character. Having given Ukrainian the status of a literary **language**, Shevchenko also laid a solid foundation for modern Ukrainian **literature**. No less important is the political aspect of his work. His passionate poetry was not restricted to mourning for the heroic past, as in the work of other Ukrainian romantics, but also awakened national feeling and projected a vision of independence. Shevchenko laid the primary blame for the enslavement of Ukraine on Russia and its tsars. Never before had a Ukrainian intellectual raised his voice so powerfully in protest against Russian subjugation. Shevchenko rejected the prevailing **Little Russian mentality,** based on the notion of the indivisibility of Little and Great Rus' and loyalty to the tsar. One of Shevchenko's major achievements was the synthesis of two contradictory aspects of the Cossack tradition—the aspirations of the rank and file and the officer stratum. Shevchenko's sensitivity to social injustice and to the dignity of ordinary people came directly from his background as a serf and a peasant, but his intellectual growth owes much to the cultural traditions of the Ukrainian gentry. Every stratum of Ukrainian society found a reflection of its concerns in Shevchenko's poetry. His appeal for both national and social liberation, as well as his fusion of the national idea with humanist ideals, became the ideological cornerstone of the Ukrainian national movement.

Shevchenko's poetic genius and his life of martyrdom made him one of the most powerful symbols of the national movement. The transfer of his coffin from St. Petersburg to Ukraine and his reburial in Kaniv (10 [22] May 1861) became one of the first mass national manifestations in Ukrainian history. Commemorations of Shevchenko anniversaries took place even during the harshest anti-Ukrainian repressions of the imperial regime. The ban on their observance in 1914 led to mass demonstrations in **Kyiv** and other Ukrainian cities. Shevchenko's name was adopted by many Ukrainian civic and political organizations, including the **Brotherhood of Taras** and the **Shevchenko Scientific Society**. All Ukrainian political groups, in greater or lesser degree, trace their ideological genealogy to Shevchenko and appropriate him as a symbol.

Using Shevchenko to legitimize Soviet rule became a fundamental aspect of Bolshevik policy in Ukraine. Before the Revolution of 1917, Bolshevik leaders formally aligned themselves with Ukrainian commemorations dedicated to Shevchenko's memory. From 1917 to 1920, when the Bolsheviks were fighting for control of Ukraine, portraits of Shevchenko and publications of his works were seen as manifestations of Ukrainian "bourgeois" nationalism and were often destroyed. However, following the stabilization of the Soviet regime, Shevchenko's image was methodically introduced into Soviet ideology. He came to be treated as a "peasant poet," "revolutionary democrat," "atheist," and "bard of two fraternal (Ukrainian and Russian) peoples." The social concerns of his poetry were stressed at the expense of national motifs. New publications of his works were subject to censorship through the exclusion or distortion of fragments or entire poems with a strongly anti-Russian character. In order to identify Shevchenko as closely as possible with Soviet rule, the Shevchenko State Prize was established in 1961, and official celebrations of his anniversaries (1961, 1964, and 1979) were staged throughout the Soviet Union. The symbolic battle for Shevchenko became one of the primary sources of resistance to the Soviet system in Ukraine. After the declaration of Ukraine's independence, Shevchenko became one of its central symbols.

Shevchenko's creative legacy consists of his poetic works, collected under the title *Kobzar*, the drama *Nazar Stodolia*, fragments of two unfinished plays, nine novellas, a diary, an autobiography, approximately 250 letters, and 835 paintings, drawings, and sketches (including 150 portraits, of which 43 are self-portraits). The manuscripts of most of Shevchenko's works are housed at the Shevchenko Institute of Literature, **Ukrainian Academy of Sciences**. His works have been translated into approximately 100 languages. The most important posthumous publications of his works are: *Poeziï Tarasa Shevchenka* (The Poems of Taras Shevchenko; Lviv, 1867), *Kobzar* (in two volumes, Prague, 1876), *Kobzar* (Geneva, 1881), *Poeziï T. Shevchenka zaboroneni v Rosiï* (The Poems of T. Shevchenko Banned in Russia; Geneva, 1890), and *Kobzar* (Leipzig, 1918–21). There have been several publications of his complete works: in 16 volumes (Warsaw, 1934–38, of which 13 volumes appeared; in the 1950s, all 16 volumes were reprinted in the United States); in 10 volumes (Kyiv, 1939–64), in six volumes (Kyiv, 1963–64), and 12 volumes (Kyiv, 1991; not yet completed). The study of Shevchenko's life and work (*Shevchenkoznavstvo*) has become a distinct field of Ukrainian studies.

SHEVELOV, GEORGE YURII (17 December 1908–12 April 2002). Linguist, philologist, literary historian, and critic. Full member of the **Shevchenko Scientific Society** (from 1949) and the **Ukrainian Academy of Arts and Sciences** (from 1945; president in 1959–61, 1981–86), foreign member of the **Ukrainian Academy of Sciences** (from 1990). Born in Łomża, Poland, he moved to **Kharkiv** as a child. He graduated from the Kharkiv Institute of Professional Education in 1931 and lectured at the Ukrainian Institute of Journalism (1933–39). In 1939, Shevelov received his candidate of sciences degree from Kharkiv University, subsequently lecturing at the university and becoming head of the department of Ukrainian philology in 1941. In 1943, he moved to **Lviv** and later to Germany, lecturing at the **Ukrainian Free University** (UVU) from 1946 to 1949 and receiving his doctorate from the UVU in 1949. He lectured at the University of Lund (1950–52) and settled in the United States in 1952, lecturing in Russian and Ukrainian at Harvard University (1952–54) before joining the faculty of Columbia University (1954–77).

Shevelov wrote more than 800 works on Slavic philology, linguistics, and literary history. His primary areas of study were phonology, morphology, syntax, lexicology, etymology, literary languages, and onomastics. His research dealt with Old Church Slavonic, Belarusian, Macedonian, Polish, Russian, Slovak, Serbo-Croatian, and especially Ukrainian. Shevelov's major works include *A Historical Phonology of the Ukrainian Language* (1979; the most detailed phonological study of any Slavic language to date; Ukr. translation, 2002), *A Prehistory of Slavic: The Historical Phonology of Common Slavic* (1964), *Narys suchasnoï ukraïns'koï literaturnoï movy* (An Outline of the Contemporary Ukrainian Literary Language, 1951), *The Syntax of Modern Literary Ukrainian: The Simple Sentence* (1963), *Die ukrainische Schriftsprache, 1798–1965* (1966), and *The Ukrainian Language in the First Half of the Twentieth Century, 1900–1941: Its State and Status* (1989). Shevelov utilized a wide range of evidence to describe the phonological development of the Ukrainian **language**, the origins of which he placed in the seventh century, up to the completion of its formative phase in the 16th century. He rejected the theory of a common origin of the three East Slavic languages in the preliterate period. Instead, Shevelov maintained that the Ukrainian, Belarusian, and Russian languages developed from separate Kyiv-Polisia, Galicia-Podilia, Polatsk-Smolensk, Novgorod-Tver, and Murom-Riazan dialects.

Shevelov was president of the MUR literary association (1945–49) and a founder of the Slovo Association of Ukrainian Writers in Exile (1954). Writing under the pseudonym Yurii Sherekh, he published four collections of articles on **literature**: *Ne dlia ditei* (Not for Children, 1964), *Druha cherha: literatura, teatr, ideolohiï* (The Second Round: Literature, Theater, Ideologies, 1978), *Tretia storozha* (The Third Watch, 1991), and *Porohy i* *zaporizhzhia*, 3 vols. (The Rapids and Beyond, 1998). A bibliography of his work was published in 1998 (*Iurii Volodymyrovych Shevel'ov: Materiialy do bibliohrafii*), and his memoirs appeared in 2001.

SHISTDESIATNYKY. "The Sixtiers." Members of a movement for the revival of the Ukrainian **language** and culture in the late 1950s and 1960s (hence the name). During the **Khrushchev** thaw, the *shistdesiatnyky*, who included young writers, artists, and scholars, strove to revitalize national consciousness, opposed **Russification**, and sought to democratize civic life.

The *shistdesiatnyky* attempted to free themselves from the ideological strictures of socialist **realism**, stressing universal values and ideals. Their world view was influenced by Western culture, which sparked interest in their own traditions, notably those of the 1920s (*see* UKRAINIZATION). In their works the *shistdesiatnyky* raised issues suppressed during the Stalin era.

The best-known members of the movement were the poets and prose writers **Ivan Drach**, Volodymyr Drozd, **Ivan Dziuba**, Vasyl Holoborodko, Yevhen Hutsalo, Roman Ivanychuk, Ihor Kalynets, Vitalii Korotych, Lina Kostenko, Borys Mamaisur, Valerii Marchenko, Yurii Mushketyk, Mykola Rudenko, Valerii Shevchuk, **Vasyl Stus**, Yevhen Sverstiuk, **Ivan Svitlychny**, **Vasyl Symonenko**, Hryhir Tiutiunnyk, and Mykola Vinhranovsky, the visual artists **Alla Horska**, Veniamin Kushnir, Liudmyla Semykina, Halyna Sevruk, Panas Zalyvakha, and Viktor Zaretsky, the film directors **Serhii Paradzhanov**, Yurii Illienko, and Leonid Osyka, and the translators Hryhorii Kochur and Mykola Lukash.

In the early 1960s, two clubs of "creative youth," Suputnyk (Satellite) in Kyiv (headed by Les Taniuk) and Prolisok (Forest Clearing) in **Lviv** (headed by Mykhailo Kosiv), became centers of *shistdesiatnyky* activity, which included literary gatherings, commemorative evenings, and theatrical productions.

Beginning in 1963, the *shistdesiatnyky* were accused of ideological deviations, especially "Ukrainian bourgeois nationalism." The authorities began persecuting the movement in the press, at meetings of writers' and artists' unions, and at various gatherings. They forbade and broke up literary and artistic activities and closed the youth clubs. Most of the *shistdesiatnyky* were denied the opportunity to publish, dismissed from their positions, and had provocations staged against them.

Under pressure, some *shistdesiatnyky* acquiesced in the official line. Most, however, remained steadfast, circulating their works in the underground if they could not publish legally. After the repressions of the mid-1960s, a number of *shistdesiatnyky* became active in Ukraine's **dissident movement**, and some, most notably Drach and Dziuba, became important public figures in the 1990s.

SHMALHAUZEN, IVAN (11 [23] April 1884–7 October 1963). Biologist, zoologist, and theorist in evolutionary studies; full member of the **Ukrainian Academy of Sciences** (VUAN) from 1922 and the **USSR** Academy of Sciences (AN SSSR) from 1935. Born in **Kyiv**, he graduated from Kyiv University in 1907 and was a professor there from 1921 to 1941. He also directed the VUAN Institute of Zoology (1930–41) and the AN SSSR Institute of Animal Morphology in Moscow (1935–48). In 1938, he was appointed professor of Darwinism at Moscow University, where he worked on a modern evolutionary theory that integrated systematics, morphology, embryology, and population genetics. For criticizing Trokhym Lysenko's "creative Darwinism," Shmalhauzen was removed from his posts in 1948 and worked at the AN SSSR Institute of Zoology, studying the origin of terrestrial vertebrates and developing cybernetic approaches to evolutionary theory.

SHUKHEVYCH, ROMAN (17 July 1907–5 March 1950). Nom de guerre: Taras Chuprynka. Political and military figure; commander in chief of the **Ukrainian Insurgent Army** (UPA, 1943–50). He was born in Krakovets, **Galicia**, the son of a district judge. Shukhevych graduated from a branch of the **Lviv** Academic Gymnasium (1925). In 1922, he joined the **Plast** youth organization, and in the following year he became a member of the **Ukrainian Military Organization** (UVO). Shukhevych studied at the Polytechnical Institute in Gdańsk, Poland (1925–26), and enrolled in the architecture department of the Lviv Polytechnical Institute (1926). In 1928–29, he served in the Polish army. He joined the **Organization of Ukrainian Nationalists** (OUN) in 1929 and headed its combat division in **western Ukraine** (1930–34). In that capacity, Shukhevych planned the assassinations of the Diet deputy Tadeusz Hołówko (1931), Police Commissioner Emilian Czechowski (1932), and Aleksei Mailov, the Soviet consul in Lviv (1933). In 1934, he was arrested in connection with the assassination of the Polish minister of internal affairs, Bronisław Pieracki, and imprisoned at the Bereza Kartuzka concentration camp. Tried in 1936, he was incarcerated in Lviv until late 1937. In the autumn of 1938, Shukhevych became an organizer of the **Carpathian Sich**. In 1939–40, he was regional leader of the OUN in the **Generalgouvernement**, a member of the OUN leadership (**Bandera** faction), and director of its communications with the Ukrainian lands.

At the beginning of **World War II**, Shukhevych was political officer and OUN(B) liaison of the Nachtigall battalion, organized in cooperation with German military circles, which entered Lviv on 30 June 1941. Shukhevych was appointed deputy minister of defense in the short-lived **Ukrainian State Administration**. The Germans merged Nachtigall with the Roland battalion, and Shukhevych served as deputy commander until most of the officers were arrested by the Gestapo in January 1943. He went underground and became head of the military division of the OUN(B) leadership (March 1943) and head of the leadership itself (August). In November, he was appointed commander in chief of the UPA. From July 1944, Shukhevych was chairman of the General Secretariat of the **Supreme Ukrainian Liberation Council**. He was killed at Bilohorshcha near Lviv in combat with Soviet secret police units.

SHULHYN, OLEKSANDER (30 July 1889–4 March 1960). Civic and political figure, diplomat, historian, and full member of the **Shevchenko Scientific Society** (from 1948). He was born in Sokhvyne, **Poltava** gubernia. The son of the historian Yakiv Shulhyn, he was descended from a **Cossack officer** family. His uncle, Vasilii Shulgin, edited the Russian newspaper *Kievlianin* (The Kyivan) and was bitterly opposed to the Ukrainian movement. Shulhyn entered the natural sciences (1908) and historical and philological (1910) departments of St. Petersburg University, remaining there after graduation (1915) to prepare for a professorship. In July 1917, he was delegated by the **Ukrainian Democratic Radical Party** to the **Ukrainian Central Rada** and served as general secretary for minority affairs until January 1918. Shulhyn was an organizer of the Congress of the Peoples of Russia in **Kyiv** (September 1917), where he advocated autonomy for Ukraine, "with no artificial reduction of its territory," within a federalized Russia. Late in 1917 he became acting minister of foreign affairs and sought unsuccessfully to obtain recognition of the **Ukrainian People's Republic** (UNR) by the Entente.

In 1918, Shulhyn was the ambassador of the **Ukrainian State** to Bulgaria; in 1919, the **Directory** appointed him a member of its delegation to the Paris peace conference. In the following year, he was a member of the UNR delegation at the First Assembly of the League of Nations in Geneva and headed the extraordinary Ukrainian diplomatic mission in Paris (1921). During the interwar period, Shulhyn was a member of the UNR government-in-exile. He was a professor at the **Ukrainian Free University** and the Ukrainian Higher Pedagogical Institute in Prague (1923–27). From 1929 to 1939, he was chairman of the Supreme Emigration Council in Paris. After **World War II**, Shulhyn founded and directed the Ukrainian

Academic Society in Paris (1946–60) and was an organizer and vice president (1952–60) of the International Free Academy of Arts and Sciences. From 1952, he was deputy chairman of the Shevchenko Scientific Society in Europe. He died in Paris and was buried in Sarcelles.

Shulhyn's scholarly work dealt with modern West European history, and his political writings concerned the history of the Ukrainian national-liberation movement.

SHUMSKY, OLEKSANDER (2 December 1890–18 September 1946). Communist political leader. He was born in Borova Rudnia, **Kyiv** region, into a poor peasant family. In 1908, he joined the **Ukrainian Social Democratic Spilka**. In 1917, Shumsky became a member of the Central Committee of the **Ukrainian Party of Socialist Revolutionaries** and of the **Ukrainian Central Rada**. Along with other leftist Socialist Revolutionaries, Shumsky planned a coup to establish Soviet rule in Ukraine (January 1918), for which he was arrested. In May 1918, he became a leader of the **Borotbists**. He fought both the **Ukrainian State** and the **Directory**. In 1919, he was commissar for **education** in the Soviet Ukrainian government of **Khristian Rakovsky**. Shumsky joined the **Communist Party of Ukraine** (CPU) in March 1920 and was elected to its Politburo and Orgburo. In the same year, he became commissar for internal affairs, and in 1921 he was the ambassador of the **Ukrainian SSR** to Poland. Following his return to Ukraine, Shumsky edited the leading journal *Chervonyi shliakh* (Red Path, 1923–34) and directed the CPU bureau of agitation and propaganda. From September 1924 to February 1927, as commissar for education in the Ukrainian SSR, he actively implemented the **Ukrainization** policy.

During a meeting with Stalin (April 1926), Shumsky sought the removal of **Lazar Kaganovich** as general secretary of the CC CPU and his replacement with a Ukrainian, **Vlas Chubar**. Stalin responded with a letter to Kaganovich and other members of the CPU Politburo in which he reproved Kaganovich for "excessive administration" and charged Shumsky with forcing Ukrainization on the Russian proletariat, as well as ignoring the danger that Ukrainization might turn into a struggle against Moscow and Russian culture. Shumsky became identified with a national-communist opposition popularly known as "Shumskyism." Under the pressure of the campaign mounted against him, Shumsky acknowledged his "errors" at a plenum of the CC CPU in 1926. Dismissed as commissar for education in 1927, he was transferred to Moscow. The circumstances surrounding Shumsky's removal were hotly debated by the **Communist Party of Western Ukraine**, leading to a split in the party.

Shumsky was arrested on 13 May 1933 on a trumped-up charge of membership in the so-called Ukrainian Military Organization. He was sentenced to 10 years' imprisonment in a forced-labor camp and spent the years 1933–35 on the Solovets Islands. He frequently appealed his case to ruling bodies and individual leaders, including Stalin. In December 1935, his imprisonment was commuted to exile in Krasnoiarsk, and Shumsky staged a hunger strike in an attempt to win full exoneration. Following the completion of his sentence (13 May 1943), he was obliged to remain in Krasnoiarsk because of illness. He worked on the monograph *Malorosy* (Little Russians), a condemnation of Ukrainian servility to Russian imperialism. He destroyed the text after deciding to commit suicide as a protest against the failure of his attempts at vindication. Shumsky wrote a letter to Stalin on 18 October 1945 informing him of this decision. His suicide attempt was unsuccessful. According to the memoirs of the senior secret police official Pavel Sudoplatov, published in 1994, Shumsky was poisoned on the orders of **Nikita Khrushchev**, and the cause of death was made to simulate heart failure.

SHUMUK, DANYLO (30 December 1914–21 May 2004). Political dissident. Born in Boremshchyna, **Volhynia**, Shumuk joined the **Communist Party of Western Ukraine**, for which he was sentenced in Kovel by a Polish court to eight years' imprisonment (1935). He was amnestied in May 1939. In May 1941, Shumuk was conscripted into a Red Army penal battalion; following his capture by the invading Germans, he spent several months in a concentration camp near **Poltava**. Shumuk escaped and returned to Volhynia, where he joined the **Ukrainian Insurgent Army**. He was captured by the Soviets in February 1945 and tried at a closed court-martial in Rivne, which sentenced him to death, commuted to 20 years' imprisonment. He was incarcerated in Norilsk, Taishet, and other Siberian camps, as well as in Vladimir Prison. Shumuk was released in 1956 after a review of his case. Rearrested in November 1957, he was charged with "anti-Soviet agitation and propaganda" after refusing to become a KGB informer and given a 10-year sentence (May 1958), which he served in Siberian labor camps. Upon his release in 1967, he began writing his memoirs, which led to another arrest in January 1972. In July of that year, he was tried in Lviv and sentenced to 10 years in strict-regime labor camps (in Mordovia and Perm oblast) and five years' exile (in Kazakhstan).

Shumuk renounced his Soviet citizenship in 1973, joined the **Ukrainian Helsinki Group** in 1979, and participated in numerous strikes and campaigns for recognition of political prisoner status. He also demanded the right to join his relatives in Canada. As a result of lengthy efforts on Shumuk's behalf by the Ukrainian **diaspora**, Amnesty International (AI), and the Canadian government, he was allowed to emigrate in April 1987 after completing his sentence. Dedicated to the ideal of an independent, democratic Ukraine, Shumuk was the longest-serving political prisoner in the history of the **USSR**. AI identified him as the world's senior prisoner of conscience. His memoirs, *Za skhidnim obriiem* (Beyond the Eastern Horizon, 1974; rev. ed. 1983), were published in English translation under the title *Life Sentence* (1984). A third edition, *Perezhyte i peredumane* (My Life and Thoughts in Retrospect), appeared in Kyiv in 1998. A documentary film, *Danylo Shumuk*, directed by Mykola Mashchenko, was released in 1994.

SHYPYNTSI LAND (Ukr. *Shypyns'ka zemlia*). Historical name for an autonomous polity in **Bukovyna**. Its beginnings have been dated to the mid-13th or mid-14th century; the first documentary mention is dated to 1359. Its territory was bounded by the Kolochyn River in the west, the Dnister Valley in the north, the Carpathian Mountains and Seret River in the south, and the Kaiutyn River in the east (roughly equivalent to present-day Chernivtsi oblast). Its political center was Shypyntsi (now in Kitsman raion, Chernivtsi oblast). The Shypyntsi land preserved the basic features of the old Rus' social order, including administrative division into *volosti* centered around Khotyn, Tsetsyna, and Khmeliv. It lay on the trade route between **Lviv** and Suceava, was home to large fairs, and had more than 100 settlements in the 14th–15th centuries. In the mid-15th century, the territory came under the control of the Moldavian Principality. The name "Shypyntsi land" was last used in documents in 1444. Owing to the prevalence of beech (*buk*) forests in the region, the Shypyntsi land and surrounding areas came to be known as Bukovyna.

SIAN REGION (Ukr. *Posiannia* or *Zasiannia*). A region situated on both sides of the Sian (Pol. San) River north of the **Lemko region** and the town of Sanok (Ukr. Sianik) along the southeastern Polish border with Ukraine. Its major centers include the towns of Przemyśl (Ukr. Peremyshl), Jarosław, and Sanok. The region was part of **Kyivan Rus'** and the Principality of **Galicia-Volhynia** until it was incorporated into Poland (1340–1772) and the Habsburg Monarchy (1772–1918). In 1918, the region became part of the **Western Ukrainian People's Republic** and, after its demise, was annexed by Poland (1923–39). The Molotov-Ribbentrop Pact of 1939 divided the region along the Sian River between Germany (in the **Generalgouvernement**) and the Soviet Union. In 1941, the entire region was occupied by the Germans; it was reoccupied by the Soviets in 1944. As a result of the Polish-Soviet treaty signed on 16 August 1945, the region was returned to Poland.

The population of the Sian region underwent extensive Polonization from the 15th century, and the boundary between Polish and Ukrainian ethnic territory was pushed gradually eastward, with Ukrainians becoming a minority. In 1945–46, most of the Ukrainian population was resettled to the **Ukrainian SSR**. In the course of **Operation Vistula** (1947), the remaining Ukrainian inhabitants were deported and dispersed throughout northwestern Poland. Today, there are very few Ukrainians in the Sian region.

SICH. Military and political organization of the Ukrainian **Cossacks**. It emerged as a result of the rapid colonization of the middle and lower reaches of the Dnipro River in the mid-16th century. The term is derived from the system of barricades used to defend fortified Cossack settlements (*zasika* or *sich*). Its first organizers were the *ukhodnyky* (foragers) engaged in fishing and hunting beyond the Dnipro Rapids.

The history of the Sich until the mid-16th century is largely legendary, and it is not until 1552, when the Sich moved to the island of Mala **Khortytsia**, that reliable historical information becomes available (*see* VYSHNEVETSKY, DMYTRO). The transformation of the Sich into a military and political formation was necessitated by the constant threat of **Tatar** and Ottoman incursions into the Cossack lands.

In the broader sense, the Sich denotes all Cossack lands, while in the narrower sense it refers to the central Cossack settlement and administrative base, called the *kish*. As the primary settlement, the Sich was well fortified. The center of the fortress was occupied by a square, with the Church of the Holy Protection in the middle. The buildings that housed the Cossacks stood in a semicircle on the square. They consisted of two long barracks, officers' buildings, the chancellery, armory, and storerooms. The fortress was surrounded by a suburb populated by Cossack tradesmen. For a variety of reasons, the Sich was moved to different locations: Khortytsia, Tomakivka, Bazavluk, Mykytyn Rih, Chortomlyk, Kamianka, Oleshky, Pidpilna (**New Sich**), and even across the Danube. The broader Sich territory was divided into eight *palanky* (districts). The Sich was governed by customary law, according to which all Cossacks were equal regardless of origin or rank. Its supreme authority was the **Cossack council**, which elected the officer staff and decided important matters. The Sich was headed by an elected **hetman**, known after 1648 as the *kish* otaman, who enjoyed unrestricted power and authority but could be deposed by the

Cossack council at any time. To expedite the administrative process, there was also an officer council. The executive body of the Sich consisted of the *kish* (camp) otaman (initially the hetman), chancellor, judge, and *osavul* (aide-de-camp). All positions were elective.

After 1648, the political center of Ukraine shifted to the **Hetmanate**. At various times, Zaporizhia was either overshadowed by the Hetmanate or interfered in Hetmanate affairs, leading to chronic antagonism between the two centers.

In early 1709, the Zaporozhian Cossacks led by *kish* otaman Kost Hordiienko supported Hetman **Ivan Mazepa** in his alliance with Sweden. In retaliation, Russian forces destroyed the Sich in May 1709. The Zaporozhians who escaped established a Sich under an Ottoman protectorate on the Kamianka River (1709–11) and later at Oleshky near the Dnipro estuary (1711–33). In 1734, the Zaporozhians returned to a Russian protectorate, since Russia was preparing for a war with the Ottoman Porte in which it wished to enlist the Cossacks. The Russian government restricted Zaporozhian freedoms in many ways, especially by establishing foreign colonies such as **New Serbia** and **Sloviano-Serbia**. The Hetmanate was gradually absorbed into the Russian Empire, leaving Zaporizhia as the last bastion of Cossack autonomy. After the signing of the Treaty of Küçük Kaynarca (1774) with the Ottomans, Gen. Petr Tekeli's armies surrounded the Sich on 4 (15) June 1775 and destroyed it. The last *kish* otaman, Petro Kalnyshevsky, and the Cossack officers were arrested and exiled. Those Zaporozhians who managed to escape established the **Transdanubian Sich** on Ottoman territory.

SICHYNSKY, MYROSLAV (11 October 1887–16 March 1979). Civic figure. Born in Chernykhivtsi, **Galicia**, into the family of a priest, he studied at the Kolomyia and Peremyshl (Przemyśl) gymnasiums, as well as at the philosophy departments of the universities of Vienna and **Lviv**. He was a member of the **Ukrainian Social Democratic Party**. In reprisal for election fraud and violence committed against Ukrainian **peasants** by local Polish authorities, Sichynsky assassinated Andrzej Potocki, the viceroy of Lviv (12 April 1908). Although no political grouping claimed responsibility for the assassination, it was approved by most Ukrainian activists, with the notable exception of Metropolitan **Andrei Sheptytsky**, who condemned it as an act of political terror. Sichynsky was arrested and sentenced to death; his sentence was later commuted to 20 years' imprisonment. Aided by Dmytro Vitovsky and Mykola Tsehlynsky, he escaped from prison (1911) to Norway and Sweden, eventually settling in the United States. He was a founder of the

Ukrainian Federation of the Socialist Party and edited its weeklies *Robitnyk* (Worker, 1914–17) and *Narod* (People, 1917). In 1920, he founded the Oborona Ukrainy (Defense of Ukraine) organization and was president of the Ukrainian Fraternal Association (1933–41). Sichynsky adopted communist views, visiting the **Ukrainian SSR** in 1928 and during the **Khrushchev** thaw. He died in Westland, Michigan. His memoirs, recorded by **Mykyta Shapoval**, are titled *Zi spomyniv Myroslava Sichyns'koho* (From the Recollections of Myroslav Sichynsky, 1928).

SIKORSKY, IGOR (13 [25] May 1889–26 October 1972). Pioneer of aviation technology, engineer, and designer. A native of **Kyiv**, Sikorsky studied at the Kyiv Polytechnical Institute (1908–12). As a student, he made some of the first helicopter designs and built a series of biplanes. Sikorsky was a member of the pioneering Kyiv Aeronautical Society, and on 29 December 1911 he set a world speed record (111 km/h) for a loaded airplane (3 passengers) using the S-6, a plane of his own design. He achieved international recognition in 1913 for his design of the first multiengine aircraft. In 1919, he emigrated to the United States, where he developed a series of aircraft that set world records for speed, range, and payload. In 1939, Sikorsky perfected the design of the first successful helicopter in the world. The Sikorsky Helicopter Co. eventually became the world leader in military and civilian helicopter design. Sikorsky died in Easton, Connecticut.

SIRKO, IVAN (ca. 1610–1 [11] August 1680). Political and military figure; *kish* otaman of the **Zaporozhian Sich**. He participated in the **Khmelnytsky Uprising** (1648–57). From 1658 to 1660, he was colonel of Vinnytsia. Sirko often changed political affiliations. In 1659, he openly opposed the Polish orientation of Hetman **Ivan Vyhovsky**. Sirko supported **Yurii Khmelnytsky** until he signed the Treaty of Slobodyshche with Poland (1660). Sirko participated in Zaporozhian campaigns to the **Crimea** (1660–61). Between 1663 and 1670, he was elected *kish* otaman eight successive times. In 1663, he organized two large-scale campaigns against Perekop. In January 1664, he fought together with Muscovite forces against the **Right-Bank** hetman **Pavlo Teteria** and Polish armies commanded by Stefan Czarniecki. Sirko initially supported **Petro Doroshenko**, but after the signing of an alliance between the **Hetmanate** and the Ottoman Empire, he withdrew his support. In 1668, he fomented an anti-Muscovite uprising in **Sloboda Ukraine**. Because of his connections with Stepan Razin, the leader of a peasant rebellion in Muscovy, Sirko was arrested and exiled to Tobolsk. With the increased threat of invasion by the Turks and **Tatars**, he was released through the efforts of the Zaporozhians and even the Polish government (summer 1673). Returning to the Sich, Sirko led several campaigns against Tatar strongholds (Ochakiv, Izmail, Perekop). In 1676, when Doroshenko resigned, Sirko accepted the hetman's insignia from him. Sirko fought Ottoman and Tatar forces and Yurii Khmelnytsky's units during the Chyhyryn campaigns (1677–78). He died at the Hrushivka homestead (now Illinka) and was buried near Kapulivka (now in Dnipropetrovsk oblast). Sirko was celebrated as a military leader in numerous Cossack dumas, folk songs, and legends.

SKOROPADSKY, IVAN (1646–3 [14] July 1722). **Hetman** of **Left-Bank Ukraine** (1708–22). Descended from a **Cossack officer** family, he was born in Uman and was well educated. In 1674, following the destruction of his native town by the Ottoman Turks, Skoropadsky moved to Left-Bank Ukraine. He was military chancellor to Hetman **Ivan Samoilovych** and carried out important missions to the tsarist government for him (1675–76). Later, Skoropadsky served as chancellor of the Chernihiv regiment (1681–94), general standard-bearer (1698), general aide-de-camp (from 1701), and colonel of the Starodub regiment (1706–8). He participated in the Crimean campaigns of 1687 and 1689. Despite his long association with **Ivan Mazepa**, Skoropadsky fought on the Russian side in the **Battle of Poltava** (1709). In November 1708, at a **Cossack council** in Hlukhiv, he was elected hetman, but Peter I never fully trusted him and delayed confirming him in office until 1710.

Skoropadsky prepared new articles of agreement between the **Hetmanate** and Muscovy (Reshetylivka Articles of 1709), intended to strengthen the Hetmanate's autonomy, but they were not ratified by Peter I. During Skoropadsky's administration, the Muscovite government considerably reduced the powers of the Hetmanate. In 1709, a Russian resident, Andrei Izmailov, was assigned to supervise and control the hetman's activities. Ten Muscovite dragoon regiments were stationed in the Hetmanate at the expense of the local population. Peter appointed Russian voevodas and magnates as general and regimental Cossack officers. Lands in Left-Bank Ukraine were redistributed among tsarist officials and personal favorites. Numerous mobilizations of Cossacks took place for military engagements in the Northern War (1700–21), as well as for heavy labor in the construction of fortresses, canals (Ladoga, Volga-Don), and the new capital, St. Petersburg. The Hetmanate was forbidden to trade with the **Zaporozhian Cossacks** and Western

Europe, and the development of Ukrainian industry was curbed; moreover, the tsarist government discriminated against Ukrainian culture and the church. Books published in a Ukrainian version of Slavic or in Middle Ukrainian could now be issued only in Russian, following a newly standardized Russian orthography (1720). In order to establish definitive control over the Hetmanate, the tsar created the **Little Russian Collegium** (1722). Skoropadsky was dissatisfied with these centralist policies, but, as one of the greatest landowners in the Hetmanate, had a large stake in the established order. He died in July 1722 and was buried at the Hamaliivka Monastery near Hlukhiv.

SKOROPADSKY, PAVLO (16 May 1873–26 or 28 April 1945). Military commander and **hetman** of Ukraine (1918); émigré political leader. He was a scion of the Skoropadsky **Cossack officer** family. Born in Wiesbaden, Germany, he grew up on his family's estate in Trostianets, Chernihiv region, and studied at the St. Petersburg Page Corps cadet school (1886–93). Skoropadsky served in a cavalry guard regiment of the Russian army and fought in the Russo-Japanese War (1904–5), during which he commanded a company of the Trans-Baikal Cossack Army. He was awarded St. George's Arms for bravery in battle. Subsequently he became an aide-de-camp to Tsar Nicholas II (December 1905) and led a cavalry regiment in the tsar's House Guard (from April 1911).

At the outbreak of **World War I**, Skoropadsky commanded the First Brigade of the First Cavalry Guard Division. In 1916, he became a lieutenant-general. He was appointed commander of the 34th Army Corps, stationed in Ukraine (January 1917). On the orders of Gen. Lavr Kornilov (July 1917), Skoropadsky began Ukrainizing the corps, which subsequently prevented pro-Bolshevik units from attacking Ukrainian territory. At the first congress of **Free Cossacks**, Skoropadsky was elected honorary otaman (commander, October 1917). The **Ukrainian Central Rada's** appointment of Yurii Kapkan as commander in chief angered Skoropadsky, who regarded Kapkan as an "extremely suspicious adventurist." He resigned in December 1917, relinquishing command of the Ukrainian Corps to Gen. Yakiv Handziuk.

Skoropadsky's dissatisfaction with the Rada was exploited by the Austro-German forces that occupied Ukraine after the **Treaty of Brest-Litovsk**. Having decided to overthrow the Rada because it was inefficient in supplying the foodstuffs promised in the treaty, the Germans sought candidates to lead a new government. On 26 April 1918, Skoropadsky met with the German chief of staff in Ukraine, Gen. Wilhelm Groener, to discuss conditions of German support for a coup d'état. The Germans demanded the unlimited export of food, manufactures, and other supplies from Ukraine to fuel their war effort; a veto on appointments to the government and control over the Ukrainian army; and the curbing of **peasant** revolts. Skoropadsky accepted these conditions, and the coup was carried out on 29 April with the support of German troops.

Skoropadsky was proclaimed hetman of Ukraine at the All-Ukrainian Agrarian Congress (29 April), composed of middle and large landowners opposed to the Rada. He immediately issued a "Charter to the Ukrainian People" that announced the dissolution of the Central Rada and its land committees, dismissed all ministers, annulled the laws and decrees of the General Secretariat and the Provisional Government on socialization, restored rights of private property, and affirmed the right of smallholders to acquire land. Skoropadsky also issued the "Laws on the Provisional State Order of Ukraine," according to which the **Ukrainian People's Republic** was replaced by the **Ukrainian State**. All executive and legislative power passed to the hetman until the convocation of the Ukrainian Soim (Diet). The hetman was empowered to appoint the otaman (premier) of the Council of Ministers. Skoropadsky became commander in chief of the Ukrainian army and navy.

Skoropadsky's assumption of the traditional Cossack leader's title of hetman indicated his desire to establish a regime based on historical tradition. He revived the designation of "Cossack" for the well-to-do peasants whom he regarded as his base of support and officially restored Cossackdom (16 October); he also accorded primacy to the Orthodox Church (although freedom of religion was guaranteed in the charter). The policies of the Hetman government, headed by the wealthy landowner **Fedir Lyzohub**, were intended to restore the prerevolutionary socioeconomic order and defend established interests (landowners, industrialists, and financiers). Most of the ministers were Russian (Constitutional Democrats and Octobrists); the only prominent Ukrainian was the minister of foreign affairs, **Dmytro Doroshenko**. As a result, former supporters of the Central Rada denounced the new government as reactionary and non-Ukrainian. They formed the **Ukrainian National-State Union** to oppose the Hetmanate (21 May 1918; later renamed the **Ukrainian National Union** [UNS]).

The Ukrainian State maintained diplomatic relations with the Central Powers and sent missions to Switzerland, Sweden, Norway, and Romania. It stabilized relations with the Don and Kuban regions and claimed the **Crimea** for Ukraine, conducting an economic blockade to obtain the peninsula's submission. Desultory peace negotiations with Russia yielded no positive result. Skoropadsky traveled to Berlin to meet with German leaders, including Kaiser Wilhelm II (4–17 September 1918).

The most enduring achievements of the short-lived Ukrainian State lay in the fields of **education** and scholarship, a sector of Skoropadsky's administration in which Ukrainian scholars were active. The government adopted a law concerning the mandatory teaching of Ukrainian **language, literature,** history, and law in secondary schools, and approximately 150 Ukrainian gymnasiums were opened. National scholarly, cultural, and educational institutions were established, including the State Ukrainian University in **Kyiv,** the Kamianets-Podilskyi Ukrainian University, the State Ukrainian Archives, the National Art Gallery, the Ukrainian Historical Museum, the Ukrainian National Library, and the Ukrainian National Theater. In November, Skoropadsky announced the founding of the **Ukrainian Academy of Sciences** and appointed its first 12 academicians.

The Hetman government, under constant pressure from the Germans to increase production, failed to establish social peace. Property and land were forcibly returned to previous owners, peasant committees dissolved, and the 12-hour workday introduced. Such measures provoked vehement resistance from peasants and workers, which was crushed by punitive expeditions of the National Guard, units of the German and Austrian armies, and Russian officer legions.

Attempting to stabilize the situation in the autumn of 1918, with the military prospects of the Central Powers clearly in decline, Skoropadsky negotiated with representatives of the UNS (**Volodymyr Vynnychenko**, Andrii Nikovsky, and Fedir Shvets), who insisted on socialist agrarian reform, a democratically elected legislature, and the inclusion of opposition forces in a reformed government. As a result, Lyzohub formed a new government including five members of the UNS: Andrii Viazlov, Volodymyr Leontovych, Oleksander Lototsky, Maksym Slavinsky, and Petro Stebnytsky (24 October 1918). This did not satisfy the UNS, which continued to plot an insurrection. When a government majority opposed the convocation of a Ukrainian National Congress, the UNS representatives resigned. Skoropadsky established a new government led by Sergei Gerbel and issued a charter announcing a federation between Ukraine and a future non-Bolshevik Russia (14 November 1918). This action, intended to curry favor with the Entente, set off the anti-hetman insurrection led by the **Directory**.

Skoropadsky held Kyiv for another month, thanks to German troops and Russian detachments, before resigning on 14 December 1918. After the Directory's forces entered Kyiv, he departed secretly for Berlin, settling in Wannsee. He belonged to the Ukrainian Union of Agrarian Statists but left because of disagreements with **Viacheslav Lypynsky** and founded the Union of Hetmanite Statists. Skoropadsky organized Hetmanite centers in various countries and helped establish the Ukrainian Scientific Institute in Berlin (1926). During **World War II**, he sought the release of the nationalist leaders **Stepan Bandera**, **Andrii Melnyk**, and **Yaroslav Stetsko**, among others, from German concentration camps. He was mortally wounded during an Allied air raid on Plattling station near Munich and was buried in Wiesbaden.

SKOVORODA, HRYHORII (22 November [3 December] 1722–29 October [9 November] 1794). Philosopher and poet. He was born in Chornukhy, **Poltava** region, and educated at the **Kyiv Mohyla Academy** (1734–53, with two interruptions). Skovoroda sang in the court capella of Empress Elizabeth in St. Petersburg (1741–44), served as music director for the Russian mission to Hungary (1745–50), and taught poetics at the Pereiaslav Collegium in 1751. In 1754 and from 1755 to 1759, he worked as a private tutor to Vasyl Tomara in the Pereiaslav region. He was a teacher of poetics, rhetoric, and Greek at the **Kharkiv** Collegium (1759–69) but was forced to abandon teaching because of disagreements with his superiors. During the final 25 years of his life, he roamed throughout Ukraine, spent time at the estates of his friends, wrote, and propagated his philosophical views. Skovoroda began writing poetry in Ukrainian and Latin that became the basis of the collection *Sad bozhestvennykh pesnei* (Garden of Divine Songs, written 1753–85). Shortly before his death, he compiled a list of his works (18 original works and seven translations, of which four have not been found). He died in Pan-Ivanivka (now Skovorodynivka in Kharkiv oblast). Skovoroda's works, written in the **baroque** dialogue genre, were published for the first time on the centenary of his death in 1894.

Skovoroda studied the Bible throughout his life, regarding it as the encoded wisdom of many generations. For this reason, he wrote on aphorisms from the Bible, striving to reveal its recondite symbolic world. On this basis, Skovoroda developed his concept of two natures and three worlds. The two natures, visible and invisible, are present in every object or phenomenon. The visible nature is apparent, but the invisible nature is the true essence, hidden from the superficial observer and perceptible only to the inquiring mind. The secrets of this hidden nature are accessible only to spiritually developed individuals who are not satisfied with transient material pleasures and strive instead to understand something higher, eternal, and immortal. In Skovoroda's opinion, the eternal exists in every object, but first and foremost in the human soul. Skovoroda did not acknowledge the superficial and ostentatious attributes of piety, believing that majestic rituals and magnificently decorated churches concealed a shallow religiosity.

Of primary importance to Skovoroda was the acknowledgement of God as the foundation of humanity, tolerance, morality, honesty, and justice. All these features are characteristic of man, whom Skovoroda compared to God. The three worlds in Skovoroda's teachings are the Cosmos, the Bible, and man. The Cosmos or Macrocosm is encoded in the symbolic world, the Bible, and is to be comprehended by man, the Microcosm. The Enlightenment ideal of progressive mastery over nature through reason and education was alien to Skovoroda, who stressed cultivation of the heart and soul. He developed the idea of "congenial labor," based on the Socratic notion of self-knowledge and uncovering one's inclinations and talents. A person will attain happiness only when he recognizes his invisible nature or essence, assumes his assigned place in the social organism, and takes satisfaction in the fruits of his labor. Skovoroda believed that this path would lead not only to individual happiness but also to the betterment of society as a whole.

Skovoroda's works, preserved in numerous manuscripts, have been published repeatedly in the original (Skovoroda wrote in a bookish Ukrainian, as well as in Latin and Greek) and in translation. On the 250th anniversary of his birth, his complete works were published in two volumes, as well as in Russian translation. A complete modern Ukrainian translation of his works first appeared in 1994. Besides *Sad bozhestvennykh pesnei*, his works include a collection of fables (*Basni Kharkovskiia* [Kharkiv Fables]), philosophical tracts and dialogues, and translations from Cicero, Plutarch, Horace, and Ovid. A memorial museum dedicated to Skovoroda was opened in Skovorodynivka in 1972 and a monument to him was erected in **Kyiv** in 1977.

SKRYPNYK, MSTYSLAV (10 April 1898–11 June 1993). Secular name: Stepan. Head of the **Ukrainian** Autocephalous **Orthodox Church** (UAOC) and patriarch of **Kyiv** and all Ukraine. Born in **Poltava**, a nephew of **Symon Petliura**, he graduated from the First Classical Gymnasium in Poltava and participated in clandestine Ukrainian youth groups. During **World War I**, he studied at the **Cossack** Officer School in Orenburg. Skrypnyk was wounded in 1917; after recovering, he became a diplomatic courier, carrying out special tasks for Petliura. After the war, he worked for cooperative organizations in **Galicia** and **Volhynia**. In the 1930s, Skrypnyk was a leading member of the Volhynian Ukrainian Alliance and studied at the School of Political Science in Warsaw. Elected to the Polish

Diet in 1930, he was active in defending the rights of Ukrainians. Skrypnyk represented the laity at eparchy councils, was a member of the ecclesiastical council headed by Metropolitan Dionisii, and initiated the Ukrainska Shkola (Ukrainian School) society in Rivne. In 1940, he was elected assistant chairman of the **Kholm** Eparchy Council, headed by Archbishop Ilarion (*see* OHIIENKO, IVAN). In April 1942, Skrypnyk was ordained a priest, later taking monastic orders, and in May he was consecrated UAOC bishop of Pereiaslav. During **World War II**, he was arrested by the Germans and imprisoned in Chernihiv and Pryluky.

After the war, Skrypnyk headed the Orthodox eparchies of Hessen and Württemberg. He immigrated to Canada in 1947 and was appointed head of the Ukrainian Greek Orthodox Church as bishop of Winnipeg and all Canada. In 1949, he became head of the Ukrainian Orthodox Church in the United States and began working toward unification with the eparchy of Archbishop Ioan Teodorovych, which was accomplished at a sobor in New York later that year. Teodorovych was elected metropolitan of the Ukrainian Orthodox Church in the United States, while Skrypnyk was appointed deputy metropolitan and head of the consistory. He built a permanent home for the consistory in South Bound Brook, New Jersey, and established a publishing house, library, and St. Sophia's Theological Seminary. Thanks to his efforts, the journal *Ukraïns'ke pravoslavne slovo* (Ukrainian Orthodox Word) began publication. In October 1965, he opened a museum and a memorial church dedicated to martyrs for the freedom of Ukraine. In 1963 and 1971, he met with the patriarch of Constantinople in order to seek official recognition for the Ukrainian Orthodox Church and the restoration of its pre-1685 autonomy. In 1969, after the death of Metropolitan Nykanor, he headed the UAOC in the United States and the diaspora. On 5 June 1990, he was elected the first UAOC patriarch of Kyiv and all Ukraine. He died in Grimsby, Canada, and was buried in South Bound Brook.

SKRYPNYK, MYKOLA (13 [25] January 1872–7 July 1933). Revolutionary, politician, and founding figure of the **Communist Party of Ukraine** (CPU). He was born in Yasynuvata, Katerynoslav gubernia (now in Donetsk oblast), into the family of a railway worker and studied at the technical school in Izium, from which he was expelled for revolutionary activity. In 1900, Skrypnyk completed a technical school equivalency exam and became a student of the St. Petersburg Technological Institute. He was expelled from the institute for organizing a demonstration and sent back to Katerynoslav (now Dnipropetrovsk). From that time onward, Skrypnyk engaged in full-time revolutionary activity. He was arrested by the tsarist police on many occasions and exiled seven times. He joined the Russian Social Democrats in 1897 and was a member of the Petrograd Military Revolutionary Committee during the October Revolution.

Lenin, who had known Skrypnyk since 1905, appointed him chairman of the People's Secretariat, the first government of the **Ukrainian SSR**, in March 1918. In April, he played a leading role at the Tahanrih (Taganrog) Bolshevik Conference, at which he advocated the creation of a Bolshevik party of Ukraine independent of the Russian Communist Party (Bolshevik). When Lenin indicated his opposition to this proposal, Skrypnyk ceased to advocate it. At the first congress of the CPU in Moscow (July 1918), he became only a candidate member of its central committee. In 1919–20, Skrypnyk headed people's commissariats of secondary importance (state control and worker-peasant inspection) in the governments of **Khristian Rakovsky**. He then became commissar for internal affairs (1921–22), commissar for justice (1922–27), and general procurator (1922–27).

In the negotiations leading to the formation of the **USSR**, Skrypnyk (with Lenin's support) clashed with Stalin, defending the rights of the Soviet republics. He became the driving force behind the **Ukrainization** policy and, by the mid-1920s, the ultimate authority on all issues of Ukrainian culture, scholarship, and the nationality question—"the Ukrainian Stalin," as the American historian **James Mace** described him.

From 1927 to 1933, Skrypnyk directed the work of the commissariat of **education**, promoting the Ukrainization of secondary and higher education and the training of teachers and instructors, assisting in the establishment of the Ukrainian press and **publishing**, and Ukrainizing education in areas of compact Ukrainian settlement throughout the USSR (especially in the Kuban region and Central Asia). In September 1928, he ratified a new Ukrainian orthography that became popularly known as the *skrypnykivka*. Under his leadership, the massive task of developing Ukrainian scientific terminology was undertaken. Skrypnyk's scholarly and publicistic legacy consists of more than 800 publications.

Skrypnyk was toppled from his post in February 1933, at the height of Stalin's **political terror** against the Ukrainian intelligentsia. Officially, his demotion was a routine reassignment; he was appointed deputy head of the Ukrainian SSR Soviet People's Commissariat and chairman of its State Planning Board. The party press then began a campaign attacking Skrypnyk's initiatives as commissar for education. In June 1933, Stalin's appointee in

Ukraine, **Pavel Postyshev**, demanded that Skrypnyk account for his "nationalist wrecking," but all his draft statements were deemed unsatisfactory. Accused of "counterrevolutionary activity," which implied a sentence of imprisonment or execution, Skrypnyk shot himself. He was the leading exponent and symbolic figure of Ukrainian "national communism" in the political arena, as **Mykola Khvyliovy** (who committed suicide two months earlier) was in the cultural sphere.

SLAVS. Large group of European peoples related by ethnicity and language. They are usually divided into the East Slavs (Belarusians, Russians, and Ukrainians), West Slavs (Czechs, Slovaks, Poles, and Wends), and South Slavs (Bulgarians, Croats, Serbs, Macedonians, and Slovenes). The Slavic languages belong to the Indo-European group.

The original homeland of the Slavs is a matter of controversy but is thought by most scholars to have comprised a territory encompassing parts of present-day central and eastern Poland, southern Belarus, and northwestern Ukraine. This was a forest-steppe zone that sheltered the agricultural Slavs from the nomads who dominated the steppes north of the Black Sea until the ninth century A.D. Besides agriculture and cattle raising, the Slavs developed crafts and engaged in trade. They were governed by clan and tribal leaders in a system that extended from local communes to tribal confederations. They practised an animistic religion (*see* PAGANISM).

In the middle of the first millennium B.C., the Slavs began a gradual migration from their original homeland. Some of them moved into what is now Ukraine, coming into contact with nomadic peoples such as the **Scythians** and **Sarmatians**, who initially held sway over them. Separate tribes, such as the Derevlianians, Siverianians, and Volhynians, emerged from the Slavic confederations; many of them were later consolidated in **Kyivan Rus'**.

Relations among modern-day Slavs have tended to revolve around the status of Russia, the largest Slavic state. Nineteenth-century **Panslavism** developed among Slavs attempting to free themselves from Austrian, Hungarian, and Ottoman rule; in the Russian Empire, this movement turned into a drive for Russian supremacy in Eastern Europe. In the 1990s, this perennial question was reopened with the fall of the Soviet Union, which gave rise mainly to independentist tendencies, as well as to some neo-Panslavist trends in Russia.

SLIPY, YOSYF (17 February 1892–7 September 1984). Head of the **Ukrainian Catholic Church** (UCC) and cardinal (from 1965). Born in Zazdrist, Ternopil region, he graduated from the Ukrainian gymnasium in Ternopil, entered the **Lviv** Theological Seminary (1911), and studied at Lviv University. In the autumn of 1912, Metropolitan **Andrei Sheptytsky** sent Slipy to study at Innsbruck University. He defended his doctoral dissertation on the teachings of the Byzantine patriarch Photios about the Holy Trinity (1918). On 30 September 1917, Slipy was ordained by Sheptytsky. In the 1920s, he continued his theological studies at the Gregorianum, Angelicum, and Oriental Institute in Rome. He graduated from the Gregorianum in 1924 with a *magister agregatus* in dogmatics.

Slipy taught theology at the Lviv Theological Seminary, edited the scholarly and theological quarterly *Bohosloviia* (Theology), and became an organizer and long-time head of the Ukrainian Theological Scholarly Society (established 1922). In 1925, he became rector of the Theological Seminary, which he reorganized as the Greek Catholic Theological Academy (1928). Slipy edited and directed a number of publications and established a museum of religious art at the Theological Academy. In 1930, he was elected a full member of the **Shevchenko Scientific Society**.

Because of his advanced age and failing health, as well as Soviet antireligious persecution, Sheptytsky named Slipy his coadjutor (deputy with the right of succession) in 1939. Slipy was named archbishop of Serres (25 November 1939) and secretly consecrated (21 December 1939). After Sheptytsky's death (1 November 1944), Slipy became metropolitan of Halych, archbishop of Lviv, and bishop of Kamianets-Podilskyi. On 11 April 1945, the Soviet authorities arrested Slipy along with all other Ukrainian Catholic bishops in **Galicia**. Initially, Slipy's fate was unknown. In March 1946, it was announced that he had been charged with "hostile acts against the **Ukrainian SSR** and collaboration with the Nazi German occupiers" and sentenced to eight years' imprisonment by a military tribunal in **Kyiv**. In the same month, the so-called Lviv Sobor proclaimed the dissolution of the UCC and its "unification" with the Moscow patriarchate. In spite of repeated proposals that he convert to Orthodoxy and promises of high ecclesiastical office, Slipy remained faithful to his church and was retried in 1957 and 1962. In all, he spent 18 years in Siberian and Mordovian forced-labor camps.

In 1963, thanks to the intervention of Pope John XXIII, U.S. President John F. Kennedy, and other prominent figures, Slipy was freed and exiled from the **USSR**. He arrived in Rome on 9 February. On 23 December 1963, the Vatican recognized Slipy as archbishop major of the UCC. That month he was appointed a member of the Congregation for Eastern-Rite Churches, and on 25

January 1965 Pope Paul VI bestowed the title of cardinal on him.

While in Rome, Slipy worked to restore the self-government of the UCC. At the Second Vatican Council he proposed the establishment of a Ukrainian patriarchate (11 October 1963). In 1969, a UCC synod ratified the proposal, and in the autumn of 1975 Slipy accepted the title of patriarch. The Vatican did not acknowledge him in that role, although Pope John Paul II ratified the statute of the UCC synod in 1983.

Slipy visited Ukrainian communities in the United States, Canada, Australia, and elsewhere to invigorate ecclesiastical and cultural life. In 1963, he founded the Ukrainian Catholic University in Rome, branches of which were subsequently opened in the United States. He built St. Sophia's Cathedral in Rome (consecrated in 1969), modeled on the Kyivan cathedral. Slipy also founded a Studite monastery in Castel Gandolfo near Rome.

A noted theologian, Slipy wrote dogmatic works on the Holy Spirit, the Trinity, and the sacraments, as well as on church history and the **Union of Brest** (1596). Thirteen volumes of his works were published (1968–84). In recognition of his scholarship, Slipy was elected to the Tiberian Academy (1965) and the St. Thomas Aquinas Pontifical Academy (1981). He died in Rome. In accordance with his will, his remains were reinterred at St. George's Cathedral in Lviv on 7 September 1992.

SLOBODA UKRAINE (Ukr. *Slobozhanshchyna*). Historical and geographic region in northeastern Ukraine that occupied the territory of present-day **Kharkiv**, Sumy, northern Donetsk, and northern Luhansk oblasts, as well as southeastern Voronezh and southern Kursk oblasts and most of Belgorod oblast in Russia. The territory of Sloboda Ukraine was settled in the early Paleolithic era. Remnants of Neolithic and Bronze Age settlements have also been found, as well as artifacts left by **Scythians**, the Cherniakhiv culture, and the Siverianians (eighth–ninth centuries). The territory was incorporated into **Kyivan Rus'** in the late ninth century. From the 11th century, it belonged to the Chernihiv Principality, and later to Pereiaslav and Novhorod-Siverskyi. The invasion of the **Golden Horde** and subsequent **Tatar** attacks turned the region into a wasteland for several centuries.

The territory came under Muscovite rule in the mid-16th century. It was settled mainly by Ukrainian **Cossacks**, **peasants**, and clergy escaping the oppressive rule of the Polish nobility. Throughout the 17th century, Cossacks founded towns and military regiments in the region. Settlements founded by Ukrainians were called *slobody* (hence Sloboda Ukraine) because of the liberties granted to the settlers. In exchange for developing the area and protecting the southern border of Muscovy from the **Crimean** and Nogai Tatars, settlers were exempted from taxes and permitted to engage in various trades, as well as to distill and sell liquor. They were given parcels of free land and allowed to retain Cossack privileges and self-government. There were five regiments (both military and administrative units) in Sloboda Ukraine.

Thanks to Orthodox **brotherhoods**, education developed in the region. By 1732, there were 124 schools in four regiments. Approximately 500 students were enrolled in the Kharkiv Collegium (est. 1722). Among those who lived and worked in the area was **Hryhorii Skovoroda**. Kharkiv, Sumy, Okhtyrka, and Ostrohozk, established as fortresses in the 17th century, became trade and manufacturing centers in the 18th century. Okhtyrka was home to the tobacco industry, Hlushkove became a center of textile manufacturing, and Kharkiv and Sumy were sites of large fairs. In order to protect the border of the Russian Empire from Ottoman and Tatar attacks, **Left-Bank** Cossacks and Sloboda Ukraine soldiers and peasants built a series of fortifications known as the Ukrainian Line (1731–33).

From the inception of the Sloboda Ukraine regiments, the tsarist administration limited their autonomy. The regiments were responsible to the War Office (mid-17th century) and later to the Foreign Office (from 1688). In 1718, the Okhtyrka and Kharkiv regiments were subordinated to the military governor of **Kyiv**, while the Izium and Ostrohozk regiments were responsible to the Voronezh military governor. Subsequently, the Cossack regiments of Sloboda Ukraine were converted into regular army regiments and placed under Russian command, the right to free landownership was abolished, the capitation tax was introduced, and free exit from Sloboda Ukraine was forbidden (1732). By the 1760s, the Cossacks had been stripped of their traditional privileges and reduced to the status of military residents subject to the capitation tax.

The Sloboda Ukraine gubernia, administered from Kharkiv, was created in 1765. It consisted of the Izium, Okhtyrka, Ostrohozk, Kharkiv, and Sumy provinces. According to the census of 1773, the gubernia was home to 660,000 people, including 390,000 military residents and 226,000 state and enserfed peasants. In 1780, the Sloboda Ukraine gubernia was abolished and became part of the Kharkiv vicegerency; in 1835 it was renamed the Kharkiv gubernia. Approximately 60 percent of the land was owned by the gentry, the government, and monasteries, while 36 percent of peasant households were landless. After the emancipation of the serfs (1861), Sloboda Ukraine began to develop as an industrial region, with more than 900 **manufacturing** enterprises. A railway connecting the

Donets Basin with the Kryvyi Rih area was built in 1884. Before the 1870s, the sugar industry predominated in Sloboda Ukraine, but was later surpassed in importance by metallurgy and machine building.

In the early 19th century, Sloboda Ukraine became the center of a Ukrainian national and cultural revival. The first university in Russian-ruled Ukraine opened in Kharkiv in 1805. The first popular journal in Ukraine, *Ukrainskii vestnik* (Ukrainian Herald), appeared in Kharkiv between 1816 and 1819 and published scholarly materials in Ukrainian. Literary activity began, with **Hryhorii Kvitka-Osnovianenko** as the most prominent author. Ukrainian literary **romanticism** developed in the region through efforts of the Kharkiv romantic school, which included Amvrosii Metlynsky, Levko Borovykovsky, and **Mykola Kostomarov**. In the second half of the 19th century, Kharkiv University became a center of research on the Ukrainian **language** (**Oleksander Potebnia** and **Mykola Sumtsov**) and history (**Dmytro Bahalii**). Kharkiv University was also home to student organizations that formed the first political party in Russian-ruled Ukraine, the **Revolutionary Ukrainian Party** (1900).

During the **Ukrainian Revolution** (1917–21), the Ukrainian Gubernia Council recognized the legitimacy of the **Ukrainian Central Rada**. Bolshevik armies invaded Sloboda Ukraine in December 1917, defeating forces loyal to the Rada. The first All-Ukrainian Congress of Soviets in Kharkiv then declared the establishment of a Soviet "Ukrainian People's Republic," the first Bolshevik government in Ukraine. By January 1919, Bolshevik forces had taken control of the region. In the 1920s, the government of the **Ukrainian SSR** sought unsuccessfully to incorporate parts of the Voronezh and Kursk regions with a Ukrainian majority. According to the 1926 census, the number of Ukrainians in the Sloboda region within the Russian SFSR constituted 64.2 percent of the **population** on ethnically Ukrainian lands and 14.1 percent in ethnically mixed areas. However, the **Russification** of those lands at the end of the 1920s (Ukrainian-language **education** was eliminated, beginning in 1927) and the man-made **famine of 1932–33** significantly reduced the Ukrainian population. By 1989, Ukrainians constituted a majority in only two raions of Voronezh oblast and one raion of Belgorod oblast.

SLOVIANO-SERBIA. Administrative unit (1753–64) that united a number of settlements along the banks of the Luhanka, Donets, and Bakhmutka Rivers (present-day Luhansk and Donetsk oblasts). The territory was home to Serbian and other South Slavic military settlers assigned to protect the southern borders of the Russian Empire. To that end, the town of Bakhmut was fortified. The new settlers were divided into two regiments, each consisting of 16 companies. Major-generals Ivan (Živan) Šević and Rajko Preradović were appointed commanders of the military units. The Sloviano-Serbia Commission, based in Bakhmut (now Artemivsk, Donetsk oblast), was responsible for administering the area. Sloviano-Serbia was under the direct supervision of the Military Collegium. Russian government plans anticipated that each regiment would consist of 2,000 men, but in 1764, the total number of military servicemen was only 1,264. In time, the Serbian officers became large landowners (the Šterić, Vojković, Preradović, and Šević families). In 1764, Sloviano-Serbia and **New Serbia** were incorporated into the **New Russia gubernia**.

SMAL-STOTSKY, STEPAN (8 January 1859–17 August 1938). Philologist, pedagogue, and civic leader in **Bukovyna**; full member of the **Shevchenko Scientific Society** (from 1899) and the **Ukrainian Academy of Sciences** (VUAN, from 1918). He was born in Nemyliv (now in **Lviv** oblast) into a peasant family. Smal-Stotsky studied at gymnasiums in Lviv (1869–74), graduated from Chernivtsi University (1883), received his doctorate from Vienna University (1884), and was professor of Ukrainian language and literature at Chernivtsi University (1885–1918). Smal-Stotsky was a leader of the Ukrainian national movement in Bukovyna. He headed the student society Soiuz in Chernivtsi (1879–82) and the Ukrainska Shkola (1887–91) and Ruska Rada (1904–14) societies. He also cofounded the People's Home, Bukovynskyi Boian, and Ruska Shkola societies. He coedited the newspaper *Bukovyna* and was editor of the *Rus'ka Rada* (Ruthenian Council) newspaper (1892–97).

A member of the **National Democratic Party**, Smal-Stotsky was a deputy to the Bukovynian Diet (1892–1911) and the Austrian Reichstag (1911–18). In late 1912, he switched from the Bukovynian to the **Galician** caucus. As a politician, he worked to achieve administrative and political equality for Ukrainians in Bukovyna and combated **Russophile** influence on the Ukrainian movement. He pressed for the expansion of Ukrainian schooling in Bukovyna and, thanks to his efforts, the phonetic orthography was introduced in secondary schools (1893). During **World War I**, he was a leader of the **Union for the Liberation of Ukraine** and engaged in cultural work among Ukrainian POWs in Freistadt, Austria. He headed the Combat Board of the **Ukrainian Sich Riflemen** (1917). In 1919, Smal-Stotsky became an envoy of the **Western Ukrainian People's**

Republic in Prague, where he remained to teach at the **Ukrainian Free University** (UVU, 1921–38) and head its arts faculty. While in Prague, he maintained close ties with the VUAN in Kyiv and published articles in its journal *Ukraïna*. Smal-Stotsky was head of the Museum of Ukraine's Struggle for Independence (1935–38) in Prague and first president of the Ukrainian Mohyla-Mazepa Academy of Sciences. He wrote numerous works on linguistics and literary criticism. In his linguistic work, Smal-Stotsky opposed the notion of a Common East Slavic language, maintaining that Ukrainian had developed directly from Proto-Slavic. He died in Prague and was buried in Cracow.

SMOLII, VALERII (b. 1 January 1950). Historian. Born in the village of Avratyn in Khmelnytskyi oblast, Smolii graduated from the Kamianets-Podilskyi Pedagogical Institute in 1970 and taught history in schools in western and central Ukraine. He joined the Institute of History at the **Ukrainian Academy of Sciences** in 1972. Smolii obtained his doctorate in 1985 and held responsible positions at the Institute of History, of which he became director in December 1993. He has headed the editorial board of *Ukraïns'kyi istorychnyi zhurnal*, Ukraine's premier forum for professional historians, since 1995. A specialist on early modern Ukraine, Smolii has published widely on the history of the Ukrainian **Cossacks** and their 17th-century leader **Bohdan Khmelnytsky**, the formation of social consciousness, and the development of the Ukrainian nation and state in the 17th and 18th centuries. His colleague from Kamianets-Podilskyi, Valerii Stepankov, has been a frequent coauthor.

Smolii served as vice-premier of Ukraine in 1997–99 and has been a presidential advisor since 1997, notably on language policy, administrative reform, and drug addiction. From 1998 to 2000, he headed the state commission for the study of the legacy and political activity of Ukraine's foremost historian of the early 20th century, **Mykhailo Hrushevsky**.

SMOTRYTSKY, MELETII (ca. 1577–17 [27] December 1633). Secular name: Maksym. Church figure, philologist, and polemical writer. Smotrytsky was born in **western Ukraine**, perhaps in the village of Smotrych in **Podilia** (now in Khmelnytskyi oblast). He studied at the Jesuit college in Vilnius (probably from the mid-1590s). Ca. 1608 he settled in Vilnius and became a monk in 1617–18. It is believed that from 1618 to 1620 he was an instructor and rector at the **Kyiv Epiphany Brotherhood** School. Smotrytsky wrote several polemical tracts in defense of Orthodoxy, the most famous of which is "Thrēnos, or Lament for the One Holy Universal

Apostolic Eastern Church" (1610). With the revival of the Orthodox hierarchy in 1620, Smotrytsky was consecrated archbishop of Polatsk. This led to a confrontation with the Uniate archbishop of that city, Yosafat Kuntsevych, who ordered the arrest of the last Orthodox priest holding clandestine services in the Vitsebsk area in October 1623. Enraged by the prohibition of their faith, a group of Orthodox burghers murdered Kuntsevych. Smotrytsky traveled to Constantinople and Palestine (1623–25), apparently seeking reassurance about the doctrinal soundness of Ruthenian Orthodoxy. Subsequent Uniate writings stressed the martyrdom of Kuntsevych as a reason for the trip, although Smotrytsky himself did not do so. In 1627, he went over to the Uniate Church (*see* UKRAINIAN CATHOLIC CHURCH) and sought unsuccessfully to unite the **Ukrainian Orthodox Church** with Rome. He was condemned at an Orthodox synod in **Kyiv** (1628) and forced to recant his pro-Union views. Smotrytsky then returned to the Derman Monastery in **Volhynia**, where he stayed until the end of his life and issued works reaffirming his commitment to the Union. His major philological work was *Hrammatiki slavenskiia pravilnoe syntagma* (Correct Syntax of Slavonic Grammar, 1619), in which he systematized Church Slavonic.

SNIEHIRIOV, YEVHEN (HELII) (14 October 1927–28 December 1978). Writer and **film** director. Sniehiriov was born in **Kharkiv** and was evacuated to Tbilisi during **World War II**. He studied at the Kharkiv Theater Institute, where he became a teacher (1950) and lecturer in **literature** and **theater** history (1951). After moving to **Kyiv** in 1956, he became an editor of the newspaper *Literaturna Ukraïna* (Literary Ukraine), as well as a film director and head of the script department at the Kyiv Documentary Film Studio. He published his first short story in 1954 and his first collection of stories, *Lito vernet'sia* (Summer Will Return), in 1957. Subsequently, he wrote the lyrical tale *Narody meni try syny* (Bear Me Three Sons), which was translated into many languages and included in an anthology of the best European novellas. In 1966, Sniehiriov was removed from his post at the film studio for filming the speeches of **Ivan Dziuba** and Viktor Nekrasov at a memorial observance for the victims of Babyn Yar. He was expelled from the **Communist Party of Ukraine**, as well as from the writers' and cinematographers' unions, and dismissed as a film director for refusing to write an incriminating article against Nekrasov (1974). He subsequently worked in **Odesa**.

Influenced by the accounts of his uncle, the writer Vadym Sobko, about his mother's negative role in the 1930 show trial of the **Union for the Liberation of Ukraine** (an organization fabricated by the GPU), Sniehiriov researched the matter and described it in the publicistic study *Naboï dlia rozstrilu (Nen'ko moia, nen'ko)* (Bullets for Execution [O Mother of Mine, Mother], 1975). Unable to publish the work in the **USSR**, Sniehiriov had it smuggled to the West, where it appeared in the journal *Kontinent* and was published in Ukrainian in Toronto. In March 1977, he wrote an open letter to U.S. President Jimmy Carter denouncing Soviet totalitarianism; in the same year, he protested the sentencing of **Ukrainian Helsinki Group** members Mykola Rudenko and **Oleksii Tykhy** by publicly renouncing his citizenship. He was arrested in September 1977. On 28 October, Sniehiriov announced a hunger strike and was subjected to force-feeding. During his imprisonment, his health deteriorated rapidly (he had been a second-category invalid). He was severely paralyzed and lost most of his eyesight. The Soviet authorities ignored Western pleas to release Sniehiriov. He was moved to the October Hospital in Kyiv, where he soon died.

SOCIAL WELFARE. The minimum standard of living in Ukraine is defined by the value of a "consumer basket" that was worth 232 *hryvni* (UAH) or U.S. $43.50 in 2002. This calculation, which covers only food and a minimum clothing allowance, does not include such essentials as housing, utilities, and **transportation**. The standard of living in Ukraine is thus much lower than that of the most developed countries of the world. According to official statistics, 30 percent of the Ukrainian population fell below the poverty line in 2001, with 17 percent living in extreme poverty. Measures to reduce poverty include the payment of pensions, family assistance, housing subsidies, and unemployment benefits.

In 2003, the average monthly wage of blue- and white-collar workers in Ukraine was 422.58 UAH (approx. U.S. $79.17). The minimum monthly wage (2004) stood at 205 UAH (U.S. $38.42), well below the sum of 356.04 UAH (U.S. $66.72) required to maintain a minimum standard of living. Some relief measures such as free **education** and **health care** and subsidized transportation and housing are provided to most citizens, although they do not significantly raise the standard of living.

The pension system in Ukraine is fairly complex. It includes the following types of pensions: old age, disability, survivor's benefits, and pension based on years of service. Pensions are normally payable to men at age 60 and to **women** at age 55. Nevertheless, some 35 percent of people aged 55–70 find themselves obliged to work for a living.

Assistance to families with children is calculated every quarter on the basis of regulations on family assistance developed by the ministries of social security, labor, education, and finance. There are

11 forms of assistance: during pregnancy and labor, at childbirth (a one-time payment, supplementary payment at birth, and work leave), for each child (under age three for working parents, under age three for nonworking parents, children aged three to 16, invalid children, and temporary assistance for children under the age of majority), and child-care assistance (for single mothers, guardians, families with three or more children, etc.).

Housing subsidies for low-income families are paid on condition that housing costs not exceed 15 percent of family income. The subsidies, however, lag behind the rising cost of housing and utilities. As a result, a considerable portion of the population refuses to pay for housing, which was almost fully subsidized during the Soviet period. Municipal budgets have become strained as local administrations struggle to find funding for subsidies.

Unemployment benefits in Ukraine are paid through the state employment fund. Workers who lose their jobs as a result of restructuring are guaranteed payment of their average monthly wage as severance pay at the expense of their former employer while they search for a new job (maximum of three months). If after three months a worker has not found a new position, he is classified as unemployed and receives unemployment benefits for the next three months in the amount of 75 percent of his former average salary, a figure reduced to 60 percent for the following six months. The state also provides other benefits and forms of compensation for laid-off workers, such as assistance to those attending training and retraining programs. Unemployment benefits are issued for a period not exceeding 12 months over the next three years. Individuals two years short of eligibility for old-age pensions may receive benefits for a maximum of 18 months. Dependent family members of the unemployed, as well as people no longer eligible for unemployment benefits, are eligible to receive assistance, including subsidies for housing, public transportation, utilities, etc. Relatively little unemployment assistance is paid in Ukraine, since the number of officially registered unemployed is low. In May 2003, the official rate of unemployment was 3.9 percent. At the same time, 11.7 percent of the workforce were on leave with little or no pay. Regulations make it inconvenient for employers to lay off workers, as they are required to pay benefits for an extended period.

The tremendous problems besetting Ukraine's social policy are most starkly apparent in the country's excess of deaths over births and the corresponding drop in its **population** (from 52.4 million at the beginning of 1993 to 48.45 million in 2001). *See also* ECONOMY.

SOCIALIST REALISM. *See* REALISM.

SOCIETY OF UKRAINIAN PROGRESSIVES/TOVARYSTVO UKRAÏNS'KYKH POSTUPOVTSIV (TUP).

Clandestine nonpartisan civic and political organization active in **eastern Ukraine** from 1908 to 1917. It was established in **Kyiv** at the initiative of members of the **Ukrainian Democratic Radical Party** (UDRP) to coordinate the activities of the Ukrainian national movement in the period of political reaction following the dissolution of the Second State Duma. In addition to members of the UDRP, TUP included social democrats (**Symon Petliura, Mykyta Shapoval**, and **Volodymyr Vynnychenko**) and liberals (**Yevhen Chykalenko**, Fedir Matushevsky, Andrii Nikovsky, and Andrii Viazlov). TUP's leading body was an annually elected council (*rada*) based in Kyiv. Approximately 60 TUP centers (**hromadas**) were active throughout Ukraine, as well as in St. Petersburg and Moscow. Prior to **World War I**, the TUP council included Chykalenko, **Dmytro Doroshenko**, Petro Kholodny, Ovksentii Korchak-Chepurkivsky, Volodymyr Leontovych, Matushevsky, Nikovsky, Viacheslav Prokopovych, **Liudmyla Starytska-Cherniakhivska**, Viazlov, Liubov Yanovska, **Serhii Yefremov**, and Leonid Zhebunev. Its unofficial publications were the newspaper *Rada* (Council) and the journal *Ukrainskaia zhizn'* (Ukrainian Life), published in Moscow under the editorship of Oleksander Salikovsky and Petliura (1912–17). At annual clandestine congresses, TUP members discussed political and cultural matters. They carried out mainly cultural work (the establishment of **Prosvita** societies, clubs, and publications), fostering national consciousness, creating united fronts with other organizations in the defense of political freedoms, participating in elections and the State Duma, and expanding the **cooperative movement**. TUP advocated the Ukrainization of schools, the legal system, and the church.

The TUP political program consisted of three basic demands: parliamentary rule, restructuring the Russian state on a federative basis, and the national and territorial autonomy of Ukraine. With the outbreak of World War I, one faction of TUP (led by Chykalenko and Nikovsky) hoped for Russia's defeat, while another (led by Yanovska) hoped for the destruction of Austria-Hungary and the unification of **western Ukraine** with the Russian Empire. In the autumn of 1914, TUP compromised by adopting neutrality. The TUP council condemned Russia's occupation of **Galicia** and issued a declaration titled "Our Position" (December 1914) demanding an end to the war, autonomy for Ukraine, guarantees of cultural, national, and political rights for the Ukrainian people, and the like. After the Revolution of February 1917, TUP and representatives of other civic and political organizations established the **Ukrainian**

Central Rada and elected **Mykhailo Hrushevsky** as its head. A TUP congress in Kyiv (25–26 March [7–8 April] 1917) included delegates from Ukraine, St. Petersburg, Ekaterinodar, and Moscow. The congress resolved to support the Provisional Government, use democratic means to achieve autonomy for Ukraine (TUP changed its name to "Union of Ukrainian Autonomist Federalists" [SUAF] to reflect this position), and safeguard the rights of ethnic minorities. TUP members were included in the Central Committee of the SUAF. In June 1917, the SUAF renamed itself the **Ukrainian Party of Socialist Federalists**.

SOCIETY OF UNITED SLAVS. (Russ. *Obshchestvo soedinennykh slavian*.) Clandestine political organization established in Novhorod-Volynskyi by the Ukrainian officers Andrii and Petro Borysov and Julian Lubliński, a member of the Polish national movement, in 1823. Its membership consisted of more than 50 officers of lower rank stationed in **Volhynia** and the **Kyiv** region. Petro Borysov was the organization's leader, while Lubliński and Ivan Horbachevsky were its ideologues. Its program (an oath and a catechism of 17 points) was based on **Panslavism**. The society aspired to free the **Slavs** from despotic rule and foreign domination, as well as to abolish serfdom and establish a federation of democratic Slavic republics. The federation was to consist of Russia, Poland, **Moldavia**, Wallachia, Moravia, Bohemia, Serbia, Dalmatia, Croatia, Transylvania, and the Slavs in Hungary. The society did not recognize the Ukrainians and Belarusians as distinct peoples, including them with the Russians.

Hoping to achieve its goals by means of an armed revolt, the society united with the Southern Society of Decembrists in September 1825, keeping its own program and a separate executive. The leader of the Southern Society, Pavel Pestel, combined his belief in radical political reform with complete opposition to independence for Ukrainians and all other peoples of the Russian Empire. The Society of United Slavs took part in preparations for an uprising and conducted propaganda within the army. Its members joined the insurrection of the Chernihiv regiment (29 December 1825 [10 January 1826]–3 [15] January 1826) and were exiled to Siberia after its defeat.

SOMKO, YAKYM (d. 18 [28] September 1663). Acting **hetman** of **Left-Bank Ukraine** (1660–63). Born in Pereiaslav into a burgher family, Somko served as a captain in the Pereiaslav **Cossack** regiment (1654) and as its acting colonel (1658). In September 1654, **Bohdan Khmelnytsky** (Somko's brother-in-law) sent him on a diplomatic mission to Moscow. In the autumn of 1659, Somko and

Col. Vasyl Zolotarenko of Nizhyn helped Muscovite armies take over Left-Bank Ukraine. Somko then swore allegiance to the tsar. An opponent of the Treaty of Slobodyshche with Poland, which **Yurii Khmelnytsky** signed in 1660, Somko advocated an alliance with Moscow. Nevertheless, his insistence on observing the **Articles of Bohdan Khmelnytsky** (1654) and efforts to preserve the autonomy of the **Hetmanate** provoked dissatisfaction on the Muscovite side. Somko was elected colonel of Pereiaslav and acting hetman of Left-Bank Ukraine at a **Cossack council** in Pereiaslav (1660). His attempts to expand the privileges of the **Cossack officers** provoked antagonism among the rank and file. During the struggle for the hetmancy, he entered into conflict with those Left-Bank officers, led by Zolotarenko and Maksym Fylymonovych, the archpriest of Nizhyn, who were oriented on Moscow. The **Sich** otaman, **Ivan Briukhovetsky**, also joined the opposition to Somko. In the spring of 1662, at an officer council in Kozelets, Somko was elected hetman of all Ukraine, but his election was not confirmed by the tsarist government. In June 1663, at a **black council** held in Nizhyn to elect a hetman, Somko, Zolotarenko, and Briukhovetsky were candidates. Briukhovetsky became hetman of Left-Bank Ukraine because of support from Muscovy and impoverished Cossack elements. In September 1663, on Briukhovetsky's orders, Somko and Zolotarenko were executed in Borzna (now in Chernihiv oblast).

SOROKA, MYKHAILO (27 March 1911–16 June 1971). **Human-rights** advocate and long-time prisoner of Polish and Soviet jails and concentration camps. He was born in Koshliaky, Ternopil region, and studied at the Ternopil gymnasium and the Prague Polytechnical Institute, becoming an architectural engineer. While at the gymnasium, Soroka joined the **Organization of Ukrainian Nationalists** (OUN), which led to his first arrest (1937). He was imprisoned in Stanyslaviv, Hrodna, and the Polish concentration camp of Bereza Kartuzka. Released at the outbreak of **World War II**, Soroka continued to work in the **Lviv** underground and belonged to the regional leadership of the OUN. In November 1939, he married **Kateryna Zarytska**. Within four months both were arrested by the NKVD, and Soroka was sentenced to eight years' imprisonment. While imprisoned in Vorkuta, he organized the OUN-North. In 1947, he arranged a communications network among the camps and, within two years, with Ukraine. As a result of his efforts, a broad network of underground organizations was established and the dominance of criminals within the camps, a form of abuse endured by political prisoners, was eliminated. In 1949, Soroka was sentenced for the third time and exiled to the Krasnoiarsk region of Siberia. In 1952, he was arrested, charged with organizing an underground in the Vorkuta camps, and sentenced to death, later commuted to 25 years' imprisonment. He spent his incarceration in Magadan, Tashkent, Karaganda, and Mordovia. In the camps he met a new generation of political prisoners, the *shistdesiatnyky*. Soroka spent nearly 35 years in Polish and Soviet prisons and concentration camps. He died in camp no. 17 in Ozernyi, Mordovia. On 28 September 1991, his remains were reburied with those of his wife at the Lychakiv Cemetery in Lviv. **Valentyn Moroz** eulogized him as an exemplar of unyielding will and principle. A memorial volume, *Mykhailo Soroka*, was published in Drohobych in 2001.

SOSIURA, VOLODYMYR (25 December 1897 [6 January 1898]–8 January 1965). Poet. Born in Debaltseve (now in Donetsk oblast) into a miner's family, Sosiura studied at the agricultural school in Yama (1914), the Artem Communist University in **Kharkiv** (1922–23), and the workers' faculty of the Kharkiv Institute of People's Education (1923–25). During the **Ukrainian Revolution**, Sosiura served in the Army of the **Ukrainian People's Republic** (winter 1918) and later joined the Red Army in battle against the Poles. He began writing poetry at the age of 14 and was first published in 1917. Sosiura belonged to the Hart literary organization. His "Chervona zyma" (Red Winter, 1922) became one of the best-known poems about the civil war in Ukraine, and Sosiura was soon extremely popular, especially among younger readers. In the following years, more books of poetry were published, revealing Sosiura as a distinguished lyricist. The collections *Chervoni troiandy* (Red Roses, 1932), *Novi poeziï* (New Poems, 1937), *Liubliu* (I Love, 1939), and *Zhuravli pryletily* (The Cranes Have Returned, 1940) are outstanding works of love poetry.

During **World War II**, Sosiura worked as a war correspondent and later for the Ukrainian radio committee in Moscow. His patriotic wartime poem "Liubit' Ukraïnu" (Love Ukraine, 1944) was later criticized as a manifestation of "bourgeois nationalism." Among works published in the last two decades of Sosiura's life, the collections *Shchob sady shumily* (So the Orchards May Rustle, 1947), *Solov'ïni dali* (The Nightingale Distance, 1956), *Lastivky na sontsi* (Swallows on the Sun, 1960), and *Osinni melodiï* (Autumn Melodies, 1964) stand out. Sosiura's poems "Rozstriliane vidrodzhennia" (The Executed Renaissance) and "Mazepa" and his autobiographical novel *Tretia rota* (The Third Company) were suppressed during his lifetime and published only in 1988. He died in **Kyiv**. Sosiura was awarded the **Shevchenko** State Prize in 1963, and a monument to him was erected in Lysychansk in 1966. *See also* LITERATURE.

SOUTHWESTERN BRANCH OF THE IMPERIAL RUSSIAN GEOGRAPHIC SOCIETY. (Russ. *Iugo-zapadnyi otdel Imperatorskogo russkogo geograficheskogo obshchestva*.) Learned society established in **Kyiv** on 13 (25) February 1873 to conduct geographic, ethnographic, economic, and statistical research. Its first president was **Hryhorii Galagan**, who was succeeded by **Volodymyr Antonovych**. **Pavlo Chubynsky**, **Mykhailo Drahomanov**, **Mykola Lysenko**, Oleksander Rusov, **Fedir Vovk**, Pavlo Zhytetsky, and other members of the Kyiv **Hromada** participated in the society's activities. It published two volumes of *Zapiski* (Notes, 1874–75). The dumas and songs of the bandura player Ostap Veresai were published as supplements to *Zapiski*. The society helped publish Ivan Rudchenko's collection of *chumak* (wagoner) songs (1874) and an anthology of historical songs collected by Antonovych and Drahomanov (1874–75). It also prepared Drahomanov's collection of Ukrainian folk legends and stories (1876) and three volumes of works by **Mykhailo Maksymovych** (1876–80) for publication. In March 1874, the society conducted a census of residents of the city of Kyiv, the results and analysis of which were published in 1875. It helped organize the Third Archaeological Congress in Kyiv (August 1874), where the research of the society's members won high praise from European scholars. In March 1875, the society participated in a geographical congress and exhibition in Paris.

In 1874, the Russian nationalist Mikhail Yuzefovich, one of the society's founders, sent two memoranda to the imperial government denouncing the society's members as seditionaries determined to bring about Ukraine's secession from the empire. This prompted the establishment of a commission to recommend measures for curbing Ukrainian activity. The result was the **Ems Ukase** (1876), which provided for the society's dissolution. Its museum was incorporated into the archaeological society at the Kyiv Theological Seminary, and part of its library passed to the Commercial Institute.

SPORT. In **Kyivan Rus'**, certain sporting activities were engaged in as part of military training, religious ceremonies, and entertainment. The **chronicles** mention that the upper classes engaged in bear hunting, capturing wild horses, wrestling, and games involving running, dancing, and singing. Duels and boxing matches were a part of funeral feasts. Little is known about competitions among the **Cossacks**, but their reputation for marksmanship, swordsmanship, and horsemanship suggests that they underwent rigorous physical training.

Sports in the modern sense were introduced into Ukraine from Western Europe in the latter half of the 19th century. The first organized Ukrainian competitions took place after the founding of physical education societies in **Galicia** at the beginning of the 20th century (*see* TRYLIOVSKY, KYRYLO). There were no organized Ukrainian sports activities in **eastern Ukraine** before 1917.

Under Soviet rule, sports were well developed as a result of the state's emphasis on physical education. In 1922, the Spartak organization was founded to unite existing sports circles and control their activities. At the 1928 All-Union Spartakiad, the Ukrainian team placed second overall and first in volleyball, handball, gymnastics, shooting, and motorcycling. The **USSR** avoided sports contacts with the West until after **World War II** and boycotted the Olympic Games until 1952. Ukraine was deprived of its own representation in international sports but always participated significantly in Soviet teams. At the 1952 Olympics, 25 athletes from Ukraine represented the USSR. By 1988, the number of Ukrainians on the Soviet team had risen to 92. Although the Soviet Union ceased to exist in 1991, the International Olympic Committee, under pressure from the Russian Olympic Federation, forced most former Soviet republics to field a "unified" team at the 1992 games. Ukraine fielded its first fully independent team at the 1994 Winter Olympics. Its athletes won 23 medals at each of the 1996, 2000, and 2004 summer games.

Traditionally, Ukrainians have excelled at athletics, artistic and rhythmic gymnastics, wrestling, and weightlifting. Noteworthy Ukrainian Olympic champions have included track-and-field athletes Volodymyr Kuts, Volodymyr Holubnychy, Valerii Brumel, Mykola Avilov, Valerii Borzov, Yurii Siedykh, Nadiia Olizarenko, Nadiia Tkachenko, Hennadii Avdieienko, Serhii Bubka, Olha Bryzhina, Tetiana Samolenko, and Inessa Kravets; swimmers Halyna Prozumenshchykova and Yana Klochkova; gymnasts Viktor Chukarin, Larysa Latynina, Borys Shakhlin, Tetiana Gutsu, Liliia Podkopaieva, Oleksandra Tymoshenko, and Kateryna Serebrianska; cyclists Volodymyr Semenets, Ihor Tselovalnykov, and Oleksandr Kyrychenko; wrestlers Oleksandr Medvid, Serhii Bielohlazov, Ivan Bohdan, Borys Hurevych, and Oleksandr Kolchynsky; weightlifters Yurii Vlasov, Leonid Zhabotynsky, and Timur Taimazov; kayakers Volodymyr Morozov, Oleksandr Shaparenko, and Yuliia Riabchynska; yachter Valentyn Mankin; fencer Hryhorii Kryss; boxer Volodymyr Klitschko; marksmen Yakiv Zhelezniak and Mykola Milchev; basketball player Oleksandr Volkov; and handballer Zinaida Turchyna.

Traditionally, Ukraine has fared less well in winter sports. There were no Ukrainians on Soviet Winter Olympic teams until 1976, and only 11 in all competed for the USSR. Since independence, however, Ukraine has produced two Olympic champions in figure skating (Viktor Petrenko and Oksana Baiul).

Among professional sports, the most popular by far is soccer. The Dynamo Kyiv soccer team won the 1975 and 1986 European Cup-Winners' Cup, more than a dozen USSR championships and cups, and the vast majority of Ukrainian championships since independence. For many years it also formed the backbone of the Soviet team. Outstanding Ukrainian soccer players have included Oleh Blokhin, Leonid Buriak, Oleh Protasov, Oleksii Mykhailychenko, and Andrii Shevchenko.

Today, more than 50 different sports are practiced in Ukraine. The most popular, in descending order, are athletics, soccer, volleyball, shooting, basketball, table tennis, skiing, handball, swimming, and gymnastics.

STAROSOLSKY, VOLODYMYR (8 January 1878–25 February 1942). Civic and political activist, sociologist, and lawyer. He was born in Jarosław (now in Poland). Starosolsky graduated from the local gymnasium and studied at the universities of Cracow, **Lviv**, and Vienna. He received his doctorate of law (1903) and did postgraduate work at the universities of Berlin (1905–6), Graz (1907), and Heidelberg (1907–8, 1911–12). Active in the Ukrainian student movement, Starosolsky became a founder of the **Moloda Ukraïna** society (1898) and an editor of its journal. To protest discrimination at Lviv University, he helped organize the secession of Ukrainian students (1901–2). Starosolsky was an executive member of the **Ukrainian Social Democratic Party** (USDP) and of the foreign bureau of the **Revolutionary Ukrainian Party**. He was a founder and the first chairman of the **Ukrainian Sich Riflemen** society (USS, 1913). From August 1914, he was a member of the **Supreme Ukrainian Council** and subsequently of the **Union for the Liberation of Ukraine**. Throughout **World War I**, Starosolsky was active in the USS and helped edit its journal *Shliakhy* (Paths). He belonged to the Ukrainian Military Committee that planned the November Uprising in Lviv (1918). During the **Ukrainian-Polish War in Galicia** (1918–19), Starosolsky was interned in Dąbie, near Cracow. Through the intercession of the International Red Cross, he was turned over to the government of the **Ukrainian People's Republic** (UNR).

In 1919, Starosolsky served as deputy foreign minister of the UNR. Later he became a professor at the Ukrainian State University in Kamianets-Podilskyi. After the defeat of the **Ukrainian Revolution**, he lived in the emigration. From 1921, he taught at the **Ukrainian Free University** in Vienna (later in Prague) and at the Ukrainian Husbandry Academy in Poděbrady. In 1927, Starosolsky returned to Lviv and resumed his legal practice. He defended members of the Ukrainian national movement and the **Organization of Ukrainian Nationalists** in court: Myroslav Sichynsky (1908), Stepan Melnychuk (1922), Vasyl Bilas (1932), Mykola Lemyk (1933), **Danylo Shumuk** (1935), and **Stepan Bandera** (1936). A lifelong social democrat (in 1933 he became president of the USDP), he was respected by representatives of all parties and political orientations. After the Soviet annexation of **western Ukraine**, Starosolsky was briefly a professor at Lviv University. In December 1939, he was arrested and sentenced to 10 years' hard labor in Siberia, where he died.

Starosolsky wrote works on sociology, history, and law. He is best remembered for his sociological treatise *Teoriia natsiï* (Theory of the Nation, 1921).

STARYTSKA-CHERNIAKHIVSKA, LIUDMYLA (17 [29] August 1868–1941). Writer, literary critic, and civic activist. She was born in **Kyiv**, the daughter of the noted Ukrainian writer **Mykhailo Starytsky**, and received a gymnasium education. She was active in the literary organization Pleiada (1888–93), and after the death of **Mykola Lysenko** she directed the Rodyna literary and artistic club. Starytska-Cherniakhivska's first poems appeared in the almanac *Pershyi vinok* (First Wreath) in **Lviv**. Her poetry was introduced by **Ivan Franko** in the anthology *Akordy* (Chords) and by **Serhii Yefremov** in *Ukraïns'ka muza* (Ukrainian Muse). Her poetic style resembles the writing of **Lesia Ukrainka**. Starytska-Cherniakhivska and her sister, Mariia, worked closely with the **Galician** literary periodicals *Zoria* (Star), *Pravda* (Truth), *Literaturno-naukovyi visnyk* (Literary and Scientific Herald), *Zhytie i slovo* (Life and Word), and others. She also contributed to the newspaper *Rada* (Council) in Kyiv.

Starytska-Cherniakhivska wrote prose works, plays, translations, and works of literary criticism, as well as the first historical study of the 19th-century Ukrainian **theater** (1907). She also published memoirs about distinguished Ukrainian cultural figures: Hanna Barvinok, Franko, Ivan Karpenko-Kary, **Mykhailo Kotsiubynsky**, Lysenko, Mykola Sadovsky, Panas Saksahansky, Volodymyr Samiilenko, Starytsky, Ukrainka, Mariia Zankovetska, and others. During **World War I**, she was active in the Kyiv Committee for the Assistance of Ukrainian Refugees and worked as a nurse in hospitals for war casualties. In April 1917, she was elected to the **Ukrainian Central Rada**. A month later, she helped establish the Ukrainian National Theater Society and was a member of its presidium. In 1919, Starytska-Cherniakhivska became a founder and deputy head of the National Council of Ukrainian **Women** in Kamianets-Podilskyi. In the 1920s, she worked at the **Ukrainian Academy of Sciences**. Arrested by the secret police in 1929, she was sentenced to five years' imprisonment during the trial of the **Union for the Liberation of Ukraine**. The sentence was commuted to internal exile in Stalino (Donetsk). Starytska-Cherniakhivska worked as a translator, notably of opera librettos, and lived in Kyiv from 1936 to 1941. In July 1941, she was arrested by the NKVD, taken to **Kharkiv**, and subsequently deported to Omsk. She died en route, but the exact place and date of her death are unknown.

STARYTSKY, MYKHAILO (2 [14] December 1840–14 [27] April 1904). Writer, **theater** director, and civic activist. He was born in Klishchyntsi (now in Cherkasy oblast) and raised by the family of **Mykola Lysenko** after his parents died. Having graduated from the **Poltava** gymnasium, he studied at **Kharkiv** University (1858–60) and **Kyiv** University (1860–66), graduating with a law degree. He worked at the Kyiv Historical Archives and the **Southwestern Branch of the Imperial Russian Geographic Society** and was one of the most active members of the Kyiv **Hromada**. With Lysenko, Starytsky organized the Society of Ukrainian Stage Actors. In 1883–84, he published two volumes of the *Rada* (Council) almanac, which helped revive Ukrainian cultural life. In 1883, he took charge of the first professional Ukrainian theater, which made a triumphant tour of Moscow and St. Petersburg in 1886–87. Because of failing health, Starytsky left the theater in 1895 and dedicated himself to writing. In 1903, he edited the almanac *Nova Rada* (New Council), which was published posthumously. He died in Kyiv.

Starytsky began his literary activity as a poet and translator, publishing several poems under a pseudonym in the **Lviv** periodicals *Nyva* (Field) and *Pravda* (Truth). Two sections of his collection of poems *Z davn'oho zshytku: pisni ta dumy* (From an Old Notebook: Songs and Dumas) were published in 1881 and 1883. Starytsky's poetry generally reflected his belief in the civic mission of **literature** for the Ukrainian national movement but also included intimate lyrics. His dramatic works bear directly on his theatrical experience and include stage adaptations from a variety of sources. Among his original works are social dramas such as *Ne sudylos'* (It Was Not Destined, 1883) and the extremely popular *Oi, ne khody, Hrytsiu, ta* *i na vechornytsi* (Don't Go to Parties, Hryts!, 1892), as well as the historical dramas *Bohdan Khmel'nyts'kyi* (1897) and *Marusia Bohuslavka* (1899). Starytsky's prose consists of some 70 short stories, novellas, and novels, most of them based on historical subjects.

STEFANYK, VASYL (14 May 1871–7 December 1936). Writer and civic activist. Born in Rusiv (now in Ivano-Frankivsk oblast) into a peasant family, Stefanyk received his secondary education at gymnasiums in Kolomyia (1883–90) and Drohobych (1890–92). He went on to study medicine at Cracow University (1892–1900). Stefanyk began his literary career in 1890 with lyrical etudes and prose poems influenced by **modernist** trends. His novellas began to appear in the newspaper *Pratsia* (Work) in Chernivtsi in 1897. Two years later he published his first collection of novellas, *Synia knyzhechka* (The Little Blue Book), to critical acclaim. Three collections followed: *Kaminnyi khrest* (The Stone Cross, 1900), *Doroha* (The Road, 1901), and *Moie slovo* (My Word, 1905). Between 1902 and 1916, Stefanyk abandoned writing in favor of civic activism. From 1908 until the collapse of Austria-Hungary, he was a member of the Austrian parliament. Stefanyk was a signatory to the **Act of Union** between the **Western Ukrainian People's Republic** and the **Ukrainian People's Republic**. In 1922, as a protest against Soviet policies, he refused a life pension from the **Ukrainian SSR**. Stefanyk returned to **literature** with a collection of novellas, *Zemlia* (Earth, 1926), which described the tragic fate of the **Galician** peasantry during the war and the defeat of the revolution. Stefanyk died in Rusiv after a long illness.

Stefanyk's literary output consisted of 59 novellas, most of them only a few pages long. He was a master of impressionist psychological prose. The protagonists of his highly dramatic, painful stories were **peasants** of his native **Pokutia**, speaking their local dialect and described against the background of poverty and war. A film based on Stefanyk's novellas, *Kaminnyi khrest* (The Stone Cross, 1968), was released by the **Dovzhenko** Film Studio in **Kyiv**. In 1971, a memorial museum dedicated to him was established in Rusiv and a monument was erected in **Lviv**.

STELMAKH, MYKHAILO (11 [24] May 1912–27 September 1983). Writer, poet, and dramatist, full member of the **Ukrainian Academy of Sciences**. He was born in Diakivtsi (now in Vinnytsia oblast) into a **peasant** family. In 1933, Stelmakh graduated from the literature department of the Vinnytsia Pedagogical Institute, and for the next six years he taught school in the **Kyiv** region. His first poems appeared in 1936, and his first collection of poetry was published in 1939. After the war (1945–53), Stelmakh worked for the Institute of Art, Folklore, and Ethnography of the Academy of Sciences and served as a deputy to the Supreme Soviet of the **USSR**. His poetry is marked by deep lyricism, the influence of folklore, and a wide variety of themes. After **World War II**, Stelmakh wrote mainly novels and plays in the socialist-**realist** vein, becoming a prominent fixture of the Soviet literary establishment. Much of his work consists of children's **literature**, of both the didactic and vividly descriptive varieties. He was awarded the Stalin Prize in 1951 and the **Shevchenko** State Prize in 1980.

STETSKO, SLAVA (née Muzyka, 14 May 1920–12 March 2003). Political figure. She was born in Romanivka (now in Ternopil oblast). During **World War II**, working with **Kateryna Zarytska**, she organized Red Cross units serving the **Ukrainian Insurgent Army**. In 1943, she was arrested and imprisoned by the Germans. After the war, she lived in Munich, where she married **Yaroslav Stetsko** in 1946. She was active in the Foreign Sections of the OUN(B) and was a member of the Central Committee of the **Anti-Bolshevik Bloc of Nations** (ABN). Stetsko edited *ABN Correspondence* (1947–91) and the quarterly *Ukrainian Review* (1965–91) and was an organizer of the European Freedom Council. In 1968, she became a member of the OUN(B) leadership in charge of its external affairs section. After the death of her husband, she assumed the leadership of the ABN (1986) and was elected leader of the OUN(B) in 1991. In 1992, Stetsko returned to Ukraine, where the OUN(B) was reconstituted under her leadership as the Congress of Ukrainian Nationalists (October 1992). In 1993, she became an honorary citizen of **Lviv**. Stetsko was elected to the **Verkhovna Rada** of Ukraine in March 1997 and reelected in 1998 and 2002.

STETSKO, YAROSLAV (19 January 1912–5 July 1986). Nationalist political leader. Born in Ternopil into the family of a priest, Stetsko graduated from the local gymnasium and studied law and philosophy at the universities of Cracow and **Lviv** (1929–34). While still a gymnasium student, he joined the clandestine Ukrainian Nationalist Youth and later became a member of the **Ukrainian Military Organization** and the **Organization of Ukrainian Nationalists** (OUN). In 1932, he became a member of the OUN executive in charge of ideology and publications. Stetsko was arrested in 1934 by the Polish authorities and sentenced to five years' imprisonment. Amnestied in 1937, he went abroad. In 1938, Stetsko was assigned by **Yevhen Konovalets** to organize the next assembly of the OUN;

it took place in Rome in August 1939 following Konovalets's assassination. The election of **Andrii Melnyk** to succeed Konovalets led to a split in the OUN in which Stetsko supported **Stepan Bandera**. In April 1941, the Bandera faction held its own assembly in Cracow, and Stetsko was elected Bandera's deputy.

Shortly after the German invasion of the **USSR**, Stetsko issued the Act of Ukrainian Statehood in Lviv (30 June 1941) and headed the **Ukrainian State Administration**. He was arrested by the Gestapo (12 July) and taken to Berlin. In September, after refusing to rescind the act of statehood, he was incarcerated in the Sachsenhausen concentration camp, where he remained until his release on 25 September 1944. In the spring of 1945, Stetsko, Bandera, **Mykola Lebed**, and others established the Foreign Center of the OUN. Stetsko was soon elected to the Leadership of the OUN (with Bandera and **Roman Shukhevych**). A founder of the Foreign Sections of the OUN(B), he took charge of their external affairs division. Stetsko also headed the **Anti-Bolshevik Bloc of Nations** (ABN, 1946–86), established an ABN representation in Taiwan in 1957 (active until 1971), and signed an agreement with the Chinese Anti-Communist League. In 1967, he helped organize the World Anti-Communist League in Tokyo. From 1968 to 1986, he was head of the OUN(B). He died and was buried in Munich.

STSIBORSKY, MYKOLA (28 March 1897–30 August 1941). Leading figure of the **Organization of Ukrainian Nationalists** (OUN). He was born in Zhytomyr. During **World War I** he served as a captain in the Russian army, then switched allegiance in 1917 to the Army of the **Ukrainian People's Republic**, becoming a lieutenant colonel. After a period of internment in Poland, Stsiborsky moved to Czechoslovakia (1922) and graduated from the Ukrainian Husbandry Academy in Poděbrady (1929) as an engineer and economist. Stsiborsky headed the **League of Ukrainian Nationalists** (1925–29) and became a member of the OUN leadership. He was active as a writer and editor of nationalist publications, notably the OUN ideological organ, *Rozbudova natsii* (Nation-Building, 1928–34), *Derzhavna natsiia* (Sovereign Nation), *Surma* (Clarion), and *Ukraïns'ke slovo* (Ukrainian Word). In the 1930s, he published pamphlets on OUN policy toward workers and **peasants**, as well as on Stalinism and the national question in the **Ukrainian SSR**. Stsiborsky was a creator of the conservative nationalist ideology of "solidarism" (i.e., corporatism), adumbrated in his *Natsiokratiia* (Natiocracy, 1935).

When the OUN became factionalized in 1940, Stsiborsky sided with **Andrii Melnyk** and compiled the OUN(M) white book on the split. The faction led by **Stepan Bandera** unsuccessfully sought Stsibosrky's expulsion, along with that of another OUN(M) leader, Omelian Senyk. Following the German invasion of the USSR, Senyk and Stsiborsky headed the OUN(M) expeditionary group whose task was to follow the Germans into Ukraine and establish an independent state. Both men were assassinated in Zhytomyr. Although responsibility for the killings has never been established, the OUN(M) immediately attributed it to the Bandera faction.

STUDIUM RUTHENUM. Official name: Provisional Ruthenian-Language Scholarly Institute. Institution of learning at **Lviv** University (1787–1809) founded by a decree of Emperor Joseph II (9 March 1787) to prepare candidates for the **Ukrainian Catholic** priesthood (in Austria, their church was officially known as Greek Catholic because of its adherence to the Eastern [Byzantine] rite). Because they did not know Latin, these candidates were unable to study theology at Lviv University, hence teaching at the Studium was conducted in a local form of Church Slavonic (*yazychiie*). The curriculum consisted of philosophy (two-year program), followed by theology (five-year program). The Studium Ruthenum was open to men who had attained the age of 17, were literate in Church Slavonic, and had certificates attesting to good health and **Galician** origin. Students were allotted living quarters in the Greek Catholic Theological Seminary. In all, 168 students from two dioceses (Peremyshl [Przemyśl] and Lviv) studied concurrently at the institute, and a total of 470 students were educated there. Its instructors included the philosopher Petro Lodii and such prominent church figures as Antin Anhelovych, Mykhailo Harasevych, and Ivan Lavrivsky.

Like the Barbareum, the Greek Catholic seminary established in Vienna in 1774 by Empress Maria Theresa, the Studium Ruthenum served to equalize the Ukrainian Catholic clergy with the dominant Polish Roman Catholic Church—an important political goal for the Austrian government, whose policy was "divide and rule." Ironically, the institute was closed in 1809 at the request of the Ukrainian students, who wanted to attend German-language lectures like their Polish counterparts. The separate religious identity created by the Studium Ruthenum helped prevent the assimilation of its graduates into Polish society; some of them became prominent in the Ukrainian revival of the 1830s and the **Revolution of 1848** in Galicia.

STUDYNSKY, KYRYLO (4 October 1868–June 1941). Literary scholar and full member of the **Shevchenko Scientific Society** (NTSh) from

1899 and the **Ukrainian Academy of Sciences** (VUAN, 1929–34). Born in Kypiachka, Ternopil county (now in Ternopil oblast), into the family of a priest, he studied at the Ternopil gymnasium and at the Academic Gymnasium in **Lviv** (1883–87). He then studied theology in Lviv and Vienna (1887–91) and Slavic philology at the University of Vienna (from 1891), receiving his doctorate in 1894. While still a student, he was elected to the Austrian parliament (1893). In the 1890s, Studynsky taught at gymnasiums in Lviv and Cracow and lectured in Ukrainian **literature** at the Jagiellonian University (1897–99). From 1906 to 1909, during **Mykhailo Hrushevsky's** directorship of the NTSh, Studynsky was his deputy. Studynsky became associate professor at Lviv University in 1900 and full professor in 1908. He worked at the university until his dismissal by the Polish authorities (1918).

Studynsky was a leading activist of the Christian Social Party in **Galicia** and coeditor of its journal, *Ruslan*. He was a member of the **Prosvita Society** and editor of its publications (1903–6), a member of the Regional School Council in Lviv (1905–14), and head of the Teachers' Association in Lviv (1916–20). He was also a member of the **Ukrainian National Rada** of the **Western Ukrainian People's Republic**. During the **Ukrainian-Polish War in Galicia** (1918–19), he was arrested and incarcerated at Polish camps in Barnów and Dąbie. From 1922 to 1925, Studynsky headed the Ukrainian Fund for War Widows and Orphans and directed a relief committee for victims of the Ukrainian **famine of 1921–23**. As head of the NTSh (1925–32), he did a great deal to establish contacts with the VUAN and scholarly institutions of various countries. In 1924, he was elected an adjunct academician of the VUAN in the department of old Ukrainian literature. In 1934, with the end of the **Ukrainization** policy, Studynsky, **Filaret Kolessa**, Vasyl Shchurat, and Mykhailo Vozniak were stripped of their academicians' rank. After the establishment of Soviet rule in **western Ukraine**, Studynsky was appointed head of the People's Assembly of Western Ukraine (October 1939). From 1939 to 1941, he was professor, dean, and prorector of Lviv University. In 1940, he was elected to the Supreme Soviet of the **USSR**. Thanks to his influential status, Studynsky saved many individuals from Soviet persecution. During the Red Army's retreat from Lviv (1941), Studynsky was forcibly taken from the city. He died under unknown circumstances, presumably executed by the NKVD.

Studynsky wrote more than 500 works, primarily in literary history, in which he employed sociological and comparative methods. He studied the monuments of 17th-century polemical literature, the 19th-century Ukrainian revival in Galicia, relations between Galicia and **eastern Ukraine**, and Polish-Ukrainian relations. Studynsky also wrote poetry, short stories, and dramatic works.

STUPKA, BOHDAN (b. 27 August 1941). Actor. Born in the town of Kulykiv in **Lviv** oblast, Stupka graduated from the Karpenko-Kary Theater Institute in Kyiv in 1961. He went on to study Ukrainian philology at Lviv University. Stupka began his career at the Mariia Zankovetska Drama Theater in Lviv, with which he was associated until 1978. He then moved to the **Ivan Franko** Drama Theater in **Kyiv**, becoming its artistic director in 2001. From 1999 to 2001, he served as Ukraine's minister of culture. Stupka has played more than 100 theatrical roles and about 50 in the cinema, winning many awards, notably the distinction of "people's artist of Ukraine" (1980). A role with which Stupka became particularly associated and played to great international acclaim was that of Tevye in the play *Tev'ie-Tevel'*, based on the works of Sholom Aleichem. He also played the **Cossack** leader **Bohdan Khmelnytsky** in the Polish **film** spectacle *Ogniem i mieczem* (With Fire and Sword, 1998), based on the 19th-century trilogy by Henryk Sienkiewicz. In 2001, Stupka played **Ivan Mazepa** in Yurii Illienko's *Molytva za het'mana Mazepu* (A Prayer for Hetman Mazepa), the first Ukrainian film epic, which was produced at the **Dovzhenko** Studio in Kyiv.

STUS, VASYL (6 January 1938–4 September 1985). Poet and **human-rights** activist. Stus was born in Rakhnivka, Vinnytsia oblast, into a **peasant** family. He studied history and philology at the Donetsk Pedagogical Institute; in 1963, he enrolled in a graduate program at the Institute of **Literature, Ukrainian Academy of Sciences**, specializing in literary theory. For his participation in protests against political repression and arrests of members of the Ukrainian intelligentsia in 1965, Stus was expelled from graduate studies. His literary activities and petitions to higher party institutions protesting human-rights violations led to his arrest in 1972. He was sentenced to five years' imprisonment and three years' exile on charges of "anti-Soviet agitation and propaganda." Stus was imprisoned in Mordovia and Magadan. While incarcerated, he renounced his citizenship. After his release, Stus returned to **Kyiv**, where he took on factory jobs. He joined the **Ukrainian Helsinki Group** (1979), continuing his human-rights activity and defending persecuted members of the group. In 1980, he was arrested a second time and sentenced to 10 years' imprisonment in a strict-regime camp and five years' internal exile. To protest the abuse of political prisoners, Stus embarked on several hunger strikes. In 1983, he was placed in solitary confinement for a year for successfully smuggling one of his poetry notebooks out of the camp. In 1985, he was nominated for the Nobel Prize for Literature. On 28 August 1985, Stus announced the beginning of a strict hunger strike; he died in a cell several days later. On 19 November 1989, the remains of Stus, **Oleksii Tykhy**, and **Yurii Lytvyn** were reinterred in Kyiv.

Stus's first poems appeared in print in 1959. While pursuing graduate studies, he published a series of critical articles and several translations of works by German and Spanish poets. He submitted two collections of poetry for publication, but none was published during his lifetime. Stus continued writing poetry in prison, but many of his poems were confiscated and destroyed by the KGB. Some of his poetry was smuggled out to the West and appeared in the collections *Zymovi dereva* (Winter Trees, 1970), *Svicha v svichadi* (A Candle in a Mirror, 1977), and *Palimpsesty: virshi 1971–1979 rokiv* (Palimpsests: Poems of 1971–79, 1986). Several collections of Stus's poetry, including works found in the KGB archives, were published in independent Ukraine. Initially, Stus's poetry was melodious and traditional in form, responding to everyday concerns. The poems written during his imprisonment were more serene and philosophical, addressing the contradictions of human existence. Stus was posthumously awarded the **Shevchenko State Prize** in 1993, and a six-volume scholarly edition of his work appeared in Kyiv in the 1990s.

SUBCARPATHIAN RUS' (Ukr. *Pidkarpats'ka Rus'*). Official name of the east-central portion of **Transcarpathia**, which constituted an administrative unit of Czechoslovakia (1919–38). From 1927, it was known as the Subcarpathian Ruthenian Land or Subcarpathian Land. According to the treaties of Saint-Germain (1919) and Trianon (1920), the territory was given autonomous status within Czechoslovakia. Ethnic Ukrainian lands in the Transcarpathian region were divided into three areas: Subcarpathian Rus', the Prešov region (incorporated into Slovakia), and the **Maramureş region** (which remained in Romania). The territory of Subcarpathian Rus' encompassed the Khust, Berehove, and Uzhhorod districts; administratively it formed one *župa* (county). Its autonomous status was defined by the General Statute (1919), which gave executive power in the region to the Directory of Subcarpathian Rus'. From 1920, the government in Prague appointed a governor for the region who was assisted by an advisory body, the Gubernatorial Council. In July 1927, Czechoslovakia was reorganized into four lands: Bohemia, Moravia-Silesia, Slovakia, and the Subcarpathian Land (Czech *Země Podkarpatoruská*). In the wake of the Munich Pact (September

1938), the Czechoslovak government, under pressure from Ukrainian nationalist forces, was compelled to agree in October to the creation of **Carpatho-Ukraine**, a new state formation on the territorial basis of Subcarpathian Rus'.

SUCHASNIST'/THE PRESENT. Monthly journal of **literature**, the arts, and public affairs established in Munich in 1961 through a merger of the newspaper *Suchasna Ukraïna* (Contemporary Ukraine), published by the External Representation of the **Supreme Ukrainian Liberation Council** (ZP UHVR), and *Ukraïns'ka literaturna hazeta* (Ukrainian Literary Gazette). Although *Suchasnist'* was issued by the ZP UHVR and published many of its materials, it also became the principal forum for belles lettres, literary criticism, and the discussion of political and historical issues in the Ukrainian **diaspora**. Beginning in 1968, the *Suchasnist'* publishing house issued some 80 volumes of literature, memoirs, and monographs. The journal was edited successively by Ivan Koshelivets, Wolfram Burghardt, Bohdan Kravtsiv, **George Y. Shevelov**, Marta Skorupska, and Taras Hunczak.

Following Ukraine's declaration of independence, *Suchasnist'* was transferred to **Kyiv**, where **Ivan Dziuba** joined Taras Hunczak as coeditor. Along with such periodicals as *Krytyka* (Criticism, est. 1997) and *Ukraïns'kyi humanitarnyi ohliad* (Ukrainian Humanities Review, est. 1999), *Suchasnist'* is a prominent intellectual journal in present-day Ukraine.

SUMTSOV, MYKOLA (6 [18] April 1854–12 September 1922). Folklorist, ethnographer, and literary scholar. He was a corresponding member of the St. Petersburg Academy of Sciences (from 1905), a full member of the **Shevchenko Scientific Society** (from 1908), an academician of the **Ukrainian Academy of Sciences** (from 1919), and a member of the Czech Academy of Arts and Sciences (from 1899). Sumtsov was born in St. Petersburg. He graduated from **Kharkiv** University (1875) and then studied in Germany. After returning to Ukraine, he taught at Kharkiv University, becoming a professor in 1888. He was head of the Kharkiv Historical and Philological Society (1897–1919) and director of the Ethnography Museum at Kharkiv University (from 1905). Sumtsov's scholarly works (approx. 800 in all) are devoted to ethnography, folklore studies, the history of Ukrainian and West European **literature**, and art history. In 1907, Sumtsov became the first scholar to lecture in Ukrainian at a university in the Russian Empire. His major ethnographic studies concern wedding rituals, the ritual use of bread, Christmas and New Year carols, Easter eggs, the duma (epic song) about Oleksii Popovych, and folk life. Sumtsov studied 17th-century Ukrainian literature (monographs on Lazar Baranovych, Ioanikii Galiatovsky, Inokentii Gizel, and **Ivan Vyshensky**) and Russian literature (works on Aleksandr Pushkin). He published studies of such writers as **Ivan Franko, Hryhorii Skovoroda, Ivan Kotliarevsky, Panteleimon Kulish, Oleksander Potebnia, Taras Shevchenko**, and **Mykhailo Starytsky**. He compiled *Khrestomatiia z istoriï ukraïns'koï literatury* (Miscellany on the History of Ukrainian Literature, 1922).

SUNDAY SCHOOLS. Tuition-free general or vocational and technical schools in Ukraine from the mid-19th to the early 20th century for children and adults who were unable to attend regular schools, mainly because of work obligations and poverty. They were established as a result of reforms instituted by Alexander II, who allowed greater initiative to local authorities in **educational** policy. The schools operated on Sundays and holidays. The first Sunday school in the Russian Empire opened in **Kyiv** on 11 (23) October 1859. Eventually there were five schools in the city, with others in **Odesa** and **Poltava**. Sunday schools also operated in Chernihiv, **Kharkiv**, Nizhyn, Yelysavethrad (now Kirovohrad), and in some larger villages. In 1859–60, there was a total of 68 Sunday schools in the Russian-ruled Ukrainian lands. Members of the intelligentsia, students, teachers, and gymnasium students, especially those active in **hromadas**, acted as instructors. The development of the Sunday-school movement was greatly facilitated by Khrystyna Alchevska, **Volodymyr Antonovych, Pavlo Chubynsky, Mykhailo Drahomanov,** and **Oleksander Konysky**. Classes were conducted in Ukrainian, although Russian was also used because of the lack of Ukrainian-**language** instructional materials. Classes lasted from one to three hours, and students were divided into groups for the illiterate and literate. They studied religion, grammar, arithmetic, and drawing, and became acquainted with Ukrainian history and culture. In 1862, as part of its anti-Ukrainian measures (*see* VALUEV CIRCULAR), the imperial government closed the Sunday schools, and some of their organizers were persecuted. The schools were reestablished in the 1870s under the auspices of churches and zemstvos. They came under the control of the Orthodox Church in 1891.

SUPREME UKRAINIAN COUNCIL/HOLOVNA UKRAÏNS'KA RADA. Multiparty organization established in **Lviv** on 1 August 1914, at the outbreak of **World War I**, by representatives of the principal **Galician** parties: the **National Democratic Party**, the

Ukrainian Radical Party, and the **Ukrainian Social Democratic Party**. It was led by **Kost Levytsky**. **Mykhailo Pavlyk** and Mykola Hankevych were elected vice presidents; Stepan Baran was secretary. The council consisted of 15 members. In a manifesto issued on 3 August, it called on Galician Ukrainians to support Austria in order to liberate Ukrainian lands from the Russian Empire. It also recruited volunteers for a Ukrainian legion that became the nucleus of the **Ukrainian Sich Riflemen**. Members of the **Union for the Liberation of Ukraine** represented **eastern Ukraine** within the council. In May 1915, it was reorganized in Vienna as the General Ukrainian Council.

SUPREME UKRAINIAN LIBERATION COUNCIL/UKRAÏNS'KA HOLOVNA VYZVOL'NA RADA (UHVR). Representative body of the Ukrainian anti-Nazi and anti-Soviet resistance. The idea of creating the UHVR was developed by the General Staff of the **Ukrainian Insurgent Army** (UPA), which was under the control of the **Bandera** faction of the **Organization of Ukrainian Nationalists** (OUN). In the spring of 1944, an initiative committee was formed under the leadership of Lev Shankovsky. On 11–15 July 1944, 20 representatives of various political orientations gathered near Nedilna in the Sambir region. This meeting, constituted as the First Great Congress of the UHVR, took place under the chairmanship of Rostyslav Voloshyn, with Mykola Duzhy as secretary. It elected a provisional executive, adopted a platform, and issued a proclamation to the Ukrainian people.

The executive included Kyrylo Osmak (president), Vasyl Mudry, the leader of the **Ukrainian National Democratic Alliance** (vice president), the Rev. Ivan Hryniokh (second vice president), Ivan Vovchuk (third vice president), **Roman Shukhevych**, commander in chief of the UPA and head of the OUN(B) in Ukraine (director of the General Secretariat), and **Mykola Lebed** (secretary for foreign affairs). The platform reflected the OUN(B)'s reorientation toward social democracy at its Third Extraordinary Great Assembly (1943). It called for democratic government, the rule of law, freedom of thought and belief, guarantees of equal educational opportunity and just working conditions, social legislation, full civil equality for ethnic minorities, and a mixed economy. The UHVR continued its struggle until the early 1950s. It initiated boycotts of elections to central and local soviets (February 1946; February and December 1947) and produced propaganda material intended for Red Army detachments reoccupying **western Ukraine**. It published the *Visnyk UHVR* (Herald of the UHVR, 1944–45), *Biuro informatsiï UHVR* (Information Bureau of the UHVR, 9 issues, 1948–51), and *Samostiinist'* (Independence, 1 issue, 1946). Most members of the UHVR were killed or arrested, leading to its disintegration in Ukraine.

Beginning in late 1944, the UHVR became more active abroad. In 1945, it established its External Representation (ZP UHVR), headed by Hryniokh, with Lebed as its general secretary. The ZP UHVR issued a series of memoranda, including one to the Paris Peace Conference (jointly with the **Ukrainian People's Republic** government-in-exile). It disseminated information through its press service, organized assistance to UPA units that made their way to the West, and maintained contact with the UHVR in Ukraine. Its efforts to consolidate Ukrainian organizations and parties in the **diaspora** were unsuccessful. With the formation of the **Ukrainian National Council** (Germany, 1948), the ZP UHVR became redundant in that capacity and concentrated on representing the insurgent movement in Ukraine. In 1954, it broke with the OUN(B) and aligned itself with the OUN (Abroad) (*see* ORGANIZATION OF UKRAINIAN NATIONALISTS). Through Lebed's Prolog Research Corporation, the ZP UHVR was highly successful in developing publishing activity, issuing more than 200 books and pamphlets and the mainstream journal *Suchasnist'*. From the mid-1960s, it strove to represent the Ukrainian **dissident movement** abroad, reissuing underground literature and disseminating information about the repression of dissent in Ukraine. Its activity came to an end following Ukraine's declaration of independence.

SURKIS, HRYHORII (b. 4 September 1949). Businessman, politician, reputed economic oligarch. He was born into the family of an **armed forces** physician in **Odesa**. In 1972, Surkis graduated from the **Kyiv** Institute of the Food Industry with a diploma in mechanical engineering. After graduation, he worked as a senior engineer at the supply office of the Central Fruit and Wine Enterprise in Kyiv. From 1975 to 1991, Surkis headed the construction supply office of Kyiv city council. As a well-connected municipal official, he accumulated sufficient venture capital to establish his own company, Dynamo-Atlantic (1991–93). At the same time, together with members of the so-called Kyiv clan, he founded the Ometa XXI Century Trust. In 1994, after the collapse of the trust, Surkis and his partners renamed it the Slavutych Industrial and Financial Concern.

In 1993, Surkis became owner and president of the top Ukrainian soccer club Dynamo Kyiv, which served as a vehicle for his political career. (In 2000, he headed the National Soccer Federation.) After the election of **Leonid Kuchma** in 1994, Surkis and his longtime associate, **Viktor Medvedchuk**, established good relations with the new president, becoming his informal advisors. Since 1995, Surkis has been an active member of the Central Council of the (United) Social Democratic Party of Ukraine and was elected to the **Verkhovna Rada** (VR) on the party's list in 1998. In 1999, he challenged **Oleksandr Omelchenko** in the Kyiv mayoral elections, only to suffer a crushing defeat. Since the mid-1990s, Surkis has gained control of the Ukrainian Credit Bank, BIG-Energiia Bank, First Investment Bank, interests in the insurance, agriculture, automobile, hotel, shipbuilding, and oil sectors, the newspapers *Biznes* and *Kievskie vedomosti* (Kyiv News), shares in the television channels 1+1, Inter, TET, and a number of FM radio stations. His companies also reportedly control eight regional electricity networks. He was reelected to the VR in 2002.

SVIATOPOLK-CHETVERTYNSKY, HEDEON (d. 6 [16] April 1690). Secular name: Hryhorii. Bishop of Lutsk and later Orthodox metropolitan of **Kyiv**. Descended from the **Riuryk line**, he served as Orthodox bishop of Lutsk and Ostrih (1663–84). When his relations with the Polish authorities deteriorated, Sviatopolk-Chetvertynsky moved first to Kyiv and then to Baturyn, the capital of the **Cossack** hetman (1685). He was favorably received by his relative, Hetman **Ivan Samoilovych**, who was then seeking a candidate to head the **Kyiv metropolitanate**. Following his election (July 1685), Sviatopolk-Chetvertynsky traveled to Moscow with a large delegation and was consecrated by Patriarch Ioakim; he swore allegiance to the patriarchate of Moscow (8 [18] November). This effectively ended the centuries-old subordination of the **Ukrainian Orthodox Church** to the patriarchate of Constantinople. In May 1686, with the help of a bribe, the Muscovite government succeeded in obtaining recognition of the transfer from Patriarch Dionysus of Constantinople. As of January 1688, the metropolitan of Kyiv was forbidden to use the title "Metropolitan of Kyiv, Halych, and all Rus'" (instead, he was called "Metropolitan of Kyiv, Halych, and Little Russia"), and his property rights were restricted. The largest monasteries (the **Kyivan Cave Monastery**, the Epiphany Monastery of Polatsk, and the Mezhyhiria Monastery) were given ecclesiastical autonomy. Along with the eparchy of Chernihiv, they were withdrawn from the metropolitan's jurisdiction and subordinated directly to the Moscow patriarchate.

SVIATOSLAV IHOREVYCH (ca. 943–72). Prince of **Kyiv** and military commander; son of Prince **Ihor** and Princess **Olha**. During his reign, Olha was primarily responsible for administering the state, as Sviatoslav spent most of his time on military campaigns. He embarked on a series of conquests vastly more ambitious than those of his predecessors. Between 964 and 966, he subjugated the Viatichians, forcing them to pay tribute to Kyiv, and defeated the Volga Bulgars. Ca. 965, he defeated the **Khazar** kaganate and destroyed its capital, Itil. Sviatoslav took the Khazar fortress of Sarkel on the lower Don and defeated the powerful Alans and Kasogians in the north Caucasus.

Having dealt with Kyiv's rivals to the east, Sviatoslav turned his attention to the Byzantine realm. In 967 or 968, he made war on the Bulgarian empire on the lower Danube at the urging of Emperor Nicephorus II Phocas of Byzantium, taking over virtually the entire state. Sviatoslav established himself in Pereiaslavets on the Danube, where he intended to transfer his capital. He had to return to Kyiv when the **Pechenegs** attacked it, probably with the connivance of the Byzantines. After the death of his mother (969), Sviatoslav, intending to continue his conquest of the Balkans, appointed his sons vicegerents of individual territories: Yaropolk in Kyiv, Oleh in the Derevlianian land, and **Volodymyr the Great** in Novgorod. Following Sviatoslav's return to Bulgaria (969), he began a war with the Bulgarians and Hungarians against Emperor John I Tzimisces of Byzantium. Defeated at Dorostolon (now Silistra, Bulgaria), Sviatoslav was forced to sign a peace treaty in which he agreed not to attack Byzantine possessions. While returning to Kyiv in the spring of 972, Sviatoslav's retinue was ambushed by the Pechenegs, probably at the instigation of the Byzantines or Bulgars, and he was killed in the attack. Legend has it that the Pecheneg kagan Kuria ordered a chalice to be made of Sviatoslav's skull.

SVIENTSITSKY, ILARION (7 April 1876–18 September 1956). Philologist, museologist, art historian, and member of the **Shevchenko Scientific Society** (from 1914). He was born in Busk, **Lviv** region, and studied at the universities of Lviv, St. Petersburg, and Vienna. Initially, Svientsitsky was a **Russophile** and published the journal *Zhivaia mysl'* (Living Thought, 1902–5), which formulated the "theoretical postulates of **Galician** Russophilism." Under the influence of **Ivan Franko**, he abandoned Russophilism (ca. 1905). Working with Metropolitan **Andrei Sheptytsky**, Svientsitsky became a founder of the National Museum in Lviv in 1905 and served as its director until 1952. He was a lecturer in Slavic philology (1913–14, 1933–39) and a professor at the **Lviv (Underground) Ukrainian University** (1921–25). From 1939 until his death, he was professor and head of the faculty of Slavic philology at Lviv University. From 1945, he was director of linguistics at the

Institute of Social Sciences, **Ukrainian Academy of Sciences**. Svientsitsky's scholarly work dealt with art history, book printing, linguistics, literary scholarship, and Slavic studies. One of his most important works was *Materialy po istorii vozrozhdeniia Karpatskoi Rusi* (Historical Materials on the Revival of Carpathian Ruthenia, 2 vols., 1905–9). He collected and described a vast amount of museum material and organized a series of exhibitions of early and modern art at the National Museum.

SVITLYCHNY, IVAN (20 September 1929–25 October 1992). Poet, linguist, literary critic, and **human-rights** activist. Born in Polovynkyne, Luhansk oblast, he graduated in Ukrainian philology from **Kharkiv** University and pursued graduate studies at the Institute of **Literature, Ukrainian Academy of Sciences**. Svitlychny began publishing literary criticism as a student. In 1955, he became head of criticism for the journal *Dnipro*, and from 1957 to 1963 he was a research associate in the department of literary theory at the Institute of Literature and an editor of the journal *Radians'ke literaturoznavstvo* (Soviet Literary Studies). He was closely associated with the *shistdesiatnyky*, opposed **Russification**, and defended young writers against political attacks. In 1965, he was arrested and imprisoned for eight months. After his release, Svitlychny was forbidden to work in his field and obliged to publish under a pseudonym. In 1972, he was rearrested and sentenced to seven years' hard labor and five years' internal exile for "anti-Soviet agitation and propaganda." He was released in 1983 and returned to **Kyiv**. In addition to literary studies, Svitlychny wrote critical and polemical works on linguistics and published translations from the French, Czech, Serbian, Polish, and Turkish. Between 1978 and 1981, he translated the *Tale of Ihor's Campaign* and wrote poetry, some of which was published in the West. In the late 1980s, his works again began to published in Ukraine, and he was awarded the **Stus** Literary Prize. His verse collection *Sertse dlia kul' i dlia rym* (A Heart for Bullets and Rhymes) was published in 1990. He died in Kyiv and was posthumously awarded the **Shevchenko** State Prize in 1994. A collection of memoirs about him was published in 1998.

SYLVESTROV, VALENTYN (SILVESTROV, VALENTIN) (b. 30 September 1937). Composer. A native of **Kyiv**, Sylvestrov studied under Borys Liatoshynsky at the Kyiv Conservatory (1958–64) and subsequently taught at a number of **music** schools. He emerged in the 1960s as a leading representative of the so-called Kyiv avant-garde, drawing unfavorable comment from the conservative Soviet music establishment. However, Sylvestrov soon began to establish his reputation abroad, winning the International Koussevitsky Prize (USA, 1967) and the Gaudeamus International Young Composers' Competition (Netherlands, 1970). He forged a highly personal stylistic idiom that incorporated tonality, atonality, modality, and audiovisual elements. The composer himself has said that "What I deal with might be termed 'poetry in music.'" His work includes six symphonies, of which the fifth is the best known and most recorded; symphonic, choral, and chamber works in a variety of forms; and film music. Among the performers who have recorded Sylvestrov's compositions are the pianist Alexei Liubimov, the violinist Gidon Kremer, and the Munich-based Rosamunde Quartet. Widely regarded in Ukraine as the country's foremost living composer, Sylvestrov has also been praised by Alfred Schnittke and Arvo Pärt as "one of the greatest composers of our time."

SYMONENKO, PETRO (b. 1 August 1952). Politician, leader of the **Communist Party of Ukraine** (CPU). He was born in Donetsk into the family of a tractor driver. In 1972, Symonenko graduated from the Donetsk Polytechnical Institute as a mining engineer. He also obtained a degree from the Kyiv Institute of Political Science (1991). From 1973, Symonenko worked as a design engineer at the Don-Dnipro Coal-Mining Machinery Institute in Donetsk. He was an instructor and later secretary of the Donetsk Communist Youth League (1975–82), then secretary of the Central Committee of the **Ukrainian SSR** Communist Youth League (1982–88). In 1988–89, he was secretary of the Mariupol CPU City Committee and, from 1990, of the Donetsk CPU Oblast Committee.

After the CPU was outlawed in 1991, Symonenko worked for two years as deputy director of the Ukrainian Coal-Mining Machinery enterprise. When the CPU was reestablished in Donetsk on 19 June 1993, Symonenko became first secretary of its Central Committee. In 1994, the party supported **Leonid Kuchma** in the second round of the presidential election. However, when Kuchma embarked on a program of market reforms, Symonenko actively opposed him. Elected to the **Verkhovna Rada** (VR) in 1994, Symonenko headed the communist opposition, fighting the president's economic reforms and initially pro-Western **foreign policy**.

In 1999, Symonenko ran for president on a program of closer cooperation with Russia and domestic political reform intended to make Ukraine a parliamentary republic without a president. He lost to Kuchma in the second round, receiving 37.8 percent of the vote. When the **Gongadze** crisis erupted in November 2000, prompting a campaign for Kuchma's impeachment, Symonenko and his party supported the president, arguing that the campaign had been initiated by anti-Ukrainian forces in the West. In 2002–3, however, Symonenko joined the opposition leaders **Viktor Yushchenko**, **Yuliia Tymoshenko**, and **Oleksandr Moroz** in an anti-Kuchma campaign. The government's constitutional reform plan, aimed at weakening the presidency and strengthening parliament, put an end to the fragile opposition alliance. Unlike Yushchenko, who favored a strong presidency, Symonenko backed the plan. In 2003, Symonenko's party voted against sending Ukrainian troops to Iraq and campaigned tirelessly to bring the contingent home. On 4 July 2004, Symonenko was nominated as the CPU candidate for president.

SYMONENKO, VASYL (8 January 1935–13 December 1963). Poet, prose writer, and journalist; representative of the *shistdesiatnyky* movement in **literature**. He was born in Biivtsi in the **Poltava** region. After graduating from his village high school, Symonenko studied at the faculty of journalism at **Kyiv** University (1952–57). From 1957, he worked for newspapers in Cherkasy. His first collection of poetry, *Tysha i hrim* (Silence and Thunder), was published in 1962. As a journalist, Symonenko exposed the shortcomings of the party and government apparatus, for which he was hounded by the authorities. In 1963, he was brutally beaten at the train station in Cherkasy and soon died.

Symonenko's overtly political poetry satirizing and condemning the Soviet system was distorted by Soviet censorship or suppressed in the **Ukrainian SSR**. Nevertheless, it had a wide appeal because of its strong national orientation and circulated in *samvydav* after his death. A portion of Symonenko's works, along with fragments of his versified diary titled *Okraitsi dumok* (Crusts of Thoughts), was published in the journal *Suchasnist'* (The Present) in Munich (1965) and in the collection *Bereh chekan'* (The Shore of Expectation, 1965). In his prose miniatures, Symonenko showed himself a master of allegory and the grotesque. In his short stories, the struggle between man's inner spirit and the degradation of everyday existence is presented romantically, as in his poetry, with good ultimately triumphant. He was posthumously awarded the **Shevchenko** State Prize in 1995.

SYNOPSIS. The first synthetic survey of Ukrainian and East European history from ancient times to the last quarter of the 17th century. Published in **Kyiv** in 1674, it is believed to have been written by Inokentii Gizel, archimandrite of the **Kyivan Cave Monastery**. The *Synopsis* attempts to enlist the Muscovite tsar as protector of the Cave Monastery and argues for its autonomy vis-à-vis the **Kyiv** metropolitanate and the Moscow patriarchate. It is also the first major work to indicate a common origin for the Eastern **Slavs** and imply that the Muscovite tsar is their legitimate ruler.

The *Synopsis* enjoyed great popularity until the mid-19th century (reprinted some 30 times), providing the expanding Russian Empire with historical and political legitimacy. The text begins with information on the origin and daily life of the early **Slavs** and ends with the mid-17th century (first edition). The second and third editions (1678 and 1681) continue the narrative to the Chyhyryn campaigns of 1677–78. The *Synopsis* is not a systematic or complete examination of Ukrainian or East European history and contains elements of legend. It focuses on the history of **Kyivan Rus'**; the struggle against the **Golden Horde**, the **Crimean** Khanate, the Ottoman Empire, and the **Polish-Lithuanian Commonwealth**; and Ukraine's domestic politics. Additions to the *Synopsis* include chronological lists of Rus' **princes**, Polish palatines in Ukraine, **Cossack** hetmans, and Kyivan metropolitans.

T

TABACHNYK, DMYTRO (b. 26 November 1963). Academic and politician. He was born in **Kyiv** into a family of engineers. In 1986, Tabachnyk graduated from Kyiv University with a degree in history. He obtained his degree of candidate of historical sciences with a thesis on "Mass Repressions in Ukraine in the Late 1930s and Early 1940s" (1991) and wrote his doctoral dissertation on "The Phenomenon of Totalitarian and Repressive Society in Ukraine from the 1920s to the Late 1950s" (1995).

Tabachnyk worked initially as a copyist and restorer at the Ukrainian Central State Archive of Cinema and Photo Documents and as a junior researcher at the Institute of Ukrainian History, **Ukrainian Academy of Sciences**. In 1991–92, he was senior consultant and then chief consultant in the **Verkhovna Rada** (VR) Secretariat. From 1992 to 1993, Tabachnyk headed the press office of the **Cabinet of Ministers**, and in 1993 he became press secretary to the Ukrainian government. He entered partisan politics in 1994, heading **Leonid Kuchma's** successful campaign for the presidency.

After Kuchma's victory, Tabachnyk's efforts were rewarded with his appointment as head of the presidential administration. He accumulated great power in this position, becoming known as the "president's shadow." His tenure of office was marked by tensions with the VR and conflict with Prime Minister **Pavlo Lazarenko** for control over government policy. Subsequently, the VR Anti-Corruption Committee investigated allegations of Tabachnyk's illegal dealings in real estate, abuse of power, and contacts with Russian politicians and businessmen, as well as with the Russian secret service. The VR appealed twice to the president to remove his chief of staff, and Tabachnyk was dismissed from that post in December 1996. Nevertheless, he continued to act as an advisor to the president and chairman of the State Awards Commission. He was elected a deputy to the VR in 1998 and 2002. In 1999, Tabachnyk was once again actively engaged in Leonid Kuchma's presidential campaign, helping him secure a second term. In November 2002, he was appointed deputy prime minister for humanitarian issues.

TALE OF BYGONE YEARS/POVIST' VREMENNYKH LIT. Most important **chronicle** of **Kyivan Rus'**, also known as the Primary Chronicle, compiled in the early 12th century. The original has not survived, but copies made in the 14th and 15th centuries have been preserved. Three redactions of the chronicle are known. The first is traditionally thought to have been compiled ca. 1111–13 by **Nestor**, a monk of the **Kyivan Cave Monastery**. The second redaction was compiled in 1116 by Sylvestr, hegumen of the Vydubychi Monastery in **Kyiv**. It survived in three copies: Laurentian, Radziwiłł (Königsberg), and Trinity (Moscow Academy). The Laurentian Chronicle was named after its copyist, the monk Lavrentii, who prepared it for Prince Dmitrii Konstantinovich of Suzdal in 1377. The Radziwiłł Chronicle dates from the 15th century. The Trinity copy was destroyed in 1812. A third redaction of the *Tale*, prepared ca. 1118 by an unknown author at the Kyivan Cave Monastery, exists in two copies: the Hypatian Chronicle, found in the Hypatian Monastery in Kostroma (compiled ca. 1425), and the Khlebnikov Chronicle (dating from the 16th century). That redaction laid the foundations for subsequent chronicle-writing in Kyiv and other Rus' lands, notably the chronicles of **Galicia-Volhynia**.

The *Tale of Bygone Years* is a compilation of previous chronicles, various historical and literary works, and legal documents. The work concentrates on political, religious, military, and dynastic events. It begins with an account of the biblical flood and Noah's division of the world among his sons (Rus' fell to Japheth). The *Tale* includes information about the origin and settlements of the Eastern **Slavs**, the founding of the Kyivan state, and its neighbors. Events up to the year 1117 are recounted in annual entries of varying length. The *Tale* is the fundamental source for the history of Kyivan Rus' and has been studied by generations of scholars. An English translation of the Laurentian text appeared in 1953. The first complete Ukrainian translation was published in 1989 by Leonid Makhnovets.

TALE OF IHOR'S CAMPAIGN/SLOVO O POLKU IHOREVI. Outstanding 12th-century epic poem depicting an unsuccessful campaign by Prince Ihor Sviatoslavych of Novhorod-Siverskyi against the **Cumans** in 1185. The manuscript was discovered in 1795 by Count Aleksei Musin-Pushkin, who published it in St. Petersburg in 1800. The manuscript and many copies of the first edition were destroyed in the fire of Moscow (1812). The *Tale's* author is unknown, but numerous hypotheses have been proposed, some suggesting that the work originated in **Kyiv** or Halych and may have been written by someone close to the prince, or perhaps by the prince himself.

The *Tale* is permeated with vivid poetic imagery. Written in the Rus' literary language, it has a larger vernacular element than the **chronicles**. It describes the three-day battle between Ihor's forces and the Cumans, blaming Ihor's defeat on feuding among the Rus' princes and calling on them to unite. "Yaroslavna's Lament" powerfully conveys the sorrow and longing of Ihor's consort. The *Tale* goes on to describe Ihor's escape from captivity and concludes with praise of the "ancient" Rus' princes and their successors. The work has been translated into many languages and is the subject of a large body of criticism. In recent times, the authenticity of the *Tale* has been challenged by such scholars as André Mazon (1940), Aleksandr Zimin (1963), and Edward Keenan (2003). *See also* LITERATURE.

TARASIUK, BORYS (b. 1 January 1949). Diplomat and politician. Born in Dzerzhynsk, Zhytomyr oblast, Tarasiuk studied at the **Kyiv** Communications College (1964–68) and graduated from Kyiv University with a diploma in international law (1975). He began work at the Ministry of Foreign Affairs of the **Ukrainian SSR** in 1975, rising from attaché to first secretary (1981). From 1981 to 1986, Tarasiuk worked at Ukraine's Permanent Mission to the **United Nations**. He then headed the department of policy analysis and coordination at the Ministry of Foreign Affairs and was promoted to first deputy minister in 1994. Tarasiuk was one of the key negotiators with Russia on the disposition of Ukraine's **nuclear weapons** and the division of the **Black Sea Fleet**. From September 1995 to April 1998, he served as ambassador to Belgium, the Netherlands, and Luxembourg. He was also Ukraine's envoy to the North Atlantic Treaty Organization (1997–98).

Tarasiuk succeeded **Hennadii Udovenko** as minister of foreign affairs on 17 April 1998 and became known for his efforts to integrate Ukraine into European and Atlantic structures. President **Leonid Kuchma** dismissed him in September 2000 under pressure from Russian leaders, who blamed Tarasiuk for conducting a pro-Western foreign policy that allegedly undermined Russo-Ukrainian relations. In June 2001, Tarasiuk founded and headed the Institute of Euro-Atlantic Cooperation in Kyiv. In the 2002 parliamentary elections, he became a deputy to the **Verkhovna Rada** (VR) as a member of **Viktor Yushchenko's** electoral bloc, Our Ukraine, and headed the VR Committee on European Integration. In May 2003, Tarasiuk was elected head of **Rukh**.

TATARS. Name designating various Turkic-speaking peoples and tribes that numbered close to five million at the breakup of the Soviet Union. Initially, the name was associated with nomadic tribes forming the western domain of the Mongol Empire in the 13th century, known as the **Golden Horde**. They were converted to Sunni **Islam** in the 14th century. With the disintegration of the Golden Horde at the end of the century, the Tatars formed four independent khanates: Kazan and Astrakhan on the Volga River, Sibir in western Siberia, and the **Crimea**. The first three khanates were conquered by Muscovy in the 16th century, while the Crimean Khanate became a vassal of the Ottoman Turks until its annexation to the Russian Empire in 1783.

During the struggle to separate from the Golden Horde, the Giray dynasty emerged. Its first representative, Haji Giray, created an independent Crimean Khanate in the early 1440s and moved its capital to Bakhchesarai (Bahçesarai). Soon after the Turks captured the southern coast of the Crimea, Khan Mengli Giray I recognized the supremacy of the sultan (1475). The Giray dynasty continued until 1783. Under the Ottoman Empire, the Crimean Tatars enjoyed significant autonomy and preserved many Mongol traditions. Their leaders were elected at *kurultays* (councils of nobles), while the Turkish sultan merely confirmed the choice. The Girays conducted an independent foreign policy, collecting tribute from Muscovy and Poland until the early 18th century. The Crimean Tatar army fought on the side of the Ottomans, but on its own terms. Having signed a peace treaty with Muscovy, the Tatar hordes sacked **Kyiv** in 1482. Throughout the 16th and 17th centuries, the Crimean Tatars raided the Ukrainian lands almost every year, plundering villages and towns, taking the local population into captivity, and selling the captives at slave markets. The **Cossacks** defended the Ukrainian population, campaigning into the Crimea from the 17th century. In 1616, Cossack armies led by Hetman **Petro Sahaidachny** captured Perekop and Kaffa.

Occasionally the Crimean Tatars entered into military and political alliances with the Ukrainian Cossacks directed against the

Ottoman Empire, Muscovy, or the **Polish-Lithuanian Commonwealth**. In 1624, Hetman Mykhailo Doroshenko supported the Crimean khan against the Ottomans. In 1648, with Tatar assistance, Hetman **Bohdan Khmelnytsky** defeated the Poles at the battles of Korsun (1648) and Zboriv (1649). However, the Tatars were unreliable allies and betrayed Khmelnytsky at the Battle of Zboriv (1649), the Battle of Berestechko (1651), and the siege of Zhvanets (1653). This forced Khmelnytsky to seek new allies and was one of the reasons for his acceptance of the **Pereiaslav Agreement** with Muscovy (1654). Alliances with the Crimean Tatars continued under Hetmans **Ivan Vyhovsky**, **Petro Doroshenko**, and Petryk Ivanenko. The final attempt at a Ukrainian-Tatar alliance occurred in 1711, when Hetman **Pylyp Orlyk** signed an agreement directed against Muscovy. Instead of providing the promised assistance, however, the Tatars conducted several campaigns against Ukraine (1711–14). The Crimean Khanate began to decline in the second half of the 17th century and, as a result of protracted Russo-Turkish wars, the Crimea was conquered in 1771. According to the Treaty of Küçük Kaynarca (1774), the Crimea was proclaimed independent of the Ottoman Empire. The last Crimean khan was forced to renounce the throne, and in 1783 the Crimea was incorporated into the Russian Empire.

Having taken the Crimea, the Russian authorities appropriated the best lands from the Tatar population and turned them over to members of the Russian nobility. This resulted in the mass emigration of Crimean Tatars to the Ottoman Empire. Throughout the 19th century, the Crimea was colonized by emigrants from other countries. Tatars constituted 34 percent of the Crimea's population in 1897, declining to 26 percent in 1921. According to various estimates, between two and five million Crimean Tatars now live in Turkey.

The late 19th century saw the national rebirth of the Crimean Tatars. Their leader, Ismail Gaspirali, attempted to modernize Crimean Tatar society and integrate it with other Turkic peoples in the Russian Empire. As a result, the Crimean Tatar literary language was standardized, and approximately 350 schools were opened. On 25 March (7 April) 1917, the First All-Crimean Islamic Congress took place, at which an Islamic executive committee led by Numan Çelebicihan was elected. Subsequently, the Crimean Tatar parliament, the *Kurultay*, was formed and held its sessions in Bakhchesarai (December 1917–January 1918). In December 1917, the Bolsheviks created the Crimean Soviet, which was supported primarily by the sailors of Sevastopol. By the end of 1917, control over the peninsula had passed to the Bolsheviks, who proclaimed the Taurida Republic in March 1918.

On 18 October 1921, the Crimean Autonomous Soviet Socialist Republic was established as part of the RSFSR. Russian and Crimean Tatar were proclaimed its official languages. During the 1920s, the prevailing policy was one of Tatarization. Under the leadership of the Crimean Tatar national communist Veli Ibrahimov, a network of cultural and educational institutions evolved (1923–28). The policy was reversed by the Stalin regime, which initiated mass repression against the local political and cultural elite, with the deportation of 35–40,000 Crimean Tatars. Thousands of Tatars died during **collectivization** and the resulting famine. In 1938, the Tatar language was forcibly converted to the Cyrillic alphabet. All remnants of Crimean autonomy were eliminated.

After the Soviet reoccupation of the peninsula toward the end of **World War II**, more than 188,000 Tatars were deported (18–20 May 1944) to special settlements in Kazakhstan and Central Asia. Moscow's decision was based on the Tatars' alleged wartime collaboration with the Nazi regime. According to various estimates, 42.5 to 50 percent of the deported Tatars died during their first years in the settlements.

In 1956, the Crimean Tatars were released from administrative supervision, without the right to return to their homeland. An organized Crimean Tatar movement developed in the 1960s. In September 1967, the Crimean Tatars were cleared of accusations of collaboration with Nazi Germany. One hundred thousand of them attempted to return to the Crimea in 1967, but only 900 families were successful in settling there. During the 1970s and 1980s, the Crimean Tatar opposition movement established close ties with Ukrainian and Russian **dissidents**.

According to the census of 1989, there were 272,000 Crimean Tatars in the **USSR** (400–500,000, according to unofficial estimates). Only 28,000 of them resided in the Crimea. In 1987–89, the movement for return to the Crimea was renewed, and in 1989 the Organization of the Crimean Tatar Movement was formed. In November 1989, the Supreme Soviet of the USSR condemned the deportation of the Crimean Tatars and permitted their return. On 12 February 1991, Crimean autonomy was restored in the **Ukrainian SSR**. At the end of June 1991, the second Kurultay (since 1917) convened in Simferopol and elected a government (*mejlis*) led by Mustafa Dzhemilev. The Kurultay declared sovereignty, adopted a national flag (which depicts the symbol of the Giray dynasty against an azure background) and a national anthem, and restored the use of the Latin alphabet. By September 1993, more than 260,000 Tatars had returned to the Crimea, and many more wanted to do so.

The Crimean Tatars have continued to press for more immigration to the Crimea, and their protests have resulted in occasional violence. They now number 248,200 and live primarily in Simferopol, Bakhchysarai, and Dzhankoi raions. They have become consolidated and politically active (notably the Kurultay parliamentary faction in the Crimean parliament). The Crimean Tatars have a national theater, art gallery, cultural fund, library, and media. They are expanding their cultural and educational network, for which teachers are being trained at the university and pedagogical school in Simferopol. Other Tatars in Ukraine are primarily Volga Tatars (73,300) living in urban centers in the **Donets Basin**.

TELIHA, OLENA (21 July [3 August] 1906–21 February 1942). Poet and political figure. She was born at Ilinskoe near Moscow into the family of the engineer Ivan Shovheniv. In 1917, Teliha moved with her parents to **Kyiv**, where she studied at one of the city's gymnasiums. In May 1920, her father, who was employed by the **Ukrainian People's Republic** (UNR), was called away from Kyiv and could not return when the city was occupied by Bolshevik forces. The family was reunited in July 1922 in Poděbrady, Czechoslovakia, where Teliha completed her secondary education later that year. In the autumn of 1923, she began studies at the Ukrainian Pedagogical Institute in Prague, specializing in Ukrainian **language** and **literature**. In 1926, she married Mykhailo Teliha, a former captain in the UNR Army. In the late 1920s, she began publishing in *Literaturno-naukovyi visnyk* (Literary and Scientific Herald) and was greatly influenced by its editor, **Dmytro Dontsov**. When he launched *Visnyk* in 1933, Teliha became one of the nationalist poets known as the *Visnyk* "quadriga" (the others were **Oleh Olzhych**, Yevhen Malaniuk, and Leonid Mosendz).

In late 1939, Teliha moved to Cracow, where she joined the **Organization of Ukrainian Nationalists** and worked with Olzhych in its cultural division, heading the Zarevo artistic society. Following the split in the OUN (1940), Teliha, like Olzhych, aligned herself with the **Melnyk** faction. In October 1941, she traveled to Kyiv with an OUN(M) expeditionary group. There she headed the Writers' Union and edited *Litavry* (Kettle-Drum), a literary and artistic supplement to the OUN(M) newspaper *Ukraïns'ke slovo* (Ukrainian Word). She also became a member of the **Ukrainian National Council**. With the onset of the Gestapo's campaign against Ukrainian nationalists, Teliha refused to leave the city. She was arrested on 9 February 1942 and shot in Babyn Yar with other OUN(M) activists. Her husband was executed in a Gestapo prison. The most complete collection of Teliha's works was published in Paris (1977).

Her poems were first reprinted in Ukraine in March 1992. A memorial cross was erected in Babyn Yar on the fiftieth anniversary of her death.

TETERIA, PAVLO (ca. 1620–April 1671). **Hetman** of **Right-Bank Ukraine** (1663–65). He was born in Pereiaslav into a family of **registered Cossacks**. After graduating from the Minsk Uniate School (ca. 1637; *see* UKRAINIAN CATHOLIC CHURCH), he served the Prażmowski family in Poland and then became a secretary at the Lutsk castle court (late 1640s). At the beginning of the **Khmelnytsky Uprising** (1648–57), he became secretary of the Pereiaslav **Cossack** regiment. In 1649, Teteria headed a legation to Prince György Rákóczi II of Transylvania and was an organizer of the Ukrainian-Transylvanian military and political alliance (1654–57). He participated in virtually all diplomatic negotiations that took place in Khmelnytsky's capital, Chyhyryn. In the summer of 1653, he became colonel of Pereiaslav. Teteria was involved in formulating the **Pereiaslav Agreement** (1654) with Muscovy; in the same year, he traveled to Moscow with General Judge Samiilo Bohdanovych-Zarudny to negotiate the **Articles of Bohdan Khmelnytsky**. After Khmelnytsky's death, Teteria supported Hetman **Ivan Vyhovsky** and took part in negotiations leading to the **Treaty of Hadiach**, intended to bring about a rapprochement with the **Polish-Lithuanian Commonwealth**. From 1658 to 1661, he lived in Warsaw, where he had considerable influence at the court of King John Casimir. He was involved in preparing the Treaty of Slobodyshche (1660) with Poland.

After the resignation of Hetman **Yurii Khmelnytsky**, Teteria was elected hetman in Chyhyryn (January 1663). Relying on the support of **Yakym Somko** and the **Cossack officers**, with the backing of the Commonwealth, Teteria strove to unite Right- and **Left-Bank Ukraine** under his control. He contended for power with Vyhovsky, whom he denounced as an insurgent, which led to Vyhovsky's execution. In October 1663, Teteria's Cossack army (approx. 24,000 men) joined the army of John Casimir (approx. 20,000) and **Tatar** units (40,000) at Bila Tserkva. The allies intended to take control of the Left Bank, as well as the Smolensk region, which had become part of Muscovy according to the Peace of Polianovka (1634). Those forces occupied most of Left-Bank Ukraine (November 1663–January 1664), but Cossack and peasant uprisings against Polish rule forced Teteria to retreat to the Right Bank. Under pressure from Muscovite forces (commanded by Grigorii Romodanovsky) and those of the Left-Bank hetman **Ivan Briukhovetsky**, the Crown Army retreated to Poland. In 1665, having seized the **Cossack insignia** and treasury, Teteria fled to

Warsaw. He soon came under pressure from Polish magnates to make restitution for their losses during the insurgency, as well as from the Right-Bank hetman **Petro Doroshenko**, who demanded the return of the treasury. After the resignation of his patron, John Casimir, Teteria's situation in Poland became untenable, and he fled to Iaşi, **Moldavia**. In 1670, Teteria met in Adrianopolis (Edirne) with Sultan Mehmed IV, whom he urged to start a war against Poland. Mehmed gave Teteria a pension and the *sancak*, or sultan's flag. Teteria was poisoned in April 1671 and was probably buried in one of Edirne's Orthodox churches.

THEATER. Nonritual Ukrainian theater began in the early 17th century with the development of secular interludes staged between the acts of religious plays. It developed further at the court of Hetman **Kyrylo Rozumovsky**, who established a serf theater troupe in 1751, and in the school drama of the 17th and 18th centuries, particularly at the **Kyiv Mohyla Academy**. This genre developed on the basis of West European school theater, especially the Jesuit theater. Academy students performed plays adapted by their teachers of poetics from the dialogic verse of the Christmas and Easter cycles. Plays with historical themes began to be written in the 18th century.

The prohibition of school performances at the Kyivan Academy in 1765 led many students to participate in the development and popularization of portable puppet theater. Known as *vertep* (referring to the crib of Bethlehem), the performance enacted Nativity scenes with comic interludes depicting secular life. It was the prevailing form of theatrical entertainment in rural areas. There were 10–40 standard *vertep* characters, with one individual operating all the hand puppets on a two-level stage in the form of a building. The religious portion of the *vertep* was performed on the upper level and the secular part on the lower. Although *vertep* performances date back to the late 16th century, they reached their height of popularity in the second half of the 18th century. One-act folk dramas based on local events were also common at the time and became the basis of 19th-century ethnographic theater.

Ukrainian secular theater became popular in the 19th century, beginning with the staging of plays by **Ivan Kotliarevsky** and **Hryhorii Kvitka-Osnovianenko** by the **Poltava** Free Theater in 1819. Serf theaters disappeared in the mid-19th century, but not before they had facilitated the emergence of professional theater in Ukraine and produced scores of well-trained actors. In **western Ukraine**, Ukrainian theatrical performances were first staged in theological seminaries, while amateur secular performances began in the late 1840s. The first professional Ukrainian theater was a touring troupe in Austrian-ruled **Galicia** and **Bukovyna** founded in 1864 under the auspices of the Ruska Besida Society. It remained active until 1914.

In Russian-ruled Ukraine in the mid-19th century, the driving forces behind the Ukrainian theater movement were **Mykhailo Starytsky** and Ivan Karpenko-Kary. The **Valuev circular** (1863) proscribed the use of Ukrainian on stage, and the **Ems Ukase** (1876) prohibited all Ukrainian-language performances, paralyzing theatrical life for some time. In 1881, Marko Kropyvnytsky founded the first touring theater in **eastern Ukraine**, which was followed by similar troupes led by Starytsky, Mykola Sadovsky, and Panas Saksahansky. Their repertoire consisted of **populist romantic** and **realist** plays. The censors did not allow performances of plays with historical and social themes and prohibited the staging of plays translated from other languages. Every performance had to include at least one Russian play, and the territory of the touring theaters was limited to Russian-ruled Ukraine.

With the relaxation of censorship after the **Revolution of 1905**, Sadovsky organized the first resident Ukrainian theater in **Kyiv** in 1907. This marked an important transition from populist ethnographic to modern Ukrainian theater. Its repertoire included Ukrainian **modernist** works, historical dramas, plays translated into Ukrainian, and Ukrainian operas.

Les Kurbas was the most important innovator of 20th-century Ukrainian theater. His Young Theater rejected the ethnographic repertoire in favor of modernism (notably the plays of **Volodymyr Vynnychenko** and **Lesia Ukrainka**) and world classics. The core of the Young Theater formed the nucleus of Kyidramte (1920–21) and the **Berezil Theater** (1922–33), the latter being openly avant-garde. Much of Kurbas's most important work was done in collaboration with the playwright **Mykola Kulish**.

From 1934, socialist realism became *de rigueur* in Ukrainian theater, resulting in isolation from European trends, the imposition of the Stanislavsky method of acting and directing, and the suppression of experimentation until the late 1980s. Few writers (notably Ivan Kocherha and Oleksander Korniichuk) wrote Ukrainian dramas, and the Soviet regime closely monitored theatrical activity. The most important Ukrainian theaters of the period were the **Ivan Franko** Theater in Kyiv (under the longtime direction of Hnat Yura), the **Taras Shevchenko** Theater in **Kharkiv**, and the Mariia Zankovetska Theater in **Lviv**.

The late 1980s saw an explosion of theatrical activity. The number of theaters in Kyiv increased from 12 to nearly 100. They presented previously banned repertoire, especially contemporary plays critical of the Soviet regime, absurdist plays from Western Europe, and Ukrainian modernist works. By the mid-1990s, however, economic decline and decreased government interest in state-funded theater resulted in markedly fewer presentations. The number of new productions staged in Kyiv fell from roughly 150 in 1989 to 50 in 1998 and about 20 at the beginning of the new millennium. Among the more important theatrical performances of the last decade are stagings by Andrii Zholdak at the Ivan Franko and Taras Shevchenko theaters, productions by Valerii Bilchenko at the Kyiv Young Theater and later at the Kyiv Experimental Theater, the work of the Les Kurbas Young Theater in Lviv under Volodymyr Kuchynsky, Iryna Volytska's productions at the Theater in a Basket in Lviv, and the large-scale happenings staged by Serhii Proskurnia. *See also* STUPKA, BOHDAN.

TIMOSHENKO, STEPHEN (11 [23] December 1878–29 May 1972). Mechanical engineer and scientist; founder of the field of strength of materials; full member and cofounder of the **Ukrainian Academy of Sciences** (UAN; from 1918); full member of the **USSR** Academy of Sciences (from 1929), the **Ukrainian Academy of Arts and Sciences** in the United States, the **Shevchenko Scientific Society**, and the Royal Society of London. Born in Shpotivka, Chernihiv gubernia, Timoshenko graduated from the St. Petersburg Institute of Civil Engineers (1901) and taught at the **Kyiv** Polytechnical Institute (1907–20, with interruptions). He was director of the UAN Institute of Mechanics (1919–20) before emigrating to the United States in 1922. He subsequently worked for the Westinghouse Co. and taught at the University of Michigan (1927–36) and Stanford University (1936–60). Timoshenko's key contributions are in the mechanics of solids and structures. He established the mathematical foundations for the discipline of strength of materials; formulated equations for calculating bending, twisting, deformation, vibrations, and collisions of solid deformable bodies, beams, membranes, and trusses; solved problems of stress concentration around corners and apertures; and devised methods for calculating the load strength of bridges, retaining walls, rails, gears, and so forth. His equations are the basis of modern design in mechanical and civil engineering. The Timoshenko Medal for major achievements in applied technological sciences was inaugurated in 1957 by the Society of American Mechanical Engineers.

TOMASHIVSKY, STEPAN (9 January 1875–21 December 1930). Historian, civic and political figure, and full member of the

Shevchenko Scientific Society (NTSh). Born in Kupnovychi, **Galicia** (now in **Lviv** oblast), Tomashivsky studied at the Sambir gymnasium and later at Lviv University, receiving his doctorate there. He taught in gymnasiums in Peremyshl (Przemyśl), Berezhany, and Lviv. From 1912 to 1914, he lectured in Austrian history at Lviv University, and in 1913–14 he was acting head of the NTSh. Tomashivsky belonged to the **National Democratic Party**. An organizer of the paramilitary Sich movement, he was a member of the Combat Board of the **Ukrainian Sich Riflemen**. From November 1918 to February 1919, he was a member of the **Ukrainian National Rada** of the **Western Ukrainian People's Republic** (ZUNR). Tomashivsky served as diplomatic advisor to the **Ukrainian People's Republic** and head of the ZUNR delegation at the Paris Peace Conference (March 1919–June 1921). In 1920, he was the ZUNR representative in London. From 1921 to 1925, he lived in Berlin, where he worked for the newspaper *Ukraïns'ke slovo* (Ukrainian Word) and edited the weekly *Litopys polityky, pys'menstva i mystetstva* (Chronicle of Politics, Literature, and Art). In 1925, Tomashivsky returned to Lviv, where he edited the periodical *Polityka* (Politics, 1925–26) and taught at a gymnasium. From 1926 to the end of his life, he lectured in Ukrainian history at the Jagiellonian University in Cracow. In the postwar period he became a leading member of the Ukrainian conservative camp, an executive member of the Ukrainian Christian Organization, and a leader of the Ukrainian Catholic People's Party.

Tomashivsky was one of the founders of the statist school in Ukrainian historiography. He studied the **Khmelnytsky Uprising** and its repercussions in Galicia, gathering a large number of source materials. He also published a monograph on the **Hetmanate** during the time of **Ivan Mazepa**. The manuscript of his two-volume history of Galicia was lost during **World War I**. In 1915, he published *Die weltpolitische Bedeutung Galiziens* (as well as a Ukrainian version). Tomashivsky also studied the history of **Transcarpathia**, especially its ethnography and the status of Ukrainians there. He published a series of important studies on the history of the Ukrainian church and began working on a comprehensive history of the subject in 1928 (four volumes were planned). His introduction to "The History of the Church in Ukraine" was published posthumously in *Analecta Ordinis S. Basilii Magni* (*Zapysky ChSVV*) (1932).

Tomashivsky outlined his conception of Ukrainian history in *Ukraïns'ka istoriia* (Ukrainian History, 1919), the first and only published section of which covered the period up to 1569. In his view, Ukraine's historical development was dominated by three fundamental themes arising from its geographical location: the struggle with the steppe nomads; the conflict with Poland, an expression of political and cultural antagonisms between West and East; and the struggle against Muscovite overlordship, based on political and economic differences between North and South. Tomashivsky considered the Principality of **Galicia-Volhynia** the first Ukrainian state and regarded the achievement of statehood as the turning point in the formation of the Ukrainian nation.

TRADE. Ukraine's geopolitical position at the crossroads of trade routes has always stimulated the exchange of goods and services. The growth of the city of **Kyiv** and the flourishing of **Kyivan Rus'** were influenced by trade along the Dnipro River, known as the highway from the **Varangian** to the Greek lands, and from Europe to Asia. From the 13th to the 16th century, the Ukrainian lands under Polish and Lithuanian rule exported grain and raw materials to Western Europe while importing textiles, household goods, and spices for the local gentry. The **Cossack** estates of the 16th and 17th centuries were known as exporters of **agricultural** goods. Ukrainian markets were gradually integrated with those of Muscovy following the **Pereiaslav Agreement** of 1654. With the Russian Empire's industrialization drive in the mid-19th century, West European investment in Ukraine's natural resources was accompanied by the import of machinery and **manufactured** goods. The construction of railroads accelerated exports of Ukrainian grain, coal, and metal ores to other parts of the empire and to Western Europe. For example, in 1913 Ukraine exported goods worth 789 million rubles but imported only 261 million rubles' worth. With the creation of the Soviet Union in 1922 and the introduction of centralized economic planning, Ukraine lost its autonomous capacity to conduct foreign trade.

Since its declaration of independence in 1991, Ukraine has established trade relations with many countries around the world. Its principal exports are ferrous and nonferrous metals, mineral products, chemicals, manufactured goods, textiles, coal, and food products. In 1991, Ukraine exported goods and services worth nearly 24 billion dollars. Exports were reduced significantly throughout the early and mid-1990s because of the economic crisis but began to rise at the end of the decade. In 2002, the value of Ukraine's exports was 22 billion dollars. The principal destinations of Ukrainian goods were Russia (18.7 percent), Germany (6 percent), Italy (5.5 percent), China (4.2 percent), Turkey (3.8 percent), Hungary (3.8 percent), Poland (3.4 percent), and the United States (3.2 percent). The fees that Ukraine charges for oil and gas transit from the Russian Federation to Western Europe are also an important source of revenue (*see* TRANSPORT).

Fuel and **energy** constitute the largest portion of Ukrainian imports, followed by chemicals, foodstuffs, and machinery. In 1991, Ukraine imported 22 billion dollars' worth of goods. Although both exports and imports declined throughout the 1990s, Ukraine maintained a negative trade balance, with imports surpassing exports. By the end of the decade, however, the **economy** had improved, and in 2002 imported goods and services were worth 18.2 billion dollars, making for a trade surplus of 3.8 billion dollars. The main sources of imports were Russia (38 percent), Germany (9.6 percent), Turkmenistan (7.7 percent), and Poland (3.5 percent).

TRANSCARPATHIA (Ukr. *Zakarpattia*). Historical name of Ukrainian ethnic territory on the southern slopes of the Carpathian Mountains and in the basin of the Tysa River. Today the area constitutes the Transcarpathian oblast of Ukraine. It borders on Romania, Hungary, Slovakia, Poland, and the **Lviv** and Ivano-Frankivsk oblasts. Its territory covers 12,800 sq. km, and its population numbers 1,252,300 (2001). Transcarpathia was settled during the late Paleolithic era and is the site of the oldest human remains discovered in Ukraine. During the final centuries B.C., Transcarpathia was settled by Celtic tribes, and the **Scythians** and **Sarmatians** raided the area. In the second century A.D., part of Transcarpathia was included in the Roman province of Dacia. It was invaded by the Huns (fourth and fifth centuries), Avars (sixth and seventh centuries), and Magyars (ninth century). From the first centuries A.D., Transcarpathia was settled by Slavic tribes, the best-known of whom were the White Croatians, whose lands were part of **Kyivan Rus'** in the 10th and 11th centuries. In 907, they participated in Prince **Oleh's** campaign to Constantinople. **Volodymyr the Great** led a campaign into Transcarpathia in 993. It was during this period that the term Rus' became entrenched in the area (later known as Hungarian Rus', **Subcarpathian Rus'**, and Carpathian Rus').

In the first half of the 11th century, Hungary began its takeover of Transcarpathia, which was completed in the 13th century. From then until the 20th century, Transcarpathia was a northern border region of the Kingdom of Hungary. Nevertheless, Ukrainian influence remained significant: in the second half of the 13th century, the town of Mukacheve and its environs were the domain of Prince Rostyslav Mykhailovych of Chernihiv, and subsequently of Prince Lev Danylovych of the Principality of **Galicia-Volhynia**. From 1393 to 1414, Prince Fedir Koriiatovych, who arrived in Transcarpathia with a sizable army from **Podilia**, was administrator of the Berehove *komitat*.

From the 13th to the 15th century, Transcarpathia was colonized by Wallachians, Germans, Slovaks, and Hungarians. The local Ukrainian population was enserfed and deprived of political rights and freedoms, its ethnic identity expressed mainly through religious allegiance. During this period, there was a separate Orthodox church organization in Transcarpathia, based in Mukacheve.

In the first half of the 16th century, Transcarpathia and a portion of Hungary passed to the Austrian Habsburgs, who were engaged in constant warfare with the Turks. The lowland areas of Transcarpathia were attacked continually by Turks and Tatars. The **opryshok** movement evolved there in the 17th century, becoming especially vigorous in the 18th century.

Early in the 17th century, efforts intensified to establish Catholicism as the official religion. In 1646, a synod in Uzhhorod ratified a religious union with Rome that became definitively established from the 1720s (*see* UZHHOROD, UNION OF).

In the late 18th and early 19th centuries, Transcarpathia experienced a significant cultural revival facilitated by contacts with other Ukrainian lands. Emigrants from the region included Petro Lodii and Ivan Zemanchyk, professors at Lviv University, Mykhailo Baluhiansky, the first rector of St. Petersburg University, and the well-known Slavist Yurii Hutsa-Venelin. Reverberations of the **Revolution of 1848** were felt in Transcarpathia. The assimilationist policies of the Hungarian revolutionary government resulted in a pro-Austrian orientation among most Ukrainian activists in the region. In April 1849, the Transcarpathian politician and publicist Adolf Dobriansky developed a project for the unification of Transcarpathia and **Galicia** into a separate crown land within the Habsburg Monarchy. With the rise of Hungarian influence and the creation of Austria-Hungary (1867), the Ukrainian population of Transcarpathia was subjected to intensive Magyarization; Ukrainian schools, newspapers, and magazines were closed, and cultural and educational societies were dissolved. In reaction to this, the **Russophile** movement grew in strength.

Economic conditions in Transcarpathia were also difficult. Constant land shortages and the slow development of industry led to mass emigration from the region, particularly to North America. After the collapse of Austria-Hungary, a movement developed for unification with the **Ukrainian People's Republic** (UNR). Two Transcarpathian delegates were members of the **Ukrainian National Rada** in Stanyslaviv and attended the **Labor Congress** in Kyiv (January 1919). On 21 January, a congress of 400 delegates in Khust declared itself in favor of union with the UNR. However, on 8 May, the Central Ruthenian (Ukrainian) People's Council, formed by representatives of the Uzhhorod, Prešov, and Khust councils, declared Transcarpathia's unification with Czechoslovakia. To a large degree, this decision was prompted by pressure from the Transcarpathian emigration in the United States, which voted in a plebiscite in favor of regional autonomy within Czechoslovakia.

By decision of the Paris Peace Conference, on the basis of the Treaty of Saint-Germain (10 September 1919), Transcarpathia became part of Czechoslovakia. It was established as a distinct region, **Subcarpathian Rus'**, administered by a governor. The Prague government kept postponing autonomous rule, the first stage of which was implemented only in 1937. Throughout the interwar period, significant socioeconomic and cultural development was achieved. Ukrainian societies such as **Prosvita** (which had 14 branches and 233 reading rooms in 1936) and the Teachers' Association (which had 1,650 members in 1925) were active. Well-known Ukrainian figures of the period included **Avhustyn Voloshyn**, Mykhailo and Yulii Brashchaiko, and Avhustyn Shtefan.

In the wake of the Munich Agreement, Voloshyn became president of an autonomous Transcarpathian government on 26 October 1938. Following the Vienna Arbitration (2 November), the southern portion of Transcarpathia was ceded to Hungary, and the government of **Carpatho-Ukraine** moved its capital to Khust.

The elections to the first parliament of Carpatho-Ukraine, which took place on 12 February 1939, were won overwhelmingly by representatives of the Ukrainian National Alliance. On 14 March, as the Nazis occupied Bohemia and Moravia, Hungarian forces overran Carpatho-Ukraine. The Seim of Carpatho-Ukraine convened on 15 March to make a symbolic declaration of independence, ratify a constitution, and elect Voloshyn president. Despite the resistance of **Carpathian Sich** units, Hungarian forces established an occupation regime that continued until October 1944.

Following the occupation of Transcarpathia by Soviet forces, a communist-organized Congress of People's Committees of Transcarpathian Ukraine was convened in Mukacheve (26 November 1944) and approved unification with the **Ukrainian SSR**. On 29 June 1945, the governments of Czechoslovakia and the **USSR** signed an agreement concerning the transfer of Transcarpathia to Ukraine. Transcarpathia oblast was established on 22 January 1946.

After the establishment of Soviet rule, the persecution of anti-Soviet Ukrainians began, the **Ukrainian Catholic Church** was suppressed (1949; it emerged from the underground in 1989), and the **collectivization** of **agriculture** was implemented (1949–50). Uzhhorod University was founded in 1946. A policy of Sovietization and Ukrainization integrated Transcarpathia into the Ukrainian SSR.

TRANSDANUBIAN SICH. Organization of former **Zaporozhian Cossacks** on Ottoman territory in the Danube River delta (1775–1828). After the destruction of the Zaporozhian **Sich** (1775), a number of Cossacks, fleeing persecution and serfdom, settled in the Dobrudja. The Ottoman government granted them lands between the Southern Buh and Danube Rivers, and they established the first Transdanubian Sich, known as Ust-Dunaiska, at the Danube estuary (1776). In 1785, as a result of conflict with Don Cossack émigrés, a number of Transdanubians (7,000 men) migrated to Silistra. In 1813, they moved the Sich to the vicinity of Katerlez. Other Transdanubians (approx. 8,000 men) moved to the Banat at the behest of Joseph II of Austria to guard the Austro-Ottoman border. In 1815, the best-known Transdanubian Sich was established on the upper Dunavets River.

The administration of the Transdanubian Sich replicated that of the Zaporozhian Sich. It was ruled by a military council that elected the officer staff. The Cossacks engaged in fishing, hunting, cattle herding, and farming. The Sich had a school and a library. The Transdanubian Cossacks were obliged to take part in Turkish military operations. In May 1828, during the Russo-Turkish War (1828–29), *kish* otaman Yosyp Hladky and a small group of Cossacks (approx. 1,500 men) switched allegiance to the Russian side at Izmail. After the war, they were organized as the Azov Cossack Host. As a result of Hladky's treachery, the Ottoman government executed Cossacks residing at the Sich; its fortifications and church were destroyed.

TRANSNISTRIA. Name for southwestern Ukraine (meaning "beyond the Dnister River") introduced by Romanian historians in the early 20th century to support Romanian claims to the territory. It was used by German and Romanian occupying forces during **World War II** to refer to lands between the Dnister, Boh, Riv, and Liadova Rivers and the Black Sea coast. After occupying a portion of southern Ukraine, the Germans transferred the territory to Romania for temporary administration (30 August 1941). Transnistria occupied a territory of 40,000 sq. km (consisting of 13 counties and 65 *volosti*) and had a population of approximately 2.2 million. Its administrative center was located first in Tyraspol (Tiraspol) and later in **Odesa**. Gheorghe Alecsianu, who governed the territory until 1944, reported to the Romanian Military-Civilian Cabinet for the Administration of **Bessarabia**, **Bukovyna**, and Transnistria. The occupation regime of Transnistria was less harsh than that of the **Reichskommissariat Ukraine**. Although Transnistria was treated as a colony, the Romanian administration was concerned not with eradicating the local population but with Romanianizing it. The authorities in Bucharest regarded Transnistria as the "Romanian Siberia"; between 1941 and 1943, 100,000 **Jews** and 23,000 Roma from Romanian ethnic lands, Bukovyna, and Bessarabia were forcibly resettled there, and many of them perished. Transnistria ceased to exist in March 1944, after the territory was occupied by the Red Army.

TRANSPORT. The transportation of passengers and goods in Ukraine is effected through an extensive network built up in the Soviet period and formerly integrated with that of the **USSR**. In 1995, the share of total freight output among the various branches was as follows: railways (36 percent); water transportation: maritime (23 percent) and river (1 percent); motor vehicle transport (6 percent); air transport (less than 1 percent); and pipeline transport (34 percent).

Pipeline transport, though limited to oil products, gas, and some chemicals, is the fastest-growing transport sector (*see* ENERGY). Transit fees for the transport of Russian gas and oil to Europe contribute significantly to state revenues. The first pipelines in Ukraine date back to the 1920s, but their rapid expansion took place only in the 1970s. The most important are the Samara (Russia)-**Odesa** and trans-European "Druzhba" oil pipelines. Natural gas is transported through two international pipelines, "Soiuz" and "Progress," as well as a large number of smaller lines with a total length of 34,400 km. The newly completed Odesa-Brody oil pipeline has the potential to connect Caspian Sea oil reserves with the Polish port of Gdańsk, reducing Ukraine's dependence on Russian oil. In 1997, the total length of all commercial pipelines in Ukraine was 45,000 km—almost twice as long as the national railways.

Railways are the major form of ground transportation in Ukraine. Their total length is 23,350 km, and they account for almost 60 percent of all passenger traffic. The first railroad line in Ukraine was built in 1861, connecting **Lviv** with Cracow and Vienna. In Russian-ruled Ukraine, the first line was built in 1865 from Balta to Odesa and extended to **Kyiv** by 1872. In 1913, Ukraine had more 15,000 km of railroad, and by 1940 its length reached 20,000 km. Considerably destroyed during **World War II**, the railroads regained their prewar capacity in 1948. As a result of network expansion and modernization initiated in the 1950s, more than one-third, or 9,250 km, of Ukrainian railroads have been electrified. They use broad-gauge rail tracks wider than those of most European countries but compatible with the rest of the former Soviet Union. By European standards, train speeds in Ukraine are quite low (55 km/h on average). Administratively, the railway network is divided into six directorates: Donets, Dnipro, Southern, Lviv, Southwestern, and Odesa.

Sea transport in Ukraine, which dates back to **Kyivan Rus'**, developed into an industry in the 18th century with the establishment of Russian control over the northern shores of the Black and Azov seas. Ports were built in Mykolaiv, Kherson, Sevastopol, and Odesa in the last quarter of the 18th century. Today, Odesa and its satellite port of Illichivsk are the main centers of Ukraine's sea transport. Other large ports are located in Mykolaiv, Kherson, Kerch, Mariupol, and Berdiansk. In 2002, the Ukrainian merchant marine consisted of more than 130 ships, including cargo transports, petroleum tankers, and passenger liners. Most of the ships were built in Ukraine's shipyards. Two international ferry lines connect Illichivsk with Varna in Bulgaria (435 km) and Poti in Georgia. Heavy year-round passenger traffic along the Crimean coast mainly serves the tourist industry.

River transport in Ukraine utilizes 4,400 km of navigable waterways. The Dnipro River has long been a major south-north route. The role of other rivers has increased significantly since the 18th century, when canals linking the basins of various rivers were built and a navigation system linking the Black Sea with the Baltic was established. The Prypiat, Dnister, Southern Buh, and Danube are other major navigable rivers. Rivers have been used mainly to transport grain, lumber, mineral building materials, cement, and, more recently, industrial materials such as coal, metal ores, and finished metals.

Motor-vehicle transport in Ukraine takes advantage of the favorable terrain, which consists mainly of plains and rolling hills. The total length of highways in Ukraine is 176,310 km, including 170,000 hard-surfaced roads that are either paved or all-weather gravel-surfaced. Expressways are relatively underdeveloped and total only 1,770 km. The highway network is most dense in regions that formerly constituted Austrian crownlands and less dense in the parts formerly belonging to the Russian Empire. Motor-vehicle transport in Ukraine, which includes freight and passenger transport, dates back to the beginning of the 20th century, when it involved mostly passenger traffic. The most intensive growth of this branch of transport occurred only after World War II.

Public transportation in Ukraine consists of subways (Kyiv, **Kharkiv**, Dnipropetrovsk), tramways, buses, and taxis. Twenty-four Ukrainian cities have tramway routes, the first of which were opened in Odesa (1880), Lviv (1886), and Kyiv (1892). Their total length exceeds 2,200 km. Since the 1980s, rapid tramway routes have gone into service in Kyiv and Kryvyi Rih. Trolley buses have been used in Ukraine since the 1930s, and today there are trolleybus lines in 46 Ukrainian cities with a total length of 4,300 km. More than 640 cities and townships have local bus services, and 610 towns and villages are serviced by taxis.

Air transportation, the most recently developed sector, has been utilized commercially in Ukraine only since World War II, and its total output is not significant as compared with other forms of transportation. Of more than 790 airports in Ukraine, 182 have paved runways, and only 17 are used for regular passenger traffic. Seven airports service regular international traffic. Boryspil International Airport near Kyiv is the main air hub, accounting for some 80 percent of all international traffic. Thirty-three foreign airlines operated regular service to Ukrainian cities in 1999.

TRIDENT. Symbol of the princely **Riuryk line** of **Kyivan Rus'**. Since 1992, it has served as the **coat of arms** of Ukraine. There are various hypotheses concerning the origin and significance of the trident (e.g., a symbol of state power, religious or military emblem, heraldic symbol, coat of arms, or geometric ornament). A trident was the symbol of Poseidon, the sea god of Greek mythology. It was used by the inhabitants of the Greek **Black Sea colonies** and served as a symbol of the Bosporan Kingdom in the first century A.D. The oldest archaeological finds of tridents in Ukraine date back to that time. Tridents have also been found at the Pereshchepyne (Poltava region) and Martynivka (**Kyiv** region) archaeological sites, which date back to the sixth-eighth centuries.

From the 10th century, the trident was used as the coat of arms of the grand **princes** of Kyivan Rus'. It appears as a bident in the seal of **Sviatoslav Ihorevych** (960–72) and on the gold and silver coins of **Volodymyr the Great** (980–1015). Later, the trident became part of the hereditary heraldic symbol of **Yaroslav the Wise** (1019–54) and his daughter, **Anna Yaroslavna**. Descendants of Yaroslav the Wise, including Iziaslav Yaroslavych (1093–1113), Yaropolk (d. 1087), Sviatopolk (1093–1113), and Vsevolod (1078–1113), used a bident in their coats of arms. **Volodymyr Monomakh** (1113–25) adopted the trident of Volodymyr the Great. In the princely period, the trident did not have official status as the state coat of arms in the modern sense but was a sign of ownership used by the ruling elite. It appeared on bricks, tiles, and stone blocks used in the construction of the Church of the Tithes in Kyiv, the Ascension Cathedral in Volodymyr-Volynskyi, and in the walls of many churches, castles, and palaces, as well as on dishes, weapons, rings, medallions, seals, and manuscripts. The trident (and bident) have been found in archaeological excavations in Halych, Zvenyhorod, and Novgorod. It was used in all principalities of the Kyivan state for several centuries. The trident was sometimes modified with the addition of a cross on one of its arms or at the side, a crescent, or ornamental decorations. It was also used as a symbolic and religious sign in Ukrainian folklore and church heraldry. Some princely families used the trident as their familial and dynastic symbol until the 15th century.

The use of the trident as the state, national, and religious symbol of Ukraine was common during the **Ukrainian Revolution** (1917–21). A trident on an azure background (designed by Vasyl Krychevsky) was adopted as the coat of arms of the **Ukrainian People's Republic** (UNR); it remained in use during the rule of the **Ukrainian State** and the **Directory**. The trident appeared on the currency of the UNR and the Ukrainian State (designed by **Heorhii Narbut** and Krychevsky). A trident with a cross on its central arm was the coat of arms of the **Black Sea Fleet** (law of 18 July 1918). Following the **Act of Union** (22 January 1919), the trident was used in the seals of the Western Province of the UNR and the emblems of the **Ukrainian Galician Army**.

Under Soviet rule, the trident was proscribed as a nationalist symbol. In the Ukrainian lands under Poland, the trident was used by political organizations, notably the **Ukrainian Military Organization**, the **Organization of Ukrainian Nationalists** (OUN), and the UNR government-in-exile. It was also adopted by Ukrainian political parties, representations, and civic organizations in the **diaspora**. On 15 March 1939, the parliament of **Carpatho-Ukraine** adopted the trident (with a cross) as its coat of arms. During **World War II**, emblems incorporating the trident were used by OUN expeditionary groups and by the **Ukrainian State Administration**. The trident was the emblem of the First Ukrainian Division of the Ukrainian National Army (*see* DIVISION GALIZIEN) and was also used in the seals, underground postal service, publications, emblems, and monetary tokens of the **Ukrainian Insurgent Army** and the **Supreme Ukrainian Liberation Council**.

There are more than 200 known variants of the trident. The central arm was depicted as a sword by the OUN and as a cross by Ukrainian Catholics and hetmanites. On 19 February 1992, the trident of Volodymyr the Great was adopted as the official small coat of arms of Ukraine by resolution of the Verkhovna Rada. According to the **Constitution** of Ukraine, ratified on 28 June 1996, it is an element of the great coat of arms of Ukraine.

TROSHCHYNSKY, DMYTRO (1754–1829). Government official and patron of Ukrainian culture. Descended from a **Cossack officer**

family, he graduated from the **Kyiv Mohyla Academy** and was employed at the **Little Russian Collegium** in Hlukhiv. He served successively as secretary to the Hadiach regiment, Prince Nikolai Repnin, and the Main Postal Administration. Troshchynsky received large estates in the **Poltava, Kyiv,** and Voronezh regions and became a senator during the reign of Paul I. Shortly after Alexander I came to power, Troshchynsky was appointed to the State Duma. In 1802–6, he was minister of appanages. On resigning his duties, he lived on his estate in Kybyntsi, Poltava gubernia. In 1812–14, he was marshal of the nobility for the gubernia. Thanks to Troshchynsky, **Nikolai Gogol** was able to study at the Nizhyn Lyceum. From 1814, he was minister of justice, before retiring in 1817.

Greatly enamored of Ukrainian history, Troshchynsky supported the autonomist ideas of his colleagues (**Vasyl Kapnist**, Pavlo Koropchevsky, Mykhailo Myklashevsky). In Kybyntsi he founded a private theater for which Gogol's father, Vasyl Hohol-Yanovsky, wrote several plays. He established a sizable library at Kaharlyk. Troshchynsky supported such Ukrainian scholars, writers, and musicians as Yakiv Markovych, Vasyl Lomykovsky, **Volodymyr Borovykovsky**, and **Artem Vedel**. He was an initiator of the publication of **Ivan Kotliarevsky's** *Eneïda* in 1798.

TRUSH, IVAN (17 January 1869–22 March 1941). Painter. Born in Vysotske (now in **Lviv** oblast), Trush studied at the Brody gymnasium and at the Cracow Academy of Fine Arts (1891–97) under Leon Wyczółkowski and Jan Stanisławski. He founded the Society for the Advancement of Ruthenian Art and the Society of Friends of Ukrainian Scholarship, Literature, and Art and published the first Ukrainian art monthly in **Galicia**, *Artystychnyi visnyk* (Artistic Herald). As a literary and art critic in Lviv, he published in the journals *Literaturno-naukovyi visnyk* (Literary and Scientific Herald), *Buduchnist'* (The Future), and *Ruthenische Rundschau* (Vienna), as well as in the newspapers *Dilo* (The Deed) and *Zoria* (Star). Trush initiated a revival of Galician painting, establishing a reputation as an impressionist noted for his innovative use of color. Most of his **paintings** are large landscapes, often inspired by his frequent travels to the Carpathian Mountains, the **Crimea**, Italy, Egypt, and Palestine. Trush's canvases also included genre paintings and some 350 portraits of contemporaries such as **Mykhailo Drahomanov, Ivan Franko, Borys Hrinchenko, Mykhailo Hrushevsky, Mykola Lysenko,** Ivan Nechui-Levytsky, **Vasyl Stefanyk,** and **Lesia Ukrainka**. His first solo exhibition was held in 1899, and he participated in exhibits by Ukrainian and Polish artists in **Kyiv, Poltava,** Cracow, Warsaw, London, Vienna, and

Sofia. In 1905, Trush initiated the first all-Ukrainian art exhibit in Lviv. The largest collections of his paintings are held at the National Museum and in his memorial museum, both in Lviv.

TRYLIOVSKY, KYRYLO (6 May 1864–19 October 1941). Civic and political figure, lawyer, journalist, and publisher. He was born in Bohutyn, **Galicia** (now Pomoriany in **Lviv** oblast), into the family of a Ukrainian Catholic priest. He attended gymnasiums in Zolochiv and Kolomyia and studied law at the universities of Chernivtsi and Lviv. As a student, he joined the **Ukrainian Radical Party** and became a member of its executive in 1898. From 1901, Tryliovsky worked as a lawyer in Kolomyia and later in Yabloniv. He participated in cultural, educational, and propaganda work among **peasants** in the Hutsul region and **Pokutia** and was an organizer of peasant strikes in 1902. He established **Prosvita** libraries and reading rooms. In Kolomyia, Tryliovsky edited and published the periodicals *Hromada* (Community, 1896–97) and *Zoria* (Star, 1904), as well as the biweekly *Khlops'ka pravda* (Peasant Truth, 1903, 1909).

In the village of Zavallia, Tryliovsky organized the first firefighting center and Sich athletic society in Galicia (5 May 1900); its name was derived from the **Sich** of **Cossack** times. The principal aims of Sich, which Tryliovsky created, were to promote national consciousness and engage in paramilitary activity. Tryliovsky composed Sich songs and marches, published **literature** on the Sich movement, and organized Sich celebrations. In April 1908, he became president of the Supreme Sich Committee, the central executive of the movement, in Stanyslaviv (now Ivano-Frankivsk). Tryliovsky became the general otaman of the Ukrainian Sich Alliance (1912) and established the paramilitary Ukrainian Sich Riflemen (1913), which gave rise to the military unit of the same name in 1914 (*see* UKRAINIAN SICH RIFLEMEN [USS]). He was elected to the Austrian Reichstag (1907 and 1911) and to the Galician Diet (1913). At the beginning of **World War I**, he became a member of the **Supreme Ukrainian Council**, and in August 1914 he headed the Combat Board of the USS. In October 1918, Tryliovsky became a member of the **Ukrainian National Rada** of the **Western Ukrainian People's Republic** (ZUNR), serving on its commissions on foreign, military, and administrative affairs. Within the Rada he chaired the Peasant Radical Club, which later became the Peasant Radical Party. In 1919, Tryliovsky published the weekly *Hromads'kyi holos*, as well as the almanacs *Zaporozhets'* (The Zaporozhian) and *Otaman*. He was the managing editor of the biweekly *Sichovyi holos* (Sich Voice, 1919).

After the downfall of the ZUNR, Tryliovsky emigrated to Vienna, where he worked in the government-in-exile of **Yevhen Petrushevych**. In 1921, he founded the Sich labor and sport society in Vienna and traveled with its delegation to the International Labor Olympics in Prague. Tryliovsky returned to Galicia in late 1927 and worked as a lawyer in Kolomyia and Hvizdka; he also resumed his journalistic activities. He died in Kolomyia. His memoirs, *Z moho zhyttia* (From My Life), were published in 1999.

TRYPILIAN CULTURE. Bronze Age culture that flourished ca. 4500–2250 B.C. It is named after a site discovered and studied in the 1890s by **Vikentii Khvoika** near the village of Trypilia in the **Kyiv** region. The culture spread eastward from present-day Moldova and **Bukovyna**, ultimately taking in part of **Left-Bank Ukraine**. Hundreds of Trypilian sites have been studied, making it the best-known archaeological culture in Ukraine.

Trypilian culture underwent three primary periods of development: early (4500–3500 B.C.), middle (3500–2750 B.C.), and late (2750–2250 B.C.). Each period is defined by social and economic developments, as well as by changes in the ceramic pottery and ornamentation for which Trypilian culture is particularly known. In the early period, settlements were small, consisting of pit and semi-pit dwellings. During the middle period, "eastern" Trypilian settlements were extensive, consisting of large surface buildings located on plateaus. Some settlements occupied 300–400 ha, had a radial-concentric street plan, and were densely built up. Some buildings had two stories, with several rooms and large clay ovens. In the late period, the Trypilians settled the middle course of the Dnipro's right bank, **Volhynia**, and the upper Dnister region. The Volhynian settlements were small, often located on high river banks and hills, and fortified by earthen walls.

During the early period, the Trypilians were engaged primarily in settled animal husbandry, as well as hoe **agriculture**, pottery-making, spinning, and weaving. In the middle period, the importance of agriculture grew significantly, particularly with the introduction of beasts of burden. The period was also distinguished by greater interaction with neighboring tribes, particularly those of the Danube-Balkan region. The late period was marked by the increased importance of animal husbandry, flint tools, and pottery making, including the building of large kilns. Trypilian society began with small clans under a matriarchal order. As animal husbandry developed and towns appeared, the Trypilians shifted to a patriarchal organization. The late period is marked by increased weapons production (flint, stone, and copper). The Trypilians had a fairly evolved spiritual culture, including various agrarian cults: cosmic myths, the cult of Mother Earth, and cults of domestic animals (primarily bulls) and fire. Trypilian art included the decoration of homes with mineral paints and the production of clay pottery. In the early and middle period, linear-incised ornaments were dominant, while in the late period, curvilinear-incised decorations were used. Trypilians also made figurines of women, animals, and houses for ritual use.

Questions about the origin and fate of the Trypilians are complex. There is a consensus that they were influenced by local Buh-Dnipro Neolithic populations and Balkan-Danube populations familiar with Near Eastern agricultural techniques. Trypilian tribes had broad contacts with Central Europe, particularly the Funnel-Beaker culture. Their decline is associated with strong external influences, particularly the appearance of the Pit-Grave culture in the Middle Dnipro region and the Globular Amphora culture in Volhynia. Trypilian cultural traditions have been preserved to some extent in Ukrainian **folk customs**, as manifested in the dwellings of the steppe regions, the decoration of homes and pottery, designs of embroideries and Easter eggs, and the like.

TSEHELSKY, LONHYN (29 August 1875–13 December 1950). Civic and political activist, diplomat, lawyer, journalist, and publisher. Born in Kamianka-Strumylova (now Kamianka-Buzka, **Lviv** oblast), he studied at the Academic Gymnasium in Lviv from 1886 and enrolled in the faculty of law at Lviv University in 1894. Tsehelsky was an organizer of a Ukrainian student congress in Lviv (1899), a student demonstration at Lviv University (1901), and peasant strikes in eastern **Galicia** (1902). He received his doctorate in international law from Lviv University and initially practiced law but soon devoted himself entirely to politics and journalism. From 1900 to 1902, he edited the literary journal *Moloda Ukraïna* (Young Ukraine). He maintained close ties with **Mykola Mikhnovsky** and published the latter's *Samostiina Ukraïna* (Independent Ukraine) in Lviv in 1900. In 1901, he published the brochure *Rus'-Ukraïna i Moskovshchyna-Rosiia* (Rus'-Ukraine and Muscovy-Russia), which asserted Ukraine's claim to the historical traditions of **Kyivan Rus'**. The work was distributed in tens of thousands of copies and had a considerable effect on Galician public opinion.

In 1907–8, Tsehelsky was publisher and managing editor of the newspaper *Dilo* and edited the newspaper *Svoboda* (Liberty). From 1915 to 1918, he edited the Lviv newspaper *Ukraïns'ke slovo* (Ukrainian Word) and was managing editor of *Literaturno-naukovyi visnyk*. He served as a deputy to the Austrian Reichstag from 1911 to 1918, representing the **National Democratic Party**, and in 1913 he became a deputy to the Galician Diet. During **World War I**, Tsehelsky belonged to every important Ukrainian organization in Galicia: the **Supreme Ukrainian Council**, the General Ukrainian Council, the Combat Board of the **Ukrainian Sich Riflemen**, and the **Union for the Liberation of Ukraine**. In October 1918, he became a member of the **Ukrainian National Rada** of the **Western Ukrainian People's Republic** (ZUNR). On 11 November, he was appointed the ZUNR secretary of internal affairs. As representatives of the Ukrainian National Rada of the ZUNR, Tsehelsky and Dmytro Levytsky signed the preliminary agreement concerning unification with the **Ukrainian People's Republic** (UNR) into a single Ukrainian state (1 December 1918). In early 1919, Tsehelsky was minister without portfolio and director of the secretariat of foreign affairs for the Western Province of the UNR in the government of Sydir Holubovych. He participated in the official proclamation of the **Act of Union** between the ZUNR and the UNR, as well as in the **Labor Congress** of the UNR. He was appointed deputy minister of foreign affairs of the UNR (22 January 1919) and made a number of diplomatic trips to Austria, Czechoslovakia, and Germany. From 1920 to 1921, he was the ZUNR representative in the United States, where he later settled. He wrote for the newspaper *Ameryka* (America) and became its editor in 1943. In his memoirs, *Vid legend do pravdy* (From Legends to Truth, 1960), he gave his interpretation of the November Uprising of 1918 in Lviv. He died in Philadelphia.

TUHAN-BARANOVSKY, MYKHAILO (20 or 21 January 1865–21 or 22 January 1919). Economist. Born in Solone, **Kharkiv** gubernia, into a gentry family, he studied in **Kyiv** and Kharkiv, obtaining a doctorate from Moscow University (1898). In 1892, he studied industrial cycles in Britain and wrote a thesis on the subject. Tuhan-Baranovsky lectured in economics in St. Petersburg and Moscow. In 1906, he became editor in chief of the journal *Vestnik kooperatsii* (Herald of Cooperation) and later edited the serial *Novye idei v èkonomike* (New Ideas in Economics, five issues). In his early years, he was an exponent of "legal Marxism" but turned against Marx's notion of inevitable class struggle. Besides general textbooks on the history and theory of political economy, he produced studies of economic **cooperation**. His monograph on paper money and metal (1917) foreshadowed Keynes's thinking on monetary policy. In 1917, Tuhan-Baranovsky moved to Kyiv, where he joined the **Ukrainian Party of Socialist Federalists**. During the **Ukrainian Revolution**, he was active in the establishment of financial institutions. He served briefly as general secretary of finance at the **Ukrainian Central Rada** and wrote the economic policy declaration of the Rada's General Secretariat (August 1917). From July 1918, he edited the journal *Ukraïns'ka kooperatsiia* (Ukrainian Cooperation). He was head of the founding congress of the Central Ukrainian Cooperative Committee (1–3 September 1918), and in early October 1918 he headed its governing council. In 1918, he contributed to legislation on the establishment of the **Ukrainian Academy of Sciences** (UAN). From November 1918, he was a full member of the UAN, and in early 1919 he became head of its socioeconomic department. He organized the Ukrainian Cooperative Institute. Under the **Directory**, Tuhan-Baranovsky was a member of a committee on monetary reform. In January 1919, he was appointed economic advisor to the delegation of the **Ukrainian People's Republic** at the Paris Peace Conference. En route to Paris, he died suddenly on a train near **Odesa**, where he was buried.

TUKALSKY-NELIUBOVYCH, YOSYF (d. 26 July [5 August] 1675 or 1676). Orthodox metropolitan of **Kyiv** (1663–75). Tonsured at an early age, he served as archimandrite of the Holy Spirit Monastery in Vilnius (1657–58). In 1661, he became bishop of Mstsislaŭ in Belarus. In November 1663, at a divided council in Korsun, Tukalsky-Neliubovych was elected metropolitan of Kyiv; elected concurrently to the same post was Bishop Antonii Vynnytsky of Peremyshl (Przemyśl), who was supported by Hetman **Pavlo Teteria**. Consequently, Tukalsky-Neliubovych presided over only part of the metropolitanate and resided in Chyhyryn, the capital of the **Hetmanate**, while the western eparchies were administered by Vynnytsky. For his opposition to Polish interference in Ukrainian church affairs, Tukalsky-Neliubovych was arrested and incarcerated at the Marienburg fortress in Prussia (1664–66). Released at the behest of Hetman **Petro Doroshenko**, he again took up residence in Chyhyryn and became Doroshenko's close advisor; his policy was to maintain the independence of the **Kyiv metropolitanate**, avoiding alliances with Muscovy or Poland. He forbade the mention of Tsar Aleksei's name in church services, ordering that Doroshenko be mentioned instead. Tukalsky-Neliubovych was buried at the Holy Trinity Monastery near Chyhyryn, and his remains were later transferred to the Mhar Transfiguration Monastery near Lubny.

TUPTALO, DYMYTRII (11 December 1651–28 October [8 November] 1709). Secular name: Danylo. Church figure, writer, and preacher. He was born in Makariv, **Kyiv** region, into a **Cossack** family and received his primary education at home. From 1662, Tuptalo studied at the **Kyiv Mohyla** Collegium with the well-known theologian Ioanikii Galiatovsky. He was tonsured in 1668 at St. Cyril's Monastery in Kyiv, and in 1669 he was consecrated a hierodeacon by Metropolitan **Yosyf Tukalsky-Neliubovych** of Kyiv. He lived at St. Cyril's Monastery until 1675. In that year Tuptalo was ordained a hieromonk at the Hustynia Trinity Monastery. Over the next three decades he served as hegumen of a number of monasteries in Ukraine and Belarus. In 1684, encouraged by Archimandrite Varlaam Yasynsky of the **Kyivan Cave Monastery**, Tuptalo undertook a major compilation of saints' lives, *Chet'i-minei* (Menaion for Daily Reading), that was issued by the Hustynia Monastery press (1689–1705). This collection, which includes accounts of many **Kyivan Rus'** saints derived from manuscripts and adaptations of Greek and Latin sources, is the most significant work of Ukrainian **baroque** hagiography. In 1701, Tuptalo was summoned to Moscow by Tsar Peter I and consecrated metropolitan of Siberia and Tobolsk (March 1701) but did not take up the post because of illness. In the following year he was appointed metropolitan of Rostov, where he founded a school. Tuptalo belonged to a group of Ukrainian hierarchs led by Stefan Yavorsky that combated the Old Believers and other traditionalist sects but also opposed Peter's subordination of the Orthodox Church to the state. The author of many theological treatises, sermons, and literary works, Tuptalo was canonized in April 1757.

TYCHYNA, PAVLO (15 [27] January 1891–16 September 1967). Poet and academician of the **Ukrainian Academy of Sciences** (from 1929). He was born in Pisky, Chernihiv region, into the family of a village precentor. Tychyna received his primary education at home and then studied at the local zemstvo school. In 1900, he moved to Chernihiv, where he sang in a monastery choir and studied at the theological seminary. In 1913, he went on to **Kyiv**, where he studied at the Commercial Institute (1913–17) and worked for the journal *Svitlo* (Light), the newspaper *Rada* (Council), and at Mykola Sadovsky's Ukrainian **theater**. In 1918, Tychyna published his first collection, *Soniashni klarnety* (Sunny Clarinets), a symbolist work that established his distinct poetic style, which was dubbed "clarinetism." His subsequent collections confirmed Tychyna's place as one of the most important Ukrainian poets of the 20th century. In 1923, he moved to **Kharkiv**, where he worked for the journal *Chervonyi shliakh* (Red Path). He was one of the most striking representatives of revolutionary **romanticism** in Ukrainian **literature** (a movement that also included **Vasyl Blakytny**, Vasyl Chumak, and Mykola Bazhan). In 1926, Tychyna joined the Free Academy of Proletarian Literature (**Vaplite**).

Tychyna's talent was deformed by the totalitarian regime. His response to Stalin's **political terror** was one of conformity. In the 1930s, his verse began to glorify Soviet patriotism and internationalism, Stalin, and the Communist Party. This conformity was sustained to the end of Tychyna's life; he did not revise his Stalin-era poetry during the **Khrushchev** thaw, as other poets did, and he was critical of the *shistdesiatnyky*. Tychyna also became a fixture of the Soviet political establishment, serving as Ukraine's minister of **education** (1943–48) and chairman of its **Verkhovna Rada** (1953–59). In 1962, he was awarded the **Shevchenko** State Prize. Having a command of many languages, Tychyna also left a significant legacy of literary translations. He died in Kyiv, where a museum devoted to him was opened in 1980.

TYHYPKO, SERHII (b. 13 February 1960). Banker and politician. Tyhypko was born in the village of Dragoneşti, **Moldavia**, into the family of a beekeeper. He graduated from the Dnipropetrovsk Metallurgical Institute in 1982 as an engineer and obtained a candidate of sciences degree in economics in 1996. After military service, he began a career in the Komsomol (Communist Youth League). From 1984 to 1989, Tyhypko held various Komsomol posts in Dnipropetrovsk; in 1989, he was appointed first secretary of the Dnipropetrovsk Komsomol city committee. After the breakup of the Soviet Union, Tyhypko reoriented his career to banking and worked as deputy chairman of the board of the Dnipro Commercial Bank (1991–92). From March 1992 to April 1997, he headed Pryvatbank in Dnipropetrovsk. During his tenure, the bank grew from a small enterprise into a leading financial institution.

Tyhypko gradually moved into politics and was appointed an adjunct consultant to President **Leonid Kuchma** on monetary reform (1994–97). From January 1996, he was a member of an interdepartmental consulting commission on banking; he also helped draft the annual presidential report on economic and social development. In July 1997, Tyhypko was appointed deputy prime minister with responsibility for the economy. From December 1999, he was minister of the economy in the government of **Viktor Yushchenko**. Tyhypko also headed the commission on restitution of funds illegally taken out of Ukraine (1998–2000). He resigned from the Yushchenko government in July 2000, stating that he was tired of "ineffective work."

In June 2000, Tyhypko was elected to the **Verkhovna Rada** (VR), where he became a close ally of **Viktor Pinchuk**, who supported Tyhypko's bid to become leader of the Labor Ukraine Party (November 2000). After the 2002 presidential elections, when the winning bloc (For a United Ukraine) fell apart, Tyhypko's political ambitions were thwarted. He left the VR in December of that year to head the National Bank of Ukraine.

TYKHY, OLEKSII (27 January 1927–6 May 1984). Poet and **human-rights** activist. He was born in Izhivka, Donetsk oblast, and graduated from the faculty of philosophy of Moscow University. From 1950, Tykhy worked as a biology teacher; from 1954, he taught history in his native village. Tykhy was first tried in 1948 by a military tribunal in Stalino (now Donetsk) oblast for criticizing a political candidate and given a suspended sentence. He was arrested again for sending a letter to the Communist Party of the Soviet Union protesting the invasion of Hungary by Warsaw Pact armies. On 18 April 1957, at a closed session of the Stalino oblast court, Tykhy was sentenced to seven years' imprisonment for "anti-Soviet agitation and propaganda." He was incarcerated in Vladimir Prison and the Dubrovlag camp in Mordovia.

Released on 15 February 1964, Tykhy was unable to obtain a position in his field and worked as a laborer. At the same time, he compiled material for a dictionary of the Ukrainian **language** and developed a method of correspondence instruction. In his publicistic writings he advocated the revival of the Ukrainian language and culture in the Donetsk region. In April 1973, he sent a letter titled "Thoughts about My Native Donetsk Region" to the Presidium of the **Verkhovna Rada** of the **Ukrainian SSR**. In 1974, he wrote an essay on "village problems," **Russification**, and the Ukrainian language. He was among the founders of the **Ukrainian Helsinki Group** (UHH).

Tykhy's literary work and human-rights activism prompted his second arrest in early February 1977. He was tried with Mykola Rudenko, the head of the UHH, in Druzhkivka (Donetsk oblast). Found guilty of "anti-Soviet agitation and propaganda" and "illegal possession of weapons," Tykhy was sentenced to 10 years' imprisonment in hard-labor camps and five years' exile. He was imprisoned at the Sosnovka camp in Mordovia. In March 1980, he was transferred to a strict-regime camp in Kuchino (Perm oblast, Russia). Tykhy undertook several hunger strikes (the longest lasted 52 days); by 1981, he was gravely ill. He died in the Perm prison hospital. By decision of the Supreme Court of the Ukrainian SSR (7 December 1990), Tykhy's sentence was overturned and his case closed "owing to absence of criminal activity." On 19 November 1989, the remains of Tykhy, **Vasyl Stus**, and **Yurii Lytvyn** were reburied at the Baikove Cemetery in **Kyiv**.

TYMOSHENKO, YULIIA (b. 27 November 1960). Businesswoman and politician. She was born into the family of a coal miner in Dnipropetrovsk. In 1984, Tymoshenko graduated from Dnipropetrovsk State University as an economist; she earned the degree of candidate of economic sciences in 1999. After graduation, she worked for five years as an economist at the Dnipropetrovsk Mechanical Engineering Plant. With the liberalization of the Soviet economy, she entered the oil business as commercial director and then general director of the Ukrainian Oil Corporation (KUB), founded in 1991. In November 1995, KUB became a major enterprise, United Energy Systems of Ukraine. Tymoshenko worked closely with **Pavlo Lazarenko**, who reportedly owned shares of the corporation. With Lazarenko's appointment as prime minister, United Energy Systems controlled more than half of Ukraine's gas exports.

In January 1997, Tymoshenko was elected to the **Verkhovna Rada** (VR) and became deputy head of the **Hromada** (Community) Party, founded by Lazarenko. She also headed Hromada's shadow cabinet in the VR. In June 1997, a group of VR deputies accused Tymoshenko of misappropriating funds earmarked for humanitarian and technical aid, which she denied. In September, the State Anti-Monopoly Committee referred several charges of dumping against United Energy Systems to the prosecutor-general's office, which attempted to lift Tymoshenko's parliamentary immunity so that charges could be filed against her. Tymoshenko was also accused of smuggling U.S. $26,000 via the Moscow airport. When the VR declined to lift Tymoshenko's immunity, she began a counterattack against the government, calling for early elections to remove President **Leonid Kuchma** from office. In 1998, Tymoshenko was reelected to the VR and headed its Budget Committee. She left the ranks of Hromada in March 1999, citing Lazarenko's "authoritarian methods" of leadership. In the same year, she founded the Batkivshchyna (Fatherland) Party and temporarily established good relations with President Kuchma.

On 30 December 1999, Tymoshenko was appointed deputy prime minister in charge of energy reform in the government of **Viktor Yushchenko**. Her efforts to establish transparency in the functioning of the energy sector brought additional revenue to the state treasury (government transfers to Ukrainian citizens rose by some 18 billion *hryvni* in 2000) and financial losses to the economic "oligarchs" **Viktor Pinchuk**, **Hryhorii Surkis**, and **Oleksandr Volkov**. In January 2001, Tymoshenko lost her cabinet position after the prosecutor-general's office initiated criminal proceedings against her. She was arrested on 13 February and incarcerated in the Lukianivka Prison in **Kyiv** on charges of bribery, fraud, and embezzlement. In March, the Pechersk District Court dismissed the charges and canceled the warrant for Tymoshenko's arrest after she had spent 42 days in prison.

In July 2001, after President Kuchma was implicated in the **Gongadze** murder case, Tymoshenko took the leadership of the National Salvation Forum, which demanded the president's dismissal. In December 2001, she created and led a new electoral bloc bearing her name that took 7.2 percent of the vote in the March 2002 parliamentary elections. Two months before the vote (29 January), Tymoshenko was involved in a car accident that she denounced as a politically motivated attempt on her life. Prior to the 2004 presidential elections, she signed an agreement with Yushchenko and supported his bid for the presidency.

U

UDOVENKO, HENNADII (b. 22 June 1931). Diplomat and politician. Udovenko was born in Kryvyi Rih into the family of a mining engineer. In 1954, he graduated from **Kyiv** University with a degree in history and international relations. From 1955 to 1958, Udovenko headed the Feliks Dzerzhinsky Collective Farm near Kyiv. Later, he joined the Ministry of Foreign Affairs, serving as first secretary (1959–65) and subsequently as an advisor on international economic organizations. In 1965, Udovenko was transferred to Geneva, where he was an administrator at the **United Nations** (UN) office. From 1971 to 1980, he held a variety of positions at the Ministry of Foreign Affairs and at UN headquarters in New York. In 1980, he was appointed deputy foreign minister.

Five years later, Udovenko returned to New York as Ukraine's permanent representative to the UN, serving as vice chairman of the UN Special Committee against Apartheid. His contribution to the eradication of apartheid in South Africa was internationally recognized. In July 1985, he served as president of the Security Council. In the General Assembly, Udovenko served as vice president (1991) and president (1997–98); he also chaired the Special Political Committee in 1989–90. From 1989 to 1991, Udovenko was vice president of the Economic and Social Council. He has also been actively involved in UN and other agencies dealing with political, economic, and financial issues, as well as development, the **environment**, and **human rights**. From September 1992 to August 1994, he was Ukraine's ambassador to Poland.

In 1994, Udovenko succeeded **Anatolii Zlenko** as Ukraine's minister of foreign affairs, a post he held until April 1998. Integration into European and Euro-Atlantic political, economic, and security structures dominated Udovenko's policy. In 1997, Ukraine signed a Charter on Distinctive Partnership with the North Atlantic Treaty Organization, providing a framework for consultation and cooperation. In 1995, Udovenko received the Honorary Award of the President of Ukraine in recognition of his contributions to the development of Ukraine's foreign policy.

Udovenko was elected to the **Verkhovna Rada** in 1998. In 1999 he was a presidential candidate, finishing seventh in a field of 13. From March 1999 to May 2003, he headed **Rukh**.

UKRAÏNA. Academic journal of Ukrainian studies published in **Kyiv** from 1914 to 1930 (except 1915–16 and 1919–23). Edited by **Mykhailo Hrushevsky**, it was issued by the Ukrainian Scientific Society and, from 1924, by the historical section of the **Ukrainian Academy of Sciences** (VUAN). Altogether, 43 issues were published.

The journal published articles on history, archaeology, economics, folklore, ethnography, **language**, **literature**, art, and regional studies. It also published annotated primary sources and documents, reviews, and bibliographies. Some issues were devoted to outstanding cultural figures, major historical events, and regional topics. Noteworthy contributors included **Dmytro Bahalii**, **Ahatanhel Krymsky**, **Ivan Krypiakevych**, **Stepan Smal-Stotsky**, **Kyrylo Studynsky**, and **Mykola Vasylenko**. Along with *Kievskaia starina* (Kyivan Antiquity) and *Literaturno-naukovyi visnyk*, *Ukraïna* was one of the most authoritative journals in its field.

Ukraïna came under heavy censorship in the late 1920s and was forced to cease publication in 1930. The last issue (no. 44) was printed but not released. It was replaced with an officially approved periodical, *Ukraïna—Zhurnal tsyklu nauk istorychnykh* (Journal of the Cycle of Historical Sciences), which attacked the "Hrushevsky School" as a "nationalist deviation." The new journal ceased publication after two issues.

UKRAINIAN ACADEMY OF ARTS AND SCIENCES/UKRAÏNS'KA VIL'NA AKADEMIIA NAUK (UVAN). The UVAN was established in November 1945 in Augsburg, Germany, to carry on the scholarly traditions of the **Ukrainian Academy of Sciences** (suppressed by Stalin's **political terror**) in the **diaspora**. Its membership consisted of approximately 150 scholars organized in 17 sections under the presidency of **Dmytro Doroshenko**. The first 24 full members of UVAN were elected in Regensburg in April 1948.

In 1949, the UVAN presidium was transferred to Winnipeg,

Canada, where Doroshenko settled; by 1989 the UVAN in Canada had more than 60 full members. It has issued a number of serials dealing with **literature** and linguistics, as well as studies on Ukrainians in Canada and other publications. UVAN members in the United States established their own organization and foundation, based in New York City, in 1950. The UVAN building in New York houses some 370 archives (a printed guide compiled by Yury Boshyk was issued in 1988), making it the most important Ukrainian archival depository outside Ukraine. The building also houses a library of ca. 55,000 volumes and museum holdings of some 500,000 items of Ukrainica. By 2000, the UVAN in the United States had more than 100 full members. It began issuing its English-language *Annals* in 1951 (48 issues by 1999) and has published more than 100 books.

UKRAINIAN ACADEMY OF SCIENCES/UKRAÏNS'KA AKADE-MIIA NAUK (UAN), also known as the All-Ukrainian Academy of Sciences (VUAN, 1921–36), Academy of Sciences of the **Ukrainian SSR** (AN UkSSR, 1936–91), and Academy of Sciences of Ukraine (1991–93); currently the National Academy of Sciences of Ukraine (NANU). The UAN was founded on 27 November 1918 by the **Ukrainian State**. It had three departments: historicophilological, physicomathematical, and socioeconomic. Its founders were the distinguished scholars **Dmytro Bahalii**, **Ahatanhel Krymsky**, Mykola Petrov, **Stepan Smal-Stotsky**, **Volodymyr Vernadsky**, Mykola Kashchenko, **Stephen Timoshenko**, Pavlo Tutkovsky, **Mykhailo Tuhan-Baranovsky**, Fedir Taranovsky, Volodymyr Kosynsky, and Orest Levytsky. New members were elected by secret ballot at general meetings. Vernadsky was elected the academy's first president.

With the establishment of Soviet rule, the estate of Countess Levashova in **Kyiv** (now the residence of the president of the NANU) was confiscated for the use of the UAN. In June 1921, the **Council of People's Commissars** ratified a resolution recognizing the academy as Ukraine's supreme scholarly institution. It was renamed the All-Ukrainian Academy of Sciences in recognition of its aspiration to unite scholars in all the Ukrainian lands under its auspices and was placed under the jurisdiction of the People's Commissariat of Education. Between 1919 and 1930, 103 academicians were elected to the VUAN. In 1924–25, the academy conducted its first election of foreign members, but the candidates were not ratified by the Commissariat of Education. In the 1920s, the VUAN maintained its original division into three departments. The first had 10 chairs in **language**, **literature**, and history, as well as 39 commissions, institutes, committees, and museums. The Archaeological Institute was established in 1921. After **Mykhailo Hrushevsky's** return to Ukraine (1924), the VUAN's research on Ukrainian history expanded considerably. The physicomathematical department consisted of 30 divisions, a number of which were involved in world-class research: applied mathematics (Heorhii Pfeiffer), mathematical physics (Mykola Krylov), experimental zoology (**Ivan Shmalhauzen**), and others. Within the socioeconomic department, the Demographic Institute, the world's first, under the directorship of **Mykhailo Ptukha**, was particularly active.

The VUAN preserved a fair degree of autonomy until the late 1920s, when it came under state control. In 1928, Krymsky, the academy's permanent secretary, was removed from his post, and a year later two academy members (**Serhii Yefremov** and Mykhailo Slabchenko) and 24 of its scholars were accused of belonging to a fictitious counterrevolutionary organization, the **Union for the Liberation of Ukraine**. They were arrested and sentenced to lengthy prison terms.

In July 1930, **Oleksander Bohomolets** became president of the academy and conducted a fundamental reorganization of its structure. In place of the former three departments, he established two new ones: a natural science and technical department and a socioeconomic department. In 1931, the VUAN consisted of 164 scholarly research institutions that employed only 242 research associates, including 79 academicians. In 1934, the VUAN came under the direct jurisdiction of the Council of People's Commissars, and in 1936 it was renamed the Academy of Sciences of the Ukrainian SSR. It incorporated institutes of Ukrainian history, literature, folklore, and economics. In the 1920s and 1930s, the academy was home to the world-class schools of **Dmitrii Grave** (algebra), Krylov (mathematical physics), **Lev Pysarzhevsky** (chemistry), Oleksander Dynnyk (mechanics and the theory of elasticity), Bohomolets (experimental pathology), **Yevhen Paton** (electrical welding), Mykhailo Fedorov (mining mechanics), Mykola Kholodny and Oleksander Fomin (botany), Shmalhauzen (zoology), and others.

In 1938, the **Kharkiv** Physico-Technical Institute, a leader in nuclear physics research, was incorporated into the Academy of Sciences. It was credited with producing the first nuclear reaction in the **USSR** (1932). In 1934, the Institute of Physical Chemistry produced heavy water (**Oleksander Brodsky**). By 1941, the AN UkSSR consisted of 26 institutes employing 3,092 scholars, including 60 academicians, 66 corresponding members, 164 doctors of science, and 325 candidates of science. Its institutes were located in Kyiv, Kharkiv, Dnipropetrovsk, and **Lviv**.

During **World War II**, the institutes were evacuated to cities in the eastern USSR. Beginning in 1944, the work of the academic institutes was gradually renewed in Ukraine and expanded rapidly in the postwar years. By 1960, 20 new institutes had been established (for a total of 44). In 1954, the academy established its Crimean branch. The academy's greatest achievements in the postwar period were in the physicomathematical and chemical sciences. Under the leadership of Sergei Lebedev, the academy built the first digital computing machine outside the United States. In 1956, a laboratory of modeling and computing technology was established under the direction of **Viktor Hlushkov**; in the following year it became the Computing Center of the AN UkSSR. Breakthroughs were also achieved in theoretical and metal physics, semiconductors, nuclear research, and rocket technology. The academy was recognized worldwide for its work in electrical welding under **Borys Paton**. The development of biological sciences was hindered by official interference, especially in genetics. The destructive influence of party ideology was felt most strongly in the humanities.

Since February 1962, Borys Paton has been president of the academy. In that time, the institutes of technology have developed most rapidly. In the 1970s, the AN UkSSR began creating research complexes consisting of institutes, construction bureaus, research facilities, and factories. In 1962, the Computing Center became the Institute of Cybernetics, which soon took on a leading role in the field of automated manufacturing systems. By 1986, 76 percent of the academy's researchers worked for the Section of Physico-Technical and Mathematical Sciences. The sections of Chemistry and Biological Sciences employed 19 percent of the academy's scholars, while the Social Sciences Section employed 5 percent. The number of research associates rose to 15,340. The academy's staff included 143 academicians and 203 corresponding members, 1,394 doctors of science, and 8,141 candidates of science. Scientists employed in many of the academy's institutes helped significantly to overcome the destructive consequences of the **Chornobyl nuclear disaster**.

After Ukraine's declaration of independence, the NANU became a truly autonomous organization for the first time in its history, with the right to own the material base at its disposal. Scholars, especially those in the humanities, were given the opportunity to pursue highly promising fields of study. Jurists, historians, sociologists, and economists became active in the process of nation-building. Communication with scholars abroad greatly improved. However, the transition from a planned to a market economy raised doubts about the feasibility of the academy's work. The collapse of the USSR severed scientific and technical ties that had developed on the basis of directives. Defense production was greatly reduced. Basic research was severely curtailed by the economic crisis. Since the early 1990s, many programs at the NANU have lost funding, and numerous young scholars began searching for employment abroad or turned away from professional research.

UKRAINIAN CANADIAN CONGRESS (UCC)/KONGRES UKRAÏNTSIV KANADY. Umbrella organization established in 1940 as the Ukrainian Canadian Committee, including five major Ukrainian-Canadian associations. The formation of the UCC was inspired by the Canadian government in order to unite the Ukrainian community behind Canada's participation in **World War II**. The UCC encouraged Ukrainian-Canadians to enlist in the armed forces and promoted the purchase of war bonds. After the war, it helped save many Ukrainian refugees in Western Europe from forced repatriation to the **USSR** and resettled them in Canada.

By 1965, the Winnipeg-based UCC consisted of 30 organizations. It promoted Ukrainian-**language** instruction in Canadian public schools and universities, as well as in Ukrainian private schools. It was also instrumental in promoting Canada's policy of official multiculturalism. In 1963, the UCC established the Ukrainian Canadian Foundation of Taras Shevchenko to support cultural activities. It helped establish the **Ukrainian World Congress** in 1967.

From its inception, the UCC was anticommunist in principle; it did not cooperate with the pro-Soviet Association of United Ukrainian Canadians until after the demise of the USSR. The UCC established a Civil Liberties Commission (1985) to respond to allegations that the government had allowed war criminals to immigrate to Canada after 1945. The UCC, which changed its name to "Congress" in 1989, has also sought compensation for Ukrainians interned in Canada during **World War I** for their supposed pro-Austrian sympathies.

UKRAINIAN CATHOLIC CHURCH/UKRAÏNS'KA KATOLYTS'KA TSERKVA. Founded as a result of the **Union of Brest** (1596), whereby part of the **Kyiv metropolitanate** renounced the jurisdiction of the patriarch of Constantinople and accepted union with Rome (hence the name "Uniate Church," which was current in the 16th–18th centuries). The Union of Brest was an attempt on the part of some Ukrainian churchmen, backed by nobles and burghers, to gain equality of status with the Roman Catholic Church of Poland. Efforts to secure equality proved unavailing: Polish Catholics saw the Uniate Church as an obstacle to their

Latinizing project in Ukraine, forcing Uniate hierarchs such as **Ipatii Potii** and **Yosyf Veliamyn Rutsky** constantly to petition for the exercise of the rights accorded their church in 1596. Moreover, the Uniates found themselves locked in internecine conflict with their countrymen who remained loyal to Orthodoxy. Among those killed in the strife was the Uniate archbishop of Polatsk, Yosafat Kuntsevych. Although the Union of Brest effectively outlawed the **Ukrainian Orthodox Church** in the **Polish-Lithuanian Commonwealth**, it received increasing support from the Ukrainian **Cossacks**: reestablishing itself in the **Kyiv** region, the Orthodox Church underwent a major cultural revival, consecrated a new hierarchy in 1620, and was relegalized in 1632. Efforts to reunite the two churches in the 1620s–30s proved unavailing, with Cossack opposition a major obstacle. In 1646, the Uniate Church expanded into **Transcarpathia** with the **Union of Uzhhorod**. The **Khmelnytsky Uprising** against Polish rule, which broke out in 1648, reasserted the dominance of Orthodoxy in Ukraine and marginalized the Uniate Church.

Following the partition of the Ukrainian lands by the **Treaty of Andrusovo** (1667) and the stabilization of Polish rule in Right-Bank Ukraine, the fortunes of the Uniate Church began to revive. It enjoyed considerable support from the Polish crown; its hierarchy and the **Basilian Order** were active on its behalf. The **Lviv** diocese acceded to the Union in 1700, followed by the Lutsk diocese (1702), the **Lviv Dormition Brotherhood** (1708), and the **Pochaiv Monastery** (1712). In the 18th century, the Uniate metropolitanate of Kyiv included nine eparchies.

After the partitions of Poland, the church developed in opposing directions under Russian and Austrian rule. In the Russian Empire, official persecution began under Catherine II and continued (with a brief respite under Paul I and Alexander I) for a century, leading to the almost complete elimination of institutional Eastern Catholicism. Four Uniate dioceses were abolished in 1795, 145 Basilian monasteries were closed, and Metropolitan Teodosii Rostotsky was confined to St. Petersburg. In the 1830s, under Tsar Nicholas II and his administrator for Uniate affairs, Yosyf Semashko, the Uniate Church was abolished in **Volhynia**, and many clergymen who refused to accept Orthodoxy were exiled to Siberia. The Union of Brest was declared null and void in February 1839. The sole remaining Uniate diocese in the empire, that of **Kholm**, was abolished in 1875.

In **Galicia**, by contrast, the new Austrian rulers promoted the Uniate Church in order to offset Polish influence and the threat of Russian expansion. Empress Maria Theresa renamed it the Greek

Catholic Church (because of its Byzantine rite) in 1774, emphasizing its equality of status with the Roman Catholic Church. This was followed by the establishment of educational institutions for Greek Catholic clergymen: the Barbareum in Vienna (1775–84), the **Studium Ruthenum** (Lviv, 1787–1809), and a general seminary in Lviv. The **Halych metropolitanate** was reestablished in 1808. Emancipated from its previously subordinate condition, the Greek Catholic clergy became heavily involved in educational activity among the Galician peasantry. It also played a leading political role in the **Revolution of 1848** in Galicia, representing the national demands of the Ukrainian population to the Habsburg authorities. While the Greek Catholic hierarchy remained politically conservative, the younger generation of priests, represented by the **Ruthenian Triad** of the 1830s and its successors, was increasingly **populist** in character. From the 1860s, priests became active in establishing reading rooms, **cooperatives**, and temperance associations; they were also involved in politics at every level. The church was adversely affected by the **Russophile** movement. Galician Russophiles played a major role in the forced conversion of the Kholm eparchy to Orthodoxy, and in 1882 the Galician village of Hnylychky applied for permission to convert. Given this apparent loss of control over the Catholic faithful, Metropolitan Yosyf Sembratovych resigned his office (1882) under pressure from the Vatican and Emperor Franz Joseph. His nephew and successor, **Sylvestr Sembratovych**, attempted to reestablish the church's authority by stabilizing relations with the dominant Poles.

Beginning in the 1890s, with the formation of the openly anticlerical **Ukrainian Radical Party**, the church's leadership of the national movement in Galicia was increasingly disputed by the secular intelligentsia. One reaction to this development, exemplified by Bishop **Hryhorii Khomyshyn** of Stanyslaviv (1904–46), was to draw closer to Rome in ecclesiastical practice and distance the church from the national movement. But the dominant tendency, represented by Metropolitan **Andrei Sheptytsky** of Lviv (1901–44), was to continue to identify the church with the national movement. A towering figure in Galician society, Sheptytsky generously subsidized Ukrainian cultural life, advanced Ukrainian political causes in the Galician Diet and the Vienna parliament, and supported the **Western Ukrainian People's Republic**. He nevertheless condemned the national movement when it resorted to violence, as in the assassination of the Galician viceroy, Andrzej Potocki (1908), or in the 1930s, when the **Organization of Ukrainian Nationalists** killed Polish officials and Ukrainians whom it considered traitors. Sheptytsky also promoted the eastward expansion of the Union, established the Russian Catholic Church, and was a leader of the ecumenical movement between the world wars.

During the interwar period, Sheptytsky and his eventual successor, **Yosyf Slipy**, propagated new religious orders and promoted the revival of theological studies and ecclesiastical scholarship. Branches of Catholic Action were established throughout Galicia in the 1930s. In the same decade, the designation "Ukrainian Greek Catholic Church" came into use. Church activity was greatly restricted during the first Soviet occupation of **western Ukraine** (1939–41), which resulted in the closing of ecclesiastical institutions, confiscation of church property, and the teaching of atheism in schools. After **World War II** and the Soviet reoccupation, the entire hierarchy of the church was arrested (April 1945) and preparations were made to suppress the institution completely. A so-called Initiative Group, led by the Rev. Havryil Kostelnyk, was recognized as the "sole provisional administrative body of the Ukrainian Catholic Church." On 8–10 March 1946, the Lviv Sobor, stage-managed by the Soviet authorities, declared the annulment of the Union of Brest and the unification of the Ukrainian Catholic Church with the Russian Orthodox Church. On 28 August 1949, a regional religious congress in Mukacheve similarly nullified the Union of Uzhhorod in Transcarpathia. In the West, the Lviv Sobor was deemed uncanonical and the abolition of the church pronounced illegal (papal encyclical of 15 December 1958). Nevertheless, the Soviet government continued to eliminate Ukrainian Catholic parishes and close their churches. Nearly 1,000 priests were arrested and sentenced to lengthy prison terms or deportation. More than 200 priests began creating a network of Ukrainian Catholic churches in the underground, where the faithful worshipped for more than 40 years, risking persecution by the authorities.

In 1956, following his release from a Soviet prison camp, Bishop Mykola Charnetsky gave permission for priests who had converted to Orthodoxy to return secretly to the Ukrainian Catholic Church. Charnetsky was succeeded upon his death by the Redemptorist hegumen Vasyl Velychkovsky. In 1963, Slipy was freed from 18 years of incarceration and allowed to travel to Rome in order to attend the Second Vatican Council. Before his departure, Slipy secretly transferred his authority over the Lviv eparchy to Velychkovsky (who was arrested in 1969). In February 1972, prior to leaving the **USSR** for Yugoslavia, Velychkovsky transferred his authority to Bishop Volodymyr Sterniuk.

Following Slipy's move to Rome, Ukrainian Catholic parishes in the **diaspora** were consolidated into a single church. A diaspora movement developed in favor of having Slipy recognized as patriarch of an autonomous Ukrainian Catholic Church, but Rome's cultivation of good relations with Eastern Orthodoxy, including the Russian Orthodox Church, prevented the granting of such status. After Slipy's death in 1984, **Myroslav Liubachivsky** became archbishop of the Ukrainian Catholic Church and was appointed cardinal in 1985.

In the late 1980s, the struggle for the legalization of the Ukrainian Catholic Church began. On 4 August 1987, church representatives in Lviv appealed to Pope John Paul II and the Soviet leader, Mikhail Gorbachev, to facilitate the church's emergence from the underground. Beginning in 1989, public meetings, demonstrations, and hunger strikes were held to demand official status. In December 1989, the Soviet government legalized the church in Ukraine, and in March 1991 its leadership, headed by Cardinal Liubachivsky, arrived in Lviv. Following Liubachivsky's death in 2000, he was succeeded as head of the church by **Lubomyr Husar**. In June 2001, John Paul II made an official visit to Ukraine that included appearances in Kyiv and Lviv; in the latter city he blessed the cornerstone of the newly established Ukrainian Catholic University.

As of 2001, there were approximately 3,300 Ukrainian Catholic communities in Ukraine with about 2,000 clergy, 78 monasteries, and 12 educational institutions. In addition to the Lviv Archeparchy, there were eight eparchies in western Ukraine: Buchach-Chortkiv, Ivano-Frankivsk, Kolomyia-Chernivtsi, Mukacheve, Sambir-Drohobych, Sokal, Stryi, and Ternopil-Zboriv. In eastern Ukraine, the church established the Kyiv-Vyshhorod and Donetsk-Kharkiv exarchates. The official transfer of the church's headquarters to Kyiv began in April 2004.

Eparchies of the Ukrainian Catholic Church are active in Argentina, Australia, Brazil, France, Germany, Great Britain, Italy, and Poland. Canada is home to five eparchies, and the United States has four. Claiming more than 5.5 million faithful, the church, now officially designated the Ukrainian Greek Catholic Church, is the largest Eastern Catholic church in the world.

UKRAINIAN CENTRAL COMMITTEE/UKRAÏNS'KYI TSEN-TRAL'NYI KOMITET (UTsK) (Ger. *Ukrainisches Hauptausschuß in Krakau*). Based in Cracow, the UTsK was the only Ukrainian civic organization permitted to exist in the **Generalgouvernement** (1939–45). It represented the interests of the Ukrainian population of southeastern Poland (and, from March 1942, of **Galicia**) to the German authorities during **World War II**. The UTsK was established in June 1940 as an alliance of Ukrainian relief committees (UDKs) helping local Ukrainians and those newly arrived from

Soviet-occupied **western Ukraine**. It was headed by **Volodymyr Kubijovyč** throughout its existence. Politically, it was influenced by the **Melnyk** faction of the **Organization of Ukrainian Nationalists**, many of whose members worked with the committee. On 1 March 1942, the Ukrainian Regional Committee (UKK) in **Lviv** was merged with the UTsK, and its president, Kost Pankivsky, became deputy head of the UTsK. The UTsK consisted of Ukrainian *okruha* (district) committees (UOKs) in Galicia, UDKs from the remainder of the Generalgouvernement, and local representatives.

The UTsK was divided into several departments, including organizational, social welfare, public health, education, financial, and youth. In order to ensure its continued existence, the UTsK was obliged to submit all its plans for approval to the German occupation authorities; it also recruited Ukrainians for labor in Germany (*see OSTARBEITER*) and promoted recruitment to the **Division Galizien**. UTsK activities were strictly regulated and focused primarily on education and social welfare. From July 1940 to June 1941, the UTsK revived Ukrainian institutions in border areas previously under Polish control, establishing schools and cooperatives in virtually every Ukrainian village. It also arranged the release of about 85,000 Ukrainians captured in the German-Polish war of 1939. In 1942, the UTsK provided large-scale assistance to victims of flooding in Subcarpathia. Its kitchens were feeding some 100,000 people by 1943. The UTsK helped arrange the resettlement of refugees, assisted Ukrainian political prisoners and laborers in Germany, and established medical clinics and disinfection centers. On 22 February 1943, Kubijovyč sent a memorandum to Governor-General Hans Frank protesting the arbitrary arrest and execution of Ukrainians in the Generalgouvernement, as well as the expropriation of property. UTsK officials made numerous efforts to intervene with the Germans to protest or prevent such abuses. The education department of the UTsK worked with the German authorities to establish new schools, provide teacher training, and develop curricula; it also provided assistance and scholarships to Ukrainian students. The cultural department established more than 800 local cultural societies, reopened **Prosvita** branches, organized choirs, theaters, and folk-arts groups, and ran the Ukrainian Publishing House in Cracow and Lviv. The youth department organized sports clubs, courses, and camps; when the Germans recruited Ukrainian youth for construction service, the UTsK managed to establish a separate organization for them. The UTsK had two publications: the irregular official *Visnyk* (Herald) *UTsK* and its unofficial organ, the newspaper *Krakivs'ki visti* (Cracow News, 1940–45, ed. Mykhailo Khomiak). Kubijovyč dissolved the UTsK in Bavaria on 17 April

1945 and turned over its assets to the Central Representation of the Ukrainian Emigration in Germany.

UKRAINIAN CENTRAL RADA/UKRAÏNS'KA TSENTRAL'NA RADA. Civic and political organization founded in **Kyiv** in 1917 to coordinate the Ukrainian movement. As the **Ukrainian Revolution** developed, the Rada took on a leading role and, after the proclamation of the **Ukrainian People's Republic** (UNR) in November 1917, became the state's supreme legislative body. The idea of establishing a coordinating center emerged in early March 1917 among the Ukrainian intelligentsia in Kyiv. On 3–7 (16–20) March, the decision to create the Central Rada as a representative body uniting "Ukrainian organizations in the pursuit of their common goal: the territorial autonomy of Ukraine with Ukrainian as the state **language**" was made during consultations among representatives of various political, civic, scholarly, cultural, and cooperative groups (**Society of Ukrainian Progressives**, Ukrainian Scientific Society, Ukrainian Technico-Agronomic Society, Ukrainian Pedagogical Society, Ukrainian social democrats, and others). The Central Rada's presidium, elected on 7 (20) March, included **Mykhailo Hrushevsky** (chairman [in absentia]), Fedir Kryzhanivsky and **Dmytro Doroshenko** (deputy chairmen), Dmytro Antonovych (assistant chairman), Serhii Veselovsky (secretary), and Volodymyr Koval (treasurer). Following Doroshenko's resignation (9 [22] March), Volodymyr Naumenko became deputy chairman (19 March [1 April]). On 9 (22) March, the Central Rada issued its first proclamation (*universal*) to the Ukrainian people, appealing for broad participation in elections to a national congress and the organization of political and civic societies, and calling for petitions to the Provisional Government to introduce the Ukrainian language into schools, courts, and government bodies. The proclamation indicated that initially the Central Rada had no broadly conceived program; hence its actions were cautious and considered.

Hrushevsky's return to Kyiv (14 [27] March) had a galvanizing effect on the Rada. He defined its primary task as the achievement of Ukraine's national and territorial autonomy within a reformed, federated, and democratic Russian state. Hrushevsky reorganized the Rada in order to make it an all-Ukrainian representative civic and political body. The first step in this process was the reelection and expansion of the Rada at the All-Ukrainian National Congress (6–8 [19–21] March). The new Rada consisted of 115 members who represented the Ukrainian gubernias, Ukrainian communities in Moscow, Petrograd, Saratov, the Kuban, the Don region, and **Bessarabia**, as well as political parties and civic, cultural, and educational organizations. Hrushevsky was elected chairman; **Volodymyr Vynnychenko** and **Serhii Yefremov** were chosen as his deputies. The All-Ukrainian National Congress and the second general assembly of the Rada voted to coopt new members; between May and July, representatives of the Ukrainian General Military Committee and the all-Ukrainian councils of workers', peasants', and soldiers' deputies were incorporated into the Rada. According to the records of the mandate commission at the Sixth General Assembly (5–9 [18–22] August), the Rada consisted of 798 seats, of which 643 were filled. Seventy-five percent of Rada seats went to Ukrainians and the remainder to ethnic minorities: Russians (14 percent), **Jews** (6 percent), Poles (2.5 percent), **Moldavians** (four seats), Germans and **Tatars** (three seats each), and Belarusians, Czechs, and Greeks (one seat each).

While the Rada was dominated by representatives of the intelligentsia and professionals, most of its new members represented the **peasantry**. The Rada included representatives of 19 political parties (of which 17 identified themselves as socialist). In addition to Ukrainian parties, Russian, Jewish, and Polish political organizations were represented. The largest Ukrainian parties were the **Ukrainian Party of Socialist Revolutionaries**, the **Ukrainian Social Democratic Labor Party** (USDRP), and the **Ukrainian Party of Socialist Federalists**. Because of their influence on the peasantry, the socialist revolutionaries had the largest representation in the Rada, although in leadership positions they were outnumbered by members of the USDRP. The social democrats Vynnychenko, **Symon Petliura**, **Mykola Porsh**, Antonovych, Borys Martos, Valentyn Sadovsky, Ivan Steshenko, Mykhailo Tkachenko, and Levko Chykalenko formed the core of the Rada until January 1918.

As the Rada's activities expanded, its structure became more complex. Its supreme body was the General Assembly, which was to meet at least once a month, although only nine such meetings actually took place. General assemblies reviewed and ratified reports on the activities of the Rada Committee, reorganized on 24 June (7 July) 1917 as the Little Rada, which prepared the most important decisions and documents. Its membership increased from 20 to 40 through the addition of representatives of ethnic minorities (by January 1918, it consisted of 80 members). Members of the Little Rada were chosen along party lines, with each party represented according to its strength in the General Assembly. However, there was no established list of Little Rada members, as it was common practice for one member to be replaced by another. The Rada's Presidium carried out day-to-day leadership functions, preparing the agenda for Rada assemblies and Little Rada meetings. It was initially elected by the All-Ukrainian National Congress and headed by Hrushevsky and his deputies, Vynnychenko and Yefremov. On 24 June (7 July) 1917, the Presidium was expanded by four deputies (Mykola Shrah, Veselovsky, Andrii Nikovsky, and Kryzhanivsky) and four secretaries (Mykola Chechel, Antin Postolovsky, Chykalenko, and Yakiv Levchenko).

On 15 (28) June 1917, the Rada Committee established its executive body, the General Secretariat, which was charged with "managing internal, financial, food-supply, land, agrarian, interethnic, and other issues in Ukraine and executing all resolutions of the Rada pertaining to these issues." After the proclamation of the UNR, the Secretariat served as its government. Following the ratification of the Fourth Universal, the General Secretariat was reorganized as the **Council of People's Ministers** of the UNR. The Rada also had many permanent and temporary commissions.

The 13-month existence of the Rada may be divided into three periods. The first, from its establishment to the All-Ukrainian National Congress, was characterized by the absence of a specific program and attempts to formulate strategic aims.

The second phase, from the All-Ukrainian National Congress to the fall of the Provisional Government, saw the Rada's emergence as the leading political force in Ukraine. The Rada sought to establish the national and territorial autonomy of Ukraine within a federated, democratic Russia, which required the mobilization of Ukrainian society and complex political maneuvering by the Rada in its relations with the Petrograd government. The mobilization of the masses took place at numerous all-Ukrainian, gubernia, and county congresses at which Rada policies, the question of national and territorial autonomy, and the Ukrainization of the army, education, and state institutions were discussed. The Rada made extensive appeals to the masses through proclamations, exhortations, and declarations. The most characteristic of these was the First Universal (10 [23] June 1917), in which the Rada called upon the Ukrainian people "to create a new order in a free, autonomous Ukraine."

The First Universal also marked a turning point in the Rada's relationship with the Provisional Government, which had refused to recognize Ukrainian autonomy. When the Rada proclaimed autonomy nevertheless, the Provisional Government sought to avoid a breach by sending a delegation consisting of Iraklii Tsereteli, Aleksandr Kerensky, and Mykhailo Tereshchenko to Kyiv. The negotiations resulted in a compromise enunciated in a special government declaration and in the Rada's Second Universal. The

Rada allotted 30 percent of its seats to members of ethnic minorities. Subsequently, the Provisional Government reneged on its commitment to recognize the legitimacy of the Rada and the General Secretariat. On 4 (17) August, it issued a "conditional instruction" declaring the secretariat its own executive body, not that of the Rada, and limiting the secretariat's authority to five gubernias (Kyiv, **Poltava**, Chernihiv, **Volhynia**, and **Podilia**).

With the Bolshevik seizure of Petrograd (25 October [7 November] 1917) and the fall of the Provisional Government, a fundamentally different political situation emerged in Ukraine. The Rada expressed its opposition to the Petrograd developments and announced that it would "combat all attempts to support this insurrection in Ukraine." On 31 October (13 November), the seventh session of the Rada expanded the jurisdiction of the General Secretariat to the Kherson, **Kharkiv**, Katerynoslav, Tavriia, Kholm (Chełm), and part of the Kursk and Voronezh gubernias. Rule over Ukraine effectively passed to the Rada. On 7 (20) November, the Third Universal declared the creation of the UNR within a federated Russia, whose government was to be established by the Constituent Assembly. This universal marked the beginning of the third and last phase of the Rada's existence, characterized by attempts at state-building and the proclamation of Ukrainian independence. The Rada ratified a series of laws and the Constitution of the UNR, introduced its own monetary system, and adopted a state **coat of arms** and a national **anthem**. It also proclaimed the nationalization of natural resources and declared that the state would take control of commerce and banking on behalf of the "toiling masses."

These initiatives met with a number of obstacles, of which the greatest were Bolshevik aggression against Ukraine in November 1917, the continuation of **World War I**, and social collapse. Because the Rada took no decisive action to redistribute land and end Ukraine's participation in the war—the two main demands of the peasant masses—the Bolsheviks outbid it in competition for popular support. In order to expel the Bolshevik forces, the Rada signed the **Treaty of Brest-Litovsk** with the Central Powers on 27 January (9 February) 1918, trading food supplies desperately needed by the Germans and Austrians for their military assistance.

Once the Bolsheviks were driven out of Ukraine, the Rada became dependent on the German and Austrian military command. Its attempt to continue its socialist policies and inability to organize deliveries of foodstuffs provoked the dissatisfaction of the occupation authorities. This allowed conservative forces to lead a coup on 29 April 1918. The "Charter to the Ukrainian People" issued by **Pavlo Skoropadsky** dissolved the Rada and annulled its laws.

The brevity of the Central Rada's career was outweighed by its historical importance. Its rule marked a transition in Ukrainian political thought from federalism to independence and a concomitant revival of Ukrainian statehood. The Rada's generous treatment of ethnic minorities and commitment to social reform proved an enduring legacy to subsequent generations of Ukrainian democrats, despite the inexperience, dilatory habits, and sectarianism that vitiated the Rada's political performance and contributed to its downfall.

UKRAINIAN COMMUNIST PARTY/UKRAÏNS'KA KOMUNISTYCHNA PARTIIA (UKP), popularly known as the Ukapisty. In January 1919, at the fourth congress of the **Ukrainian Social Democratic Labor Party** (USDRP), a group known as the **USDRP (Independentists)** split away, advocating a national communist regime in Ukraine and repudiating both the **Directory** of the **Ukrainian People's Republic**, which it considered excessively nationalist, and the Moscow-controlled **Communist Party of Ukraine** (CPU). In August 1919, the Independentists split; the left faction joined the **Borotbists**, while the majority went on to establish the UKP at a founding congress in **Kyiv** on 22–25 January 1920. In contrast to the **peasant**-based Borotbists, the UKP never became a mass organization (its membership did not exceed 250), as it sought its base of support among the urban proletariat, which was highly **Russified**. In the tradition of European social democracy, the UKP emphasized the importance of theoretical study and the education of its members. Its press organ, *Chervonyi prapor* (Red Flag), was coedited by the UKP's well-known publicist and ideologue, Andrii Richytsky. The UKP's most prominent activists were Mykhailo Avdiienko, Antin Drahomyretsky, Yurii Lapchynsky, Yurii Mazurenko, and Mykhailo Tkachenko.

Like the Borotbists, the UKP sent a memorandum to the Comintern stressing the need for the Russian Bolsheviks to acknowledge their Ukrainian comrades as equals. Neither group was admitted to the Comintern. **Volodymyr Vynnychenko**, who had resigned from the Directory in 1919, organized a foreign representation of the UKP in Vienna in February 1920 and returned to Ukraine, seeking an accommodation with the Soviet regime. On realizing that the Soviets were exploiting him as a figurehead to advertise the putative collapse of the Directory, Vynnychenko emigrated again, ending his association with the UKP.

After this episode, the UKP was increasingly marginalized. Members began defecting to the CPU, which attempted to subvert the UKP from within by sponsoring a left faction in 1923. In August 1924, the UKP applied once again to the Comintern, proposing to dissolve itself if the Comintern admitted an independent Ukrainian communist party to represent the **Ukrainian SSR**. The Comintern responded that the Ukrainian SSR was a sovereign state and the CPU a member party. Under pressure from the CPU, the UKP had little choice but to dissolve itself (January 1925). Many of its members joined the CPU and were active in the **Ukrainization** drive. Most of them perished in Stalin's **political terror** of the 1930s.

UKRAINIAN CONGRESS COMMITTEE OF AMERICA (UCCA)/ UKRAÏNS'KYI KONGRESOVYI KOMITET AMERYKY. Umbrella organization established in 1940 by four Ukrainian-American fraternal insurance associations. By 1980, the UCCA had 65 branches representing about 70 community organizations.

From its inception, the UCCA championed the cause of Ukrainian independence and promoted the interests of Ukrainians in the United States. After **World War II**, like the **Ukrainian Canadian Congress**, it opposed the forced repatriation of Ukrainian refugees to the **USSR** and established the United Ukrainian American Relief Committee, which helped refugees settle in the United States. The UCCA began to publish the *Ukrainian Quarterly* in 1944. It also promoted the formation of an Educational Council to establish standards for Ukrainian Saturday schools and publish textbooks for them.

As a result of UCCA lobbying, the U.S. government annually proclaimed Captive Nations Week, beginning in the 1950s. The UCCA helped establish the Pan-American Ukrainian Conference and the World Congress of Free Ukrainians (now the **Ukrainian World Congress**). Its role as an umbrella organization was seriously undermined in 1980, when the organizations of the Ukrainian Liberation Front and their allies (representing the **Bandera** faction of the **Organization of Ukrainian Nationalists**) exploited their majority at the UCCA convention to override the organization's statute and procedures. Two fraternal associations and 25 organizations left the convention to form the Committee for Law and Order in the UCCA, which gave rise to the Ukrainian American Coordinating Council two years later. By 1990, UCCA membership was reduced to 42 organizations in 67 local branches.

UKRAINIAN DEMOCRATIC AGRARIAN PARTY/UKRAÏNS'KA DEMOKRATYCHNO-KHLIBOROBS'KA PARTIIA (UDKhP). Conservative political party (initially known as the Ukrainian Democratic Party) established by Mykhailo Boiarsky, Serhii Shemet, Vasyl Shkliar, Ivan Korniienko, and others. Its constituent assembly, held on 29 June (12 July) 1917 in Lubny, was attended by 1,500 well-to-do peasants and 20 landowners. Its basic principles included the achievement of Ukrainian sovereignty, the preservation of private property, and the resolution of the land question by state purchase and leasing, as well as cooperative farming. Viktor Andriievsky, Shemet, and **Viacheslav Lypynsky** developed the party's platform. Lypynsky's draft, which gave the party its name, was accepted as the official program in October 1917. The program advocated Ukrainian independence, the formation of a ruling elite with a statist orientation, and a democratic state order (although Lypynsky was a monarchist, he yielded the principle for the sake of independence). The program declared general civil rights and the autocephaly of religious denominations in Ukraine.

In March 1918, the party leadership negotiated unsuccessfully for admission to the **Ukrainian Central Rada**. It supported **Pavlo Skoropadsky's** coup but subsequently grew wary of his policies. In May 1918, the UDKhP joined the **Ukrainian National-State Union**, which opposed Skoropadsky. Under the **Directory**, the party split. In February 1920, some of its leaders (Shemet, Lypynsky, and Oleksander Skoropys-Yoltukhovsky) established a monarchist organization, the Ukrainian Union of Agrarian Statists, in Vienna, while others supported the **Ukrainian People's Republic** in exile.

UKRAINIAN DEMOCRATIC RADICAL PARTY/UKRAÏNS'KA DEMOKRATYCHNO-RADYKAL'NA PARTIIA (UDRP). Party of a liberal-democratic orientation established in **Kyiv** on 30 December 1905 (12 January 1906) through the merger of the Ukrainian Democratic Party (UDP) and the Ukrainian Radical Party (URP). A joint commission representing both parties (from the UDP: **Yevhen Chykalenko**, Yevhen Tymchenko, and Illia Shrah; from the URP: **Borys Hrinchenko** and Mykola Levytsky) developed a program and name for the new party. Its leaders included Chykalenko, Hrinchenko, Levytsky, Fedir Matushevsky, and **Serhii Yefremov**. **Hromadas** were the first centers of the party. Its program, based on parliamentary democracy and federalism, was adopted at its first congress in 1906. The UDRP envisioned the reformed Russian state as a "federation of equal, territorially autonomous units." Autonomous Ukraine was to be administered by an elected Ukrainian Popular Council (Soim). In the socioeconomic sphere, the UDRP declared war on "all exploitation," maintaining that land and industry should eventually become communal property. Land was to be nationalized and redistributed to **peasants** for a redemption fee. The party advocated harmonizing relations between management and labor by introducing the eight-hour workday, regulating hiring practices, and so on.

The similarity of the UDRP's program to that of the Constitutional Democratic Party (Cadets) during the **Revolution of 1905** led many UDRP members to join the Cadets as well, creating a danger of absorption by the stronger party. Consequently, in October 1906 the UDRP forbade simultaneous membership. After the revolution, the UDRP attempted to realize its primary aim of cultural and political autonomy for Ukraine, propagating it at various congresses, in the press, and in municipal councils, zemstvos, and civic organizations. UDRP members constituted three-quarters of the Ukrainian caucus in the Second State Duma. The publications of the UDRP and its predecessors were the weekly *Ridnyi krai* (Native Land, 1900) and the newspaper *Hromads'ka dumka* (Civic Thought, 1905–6). Efforts to keep the UDRP apart from the Cadets proved unavailing, and in 1908 it dissolved. Many of the remaining members then established the **Society of Ukrainian Progressives**.

UKRAINIAN FREE UNIVERSITY/UKRAÏNS'KYI VIL'NYI UNIVERSYTET (UVU). First institution of higher learning and scholarship established in the Ukrainian **diaspora**. It was inaugurated in Vienna on 17 January 1921 at the initiative of the Union of Ukrainian Journalists, the Society of Friends of Education, and the Ukrainian Sociological Institute. At the university's founding, divergences concerning its structure emerged between Oleksander Kolessa, who preferred the traditional university structure, and **Mykhailo Hrushevsky**, who favored a people's university. As a result, Hrushevsky abandoned the university in its organizational phase. Initially the UVU had 90 students, 12 professors, and three lecturers. After the defeat of the **Ukrainian Revolution**, Prague became the center of the Ukrainian political emigration, and with the consent of the Czechoslovak authorities, who provided financial assistance, the university moved there. The UVU's official opening took place on 23 October 1921. Its administration was located at the embassy of the **Western Ukrainian People's Republic**, and lectures were held at Charles University. Ukrainian was the language of instruction, although individual subjects were taught in other languages. During the Prague period, the UVU had faculties of arts and law. Rotation of the university administration took place annually. Between 1921 and 1945, the UVU's rectors were Kolessa (1921–22, 1925–28, 1935–37, 1943–44), Stanislav Dnistriansky (1922–23), **Ivan Horbachevsky** (1923–24, 1931–35), Fedir Shcherbyna (1924–25), Dmytro Antonovych (1928–30, 1937–38), Andrii

Yakovliv (1930–31, 1944–45), Oleksander Mytsiuk (1938–39, 1940–41), Ivan Borkovsky (1939–40, 1941–43), and **Avhustyn Voloshyn** (1945).

The UVU accepted 325 students annually: 221 to the faculty of arts and 104 to the faculty of law. At its peak in 1933–34, it employed 46 instructors, including 30 professors. During the interwar period, UVU instructors included some of the best-known Ukrainian scholars of the day (in addition to those who also worked as administrators): Opanas Andriievsky, Ahenor Artymovych, Vasyl Bidnov, Leonyd Biletsky, Serhii Borodaievsky, **Dmytro Chyzhevsky**, **Dmytro Doroshenko**, Borys Krupnytsky, **Volodymyr Kubijovyč**, Zenon Kuzelia, Rostyslav Lashchenko, **Viacheslav Lypynsky**, Mykhailo Lozynsky, Ivan Mirchuk, Oleksander Orlov, **Stepan Rudnytsky**, Vadym Shcherbakivsky, Leontii Shramchenko, **Oleksander Shulhyn**, Vasyl Simovych, Fedir Sliusarenko, **Volodymyr Starosolsky**, and others. They lectured and published courses on the history and geography of Ukraine, Ukrainian historiography and the study of historical sources, the history of Ukrainian law, church history, art history, ethnology, archaeology, Ukrainian **language** and **literature**, philosophy, and pedagogy. In the first decade of its existence, the UVU published 27 scholarly volumes. UVU instructors represented Ukrainian scholarship at international and regional congresses, conferences, and symposia, maintained ties with Ukrainian and foreign scholarly institutions, and were elected members of the **Ukrainian Academy of Sciences** and honorary members of foreign academies of sciences, universities, and institutes. They worked at the universities of Prague, Poděbrady, Warsaw, Lviv, and in the United States. In its first two decades of existence, the UVU conferred 132 doctorates.

During the interwar period, the UVU worked under difficult conditions. In the 1920s, subsidies from the Czechoslovak ministry of foreign affairs were steadily reduced, but another subsidy was provided by President Thomas Masaryk. The UVU was also threatened by closer political relations between Czechoslovakia and the USSR and Poland, which reduced the rights of the Ukrainian political emigration in Czechoslovakia. During **World War II**, the UVU was placed under the jurisdiction of the rector of Charles University, its statute and program of instruction were altered, and instructors were subject to intense scrutiny to verify their "Aryan" origins. Following the Red Army's occupation of Prague in May 1945, most instructors and students managed to escape to the West, but those who stayed behind, led by Voloshyn, were persecuted or killed. The property and archives of the UVU were confiscated or looted by the Soviet occupiers.

At the initiative of Shcherbakivsky, who was joined by a group of scholars from the Ukrainian Scientific Institute in Berlin (headed by Mirchuk), the UVU was reopened in Munich. Younger scholars who had emigrated to escape Soviet repression joined the staff, and instruction resumed in 1946–47. In 1947, the university had 493 students, 44 professors, 16 lecturers, and 18 instructors and assistants. The UVU's activities were supported financially by the Congregation of Eastern Churches (Bishop Ivan Buchko became the UVU's curator). However, in the immediate postwar years, the UVU's financial status remained uncertain, especially in the wake of monetary reform in West Germany (1948). The UVU had 272 students in 1949 and 137 in 1950; in 1956, classroom instruction was eliminated. In the first decade after the war, the university conferred 206 doctorates and 103 master's degrees. On 16 September 1950, the Bavarian government granted the UVU the status of a private university.

In 1957 the UVU began publishing *Zapysky Ukraïns'koho vil'noho universytetu* (Memoirs of the UVU) and expanded its correspondence instruction program. Its circumstances improved following the establishment of the Association for the Advancement of Ukrainian Studies (1962), which allowed it to resume instruction in 1965. The UVU also introduced courses in Ukrainian and East European studies and English-language courses. The teaching staff increased to 56 in 1965 and to 92 in 1990. Thanks to a donation from Cardinal **Yosyf Slipy**, the UVU acquired a building to house lecture halls, offices, and a library. It conducted scholarly conferences, commemorated Ukrainian anniversaries, and organized art exhibits. In 1981, the Institute for the Study of Nationality Problems was established at the UVU. Between 1966 and 1989, the UVU conferred 116 doctorates and 44 master's degrees. It issued more than 230 publications after becoming established in Munich.

Opportunities to work with scholarly and educational institutions in Ukraine came after the declaration of Ukrainian independence (1991). The UVU initiated exchanges of scholarly delegations, scholars from Ukraine did research at the UVU, and joint projects were undertaken. The university continues to receive funding from the Bavarian government and provides an outlet to the West for scholars from Ukraine.

UKRAINIAN GALICIAN ARMY/UKRAÏNS'KA HALYTS'KA ARMIIA (UHA). Regular army of the **Western Ukrainian People's Republic** (ZUNR), which adopted a law on military service on 13 November 1918. Its State Secretariat for Military Affairs was headed by Col. Dmytro Vitovsky (until 13 February

1919) and then by Col. Viktor Kurmanovych. The principal commanders of the UHA were Gen. Mykhailo Omelianovych-Pavlenko (10 December 1918–9 June 1919), Gen. Oleksander Hrekov (9 June-5 July), Gen. Myron Tarnavsky (5 July-7 November), and Gen. Osyp Mykytka (7 November-10 February 1920). The nucleus of the UHA was the Legion of **Ukrainian Sich Riflemen**, as well as other Ukrainian detachments in the army of the Habsburg Monarchy; these were joined by a variety of insurgents upon the outbreak of the **Ukrainian-Polish War in Galicia**, in which the UHA was engaged until its forced retreat across the Zbruch River on 16–17 July 1919.

At the beginning of 1919, the UHA was organized into three corps. Its maximum strength, attained in June 1919, was approximately 75,000 men (67 percent infantry and 10 percent artillery). The UHA also had a cavalry brigade and 30–40 airplanes. Because of the critical shortage of Ukrainian officers (only 2.4 percent of the UHA), senior UHA personnel were often recruited from the Habsburg forces and the Army of the **Ukrainian People's Republic** (UNR). The UHA was chronically short of arms, ammunition, and equipment.

After its retreat across the Zbruch, the UHA joined the Army of the UNR in an unsuccessful drive on **Kyiv** and **Odesa**. The ZUNR was politically at odds with the UNR; the dictator of the ZUNR, **Yevhen Petrushevych**, was opposed to antagonizing the White Army of Gen. Anton Denikin because of its ties with the Entente, while **Symon Petliura**, the president of the UNR, sought Polish assistance against the Whites and Bolsheviks. By November 1919, the Ukrainian forces had been driven into a small corner of **Podilia** near Vinnytsia, where they were threatened by all three enemies. An epidemic of typhus reduced the effective strength of the UHA to 7,000 men. Under these circumstances, Gen. Tarnavsky made an unauthorized truce with Denikin on 6 November, for which he was promptly dismissed (a subsequent court-martial exonerated him). His successor, Gen. Mykytka, made a similar truce on 19 November.

The subsequent destruction of Denikin's forces by the Red Army reduced the remaining UHA forces to the desperate expedient of negotiating a merger with the Bolshevik forces in Kyiv. In January 1920, under the direction of **Volodymyr Zatonsky**, the UHA was reorganized as the Red Ukrainian Galician Army, consisting of three brigades. Mykytka and his chief of staff, Gen. Gustav Ziritz, were arrested and shot in August. In mid-April 1920, a joint Polish-Ukrainian offensive against Soviet forces was launched under the terms of the **Treaty of Warsaw**. On 23–24

April, the second and third brigades of the Red UHA deserted to the invading forces, while the first brigade was surrounded by them several days later. The deserters and captured soldiers were interned in Warsaw, while most of the remainder were imprisoned and shot by the Soviet authorities.

Like the Ukrainian Sich Riflemen, the UHA became the object of a patriotic cult and an extensive memoir literature in interwar western Ukraine and the **diaspora**.

UKRAINIAN HELSINKI GROUP/UKRAÏNS'KA HEL'SINS'KA HRUPA (UHH). Ukrainian Civic Group to Promote the Implementation of the Helsinki Accords. First public **human-rights** organization in the **Ukrainian SSR**, established in **Kyiv** on 9 November 1976. Its activities were based on the **United Nations'** General Declaration of Human Rights (10 December 1948) and the human-rights provisions of the Final Act of the Council for Security and Cooperation in Europe (Helsinki Accords, 1 August 1975), signed by 33 European states, including the **USSR**. The founders of the UHH were the writers Mykola Rudenko (president) and Oles Berdnyk, the teachers Oksana Meshko and **Oleksii Tykhy**, the lawyers **Levko Lukianenko** and Ivan Kandyba, Maj.-Gen. Petr Grigorenko (Petro Hryhorenko), the historian Mykola Matusevych, the engineer Myroslav Marynovych, and the microbiologist Nina Strokata-Karavanska. The UHH became the second such group in the USSR, following the Moscow Helsinki Group (founded on 12 May 1976; the Lithuanian group was formed on 25 November 1976, the Georgian group on 14 January 1977, and the Armenian group on 1 April 1977). The Declaration of the UHH stated that its aim was to monitor the implementation of the Helsinki Accords in Ukraine and inform signatories and the international community of human-rights abuses. In its open letter "To People of Good Will" (14 November 1976), the UHH declared its willingness to cooperate with the Moscow group but asserted its autonomy. Grigorenko became the group's representative in Moscow. The UHH made several unsuccessful attempts to register officially as a civic organization.

In its public memoranda, the group condemned the crimes of the communist regime and expressed its commitment to fight for human rights "until these rights become the everyday norm." It issued a list of Ukrainian political prisoners incarcerated in forced-labor camps and special psychiatric hospitals. The group demanded freedom of exit from and entry into the country, the free circulation of ideas, the creation of organizations not controlled by the state, the elimination of censorship, the liberation of political prisoners, and the abolition of the death penalty. It also addressed the national question, demanding the "decolonization" of the USSR and Ukraine's legal secession from it. By the end of 1980 it had published 30 memoranda, declarations, manifestos, appeals, and information bulletins.

The Communist Party began a campaign to crush the Helsinki movement, arresting Rudenko; the leaders of the Moscow group, Yurii Orlov and Aleksandr Ginzburg; and the leader of the Lithuanian group, Tomas Venclova. In 1977, Rudenko, Tykhy, Marynovych, Matusevych, and Lukianenko were arrested and sentenced to lengthy prison terms. (Following Rudenko's arrest, Berdnyk assumed leadership of the UHH.) In the same year, Georgii Vins, Olha Heiko-Matusevych, Vitalii Kalynychenko, **Leonid Pliushch**, and Vasyl Striltsiv joined the UHH. They were followed by Vasyl Sichko, Petro Sichko, **Yurii Lytvyn**, Nadiia Svitlychna, Volodymyr Malynkovych, Mykhailo Melnyk, and Vasyl Ovsiienko in 1978, and Sviatoslav Karavansky, Oksana Popovych, Bohdan Rebryk, **Vasyl Romaniuk**, Iryna Senyk, Stefaniia Shabatura, **Danylo Shumuk**, Yurii Shukhevych, **Viacheslav Chornovil**, Yosyf Zisels, Zinovii Krasivsky, Yaroslav Lesiv, Petro Rozumny, Ivan Sokulsky, **Vasyl Stus**, and Mykola Horbal in 1979 (some of whom were already imprisoned or in exile). In 1979, most UHH members were imprisoned or sentenced to forced-labor camps. The Soviet regime fabricated charges against UHH members not only of the "political" variety but also of a purely criminal nature in an attempt to discredit them. (Following Berdnyk's arrest, Meshko became president of the group on 6 March 1979.) By March 1981, all group members were either imprisoned or exiled.

As a result of persecution, the Moscow group announced its dissolution in 1982, followed shortly thereafter by other groups in the USSR. Only the Ukrainian group continued its activities in the labor camps.

Despite political terror, new members continued to join the UHH. In 1982, Mykhailo Horyn joined at the camp in Kuchino, followed by the Estonian human-rights activist Mart Niklus and the Lithuanian Viktoras Petkus. Valerii Marchenko joined in 1983 and Petro Ruban in 1985. Lytvyn, Marchenko, and Ovsiienko were given 15–year prison terms in 1982 and 1983. That year, Heiko-Matusevych, Kalynychenko, and V. Sichko were sentenced a second time (three years each). In 1984, Zisels was arrested, followed by Ruban (13 years), Horbal, and Sokulsky (again) in 1985.

The foreign representation of the UHH, consisting of Grigorenko, Pliushch, Svitlychna (who emigrated in October 1978), and Strokata-Karavanska (who emigrated with her husband on 30 November 1979), remained active. It published *Visnyk represii v Ukraïni* (Herald of

Repressions in Ukraine, 1979–85) in Ukrainian and English.

Group members who died in Soviet concentration camps were Tykhy (1984), Lytvyn (1984), Marchenko (1984), and Stus (1985). Threatened with arrest, Melnyk committed suicide on 9 March 1979.

UHH activities were supported by democratic organizations in various countries, notably Amnesty International (London), the Washington Group for the Helsinki Guarantees in Ukraine (founded in November 1976), and Americans in Defense of Human Rights in Ukraine (1980). By resolution no. 205, dated 21 June 1982, the U.S. Congress declared 9 November 1982 Ukrainian Helsinki Group Day, and an announcement to that effect was made by President Ronald Reagan. The Congress passed a similar resolution to commemorate the group's 10th anniversary (1986) and called on the president and secretary of state to demand the immediate release of UHH members.

In 1987, group members released from imprisonment renewed UHH activities, and the editorial board of *Ukraïns'kyi visnyk* (Ukrainian Herald; Chornovil, Vasyl Barladianu, Horyn, and Pavlo Skochok) declared the publication to be an organ of the group. The UHH was reorganized as the Ukrainian Helsinki Association (UHA), a broad civic union (7 July 1988). The meeting adopted a declaration of principles and a statute. Lukianenko, then in exile (he returned to Ukraine in January 1989), was elected president. The UHA executive committee included Chornovil, Horbal, Horyn, Yevhen Proniuk, and Stepan Khmara. The association's primary function was the defense of Ukrainian national rights. In addition to Kyiv, the UHA had press centers in Moscow and **Lviv**. Its foreign representation was headed by Rudenko, who emigrated to the United States in December 1987, and included Pliushch and Svitlychna. Soon the association became a significant political force whose members promoted unofficial associations (the Shevchenko Ukrainian Language Society, Memorial, **Rukh**, and the All-Ukrainian Society of the Persecuted), the creation of an independent press, the organization of demonstrations and labor strikes, and the legalization of the **Ukrainian Catholic Church**. Twelve UHA members were elected to the **Verkhovna Rada** of the Ukrainian SSR in March 1990, and many others were elected to local councils. By April 1990, the UHA had 2,300 members and branches throughout Ukraine. It provided the main cadres of the Ukrainian Republican Party, which superseded the UHA in 1990.

UKRAINIAN INSURGENT ARMY/UKRAÏNS'KA POVSTANS'KA ARMIIA (UPA). Military force that fought the German and Soviet occupation of Ukraine (1942–49) with the goal of establishing an independent state. Its origins are associated with popular resistance to German depredations in **Volhynia** and **Polisia**, which were part of the **Reichskommissariat Ukraine**. The first formation to adopt the name "Ukrainian Insurgent Army" was organized in western Volhynia in the summer of 1941 by **Taras Borovets**. Other formations active in 1942 were the "Front of Ukrainian Revolution" in the Kremianets region, units of the **Melnyk** faction of the **Organization of Ukrainian Nationalists** (OUN) commanded by Mykola Nedzvetsky, a unit in Polisia led by Serhii Kachynsky, and another in Volhynia commanded by Hryhorii Perehiiniak. The majority **Bandera** faction of the OUN avoided resistance activity after having been driven underground in July 1941, considering it premature. **Mykola Lebed**, who led the OUN(B) underground network, changed course in late 1942, when resistance to the Germans in northwestern Ukraine became so widespread as to require organization. By mid-1943, the OUN(B) had managed to bring the smaller insurgent units under its control, not without armed confrontations and infighting, and adopted the UPA name as its own. The UPA formations in Volhynia and Polisia became known as UPA-North. The **Ukrainian People's Self-Defense**, which became active in **Galicia** in the summer of 1943, was renamed UPA-West in December 1943. UPA-South included units in the Vinnytsia and Kamianets-Podilskyi oblasts, while the planned UPA-East failed to develop because of the advance of Soviet forces. The UPA Supreme Command, comprising seven sections—operations, intelligence, logistics, personnel, training, political education, and inspection—was established in November 1943, and **Roman Shukhevych**, who headed the OUN(B) during Bandera's incarceration, was appointed commander in chief. In 1944, the OUN(B) and UPA established the **Supreme Ukrainian Liberation Council** (UHVR) as a national body to lead the struggle for independence.

The UPA's basic unit was the company (120–180 men), divided into three platoons, each consisting of three squads. Squads were armed with a light machine gun, two to three automatic weapons, and seven or more rifles. During its period of greatest activity (1943-45), the UPA organized two to four companies into kurins (a traditional **Cossack** term), which in turn could form a brigade (*zahin*). All weapons, ammunition, uniforms, and supplies had to be taken from enemy forces. A Ukrainian Red Cross staffed by women in the OUN(B) underground was established (*see* ZARYTSKA, KATERYNA), and **Jewish** doctors who took refuge from the Gestapo provided medical care. The UPA had a chronic shortage of trained personnel; its officer candidate school produced some 690 graduates, while NCOs were trained at district schools. All ranks fought without any remuneration. In January 1944, the UPA introduced military decorations: the Gold Cross of Combat Merit first and second class; the Silver Cross, first and second class; the Bronze Cross; and lesser distinctions.

While OUN(B) members formed more than half of the UPA, it was also joined by Ukrainian auxiliary units that deserted the German forces (notably the **Division Galizien**, especially after its defeat at Brody in 1944), as well as by young men avoiding forced labor as *Ostarbeiter*. In 1943, the UPA's strength was estimated by Soviet partisans at about 20,000. Beginning in August 1943, small units of Armenians, Azeris, Georgians, Kazakhs, Lithuanians, **Tatars**, and Uzbeks, totaling between 1,000–2,000 men, were formed as part of the UPA, and a Conference of Subjugated Peoples of Eastern Europe and Asia was held in November 1943 (*see* ANTI-BOLSHEVIK BLOC OF NATIONS). The UPA also reached neutrality agreements with Hungarian and Romanian units stationed in Ukraine (autumn 1943).

The UPA's political education section published such journals as *Do zbroï* (To Arms, 1943), *Povstanets'* (Insurgent, 1944–45), *Ukraïns'kyi perets'* (Ukrainian Pepper, 1943–45), *Ideia i chyn* (Idea and Action, 1942–46), and *Oseredok informatsiï i propahandy* (Center of Information and Propaganda, 1948–51). Local publications included *Za samostiinu Ukraïnu* (For an Independent Ukraine, 1942), *Biuleten'* (Bulletin, 1942), *Informator* (Informer, 1942), *Za ukraïns'ku derzhavu* (For a Ukrainian State, 1944), *Na chatakh* (On Guard, 1946), *Na zminu* (On Duty, 1946), and *Molodyi revoliutsioner* (Young Revolutionary, 1948). Some tactical units also had their own publications: *Shliakh peremohy* (Path of Victory, published by the Hoverlia division), *Strilets'ki visti* (Riflemen's News, published by the Buh division), *Lisovyk* (Forester, published by the Sian division), and *Chornyi lis* (Black Forest, published by the Stanyslaviv tactical division). The UPA published a large number of brochures, handbooks, pamphlets, propaganda leaflets, and the like. Its leading publicists were Yakiv Busel (Halyna), Mykhailo Diachenko (Marko Boieslav), Osyp Diakiv (Hornovy), **Petro Poltava**, and Yaroslav Starukh. For a time, an underground radio station, *Afrodita* (Aphrodite), headed by Starukh, was active in the Carpathians.

The UPA began its operations with an attack on German posts in the town of Volodymyrets on 7 February 1943. In the course of that year, it firmly established itself in the Volhynian and Polisian countryside, forcing the Germans to limit their movements outside major centers to daylight hours, with large military escorts for protection. The Germans responded with mass terror against the population, killing many civilian hostages (in Galicia alone, between 10 October 1943 and 30 June 1944, approximately 16,700 Ukrainian hostages were publicly executed). There was a price of 50,000 marks on Lebed's head. For a time, large-scale anti-insurgent operations in Volhynia were commanded by Gen. Erich von dem Bach, whose forces included 50 tanks and armed cars, 27 airplanes, and·five armored trains. Between June and August 1943, the UPA fought some 60 battles against the Germans.

As the Red Army approached, the Germans and the UPA were forced into mutual neutrality and a degree of cooperation. Local agreements were reached to barter German arms and ammunition for UPA intelligence about Soviet forces, and in 1944 the UPA strove to avoid battles against the retreating Germans (except to capture weapons and supplies) in order to conserve its strength. In 1943, the UPA attacked Soviet partisans in Volhynia and Polisia, hampering their operations. Such actions were intended to weaken the Soviet advance and mobilize the Ukrainian population to revolt, as the UPA believed that the Western Allies would not permit Stalin to establish control over Eastern Europe and hoped for a general uprising of non-Russians that would put an end to Soviet rule.

UPA clashes with the Red Army (RA) began even before the latter reached **western Ukraine**. As early as 12 February 1944, **Nikita Khrushchev** signed the first of six appeals to the UPA to lay down its arms. This had no effect; the Supreme Command ordered UPA units to bypass the advancing Soviet front and attack its rear guard, as well as secret police (NKVD) units. In late February, the UPA mortally wounded Gen. Nikolai Vatutin, commander of the RA 1st Ukrainian Front. This led Stalin to send Marshal Georgii Zhukov to western Ukraine in order to destroy UPA resistance. A large battle was fought near the village of Hurby, south of Rivne, on 24 April (about 30,000 RA soldiers against some 5,000 insurgents), with the UPA suffering about 2,000 casualties and 1,500 troops captured by the enemy. Further battles with the RA greatly reduced UPA forces, forcing it to operate on a local scale with smaller units. The Supreme Command was moved from Volhynia to the Carpathian Mountains in the spring of 1944, while operations began to be centered in Galicia, where the OUN(B) underground was strongest. By the end of the year, Soviet military and administrative forces were well established in western Ukraine, although the UPA still dominated the countryside. According to NKVD statistics, between February 1944 and November 1945, a total of 26,685 operations were undertaken against the OUN-UPA (many of them futile), with the insurgents having a strength of 5,831 men organized in 379 units that completed 6,148 operations.

The overall strength of the UPA remains a disputed issue. Its leading American historian, Petro Sodol, estimates that at its peak in 1944, the UPA had some 25,000–30,000 soldiers at any one time. Historians in Ukraine suggest that as many as 90,000 men passed through the ranks of the UPA during its existence, and some estimates range as high as 300–400,000. The OUN(B) underground and its supporters comprised scores of thousands.

Following the end of **World War II** in May 1945, the Soviet regime proclaimed another amnesty with a deadline of 20 July. This led to defections, and the UPA made use of the amnesty to divest itself of ill or unreliable insurgents, leaving only battle-hardened veterans. The UPA's non-Ukrainian cadres deserted it after the reoccupation of Ukraine. A further blow to the UPA was the Carpathian blockade of January-April 1946, during which NKVD troops continually swept the UPA's entire area of operations, forcing its troops to remain continually on the move in extremely cold weather, without adequate food or supplies. UPA losses totaled 40 percent of its strength, and in July 1946 the UHVR decided on a gradual demobilization. By the end of that year, only elements of the Fourth "Hoverlia" Division, operating in the Carpathians, and the Sixth "Sian" Division, posted on Ukrainian ethnic territory in southeastern Poland, were still active. The latter carried out the UPA's last battalion-strength operation against Polish army and police units in Hrubeshiv (Hrubieszów) on 27 May 1946. The 6th Division attempted unsuccessfully to prevent the forced resettlement of Ukrainians on Polish territory (*see* OPERATION VISTULA). On 29 August 1949, the UHVR ordered the cessation of UPA activity. Sporadic resistance continued into the mid-1950s, as the OUN(B) underground and some UPA insurgents remained active but no longer subject to a central command. Company 95 fought its way across Czechoslovakia and surrendered to the US Army in Germany on 11 September 1947.

Despite the vast preponderance of Soviet strength after 1945, the destruction of the OUN-UPA underground in western Ukraine and southeastern Poland took a protracted effort. In western Ukraine, according to Soviet records, a total of 212 extermination battalions (23,906 men) were formed, supported by 2,336 auxiliary groups (24,025 men). A report of 22 October 1945 signed by the Ukrainian deputy head of the NKVD, Tymofii Strokach, indicates that there was a large secret police network in western Ukraine in 1944–45: 359 residents, 1,473 agents, and 13,085 informers. Captured UPA soldiers were publicly hanged to deter recruitment, and NKVD units disguised as UPA insurgents terrorized the population. According to a report sent by **Mykola Pidhorny** to the CC CPSU on 25 September 1956, the nationalist underground killed some 22,400 Soviet officials in western Ukraine (many of them transferred from **eastern Ukraine** in order to ensure loyalty to the central authorities), while the insurgents suffered 150,000 casualties and 103,000 arrests, and 65,000 families of insurgents (203,662 persons) were deported to Siberia.

Controversy surrounds the UPA's role in the struggle against the Polish colonization of western Ukraine, which began to be seriously researched in Poland following the collapse of the communist regime in 1989 (*see* UKRAINIAN-POLISH CONFLICT, 1943–47).

After Ukraine's declaration of independence in 1991, when UPA veterans began to apply for official recognition, the history of the UPA became a public issue, leading to a split in World War II veterans' organizations. In 1997, the government organized a historical commission to study the OUN-UPA: it received tens of thousands of letters, the most significant of which were published in 1999. Essentially, western Ukrainians wrote to express support for the OUN-UPA as a patriotic movement that had fought for independence and prevented the complete **Russification** of the country. Eastern Ukrainians, who identified themselves with the RA's anti-Nazi struggle and bore the brunt of its huge cost in civilian and military casualties, tended to regard the UPA insurgents as collaborators with the Germans, as they had long been depicted in Soviet propaganda. The issue remains a divisive one, both in public opinion and in historiography. In 1976, UPA veterans in Canada began to publish the documentary series *Litopys UPA* (UPA Chronicle), which was transferred to Ukraine in the mid-1990s and comprises more than 40 volumes.

The U.S. political scientist John A. Armstrong, summarizing the UPA's achievements in his book *Ukrainian Nationalism* (2d ed., 1963), wrote that "If one takes into account duration, geographical extent, and intensity of activity, the UPA very probably is the most important example of forceful resistance to Communist rule."

UKRAINIAN LIBERATION ARMY/UKRAÏNS'KE VYZVOL'NE VIIS'KO (UVV). General designation of Ukrainian auxiliary formations in the German armed forces during **World War II**. The UVV was made up of Ukrainian companies attached to the Wehrmacht; their members were known as *Hiwi* (volunteer assistants, from the German *Hilfswillige*). From the autumn of 1941, *Hiwi* units consisting mainly of captured Red Army soldiers were employed as support staff and guards; later, they were also used in combat. In 1942, 74 mostly Ukrainian *Hiwi* battalions were formed within the

Wehrmacht. As the tide of battle turned against the Germans, it was decided in February 1943 that Ukrainian units would be identified as the UVV. In May 1943, the first issue of the UVV publication *Ukraïns'kyi dobrovolets'* (Ukrainian Volunteer) was published in Berlin. Recruitment into the UVV was conducted in the **Reichskommissariat Ukraine** and adjacent territories, resulting in the creation of several units. In August 1943, Hitler ordered a halt to UVV recruitment on the grounds that Slavs should not be allowed to bear arms.

In early 1944, some Ukrainian members of UVV units were forcibly incorporated into Gen. Andrei Vlasov's Russian Liberation Army (ROA), a Wehrmacht formation. As a result of numerous protests, most Ukrainian units (but not all Ukrainians) were removed from the ROA and incorporated into the UVV (spring 1944). At its height, the UVV had a total of some 75,000 men. It was active primarily in Ukraine, Belarus, and France (where the Ivan Bohun battalion defected to the French Resistance). UVV soldiers used arms and uniforms of Soviet or German manufacture bearing no special identifying marks, with the exception of blue-and-yellow sleeve emblems with the Cyrillic letters "YBB" and **trident** cap badges. In March 1945, remnants of the UVV were incorporated into the nascent Ukrainian National Army, commanded by Gen. **Pavlo Shandruk**. At the end of the war, some former UVV soldiers found themselves in displaced-persons camps in occupied Germany, while others were forcibly "repatriated" to the **USSR** and sent to concentration camps as collaborators.

UKRAINIAN MILITARY ORGANIZATION/UKRAÏNS'KA VIIS'KOVA ORHANIZATSIIA (UVO). Revolutionary underground organization in interwar **western Ukraine**. It was created at the initiative of former officers of the **Ukrainian Galician Army** and members of the **Ukrainian Sich Riflemen** (USS) in order to continue the struggle for independence after the defeat of the **Ukrainian Revolution**. The Supreme Collegium of the UVO was formed in September 1920 (head, Osyp Navrotsky; members: Yaroslav Chyzh, Mykhailo Matchak, Yurii Poliansky, and Volodymyr Tselevych). On 20 July 1921, **Yevhen Konovalets**, the former commander of the USS, took command of the UVO and remained in that post, with a brief interruption in 1924–25, until 1931. Yurii Otmarshtain was appointed chief of staff. Konovalets organized a Supreme Command and established organizational, intelligence, operations, and propaganda divisions. **Galicia**, the territory of the UVO's primary activity, was divided into 13 military districts comprised of 58 counties, each with its own UVO cell.

During the first year of its existence, the UVO made an unsuccessful attempt on the life of the Polish head of state, Józef Piłsudski, conducted a campaign of arson against Polish landowners and colonists, and assassinated Sydir Tverdokhlib, a writer who defied the general Ukrainian boycott of the 1922 elections to the Polish Diet.

In early 1923, the Supreme Command of the UVO was moved to Berlin, while the home command, led by **Andrii Melnyk**, supervised UVO actions in western Ukraine. Melnyk's successors were Yuliian Holovinsky, Roman Sushko, Omeliian Senyk, Bohdan Hnatevych, and Volodymyr Horbovy. The UVO's relations with its nominal political sponsor, the government-in-exile of the **Western Ukrainian People's Republic**, led by **Yevhen Petrushevych**, were difficult. Petrushevych saw Konovalets as a dangerous rival, and the struggle for control of the UVO intensified after March 1923, when the Council of Allied Ambassadors recognized Poland's sovereignty over Galicia. The conflict within the UVO continued for two more years, until the Petrushevych faction was expelled and formed its own short-lived Western Ukrainian National Revolutionary Organization, led by Osyp Dumin.

In the **diaspora**, Konovalets developed ties with countries hostile to Poland; German military circles financed UVO training, while Lithuania funded UVO publications. Its journal *Surma* (Clarion, published in Berlin in 1927–28 and in Kaunas from 1928 to 1934; ed. Volodymyr Martynets), which was illegally distributed in western Ukraine, had a press run of 10,000.

In 1924, the Polish police arrested many leading members of the UVO following their interrogation of **Olha Basarab**, an UVO courier who died under torture. In 1925, the UVO unsuccessfully attempted to kill President Stanisław Wojciechowski of Poland. It held up mail trucks and post offices to obtain cash for its operations. In 1926, the UVO assassinated the Lviv school superintendent, Stanisław Sobiński, in retaliation for the government's closing of many Ukrainian schools.

In 1927–28, the UVO began to consolidate its relations with other nationalist groups, which merged into the **Organization of Ukrainian Nationalists** in 1929. The UVO ceased to exist as an separate organization in 1931, although the name continued to be used for political purposes for several more years.

UKRAINIAN NATIONAL ALLIANCE/UKRAÏNS'KE NATSIO-NAL'NE OB'IEDNANNIA (UNO). Ukrainian community organization established in Berlin in 1933. Along with the Ukrainian **Hromada**, it was tolerated by the Nazi regime. UNO membership increased considerably after it espoused the Ukrainian nationalist cause in 1937. Despite official restrictions, the UNO had 42,000 members in more than 1,200 branches and centers (1942). It operated an information bureau in Berlin and a publishing house in Prague. Aside from organizing classes and lectures, the UNO defended the interests of Ukrainian *Ostarbeiter* in Germany and provided assistance to Ukrainian students and prisoners of war from Soviet and Polish units. In 1943, the Gestapo began to persecute the UNO, whose activities were terminated by the Soviet occupation of Berlin.

UKRAINIAN NATIONAL COMMITTEE/UKRAÏNS'KYI NATSIO-NAL'NYI KOMITET (UNK). Civic and political body established in Germany in the autumn of 1944 to defend Ukrainian interests before the German authorities. Its formation was made possible by the release from Sachsenhausen in September and October 1944 of leaders of the **Organization of Ukrainian Nationalists** (OUN), notably **Stepan Bandera** and **Andrii Melnyk**, whom the Germans hoped to exploit for their foundering war effort. Following initial talks, the OUN leaders refused to participate in a German-sponsored committee. The UNK was headed by Gen. **Pavlo Shandruk**. In large measure, it was a successor to the **Ukrainian Central Committee**, whose members had been forced to flee the **General-gouvernement**, but also included the president-in-exile of the **Ukrainian People's Republic**, **Andrii Livytsky**, and members of the Ukrainian Civic Committee, which consisted largely of eastern Ukrainian émigrés. On 12 March 1945, without seeking authorization from Hitler, *Reichsminister* Alfred Rosenberg recognized the UNK as the sole representative of Ukrainians in Germany (the Germans had demanded the UNK's merger with Gen. Andrei Vlasov's Committee for the Liberation of the Peoples of Russia, but the Ukrainians refused). In the last weeks of the war, the UNK undertook the formation of a Ukrainian National Army under Shandruk's command. Its First Division, comprising the **Division Galizien** and other Ukrainian units serving with the Germans, was to fight the Red Army, while irregulars (a battalion of whom was formed) were to conduct partisan activity behind enemy lines. The UNK ceased to exist at the end of **World War II**.

UKRAINIAN NATIONAL COUNCIL/UKRAÏNS'KA NATSIO-NAL'NA RADA (GERMANY, 1948). Legislative body of the State Center established by the government-in-exile of the **Ukrainian People's Republic** (UNR). It was created after **World War II** in order to consolidate **diaspora** political parties dedicated to the restoration of an independent Ukrainian state. Preliminary work was performed by a commission headed by **Isaak Mazepa**, and the council's first session took place on 16–20 July 1948 in Augsburg, Bavaria. The following organizations took part in the session: the **Organization of Ukrainian Nationalists (Bandera** and **Melnyk** factions), the **Ukrainian National Democratic Alliance**, the Ukrainian National-State Union, the **Ukrainian Revolutionary Democratic Party**, the **Ukrainian Party of Socialist Revolutionaries**, the **Ukrainian Social Democratic Labor Party**, and the Union of Lands of United Ukraine (Peasant Party).

The council established an executive organ and elected the president of the UNR-in-exile. It worked in sessions lasting five years each and conducted 10 sessions in all. The council performed an important symbolic function, demonstrating the refusal of diaspora Ukrainians to recognize the legitimacy of the **Ukrainian SSR**.

The extraordinary session of 14–15 March 1992 passed a resolution whereby the last president of the UNR-in-exile, Mykola Plaviuk, transferred the council's charter, declaration, presidential insignia and seal, and national flag to the first democratically elected president of Ukraine, **Leonid Kravchuk**, at the Mariinsky Palace in **Kyiv** on 24 August 1992.

UKRAINIAN NATIONAL COUNCIL/UKRAÏNS'KA NATSIO-NAL'NA RADA (KYIV, 1941). Political and civic body established on 5 October 1941 at the initiative of the **Melnyk** faction of the **Organization of Ukrainian Nationalists** (OUN-M). Its chief organizer was **Oleh Olzhych**. The intended head of the council, the academician **Ahatanhel Krymsky**, was arrested by the Soviet secret police. Instead, Mykola Velychkivsky, rector of the **Kyiv** Polytechnical Institute, became the council's chairman, while its secretaries were the geologist Ivan Dubyna, subsequently a leading figure in the **Ukrainian Revolutionary Democratic Party**, and Osyp Boidunyk, a leader of the OUN(M). Altogether the council had approximately 130 members, most of whom were politically unaffiliated, although some were members of the OUN(M), while others were former supporters of the **Ukrainian State** and the **Ukrainian People's Republic** (UNR). Metropolitan **Andrei Sheptytsky** sent a letter to Velychkivsky in November 1941 recognizing the council's authority, and the president of the UNR in exile, **Andrii Livytsky**, delegated a representative. The council began organizing local administrative bodies. In Kyiv, it published the newspaper *Ukraïns'ke slovo* (Ukrainian Word, ed. Ivan Rohach), which had a circulation of more than 50,000. Council members were briefly successful in taking control of the Kyiv city administration and reviving the city's cultural and artistic life. The Union of Ukrainian Writers, headed by **Olena Teliha**, was established in Kyiv.

In November, the Gestapo began to arrest and execute members of the OUN(M) in Kyiv, and the council went underground. It reemerged briefly in 1944, with Velychkivsky reelected president, as the All-Ukrainian National Council. Its efforts to establish cooperation with the **Supreme Ukrainian Liberation Council**, dominated by the **Bandera** faction of the OUN, were unsuccessful, and the council ceased its activities in 1946.

UKRAINIAN NATIONAL COUNCIL/UKRAÏNS'KA NATSIONAL'NA RADA (LVIV, 1941). Civic body established at the initiative of the **Bandera** faction of the **Organization of Ukrainian Nationalists**. Initially, a Council of Seniors was convened in **Lviv** (6 July 1941) under the chairmanship of one of Galicia's most eminent politicians, **Kost Levytsky**, with Metropolitan **Andrei Sheptytsky** acting as its patron and honorary chairman. It was intended to function as a quasi-senate for the **Ukrainian State Administration**, which the OUN(B) had established the previous day.

When the Gestapo arrested the administration's leading OUN(B) members, it ceased to function. The Council of Seniors reconstituted itself on 30 July as the Ukrainian National Council, adding a number of lawyers and representatives of the **cooperative movement** to its membership, which eventually rose to 45. Before the war, most of its members had belonged to the moderate **Ukrainian National Democratic Alliance**. On 31 July, the council established a General Secretariat headed by the lawyer Kost Pankivsky. It saw its task as representing the interests of the Ukrainian population of **Galicia** to the German occupation authorities. Shortly after the annexation of Galicia to the **Generalgouvernement** (1 August), headed by Hans Frank, the council addressed a memorandum to Frank maintaining that Galicia was an integral part of Ukrainian territory and that the annexation could be regarded only as a temporary measure. It also demanded the recognition of Ukrainian authority over the Ukrainian portion of the Generalgouvernement. Frank responded by announcing the formation of the Ukrainian Regional Committee as the sole representative body for Ukrainians in Galicia. Pankivsky was recognized as its head. Following Levytsky's death on 12 November, the council's activity ceased, although it formally continued to exist until February 1942. When Metropolitan Sheptytsky addressed a protest to Heinrich Himmler against the extermination of the **Jews** and the use of Ukrainian auxiliary police in that capacity, the district head of the German Security Service in Lviv, Alfred Kolf, summoned the presidium of the National Council and demanded its dissolution. On 1 March 1942, the Regional Committee was merged with the **Ukrainian Central Committee**.

UKRAINIAN NATIONAL DEMOCRATIC ALLIANCE/UKRAÏNS'KE NATSIONAL'NO-DEMOKRATYCHNE OB'IEDNANNIA (UNDO). Largest **Galician** political party of the interwar period (1925–39); successor to the **National Democratic Party**. It was established in **Lviv** on 11 July 1925 through a merger of the Ukrainian Labor Party, the **Ukrainian Party of National Work**, and Ukrainian deputies to the Polish Diet. The UNDO program and statute were adopted at its second congress (Lviv, 19–20 November 1925). A Christian democratic party, the UNDO stood for parliamentary democracy, organic work carried on by legal methods, redistribution of land to the **peasants**, and the development of national industry, trade, and **cooperatives**. Its ultimate goal was an independent Ukrainian state. The UNDO put pressure on the Polish government to fulfill its international and constitutional obligations to recognize Ukrainian autonomy in Galicia. Its ruling body was the People's Convention, which met every two years to elect the Central (People's) Committee. On the local level, county committees were elected and "men of trust" chosen in the villages. The chairman of the UNDO was Dmytro Levytsky; leading figures included Volodymyr Bachynsky, Mykhailo Halushchynsky, Ivan Kedryn-Rudnytsky, Ostap Lutsky, Vasyl Mudry, Stepan Vytvytsky, and Volodymyr Zahaikevych.

The UNDO was not so much a political organization as a broad national movement, lacking a registered membership or regular membership dues (except in the city of Lviv). It influenced large economic, cultural and educational, and sports organizations, as well as the largest Galician daily, *Dilo* (The Deed). From 1925, the party's official organ was the weekly *Svoboda* (Liberty, eds. Mykhailo Strutynsky and Oleksa Kuzma). In the late 1920s, it extended its influence to **Volhynia**. The UNDO participated in the 1928 elections to the Polish Diet and won 26 seats (of the 48 seats won by Ukrainians) and nine seats in the Senate (out of 11). During the **Pacification**, the Polish authorities arrested 19 UNDO deputies. In 1930, the party won 17 (of 27) Ukrainian mandates in the Diet; in 1935, it took 13 seats in the Diet and four in the Senate.

In 1935, the UNDO leadership, attempting to normalize Ukrainian-Polish relations, reached an accommodation with the Polish government that assured it 19 seats in the Diet. The policy of "normalization" was controversial, leading to a split in the party. Levytsky was expelled, and Mudry, the editor of *Dilo*, became head of the party (and vice-marshal of the Diet, as a result of "normalization"). A group led by Dmytro Paliiv left the party and founded the **Front of National Unity**. An internal opposition formed within the UNDO, centering around *Dilo* and the **women's** organization Retinue of Princess Olha, led by Milena Rudnytska. The **Organization of Ukrainian Nationalists** campaigned against UNDO policies. In 1938, Mudry abandoned the normalization policy as ineffectual, which stabilized the party but did not halt the radicalization of Galician politics. In September 1939, with the Soviet occupation of **western Ukraine**, the UNDO ceased its activity. In 1947, a group of its former members revived the party abroad and joined the **Ukrainian National Council** (1948) and its executive body, the State Center of the **Ukrainian People's Republic**.

UKRAINIAN NATIONAL PARTY/UKRAÏNS'KA NATSIONAL'NA PARTIIA (UNP). The only legal Ukrainian political party in Romanian-ruled **Bukovyna** after the dissolution of the Ukrainian section of the Social Democratic Party of Bukovyna. Active from 1927 to 1938, the party was based in Chernivtsi. It opposed the official policy of Romanianization, striving to promote the use of Ukrainian in schools and churches, as well as agrarian reform. The UNP lacked a permanent organization and staff, relying on local "men of trust" in its day-to-day operations. The party had an electoral base of some 32,000 voters, but according to Romanian electoral law, it could only stand for election in coalitions with Romanian parties. Its leader was Volodymyr Zalozetsky-Sas, who served as a senator and member of parliament, as well as a delegate to the national minorities section of the League of Nations (1928–38). The UNP's official organ was *Rada* (1934–38); other publications associated with it were *Ridnyi krai* (1926–30) and *Chas* (1928–40). It was banned in 1938 together with all political parties in Romania.

UKRAINIAN NATIONAL RADA/UKRAÏNS'KA NATSIONAL'NA RADA (UNRada). Legislative body of the **Western Ukrainian People's Republic** (ZUNR). It was established in **Lviv** on 18 October 1918 as the Constituent Assembly of Ukrainians in the Austro-Hungarian Empire. The UNRada included all Ukrainian deputies in both houses of the Austrian Reichstag, Ukrainian deputies from the **Galician** and **Bukovynian** diets, and three representatives each from the Ukrainian political parties in those lands. Student representatives from Galicia also took part. On 19 October, the UNRada passed a resolution concerning the establishment of the ZUNR on Ukrainian ethnic territory in Austria-Hungary. It also called upon ethnic minorities to send representatives, but they were never delegated. **Yevhen Petrushevych** became the UNRada's president. Three delegations of the UNRada were created: the executive (provisional government), chaired by Petrushevych in Vienna (25 October); the delegation for Galician and **Transcarpathian** affairs in Lviv (chaired by **Kost Levytsky**); and the Bukovynian delegation in Chernivtsi (chaired by Omelian Popovych).

On 29 October, the Lviv delegation established the UNRada Central Bureau in Lviv (headed by Roman Perfetsky) and the Food Supply Office (headed by Stepan Fedak). Following the seizure of power in Lviv by the Military Commissariat on 1 November, the newly appointed vicegerent, Volodymyr Detsykevych, officially transferred power to Levytsky. On 9 November, the UNRada established an executive body, the Rada of State Secretaries (State Secretariat), headed by Levytsky. On the following day, it instructed the State Secretariat to undertake measures to unite all Ukrainian lands in a single state. It then ratified laws on the independence of Ukrainian lands in the former Habsburg Monarchy and on the administration of the ZUNR. After the Poles captured Lviv, the State Secretariat and members of the Rada left the city (21 November) for Ternopil. The Rada members Lev Hankevych, Volodymyr Okhrymovych, and **Stepan Tomashivsky** were delegated to defend the interests of the Ukrainian population in Lviv.

In late November and early December 1918, elections to the UNRada were held in Galicia. In 1919, the Rada continued its work in Stanyslaviv (now Ivano-Frankivsk), where three sessions were held. Augmented by new representatives from the counties and towns, the UNRada nominally consisted of more than 150 members; some 130 actually participated. On 2–4 January 1919, nine commissions of the UNRada were created: land, military, legislative, technical reconstruction, finance, education, foreign affairs, social welfare, and communications. On 15 February, an administrative commission was formed.

On 4 January, the UNRada elected an executive (nine members and a president), whose decisions were taken by majority vote and required a quorum of six. The executive included Petrushevych (president), **Lev Bachynsky**, Hryhorii Duvirak, Antin Horbachevsky, Mykhailo Novakovsky, Teofil Okunevsky, Popovych, Andrii Shmigelsky, Semen Vityk, and Stepan Yuryk.

On 3 January, the UNRada ratified a preliminary agreement on and voted unanimously for the union of the ZUNR with the

Ukrainian People's Republic (UNR). A delegation of the UNRada (36 persons) participated in the official proclamation of the **Act of Union** in Kyiv on 22 January 1919. The act was ratified on the following day by the **Labor Congress** of Ukraine, in which the Rada delegation participated. UNRada members were elected to the presidium of the congress and were members of its commissions. After unification, the ZUNR was renamed the Western Province of the Ukrainian People's Republic (ZO UNR) and received full territorial autonomy. Petrushevych joined the **Directory**, and the Rada members Antin Krushelnytsky, **Osyp Nazaruk, Lonhyn Tsehelsky,** Yosyp Bezpalko, and Volodymyr Temnytsky became ministers of the UNR.

During the Stanyslaviv sessions, the Rada adopted a number of important statutes, including laws on land reform, schooling, language use, and citizenship. On 15 April, the Rada passed laws on the Diet of the ZO UNR and its election. It introduced universal suffrage for citizens aged 20 years and older. Voting was to be direct, secret, and proportional. Any individual 28 years of age and older was eligible to run for office. The unicameral Diet, to be elected in June 1919, was to consist of 226 delegates: 160 Ukrainians (70.8 percent of the total), 33 Poles (14.6 percent), 27 **Jews** (11.9 percent), and six Germans (2.7 percent). Following the election, the UNRada was to dissolve itself. The **Ukrainian-Polish War in Galicia** prevented the election from taking place.

On 9 June, prior to the retreat of the government of the ZO UNR and the **Ukrainian Galician Army** across the Zbruch River, the Presidium of the Executive of the UNRada and the State Secretariat jointly transferred their constitutional authority to Petrushevych, granting him dictatorial powers. After the occupation of western Ukraine by Poland, individual UNRada meetings took place in Vienna and Lviv between 1919 and 1923.

UKRAINIAN NATIONAL-STATE UNION/UKRAÏNS'KYI NATSIONAL'NO-DERZHAVNYI SOIUZ (UNDS). Coordinating center of centrist and center-right political parties and professional organizations, active from May to July 1918. It was established in Kyiv on 21 May 1918, after Hetman **Pavlo Skoropadsky** became head of state. Participating organizations included the **Ukrainian Party of Socialist Independentists,** the **Ukrainian Party of Socialist Federalists,** the **Ukrainian Democratic Agrarian Party,** the Ukrainian Labor Party, the United Council of Railway Workers of Ukraine, and the Main Council of the All-Ukrainian Postal and Telegraphic Union. Its main goal was to defend Ukrainian statehood against the threat of a Russian restoration. On 24 May, the UNDS submitted a statement to Skoropadsky expressing its distrust of the government of **Fedir Lyzohub**, which consisted primarily of representatives of Russian parties (Constitutional Democrats, Octobrists), and accused some ministers of anti-Ukrainian activities. Protesting the government's ban on zemstvo, worker, and **peasant** congresses, the statement condemned the dissolution of local agencies of self-government and the restoration of prerevolutionary administrative bodies. The UNDS proposed the creation of a "national-democratic cabinet" incorporating its representatives. There was no reply to this or subsequent UNDS appeals to the Hetman government. In early August 1918, the UNDS was reorganized as the **Ukrainian National Union**.

UKRAINIAN NATIONAL UNION/UKRAÏNS'KYI NATSIONAL'NYI SOIUZ (UNS). Umbrella organization of political parties and civic and professional organizations opposed to the administration of Hetman Pavlo Skoropadsky. It was organized in early August 1918 as a successor to the **Ukrainian National-State Union**, following the departure of the **Ukrainian Democratic Agrarian Party** from the organization and the addition of leftist Ukrainian parties. It included the **Ukrainian Social Democratic Labor Party**, the **Ukrainian Party of Socialist Independentists**, the **Ukrainian Party of Socialist Federalists**, the Ukrainian Labor Party, the **Ukrainian Party of Socialist Revolutionaries**, the Peasant Union, the Medical Union, **Prosvita**, and others. The union advocated the establishment of an independent, democratic Ukrainian republic. Andrii Nikovsky was the union's president, succeeded on 18 September by **Volodymyr Vynnychenko**. Branches were established in Vinnytsia, **Poltava**, Kremenchuk, **Odesa**, and Kamianets-Podilskyi. Working selectively with organizations of the **Ukrainian State** and maintaining contact with the Bolsheviks, the UNS sought to bring down the Hetmanate and restore the **Ukrainian People's Republic** (UNR).

On 5 October, a UNS delegation met with Skoropadsky, argued the need for agrarian reform and democratic elections, and proposed the addition of UNS representatives to the cabinet. Faced with a political crisis, Skoropadsky agreed, and five UNS candidates briefly joined Fedir Lyzohub's cabinet (*see* SKOROPADSKY, PAVLO). On 14 November, Skoropadsky formed a new government and announced Ukraine's entry into a federation with a future non-Bolshevik Russia. He was opposed by the **Directory** of the UNR, created at a UNS meeting on the night of 13–14 November, which initiated a successful uprising. After the fall of the Skoropadsky regime, **Mykyta Shapoval** headed the UNS (14 November 1918–January 1919).

UKRAINIAN ORTHODOX CHURCH/UKRAÏNS'KA PRAVO-SLAVNA TSERKVA. Like Ukraine's other Christian churches (*see* UKRAINIAN CATHOLIC CHURCH; PROTESTANT CHURCHES IN UKRAINE), the Ukrainian Orthodox Church traces its roots back to the **Christianization of Rus'** during the first millennium A.D., which culminated in the official adoption of Christianity by Prince **Volodymyr the Great** in 988–89. Christianity came to **Kyivan Rus'** from Byzantium, and many hierarchs of the Rus' church were Greeks. In the first half of the 11th century, under the rule of **Yaroslav the Wise**, the church was headed by its first native metropolitan, **Ilarion**, the construction of **St. Sophia's Cathedral** began in **Kyiv**, and the **Kyivan Cave Monastery** developed into a preeminent center of worship and learning. Following the schism in the universal church in 1054, the Rus' church identified itself with Byzantine Orthodoxy, recognizing the patriarch of Constantinople as its head.

The invasion of the **Golden Horde** (1237–40), which resulted in the disintegration of Rus', eclipsed Kyiv's status as an ecclesiastical center until the early 17th century. Metropolitan Cyril II (1251–81) moved his residence from Kyiv to Vladimir on the Kliazma, and his successor, Maximos, confirmed the transfer of the **Kyiv metropolitanate** to Vladimir in 1299–1300. A separate **Halych metropolitanate** was established in 1303 in the Principality of **Galicia-Volhynia**, with Niphont as the first metropolitan. It was abolished in 1401, following the Polish annexation of **Galicia**, not to be restored until 1808 (under Habsburg auspices, as a Ukrainian Catholic metropolitanate).

From the late 14th century, when most of the Ukrainian lands came under the rule of Lithuania, competition developed between candidates backed by the Muscovite and Lithuanian political authorities for the Kyivan metropolitan see. The Orthodox Church, culturally isolated and often ruled by appointees whose primary interests were political and secular, entered a long period of decline. In the 16th century, it was sharply challenged by Polish Roman Catholicism and Protestantism, both of which gained many converts among the Ukrainian elite. The Orthodox laity, organized in religious **brotherhoods**, began to play an increasing role in ecclesiastical life from the 1580s, sometimes challenging the authority of local bishops and successfully appealing to the Eastern patriarchs for the right of stauropegion (autonomy from local episcopal rule).

The crisis of Orthodoxy in the Ukrainian lands led to a schism in the church. Part of the hierarchy, supported by nobles and burghers, opted for union with Rome, and the Uniate Church (subsequently renamed the Greek Catholic and then **Ukrainian Catholic Church**) was established at the **Union of Brest** in 1596. The Orthodox loyalists, who had initiated an academic and cultural revival in Ostrih under the auspices of Prince **Kostiantyn Ostrozky** in the 1580s, withdrew to Kyiv, which was distant enough from the Polish authorities to afford a large measure of autonomy. With crucial support from the Ukrainian **Cossacks**, notably Hetman **Petro Sahaidachny** (who enrolled the entire Cossack Host in the Kyiv Brotherhood), a new Orthodox hierarchy was consecrated in 1620. The church was relegalized in the **Polish-Lithuanian Commonwealth** in 1632, and a full-scale Orthodox revival developed under the leadership of **Petro Mohyla**, who served as metropolitan of Kyiv from 1633 to 1647. He established a college that grew into an outstanding center of learning, the **Kyiv Mohyla Academy**, revised ecclesiastical service books, and compiled a profession of faith and a catechism that long served as standard Orthodox religious manuals.

After the **Khmelnytsky Uprising** against Polish rule, which broke out in 1648, Orthodoxy became the established religion in the **Hetmanate**. The church regained many of the shrines and monasteries that had previously been lost to the Uniates and was patronized by Cossack officers and hetmans, especially **Petro Doroshenko**, **Ivan Samoilovych**, and **Ivan Mazepa**. The Hetmanate, however, came increasingly under the control of Muscovy after the **Pereiaslav Agreement** of 1654, as did the Orthodox Church in Ukraine—a process facilitated by the large influx of Ukrainian clergymen into the Muscovite church, where they served as teachers and administrators. In 1685, the bishop of Lutsk and Ostrih, **Hedeon Sviatopolk-Chetvertynsky**, was consecrated in Moscow as metropolitan of Kyiv, breaking the tradition of the church's subordination to Constantinople. As the Ukrainian church came under the authority of the Moscow patriarchate, it initially retained a significant measure of autonomy; the metropolitan of Kyiv was to be elected for life by the Kyivan clergy, the Mohyla Academy remained self-governing, and the church was free to authorize its own publications. These liberties were taken away after Mazepa's unsuccessful rebellion against Tsar Peter I in 1708–9. The Ukrainian church was obliged to participate in the ritual anathematization of Mazepa, and after Peter's abolition of the Moscow patriarchate (replaced by the Holy Synod) in 1721, the Kyivan metropolitan was reduced to the status of an archbishop. Although the Holy Synod was headed by Ukrainian clergymen—Stefan Yavorsky, Teodosii Yanovsky, and **Teofan Prokopovych**—they were devoted to Peter's imperial project and did little to assert Ukrainian autonomy. The subordination of the Ukrainian church to Moscow was completed during the reign of Catherine II, who ignored a petition of the Ukrainian clergy for the restoration of its traditional rights, secularized monastic properties and made monasteries financially dependent on the state, and introduced Russian as the language of instruction at the Mohyla Academy. The academy had to submit its publications to censorship in order to ensure their conformity to Russian standards.

During the 19th century, the Orthodox Church in Ukraine was ruled by a succession of Russian metropolitans and became an agency of cultural **Russification**. The metropolitan of Kyiv had no jurisdiction outside his own eparchy. Theological education was Russified, as was the pronunciation of liturgical texts. Even the building of churches in the Ukrainian Cossack **baroque** style was prohibited after 1800. By the early 20th century, much of the clergy and hierarchy of the Orthodox Church in Ukraine identified itself with such reactionary organizations as the Union of the Russian People.

Ukrainian religious traditions were preserved by the peasants and the rural clergy, which passed on parishes from father to son. Moreover, with the growth of the Ukrainian intelligentsia during the 19th century, clandestine Ukrainian groups were formed at theological seminaries, most notably in **Poltava** and Kamianets-Podilskyi. It was this element that came to the fore during the **Ukrainian Revolution** (1917–21) to demand the Ukrainization of the Orthodox Church. An All-Ukrainian Orthodox Church Sobor (Council) headed by a military chaplain, Oleksander Marychiv, and the retired Archbishop Oleksii Dorodnytsyn was established in December 1917. With the conditional approval of Patriarch Tikhon of Moscow, it summoned the First All-Ukrainian Church Sobor in Kyiv in January 1918, but its deliberations were interrupted by the first Bolshevik invasion of Ukraine. Under the government of **Pavlo Skoropadsky**, the Russian element regained its dominance; Antonii Khrapovitsky, a strong opponent of the Ukrainian movement, became metropolitan of Kyiv, and demands for Ukrainian Orthodox autocephaly (complete ecclesiastical independence) were rejected at the second session of the sobor (July 1918). Not until the dying days of the Skoropadsky regime did its new minister of confessions, Oleksander Lototsky, express official backing for autocephaly. The **Directory** of the **Ukrainian People's Republic**, which came to power in December 1918, dismissed Khrapovitsky and issued a law on 1 January 1919 providing for autocephaly of the Orthodox Church in Ukraine. Lototsky was dispatched to Istanbul in an unsuccessful attempt to gain recognition from the ecumenical patriarchate.

In 1920, as Soviet rule began to be established, the church split into two opposing factions: the Russian (Patriarchal) Orthodox Church, encompassing most of the hierarchy and traditional believers, and the Ukrainian Autocephalous Orthodox Church (UAOC), backed by the nationally conscious intelligentsia and faithful. At its first all-Ukrainian sobor (14–30 October 1921), the UAOC, bereft of ecclesiastical leadership, resolved to consecrate its own hierarchs according to the ancient Alexandrine practice of the laying on of hands by participants in the council. **Vasyl Lypkivsky** was ordained metropolitan of Kyiv and all Ukraine, and Nestor Sharaivsky was ordained as his deputy. The UAOC expanded rapidly in central Ukraine, with more than 1,100 parishes established by 1924. It also attracted adherents among émigrés in Western Europe and North America: from 1924, the UAOC in the United States was headed by Archbishop Ivan Teodorovych, whose spiritual authority was also recognized by Ukrainian Orthodox faithful in Canada.

The UAOC soon found itself at odds with the Soviet regime, which initially sought to divide it by promoting an Active Church of Christ and a Renovationist Church. From 1927, however, the political authorities went over to direct repression. Lypkivsky was arrested in 1926, and his dismissal was engineered at the Second All-Ukrainian Church Sobor (October 1927). In connection with the trial of the trumped-up **Union for the Liberation of Ukraine**, where the principal ideologist of the UAOC, **Volodymyr Chekhivsky**, was sentenced to death, the regime forced the convocation of an "extraordinary sobor" (January 1930) that dissolved the UAOC. A much smaller Ukrainian Orthodox Church, reconstituted at the end of 1930, was incessantly persecuted and finally destroyed in 1936. It is estimated that the regime was responsible for the deaths of more than 1,150 priests, 54 deacons, and 20,000 members of local UAOC councils, as well as many thousands of its faithful.

Ukrainian Orthodoxy continued to develop in **Volhynia** and the **Kholm region** (incorporated into the Second Polish Republic) during the interwar period, where the Orthodox Church under Metropolitan Dmitrii Valedinsky was granted independence of Moscow by the ecumenical patriarchate in 1924. However, the Polonizing policies of the authorities, as well as their confiscation and destruction of Orthodox churches, created serious difficulties for the Ukrainian Orthodox. The German occupation of Ukraine in **World War II** witnessed a spontaneous revival of ecclesiastical life, with two contending Orthodox churches: the UAOC led by Archbishop Polikarp Sikorsky and the Autonomous Orthodox Church under Archbishop Oleksii Hromadsky. **Mstyslav Skrypnyk**, consecrated UAOC bishop of Pereiaslav in 1942, emerged after the war as a leading Orthodox hierarch of the Ukrainian **diaspora**.

During the war, the Stalin regime permitted a controlled revival of the Russian Orthodox Church (ROC) in order to help mobilize patriotic sentiment and appease the West. With the Soviet suppression of the Ukrainian Catholic Church in 1946, the ROC became the only officially recognized Eastern Christian church in Ukraine—a status that it guarded jealously, since its Ukrainian exarchate (headed from 1968 by Metropolitan **Filaret Denysenko**) accounted for more than half the churches and monasteries in the USSR.

The ROC monopoly was first challenged in 1989, when an Initiative Committee for the Revival of the UAOC was formed and UAOC communities began to declare themselves in traditionally Catholic western Ukraine, recognizing Mstyslav Skrypnyk as their superior. This prompted the ROC to rename its Ukrainian exarchate the "Ukrainian Orthodox Church" (UOC) in order to emphasize its autonomy. A conflict ensued between the UOC and the ROC in 1991 when Filaret Denysenko, having failed to be elected head of the ROC, attempted to gain canonical autocephaly for the UOC. The ROC refused to grant autocephaly and dismissed Denysenko from his post; he was replaced in May 1992 by **Volodymyr Sabodan**, who was appointed Metropolitan of Kyiv and All Ukraine, with a residence at the Kyivan Cave Monastery. Denysenko, backed by the administration of President **Leonid Kravchuk**, went on to create the Ukrainian Orthodox Church (Kyiv Patriarchate) in June 1992. For three years, an internecine struggle went on between the UOC-KP and the UAOC, which came under strong pressure to subordinate itself to Denysenko's authority. In June 1995, the statute of the UAOC was finally registered by the authorities, but tensions with the UOC-KP remained high. They exploded in July 1995, when **Vasyl Romaniuk**, who had succeeded Skrypnyk as metropolitan of the UAOC in 1993, died unexpectedly. His followers' spontaneous attempt to bury him on the grounds of St. Sophia's Cathedral led to a bloody confrontation with the police. The administration of **Leonid Kuchma** subsequently adopted a hands-off policy in religious affairs. In October 1995, Denysenko was elected head of the UOC-KP with the title of Patriarch of Kyiv and All Rus'-Ukraine, while Patriarch Dmytro Yarema of **Lviv** headed the UAOC until his death in 2000, when he was succeeded by Metropolitan Mefodii Kudriakov of Ternopil under the jurisdiction of Metropolitan Constantine (based in the United States).

At the beginning of the new millennium, the UOC remained by far the largest Orthodox church in Ukraine, with more than 9,000 communities; it was followed by the UOC-KP, with more than 2,700 communities, and the UAOC, largely restricted to western Ukraine, with more than 1,000 communities. Indications that Patriarch Bartholomew of Constantinople might be prepared to grant canonical recognition to a united Ukrainian Orthodox Church led to exploratory talks between the UOC-KP and the UAOC, but these appeared unlikely to yield any immediate results.

UKRAINIAN PARTY OF LABOR/UKRAÏNS'KA PARTIIA PRATSI (UPP). Sovietophile political party in **Galicia** (1927–30). It was founded in Lviv on 7 May 1927 by former members of the **Ukrainian National Democratic Alliance**. Ideologically, the UPP was based on the "independent group" of the earlier Ukrainian Labor Party (est. 1919), which supported the government-in-exile of the **Western Ukrainian People's Republic**, rejected the decision of the Council of Allied Ambassadors concerning the incorporation of Galicia into the Polish state (1923), and condemned all attempts to normalize Ukrainian-Polish relations. The UPP supported the **Ukrainian SSR** because of its policy of **Ukrainization**, but the show trial of the **Union for the Liberation of Ukraine** in Kharkiv (March-April 1930) rendered that orientation untenable. The party was headed by Viacheslav Budzynovsky and was represented in the Polish Diet by Mykhailo Zakhidny. Its publications were the biweekly *Rada* (Council) and the weekly *Pratsia* (Work). The UPP dissolved itself in 1930.

UKRAINIAN PARTY OF NATIONAL WORK/UKRAÏNS'KA PARTIIA NATSIONAL'NOÏ ROBOTY (UPNR). Also known as the Ukrainian Party of National Revolution. It was founded in Lviv on 24 April 1924 by a faction of the Ukrainian Labor Party (UPP), which was joined by nationalists associated with the journal *Zahrava* (Glow), edited by **Dmytro Dontsov**. The party's program declared the supremacy of the national idea over socialism and internationalism; its slogan was "Ukraine for Ukrainians." The leadership included Samiilo Pidhirsky, a representative to the Polish Diet from **Volhynia** (president), Volodymyr Kuzmovych, Ostap Lutsky, and Dmytro Paliiv (secretary). District executive committees were formed in Lviv, Ternopil, Lutsk, Dubno, Kovel, and Pynsk (Pinsk). In 1925, as a result of negotiations between the UPNR and the Volhynian group of the Ukrainian Parliamentary Representation (UPR), the two groups merged into a single party. On 11 July 1925, at a congress in Lviv, representatives of the UPNR, UPP, the Volhynian UPR, and others merged to establish the **Ukrainian National Democratic Alliance**. The UPNR was notable as the first political expression of Ukrainian integral nationalism in **Galicia**. *See also* ORGANIZATION OF UKRAINIAN NATIONALISTS.

UKRAINIAN PARTY OF SOCIALIST FEDERAL-ISTS/UKRAÏNS'KA PARTIIA SOTSIIALISTIV-FEDERALISTIV (UPSF). Political party founded in Kyiv in April 1917 (initially under the name Ukrainian Party of Autonomist Federalists) by former members of the **Ukrainian Democratic Radical Party** (UDRP) and the **Society of Ukrainian Progressives**. The party revived the liberal-democratic program of the UDRP. Of all the post-1905 Ukrainian parties, it had the largest number of veteran politicians and members of the intelligentsia. Its leader was **Serhii Yefremov**, and members included Makar Kushnir, Oleksander Lototsky, Fedir Matushevsky, Ivan Mirny, Andrii Nikovsky, Viacheslav Prokopovych, Serhii Shelukhyn, Illia Shrah, Petro Stebnytsky, and Andrii Viazlov. Its newspaper was the daily *Nova rada* (New Council).

UPSF members were prominent in the **Ukrainian Central Rada** and were members of governments of the **Ukrainian People's Republic** (UNR) (Yefremov, **Oleksander Shulhyn**, Ivan Feshchenko-Chopivsky, Lototsky, Mirny, Prokopovych, Shelukhyn, and Stebnytsky) and of the **Ukrainian State** (Lototsky, Maksym Slavinsky, Stebnytsky, and Viazlov). In 1918, the UPSF participated in the **Ukrainian National-State Union** and the **Ukrainian National Union**, which opposed the rule of **Pavlo Skoropadsky**. In November 1918, the party helped establish the **Directory**, in which UPSF members held ministerial posts (Shelukhyn, **Ivan Ohiienko**, Feshchenko-Chopivsky, Petro Kholodny, Ovksentii Korchak-Chepurkivsky, Mykhailo Korchynsky, Mykhailo Kryvetsky, Dmytro Markovych, and Kost Matsiievych). In May 1920, Prokopovych headed the cabinet.

In the Prague emigration, the UPSF was renamed the Ukrainian Radical Democratic Party, headed by Lototsky (1923). Party leaders Matsiievych, Prokopovych, Oleksander Salikovsky, Shulhyn, Slavinsky, and Andrii Yakovliv cooperated with the UNR government-in-exile. The radical democrats did not reestablish their party after **World War II**.

UKRAINIAN PARTY OF SOCIALIST INDEPENDENTISTS/UKRAÏNS'KA PARTIIA SOTSIIALISTIV-SAMOSTIINYKIV (UPSS). Party of a radical nationalist orientation established on 17 (30) December 1917 at the All-Ukrainian Congress of Independentists in **Kyiv**. It included members of the **Ukrainian People's Party**, military servicemen, and previously unaligned individuals connected with the Union of Ukrainian Statehood (formed in 1917). Despite the word "socialist" in its name, intended to lend respectability at a time when socialism was the dominant ideology, the UPSS was dedicated to the nationalist program of **Mykola Mikhnovsky**. It demanded the immediate proclamation of an independent Ukraine and opposed the **Ukrainian Central Rada's** policy of socializing land, as well as its positive attitude toward ethnic minorities. UPSS leaders included Opanas Andriievsky, Petro Bolbochan, Ivan Lutsenko, Oleksander Makarenko, Pavlo Makarenko, and Oleksander Stepanenko.

In late 1917, the UPSS proposed the establishment of a national military dictatorship. Under the **Ukrainian State**, however, it opposed the policies of **Pavlo Skoropadsky**, joining the **Ukrainian National-State Union**. After Skoropadsky's downfall, Andriievsky became a member of the **Directory**, and individual UPSS members—notably Mykhailo Bilynsky, Ivan Lypa, Oleksander Osetsky, Oleksander Shapoval, and Dmytro Symoniv—were members of the governments of **Volodymyr Chekhivsky** and Serhii Ostapenko. Dissatisfied with the Directory's policies and advocating a military dictatorship to fight Soviet Russia, the UPSS made an unsuccessful coup attempt led by Volodymyr Oskilko on 29 April 1919. The party split and, following the defeat of the Directory, ceased its activities. In the early 1920s, the UPSS was revived in Vienna, and in 1922 it used the name Ukrainian People's Party. It was active for some time in **Volhynia** but remained marginal because it favored cooperation with the Polish authorities. UPSS periodicals were the weekly *Samostiinyk* (Independentist, Kyiv) and the dailies *Samostiina Ukraïna* (Independent Ukraine), *Ukraïna* (Ukraine), *Ukraïns'ki visti* (Ukrainian News, Ternopil), and *Ukraïns'ka sprava* (The Ukrainian Cause, Rivne).

UKRAINIAN PARTY OF SOCIALIST REVOLUTIONARIES/UKRAÏNS'KA PARTIIA SOTSIIALISTIV-REVOLIUTSIONERIV (UPSR). Mass-based **peasant** party established in **Kyiv** on 4–5 (17–18) April 1917 through a merger of individual socialist revolutionary groups that had existed in Ukraine since 1905. Notable among its leaders, who came from the intelligentsia, were **Pavlo Khrystiuk**, Mykola Kovalevsky, Levko Kovaliv, **Oleksander Sevriuk**, Mykola Shrah, and Volodymyr Zalizniak. **Mykhailo Hrushevsky** worked closely with the party. The UPSR advocated cultural and political autonomy for Ukraine and the socialization of land without compensation to landowners. It became the leading advocate of peasant interests, relying on the Peasant Union, which it established, for organizational strength. By November 1917, the party had approximately 75,000 members. Its publications were the **cooperative** daily newspaper *Narodna volia* (People's Will) and the daily *Borot'ba* (Struggle).

During the early phase of the **Ukrainian People's Republic** (UNR), the UPSR held a majority in the **Ukrainian Central Rada**, and its members served in the General Secretariat and the **Council of People's Ministers**. In the governments of **Volodymyr Vynnychenko**, the Socialist Revolutionaries controlled the secretariats of supply (Kovalevsky), industry and trade (Vsevolod Holubovych), and the postal and telegraph service (Mykyta Shapoval). Khrystiuk was state secretary. From January to April 1918, when Holubovych was the president of the Council of People's Ministers, most ministries were headed by UPSR members.

Following the establishment of the **Ukrainian State**, the party split into right and left wings at its clandestine fourth congress (13–16 May 1918). The right wing (the so-called central current: Holubovych, Ivan Lyzanivsky, Shapoval, Mykola Chechel, Nykyfor Hryhoriiv, Oleksander Zhukovsky, Sevriuk, Khrystiuk, and others), which considered the revolution complete, advocated legal opposition to the government of Hetman **Pavlo Skoropadsky**. The left wing (Kovaliv, Mykhailo Poloz, Hnat Mykhailychenko, **Oleksander Shumsky**, **Vasyl Blakytny**, Antin Prykhodko, Panas Liubchenko, and others) propagated a government based on councils (i.e., soviets), cooperation with the Bolsheviks, organization of underground resistance, and preparation of an uprising against Skoropadsky. After gaining control of the central committee, the left wing ousted the right and took the party underground. Subsequently, this branch came to be known as the **Borotbists** (from their newspaper *Borot'ba* [Struggle]) and constituted itself in March 1919 as the Ukrainian Party of Socialist Revolutionary Borotbists (Communists). The right wing established its own organizational center (January 1919), which assumed the party's old name in April 1919. It belonged to the **Ukrainian National Union** and participated in the anti-Skoropadsky uprising. Its publications were the journal *Trudova respublika* (Labor Republic, 1918–19) and the newspaper *Trudova hromada* (Labor Community, 1917–19).

Under the **Directory**, representatives of the UPSR were members of the governments of **Volodymyr Chekhivsky**, Borys Martos, and **Isaak Mazepa**. In late 1919, some members emigrated and propagated the principle of "dictatorship of the working masses" abroad (Shapoval, Hryhoriiv). In 1920, the Foreign Delegation of the UPSR was established in Vienna (Hrushevsky, Shrah, Khrystiuk, Chechel, Dmytro Isaievych, and others). It published the journal *Boritesia—poborete!* (Struggle—You Will Overcome!, ed. Hrushevsky) in 1920–22, advocating the transformation of the UNR into a "soviet republic." In the 1920s, the party underwent further divisions in the emigration and ceased to exist as a single organization. A show trial of UPSR central committee members arrested by the Bolsheviks took place in **Kharkiv** in 1921. In 1924, most members of the Foreign Delegation returned to the **Ukrainian SSR**, where they faced persecution in the 1930s. After Shapoval's death, Socialist Revolutionary organizations abroad merged and created a joint central committee in Prague. From 1932 to 1939, it published *Trudova Ukraïna* (Labor Ukraine), edited by Hryhoriiv and Pavlo Bohatsky. In 1950, members of the UPSR and other émigré socialists formed the Ukrainian Socialist Party.

UKRAINIAN PEOPLE'S PARTY/UKRAÏNS'KA NARODNA PARTIIA (UNP). First independentist party in **eastern Ukraine**. Founded by **Mykola Mikhnovsky** in **Kharkiv** in 1902, it included former members of the **Revolutionary Ukrainian Party** and young representatives of the **hromadas** who supported Ukrainian independence. Its leaders included Mykola Shemet, Serhii Shemet, Oleksander Makarenko, and Oleksander Stepanenko. The program of the UNP, set forth in Mikhnovsky's "Ten Commandments," was summarized in the slogan "Ukraine for Ukrainians." In 1904, the 250th anniversary of the political union of Ukraine with Muscovy (*see* PEREIASLAV AGREEMENT), members of the UNP attempted unsuccessfully to destroy the Pushkin monument in Kharkiv and tsarist monuments in **Kyiv**, Kharkiv, and **Odesa** as a protest against Russian tyranny.

The UNP garnered very little support, since its advocacy of independence was illegal and ran counter to the well-established federalist tradition in Ukrainian political thought. After the **Revolution of 1905**, the UNP participated in elections to the State Duma but failed to win a seat. UNP materials were printed in **Lviv** and Chernivtsi and smuggled into eastern Ukraine. Its publications were *Samostiina Ukraïna* (Independent Ukraine, one issue published in Lviv, 1906) and *Slobozhanshchyna* (**Sloboda Ukraine**, one issue published in Kharkiv, 1906). After Mikhnovsky's withdrawal in 1907, the UNP declined. In December 1917, UNP members established the **Ukrainian Party of Socialist Independentists**.

UKRAINIAN PEOPLE'S REPUBLIC/UKRAÏNS'KA NARODNA RESPUBLIKA (UNR). Ukrainian state (1917–20). The establishment of the UNR on the territory of **eastern Ukraine** in federation with Russia was proclaimed in the Third Universal of the **Ukrainian Central Rada** (7 [20] November 1917). After the Bolsheviks seized power and Soviet Russian forces invaded Ukraine, the Rada declared the independence of the UNR (9 [22] January 1918). In February 1918, the UNR signed the **Treaty of Brest-Litovsk** and was recognized as an independent state by the Central Powers. German and Austrian armies drove out the Bolsheviks, but the UNR did not satisfy its allies' demand for regular delivery of foodstuffs. In April 1918, as a result of **Pavlo Skoropadsky's** coup, the **Ukrainian State** was declared in place of the UNR. The UNR was restored by the **Directory** in December 1918. With the proclamation of the **Act of Union** (22 January 1919), the UNR incorporated the territory of the **Western Ukrainian People's Republic**. The UNR ceased to exist in Ukraine in late November 1920, following the renewed invasion of Ukraine by Bolshevik forces and the emigration of the Directory and the **Council of People's Ministers** of the UNR. The UNR government-in-exile continued to function until 1992 (*see* LIVYTSKY, ANDRII; PETLIURA, SYMON; UKRAINIAN NATIONAL COUNCIL [GERMANY, 1948]).

UKRAINIAN PEOPLE'S SELF-DEFENSE/UKRAÏNS'KA NARODNA SAMOOBORONA (UNS). Armed underground formation active in **Galicia** in 1943. The **Bandera** faction of the **Organization of Ukrainian Nationalists** conducted clandestine military training of its members in Galicia from September 1941 to June 1943. Since Galicia was part of the **Generalgouvernement**, where the German occupation regime was less severe than in the **Reichskommissariat Ukraine**, the OUN(B) avoided clashes with the Germans so as not to provoke repressive measures. Two developments led to active UNS resistance under the command of Lieut. Oleksander Lutsky: the beginning of recruitment to the Waffen-SS **Division Galizien** in April 1943 and the Carpathian raid of the Soviet partisan leader **Sydir Kovpak** (July-August). The UNS fought the remains of Kovpak's units as well as detachments of the German police, which began to execute captured UNS members and hostages in October, when martial law was declared in Galicia. In December 1943, the UNS merged with the **Ukrainian Insurgent Army** (UPA), becoming known as UPA-West.

UKRAINIAN-POLISH CONFLICT (1943–47). War of ethnic cleansing in **western Ukraine** and southeastern Poland that took the lives of between 50,000 and 100,000 Poles and Ukrainians and forced another 1.5 million to leave their homes. Research on the subject was forbidden by the communist regimes in Poland and Ukraine; since 1989, a large (mainly Polish-language) literature has been produced. Recently, such Ukrainian scholars as Ihor Iliushyn, Anatolii Rusnachenko, and Yurii Shapoval have addressed the issue.

The conflict, rooted in competing historical claims to sovereignty and territory, was greatly exacerbated by tensions that built up during the interwar period. Defeated in the **Ukrainian-Polish War in Galicia** (1918–19), which gave Poland sovereignty over most of western Ukraine until the outbreak of **World War II**, Ukrainians faced systematic discrimination (*see* GALICIA), against which their legal political parties were powerless (*see* UKRAINIAN NATIONAL DEMOCRATIC ALLIANCE). Moreover, the Polish government promoted colonization, distributing land in western Ukraine to war veterans and peasants from western Poland. This situation led to the rise of the clandestine **Organization of Ukrainian Nationalists** (OUN), which conducted a terrorist campaign against Polish rule in the 1930s and emerged as the strongest Ukrainian political force during the war. In 1942, the radical **Bandera** wing of the OUN proceeded to organize the underground **Ukrainian Insurgent Army** (UPA) in **Volhynia**, while the conservative **Melnyk** faction of the OUN remained dominant in Galicia.

The Polish underground attacked Ukrainians in the **Kholm** (Chełm) **region** in 1942 and early 1943, killing numerous members of the intelligentsia and community leaders, apparently in reaction to the revival of Ukrainian activity stimulated by the **Ukrainian Central Committee** and the settlement of post-1939 émigrés from Galicia. In the Hrubeshiv (Hrubieszów) region, the Germans' deportation of Poles and settlement of Ukrainians in their place provoked further Polish attacks in 1942–43. According to a statement issued in 1944 by Bishop Ilarion (**Ivan Ohiienko**), some 7,000 Ukrainians were killed in these attacks.

While the OUN-UPA was committed to establishing an independent state on all Ukrainian ethnic territory, the London-based Polish government-in-exile and its military arm, the underground Armia Krajowa (AK, Home Army), was adamant about restoring the Second Polish Republic within its borders of 1939. In negotiations with Ukrainian representatives, the London Poles offered no more than political autonomy and full civil rights to Ukrainians in a restored Polish state. Realizing that AK war plans made provision for a conflict with Ukrainian forces and anticipating a postwar transfer of reinforcements and colonists from central Poland to western Ukraine, the Ukrainian nationalists considered it vital to act swiftly and decisively. The OUN-UPA sought to establish its territorial claims by driving Polish settlers out of western Ukraine, starting with its Volhynian base of operations. Recent research suggests that there was a split in the OUN leadership on this issue; **Mykola Lebed**, who considered an armed rising premature and opposed attacks on civilians, was maneuvered out of the OUN (Bandera) leadership in February 1943, while the Volhynian UPA commander, Dmytro Kliachkivsky, and his associates resolved to drive the Poles out of Volhynia.

Polish-Ukrainian tensions in Volhynia had run high since 1935, when a military regime took power in Poland. The regime increased assimilatory pressure on Ukrainians and dismissed the conciliatory Volhynian governor, Henryk Józewski, in 1938. In the Kholm region, which bordered on Volhynia, Orthodox churches were destroyed en masse in the late 1930s, while armed gangs attacked Ukrainian homes with the tacit support of the regime. During the German occupation, Poles firmly entrenched themselves in the administrative and economic apparatus of Volhynia, expecting to consolidate their status definitively after Germany's defeat. Beginning in April 1943, UPA forces, which included many armed deserters from the German-controlled Ukrainian auxiliary police, killed many thousands of Polish civilians in Volhynia (Poles accounted for approx. 16 percent of the population at the time). They were assisted by land-hungry peasants attracted by the prospect of taking over the farms of Polish colonists. According to a massive collection of Polish testimonies (many of them prepared decades after the events) compiled by Władysław and Ewa Siemaszko and published in 2000, a total of 36,750 Polish civilians were killed, of whom 19,500 have been identified by name.

About 250,000 Poles fled to the **Generalgouvernement** (German-occupied ethnic Poland), while thousands more formed self-defense units or joined German and Soviet units that were fighting the Ukrainian underground (the better to secure their dominance, both the Germans and the Soviets played Ukrainians and Poles off against each other). The AK and other Polish partisan formations also went over to the attack, burning Ukrainian villages and killing their inhabitants, as well as assassinating prominent Ukrainians. No detailed statistics of Ukrainian losses are available, although work has begun in Lutsk and **Lviv** to collect survivors' testimonies and establish figures. In 2003, the Polish historian Grzegorz Motyka, a leading specialist on the conflict, estimated total Ukrainian losses at 15–20,000. In Galicia, where the UPA and AK fought each other in 1944, some 20–30,000 Poles and several thousand Ukrainians were killed. Polish survivors' accounts note that many Ukrainians disapproved of ethnic cleansing and assisted or sheltered Poles.

The Soviet occupation of western Ukraine in mid-1944 brought the Polish-Ukrainian conflict to an end as both underground armies concentrated on fighting their principal enemy (in 1945, there was even limited cooperation between Polish and Ukrainian partisans against Soviet forces). A secret accord of 27 July 1944 between

Stalin and the Polish communists (subsequently approved by the Western Allies at the **Yalta Conference**) shifted Poland's borders westward, with the eastern border approximating the **Curzon Line**. The victorious Soviets, intent on destroying the Ukrainian underground and bringing all Ukrainian lands under their control, concluded an agreement on population transfer with Poland on 9 September 1944. Some 788,000 Poles left western Ukraine as a result.

The 700,000 Ukrainians remaining in southeastern Poland were much less willing to leave their ancestral lands for "repatriation" to Ukraine, given the viciously anti-Ukrainian policies implemented by the Stalin regime in the 1930s (*see* FAMINE; POLITICAL TERROR) and during their occupation of western Ukraine in 1939–41. Early in 1945, Polish forces began a campaign to drive Ukrainians out of Poland, burning their villages and killing thousands of civilians. The UPA sought to prevent these deportations by defending Ukrainian villagers and attacking Polish settlements. These countermeasures were unavailing, as approximately 208,000 Ukrainians were expelled between January and August 1945. In September, the Soviet official in charge of the population transfer, **Mykola Pidhorny**, asked that force be used to complete the task, to which three Polish infantry divisions were duly assigned. This resulted in the expulsion of another quarter million Ukrainians in the spring of 1946. According to the U.S. historian Timothy Snyder, a total of 482,000 Ukrainians were resettled to Ukraine between 1944 and 1946, with about 300,000 transferred by force. The depopulation of Ukrainian settlements in southeastern Poland was completed by **Operation Vistula** in 1947.

The conflict embittered Ukrainian-Polish relations for decades, giving rise to polemics in the **diaspora**. In Poland, an extensive literature on the "reactionary underground" helped foster a relentlessly negative stereotype of Ukrainians in general. Nevertheless, the population transfer resolved the last major dispute between Poland and Ukraine, leading both sides to acknowledge the prevalence of common interests. Poland was the first nation to recognize Ukrainian independence in 1991. On 21 May 1997, Presidents **Leonid Kuchma** and Aleksander Kwaśniewski signed a joint declaration in **Kyiv** calling for the frank acknowledgement of past wrongs, including the mass murders and forced population transfers of 1943–47, as a precondition of mutual understanding. On 11 July 2003, a monument to Polish and Ukrainian victims was unveiled by both presidents in the Volhynian village of Pavlivka, and the parliaments of Poland and Ukraine passed an identically worded resolution calling for remembrance and reconciliation. Sustained research on the conflict was undertaken jointly in 1996 by the Association of Ukrainians in Poland and the World Association of AK Veterans, leading to the publication of the serial *Ukraïna-Pol'shcha: vazhki pytannia* (Ukraine-Poland: Difficult Questions, eight issues, 1998–2001) and the development of a statistical database of casualties.

UKRAINIAN-POLISH WAR IN GALICIA (1918–19). Armed conflict between the **Western Ukrainian People's Republic** (ZUNR) and the Second Polish Republic. As a result of the November Uprising (1 November 1918), led by Capt. Dmytro Vitovsky with a force of some 1,500 **Ukrainian Sich Riflemen**, the **Ukrainian National Rada** (UNRada) assumed sovereignty over **Lviv** and later all of western Ukraine. In response, Polish military units (383 officers and approximately 4,000 men) commanded by Capt. Czesław Mączyński launched an immediate uprising in Lviv. Armed Polish revolts also broke out in other western Ukrainian towns, notably Drohobych, Peremyshl (Przemyśl), and Sambir.

The battle for Lviv lasted three weeks. Polish reinforcements (140 officers and approximately 1,220 men) arrived from Peremyshl on 20 November. Although the UNRada announced the formation of the **Ukrainian Galician Army** (UHA) on 13 November, the Ukrainian forces in Lviv, inexperienced in street fighting and poorly coordinated, were driven out of the city on 21 November.

The UNRada retreated to Ternopil and, in late December, to Stanyslaviv. By mid-January 1919, the UHA had mobilized some 50,000–60,000 men under the command of an eastern Ukrainian, Gen. Mykhailo Omelianovych-Pavlenko. On 17 February, it undertook the Vovchukhy operation, hoping to gain control of the Lviv-Peremyshl railway, capture those cities, and reach the Sian (San) River, which divided eastern (Ukrainian) **Galicia** from western (Polish) Galicia. The offensive was initially successful but was halted on 25 February at the demand of the Entente.

The Ukrainian side agreed to a truce and entered into negotiations with an Entente mission led by Gen. Joseph Berthélemy. The mission demanded that the Ukrainians retreat east of the "Berthélemy line" and cede 40 percent of eastern Galicia, including Lviv and the Drohobych oil fields, to Poland. Although **Symon Petliura**, who headed the **Ukrainian People's Republic** (with which the ZUNR had united on 22 January), urged acceptance of these terms, the ZUNR rejected them on 4 March. The Poles brought in further reinforcements and broke through the UHA lines on 19 March, retaking Lviv and the railway line to Peremyshl.

In May 1919, another Entente commission headed by Gen. Louis Botha proposed a territorial division that would have given Lviv to Poland and the Drohobych oil fields to the ZUNR, with a limit of 20,000 on the armies of both sides. While the ZUNR accepted these terms, the Polish side, having gained a crushing advantage in manpower with the formation in France of a well-equipped army commanded by Gen. Józef Haller (six divisions, approx. 68,000 men), rejected them. Although the Entente authorized Haller's army only to combat the Bolsheviks, Polish representatives at the Paris Peace Conference evaded this restriction, claiming that there were Bolsheviks among the Ukrainian forces. On 14 May, Haller's army began an assault along the entire front, driving the UHA eastward. Part of it lost contact with the main UHA forces and retreated to **Transcarpathia**, where its soldiers were interned by the Czechoslovak authorities. In late May, Romanian armies began occupying the southeastern counties of Pokutia. The UHA retreated to a corner of southeastern Galicia between the Zbruch and Dnister Rivers.

After regrouping, the UHA, now commanded by Gen. Oleksander Hrekov (Omelianovych-Pavlenko was dismissed on 9 June), began an advance on Chortkiv and Lviv. It regained about half the territory occupied by the Polish forces but was constantly hampered by a lack of weapons, ammunition, and equipment. On 28 June, the Poles counterattacked, and on 16–17 July the UHA retreated across the Zbruch, where it joined the UNR forces.

Although Petliura arranged a last-ditch alliance with the Poles against the Bolsheviks (*see* TREATY OF WARSAW), it proved unsuccessful. The western Ukrainian lands were occupied by Poland, which ruled them until **World War II**. Throughout that period, the western Ukrainian population resisted Polish rule both by legal means (demands for autonomy) and underground struggle (*see* ORGANIZATION OF UKRAINIAN NATIONALISTS). Most Poles regarded the victory of 1919 as a vindication of their country's historical claim to the eastern borderlands (*kresy*). The defense of Lviv in November 1918 by Mączyński's "eaglets" entered the annals of Polish martial legend. The Soviet destruction of the Lviv cemetery in which the fallen Polish soldiers were buried, which began in the 1950s and culminated in August 1971, was bitterly resented. The cemetery was restored in the 1990s.

UKRAINIAN RADICAL PARTY/UKRAÏNS'KA RADYKAL'NA PARTIIA (URP). Initially the Ruthenian-Ukrainian Radical Party; from 1926, the Ukrainian Socialist Radical Party. First Ukrainian political party, established in **Lviv** on 4 October 1890. Its founders and leaders included **Ivan Franko** (until 1898), **Mykhailo Pavlyk** (until 1914), Viacheslav Budzynovsky, Severyn Danylovych, and Yevhen Levytsky. **Mykhailo Drahomanov** had a great influence on the ideological formation of the radical movement, and the URP was programmatically socialist and anticlerical. In its activities, the party strove to represent the interests of the **Galician peasantry**, with lesser attention to the small Ukrainian proletariat. As a result of discussions between older members (notably Franko and Pavlyk) and younger ones (Budzynovsky, Levytsky, Volodymyr Okhrymovych, and others), the postulate of Ukrainian political independence was advanced for the first time in **Yuliian Bachynsky's** book *Ukraïna irredenta* and in the second URP program, both published in 1895. Because of their insistence on social reform, the radicals generally opposed the conservative **populists** who dominated Ukrainian politics in Galicia. After a split in the Radical Party (1899), most of the membership left to establish the **National Democratic Party** (NDP) together with the populists; others founded the **Ukrainian Social Democratic Party**. An unofficial two-party system arose in Galician politics, with the URP acting as the leftist, peasant-based opposition to the centrist NDP. The URP elected five deputies to the Austrian Reichstag (1911) and six to the Galician Diet (1913). Party activists played an important role in organizing peasant strikes in Galicia (1902) and the Sich movement (*see* TRYLIOVSKY, KYRYLO). They also held leading posts in the government of the **Western Ukrainian People's Republic** (**Lev Bachynsky**, Hryhorii Duvirak, Ivan Makukh, Andrii Shmigelsky, and Dmytro Vitovsky).

From 1919 to 1939, when Galicia was under Polish rule, the URP was one of the most influential Ukrainian parties. In 1926, it merged with the Ukrainian Socialist Revolutionary Party of **Volhynia** to form the Ukrainian Socialist Radical Party. Party membership approached 20,000, and in the 1931 elections, which it contested in tandem with the **Ukrainian National Democratic Alliance**, the USRP won a quarter of the parliamentary seats taken by the coalition. In the same year, it joined the Second Socialist International. The party's leaders during **World War I** and the interwar period were Mykola Lahodynsky (1914–19), Lev Bachynsky (1924–30), and Makukh (1930–39). Its main publications were *Narod* (The People, 1890–95, 1918), *Khliborob* (The Agrarian, 1891–95), and *Hromads'kyi holos* (Civic Voice, 1895–1939, with interruptions). After **World War II**, it was active in the **diaspora**. In 1950, it merged with like-minded parties to form the Ukrainian Socialist Party.

UKRAINIAN REVOLUTION (1917–21). Political and social upheaval, precipitated by **World War I**, that determined the status of the Ukrainian lands until **World War II**. The revolution of February 1917 in Russia, which brought down the Romanov dynasty, led to the formation of the **Ukrainian Central Rada** in **Kyiv** (7 [20] March 1917), a representative body led by the historian **Mykhailo Hrushevsky**. The Rada, dominated by political parties composed of **populist** and socialist intellectuals, challenged the Provisional Government in St. Petersburg for the right to govern the Ukrainian lands of the former Russian Empire. In its Third Universal, issued on 7 (20) November 1917, it asserted Ukraine's autonomy within a future democratic all-Russian federation. The Bolshevik Revolution of October 1917 promptly led to conflict with the Central Rada, as the new Soviet government needed Ukrainian grain and industry to survive. The Bolsheviks attacked the Central Rada and proclaimed a Soviet Ukrainian republic. This prompted the Rada to declare the independence of the **Ukrainian People's Republic** (UNR) in its Fourth Universal (9 [22] January 1918).

As the Ukrainian population consisted overwhelmingly of **peasants**, their attitude was all-important for the prospects of any government. The Central Rada did not move quickly enough to satisfy the two major demands of the Ukrainian peasantry: to end Ukraine's participation in the world war and expropriate the holdings of large landowners in order to redistribute them. This left the Rada sorely lacking in peasant recruits to fight the invading Bolsheviks, who adopted the popular slogan "Peace, land, and bread." The Rada signed the **Treaty of Brest-Litovsk** (February 1918) with the Central Powers, who drove the Bolsheviks out of Ukraine in the spring of 1918. Dissatisfied with the Rada's inefficiency in supplying the foodstuffs and resources that were the quid pro quo of this arrangement, the Germans began casting about for a leader of a new Ukrainian regime.

They found him in **Pavlo Skoropadsky**, a career officer descended from a Ukrainian **Cossack** family. The German-sponsored coup of 29 April 1918 brought down the Rada almost without a shot, and Skoropadsky was proclaimed **hetman** of the **Ukrainian State**, which drew its support largely from Russian-oriented landowners and industrialists. His regime antagonized the peasantry with punitive expeditions intended to requisition grain and take back expropriated property. It also estranged the Ukrainian intelligentsia with its ideological opposition to socialism and its markedly pro-Russian character. As the Central Powers neared military collapse on the Western front, the Ukrainian socialists, led by **Symon Petliura** and **Volodymyr Vynnychenko**, formed the **Directory** of the UNR, which led a revolt against Skoropadsky in November 1918 and took power a month later.

The Directory, which restored the UNR and convoked a **Labor Congress** in January 1919 as a representative body of Ukrainian workers and peasants, was immediately faced with a new Bolshevik invasion led by **Volodymyr Antonov-Ovsiienko**. Like the Rada, the Directory had little in the way of a regular army and was dependent on such fickle peasant warlords as **Nestor Makhno** and **Nykyfor Hryhoriiv**, who opposed all restrictions on the peasantry. Throughout 1919, which became a year of anarchy in Ukraine, the Directory battled for power with the Bolsheviks and the Russian White (protsarist) armies. The Bolsheviks faced violent opposition from the Ukrainian peasants because of their incessant requisitioning of grain for the Red Army and the home front in the Civil War.

The **Western Ukrainian People's Republic** (ZUNR), which had come into being in October 1918 on the Ukrainian territories of the former Austro-Hungarian Empire, concluded an **Act of Union** with the UNR under the Directory's auspices in January 1919. Until July of that year, the regular **Ukrainian Galician Army** (UHA) of the ZUNR fought the newly established Second Polish Republic for control of its territory (*see* UKRAINIAN-POLISH WAR IN GALICIA). The Poles gained a decisive advantage when an army of 68,000 men, formed in France and armed by the Entente, was transferred to the Galician front. When the UHA was driven eastward across the Zbruch River on 16–17 July, the ZUNR administration, led by **Yevhen Petrushevych**, established itself in Kamianets-Podilskyi together with Petliura's UNR government. Unable to agree on a strategy—Petrushevych hoped for an alliance with the Entente by means of a truce with Anton Denikin's White Army, while Petliura sought assistance from the Poles—the joint forces were defeated in November 1919. Petliura escaped to Warsaw, while Petrushevych settled in Vienna.

In April 1920, Petliura signed the **Treaty of Warsaw**, which arranged for a Polish-Ukrainian campaign to retake eastern Ukraine at the price of ceding western Ukraine to Poland. Although the Polish-Ukrainian forces briefly succeeded in taking Kyiv, the Red Army, which now numbered approximately a million men, drove them back almost to the gates of Warsaw. The Poles then made a separate peace (**Treaty of Riga**, March 1921) with Russia and the **Ukrainian SSR**. That treaty, as well as the failure of Petliura's **Winter Campaigns** of 1920–21, marked the definitive military victory of Soviet forces in the struggle for eastern Ukraine. Peasant resistance to Soviet rule remained very strong in the Ukrainian SSR until the introduction of the New Economic Policy and was not fully overcome until the mid-1920s (*see* INSURGENT MOVEMENT).

Transcarpathia was annexed to Czechoslovakia in 1919 and **Bukovyna** to Romania in 1920. Last to be determined was the status of Galicia, which was awarded to Poland in March 1923 on condition (officially ignored throughout the interwar period) that it be treated as an autonomous region.

UKRAINIAN REVOLUTIONARY DEMOCRATIC PARTY/UKRAÏNS'KA REVOLIUTSIINO-DEMOKRATYCHNA PARTIIA (URDP). Émigré political party dedicated to the overthrow of the **USSR** and the establishment of an independent social-democratic Ukrainian state. It was the only political party in the **diaspora** whose membership was overwhelmingly eastern Ukrainian. The URDP was founded in Regensburg, Germany, in August 1947 by emigrants from the **Ukrainian SSR** who embraced the social ideals of the **Ukrainian Revolution** and by former members of the **Organization of Ukrainian Nationalists** who supported Ivan Mitrynga's faction. Its first president was the literary scholar Hryhorii Kostiuk, who broke with the party in 1948 to form the Left URDP (which eventually dissolved). The writer Ivan Bahriany was president from 1948 to 1963. The URDP helped establish the **Ukrainian National Council** (Germany, 1948), in which it participated until 1968. Branches were established in the United States, Canada, Britain, Belgium, Germany, Australia, and Argentina, with a variety of publications. In 1979, a splinter group formed the Right URDP. The URDP renamed itself the Ukrainian Democratic Republican Party in 1990.

UKRAINIAN SICH RIFLEMEN/UKRAÏNS'KI SICHOVI STRIL'TSI (USS). Sole Ukrainian military unit in the Austrian army, active on the Russian front from 1914 to 1918. On 6 August 1914, the **Supreme Ukrainian Council** in **Lviv** established the Combat Board of the USS, which appealed to the Austrian government for permission to form the Legion of the USS. The imperial command responded favorably but allotted only 60 Ukrainian officers, among them Vasyl Didushok, Semen Horuk, Hryhorii Kossak, and Dmytro Vitovsky. Arms allocated to the USS consisted of 1,000 heavy single-loading muskets that had been decommissioned in 1888. In total, 28,000 **Galicians** volunteered for the USS, sufficient numbers for two infantry divisions, but the government and Polish political circles, fearing the creation of a Ukrainian army, restricted the legion's numbers to 2,000. Its core consisted of activists of the paramilitary Sich (*see* TRYLIOVSKY,

KYRYLO), Sokil, and **Plast** movements, until recently gymnasium and university students. The new recruits included the female students Hanna Dmyterko, Sofiia Halechko, Iryna Kuz, and Olena Stepaniv. Most mobilized Galicians (more than 100,000 men) were stationed far from Ukraine on the Italian front.

The Austrian command decided to pitch the poorly trained USS riflemen against the advancing Russian armies, ensuring large casualties. The first battles against Russian Cossack units were fought in late September 1914 in the vicinity of the Veretskyi and Uzh mountain passes. As part of the 55th Austrian Division, the riflemen engaged in a counteroffensive and recaptured Boryslav, Drohobych, and Stryi in October. The Russian commander, Gen. Aleksei Brusilov, was able to retake the area only after transferring reserves from the Peremyshl (Przemyśl) region, forcing the USS to retreat to the Carpathian Mountains.

In early March 1915, the Sich Riflemen took up positions on the slopes of Makivka in the Carpathians, joining the 129th and 130th Austrian brigades. The Russian assault began on the night of 28–29 April and lasted until 2 May; after fierce battles, the Russian armies were driven back. After this significant victory, the USS fought on the **Podilian** plains and, on 2 November, stopped the Russian breakthrough at Berezhany. These battlefield achievements won praise from the Austrian military, but the political authorities continued to regard the USS as unreliable.

The regiment spent the winter of 1915–16 on the home front, engaged in military training and cultural and educational work. During the Brusilov offensive (summer 1916), the imperial command once again used the USS to cover the most important segment of the front (the route from Pidhaitsi to Berezhany). On the slopes of Lysonia, the newly reorganized USS regiment (commanded by Kossak) suffered more than 1,000 casualties (2–4 September). The survivors were pulled back from the front, reformed, and given a new commander, Franz Kikal. In the autumn of 1916, USS officers led by Vitovsky began large-scale cultural and educational activity in **Volhynia**, where they had been transferred to gather recruits. In a brief period they established nearly 100 Ukrainian schools, at which 16 officers and riflemen worked as teachers. With the help of **Kyrylo Studynsky**, Luka Myshuha, and **Ivan Krypiakevych**, the riflemen acquired 1,500 textbooks for the Volhynian schools, as well as a considerable quantity of supplies.

The regiment returned to the front near Berezhany in February 1917. At the cost of many casualties, it held the front near Koniukhy against a new Russian advance. In accordance with the **Treaty of Brest-Litovsk**, the USS advanced with Austro-German forces into

eastern Ukraine (March–October 1918). The regiment devoted most of its attention to cultural and educational work. The Reserve Section was active in recruiting and training riflemen. It also had a library, a riflemen's choir and orchestra, and a press bureau. In early October 1918, the USS was transferred from the Kherson region to Chernivtsi in **Bukovyna**. After the establishment of the **Western Ukrainian People's Republic** (November 1918), the regiment proceeded to Lviv, where it became the basis of the **Ukrainian Galician Army** (UHA).

Another corps of Sich Riflemen made up one of the most disciplined and battle-ready formations in the Army of the **Ukrainian People's Republic** (UNR) during the **Ukrainian Revolution** (1917–21). In early November 1917, Galician and Bukovynian POWs in **Kyiv** organized a battalion of Sich Riflemen. On 6 (19) January 1918, **Yevhen Konovalets** was appointed its commander, and **Andrii Melnyk** became chief of staff. The battalion consisted of two infantry companies, a reserve company, a machine-gun company, and a battery of cannon. It had approximately 600 soldiers. In January and February 1918, the battalion fought Bolshevik units commanded by Mikhail Muraviev on the outskirts of Kyiv and in the city itself. On 20–22 January (2–4 February), the USS and the **Haidamaka** Battalion of **Sloboda Ukraine** quelled a Bolshevik-inspired uprising against the UNR at the Kyiv Arsenal. The Sich Riflemen protected the UNR government, which was forced to retreat from Kyiv to Volhynia in February. In early March, the Sich Riflemen, the Haidamaka Battalion, and the Separate Zaporozhian Detachment drove the Bolsheviks out of Kyiv. On 10 March, the battalion of Sich Riflemen, augmented by new volunteers, expanded into a regiment including three infantry battalions (each consisting of four companies), two machine-gun companies, an infantry scouting company, and an artillery unit. The regiment consisted of 3,000 soldiers under the command of Konovalets.

When **Pavlo Skoropadsky** seized power, the Sich Riflemen's barracks were surrounded by German forces and disarmed (30 April 1918). Most riflemen joined the Zaporozhian Corps of the Army of the UNR, where they were organized as a battalion of the Second Zaporozhian Infantry Regiment (commanded by Col. Petro Bolbochan).

Following negotiations with a USS delegation, Skoropadsky agreed to the formation of a rifle division (August 1918) and issued an order for the creation of a Separate Detachment of Sich Riflemen (23 August) to be stationed at Bila Tserkva. During the uprising against Skoropadsky in November, the Sich Riflemen played a decisive role in defeating his forces at the Battle of Motovylivka.

In the course of the fighting for Kyiv (November–December 1918), the Separate Detachment of Sich Riflemen expanded first into a division and, on 12 December, into the Standing Corps of Sich Riflemen (approx. 20,000 soldiers and officers). Under the influence of Bolshevik agitation, much of the corps virtually demobilized itself in early January 1919, but a 7,000-strong division remained battle-ready. After suffering heavy losses at the hands of the Red Army, most USS units fell back on Proskuriv and Starokostiantyniv to regroup (late February). On orders of the UNR Army, all Sich Riflemen units of the former Standing Corps were incorporated into a new Corps of Sich Riflemen, commanded by Konovalets. The corps consisted of five or six infantry regiments, an artillery brigade (six regiments), a cavalry division, a technical company, an armored division, and technical and transport units. The unit was supplied by four armored trains: Sichovyi, Strilets, Zaporozhets, and Pomsta. At various times, the corps consisted of infantry (500 officers and approx. 7,000 soldiers, March 1919; 319 officers and 8,067 soldiers, June 1919) and cavalry (15 officers and 297 soldiers, March 1919; 15 officers and 242 soldiers, June 1919).

In March and April 1919, the corps suffered heavy losses in battles with Bolshevik forces for Berdychiv and Shepetivka. Part of the corps consolidated and fought Bolshevik forces in the vicinity of Bazaliia and Chornyi Ostriv (June). At this time the corps was renamed the Sich Riflemen Group, and rifle units were reformed into two divisions.

As the UNR Army and the UHA approached Kyiv, USS units in the Second Corps of the UHA took Shepetivka (16 August), Novohrad-Volynskyi (20 August), and Korosten. After the **Directory** declared war on the Russian White armies of Gen. Anton Denikin (24 September), the riflemen fought in the vicinity of Zhmerynka and Proskuriv (October-November). In early December, the UNR Army, including the Sich Riflemen, was surrounded by Bolshevik, Polish, and Denikinite forces in the vicinity of Ostropil—Liubar—Chortoryia. The riflemen were demobilized on 6 December. Some of them joined the Army of the UNR, which set out on its first **Winter Campaign** at that time. Others remained in the UHA when it was reorganized as the Red Ukrainian Galician Army and fought against the Poles, suffering heavy casualties.

During the interwar period, a large memoir literature was published by veterans of the USS, firmly establishing it in western Ukrainian public consciousness as the first military force since **Cossack** times to have dedicated itself to the struggle for Ukrainian independence. *See also* WORLD WAR I.

UKRAINIAN SOCIAL DEMOCRATIC LABOR PARTY/UKRAÏNS'KA SOTSIIAL-DEMOKRATYCHNA ROBITNYCHA PARTIIA (USDRP).

Political party of the revolutionary intelligentsia in **eastern Ukraine**, founded in **Kyiv** in early December 1905 to supersede the **Revolutionary Ukrainian Party**. Its platform was based on the Erfurt program of the German social democrats. In 1908, it had approximately 3,000 members, and its leaders were **Symon Petliura**, **Mykola Porsh**, **Volodymyr Vynnychenko**, Dmytro Antonovych, Mykola Kovalsky, Mykhailo Tkachenko, and Lev Yurkevych. It published the newspapers *Borot'ba* (Struggle, 1906) and *Slovo* (Word, 1907–9) in Kyiv and *Pratsia* (Work, 1909–10), *Robitnyk* (Worker, 1910), and *Nash holos* (Our Voice, 1910–11) in **Lviv**. The USDRP sought recognition from the Russian social democrats as the representative body of the Ukrainian proletariat and supported Ukrainian autonomy. Yurkevych polemicized with Lenin on the national question, criticizing the latter as a centralist whose avowed support for the national movements of the empire's non-Russian peoples was mere political opportunism.

Under the **Ukrainian Central Rada**, the social democrats held leading posts in Vynnychenko's governments (June 1917–January 1918). Because of its reluctance to approve the socialization of land, the USDRP lost support among the **peasantry**, and after the Rada's fourth universal, only two of its members remained in the government (Antonovych and Tkachenko).

Under the **Ukrainian State**, the USDRP opposed **Pavlo Skoropadsky**, and its leaders were temporarily jailed. The party initiated the creation of the **Ukrainian National Union** and took part in preparations for an uprising against Skoropadsky. It then helped establish the **Directory**, led by Vynnychenko and Petliura. Between 1918 and 1920, the Council of People's Ministers was headed by the USDRP members **Volodymyr Chekhivsky**, Borys Martos, and **Isaak Mazepa**.

At its fourth congress (10–12 January 1919), the party split into two factions: right ("official") and left ("independentists"). The right wing (led by Mazepa, Petliura, Porsh, and Vynnychenko) supported the Directory, advocating "labor democracy" and gradual socialization of major industries. The independentists supported soviet rule in an independent Ukrainian socialist republic.

In early February 1919, in order to facilitate an expected agreement between the Directory and the Entente, the USDRP members of the government resigned, allowing Prime Minister Serhii Ostapenko to begin negotiations with the French command in **Odesa**. Simultaneously, Petliura left the party and Vynnychenko resigned from the Directory, yielding his authority to Petliura. In late

1919, as the Directory's rule collapsed, most party leaders emigrated.

In January 1920, the "independentists" established the **Ukrainian Communist Party**, which championed the independence of the **Ukrainian SSR** until it was forced to dissolve in 1925. The Foreign Delegation of the USDRP (led by Yosyp Bezpalko, Panas Fedenko, Borys Matiushenko, Mazepa, and Volodymyr Starosolsky) was active in the **diaspora** as a member of the Socialist International. It published its periodicals, *Sotsiialistychna dumka* (Socialist Thought, 1921–23) and *Sotsiialist-Demokrat* (Socialist Democrat, 1925–39), in Czechoslovakia. After **World War II**, the USDRP participated in the creation of the **Ukrainian National Council** in Germany, and in 1950 it joined like-minded parties to form the Ukrainian Socialist Party.

UKRAINIAN SOCIAL DEMOCRATIC LABOR PARTY (INDEPENDENTISTS)/UKRAÏNS'KA SOTSIIAL-DEMOKRATYCHNA ROBITNYCHA PARTIIA (NEZALEZHNYKY). Left wing of the **Ukrainian Social Democratic Labor Party** (USDRP), formed at the fourth congress of the USDRP (10–12 January 1919). It advocated the establishment of soviet rule in Ukraine in the form of "workers' and peasants' soviets," the proclamation of an independent Ukrainian socialist republic, immediate peace with the Bolsheviks, and continuation of military action against Entente interventionists in southern Ukraine. Members of the Independentists included Mykhailo Avdiienko, Antin Drahomyretsky, Yurii Mazurenko, Antin Pisetsky, and Mykhailo Tkachenko. The independentists' official publication was *Chervonyi prapor* (Red Flag). From the beginning of the Bolshevik occupation of Ukraine, they sought to function as an opposition party, but Bolshevik policies soon drove them to outright revolt. An All-Ukrainian Revolutionary Committee led by Drahomyretsky was created to lead the rebellion, and Mazurenko commanded the insurgent units. The left wing of the USDRP (Independentists), which did not support the insurrection, created the USDRP (Left Independentists). In August 1919, the Left Independentists merged with the **Borotbists**. In January 1920, the majority faction of the Independentists proclaimed the establishment of the **Ukrainian Communist Party**.

UKRAINIAN SOCIAL DEMOCRATIC PARTY/UKRAÏNS'KA SOTSIIAL-DEMOKRATYCHNA PARTIIA (USDP). Reformist party active in **Galicia** and **Bukovyna** as an autonomous section of the Social Democratic Labor Party of Austria and later as an independent party in the western Ukrainian lands. The party was established in **Lviv** on 17 September 1899 by Ukrainian members of the Polish Social Democratic Party of Galicia and Silesia (PPSD) and young socialists who had left the **Ukrainian Radical Party**, including **Yuliian Bachynsky**, Mykola Hankevych, Stepan and Mykhailo Novakovsky, Yatsko Ostapchuk, Andrii Shmigelsky, Semen Vityk, and Ivan Vozniak. It did trade-union work among the Ukrainian rural proletariat and organized strike committees during the **peasant** strikes of 1902. It also advocated the unity and independence of Ukraine. In 1907, the USDP became independent of the PPSD, winning approximately eight per cent of the Ukrainian vote and two seats (Ostapchuk and Vityk) in elections to the Reichstag that year. In 1911, the party had 1,366 members and local committees in 13 towns; its educational society, Volia (Freedom), had 13 branches. In the 1911 elections, the USDP won a single mandate (Vityk). Mykola Havryshchuk became a deputy to the Bukovynian Diet.

Because of continuing conflict about relations with the PPSD, the USDP split into "centrist" or pro-PPSD (M. Hankevych, Vityk, Teofil Melen) and "autonomist" (Volodymyr Levynsky, Lev Hankevych, Porfyr Buniak) groups at its fourth congress (3–4 December 1911). Unity was restored at its fifth congress (1–2 March 1914).

During **World War I**, the USDP cooperated with the **Union for the Liberation of Ukraine** and participated in the founding of the **Supreme Ukrainian Council**. It also helped establish the **Ukrainian National Rada** of the **Western Ukrainian People's Republic** (ZUNR). From January 1919, the USDP opposed the ZUNR government and supported the socialist government of the **Directory**, which included the USDP members Yosyp Bezpalko, Volodymyr Temnytsky, **Volodymyr Starosolsky**, and Vityk. In 1920, it adopted a Sovietophile orientation, and in 1922 it demanded the unification of **western Ukraine** with the **Ukrainian SSR**. At the party's sixth congress, it became officially communist (March 1923), and the leading members Buniak, M. and L. Hankevych, Ivan Kvasnytsia, and Starosolsky were removed from their posts. In 1923, the party had 4,200 members. It was banned by the Polish authorities on 30 January 1924. Some members joined the **Communist Party of Western Ukraine**, and its four deputies in the Polish Diet (Andrii Pashchuk, Khoma Prystup, Yosyp Skrypa, and Yakiv Voitiuk) joined the parliamentary communist faction.

Former USDP members who maintained their social-democratic views created the Vpered (Onward) movement under L. Hankevych's leadership. The gradual reconstruction of the party on a social-democratic basis was completed at a congress in Lviv (8–9

December 1928). The USDP participated in attempts to consolidate Ukrainian statist forces and condemned the policy of "normalization" of relations with the Polish government. In the 1930s, it participated in the Second Socialist International. By that time, the party had declined very considerably; it ceased operations at the beginning of **World War II**.

USDP leaders were Vozniak (until 1907), M. Hankevych (1907–14), Temnytsky (1914–19), L. Hankevych (1920–22 and 1928–37), Ivan Kushnir (1922–23), O. Panas (1923–24), and Starosolsky (1937–39). Its newspapers included *Volia* (Freedom, 1900–6, 1919), *Zemlia i volia* (Land and Freedom, 1906–24, with interruptions), *Borba* (Struggle, 1908–14, 1918, in Bukovyna), *Vpered* (Onward, 1911–34, with interruptions), and *Robitnychyi holos* (Labor Voice, 1938–39).

UKRAINIAN SOCIAL DEMOCRATIC SPILKA/UKRAÏNS'KA SOTSIIAL-DEMOKRATYCHNA SPILKA. Political party in **eastern Ukraine** founded in December 1904 as a result of a split in the **Revolutionary Ukrainian Party** (RUP). In January 1905, it joined the Russian Social Democratic Labor Party (RSDLP) as an autonomous unit. The split in the RUP occurred because of differences of opinion on the Ukrainian national question; the Spilka (Association) opposed RUP's demands for political and cultural autonomy for Ukraine, which Spilka members regarded as "bourgeois radicalism" at odds with the interests of the international working class. Aspiring to the creation of a proletarian party for the whole Russian Empire, the Spilka worked closely with the RSDLP and the Jewish Bund. The Spilka was initially better organized and more influential among the **peasant** masses than the RUP. In addition to nationally conscious Ukrainians, Spilka members included Ukrainians indifferent to the national movement (Pavlo Tuchapsky) and others negatively disposed to it (Ivan Kyriienko), as well as Russians and **Jews**. The party's leaders included Mariian Melenevsky, Oleksander Skoropys-Yoltukhovsky, Petro Kanivets, Hryhorii Dovzhenko, Pavlo Krat, Vasyl Mazurenko, and Tuchapsky, as well as non-Ukrainians: Yurii Larin, Arnold Rish, A. Podolsky (Hoikhberg), S. Sokolov, S. Zavadsky, and V. Perekrestov.

During the **Revolution of 1905**, the Spilka extended its influence among peasant laborers, leading peasant and worker strikes. Having attracted many former RUP members to its ranks, it opposed the **Ukrainian Social Democratic Labor Party** (USDRP), as the other RUP faction now styled itself. The Spilka had its greatest success in the elections to the First and Second State Dumas, taking 14 seats in the Second Duma to the USDRP's one.

Its publication was the monthly *Pravda* (Truth, 1905); it also published many propaganda brochures in Ukrainian and Russian.

In 1907, as political reaction set in, many Spilka members were arrested and leading figures exiled (Rish, R. Rabinovich, Y. Soroker, Hryhorii Tkachenko, and others). In 1908, the party moved its headquarters abroad, creating "facilitating groups" in **Lviv**, Vienna, Paris, Geneva, and Zurich. From 1908 to 1912, it published the journal *Pravda*, first in **Lviv** and later in Vienna. In the years prior to **World War I**, the Spilka continued to lose influence in eastern Ukraine owing to its leaders' concessions to centralist tendencies in the RSDLP and the rise of national consciousness among the Ukrainian peasantry. Its nationally conscious members joined Ukrainian national parties, and in 1913 the Spilka ceased to exist.

UKRAINIAN SOVIET SOCIALIST REPUBLIC (UkSSR)/UKRAÏN-S'KA RADIANS'KA SOTSIALISTYCHNA RESPUBLIKA (URSR). Until 1937, the Ukrainian Socialist Soviet Republic. Surrogate state that existed from 1917 to 1991. It arose as a consequence of the civil war that erupted in the Russian Empire after the fall of the autocracy. After the February Revolution (1917), the **Ukrainian Central Rada** was established in Kyiv as a representative body that sought cultural and political autonomy for Ukraine in a democratized Russian federation. Such an arrangement was not achieved with the Provisional Government, whose fall in the October Revolution left the Rada facing two illiberal opponents—the Whites, who wanted to restore the prewar empire, and the Bolsheviks, who opposed national autonomy on the grounds that it weakened the "unity of the working class," which was to be led from Moscow.

The Bolsheviks proved stronger than the Whites. They tried to stage a coup in **Kyiv** on 29 November (12 December) 1917 but were disarmed by forces loyal to the Central Rada. An attempt to organize an All-Ukrainian Congress of Soviets in Kyiv on 4 (17) December proved a fiasco when **peasant** delegates supporting the Central Rada outvoted the Bolsheviks. The latter retreated to **Kharkiv**, which had just been occupied by the forces of **Volodymyr Antonov-Ovsiienko**. There the Bolsheviks organized another gathering, officially known in Soviet historiography as the First All-Ukrainian Congress of Soviets (11–12 [24–25] December 1917), which declared a parallel "Ukrainian People's Republic" and formed a government, the People's Secretariat. Since virtually all members of the People's Secretariat were Bolsheviks subject to party discipline, the secretariat was firmly under the control of Moscow. The Council of People's Commissars in Moscow then sent its armies into Ukraine and drove the Central Rada out of Kyiv. However, the Bolsheviks were expelled from the **Ukrainian People's Republic** (UNR) in the spring of 1918 by Austro-German and UNR forces.

The second Bolshevik invasion of Ukraine began in November 1918 (as the fall of the **Ukrainian State** became imminent) with the formation of the **Provisional Workers' and Peasants' Government of Ukraine** in Sudzha (now in Kursk oblast, Russia). On 6 January 1919, the Provisional Government rejected the name Ukrainian People's Republic and replaced it with a term based on the Russian model: Ukrainian Socialist Soviet Republic (UkSSR). On 29 January, the provisional government was renamed the **Council of People's Commissars** (RNK) on the Russian model. The Third All-Ukrainian Congress of Soviets ratified the first constitution of the UkSSR, explicitly based on that of Soviet Russia, on 10 March 1919. The Bolshevik victory of 1920 (following a third invasion of Ukraine in December 1919) led to the emergence of two models for the new Soviet state: Stalin favored incorporating the Soviet republics into Russia, while Lenin backed a federation. The **Union of Soviet Socialist Republics** (USSR), proclaimed on 30 December 1922, was nominally a federation, but real power remained in the hands of the Communist Party, whose structure was centralized in Moscow. This made it possible for Stalin, as secretary-general of the All-Union Communist Party (Bolshevik), to consolidate dictatorial power (1928–34) in the USSR.

Until the mid-1930s, the supreme government body of the UkSSR was the All-Ukrainian Congress of Soviets, which elected the All-Ukrainian Central Executive Committee to govern between sessions of the congress and appointed the RNK as its executive organ. The Stalin constitution of the USSR (December 1936) and the new constitution of the UkSSR (January 1937) established the **Verkhovna Rada** (VR; Supreme Council), with its Presidium, in place of the Congress of Soviets. In 1946, the RNK was renamed the **Council of Ministers**. In practice, all these government bodies were subordinate to the **Communist Party of Ukraine** (CPU).

Only in the 1920s, before the rise of Stalin, did the authorities of the UkSSR follow an independent line, introducing the policy of **Ukrainization**. Such prominent Ukrainian "national communists" as **Mykola Skrypnyk** and **Mykola Khvyliovy** made the UkSSR a voice to be reckoned with in Soviet affairs, but they and their followers were destroyed by Stalin's dictatorship. Soviet Ukraine's diplomatic activities ended in 1923 after it became a constituent republic of the USSR. In 1945, the UkSSR and the Belarusian SSR became founding members of the **United Nations** (Stalin had originally sought separate membership for each republic of the USSR in order to increase the number of Soviet votes). The central government in Moscow allowed the UkSSR to join international organizations and maintain a small ministry of foreign affairs but prohibited bilateral relations with other states. From the 1930s on, the government and the CPU exercised no effective sovereignty: the only Ukrainian first secretary to attempt a limited assertion of autonomy, **Petro Shelest**, was removed in 1972 and replaced by the rigidly subservient **Volodymyr Shcherbytsky**, who remained in office until 1989. The UkSSR ceased to exist on 24 August 1991, when the VR declared the independence of Ukraine. An all-Ukrainian referendum took place on 1 December 1991, during which 28,804,100 or 90.3 percent of voters endorsed Ukraine's Act of Independence.

UKRAINIAN STATE/UKRAÏNS'KA DERZHAVA. Official name of the **Hetman** state in Ukraine (29 April–14 December 1918). A German-sponsored coup led by Gen. **Pavlo Skoropadsky** abolished the **Ukrainian People's Republic** (UNR), eliminated the **Ukrainian Central Rada**, and canceled the mandates of delegates to the planned Ukrainian Constituent Assembly. (For the history of the state, *see* SKOROPADSKY, PAVLO.)

UKRAINIAN STATE ACADEMY OF ARTS/UKRAÏNS'KA DERZHAVNA AKADEMIIA MYSTETSTV. First postsecondary art school in Ukraine, founded in **Kyiv** in August 1917 by a commission headed by Hryhorii Pavlutsky on the instructions of the general secretary of education, Ivan Steshenko. The academy's statute was confirmed by the **Ukrainian Central Rada** on 18 November 1917, and its official opening took place on 22 November (5 December). Its governing council consisted of Dmytro Antonovych, Danylo Shcherbakivsky, and Pavlo Zaitsev. Its rectors were Vasyl Krychevsky (1917–18), Fedir Krychevsky (1918, 1920–22), **Heorhii Narbut** (1919–20), and **Mykhailo Boichuk** (1920). Professors at the academy included Boichuk (frescoes and mosaics), Mykola Burachek (landscape **painting**), F. Krychevsky (portraiture, **sculpture**, and historical painting), V. Krychevsky (folk art, ornament, **architecture**, and composition), Abram Manevich (landscape painting), Oleksander Murashko (genre painting), Narbut (graphic art), and Mykhailo Zhuk (portraiture). The academy accepted students of both sexes over the age of 14, each of whom had an individual program of study. It had a library, museum, and photographic archive. In April 1919, the Bolshevik authorities closed the academy, but teaching continued in the instructors' homes until

October. The academy was subsequently reopened, but its statute and pedagogical principles were changed and new staff members hired. Other artists who joined the faculty included Lev Kramarenko (monumental painting), Bernard Kratko (sculpture), Vadym Meller (theatrical design), Sofiia Nalepinska-Boichuk (woodworking), Yevhen Sahaidachny (sculpture), and Andrii Taran (mosaics). In 1918–19, the academy had 140 students, rising to 253 in 1919 and approximately 400 in 1921–22. Its graduates included Tymofii Boichuk, Serhii Kolos, Pavlo Kovzhun, Oleksander Lozovsky, Ivan Padalka, Oksana Pavlenko, and **Vasyl Sedliar**. In late 1922, the academy was renamed the Kyiv Institute of Plastic Arts, and in 1924 it was merged with the Kyiv Architecture Institute and renamed the Kyiv Art Institute. The new institute's first rector was Ivan Vrona.

UKRAINIAN STATE ADMINISTRATION/UKRAÏNS'KE DERZHAVNE PRAVLINNIA. Provisional regional government formed in **Lviv** by the Bandera faction of the **Organization of Ukrainian Nationalists** (OUN-B) following its proclamation of Ukrainian statehood (30 June 1941). At a public meeting in the **Prosvita** building in Lviv on 30 June, eight days after the German invasion of the **USSR**, a Ukrainian state was proclaimed on **western Ukrainian** territory (to be superseded by a future state with its capital in Kyiv). Acting as **Stepan Bandera's** deputy, **Yaroslav Stetsko** proceeded to establish the state administration (5 July). According to the list given in Stetsko's book *30 chervnia 1941* (30 June 1941, 1967), the administration included 11 OUN(B) members, eight members of established **Galician** parties (the **Ukrainian National Democratic Alliance**, the **Front of National Unity**, and the **Ukrainian** Socialist **Radical Party**), and 10 politically unaffiliated members.

The OUN(B) strategy was to confront the invading Germans with a *fait accompli*, gambling that they would tolerate the state administration because they needed Ukraine as an ally against Russia. In line with this strategy, Stetsko and his associates also endeavored to convince the newly appointed non-OUN ministers and the Galician public at large that they were acting with German approval. That impression was reinforced by the arrival of the OUN(B) Nachtigall unit, formed with the approval of German military circles and garbed in German uniforms. A letter of recognition from the bedridden Metropolitan **Andrei Sheptytsky** also provided crucial moral support. Moreover, the administration established an advisory body, the Council of Seniors, chaired by one of Galicia's most eminent politicians, **Kost Levytsky** (*see* UKRAINIAN NATIONAL COUNCIL [LVIV, 1941]). Numerous Galician towns greeted the administration (news of its formation was broadcast from the Lviv radio station on 30 June).

The OUN(B)'s calculation proved erroneous; in the first two weeks of July Bandera, Stetsko, and other OUN(B) members of the administration were arrested, taken to Berlin, and confronted with the demand to rescind the proclamation of 30 June. When they refused to do so, they were incarcerated in the Sachsenhausen concentration camp.

After the war, the state administration became the subject of intense polemics in the Ukrainian **diaspora**. The case against it was best presented by Kost Pankivsky, an apolitical lawyer who found himself appointed deputy minister of internal affairs in the Stetsko administration and subsequently worked with **Volodymyr Kubijovyč** in the **Ukrainian Central Committee**. In the first volume of his memoirs, *Vid derzhavy do komitetu* (From State to Committee, 1957, 2d ed. 1970), Pankivsky maintains that the proclamation of 30 June included the phrase "Glory to the heroic German Army and its Führer, Adolf Hitler!" and that Sheptytsky's letter included greetings to the German army as a "liberator from the enemy." This would indicate that at the time the OUN(B) was attempting to create the impression of a united front with the Germans, contrary to its later claims of acting independently. In his *30 chervnia 1941*, which contains an extensive polemic with Pankivsky, Stetsko rejects the quoted phrases as inauthentic. Pankivsky also claims that non-OUN(B) members were appointed to the administration with no preliminary consultation and that the OUN(B) not only created the misleading impression of German approval for the administration but generally acted in a domineering and tactless manner. These charges are also rejected by Stetsko, who terms Pankivsky's work "defamatory." Stetsko acknowledges that he drafted the proclamation in haste following his meeting with Sheptytsky and that the OUN(B) "may have overemphasized its responsibility" in taking it upon itself to proclaim the revival of Ukrainian statehood.

The German arrests forced the OUN(B) into the underground and led it to form the **Ukrainian Insurgent Army**, which fought both German and Soviet forces.

UKRAINIAN WORLD CONGRESS (UWC)/SVITOVYI KONGRES UKRAÏNTSIV. Umbrella organization of the Ukrainian **diaspora**. The idea of creating a worldwide nonpartisan Ukrainian association emerged after **World War II**, and a proposal to that effect was made by **Andrii Melnyk** in 1957. The first convention of the World Congress of Free Ukrainians (WCFU), attended by more than 1,000 delegates from 17 countries, was held in New York in November 1967. The WCFU saw its primary mission as uniting the diaspora's efforts in aiding the Ukrainian struggle for independence. It included more than 150 organizations, notably the **Ukrainian Congress Committee of America**, the **Ukrainian Canadian Congress**, the Coordinating Center of Ukrainian Community, Central, and National Institutions in Europe, the Federation of Ukrainian Organizations in Australia, the Ukrainian Central Representation in Argentina, and the Ukrainian Brazilian Central Representation. The organization's name was changed after Ukraine became independent in 1991, and in 1992 the UWC congress was held in **Kyiv** for the first time. UWC congresses take place every five years; between congresses UWC business is handled by a secretariat based in Toronto, Canada. The UWC is active in the fields of **human rights**, social services, economic cooperation, culture, and education.

UKRAINIAN YOUTH ASSOCIATION/SPILKA UKRAÏNS'KOÏ MOLODI (SUM). Emigrant youth organization established in Germany in 1946 by the **Bandera** faction of the **Organization of Ukrainian Nationalists**. The name was inspired by that of a fictitious nationalist organization invented by the Soviet secret police in order to indict Mykola Pavlushkov and Borys Matushevsky, defendants at the show trial of the **Union for the Liberation of Ukraine** (Kharkiv, 1930). Branches of SUM were established in Belgium, France, Great Britain, the United States, Canada, Brazil, Paraguay, and Australia. Like **Plast**, with which it competed for membership in the **diaspora**, SUM developed a program of education and recreation based on the principles of Christian morality and Ukrainian patriotism.

UKRAINIZATION. Communist Party policy implemented in Ukraine from 1923 to 1933. It was the Ukrainian version of the policy of indigenization, announced in April 1923 at the twelfth congress of the Russian Communist Party with the intention of rooting Soviet power in the USSR's non-Russian republics. Party and government workers were to learn the **language** of the local population and recruit new personnel from it.

Because the **Communist Party of Ukraine** (CPU) and the government apparatus subordinate to it were largely non-Ukrainian, they strongly resisted Ukrainization. The state bureaucracy was no more than 35 percent Ukrainian and, in the **Council of People's Commissars** (RNK), Russians comprised 47 percent, **Jews** 26 percent, and Ukrainians 12 percent. In 1923, only 797 of 11,826 officials in these structures spoke Ukrainian. Dmitrii Lebed, second secretary of the CPU Central Committee, posited a "struggle of two cultures": progressive proletarian Russian culture was to overcome backward **peasant** Ukrainian culture.

Ukrainization gained momentum with the appointment of **Vlas Chubar** as chairman of the RNK on 16 July 1923. On 27 July, the council ordered the school system Ukrainized in two years, and on 1 August it decreed that all official business be transacted in Ukrainian and that all officials master the language within two years. Further support for Ukrainization came with the arrival in Ukraine of **Lazar Kaganovich**, whom Stalin appointed first secretary of the CPU. During his struggle for power in the Kremlin, Stalin endeavored to gain the support of local party structures, particularly in Ukraine, the largest non-Russian republic. This created an opportunity for Ukrainian "national communists," most notably the commissar for **education, Mykola Skrypnyk**, to transform Ukrainization into a drive for national revival.

There was a large influx of Ukrainians into the cities: between 1923 and 1933, their numbers in **Kharkiv** grew from 38 to 50 percent; in **Kyiv**, from 27 to 42 percent; in Dnipropetrovsk, from 16 to 48 percent; and in **Odesa**, from 7 to 17 percent. The number of Ukrainians in the state apparatus grew from 35 to 54 percent (1923–27). Ukrainian-language instruction was implemented in higher educational institutions (19.5 percent in 1923; 69 percent in 1929), 55 percent of technical schools, and 97 percent of public schools (late 1920s). A mass literacy campaign, conducted mainly in Ukrainian, raised adult literacy to 74 percent by 1929. Most books (more than 50 percent in 1927) and newspapers (373 of 426 in 1933) were published in Ukrainian. Radio programs and **film** production were also largely Ukrainized. At Skrypnyk's initiative, Ukrainian was introduced into army officer schools and in some Red Army divisions. In areas of Ukrainian settlement in the Kuban region and Kazakhstan, Ukrainian schools, newspapers, and radio programs were introduced.

Ukrainians were favored in mass recruitment into the party. In 1923, they comprised only 23 percent of CPU membership, but by 1927 they made up 52 percent, and 60 percent by 1933. However, Ukrainian representation in the Central Committee did not exceed 25 percent. The first secretaries were all non-Ukrainian.

For the All-Union CP, Ukrainization raised the specter of loss of control over the CPU and Ukraine. Accordingly, in the mid-1920s, Stalin and Kaganovich found it necessary to attack such prominent Ukrainian communists as **Mykola Khvyliovy** and **Oleksander Shumsky** for "national deviationism." Large-scale persecution of the Ukrainian intelligentsia began in 1930, especially through the invention of "counterrevolutionary" organizations such as the **Union for the Liberation of Ukraine**. Following the appointment of **Pavel Postyshev** as Stalin's representative in Ukraine (January 1933), Ukrainization was eliminated (November 1933). As a result of **political terror**, many activists of Ukrainization were either executed or silenced. The gains of the policy were then reversed by thoroughgoing **Russification**.

UKRAINKA, LESIA (13 [25] February 1871–19 July [1 August] 1913). Pseudonym of Larysa Kosach-Kvitka. Poet, prose writer, playwright, translator, literary critic, and folklorist. She was the daughter of the well-known writer and civic activist Olena Pchilka. Born in Zviahel (now Novohrad-Volynskyi), Ukrainka spent her childhood in Kolodiazhne (now in **Volhynia** oblast). Because she suffered from tuberculosis, she received her education at home, learning history, **literature**, and foreign languages.

She made her debut as a lyric poet in 1884 in the **Lviv** journal *Zoria* (Star), where she published "Konvaliia" (Lily of the Valley) and "Safo" (Sappho) under the pseudonym Lesia Ukrainka. She went on to publish the collections *Na krylakh pisen'* (On Wings of Songs, 1893), *Dumy i mriï* (Thoughts and Dreams, 1899), and *Vidhuky* (Echoes, 1902). Her poetry is filled with great emotional tension and deep patriotic feeling. Ukrainka's greatest accomplishments were her plays (she wrote more than 20 dramas). Her first work in this genre was the psychological drama *Blakytna troianda* (The Azure Rose, 1896). She wrote both dramatic poems and social dramas: *Oderzhyma* (A Woman Possessed, 1901), *Osinnia kazka* (Autumn Tale, 1905), *U katakombakh* (In the Catacombs, 1905), *Kassandra* (Cassandra, 1907), *U pushchi* (In the Wilderness, 1897–1909), *Boiarynia* (The **Boyar** Woman, 1910), *Advokat Martiian* (The Lawyer Martiian, 1911), *Kaminnyi hospodar* (The Stone Host, 1912), *Orhiia* (The Orgy, 1913), and *Na poli krovy* (On a Field of Blood, 1910). Her greatest play is *Lisova pisnia* (The Forest Song, 1911), which affirms the value of human dreams, elevated feelings, and the triumph of life over soullessness. Ukrainka borrowed images and stories from world literature, history, and mythology in order to explore the concerns of contemporary Ukrainian society. She modernized the poetics of Ukrainian drama by employing more penetrating dialogue, greater complexity, and symbolic stage settings, as well as by shifting emphasis from external action to inner conflict. Together with **Filaret Kolessa** and Klyment Kvitka, she organized ethnographic expeditions to record performances of Ukrainian epic songs (1908). She was also a prolific translator and critic of contemporary Ukrainian, Italian, and Polish literature. Ukrainka died in Surami, Georgia. Monuments to her have been erected in **Kyiv**, Surami, Cleveland, Toronto, and Saskatoon.

UKRAINOPHILISM. Term for the Ukrainian national movement in the Russian Empire from the 1860s to the 1880s. As many Ukrainian activists limited themselves to pursuing cultural goals, the word came to imply nonpolitical activity. In the late 19th and early 20th centuries, "Ukrainophile" became a term of opprobrium for Ukrainians who sought to avoid the political implications of their cultural activity.

*UKRAÏNS'KA KHATA/***UKRAINIAN HOUSE.** Monthly journal of literary criticism and politics published by the democratic, nationally conscious Ukrainian intelligentsia after the **Revolution of 1905**. It appeared in **Kyiv** from March 1909 until the autumn of 1914 (a total of 66 issues) under the editorship of Pavlo Bohatsky and **Mykyta Shapoval**. The journal attacked its **Ukrainophile** predecessors for their political compromises and orientation on Russian and Polish culture; it bitterly polemicized with the liberal *Rada*. *Ukraïns'ka khata* promoted Nietzschean individualism, cultural **modernism**, and a self-reliant Ukrainian literary culture. The journal published contributions by Oleksander Oles, **Olha Kobylianska, Maksym Rylsky, Mykhail Semenko, Pavlo Tychyna**, Mykola Vorony, and **Volodymyr Vynnychenko**, as well as translations of European works. It was banned by the tsarist government at the beginning of **World War I**.

UMANETS, FEDIR (5 March 1841–1908). Writer, historian, and civic activist. A descendant of an old **Cossack** family from the Hlukhiv region, Umanets worked in the Hlukhiv county zemstvo administration (1887–95) and the Chernihiv gubernia administration (from 1895). He obtained employment for **Borys Hrinchenko, Mykhailo Kotsiubynsky**, Mykola Vorony, and Volodymyr Samiilenko in the Chernihiv zemstvo. Umanets wrote a number of works on 16th-century Ukrainian and Polish history, as well as a book on public **education** in the Russian Empire (1861). His study of Hetman **Ivan Mazepa** (1897), based on the archives and collections of the **Doroshenko** and Markovych families, was the first historical work to portray Mazepa positively as an individual and as a statesman. Since Mazepa's name was synonymous with Ukrainian separatism, no liberal Russian journal would publish the work, and Umanets had to print it at his own expense.

UNIATE CHURCH. *See* UKRAINIAN CATHOLIC CHURCH.

UNION FOR THE LIBERATION OF UKRAINE/SOIUZ VYZVO-LENNIA UKRAÏNY (SVU, 1914). Political organization of socialist émigrés from **eastern Ukraine** established in **Lviv** on 14 August 1914. It was based in Vienna throughout **World War I**. The SVU consisted of leaders of the **Revolutionary Ukrainian Party**, the **Ukrainian Social Democratic Labor Party**, and the **Ukrainian Social Democratic Spilka** who had emigrated or been deported from Russian-ruled Ukraine during the Stolypin reaction. SVU activities were organized by a presidium that included **Dmytro Dontsov**, Volodymyr Doroshenko, Mariian Melenevsky, Oleksander Skoropys-Yoltukhovsky, and Andrii Zhuk. Its primary goal was the establishment of an independent Ukrainian state through the defeat of the Russian Empire. In the Central Powers and in some neutral European countries, the SVU was active in publishing and diplomatic activity. Its major publication was the weekly *Visnyk Soiuzu vyzvolennia Ukraïny* (Herald of the Union for the Liberation of Ukraine, Vienna, 1915–18); in 1918 it was renamed *Visnyk polityky, literatury i zhyttia* (Herald of Politics, Literature, and Life). The SVU also published *Ukrainische Nachrichten* (Vienna) and *La Revue ukrainienne* (Lausanne). Information about Ukraine was issued in English, French, German, Italian, Swedish, Bulgarian, Croatian, Czech, and Turkish; there were also publications by Dontsov, **Mykhailo Hrushevsky**, **Kost Levytsky**, **Stepan Rudnytsky**, **Fedir Vovk**, Mykhailo Vozniak, and others. Its representatives were active in Germany, Italy, Bulgaria, Turkey, Norway, and Sweden. The SVU worked closely with the major wartime **Galician** political organizations, the **Supreme Ukrainian Council** and its successor, the General Ukrainian Council (Doroshenko, Melenevsky, and Skoropys-Yoltukhovsky were members of the latter).

One of the SVU's most important missions was to protect Ukrainians in the Russian army who became Austrian POWs. Thanks to the SVU, many of them were moved to separate camps in Austria-Hungary (Freistadt, Duna-Serdahel) and Germany (Wetzlar, Salzwedel, Rastatt). With the help of scholars and cultural figures, various forms of cultural, political, and educational activity were conducted in the camps. The SVU opened reading rooms and schools, organized choirs, and held courses on **cooperatives** and husbandry. It published Ukrainian newspapers in the camps, produced the weekly *Ridne slovo* (Native Word) in **Podlachia**, and issued **Taras Shevchenko's** *Kobzar* in a large press run. With the SVU's assistance, the POWs helped collect funds to open Ukrainian schools in **Volhynia** and Podlachia. From 1916 to 1918, the SVU and its Lviv office were involved in cultural and educational work in Volhynia and opened some 100 Ukrainian-language schools in

Podlachia. In 1918, the SVU helped recruit two divisions made up of Ukrainian POWs, the Graycoats and the Bluecoats, who initially fought under the command of the Central Powers and were later incorporated into the Army of the **Ukrainian People's Republic**. The SVU was dissolved on 1 May 1918.

UNION FOR THE LIBERATION OF UKRAINE/SPILKA VYZVO-LENNIA UKRAÏNY (SVU, 1930). Fictitious anti-Soviet organization invented by the State Political Administration (GPU; i.e., secret police) in order to stage a show trial of Ukrainian intellectuals, politicians, and church figures. The trial was held at the **Kharkiv** Opera House from 9 March to 19 April 1930.

In the late 1920s, as Stalin began to consolidate power, the Soviet authorities launched a broad campaign to discredit the non-Soviet Ukrainian elite, including political and cultural figures and clergymen of the **Ukrainian** Autocephalous **Orthodox Church**. The campaign included a number of show trials, beginning with the **Shakhty trial** (1928).

The first victim of this **political terror** was the Ukrainian intelligentsia. The 45 defendants at the SVU trial included two academicians (**Serhii Yefremov** and Mykhailo Slabchenko), the former premier of the **Ukrainian People's Republic** (UNR), Volodymyr Chekhivsky, three writers, including **Liudmyla Starytska-Cherniakhivska**, professors, lawyers, clergymen, secondary and postsecondary teachers, and students. They were charged with belonging to the counterrevolutionary SVU, supposedly established at the behest of the government-in-exile of the UNR in order to carry out an uprising in Ukraine with the help of foreign powers, detach it from the **USSR**, and reestablish capitalism.

The principal "conductors" of the trial were the head of the Secret Division of the Ukrainian GPU, Valerii Gorozhanin, and his subordinate Boris Kozelsky, who coordinated their actions with Stalin (as evidenced by Stalin's coded telegram of 2 January 1930 to **Stanislav Kosior**, head of the **Communist Party of Ukraine** [CPU], and **Vlas Chubar**, head of the Ukrainian government). In order to build up antagonism against the defendants, a press campaign preceded the trial. They were also "exposed" in speeches by Vsevolod Balytsky, head of the Ukrainian GPU, Vlas Chubar, and Panas Liubchenko, secretary of the CC CPU.

The trial was adjudicated by an extraordinary jury of the Supreme Court of the **Ukrainian SSR**. Most of the testimony about the existence and activities of the SVU was obtained through physical and psychological coercion. Evidence adduced at the trial was marked by many contradictions and inconsistencies. Daily reports appeared in *Komunist* (Communist, an organ of the CPU) and in the government *Visti* (News), and discussions of the trial were organized at workplaces.

Four of the most prominent defendants, including Yefremov and Chekhivsky, were given 10-year sentences; six were sentenced to eight-year terms, and the rest were allotted terms between three and six years (a few sentences were suspended). The sentences were not subject to appeal. Over the next several years, almost all the defendants were rearrested and perished in prisons or concentration camps. A further 700 individuals were arrested in connection with the SVU trial. According to some estimates, the total of those arrested, killed, and exiled in connection with the trial exceeded 30,000.

UNION OF SOVIET SOCIALIST REPUBLICS (USSR). Eurasian state that existed from 1922 to 1991. It was built out of the remnants of the Russian Empire by the Russian Communist Party (Bolshevik) (RCP[B]). Five constituents of the former empire—Finland, Poland, Estonia, Latvia, and Lithuania—remained independent during the interwar period. The core of the USSR was the Russian Socialist Federative Soviet Republic (RSFSR), established in 1918, whose government was subordinate to the RCP(B). The Bolsheviks won the civil war (1918–21) and conquered most of the former Russian Empire, defeating the Russian Whites (who wanted to reestablish the empire) and overthrowing the new states established by the non-Russian peoples. While Stalin favored the establishment of a unitary state, integrating the non-Russian peoples into the RSFSR, Lenin, compromising with the non-Russians' desire for independence, insisted on a federal structure. The USSR was established on 30 December 1922 by the RSFSR and the Ukrainian, Belarusian, and Transcaucasian Soviet republics. On that date, the first Congress of Soviets ratified the agreement on the formation of the USSR. The second congress ratified the Union's constitution (31 January 1924). The RCP(B), which retained a monopoly of power in the USSR, was renamed the All-Union CP(B) in 1925, becoming the Communist Party of the Soviet Union in 1952.

Only in the 1920s did the non-Russian republics enjoy a degree of autonomy as the RCP(B) sought to "root" Soviet power in the republics (*see* UKRAINIZATION). As Stalin consolidated dictatorial power, the USSR became a federation in name only; central control from Moscow and Russian dominance became permanent features of Soviet life.

The eighth extraordinary Congress of Soviets adopted a new constitution (5 December 1936) that proclaimed many democratic freedoms but did not change the structure of power. The Transcaucasian SSR was dismantled, making Azerbaijan, Armenia, and Georgia union republics; the same status was given to Kazakhstan, Kyrgyzstan, and Tajikistan. As a consequence of the Molotov-Ribbentrop Pact with Nazi Germany (August 1939), Stalin extended the Soviet border westward (1939–40), incorporating western Ukraine and western Belarus. Five new union republics were created: Estonia, Karelia-Finland, Latvia, Lithuania, and Moldavia.

Under Stalin, the USSR became a tyranny that killed millions of its own citizens in a system of forced-labor camps known as the GULAG (Main Administration of Labor Camps). For Ukraine, Stalin's rule brought **political terror**, the destruction of the national movement, the catastrophic man-made **famine of 1932–33**, and unrelenting **Russification**. Stalin's buildup of the Soviet military machine and postwar establishment of satellite regimes in Eastern Europe made the USSR a world power. The attempted liberalization of the Soviet regime initiated in the 1950s by Stalin's successor, **Nikita Khrushchev**, was reversed under the regime of Leonid Brezhnev (1964–82). The CPSU's monopoly of power and intolerance of dissent (*see* DISSIDENT MOVEMENT; *SHISTDESIATNYKY*; UKRAINIAN HELSINKI GROUP) increasingly isolated the USSR from world socioeconomic developments, leading to stagnation of the Soviet system.

The Union's collapse was precipitated by the reforms of Mikhail Gorbachev, who took office in 1985. His reforms of the CPSU, announced at the 19th party congress (July 1988), encroached for the first time on its monopoly of power. During elections in the spring of 1989, candidates from the "bloc of communists and the nonaligned" suffered significant defeats for the first time in more than 70 years (especially in the Baltic region, Moscow, St. Petersburg, **Kyiv**, and western Ukraine). Two parallel systems of power emerged—party and soviet—particularly in the Baltics, the Caucasus, and Ukraine, where national movements catalyzed decentralizing tendencies. In March 1990, Gorbachev introduced the post of president of the USSR in an attempt at stabilization, but elections to the Supreme Soviets of the union republics created 15 new centers of power independent of Moscow. On 12 June 1990, at the initiative of Boris Yeltsin, the Russian Federation declared its sovereignty. Other republics followed, and on 16 July 1990, the **Verkhovna Rada** of Ukraine ratified the declaration of Ukraine's sovereignty. The unsuccessful coup of 19–21 August 1991 in Moscow accelerated the USSR's collapse. In the non-Russian republics, local bureaucrats came to power, supported by popular demands for independence. After Ukraine declared independence (24 August 1991), the USSR essentially ceased to exist. Its collapse was confirmed by the establishment of the Commonwealth of Independent States (CIS, 8 December 1991) at the initiative of President Yeltsin of Russia, President **Leonid Kravchuk** of Ukraine, and the chairman of the Supreme Soviet of Belarus, Stanislaŭ Shushkevich. Gorbachev resigned as president of the USSR on 25 December, and on the following day the Supreme Soviet passed a formal declaration of the USSR's dissolution.

UNION OF UKRAINIAN WOMEN/SOIUZ UKRAÏNOK (SU). Largest Ukrainian **women's** organization, established in **Lviv** at a Women's Congress on 22–23 December 1921 following the reorganization of the Women's **Hromada** of Lviv. It strove to increase social activism among women, raise their educational and professional qualifications, and expand their participation in cultural, educational, and charity work. Ideologically, the SU was based on the idea of Ukrainian statehood and belief in the social equality of women. It had a three-tiered structure: a central executive in Lviv, branches in cities and towns, and village circles. By the mid-1930s, the organization's membership approached 50,000. Its presidents were Yevheniia Makarushka (1921–22), Katria Hrynevych (1923–24), Mariia Biletska (1924–25), Olena Fedak-Sheparovych (1925–26), Mariia Dontsova (1926–27), and Milena Rudnytska (1928–39). The SU devoted considerable attention to working with **peasant** women, involving them in the **cooperative movement** and the process of rationalizing peasant farms. It organized courses on business, cooperatives, home economics, child care, etc., and supported the development of folk arts. The SU worked closely with the **Prosvita**, **Ridna Shkola**, and Silskyi Hospodar (agricultural) societies, among others. The Congress of Ukrainian Women in Stanyslaviv (23–27 June 1934) was attended by thousands of participants, demonstrating the increased social importance of the women's movement.

The SU was nonpartisan but collaborated with Ukrainian democratic parties and supported women's participation in politics. Rudnytska was a deputy to the Polish Diet, while Olena Kysilevska and Olena Levchanivska were members of the Senate. The political activism of the SU led the Polish authorities to suspend it in 1929, but protests forced its reinstatement. In 1934, the SU founded a **publishing** cooperative in Lviv that issued a biweekly periodical for the intelligentsia, *Zhinka* (Woman, 1935–39), and a periodical for peasant women, *Ukraïnka* (Ukrainian Woman, 1938–39).

The SU established ties with international women's organizations, joining the International Women's Union in 1923 and sending delegates to congresses in Rome (1923), Paris (1926), Berlin (1929), and Marseille (1933). It sought to draw international attention to Ukrainian problems. In 1924, Rudnytska raised the death of **Olha Basarab** at the hands of the Polish police in the international press. The SU condemned the **Pacification** at the League of Nations (1930) and protested the man-made **famine of 1932–33**. In 1938, Polish authorities banned the SU, and a new organization, the Retinue of Princess Olha, was temporarily established. The Soviet annexation of **western Ukraine** ended the SU's activities.

The Union of Ukrainian Women of **Volhynia** was active primarily in cultural, educational, and charity work from 1927 to 1938. Women's organizations were formed in the **diaspora**, notably in the United States (1925), Canada (1925), France (1945), Australia, and Argentina (both 1949). In the 1920s, the Union of Ukrainian Women Emigrants was established in Poland and Romania. In 1990, the SU renewed its activities in Ukraine, becoming one of the country's largest women's organizations.

UNITED HETMAN ORGANIZATION/SOIUZ HET'MANTSIV-DERZHAVNYKIV (SHD). Monarchist organization dedicated to the restoration of the **Ukrainian State** ruled by **Pavlo Skoropadsky**. It developed in Canada and the United States during the interwar period, growing out of Sich sporting societies formed there early in the 20th century (*see* TRYLIOVSKY, KYRYLO). The impetus to establish the SHD came from **Osyp Nazaruk**, a conservative ideologue who spent several years in North America (1922–27). The movement had the implicit support of the **Ukrainian Catholic Church**.

The Canadian Sitch organization reconstituted itself as the SHD in 1934. Its development was stimulated by the visit of Danylo Skoropadsky, the **hetman's** son and successor, to North America in 1937–38. In 1940, the SHD helped establish the **Ukrainian Canadian Congress**, but declined during the war. It was further weakened by a split in 1952.

In the United States, the Sich societies elected Stepan Hrynevetsky as supreme otaman in 1922 and proceeded to recruit a Ukrainian "liberation army." The societies constituted themselves as the SHD in 1930, and in that year hundreds of members joined the American militia (now the National Guard), in which they were permitted to form their own companies. Because Skoropadsky resided in Berlin and the SHD opposed the Versailles peace settlement, American communists and their sympathizers imputed pro-fascist motives to the organization. In 1938, the SHD was investigated for subversive activity by the Dies Committee of the

U.S. Congress and in 1940 by the FBI. Although no charges were laid, the investigations severely undermined support for the SHD and led to its dissolution in 1942.

UNITED NATIONS (UN). Ukraine became a founding member of the United Nations Organization in June 1945 when Dmytro Manuilsky, people's commissar for international affairs of the **Ukrainian SSR** and head of the Ukrainian delegation at the UN Conference in San Francisco, signed the UN Charter. Initially, Stalin had wanted all 15 republics of the **USSR** to become members so as to increase Soviet voting power, but when Roosevelt countered with the idea of enlisting all 48 American states, Stalin agreed to member status for the USSR, the Belarusian SSR, and the Ukrainian SSR (ostensibly in recognition of the two republics' contribution to the victory over fascism in **World War II**). Although Ukraine's UN participation was wholly determined by decisions made in Moscow, it was a member of the Security Council twice during the Soviet period (1948–49 and 1984–85), and representatives of Ukraine were repeatedly appointed to governing offices in major committees of the UN General Assembly (*see* UDOVENKO, HENNADII).

Following Ukraine's declaration of independence, participation in all aspects of UN activity became one of its **foreign-policy** priorities. In 2000–1, Ukraine served as a nonpermanent member of the Security Council, focusing its efforts on enhancing the council's role in resolving conflicts in the former Soviet Union (Abkhazia, Georgia), the Balkans, and the Middle East. The 2001 ministerial meeting of the Security Council on measures to combat terrorism was initially proposed by the foreign minister of Ukraine, **Anatolii Zlenko**. Ukraine also declared its support for the reform of participation in the Security Council by increasing the number of permanent and nonpermanent members.

In the General Assembly, Ukraine made significant efforts to maintain international peace and security by advocating measures for the nonproliferation of **nuclear weapons** and peaceful exploration/use of outer space. Ukrainian representatives raised concerns about illicit trafficking and accumulation of small arms. Ukraine also pledged to cooperate with international economic and ecological organizations in order to accelerate its integration into the world economy and tackle acute **environmental** issues. Ukraine initiated a special session on combating HIV/AIDS (June 2001).

Ukraine actively supports UN peacekeeping activities. Since independence, it has contributed more than 14,000 military and civilian personnel to 18 UN peacekeeping operations and missions in Afghanistan, Angola, Bosnia and Herzegovina (where 19

Ukrainian peacekeepers were killed and more than 60 wounded), the Congo, Croatia, East Timor, Georgia, Guatemala, Macedonia, Tajikistan, and Yugoslavia. In addition, Ukraine provided airlift services for UN humanitarian operations in Africa.

Since 1993, a UN Mission has been active in Ukraine, implementing a number of programs of the UN, its bodies, and specialized agencies in the areas of socioeconomic reform; environmental protection, mitigating the consequences of the **Chornobyl nuclear disaster**; and assisting in the settlement of peoples previously deported from the Ukrainian SSR (*see* TATARS). Ukraine has received considerable assistance from the UN Development Program, the Global Ecological Fund, the International Labor Organization, and the UN Conference on Trade and Development.

USSR. *See* UNION OF SOVIET SOCIALIST REPUBLICS.

UZHHOROD, UNION OF. Union between the Orthodox Church in **Transcarpathia** and the Catholic Church initiated by the **Basilian Order** under the leadership of Bishop Petro Partenii on the model of the **Union of Brest**. It was signed on 24 April 1646 at the castle chapel of the Drugeth family in Uzhhorod, where 63 Orthodox priests made a profession of faith before the Roman Catholic bishop of Eger. The Byzantine rite was to be preserved, and Uniate priests were to enjoy equality of status with their Roman Catholic counterparts. The act was confirmed by the primate of Hungary, György Lippay, on 14 May 1648 and by a synod of Hungarian bishops in Trnava in the autumn. Rome did not ratify the Union until 1655, as Partenii had been consecrated by an Orthodox metropolitan. The Union did not gain general acceptance among the Orthodox faithful of Transcarpathia until 1721. The Uniate Church of Transcarpathia resisted the Magyarization of the Ukrainian population, helping to preserve its language, customs and rites, and ethnic identity. The Union of Uzhhorod was abolished by the Soviet authorities in 1947–49, but the **Ukrainian Catholic Church** continued to exist in the underground. It was reestablished in Transcarpathia in 1989.

V

VAHYLEVYCH, IVAN (2 September 1811–10 June 1866). Poet, philologist, folklorist, and civic activist. He was born in Yaseniv-Horishnia in the Stanyslaviv region (now in Ivano-Frankivsk oblast) into the family of a priest and graduated from the **Lviv** Theological Seminary. He was ordained in 1846. A member of the **Ruthenian Triad**, Vahylevych helped publish the literary miscellany *Rusalka*

Dnistrovaia (Dnister Nymph, 1837), which included folk songs that he had collected. Vahylevych and **Markiian Shashkevych** translated the *Tale of Ihor's Campaign* into Ukrainian. With August Bielowski, Vahylevych translated the *Tale of Bygone Years* into Polish (published in 1864). In a treatise written in the 1840s, Vahylevych became one of the first scholars to treat the Ukrainian ("Southern Ruthenian") **language** as a separate entity and wrote one of the earliest surveys of Ukrainian **literature**. He also collected a great deal of ethnographic material.

In 1848, Vahylevych propagated a democratic Polish-Ukrainian federation and edited the newspaper *Dnewnyk Ruskij* (Ruthenian Daily, 1848), which was published by the pro-Polish Ruthenian Congress. This led to a conflict with the Greek Catholic Church (*see* UKRAINIAN CATHOLIC CHURCH), and Vahylevych converted to Lutheranism. He was unable to obtain steady employment until 1862, when he became the municipal archivist of Lviv. Vahylevych left a considerable number of unpublished works on linguistics and ethnography; a bibliographic guide to these manuscripts appeared in 1986.

VALUEV CIRCULAR. Secret instruction of the tsarist government, issued on 18 (30) July 1863, forbidding the printing of books in Ukrainian. It was written by the imperial minister of internal affairs, Count Petr Valuev, who declared in the instruction that "a separate Little Russian [i.e., Ukrainian] **language** has not, does not, and cannot exist." The circular was prompted by an application to print Pylyp Morachevsky's Ukrainian translation of the Bible. One of the official reviewers was Nikolai Annenkov, the former governor-general of the **Kyiv, Podilia,** and **Volhynia** gubernias, who argued that the Ukrainian language could not express abstractions or the wisdom of Providence and that the translation would serve no useful purpose. He further maintained that it would be impolitic to permit publication, as this would give the Ukrainian language independent status, which in turn would allow Ukrainians to demand political autonomy. Tsar Alexander II was persuaded by these arguments. Another factor that prompted the circular was the Polish insurrection of 1863, which heightened fears of Ukrainian separatism (ultranationalist Russian newspapers promoted the view that the Ukrainian movement was a Polish intrigue). The Valuev circular banned the publication of all works in Ukrainian except belles-lettres. It was a prelude to the even more oppressive **Ems Ukase** (1876).

VAPLITE. Vil'na akademiia proletars'koï literatury (Free Academy of Proletarian Literature). Literary organization based in **Kharkiv** from

1926 to 1928. Despite its official name, which implied dedication to officially approved working-class culture, Vaplite advocated the creation of a new Ukrainian **literature** by assimilating the finest achievements of Western Europe. The acknowledged leader of Vaplite was **Mykola Khvyliovy**; members included Mykola Bazhan, Ivan Dniprovsky, Oles Dosvitnii, Hryhorii Epik, Oleksander Kopylenko, Hordii Kotsiuba, **Mykola Kulish**, Arkadii Liubchenko, Ivan Senchenko, Oleksa Slisarenko, Yurii Smolych, **Pavlo Tychyna**, Mykhailo Yalovy, **Yurii Yanovsky**, and Maik Yohansen. In 1927, the organization published the journal *Vaplite* (five issues). Vaplite's program provoked criticism from the party and government, which demanded mass participation in literary activity. Owing to constant persecution, Vaplite was forced into "self-dissolution" in January 1928. Its members continued their activities in the almanac *Literaturnyi iarmarok* (Literary Fair, 1928–30) and the Prolitfront literary organization.

VARANGIANS. Old **Kyivan Rus'** and Byzantine name for Scandinavians, from Old Scandinavian *væring*, meaning "one who has taken an oath of allegiance." In Western Europe, the Varangians were known as Normans or Vikings. They began to trade with the **Khazars** and the Orient generally in the eighth century, establishing trading posts in what is now European Russia. The main historical **chronicle** of Kyivan Rus', the *Tale of Bygone Years*, includes a narrative about an "invitation to the Varangians" to rule the inhabitants of Rus'. In the 18th century, this became the basis for the **Norman theory** of the origin of the Kyivan state. The Varangians gave rise to the ruling **Riuryk line** and, establishing themselves in **Kyiv** in the ninth century, built it up into the capital of Rus'. From the ninth to the 11th century, Varangians served as mercenaries to the Rus' **princes** and participated in campaigns against Byzantium and nomadic invaders. They also served the princes as ambassadors and engaged in trade on the route "from the Varangians to the Greeks" (from Scandinavia to Byzantium via the Dnipro River and the Black Sea). Many of them adopted the language and culture of the **Slavs** and were assimilated. They are last mentioned in the *Tale* entry for 1036.

VASYLENKO, MYKOLA (20 March [1 April] 1867–3 October 1935). Civic leader, historian, academician of the **Ukrainian Academy of Sciences** (from 1920), full member of the **Shevchenko Scientific Society** (from 1911), husband of **Nataliia Polonska-Vasylenko**. He was born in Yesman, Hlukhiv county (now Chervone, Sumy oblast), and studied at the faculty of history and philology of Dorpat (Tartu) University, after which he worked as a teacher and journalist in

Kyiv. Participating actively in the Ukrainian national movement, Vasylenko was a member of the Kyiv **Hromada**, later of the **Society of Ukrainian Progressives**, and an editor of the journal *Kievskaia starina* (Kyivan Antiquity). In 1905, he edited the **Ukrainophile** newspaper *Kievskie otkliki* (Kyiv Echoes), for which he was arrested and sentenced to a year's imprisonment. Upon his release, he passed his examinations at the faculty of law of Novorossiisk (Odesa) University. Vasylenko became one of the most active members of the Ukrainian Scientific Society, founded in Kyiv in 1907, and editor of its *Zapysky* (Memoirs). In 1909, he became a lecturer at Kyiv University. Vasylenko was appointed curator of the Kyiv school district (1917) and became a member of the General Court of the **Ukrainian People's Republic** (January 1918). He belonged to the Constitutional Democratic Party.

In May 1918, Hetman **Pavlo Skoropadsky** appointed Vasylenko minister of **education** and acting minister of foreign affairs of the **Ukrainian State**. He was confirmed as president of the State Senate (July 1918). Vasylenko proceeded to Ukrainize educational institutions. He was a founder of the Kyiv State Ukrainian University, the Kamianets-Podilskyi State Ukrainian University, and the Ukrainian Academy of Sciences. In 1921, he was elected president of the academy, but the Soviet authorities dismissed him in February 1922. In the 1920s, he chaired the academy's Commission on the Study of Ukrainian Law and edited its publications. He was arrested in 1924 on trumped-up charges of "counterrevolutionary activity" and sentenced to 10 years' imprisonment but amnestied a year later owing to protests from such figures as the French prime minister, Raymond Poincaré. Beginning in 1929, he was again subjected to harsh official criticism and forbidden to publish.

Vasylenko was a pioneer in the study of the history of Ukrainian law and wrote important works on land tenure in Ukraine from the 16th to the 18th century, as well as on the **Hetmanate**. He also published numerous studies on 19th-century historiography.

VEDEL, ARTEM (ca. 1767–14 [26] July 1808). Composer, choral director, and singer. Born in **Kyiv**, Vedel studied at the **Kyiv Mohyla Academy**, where he was a soloist. From 1787 to 1790, he was conductor and music director of the choir of the governor-general of Moscow, Petr Eropkin. In 1790, he returned to Ukraine, and from 1793 he lived in Kyiv, where he directed the choir of the Kyiv Mohyla Academy (1793–94) and the choir of Gen. A. Levanidov. In 1796, Vedel moved to **Kharkiv**, where he directed the gubernia choir and taught **music** at the Kharkiv Collegium. In 1798, he became a novice at the **Kyivan Cave Monastery**. Arrested by Russian government agents in 1799, he was declared mentally ill and incarcerated at the insane asylum of St. Cyril's Monastery in Kyiv. Vedel's legacy consists of more than 80 compositions of church music for a cappella choir in the **baroque** style.

VERKHOVNA RADA (VR)/SUPREME COUNCIL. Parliament of Ukraine. It was established in the **Ukrainian SSR** in 1937, following the enactment of the Stalin Constitution (1936), to replace the Congress of Soviets as the supreme governing body of the republic. While the Soviet Union existed, the VR was known in English as the "Supreme Soviet of the Ukrainian SSR," given the Western practice of applying the Russian word *sovet* (council) to all governing councils in the **USSR**, regardless of ethnic considerations.

The unicameral VR consists of 450 deputies elected by secret ballot to four-year terms on a mixed (majority and proportional) basis in universal, equal, and direct elections. Thus, 225 deputies are elected in single-mandate electoral districts on the basis of absolute majority, while the other 225 deputies are elected from lists of candidates nominated by **political parties** and electoral blocs on the basis of proportional representation. *See also* GOVERNMENT.

VERNADSKY, VOLODYMYR (VLADIMIR) (28 February [12 March] 1863–6 January 1945). Natural scientist, mineralogist, crystallographer, a founder of geochemistry, biogeochemistry, hydrogeochemistry, and the study of the noosphere and biosphere, academician (from 1918) and first president (1918–19) of the **Ukrainian Academy of Sciences** (UAN). Born to Ukrainian parents in St. Petersburg, Vernadsky graduated from the physics and mathematics faculty of St. Petersburg University (1885) and studied abroad (1888–90). From 1890 to 1911, he worked at Moscow University (professor from 1898). In 1918, he became an organizer of the Commission for the Study of Russia's Natural Resources, which gave rise to a number of institutes.

In the spring of 1917, owing to a lung illness, Vernadsky moved to Ukraine. In June 1918, on the proposal of the minister of education of the **Ukrainian State**, **Mykola Vasylenko**, Vernadsky chaired a commission preparing the draft law on the founding of the UAN and became its first president. He was professor at Tavriia University in Simferopol (1920–21); from 1922 to 1941, he was based in Leningrad, where he directed the Radium Institute, which he founded, and other scientific institutions. During this period, Vernadsky worked in Prague (Charles University) and Paris (the Sorbonne) and was a member of the Czechoslovak (from 1926) and Paris (from 1928) academies of sciences, as well as many foreign scientific societies. He wrote approximately 400 works.

Vernadsky's ideas provided the foundations for new research in geology, mineralogy, and hydrogeology. During **World War II**, he wrote a study of the chemical structure of the earth's biosphere, a summary of his life's work that was issued in a censored edition in 1965. There have been many posthumous editions of his works, and much has been written about him in Ukraine and Russia. The National Library of Ukraine is named after him.

VICHE. Popular assembly in **Kyivan Rus'** convoked to discuss important issues. It originated in East Slavic tribal assemblies and was first chronicled in the late 10th century. The *viche* was called irregularly at the initiative of a **prince** or **boyar** or of a group of residents. The power of the *viche* depended on the political situation; it had no established rules of procedure. Among the matters considered at its meetings were war and peace, the election or expulsion of a prince and senior officials, negotiations with foreign traders, and the ratification of laws. The *viche* declined in importance as the Rus' lands were absorbed by the **Grand Duchy of Lithuania** and the Kingdom of Poland.

VOLHYNIA (Ukr. *Volyn'*). Historical and geographic region in northwestern Ukraine located in the basin of the Prypiat and Western Buh Rivers. Its name is derived from the early fortified town of Volyn (Velyn) near Volodymyr-Volynskyi, mentioned in the **chronicles** under the year 1018. From the late seventh to the early 10th century, the area was populated by tribes of Dulibians, Buzhanians, and Volhynians. In the 10th century, its most prominent centers were Busk, Lutsk, Cherven, Belz, and later Berestia (Brest), Dorohychyn, Peresopnytsia, Kholm (Chełm), and Kremianets. Ca. 988 Prince **Volodymyr the Great** of **Kyiv** founded the town of Volodymyr (now Volodymyr-Volynskyi), which became the center of the eponymous principality. In the 11th and 12th centuries, Volhynia was ruled by various princes, mainly descendants of **Yaroslav the Wise** and **Volodymyr Monomakh**. The Volhynian land separated from **Kyivan Rus'** in the mid-12th century. Having taken control of Halych, Prince **Roman Mstyslavych** of Volodymyr-Volynskyi united the Galician and Volhynian lands into a single Principality of **Galicia-Volhynia** (1199).

In 1349, the principality was partitioned between Poland and Lithuania; armed conflict between them culminated in the signing of a treaty incorporating Volhynia into the **Grand Duchy of Lithuania** (1352). In 1366, Poland seized western Volhynia, including the towns of Kholm and Belz. Within Lithuania, Volhynia maintained the title of principality until 1452, when it was reduced to an ordinary province of Lithuania. After the **Union of Lublin** (1569), Poland took over all of Volhynia. The struggle against Roman Catholicism and Polonization gave rise to a national and cultural movement in the late 16th and early 17th centuries, manifested in the activities of Orthodox **brotherhoods** in Ostrih, Volodymyr, and Lutsk, the founding of the **Ostrih Academy** and schools in Dubno, Lutsk, and Volodymyr, and the development of book printing in Pochaiv, Kremianets, Kostiantyniv, and other towns. Volhynia became the site of bloody struggles against Polish overlordship during the **Khmelnytsky Uprising** (1648–57) and the **haidamaka** rebellions (1730s–60s).

After the partitions of Poland in the late 18th century, Volhynia, with the exception of Kremianets county, was annexed to the Russian Empire. It was initially constituted as the Volhynian vicegerency (called the Iziaslav vicegerency until 1795), which became the Volhynia gubernia in 1797 (with its administrative center in Novohrad-Volynskyi, moved to Zhytomyr in 1804). Russian policies, especially the abolition of the Uniate Church (*see* UKRAINIAN CATHOLIC CHURCH) in 1838 and the abrogation of the **Lithuanian Statute** in 1840, weakened the Ukrainian national movement in the region. Volhynia suffered huge losses in the course of **World War I**. During the **Ukrainian Revolution** (1917–21), it was an arena of conflict between Polish and Bolshevik forces. In February 1918, Zhytomyr was the temporary seat of the **Ukrainian Central Rada**, and in April 1919 the government of the **Directory** was based in Rivne. In May 1919, western Volhynia was occupied by the Poles, and the Red Army occupied eastern Volhynia in 1920. The Volhynian group of the Directory's Army, commanded by Yurii Tiutiunnyk, conducted a raid through Volhynia in November 1921 (*see* WINTER CAMPAIGNS).

In accordance with the Polish-Soviet **Treaty of Riga** (1921), eastern Volhynia was incorporated into the **Ukrainian SSR**, while the western part went to Poland. Economic and sociopolitical developments of the interwar period in eastern Volhynia were typical of those of the rest of the Ukrainian SSR. In western Volhynia, the Polish government strove to divide Ukrainians into discrete groups so as to implement its policy of Polonization. To this end, it established the so-called Sokal border between **Galicia** and Volhynia, intended to put an end to political and cultural ties between those Ukrainian territories. The collaborationist policy of the Volhynian Ukrainian Alliance and the **Pacification** of 1930 considerably weakened the national movement in Volhynia. Between 1928 and 1932, centers of the **Prosvita** society were abolished in

Rivne, Ostrih, Kovel, Volodymyr, and Kremianets. In 1922–23, there were 443 Ukrainian elementary schools in Volhynia; by 1939, these had been reduced to eight (the number of Polish schools was 1,459), and there were no Ukrainian secondary schools in the region. Resistance to Polonization came mainly from the Galician-based **Organization of Ukrainian Nationalists**. Ukrainian deputies to the Polish Diet also voiced opposition to government policies in Volhynia.

In September 1939, Volhynia was occupied by Soviet forces and incorporated into the Ukrainian SSR. On 4 December 1939, Volhynia oblast (administered from Lutsk) and Rivne oblast (centered in Rivne) were established, while the Kremianets region was incorporated into Ternopil oblast. The retreat of the Red Army from Volhynia in 1941 was accompanied by mass terror against the civilian population and the execution of members of Ukrainian organizations in the jails of Lutsk, Dubno, and other towns.

During the Nazi occupation, Volhynian lands were incorporated into the **Reichskommissariat Ukraine**, which was administered from Rivne. The policies of the occupation regime, whose chief task was maximum extraction of produce and resources from the area, faced growing resistance. Between 1942 and 1944 Ukrainian military formations, the Polisian Sich and the **Ukrainian Insurgent Army** (UPA), and Soviet partisans were active in Volhynia. The UPA continued its underground struggle against the Soviet regime into the 1950s. There were also violent clashes and mass murders of civilians in Volhynia during the **Ukrainian-Polish Conflict** (1943–47).

Today, the historical region of Volhynia consists of the Volhynia, Rivne, and parts of the Zhytomyr and Ternopil oblasts (total area: 40,300 sq. km). The vast majority of its **population** is Ukrainian (96.9 percent), with a Russian minority (2.4 percent).

VOLKOV, OLEKSANDR (b. 30 April 1948). Politician, reputed economic oligarch. He was born in **Kyiv** into the family of a Hero of the Soviet Union (*see* WORLD WAR II). Volkov graduated from the Kyiv Institute of Commerce and Economics (1972). In 2002, he earned a candidate degree in political science from the State Tax Administration Academy of Ukraine. After graduation, Volkov worked in the agro-industrial complex. From 1989 to 1991, he was president of the Decor production cooperative, then headed the VGV and VAM commercial associations (1991–92) and a number of joint-venture firms. He founded and headed the Gravis television company in Kyiv (1992–94). Volkov's influence in the **media** gave him political prominence and allowed him to establish friendly relations with Prime Minister **Leonid Kuchma**. In 1993, Volkov became a member of the Prime Minister's Council of Industrialists and Entrepreneurs and a board member of the Union of Industrialists and Entrepreneurs. He was a major contributor to Kuchma's successful presidential campaign in 1994 and was appointed a presidential assistant. Thanks to his influential connections, Volkov became a major figure in Ukrainian business. In 1995, together with **Vadym Rabynovych**, he launched two highly successful projects, the Ukraine-Israel Chamber of Commerce and the television channel 1+1. In May 1997, Volkov was accused of money-laundering by two members of the **Verkhovna Rada** (VR) but denied all charges. In 1998, he was elected to the VR, where he worked in the Committee on Health Care, Maternity, and Childhood. At the same time, he was appointed adjunct presidential advisor and deputy head of the presidential Coordinating Council on Domestic Policy. In the VR, he headed the Renaissance of Regions group.

Prior to the 1999 presidential elections, Volkov established the Social Protection Foundation, which served as Kuchma's informal campaign headquarters and generously supported his candidacy. Volkov is known for his close connections with the businessman Ihor Bakai, a former head of the government-owned firm Naftohaz Ukrainy, who collected major funds for Kuchma's election campaign by selling Russian gas and oil piped across Ukrainian territory. In 2000, Volkov became vice president of the National Soccer Federation and of the Dynamo Kyiv Soccer Club.

In March 1999, a Brussels court froze Volkov's bank accounts in Belgium, seized his real-estate holdings on Belgian territory, and opened an investigation of his alleged money-laundering activities. The VR established a commission in June of the same year to investigate Volkov, who was accused of having transferred funds to bank accounts in Belgium, the United Kingdom, France, Luxembourg, Germany, Switzerland, and Latvia. Prosecutor-General Mykhailo Potebenko of Ukraine stated that there were no grounds for a criminal investigation.

As a major contributor to Kuchma's presidential campaign, Volkov acquired great power in the VR and became known as "director of parliament." In 1999, he formed a political party, the Democratic Union, and became its leader. He also directed Kuchma's national referendum of 2000, which increased presidential power. Wary of Volkov's growing influence, the World Bank advised Kuchma to distance himself from his political ally. In 2000, Volkov's activities and connections became a major focus of investigation by the journalist **Heorhii Gongadze**, whose murder in the same year turned into a political scandal.

Volkov stepped down as leader of the Democratic Union in December 2001, declaring himself an "ordinary party member." He was reelected to the VR in 2002 and joined the Committee on Ecological Policy.

VOLOBUIEV, MYKHAILO (24 January 1903–20 June 1972). Economist of Russian origin. He was born in Mykolaiv, Kherson gubernia. Volobuiev joined the **Communist Party of Ukraine** in 1920. In 1923, he began working at Holovpolitosvita (a branch of the commissariat of **education** in charge of adult learning and literacy programs), becoming its deputy director in 1927. In 1928, he published an article in the journal *Bil'shovyk Ukraïny* (Bolshevik of Ukraine) titled "Do problemy ukraïns'koï ekonomiky" (On the Problem of the Ukrainian Economy), arguing that Ukraine under Soviet rule, as under the Russian Empire, remained an economic colony of Russia. Volobuiev supported his thesis with statistical data supplied by the economist Viktor Dobrohaiev, arguing that by developing industry in central Russia, the Soviet government was making Ukraine even more dependent on the Russian metropolis. It was in the interests of Soviet economic development to eliminate this inequality, maintained Volobuiev.

His analysis complemented the views of such "national communists" as **Mykola Khvyliovy** and **Oleksander Shumsky**. An official campaign was immediately launched against his "nationalist deviation," and Volobuiev was forced to recant his views in another article in *Bil'shovyk Ukraïny*, "Proty ekonomichnoï platformy natsionalizmu (Do krytyky volobuïvshchyny)" (Against the Economic Platform of Nationalism [Toward a Critique of Volobuievism], 1930). In 1934, after the eradication of the leaders of Ukrainian "national communism," Volobuiev was arrested and sentenced to a five-year term in a concentration camp. He was rehabilitated in 1957, worked in a trade institute in Donetsk in the 1960s, and spent his last years in Rostov-na-Donu.

VOLODYMYR MONOMAKH (1053–1125). Prince of **Kyivan Rus'** and grand prince of **Kyiv** (1113–25). He was the son of Prince Vsevolod Yaroslavych; his mother was the daughter of the Byzantine emperor Constantine Monomachos. In 1078, his father became grand prince of Kyiv, while Volodymyr ruled the Smolensk and Chernihiv principalities. From 1093, he battled the **Cumans**, who were allied with Monomakh's cousin Oleh Sviatoslavych. Monomakh was forced to surrender Chernihiv to Oleh in 1094 but won it back in 1096. A ruler of great moral authority, he sought an end to internecine wars between the **princes** and the consolidation of their forces against the Cumans. For that purpose, he initiated the congresses of **Liubech** (1097), Vytychiv (1100), and Dolobsk (1103). In 1103, 1107, and 1111, he organized joint campaigns against the Cumans, putting an end to their raids on Rus' for an extended period. He was invited to rule over Kyiv during a rebellion there in 1113. Seeking to ease social tensions, Monomakh outlawed servitude as a means of debt repayment and decreased lending rates. He was the last Kyivan ruler to succeed in uniting most of the Rus' lands. Monomakh was the author of the "Poucheniie" (Instruction; text in the *Tale of Bygone Years*, Laurentian redaction), addressed to his children, in which he called for just rule and harmony among the princes. He attempted to establish dynastic rule, placing his eldest son, Mstyslav, on the Kyivan throne and his younger sons in other principalities, but the system broke down after Mstyslav's death (1132). Monomakh was buried in **St. Sophia's Cathedral** in Kyiv.

VOLODYMYR THE GREAT (Norse Valdemar; Russ. Vladimir, d. July 1015). Grand prince of **Kyiv** (ca. 980–1015), one of the most distinguished rulers of **Kyivan Rus'**, and son of **Sviatoslav Ihorevych**. From 969 to 978, he ruled in Novgorod. Having defeated his half-brother, Yaropolk, who was treacherously murdered by Volodymyr's retinue, he established himself in Kyiv (ca. 980). Volodymyr greatly expanded and strengthened the boundaries of Kyivan Rus'. In 981, he led a campaign against the Poles, capturing Peremyshl (Przemyśl) and the Cherven towns. He fought the Viatichians (982), Yatvingians (983), Radimichians (984), Volga Bulgars (985), and Croatians (993). In order to defend his territory against the nomadic **Pechenegs**, he built a series of fortified towns along the Stuhna, Desna, Irpin, Trubizh, and Sula Rivers. He united the Rus' lands under the rule of Kyiv.

Volodymyr is best known for the **Christianization of Rus'** (988–89), which linked his realm with the preeminent power of Byzantium and promoted its cultural and economic development. When asked by the Byzantine emperor Basil II to help crush the rebellion of Bardas Phocas in Asia Minor, Volodymyr demanded a political alliance, to be consolidated by his marriage to the emperor's daughter, Anna. This was achieved when Volodymyr's armies captured Chersonesus (now Sevastopol) in the **Crimea** (989), crushing the rebellion. Volodymyr also developed political, economic, and cultural ties with Poland, Hungary, Bohemia, and Scandinavia. He was canonized after his death. The statue of Volodymyr overlooking the Dnipro River is one of Kyiv's best-known landmarks.

VOLOSHYN, AVHUSTYN (17 March 1874–19 July 1945). Pedagogue, civic leader, and president of **Carpatho-Ukraine** (1939). He was born in the village of Kelechyn (now in **Transcarpathia** oblast) into a clerical family. Voloshyn graduated from the Uzhhorod gymnasium (1892) and the Uzhhorod theological seminary (1896), becoming a **Ukrainian Catholic** priest. In 1900, he obtained a teaching diploma from the Higher Pedagogical School in Budapest. Voloshyn worked at the Uzhhorod Teachers' Seminary as an instructor from 1897 and as director from 1912 to 1938. From 1903 to 1914, he edited the only Ukrainian newspaper in Ukrainian lands under Hungarian rule, *Nauka* (Learning). Voloshyn was a prolific writer of textbooks and helped establish many Ukrainian schools in Transcarpathia. He also turned **Prosvita** into a mass **educational** organization there during the interwar period. In 1918, Voloshyn became a founding member of the Ruthenian People's Council and later head of the Central Ruthenian (Ukrainian) People's Council in Uzhhorod. In 1923, he helped organize the Christian People's Party, serving as its president until 1939. From 1925 to 1929, he was a deputy to the Czechoslovak parliament.

When Germany began the dismemberment of Czechoslovakia after the Munich Agreement (29 September 1938), the Prague authorities were constrained to grant autonomy to **Subcarpathian Rus'**. Voloshyn became its premier on 26 October. During his brief tenure, the educational system and the press were Ukrainized and a defense force, the **Carpathian Sich**, was established. On 12 February 1939, elections were held to the Diet of Subcarpathian Rus', resulting in an overwhelming victory for the Ukrainian National Alliance (92.4 percent of the vote). As Voloshyn had little choice but to cultivate good relations with Germany, he promoted the interests of the local German population. He was unprepared for Hitler's acquiescence in Hungary's invasion of the territory on 14 March 1939. On the same day, Voloshyn proclaimed the independence of Carpatho-Ukraine and was elected its president at a session of the Diet on 15 March. As Hungarian forces overran Carpatho-Ukraine, Voloshyn and other members of the government fled to escape arrest. Voloshyn settled in Prague, heading the chair of pedagogy at the **Ukrainian Free University**; he subsequently became its rector. Arrested by the Soviet secret police in May 1945, he was deported and incarcerated at the Lefortovo Prison in Moscow, where he died.

VORONETS, PETRO (8 July 1871–27 October 1923). Mathematician and physicist. Voronets studied at **Kyiv** University and taught there upon graduating in 1896. He specialized in mechanics, especially differential equations, vector analysis, dynamics, and analytic mechanics. His work in nonholonomic mechanics—the study of motion in which the differential equations of constraints are not integrable (e.g., a sphere slipping and rolling on a plane)—found applications in robotic manipulation and nonlinear control. He is best known for his equation of motion of nonholonomic systems (1909), which included functions depending only on time, generalized coordinates, and certain linear functions of generalized velocity. Voronets arrived at the equation by generalizing the Hamilton-**Ostrohradsky** principle for nonholonomic systems and applied it to solve problems in mechanics.

VORONY, HEORHII (16 [28] April 1868–7 [20] November 1908). Mathematician. Born in Zhuravka, **Poltava** gubernia (now in Chernihiv oblast), Vorony graduated from the Pryluky Gymnasium and St. Petersburg University. In 1894, he received a master's degree from that university for a thesis on the algebraic integers associated with the roots of an irreducible cubic equation. He subsequently wrote a doctoral dissertation on algorithms for continued fractions. His thesis and dissertation were both awarded the **Buniakovsky** prize by the St. Petersburg Academy of Sciences, of which he became a corresponding member in 1907. From 1894, he taught mathematics at Warsaw University. Vorony's fundamental works pertain to number theory, particularly algebraic numbers and the geometry of numbers. He made significant contributions to the arithmetical theory of quadratic forms and the analytical theory of numbers. Together with Hermann Minkowski, Vorony is considered the founder of the geometric theory of numbers. Many of his ideas were developed further by members of **Dmitrii Grave's Kyiv** school of algebra. However, most of his works were not published until the 1950s and have gained recognition only recently.

VOVK, FEDIR (5 [17] March 1847–30 June 1918). Anthropologist, ethnographer, and archaeologist. He was born in Kriachivka (now in **Poltava** oblast) and studied at Novorossiisk (**Odesa**) and **Kyiv** universities, as well as at the Sorbonne. With **Volodymyr Antonovych**, he participated in archaeological digs in the Kyiv region and **Volhynia**. He was a member of the **Southwestern Branch of the Imperial Russian Geographic Society**, which published five volumes of his works (1873–76). In 1879, the tsarist campaign against Ukrainian culture (*see* EMS UKASE) led Vovk to emigrate to France, where he remained until 1905. There he published his "Rites et usages nuptiaux en Ukraine." From 1904 to 1906, he took part in anthropological and ethnographic expeditions in **Galicia** and **Bukovyna**. Vovk was privat-docent (from 1907) and later professor (1917) of St. Petersburg University. In late 1917, Kyiv University appointed him professor of geography and anthropology. He died in Homel en route to Ukraine.

Vovk collected a great deal of anthropological material that laid the foundations for his scholarly works, which number approx. 450. In them he reached the conclusion that Ukrainians constitute an anthropological type distinct from the Eastern **Slavs** and similar to the Southern Slavs. He was a full member of the **Shevchenko Scientific Society** (from 1893), the Imperial Russian Geographic Society in St. Petersburg, the Historical and Anthropological Society in Paris, and many other learned societies.

VYHOVSKY, IVAN (d. 16 [26] March 1664). Military leader; **hetman** of Ukraine (1657–59). He studied at the **Kyiv Mohyla Academy**, worked as a lawyer in the Lutsk castle court, and was later deputy to the Lutsk starosta. At the beginning of the **Khmelnytsky Uprising** (1648–57), he served in the Polish army. During the Battle of Zhovti Vody (April-May 1648), Vyhovsky was captured by the **Tatars** and ransomed by **Bohdan Khmelnytsky**, who valued his knowledge and experience. In 1648, Vyhovsky was appointed Khmelnytsky's general chancellor and became one of his closest advisors. He conducted negotiations with Poland, Muscovy, Sweden, and the **Crimean** Khanate.

After Khmelnytsky's death, Vyhovsky was elected hetman of Ukraine at a **Cossack council** in Korsun (15 [25] October 1657). On the following day, he signed the Ukrainian-Swedish **Treaty of Korsun**, which had been developed with Khmelnytsky's participation. At the same time, he renewed the alliance with the Crimean Khanate that had been severed by the **Articles of Bohdan Khmelnytsky** (1654) and began negotiations with Poland. Vyhovsky's domestic policy, which sought to strengthen the **Cossack officer** stratum, provoked dissatisfaction among the rank and file. Agitation among the peasantry and Cossacks by tsarist agents helped bring about a rebellion against the hetman led by the colonel of Poltava, Martyn Pushkar, and Yakiv Barabash, the **Zaporozhian** otaman (1658). Vyhovsky quelled the rebellion at a considerable cost in lives.

Relations with Muscovy now reached the breaking point. Vyhovsky signed the **Treaty of Hadiach** with the **Polish-Lithuanian Commonwealth** (6 [16] September 1658). In 1659, Muscovy sent an army led by Aleksei Trubetskoi to occupy **Left-Bank Ukraine**. At the **Battle of Konotop**, the Ukrainian forces

commanded by Vyhovsky destroyed the Muscovite army.
Vyhovsky was unable to profit from his victory. A Cossack officer opposition led by the pro-Muscovite colonels Ivan Bezpaly, Tymish Tsiutsiura, and Vasyl Zolotarenko resisted the hetman's policies. Exploiting this new insurgency, as well as widespread dissatisfaction with the Treaty of Hadiach, Muscovite armies commanded by Grigorii Romodanovsky seized Left-Bank Ukraine. Vyhovsky resigned in September 1659 and fled to Poland. Some time later, he was appointed senator and palatine of Kyiv. From 1662, he participated actively in the **Lviv Dormition Brotherhood**. In early 1664, he was denounced as an insurrectionist by **Pavlo Teteria** and executed.

VYNNYCHENKO, VOLODYMYR (26 July [7 August] 1880–6 March 1951). Writer and politician. He was born in Veselyi Kut (now in Kirovohrad oblast). After completing the Yelysavethrad gymnasium, Vynnychenko enrolled in the faculty of law at **Kyiv** University. While studying, he belonged to the Kyiv **Hromada** and became a founder of the **Revolutionary Ukrainian Party**. He conducted propaganda work among **peasants** in the **Poltava** region and workers in Kyiv, for which he was arrested, expelled from the university, and banned from entering any other educational institution.

In 1905, Vynnychenko helped establish the **Ukrainian Social Democratic Labor Party** (USDRP), was a member of its executive, and edited its publication *Borot'ba* (Struggle). To escape continual police surveillance, Vynnychenko lived as an émigré (1906–14). He was a member of the Ukrainian Hromada in Paris (1910), edited the journal *Dzvin* (Bell) with **Dmytro Dontsov** and Lev Yurkevych in **Lviv** (1913–17), and worked for the periodical *Ukrainskaia zhizn'* (Ukrainian Life) in Moscow (1914).

From 1917 to 1919, as leader of the USDRP, Vynnychenko played a significant role in the **Ukrainian Revolution**. He was elected vice president of the **Ukrainian Central Rada** (March 1917) and later vice chairman of the Little Rada. In late May 1917, he headed the Ukrainian delegation in negotiations with the Provisional Government in Petrograd. On 15 (28) June 1917, he was appointed head of the Rada's General Secretariat (government), simultaneously acting as general secretary of internal affairs. Vynnychenko helped draft all four proclamations of the Rada. In December 1917, he was instrumental in rejecting the ultimatum of the Bolshevik Council of People's Commissars, which led to war between Ukraine and Russia. In January 1918, Vynnychenko headed the **Council of People's Ministers** and the Ministry of Internal Affairs. Because of interparty discord, he resigned on 17 (30)

January 1918. From 18 September to 14 November 1918, he headed the **Ukrainian National Union** and became a leader of the rebellion against Hetman **Pavlo Skoropadsky**. On 14 November, Vynnychenko was elected chairman of the **Directory**. Opposed to its policy toward the Entente, he resigned in February 1919.

Together with a group of like-minded individuals, Vynnychenko organized a foreign group of the **Ukrainian Communist Party** in Vienna and founded its publication, the newspaper *Nova doba* (New Era). Unable to reach an agreement with the Bolshevik government in 1920, he returned to Vienna and harshly criticized the nationality policies of the Bolsheviks and the **Communist Party of Ukraine**. In the 1920s, Vynnychenko settled in France, where he spent the rest of his life, devoting himself mainly to writing. During the Nazi occupation, he was imprisoned in a concentration camp. He died in Mougins near Cannes.

Vynnychenko was a major writer who gained broad recognition for his racy stories of working-class life—a new theme in Ukrainian literature at the time. He also became a popular and controversial playwright, engaging in the radical exploration of moral questions. These included the notion of spiritual love in *Dysharmoniia* (Disharmony, 1906), equality of the sexes in *Bazar* (Bazaar, 1910), the view that ends justify means in *Hrikh* (The Sin, 1920), and surrogate motherhood in *Zakon* (The Law, 1923). Many of Vynnychenko's plays were translated and staged throughout Europe. He arrived at the notion of "honesty with oneself" as his guiding principle and later developed a view of moral order that he termed "concordism." Throughout his adult life he kept a diary, the first two volumes of which (covering the years 1911–25) have been published. His three-volume memoir of the Ukrainian Revolution, titled *Vidrodzhennia natsiï* (Rebirth of a Nation), appeared in 1920.

VYSHENSKY, IVAN (ca. 1545–50–after 1620). Orthodox monk, writer, and polemicist. Born in Sudova Vyshnia (now in **Lviv** oblast), he participated in the activities of the **Lviv Dormition Brotherhood** and was associated with the **Ostrih Academy**. From the late 1580s, he lived on Mt. Athos (Greece), the center of Eastern Orthodox monasticism. After being tonsured, Vyshensky settled in a cave and lived as a hermit. He sent impassioned epistles against the **Union of Brest** to Prince **Kostiantyn Ostrozky**, as well as to church **brotherhoods** and clergymen. Transcriptions of these works, of which 15 have been preserved, circulated widely in Ukraine. In 1605, Vyshensky visited Ukraine and stayed at the **Maniava Hermitage**. Preaching radical asceticism, he rejected both the secular **education** of his day and pre-Christian ways of life.

Denouncing the moral decadence of the nobility and clergy, he exalted primitive Christianity and the piety of simple **peasants** and monks. His writings, whose style draws on Byzantine sermons, as well as on Ukrainian and Polish polemics of the day, are considered to be among the finest examples of Ukrainian **baroque** prose. *See also* LITERATURE.

VYSHNEVETSKY, DMYTRO (d. 29 October 1563). Prince and first known **Cossack hetman** (ca. 1552–63). A landowner in Kremianets county, **Volhynia**, he was descended from the Lithuanian ruling clan of Gediminas. From 1550 to 1553, he was starosta of Cherkasy and Kaniv counties. Ca. 1552, he built a castle on the island of Mala **Khortytsia** that became the prototype of the **Zaporozhian Sich** and assembled several hundred Cossacks to fight the Crimean **Tatars**. In October 1557, Vyshnevetsky led a Cossack force to the Ottoman fortress of Islam Kerman and seized its cannon. He attempted to organize an alliance between Poland and Muscovy, with Zaporozhian participation, to fight the Ottoman Empire and the Crimean Khanate. In early 1559, he led a successful campaign into the **Crimea**, liberating several thousand Ukrainian prisoners. In 1563, Vyshnevetsky became embroiled in the struggle for **Moldavia** and was defeated near Suceava by Ştefan Tomşa, pretender to the Moldavian throne. Vyshnevetsky was captured and turned over to the Ottoman government. According to the *Chronicle of Marcin Bielski*, Vyshnevetsky was tortured and executed in Constantinople at the command of Sultan Süleyman II by being thrown from a tower onto a bed of iron spikes. He is the hero of the Ukrainian epic song (duma) about the Cossack Baida.

W

WARSAW, TREATY OF. Agreement between the **Ukrainian People's Republic** (UNR) and Poland, concluded in Warsaw on 21 April 1920. On 2 December 1919, a diplomatic mission headed by the deputy foreign minister of the UNR, **Andrii Livytsky**, and Stepan Vytvytsky, representative of the Western Province of the UNR, issued a statement declaring the willingness of the UNR to relinquish Ukrainian territories west of the Zbruch River (Vytvytsky subsequently resigned in protest over this point). On 21 April 1920, a political and economic convention was signed by Livytsky and the Polish deputy minister of foreign affairs, Jan Dąbski. Under its terms, the Polish government recognized the independence of the UNR and the **Directory**, headed by **Symon Petliura**, as Ukraine's supreme political authority. The Ukrainian-Polish border was established along the Zbruch River, continuing northeast to Vyshhorodok and further east from Zdolbuniv, along the eastern boundary of Rivne county to the Prypiat River. Both governments were forbidden to make third-party agreements contrary to the treaty, and both were to guarantee the national and cultural rights of their ethnic minorities. The treaty included a military convention signed on 24 April by Gen. Volodymyr Sinkler for the UNR and a representative of the Polish War Department, Walery Sławek, which provided for joint Polish-Ukrainian military action against Bolshevik armies on Ukrainian territory. The conditions of the treaty, especially official UNR recognition of Poland's annexation of **Galicia**, western **Volhynia**, parts of **Polisia**, the **Lemko region**, **Podlachia**, and the **Sian** and **Kholm regions**, led to a political breach between eastern and western Ukrainians. The treaty was unequivocally opposed by the government-in-exile of the **Western Ukrainian People's Republic** and the population of western Ukraine. It resulted in a Polish-Ukrainian campaign that briefly recaptured **Kyiv** for the UNR, but the subsequent near-victory of Bolshevik forces in the Polish-Soviet War (1920) led Poland to break the terms of the Treaty of Warsaw and conclude a separate peace—the **Treaty of Riga** (1921)—with the Russian SFSR and the **Ukrainian SSR**.

WESTERN UKRAINE (Ukr. *Zakhidna Ukraïna*). Term used to denote Ukrainian lands under Austrian rule before 1918, as contrasted with **eastern Ukraine**. It was also the popular name of the **Western Ukrainian People's Republic**. From 1919 to 1939, it referred to Ukrainian lands within Poland, Czechoslovakia, and Romania. It was also used to designate Ukrainian lands annexed to the **Ukrainian SSR** in 1939–40. Today it is sometimes used to refer to the territory of the Chernivtsi, Ivano-Frankivsk, **Lviv**, Rivne, Ternopil, **Transcarpathia**, and **Volhynia** oblasts. Its total territory is 110,700 sq. km and its population is 9.6 million. Ethnic Ukrainians constitute 91.8 percent of the **population** of western Ukraine and ethnic Russians 2.7 percent.

WESTERN UKRAINIAN PEOPLE'S REPUBLIC/ZAKHIDNO-UKRAÏNS'KA NARODNA RESPUBLIKA (ZUNR). State established in October 1918 in the **western Ukrainian** lands that had been part of the Austro-Hungarian Empire (*see* WORLD WAR I). In late September 1918, the Ukrainian General Military Commissariat was formed in **Lviv** and began making preparations for armed insurrection. Dmytro Vitovsky, a captain in the Legion of the **Ukrainian Sich Riflemen**, was elected chairman of the commissariat (October 1918). As Austria-Hungary disintegrated, the Ukrainian members of the **Galician** and **Bukovynian** diets, representatives of Galician and Bukovynian political parties, the clergy, and students established the **Ukrainian National Rada** (UNRada) in Lviv (18 October). On the following day, the UNRada declared a Ukrainian state on all Ukrainian ethnic territory in Galicia, Bukovyna, and **Transcarpathia**. It was decided to develop a democratic constitution, and **Yevhen Petrushevych** was elected president of the UNRada.

On 31 October, it became known that the Polish Liquidation Commission (created on 28 October in Cracow) was to arrive in Lviv the next day with the intention of incorporating Galicia into Poland. When the UNRada appealed to the Austrian vicegerent, Gen. Karl Huyn, to transfer control of Galicia and Bukovyna to the Rada, he refused to do so. On the same day, independently of the UNRada, the Military Commissariat decided to take control of Lviv. On the night of 31 October-1 November, units of riflemen commanded by Vitovsky seized the major government buildings.

The State Secretariat of the ZUNR was established on 13 November 1918. The constitutional foundations of the newly created state were ratified and its name officially adopted. The Provisional Basic Law defined the territory of the ZUNR, which incorporated Ukrainian ethnic lands in Galicia, Bukovyna, and Transcarpathia (70,000 sq. km), with a population of six million. The state **coat of arms** (a golden lion on a blue background) and **flag** (azure and gold) were also adopted. Ethnic minorities in the ZUNR were guaranteed equal rights with the Ukrainian population. The basic law was augmented by legislation on the organization of the army (13 November), provisional administration (15 November), provisional organization of the court system (16 and 21 November 1918), state language (1 February 1919), schooling (13 February), citizenship (8 April), and land reform (14 April). The ZUNR opened diplomatic representations in Austria, Germany, and Hungary; it also sent missions to Brazil, Canada, Czechoslovakia, Italy, and the United States. The German and **Jewish** population proved loyal to the new state, but the Poles began immediate military action against it (*see* UKRAINIAN-POLISH WAR IN GALICIA). At the same time, Romanian armies crossed the ZUNR border and, despite popular resistance, occupied Chernivtsi (11 November) and the remainder of northern Bukovyna. On 21 November, after three weeks of fighting, the Poles took control of Lviv.

The government of the ZUNR moved to Ternopil and then, in late December, established itself in Stanyslaviv (now Ivano-Frankivsk). Elections were held to form a government, which took office on 4 January 1919, and an Executive Committee of the UNRada (consisting of nine members) was formed under the leadership of

Petrushevych. On 1 December 1918, a delegation of the UNRada and representatives of the **Directory** of the **Ukrainian People's Republic** (UNR) signed a preliminary agreement concerning the unification of the ZUNR with the UNR, ratified on 3 January 1919. On 22 January 1919, the **Act of Union** between the ZUNR and the UNR was proclaimed in Kyiv. The ZUNR was renamed the Western Province of the UNR (ZO UNR). However, the administrative unification of the two Ukrainian states was not realized, nor were their differing political views reconciled.

The political culture of the ZUNR, shaped by decades of Austrian constitutionalism, made for a stable and orderly administration whose institutions functioned reliably. The **National Democratic** and **Ukrainian Radical** parties shared power in a coalition government. Unlike in **eastern Ukraine**, there were no anti-Jewish pogroms. The land legislation of the ZUNR differed fundamentally from that of the UNR; private landholdings were not nationalized, and even though peasant holdings in the ZUNR were generally much smaller than in eastern Ukraine, **peasants** there tended to respect the institution of private property. Accordingly, a considerable number of peasant deputies to the UNRada favored compensation for landowners whose holdings exceeded the norm that was to be legislated by the Rada.

By early June 1919, Polish armies had overwhelmed the **Ukrainian Galician Army** (UHA) and occupied virtually all of Galicia, with the exception of a triangle between the Dnister and Zbruch Rivers and the town of Zalishchyky. The government resigned (9 June 1919), and the Executive Committee of the UNRada transferred its powers to Petrushevych, who became dictator of the ZO UNR. He established a provisional executive body, a Council of Plenipotentiaries, and a Military Chancellery. The UHA retreated across the Zbruch in mid-July, where it joined the Army of the UNR. From July to November 1919, Petrushevych and his administration were based in Kamianets-Podilskyi with the UNR government.

In November 1919, military defeat forced Petrushevych and the ZUNR government to emigrate; with Vienna as their base, they continued diplomatic activity. On 8 December, the Supreme Council of the Entente, recognizing the **Curzon Line** as the eastern border of Poland, ratified the Polish administration of the western Ukrainian lands. From 1920 to 1923, the ZUNR government-in-exile lobbied continually with the League of Nations and the Entente for recognition of an independent ZUNR. The Entente, however, favored a strong Polish state as a counterweight to Soviet Russia. In March 1921, a ZUNR delegation (including **Kost Levytsky** and **Osyp**

Nazaruk) protested the **Treaty of Riga** between Russia, the **Ukrainian SSR**, and Poland, which ratified the Polish annexation of western Ukraine. On 14 March 1923, the Council of Allied Ambassadors recognized the existing eastern border of Poland on condition that **eastern Galicia** be granted autonomy. Attempting to change the council's decision, Metropolitan **Andrei Sheptytsky** met with Premier Raymond Poincaré of France, to no avail. On 15 March, the Government-in-exile of the ZUNR ceased to exist, and Petrushevych resigned his post. In accordance with the Treaty of Saint-Germain (10 September 1919), the Treaty of Sèvres (10 August 1920), and the Treaty of Trianon (28 October 1920), Bukovyna and part of **Bessarabia** were annexed by Romania, while Transcarpathia was ceded to Czechoslovakia. These political arrangements prevailed until **World War II**.

WINTER CAMPAIGNS. Military campaigns of the Army of the **Directory** of the **Ukrainian People's Republic** in 1919–20 and 1921, consisting of raids behind Bolshevik and White lines in western and central Ukraine. The First Winter Campaign lasted from 6 December 1919 to 6 May 1920. In December 1919, the Red Army seized a significant portion of **western Ukraine**, the Volunteer White Army of Gen. Anton Denikin was in southern Ukraine, and Polish units occupied **Volhynia** and western **Podilia**. The Army of the UNR controlled an insignificant territory in the vicinity of Chortoryia (now in Zhytomyr oblast) on the Sluch River in Volhynia, surrounded by Bolshevik, Polish, and Denikinite armies. Under these circumstances, it became impossible to continue the struggle with regular armed forces. On 5 December, at a meeting of the government of the UNR and the command of the UNR Army in Chortoryia, it was decided to eliminate the regular front and turn to partisan warfare. On 6 December, 5,000 men commanded by Gen. Mykhailo Omelianovych-Pavlenko set out on the First Winter Campaign. The premier of the UNR, **Isaak Mazepa**, also participated.

The military grouping consisted of three units—Zaporozhian, **Kyiv**, and Volhynian. Andrii Dolud was appointed chief of staff. In December 1919 and January 1920, the Ukrainian armies operated in the Yelysavethrad (now Kirovohrad) region, destroying enemy garrisons and individual units. In February, they crossed the Dnipro River and reached the vicinity of Zolotonosha (now in Cherkasy oblast). Battles were fought for Lypovets, Uman, Cherkasy, Kaniv, Smila, Zolotonosha, and Balta. In April 1920, the guerrilla units began to break through to the west in order to join Ukrainian units on the Polish-Soviet front, which they reached in the vicinity of Yampil (now in Khmelnytskyi oblast) on 6 May.

The Second Winter Campaign (Ice Campaign or November Raid) took place in November 1921. In November 1920, units of the Army of the UNR that had returned to western Ukraine were interned in POW camps on orders of the Polish government. Insurgent units continued to fight the Bolsheviks in Podilia and in the Kyiv, Katerynoslav (now Dnipropetrovsk), and **Poltava** regions. In October 1921, the UNR government-in-exile developed a plan to unite the partisans and topple the Bolshevik regime. A Ukrainian Insurgent Army was recruited from among the internees. It consisted of three groups: Volhynian (800 soldiers), Bessarabian (approx. 300 soldiers), and Podilian (400 soldiers), all poorly armed and supplied. Yurii Tiutiunnyk was commander of the Insurgent Army, while Col. Yurii Otmarshtain served as chief of staff. The three groups crossed the Soviet border at different points. The Bessarabian group retreated to Romanian territory after a few days. The Podilian group set out on 25 October from Husiatyn in the Ternopil region. In its first battles, it defeated a Red cavalry regiment and became a cavalry group. It reached the vicinity of Vakhnivka (60 km from Kyiv), then turned west and crossed the Polish border on 29 November. The Volhynian group commenced its raid on 4 November and took Korosten on 7 November but lacked the strength to hold it. The insurgents were surrounded by the Bolshevik cavalry of Hryhorii Kotovsky and defeated near Mali Mynky on 17 November. Following their refusal to join the Red Army, 359 soldiers of the Insurgent Army were executed near Bazar (now in Zhytomyr oblast) on 23 November. Only a small unit of 120 men from the Volhynian group managed to escape and return to western Ukraine. The Second Winter Campaign was the last attempt of the Ukrainian armed forces to attain independence by military means during the **Ukrainian Revolution** (1917–21).

WOMEN. Women have constituted a majority of Ukraine's **population** (54 percent in 2001) throughout the 20th century. The imbalance between the number of men and women in Ukraine is a direct result of disproportionate losses of male lives in two world wars, as well as **famines** and other Soviet repressive measures. The life expectancy for women is 74.4 years—more than 10 years longer than for men.

There is strong evidence that matriarchy was a dominant social structure in prehistoric times on what is now Ukrainian territory. Archaeological findings of female cult statues dating back to the **Trypilian culture** suggest that worship of goddesses was the primary form of religious expression.

Under the patriarchal order that followed primitive society, women became subordinate to men and were treated as chattel. This changed with the **Christianization of Rus'** and the transition from tribal society to the medieval state of **Kyivan Rus'**, in which monogamous relationships were established between men and women. The prevailing law code, the *Ruskaia Pravda*, was based on customary law and was relatively liberal in its treatment of women. Unlike Germanic and Roman law, it did not delimit women's status or privileges on the basis of gender but linked the legal status of women with their socioeconomic position. Noblewomen had considerable influence in the politics of Rus', and some, like Princess **Olha**, ruled as regents. **Anna Yaroslavna**, queen of France from 1049, was one of several Kyivan princesses who married foreign monarchs.

In the Lithuanian-Ruthenian state, women's legal status was defined by the **Lithuanian Statute**. Its criminal and civil articles adopted the principle of gender equality, and women enjoyed legal rights with no basic restrictions. In the **Cossack** period, the absence of most men during constant wars and uprisings made women responsible not only for running households, farming, and raising children, but also for defending their families with arms. The burden of corvée labor also fell on the shoulders of **peasant** women. During the frequent **Tatar** raids of the period, women were often abducted and sold as slaves to Turkish harems (*see* ROKSOLIANA). The **Code of Laws of 1743** provided harsh penalties for crimes against women. However, the economic and legal status of women depended very much on their social standing. Free peasant women, for example, were treated as equal with their husbands, but serf women had no legal protection and were subject to exploitation.

The independence and leadership role of women in Cossack society declined under Russian rule. The native Ukrainian elite was severely depleted through Polonization and **Russification**, and the preservation of national consciousness fell to the peasantry. The transmission of **language**, customs, and basic historical knowledge from generation to generation was overseen mainly by women.

In the 19th century, middle-class women began to play an important role in the Ukrainian social and cultural revival, forming community-oriented groups from the 1880s. Initially they were not oriented toward feminism or suffrage, but began to develop an interest in these issues as a result of their activism. The early organizations focused on the struggle to alleviate poverty, disease, and illiteracy in the general population and developed programs to educate women, establish day-care centers, and assist peasant girls adapting to urban life. Although middle-class women did not earn an income outside the home and depended on their families, they began to achieve prominence as artists and cultural activists. For example, **Lesia Ukrainka** became a poet and dramatist, **Olha Kobylianska** an outstanding novelist, and **Solomiia Krushelnytska** a world-renowned opera singer.

Suffrage was granted to women only in 1914 in Austrian-ruled **western Ukraine** and in 1917 in the Russian Empire. The constitution of the short-lived **Ukrainian People's Republic** declared complete gender equality in 1918. Although various redactions of the Soviet constitution proclaimed equality between men and women, guaranteeing women equal access to higher **education** and equal opportunity for professional advancement, in reality women played a subordinate role in the **USSR**. The Soviet government was interested mainly in exploiting their labor power, which was badly needed after the devastation of **World War I** and the revolution. In addition to the traditional role of mother and homemaker, women were expected to hold full-time jobs; they constituted 52 percent of the labor force. Moreover, 80 percent of jobs requiring heavy physical labor were held by women who had little education and were paid low wages.

The early 1920s also saw the legalization of abortion and the spread of ideas of sexual liberation. With the adoption of a policy of forced industrialization in 1928, the Soviet state rejected such notions and promoted a cult of large families and heroic motherhood. Women who bore many children qualified for the status of "mother-heroine" and were awarded state prizes. A support system in which women could combine maternity and work included extended paid maternity leaves, shorter workdays for mothers with infants, and affordable day-care facilities. Despite such social benefits, the level of women's health education and access to birth control was low. Abortion was often the only method of birth control available. The government banned abortion in 1936 but reinstated it in 1955. At the end of the Soviet period, Ukraine had one of the highest abortion rates in the world; the average abortion rate rose from five per 1,000 women aged 15–49 in 1925–27 to 90 per 1,000 in 1980–88.

The **collectivization** of agriculture and the man-made **famine of 1932–33**, as well as the **political terror** of the 1930s, took a heavy toll on women. Not only did they suffer the same depredations as men, but they were responsible for their large families when men were deported or executed. Opposition to collectivization came from women in the form of so-called *babs'ki bunty* or women's uprisings. In western Ukraine, women fought in World War I and engaged in civic and political activism during the interwar period and in **World War II**; **Olha Basarab** was tortured to death in interwar Poland for her membership in the **Ukrainian Military**

Organization, **Kateryna Zarytska's** involvement in the **Organization of Ukrainian Nationalists** resulted in her lengthy incarceration in Polish and Soviet prisons, and **Slava Stetsko** became a lifelong champion of Ukrainian sovereignty and anticommunist activism. The **Union of Ukrainian Women**, established in 1921, was the largest organization of its kind in Ukraine. In the 1960s, Ukrainian women took a notable part in the **dissident movement**. Many, including Oksana Meshko, Iryna Stasiv-Kalynets, Nina Strokata-Karavanska, and Nadiia Svitlychna, were persecuted and incarcerated for their beliefs; the dissident artist **Alla Horska** was murdered.

In the **Ukrainian SSR**, relatively few women held political and economic leadership positions. In 1990, women made up only 28.5 percent of the membership of the **Communist Party of Ukraine**, and at its final congress women constituted only 7 percent of delegates. The representation of women was even lower (5.3 percent) in senior managerial positions in Ukrainian industry.

In the wake of Ukrainian independence, the condition of women remains difficult. The ensuing economic crisis put a strain on Ukrainian families and severely affected women, who make up more than 70 percent of the unemployed. Large numbers of Ukrainian women have gone abroad to take low-paying jobs in order to support their families; many have fallen victim to the sex-trade traffic. Although in level of **education** and professional training Ukrainian women are equal to men, they earn only about 70 percent of men's salaries. The proportion of women in decision-making positions is very low. They are not represented at all in the **Cabinet of Ministers** and constitute only 5 percent of the 450-seat Verkhovna Rada.

The process of changing cultural patterns and gender stereotypes is a slow one; there are no feminist organizations in Ukraine, and the question of political parity is not raised. Women take part in the democratization process through involvement in political, social, and ecological movements. A major political opposition bloc is led by a former deputy premier, **Yuliia Tymoshenko**, numerous non-governmental organizations rely on women as leaders, and women are becoming increasingly visible in opinion-forming professions such as journalism and scholarship.

WORLD WAR I. Conflict between the Entente (England, France, and Russia, joined by the United States in 1917) and the Central Powers (Germany, Austria-Hungary, Turkey, and Bulgaria) from 1914 to 1918 in which Ukraine was a major battleground. The war was touched off by long-standing Austro-Russian rivalry in the Balkans, and Ukrainians were involved on both sides of the conflict. In the western Ukrainian lands under Austrian rule, some 300,000 Ukrainians fought in the Austrian forces. The **Supreme Ukrainian Council**, established in **Lviv** at the outbreak of the war, called on Ukrainians to support the Central Powers in order to defeat the Russian Empire, their greatest enemy. The **Ukrainian Sich Riflemen** fought on the Austrian side, proving their battle-worthiness against Russian forces at Makivka and Lysonia. Ukrainian service to the Austrian cause yielded no political concessions, as the Central Powers were concerned with placating the more powerful Poles. On 5 November 1916, they proclaimed an independent Polish kingdom and granted **Galicia** complete autonomy, which meant that it would be dominated by the Poles. Only in 1918, when the Central Powers desperately needed Ukrainian grain for the home front, did they secretly agree to the establishment of a Ukrainian crown land within Austria consisting of eastern Galicia and **Bukovyna**. This agreement, an annex to the **Treaty of Brest-Litovsk**, was also nullified by Polish pressure.

Approximately 3.5 million Ukrainians fought in World War I in the armies of the Russian Empire. The outbreak of war provided the tsarist authorities with a pretext to close down all Ukrainian institutions that had survived the reaction to the **Revolution of 1905** on grounds of alleged disloyalty to the imperial cause. A declaration of loyalty by **Symon Petliura**, editor of the newspaper *Ukrainskaia zhizn'* (Ukrainian Life), was of no avail. The major Ukrainian organization in the empire, the **Society of Ukrainian Progressives**, remained neutral.

The Russian offensive of August and September 1914 led to the occupation of Galicia, Bukovyna, **Transcarpathia**, and eastern Slovakia. Since the tsarist government regarded the Ukrainian lands as "ancient Russian territories," it began a program of thoroughgoing **Russification**. Ukrainian institutions were closed and Ukrainian-language schooling and publishing prohibited. Ukrainian Catholic clerics, including Metropolitan **Andrei Sheptytsky**, were exiled to Russia, while Russian Orthodox priests were brought in to convert the population to Orthodoxy. Members of the Ukrainian elite were deported to Russia en masse. Corruption, vandalism, and robbery became so prevalent under the occupation regime as to arouse protests in the State Duma itself. The **Russophiles** were the only group that prospered under the occupation; their leaders were given administrative posts and their institutions, closed by the Austrian authorities before the war, now flourished.

The Russian advance led the Austrian authorities and armed forces to believe that the western Ukrainians (most of whom still referred to themselves as *rusyny*, easily confused with "Russians") were abetting the occupying forces. Many Ukrainians were deported to concentration camps in Austria on suspicion of espionage or disloyalty, where thousands were held without trial in unsanitary conditions. The most infamous of these camps was Thalerhof, where some 1,767 Ukrainians were officially registered as having died of epidemic disease (the actual figure was probably much higher). Others were summarily executed, often by Poles in administrative positions, or beaten and murdered, especially by Hungarian forces. The **Union for the Liberation of Ukraine**, established by eastern Ukrainian exiles to promote Ukrainian independence, was active in Austria until 1918. It did considerable cultural and educational work, especially with Ukrainian POWs captured by the Central Powers, but its extensive propaganda in support of Ukrainian sovereignty gained no broad sympathy.

An Austro-German offensive in the spring of 1915 pushed the Russian forces out of Galicia and Bukovyna, but much of this territory was retaken in the Brusilov offensive (summer 1916). The new occupation, which lasted several months, was less severe than that of 1914–15, largely because the Committee for the Southwestern Front attached to the All-Russian Union of Towns was under the control of the eastern Ukrainian intelligentsia. The historian **Dmytro Doroshenko** became governor-general of Bukovyna and part of eastern Galicia.

The revolution of February 1917 in the Russian Empire, the result of social collapse engendered by the war, also marked the beginning of the **Ukrainian Revolution** of 1917–21. The war served as something of a catalyst for the Ukrainian national movement, bringing together large numbers of Ukrainians from different political jurisdictions for the first time, providing an opportunity for independentists to assert their claims, and uprooting apolitical **peasant** traditionalism by means of mass mobilization and deportation. Outweighing these effects, however, was the tremendous destruction wrought by three years of intensive warfare in western Ukraine and the rise of new states—Poland, Czechoslovakia, Romania, and Bolshevik Russia—all with designs on Ukraine, which failed to develop a stable political order of its own.

WORLD WAR II. In Eastern Europe, the war was essentially a four-year struggle between Nazi Germany and the **USSR**. The two states, which had been mutually hostile in the 1930s, stunned the world on 23 August 1939 by signing a nonaggression pact that allowed the Nazis to attack and overrun most of Poland. Under the terms of the pact's secret protocol, whose existence the USSR denied until 1989, the Red Army took over **western Ukraine** and western Belarus in September 1939. On 28 September, the Nazi-Soviet understanding was sealed with an agreement (whose existence the USSR also denied until 1989) on cooperation and the demarcation of borders. The Soviet occupation of northern **Bukovyna** and **Bessarabia** followed in June 1940.

Stalin collaborated faithfully with Hitler, supplying Germany with large quantities of strategic goods and handing over more than 90,000 anti-Nazi refugees from occupied Poland to the Gestapo. Expecting a lengthy war in Western Europe in which the USSR would intervene at its convenience, Stalin ignored more than 80 warnings of impending German aggression. Given the prevailing **political terror**, which took the lives of no less than 44,000 Soviet officers in the late 1930s (including one-third of the **Kyiv** special military district command), no one dared to challenge Stalin's complacency. The new officer cadres were poorly educated and often incompetent, border defenses were weak, and more than 80 percent of Soviet weapons were obsolete, while the production of technologically advanced weapons was neglected.

As a result, the German attack of 22 June 1941 had the advantage of total surprise, and blitzkrieg tactics allowed the invaders to advance very swiftly, occupying almost all of Ukraine within four months. Whole Soviet divisions were surrounded and their personnel taken prisoner; the Red Army captives included 20 generals and more than 180,000 officers. Moreover, the brutal two-year Soviet occupation of western Ukraine, which ended with the wholesale slaughter of at least 15,000 prisoners to save the trouble of evacuating them, turned the population decisively against the USSR; thus, many western Ukrainians initially welcomed the Germans as liberators from Soviet tyranny. The **Bandera** faction of the **Organization of Ukrainian Nationalists** (OUN), which sought to establish an independent state, proclaimed a **Ukrainian State Administration** in Lviv on 30 June under the leadership of **Yaroslav Stetsko**. It also established a **Ukrainian National Council**. The Germans immediately arrested Bandera, Stetsko, and other OUN leaders, making it clear that they had come to Ukraine as occupiers. The rival **Melnyk** faction of the OUN, whose leaders included **Oleh Olzhych** and **Olena Teliha**, established its own Ukrainian National Council in Kyiv in the autumn of 1941; like their rivals in the OUN(B), they were hunted down and killed by the Gestapo.

Hitler and the Nazi leaders, who regarded the **Slavs** as racially inferior and held the Red Army in contempt, expected to destroy the Soviet armed forces in a maximum of five months. They saw

Ukraine as a breadbasket, a source of raw material for the war effort, and a future colony for German settlement. Their policy was one of blatant exploitation, particularly in the **Reichskommissariat Ukraine**, which encompassed most of occupied Ukraine and whose administrator, Erich Koch, described himself as a "brutal dog." The Ministry for the Occupied Eastern Territories under Alfred Rosenberg attempted to moderate Nazi policy but achieved very little. A sizable portion of southwestern Ukraine was constituted as **Transnistria** and turned over to the Nazis' Romanian allies.

Only in Galicia, which was renamed the Distrikt Galizien and annexed to the **Generalgouvernement** of Poland, did the Germans allow their Ukrainian subjects minimal freedom of action, seeking to set them at odds with the Poles. The **Ukrainian Central Committee** (UCC), led by **Volodymyr Kubijovyč**, was the only Ukrainian representative body tolerated by the Germans in the course of the occupation. The UCC carried out extensive relief work among the western Ukrainian population and prisoners of war. In 1943, following the German defeat at Stalingrad, it helped recruit the Waffen-SS **Division Galizien**, hoping to create the nucleus of a well-trained Ukrainian army for the chaotic period expected to ensue after the German defeat. Most of the division was destroyed in battle against the Red Army in July 1944.

The reserve of good will that the Germans could have mobilized for their war effort against the USSR was squandered by 1942 because of their ruthless occupation policy. Of an estimated 5.7 million prisoners of war in German hands, some 3.7 million died of starvation and disease in concentration camps (in **World War I**, by contrast, about 5.4 percent of those taken prisoner by the Germans died in captivity). Of that total, almost 1.4 million died in 180 concentration camps in Ukraine. Retribution for aiding partisans or prisoners of war was extremely severe; hundreds of punishment details burned and looted villages, shooting their inhabitants indiscriminately or burning them alive, in an effort to put down popular resistance. Thousands of hostages were shot in the cities, whose population was drastically reduced by malnutrition, disease, unemployment, and general neglect. Ukrainian industry and natural resources were exploited to the utmost in accordance with Hermann Göring's injunction to "rob everything, and rob it effectively"; some 16,000 enterprises employing 2.3 million Ukrainian workers were pillaged and put out of commission. Agriculture was exploited even more thoroughly; in the first three months of the occupation alone, some 11.6 million food parcels were sent to Germany from Ukraine. Peasants were burdened with heavy taxes and forced to deliver produce on pain of severe punishment; the hated Soviet collective farms were kept in place to guarantee food supplies for the German war effort. Some 2.2 million slave laborers, designated as *Ostarbeiter*, were transported from Ukraine to Germany to work in agriculture and industry. Ukrainian cultural institutions were plundered on a massive scale, suffering damages of an estimated 11 billion *karbovantsi* (in 1940 prices). This was due less to vandalism than to organized theft; special German details confiscated, catalogued, and transported to Germany some 330,000 museum pieces, 120,000 books, and 11,500 runs of journals, among other cultural properties. Finally, the arrogance, thievery, and corruption that characterized the behavior of many rank-and-file German soldiers made them a despised presence in Ukraine.

The German occupation authorities were assisted by Ukrainian collaborators. The broadest category of these, known as *Hilfswillige*, were employed as support staff and guards and designated as the **Ukrainian Liberation Army**. In wartime conditions, such service was often the only alternative to starvation. The Ukrainian auxiliary police (whose ranks also included Russians, Belarusians, and members of Caucasian nationalities), numbering about 250,000, carried out the most odious tasks, guarding prisoners of war and rounding up **Jews** for execution. With the development of OUN resistance to the occupation, many policemen deserted to the nationalist underground. Late in 1944, hoping to involve Ukrainians in resisting the Red Army's advance, the Germans released the OUN leaders from prison and allowed the formation of a **Ukrainian National Committee** led by Gen. **Pavlo Shandruk**, but its planned participation in the war never materialized, not least because of Hitler's stubborn refusal to permit Slavs to bear weapons.

Soviet resistance to the invasion was slow to develop. Initially, Stalin and the Soviet leaders were totally at a loss; a state defense committee was put in place only eight days following the invasion and a commander in chief appointed on 10 July; Stalin's first public address of the war was delivered 12 days after the invasion. Soon afterward, the secret police began arresting and executing those on whom Stalin blamed the disaster, including Gen. Dmitrii Pavlov, commander of the Western front, and his staff. More than 75,000 servicemen, including many commanders, were arrested for "panic desertion." On 12 September, Stalin issued a secret order creating NKVD units behind Soviet lines to kill any serviceman attempting to desert. Stalin's order to hold Kyiv at all costs led to a military disaster, as the Germans surrounded and captured more than 450,000 troops; **Nikita Khrushchev**, whom Stalin accused of planning to surrender the city, had little choice but to promise an effective defense even though he lacked the resources to mount one.

The Soviet system of command administration, whose concentration of power in Stalin's hands was ultimately responsible for the disaster of 1941, was now called upon to save the country. It did so by squeezing every ounce of effort from a population that had no alternative but to resist the invaders. Civilians were mobilized to dig trenches and build defensive works that had not been prepared in advance, as Soviet military doctrine maintained that any war with Germany would be fought on foreign territory. Industrial equipment and personnel were evacuated from Ukraine on a vast scale and reinstalled behind the lines; almost half the new Soviet military-industrial complex operated with machinery from Ukraine. Half-starved, poorly housed, and working 14- and 16-hour days, often in appalling conditions, Soviet workers managed to outproduce the German war machine. A large contribution was made by prisoners of the GULAG, who died by the thousands as they supplied metal ores and built some 700 large defensive installations. These in turn were guarded by NKVD troops that were badly needed at the front.

Red Army soldiers fared no better than their civilian counterparts behind the lines. They were poorly equipped; often there was only one rifle, with 5–6 rounds of ammunition, for every two soldiers, who were constantly enjoined to capture weapons in battle. Rations were insufficient, and about one-quarter of the Red Army was chronically ill or frostbitten because of exposure. While equipment was prized and safeguarded, manpower was squandered recklessly; at the height of the fighting in Ukraine (January 1943 October 1944), Soviet losses averaged 68,000 per day. The badly organized crossing of the Dnipro to recapture Kyiv cost some 417,000 casualties—so many that military burial squads could not cope and had to enlist civilians to help them. In Ukraine alone, close to 250,000 16- and 17-year-old boys were mobilized and sent into battle as unarmed cannon fodder. The ever-vigilant secret police arrested the equivalent of a regiment per month for "desertion" and other crimes, executing those convicted or consigning them to punishment details and forced-labor camps. Red partisan detachments (*see* KOVPAK, SYDIR), consisting largely of Red Army soldiers who had managed to avoid capture, began to harass the Germans seriously in 1943; they numbered some 200,000—a figure that was arbitrarily tripled in Soviet historiography of the 1960s.

Ukraine was by far the most important East European front of World War II; almost half the Red Army was concentrated there in 1943–44, 607 Wehrmacht divisions were defeated there, and particularly fierce battles were waged in more than 100 settlements. More than 700 towns and 28,000 villages were partly or totally destroyed, leaving some 10 million people homeless. Ukraine was devastated by the scorched-earth policy of the retreating Soviet forces in 1941 and of the retreating Germans in 1943–44: it accounted for more than 40 percent of total Soviet war losses. Approximately 5,264,000 civilians and prisoners of war were killed by the invading Germans. Close to a million Jews from Ukraine perished in the Holocaust. Red Army losses in Ukraine totaled 3.5 million (of these, Ukrainians accounted for 50–70 percent). Tens of thousands of Ukrainians also served in various Allied armies.

In **eastern Ukraine**, the return of the Red Army was hailed as a liberation from three years of German depredations; moreover, there was widespread hope that the postwar Stalin regime would be less oppressive. Such hopes proved unavailing; as early as August 1941, Stalin and the General Staff of the Red Army signed order no. 270 (whose existence was not revealed until 1988), blaming the German breakthrough on the cowardice and desertion of commanding officers. They were to be shot without trial and their families to be treated as coresponsible for their "crimes." In May 1945, Stalin ordered the establishment of 100 inspection camps where returning prisoners of war were to be screened by Soviet counterintelligence; by December 1946, some 1,834,000 POWs (at least one-third of whom were Ukrainians) passed through these camps. Many were found unreliable and sentenced to years of hard labor or terms in the GULAG; not until 1956 did a government commission headed by Marshal Georgii Zhukov issue a secret order to make amends to these people, who were amnestied and released. Almost all those who had spent the war on occupied territory were regarded as traitors and punished accordingly; similar treatment was meted out to returning *Ostarbeiter*. In May 1944, there were mass deportations from the Crimea of ethnic groups accused of collaboration; more than 188,000 **Tatars**, 14,700 Greeks, 12,400 Bulgarians, and 8,500 Armenians were forcibly resettled. The postwar reconstruction of eastern Ukraine depended on the large-scale exploitation of virtually unpaid labor. In 1943–45, state contributions to reconstruction amounted to only 7 percent of the wartime damage inflicted on Ukraine. Close to a million workers were mobilized for reconstruction; in July and August 1944 alone, more than 30,000 were charged with criminal desertion of productive labor.

In western Ukraine, by contrast, the return of Soviet forces was met with determined resistance that amounted to a full-scale war until the late 1940s and continued sporadically until the mid-1950s. The **Ukrainian Insurgent Army** (UPA), dominated by the Bandera faction of the OUN and commanded by **Roman Shukhevych**, was originally formed in **Volhynia** in 1942 to counteract German depredations against the Ukrainian population; as the Germans began to retreat, it concentrated on harassing the advancing Soviet forces. The **Supreme Ukrainian Liberation Council** was formed in 1944 to coordinate the struggle. Having experienced the devastating Soviet occupation of 1939–41, the UPA and much of the western Ukrainian populace were determined to resist the reoccupation at all costs. Although the **Yalta Conference** (March 1945) appeared to confirm Soviet dominance in Eastern Europe, the onset of the Cold War raised OUN-UPA hopes of a conflict between the Western Allies and the USSR. UPA forces killed thousands of Soviet officials and collaborators; destroying the UPA in order to reimpose Soviet control of western Ukraine took a prolonged effort on the part of Red Army and NKVD troops, as well as Polish and Czechoslovak forces.

In geopolitical terms, the most important consequence of World War II for Ukraine was the unification of its ethnic territory. The **Ukrainian-Polish Conflict** of 1943–47, which was waged for control of territories settled mainly by Ukrainians but long ruled by Poland, resulted in tens of thousands of civilian casualties and a massive population transfer that removed the last major bone of contention between Poland and Ukraine. Northern Bukovyna, taken over in 1940, remained part of the **Ukrainian SSR**, and **Transcarpathia** was annexed in 1945. Thus there remained no Ukrainian irredenta that could serve as a base for anti-Soviet resistance. The Soviet authorities repatriated some 5.2 million displaced persons from Eastern Europe, largely by force, including many Ukrainians (who represented 52.6 percent of the total); initially the Western Allies sent refugees back to the USSR against their will. Ukraine also became a founding member of the **United Nations**, although it played no independent role there until after the collapse of the USSR.

A more general consequence of the war was that the Soviet dictatorship, unlike its Axis counterparts, emerged victorious. The USSR was among the powers that prosecuted Nazi war criminals at Nuremberg: its own prewar collaboration with Nazi Germany was studiously ignored, while the crimes of the Stalin regime went officially undocumented and unpunished. On the international scene, the victory greatly enhanced the status of the USSR, making it a world power with a network of satellites and client states. For decades, the authoritarian system reaped massive propaganda benefits from its wartime victory, which was presented at home and abroad as evidence of its efficiency, productivity, and dedication to democratic values. This served as a major rationale for keeping the system in place, leading to decades of stagnation.

In Ukraine, the legacy of the war remains divisive. While eastern Ukraine continues to commemorate 9 May as Victory Day, in western Ukraine it has become an occasion for remembering the anti-Soviet struggle of the OUN-UPA. In 1997, following demands from veterans and political groups to recognize the OUN-UPA as a patriotic organization, a government commission was formed to study its record. The commission's publications include two collections of memoranda from the Ukrainian public arguing both sides of the issue. The state of current opinion is well represented in the title of a monograph issued in 1999 by one of Ukraine's foremost specialists on the subject, the late historian Mykhailo Koval—*Ukraine in the Second World War and the Great Patriotic War (1939–1945)*.

Y

YAKOVENKO, NATALIA (b. 16 October 1942). Historian. Born in the village of Aprelivka in Kirovohrad oblast, Yakovenko studied at **Lviv** University, specializing initially in classical philology (she has published a Latin textbook for historians). Yakovenko obtained her doctorate in 1994, became head of the Institute of East European Research at the **Ukrainian Academy of Sciences** in 1995, and was appointed professor at the **Kyiv Mohyla Academy** National University, where she now heads the department of history. Yakovenko has specialized in the late medieval and early modern periods. Her initial years of archival research and publication of documentary sources prepared the way for her first monograph, *Ukraïns'ka shliakhta z kintsia XIV do seredyny XVII stolittia (Volyn' i Tsentral'na Ukraïna)* (The Ukrainian Nobility from the Late 14th to the Mid-17th Century: **Volhynia** and Central Ukraine, 1993). Not since the days of **Viacheslav Lypynsky** had a historian in Ukraine seriously studied the social elite, to which both the Soviet regime and the older **populist** tradition were hostile. Yakovenko went on to produce a survey of Ukrainian history to the end of the 18th century under the title *Narys istoriï Ukraïny z naidavnishykh chasiv do kintsia XVIII stolittia* (1997; a companion volume covering the later centuries was written by **Yaroslav Hrytsak**). In this work, based on the latest Ukrainian and Western research, Yakovenko declared her intention to go beyond not only Soviet and populist historical schemes but also the statist school associated with Lypynsky and his followers. Without neglecting distinctive features of the Ukrainian past, she proposed to coordinate its periodization with that of European history in general.

Yakovenko continued to challenge historical stereotypes in her collection of essays *Paralel'nyi svit* (The Parallel World, 2002), which focuses on early modern social views and ideas. Here she disputes the notion that Ukrainian and Polish nobles were polar opposites, noting that they held many political and cultural beliefs in common and shared a "warrior ethos." Yakovenko advances a differentiated view of the Ukrainian nobility, pointing out that the **princes** were fairly pragmatic in their view of conversion to Roman Catholicism, while the lesser nobles tended to remain Orthodox. The traditional view of Ukrainian nobles and **Cossacks** as fighters for religion and nationality is also challenged with counterexamples drawn from recent research.

In addition to her own writing, Yakovenko has pursued her goal of conceptual and methodological innovation in two influential journals; she was coeditor of *Mediaevalia Ucrainica* (1992–98), which concentrated on the history of ideas and mentalities, and in 1999 she founded *Ukraïns'kyi humanitarnyi ohliad* (Ukrainian Humanities Review), of which she remains editor in chief.

YALTA CONFERENCE. Diplomatic meeting of the "Big Three" Allied states held near Yalta in the **Crimea** from 4 to 11 February 1945. The delegations were headed by Joseph Stalin (**USSR**), Franklin D. Roosevelt (United States), and Winston Churchill (Great Britain). The conference considered the basic principles of the postwar settlement in Europe. Germany was to be occupied by the Allies (including France), denazified, and demilitarized. Stalin insisted that Germany's "dismemberment" be mentioned in the terms of surrender, as he feared that the Western Allies might otherwise collude with the Nazis to prevent a postwar Soviet presence in Germany. The question was referred to the Allied foreign ministers, and Stalin achieved his goal after the conference through the Soviet occupation of eastern Germany.

Concerning the Polish state—the most important East European question decided at the conference—the conference participants expressed their "common desire to see established a strong, free, independent and democratic Poland." Its eastern border was defined as the **Curzon Line**, with small deviations in favor of Poland. In the west, Poland was to receive significant territorial compensation at the expense of Germany. This settlement legitimized the Soviet annexation of **western Ukraine** and western Belarus according to the terms of the secret protocol to the Molotov-Ribbentrop Pact (1939). In determining Poland's political status, Roosevelt and Churchill agreed to Stalin's proposal that the communist government in Warsaw be "enlarged" with "democratic leaders" from the Polish emigration, which prevented the London-based Polish government-in-exile from returning to power. Stalin thus achieved his principal objectives in Eastern Europe—dominance over Poland and control of a significant part of Germany.

In order to prevail on the Polish issue, Stalin abandoned his previous demand that the USSR be given 16 votes in the proposed **United Nations** Organization, whose establishment was Roosevelt's major preoccupation. Stalin's new proposal, whereby the USSR, the **Ukrainian SSR**, and the Belarusian SSR would be given seats in the UN, was accepted by the Western Allies.

The conference adopted a "Declaration on Liberated Europe" that stressed the Allies' commitment to establish postwar governments "broadly representative of all democratic elements in the population" and consult with one another to that end. This diplomatic formula concealed a fundamental difference of opinion; within a few weeks after the conference, the Western Allies, interpreting democracy as political pluralism, were taken aback by Stalin's installation of Soviet-backed "democratic" governments in Eastern Europe. Consequently, during the Cold War, the Yalta conference was widely criticized in the West as a diplomatic fiasco that made possible the reduction of Eastern Europe to satellite status.

YANOVSKY, YURII (14 [27] August 1902–25 February 1954). Writer. Born on the Maierove estate (now in Kirovohrad oblast), Yanovsky graduated from the Yelysavethrad (now Kirovohrad) technical school (1919) and the **Kyiv** Polytechnical Institute (1922). He contributed to the development of the Ukrainian **film** industry, working as an editor at the **Odesa** film studio (1925–26). Subsequently he lived and worked in **Kharkiv** (1927–39) and Kyiv. Yanovsky's first poems began to appear in print in 1922 and were marked by extensive formal experimentation. In his first collections of novellas, *Mamutovi byvni* (The Mammoth's Tusks, 1925) and *Krov zemli* (Blood of the Earth, 1927), Yanovsky depicted the psychology of heroic, quasi-mythical characters. Along with **Mykola Khvyliovy**, Yanovsky was one of the most prominent neoromantics of the 1920s. The novel *Maister korablia* (The Figurehead, 1928), often considered his masterpiece, centers on his **romantic** obsession with the sea. The peasant insurgency of the **Ukrainian Revolution** (1917–21), as well as the tragedy of Ukrainian fratricide, was the primary theme of Yanovsky's novels *Chotyry shabli* (Four Sabers, 1931) and *Vershnyky* (The Horsemen, 1935).

During **World War II**, Yanovsky lived in Ufa, edited the journal *Ukraïns'ka literatura* (Ukrainian **Literature**, 1941–46, now *Vitchyzna* [Fatherland]), and served as a war correspondent. In 1945–46, he covered the Nuremberg trials, which inspired his *Lysty z Niurenberha* (Letters from Nuremberg). His outstanding postwar work is the novel *Zhyva voda* (Living Water, 1947), dealing with events in Ukraine in 1945, in which he depicted the Ukrainian nation reborn. The novel was harshly criticized by the authorities, and Yanovsky was accused of "nationalism." Under pressure from party censors, he reworked the novel, which was published posthumously as *Myr* (Peace, 1956).

YANUKOVYCH, VIKTOR (b. 9 July 1950). Twelfth prime minister of independent Ukraine. Doctor of economics (2001), professor, full member of the Academy of Economic Sciences of Ukraine. Yanukovych was born in the town of Yenakiieve, Donetsk oblast, into the family of a metalworker. Orphaned at the age of five, he was raised by his grandmother. The Yenakiieve court convicted Yanukovych of theft in 1967 and assault and battery in 1970, but both verdicts were overturned by the Donetsk oblast court for lack of evidence of criminal intent. In 1973, Yanukovych graduated from the Yenakiieve mining technical school, and in 1980, he earned a degree in mechanical engineering from the Donetsk Polytechnical Institute. Yanukovych began his career as a gas worker at the Yenakiieve Metal Works in 1969. Over the years, he advanced to executive positions in major enterprises, such as Donbas Transport Repair and Ukrainian Coal Industry Transport. In August 1996, Yanukovych was appointed deputy head of the Donetsk oblast administration; he was promoted to head of administration (i.e., governor of Donetsk oblast) in May 1997 and held the post until November 2002. He was a consistent supporter of President **Leonid Kuchma**.

Yanukovych is generally considered a representative of the powerful "Donetsk clan," headed by **Rinat Akhmetov**. The clan's resources and Akhmetov's lobbying secured Yanukovych's position as regional leader, and Kuchma appointed him prime minister on 21 November 2002. A leading contender for the presidency in 2004, he was defeated by **Viktor Yushchenko** (*see* INTRODUCTION) and resigned as prime minister on 31 December 2004.

YAROSLAV THE WISE (ca. 978–20 February 1054). Ruler of **Kyivan Rus'** and grand prince of **Kyiv** (1019–54). He was the son of **Volodymyr the Great** and Princess Rahneda (Rohnida) of Polatsk. During his father's lifetime, Yaroslav ruled Rostov and later Novgorod. In 1014, he refused to pay tribute to Kyiv, and only Volodymyr's death prevented a war. From 1015 to 1019, Yaroslav engaged in a struggle for the throne of Kyiv with his half-brother Sviatoslav, defeating him in battle on the Alta River. Yaroslav also fought his half-brother Mstyslav Volodymyrovych, prince of Tmutorokan (from 988). Yaroslav was defeated by Mstyslav at the Battle of Lystven (1024) and forced to cede Chernihiv and lands east of the Dnipro River. He reclaimed them only in 1036, after Mstyslav's death.

Under Yaroslav, the Kyivan state attained the height of its power and prestige. In 1030–31, the armies of Yaroslav and Mstyslav captured the Chervcn towns, which had been seized by Bolesław I of Poland in 1018. He formed an alliance with Casimir I of Poland by marrying his sister, Dobroniha, to Casimir and his eldest son, Iziaslav, to Casimir's sister. In 1031, he founded the city of Yaroslav (Jarosław) on the Sian River, which became the Kyivan state's western frontier outpost. Yaroslav conducted campaigns against the Ests (1030) and Yatvingians (1038), and in 1030 he founded the city of Yurev (now Tartu) on Lake Chud (Lake Peipus). He secured his southern border against nomadic raiders, building fortifications along the Sula, Stuhna, Ros, and Trubizh Rivers. In 1036, Rus' armies defeated the **Pechenegs** near Kyiv. To commemorate that victory, Yaroslav began the building of **St. Sophia's Cathedral** in 1037—part of an extensive construction program intended to rival the magnificence of Constantinople. In 1043, Yaroslav organized a campaign against Byzantium (the last initiated by a Kyivan prince) that ended in defeat.

During Yaroslav's reign, Kyivan Rus' maintained ties with Byzantium, Germany, Hungary, France, and the Scandinavian countries. Yaroslav established dynastic ties with many European rulers. He himself was married to Ingigerd, daughter of King Olaf of Sweden. Yaroslav's daughter Yelysaveta was married to Harald III of Norway, his daughter **Anna Yaroslavna** to Henry I of France, and his daughter Anastasia to Andrew I of Hungary. Yaroslav's reputation for wisdom is associated with his codification of Rus' law and promotion of learning. The oldest section of the ***Ruskaia Pravda*** (Rus' Justice) was compiled at Yaroslav's initiative. Christianity consolidated its dominance in the Kyivan state; in 1051, Yaroslav appointed **Ilarion** as metropolitan (the first native of Rus' to hold the office; *see* KYIV METROPOLITANATE). The first monasteries in Kyivan Rus' (St. George's, St. Irene's, and the **Kyivan Cave Monastery**) were founded during his reign. Yaroslav promoted the collection and copying of manuscripts, establishing the foundations of Kyivan learning. Seeking to end the internecine warfare that had plagued his reign, Yaroslav introduced a system of primogeniture (*see* LIUBECH CONGRESS OF PRINCES). He died in Vyshhorod and was buried at St. Sophia's Cathedral, where his marble sarcophagus has been preserved.

YAVORNYTSKY, DMYTRO (25 October [6 November] 1855–5 August 1940). Historian, archaeologist, ethnographer, folklorist, writer, and academician of the **Ukrainian Academy of Sciences** (from 1929). He was born in Sontsivka (now Borysivka, **Kharkiv**

oblast) into the family of the village deacon. Yavornytsky enrolled in the Kharkiv Theological Seminary (1874), which he did not complete. From 1877 to 1881, he studied at the faculty of history and philology of Kharkiv University. He was influenced by the philologists **Oleksander Potebnia** and **Mykola Sumtsov** and by the works of **Nikolai Gogol**.

Yavornytsky researched the history of the **Zaporozhian Cossacks** from his student years, despite an unofficial ban on the subject. At the site of the former Zaporozhian **Sich**, he collected archaeological, folkloric, ethnographic, and archival materials. Because of his **Ukrainophilism**, Yavornytsky was obliged to move to St. Petersburg (1885), where he was kept under surveillance. He taught history at a gymnasium while continuing to study the Zaporozhians. In 1892, he was exiled to Tashkent, where he studied the Central Asian peoples, publishing an archaeological and historical guide on the subject (1893).

From the autumn of 1896, Yavornytsky taught history at Moscow University. In this period he published *Istoriia zaporozhskikh kazakov* (History of the Zaporozhian Cossacks, 1892–97), a three-volume account of his work on the subject, followed by a two-volume collection of sources on Cossack history (1903). Yavornytsky also published a collection of Ukrainian songs that he had gathered in the course of three decades (1906) and contributed to **Borys Hrinchenko's** Ukrainian dictionary, issuing a supplement to it in 1920. Every summer, Yavornytsky conducted archaeological digs and ethnographic expeditions in Ukraine, particularly in Zaporizhia. In 1902, he was invited to head the newly established Katerynoslav Regional Museum of History. Supplementing the museum's collection with materials from his expeditions, as well as donated and acquired items (manuscripts, paintings, weapons, Zaporozhian clothing, and the like), Yavornytsky created a unique collection of the material culture of Zaporizhia and southern Ukraine, numbering some 75,000 artifacts. From 1920 to 1933, he also worked at the Katerynoslav (Dnipropetrovsk) Institute of People's Education, where he headed the department of Ukrainian studies. From 1927 to 1932, he directed the work of the Dnipro Hydroelectric Station archaeological expedition in the area scheduled for flooding. He published a large collection of historical sources, *Do istoriï Stepovoï Ukraïny* (On the History of Steppe Ukraine, 1929), as well as ethnographic studies of the region. When the Stalin regime unleashed its **political terror**, Yavornytsky was accused of idealizing the Cossacks and of "bourgeois nationalism." Dismissed from his post, he was forbidden to engage in scholarship. He died in 1940 and was buried near the historical museum that now bears his name. A memorial museum was opened in his Dnipropetrovsk home in 1946.

Yavornytsky published more than 200 research studies and a number of literary works. He was as much a popularizer as a scholar, which led specialists to criticize his publications. His works inspired many Ukrainian artists, composers, and poets, and the cultural revival of the 1980s–90s led to an upsurge of interest in his writings. In 1995, a bronze monument to Yavornytsky was erected at his gravesite.

YAVORSKY, MATVII (28 November 1884–3 November 1937). Historian. Born in Korchmyn, **Galicia**, into a **peasant** family, he graduated from the faculty of law of **Lviv** University (1910) and studied at Vienna University. In 1912, he was awarded a doctorate in political science. During **World War I**, Yavorsky was a second lieutenant in the Austrian army. In 1917, he became a translator on the staff of the Austrian military representative to the **Ukrainian Central Rada**. Later he worked for the government of Hetman **Pavlo Skoropadsky**. In November 1918, following the establishment of the **Western Ukrainian People's Republic**, Yavorsky returned to Galicia. He was among the officers of the **Ukrainian Galician Army** who planned its defection to the Red Army and became director of the political school for Red Army officers in **Kyiv**. He traveled to Moscow and then to Kazan, where he joined the Bolshevik Party. In August 1920, Yavorsky returned to Ukraine, where he lectured at the Institute of People's Education and the Central Party School in **Kharkiv**. From December 1922, he worked at the Ukrainian University of Marxism and Marx Studies in Kharkiv. In 1924, Yavorsky was appointed deputy director of the Administration of Scholarly Institutions in Ukraine (Ukrnauka), serving as its acting director from 1926 to 1929. An organizer of the Ukrainian Society of Marxist Historians, he was the first historian to put forward an interpretation of Ukrainian history based on Marxist methodological foundations.

Yavorsky wrote the first Ukrainian Marxist history textbooks: *Narys istoriï Ukraïny* (Outline History of Ukraine, 2 vols., 1923–24), *Korotka istoriia Ukraïny* (Short History of Ukraine, 1927), and *Istoriia Ukraïny u styslomu narysi* (The History of Ukraine in Concise Outline, 1928–29). He also wrote *Ukraïna v epokhu kapitalizmu* (Ukraine in the Epoch of Capitalism, 3 vols., 1924–25), *Narysy z istoriï revoliutsiinoï borot'by na Ukraïni* (Sketches of the History of the Revolutionary Struggle in Ukraine, 2 vols., 1928–29), and numerous articles for specialized journals. He led the campaign against "Ukrainian bourgeois historiography," which was primarily directed against **Mykhailo Hrushevsky**. In 1928, Yavorsky was awarded a doctorate in history on the basis of his published works. He was elected a full member of the **Ukrainian Academy of Sciences** in 1929.

Beginning in 1928, when Stalin took power, even Marxist interpretations of Ukrainian history were proscribed for contributing to a distinct Ukrainian identity. Yavorsky was criticized by Russian Marxist historians, notably Mikhail Pokrovsky, for "nationalist distortion." He was accused of replacing the class-struggle approach with a "formalist nationalist" method and depicting the history of Ukraine as a "distinct process" (i.e., separate from Russian history). Yavorsky was also criticized for exaggerating the importance of the Ukrainian bourgeoisie, treating non-Bolshevik Ukrainian socialists as revolutionaries, and minimizing the activities of the Bolsheviks in Ukraine prior to the October Revolution. The campaign against *yavorshchyna* (Yavorskyism) was employed to destroy Ukrainian historiography in the **Ukrainian SSR**. In February 1930, Yavorsky was expelled from the party and dismissed from his position at the Academy of Sciences. He subsequently moved to Leningrad and was arrested in March 1931. In 1932, he was accused of participating in the fictitious Ukrainian National Center and sentenced to six years' imprisonment on the Solovets Islands. During his incarceration, Yavorsky condemned the Communist Party and Stalin for their policies, particularly toward Ukraine. He was accused of creating an underground organization at the prison camp and executed.

YAZYCHIIE. Derogatory term for the **language** used by **Russophiles** in the **western Ukrainian** lands (**Galicia**, **Bukovyna**, and **Transcarpathia**) in the late 19th and early 20th centuries. The Russophiles proclaimed the ethnic, cultural, and linguistic unity of Ukrainians and Russians. *Yazychiie* was based on Church Slavonic with elements of Russian but also incorporated Ukrainianisms and Polonisms and used Ukrainian pronunciation. It fell out of use around the turn of the century, after Russophile publications switched to standard literary Russian.

YEFREMOV, SERHII (6 [18] October 1876–31 March 1939). Literary historian, academician of the **Ukrainian Academy of Sciences** (from 1919), full member of the **Shevchenko Scientific Society** (from 1923), and political figure. He was born in the village of Palchyk in the **Kyiv** region into the family of a priest. From 1891 to 1896 he studied at the Kyiv Theological Seminary, then graduated from the law faculty of Kyiv University. In 1904, Yefremov became a cofounder of the Ukrainian Radical Party and helped initiate the merger that produced the **Ukrainian Democratic Radical Party**. He was a leading member of the **Society of Ukrainian Progressives** (est. 1908). Yefremov contributed to many Ukrainian periodicals, such as *Kievskaia starina* (Kyivan Antiquity), ***Literaturno-naukovyi visnyk***, *Pravda* (Truth), *Hromads'ka dumka* (Civic Thought), and *Rada*, publishing articles on **literature** and current affairs. He was twice incarcerated by the Russian authorities for his articles in defense of Ukrainian culture and political freedom. In 1917, he was elected vice chairman of the **Ukrainian Central Rada** and became its secretary for interethnic affairs. From September 1917, he headed the **Ukrainian Party of Socialist Federalists**. After the Bolshevik Revolution, Yefremov became preoccupied with establishing a national front against the Bolsheviks and remained an uncompromising opponent of Soviet rule to the end of his life. When Soviet forces took Kyiv, Yefremov went into hiding but was amnestied at the request of the Ukrainian Academy of Sciences. As vice president of the academy (1922–28) and head of its executive (1924–28), he accomplished a great deal of organizational and scholarly work, heading commissions in charge of publishing major works of modern Ukrainian literature, compiling a Ukrainian biographical dictionary, augmenting and publishing **Borys Hrinchenko's** dictionary of the Ukrainian language, and the like. With the onset of Stalin's **political terror**, Yefremov was barred from all further work at the academy in 1928. On 21 July 1929, he was arrested in connection with the show trial of the **Union for the Liberation of Ukraine**, which he was accused of heading, and sentenced to 10 years' solitary confinement. He died in a GULAG camp.

A **populist** and an inveterate opponent of **modernism**, Yefremov regarded the idea of national liberation as the leitmotif of Ukrainian **literature**. His influential *Istoriia ukraïns'koho pys'menstva* (History of Ukrainian Literature) appeared in 1911 (4th ed., 1924). Yefremov published monographs on **Taras Shevchenko** (1914), **Ivan Franko** (1913; 2d ed. 1926), **Mykhailo Kotsiubynsky** (1922), Ivan Nechui-Levytsky, Ivan Karpenko-Kary (both 1924), Panas Myrny (1928), and others. In 1927–28, he edited and published Shevchenko's diary and correspondence. Yefremov's diaries for 1923–29, published in 1997, are an important source on the period.

YURII II BOLESLAV (BOLESŁAW TROJDENOWICZ) (ca. 1306–7 April 1340). Prince of **Galicia-Volhynia** (1323–40). The son of a Polish prince, Trojden II of Mazovia, and Maria, a descendant of the Romanovych princes, he was elected prince of Volhynia by its **boyars** in 1323. Initially a Catholic, he converted to Orthodoxy and adopted the name Yurii. Attempting to oppose the expansion of Poland and Hungary, he maintained good relations with the Teutonic Order and married the daughter of Grand Prince Gediminas of Lithuania. He supported colonization by German settlers and introduced **Magdeburg law** in Sianik (Sanok) in 1339. These actions reduced the power of the boyars, who conspired against Yurii and poisoned him in Volodymyr. Yurii II was the last representative of the Romanovych dynasty, and soon after his death, Galicia-Volhynia lost its independence.

YUSHCHENKO, VIKTOR (b. 23 February 1954). Tenth prime minister and third president of independent Ukraine. Yushchenko was born in the village of Khoruzhivka, Sumy oblast, into the family of a teacher. He studied accounting at the Ternopil Financial and Economic Institute (1970–75). He earned the degree of candidate of sciences in 1998 and won a state prize in science and technology (1999). Yushchenko began his career as an economist at a collective farm in Ternopil oblast. From 1977 to 1985, he headed a branch of the **Ukrainian SSR** State Bank in the township of Ulianivka, Sumy oblast. He then worked as a deputy department head in the State Bank itself (1985–87).

In 1987, Yushchenko moved to Agroprombank, headed by **Vadym Hetman**, who became an active patron of Yushchenko's financial and political career. In January 1989, Yushchenko became deputy chairman of the board of Agroprombank and, three years later, when it was reorganized as the Ukraina Agroindustrial Bank, he was appointed first deputy chairman. Only a few weeks after Hetman became head of the National Bank of Ukraine, Yushchenko succeeded him as chairman of the Ukraina Bank. In December 1993, Hetman resigned his post and proposed Yushchenko as his successor. Despite gloomy economic prospects, Yushchenko launched a program of reform at the National Bank. He successfully implemented a currency reform in 1996, introducing the *hryvnia* (and was later credited with maintaining its stability during the Russian ruble crisis of 1998).

Yushchenko was appointed prime minister on 22 December 1999. During his tenure, Ukraine experienced economic growth of 5.5 percent after nine years of consistent decline, gaining approval from the International Monetary Fund and the World Bank. The Yushchenko government's ambitious reform program was approved by the **Verkhovna Rada** (VR) on 17 April 2000. The government improved tax-collection policies in order to pay arrears of pensions and wages and sought to eliminate corruption and tax evasion in the energy sector. These actions aroused opposition to Yushchenko and his key ministers among powerful "oligarchs" in profitable sectors of the economy. In January 2001, Deputy Prime Minister **Yuliia Tymoshenko**, who was in charge of energy reform, was arrested, dismissed from office by President **Leonid Kuchma**, and imprisoned on charges of fraud and embezzlement. Yushchenko's former first deputy at the National Bank, Volodymyr Bondar, was detained in March 2001 and indicted for malfeasance involving loss of state funds deposited with a Cyprus-based bank. Yushchenko termed the case a "settlement of political scores." His government fell under the pressure of an ad hoc coalition in the VR, which forced a vote of nonconfidence on 26 May 2001.

In 2002, Yushchenko headed the Our Ukraine electoral bloc, which took 23.6 percent of the vote and came first in the parliamentary election that year, forming an opposition in the VR. Yushchenko was subsequently criticized for failing to confront President Kuchma and the "oligarchic" parties on such issues as the appointment of **Viktor Yanukovych** as prime minister in 2002 and the dispatch of Ukrainian troops to Iraq in 2003. Nevertheless, his reform program and charismatic personality made Yushchenko a leading candidate in the 2004 presidential election. He won the presidency as a result of the Orange Revolution (*see* INTRODUCTION) and was inaugurated on 23 January 2005.

Z

ZABOLOTNY, DANYLO (16 [28] December 1866–15 December 1929). Microbiologist and epidemiologist, full member of the **Ukrainian Academy of Sciences** (VUAN) from 1922 and its president in 1928–29, and full member of the **USSR** Academy of Sciences from 1929. Born in Chobotarka, **Podilia** gubernia (now Zabolotne in Vinnytsia oblast), he studied physics and mathematics at **Odesa** University and medicine at **Kyiv** University. He founded and directed a number of medical facilities, including the first bacteriological department in the Russian Empire at the St. Petersburg Women's Medical Institute (1898), the world's first epidemiology department at Odesa University (1920), and the VUAN Institute of Microbiology and Virology (1928). Zabolotny's research advanced the study of plague, cholera, syphilis, gangrene, diphtheria, typhus, and dysentery. With Ivan Savchenko, he discovered bacilli-carrying and vibrio cholera (1893), proving that plague-causing bacteria are transmitted to humans by wild rodents (1911). Zabolotny was a cofounder of the International Society of Microbiologists.

ZALIZNIAK, MAKSYM (b. early 1740s, d. ?). Leader of the **Koliivshchyna Rebellion** (1768) against Polish rule in **Right-Bank Ukraine**.

He was born in Medvedivka in the Chyhyryn region. From the age of 13, after the death of his father, he lived at the **Zaporozhian Sich**. The actions of the Confederation of Bar in **Podilia**, the **Kyiv** region, and **Volhynia**, including the abuse and plunder of the Ukrainian population, spawned a rebellion against the Poles led by Zalizniak. In the spring of 1768, he gathered a **haidamaka** unit in Kholodnyi Yar, near Chyhyryn, that began fighting the Polish nobility in late May. It soon captured Zhabotyn, Smila, Cherkasy, Kaniv, Korsun, Lysianka, Bohuslav, and Moshny. On 9–10 (20–21) June 1768, Zalizniak's rebels and a **Cossack** unit commanded by **Ivan Gonta** captured Uman and massacred its Polish and **Jewish** inhabitants. The rebels declared Zalizniak **hetman** and prince of Smila. The haidamaka movement engulfed the Kyiv and Bratslav palatinates, where the rebels introduced a Cossack administration. Alarmed by the rebellion's growth, the Russian government ordered its forces, which were fighting the confederates, to help the Polish army crush the rebellion. On 27 June (8 July), Zalizniak and Gonta were seized near Uman. The Russian command sentenced Zalizniak to flogging, branding, and a life sentence of hard labor in Nerchinsk, where he died. Zalizniak was celebrated as a fighter for Ukrainian liberty in songs and poems, including works by **Taras Shevchenko**.

ZAPOROZHIAN HOST/VIIS'KO ZAPOROZ'KE. First **Cossack** army, established in the mid-16th century below the rapids (*za porohamy*) of the Dnipro River (*see* **VYSHNEVETSKY, DMYTRO**). It constituted a semiautonomous entity on the borderlands of the **Polish-Lithuanian Commonwealth**. In 1572, some of the Zaporozhian Cossacks were recruited by Sigismund II Augustus of Poland for the defense of the southern borders against Ottoman and Crimean **Tatar** attacks. The number of **registered Cossacks** in the king's service changed frequently (from 300 men in 1572 to 8,000 in 1638–39). These registered Cossacks were referred to as the Zaporozhian Host. However, thousands of unregistered Cossacks—runaway serfs, burghers, impoverished gentry, and adventurers of various backgrounds—who chose to live at the Zaporozhian **Sich** were also known as the Zaporozhian Host. The Zaporozhians of the Lower Dnipro, who took part in several major **Cossack rebellions** against Poland, conducted raids and wars against the Tatars and Ottoman Turks, Poland, Muscovy, and **Moldavia**. After the **Khmelnytsky Uprising** (1648), the Zaporozhians helped shape the political outlook, symbols, and organizational structure of a new Cossack polity, the **Hetmanate**. The Zaporozhian Host, which increasingly found itself at odds with the better-established and more conservative leadership of the Hetmanate, continued to exist as a borderland Cossack republic that was finally destroyed by Russian imperial forces in 1775.

ZAPOROZHIAN SICH. *See* SICH.

ZARYTSKA, KATERYNA (5 November 1914–29 August 1986). Political activist. Born near Zbarazh in the Ternopil region, she was the daughter of a mathematician. A member of the **Organization of Ukrainian Nationalists** (OUN), Zarytska participated in planning the assassination of Bronisław Pieracki, Poland's minister of internal affairs (1934), and helped his assassin, Hryhorii Matseiko, escape to Czechoslovakia. Tried in 1936, she was sentenced to eight years' imprisonment. With the outbreak of **World War II**, Zarytska regained her freedom and married **Mykhailo Soroka**, who later became well known for organizing an OUN underground in Soviet concentration camps. In 1943–44, Zarytska organized the underground Red Cross attached to the **Ukrainian Insurgent Army**. Arrested by the Soviet secret police in October 1947, she was sentenced in 1949 to 25 years' imprisonment. Until 1969, she was held at Verkhneuralsk and Vladimir, then at the Mordovian forced-labor camps. After her release, Zarytska was denied permission to live in **Galicia** and settled in Volochysk, Khmelnytskyi oblast. She died in **Lviv**. On 28 September 1991, the reburial of Zarytska's and Soroka's remains took place at the Lychakiv Cemetery in Lviv.

ZATONSKY, VOLODYMYR (27 July [8 August] 1888–29 July 1938). Bolshevik leader. He was born in Lysets, **Podilia** gubernia (now in Khmelnytskyi oblast), graduated from the department of physics and mathematics at **Kyiv** University (1912), and taught physics at the Kyiv Polytechnical Institute (from 1913). Zatonsky joined the Russian Social Democratic Labor Party in 1905. Along with **Georgii Piatakov**, he was a Bolshevik representative in the **Ukrainian Central Rada** and the Regional Committee for the Defense of the Revolution in Ukraine (1917). Zatonsky was commissar for **education** in the **Provisional Workers' and Peasants' Government of Ukraine** and head of the Bolshevik Central Executive Committee in Ukraine (March-April 1918), as well as a leading organizer of the **Communist Party of Ukraine** (CPU). In early 1920, he was responsible for reorganizing and expanding the Red **Ukrainian Galician Army**. He became a prominent official in the 1920s, serving as head of the Galician Revolutionary Committee (July-September 1920), people's commissar for education of the **Ukrainian SSR** (1922–23 and 1933–38, following the suicide of **Mykola Skrypnyk**), and a member of the CC CPU Politburo.

Zatonsky also edited the major literary journal *Chervonyi shliakh* (Red Path, 1926–30). A follower of the party line, he gave limited support to **Ukrainization**. In the purge of 1937–38, he and his wife were executed by the secret police.

ZLENKO, ANATOLII (b. 2 June 1938). Diplomat. Zlenko was born in the township of Stavyshche, **Kyiv** oblast. In 1959, he graduated from the Kyiv Mining College and began to work as a foreman at the Maksymivka-Poloha coal mine in Kadiivka. In 1967, he graduated from Kyiv University. For six years after graduation, Zlenko served as attaché and then as second secretary of the international organizations department at the Ministry of Foreign Affairs of the **Ukrainian SSR**. From March 1973, he was a staff member of the **United Nations** (UN) Educational, Scientific, and Cultural Organization (UNESCO) Secretariat in Paris. Upon returning to Kyiv in 1979, he became a counsellor in the UNESCO division of the international organizations department. From 1983 to 1987, Zlenko held the post of permanent representative of the Ukrainian SSR to UNESCO.

Zlenko served as deputy minister of foreign affairs from April 1987, becoming first deputy minister two years later. In July 1990, he was appointed minister of foreign affairs. During his tenure, Ukraine took its first steps toward renouncing **nuclear weapons**. In May 1992, Zlenko headed the Ukrainian delegation at disarmament negotiations in Lisbon, resulting in the signing of the Lisbon Protocol, which made Ukraine a party to the START Treaty. In February 1994, Zlenko signed Ukraine's Partnership for Peace agreement with the North Atlantic Treaty Organization (NATO). After the election of President **Leonid Kuchma** in 1994, Zlenko was replaced as foreign minister by **Hennadii Udovenko**.

Subsequently, Zlenko served as Ukraine's permanent representative to the UN (September 1994–September 1997) and as ambassador to France (1997–2000) and to Portugal (1998–2000). In this period, he also resumed his role as Ukraine's permanent representative to UNESCO. On 2 October 2000, following the dismissal of **Borys Tarasiuk**, President Kuchma reappointed Zlenko minister of foreign affairs. In September 2002, when the United States accused Ukraine of selling Kolchuga radar systems to Iraq in violation of UN sanctions, Zlenko actively rebutted the charge at the UN, NATO, and other international forums, seeking to avoid the diplomatic isolation of Ukraine. He resigned his office in September 2003, having attained retirement age. Since October 2003, Zlenko has served as a presidential advisor on international issues and as Ukraine's representative to the UN Commission on Human Rights.

ZVIAHILSKY, YUKHYM (b. 20 February 1933). Fourth prime minister of independent Ukraine; prominent politician and businessman. He was born into the family of a civil servant in Donetsk. In 1956, Zviahilsky graduated from the Donetsk Industrial Institute as a mining engineer. He earned his candidate of sciences degree from the Moscow Mining Institute and completed doctoral studies at the Institute of Geotechnical Mechanics, **Ukrainian Academy of Sciences**. Having begun his career in the coal-mining industry as an assistant section manager in Donetsk (1957), Zviahilsky was promoted to section manager, head engineer, and then head of Mine no. 13. From June 1970, he was in charge of the Kuibyshev Mining Authority in Donetsk, and from 1979 to 1992, he was director of the Zasiadko Mine in the same city. In the March 1990 elections, Zviahilsky's popularity among Donetsk miners and the great resources under his control secured him a seat in the **Verkhovna Rada** (VR). Two years later, he became mayor of Donetsk.

In early 1993, when the socially devastating impact of Prime Minister **Leonid Kuchma's** market reforms led to a mass miners' strike, Zviahilsky was their greatest advocate. In June, he was appointed first deputy prime minister to deal with the strike, and after Kuchma's resignation in September, Zviahilsky was acting prime minister (until June 1994). He was reelected to the VR in 1994, but accusations of corruption and illegal economic activity during his tenure as acting prime minister forced him to leave Ukraine. From November 1994 to March 1997, Zviahilsky lived in Israel. In 1995, the prosecutor-general of Ukraine opened an investigation of Zviahilsky's activities. Zviahilsky's mandate as deputy to the VR was suspended. In 1997, the prosecutor-general closed the investigation for lack of evidence. Following this decision, Zviahilsky returned to Ukraine and was reappointed head of the Zasiadko Mine. He was reelected to the VR in 1998 and 2002. In April 1999, Zviahilsky became copresident of the **Jewish Confederation of Ukraine**. In 2003, President Kuchma honored him with the title of Hero of Ukraine.

Bibliography

Contents

Introduction

I. GENERAL
    1. Bibliographies and Dictionaries
    2. Encyclopedias and Interdisciplinary Works
    3. Descriptions, Guidebooks, and Travel
    4. Internet Sites

II. CULTURAL
    1. Art and Architecture
    2. Literary History, Linguistics, Language Textbooks, and Literature
        a. Literary History and Theory
        b. Linguistics, Language Politics
        c. Language Textbooks
        d. Literature
            (1) Prose, Criticism
            (2) Poetry
    3. Performing Arts
        a. Music
        b. Theater
        c. Film

III. ECONOMIC

IV. HISTORICAL
    1. General
    2. Historiography
    3. Archaeology and Early History
    4. Medieval History
    5. Cossackdom and the Hetmanate
    6. Ukraine under Russian and Austrian Rule

	7. Western Ukraine, 1918–53
	8. The Ukrainian Revolution, 1917–21
	9. Ukraine under Soviet Rule (General Works)
	10. Interwar Ukraine under Soviet Rule
	11. Ukraine in World War II
	12. Ukraine, 1945–91

V. JURIDICAL

VI. POLITICAL
	1. General
	2. Ethnic Minorities, Crimean Affairs
	3. Foreign Policy
	4. Nuclear Weapons
	5. Security Studies

VII. SCIENTIFIC
	1. General
	2. Demography, Ecology

VIII. SOCIAL
	1. Anthropology and Ethnology
	2. Education
	3. Health, Social Welfare
	4. Diaspora, Ukrainian Minorities
	5. Sociology
	6. Religion
	7. Philosophy, Intellectual Life

Introduction

With very few exceptions, the present bibliography is limited to English-language publications. Histories of Ukraine began to appear in English during the 1930s, as the looming conflict between Nazi Germany and the Soviet Union attracted public attention to Eastern Europe. In the decades following World War II, an extensive literature on Ukraine appeared in the West, produced largely by Ukrainian émigrés and scholars of Ukrainian descent. Since Ukraine's declaration of independence in 1991, it has attracted the attention of Western scholars—many of them non-Ukrainian—in a variety of disciplines.

The reader seeking a brief scholarly outline of Ukrainian history may turn to "History of Ukraine" by Orest Subtelny and Arkadii Zhukovsky in the *Encyclopedia of Ukraine*, vol. 2 (Toronto, 1988), pp. 161–93. Recent book-length introductions to Ukraine are Andrew Wilson, *The Ukrainians: Unexpected Nation*, 2d ed. (New Haven, Conn., 2002) and Anna Reid, *Borderland* (London, 1997). A useful German-language survey of Ukrainian history is Andreas Kappeler's *Kleine Geschichte der Ukraine*, 2d ed. (Munich, 2000); the first edition was translated into French as *Petite histoire de l'Ukraine* (Paris, 1997). Also noteworthy is Kappeler's *The Russian Empire: A Multiethnic History*, trans. Alfred Clayton (Harlow, 2001).

Two full-length histories of Ukraine (with extensive bibliographies) have recently appeared in English: Orest Subtelny, *Ukraine: A History*, 3d ed. (Toronto, 2000), and Paul R. Magocsi, *A History of Ukraine* (Toronto, 1996). Ivan L. Rudnytsky's *Essays in Modern Ukrainian History* (Edmonton and Toronto, 1987) have proved influential in Ukraine and abroad. For an English-language treatment of historical writing about Ukraine, the reader may consult Dmytro Doroshenko, *A Survey of Ukrainian Historiography*, supplemented for the period 1917–56 by Olexander Ohloblyn (New York, 1957), as well as two monographs by Stephen Velychenko, *National History as Cultural Process: A Survey of the Interpretations of Ukraine's Past in Polish, Russian, and Ukrainian Historical Writing from the Earliest Times to 1914* (Edmonton and Toronto, 1992), and *Shaping Identity in Eastern Europe and Russia: Soviet-Russian and Polish Accounts of Ukrainian History, 1914–1991* (New York, 1993). Nineteenth-century Ukrainian historiography is discussed in *Historiography of Imperial Russia: The Profession and Writing of History in a Multinational State*, ed. Thomas Sanders (Armonk, N.Y., 1999).

Historical maps are available in Magocsi's *Ukraine: A Historical Atlas*, cartography by Geoffrey J. Matthews, revised ed. (Toronto, 1987), and his *Historical Atlas of Central Europe* (Seattle, 2002).

For annotated bibliographic guides, see Bohdan S. Wynar, ed., *Ukraine: A Bibliographic Guide to English-language Publications* (Englewood, Colo., 1990); idem, ed., *Independent Ukraine: A Bibliographic Guide to English-language Publications, 1989–1999* (Englewood, Colo., 2000). Online addenda to the latter work are available at http://www.lu.com/lu/ukrain-updates.htm.

Most subjects discussed in this dictionary are treated in detail in the six-volume *Encyclopedia of Ukraine* (Toronto, 1984–2001), augmented since 2001 by an Internet version (www.encyclopediaofukraine.com)—the most important reference work on Ukraine in English. Like its predecessor, the two-volume *Concise Encyclopaedia of Ukraine* (Toronto, 1963–71), the *EU* is based on the Ukrainian-language *Entsyklopediia ukraïnoznavstva* (Munich, 1949–95), published in 14 volumes by the

Shevchenko Scientific Society. The *Ukraïns'ka radians'ka entsyklopediia* (Ukrainian Soviet Encyclopedia), published in Kyiv in two editions (18 vols., 1959–68; 12 vols., 1977–85), was in part a response to the émigré *EU*. The four-volume *Radians'ka entsyklopediia istoriï Ukraïny* (Soviet Encyclopedia of the History of Ukraine; Kyiv, 1972) was the major Soviet-era compendium on the subject. Following Ukraine's declaration of independence, a three-volume *Dovidnyk z istoriï Ukraïny* (Handbook of Ukrainian History; Kyiv, 1993–99; revised one-volume ed., Kyiv, 2001) appeared under the editorship of Ihor Pidkova and Roman Shust. In 2001, the *Entsyklopediia suchasnoï Ukraïny* (Encyclopedia of Contemporary Ukraine), whose editorial board is headed by Ivan Dziuba, began publication in Kyiv.

Postindependence Ukraine has witnessed an explosion of publishing on historical subjects, involving both the reissue of previously banned publications and writing based on newly accessible archives and publications. A 15-volume series titled *Ukraïna kriz' viky* (Ukraine through the Ages), edited by Valerii Smolii, the director of the Institute of Ukrainian History, National Academy of Sciences of Ukraine, was issued in 1998–99 by the Al'ternatyvy publishing house in Kyiv. Featuring contributions by some of Ukraine's leading historians and intended for a broad audience, it is the most extensive postindependence synthesis of Ukrainian history published to date. An important two-volume work based on recent scholarship and Western historical paradigms, *Narys istoriï Ukraïny* (Outline History of Ukraine), was issued in 1996–97 by the Heneza publishing house in Kyiv. The first volume, by Natalia Yakovenko, covers the subject from the earliest times to the late 18th century; the second, by Yaroslav Hrytsak, brings the account up to the postindependence period. Polish translations of these volumes were issued in 2000 by the Institute of East-Central Europe in Lublin; as of this writing, they are not available in English.

A comprehensive English-language guide to Ukrainian archives is Patricia K. Grimsted, *Archives and Manuscript Repositories in the USSR: Ukraine and Moldavia*, Book 1, *General Bibliography and Institutional Directory* (Princeton, N.J., 1988). This should be supplemented with her recent *Trophies of War and Empire: The Archival Heritage of Ukraine, World War II, and the International Politics of Restitution* (Cambridge, Mass., 2001), which takes account of archival reorganization since the fall of the Soviet Union. Yury Boshyk's *Guide to the Archival and Manuscript Collection of the Ukrainian Academy of Arts and Sciences in the U.S., New York City: A Detailed Inventory* (Edmonton: Canadian Institute of Ukrainian Studies Press, Research Report no. 30, 1988) describes the most important Ukrainian archive outside Ukraine. The Shevchenko Scientific Society also maintains a library and archive at its New York

City headquarters (described on the Internet at www.shevchenko.org). Other archives are held at the Harvard Ukrainian Research Institute (www.huri.harvard.edu), the Library and Archives of Canada in Ottawa (www.archives.ca), the Ukrainian Cultural and Educational Centre of Winnipeg (www.oseredok.org), and the Canadian Institute of Ukrainian Studies in Edmonton (www.ualberta.ca/ARCHIVES).

A detailed analysis of present-day Ukrainian politics is presented in Bohdan Harasymiw, *Post-Communist Ukraine* (Edmonton and Toronto, 2002), and in Paul D'Anieri, Robert Kravchuk, and Taras Kuzio, *Politics and Society in Ukraine* (Boulder, Colo., 1999). A recent monograph by Roman Wolczuk offers a comprehensive review of *Ukraine's Foreign and Security Policy, 1991–2000* (New York, 2003). Relations with Russia are covered in Roman Szporluk, *Russia, Ukraine, and the Breakup of the Soviet Union* (Stanford, Calif., 2000), and Roman Solchanyk, *Ukraine and Russia: The Post-Soviet Transition* (Lanham, Md., 2001), and relations with Poland in Kataryna Wolczuk and Roman Wolczuk, *Poland and Ukraine: A Strategic Partnership in a Changing Europe?* (London, 2002). For a survey of economic developments, see King Banaian, *The Ukrainian Economy since Independence* (Aldershot, 1999).

Ukrainian literature is surveyed at length in Dmytro Čyževs'kyj, *A History of Ukrainian Literature (From the 11th to the End of the 19th Century)*, ed. George S. N. Luckyj, 2d ed. (New York, 1997). George G. Grabowicz offers a critical evaluation of this work in his *Toward a History of Ukrainian Literature* (Cambridge, Mass., 1981). Subsequent literary developments are discussed in George Luckyj's *Ukrainian Literature in the Twentieth Century: A Reader's Guide* (Toronto, 1992). On the Ukrainian language, the reader may consult George Y. Shevelov's magisterial *Historical Phonology of the Ukrainian Language* (Heidelberg, 1979). Shevelov also gave an account of *The Ukrainian Language in the First Half of the Twentieth Century, 1900–1941* (Cambridge, Mass., 1989). A widely used language textbook is Assya Humesky, *Modern Ukrainian*, 3d ed. (Edmonton and Toronto, 1999). English-Ukrainian dictionaries are listed in the "Bibliographies and Dictionaries" section below. The most comprehensive dictionary of the Ukrainian language is the 11-volume *Slovnyk ukraïns'koï movy*, issued by the O. O. Potebnia Institute of Linguistics in Kyiv (1970–80).

The development of Ukrainian culture, with considerable attention to politics and religion, is discussed in Ihor Ševčenko, *Ukraine between East and West: Essays on Cultural History to the Early Eighteenth Century* (Edmonton and Toronto, 1996). More specialized is David Saunders, *The Ukrainian Impact on Russian Culture, 1750–1850* (Edmonton and Toronto, 1985). Sviatoslav Hordynsky's *The Ukrainian Icon of the XIIth to XVIIIth Centuries* (Philadelphia, 1973) offers an account of the dominant genre of Ukrainian religious art, while the history of Ukrainian painting is surveyed in Daria Darewych et al., *Spirit of Ukraine: 500 Years of Painting. Selections from the State Museum of Ukrainian Art* (Winnipeg, 1991). *100 Films of the Ukrainian Cinema* (Kyiv, 1996) is a UNESCO-sponsored introduction to a subject that lacks an English-language survey. For a brief account of the arts, see Ihor Verba et al., *This Is Ukraine* (Kyiv, 1995).

The history of Ukrainian Orthodoxy to the end of the 17th century is covered in Ivan Wlasowsky, *Outline History of the Ukrainian Orthodox Church*, 2 vols. (New York, 1956–79), and Sophia Senyk has published the first volume of her *History of the Church in Ukraine* (to the end of the 13th century; Rome, 1993). The interaction of religion and politics is examined in Serhii Plokhy and Frank E. Sysyn, *Religion and Nation in Modern Ukraine* (Edmonton and Toronto, 2003).

The following abbreviations are used for journal titles:

AUAAS *Annals of the Ukrainian Academy of Arts and Sciences in the U.S.*
CSP   *Canadian Slavonic Papers*
HUS   *Harvard Ukrainian Studies*
JUS   *Journal of Ukrainian Studies*
UQ   *Ukrainian Quarterly*
UR   *Ukrainian Review* (London)

The Canadian Institute of Ukrainian Studies Press is abbreviated as CIUS Press and the Harvard Ukrainian Research Institute as HURI.

I. General

1. Bibliographies and Dictionaries

The American Bibliography of Slavic and East European Studies. Stanford, Calif.: Library of Congress for the American Association for the Advancement of Slavic Studies, 1967– . Annual.

Andrusyshen, C. H., and J. N. Krett. *Ukrainian-English Dictionary.* Toronto: University of Toronto Press, 1957.

Boshyk, Yury, and Boris Balan, comps. *Political Refugees and "Displaced Persons," 1945–1954: A Selected Bibliography and Guide to Research with Special Reference to the Ukrainians.* Edmonton and Toronto: CIUS Press, 1982.

Boshyk, Yury, and Włodzimierz Kiebalo. *Publications by Ukrainian "Displaced Persons" and Political Refugees, 1945–1954 in the John Luczkiw Collection, Thomas Fisher Rare Book Library, University of Toronto.* Edmonton and Toronto: CIUS Press, 1988.

Cooper, Henry R. *The Igor Tale: An Annotated Bibliography of 20th*

Century Non-Soviet Scholarship on the "Slovo o Polku Igoreve." White Plains, N.Y.: M. E. Sharpe, 1978.

Crowther, Peter A. *A Bibliography of Works in English on Early Russian History to 1800.* New York: Barnes and Noble, 1969.

Danko, Joseph. "A Bibliography of Western-Language Writings on the Ukrainian Economy, 1919–1975. A Preliminary Attempt." *AUAAS* 13, 35/36 (1973–77): 257–313.

Dobczansky, Jurij. *Chernobyl and Its Aftermath: A Selected Bibliography.* Edmonton and Toronto: CIUS Press, 1988.

Dorosh, John T. *Guide to Soviet Bibliographies: A Selected List of References.* Washington, D.C.: Library of Congress, 1950.

Essar, D. F., and A. B. Pernal. "Beauplan's *Description d'Ukranie*: A Bibliography of Editions and Translations." *HUS* 6, 4 (Dec. 1982): 485–99.

Friesen, Paul T. *"Ukrainian Lands" Maps in the University of Alberta Map Collection: A Cartobibliography.* Edmonton and Toronto: CIUS Press, 1988.

Gregorovich, Andrew. *Jewish-Ukrainian Bibliography: A Selected Annotated Bibliography of Resources in English.* 2d ed. Toronto and Scranton, Pa.: Forum, 1999.

———. *Ukraine, Rus', Russia and Muscovy: A Selected Bibliography of the Names.* Toronto: New Review Books, 1971.

Grimsted, Patricia Kennedy. *Archives and Manuscript Repositories in the USSR: Ukraine and Moldavia.* Book 1, *General Bibliography and Institutional Directory.* Princeton, N.J.: Princeton University Press, 1988.

Horak, Stephan M. *Russia, the USSR, and Eastern Europe: A Bibliographic Guide to English Language Publications, 1964–1974.* Littleton, Colo.: Libraries Unlimited, 1978.

———. *Russia, the USSR, and Eastern Europe: A Bibliographic Guide to English Language Publications, 1975–1980.* Littleton, Colo.: Libraries Unlimited, 1982.

———. *Russia, the USSR, and Eastern Europe: A Bibliographic Guide to English Language Publications, 1981–1985.* Littleton, Colo.: Libraries Unlimited, 1987.

Horecky, Paul L., ed. *Russia and the Soviet Union: A Bibliographic Guide to Western-Language Publications.* Chicago: University of Chicago Press, 1965.

———. *Russian, Ukrainian, and Belorussian Newspapers, 1917–1953: A Union List.* Washington, D.C.: Library of Congress, 1953.

Horecky, Paul L., and Robert G. Carlton. *The USSR and Eastern Europe: Periodicals in Western Languages.* 3d rev. ed. Washington, D.C.: Library of Congress, 1967.

Jones, Lesia, and Luba Pendzey. "Dissent in Ukraine: Bibliography." *Nationalities Papers* 6, 1 (spring 1978): 64–70.

Lawrynenko, Jurij. *Ukrainian Communism and Soviet Russian Policy toward the Ukraine: An Annotated Bibliography, 1917–1953.* New York: Research Program on the USSR, 1953.

Lewanski, Richard C. *A Bibliography of Slavic Dictionaries.* 2d ed. 4 vols. Bologna: Editrice Compositori, 1972–73.

Liber, George, and Anna Mostovych. *Nonconformity and Dissent in the Ukrainian SSR, 1955–1975: An Annotated Bibliography.* Cambridge, Mass.: HURI, 1978.

Madden, Cheryl A. *The Ukrainian Famine (Holodomor) of 1932–33, and Aspects of Stalinism: An Annotated Bibliography-in-Progress in the English Language.* www.shevchenko.org/famine/index.htm

Niniovs'kyi, W. *Ukrainian-English and English-Ukrainian Dictionary.* Edmonton: Ukrainian Bookstore, 1985.

Pelenskyj, Eugene J. *Ucrainica: Ausgewählte Bibliographie über die Ukraine in west-europäischen Sprachen.* Munich: Bystrytsia, 1948; repr. Edmonton and Toronto: CIUS Press, 1990.

Petryshyn, W. Roman, and Natalia Chomiak, comps. *Political Writings of Post-World War Two Ukrainian Émigrés: Annotated Bibliography and Guide to Research.* Edmonton and Toronto: CIUS Press, 1984.

Piaseckyj, Oksana. *Bibliography of Ukrainian Literature in English and French: Translations and Critical Works (1950–1986).* Ottawa: University of Ottawa Press, 1989.

Pidhainy, Oleh S., and Alexandra I. Pidhainy. *The Ukrainian Republic in the Great East European Revolution: A Bibliography.* Vols. 5 and 6, pt. 2. Toronto: New Review Books, 1971–75.

Podvesko, M. L. *Ukrainian-English Dictionary.* 2d ed. Kyiv: Radians'ka shkola, 1957.

Podvesko, M. L., and M. I. Balla. *English-Ukrainian Dictionary.* Kyiv: Radians'ka shkola, 1974; repr. Edmonton and Toronto: CIUS Press, 1988.

Rudnyc'kyj, Jaroslav Bohdan. *An Etymological Dictionary of the Ukrainian Language.* 2d ed. Winnipeg: Ukrainian Free Academy of Sciences, 1966–72.

———. *Ukrainian Linguistics in Exile: A Bibliographic Survey, 1918–1988.* Winnipeg: Ukrainian Language Association, 1989.

Shapiro, David. *A Select Bibliography of Works in English and Russian History, 1801–1917.* Oxford: Blackwell, 1962.

Slavutych, Yar. *An Annotated Bibliography of Ukrainian Literature in Canada: Canadian Book Publications, 1908–1986.* 2d ed. Edmonton: Slavuta, 1986.

Sokolyszyn, Aleksander, and Vladimir Wertsman. *Ukrainians in Canada and the United States: A Guide to Information Sources.* Detroit: Gale, 1981.

Sullivan, Helen F., and Robert H. Burger. *Russia and the Former Soviet Union: A Bibliographic Guide to English Language Publications, 1986–1991.* Englewood, Colo.: Libraries Unlimited, 1994.

Tarnawsky, Marta. *Ukrainian Literature in English: Articles in Journals and Collections, 1840–1965.* Edmonton and Toronto: CIUS Press, 1992.

———. *Ukrainian Literature in English: Books and Pamphlets, 1890–1965. An Annotated Bibliography.* Edmonton and Toronto: CIUS Press, 1988.

———. *Ukrainian Literature in English, 1980–1989: An Annotated Bibliography.* Edmonton and Toronto: CIUS Press, 1999.

Weres, Roman. *Ukraine: Selected References in the English Language.* 2d ed. Chicago: Ukrainian Research and Information Institute, 1974.

Wynar, Bohdan S. *Doctoral Dissertations on Ukrainian Topics in English Prepared during the Years 1928–1978.* Englewood, Colo.: Ukrainian Research Foundation, 1980.

———. *Independent Ukraine: A Bibliographic Guide to English-Language Publications, 1989–1999.* Englewood, Colo.: Ukrainian Academic Press, 2000.

———. *Ukraine: A Bibliographic Guide to English-Language Publications.* Englewood, Colo.: Ukrainian Academic Press, 1990.

Wynar, Lubomyr, ed. *Mykhailo Hrushevs'kyi, 1866–1934. Bibliographic Sources.* New York: Ukrainian Historical Association, 1985.

Zubkov, Mykola, comp. *Velykyi anhlo-ukraïns'kyi slovnyk* [Comprehensive English-Ukrainian Dictionary]. Kharkiv: Folio, 2003.

2. Encyclopedias and Interdisciplinary Works

Aspects of Contemporary Ukraine. Chicago: University of Chicago. Division of Social Sciences, 1955.

Kubijovyč, Volodymyr, ed. *Ukraine: A Concise Encyclopaedia.* 2 vols. Toronto: University of Toronto Press, 1963–71.

Kubijovyč, Volodymyr, and Danylo Husar Struk, eds. *Encyclopedia of Ukraine.* 6 vols. Toronto: University of Toronto Press, 1984–2001.

Mirchuk, I., ed. *Ukraine and Its People: A Handbook with Maps, Statistical Tables, and Diagrams.* Munich: Ukrainian Free University Press, 1949.

Pawliczko, Ann Lencyk, ed. *Ukraine and Ukrainians throughout the World: A Demographic and Sociological Guide to the Homeland and Its Diaspora.* Toronto: University of Toronto Press, 1994.

Soviet Ukraine. Ed. M. P. Bazhan et al. Kyiv: Ukrainian Soviet Encyclopedia, 1970.

Ukraine: A Concise Encyclopedia. Clifton, N.J.: Ukrainian Orthodox Church of the U.S.A., 1987.

Weber, Harry B. et al., eds. *The Modern Encyclopedia of Russian and Soviet Literatures. Including Non-Russian and Emigre Literatures.* Gulf Breeze, Fla.: Academic International Press, 1977–.

3. Descriptions, Guidebooks, and Travel

Beauplan, Guillaume Le Vasseur Sieur de. *A Description of Ukraine.* Cambridge, Mass.: HURI, 1991.

Biryulov, Yu. et al. *Lviv: Sightseeing Guide.* Lviv: Tsentr Ievropy, 1999.

Hodges, Linda, and George Chumak. *Hippocrene Language and Travel Guide to Ukraine.* 2d ed. New York: Hippocrene Books, 1996.

Kal'nyts'kyi, M. et al. *Kyiv: Sightseeing Guide.* Lviv: Tsentr Ievropy, 2001.

Kardash, Peter. *Ukraine and Ukrainians.* Melbourne: Fortuna, 1988.

Kordan, Bohdan S. *Black Sea, Golden Steppes: Antiquarian Maps of the Black Sea Coast and the Steppes of Old Ukraine.* Saskatoon: Heritage Press, 2001.

Kubijovyč, Volodymyr, and Arkadii Zhukovsky. *Map and Gazetteer of Ukraine.* Toronto: University of Toronto Press, 1984. [Supplement to *Encyclopedia of Ukraine.*]

Pernal, Andrew B., and Dennis F. Essar. "The 1652 Beauplan Maps of the Ukraine." *HUS* 9, 1/2 (June 1985): 61–84.

Sichynsky, Volodymyr. *Ukraine in Foreign Comments and Descriptions: From the VIth to the XXth Century.* New York: Ukrainian Congress Committee of America, 1953.

Smolii, V. A. et al. *Vse pro Ukraïnu/All about Ukraine.* 2 vols. Kyiv: Al'ternatyvy, 1998.

Somko, Nadia, and Serhij Makarenko. *Ukraine in Pictures.* New York: East European Research Institute, 1971.

Zinkewycz, Osyp, and Volodymyr Hula. *Ukraine: A Tourist Guide.* Ed. and trans. Marta D. Olynyk. Kyiv and Baltimore: Smoloskyp, 1993.

4. Internet Sites

President of Ukraine: http://www.president.gov.ua
Cabinet of Ministers of Ukraine: http://www.kmu.gov.ua
Ministry of Agriculture: http://www.minagro.gov.ua
Ministry of Defense: http://www.mil.gov.ua
Ministry of Energy: http://mpe.energy.gov.ua
Ministry of the Environment: http://www.menr.gov.ua
Ministry of Finance: http://www.minfin.gov.ua
Ministry of Foreign Affairs: http://www.mfa.gov.ua

Ukrainian Embassy in the United States: http://www.ukremb.com

Brama: http://www.brama.com
Infoukes: http://www.infoukes.com
Transitions Online: http://knowledgenet.tol.cz
Ukrainian Literature: http://www.ukrainianliterature.org

Den' Digest: http://www.day.kiev.ua/DIGEST
Mirror Weekly: http://www.mirror-weekly.com
Ukrainian Weekly: htp://www.ukrweekly.com

Canadian Institute of Ukrainian Studies: http://www.ualberta.ca/cius
Harvard Ukrainian Research Institute: http://www.huri.harvard.edu

Ukrainian Canadian Congress: http://www.ucc.ca
Ukrainian Congress Committee of America: http://ucca.org

II. Cultural

1. Art and Architecture

"Alla Horska, 1929–70—A Tribute." *UR* 42, 4 (winter 1995): 51–55.
Beletsky, P., and L. Vladich. *Ukrainian Painting*. Leningrad: Aurora Publishers, 1976.
Białostocki, Jan. "At the Crossroads of Classicism and Byzantinism: Leopolitan Architectural Achievements ca. A.D. 1600." *HUS* 7 (1983): 51–65.
Boris Kriukow. Buenos Aires: Olga Gurski, 1970.
Darevych, Daria. *Myron Levytsky*. Toronto: Ukrainian Artists' Association, 1985.
Darewych, Daria et al. *Spirit of Ukraine: 500 Years of Painting. Selections from the State Museum of Ukrainian Art*. Winnipeg: Winnipeg Art Gallery, 1991.
Dmytriw, Olya. *Ukrainian Arts*. New York: Ukrainian Youth's League of North America, 1952.
Feodosiy Humeniuk. Kyiv: ArtEc Publishers, 1995.
Gregor Kruk. Munich: Ukrainian Free University and Südwest Verlag, 1975.
Hewryk, Titus D. *The Lost Architecture of Kiev*. New York: Ukrainian Museum, 1982.
———. *Masterpieces in Wood: Houses of Worship in Ukraine*. New York: Ukrainian Museum, 1987.
Hnatenko, Stefania. *Treasures of Early Ukrainian Art. Religious Art of the*

16th–18th Centuries. New York: Ukrainian Museum, 1989.
Hordynsky, Sviatoslav. *Peter Andrusiw: Painter and Graphic Artist.* New York: Ukrainian Academy of Arts and Sciences in the U.S., 1980.
———. *The Ukrainian Icon of the XIIth to XVIIIth Centuries.* Philadelphia: Providence Association, 1973.
———. *Victor Cymbal.* New York: Ukrainian Academy of Arts and Sciences in the U.S., 1972.
Hvozda, John. *Wooden Architecture of the Ukrainian Carpathians.* New York: Lemko Research Foundation, 1978.
Karshan, Donald H. *Archipenko: International Visionary.* Washington, D.C.: Smithsonian Institution Press, 1969.
———. *Archipenko: The Sculpture and Graphic Art.* Boulder, Colo.: Westview Press, 1975.
Keywan, Ivan. *Taras Shevchenko: The Artist.* Winnipeg: Ukrainian Canadian Committee, 1964.
Kmit, Ann, Johanna Luciow, and Loretta Luciow. *Ukrainian Embroidery.* New York: Van Nostrand Reinhold, 1978.
Kurelek, William. *Someone with Me: An Autobiography.* Toronto: McClelland and Stewart, 1980.
Logvin, Grigori. *Kiev: Architectural Landmarks, Places of Interest.* Leningrad: Aurora Art Publishers, 1980.
Magocsi, Paul Robert. *Wooden Churches in the Carpathians: The Photographs of Florian Zapletal.* Vienna: Wilhelm Braumüller, 1982.
Markovyč, Pavlo. *Rusyn Easter Eggs from Eastern Slovakia.* Vienna: Wilhelm Braumüller, 1987.
Mehyk, Petro. *Ukrainian Art in the Diaspora.* Philadelphia: Ukrainian Art Digest, 1981.
Mezentsev, Volodymyr. "The Masonry Churches of Medieval Chernihiv." *HUS* 11, 3/4 (Dec. 1987): 365–83.
Michaelsen, Katherine Jánszky. *Alexander Archipenko: A Centennial Tribute.* Washington, D.C.: National Gallery of Art, 1987.
———. *Alexander Archipenko: A Study of the Early Works, 1908–1920.* New York: Garland, 1977.
Milyaeva, Liudmilla. *The Ukrainian Icon: 11th–18th Centuries. From Byzantine Sources to the Baroque.* Bournemouth, England: Parkstone Press; St. Petersburg: Aurora Art Publishers, 1996.
Ohloblyn, Oleksander. "Western Europe and the Ukrainian Baroque." *AUAAS* 1, 2 (Feb. 1951): 127–37.
Pavlovsky, Vadim. *Vasyl H. Krychevsky: Life and Work.* New York: Ukrainian Academy of Arts and Sciences in the U.S., 1974.
Pekarska, Ludmyla. "The Mystery of the First Kyiv Treasure." *UR* 41, 2 (summer 1994): 14–23.
Powstenko, Olexa. *The Cathedral of St. Sophia in Kiev.* New York:

Ukrainian Academy of Arts and Sciences in the U.S., 1954.
Prystalenko, Nelli. "Ielyzaveta Piskorska: A Rediscovered 'Boichukist.'" *JUS* 25, 1/2 (summer-winter 2000): 73–90.
Rogers, Alla. "Out of Isolation: Ukrainian Artists Pioneer Contact with the West." *The World and I* 9, 8 (Aug. 1994): 221–31.
Shymchuk, Yevstakhia. "The Art of Glass in Ukraine." *UR* 43, 1 (spring 1996): 71–76.
Sydor, Oleh, and Taras Lozynskyj. *Ukrainian Icons, 13th–18th Centuries, from Private Collections.* Kyiv: Rodovid, 2003.
Tahir, Abe M., Jr. *Jacques Hnizdovsky: Woodcuts and Etchings.* New York: Pelican Publishing, 1987.
Verba, Ihor et al. *This Is Ukraine.* Kyiv: Computer Systems Publishing House, 1995.
Wight, Frederick S., Katherine Kuh, and Donald Karshan. *Alexander Archipenko: A Memorial Exhibition, 1967–1969.* Los Angeles: University of California, 1967.

2. Literary History, Linguistics, Language Textbooks, and Literature

a. Literary History and Theory
Aheieva, Vira. "Mykola Khvylovy and Expressionism." *JUS* 25, 1/2 (summer-winter 2000): 45–60.
Andreev, Michael. "The Party and the Literature of Non-Russian Peoples." *Studies of the Soviet Union* 3, 1 (1963): 109–18.
Asher, Oksana Dray-Khmara. "Dray-Khmara's Poetical Creativeness." *UQ* 13, 4 (1957): 355–65; 14, 1 (1958): 77–83.
———. *Letters from the Gulag: The Life, Letters, and Poetry of Michael Dray-Khmara.* New York: R. Speller, 1983.
———. *A Ukrainian Poet in the Soviet Union.* New York: Svoboda, 1959.
Babinski, Hubert F. *The Mazeppa Legend in European Romanticism.* New York: Columbia University Press, 1974.
Bahrij, Romana. "Sir Walter Scott and Panteleimon Kulish." *AUAAS* 16, 41/42 (1984–85): 135–73.
Bahrij-Pikulyk, Romana. "The Expressionist Experiment in Berezil: Kurbas and Kulish." *CSP* 14, 2 (summer 1972): 324–43.
———. "The Individual and History in the Historical Novel: P. Kulish's *The Black Council*." *CSP* 24, 2 (June 1982): 152–60.
———. "Superheroes, Gentlemen or Pariahs? The Cossacks in Nikolai Gogol's *Taras Bulba* and Panteleimon Kulish's *Black Council*." *JUS* 5, 2 (fall 1980): 30–47.
———. "The Use of Historical Sources in *Taras Bul'ba* and *The Black Council*." *Studia Ukrainica* 2 (1984): 49–64.

Balinska-Ourdeva, Vessela. "The Act of Reading as a Rite of Passage: Iurii Andrukhovych's *Rekreatsiï.*" *CSP* 40, 3/4 (Sep.–Dec. 1998): 209–32.

Bednarsky, Dushan. "*Ex abundantia enim cordis os loquitor*: Dymytrij Tuptalo's Ukrainian Sermons and the Kievan Rhetorical Model." *JUS* 17, 1/2 (summer–winter 1992): 217–43.

Bereshko-Hunter, Ludmilla. "The Search for the Ideal Place in Panteleimon Kulish's *Chorna Rada.*" *Journal of Ukrainian Graduate Studies* 1, 1 (fall 1976): 3–11.

Besharov, Justinia. *Imagery of the Igor Tale in the Light of Byzantino-Slavic Poetic Theory.* Leiden: E. J. Brill, 1956.

Bida, Constantine. *Lesya Ukrainka: Life and Work.* Toronto: University of Toronto Press, 1968.

Boyko, Jurij. "Taras Shevchenko and West European Literature." *Slavonic and East European Review* 34 (1956): 77–98.

Burianyk, Natalia. "Painting with Words: Mykhail' Semenko's Poetic Experiments." *CSP* 37, 3/4 (Sep.–Dec. 1995): 467–83.

Carynnyk, Marco. "Vasyl Stus." *Journal of Ukrainian Graduate Studies* 1, 1 (fall 1976): 62–67.

Chernetsky, Vitaly. "Opening the Floodgates: The New Ukrainian Writing." *Slavic and East European Journal* 41, 4 (winter 1997): 674–77.

Chyzhevsky (Čyževs'kyj), Dmytro. *A History of Ukrainian Literature (From the 11th to the End of the 19th Century).* Ed. George S. N. Luckyj. 2d ed. New York: Ukrainian Academic Press, 1997.

———. (Čiževsky, Dmitry). "Ivan Vyšenśkyj." *AUAAS* 1, 2 (1951): 113–26.

———. "The Soviet History of Ukrainian Literature." *Ukrainian Review* (Munich) 1 (1955): 53–64.

Cundy, Percival. "Marko Vovchok." *UQ* 3, 2 (winter 1947): 116–25.

Derzhavyn, Volodymyr. "The Coryphaeus of Ukrainian Literature." *UR* 29, 4 (winter 1981): 45–53.

———. "Postwar Ukrainian Literature in Exile." *UR* 4, 3 (autumn 1957): 13–24; 2 (winter 1957): 56–66; 5, 3 (autumn 1958): 30–40; 4 (winter 1958): 50–60; 7, 1 (spring 1960): 17–29.

Doroshenko, Volodymyr. "Ivan Franko as a Scholar." *UQ* 12, 2 (June 1956): 144–51.

Duć-Fajfer, Olena. "Ukrainian Literature in Poland, 1956–1993." *JUS* 23, 1 (summer 1998): 61–82.

Ferguson, Dolly M. "Lyricism and the Internal Landscape in the Early Creative Prose of Mykola Khvylovyi." *CSP* 18, 4 (Dec. 1976): 427–41.

———. "Yuriy Yanovs'ky's *Four Sabres*: A Re-examination of the

Concept of Faustian Man." In *In Working Order: Essays Presented to G. S. N. Luckyj*, ed. E. N. Burstynsky and R. Lindheim, 103–12. Edmonton and Toronto: CIUS Press, 1990.

Fizer, John. *Alexander A. Potebnja's Psycholinguistic Theory of Literature: A Metacritical Inquiry*. Cambridge, Mass.: HURI, 1986.

Frick, David A. "Meletij Smotryc'kyj's *Threnos* of 1610 and its Rhetorical Models." *HUS* 11, 3/4 (Dec. 1987): 462–86.

——. "The Uses of Authority and the Authority of Use: Philological Praise and Blame in Early Modern Rus'." *HUS* 18, 1/2 (June 1994): 76–93.

Gehrt-Wynar, Christine. "Ukrainian Children's Literature in North America." *Phaedrus. An International Journal of Children's Literature Research* 6, 1 (spring 1979): 6–21.

Gitin, Vladimir. "The Reality of the Narrator: Typological Features of Ševčenko's Prose." *HUS* 9, 1/2 (June 1985): 85–117.

Goldblatt, Harvey. "Notes on the Text of Ivan Vyšens'kyj's *Epistle to the Renegade Bishops*." *HUS* 18, 1/2 (June 1994): 47–75.

——. "On the Language Beliefs of Ivan Vyšens'kyj and the Counter-Reformation." *HUS* 15, 1/2 (June 1991): 7–34.

Grabowicz, George G. "Commentary: Exorcising Ukrainian Modernism." *HUS* 15, 3/4 (Dec. 1991): 273–83.

——. "Insight and Blindness in the Reception of Ševčenko: The Case of Kostomarov." *HUS* 17, 3/4 (Dec. 1993): 279–340.

——. *The Poet as Mythmaker: A Study of Symbolic Meaning in Taras Ševčenko*. Cambridge, Mass.: HURI, 1982.

——— "The Question of Authority in Ivan Vyšens'kyj: A Dialectics of Absence." *HUS* 12/13 (1988–89): 781–94.

——. "Three Perspectives on the Cossack Past: Gogol, Ševčenko, Kuliš." *HUS* 5, 2 (June 1981): 171–94.

——. *Toward a History of Ukrainian Literature*. Cambridge, Mass.: HURI, 1981.

——. "Ukrainian Elements in Russian Literature." In *Handbook of Russian Literature*, ed. Victor Terras, 493–96. New Haven, Conn.: Yale University Press, 1985.

——. "Ukrainian Poetry." In *The New Princeton Encyclopedia of Poetry and Poetics*, ed. Alex Preminger and T. V. F. Brogan, 1334–37. New York: MJF Books, 1993.

——. "The Voices of Ukrainian Emigre Poetry." *CSP* 28, 2 (June 1986): 157–73.

Graham, Hugh F. "The Travestied Aeneid and Ivan P. Kotliarevs'kyi, the Ukrainian Vergil." *Vergilius* 5 (1959): 5–11.

Hlobenko, M. "The Official History of Ukrainian Soviet Literature." *Ukrainian Review* (Munich) 5 (1957): 19–37.

Horban-Carynnyk, Marta. "Ivan Franko and *Moloda Muza*." In *In Working Order: Essays Presented to G. S. N. Luckyj*, ed. E. N. Burstynsky and R. Lindheim, 80–89. Edmonton and Toronto: CIUS Press, 1990.

Hudzii, Nikolai K. *History of Early Russian Literature*. New York: Macmillan, 1949.

Ilnytzkyj, Oleh S. "Antonych: Intimations of Mortality." *Journal of Ukrainian Graduate Studies* 1, 1 (fall 1976): 12–17.

———. "The Cossack and Peasant Ethos in Conflict: Reflections on *Khiba revut' voly, iak iasla povni?*" *JUS* 13, 1 (summer 1988): 43–54.

———. "The Modernist Ideology and Mykola Khvyl'ovyi." *HUS* 15, 3/4 (Dec. 1991): 257–62.

———. *Ukrainian Futurism, 1914–1930*. Cambridge, Mass.: HURI, 1997.

———. "Ukrainian Symbolism and the Problem of Modernism." *CSP* 34, 1/2 (Mar.–June 1992): 113–30.

———. "*Ukrainska khata* and the Paradoxes of Ukrainian Modernism." *JUS* 19, 2 (winter 1994): 5–30.

Jefremov, Serhii. "Historiography of Ukrainian Literature." *AUAAS* 1, 1 (1951): 4–20.

Klynovy, Y. "Vasyl Stefanyk's Heroes in the Reality." *UQ* 28 (1972): 28–36.

Kononenko, Natalie. "Widows and Sons: Heroism in Ukrainian Epic." *HUS* 14, 3/4 (Dec. 1990): 388–414.

Koropeckyj, R. "T. Ševčenko's 'Davydovi psalmy': A Romantic Psalter." *Slavic and East European Journal* 27, 2 (1983): 228–44.

Lewin, Paulina. "Polish-Ukrainian-Russian Literary Relations of the Sixteenth–Eighteenth Centuries: New Approaches." *Slavic and East European Journal* 24, 3 (1980): 256–69.

Lord, Albert B. "Comparative Slavic Epic." *HUS* 5, 4 (Dec. 1981): 415–29.

———. "The Opening Scenes of the *Dumy* on Holota and Andyber: A Study of the Technique of Oral Traditional Narrative." *HUS* 3/4 (1979–80): 569–94.

Luckyj, George S. N. *Between Gogol' and Ševčenko: Polarity in the Literary Ukraine, 1798–1847*. Munich: Wilhelm Fink Verlag, 1971.

———, ed. *Discordant Voices: The Non-Russian Soviet Literatures, 1953–1973*. Oakville, Ont.: Mosaic Press, 1975.

———. *Keeping a Record. Literary Purges in the Soviet Ukraine (1930s): A Bio-Bibliography*. Edmonton and Toronto: CIUS Press, 1987.

———. *Literary Politics in the Soviet Ukraine, 1917–1934*. New York:

Columbia University Press, 1956. 2d ed. Durham, N.C.: Duke University Press, 1990.
———. *Panteleimon Kulish: A Sketch of His Life and Times.* Boulder, Colo.: East European Monographs, 1983.
———. "Ševčenko and Blake." *HUS* 2, 1 (Mar. 1978): 94–115.
———, ed. *Shevchenko and the Critics, 1861–1980.* Toronto: University of Toronto Press, 1980.
———. "The Ukrainian Literary Scene Today." *Slavic Review* 31, 4 (Dec. 1972): 863–69.
———. *Ukrainian Literature in the Twentieth Century: A Reader's Guide.* Toronto: University of Toronto Press, 1992.
Manning, Clarence A. "Ivan Kotliarevsky." *UQ* 26, 2 (summer 1970): 164–70.
———. *Ukrainian Literature. Studies of the Leading Authors.* Jersey City, N.J.: Ukrainian National Association, 1944.
McMillin, Arnold. "Byelorussian-Ukrainian Literary Relations before 1917." *AUAAS* 16, 41/42 (1984–85): 175–90.
Mihaychuk, George. "The Role of the 1920s Form and Content Debate in Ukraine." *CSP* 37, 1/2 (Mar.–June 1995): 107–26.
Mijakovs'kyj, Volodymyr, and George Y. Shevelov, eds. *Taras Shevchenko, 1814–1861: A Symposium.* The Hague: Mouton, 1962.
Modern Slavic Literatures. Comp. and ed. Vasa D. Mihailovich. Volume 2, *Bulgarian, Czechoslovak, Polish, Ukrainian and Yugoslav Literatures.* New York: Frederick Ungar, 1976.
Mudrak, Myroslava M. *The New Generation and Artistic Modernism in the Ukraine.* Ann Arbor, Mich.: U.M.I. Research Press, 1986.
Naydan, Michael M. "Ukrainian Prose of the 1990s as It Reflects Contemporary Social Structures." *UQ* 51, 1 (spring 1995): 45–61.
Nazarenko, Tatiana. "To Pass Through on One's Wings: The Poetry of Oleh Zujewskyj." *CSP* 38, 1/2 (Mar.–June 1996): 23–46.
Nowosad, Myron E. "Mysterious and Irrational Elements in the Works of Mykhailo Kotsiubyns'kyi and Theodor Storm." In *East European Literature: Selected Papers from the Second World Congress for Soviet and East European Studies*, ed. Evelyn Bristol, 43–56. Berkeley, Calif.: Slavic Specialties, 1982.
Ovcharenko, Maria. "Lina Kostenko—the Poet of the Freedom of Spirit and of the Truth of the Word." *UR* 23, 1 (1976): 21–30.
Pavlyshyn, Marko. "Anatomizing Melancholy: The Poetry of Ihor Kalynets." *JUS* 18, 1/2 (summer–winter 1993): 185–215.
———. "From Osadchy to the 'Koleso' Controversy: Modernity and Its Meanings in Ukrainian Culture since the 1960s." *JUS* 20, 1/2 (summer–winter 1995): 69–78.
———. "The Rhetoric and Politics of Kotliarevsky's *Eneida*." *JUS* 10,

1 (summer 1985): 9–24.

———. "The Soviet Ukrainian Whimsical Novel." *JUS* 25, 1/2 (summer–winter 2000): 103–20.

———. "Ukrainian Literature and the Erotics of Postcolonialism: Some Modest Propositions." *HUS* 17, 1/2 (June 1993): 110–26.

Pazuniak, Natalia. "Lesya Ukrainka—Ukraine's Greatest Poetess." *UQ* 27, 3 (autumn 1971): 237–52.

Picchio, Riccardo. "Notes on the Text of the *Igor' Tale*." *HUS* 2, 4 (Dec. 1978): 393–422.

Pinchuk, Jaroslav R. "The Concept of 'Urbanism' in V. Pidmohylnyi's *Misto*." *Studia Ucrainica* 1 (1978): 129–32.

Pylypiuk, Natalia. "*Eucharisterion. Albo, Vdjačnost'*: The First Panegyric of the Kiev Mohyla School." *HUS* 8, 1/2 (June 1984): 45–70.

———. "The Primary Door: At the Threshold of Skovoroda's Theology and Poetics." *HUS* 14, 3/4 (Dec. 1990): 551–83.

———. "Skovoroda's Divine Narcissism." *JUS* 22, 1/2 (summer–winter 1997): 13–50.

———. "Vasyl' Stus, Mysticism, and the Great Narcissus." In *A World of Slavic Literatures*, ed. Paul D. Morris, 173–210. Bloomington, Ind.: Slavica, 2002.

Revutsky, Valerian. "How to Save Your Marriage and Other Matters of Love: Vynnyčenko and Maugham." *AUAAS* 16, 41/42 (1984–85): 353–60.

Rich, Vera. "Ivan Kotlyarevsky: An Appreciation." *UQ* 25, 4 (fall 1969): 331–34.

Romanenchuk, Bohdan. "Lesia Ukrainka and French Literature." *UQ* 41, 3 (fall–winter 1985): 224–31.

Rosalion, Olesia. "The Dramaturgy of Grief: Vasyl Stefanyk's *Syny*." *JUS* 10, 1 (summer 1985): 39–48.

Rozumnyj, Jaroslav. "Byzantinism and Idealism in the Aesthetic Views of Taras Shevchenko." *CSP* 19, 2 (June 1977): 193–207.

Rubchak, Bohdan. "Because We Have No Time: Recent Ukrainian Poetry." *Agni* 33 (1991): 278–304.

———. "Images of Center and Periphery in the Poetry of Taras Shevchenko." *AUAAS* 16, 41/42 (1984–85): 81–118.

———, ed. *Studies in Ukrainian Literature*. *AUAAS* 16, 41/42 (1984–85).

———. "Taras Shevchenko as an Émigré Poet." In *In Working Order: Essays Presented to G. S. N. Luckyj*, ed. E. N. Burstynsky and R. Lindheim, 21–56. Edmonton and Toronto: CIUS Press, 1990.

Rudnytzky, L. D. "Franko's *Pans'ki zharty* in Light of German Literary Theories." In *Symbolae in Honorem Volodymyri Janiw*, ed. Oleksa Horbach et al., 800–809. Munich: Ukrainian Free University, 1983.

———. "The Image of Austria in the Works of Ivan Franko." In *Nationbuilding and the Politics of Nationalism*, ed. Andrei S. Markovits and Frank E. Sysyn, 239–54. Cambridge, Mass.: HURI, 1982.
Sawczak, Peter. "The Novelization of the Pamphlet: Aesthetic Compromise as Argument in Mykola Khvylovy's *Woodcocks*." *JUS* 20, 1/2 (summer–winter 1995): 53–60.
Schneider, Lisa E. "An Examination of Shevchenko's Romanticism." *Journal of Ukrainian Graduate Studies* 3, 1 (spring 1978): 5–28.
Shabliovsky, Yevhen. *Ukrainian Literature through the Ages*. Kyiv: Mystetstvo, 1970.
Shakhovs'kyi, Semen M. *Lesya Ukrainka: A Biographical Sketch*. Kyiv: Dnipro Publishers, 1975.
Shankovsky, Igor. *Symonenko: A Study in Semantics*. Munich: Ukrainisches Institut für Bildungspolitik, 1977.
Shevelov, George Y. "Iak sklo: On and Around a Simile in Ševčenko's Poetry." In *In Working Order: Essays Presented to G. S. N. Luckyj*, ed. E. N. Burstynsky and R. Lindheim, 9–20. Edmonton and Toronto: CIUS Press, 1990.
———. "Ševčenko contra Pushkin." *AUAAS* 16, 41/42 (1984–85): 119–34.
Shkandrij, Myroslav. "Fiction by Formula: The Worker in Early Soviet Ukrainian Prose." *JUS* 7, 2 (fall 1982): 47–60.
———. "Irony in the Works of Mykola Khvyl'ovy." In *In Working Order: Essays Presented to G. S. N. Luckyj*, ed. E. N. Burstynsky and R. Lindheim, 90–102. Edmonton and Toronto: CIUS Press, 1990.
———. *Modernists, Marxists and the Nation: The Ukrainian Literary Discussion of the 1920s*. Edmonton and Toronto: CIUS Press, 1992.
———. "Polarities in Contemporary Ukrainian Literature." *Dalhousie Review* 72, 2 (summer 1992): 236–50.
———. *Russia and Ukraine: Literature and the Discourse of Empire from Napoleonic to Postcolonial Times*. Montreal: McGill-Queen's University Press, 2001.
Shtohryn, Dmytro M. "Ukrainian Literature in the United States: Trends, Influences, Achievements." In *Ethnic Literature since 1776: The Many Voices of America*, ed. Wolodymyr T. Zyla and Wendell M. Aycock, 569–90. Lubbock: Texas Tech Press, 1979.
Sirka, Josef. *The Development of Ukrainian Literature in Czechoslovakia, 1945–1975: A Survey of Social, Cultural and Historical Aspects*. Frankfurt/Main: Peter Lang, 1978.
Slavutych, Yar. "Marko Vovchok: A Ukrainian Scourge of Russian Serfdom." *UQ* 14, 4 (1958): 363–67.
———. "The Ukrainian Literary Renaissance of the 1920s." *UR* 4, 1

(1957): 9–22.

———. "Ukrainian Poetry in Canada: A Historical Account." *UR* 22, 1 (spring 1975): 109–24.

Smal-Stocki, Stepan. "Shevchenko's Mind and Thought." *AUAAS* 2, 4 (1952): 227–38.

Smyrniw, Walter. "The First Utopia in Ukrainian Belles Lettres: Pavlo Krat's *Koly ziishlo sontse.*" *CSP* 38, 3/4 (Sep.–Dec. 1996): 405–18.

———. "Prediction and Progress in Vynnyčenko's *Sonjašna mašyna.*" *AUAAS* 16, 41/42 (1984–85): 327–40.

———. "The Theme of Man-godhood in Oles Berdnyk's Science Fiction." *JUS* 6, 1 (spring 1981): 3–19.

———. "The Treatment of the Ballad of Shevchenko and His Contemporaries in Relation to Western Balladry." *CSP* 12, 2 (1970): 142–74.

Stetkevych, Jaroslav. "Encounter with the East: The Orientalist Poetry of Ahatanhel Kryms'kyj." *HUS* 8, 3/4 (Dec. 1984): 321–50.

Struk, Danylo Husar. "Andievs'ka's Concept of Round Time." *CSP* 27, 1 (Mar. 1985): 65–73.

———. "The How, the What and the Why of *Marusia Churai*: A Historical Novel in Verse by Lina Kostenko." *CSP* 32, 2 (June 1990): 148–65.

———. "The Journal *Svit*: A Barometer of Modernism." *HUS* 15, 3/4 (Dec. 1991): 245–56.

———. "A Novel about Human Destiny, or the Andiievska Chronicle." *JUS* 18, 1/2 (summer–winter 1993): 151–60.

———. *A Study of Vasyl' Stefanyk: The Pain at the Heart of Existence.* Littleton, Colo.: Ukrainian Academic Press, 1973.

———. "The Summing-up of Silence: The Poetry of Ihor Kalynets'." *Slavic Review* 38, 1 (Mar. 1979): 17–29.

———. "Tupyk or Blind Alley: *Val'dshnepy* of M. Khvyl'ovyj." *Canadian Slavic Studies* 2 (1968): 239–51.

———. "Vynnychenko's Moral Laboratory." *AUAAS* 16, 41/42 (1984–85): 275-88.

———. "What Is the Meaning of 'Sin' in V. Vynnychenko's *Hrikh*?" *CSP* 31, 1 (Mar. 1989): 57–66.

Sverstiuk, Ievhen. *Clandestine Essays.* Trans. George S. N. Luckyj. Littleton, Colo.: Ukrainian Academic Press, 1976.

Svitlychnyi, Ivan. "Steel Does Not Rust." *UR* 18, 2 (summer 1971): 39–44.

Svoboda, V., and R. Martin. "Shevchenko and Belinsky Revisited." *Slavonic and East European Review* 45, 4 (Oct. 1978): 546–62.

Tarnawsky, Maxim. *Between Reason and Irrationality: The Prose of Valerijan Pidmohyl'nyj.* Toronto: University of Toronto Press, 1994.

———. "European Influence in Ukrainian Modernist Prose." *CSP* 34, 1/2

(Mar.–June 1992): 131–42.
———. "Feminism, Modernism, and Ukrainian Women." *JUS* 19, 2 (winter 1994): 31–41.
———. "Modernism in Ukrainian Prose." *HUS* 15, 3/4 (Dec. 1991): 263–72.
———. "The Paradox of Populism: The Realism of Ivan Nečuj-Levyc'kyj." *HUS* 14, 3/4 (Dec. 1990): 608–22.
Tarnawsky, Ostap. "Dissident Poets in Ukraine." *JUS* 6, 2 (fall 1981): 17–27.
Vladiv-Glover, Slobodanka M. "Iurii Andrukhovych's *Recreations* and Ukrainian Postmodernism." *JUS* 20, 1/2 (summer–winter 1995): 79–86.
Wilcher, Asher. "Ivan Franko and Theodor Herzl: To the Genesis of Franko's *Mojsej*." *HUS* 6, 2 (June 1982): 233–43.
Yekelchyk, Serhy. "Celebrating the Soviet Present: The Zhdanovshchina Campaign in Ukrainian Literature and the Arts, 1946–48." In *Provincial Landscapes: Local Dimensions of Soviet Power, 1917–1953*, ed. Donald J. Raleigh, 255–75. Pittsburgh: University of Pittsburgh Press, 2001.
Zabuzhko, Oksana. "Reinventing the Poet in Modern Ukrainian Culture." *Slavic and East European Journal* 39, 2 (summer 1995): 270–75.
Zaitsev, Pavlo. *Taras Shevchenko: A Life*. Edited, abridged, and translated by George S. N. Luckyj. Toronto: University of Toronto Press, 1988.
Zerov, Mykola. "Modern Ukrainian Literature." *UR* 35, 4 (winter 1987): 35–49.
Zinkewych, Osyp. *Svitlychny and Dzyuba: Ukrainian Writers under Fire*. Baltimore: Smoloskyp, 1966.
Znayenko, M. T. "Restoration of the Self through History and Myth in Lina Kostenko's 'Marusia Churai.'" *CSP* 32, 2 (June 1990): 166–76.
Zyla, Wolodymyr. "A Prophetess Fated to Be Disbelieved: Lesya Ukrainka's 'Cassandra.'" *UQ* 38, 3 (1982): 281–89.
———. "*Svyns'ka konstytucija*: A Notable Satirical Work by Ivan Franko." *UR* 30, 2 (summer 1982): 47–55.
———. "A Ukrainian Version of 'The Aeneid': Ivan Kotliarevskyi's 'Enejida.'" *Classical Journal* 67, 3 (1972): 193–97.

b. Linguistics, Language Politics
Altshuler, Mordechai. "Some Soviet and Post-Soviet National and Linguistic Problems in the Slavic Republics (States): Russia, Ukraine, Belorus." In *Quest for Models of Coexistence: National and Ethnic Dimensions of Changes in the Slavic Eurasian World*, ed. Koichi Inoue and Tomohiko Uyama, 111–31. Sapporo: Slavic Research Center, Hokkaido University, 1998.

Anderson, Henning. "The Ukrainian Fourth Declension." *HUS* 18, 1/2 (June 1994): 154–66.

Arel, Dominique. "Language Politics in Independent Ukraine: Towards One or Two State Languages?" *Nationalities Papers* 23, 3 (Sep. 1995): 597–622.

———. "A Lurking Cascade of Assimilation in Kiev?" *Post-Soviet Affairs* 12, 1 (Jan.–Mar. 1996): 73–90.

Barnstead, John. "Ambiguities in the Universal Noun Phrase Accessibility Hierarchy: The Ukrainian Evidence." *Studia Ucrainica* 2 (1984): 145–56.

Becker, Lee A. "On the Phonetic Nature of the Origin of Ukrainian Ikavism." *CSP* 22, 3 (Sep. 1980): 400–407.

Birnbaum, David J. "Sisters, Wives, and Grandmothers: Stress Patterns in Ukrainian." *HUS* 14, 3/4 (Dec. 1990): 268–92.

Birnbaum, Henrik. "Potebnja's Conception of East Slavic Morphosyntax Viewed in Its Historical Context." *HUS* 18, 1/2 (June 1994): 117–24.

Carlton, T. R. "Compensatory Lengthening, Rounding, and Sharping in Ukrainian." *CSP* 38, 3/4 (Sep.–Dec. 1996): 385–404.

Clarke, J. E. M. "Towards a Systematic Account of Nominal Word-Transformation through Suffixation in Ukrainian." *JUS* 20, 1/2 (summer–winter 1995): 111–22.

De Vincenz, A. "West Slavic Elements in the Literary Language of Kievan Rus'." *HUS* 12/13 (1988–89): 262–75.

Farmer, Kenneth C. "Language and Linguistic Nationalism in the Ukraine." *Nationalities Papers* 6, 2 (fall 1978): 125–49.

Flier, Michael. "Segmentation, Rank, and Natural Class in Ukrainian Dialectology." *HUS* 18, 1/2 (June 1994): 137–53.

Frick, David. "Meletij Smotryc'kyj and the Ruthenian Language Question." *HUS* 9, 1/2 (June 1985): 25–52.

Gasparov, Boris. "From the Romantic Past to the Modern World: Historical-Cultural Underpinnings of Potebnia's Thought on Language." *HUS* 18, 1/2 (June 1994): 94–103.

Gerus-Tarnawecka, Iraida. "Interference of Standard Literary Ukrainian in the Speech of Canadian Ukrainians." *CSP* 25, 1 (Mar. 1983): 163–79.

Harchun, Yaroslav. "French Loan-Words in the Work of 19th Century and Early 20th Century Ukrainian Writers." *JUS* 15, 2 (winter 1990): 75–84.

Holutiak-Hallick, Stephen P. *Slavic Toponymic Atlas of the United States*. Volume 1, *Ukrainian*. New York: Slavic Onomastic Research Group, 1982.

Hornjatkevyč, Andrij. "What or Who Is Really a Threat to the Ukrainian Language?" *JUS* 25, 1/2 (summer–winter 2000): 219–29.

Hursky, Jacob P., ed. *Studies in Ukrainian Linguistics in Honor of George Y. Shevelov. AUAAS* 15, 39/40 (1981–83).
Karavanskyi, Svyatoslav. "Political Aspect of Linguistic Processes in Ukraine." *UR* 45, 3 (autumn 1998): 39–47.
Kossak, Orest. "Problems of Ukrainian Terminology and the Compilation of Dictionaries of Computer Science and Telecommunications." *UR* 42, 4 (winter 1995): 15–20.
Kovaliv, Panteleymon. "Problems of the Ukrainian Literary Language." *AUAAS* 3, 7 (1953): 571–83.
Kuligowska, Jadwiga. "Non-deverbative Formation of Verbs in Modern Ukrainian and Polish." *JUS* 10, 1 (summer 1985): 49–66.
Lewis, Glyn E. *Multiculturalism in the Soviet Union: Aspects of Language Policy and Its Implementation.* Paris: Mouton, 1972.
Lunt, Horace G. "The Language of Rus' in the Eleventh Century: Some Observations about Facts and Theories." *HUS* 12/13 (1988–89): 276–313.
———. "Lexical Variation in the Copies of the Rus' *Primary Chronicle*: Some Methodological Problems." *HUS* 18, 1/2 (June 1994): 10–28.
Lunt, Horace G., and Moshe Taube. *The Slavonic Book of Esther: Text, Lexicon, Linguistic Analysis, Problems of Translation.* Cambridge, Mass.: HURI, 1998.
Lychyk, Victor. "Productive Deverbal Derivation in Modern Ukrainian." *JUS* 18, 1/2 (summer–winter 1993): 161–83.
Magocsi, Paul Robert. "The Language Question in Nineteenth-Century Galicia." In *Aspects of the Slavic Language Question.* Volume II, *East Slavic*, ed. Riccardo Picchio and Harvey Goldblatt, 49–64. New Haven, Conn.: Yale Concilium on International and Area Studies, 1984.
———. *Ukrainian Heritage Notes: The Language Question in Galicia.* Cambridge, Mass.: Ukrainian Studies Fund, 1978.
Minissi, Nullo. "What Does 'Indo-European' Mean in Reference to the Slavic Languages?" *HUS* 12/13 (1988–89): 587–92.
Orel, Vladimir. "Old Slavic Graffiti of Kyiv: Problems of Linguistic History." *HUS* 17, 3/4 (Dec. 1993): 209–18.
Pavliuc, N. "Dual Forms in Literary Ukrainian and Dialects." In *In Working Order: Essays Presented to G. S. N. Luckyj*, ed. E. N. Burstynsky and R. Lindheim, 158–73. Edmonton and Toronto: CIUS Press, 1990.
Perfecky, George A. "An English-Ukrainian Dictionary for the Western User: Past and Future." *UR* 27, 2 (summer 1979): 15–28.
———. "The Status of the Ukrainian Language in the Ukrainian SSR." *East European Quarterly* 21, 2 (June 1987): 207–30.
Pritsak, Omeljan. "A Historical Perspective on the Ukrainian Language

Question." In *Aspects of the Slavic Language Question*. Volume II, *East Slavic*, ed. Riccardo Picchio and Harvey Goldblatt, 1–8. New Haven, Conn.: Yale Concilium on International and Area Studies, 1984.

Pugh, Stefan M. "The Ruthenian Language of Meletij Smotryc'kyj: Phonology." *HUS* 9, 1/2 (June 1985): 53–60.

———. *Testament to Ruthenian: A Linguistic Analysis of the Smotryc'kyj Variant*. Cambridge, Mass.: HURI, 1996.

Rieger, Janusz A. *A Lexical Atlas of the Hutsul Dialects of the Ukrainian Language*. Cambridge, Mass.: HURI, 1996.

Rosalion, Olesia. "Prefixation in the Ukrainian Verbal System." *JUS* 20, 1/2 (summer–winter 1995): 123–38.

Rothstein, Robert A. "Baudouin de Courtenay and the Ukrainian Question." *HUS* 16, 3/4 (Dec. 1992): 315–24.

Rudnyckyj, Jaroslav Bohdan. "Carpatho-Ukraine and Its Ethnolinguistic Problems." *UR* 27, 4 (1979): 78–82.

———. "The Ems Ukase of 1876 and the Problem of Linguicide." *Nationalities Papers* 4, 2 (fall 1976): 113–24.

———. *Linguicide*. Winnipeg: Ukrainian Technological University, 1976.

———. "Linguicide." *UR* 26, 4 (fall 1978): 24–42.

Shevelov, George Y. "Alexander Potebnia as a Linguist." *AUAAS* 5, 16/17 (1956): 1112–27.

———. *A Historical Phonology of the Ukrainian Language*. Heidelberg: Carl Winter Verlag for the CIUS Press, 1979.

———. "Homer's Arbitration in a Ukrainian Linguistic Controversy: Alexander Potebnja and Peter Niščyns'kyj." *HUS* 18, 1/2 (June 1994): 104–16.

———. *In and Around Kiev: Twenty-Two Studies and Essays in Eastern Slavic and Polish Linguistics and Philology*. Heidelberg: Carl Winter Universitätsverlag, 1991.

———. "On the Chronology of h and the New g in Ukrainian." *HUS* 1, 2 (June 1977): 137–52.

———. *A Prehistory of Slavic: The Historical Phonology of Common Slavic*. New York: Columbia University Press, 1965.

———. "Prosta Čad' and Prostaja Mova." *HUS* 12/13 (1988–89): 593–624.

———. *The Syntax of Modern Literary Ukrainian: The Simple Sentence*. The Hague: Mouton, 1963.

———. *Teasers and Appeasers: Essays and Studies on Themes of Slavic Philology*. Munich: Wilhelm Fink Verlag, 1971.

———. "Ukrainian." In *The Slavic Literary Languages: Formation and Development*, ed. Alexander M. Schenker and Edward Stankiewicz, 143–60. New Haven, Conn.: Yale Concilium on International and

Area Studies, 1980.

———. *The Ukrainian Language in the First Half of the Twentieth Century, 1900–1941*. Cambridge, Mass.: HURI, 1989.

———. "Why in Ukrainian *sl'ozy* 'Tears' but *zelenyj* 'Green', While in Russian *sljozy* and *zeljonyj*? An Unresolved Problem of Ukrainian Historical Phonology." *Slavonic and East European Review* 57, 1 (Jan. 1979): 1–15.

Shevelov, George Y., and Fred Holling. *A Reader in the History of the Eastern Slavic Languages: Russian, Belorussian, Ukrainian*. New York: Columbia University Press, 1958.

Shymkiw, Anna. "Some Phonological Innovations and the Canadian Variant of the Ukrainian Language." *CSP* 24, 1 (1982): 50–66.

Silver, Brian. "The Impact of Urbanization and Geographic Dispersion on the Linguistic Russification of Soviet Nationalities." *Demography* 9, 1 (Feb. 1974): 89–103.

Slavutych, Yar. "Soviet Language Policy: The Case of Ukrainian." In *Symbolae in Honorem Volodymyri Janiw*, ed. Oleksa Horbach et al., 819–32. Munich: Ukrainian Free University, 1983.

Slonek, Robert. "Certain Paradigmatic Anomalies in the History of Ukrainian Accentuation." *JUS* 10, 1 (summer 1985): 67–72.

Solchanyk, Roman. "Language Politics in the Ukraine." In *Sociolinguistic Perspectives on Soviet National Languages: Their Past, Present, and Future*, ed. I. T. Kreindler, 57–105. New York: Mouton, 1985.

Strumiński, Bohdan. *Linguistic Interrelations in Early Rus'. Northmen, Finns, and East Slavs (Ninth to Eleventh Centuries)*. Edmonton and Toronto: CIUS Press, 1996.

Struminsky, Bohdan. "Linguistics in Ukraine, 1980–85." *JUS* 11, 2 (winter 1986): 47–61.

———. *Pseudo-Meleško: A Ukrainian Apocryphal Parliamentary Speech of 1615–1618*. Cambridge, Mass.: HURI, 1984.

Strumins'kyj, Bohdan. "The Influence of Populists on Ukrainian Grammar: The Plight of Active Present Adjectival Participles in Ukrainian." *JUS* 5, 1 (spring 1980): 3–14.

———. "Ukrainian between Old Bulgarian, Polish, and Russian." *Journal of Ukrainian Graduate Studies* 3, 2 (fall 1978): 40–56.

Swoboda, Victor. "Ukrainian in the Slavic Element of Yiddish Vocabulary." *HUS* 3/4 (1979–80): 818–25.

Tkachenko, Sergei I. "The Perestroika of Language Policy in Ukraine." In *Language as Barrier and Bridge*, ed. Kurt E. Muller, 67–71. Lanham, Md.: University Press of America, 1992.

Vetukhiv, O. "Towards an Understanding of Potebnja." *AUAAS* 5, 16/17 (1956): 1079–1111.

Wexler, Paul. *Purism and Language: A Study of Modern Ukrainian and*

Belorussian Nationalism, 1940–1967. Bloomington, Ind.: Indiana University Press, 1974.

Worth, Dean S. "The Dative Absolute in the *Primary Chronicle*: Some Observations." *HUS* 18, 1/2 (June 1994): 29–46.

———. "Phraseology in the Galician-Volhynian Chronicle." *AUAAS* 8, 25/26 (1960): 55–69.

Zilyns'kyj, Ivan. *A Phonetic Description of the Ukrainian Language.* Cambridge, Mass.: HURI, 1979.

Zyla, Wolodymyr. "George Shevelov: His Contribution to the Prehistory of Slavic." *Nationalities Papers* 4, 2 (fall 1976): 113–24.

———. "Ivan Franko's Studies in Ukrainian Onomastics." *AUAAS* 12, 33/34 (1969–72): 151–57.

c. Language Textbooks

Barantsev, K. T. *English-Ukrainian Phrase-Book.* Kyiv: Radians'ka shkola, 1969.

Bekh, Olena, and James Dingley. *Teach Yourself Ukrainian.* London: Hodder & Stoughton, 1997.

De Lossa, Robert A. "Collegiate Ukrainian Language Teaching and Material Development in the United States in the Late 1990s." In *The Learning and Teaching of Slavic Languages*, ed. Olga Kagan and Benjamin Rifkin, 627–54. Bloomington, Ind.: Slavica, 2000.

Derlycia, Zirka. *Everyday Ukrainian: A Practical Basic Course.* Guilford, Conn.: Audio-Forum, 1993.

Dingley, Jim, and Olena Bekh. *Ukrainian Phrasebook.* Hawthorne, Australia: Lonely Planet, 1996.

Duravetz, G. *Ukrainian: Conversational and Grammatical.* 3d ed. Toronto: Ukrainian Teachers' Committee, 1981.

Hornjatkevyč, Andrij. *530 Ukrainian Verbs Fully Conjugated in All Tenses* [electronic book]. Edmonton: Ukrainian Multimedia Publishing, University of Alberta, 2001.

Humesky, Assya. *Modern Ukrainian.* 3d ed. Edmonton and Toronto: CIUS Press, 1999.

Luckyj, George, and Jaroslav B. Rudnyckyj. *A Modern Ukrainian Grammar.* Winnipeg: Ukrainian Language Association, 1978.

Makarova, H. I., L. P. Palamar, and N. K. Prisyazhnyuk. *Learn Ukrainian: An Elementary Practical Course in Conversational Ukrainian.* Kyiv: Vyshcha shkola, 1975.

Medushevsky, A., and R. Zyatkovska. *Ukrainian Grammar.* Kyiv: Radians'ka shkola, 1978.

Press, Ian, and Stefan Pugh. *Colloquial Ukrainian.* London: Routledge, 1994.

Slavutych, Yar. *Conversational Ukrainian.* Edmonton: Gateway, 1987.

———. *Standard Ukrainian Grammar*. Edmonton: Slavuta, 1987.
———. *Ukrainian for Beginners*. Edmonton: Slavuta, 1980.
———. *Ukrainian in Pictures*. Edmonton: Gateway, 1965.
Smyrniw, Walter. *Ukrainian Prose Manual: A Text for Intermediate Language Students*. Oakville, Ont.: Mosaic Press, 1977; repr. CIUS Press, 1991.
Struk, Danylo Husar. *Ukrainian for Undergraduates*. 2d rev. ed. Edmonton and Toronto: CIUS Press, 1998.

d. Literature

(1) Prose, Criticism
Andijewska, Emma. "The Journey." Trans. Marta D. Olynyk. *Journal of Ukrainian Graduate Studies* 2, 2 (fall 1977): 18–30.
Andrukhovych, Yuri. *Perverzion*. Trans. Michael Naydan. Evanston, Ill.: Northwestern University Press, 2004.
———. *Recreations*. Trans. Marko Pavlyshyn. Edmonton and Toronto: CIUS Press, 1998.
Bahriany, Ivan. *The Hunters and the Hunted*. London: Macmillan, 1956.
Bain, Robert Nisbet. *Cossack Fairy Tales and Folk Tales*. New York: F. A. Stokes, 1916.
Balan, Jars, ed. *Identifications: Ethnicity and the Writer in Canada*. Edmonton and Toronto: CIUS Press, 1982.
Berdnyk, Oles. *Apostle of Immortality: Ukrainian Science Fiction*. Trans. Yuri Tkach. Toronto: Bayda Books, 1984.
———. "The Testament of Christ (Letter to a Friend)." Trans. Wolodymyr Slez. *UR* 28, 3 (fall 1980): 28–40.
Dibrova, Volodymyr. *Peltse* and *Pentameron*. Trans. Halyna Hryn. Evanston, Ill.: Northwestern University Press, 1996.
Dovzhenko, Alexander. *The Enchanted Desna: A Film Story by Alexander Dovzhenko*. Trans. Anatole Bilenko. Kyiv: Dnipro Publishers, 1979.
The Edificatory Prose of Kievan Rus'. Trans. William R. Veder. Cambridge, Mass.: HURI, 1994.
Franko, Ivan. *Boa Constrictor and Other Stories*. Trans. Fainna Solasko. Moscow: Foreign Languages Publishing House, 1957.
———. *Fox Mykyta: Ivan Franko's Ukrainian Classic*. Trans. Bohdan Melnyk. Montreal: Tundra, 1978.
———. *Short Stories*. Kyiv: Dnipro Publishers, 1977.
———. *Stories*. Kyiv: Mystetstvo, 1972.
———. *When the Animals Could Talk. Fables*. Kyiv: Dnipro Publishers, 1987.
———. *Zakhar Berkut*. Kyiv: Dnipro Publishers, 1987.
Gzhytsky, Volodymyr. *Night and Day*. Trans. Ian Press. Edmonton and

Toronto: CIUS Press, 1988.
The Hagiography of Kievan Rus'. Trans. Paul Hollingsworth. Cambridge, Mass.: HURI, 1992.
Hogan, Ed, ed. *From Three Worlds: New Ukrainian Writing*. Boston: Zephyr Press, 1996.
Honchar, Oles. "The Cathedral." Trans. Marta Olynyk. *Journal of Ukrainian Graduate Studies* 1, 1 (fall 1976): 51–61.
———. *The Cyclone*. Trans. Alice Ingman. Moscow: Progress Publishers, 1972.
———. *Man and Arms*. Trans. Anatole Bilenko. Kyiv: Dnipro Publishers, 1985.
———. *The Shore of Love*. Trans. David Sinclair-Loutit. Moscow: Progress Publishers, 1980.
———. *The Standard-Bearers*. Trans. N. Jochel. Moscow: Foreign Languages Publishing House, 1955.
Khvylovy (Khvyliovy), Mykola. *Stories from the Ukraine*. Trans. George S. N. Luckyj. New York: Philosophical Library, 1960.
Kiriak, Illia. *Sons of the Soil*. Winnipeg: St. Andrew's College, 1983.
Kobylians'ka, Ol'ha. *On Sunday Morning She Gathered Herbs*. Trans. Mary Skrypnyk. Edmonton and Toronto: CIUS Press, 2001.
Kotsiubynsky, Mykhailo. *The Birthday Present and Other Stories*. Trans. Abraham Mistetsky. Kyiv: Dnipro Publishers, 1973.
———. *Chrysalis and Other Stories*. Trans. J. Guralsky. Moscow: Foreign Languages Publishing House, 1958.
———. *Fata Morgana and Other Stories*. Trans. Arthur Bernhard. Kyiv: Dnipro Publishers, 1980.
———. *Shadows of Forgotten Ancestors*. Trans. Marco Carynnyk. Littleton, Colo.: Ukrainian Academic Press, 1981.
Kulish, Panteleimon. *The Black Council*. Trans. George and Moira Luckyj. Littleton, Colo.: Ukrainian Academic Press, 1973.
Lev Krevza's "Defense of Church Unity" (1617) and Zaxarija Kopystens'kyj's "Palinodija or Book of Defense of the Holy Apostolic Eastern Catholic Church and Holy Patriarchs" (1620–1623). Trans. Bohdan Struminsky. Cambridge, Mass.: HURI, 1995.
The Life of Paisij Velyčkovs'kyj. Trans. Jeffrey Featherstone. Cambridge, Mass.: HURI, 1989.
Luchkovich, Michael, and Clarence A. Manning, eds. *Their Land: An Anthology of Ukrainian Short Stories*. Jersey City, N.J.: Svoboda Press, 1964.
Luckyj, George, ed. *Before the Storm: Soviet Ukrainian Fiction of the 1920s*. Trans. Yuri Tkach. Ann Arbor, Mich.: Ardis, 1986.
———. *Modern Ukrainian Short Stories*. Littleton, Colo.: Ukrainian Academic Press, 1973.

Mandryka, M. I. *History of Ukrainian Literature in Canada.* Winnipeg and Ottawa: Ukrainian Free Academy of Sciences, 1968.
On the Fence: An Anthology of Ukrainian Prose in Australia. Melbourne: Lastivka Press, 1985.
Osmachka, Theodosii. *Red Assassins.* Minneapolis: T. S. Denison, 1959.
The Paterik of the Kievan Caves Monastery. Trans. Muriel Heppell. Cambridge, Mass.: HURI, 1989.
Pidmohylny, Valerian. *A Little Touch of Drama.* Trans. George and Moira Luckyj. Littleton, Colo.: Ukrainian Academic Press, 1972.
Sermons and Rhetoric of Kievan Rus'. Trans. Simon Franklin. Cambridge, Mass.: HURI, 1991.
Soviet Ukrainian Short Stories. 2 vols. Kyiv: Dnipro Publishers, 1983–85.
Stefanyk, Vasyl. *Maple Leaves and Other Stories.* Trans. Mary Skrypnyk. Kyiv: Dnipro Publishers, 1988.
———. *The Stone Cross.* Toronto: McClelland and Stewart, 1991.
Stelmakh, Mykhailo. *Let the Blood of Man Not Flow.* Moscow: Foreign Languages Publishing House, 1962.
Stories of the Soviet Ukraine. Moscow: Progress Publishers, 1970.
Symonenko, Vasyl. "Diary. Crusts of Thoughts." *UR* 42, 1 (spring 1995): 56–61.
Ukrainian Authors. Winnipeg: Ukrainian Canadian Committee, 1946.
Vovchok, Marko. *Marusia: A Maid of Ukraine.* Translated from the French of P. J. Stahl by Cornelia W. Cyr. New York: Dodd Mead, 1890.
Yanovsky, Yurii. *The Horsemen.* Kyiv: Dnipro Publishers, 1989.

(2) Poetry
Anthology of Soviet Ukrainian Poetry. Kyiv: Dnipro Publishers, 1982.
Antonych, Bohdan. *Square of Angels: Poems.* Trans. Mark Rudman and Paul Nemser with Bohdan Boychuk. Ann Arbor, Mich.: Ardis, 1977.
Drach, Ivan. *Orchard Lamps.* New York: Sheep Meadow Press, 1978.
Ewach, Honore. *Ukrainian Songs and Lyrics: A Short Anthology of Ukrainian Poetry.* Winnipeg: Ukrainian Publishing, 1933.
Four Ukrainian Poets: Drach, Korotych, Kostenko, Symonenko. Trans. Martha Bohachevsky-Chomiak and Danylo Struk. New York: Quixote, 1969.
Franko, Ivan. "Ivan Franko—A Selection of Poems." *UR* 40, 4 (winter 1992): 40–48.
———. *Ivan Franko: The Poet of Western Ukraine. Selected Poems.* Trans. Percival Cundy. New York: Greenwood Press, 1968.
———. *Ivan Vyshensky: A Poem.* Trans. Roman Tatchyn. New York: Shevchenko Scientific Society, 1983.
———. *The Master's Jests.* Trans. Roman Tatchyn. New York: Shev-

chenko Scientific Society, 1979.

———. *Moses and Other Poems*. Trans. Vera Rich and Percival Cundy. New York: Shevchenko Scientific Society, 1973.

———. *Selections, Poems and Stories*. Trans. John Weir. Kyiv: Dnipro Publishers, 1986.

Honcharuk, Zakhar, ed. *Anthology of Soviet Ukrainian Poetry*. Kyiv: Dnipro Publishers, 1982.

Invincible Spirit: Art and Poetry of Ukrainian Women Political Prisoners in the USSR. Baltimore: Smoloskyp, 1977.

Kostenko, Lina. "Four Poems." *UR* 15, 3 (1968): 55–58.

Livesay, Florence Randall. *Songs of Ukraina with Ruthenian Poems*. London: Dent, 1916.

Luchuk, Olha, and Michael M. Naydan, eds. *A Hundred Years of Youth: A Bilingual Anthology of 20th Century Ukrainian Poetry*. Lviv: Litopys, 2000.

Lypa, Yurii. "Curse." *UR* 41, 3 (autumn 1994): 66.

Oles, Oleksander. "The Asters." *UR* 41, 2 (summer 1994): 59.

———. "Daybreak, daybreak . . . " *UR* 41, 2 (summer 1994): 60.

Olzhych, Oleh. "Evening, I look on the blue rock-faces . . . " *UR* 41, 3 (autumn 1994): 62.

———. "Morning Prayer." *UR* 41, 3 (autumn 1994): 62.

———. "The Prophet." *UR* 41, 3 (autumn 1994): 62–63.

Osmachka, Todos. "Elegy." *UR* 42, 4 (winter 1995): 67–68.

Rudenko, Mykola. *Khrest: poema/The Cross: A Poem*. Kyiv: Smoloskyp, 1996.

Rylsky, Maksym. *Selected Poetry*. Kyiv: Dnipro Publishers, 1980.

Shevchenko, Taras. "Five Political Poems." *UR* 41, 1 (spring 1994): 54–65.

———. *The Kobzar: The Poetical Works of Taras Shevchenko*. Trans. C. H. Andrusyshen and Watson Kirkconnell. Toronto: University of Toronto Press, 1964.

———. *Selected Works: Poetry and Prose*. Moscow: Progress Publishers, 1964.

———. *Selections*. Trans. John Weir. Toronto: Ukrainian Canadian, 1961.

———. *Selections, Poetry and Prose*. Kyiv: Dnipro Publishers, 1988.

———. *Song out of Darkness: Selected Poems*. Trans. Vera Rich. London: Mitre Press, 1961.

———. *Taras Shevchenko: Selected Poetry. Illustrated with Reproductions of Drawings, Sketches, Outlines, Etchings by Taras Shevchenko*. Kyiv: Dnipro Publishers, 1972.

Skovoroda, Hryhorii. "Little Bird, Whose Flanks Shine Goldly." *UR* 41, 4 (winter 1994): 67.

The Song of Igor's Campaign: An Epic of the Twelfth Century. Trans. Vladimir Nabokov. New York: Vintage Books, 1960.

Stus, Vasyl. "From the Cycle *Palimpsests.*" *UR* 42, 4 (winter 1995): 57–59.

———. "In Memory of Alla Horska." *UR* 42, 4 (winter 1995): 55.

———. *Selected Poems.* Trans. Jaropolk Lassovsky. Munich: Ukrainian Free University, 1987.

Symonenko, Vasyl. "From the Prohibited Works of Vasyl Symonenko." *UR* 42, 1 (spring 1995): 62–65.

———. *Granite Obelisks.* Trans. Andriy M. Fr.-Chirovsky. Jersey City, N.J.: Svoboda, 1975.

Szporluk, Mary Ann, and I. R. Titunik. "Ukrainian Baroque Poetry and Drama in Translation." *JUS* 13, 1 (summer 1988): 3–42.

Teliha, Olena. *Boundaries of Flame: A Complete Collection of Poetry.* Trans. Orysia Prokopiw. Baltimore: Smoloskyp Publishers, 1977.

Tychyna, Pavlo. *The Complete Early Poetry Collections of Pavlo Tychyna.* Trans. Michael M. Naydan. Lviv: Litopys, 2000.

———. *Selected Poetry.* Trans. Gladys Evans et al. Kyiv: Dnipro Publishers, 1987.

Ukrainian Dumy: Editio Minor. Trans. George Tarnawsky and Patricia Kilina. Edmonton and Toronto: CIUS Press, 1979.

The Ukrainian Poets, 1182–1962. Trans. C. H. Andrusyshen and Watson Kirkconnell. Toronto: University of Toronto Press, 1963.

"Ukrainian Poets and World War II." *UR* 42, 2 (summer 1995): 42–52.

Ukrainka, Lesia. *Hope: Selected Poetry.* Kyiv: Dnipro Publishers, 1975.

———, *Spirit of Flame: A Collection of the Works of Lesya Ukrainka.* Trans. Percival Cundy. New York: Bookman Associates, 1950.

Zabuzhko, Oksana. *A Kingdom of Fallen Statues: Poems and Essays.* Toronto: Wellspring, 1996.

3. Performing Arts

a. Music

Antonovych, Myroslav. *The Chants from Ukrainian Heirmologia.* Bilthoven: A. B. Creyghton, 1974.

———. and Irene R. Makaryk. "Musical Brain-Drain: The Ukrainian Influence on Russian Liturgical Music." *Studia Ukrainica* 2 (1984): 121–39.

Bahry, Romana. "Rock Culture and Rock Music in Ukraine." In *Rocking the State: Rock Music and Politics in Eastern Europe and Russia*, ed. Sabrina Petra Ramet, 243–96. Boulder, Colo.: Westview Press, 1994.

Baley, Virko. "Boris Lyatoshynsky and Ukrainian Opera: Etudes toward an Essay." *Opera Journal* 27, 3 (Sep. 1994): 12–18.

Filenko, Taras, and Tamara Bulat. *The World of Mykola Lysenko.* Edmonton: Ukraine Millennium Foundation, 2001.
Kononenko, Natalie O. *Ukrainian Minstrels: And the Blind Shall Sing.* Armonk, N.Y.: M. E. Sharpe, 1998.
Kulikovič, M. "Stalin and Post-Stalin Elements in Soviet Ukrainian Music." *Ukrainian Review* (Munich) 7 (1959): 83–92.
Kytasty, Hryhoriy. *A Few Reflections on Ukrainian Music under Soviet Rule.* New York: Eastern European Fund, 1954.
Lutsiv, Volodymyr. "Kobza-Bandura and 'Dumy' and Their Significance in the History of the Ukrainian People." *UR* 13, 1 (spring 1966): 53–70.
Noll, William. "The Social Role and Economic Status of Blind Peasant Minstrels in Ukraine." *HUS* 17, 1/2 (June 1993): 45–71.
Olkhovsky, Andrey. *Music under the Soviets.* London: Routledge and Kegan Paul, 1955.
Pauls, John P. "Musical Works Based on the Legend of Mazepa." *UR* 11, 4 (winter 1964): 57–65.
Roccasalvo, Joan L. *The Plainchant Tradition of Southwestern Rus'.* Boulder, Colo.: East European Monographs, 1986.
Shatulsky, Myron. *The Ukrainian Folk Dance.* Toronto: Kobzar Publishing Company, 1986.
Shtokalko, Zinovii. *A Kobzar Handbook.* Trans. Andrij Hornjatkevyč. Edmonton and Toronto: CIUS Press, 1989.
Sichynskyi, Denys. *Ukrainian Christmas Carols.* New York: Surma Books and Music, 1960.
Soroker, Yakov. *Ukrainian Musical Elements in Classical Music.* Edmonton and Toronto: CIUS Press, 1995.
Two Hundred and One Ukrainian Folk Songs. New York: Surma Books and Music, 1971.
Yekelchyk, Serhy. "Diktat and Dialogue in Stalinist Culture: Staging Patriotic Historical Opera in Soviet Ukraine (1936–1954)," *Slavic Review* 59, 3 (fall 2000): 597–624.

b. Theater

About the Harrowing of Hell: A Seventeenth-Century Ukrainian Play in Its European Context. Trans. Irena R. Makaryk. Ottawa: Dovehouse Editions, 1989.
Bahry, Romana. "Les' Kurbas' *Jimmie Higgins*: An Expressionist Avant-garde Drama." *CSP* 36, 3/4 (Sep.–Dec. 1994): 349–62.
Bowlt, John, ed. *Twentieth-Century Russian and Ukrainian Stage Design.* Temple, Ariz.: Charles Schlacks, 1981.
Chorney, Stephen. "Don Juanian Motif in Lesya Ukrainka's Dramaturgy." *UQ* 35, 2 (summer 1979): 156–66.

Derzhavyn, Volodymyr. "The Dramatic Works of Lesya Ukrainka." *UR* 3, 2 (1956): 34–42.

Dyky, Luba M. "Some Aspects of the *Sonata Pathetique* by Mykola Kulish." *AUAAS* 12, 33/34 (1969–72): 158–91.

Hirniak, Yosyp. "Birth and Death of the Modern Ukrainian Theater." In *Soviet Theaters, 1917–1941*, ed. Martha Bradshaw, 250–338. New York: Research Program on the USSR, 1954.

Karpiak, Robert. "Don Juan: A Universal Theme in Ukrainian Drama." *CSP* 24, 1 (spring 1982): 25–31.

Kiselyov, Yosip. *Dramatic Art in the Soviet Ukraine*. Kyiv: Dnipro Publishers, 1979.

Kocherha, Ivan. *Yaroslav the Wise*. Kyiv: Dnipro Publishers, 1982.

Korniichuk, Oleksandr. *Wings: A Play in Four Acts*. Moscow: Foreign Languages Publishing House, 1954.

Kotovich, P. "Contemporary Drama in the Ukrainian SSR." *Ukrainian Review* (Munich) 2 (1956): 70–83.

Kulish, Mykola. *Sonata pathetique*. Trans. George and Moira Luckyj. Littleton, Colo.: Ukrainian Academic Press, 1975.

Lewin, Paulina. "Drama and Theater at Ukrainian Schools in the Seventeenth and Eighteenth Centuries: The Bible as Inspiration of Images, Meanings, Style, and Stage Productions." *HUS* 8, 1/2 (June 1984): 93–122.

———. "Early Ukrainian Theater and Drama." *Nationalities Papers* 8, 2 (fall 1980): 219–32.

———. "The Staging of Plays at the Kiev Mohyla Academy in the Seventeenth and Eighteenth Centuries." *HUS* 5, 3 (Sep. 1981): 320–34.

———. "The Ukrainian Popular Religious Stage of the Seventeenth and Eighteenth Centuries on the Territory of the Polish Commonwealth." *HUS* 1, 3 (Sep. 1977): 308–29.

———. "The Ukrainian School Theater in the Seventeenth and Eighteenth Centuries: An Expression of the Baroque." *HUS* 5, 1 (Mar. 1981): 54–65.

Luzhnytsky, Hryhor H. "Liturgical Elements in the History of Ukrainian Theater." *UQ* 43, 3/4 (fall–winter 1987): 200–209.

Makaryk, Irena R. *Shakespeare in the Undiscovered Bourn: Les Kurbas, Ukrainian Modernism, and Early Soviet Cultural Politics*. Toronto: University of Toronto Press, 2004.

Onyshkevych, Larissa M. L. Z. "Exponents of Traditions and Innovations in Modern Ukrainian Drama." *Slavic and East European Journal* 43, 1 (spring 1999): 49–63.

Revutsky, Valerian. "The Act of Ems (1876) and Its Effect on Ukrainian Theatre." *Nationalities Papers* 5, 1 (spring 1977): 67–78.

———. "Between *Sonata Pathetique* and *Optimistic Tragedy*." *Studia Ucrainica* 1 (1978): 111–16.

———. "Mykola Kulish in the Modern Ukrainian Theatre." *Slavonic and East European Review* 49, 116 (1971): 355–64.

———. "A Survey of the Ukrainian Post-War Drama." *CSP* 14, 2 (summer 1972): 251–68.

Rozumnyj, Jaroslav. "Conflicting Ideas in Lesya Ukrainka's 'Stone Host.'" *CSP* 15, 3 (1973): 382–89.

Slez, Wolodymyr. "Les Kurbas and the Modern Ukrainian Theater." *UR* 37, 1 (spring 1989): 24–37.

Smyrniw, Walter. "The Symbolic Design of Narodnyy Malakhiy." *Slavonic and East European Review* 61, 2 (1983): 184–96.

Tkacz, Virlana. "The Birth of a Director: The Early Development of Les Kurbas and His First Season with the Young Theatre." *JUS* 12, 1 (summer 1987): 22–54.

———. "Les Kurbas's Use of Film Language in His Stage Productions of *Jimmie Higgins* and *Macbeth*." *CSP* 32, 1 (Mar. 1990): 59–76.

Ukrainka, Lesia. *Forest Song*. In *UR* 41, 1 (spring 1994): 66–73; 2 (summer 1994): 33–58; 3 (autumn 1994): 40–60; 4 (winter 1994): 48–64.

———. *Her Excellency: A Dramatic Poem in Five Acts*. In *UR* 40, 1 (spring 1992): 28–54; 2 (summer 1992): 23–40; 3 (autumn 1992): 37–44.

c. Film

Carynnyk, Marco, ed. *Alexander Dovzhenko: The Poet as Filmmaker*. Cambridge, Mass.: MIT Press, 1973.

———. "Sergo Paradzhanov in Prison." *Journal of Ukrainian Graduate Studies* 3, 1 (spring 1978): 47–55.

Halchenko, L. "The Soviet Film Industry in the Ukrainian SSR." *Ukrainian Review* (Munich) 8 (1959): 57–68.

Kepley, Vance, Jr. *In the Service of the State: The Cinema of Alexander Dovzhenko*. Madison: University of Wisconsin Press, 1986.

Liber, George. *Alexander Dovzhenko: A Life in Soviet Film*. London: BFI Publishers, 2002.

Nebesio, Bohdan Y. *Alexander Dovzhenko: A Guide to Published Sources*. Edmonton and Toronto: CIUS Press, 1995.

———. "*Zaporozhets za Dunaiem* (1938): The Production of the First Ukrainian-Language Feature Film in Canada." *JUS* 16, 1/2 (summer–winter 1991): 115–29.

———, ed. *JUS* 19, no. 1 (summer 1994). *Special Issue: The Cinema of Alexander Dovzhenko*.

100 Films of the Ukrainian Cinema. Kyiv: Spalakh, 1996.

Sawycky, Roman. *Ukrainian Film Guide*. Cranford, N.J.: The Keys Publishing Association, 1980.
Zaporzan, Shirley, and Robert B. Klymasz. *Film and the Ukrainians in Canada, 1921–1980*. Edmonton and Toronto: CIUS Press, 1982.

III. ECONOMIC

Arkhymovych, O. "Grain Crops in the Ukraine." *Ukrainian Review* (Munich) 2 (1956): 21–34.
Balmaceda, Margarita Mercedes. "Gas, Oil and the Linkages between Domestic and Foreign Policies: The Case of Ukraine." *Europe-Asia Studies* 50, 2 (Mar. 1998): 257–86.
Banaian, King. *The Ukrainian Economy since Independence*. Aldershot: Edward Elgar, 1999.
Bandera, V., and Z. L. Melnyk, eds. *The Soviet Economy in Regional Perspective*. New York: Praeger, 1973.
Bekkers, Angela et al., eds. *Taming the Wild West? A Business Study of the Ukraine*. Rotterdam: Erasmus University, 1993.
Bohatiuk, Nicholas G. "The Economy of Kiev under Foreign Conquerors, 1941–1944." *UQ* 42, 1/2 (spring–summer 1986): 35–58.
Boss, Helen. "Ukraine's First Year of Economic Statehood." In *Economic Transformation in East-Central Europe and in the Newly Independent States*, ed. Gábor Hunya, 243–75. Boulder, Colo.: Westview Press, 1994.
Buck, Trevor et al. "The Process and Impact of Privatization in Russia and Ukraine." *Comparative Economic Studies* 38, 2/3 (summer–fall 1996): 45–67.
Burmistenko, Milada. "Female Unemployment: Ukraine and Great Britain—A Comparison." *UR* 43, 2 (summer 1996): 13–20.
Chirovsky, Nicholas L. *Old Ukraine: Its Socio-Economic History prior to 1781*. Madison, N.J.: Florham Park Press, 1963.
Cowley, Andrew. "Unruly Child: A Survey of Ukraine." *Economist* 331 (7 May 1994): 1–18.
Csaki, Csaba. *Land Reform in Ukraine: The First Five Years*. Washington, D.C.: World Bank, 1997.
Dabrowski, Marek. "The Ukrainian Way to Hyperinflation." *Communist Economies and Economic Transformation* 6, 2 (1994): 115–37.
D'Anieri, Paul. *Economic Interdependence in Ukrainian-Russian Relations*. New York: State University of New York Press, 1999.
Deal, Zack. "Ukrainian Regional Agrarian History: A Review of the Findings of T. D. Lipovskaia on the Crisis of the Serf Economy in the Left-Bank Ukraine." *HUS* 1, 4 (Dec. 1977): 524–49.
Dienes, Susan F. "Economic Geographic Relations in the Post-Soviet

Republics." *Post-Soviet Geography* 34, 8 (Oct. 1993): 497–529.
Friesen, Leonard G. "Toward a Market Economy: Fruit and Vegetable Production by the Peasants of New Russia, 1850–1900." *CSP* 40, 1/2 (Mar.–June 1998): 27–42.
Fuxman, Leonora. "Ethical Dilemmas of Doing Business in Post-Soviet Ukraine." *Journal of Business Ethics* 16, 12/13 (Sep. 1997): 1273–82.
Glowinskyj, E. "Agriculture in the Ukraine." *Ukrainian Review* (Munich) 2 (1956): 5–20.
Havrylyshyn, Oleh, Marcus Miller, and William Perraudin. "Deficits, Inflation and the Political Economy of Ukraine." *Economic Policy* 9 (Oct. 1996): 354–401.
Holubnychy, Vsevolod. *The Industrial Output of the Ukraine, 1913–1956: A Statistical Analysis.* Munich: Institute for the Study of the USSR, 1957.
———. *Soviet Regional Economics: Selected Works of Vsevolod Holubnychy*, ed. I. S. Koropeckyj. Edmonton and Toronto: CIUS Press, 1982.
———. "The Views of M. Volobuyev and V. Dobrohayev and the Party Criticism." *Ukrainian Review* (Munich) 3 (1956): 5–12.
Ivanytsky, Borys. "Ukrainian Forestry." *AUAAS* 3, 7 (1953): 553–70.
Johnson, S. R. "Production Efficiency and Agricultural Reform in Ukraine." *American Journal of Agricultural Economics* 76, 3 (Aug. 1994): 629–65.
Kamiński, Bartłomiej, ed. *Economic Transition in Russia and the New States of Eurasia.* Armonk, N.Y.: M. E. Sharpe, 1996.
Kononenko, Konstantyn. *Ukraine and Russia: A History of the Economic Relations between Ukraine and Russia, 1654–1917.* Milwaukee: Marquette University Press, 1958.
Koropeckyj, Iwan S. "A Century of Moscow-Ukraine Economic Relations: An Interpretation." *HUS* 5, 4 (Dec. 1981): 467–96.
———. *Development in the Shadow: Studies in Ukrainian Economics.* Edmonton and Toronto: CIUS Press, 1990.
———. "The Economic Profession in the Ukraine." *AUAAS* 13, 35/36 (1973–77): 173–88.
———. *Location Problems in Soviet Industry Before World War II: The Case of the Ukraine.* Chapel Hill, N.C.: University of North Carolina Press, 1971.
———. *Selected Contributions of Ukrainian Scholars to Economics.* Cambridge, Mass.: HURI, 1984.
———, ed. *The Ukraine within the USSR: An Economic Balance Sheet.* New York: Praeger, 1977.
———, ed. *Ukrainian Economic History: Interpretive Essays.* Edmonton and Toronto: CIUS Press, 1991.

———, ed. *The Ukrainian Economy: Achievements, Problems, Challenges*. Cambridge, Mass.: HURI, 1992.
Kowal, Lubomyr M. "Mykhailo Ivanovich Tuhan-Baranovsky: His Political, Teaching, Scientific and Cooperative Activity in Ukraine, 1917–1919." *Wissenschaftliche Mitteilungen* (Munich) 18 (1968–69): 52–68.
Krasnov, Gregory V., and Josef C. Brada. "Implicit Subsidies in Russian-Ukrainian Energy Trade." *Europe-Asia Studies* 49, 5 (July 1997): 825–43.
Kravchuk, Robert S. *Ukrainian Political Economy: The First Ten Years*. New York: Palgrave Macmillan, 2002.
Krawec, Roman. "Ukrainian Space Policy: Contributing to National Economic Development." *Space Policy* 11, 2 (May 1995): 105–14.
Kushnirsky, Fyodor. "Free Economic Zones in Ukraine: The Case of Odessa." *Ukrainian Economic Review* 2, 3 (1996): 117–24.
———. "Ukraine's Industrial Enterprise: Surviving Hard Times." *Comparative Economic Studies* 36, 4 (winter 1994): 21–39.
Lyashchenko, Peter I. *History of the National Economy of Russia to the 1917 Revolution*. New York: Octagon Books, 1970.
Marples, David. "The Post-Soviet Nuclear Power Program." *Post-Soviet Geography* 34, 3 (Mar. 1993): 172–84.
Melnyk, Zinowij Lew. *Soviet Capital Formation in Ukraine, 1928–1932*. Munich: Ukrainian Free University Press, 1965.
Ohloblyn, Oleksander. "Ukrainian Economics in Scholarly and Public Thought in the 19th–20th Centuries." *AUAAS* 13, 35/36 (1973–77): 5–22.
Poplujko, A. "The Economy of the Ukraine Today." *Ukrainian Review* (Munich) 3 (1956): 54–87.
Prociuk, S. G. "Transportation in Ukraine." *UQ* 13, 1 (Mar. 1957): 67–76.
Pukhtayevych, Halyna. "The Current State of the Ukrainian Economy: Strategy and Reform." *UR* 41, 2 (summer 1994): 5–13.
Rose, Richard. *Adaptation, Resilience and Destitution: Alternatives in Ukraine*. Glasgow: University of Strathclyde, 1995.
Shen, Raphael. *Ukraine's Economic Reform: Obstacles, Errors, Lessons*. Westport, Conn.: Praeger, 1996.
Siedenberg, Axel, and Lutz Hoffmann, eds. *Ukraine at the Crossroads: Economic Reforms in International Perspective*. Heidelberg: Physica-Verlag, 1999.
Smolansky, Oles M. "Ukraine's Quest for Independence: The Fuel Factor." *Europe-Asia Studies* 47, 1 (1995): 67–90.
Tedstrom, John E. "Ukraine: A Crash Course in Economic Transition." *Comparative Economic Studies* 37, 4 (winter 1995): 49–67.
Timoshenko, Vladimir P. *Agricultural Russia and the Wheat Problem*.

Stanford, Calif.: Food Research Institute and the Committee on Russian Research of the Hoover War Library, 1932.

———. "Soviet Agricultural Policy and the Nationalities Problem in the USSR." *Report on the Soviet Union in 1956: A Symposium of the Institute for the Study of the USSR*. Munich, 1956.

The Ukrainian Challenge: Reforming Labour Market and Social Policy. Budapest: Central European University Press, 1995.

Wilson, Andrew, and Ihor Burakovsky. *Economic Reform in Ukraine*. London: Royal Institute of International Affairs, 1996.

———. *The Ukrainian Economy under Kuchma*. London: Royal Institute of International Affairs, 1996.

Wolf, Charles, ed. *The Role of the Military Sector in the Economies of Russia and Ukraine*. Santa Monica, Calif.: Rand, 1993.

Woroby, Tamara, and Andrew Bihun. "The Ukrainian Economy: One Year After Independence." *Eurasian Reports* 3, 1 (winter 1992–93): 43–50.

Wynar, Bohdan S. "Ukrainian Economy—Spoil of Russian Occupation and Victim of War, 1930–1954." *UQ* 14, 3 (Sep. 1958): 240–52.

IV. HISTORICAL

1. General

Adams, Arthur E., Ian M. Matley, and William O. McCagg. *An Atlas of Russian and East European History*. New York: Praeger, 1966.

Allen, W. E. D. *The Ukraine: A History*. Cambridge: University Press, 1940.

Aster, Howard, and Peter J. Potichnyj. *Jewish-Ukrainian Relations: Two Solitudes*. Oakville, Ont.: Mosaic Press, 1983.

Brégy, Pierre, and Serge Obolensky. *The Ukraine—A Russian Land*. London: Selwyn & Blount, 1940.

Chamberlin, William Henry. *The Ukraine: A Submerged Nation*. New York: Macmillan, 1944.

Doroshenko, Dmytro. *A Survey of Ukrainian History*. Ed. and updated by Oleh W. Gerus. Winnipeg: Humeniuk Publication Foundation, 1975.

Dvornik, Francis. *The Slavs in European History and Civilization*. New Brunswick, N.J.: Rutgers University Press, 1962.

Himka, John-Paul. *Galicia and Bukovina: A Research Handbook about Western Ukraine, Late 19th and 20th Centuries*. Edmonton: Alberta Culture and Multiculturalism, 1990.

Hrushevsky, Michael. *A History of Ukraine*. New Haven, Conn.: Yale University Press, 1941.

Hrushevsky, Mykhailo. *The Historical Evolution of the Ukrainian*

Problem. London: SVU, 1915; repr. Cleveland: John T. Zubal Publishers, 1981.

———. *History of Ukraine-Rus'*. Edmonton and Toronto: CIUS Press, 1997– (volumes 1, 7, 8, 9 [pt. 1] published to date).

Hryhorijiv, N. Y. *The War and Ukrainian Democracy: A Compilation of Documents from the Past and Present*. Toronto: Industrial and Educational Publishing, 1945.

Kappeler, Andreas. *"Great Russians" and "Little Russians." Russian-Ukrainian Relations and Perceptions in Historical Perspective*. Donald W. Treadgold Papers, no. 39. Seattle: University of Washington Press, 2003.

Kappeler, Andreas, Zenon E. Kohut, Frank E. Sysyn, and Mark von Hagen, eds. *Culture, Nation, and Identity: The Ukrainian-Russian Encounter, 1600–1945*. Edmonton and Toronto: CIUS Press, 2003.

Kondufor, Yuri, ed. *A Short History of the Ukraine*. Kyiv: Naukova dumka, 1986.

Kotliar, N., and S. Kulchitsky. *Kiev: Ancient and Modern City*. Kyiv: Politvydav Ukrainy, 1983.

Magocsi, Paul Robert. *Galicia: A Historical Survey and Bibliographic Guide*. Toronto: University of Toronto Press, 1983.

———. *Historical Atlas of Central Europe*. Seattle: University of Washington Press, 2002.

———. *A History of Ukraine*. Toronto: University of Toronto Press, 1996.

———. *Ukraine: A Historical Atlas*. Toronto: University of Toronto Press, 1985; repr. with corrections, 1987.

Manning, Clarence A. *The Story of the Ukraine*. New York: Philosophical Library, 1947.

Morozov, Kostiantyn et al. *The Military Tradition in Ukrainian History: Its Role in the Construction of Ukraine's Armed Forces*. Cambridge, Mass.: HURI, 1995.

Potichnyj, Peter J., ed. *Poland and Ukraine: Past and Present*. Edmonton and Toronto: CIUS Press, 1980.

Potichnyj, Peter J., and Howard Aster, eds. *Ukrainian-Jewish Relations in Historical Perspective*. 2d ed. Edmonton and Toronto: CIUS Press, 1990.

Potichnyj, Peter J., Marc Raeff, Jaroslaw Pelenski, and Gleb N. Žekulin, eds. *Ukraine and Russia in Their Historical Encounter*. Edmonton and Toronto: CIUS Press, 1992.

Reid, Anna. *Borderland: A Journey through the History of Ukraine*. London: Weidenfeld & Nicolson, 1997.

Rudnytsky, Ivan L. *Essays in Modern Ukrainian History*. Edmonton and Toronto: CIUS Press, 1987.

Saunders, David. "What Makes a Nation a Nation? Ukrainians since 1600." *Ethnic Groups* 10 (1993): 196–207.
Ševčenko, Ihor. *Ukraine between East and West: Essays on Cultural History to the Early Eighteenth Century.* Edmonton and Toronto: CIUS Press, 1996.
Subtelny, Orest. *Ukraine: A History.* Toronto: University of Toronto Press, 1988. 3d ed. Toronto, 2000.
Szporluk, Roman. *Ukraine: A Brief History.* 2d ed. Detroit: Ukrainian Festival Committee, 1982.
———. "The Ukraine and Russia." In *The Last Empire: Nationality and the Soviet Future,* ed. Robert Conquest, 151–82. Stanford, Calif.: Hoover Institution Press, 1986.
———. "The Ukraine and the Ukrainians." In *Handbook of Major Soviet Nationalities,* ed. Zev Katz et al., 21–48. New York: Free Press and Collier Macmillan, 1975.
Torke, Hans-Joachim, and John-Paul Himka, eds. *German-Ukrainian Relations in Historical Perspective.* Edmonton and Toronto: CIUS Press, 1994.
Ukrainians and Jews: Articles, Testimonies, Letters and Official Documents Dealing with Interrelations of Ukrainians and Jews in the Past and Present. A Symposium. Ed. Walter Dushnyck. New York: Ukrainian Congress Committee of America, 1966.
Vernadsky, George, and Michael Karpovich. *A History of Russia.* 5 vols. New Haven, Conn.: Yale University Press, 1943–69.
Wilson, Andrew. *The Ukrainians: Unexpected Nation.* 2d ed. New Haven, Conn.: Yale University Press, 2002.

2. Historiography

Abramson, Henry. "Historiography on the Jews and the Ukrainian Revolution." *JUS* 15, 2 (winter 1990): 33–45.
Baker, Mark. "Beyond the National: Peasants, Power, and Revolution in Ukraine." *JUS* 24, 1 (summer 1999): 39–68.
Basile, Giovanni Maniscalco. "The Christian Prince through the Mirror of the Rus' Chronicles." *HUS* 12/13 (1988–89): 672–88.
Bercoff, Giovanna Brogi. "The History of Christian Rus' in the *Annales Ecclesiastici* of Caesar Baronius." *HUS* 12/13 (1988–89): 551–75.
Bojcun, Marko. "Approaches to the Study of the Ukrainian Revolution." *JUS* 24, 1 (summer 1999): 21–38.
Burant, Stephen R., and Voytek Zubek. "Eastern Europe's Old Memories and New Realities: Resurrecting the Polish-Lithuanian Union." *East European Politics and Societies* 7, 2 (spring 1993): 370–93.
Chubaty, Nicholas. "Kievan Christianity Misinterpreted." *Ukraïns'kyi istoryk* 9, 1/2 (1972): 100–109.

Cracraft, James. "Did Feofan Prokopovich Really Write *Pravda Voli Monarshei*?" *Slavic Review* 40, 2 (summer 1981): 173–93.

———. "Prokopovyč's Kiev Period Reconsidered." *HUS* 2, 2 (1978): 138–57.

Dashkevych, Yaroslav. "East Galicia: Ethnic Relations, National Myths and Mentality." *UR* 43, 2 (summer 1996): 45–54.

Diadychenko, V. A., F. E. Los, and V. G. Sarbey. *Development of Historical Science in the Ukrainian SSR*. Kyiv: Naukova dumka, 1970.

Doroshenko, Dmytro. *A Survey of Ukrainian Historiography*. Supplement: Olexander Ohloblyn, *Ukrainian Historiography, 1917–1956*. New York: Ukrainian Academy of Arts and Sciences in the U.S., 1957.

Grabowicz, George G. "Some Further Observations on 'Non-historical' Nations and 'Incomplete' Literatures: A Reply." *HUS* 5, 3 (Sep. 1981): 358–68.

———. "Ukrainian Studies: Framing the Contexts." *Slavic Review* 54, 3 (fall 1995): 674–90.

Graziosi, Andrea. "Stalin's War against the Peasants: Questions and Meanings." *JUS* 24, 1 (summer 1999): 85–94.

Grimsted, Patricia Kennedy. "Archeography in the Service of Imperial Policy: The Foundation of the Kiev Archeographic Commission and the Kiev Central Archive of Early Record Books." *HUS* 17, 1/2 (June 1993): 27–44.

———. *Trophies of War and Empire: The Archival Heritage of Ukraine, World War II, and the International Politics of Restitution*. Cambridge, Mass.: HURI, 2001.

Horak, Stephan M. "Michael Hrushevsky: Portrait of an Historian." *CSP* 10, 3 (autumn 1968): 341–56.

———. "Periodization and Terminology of the History of Eastern Slavs: Observations and Analyses." *Slavic Review* 31, 4 (Dec. 1972): 853–62.

———. "Ukrainian Historiography, 1953–1963." *Slavic Review* 24, 2 (June 1965): 258–72.

Hrushevsky, Michael. *The Traditional Scheme of "Russian" History and the Problem of a Rational Organization of the History of the East Slavs*. Ed. Andrew Gregorovich. 2d ed. Winnipeg: Ukrainian Free Academy of Sciences, 1966.

Ilnytzkyj, Oleh S. "Russian and Ukrainian Studies and the New World Order." *CSP* 34, 4 (Dec. 1992): 445–58.

Isaievych, Iaroslav. "Ukrainian Studies—Exceptional or Merely Exemplary?" *Slavic Review* 54, 3 (fall 1995): 702–8.

———. "Ukrainians and Poles: Recent Developments in Politics and National Historiographies." *JUS* 21, 1/2 (summer–winter 1996):

67–79.
Kappeler, Andreas. "Ukrainian History from a German Perspective." *Slavic Review* 54, 3 (fall 1995): 691–701.
Klid, Bohdan. "The Struggle over Mykhailo Hrushevs'kyi: Recent Soviet Polemics." *CSP* 33, 1 (Mar. 1991): 32–45.
———. "Volodymyr Antonovych: Ukrainian Populist Historiography and the Cultural Politics of Nation Building." In *Historiography of Imperial Russia: The Profession and Writing of History in a Multinational State*, ed. Thomas Sanders, 373–93. Armonk, N.Y.: M. E. Sharpe, 1999.
Knysh, George D. "Some Problems in Omeljan Pritsak's Reconstruction of Ninth Century Ukrainian and East European History." *Ukraïns'kyi istoryk* 20, 2–4 (1983): 93–102.
Kohut, Zenon E. "The Development of a Ukrainian National Historiography in Imperial Russia." In *Historiography of Imperial Russia: The Profession and Writing of History in a Multinational State*, ed. Thomas Sanders, 453–77. Armonk, N.Y.: M. E. Sharpe, 1999.
———. "History as a Battleground: Russian-Ukrainian Relations and Historical Consciousness in Contemporary Ukraine." In *The Legacy of History in Russia and the New States of Eurasia*, ed. S. Frederick Starr, 123–45. Armonk, N.Y.: M. E. Sharpe, 1994.
———. "In Search of Early Modern Ukrainian Statehood: Post-Soviet Studies of the Cossack Hetmanate." *JUS* 24, 2 (winter 1999): 101–12.
———. "Myths Old and New: The Haidamak Movement and the *Koliivshchyna* (1768) in Recent Historiography." *HUS* 1, 3 (Sep. 1977): 359–78.
Korduba, Myron. *La littérature historique soviétique-ukrainienne*. Warsaw, 1938; repr. Munich: Wilhelm Fink Verlag, 1972.
Krupnytsky, Borys. "Mazepa and Soviet Historiography." *Ukrainian Review* (Munich) 3 (1956): 49–53.
———. "Trends in Modern Ukrainian Historiography." *UQ* 6, 4 (autumn 1950): 337–45.
Lypynsky, Vyacheslav. "The Ukraine at the Turning Point." *AUAAS* 3, 7 (1953): 605–19.
Mazour, Anatole G. *Modern Russian Historiography*. Rev. ed. Westport, Conn.: Greenwood Press, 1975.
Miller, David B. "The Kievan Principality in the Century before the Mongol Invasion: An Inquiry into Recent Research and Interpretation." *HUS* 10, 1/2 (June 1986): 215–40.
Ostapchuk, Victor. "An Ottoman Ġazānāme on Halīl Paša's Naval Campaign against the Cossacks (1621)." *HUS* 14, 3/4 (Dec. 1990):

482–521.

———. "The Publication of Documents on the Crimean Khanate in the Topkapı Sarayı: New Sources for the History of the Black Sea Basin." *HUS* 6, 4 (Dec. 1982): 500–528.

Ostrowski, Donald. "The Christianization of Rus' in Soviet Historiography: Attitudes and Interpretations (1920–1960)." *HUS* 11, 3/4 (Dec. 1987): 444–461.

———. "Textual Criticism and the *Povest' vremennykh let*: Some Theoretical Considerations." *HUS* 5, 1 (Mar. 1981): 11–31.

Pelenski, Jaroslaw. "Soviet Ukrainian Historiography after World War II." *Jahrbücher für Geschichte Osteuropas* 12 (Oct. 1964): 375–418.

Perfecky, George A. "The Slavic and Non-Slavic Sources of the 13th Century Galician-Volhynian Chronicle." *East European Quarterly* 19, 2 (June 1985): 129–38.

———. "Studies on the Galician Volhynian (Volhynian) Chronicle." *AUAAS* 12, 33/34 (1969–72): 62–112.

Pidhainy, Oleh. *Ukrainian Historiography and the Great East-European Revolution: A Propos Symonenko's Polemics.* Toronto: New Review Books, 1968.

Plokhy, Serhii M. "The Ghosts of Pereyaslav: Russo-Ukrainian Historical Debates in the Post-Soviet Era." *Europe-Asia Studies* 53, 3 (May 2001): 489–505.

———. "Historical Debates and Territorial Claims: Cossack Mythology in the Russian-Ukrainian Border Dispute." In *The Legacy of History in Russia and the New States of Eurasia*, ed. S. Frederick Starr, 147–70. Armonk, N.Y.: M. E. Sharpe, 1994.

———. "The History of a 'Non-Historical' Nation: Notes on the Nature and Current Problems of Ukrainian Historiography." *Slavic Review* 54, 3 (fall 1995): 709–16.

———. "Ukraine and Russia in Their Historical Encounter." *CSP* 35, 3/4 (Sep.–Dec. 1993): 333–44.

———. *Unmaking Imperial Russia: Mykhailo Hrushevsky and the Writing of Ukrainian History.* Toronto: University of Toronto Press, 2005.

Polonska-Vasylenko, Nataliia. *Two Conceptions of the History of Ukraine and Russia.* London: Association of Ukrainians in Great Britain, 1968.

Pritsak, Omeljan. "Kiev and All of Rus': The Fate of a Sacral Idea." *HUS* 10, 3/4 (Dec. 1986): 279–300.

———. "On the Chronology of Óláfr Tryggvason and Volodimer the Great: The Saga's Relative Chronology as a Historical Source." *HUS* 16, 1/2 (June 1992): 7–36.

———. and John S. Reshetar, Jr. "The Ukraine and the Dialectics of

Nation-Building." *Slavic Review* 22, 2 (June 1963): 224–55.
Prymak, Thomas M. *Mykhailo Hrushevsky: The Politics of National Culture*. Toronto: University of Toronto Press, 1987.
———. *Mykola Kostomarov: A Biography*. Toronto: University of Toronto Press, 1996.
Rothe, Hans, ed. *Sinopsis, Kiev 1681: Facsimile*. Cologne: Böhlau Verlag, 1983.
Rudnytsky, Ivan L. "Observations on the Problem of 'Historical' and 'Non-historical' Nations." *HUS* 5, 3 (Sep. 1981): 358–68.
———. "The Role of the Ukraine in Modern History." *Slavic Review* 22, 2 (June 1963): 199–216; "Reply," ibid., 256–62.
———. and John-Paul Himka, eds. *Rethinking Ukrainian History*. Edmonton and Toronto: CIUS Press, 1981.
Šaskol'skij, I. P. "Recent Developments in the Normanist Controversy." *Scando-Slavica*, suppl. 1, *Varangian Problems* (1970): 21–38.
Solchanyk, Roman. "An Interview with Stanislav V. Kulchyts'kyi." *JUS* 15, 1 (summer 1990): 39–52.
Subtelny, Orest. "The Current State of Ukrainian Historiography." *JUS* 18, 1/2 (summer–winter 1993): 33–54.
Sulimirski, Tadeusz. "Late Bronze Age and Earliest Iron Age in the USSR. A Guide to Recent Literature on the Subject." *Bulletin of the Institute of Archaeology in London* 8/9 (1968–69): 117–50.
Sysyn, Frank E. "Concepts of Nationhood in Ukrainian History Writing, 1620–1690." *HUS* 10, 3/4 (Dec. 1986): 393–423.
———. "The Cossack Chronicles and the Development of Modern Ukrainian Culture and National Identity." *HUS* 14, 3/4 (Dec. 1990): 593–607.
———. "The Jewish Massacres in the Historiography of the Khmelnytsky Uprising." *JUS* 23, 1 (summer 1998): 83–89.
———. "Peter Mohyla and the Kiev Academy in Recent Western Works: Divergent Views on Seventeenth-Century Ukrainian Culture." *HUS* 8, 1/2 (June 1984): 155–87.
———. "The Reemergence of the Ukrainian Nation and Cossack Mythology." *Social Research* 58, 4 (winter 1991): 845–64.
———. "Seventeenth-Century Views on the Causes of the Khmel'nyts'kyi Uprising: An Examination of the 'Discourse on the Present Cossack or Peasant War.'" *HUS* 5, 4 (Dec. 1981): 430–66.
Szporluk, Roman. "Belarus', Ukraine and the Russian Question: A Comment." *Post-Soviet Affairs* 9, 4 (Oct.–Dec. 1993): 366–74.
———. "National History as a Political Battleground: The Case of Ukraine and Belorussia." In *Russian Empire: Some Aspects of Tsarist and Soviet Colonial Practices*, ed. Michael Pap, 131–50. Cleveland: Institute for Soviet and East European Studies, John Carroll Univer-

sity, 1985.
Tillett, Lowell. *The Great Friendship: Soviet Historians on the Non-Russian Nationalities*. Chapel Hill, N.C.: University of North Carolina Press, 1969.
Tolotchko, Oleksij. "Roman Mstyslavič's Constitutional Project of 1203: Authentic Document or Falsification?" *HUS* 18, 3/4 (Dec. 1994): 249–74.
Varvartsev, Nikolai N. *Ukrainian History in the Distorting Mirror of Sovietology*. Kyiv: Naukova dumka, 1987.
Velychenko, Stephen. *National History as Cultural Process: A Survey of the Interpretations of Ukraine's Past in Polish, Russian, and Ukrainian Historical Writing from the Earliest Times to 1914*. Edmonton and Toronto: CIUS Press, 1992.
———. "The Official Soviet View of Ukrainian Historiography." *JUS* 10, 2 (winter 1985): 81–93.
———. *Shaping Identity in Eastern Europe and Russia: Soviet-Russian and Polish Accounts of Ukrainian History, 1914–1991*. New York: St. Martin's, 1993.
———. "Tsarist Censorship and Ukrainian Historiography, 1828–1906." *Canadian-American Slavic Studies* 23, 4 (1989): 385–408.
Vernadsky, George et al., eds. *A Source Book for Russian History from Early Times to 1917*. New Haven, Conn.: Yale University Press, 1972.
Verstiuk, Vladyslav. "Conceptual Issues in Studying the History of the Ukrainian Revolution." *JUS* 24, 1 (summer 1999): 5–20.
Von Hagen, Mark. "Does Ukraine Have a History?" *Slavic Review* 54, 3 (fall 1995): 658–73.
Wilson, Andrew. "The Donbas between Ukraine and Russia: The Use of History in Political Disputes." *Journal of Contemporary History* 30, 2 (Apr. 1995): 265–89.
———. "Myths of National History in Belarus and Ukraine." In *Myths and Nationhood*, ed. Geoffrey Hosking and George Schöpflin, 182–97. London: Hurst, 1997.
Wolff, Lawrence. "Voltaire's Eastern Europe: The Mapping of Civilization on the Itinerary of Charles XII." *HUS* 14, 3/4 (Dec. 1990): 623–47.
Wynar, Lubomyr R. "Michael Hrushevsky's Scheme of Ukrainian History in the Context of the Study of Russian Colonialism and Imperialism." In *Russian Empire: Some Aspects of Tsarist and Soviet Colonial Practices*, ed. Michael Pap, 19–39. Cleveland: Institute for Soviet and East European Studies, John Carroll University, 1985.
———. *Mykhailo Hrushevsky: Ukrainian-Russian Confrontation in Historiography*. New York: Ukrainian Historical Association, 1988.

———. "The Present State of Ukrainian Historiography in Soviet Ukraine: A Brief Overview." *Nationalities Papers* 7, 1 (spring 1979): 1–23.

———. "Ukrainian-Russian Confrontation in Historiography: Michael Hrushevsky versus the Traditional Scheme of 'Russian' History." *UQ* 30, 1 (spring 1974): 13–25.

Yekelchyk, Serhy. "Cossack Gold: History, Myth, and the Dream of Prosperity in the Age of Post-Soviet Transition." *CSP* 40, 3/4 (Sep.–Dec. 1998): 311–26.

———. "The Revolution at Eighty: Reconstructing Past Identities after the 'Linguistic Turn.'" *JUS* 24, 1 (summer 1999): 69–84.

3. Archaeology and Early History

Baran, Volodymyr, and Bohdan Tomenchuk. "Archaeological Survey of Ancient Halych, 1991–1996." *UR* 45, 3 (autumn 1998): 48–62.

Callmer, Johan. "The Archaeology of Kiev to the End of the Earliest Urban Phase." *HUS* 11, 3/4 (Dec. 1987): 323–64.

From the Lands of the Scythians: Ancient Treasures from the Museums of the USSR, 3000 B.C.-100 B.C. New York: Metropolitan Museum of Art [1975].

Klein, Richard D. *Ice-Age Hunters of the Ukraine*. Chicago: University of Chicago Press, 1973.

Kordysh, Neonila. "Settlement Plans of the Trypillyan Culture." *AUAAS* 3, 7 (1953): 535–51.

Kovalev, Roman K. "Zvenyhorod in Galicia: An Archaeological Survey (Eleventh–Mid-Thirteenth Century)." *JUS* 24, 2 (winter 1999): 7–36.

Maksymiv, Yevhen. "The East Slavs in the Time of Julius Caesar." *UR* 41, 2 (summer 1994): 24–32.

Mezentsev, Volodymyr I. "The Emergence of the Podil and the Genesis of the City of Kiev: Problems of Dating." *HUS* 10, 1/2 (June 1986): 48–70.

Reeder, Ellen D. et al. *Scythian Gold: Treasures from Ancient Ukraine*. New York: Abrams, 1999.

Rice, Tamara. *The Scythians*. London: Thames and Hudson, 1957.

Strumins'kyj, Bohdan. "Were the Antes Eastern Slavs?" *HUS* 3/4 (1979–80): 786–96.

4. Medieval History

Antonovych, M. "Comparative Notes on the Earliest Slavic Chronicles." *The New Review* 5 (1965): 44–53.

Backus, Oswald P., III. "The Problem of Unity in the Polish-Lithuanian State." *Slavic Review* 22, 3 (Sep. 1963): 411–31; "Reply," ibid., 450–55.

Boba, Imre. *Nomads, Northmen and Slavs: Eastern Europe in the Ninth Century.* The Hague: Mouton, 1967.
Carile, Antonio. "Byzantine Political Ideology and the Rus' in the Tenth-Twelfth Centuries." *HUS* 12/13 (1988–89): 400–13.
Chekin, Leonid S. "Lower Scythia in the Western European Geographical Tradition at the Time of the Crusades." *HUS* 15, 3/4 (Dec. 1991): 289–339.
Colucci, Michele. "The Image of Western Christianity in the Culture of Kievan Rus'." *HUS* 12/13 (1988–89): 576–86.
Constantine VII Porphyrogenitus. *De administrando imperio.* Trans. G. Moravcsik. Washington, D.C.: Dumbarton Oaks Center for Byzantine Studies, 1967. Vol. 2, R. J. H. Jenkins et al. *Commentary.* London: Athlone Press, 1962.
Dimnik, Martin. *The Dynasty of Chernigov.* Toronto: Pontifical Institute of Mediaeval Studies, 1994.
———. *Mikhail, Prince of Chernigov and Grand Prince of Kiev, 1224–1246.* Toronto: Pontifical Institute of Medieval Studies, 1981.
———. "The 'Testament' of Iaroslav 'The Wise': A Re-examination." *CSP* 29, 4 (Dec. 1987): 369–86.
Dmytryshyn, Basil. *Medieval Russia: A Source Book, 900–1700.* Hinsdale, Ill.: Dryden Press, 1973.
Featherstone, Jeffrey. "Ol'ga's Visit to Constantinople." *HUS* 14, 3/4 (Dec. 1990): 293–312.
Franklin, Simon. *Writing, Society and Culture in Early Rus, c. 950–1300.* Cambridge and New York: Cambridge University Press, 2002.
Franklin, Simon, and Jonathan Shepard. *The Emergence of Rus, 750–1200.* London: Longman, 1996.
Friedman, Philip. "The First Millennium of Jewish Settlement in the Ukraine and the Adjacent Areas." *AUAAS* 7, 23/24 (1959): 1483–1516.
Goldblatt, Harvey. "Orthodox Slavic Heritage and National Consciousness: Aspects of the East Slavic and South Slavic National Revivals." *HUS* 10, 3/4 (Dec. 1986): 336–54.
Golden, Peter B. "The *Polovci Dikii.*" *HUS* 3/4 (1979–80): 296–309.
Grekov, Boris D. *Kiev Rus.* Moscow: Foreign Languages Publishing House, 1959.
Grimsted, Patricia Kennedy, and Irene Sułkowska-Kurasiowa. *The "Lithuanian Metrica" in Moscow and Warsaw: Reconstructing the Archives of the Grand Duchy of Lithuania.* Cambridge, Mass.: HURI, 1984.
The Hypatian Codex, Part II: The Galician-Volhynian Chronicle. Trans. George A. Perfecky. Munich: Wilhelm Fink Verlag, 1973.
Inalcik, Halil. *Sources and Studies on the Ottoman Black Sea.* Volume 1,

The Customs Register of Caffa, 1487–1490. Cambridge, Mass.: HURI, 1996.
Jakstas, Joseph. "How Firm Was the Polish-Lithuanian Federation?" *Slavic Review* 22, 3 (Sep. 1963): 442–49.
Kaiser, Daniel H. *The Laws of Rus'—Tenth to Fifteenth Centuries.* Salt Lake City: Charles Schlacks, Jr., 1992.
Kazhdan, Alexander. "Rus'-Byzantine Princely Marriages in the Eleventh and Twelfth Centuries." *HUS* 12/13 (1988–89): 414–29.
Kollmann, Nancy Shields. "Collateral Succession in Kievan Rus'." *HUS* 14, 3/4 (Dec. 1990): 377–87.
Labunka, Miroslav. "Religious Centers and Their Missions to Kievan Rus': From Ol'ga to Volodimer." *HUS* 12/13 (1988–89): 159–93.
The Lithuanian Statute of 1529. Trans. and ed. Karl von Loewe. Leiden: E. J. Brill, 1976.
Lunt, Horace G. "What the Rus' Primary Chronicle Tells Us about the Origin of the Slavs and of Slavic Writing." *HUS* 19 (1995): 335–57.
Manz, Beatrice Forbes. "The Clans of the Crimean Khanate, 1466–1532." *HUS* 2, 3 (Sep. 1978): 282–309.
Martin, Janet. *Medieval Russia, 980–1584.* Cambridge: Cambridge University Press, 1995.
Medieval Russian Laws. Trans. George Vernadsky. New York: Columbia University Press, 1947.
Mezentsev, Vladimir I. "The Territorial and Demographic Development of Medieval Kiev and Other Major Cities of Rus'." *Russian Review* 48, 2 (1989): 145–70.
Noonan, Thomas S. "Fluctuations in Islamic Trade with Eastern Europe during the Viking Age." *HUS* 16, 3/4 (Dec. 1992): 237–60.
———. "The Monetary History of Kiev in the Pre-Mongol Period." *HUS* 11, 3/4 (Dec. 1987): 384–443.
———. "When Did Dirhams First Reach the Ukraine?" *HUS* 2, 1 (Mar. 1978): 26–40.
———. "Why the Vikings First Came to Russia." *Jahrbücher für Geschichte Osteuropas* 34, 3 (1986): 321–48.
Obolensky, Dimitri. *The Byzantine Commonwealth: Eastern Europe, 500–1453.* New York: Praeger, 1971.
———. *Byzantium and the Slavs.* Crestwood, N.Y.: St. Vladimir's Seminary Press, 1994.
———. "Ol'ga's Conversion: The Evidence Reconsidered." *HUS* 12/13 (1988–89): 145–58.
Pelenski, Jaroslaw. *The Contest for the Legacy of Kievan Rus'.* Boulder, Colo.: East European Monographs, 1998.
Picchio, Riccardo. "From Boris to Volodimer: Some Remarks on the Emergence of Proto-Orthodox Slavdom." *HUS* 12/13 (1988–89):

200–213.

Pliguzov, Andrei. "On the Title 'Metropolitan of Kiev and All Rus'.'" *HUS* 15, 3/4 (Dec. 1991): 340–53.

Poppe, Andrzej. "How the Conversion of Rus' Was Understood in the Eleventh Century." *HUS* 11, 3/4 (Dec. 1987): 287–302.

———. *The Rise of Christian Russia*. London: Variorum Reprints, 1982.

———. "Two Concepts of the Conversion of Rus' in Kievan Writings." *HUS* 12/13 (1988–89): 488–504.

Pritsak, Omeljan. "At the Dawn of Christianity in Rus': East Meets West." *HUS* 12/13 (1988–89): 87–113.

———. "The Invitation to the Varangians." *HUS* 1, 1 (Mar. 1977): 7–22.

———. "The Khazar Kingdom's Conversion to Judaism." *HUS* 2, 3 (Sep. 1978): 261–81.

———. *The Origin of Rus': An Inaugural Lecture, October 24, 1975*. Cambridge, Mass.: HURI, 1976.

———. *The Origin of Rus'*. Volume 1, *Old Scandinavian Sources other than the Sagas*. Cambridge, Mass.: Harvard University Press, 1981.

———. *The Origins of Old Rus' Weights and Monetary Systems*. Cambridge, Mass.: HURI, 1998.

———. "The System of Government under Volodimer the Great and His Foreign Policy." *HUS* 19 (1995): 573–93.

———. "When and Where Was Ol'ga Baptized?" *HUS* 9, 1/2 (June 1985): 5–24.

Rowell, S. C. *Lithuania Ascending: A Pagan Empire within East-Central Europe, 1295–1345*. Cambridge: Cambridge University Press, 1994.

The Russian Primary Chronicle: Laurentian Text. Trans. and ed. Samuel Hazzard Cross and Olgerd P. Sherbowitz-Wetzor. Cambridge, Mass.: Medieval Academy of America, 1963.

Rusyna, O. V. "On the Kyivan Princely Tradition from the Thirteenth to the Fifteenth Centuries." *HUS* 18, 3/4 (Dec. 1994): 175–90.

Stone, Daniel. *The Polish-Lithuanian State, 1386–1795*. Seattle: University of Washington Press, 2001.

Tachiaos, Anthony-Emil. "The Greek Metropolitans of Kievan Rus': An Evaluation of Their Spiritual and Cultural Activity." *HUS* 12/13 (1988–89): 430–45.

Thompson, Francis J. "The Bulgarian Connection to the Reception of Byzantine Culture in Kievan Rus': The Myths and the Enigma." *HUS* 12/13 (1988–89): 214–61.

Tolochko, Petro P. "Religious Sites in Kiev during the Reign of Volodimer Sviatoslavich." *HUS* 11, 3/4 (Dec. 1987): 317–22.

———. "Volodimer Svjatoslavič's Choice of Religion: Fact or Fiction?" *HUS* 12/13 (1988–89): 816–29.

Treadgold, Warren. "Three Byzantine Provinces and the First Byzantine

Contacts with the Rus'." *HUS* 12/13 (1988–89): 132–44.
Váňa, Zdeněk. *The World of the Ancient Slavs.* London: Orbis, 1983.
Zdan, Michael B. "The Dependence of Halych-Volyn' Rus' on the Golden Horde." *Slavonic and East European Review* 35, 2 (June 1957): 505–22.

5. Cossackdom and the Hetmanate

Baran, Alexander, and George Gajecky. *The Cossacks in the Thirty Years War.* 2 vols. Rome: Basiliani, 1969–83.
Baron, Samuel H., and Nancy Shields Kollman, eds. *Religion and Culture in Early Modern Russia and Ukraine.* DeKalb, Ill.: Northern Illinois University Press, 1997.
Basarab, John. *Pereiaslav 1654: A Historical Study.* Edmonton and Toronto: CIUS Press, 1982.
Borschak, Elie. *Hryhor Orlyk, France's Cossack General.* Toronto: Burns and McEachern, 1956.
Braichevskyi, Mykhailo I. *Annexation or Reunification: Critical Notes on One Conception.* Trans. and ed. George P. Kulchycky. Munich: Ukrainisches Institut für Bildungspolitik, 1974.
Chubaty, N. "The Ukrainian Independence Movement at the Time of the American Revolution." *UQ* 5, 3 (summer 1949): 226–37.
Chynczewska-Hennel, Teresa. "The National Consciousness of Ukrainian Nobles and Cossacks from the End of the Sixteenth to the Mid-Seventeenth Century." *HUS* 10, 3/4 (Dec. 1986): 377–92.
Dashkevych, Yaroslav. "Armenians in the Ukraine at the Time of Hetman Bohdan Xmel'nyc'kyj (1648–1657)." *HUS* 3/4 (1979–80): 166–88.
Dmytryshyn, Basil. *Imperial Russia: A Source Book, 1700–1917.* Hinsdale, Ill.: Dryden Press, 1974.
Ettinger, Shmuel. "The Legal and Social Status of the Jews of Ukraine from the Fifteenth Century to the Cossack Uprising of 1648." *JUS* 17, 1/2 (summer–winter 1992): 107–40.
Fischer, Alan. "The Ottoman Crimea in the Mid-Seventeenth Century: Some Problems and Preliminary Considerations." *HUS* 3/4 (1979–80): 215–26.
———. "The Ottoman Crimea in the Sixteenth Century." *HUS* 5, 2 (June 1981): 135–70.
Frick, David A. "The Circulation of Information about Ivan Vyhovs'kyj." *HUS* 17, 3/4 (Dec. 1993): 251–78.
———. "'Foolish Rus'": On Polish Civilization, Ruthenian Self-Hatred, and Kasijan Sakovyč." *HUS* 18, 3/4 (Dec. 1994): 210–48.
Gajecky, George. *The Cossack Administration of the Hetmanate.* 2 vols. Cambridge, Mass.: HURI, 1978.
———. "The Kiev Mohyla Academy and the Hetmanate." *HUS* 8, 1/2

(June 1984): 81–92.
Gerus, O. W. "Manifestations of the Cossack Legacy and Its Impact." *Ukraïns'kyi istoryk* 19, 1/2 (1982): 22–39.
Gordon, Linda. *Cossack Rebellions: Social Turmoil in the Sixteenth-Century Ukraine.* Albany, N.Y.: State University of New York Press, 1983.
Grimsted, Patricia Kennedy. "The Ruthenian (Volhynian) Metrica: Polish Crown Chancery Records for Ukrainian Lands, 1569–1673." *HUS* 14, 1/2 (June 1990): 7–83.
Huttenbach, Henry R. "The Ukraine and Muscovite Expansion." In *Russian Imperialism from Ivan the Great to the Revolution*, ed. Taras Hunczak, 167–97. New Brunswick, N.J.: Rutgers University Press, 1974.
Inalcik, Halil. "The Khan and the Tribal Aristocracy: The Crimean Khanate under Sahib Giray I." *HUS* 3/4 (1979–80): 445–466.
Ivan Mazepa: Hetman of Ukraine. New York: Ukrainian Congress Committee of America, 1960.
Kamiński, Andrzej. "The Cossack Experiment in *Szlachta* Democracy in the Polish-Lithuanian Commonwealth: The Hadiach (*Hadziacz*) Union." *HUS* 1, 2 (June 1977): 178–97.
———. *Republic vs. Autocracy: Poland-Lithuania and Russia, 1686–1697.* Cambridge, Mass.: HURI, 1993.
Kentrschynskyi, Bohdan. "The Political Struggle of Mazepa and Charles XII for Ukrainian Independence." *UQ* 15, 3 (Sep. 1959): 241–59.
Kohut, Zenon E. "Belarus, Russia, and Ukraine from the Sixteenth to the Eighteenth Century: An Agenda for the Study of Politics." *JUS* 17, 1/2 (summer–winter 1992): 3–16.
———. "The Development of a Little Russian Identity and Ukrainian Nationbuilding." *HUS* 10, 3/4 (Dec. 1986): 559–76.
———. "A Gentry Democracy within an Autocracy: The Politics of Hryhorii Poletyka (1723/25–1784)." *HUS* 3/4 (1979–80): 507–19.
———. *Russian Centralism and Ukrainian Autonomy: Imperial Absorption of the Hetmanate, 1760s–1830s.* Cambridge, Mass.: HURI, 1988.
Kołodziejczyk, Dariusz. "Ottoman Podillja: The *Eyalet* of Kam'janec', 1672–1699." *HUS* 16, 1/2 (June 1992): 87–101.
Koropeckyj, Roman. "The Slap, The Feral Child, and the Steed: Pasek Settles Accounts with Mazepa." *HUS* 14, 3/4 (Dec. 1990): 415–26.
Krupnytsky, Borys. "General Characteristics of Pylyp Orlyk." *AUAAS* 6, 21/22 (1958): 1247–59.
———. "The Swedish-Ukrainian Treaties of Alliance, 1708–1709." *UQ* 12, 1 (winter 1956): 47–57.
Levy, Avigdor. "The Contribution of Zaporozhian Cossacks to Ottoman Military Reform: Documents and Notes." *HUS* 6, 3 (Sep. 1982):

372–413.

Mackiw, Theodore. "England, Russia and the Ukrainian Question during the Great Northern War." *UR* 39, 1 (spring 1991): 26–34; 2 (summer 1991): 29–41; 3 (autumn 1991): 27–41.

———. "English Press on Liberation War in Ukraine, 1648–49." *UQ* 42, 1/2 (spring–summer 1986): 102–26; 3/4 (fall–winter 1986): 239–59.

———. *English Reports on Mazepa: Hetman of Ukraine and Prince of the Holy Roman Empire, 1687–1709*. Munich and Toronto: Ukrainian Historical Association, 1983.

Prince Mazepa, Hetman of Ukraine, in Contemporary English Publications, 1687–1709. Chicago: Ukrainian Research and Information Institute, 1967.

———. "*Promoveatur ut Amoveatur*, or How Hetman Mazepa Became Prince of the Holy Roman Empire." *UR* 42, 1 (spring 1995): 27–31.

———. "Ukrainian-Polish Peace Treaty of Zboriv in the English and German Press of 1649 and Its Background." *UR* 40, 2 (summer 1992): 12–22; 3 (autumn 1992): 24–36.

Manning, Clarence A. *Hetman of Ukraine: Ivan Mazeppa*. New York: Bookman Associates, 1957.

Nadav, Mordekhai. "The Jewish Community of Nemyriv in 1648: Their Massacre and Loyalty Oath to the Cossacks." *HUS* 8, 3/4 (Dec. 1984): 376–95.

O'Brien, C. Bickford. *Muscovy and the Ukraine: From the Pereiaslavl Agreement to the Truce of Andrusovo, 1654–1667*. Berkeley and Los Angeles: University of California Press, 1963.

Ohloblyn, Oleksander. "American Revolution and Ukrainian Liberation Ideas during the Late 18th Century." *UQ* 11, 2 (spring 1955): 203–12.

———. *Treaty of Pereyaslav 1654*. Toronto and New York: Canadian League for Ukraine's Liberation and Organization for Defense of Four Freedoms for Ukraine, 1954.

Okinshevich, Leo. *Ukrainian Society and Government, 1648–1781*. Munich: Ukrainian Free University, 1978.

Pelenski, Jaroslaw. "The Haidamak Insurrections and the Old Regimes in Eastern Europe." In *The American and European Revolutions, 1776–1848*, ed. Jaroslaw Pelenski, 228–42. Iowa City: University of Iowa Press, 1980.

Plokhy, Serhii. *The Cossacks and Religion in Early Modern Ukraine*. Oxford: Oxford University Press, 2001.

———. *Tsars and Cossacks: A Study in Iconography*. Cambridge, Mass.: HURI, 2002.

Poe, Marshall. "The Zaporozhian Cossacks in Western Print to 1600." *HUS* 19 (1995): 531–47.

Prokopovych, Vyacheslav. "The Problem of the Judicial Nature of the Ukraine's Union with Muscovy." *AUAAS* 4, 13 (1955): 917–80.
Raba, Joel. *Between Remembrance and Denial: The Fate of the Jews in the Wars of the Polish Commonwealth during the Mid-Seventeenth Century as Shown in Contemporary Writings and Historical Research.* Boulder, Colo.: East European Monographs, 1995.
Rosman, M. J. *The Lord's Jews: Magnate-Jewish Relations in the Polish-Lithuanian Commonwealth during the 18th Century.* Cambridge, Mass.: HURI and Center for Jewish Studies, Harvard University, 1990.
Rustemeyer, Angela. "Ukrainians in Seventeenth-Century Political Trials." *JUS* 24, 2 (winter 1999): 37–58.
Serczyk, Władysław A. "The Commonwealth and the Cossacks in the First Quarter of the Seventeenth Century." *HUS* 2, 1 (Mar. 1978): 73–93.
Struminsky, Bohdan A. "Ukrainian Hetmans' *Universaly* (1678–1727) at the Lilly Library of Indiana University." *HUS* 5, 3 (Sep. 1981): 335–50.
Subtelny, Orest. *Domination of Eastern Europe: Native Nobilities and Foreign Absolutism, 1500–1715.* Kingston and Montreal: McGill-Queen's University Press, 1986.
———. "Mazepa, Peter I, and the Question of Treason." *HUS* 2, 2 (1978): 158–83.
———. *The Mazepists: Ukrainian Separatism in the Early Eighteenth Century.* Boulder, Colo.: East European Monographs, 1981.
———, ed. *On the Eve of Poltava: The Letters of Ivan Mazepa to Adam Sieniawski, 1704–1708.* New York: Ukrainian Academy of Arts and Sciences in the U.S., 1975.
———. "Pylyp Orlyk in Exile: The Religious Dimension." *HUS* 14, 3/4 (Dec. 1990): 584–92.
———. "The Ukrainian-Crimean Treaty of 1711." *HUS* 3/4 (1979–80): 808–17.
Sysyn, Frank E. *Between Poland and the Ukraine: The Dilemma of Adam Kysil, 1600–1653.* Cambridge, Mass.: HURI, 1985.
———. "A Contemporary's Account of the Causes of the Khmel'nyts'kyi Uprising." *HUS* 5, 2 (June 1981): 245–57.
———. "The Khmelnytsky Uprising and Ukrainian Nation-Building." *JUS* 17, 1/2 (summer–winter 1992): 141–70.
Tazbir, Janusz. "The Political Reversals of Jurij Nemyryč." *HUS* 5, 3 (Sep. 1981): 306–19.
Velychenko, Steven. "Bohdan Khmelnytsky and the Rákóczis of Transylvania during the Polish Election of 1648." *JUS* 8, 2 (winter 1983): 3–12.

———. "The Origins of the Ukrainian Revolution of 1648." *Journal of Ukrainian Graduate Studies* 1, 1 (fall 1976): 18–26.
Vernadsky, George. *Bohdan, Hetman of Ukraine*. New Haven: Yale University Press, 1941.
Weinryb, Bernard D. "The Hebrew Chronicles on Bohdan Khmel'nyts'kyi and the Cossack-Polish War." *HUS* 1, 2 (June 1977): 153–77.
Wójcik, Zbigniew. "The Early Period of Pavlo Teterja's Hetmancy in the Right-Bank Ukraine (1661–1663)." *HUS* 3/4 (1979–80): 958–72.
Wynar, Lubomyr. "The Question of Anglo-Ukrainian Relations in the Middle of the 17th Century." *AUAAS* 6, 21/22 (1958): 1411–18.
———, ed. *Habsburgs and Zaporozhian Cossacks: The Diary of Erich Lassota von Steblau, 1594*. Trans. Orest Subtelny. Littleton, Colo.: Ukrainian Academic Press, 1975.

6. Ukraine under Russian and Austrian Rule

Andriewsky, Olga. "*Medved' iz berlogi*: Vladimir Jabotinsky and the Ukrainian Question, 1904–1914." *HUS* 14, 3/4 (Dec. 1990): 249–67.
Baker, Mark. "Lewis Namier and the Problem of Eastern Galicia." *JUS* 23, 2 (winter 1998): 59–104.
Banac, Ivo, and Paul Bushkovitch, eds. *The Nobility in Russia and Eastern Europe*. New Haven, Conn.: Yale Concilium of International and Area Studies, 1983.
Banac, Ivo, and Frank E. Sysyn, eds. *Concepts of Nationhood in Early Modern Eastern Europe*. *HUS* 10, 3/4 (Dec. 1986).
Beauvois, Daniel. *The Noble, the Serf, and the Revizor: The Polish Nobility between Tsarist Imperialism and the Ukrainian Masses, 1831–1863*. New York: Harwood Academic Publishers, 1991.
Bilinsky, Yaroslav. "Mykhailo Drahomanov, Ivan Franko, and the Relations between the Dnieper Ukraine and Galicia in the Last Quarter of the 19th Century." *AUAAS* 7, 23/24 (1959): 1542–66.
Brock, Peter. "Ivan Vahylevych (1811–1866) and the Ukrainian National Identity." *CSP* 14, 2 (summer 1972): 153–90.
Ciuciura, Theodore B. "Galicia and Bukovina as Austrian Crown-Provinces: Ukrainian Experience in Representative Institutions, 1861–1918." *Studia Ukrainica* 2 (1984): 175–96.
———. "Provincial Politics in the Habsburg Empire: The Case of Galicia and Bukovina." *Nationalities Papers* 13, 2 (fall 1985): 247–73.
———. "Ukrainian Deputies in the Old Austrian Parliament, 1861–1918." *Mitteilungen* (Munich) 14 (1977): 38–56.
Edelman, Robert. *Proletarian Peasants: The Revolution of 1905 in Russia's Southwest*. Ithaca, N.Y.: Cornell University Press, 1987.
Gerus, Oleh W. "The Ukrainian Question in the Russian Duma, 1906–1917: An Overview." *Studia Ucrainica* 2 (1984): 157–74.

Haczynsky, Leo J. "Two Contributions to the Problem of Galicia." *East European Quarterly* 4, 1 (Mar. 1970): 94–104.
Hamm, Michael F. *Kiev: A Portrait, 1800–1917*. Princeton, N.J.: Princeton University Press, 1993.
Herlihy, Patricia. *Odessa: A History, 1794–1914*. Cambridge, Mass.: HURI, 1986.
Heuman, Susan. *Kistiakovsky: The Struggle for National and Constitutional Rights in the Last Years of Tsarism*. Cambridge, Mass.: HURI, 1998.
Himka, John-Paul. "The Construction of Nationality in Galician Rus': Icarian Flights in Almost All Directions." In *Intellectuals and the Articulation of the Nation*, ed. Michael D. Kennedy and Ron Suny, 109–64. Ann Arbor: University of Michigan Press, 1999.
———. *Galician Villagers and the Ukrainian National Movement in the Nineteenth Century*. Edmonton and Toronto: CIUS Press; New York: St. Martin's, 1988.
———. "Serfdom in Galicia." *JUS* 9, 2 (winter 1984): 3–28.
———. *Socialism in Galicia. The Emergence of Polish Social Democracy and Ukrainian Radicalism, 1860–1890*. Cambridge, Mass.: HURI, 1983.
———. "The Transformation and Formation of Social Strata and Their Place in the Ukrainian National Movement in Nineteenth-Century Galicia." *JUS* 23, 2 (winter 1998): 3–22.
———. "Young Radicals and Independent Statehood: The Idea of a Ukrainian Nation-State, 1890–1895." *Slavic Review* 41, 2 (summer 1982): 219–35.
Isaievych, Iaroslav. "Galicia and Problems of National Identity." In *The Habsburg Legacy: National Identity in Historical Perspective*, ed. Ritchie Robertson and Edward Timms, 37–45. Edinburgh: Edinburgh University Press, 1994.
Kappeler, Andreas. "A 'Small People' of Twenty-Five Million: The Ukrainians circa 1900." *JUS* 18, 1/2 (summer–winter 1993): 85–92.
Klier, John D. "*Kievlianin* and the Jews: A Decade of Disillusionment, 1864–1873." *HUS* 5, 1 (Mar. 1981): 83–101.
Kostomariv, Mykola Ivanovych. *Books of Genesis of the Ukrainian People*. New York: Research Program on the USSR, 1954.
Kozak, Stefan. "On the Tradition of Cyril and Methodius in Ukraine." *JUS* 13, 2 (winter 1988): 29–51.
Kozik, Jan. *The Ukrainian National Movement in Galicia, 1815–1849*. Edmonton and Toronto: CIUS Press, 1986.
Luciw, Wasyl. *Ukrainians and the Polish Revolt of 1863*. New Haven, Conn.: Slavia Library, 1961.
Luckyj, George S. N. *Young Ukraine: The Brotherhood of Saints Cyril*

and Methodius, 1845–1847. Ottawa: University of Ottawa Press, 1991.

Lviv: *A City in the Crosscurrents of History.* Ed. John Czaplicka. *HUS* 24 (2000).

Lviv: *A Symposium on Its 700th Anniversary.* Ed. Vasyl Mudry. New York: Shevchenko Scientific Society, 1962.

Magocsi, Paul Robert. "The Kachkovs'kyi Society and the National Revival in Nineteenth-Century East Galicia." *HUS* 15, 1/2 (June 1991): 48–87.

———. *The Shaping of a National Identity: Subcarpathian Rus', 1848–1948.* Cambridge, Mass.: Harvard University Press, 1978.

———. "Ukrainians and the Habsburgs." *JUS* 21, 1/2 (summer–winter 1996): 55–66.

Markovits, Andrei S., and Frank E. Sysyn, eds. *Nationbuilding and the Politics of Nationalism: Essays on Austrian Galicia.* Cambridge, Mass.: HURI, 1982.

Nowosiwsky, I. M. *Bukovinian Ukrainians: A Historical Background and Their Self-Determination in 1918.* New York: Shevchenko Scientific Society, 1970.

Ohloblyn, Olexander. "Ukrainian Autonomists of the 1780s and 1790s and Count P. A. Rumyantsev-Zadunaysky." *AUAAS* 6, 21/22 (1958): 1313–26.

Pękacz, Jolanta T. "Galician Society as a Cultural Public, 1771–1914." *JUS* 23, 2 (winter 1998): 23–44.

Pelech, Orest. "The State and the Ukrainian Triumvirate in the Russian Empire, 1831–47." In *Ukrainian Past, Ukrainian Present*, ed. Bohdan Krawchenko, 1–17. New York: St. Martin's Press, 1993.

Pipes, Richard. "Peter Struve and Ukrainian Nationalism." *HUS* 3/4 (1979–80): 675–83.

Polonska-Vasylenko, N. D. *The Settlement of the Southern Ukraine, 1750–1775.* New York: Ukrainian Academy of Arts and Sciences in the U.S., 1955.

Pritsak, Omeljan. "The Pogroms of 1881." *HUS* 11, 1/2 (June 1987): 8–43.

Prymak, Thomas M. "Herzen on Poland and Ukraine." *JUS* 7, 1 (spring 1982): 31–49.

Pyziur, E. "Taras Shevchenko and Edmund Burke: Similarities and Contrasts in Their Ideas of Nations." *AUAAS* 14, 37/38 (1978–80): 11–38.

Rudnytsky, Ivan L., ed. *Mykhailo Drahomanov. A Symposium and Selected Writings.* New York: Ukrainian Academy of Arts and Sciences in the U.S., 1952.

Ryabchuk, Mykola. "The Nativist-Westernizer Controversy in Ukraine:

The End or the Beginning?" *JUS* 21, 1/2 (summer–winter 1996): 27–54.
Saunders, David. "Mikhail Katkov and Mykola Kostomarov: A Note on Pëtr A. Valuev's Anti-Ukrainian Edict of 1863." *HUS* 17, 3/4 (Dec. 1993): 365–83.
Sonevytsky, Leonid C. "Bukovina in the Diplomatic Negotiations of 1914." *AUAAS* 7, 23/24 (1959): 1586–1629.
Steblii, Feodosii. "Vasyl Podolynsky's *Słowo przestrogi* and Ukrainian-Polish Relations in Nineteenth-Century Galicia." *JUS* 23, 2 (winter 1998): 45–58.
Velychenko, Stephen. "Identities, Loyalties, and Service in Imperial Russia: Who Administered the Borderlands?" *Russian Review* 54, 2 (1995): 188–208.
Wandycz, Piotr S. *The Lands of Partitioned Poland, 1795–1918*. Seattle: University of Washington Press, 1974.
Wynn, Charters. *Workers, Strikes, and Pogroms: The Donbass-Dnepr Bend in Late Imperial Russia, 1870–1905*. Princeton, N.J.: Princeton University Press, 1992.
Yakovliv, Andriy. "Istoriya Rusov and Its Author." *AUAAS* 3, 8 (1953): 620–69.
Yekelchyk, Serhy. "The Body and National Myth: Motifs from the Ukrainian National Revival in the Nineteenth Century." *Australian Slavonic and East European Studies* 7, 2 (1993): 31–59.
Zipperstein, Steve Jeffrey. *The Jews of Odessa: A Cultural History, 1794–1871*. Stanford, Calif.: Stanford University Press, 1986.

7. Western Ukraine, 1918–53

Budurowycz, Bohdan. "Poland and the Ukrainian Problem, 1921–1939." *CSP* 25, 4 (Dec. 1983): 473–500.
Burds, Jeffrey. "AGENTURA: Soviet Informants' Networks and the Ukrainian Underground in Galicia, 1944–48." *East European Politics and Societies* 11, 1 (winter 1997): 89–130.
Caballero Jurado, Carlos. *Breaking the Chains: 14 Waffen-Grenadier-Division der SS and Other Ukrainian Volunteer Formations, Eastern Front, 1942–45*. Trans. Roberts Haigh. Halifax, UK: Shelf Books, 1998.
Danko, Joseph. "Plebiscite of Carpatho-Ruthenians in the United States Recommending Union of Carpatho-Ruthenia with the Czechoslovak Republic." *AUAAS* 11, 31/32 (1964–68): 184–207.
Diakiv-Hornovy, Osyp. *The USSR Unmasked: A Collection of Articles and Essays on Soviet-Russian Repression in Ukraine*. New York: Vantage Press, 1976.
Dmytryshyn, Basil. "The Nazis and the SS Volunteer Division Galicia."

American Slavic and East European Review 15, 1 (Feb. 1956): 1–10.

Gelber, Nahum M. "The National Autonomy of Eastern Galician Jewry in the West Ukrainian Republic, 1918–1919." In Isaac Lewin et al., *A History of Polish Jewry during the Revival of Poland*, 221–326. New York: Shengold Publishers, 1990.

Hann, Chris. "Ethnic Cleansing in Eastern Europe: Poles and Ukrainians beside the Curzon Line." *Nations and Nationalism* 2, 3 (1996): 389–406.

Heike, Wolf-Dietrich. *The Ukrainian Division 'Galicia,' 1943–1945: A Memoir*. Toronto: Shevchenko Scientific Society, 1988.

Himka, John-Paul. "Western Ukraine in the Interwar Period." *Nationalities Papers* 20, 2 (1994): 347–64.

Horak, Stephan. *Poland and Her National Minorities, 1919–1939: A Case Study*. New York: Vantage Press, 1961.

Hunczak, Taras. *On the Horns of a Dilemma: The Story of the Ukrainian Division Halychyna*. Lanham, Md.: University Press of America, 2000.

———. "Sir Lewis Namier and the Struggle for Eastern Galicia, 1918–1920." *HUS* 1, 2 (June 1977): 198–210.

Karaczko, Lucijan. "An Outline of the Tragic Polish-Ukrainian Relations." *UQ* 38, 1 (spring 1982): 31–60.

Kubijovych, Volodymyr. *Western Ukraine within Poland, 1920–1939*. Chicago: Ukrainian Research and Information Institute, 1963.

Logusz, Michael O. *Galicia Division: The Waffen-SS 14th Grenadier Division, 1943–1945*. Atglen, Pa.: Schiffer Publishing, 1997.

Marples, David R. "Toward a Thematic Approach to the Collectivization Campaign in the Soviet West (1948–56)." *CSP* 33, 3/4 (Sep.–Dec. 1991): 285–300.

Martowych, Oleh. *The Ukrainian Insurgent Army (UPA)*. Munich: Ukrainian Information Service, 1950.

Mirchuk, Petro. *In the German Mills of Death, 1941–1945*. New York: Vantage Press, 1976.

Motyl, Alexander J. "The Problem of Bessarabia and Bukovyna: The Intersection of the Sino-Soviet and Soviet-Rumanian Disputes." *Journal of Ukrainian Graduate Studies* 2, 1 (spring 1977): 32–48.

———. "The Rural Origins of the Communist and Nationalist Movements in Wołyn Województwo 1919–1939." *Slavic Review* 38, 3 (Sep. 1978): 412–20.

———. *The Turn to the Right: The Sociological Origins and Development of Ukrainian Nationalism, 1919–1929*. Boulder, Colo.: East European Monographs, 1980.

———. "Ukrainian Nationalist Political Violence in Inter-War Poland, 1921–1939." *East European Quarterly* 19, 1 (March 1985): 45–55.

Pavliuk, Oleksandr. "Ukrainian-Polish Relations in Galicia in 1918–1919." *JUS* 23, 1 (summer 1998): 1–23.
Petelycky, Stefan. *Into Auschwitz, for Ukraine*. Kingston, Ont.: Kashtan Press, 1999.
Potichnyj, Peter J., and Yevhen Shtendera, eds. *Political Thought of the Ukrainian Underground, 1943–1951*. Edmonton and Toronto: CIUS Press, 1986.
Radziejowski, Janusz. *The Communist Party of Western Ukraine, 1919–1929*. Trans. Alan Rutkowski. Edmonton and Toronto: CIUS Press, 1983.
Raschhofer, Hermann. *Political Assassination: The Legal Background of the Oberländer and Stashinsky Cases*. Tübingen: Fritz Schlichtenmayer, 1964.
Revyuk, Emil, ed. *Polish Atrocities in Ukraine*. New York: United Ukrainian Organizations of the U.S., 1931.
Shandor, Vincent. *Carpatho-Ukraine in the Twentieth Century: A Political and Legal History*. Cambridge, Mass.: HURI, 1997.
Shandruk, Pavlo. *Arms of Valor*. New York: Robert Speller, 1959.
Shapoval, Yuri. "The Tragic Fate of Iuliian Bachynsky." *JUS* 23, 1 (summer 1998): 25–39.
Shumuk, Danylo. *Life Sentence: Memoirs of a Ukrainian Political Prisoner*. Edmonton and Toronto: CIUS Press, 1984.
Sluzhynska, Zynoviya. "The High Price of Liberation: The Return of Soviet Occupation to Western Ukraine." *UR* 42, 3 (autumn 1995): 16–23.
Snyder, Timothy. "'To Resolve the Ukrainian Problem Once and for All': The Ethnic Cleansing of Ukrainians in Poland." *Journal of Cold War Studies* 1, 2 (1999): 86–120.
Sodol, Petro R. *UPA: They Fought Hitler and Stalin*. New York: Committee for the World Convention and Reunion of Soldiers in the Ukrainian Insurgent Army, 1987.
Solchanyk, Roman. "The Comintern and the Communist Party of Western Ukraine, 1919–1928." *CSP* 23, 2 (June 1981): 181–97.
Stachiw, Matthew, and Jaroslaw Sztendera. *Western Ukraine at the Turning Point of Europe's History, 1918–1923*. 2 vols. New York: Shevchenko Scientific Society, 1969–71.
Stercho, Peter G. *Diplomacy of Double Morality: Europe's Crossroads in Carpatho-Ukraine, 1919–1939*. New York: Carpathian Research Center, 1971.
Tys-Krokhmaliuk, Yuriy. *UPA Warfare in Ukraine: Strategical, Tactical and Organizational Problems of Ukrainian Resistance in World War II*. Trans. Walter Dushnyck. New York: Society of Veterans of Ukrainian Insurgent Army of the United States and Canada, 1972.

Winch, Michael. *Republic for a Day: An Eyewitness Account of the Carpatho-Ukraine Incident*. London: Robert Hale, 1939.
Wynot, Edward, Jr. "The Ukrainians and the Polish Regime, 1937–1939." *Ukraïns'kyi istoryk* 7, 4 (1970): 44–60.

8. The Ukrainian Revolution, 1917–21

Abramson, Henry. *A Prayer for the Government: Jews and Ukrainians in Revolutionary Times, 1917–1920*. Cambridge, Mass.: HURI, 1999.
Adams, Arthur E. *Bolsheviks in the Ukraine: The Second Campaign, 1918–1919*. New Haven, Conn.: Yale University Press, 1963.
Brinkley, George A. *The Volunteer Army and Allied Intervention in South Russia, 1917–1921: A Study of the Politics and Diplomacy of the Russian Civil War*. Notre Dame, Ind.: University of Notre Dame Press, 1966.
Czajkowskyj, Melanie. "Volodymyr Vynnychenko and His Mission to Moscow and Kharkiv." *Journal of Ukrainian Graduate Studies* 3, 2 (fall 1978): 3–24.
Desroches, Alain. *The Ukrainian Problem and Symon Petlura*. Chicago: Ukrainian Research and Information Institute, 1970.
Doroshenko, Dmytro. *History of Ukraine, 1917–1923*. Volume 2, *The Ukrainian Hetman State of 1918*. Trans. D. M. Elcheshen. Winnipeg: Basilian Press, 1973.
Eichenbaum, Vsevolod. *The Unknown Revolution (Kronstadt 1921— Ukraine 1918–1921)*. London: Freedom Press, 1955.
Fedyshyn, Oleh S. *Germany's Drive to the East and the Ukrainian Revolution, 1917–1918*. New Brunswick, N.J.: Rutgers University Press, 1971.
Friedgut, Theodore H. *Iuzovka and the Revolution*. 2 vols. Princeton, N.J.: Princeton University Press, 1989–94.
Goldelman, Solomon I. *Jewish National Autonomy in Ukraine, 1917–1920*. Chicago: Ukrainian Research and Information Institute, 1968.
Guthier, Stephen. "The Popular Base of Ukrainian Nationalism in 1917." *Slavic Review* 38, 1 (1979): 30–47.
Horak, Stephan. *The First Treaty of World War I: Ukraine's Treaty with the Central Powers of February 9, 1918*. Boulder, Colo.: East European Monographs, 1988.
Hunczak, Taras. "A Reappraisal of Symon Petliura and Ukrainian-Jewish Relations, 1917–1921." *Jewish Social Studies* 31, 3 (July 1969): 163–83.
———, ed. *The Ukraine, 1917–1921: A Study in Revolution*. Cambridge, Mass.: HURI, 1977.
Jurczenko, O. "The Bolshevik Conquest of the Ukraine." *Ukrainian Review* (Munich) 1 (1955): 5–28.

Kamenetsky, Ihor. "The Ukrainian Central Rada and the Status of the German and Austrian Troops Following the Peace Treaty of Brest Litovsk." *Ukraïns'kyi istoryk* 19–20 (1982–83): 119–27.
Kenez, Peter. *Civil War in South Russia, 1918–1920*. 2 vols. Berkeley: University of California Press, 1971–77.
Kleiner, Israel. *From Nationalism to Universalism: Vladimir (Ze'ev) Jabotinsky and the Ukrainian Question*. Edmonton and Toronto: CIUS Press, 2000.
Liber, George. "Ukrainian Nationalism and the 1918 Law on National-Personal Autonomy." *Nationalities Papers* 15, 1 (1987): 22–42.
Majstrenko, Iwan. *Borotbism: A Chapter in the History of Ukrainian Communism*. New York: Research Program on the U.S.S.R., 1954.
Malet, Michael. *Nestor Makhno in the Russian Civil War*. London: London School of Economics and Political Science, 1982.
Margolin, Arnold. *From a Political Diary: Russia, Ukraine and America, 1905–1945*. New York: Columbia University Press, 1946.
———. *Ukraine and Policy of the Entente*. New York: L. A. Margolena, 1977.
Mark, Rudolf A. "Social Questions and National Revolution: The Ukrainian National Republic in 1919–1920." *HUS* 14, 1/2 (June 1990): 113–31.
Mazlakh, Serhii, and Vasyl' Shakrai. *On the Current Situation in the Ukraine*. Ann Arbor: University of Michigan Press, 1970.
Mintz, M. "The Secretariat of Internationality Affairs (*Sekretariiat mizhnatsional'nykh sprav*) of the Ukrainian General Secretariat (1917–1918)." *HUS* 6, 1 (Mar. 1982): 25–42.
Neufeld, Dietrich. *A Russian Dance of Death: Revolution and Civil War in the Ukraine*. Trans. Al Reimer. Winnipeg: Hyperion Press, 1977.
Palij, Michael. *The Anarchism of Nestor Makhno, 1918–1921: An Aspect of the Ukrainian Revolution*. Seattle: University of Washington Press, 1976.
———. *The Ukrainian-Polish Defensive Alliance, 1919–1921: An Aspect of the Ukrainian Revolution*. Edmonton and Toronto: CIUS Press, 1995.
Pidhainy, Oleh S. *The Formation of the Ukrainian Republic*. Toronto: New Review Books, 1966.
Procyk, Anna M. *Russian Nationalism and Ukraine: The Nationality Policy of the Volunteer Army during the Civil War*. Edmonton and Toronto: CIUS Press, 1995.
Prymak, Thomas M. "The First All-Ukrainian Congress of Soviets and Its Antecedents." *Journal of Ukrainian Graduate Studies* 4, 1 (spring 1979): 3–19.
Reshetar, John S. *The Ukrainian Revolution, 1917–1920: A Study in*

Nationalism. Princeton, N.J.: Princeton University Press, 1952; repr. New York: Arno Press, 1972.

———. "The Ukrainian Revolution in Retrospect." *CSP* 10, 2 (summer 1968): 116–32.

Silberfarb, Moses. *The Jewish Ministry and Jewish National Autonomy in Ukraine.* New York: Aleph Press, 1993.

Stachiw, Matthew. *Ukraine and Russia: An Outline of History of Political and Military Relations (December 1917–April 1918).* Trans. Walter Dushnyck. New York: Ukrainian Congress Committee of America, 1967.

Stachiw, Matthew, Peter G. Stercho, and Nicolas L. F. Chirovskyj. *Ukraine and the European Turmoil, 1917–1919.* 2 vols. New York: Shevchenko Scientific Society, 1973.

Texts of the Ukraine "Peace" (1918). Introduction and comments by Paul R. Magocsi. Cleveland: John T. Zubal Publishers, 1981.

Yakymovych, Bohdan. "The Ukrainian Navy in 1917–1920." *UR* 40, 2 (summer 1993): 47–53.

Yurkevych, Lev. "The Russian Social Democrats and the National Question." *JUS* 7, 1 (spring 1982): 57–78.

9. Ukraine under Soviet Rule (General Works)

Applebaum, Anne. *Gulag: A History.* New York: Doubleday, 2003.

Bohdaniuk, Volodymyr, ed. *The Real Face of Russia.* London: Ukrainian Information Service, 1967.

Courtois, Stéphane et al. *The Black Book of Communism: Crimes, Terror, Repression.* Cambridge, Mass.: Harvard University Press, 1999.

Dmytryshyn, Basil. *Moscow and the Ukraine, 1918–1953: A Study of Russian Bolshevik Nationality Policy.* New York: Bookman Associates, 1956.

Holubnychny, Vsevolod. "Outline History of the Communist Party of the Ukraine." *Ukrainian Review* (Munich) 6 (1958): 68–127.

Kohn, Hans. *Nationalism in the Soviet Union.* New York: Columbia University Press, 1933.

Krawchenko, Bohdan. *Social Change and National Consciousness in Twentieth-Century Ukraine.* Houndmills and London: Macmillan, 1985; repr. Edmonton and Toronto: CIUS Press, 1987.

Manning, Clarence A. *Twentieth-Century Ukraine.* New York: Bookman Associates, 1951.

———. *Ukraine under the Soviets.* New York: Bookman Associates, 1953.

Russian Oppression in Ukraine: Reports and Documents. London: Ukrainian Publishers, 1962.

Shelukhyn, Serhii. *Ukraine, Poland, and Russia and the Right of the Free*

Disposition of the Peoples. Washington, D.C.: Friends of Ukraine, 1919.
Shulhyn, Olexander. *Ukraine against Moscow.* New York: Speller, 1959.
Simon, Gerhard. *Nationalism and Policy toward the Nationalities in the Soviet Union: From Totalitarian Dictatorship to Post-Stalinist Society.* Boulder, Colo.: Westview Press, 1991.
Smal-Stocki, Roman. *The Nationality Problem of the Soviet Union and Russian Communist Imperialism.* Milwaukee: Bruce Publishing, 1952.
Sullivant, Robert S. *Soviet Politics and the Ukraine,1917–1957.* New York: Columbia University Press, 1962.
Vynnychenko, Ihor. "The Deportation, Incarceration, and Forced Resettlement of Ukrainians in the Soviet Period." *JUS* 18, 1/2 (summer–winter 1993): 55–68.

10. Interwar Ukraine under Soviet Rule

Ammende, Ewald. *Human Life in Russia.* London: Allen & Unwin, 1936; repr. Cleveland: John T. Zubal Publishers, 1984.
The Black Deeds of the Kremlin: A White Book. Volume 1, *Book of Testimonies.* Volume 2, *The Great Famine in Ukraine, 1932–1933.* Detroit and Toronto: DOBRUS and Ukrainian Association of Victims of Russian Communist Terror, 1953–55.
Borys, Jurij. *The Sovietization of Ukraine, 1917–1923: The Communist Doctrine and Practice of National Self-Determination.* Rev. ed. Edmonton and Toronto: CIUS Press, 1980.
———. "Who Ruled the Soviet Ukraine in Stalin's Time (1917–1939)?" *CSP* 14, 2 (summer 1972): 213–33.
Carynnyk, Marco. "The Famine the 'Times' Couldn't Find." *Commentary* 76, 5 (Nov. 1983): 32–40.
Carynnyk, Marco, Lubomyr Y. Luciuk, and Bohdan S. Kordan, eds. *The Foreign Office and the Famine: British Documents on Ukraine and the Great Famine of 1932–1933.* Kingston, Ont.: Limestone Press, 1988.
Commission on the Ukraine Famine. *Investigation of the Ukrainian Famine, 1932–1933. Report to Congress.* Ed. James E. Mace and Leonid Heretz. Washington, D.C.: Government Printing Office, 1988.
———. *Oral History Project of the Commission on the Ukraine Famine.* Ed. James E. Mace and Leonid Heretz. 3 vols. Washington, D.C.: Government Printing Office, 1990.
Conquest, Robert. *The Great Terror: A Reassessment.* New York: Oxford University Press, 1990.
———. *The Harvest of Sorrow: Soviet Collectivization and the Terror-Famine.* New York: Oxford University Press, 1986.
———. *Kolyma: The Arctic Death Camps.* New York: Viking Press,

1978.

Dolot, Miron. *Execution by Hunger: The Hidden Holocaust.* New York: Norton, 1985.

Famine in the Soviet Ukraine, 1932–1933: A Memorial Exhibition, Widener Library, Harvard University. Ed. Oksana Procyk et al. Cambridge, Mass.: Harvard College Library, 1986.

Fedenko, Panas. "Mykola Skrypnyk: His National Policy, Conviction and Rehabilitation." *Ukrainian Review* (Munich) 5 (1957): 56–72.

Graziosi, Andrea. "G. L. Piatakov (1890–1937): A Mirror of Soviet History." *HUS* 16, 1/2 (June 1992): 102–66.

———. *The Great Soviet Peasant War: Bolsheviks and Peasants, 1917–1933.* Cambridge, Mass.: HURI, 1996.

The Great Famine in Ukraine: The Unknown Holocaust. Jersey City, N.J.: Ukrainian National Association, 1983.

Hewryk, Titus D. "Planning of the Capital in Kharkiv." *HUS* 16, 3/4 (Dec. 1992): 325–59.

Hryshko, Vasyl. *Experience with Russia.* New York: Ukrainian Congress Committee of America, 1956.

———. *The Ukrainian Holocaust of 1933.* Ed. and trans. Marco Carynnyk. Toronto: Bahriany Foundation, 1983.

Hunter, Ian A. "Putting History on Trial: The Ukrainian Famine of 1932–33." *JUS* 15, 2 (winter 1990): 47–74.

Kagedan, Allan L. "Soviet Jewish Territorial Units and Ukrainian-Jewish Relations." *HUS* 9, 1/2 (June 1985): 118–32.

Kamenetsky, Ihor, ed. *The Tragedy of Vinnytsia: Materials on Stalin's Policy of Extermination in Ukraine during the Great Purge, 1936–1938.* Toronto and New York: Ukrainian Historical Association, 1989.

Kopelev, Lev. *The Education of a True Believer.* Trans. Gary Kern. New York: Harper & Row, 1980.

Kostiuk, Hryhory. *Stalinist Rule in the Ukraine: A Study of the Decade of Mass Terror, 1929–1939.* New York: Praeger, 1960.

Kuromiya, Hiroaki. *Freedom and Terror in the Donbas: A Ukrainian-Russian Borderland, 1870s–1990s.* Cambridge: Cambridge University Press, 1998.

———. "Ukraine and Russia in the 1930s." *HUS* 18, 3/4 (Dec. 1994): 327–41.

Levytsky, Borys. *The Stalinist Terror in the Thirties: Documentation from the Soviet Press.* Stanford, Calif.: Hoover Institution Press, 1974.

Mace, James E. *Communism and the Dilemmas of National Liberation: National Communism in Soviet Ukraine, 1918–1933.* Cambridge, Mass.: HURI and Ukrainian Academy of Arts and Sciences in the U.S., 1983.

———. "The Famine of 1932–1933: A Watershed in the History of Soviet Nationality Policy." In *Soviet Nationality Policies: Ruling Ethnic Groups in the USSR*, ed. Henry R. Huttenbach, 177–205. London: Mansell, 1990.

———. "The Man-Made Famine of 1933 in the Soviet Ukraine: What Happened and Why?" In *Toward the Understanding and Prevention of Genocide*, ed. Israel W. Charny, 67–83. Boulder, Colo.: Westview Press, 1984.

Martin, Terry. *The Affirmative Action Empire: Nations and Nationalism in the Soviet Union, 1923–1939*. Ithaca, N.Y.: Cornell University Press, 2001.

Mykula, Volodymyr. "Soviet Nationalities Policy in Ukraine, 1920–1930." *UR* 18, 4 (winter 1971): 2–38; 19, 1 (spring 1972): 21–65; 3 (autumn 1972): 36–54; 4 (winter 1972): 56–77; 20, 1 (spring 1973): 44–56; 2 (summer 1973): 59–65; 3 (autumn 1973): 44–55; 4 (winter 1973): 37–54; 21, 1 (spring 1974): 46–52; 2 (summer 1974): 31–41.

Nahaylo, Bohdan. "Ukrainian National Resistance in Soviet Ukraine during the 1920s." *JUS* 15, 2 (winter 1990): 1–18.

Nakai, Kazuo. "Soviet Agricultural Policies in the Ukraine and the 1921–1922 Famine." *HUS* 6, 1 (Mar. 1982): 43–61.

Pidhainy, Semen. "Ukrainian National Communism." *Ukrainian Review* (Munich) 7 (1959): 45–64.

Pipes, Richard. *The Formation of the Soviet Union: Communism and Nationalism, 1917–1923*. Rev. ed. Cambridge, Mass.: Harvard University Press, 1964.

Prychodko, Nicholas. *One of the Fifteen Million*. Boston: Little & Brown, 1952.

Radziejowski, Janusz. "The Last Years of Mykhailo Slabchenko." *JUS* 8, 2 (winter 1983): 81–84.

Rakovsky, Christian. *Selected Writings on Opposition in the USSR, 1923–30*. Ed. Gus Fagan. London and New York: Allison and Busby, 1980.

Rassweiler, Anne D. *The Generation of Power: The History of Dneprostroi*. Oxford: Oxford University Press, 1988.

Rich, Vera. "'No Ripe Plums': British Diplomatic Perceptions of Ukrainian Independence Movements, 1938–40." *UR* 42, 3 (autumn 1995): 24–58.

Serbyn, Roman, and Bohdan Krawchenko, eds. *Famine in Ukraine, 1932–1933*. Edmonton and Toronto: CIUS Press, 1986.

Shapoval, Yuri. "Mykhailo Hrushevsky in Moscow and His Death (1931–34): New Revelations." *JUS* 24, 2 (winter 1999): 79–100.

———. "Oleksander Shumsky: His Last Thirteen Years." *JUS* 18, 1/2 (summer–winter 1993): 69–84.

———. "'On Ukrainian Separatism': A GPU Circular of 1926." *HUS* 18, 3/4 (Dec. 1994): 275–302.
Somchynsky, Bohdan. "National Communism and the Politics of Industrialization in Ukraine, 1923–1928." *JUS* 13, 2 (winter 1988): 52–69.
Taubman, William. *Khrushchev: The Man and His Era.* New York: Norton, 2003.
Yekelchyk, Serhy. *Stalin's Empire of Memory: Russian-Ukrainian Relations in the Soviet Historical Imagination.* Toronto: University of Toronto Press, 2004.

11. Ukraine in World War II

Armstrong, John A. "Collaborationism in World War II: The Integral Nationalist Variant in Eastern Europe." *Journal of Modern History* 40, 3 (1968): 396–410.
———. *Ukrainian Nationalism, 1939–1945.* 2d ed. New York: Columbia University Press, 1963.
Berkhoff, Karel C. *Harvest of Despair: Life and Death in Ukraine under Nazi Rule.* Cambridge, Mass.: Harvard University Press, 2004.
Bilinsky, Yaroslav. "The Impact of World War II on the Nationality Question. An Essay." *UQ* 42, 3/4 (fall–winter 1986): 197–213.
Boshyk, Yury, ed. *Ukraine during World War II: History and Its Aftermath. A Symposium.* Edmonton and Toronto: CIUS Press, 1986.
Burleigh, Michael. *Germany Turns Eastwards: A Study of Ostforschung in the Third Reich.* Cambridge: Cambridge University Press, 1988.
Chirovsky, Nicholas L. Fr. *Ukraine and the Second World War.* New York: Ukrainian Congress Committee of America, 1985.
Dallin, Alexander. *German Rule in Russia, 1941–1945: A Study of Occupation Policies.* 2d ed. Boulder, Colo.: Westview Press, 1981.
Denisov, V. N., and G. I. Changuli, eds. *Nazi Crimes in Ukraine, 1941–1944: Documents and Materials.* Kyiv: Naukova dumka, 1987.
Dima, Nicholas. *Bessarabia and Bukovina: The Soviet-Romanian Territorial Dispute.* Boulder, Colo.: East European Monographs, 1983.
Dyczok, Marta. *The Grand Alliance and Ukrainian Refugees.* Basingstoke: Macmillan, 2000.
Elliott, Mark R. *Pawns of Yalta: Soviet Refugees and America's Role in Their Repatriation.* Urbana: University of Illinois Press, 1982.
Epstein, Julius. *Operation Keelhaul: The Story of Forced Repatriation from 1944 to the Present.* Old Greenwich, Conn.: Devin-Adair, 1973.
Friedman, Philip. *Roads to Extinction: Essays on the Holocaust.* New York: Jewish Publication Society of America, 1980.
Gross, Jan T. *Revolution from Abroad: The Soviet Conquest of Poland's*

Western Ukraine and Western Belorussia. Expanded ed. Princeton, N.J.: Princeton University Press, 2002.

Himka, John-Paul. "*Krakivski visti* and the Jews, 1943: A Contribution to the History of Ukrainian-Jewish Relations during the Second World War." *JUS* 21, 1/2 (summer–winter 1996): 81–95.

Homze, Edward L. *Foreign Labor in Nazi Germany*. Princeton, N.J.: Princeton University Press, 1967.

Hunczak, Taras. "Between Two Leviathans: Ukraine during the Second World War." In *Ukrainian Past, Ukrainian Present*, ed. Bohdan Krawchenko, 97–106. New York: St. Martin's Press, 1993.

Kahane, David. *Lvov Ghetto Diary*. Trans. Jerzy Michalowicz. Amherst: University of Massachusetts Press, 1990.

Kamenetsky, Ihor. *Secret Nazi Plans for Eastern Europe: A Study of Lebensraum Policies*. New York: Bookman Associates, 1961.

———. Kamenetsky, Ihor. *Hitler's Occupation of Ukraine, 1941–1945: A Study of Totalitarian Imperialism*. Milwaukee: Marquette University Press, 1956.

Kosyk, Volodymyr. *The Third Reich and the Ukrainian Question: Documents, 1934–1944*. London: Ukrainian Central Information Service, 1991.

———. *The Third Reich and Ukraine*. New York: Peter Lang, 1993.

———. "Ukraine's Losses during the Second World War." *UR* 33, 2 (summer 1985): 9–19.

Luciuk, Lubomyr Y., and Bohdan S. Kordan. *Anglo-American Perspectives on the Ukrainian Question, 1938–1951: A Documentary Collection*. Kingston, Ont.: Limestone Press, 1987.

Mulligan, Timothy Patrick. *The Politics of Illusion and Empire: German Occupation Policy in the Soviet Union, 1942–1943*. New York: Praeger, 1988.

Neufeldt, Colin P. "Fifth Column? New Light on the Soviet Germans and Their Relationship to the Third Reich." *JUS* 13, 1 (summer 1988): 65–81.

Pyskir, Maria Sawchyn. *Thousands of Roads: A Memoir of a Young Woman's Life in the Ukrainian Underground during and after World War II*. Trans. Ania Savage. Jefferson, N.C.: McFarland, 2001.

Rich, Norman. *Hitler's War Aims*. 2 vols. New York: Norton, 1973.

Sydorenko, Natalya. "Ukrainian PoW Press in Italy, 1945–47." *UR* 42, 2 (summer 1995): 30–36.

"Symposium: Ukrainians in World War II, Views and Points." *Nationalities Papers* 10, 1 (spring 1982): 1–40.

Tolstoy, Nikolai. *Stalin's Secret War*. London: Jonathan Cape, 1981.

Troper, Harold, and Morton Weinfeld. *Old Wounds: Jews, Ukrainians and the Hunt for Nazi War Criminals in Canada*. Toronto: Viking, 1988.

Weerd, Hans de. "Erich Koch and Ukraine." *UQ* 11, 1 (winter 1955): 29–34.
Wytwycky, Bohdan. *The Other Holocaust: Many Circles of Hell. A Brief Account of 9–10 Million Persons Who Died with the 6 Million Jews under Nazi Racism*. Washington, D.C.: Novak Report, 1980.

12. Ukraine, 1945–91

Alekseeva, Liudmila. *Soviet Dissent: Contemporary Movements for National, Religious, and Human Rights*. Trans. Carol Pearce and John Glad. Middletown, Conn.: Wesleyan University Press, 1985.
Allworth, Edward, ed. *Soviet Nationality Problems*. New York: Columbia University Press, 1971.
Amnesty International. *Prisoners of Conscience in the USSR: Their Treatment and Conditions*. 2d ed. London: Amnesty International, 1980.
Antonov, B. *"Prisoners of Conscience" in the USSR and Their Patrons*. Moscow: Novosti, 1988.
Armstrong, John A. *The Soviet Bureaucratic Elite: A Case Study of the Ukrainian Apparatus*. New York: Praeger, 1959.
Azrael, Jeremy R., ed. *Soviet Nationality Policies and Practices*. New York: Praeger, 1978.
Badzo, Iurii. "An Open Letter to the Presidium of the Supreme Soviet of the USSR and the Central Committee of the CPSU." Trans. Roman Senkus. *JUS* 9, 1 (summer 1984): 74–94; 2 (winter 1984): 47–70.
Bilinsky, Yaroslav. "The Concept of the Soviet People and Its Implications for Soviet Nationality Policy." *AUAAS* 14, 37/38 (1978–80): 87–133.
———. *The Second Soviet Republic: The Ukraine after World War II*. New Brunswick, N.J.: Rutgers University Press, 1964.
———. "Shcherbytsky, Ukraine, and Kremlin Politics." *Problems of Communism* 32, 4 (July–Aug. 1983): 1–20.
Bilinsky, Yaroslav, and Tönu Parming. "Helsinki Watch Committees in the Soviet Republics: Implications for Soviet Nationality Policy." *Nationalities Papers* 9, 1 (spring 1981): 1–25.
Bilocerkowycz, Jaroslaw. *Soviet Ukrainian Dissent: A Study of Political Alienation*. Boulder, Colo.: Westview Press, 1988.
Bloch, Sidney, and Peter Reddaway. *Soviet Psychiatric Abuse: The Shadow over World Psychiatry*. London: Victor Gollancz, 1984.
———. *Psychiatric Terror: How Soviet Psychiatry Is Used to Suppress Dissent*. New York: Basic Books, 1977.
Bothwell, Robert, and J. L. Granatstein, eds. *The Gouzenko Transcripts: The Evidence Presented to the Kellock-Taschereau Royal Commis-*

sion of 1946. Ottawa: Deneau Publishers, 1982.
Browne, Michael, ed. *Ferment in the Ukraine: Documents by V. Chornovil, I. Kandyba, L. Lukyanenko, V. Moroz and Others.* New York: Praeger, 1971.
Chornovil, Vyacheslav. *The Chornovil Papers.* New York and Toronto: McGraw-Hill, 1968.
Dushnyck, Walter, ed. *Ukraine in a Changing World.* New York: Ukrainian Congress Committee of America, 1977.
Dzyuba, Ivan. *Internationalism or Russification? A Study in the Soviet Nationalities Problem.* Ed. M. Davies. 2d ed. London: Weidenfeld and Nicolson, 1970.
Farmer, Kenneth C. *Ukrainian Nationalism in the Post-Stalin Era: Myth, Symbols and Ideology in Soviet Nationalities Policy.* The Hague: Martinus Nijhoff, 1980.
Grigorenko, Petr Grigor'evich. *The Grigorenko Papers. Writings by General P. G. Grigorenko and Documents on His Case.* Boulder, Colo.: Westview Press, 1973.
Grigorenko, Petro G. *Memoirs.* New York and London: Norton, 1982.
Hodnett, Grey. *Leadership in the Soviet National Republics: A Quantitative Study of Recruitment Policy.* Oakville, Ont.: Mosaic Press, 1978.
―――. "The Views of Petro Shelest." *AUAAS* 14, 37/38 (1978–80): 209–43.
Hodnett, Grey, and Peter J. Potichnyj. *The Ukraine and the Czechoslovak Crisis.* Canberra: Australian National University, 1970.
Kamenetsky, Ihor, ed. *Nationalism and Human Rights: Processes of Modernization in the USSR.* Littleton, Colo.: Libraries Unlimited, 1977.
Khodorovich, Tatyana, ed. *The Case of Leonid Plyushch.* Boulder, Colo.: Westview Press, 1976.
Kis, Theofil I. *Nationhood, Statehood and the International Status of the Ukrainian SSR/Ukraine.* Ottawa: University of Ottawa Press, 1989.
Klejner, Israel. "The Present-Day Ukrainian National Movement in the USSR and the Jewish Question." *Soviet Jewish Affairs* 11, 3 (1981): 3–14.
Kolasky, John. *Two Years in Soviet Ukraine: A Canadian's Personal Account of Russian Oppression and the Growing Opposition.* Toronto: Peter Martin Associates, 1970.
Kosyk, Volodymyr. *Concentration Camps in the USSR.* London: Ukrainian Publishers, 1962.
Krawchenko, Bohdan. "National Memory in Ukraine: The Role of the

Blue and Yellow Flag." *JUS* 15, 1 (summer 1990): 1–21.

———, ed. *Ukraine after Shelest*. Edmonton and Toronto: CIUS Press, 1983.

Kuzio, Taras. *Ukraine: Perestroika to Independence*. 2d ed. New York: St. Martin's, 2000.

Lewytzkyj, Borys. *Politics and Society in Soviet Ukraine, 1953–1980*. Edmonton and Toronto: CIUS Press, 1984.

Marples, David R. *Stalinism in Ukraine in the 1940s*. Edmonton: University of Alberta Press, 1992.

Moroz, Valentyn. *Boomerang: The Works of Valentyn Moroz*. Ed. Yaroslav Bihun. Baltimore: Smoloskyp, 1974.

———. *Report from the Beria Reserve: The Protest Writings of Valentyn Moroz, a Ukrainian Political Prisoner in the USSR*. Ed. and trans. John Kolasky. Toronto: Peter Martin Associates, 1974.

Motyl, Alexander J. *Will the Non-Russians Rebel? State, Ethnicity, and Stability in the USSR*. Ithaca, N.Y.: Cornell University Press, 1987.

Osadchy, Mykhaylo. *Cataract*. Trans. Marco Carynnyk. New York: Harcourt Brace Jovanovich, 1976.

The Persecution of the Ukrainian Helsinki Group. 2d ed. Toronto: World Congress of Free Ukrainians, 1981.

Plyushch, Leonid. *History's Carnival: A Dissident's Autobiography*. Ed. and trans. Marco Carynnyk. New York: Harcourt Brace Jovanovich, 1979.

Potichnyj, Peter J. "The Referendum and Presidential Elections in Ukraine." *CSP* 33, 2 (June 1991): 123–38.

———, ed. *Ukraine in the Seventies*. Oakville, Ont.: Mosaic Press, 1975.

Sawczuk, Konstantyn. *The Ukraine in the United Nations Organization: A Study in Soviet Foreign Policy, 1944–1950*. Boulder, Colo.: East European Quarterly, 1975.

Shymko, Yuri R., ed. *For This Was I Born...: The Human Conditions in USSR Slave Labor Camps*. Toronto: Ukrainica Research Institute, 1973.

Simmonds, George W., ed. *Nationalism in the USSR and Eastern Europe in the Era of Brezhnev and Kosygin*. Detroit: University of Detroit Press, 1977.

Solchanyk, Roman. "Chernobyl: The Political Fallout in Ukraine." *JUS* 11, 1 (summer 1986): 20–34.

———, ed. *Ukraine: From Chernobyl' to Sovereignty*. Edmonton and Toronto: CIUS Press; New York: St. Martin's, 1992.

Solovey, D. "Fresh Light on the Nationality Policy of the Communist Party and the Soviet Government." *Ukrainian Review* (Munich) 6 (1957): 67–122.

Sorokowsky, Andrew. "National Discrimination in Ukraine." *UQ* 41, 3/4 (fall–winter 1985): 184–95.
Stenchuk, Bohdan [pseud.]. *What I. Dziuba Stands For and How He Does It.* Kyiv: UkrSSR Association for Cultural Relations with Ukrainians Abroad, 1969.
Sullivant, Robert S. "The Agrarian-Industrial Dichotomy in the Ukraine as a Factor in Soviet Nationality Policy." *AUAAS* 9, 27/28 (1961): 110–25.
Szporluk, Roman, ed. *The Influence of East Europe and the Soviet West on the USSR.* New York: Praeger, 1976.
Tillett, Lowell. "Ukrainian Nationalism and the Fall of Shelest." *Slavic Review* 34, 4 (1975): 752–68.
The Ukrainian Herald, Issue 6: Dissent in Ukraine. Ed. and trans. Lesya Jones and Bohdan Yasen. Baltimore: Smoloskyp Publishers, 1977.
The Ukrainian Herald, Issue 7–8: Ethnocide of Ukrainians in the U.S.S.R. (Spring 1974). An Underground Journal from Soviet Ukraine. Comp. Maksym Sahaydak. Ed. and trans. Olena Saciuk and Bohdan Yasen. 2d ed. Baltimore: Smoloskyp Publishers, 1981.
Verba, Lesya, and Nina Strokata, eds. *The Human Rights Movement in Ukraine: Documents of the Ukrainian Helsinki Group, 1976–1980.* Baltimore: Smoloskyp Publishers, 1980.

V. JURIDICAL

"Constitution of Ukraine (Official English Translation)." *UR* 43, 4 (winter 1996): 3–48.
Dingley, James. "The Constitutions of Ukraine and Belarus: Increasing Cooperation *versus* Confrontation." *UR* 43, 3 (autumn 1996): 35–45.
Futey, Bohdan. "Comments on the Constitution of Ukraine." *East European Constitutional Review* 5, 2/3 (spring–summer 1996): 29–34.
———. "Comments on the Law on the Constitutional Court of Ukraine." *East European Constitutional Review* 6, 2/3 (spring–summer 1997): 56–63.
Matkovskyi, Oleh. "A Criminal Code for Ukraine." *UR* 43, 1 (spring 1996): 3–7.
Wilson, Andrew. "The New Ukrainian Constitution." *UR* 43, 4 (winter 1996): 49–54.
Wolczuk, Kataryna. "Constituting Statehood: The New Ukrainian Constitution." *UR* 45, 3 (autumn 1998): 17–38.

VI. POLITICAL

1. General

Arel, Dominique. "Ukraine: The Temptation of the Nationalizing State." In *Political Culture and Civil Society in Russia and the New States of Eurasia*, ed. Vladimir Tismaneanu, 157–88. Armonk, N.Y.: M. E. Sharpe, 1995.

―――. "Voting Behavior in the Ukrainian Parliament: The Language Factor." In *Parliaments in Transition: The New Legislative Politics in the Former USSR and Eastern Europe*, ed. Thomas F. Remington, 125–58. Boulder, Colo.: Westview Press, 1994.

Arel, Dominique, and Valeri Khmelko. "The Russian Factor and Territorial Polarization in Ukraine." *Harriman Review* 9, 1/2 (spring 1996): 81–91.

Armstrong, John A. "Persistent Patterns of the Ukrainian Apparatus." *Soviet and Post-Soviet Review* 20, 2/3 (1993): 213–31.

―――. "Whither Ukrainian Nationalism?" *Canadian Review of Studies in Nationalism* 23, 1/2 (1996): 111–24.

Åslund, Anders. "Eurasia Letter: Ukraine's Turnaround." *Foreign Policy* 100 (fall 1995): 125–43.

Bach, Stanley. "From Soviet to Parliament in Ukraine: The Verkhovna Rada during 1992–94." In *The New Parliaments of Central and Eastern Europe*, ed. David M. Olson and Philip Norton, 213–30. London: Cass, 1996.

Barrington, Lowell. "The Domestic and International Consequences of Citizenship in the Soviet Successor States." *Europe-Asia Studies* 47, 5 (July 1995): 731–53.

Bilinsky, Yaroslav. "Are the Ukrainians a State Nation?" *Problems of Communism* 41, 1/2 (Jan.–Apr. 1992): 134–35.

―――. "Primary Language of Communication as a Secondary Indicator of National Identity: The Ukrainian Parliamentary and Presidential Elections of 1994 and the 'Manifesto of the Ukrainian Intelligentsia' of 1995." *Nationalities Papers* 24, 4 (Dec. 1996): 661–78.

―――. "Ukraine: The Multiple Challenges to Independence." *Harriman Institute Forum* 7, 1/2 (Sep.–Oct. 1993): 27–31.

Birch, Julian. "Ukraine—a Nation State or a State of Nations?" *JUS* 21, 1/2 (summer-winter 1996): 109–24.

Birch, Sarah. "Electoral Behaviour in Western Ukraine in National Elections and Referendums, 1989–91." *Europe-Asia Studies* 47, 7 (Nov. 1995): 1145–76.

―――. "The Ukrainian Parliamentary and Presidential Elections of 1994." *Electoral Studies* 14, 1 (1995): 93–99.

Bojcun, Marko. "Leonid Kuchma's Presidency in Its First Year." *JUS* 20, 1/2 (summer–winter 1995): 177–93.
———. "Ukraine under Kuchma." *Labour Focus on Eastern Europe* 52 (autumn 1995): 70–83.
———. "The Ukrainian Parliamentary Elections in March–April 1994." *Europe-Asia Studies* 47, 2 (Mar. 1995): 229–49.
Boukhalov, Oleksandr, and Serguei Ivannikov. "Ukrainian Local Politics after Independence." *Annals of the American Academy of Political and Social Science* 540 (July 1995): 126–36.
Brzezinski, Ian. "Ukraine: The Geopolitical Dimension." *National Interest* 27 (spring 1992): 48–52.
Brzezinski, Zbigniew. "Ukraine's Critical Role in the Post-Soviet Space." *HUS* 20 (1996): 3–8.
Campbell, Adrian. "Regional and Local Government in Ukraine." In *Local Government in Eastern Europe: Establishing Democracy at the Grassroots*, ed. Andrew Coulson, 115–27. Aldershot: Elgar, 1995.
Carrère d'Encausse, Hélène. *The End of the Soviet Empire: The Triumph of the Nations*. Trans. Franklin Philip. New York: Basic Books, 1993.
Chandler, Andrea. "State Building and Social Obligations in Post-Communist Systems: Assessing Change in Russia and Ukraine." *CSP* 38, 1/2 (Mar.–June 1996): 1–22.
———. "Statebuilding and Political Priorities in Post-Soviet Ukraine: The Role of the Military." *Armed Forces and Society* 22, 4 (summer 1996): 573–97.
Chudowsky, Victor. "The Ukrainian Party System." In *State and Nation Building in East Central Europe: Contemporary Perspectives*, ed. John S. Micgiel, 305–21. New York: Columbia University, 1996.
Churilov, Nikolay, and Tatyana Koshechkina. "Public Attitudes in Ukraine." In *Perceptions of Security: Public Opinion and Expert Assessments in Europe's New Democracies*, ed. Richard Smoke, 189–208. New York: Manchester University Press, 1996.
D'Anieri, Paul, Robert Kravchuk, and Taras Kuzio. *Politics and Society in Ukraine*. Boulder, Colo.: Westview Press, 1999.
Darski, Józef. "Quo Vadis Ukraine." *Uncaptive Minds* 5, 1 (spring 1992): 59–74.
———. "Which Way Independence?" *Uncaptive Minds* 7, 3 (fall–winter 1994): 117–28.
Diuk, Nadia, and Adrian Karatnycky. *New Nations Rising: The Fall of the Soviets and the Challenge of Independence*. New York: Wiley, 1993.
Dobriansky, Paula J. "Ukraine: A Question of Survival." *National*

Interest 36 (summer 1994): 65–72.

Dyczok, Marta. *Ukraine: Movement without Change, Change without Movement*. Amsterdam: Harwood Academic Publishers, 2000.

Friedgut, Theodore. "Perestroika in the Provinces: The Politics of Transition in Donets'k." In *Local Power and Post-Soviet Policies*, ed. Theodore H. Friedgut and Jeffrey W. Hahn, 162–83. Armonk, N.Y.: M. E. Sharpe, 1994.

———. "Pluralism and Politics in an Urban Soviet: Donetsk, 1990–1991." In *In Search of Pluralism: Soviet and Post-Soviet Politics*, ed. Carl R. Saivetz and Anthony Jones, 45–61. Boulder, Colo.: Westview Press, 1994.

———. "Popular Efforts toward Self-Government: Political, Social and Economic Initiatives in Donetsk." In *Trials of Transition: Economic Reform in the Former Communist Bloc*, ed. Michael Keren and Gur Ofer, 39–50. Boulder, Colo.: Westview Press, 1992.

Gibson, James L. "Political and Economic Markets: Changes in the Connections between Attitudes toward Political Democracy and a Market Economy within the Mass Culture of Russia and Ukraine." *Journal of Politics* 58, 4 (Nov. 1996): 954–85.

———. "The Resilience of Mass Support for Democratic Institutions and Processes in the Nascent Russian and Ukrainian Democracies." In *Political Culture and Civil Society in Russia and the New States of Eurasia*, ed. Vladimir Tismaneanu, 53–111. Armonk, N.Y.: M. E. Sharpe, 1995.

Golovakha, Evgenii. "Elites in Ukraine: Evaluation of the Project's Elite Survey." In *Emerging Societal Actors—Economic, Social and Political Interests, Theories, Methods and Case Studies*, ed. Segbers Klaus and Stephan De Spiegeleire, 167–242. Baden-Baden: Nomos, 1995.

Golovakha, Evhen I., and Nataliya V. Panina. "The Development of a Democratic Political Identity in Contemporary Ukrainian Political Culture." In *Nationalism, Ethnicity, and Identity: Cross National and Comparative Perspectives*, ed. Russell F. Farnen, 403–25. New Brunswick: Transaction, 1994.

Hague, Judy, Rose Aidan, and Marko Bojcun. "Rebuilding Ukraine's Hollow State: Developing a Democratic Public Service in Ukraine." *Public Administration and Development* 15, 4 (Oct. 1995): 417–33.

Harasymiw, Bohdan. *Post-Communist Ukraine*. Edmonton and Toronto: CIUS Press, 2002.

———. "Ukrainian Nationalism and the Future." In *Nationalism and the Breakup of an Empire: Russia and Its Periphery*, ed. Miron Rezun, 57–70. New York: Praeger, 1992.

Hemans, Simon. "Ukraine's Place in Europe." *RUSI Journal* 139, 6

(Dec. 1994): 54–57.
Hesli, Vicki L. "Public Support for the Devolution of Power in Ukraine: Regional Patterns." *Europe-Asia Studies* 47, 1 (1995): 91–121.
Hesli, Vicki L., and Arthur H. Miller. "The Gender Base of Institutional Support in Lithuania, Ukraine and Russia." *Europe-Asia Studies* 45, 3 (1993): 505–32.
Himka, John-Paul. "Ukrainians, Russians, and Alexander Solzhenitsyn." *Cross Currents: A Yearbook of Central European Culture* 11 (1992): 193–204.
Holdar, Sven. "Torn between East and West: The Regional Factor in Ukrainian Politics." *Post-Soviet Geography* 36, 2 (Feb. 1995): 112–32.
Holovaty, Serhiy. "Politics after Communism. Ukraine: A View from Within." *Journal of Democracy* 4, 3 (July 1993): 110–13.
Horak, Stephen. "Studies of Non-Russian Nationalities of the USSR in the United States: An Appraisal." *Canadian Review of Studies in Nationalism* 2, 1 (autumn 1974): 117–31.
Khomchuk, Oksana. "The Far Right in Russia and Ukraine." *Harriman Review* 8, 2 (July 1995): 40–44.
Kis, Theofil et al., eds. *Towards a New Ukraine* 1. *Ukraine and the New World Order, 1991–1996*. Ottawa: University of Ottawa, 1997.
———. 2. *Meeting the New Century*. Ottawa: University of Ottawa, 1999.
———. 3. *Geopolitical Imperatives of Ukraine*. Ottawa: Legas, 2001.
Kistersky, Leonid. "Economic Reasons for the Political Crisis in Ukraine." *Brown Journal of Foreign Affairs* 1, 1 (winter 1993–94): 171–76.
Korotich, Vitaly. "The Ukraine Rising." *Foreign Policy* 85 (winter 1991–92): 73–82.
Kravchuk, Robert S. *Ukrainian Politics, Economics and Governance, 1991–96*. Basingstoke: Macmillan, 1999.
Krawchenko, Bohdan. "Ukraine: The Politics of Independence." In *Nations and Politics in the Soviet Successor States*, ed. Ian Bremmer and Ray Taras, 75–98. Cambridge: Cambridge University Press, 1993.
Kubicek, Paul. "Delegative Democracy in Russia and Ukraine." *Communist and Post-Communist Studies* 27, 4 (Dec. 1994): 423–41.
———. "Dynamics of Contemporary Ukrainian Nationalism: Empire-Breaking to State Building." *Canadian Review of Studies in Nationalism* 23, 1/2 (1996): 39–50.
Kuzio, Taras, ed. *Contemporary Ukraine: Dynamics of Post-Soviet Transformation*. Armonk, N.Y.: M. E. Sharpe, 1998.
———. "The Emergence of Ukraine." *Contemporary Review* 268, 1562

(Mar. 1996): 119–25; 1563 (Apr. 1996): 182–87.

———. "Kravchuk to Kuchma: The 1994 Presidential Elections in Ukraine." *Journal of Communist Studies and Transition Politics* 12, 2 (June 1996): 117–44.

———. "National Identity in Independent Ukraine: An Identity in Transition." *Nationalism and Ethnic Politics* 2, 4 (winter 1996): 582–608.

———. "Radical Nationalist Parties and Movements in Contemporary Ukraine before and after Independence: The Right and Its Politics, 1989–1994." *Nationalities Papers* 25, 2 (June 1997): 211–42.

———. "Radical Right Parties and Civic Groups in Belarus and the Ukraine." In *The Revival of Right-Wing Extremism in the Nineties*, ed. Peter H. Merkl and Leonard Weinberg, 203–30. London: Cass, 1997.

———. *Ukraine: State and Nation Building*. London and New York: Routledge, 1998.

———. *Ukraine under Kuchma: Political Reform, Economic Transformation and Security Policy in Independent Ukraine*. Basingstoke: Macmillan, 1997.

———. "Ukrainian Nationalism." *Journal of Area Studies* 4 (1994): 79–95.

———, ed. *Ukraine: A Decade of Independence*. Special issue of *JUS* 26, 1/2 (summer–winter 2001).

Kuzio, Taras, and Paul D'Anieri, eds. *Dilemmas of State-Led Nation Building in Ukraine*. Westport, Conn.: Praeger, 2002.

Kuzio, Taras, Robert Kravchuk, and Paul D'Anieri, eds. *State and Institution Building in Ukraine*. New York: St. Martin's, 1999.

Maryniak, Iryna. "Belarus and Ukraine: Nation Building in Babel." *Index on Censorship* 22, 2 (Mar. 1993): 20–33.

Miller, Arthur H., Vicki L. Hesli, and William M. Reisinger. "Comparing Citizen and Elite Belief Systems in Post-Soviet Russia and Ukraine." *Public Opinion Quarterly* 59, 1 (spring 1995): 1–40.

Motyl, Alexander J. "The Conceptual President: Leonid Kravchuk and the Politics of Surrealism." In *Patterns in Post-Soviet Leadership*, ed. Timothy J. Colton and Robert C. Tucker, 103–21. Boulder, Colo.: Westview Press, 1995.

———. *Dilemmas of Independence: Ukraine after Totalitarianism*. New York: Council on Foreign Relations Press, 1993.

———, ed. *The Post-Soviet Nations: Perspectives on the Demise of the USSR*. New York: Columbia University Press, 1992.

———. *Sovietology, Rationality, Nationality: Coming to Grips with Nationalism in the USSR*. New York: Columbia University Press, 1990.

———. "Structural Constraints and Starting Points: The Logic of Systemic Change in Ukraine and Russia." *Comparative Politics* 29, 4 (July 1997): 433–47.

———, ed. *Thinking Theoretically about Soviet Nationalities: History and Comparison in the Study of the USSR*. New York: Columbia University Press, 1992.

Motyl, Alexander J., and Bohdan Krawchenko. "Ukraine: From Empire to Statehood." In *New States, New Politics: Building the Post-Soviet Nations*, ed. Ian Bremmer and Ray Taras, 235–75. Cambridge: Cambridge University Press, 1997.

Mroz, John Edwin, and Oleksandr Pavliuk. "Ukraine: Europe's Linchpin." *Foreign Affairs* 75, 3 (May–June 1996): 52–62.

Nahaylo, Bohdan. *The Ukrainian Resurgence: Ukraine's Road to Independence*. Toronto: University of Toronto Press, 1998.

Oosterbaan, Gwynne. "Clan Based Politics in Ukraine and the Implications for Democratization." In *Perspectives on Political and Economic Transitions after Communism*, ed. John S. Micgiel, 213–33. New York: Columbia University, 1997.

Pakulski, Jan. "Poland and Ukraine: Elite Transformations and Prospects for Democracy." *JUS* 20, 1/2 (summer–winter 1995): 195–208.

Pavlychko, Solomea. *Letters from Kiev*. Trans. Myrna Kostash. Edmonton and Toronto: CIUS Press; New York: St. Martin's Press, 1992.

Peoples, Nations, Identities: The Russian-Ukrainian Encounter. Harriman Review 9, 1/2 (spring 1966).

Pirie, Paul S. "National Identity and Politics in Southern and Eastern Ukraine." *Europe-Asia Studies* 48, 7 (Nov. 1996): 1079–1104.

Polokhalo, Volodymyr, ed. *The Political Analysis of Postcommunism: Understanding Postcommunist Societies*. Kyiv: Political Thought, 1995.

Pond, Elizabeth. "Is Ukraine European?" *Europe* 344 (Mar. 1995): 26–27.

———. "Poland Is Not Yugoslavia. Neither Is Ukraine." *Harriman Review* 8, 2 (July 1995): 1–4.

Potichnyj, Peter J. "Formation of Political Parties in Ukraine." *Berichte des Bundesinstituts für ostwissenschaftliche und internationale Studien* 1 (1994).

———. "The Referendum and Presidential Elections in Ukraine." *CSP* 33, 2 (June 1991): 123–38.

Prisiajniouk, Oxana. "The State of Civil Society in Independent Ukraine." *JUS* 20, 1/2 (summer–winter 1995): 161–76.

Prizel, Ilya. "Ukraine between Proto-Democracy and 'Soft' Authoritarianism." In *Democratic Changes and Authoritarian Reactions in Russia, Ukraine, Belarus, and Moldova*, ed. Karen Dawisha and Bruce Parrott, 330–69. Cambridge: Cambridge University Press, 1997.

Rakhmanny, Roman. *In Defense of the Ukrainian Cause*. North Quincy, Mass.: Christopher Publishing House, 1979.

Reisinger, William L., Arthur H. Miller, and Vicki L. Hesli. "Public Behavior and Political Change in Post-Soviet States." *Journal of Politics* 57, 4 (Nov. 1995): 941–70.

Reshetar, John S., Jr. "Imperial Decline and Collapse as a Problem in the Social Sciences." *JUS* 21, 1/2 (summer–winter 1996): 9–25.

Robinson, John P., et al. "Ethnonationalist and Political Attitudes among Post-Soviet Youth: The Case of Russia and Ukraine." *PS: Political Science and Politics* 26, 3 (Sep. 1993): 516–21.

Rusnachenko, Anatolii. "The Workers' and National-Democratic Movements in Contemporary Ukraine." *JUS* 18, 1/2 (summer–winter 1993): 123–49.

Ryabchuk, Mykola. "Between Civil Society and the New Etatism: Democracy in the Making and State Building in Ukraine." In *Envisioning Eastern Europe: Postcommunist Cultural Studies*, ed. Michael D. Kennedy, 125–48. Ann Arbor: University of Michigan Press, 1994.

———. "Democracy and the So-Called 'Party of Power' in Ukraine." *Politychna dumka* 3 (spring 1995): 154–59.

———. "Two Ukraines?" *East European Reporter* 4 (1992): 18–22.

———. "Ukraine: Authoritarianism with a Human Face." *East European Reporter* 5, 6 (Nov.–Dec. 1992): 52–56.

Shaw, Denis J. B., and Michael J. Bradshaw. "Problems of Ukrainian Independence." *Post-Soviet Geography* 33, 1 (Jan. 1992): 10–20.

Sherr, James. "Ukraine's Parliamentary Elections: The Limits of Manipulation." Conflict Studies Research Centre (Camberley, UK) Occasional Brief, 21 April 2002.

Shevchuk, Yuri I. "Citizenship in Ukraine: A Western Perspective." In *State and Nation Building in East Central Europe: Contemporary Perspectives*, ed. John S. Micgiel, 351–69. New York: Columbia University, 1996.

Shulga, Nikolai. "Regionalisation, Federalisation and Separatism in Ukraine: Historical Roots, New Realities and Prospects." In *Emerging Geopolitical and Territorial Units: Theories, Methods and Case Studies*, ed. Klaus Segbers and Stephan De Spiegeleire, 467–88. Baden-Baden: Nomos, 1995.

Simon, Gerhard. "Problems Facing the Formation of the Ukrainian State." *Aussenpolitik* 45, 1 (1994): 61–67.

Smith, Graham, et al. *Nation-building in the Post-Soviet Borderlands: The Politics of National Identities*. Cambridge: Cambridge University Press, 1998.

Sochor, Zenovia A. "August 1991 in Comparative Perspective: Moscow and Kiev." In *The Legacy of the Soviet Bloc*, ed. Jane Shapiro Zacek and Ilpyong J. Kim, 91–105. Gainsville, Fla.: University Press of Florida, 1997.

———. "From Liberalization to Post-Communism: The Role of the Communist Party in Ukraine." *JUS* 21, 1/2 (summer–winter 1996): 147–63.

Solchanyk, Roman. "The Politics of State Building: Center-Periphery Relations in Post-Soviet Ukraine." *Europe-Asia Studies* 46, 1 (1994): 47–68.

———. "Ukraine: The Politics of Reform." *Problems of Post-Communism* 42, 6 (Nov.–Dec. 1995): 46–51.

Stent, Angela. "Ukraine's Fate." *World Policy Journal* 11, 3 (fall 1994): 83–87.

Subtelny, Orest. "Imperial Disintegration and Nation-State Formation: The Case of Ukraine." In *The Successor States to the USSR*, ed. John W. Blaney, 184–95. Washington, D.C.: Congressional Quarterly, 1995.

———. "Russocentrism, Regionalism, and the Political Culture of Ukraine." In *Political Culture and Civil Society in Russia and the New States of Eurasia*, ed. Vladimir Tismaneanu, 189–207. Armonk, N.Y.: M. E. Sharpe, 1995.

Szporluk, Roman. "The National Question." In *After the Soviet Union: From Empire to Nations*, ed. Timothy J. Colton and Robert Legvold, 84–112. New York: Norton, 1992.

———. *Russia, Ukraine, and the Breakup of the Soviet Union*. Stanford, Calif.: Hoover Institution Press, 2000.

———. "The Strange Politics of Lviv: An Essay in Search of an Explanation." In *The Politics of Nationality and the Erosion of the USSR*, ed. Zvi Gitelman, 215–31. London: Macmillan, 1992.

Tabachnyk, D. V., Volodymyr Lytvyn, and Irina Ilyuschenko. *Ukraine: 5 Years of Independence*. Kyiv: Arc-Ukraine, 1996.

Ukraine's New Parliament. Kyiv: International Foundation for Election Systems, 1994.

Ukraine's Parliamentary Election: March 29, 1998. Washington, D.C.: Commission on Security and Cooperation in Europe, 1998.

Urban, George. "Ukraine: The Awakening." *National Interest* 27 (spring 1992): 39–47.

Vydrin, Dmytro, and Dmytro Tabachnyk. *Ukraine on the Threshold of the XXI Century: Political Aspect*. Kyiv: Lybid, 1995.

Wilson, Andrew. "Parties and Presidents in Ukraine and Crimea, 1994." *Journal of Communist Studies and Transition Politics* 11, 4 (Dec. 1995): 362–71.
———. "Ukraine." In *Political Parties of Eastern Europe, Russia and the Successor States*, ed. Bogdan Szajkowski, 577–604. London: Longman, 1994.
———. "Ukraine in 1993." *Russia and the Successor States Briefing Service* 2, 1 (Feb. 1994): 2–31.
———. "Ukraine: Two Presidents and Their Powers." In *Postcommunist Presidents*, ed. Ray Taras, 67–105. Cambridge: Cambridge University Press, 1997.
———. "Ukraine under Kuchma." *Russia and the Successor States Briefing Service* 3, 6 (Dec. 1995): 2–17.
———. *Ukrainian Nationalism in the 1990s: A Minority Faith*. Cambridge: Cambridge University Press, 1997.
Wilson, Andrew, and Artur Bilous. "Political Parties in Ukraine." *Europe-Asia Studies* 45, 4 (1993): 693–703.
Wolchik, Sharon L., and Volodymyr Zviglyanich, eds. *Ukraine: The Search for a National Identity*. Lanham, Md.: Rowman & Littlefield, 2000.
Yakovenko, Natalya. *Independent Ukraine, 1991–1995: A Difficult Stage of Development*. Lancaster: Centre for Defence and International Security Studies, 1995.
Zwarych, Roman. "Ukrainian Revolutionary Nationalism: A Conceptual Survey." *UR* 28, 4 (winter 1980): 11–24.

2. Ethnic Minorities, Crimean Affairs

Allworth, Edward A., ed. *The Tatars of Crimea: Return to the Homeland*. 2d ed. Durham, N.C.: Duke University Press, 1998.
Bekirov, Nadir. "We Prefer Ukraine." *Uncaptive Minds* 8, 2 (summer 1995): 55–61.
Bremmer, Ian. "The Politics of Ethnicity: Russians in the New Ukraine." *Europe-Asia Studies* 46, 2 (1994): 261–83.
Brym, Robert J., and Rozalina Ryvkina. *The Jews of Moscow, Kiev and Minsk: Identity, Antisemitism, Emigration*. New York: New York University Press, 1994.
Butkevych, Volodymyr. "Who Has a Right to Crimea?" *UR* 41, 3 (autumn 1994): 22–39; 4 (winter 1994): 27–47.
Casanova, José. "Ethno-Linguistic and Religious Pluralism and Democratic Construction in Ukraine." In *Post-Soviet Political Order: Conflict and State Building*, ed. Barnett R. Rubin and Jack Snyder, 81–103. London: Routledge, 1998.
Crimean Tatars: Repatriation and Conflict Prevention. New York:

Open Society Institute, 1996.
Developments in Crimea: Challenges for Ukraine and Implications for Regional Security. Washington, D.C.: American Association for the Advancement of Science, 1995.
Deychakiwsky, Orest. "National Minorities in Ukraine." *UQ* 50, 4 (winter 1994): 371–89.
Drohobycky, Maria, ed. *Crimea: Dynamics, Challenges, and Prospects.* Lanham, Md.: Rowman & Littlefield, 1995.
Fischer, Alan W. *The Crimean Tatars.* Stanford, Calif.: Hoover Institution Press, 1978.
Golovakha, Evgenii, Natalya Panina, and Nikolai Churilov. "Russians in Ukraine." In *The New Russian Diaspora: Russian Minorities in the Former Soviet Republics,* ed. Vladimir Shlapentokh, Munr Sendich, and Emil Payin, 59–71. Armonk, N.Y.: M. E. Sharpe, 1994.
Guboglo, M. N., and S. M. Chervonnaia. "The Crimean Tatar Question and the Present Ethnopolitical Situation in Crimea." *Russian Politics and Law* 33, 6 (Nov.–Dec. 1995): 31–60.
Hesli, Vicki L., Arthur H. Miller, William H. Reisinger, and Kevin L. Morgan. "Social Distance from Jews in Russia and Ukraine." *Slavic Review* 53, 3 (fall 1994): 807–28.
Kuzio, Taras. "The Crimea and European Security." *European Security* 3, 4 (winter 1994): 734–74.
———. *Russia—Crimea—Ukraine: Triangle of Conflict.* London: Research Institute for the Study of Conflict and Terrorism, 1994.
Lazzerini, Edward J. "Crimean Tatars." In *The Nationalities Question in the Post-Soviet States,* ed. Graham Smith, 412–35. London: Longman, 1996.
Marples, David R., and David F. Duke. "Ukraine, Russia, and the Question of Crimea." *Nationalities Papers* 23, 2 (June 1995): 261–89.
Melvin, Neil. *Russians beyond Russia: The Politics of National Identity.* London: Royal Institute of International Affairs, 1995.
Meyer, David J. "Why Have Donbas Russians Not Ethnically Mobilized Like Crimean Russians Have? An Institutional/Demographic Approach." In *State and Nation Building in East Central Europe: Contemporary Perspectives,* ed. John S. Micgiel, 317–30. New York: Columbia University, 1996.
Mirsky, Rudolf. "Antisemitism in Post-Soviet Ukraine." *East European Jewish Affairs* 24, 2 (winter 1994): 141–46.
Monyak, Robert, and Valentin Sazhin. "Contemporary Relations among Nationalities in Ukraine." *Nationalities Papers* 21, 2 (fall 1993): 160–62.

Naboka, Serhiy. "Nationalities Issues in Ukraine." *Uncaptive Minds* 5, 1 (spring 1992): 75–80.
Panina, Natalya. "Interethnic Relations and Ethnic Tolerance in Ukraine. An In-Depth Analytical Report." In *The Emancipation of Society as a Reaction to Systematic Change: Survival, Adaptation to New Rules and Ethnopolitical Conflicts*, ed. Klaus Segbers and Stephan De Spiegeleire, 101–21. Baden-Baden: Nomos, 1995.
Plokhy, Serhii. "The City of Glory: Sevastopol in Russian Historical Mythology." *Journal of Contemporary History* 35, 3 (2000): 369–83.
Popadiuk, Roman. "Crimea and Ukraine's Future." *Mediterranean Quarterly* 5, 4 (fall 1994): 30–39.
Resler, Tamara J. "Dilemmas of Democratisation: Safeguarding Minorities in Russia, Ukraine, and Lithuania." *Europe-Asia Studies* 49, 1 (1997): 89–106.
Sasse, Gwendolyn. "The Crimean Issue." *Journal of Communist Studies and Transition Politics* 12, 1 (Mar. 1996): 83–100.
Shaw, Denis J. B. "Crimea: Background and Aftermath of Its 1994 Presidential Election." *Post-Soviet Geography* 35, 4 (Apr. 1994): 221–34.
Shved, V'iacheslav. "The Conceptual Approaches of Ukrainian Political Parties to Ethno-Political Problems in Independent Ukraine." *JUS* 19, 2 (winter 1994): 69–83.
Tolstov, Serhiy. "Dimensions of Inter-Ethnic Relations in Ukraine." *UR* 40, 2 (summer 1993): 28–46.
Williams, Brian G. "A Community Reimagined. The Role of 'Homeland' in the Forging of National Identity: The Case of the Crimean Tatars." *Journal of Muslim Minority Affairs* 17, 2 (Oct. 1997): 225–52.
———. *The Crimean Tatars: The Diaspora Experience and the Forging of a Nation*. Leiden and Boston: Brill, 2001.
Wilson, Andrew. *The Crimean Tatars*. London: International Alert, 1994.
Yakovenko, Natalya. *Crimea and Ukraine: Together or Apart?* Lancashire: Centre for Defence and International Security Studies, 1995.

3. Foreign Policy

Bilinsky, Yaroslav. "Basic Factors in the Foreign Policy of Ukraine: The Impact of the Soviet Experience." In *The Legacy of History in Russia and the New States of Eurasia*, ed. S. Frederick Starr, 171–91. Armonk, N.Y.: M. E. Sharpe, 1994.
———. "The Ukrainian SSR in International Affairs after World War II." *AUAAS* 9, 27/28 (1961): 147–66.

Bodie, William C. "Ukraine and Russian-American Relations." In *Russia and America: From Rivalry to Reconciliation,* ed. George Ginsburgs, Alvin Z. Rubinstein, and Oles M. Smolansky, 103–25. Armonk, N.Y.: M. E. Sharpe, 1993.
Brzezinski, Ian. "Polish-Ukrainian Relations: Europe's Neglected Strategic Axis." *Survival* 35, 3 (autumn 1993): 26–37.
Burant, Stephen R. "Foreign Policy and National Identity: A Comparison of Ukraine and Belarus." *Europe-Asia Studies* 47, 7 (Nov. 1995): 1125–44.
Clark, Dick, ed. *Russia, Ukraine and the U.S. Response.* Queenstown, Md.: Aspen Institute, 1993.
D'Anieri, Paul. "Dilemmas of Interdependence: Autonomy, Prosperity, and Sovereignty in Ukraine's Russia Policy." *Problems of Post-Communism* 44, 1 (Jan.–Feb. 1997): 16–26.
———. "Interdependence and Sovereignty in the Ukrainian-Russian Relationship." *European Security* 4, 4 (winter 1995): 603–21.
———. "Nationalism and International Politics: Identity and Sovereignty in the Russian-Ukrainian Conflict." *Nationalism and Ethnic Politics* 3, 2 (summer 1997): 1–28.
Dawisha, Karen, and Bruce Parrott. *Russia and the New States of Eurasia: The Politics of Upheaval.* Cambridge: Cambridge University Press, 1994.
Ehrhart, Hans-Georg, and Oliver Thränert. *European Conflicts and International Institutions: Cooperating with Ukraine.* Baden-Baden: Nomos, 1998.
Ellis, Jason. "The 'Ukraine Dilemma' and U.S. Foreign Policy." *European Security* 3, 2 (summer 1994): 251–80.
Forsberg, Tuomas, ed. *Contested Territory: Border Disputes at the Edge of the Former Soviet Empire.* Aldershot: Elgar, 1995.
Furtado, Charles F., Jr. "Nationalism and Foreign Policy in Ukraine." *Political Science Quarterly* 109, 1 (spring 1994): 81–104.
The Future of Ukrainian-American Relations: Joint Policy Statement with Joint Policy Recommendations. Washington, D.C.: Atlantic Council of the U.S., 1995.
Garnett, Sherman W. "The Ukrainian Question and the Future of Russia." *Political Thought* 3 (1994): 169–77.
Goncharenko, Alexander. *Ukrainian-Russian Relations: An Unequal Partnership.* London: Royal United Services Institute for Defence Studies, 1995.
Hajda, Lubomyr A., ed. *Ukraine in the World: Studies in the International Relations and Security Structure of a Newly Independent State. HUS* 20 (1996).
Haran, Olexiy. *Disintegration of the Soviet Union and the US Position*

on the Independence of Ukraine. Cambridge, Mass.: Belfer Center for Science and International Affairs, Harvard University, 1995.

Isaievych, Iaroslav. "Ukraine and Russia: The Burden of Historical Tradition and Contemporary Realities." *JUS* 20, 1/2 (summer–winter 1995): 5–14.

Jensen, Jens-Jørgen. *The Foreign Policy of Ukraine*. Esbjerg: Sydjysk Univversitetsforlag, 1997.

Jonson, Lena, ed. *Ukraine and Integration in the East: Economic, Military and Military-Industrial Relations*. Stockholm: Utrikespolitiska Institutet, 1995.

Kaiser, Robert J. *The Geography of Nationalism in Russia and the USSR*. Princeton, N.J.: Princeton University Press, 1994.

Karatnycky, Adrian. "The 'Nearest Abroad': Russia's Relations with Ukraine and Belarus'." In *Russia: A Return to Imperialism?*, ed. Uri Ra'anan and Kate Martin, 69–86. New York: St. Martin's, 1996.

———. "The Ukrainian Factor." *Foreign Affairs* 71, 3 (summer 1992): 90–107.

Kreutz, Andrzej. "Polish-Ukrainian Dilemmas: A Difficult Partnership." *CSP* 39, 1/2 (Mar.–June 1997): 209–21.

Kuzio, Taras. "The Polish Opposition and the Ukrainian Question." *JUS* 12, 2 (winter 1987): 26–58.

———. "Ukraine and the Yugoslav Conflict." *Nationalities Papers* 25, 3 (Sep. 1997): 587–600.

Lester, Jeremy. "Russian Political Attitudes to Ukrainian Independence." *Journal of Communist Studies and Transition Politics* 10, 2 (June 1994): 193–232.

Mhitaryan, Nataliya. "Turkish-Ukrainian Relations." *Eurasian Studies* 3, 2 (summer 1996): 2–13.

Molchanov, Mikhail A. "Borders of Identity: Ukraine's Political and Cultural Significance for Russia." *CSP* 38, 1/2 (Mar.–June 1996): 177–94.

———. *Political Culture and National Identity in Russian-Ukrainian Relations*. College Station: Texas A&M University Press, 2002.

Moroney, Jennifer D. P., Taras Kuzio, and Mikhail Molchanov, eds. *Ukrainian Foreign and Security Policy: Theoretical and Comparative Perspectives*. Westport, Conn.: Praeger, 2002.

Morrison, John. "Pereyaslav and After: The Russian-Ukrainian Relationship." *International Affairs* 69, 4 (Oct. 1993): 677–703.

Motyl, Alexander J. "The Foreign Relations of the Ukrainian SSR." *HUS* 6, 1 (Mar. 1982): 62–78.

Pavliuk, Oleksandr. "Ukraine and Regional Cooperation in Central and Eastern Europe." *Security Dialogue* 28, 3 (Sep. 1997): 347–62.

———. "Ukrainian-Polish Relations: A Pillar of Regional Stability?"

In *The Effects of Enlargement on Bilateral Relations in Central and Eastern Europe*, ed. Monika Wohlfeld, 43–62. Paris: Institute for Security Studies, 1997.

———. "An Unfulfilling Partnership: Ukraine and the West, 1991–2001." *European Security* 11, 1 (spring 2002): 81–101.

Prizel, Ilya. "The Influence of Ethnicity on Foreign Policy: The Case of Ukraine." In *National Identity and Ethnicity in Russia and the New States of Eurasia*, ed. Roman Szporluk, 103–28. Armonk, N.Y.: M. E. Sharpe, 1994.

———. *National Identity and Foreign Policy: Nationalism and Leadership in Poland, Russia, and Ukraine*. Cambridge: Cambridge University Press, 1998.

———. "Ukraine's Foreign Policy as an Instrument of Nation Building." In *The Successor States to the USSR*, ed. John W. Blaney, 196–207. Washington, D.C.: Congressional Quarterly, 1995.

Sezer, Duygu Bazoglu. "From Hegemony to Pluralism: The Changing Politics of the Black Sea." *SAIS Review* 17, 1 (winter–spring 1997): 1–29.

Shcherbak, Yuri. *The Strategic Role of Ukraine: Diplomatic Addresses and Lectures (1994–1997)*. Cambridge, Mass.: HURI, 1998.

Shulman, Stephen. "Cultures in Competition: Ukrainian Foreign Policy and the 'Cultural Threat' from Abroad." *Europe-Asia Studies* 50, 2 (Mar. 1998): 287–303.

Smith, Graham, and Andrew Wilson. "Rethinking Russia's Post-Soviet Diaspora: The Potential for Political Mobilisation in Eastern Ukraine and North-East Estonia." *Europe-Asia Studies* 49, 5 (July 1997): 845–64.

Sochor, Zenovia. A. "Political Culture and Foreign Policy: Elections in Ukraine 1994." In *Political Culture and Civil Society in Russia and the New States of Eurasia*, ed. Vladimir Tismaneanu, 208–26. Armonk, N.Y.: M. E. Sharpe, 1995.

Solchanyk, Roman. "Russia, Ukraine, and the Imperial Legacy." *Post-Soviet Affairs* 9, 4 (Oct.–Dec. 1993): 337–65.

———. *Ukraine and Russia: The Post-Soviet Transition*. Lanham, Md.: Rowman & Littlefield, 2001.

———. "Ukraine, The (Former) Center, Russia and 'Russia.'" *Studies in Comparative Communism* 25, 1 (Mar. 1992): 31–45.

Wolczuk, Kataryna, and Roman Wolczuk. *Poland and Ukraine: A Strategic Partnership in a Changing Europe?* London: Royal Institute of International Affairs, 2002.

Wolczuk, Roman. *Ukraine's Foreign and Security Policy, 1991–2000*. New York: Routledge Curzon, 2003.

Yakovenko, Natalya. *The Russian Dimension in Ukraine Foreign*

Policy. Lancaster: Centre for Defence and International Security Studies, 1998.

Zviglyanich, Volodymyr. "The Specter of Integration in Russia: Lessons for the West and Ukraine." *Demokratizatsiya* 4, 4 (fall 1996): 502–18.

4. Nuclear Weapons

DeWing, Martin J. *The Ukrainian Nuclear Arsenal: Problems of Command, Control, and Maintenance.* Program for Nonproliferation Studies, Working Paper no. 3. Monterey, Calif.: Institute of International Studies, 1993.

Garnett, Sherman W. "The Sources and Conduct of Ukrainian Nuclear Policy: November 1992 to January 1994." In *The Nuclear Challenge in Russia and the New States of Eurasia,* ed. George Quester, 125–51. Armonk, N.Y.: M. E. Sharpe, 1995.

———. "Ukraine's Decision to Join the NPT." *Arms Control Today* 25, 1 (Jan.–Feb. 1995): 7–12.

Hopkins, Arthur T. *Unchained Reactions: Chernobyl, Glasnost, and Nuclear Deterrence.* Washington, D.C.: National Defense University Press, 1993.

Jalonen, Olli-Pekka. *Captors of Denuclearization? Belarus, Kazakhstan, Ukraine, and Nuclear Disarmament.* Tampere: Tampere Peace Research Institute, 1994.

Kuzio, Taras. "Nuclear Weapons and Military Policy in Independent Ukraine." *Harriman Institute Forum* 6, 9 (May 1992): 1–14.

Lindskog, Lars G., and Alec Hoatson, eds. *Nuclear Weapons and the Security of Ukraine.* Stockholm: Olof Palme International Center, 1994.

Matiaszek, Petro. "International Legal Aspects of Ukraine's Claim to the Soviet Nuclear Legacy." *UQ* 49, 3 (fall 1993): 252–93.

Miller, Steven E. "The Case against a Ukrainian Nuclear Deterrent." *Foreign Affairs* 72, 3 (summer 1993): 67–80.

Tolstov, Serhiy. "International Factors of Nuclear Disarmament of Ukraine." *UR* 41, 1 (spring 1994): 5–20.

Zyla, Roman P. "Ukraine as a Nuclear Weapons Power." In *Nuclear Energy and Security in the Former Soviet Union,* ed. David R. Marples and Marilyn J. Young, 121–37. Boulder, Colo.: Westview Press, 1997.

5. Security Studies

Alexandrova, Olga. "Russia as a Factor in Ukrainian Security Concepts." *Aussenpolitik* 45, 1 (1994): 68–78.

Balmaceda, Margarita M. "'Two's Company, Three's a Crowd': The Role of Central Europe in Ukrainian Security." *East European Quarterly* 32, 3 (fall 1998): 335–51.

———. "Ukraine, Russia, and European Security: Thinking beyond NATO Expansion." *Problems of Post-Communism* 45, 1 (Jan.–Feb. 1998): 21–29.

Bilinsky, Yaroslav. *Endgame in NATO's Enlargement: The Baltic States and Ukraine.* Westport, Conn.: Praeger, 1999.

———. "Ukraine, Russia, and the West: An Insecure Security Triangle." *Problems of Post-Communism* 44, 1 (Jan.–Feb. 1997): 27–34.

Blank, Stephen. *Russia, Ukraine and European Security.* Carlisle Barracks, Pa.: U.S. Army War College, 1993.

Bukkvoll, Tor. *Ukraine and European Security.* London: Royal Institute of International Affairs, 1997.

———. "Ukraine and NATO: The Politics of Soft Cooperation." *Security Dialogue* 28, 3 (Sep. 1996): 363–74.

Garnett, Sherman W. *Keystone in the Arch: Ukraine in the Emerging Security Environment of Central and Eastern Europe.* Washington, D.C.: Carnegie Endowment for International Peace, 1997.

Goldstein, Lyle, and Blake Loveless. "Keeping the Bear at Bay: The Dilemmas of Ukrainian Security Policy." *Harvard International Review* 14, 4 (summer 1992): 46–48.

Goncharenko, Alexander. "Ukraine: National Interests between the CIS and the West." In *Security Dilemmas in Russia and Eurasia*, ed. Roy Allison and Christoph Bluth, 121–33. London: Royal Institute of International Affairs, 1998.

Gow, James. "Independent Ukraine: The Politics of Security." *International Relations* 11, 3 (Dec. 1992): 253–67.

Grytsenko, Anatoliy S. "Defense Reform in Ukraine: Chronology of the First Five Years." *Berichte des Bundesinstituts für ostwissenschaftliche und internationale Studien* 29 (1998).

Jaworsky, John. *Ukraine: Stability and Instability.* Washington, D.C.: National Defense University, 1995.

Kistersky, Leonid, Michael C. Soussan, and Daniel L. Cruise. *Security in Eastern Europe: The Case of Ukraine.* Providence, R.I.: Brown University, 1994.

Kolstø, Pål, Andrei Edemsky, and Natalya Kalashnikova. "The Dniester Conflict: Between Irredentism and Separatism." *Europe-Asia Studies* 45, 6 (Nov. 1993): 973–1000.

Krawciw, Nicholas S. H. "Ukrainian Perspectives on National Security and Ukrainian Military Doctrine." In *State Building and Military Power in Russia and the New States of Eurasia*, ed. Bruce Parrott,

134–56. Armonk, N.Y.: M. E. Sharpe, 1995.

Kulinich, Nikolai A. "Ukraine in the New Geopolitical Environment: Issues of Regional and Subregional Security." In *The Making of Foreign Policy in Russia and the New States of Eurasia*, ed. Adeed Dawisha and Karen Dawisha, 113–39. Armonk, N.Y.: M. E. Sharpe, 1995.

Kuzio, Taras. "Civil-Military Relations in Ukraine, 1989–1991." *Armed Forces and Society* 22, 1 (fall 1995): 25–48.

———. "Ukrainian Civil-Military Relations and the Military Impact of the Ukrainian Economic Crisis." In *State Building and Military Power in Russia and the New States of Eurasia*, ed. Bruce Parrott, 157–92. Armonk, N.Y.: M. E. Sharpe, 1995.

———. *Ukrainian Security Policy*. Westport, Conn.: Praeger, 1995.

Laba, Roman. "The Russian-Ukrainian Conflict: State Nation and Identity." *European Security* 4, 3 (autumn 1995): 457–87.

Lepingwell, John W. R. "The Russian Military and Security Policy in the 'Near Abroad.'" *Survival* 36, 3 (autumn 1994): 70–93.

Lupiy, Bohdan. *Ukraine and European Security: International Mechanisms as Non-Military Security Options for Ukraine*. Frankfurt: Lang, 1996.

Mihalisko, Kathleen. "Security Issues in Ukraine and Belarus." In *Central and Eastern Europe: The Challenge of Transition*, ed. Regina Cowen Karp, 225–57. Oxford: Oxford University Press, 1993.

Molchanov, Mikhail. "Ukraine between Russia and NATO: Politics and Security." *UR* 45, 3 (autumn 1998): 3–16.

Morozov, Kostiantyn. *Above and Beyond: From Soviet General to Ukrainian State Builder*. Cambridge, Mass.: HURI, 2000.

———. "The Formation of the Ukrainian Army, 1991–95." *UR* 43, 1 (spring 1996): 8–17.

Olynyk, Stephen D. "Ukraine as a Post-Cold War Military Power." *Joint Force Quarterly* (spring 1997): 87–94.

Popadiuk, Roman. *Ukraine, the Security Fulcrum of Europe*. Washington, D.C.: National Defense University, 1996.

Pyrozhkov, Serhiy, and Volodymyr Chumak. "Ukraine and NATO." *UR* 42, 3 (autumn 1995): 9–15.

Pyskir, Bohdan. "The Silent Coup: The Building of Ukraine's Military." *European Security* 2, 1 (spring 1993): 140–60.

Rahr, Alexander. "The Ukraine between Russia and the West." In *Crises Policies in Eastern Europe: Imperatives, Problems and Perspectives*, ed. Reimund Seidelmann, 83–94. Baden-Baden: Nomos, 1996.

Sherr, James. "Russia-Ukraine Rapprochement? The Black Sea Fleet

Accords." *Survival* 39, 3 (autumn 1997): 33–50.
Strekal, Oleg. "Conflict Potential in Modern Ukraine: Sources and Developments." In *Crises Policies in Eastern Europe: Imperatives, Problems and Perspectives*, ed. Reimund Seidelmann, 95–112. Baden-Baden: Nomos, 1996.
Tolstov, Serhiy. "NATO Enlargement: The Ukrainian Position." *UR* 43, 2 (summer 1996): 21–25.
Udovenko, Hennadiy. "European Stability and NATO Enlargement: Ukraine's Perspective." *NATO Review* 6 (Nov. 1995): 15–18.
Van Ham, Peter. *Ukraine, Russia, and European Security: Implications for Western Policy*. Paris: Institute for Security Studies, 1994.
Vydrin, Dmytro. "Ukraine and Russia." In *Damage Limitation or Crisis? Russia and the Outside World*, ed. Robert D. Blackwill and S. Karaganov, 123–37. Washington, D.C.: CSIA, 1994.
Yakovenko, Natalya. *Ukraine, NATO and European Security*. Lancaster: Centre for Defence and International Security Studies, 1998.

VII. SCIENTIFIC

1. General

Egorov, Igor. "Painful Transition: Trends in Transforming R and D Potential in Russia and Ukraine in the Early 1990s." *Science and Public Policy* 23, 4 (Aug. 1996): 202–14.
Holowinsky, Ivan Z. "Contemporary Psychology in the Ukrainian Soviet Socialist Republic." *American Psychologist* 33, 2 (1976): 185–89.
Josephson, Paul, and Igor Egorov. "The Deceptive Promise of Reform: Ukrainian Science in Crisis." *Minerva* 35, 4 (winter 1997): 321–47.
Josephson, Paul, and Igor Egorov. "Ukraine's Declining Scientific Research Establishment." *Problems of Post-Communism* 49, 4 (Jul.–Aug. 2002): 43–51.
Josephson, Paul, and Irina Dezhina. "The Slow Pace of Reform of Fundamental Science in Russia and Ukraine." *Problems of Post-Communism* 45, 5 (Sep.–Oct. 1998): 48–62.

2. Demography, Ecology

Allsen, Thomas T. "Mongol Census Taking in Rus', 1245–1275." *HUS* 5, 1 (Mar. 1981): 32–53.
Anderson, Barbara A., and Brian D. Silver. "Demographic Analysis and Population Catastrophes in the USSR." *Slavic Review* 44, 3 (fall 1985): 517–36.

Bass, Corin Fairburn, and Janet Kenny. *Beyond Chernobyl: Women Respond.* Sydney: Envirobook, 1993.
Bohatiuk, Yurii. "The Chornobyl Disaster." *UQ* 42, 1/2 (spring–summer 1986): 5–21.
Dawson, Jane I. *Eco-Nationalism: Anti-Nuclear Activism and National Identity in Russia, Lithuania, and Ukraine.* Durham, N.C.: Duke University Press, 1996.
Ebel, Robert E. *Chernobyl and Its Aftermath: A Chronology of Events.* Washington, D.C.: Center for Strategic and International Studies, 1994.
Edwards, Mike, and Gerd Ludwig. "Living with the Monster: Chornobyl." *National Geographic* 186, 2 (Aug. 1994): 100–115.
Goldin, Milton. "Forgotten Victims." *The Humanist* 56, 4 (July–Aug. 1996): 20–23.
Hajda, Lubomyr. "Nationality and Age in Soviet Population Change." *Soviet Studies* 32, 4 (Oct. 1980): 475–99.
Herlihy, Patricia. "The Ethnic Composition of the City of Odessa in the Nineteenth Century." *HUS* 1, 1 (Mar. 1977): 53–78.
Huda, Walter. "Medical Consequences of Chernobyl." *JUS* 11, 1 (summer 1986): 35–52.
Kaczmarskyj, Vera L. "The State of Demography in Ukraine: The Post War Period." *Visti ukraïns'kykh inzheneriv* 21, 1–4 (Jan.–Dec. 1980): 18–20.
Komarov, Boris. *The Geography of Survival: Ecology in the Post-Soviet Era.* Armonk, N.Y.: M. E. Sharpe, 1994.
Kubijovyč, Volodymyr. "Changes in the Population of the Ukrainian SSR, 1927–1958." *Ukrainian Review* (Munich) 8 (1959): 6–20.
———. *Ethnic Groups of the South-Western Ukraine: Halyčyna—Galicia 1.I.1939.* Wiesbaden: Otto Harrassowitz, 1983.
Launer, Michael K., and Marilyn J. Young. "Ukraine, Russia, and the Question of Nuclear Safety." In *Nuclear Energy and Security in the Former Soviet Union*, ed. David R. Marples and Marilyn J. Young, 45–82. Boulder, Colo.: Westview Press, 1997.
The Legacy of Chornobyl, 1986 to 1996 and Beyond. Washington, D.C.: Commission on Security and Cooperation in Europe, 1996.
Lenssen, Nicholas. "Meltdown: The Worst Industrial Accident Ever to Befall Humanity Left a Wound That Has Not Healed with Time." *World Watch* 9 (May–June 1996): 22–31.
Lewis, Robert A., and Richard B. Rowland. *Population Redistribution in the USSR: Its Impact on Society, 1897–1917.* New York: Praeger, 1979.
Marples, David R. "Chernobyl: A Six-Month Review." *JUS* 11, 1 (summer 1986): 3–19.

———. *Chernobyl and Nuclear Power in the USSR.* Edmonton and Toronto: CIUS Press, 1986.
———. "Nuclear Power in Ukraine in the Late 1990s." *Post-Soviet Geography and Economics* 39, 6 (June 1998): 359–69.
———. *The Social Impact of the Chernobyl Disaster.* New York: St. Martin's, 1988.
Medvedev, Grigori. *No Breathing Room: The Aftermath of Chernobyl.* Trans. Evelyn Rossiter. New York: Basic Books, 1993.
Medvedev, Zhores. "Chernobyl: Ten Years Later." *International Affairs* 42, 3 (1996): 212–18.
Page, G. William et al. "Environmental Health Policy in Ukraine after the Chernobyl Accident." *Policy Studies Journal* 23, 1 (spring 1995): 141–51.
Petryna, Adriana. *Life Exposed: Biological Citizens after Chernobyl.* Princeton, N.J.: Princeton University Press, 2002.
Pirozhkov, Serhii. "Population Loss in Ukraine in the 1930s and 1940s." In *Ukrainian Past, Ukrainian Present,* ed. Bohdan Krawchenko, 84–96. New York: St. Martin's Press, 1993.
Prociuk, Stephan G. "Human Losses in the Ukraine in World War I and II." *AUAAS* 13, 35/36 (1973–77): 23–50.
Pryde, Philip R., ed. *Environmental Resources and Constraints in the Former Soviet Republics.* Boulder, Colo.: Westview Press, 1995.
Rapawy, Stephen. "Nationality Composition of the Soviet Population." *Nationalities Papers* 13, 1 (spring 1985): 70–83.
Read, Piers Paul. *Ablaze: The Story of the Heroes and Victims of Chernobyl.* New York: Random House, 1993.
Rich, Vera. "Chornobyl—Ten Years On." *UR* 43, 1 (spring 1996): 21–26.
Rosen, Seth B. "Balancing Economics and Ecology: Financing Mechanisms for the Cleanup of Ukraine." *Harvard Environmental Law Review* 18, 1 (1994): 235–47.
Saunders, David. "Russia's Ukrainian Policy (1847–1905): A Demographic Approach." *European History Quarterly* 25, 2 (1995): 181–208.
Shabad, Theodore. "Ethnic Results of the 1979 Soviet Census." *Soviet Geography* 21, 7 (Sep. 1980): 440–88.
Shcherbak, Iurii. *Chernobyl: A Documentary Story.* Edmonton and Toronto: CIUS Press, 1989.
Sluzhynska, Zynoviya. "Ukraine's Demographic Losses during World War II." *UR* 42, 2 (summer 1995): 25–29.
Solchanyk, Roman. "Ukraine and the Ukrainians in the USSR: Nationality and Language Aspects of the 1979 Census." *UQ* 36, 3 (autumn 1980): 271–81.

———. "Ukraine and the Ukrainians in the USSR: Nationality and Language Aspects of the 1979 Soviet Census in the Ukrainian SSR." *UR* 28, 2 (summer 1980): 37–41.
Stebelsky, Ihor. "Soil Management in Ukraine: Responding to Environmental Degradation." *CSP* 31, 3/4 (Sep.–Dec. 1989): 247–66.
Szporluk, Roman. "Kiev as the Ukraine's Primate City." *HUS* 3/4 (1979–80): 843–49.
Vallin, Jacques, France Meslé, Serguei Adamets, and Serhii Pyrozhkov. "A New Estimate of Ukrainian Population Losses during the Crises of the 1930s and 1940s." *Population Studies* 56 (2002): 249–64.
Weisman, Alan. "Journey through a Doomed Land: Exploring Chernobyl's Still-Deadly Ruins." *Harper's* 289, 1731 (Aug. 1994): 45–53.

VIII. SOCIAL

1. Anthropology and Ethnology

Klymash, Robert B. *Folk Narrative among Ukrainian-Canadians in Western Canada*. Ottawa: Canadian Centre for Folk Culture Studies, 1973.
———. *Ukrainian Folklore in Canada*. New York: Arno Press, 1980.
———. "Ukrainian Folklore in Canada: The Big Put-Down." *Journal of Ukrainian Graduate Studies* 3, 1 (spring 1978): 66–77.
Magocsi, Paul Robert, ed. *The Persistence of Regional Cultures: Rusyns and Ukrainians in Their Carpathian Homeland and Abroad*. Boulder, Colo.: East European Monographs, 1993.
Pomorska, Krystyna. "Observations on Ukrainian Erotic Folk Songs." *HUS* 1, 1 (Mar. 1977): 115–29.
Rudnyckyj, J. B. *Ukrainian-Canadian Folklore: Texts in English Translation*. Winnipeg: Ukrainian Free Academy of Sciences, 1960.
Ukrainian Folk Tales. Kyiv: Dnipro Publishers, 1986.
Wanner, Catherine. *Burden of Dreams: History and Identity in Post-Soviet Ukraine*. University Park, Pa.: Pennsylvania State University Press, 1998.
———. "Crafting Identity, Marking Time: An Anthropological Perspective on Historical Commemoration and Nation-Building in Ukraine." *HUS* 23, 3/4 (Dec. 1999): 105–31.
Wixman, Ronald. *The Peoples of the USSR: An Ethnographic Handbook*. Armonk, N.Y.: M. E. Sharpe, 1984.

2. Education

Bahry, Romana. "J. J. Rousseau's *Émile* and P. Kulish's Views on

Education." In *In Working Order: Essays Presented to G. S. N. Luckyj*, ed. E. N. Burstynsky and R. Lindheim, 57–79. Edmonton and Toronto: CIUS Press, 1990.
Bilinsky, Yaroslav. "Education of the Non-Russian Peoples of the USSR, 1917–1967: An Essay." *Slavic Review* 27, 3 (1968): 411–37.
Bohachevsky-Chomiak, Martha. "The Ukrainian University in Galicia: A Pervasive Issue." *HUS* 5, 4 (Dec. 1981): 497–545.
Canadian Institute of Ukrainian Studies: 25 Years. Edmonton and Toronto: CIUS Press, 2001.
Holowinsky, Ivan Z. "Developmental and Preschool Psychology in the Ukrainian SSR." *Nationalities Papers* 15, 2 (fall 1987): 184–93.
———. "Research and Education of Exceptional Children in the Ukrainian SSR." *Journal of Special Education* 1 (1981): 91–96.
Horak, Stephan. "The Kiev Academy: A Bridge to Europe in the Seventeenth Century." *East European Quarterly* 2, 1 (1968): 117–37.
The Kiev Mohyla Academy: Commemorating the 350th Anniversary of Its Founding (1632). HUS 8, 1/2 (June 1984).
Kolasky, John. *Education in Soviet Ukraine: A Study in Discrimination and Russification.* Toronto: Peter Martin Associates, 1968.
Lupul, Manoly R. "The Canadian Institute of Ukrainian Studies." *Ukrainian Canadian Review* 6 (May 1977): 5–9.
———, ed. *Osvita: Ukrainian Bilingual Education.* Edmonton and Toronto: CIUS Press, 1985.
Petheridge-Hernandez, Patricia, and Rosalind Latiner Raby. "Twentieth-Century Transformations in Catalonia and the Ukraine: Ethnic Implications in Education." *Comparative Education Review* 37, 1 (Feb. 1993): 31–49.
Public Education in the Ukrainian SSR. Kyiv: Radians'ka shkola, 1970.
Randall, David. "Higher Education in Ukraine—International Collaboration in Development." *UR* 40, 3 (autumn 1993): 28–32.
Shamshur, Oleg, and Tetiana Izhevska. "Multilingual Education as a Factor of Inter-Ethnic Relations: The Case of the Ukraine." *Current Issues in Language and Society* 1, 1 (1994): 29–39.
Sirka, Ann. *The Nationality Question in Austrian Education: The Case of Ukrainians in Galicia, 1867–1914.* Frankfurt/Main: Lang, 1980.
Stakhanov, Irina. "Reforms in the System of Higher Education in Ukraine." *East/West Education* 13, 2 (fall 1992): 153–59.
Sydorenko, Alexander. *The Kievan Academy in the Seventeenth Century.* Ottawa: University of Ottawa, 1977.
The Ukrainian Research Institute: Twenty Years. Cambridge, Mass.: Ukrainian Research Institute, Harvard University, 1993.
Vetukhiv, Michael. "A Hundred and Fifty Years of Kharkiv Univer-

sity." *AUAAS* 5–6, 16/17 (1955): 1140–59.

3. Health, Social Welfare

Chandler, Andrea. "Social Policy and Political Discourse in Post-Soviet Ukraine." *JUS* 21, 1/2 (summer–winter 1996): 191–211.
Chernobyl—Ten Years On: Radiological and Health Impact. Paris: OECD, 1995.
Iskiv, B. H. "The State of the Ukrainian Health Service." *UR* 40, 3 (autumn 1993): 23–27.
Kupryashkina, Svetlana. "Women's Health in Ukraine: Facts and Opinions." *Surviving Together* 13, 2 (summer 1995): 26–28.
Malarek, Victor. *The Natashas: The New Global Sex Trade.* Toronto: Viking Canada, 2003.

4. Diaspora, Ukrainian Minorities

Balan, Jars. *Salt and Braided Bread: Ukrainian Life in Canada.* Toronto: Oxford University Press, 1984.
Boshyk, Yury. "A Chapter from the History of the Ukrainian Diaspora: M. Drahomanov's *Hromada*, the Ukrainian Printing House in Geneva, and A. M. (Kuzma) Liakhotsky." *Journal of Ukrainian Graduate Studies* 3, 2 (fall 1978): 25–39.
Burke, Marguerite. *The Ukrainian Canadians.* Toronto: Van Nostrand Reinhold, 1978.
Cipko, Serge. "The Legacy of the 'Brazilian Fever': The Ukrainian Colonization of Parana." *JUS* 11, 2 (winter 1986): 19–32.
Cipko, Serge, and Oleh Leszczyszyn. "Survey of Second-Generation Ukrainians in Britain." *JUS* 11, 2 (winter 1986): 41–46.
Darcovich, William, and Paul Yuzyk, eds. *A Statistical Compendium on the Ukrainians in Canada, 1891–1976.* Ottawa: University of Ottawa Press, 1980.
———. *Ukrainian Canadians and the 1981 Canada Census: A Statistical Compendium.* Edmonton and Toronto: CIUS Press, 1988.
Dutka, June. *The Grace of Passing. Constantine H. Andrusyshen: The Odyssey of a Slavist.* Edmonton and Toronto: CIUS Press, 2000.
Ewanchuk, Michael. *Hawaiian Ordeal: Ukrainian Contract Workers, 1897–1910.* Winnipeg: Author, 1986.
Gerus, Oleh W. "Ukrainians in Argentina: A Canadian Perspective." *JUS* 11, 2 (winter 1996): 3–18.
Gory, Duane. "Ukrainian-Americans and the 1990 Census: Some Demographic Considerations." *UR* 42, 3 (autumn 1995): 3–8.
Halich, Wasyl. *Ukrainians in the United States.* Chicago: University of Chicago Press, 1937.

Hryniuk, Stella. *Peasants with Promise: Ukrainians in Southeastern Galicia, 1880–1990*. Edmonton and Toronto: CIUS Press, 1991.

Isajiw, Wsevolod W., ed. *Ukrainians in American and Canadian Society*. Jersey City, N.J.: M. P. Kots Publishing, 1976.

Isajiw, Wsevolod W., Yury Boshyk, and Roman Senkus, eds. *The Refugee Experience: Ukrainian Displaced Persons after World War II*. Edmonton and Toronto: CIUS Press, 1992.

Kaye, Vladimir J., ed. *Dictionary of Ukrainian Canadian Biography of Pioneer Settlers of Alberta, 1891–1900*. [Edmonton]: Ukrainian Pioneers' Association, 1984.

———. *Dictionary of Ukrainian Canadian Biography: Pioneer Settlers of Manitoba, 1891–1900*. Toronto: Ukrainian Canadian Research Foundation, 1975.

———. *Early Ukrainian Settlements in Canada, 1895–1900: Dr. Josef Oleskow's Role in the Settlement of the Canadian Northwest*. Toronto: University of Toronto Press, 1964.

Keywan, Zonia, and Martin Coles. *Greater Than Kings: Ukrainian Pioneer Settlement in Canada*. Montreal: Harvest House, 1977.

Kolasky, John, ed. *Prophets and Proletarians: Documents on the History of the Rise and Decline of Ukrainian Communism in Canada*. Edmonton and Toronto: CIUS Press, 1990.

———. *The Shattered Illusion: The History of Ukrainian Pro-Communist Organizations in Canada*. Toronto: Peter Martin Associates, 1979.

Kordan, Bohdan. *Canada and the Ukrainian Question, 1939–45: A Study in Statecraft*. Montreal: McGill-Queen's University Press, 2001.

———. *Enemy Aliens, Prisoners of War: Internment in Canada during the Great War*. Montreal: McGill-Queen's University Press, 2002.

———. "Ukrainians in Canada: 1981 Census Profile." *JUS* 13, 2 (winter 1988): 70–104.

Kordan, Bohdan, and Peter Melnycky, eds. *In the Shadow of the Rockies: Diary of the Castle Mountain Internment Camp, 1915–1917*. Edmonton and Toronto: CIUS Press, 1991.

Kostash, Myrna. *All of Baba's Children*. Edmonton: Hurtig Publishers, 1977.

Kuropas, Myron B. *The Ukrainian Americans: Roots and Aspirations, 1884–1954*. Toronto: University of Toronto Press, 1991.

Luciuk, Lubomyr. *Searching for Place: Ukrainian Displaced Persons, Canada, and the Migration of Memory*. Toronto: University of Toronto Press, 2000.

Luciuk, Lubomyr, and Stella Hryniuk, eds. *Canada's Ukrainians: Negotiating an Identity*. Toronto: Ukrainian Canadian Centennial

Committee and University of Toronto Press, 1991.
Luciw, Theodore. *Father Agapius Honcharenko, First Ukrainian Priest in the United States.* New York: Ukrainian Congress Committee of America, 1970.
Luciw, Wasyl, and Theodore Luciw. *Ahapius Honcharenko and the Alaska Herald: The Editor's Life and an Analysis of His Newspaper.* Toronto: Slavia Library, 1963.
Lupul, Manoly R., ed. *Continuity and Change: The Cultural Life of Alberta's First Ukrainians.* Edmonton and Toronto: CIUS Press, 1988.

———, ed. *A Heritage in Transition: Essays in the History of Ukrainians in Canada.* Toronto: McClelland and Stewart, 1982.

———, ed. *Ukrainian Canadians, Multiculturalism, and Separatism: An Assessment.* Edmonton and Toronto: University of Alberta Press, 1978.

———, ed. *Visible Symbols: Cultural Expression among Canada's Ukrainians.* Edmonton and Toronto: CIUS Press, 1984.
Magocsi, Paul Robert. *Our People: Carpatho-Rusyns and Their Descendants in North America.* Toronto: Multicultural History Society of Ontario, 1985.

———. *The Rusyn-Ukrainians of Czechoslovakia: An Historical Survey.* Vienna: Wilhelm Braumüller, 1983.

———, ed. *The Ukrainian Experience in the United States: A Symposium.* Cambridge, Mass.: HURI, 1979.
Mandryka, M. I. *Ukrainian Refugees.* Winnipeg: Ukrainian Canadian Committee, 1946.
Martynowych, Orest T. "The Ukrainian Socialist Movement in Canada, 1900–1918." *Journal of Ukrainian Graduate Studies* 1, 1 (fall 1976): 27–44; 2, 1 (spring 1977): 22–31.

———. *Ukrainians in Canada: The Formative Period, 1891–1924.* Edmonton and Toronto: CIUS Press, 1991.
Marunchak, Mykhaylo. *The Ukrainian Canadians: A History.* 2d ed. Winnipeg: Ukrainian Academy of Arts and Sciences in Canada, 1982.
Mazur, Lubomyr. "Fifty Years of the Association of Ukrainians in Great Britain." *UR* 43, 3 (autumn 1996): 3–8.
Naulko, Vsevolod, Ihor Vynnychenko, and Rostyslav Sossa. *Ukrainians of the Eastern Diaspora: An Atlas.* Edmonton and Toronto: CIUS Press, 1993.
New Soil—Old Roots: The Ukrainian Experience in Canada. Ed. Jaroslav Rozumnyj et al. Winnipeg: Ukrainian Academy of Arts and Sciences in Canada, 1983.
Paprocki, S. J. "Political Organization of the Ukrainian Exiles after the

Second World War." *Eastern Quarterly* 5 (Jan.–Apr. 1952): 41–50.
Petryshyn, W. Roman, ed. *Changing Realities: Social Trends among Ukrainian Canadians.* Edmonton and Toronto: CIUS Press, 1980.
Piniuta, Harry. *Land of Pain, Land of Promise: First Person Accounts by Ukrainian Pioneers, 1891–1914.* Saskatoon, Sask.: Western Producer Prairie Books, 1978.
Potrebenko, Helen. *No Streets of Gold: A Social History of Ukrainians in Alberta.* Vancouver: New Star Books, 1977.
Procko, Bohdan P. "The Establishment of the Ruthenian Church in the United States, 1854–1907." *Pennsylvania History* 42, 2 (Apr. 1975): 136–54.
———. *Ukrainian Catholics in America: A History.* Washington, D.C.: University Press of America, 1982.
Prymak, Thomas M. "Ivan Franko and Mass Immigration to Canada." *CSP* 26, 4 (Dec. 1984): 307–17.
———. *Maple Leaf and Trident: The Ukrainian Canadians during the Second World War.* Toronto: Multicultural History Society of Ontario, 1988.
Rotoff, Basil, Roman Yereniuk, and Stella Hryniuk. *Monuments to Faith: Ukrainian Churches in Manitoba.* Winnipeg: University of Manitoba Press, 1990.
Seneta, Eugene. "On the Number of Ukrainians in Australia in 1979." *JUS* 11, 2 (winter 1986): 33–39.
Shtohryn, Dmytro M. *Ukrainians in North America: A Biographical Directory of Noteworthy Men and Women of Ukrainian Origin in the United States and Canada.* Champaign, Ill.: Association for the Advancement of Ukrainian Studies, 1975.
Slavs in Canada: Proceedings of the First National Conference of Canadian Slavs. Edmonton: Inter-University Committee on Canadian Slavs, 1966.
Smyrniw, Walter. "At the Crossroads of Socialism, Nationalism, and Christianity: The Intriguing Biography/Autobiography of Pavlo Krat." *JUS* 23, 1 (summer 1998): 41–59.
Subtelny, Orest. *Ukrainians in North America.* Toronto: University of Toronto Press, 1991.
Swyripa, Frances. *Ukrainian Canadians: A Survey of Their Portrayal in English-Language Works.* Edmonton and Toronto: CIUS Press, 1978.
———. *Wedded to the Cause: Ukrainian-Canadian Women and Ethnic Identity, 1881–1991.* Toronto: University of Toronto Press, 1993.
———, ed. *Special Issue: Ukrainians in Canada. JUS* 16, 1/2 (summer–winter 1991).
Swyripa, Frances, and John Herd Thompson, eds. *Loyalties in Conflict:*

Ukrainians in Canada during the Great War. Edmonton and Toronto: CIUS Press, 1983.

Weres, Roman. *Directory of Ukrainian Publishing Houses, Periodicals, Bookstores, Libraries, and Library Collections of Ukrainica in Diaspora.* Chicago: Ukrainian Bibliographical-Reference Center, 1976.

Wertsman, Vladimir, ed. *The Ukrainians in America: A Chronology and Fact Book.* Dobbs Ferry, N.Y.: Oceana Publications, 1976.

Wolowyna, Oleh, ed. *Ethnicity and National Identity: Demographic and Socioeconomic Characteristics of Persons with Ukrainian Mother Tongue in the United States.* Cambridge, Mass.: HURI, 1986.

Woycenko, Ol'ha. *The Ukrainians in Canada.* 2d ed. Winnipeg: Trident Press, 1968.

Yuzyk, Paul. *The Ukrainians in Manitoba: A Social History.* Toronto: University of Toronto Press, 1953.

5. Sociology

Bohachevsky-Chomiak, Martha. "Feminism in Ukrainian History." *JUS* 7, 1 (spring 1982): 16–30.

———. *Feminists Despite Themselves: Women in Ukrainian Community Life, 1884–1939.* Edmonton and Toronto: CIUS Press, 1988.

———. *Political Communities and Gendered Ideologies in Contemporary Ukraine.* Cambridge, Mass.: HURI, 1994.

Chandler, Andrea. "State Building and Social Obligations in Post-Communist Systems: Assessing Change in Russia and Ukraine." *CSP* 38, 1/2 (Mar.–June 1996): 1–21.

Duncan, Peter J. S. "Ukraine and Ukrainians." In *The Nationalities Question in the Post-Soviet States*, ed. Graham Smith, 188–209. London: Longham, 1996.

Golovakha, Evgenii, and Natalya Panina. "Ukraine's Population under Conditions of Socio-Economic Crisis: Psychological State and Factors of Survival." In *The Emancipation of Society as a Reaction to Systematic Change*, ed. Klaus Segbers and Stephan De Spiegeleire. Baden-Baden: Nomos, 1995.

Guthier, Steven L. "Ukrainian Cities during the Revolution and the Interwar Era." In *Rethinking Ukrainian History*, ed. Ivan L. Rudnytsky, 156–79. Edmonton and Toronto: CIUS Press, 1981.

Herlihy, Patricia. "Ukrainian Cities in the Nineteenth Century." In *Rethinking Ukrainian History*, ed. Ivan L. Rudnytsky, 135–55. Edmonton and Toronto: CIUS Press, 1981.

Isajiw, Wsevolod W. "Urban Migration and Social Change in Contemporary Soviet Ukraine." *CSP* 22, 1 (Mar. 1980): 58–66.

———, ed. *Society in Transition: Social Change in Ukraine in*

Western Perspectives. Toronto: Canadian Scholars' Press, 2003.
Kipp, Jacob W. "The Ukraine's Socio-Economic Crisis." *Military Review* 74, 3 (Mar. 1994): 32–37.
Kohn, Melvin L., et al. "Social Structure and Personality under Conditions of Radical Social Change: A Comparative Analysis of Poland and Ukraine." *American Sociological Review* 62, 4 (Aug. 1997): 614–38.
Kolstø, Pål. *Russians in the Former Soviet Republics.* Bloomington: Indiana University Press, 1995.
Krawchenko, Bohdan. "Changes in the National and Social Composition of the Communist Party of Ukraine from the Revolution to 1976." *JUS* 9, 1 (summer 1984): 33–54.
———. "The Impact of Industrialization on the Social Structure of Ukraine." *CSP* 22, 3 (Sep. 1980): 338–57.
———. "The Social Structure of the Ukraine in 1917." *HUS* 14, 1/2 (June 1990): 97–112.
———. "The Social Structure of Ukraine at the Turn of the Twentieth Century." *East European Quarterly* 16, 2 (June 1982): 171–81.
Kupryashkina, Svetlana. "Women in the Ukraine: Trends and Tendencies in the Labour Market." *Canadian Woman Studies* 16, 1 (winter 1995): 60–63.
Liber, George. *Soviet Nationality Policy, Urban Growth, and Identity Change in the Ukrainian SSR, 1923–1934.* Cambridge: Cambridge University Press, 1992.
Mace, James E. "The *Komitety nezamozhnykh selian* and the Structure of Soviet Rule in the Ukrainian Countryside, 1920–1933." *Soviet Studies* 35, 4 (Oct. 1983): 487–503.
Nemirya, Grigorii. "A Qualitative Analysis of the Situation in the Donbass." In *Emerging Geopolitical and Territorial Units: Theories, Methods and Case Studies,* ed. Klaus Segbers and Stephan De Spiegeleire, 451–66. Baden-Baden: Nomos, 1995.
Pavlychko, Solomea. "Between Feminism and Nationalism: New Women's Groups in Ukraine." In *Perestroika and Soviet Women,* ed. Mary Buckley, 82–96. Cambridge: Cambridge University Press, 1992.
———. "Feminism and Post-Communist Ukrainian Society." In *Women in Russia and Ukraine,* ed. Rosalind Marsh, 305–14. Cambridge: Cambridge University Press, 1996.
———. "Progress on Hold: The Conservative Faces of Women in Ukraine." In *Post-Soviet Women: From the Baltic to Central Asia,* ed. Mary Buckley, 219–34. Cambridge: Cambridge University Press, 1997.
Rubchak, Marian J. "Christian Virgin or Pagan Goddess: Feminism

versus the Eternally Feminine in Ukraine." In *Women in Russia and Ukraine*, ed. Rosalind Marsh, 315–30. Cambridge: Cambridge University Press, 1996.

Senkiw, Roman. "Ukrainian National Revolutionary Tendencies in the Light of Structural Shifts in the Urban Network during 1897–1979." *UR* 28, 4 (winter 1980): 36–48.

Shevchuk, Yuri I. "Dual Citizenship in Old and New States." *Archives européennes de sociologie* 37, 1 (1996): 47–73.

Shevtsova, Lilia. "Ukraine in the Context of New European Migrations." *International Migration Review* 26, 2 (summer 1992): 258–68.

Siegelbaum, Lewis H., and Daniel J. Walkowitz. *Workers of the Donbass Speak: Survival and Identity in the New Ukraine, 1989–1992*. Albany, N.Y.: State University of New York Press, 1995.

Stepanenko, Victor. "The Social Construction of Identities in Ukraine." *UR* 42, 2 (summer 1995): 9–24.

Walker, W. Michael. "Changing Lives: Social Change and Women's Lives in East Ukraine." *Interface: Bradford Studies in Language, Culture and Society* 1 (1996): 94–116.

Woroby, Peter. "Effects of Urbanization in the Ukraine." *AUAAS* 13, 35/36 (1973–77): 51–115.

———. "The Role of the City in Ukrainian History." In *Rethinking Ukrainian History*, ed. Ivan L. Rudnytsky, 203–15. Edmonton and Toronto: CIUS Press, 1981.

Yekelchyk, Serhy. "The Making of a 'Proletarian Capital': Patterns of Stalinist Social Policy in Kiev in the Mid-1930s." *Europe-Asia Studies* 50, 7 (November 1998): 1229–44.

Zon, Hans van, Andre Batako, and Anna Kreslavska. *Social and Economic Change in Eastern Ukraine: The Example of Zaporizhzhya*. Aldershot: Ashgate, 1998.

6. Religion

Anderson, John. "Religion, State and Politics into the 1990s." In *Religion, State and Politics in the Soviet Union and Successor States*, ed. John Anderson, 182–214. Cambridge: Cambridge University Press, 1994.

Andrijisyn, Joseph, ed. *Millennium of Christianity in Ukraine: A Symposium*. Ottawa: Saint Paul University, 1987.

Andrusiak, N. "Selected Problems of Christianity in Rus'-Ukraine." *UQ* 39, 1 (spring 1983): 60–68.

Avenarius, Alexander. "Metropolitan Ilarion on the Origin of Christianity in Rus': The Problem of the Transformation of Byzantine

Influence." *HUS* 12/13 (1988–89): 689–701.
Batalden, Stephen K., ed. *Seeking God: The Recovery of Religious Identity in Orthodox Russia, Ukraine, and Georgia.* DeKalb: Northern Illinois University Press, 1993.
Bilokin, Serhiy. "The Kiev Patriarchate and the State." In *The Politics of Religion in Russia and the New States of Eurasia*, ed. Michael Bourdeaux, 182–201. Armonk, N.Y.: M. E. Sharpe, 1995.
Blazejowskyj, Dmytro. *Schematism of the Ukrainian Catholic Church: A Survey of the Church in Diaspora.* Rome: Analecta OSBM, 1988.
Bociurkiw, Bohdan R. "The Catacomb Church: Ukrainian Greek Catholics in the USSR." *Religion in Communist Lands* 5, 1 (spring 1977): 26–34.
———. "Church-State Relations in the USSR." *Survey* 66 (Jan. 1969): 4–32.
———. "The Orthodox Church and the Soviet Regime in the Ukraine, 1953–1971." *CSP* 14, 2 (summer 1972): 191–211.
———. "Politics and Religion in Ukraine: The Orthodox and the Greek Catholics." In *The Politics of Religion in Russia and the New States of Eurasia*, ed. Michael Bourdeaux, 131–62. Armonk, N.Y.: M. E. Sharpe, 1995.
———. *The Politics of Religion in Ukraine: The Orthodox Church and the Ukrainian Revolution.* Washington, D.C.: Wilson Center, 1986.
———. "The Renovationist Church in the Soviet Ukraine, 1922–1939." *AUAAS* 9, 27/28 (1961): 41–74.
———. "The Soviet Destruction of the Ukrainian Orthodox Church, 1929–1936." *JUS* 12, 1 (summer 1987): 3–21.
———. *Ukrainian Churches under Soviet Rule: Two Case Studies.* Cambridge, Mass.: Harvard Ukrainian Studies Fund, 1984.
———. *The Ukrainian Greek Catholic Church and the Soviet State (1939–1950).* Edmonton and Toronto: CIUS Press, 1996.
———. "The Ukrainian Greek Catholic Church in the Contemporary USSR." *Nationalities Papers* 20, 1 (spring 1992): 17–30.
———. "Ukrainization Movements within the Russian Orthodox Church and the Ukrainian Autocephalous Church." *HUS* 3/4 (1979–80): 92–111.
Bociurkiw, Bohdan R., and John Strong, eds. *Religion and Atheism in the U.S.S.R. and Eastern Europe.* London: Macmillan, 1975.
Borenstein, Eliot. "Articles of Faith: The Media Response to Maria Devi Khristos." *Religion* 25, 3 (July 1995): 249–66.
Chirovsky, Nicholas L., ed. *The Millennium of Ukrainian Christianity.* New York: Philosophical Library, 1988.
Chopyk, D. "Meletii Smotryts'kyi's Threnos." *UQ* 43, 3/4 (fall–winter 1987): 179–86.

Coulter, Debra. "Saints and State-Building in Kyivan Rus', 988–1240." *UR* 42, 4 (winter 1995): 23–32.
———. "Ukrainian Pilgrimage to the Holy Land, 988–1914." *UR* 43, 3 (autumn 1996): 62–77.
Cracraft, James. "Theology at the Kiev Academy during Its Golden Age." *HUS* 8, 1/2 (June 1984): 71–80.
Czubatyj, Nicholas. "Russian Church Policy in Ukraine." *UQ* 2, 1 (spring 1946): 1–15.
Dmitriev, Mikhail. "The Religious Programme of the Union of Brest in the Context of the Counter-Reformation in Eastern Europe." *JUS* 17, 1/2 (summer–winter 1992): 29–43.
Dushnyck, Walter, ed. *The Ukrainian Catholic Church at the Ecumenical Council, 1962–1965*. New York: Shevchenko Scientific Society, 1967.
Ericsson, V. "The Earliest Conversion of the Rus' to Christianity." *Slavonic and East European Review* 44, 1 (Jan. 1961): 98–122.
Fedoriw, George. *History of the Church in Ukraine*. Trans. Petro Krawchuk. St. Catharines, Ont.: St. Sophia Religious Association of Ukrainian Catholics in Canada, 1983.
Frick, David A. "*Fides Meletiana*: Marcantonio de Dominis and Meletij Smotryc'kyj." *HUS* 15, 3/4 (Dec. 1991): 383–414.
———. *Meletij Smotryc'kyj*. Cambridge, Mass.: HURI, 1995.
———. "Zyzanij and Smotryc'kyj (Moscow, Constantinople, and Kiev): Episodes in Cross-Cultural Misunderstanding." *JUS* 17, 1/2 (summer–winter 1992): 67–93.
Gee, Gretchen Knudson. "Geography, Nationality, and Religion in Ukraine: A Research Note." *Journal for the Scientific Study of Religion* 34, 3 (Sep. 1995): 383–90.
Gerus, Oleh W. "The Christian Experience in the Soviet Empire: Church-State Relations in Eastern Europe, 1917–1991." *JUS* 25, 1/2 (summer–winter 2000): 159–80.
Gerus, Oleh W., and Alexander Baran, eds. *Millennium of Christianity in Ukraine, 988–1988*. Winnipeg: Ukrainian Academy of Arts and Sciences in Canada, 1989.
Goa, David J., ed. *The Ukrainian Religious Experience: Tradition and the Canadian Cultural Context*. Edmonton and Toronto: CIUS Press, 1989.
Goldblatt, Harvey. "Ivan Vyšens'kyj's Conception of St. John Chrysostom and His Idea of Reform for the Ruthenian Lands." *HUS* 16, 1/2 (June 1992): 37–66.
———. "On the Reception of Ivan Vyšens'kyj's Writings among the Old Believers." *HUS* 15, 3/4 (Dec. 1991): 354–82.
Gudziak, Borys A. *Crisis and Reform: The Kyivan Metropolitanate, the*

Patriarchate of Constantinople, and the Genesis of the Union of Brest. Cambridge, Mass.: Harvard Institute of Ukrainian Studies, 1998.

Halecki, Oskar. *From Florence to Brest (1439–1596).* 2d ed. Hamden, Conn.: Archon Books, 1968.

Hayova, Oksana. "Andrey Sheptytskyi and the Social Role of the Church under the Occupational Regimes." *UR* 41, 4 (winter 1994): 9–22.

Herlihy, Patricia. "Crisis in Society and Religion in Ukraine." *Religion in Eastern Europe* 14 (Apr. 1994): 1–13.

Himka, John-Paul. "The Conflict between the Secular and the Religious Clergy in Eighteenth-Century Western Ukraine." *HUS* 15, 1/2 (June 1991): 35–47.

———. "The Greek Catholic Church and Nation-Building in Galicia, 1772–1918." *HUS* 8, 3/4 (Dec. 1984): 426–52.

———. "Priests and Peasants: The Greek Catholic Pastor and the Ukrainian National Movement in Austria, 1867–1900." *CSP* 21, 1 (Mar. 1979): 1–14.

———. *Religion and Nationality in Western Ukraine: The Greek Catholic Church and the Ruthenian National Movement in Galicia, 1867–1900.* Montreal: McGill-Queen's University Press, 1999.

Hosking, Geoffrey A., ed. *Church, Nation and State in Russia and Ukraine.* London: Macmillan; Edmonton and Toronto: CIUS Press, 1990.

Hunczak, Taras. "The Politics of Religion: The Union of Brest, 1596." *Ukraïns'kyi Istoryk* 9, 3/4 (1972): 97–106.

Hvat, Ivan. *The Catacomb Ukrainian Catholic Church and Pope John Paul II.* Cambridge, Mass.: HURI, 1984.

Jerabek, B. "Church Slavonic Documents and Early Relations between Bohemia-Moravia and Kievan Rus'-Ukraine." *UQ* 42, 3/4 (fall–winter 1986): 214–21.

Karatnycky, Adrian. "Christian Democracy Resurgent: Raising the Banner of Faith in Eastern Europe." *Foreign Affairs* 77, 1 (Jan.–Feb. 1998): 13–18.

Kohut, Zenon E. "The Problem of Ukrainian Orthodox Church Autonomy in the Hetmanate (1654–1780s)." *HUS* 14, 3/4 (Dec. 1990): 364–76.

Kolodny, Anatoly. "Church and State in Ukraine Past and Present." *UR* 42, 4 (winter 1995): 33–44.

———. "Kyiv-Mohyla Academy: The Cradle of Ukrainian Theological Thought." *UR* 43, 1 (spring 1996): 33–43.

Korolevsky, Cyril. *Metropolitan Andrew (1865–1944).* Trans. and rev. Serge Keleher. Lviv: Stauropegion, 1993.

Kortschmaryk, F. B. *Christianization of the European East and Messianic Aspirations of Moscow as the "Third Rome."* Toronto: Studium Research Institute, 1971.

Krawchuk, Andrii. *Christian Social Ethics in Ukraine: The Legacy of Andrei Sheptytsky.* Edmonton and Toronto: CIUS Press, 1997.

Kuzio, Taras. "In Search of Unity and Autocephaly: Ukraine's Orthodox Churches." *Religion, State and Society* 25, 4 (Dec. 1997): 393–415.

Labunka, Miroslav, and Leonid Rudnytzky, eds. *The Ukrainian Catholic Church, 1945–1975.* Philadelphia: St. Sophia Religious Association of Ukrainian Catholics, 1976.

Lacko, Michael. "The Forced Liquidation of the Union of Užhorod." *Slovak Studies* (Rome) 1 (1961): 145–85.

Lencyk, Wasyl. *The Eastern Catholic Church and Czar Nicholas I.* Rome: Centro di Studi Universitari Ucraini a Roma, 1966.

———. "The Question of a Ukrainian Patriarchate." *UQ* 43, 3/4 (fall–winter 1987): 154–78.

Lewin, Kurt I. "Andreas Count Sheptytsky, Archbishop of Lviv, Metropolitan of Halych, and the Jewish Community in Galicia during the Second World War." *AUAAS* 7, 23/24 (1959): 1656–67.

Lewin, Paulina, and Frank E. Sysyn. "The *Antimaxia* of 1632 and the Polemic over Uniate-Orthodox Relations." *HUS* 9, 1/2 (June 1985): 145–65.

Libackyj, Anfir. *The Ancient Monasteries of Kiev Rus'.* New York: Vantage Press, 1978.

Magocsi, Paul R., ed. *Morality and Reality: The Life and Times of Andrei Sheptyts'kyi.* Edmonton and Toronto: CIUS Press, 1989.

Markus, Vasyl. "Politics and Religion in Ukraine: In Search of a New Pluralistic Dimension." In *The Politics of Religion in Russia and the New States of Eurasia*, ed. Michael Bourdeaux, 163–81. Armonk, N.Y.: M. E. Sharpe, 1995.

———. "Religion and Nationalism in Soviet Ukraine after 1945." In *Nationalism and Human Rights*, ed. I. Kamenetsky, 155–67. Littleton, Colo.: Libraries Unlimited, 1977.

———. "Religion and Nationalism in Ukraine." In *Religion and Nationalism in Soviet and East European Politics*, ed. Pedro Ramet, 138–70. Durham, N.C.: Duke University Press, 1989.

———. "The Suppressed Church: Ukrainian Catholics in the Soviet Union." In *Marxism and Religion in Eastern Europe*, ed. Richard T. De George and James P. Scanlan, 119–32. Boston: D. Reidel, 1976.

Michels, Georg. "The First Old Believers in Ukraine: Observations about Their Social Profile and Behavior." *HUS* 16, 3/4 (Dec. 1992):

289–314.
Miller, M. "Bolshevik Persecution of the Orthodox Church in the Ukraine." *Ukrainian Review* (Munich) 7 (1959): 10–21.
Mirchuk, Ivan. "The Ukrainian Uniate Church." *Slavonic and East European Review* 10, 3 (fall 1932): 377–85.
Mončak, Ihor. *Florentine Ecumenism in the Kyivan Church*. Rome: Editiones Universitatis Catholicae Ucrainorum S. Clementis Papae, 1987.
Ohiienko, Ivan (Metropolitan Ilarion). *The Ukrainian Church*. Trans. Orysia Ferbey. Winnipeg: Ukrainian Orthodox Church of Canada, 1986.
Pekar, Atanasii V. *The History of the Church in Carpathian Rus'*. Trans. Marta Skorupsky. Fairview, N.J.: Carpatho-Rusyn Research Center, 1992.
Pekarska, Ludmyla. "The Millennium of the Church of the Tithes." *UR* 43, 2 (summer 1996): 63–75.
Pelikan, Jaroslav. *Confessor between East and West: A Portrait of Ukrainian Cardinal Josyf Slipyj*. Grand Rapids, Mich.: Eerdmans, 1990.
Plokhy, Serhii, and Frank E. Sysyn. *Religion and Nation in Modern Ukraine*. Edmonton and Toronto: CIUS Press, 2003.
Podskalsky, Gerhard. "Principal Aspects and Problems of Theology in Kievan Rus'." *HUS* 11, 3/4 (Dec. 1987): 270–86.
Polonska-Vasylenko, N. "The Distinguishing Characteristics of the Ukrainian Church." *Ukrainian Review* (Munich) 8 (1959): 78–94.
Poppe, Andrzej. "How the Conversion of Rus' Was Understood in the Eleventh Century." *HUS* 11, 3/4 (Dec. 1987): 287–302.
Pospishil, J. Victor, and Hryhor M. Luzhnycky. *The Quest for an Ukrainian Catholic Patriarchate*. Philadelphia: Ukrainian Publications, 1971.
Reshetar, J. "Ukrainian Nationalism and the Orthodox Church." *American Slavic and East European Review* 10, 1 (Feb. 1951): 38–49.
Sadkowski, Konrad. "From Ethnic Borderland to Catholic Fatherland: The Church, Christian Orthodox, and State Administration in the Chełm Region, 1918–1939." *Slavic Review* 57, 4 (winter 1998): 813–39.
Senyk, Sophia. *A History of the Church in Ukraine*. Volume 1, *To the End of the Thirteenth Century*. Rome: Pontificio Istituto Orientale, 1993.
———. *Women's Monasteries in Ukraine and Belorussia to the Period of Suppressions*. Rome: Pontificium Institutum Studiorum Orientalium, 1983.

———, trans. *Manjava Skete: Ukrainian Monastic Writings of the Seventeenth Century*. Kalamazoo: Cistercian Publications, 2001.

Senyshyn, Ambrose. *Catholics of the Byzantine-Slavonic Rite and Their Divine Liturgy*. Stamford, Conn.: Ukrainian Catholic Seminary, 1946.

Shein, Louis J. "Ivan Franko's Religious *Weltanschauung*." *UQ* 35, 4 (winter 1979): 381–89.

Shevelov, George Y. *Two Orthodox Ukrainian Churchmen of the Early Eighteenth Century: Teofan Prokopovych and Stefan Iavors'kyi*. Cambridge, Mass.: Harvard Ukrainian Studies Fund, 1985.

Solovey, Meletius Michael. *The Byzantine Divine Liturgy: History and Commentary*. Washington, D.C.: Catholic University of America Press, 1970.

Sorokowski, Andrew. *Ukrainian Catholics and Orthodox in Poland and Czechoslovakia*. Cambridge, Mass.: HURI, 1988.

———, et al., eds. *A Millennium of Christian Culture in Ukraine*. London: Ukrainian Millennium Committee in Great Britain, 1988.

Stehle, Hansjakob. *Eastern Politics of the Vatican, 1917–1979*. Athens, Ohio: Ohio University Press, 1981.

Stojko, Wolodymyr. "The Ukrainian Catholic Church in the Catacombs." *UQ* 43, 1/2 (spring–summer 1987): 5–22.

Sutton, Jonathan. *Traditions in New Freedom: Christianity and Higher Education in Russia and Ukraine Today*. Nottingham: Bramcote Press, 1996.

Theodorovich, John. *American-Ukrainian Orthodox Catechism*. South Bound Brook, N.J.: Ukrainian Orthodox Church in the U.S., 1946.

Tolochko, Petro P. "Religious Sites in Kiev during the Reign of Volodimer Sviatoslavich." *HUS* 11, 3/4 (Dec. 1987): 317–22.

Turchyn, Andrew. "The Ukrainian Catholic Church during WWII." *UQ* 41, 1/2 (spring–summer 1985): 57–67.

Vlasto, A. P. *The Entry of the Slavs into Christendom: An Introduction to the Medieval History of the Slavs*. London: Cambridge University Press, 1970.

Waugh, Daniel Clarke. "Ioannikii Galiatovs'kyi's Polemics against Islam and Their Muscovite Translations." *HUS* 3/4 (1979–80): 908–19.

Williams, George H. "Francis Stancaro's Schismatic Reformed Church, Centered in Dubets'ko in Ruthenia." *HUS* 3/4 (1979–80): 931–57.

———. "Protestants in the Ukraine during the Period of the Polish-Lithuanian Commonwealth." *HUS* 2, 1 (Mar. 1978): 41–72; 2, 2 (June 1978): 184–210.

Wlasowsky, Ivan. *Outline History of the Ukrainian Orthodox Church*. Volume 1, *The Baptism of Ukraine to the Union of Berestye (988–1596)*. Volume 2, *XVII Century*. New York and South Bound

Brook, N.J.: Ukrainian Orthodox Church of the USA, 1956–79.
Wolff, Lawrence. "Vatican Diplomacy and the Uniates of the Ukraine after the First Partition of the Polish-Lithuanian Commonwealth." *HUS* 8, 3/4 (Dec. 1984): 396–425.
Yuzyk, Paul. *The Ukrainian Greek Orthodox Church of Canada, 1918–1951.* Ottawa: University of Ottawa Press, 1981.
Zinkewych, Osyp, and Andrew Sorokowski, eds. *A Thousand Years of Christianity in Ukraine: An Encyclopedic Chronology.* New York: Smoloskyp Publishers, 1988.

7. Philosophy, Intellectual Life

Adelphotes: A Tribute to Omeljan Pritsak by His Students. HUS 14, 3/4 (Dec. 1990).
Andrusyshen, Constantine. "Skovoroda, The Seeker of the Genuine Man." *UQ* 2, 4 (summer 1946): 317–30.
Buyniak, Victor. "Doukhobors, Molokans and Skovoroda's Teachings." In *Roots and Realities among Eastern and Central Europeans*, ed. Martin L. Kovacs, 13–23. Edmonton: Central and East European Studies Association, 1983.
Čiževsky, Dmitri. "The Influence of the Philosophy of Schelling (1775–1854) in the Ukraine." *AUAAS* 5, 16/17 (1955): 1128–39.
Cultures and Nations of Central and Eastern Europe: Essays in Honor of Roman Szporluk. HUS special volume, 22 (1998).
Cymbalisty, Petro. "Ukrainian Religious and Cultural Influences on Muscovy in the 17th and 18th Centuries." *UR* 41, 4 (spring 1994): 33–53.
Dushnyck, Walter, ed. *Professor Roman Smal-Stocki and His Contributions to the Ukrainian Nation: Collected Papers.* New York: Shevchenko Scientific Society, 1970.
Eucharisterion: Essays Presented to Omeljan Pritsak on His Sixtieth Birthday by His Colleagues and Students. HUS 3/4 (1979–80).
Fizer, John. "Skovoroda's and Socrates' Concepts of Self-Cognition: A Comparative View." *JUS* 22, 1/2 (summer–winter 1997): 65–73.
Franklin, Simon. "Booklearning and Bookmen in Kievan Rus': A Survey of an Idea." *HUS* 12/13 (1988–89): 830–48.
Grimsted, Patricia Kennedy. "Lviv Manuscript Collections and Their Fate." *HUS* 3/4 (1979–80): 348–75.
Haigh, Elizabeth Luchka. "Was V. I. Vernadsky a Ukrainian Nationalist?" *UR* 43, 2 (summer 1996): 55–62.
Horak, Stephen M. "The Shevchenko Scientific Society, 1873–1973: Contributor to the Birth of a Nation." *East European Quarterly* 7, 3 (fall 1973): 249–64.
Innis, Robert E. "Rosdolsky's Reconstruction of Marx: From the

Abstract to the Concrete." *Philosophy and Social Criticism* 6, 3 (fall 1979): 327–47.
Isaievych, Iaroslav. "Books and Book Printing in Ukraine in the 16th and First Half of the 17th Centuries." *Solanus* (London), n.s. 7 (1993): 69–93.
———. "Early Modern Belarus, Russia, and Ukraine: Culture and Cultural Relations." *JUS* 17, 1/2 (summer–winter 1992): 17–28.
Jarmus, Stephan. *Pamphil D. Yurkevych and His Philosophical Legacy*. Winnipeg: St. Andrew's College, 1979.
Kasinec, Edward. "Ivan Ohienko (Metropolitan Ilarion) as Bookman and Book Collector: The Years in the Western Ukraine and Poland." *HUS* 3/4 (1979–80): 474–483.
Khvylovy (Khvyliovy), Mykola. *The Cultural Renaissance in Ukraine: Polemical Pamphlets, 1925–1926*. Ed. and trans. Myroslav Shkandrij. Edmonton and Toronto: CIUS Press, 1986.
Kline, George L. "Skovoroda: *In* but Not *of* the Eighteenth Century." *JUS* 22, 1/2 (summer–winter 1997): 117–23.
Lashchyk, E. "Vynnyčenko's Philosophy of Happiness." *AUAAS* 16, 41/42 (1984–85): 289–326.
Lindheim, Ralph, and George S. Luckyj, eds. *Towards an Intellectual History of Ukraine: An Anthology of Ukrainian Thought from 1710 to 1993*. Toronto: University of Toronto Press, 1996.
Magocsi, Paul R. "Nationalism and National Bibliography: Ivan E. Levyts'kyi and 19th-Century Galicia." *Harvard Library Bulletin* 28, 1 (1980): 81–109.
Marshall, Richard H., Jr., and Thomas E. Bird, eds. *Hryhorij Savyč Skovoroda: An Anthology of Critical Articles*. Edmonton and Toronto: CIUS Press, 1994.
McDonald, David. "Nationhood and Its Discontents: Ukrainian Intellectual History at Empire's End. A Review Article." *JUS* 23, 2 (winter 1998): 105–16.
Mirtschuk, Ivan. "History of Ukrainian Culture." *UR* 29, 2 (summer 1981): 72–81; 4 (winter 1981): 35–44; 30, 1 (spring 1982): 40–46; 2 (summer 1982): 56–65; 3 (autumn 1982): 19–37.
Okeanos: Essays Presented to Ihor Ševčenko on His Sixtieth Birthday by His Colleagues and Students. HUS 7 (1983).
Pavlyshyn, Marko. "Post-Colonial Features in Contemporary Ukrainian Culture." *Australian Slavonic and East European Studies* 6, 2 (1992): 41–55.
Pelenski, Jaroslaw, ed. *The Political and Social Ideas of Vjačeslav Lypyns'kyj. HUS* 9, 3/4 (Dec. 1985).
Saunders, D. B. *The Ukrainian Impact on Russian Culture, 1750–1850*. Edmonton and Toronto: CIUS Press, 1985.

Scherer, Stephen. "Beyond Morality: The Moral Teaching and Practice of H. S. Skovoroda (1722–94)." *Ukraïns'kyi istoryk* 18, 1–4 (1981): 60–73.
———. "*The Narcissus*: Skovoroda's 'First-Born Son.'" *JUS* 22, 1/2 (summer–winter 1997): 51–64.
Ševčenko, Ihor. *Byzantium and the Slavs in Letters and in Culture.* Cambridge, Mass.: HURI; Naples: Istituto Universitario Orientale, 1991.
Shein, Louis. "An Examination of Hryhory Skovoroda's Philosophical System." *UQ* 39, 2 (summer 1983): 171–78.
Slez, Wolodymyr. "D. P. Yurkevych—The Neglected Philosopher." *UR* 35, 2 (summer 1987): 51–64; 3 (autumn 1987): 39–56.
Tonkal, V. E. et al. *Academy of Sciences of the Ukrainian SSR.* Kyiv: Naukova dumka, 1980.
Wynar, Lubomyr. *History of Early Ukrainian Printing, 1491–1600.* Denver: University of Denver, 1962.
———. "Ukrainian Scholarship in Exile: The DP Period, 1945–1952." *Ethnic Forum* 8, 1 (1988): 40–72.
Zakydalsky, Taras D. "Skovoroda as *Philosophus Ludens*." *JUS* 22, 1/2 (summer–winter 1997): 3–11.

About the Authors

Zenon E. Kohut, who holds his doctorate from the University of Pennsylvania, has taught there and at Michigan State University. He has been a longtime associate of the Ukrainian Research Institute at Harvard University, compiler and editor of the *American Bibliography of Slavic and East European Studies*, and senior research specialist for Eastern Europe and the Soviet Union at the Library of Congress. Since 1994, he has been director of the Canadian Institute of Ukrainian Studies at the University of Alberta. His many works on early modern Ukraine, historiography, and the development of Ukrainian identity include *Russian Centralism and Ukrainian Autonomy: Imperial Absorption of the Hetmanate, 1760s–1830s* (English version, 1988; revised Ukrainian version, 1996) and *Korinnia identychnosty: Studiï z rann'omodernoï ta modernoï istoriï Ukraïny* (Roots of Identity: Studies on Early Modern and Modern Ukraine; Kyiv, 2004).

Bohdan Y. Nebesio teaches film in the Department of English and Film Studies at the University of Alberta and serves as assistant editor of *Canadian Slavonic Papers*. He received an undergraduate degree in film studies and a master's degree in Slavic languages and literatures from the University of Toronto. His doctorate in modern languages and comparative studies was conferred by the University of Alberta. Subsequently, he held a postdoctoral fellowship from the Social Sciences and Humanities Research Council of Canada at the Communications Arts Department, University of Wisconsin-Madison. His publications focus on the films of Alexander Dovzhenko, East European cinema, and the history of film theory. His articles and reviews have appeared in *Film Criticism, Literature/Film Quarterly, Slavic Review, Canadian Review of Comparative Literature, Canadian Slavonic Papers*, and the *Journal of Ukrainian Studies*. He compiled *Alexander Dovzhenko: A Guide to Published Sources* (Edmonton, 1995).

About the Authors

Myroslav Yurkevich is senior editor of the Canadian Institute of Ukrainian Studies Press and has participated in the CIUS project to translate Mykhailo Hrushevsky's 10-volume *History of Ukraine-Rus'* since its inception. He received an undergraduate degree in English language and literature from the University of Toronto and a master's degree in East European history from the University of Michigan. In 1992 he established the Kyiv office of CIUS, which brought out 15 Ukrainian-language books and several other publications. He has been an editor of the *Encyclopedia of Ukraine* and of the *Journal of Ukrainian Studies*, as well as a translator of academic articles and government documents. Books that he has edited have been published by CIUS Press, Oxford University Press, the Ukrainian Research Institute at Harvard University, and the University of Toronto Press.